Real World Psychology w/Myths Paperback

KAREN HUFFMAN • CATHERINE A. SANDERSON

Wiley Custom Learning Solutions

Cover Image © Kirsten Hinte/Shutterstock

To order books or for customer service, please call 1(800)-CALL-WILEY (225-5945).

Printed in the United States of America.

ISBN 978-1-119-01489-8
Printed and bound by LSC Communications.

10 9 8 7 6 5 4

Brief Contents

REAL WORLD PSYCHOLOGY

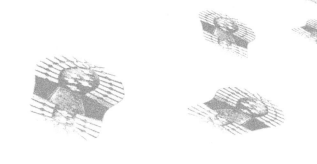

Karen Huffman
Palomar College

Catherine A. Sanderson
Amherst College

WILEY

VICE PRESIDENT AND EXECUTIVE PUBLISHER	George Hoffman
EXECUTIVE EDITOR	Christopher Johnson
PRODUCT DESIGNER	Beth Tripmacher
EDITORIAL ASSISTANT	Kristen Mucci
SENIOR CONTENT MANAGER	Micheline Frederick
SENIOR PRODUCTION EDITOR	Janet Foxman
SENIOR PHOTO EDITOR	Mary Ann Price
MEDIA SPECIALIST	Anita Castro
CREATIVE DIRECTOR	Harry Nolan
SENIOR DESIGNER	Maureen Eide
SENIOR MARKETING MANAGER	Margaret Barrett
PRODUCTION SERVICES	Furino Production
PRODUCTION ASSISTANT	John Du Val

Cover photos: Chameleon © GlobalP/iStockphoto, Footprints © TPopova/iStockphoto
This book was set in Garamond 10/12 pts by MPS Limited, and printed and bound by Quad Graphics/Versailles.

This book is printed on acid-free paper. ∞

Founded in 1807, John Wiley & Sons, Inc. has been a valued source of knowledge and understanding for more than 200 years, helping people around the world meet their needs and fulfill their aspirations. Our company is built on a foundation of principles that include responsibility to the communities we serve and where we live and work. In 2008, we launched a Corporate Citizenship Initiative, a global effort to address the environmental, social, economic, and ethical challenges we face in our business. Among the issues we are addressing are carbon impact, paper specifications and procurement, ethical conduct within our business and among our vendors, and community and charitable support. For more information, please visit our website: *www.wiley.com/go/citizenship.*

978-1-118-79777-8 (Binder-Ready Version ISBN)

Printed in the United States of America

10 9 8 7 6 5 4 3 2 1

brief contents

contents

Chapter Four
Sensation and Perception 90

Chapter Five
States of Consciousness 122

Chapter Six
Learning 150

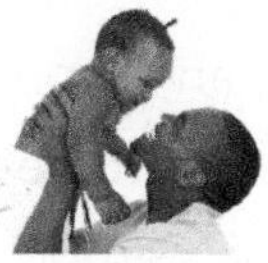

Chapter Seven
Memory 178

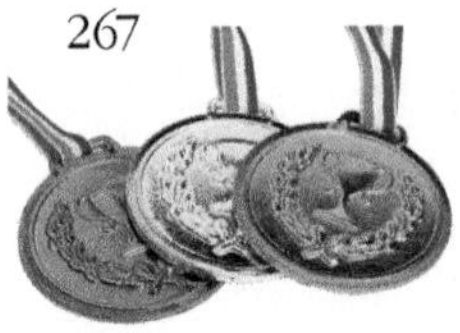

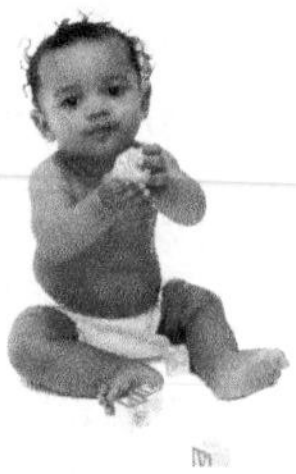

Chapter Eleven
Personality 300

Chapter Twelve
Psychological Disorders 332

Chapter Thirteen
Therapy 366

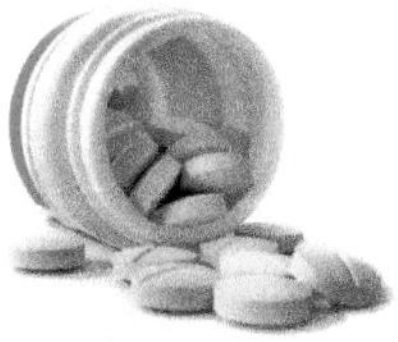

Chapter Fourteen
Social Psychology 396

CHAPTERS 15 AND 16 AVAILABLE SEPARATELY UPON REQUEST.

Chapter Fifteen
Gender and Human Sexuality 428

Chapter Sixteen
Industrial/Organizational Psychology 458

preface

"I have made this letter longer than usual, only because I have not had the time to make it shorter."

This quote, attributed to philosopher Blaise Pascal (among others), provides one key rationale for this new text, ***Real World Psychology (RWP)***. After a combined total of 49 years of teaching introductory psychology, and reading thousands of essay exams, we firmly believe that *brevity matters*! Given the time constraints for today's instructors and students, we need a brief book now more than ever.

In addition to being brief, this text will provide the latest up-to-date coverage and real world applications of the core concepts in psychology. Designed for introductory psychology teachers and their students, this text is:

- **CONCISE** When textbook chapters (or classroom lectures) are too long, attention strays and educational goals are lost. But brevity is more than just fewer words. The true goal of concise writing is clarity. Textbooks and teachers must be as brief and clear as possible because *brevity with clarity matters*!
- **COMPREHENSIVE** Knowing that the overarching goal of all instructors is to present the essentials of our field, this text is dedicated to comprehensive coverage of all the core concepts because *content matters!* For example, given that the scientific method and its various components is one of the most common learning objectives in psychology, we believe students need more practice and exposure than just the basic introductory material most texts traditionally provide. Therefore, we include a special **Psych Science** feature that offers an expanded discussion of the latest research on various "Hot Topics," such as the influence of media images of women on preschool girls' body-shape preferences, the impact of cell phone use on driving errors, and whether animals have distinct personalities. The detailed example is then followed by a special, interactive **Research Challenge,** which asks the reader to identify the research method, independent variable (IV), dependent variable (DV), and so on. This exercise helps reinforce the core learning objective on research methods, while also building student appreciation and engagement with the latest research. Answers are provided in Appendix B. (See sample **Psych Science** to the right.)
- **COMPREHENSIBLE** A good textbook must be more than concise and comprehensive. It must organize and present complex topics in a manner that is easily read and understood by the reader. However, comprehension without real world application is fairly useless. Therefore, ***RWP*** will use real world examples and real world applications to scaffold the content of psychology onto the reader's existing schemas, thus increasing comprehension, while at the same time showing students why *studying psychology matters*!

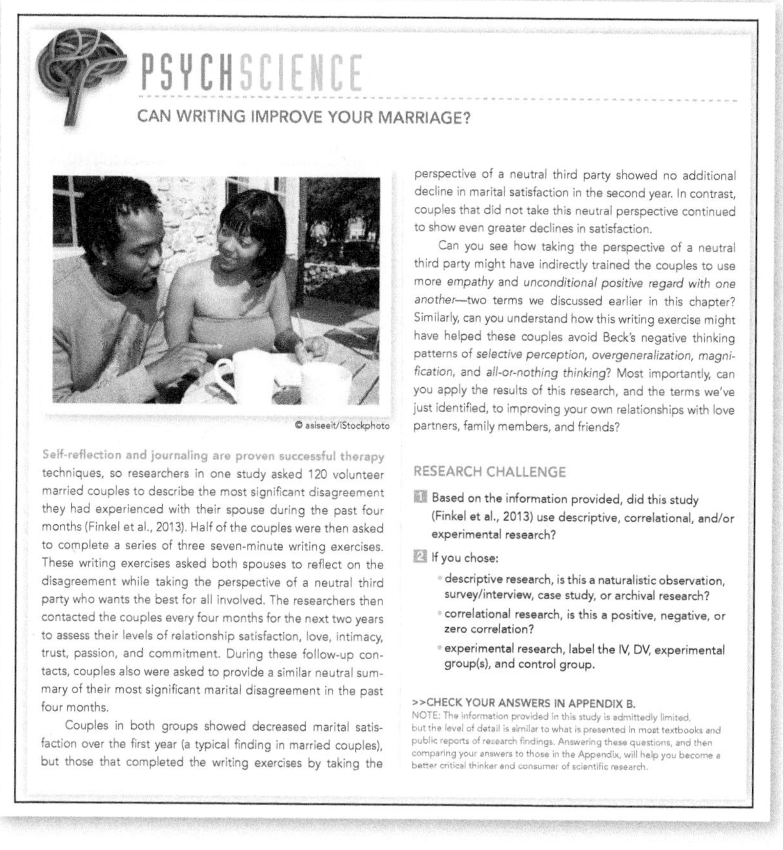

PSYCHSCIENCE

CAN WRITING IMPROVE YOUR MARRIAGE?

© asiseeit/iStockphoto

Self-reflection and journaling are proven successful therapy techniques, so researchers in one study asked 120 volunteer married couples to describe the most significant disagreement they had experienced with their spouse during the past four months (Finkel et al., 2013). Half of the couples were then asked to complete a series of three seven-minute writing exercises. These writing exercises asked both spouses to reflect on the disagreement while taking the perspective of a neutral third party who wants the best for all involved. The researchers then contacted the couples every four months for the next two years to assess their levels of relationship satisfaction, love, intimacy, trust, passion, and commitment. During these follow-up contacts, couples also were asked to provide a similar neutral summary of their most significant marital disagreement in the past four months.

Couples in both groups showed decreased marital satisfaction over the first year (a typical finding in married couples), but those that completed the writing exercises by taking the perspective of a neutral third party showed no additional decline in marital satisfaction in the second year. In contrast, couples that did not take this neutral perspective continued to show even greater declines in satisfaction.

Can you see how taking the perspective of a neutral third party might have indirectly trained the couples to use more *empathy* and *unconditional positive regard with one another*—two terms we discussed earlier in this chapter? Similarly, can you understand how this writing exercise might have helped these couples avoid Beck's negative thinking patterns of *selective perception*, *overgeneralization*, *magnification*, and *all-or-nothing thinking*? Most importantly, can you apply the results of this research, and the terms we've just identified, to improving your own relationships with love partners, family members, and friends?

RESEARCH CHALLENGE

1. Based on the information provided, did this study (Finkel et al., 2013) use descriptive, correlational, and/or experimental research?
2. If you chose:
   - descriptive research, is this a naturalistic observation, survey/interview, case study, or archival research?
   - correlational research, is this a positive, negative, or zero correlation?
   - experimental research, label the IV, DV, experimental group(s), and control group.

>>CHECK YOUR ANSWERS IN APPENDIX B.

NOTE: The information provided in this study is admittedly limited, but the level of detail is similar to what is presented in most textbooks and public reports of research findings. Answering these questions, and then comparing your answers to those in the Appendix, will help you become a better critical thinker and consumer of scientific research.

For instance, many students have difficulty understanding the differences between positive and negative reinforcement and/or positive and negative punishment. This is how ***RWP*** handles these topics:

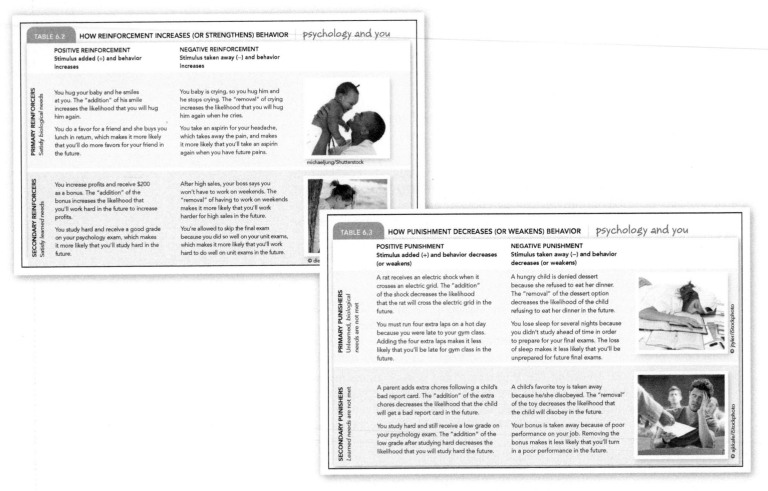

TABLE 6.2 HOW REINFORCEMENT INCREASES (OR STRENGTHENS) BEHAVIOR psychology and you

	POSITIVE REINFORCEMENT **Stimulus added (+) and behavior increases**	NEGATIVE REINFORCEMENT **Stimulus taken away (–) and behavior increases**
PRIMARY REINFORCERS *Satisfy biological needs*	You hug your baby and he smiles at you. The "addition" of his smile increases the likelihood that you will hug him again. You do a favor for a friend and she buys you lunch in return, which makes it more likely that you'll do more favors for your friend in the future.	You baby is crying, so you hug him and he stops crying. The "removal" of crying increases the likelihood that you will hug him again when he cries. You take an aspirin for your headache, which takes away the pain, and makes it more likely that you'll take an aspirin again when you have future pains.
SECONDARY REINFORCERS *Satisfy learned needs*	You increase profits and receive $200 as a bonus. The "addition" of the bonus increases the likelihood that you'll work hard in the future to increase profits. You study hard and receive a good grade on your psychology exam, which makes it more likely that you'll study hard in the future.	After high sales, your boss says you won't have to work on weekends. The "removal" of having to work on weekends makes it more likely that you'll work harder for high sales in the future. You're allowed to skip the final exam because you did so well on your unit exams, which makes it more likely that you'll work hard to do well on unit exams in the future.

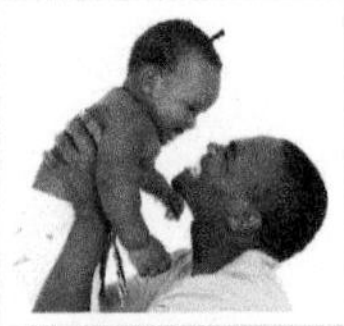
michaeljung/Shutterstock

© die

TABLE 6.3 HOW PUNISHMENT DECREASES (OR WEAKENS) BEHAVIOR psychology and you

	POSITIVE PUNISHMENT **Stimulus added (+) and behavior decreases (or weakens)**	NEGATIVE PUNISHMENT **Stimulus taken away (–) and behavior decreases (or weakens)**
PRIMARY PUNISHERS *Unlearned, biological needs are not met*	A rat receives an electric shock when it crosses an electric grid. The "addition" of the shock decreases the likelihood that the rat will cross the electric grid in the future. You must run four extra laps on a hot day because you were late to your gym class. Adding the four extra laps makes it less likely that you'll be late for gym class in the future.	A hungry child is denied dessert because she refused to eat her dinner. The "removal" of the dessert option decreases the likelihood of the child refusing to eat her dinner in the future. You lose sleep for several nights because you didn't study ahead of time in order to prepare for your final exams. The loss of sleep makes it less likely that you'll be unprepared for future final exams.
SECONDARY PUNISHERS *Learned needs are not met*	A parent adds extra chores following a child's bad report card. The "addition" of the extra chores decreases the likelihood that the child will get a bad report card in the future. You study hard and still receive a low grade on your psychology exam. The "addition" of the low grade after studying hard decreases the likelihood that you will study hard the future.	A child's favorite toy is taken away because he/she disobeyed. The "removal" of the toy decreases the likelihood that the child will disobey in the future. Your bonus is taken away because of poor performance on your job. Removing the bonus makes it less likely that you'll turn in a poor performance in the future.

© jtyler/iStockphoto

© ajkkafe/iStockphoto

We also scatter numerous *Real World Psychology* and *Psychology and You* examples, like these throughout our text because research shows that tying everyday examples to new material not only provides the scaffolding necessary for mastering complex topics, it also helps today's busy students see how the terms and concepts they're learning in this text can help improve their everyday lives.

realworldpsychology **Short-Term Stress** Just as flashbulb memories affect our memories for highly emotional events, short-term stress can affect the retrieval of existing memories, the laying down of new memories, and general information processing (Almela et al., 2011; Guenzel et al., 2013; Pechtel & Pizzagalli, 2011; Schwabe & Wolf, 2013). This interference with cognitive functioning helps explain why you may forget important information during a big exam and why people may become dangerously confused during a fire and be unable to find the fire exit. The good news is that once the cortisol washes out, memory performance generally returns to normal levels.

tty Images

psychology and you **Spontaneous Recovery** Have you ever felt renewed excitement at the sight of a former girlfriend or boyfriend, even though years have passed, you have a new partner, and extinction has occurred? This may be an example of spontaneous recovery. It also may help explain why people might misinterpret a sudden flare-up of feelings and be tempted to return to unhappy relationships. To make matters worse, when a conditioned stimulus is reintroduced after extinction, the conditioning occurs much faster the second time around—a phenomenon known as *reconditioning*.

The good news is that those who have taken general psychology (or read this book) are far less likely to make this mistake. Looking at **Figure 6.5**, you can see that even if you experience spontaneous recovery, your sudden peak of feelings for the old love partner will gradually return to their previously extinguished state. So don't overreact.

Finally, we've added a new feature, **Voices from the Classroom**, which provides real life examples from professors across the nation, which illustrate how psychology can help us *describe, explain, predict,* and *change* our personal worlds--and maybe even the world around us:

> **Voices from the Classroom**
>
> **Operant Conditioning and Driving with Kids** I have two children, who used to fight like cats and dogs, especially in the confined area of the car. Rather than punish them, I decided to ignore their bickering (as long as no arms or legs flew out the window). If we made it all the way to the shopping mall without an argument, I immediately praised them highly, showed excitement, and told them how great I felt. Another time when they made it to the mall without bickering, I stopped and we had ice cream on the way home. (Trips with bickering were ignored; no reinforcement.) Happily, within about five or six trips to the mall, there was virtually no bickering. It was awesome!
>
> Professor Barbara Kennedy
> Brevard Community College
> Palm Bay, Florida

- **CONVENIENT** Today's instructors and students are busier than ever, so ***RWP*** will provide them with the most essential, educationally sound assets in the most easily accessible and user-friendly manner because *convenience matters*!

As you can see, we feel passionate about our new text and believe that our B (Brevity) and four C's (Concise, Comprehensive, Comprehensible, and Convenient) can turn "B" and "C" students into "A"s! Even more important than high grades, the study of psychology offers an incomparable window into not only ourselves, but also to the world around us. We're eager to share our passion for psychology with all instructors and their students. If you have suggestions or comments, please feel free to contact us directly: Karen Huffman (khuffman@palomar.edu) and Catherine Sanderson (casanderson@amherst.edu).

SUPPLEMENTS TEACHING AND LEARNING PROGRAM

Real World Psychology is accompanied by a full menu of ancillary materials designed to facilitate the mastery of psychology.

WileyPlus with ORION

WileyPLUS is a research-based online environment for the most effective and efficient teaching and learning. From multiple study paths, to self-assessment, to a wealth of interactive resources—including the complete online textbook—*WileyPLUS* gives you everything you need to personalize the teaching and learning experience while giving your students more value for their money. Students achieve concept mastery in a rich environment that is available 24/7. Instructors personalize and manage their course more effectively with assessment, assignments, grade tracking, and more. Powered by a proven technology, *WileyPLUS* has enriched the education of millions of students in over 20 countries around the world.

WileyPLUS is now equipped with a NEW interactive teaching and learning module called ORION. Based on the latest findings in cognitive science, *WileyPLUS* with ORION, provides students with a personal, *adaptive* learning experience, which personalizes (adapts) the educational material according to their specific learning needs. With this individualized, immediate feedback, students can build on their strengths, overcome their weaknesses, and maximize their study time.

***WileyPLUS* with ORION** is great as:

- an adaptive **pre-lecture tool** that assesses your students' conceptual knowledge so they to come to class better prepared;
- a **personalized study guide** that helps students understand their strengths, as well as areas where they need to invest more time, especially in preparation for quizzes and exams.

Unique to ORION, students begin their study of each chapter with a quick diagnostic test. This test provides invaluable feedback to each student regarding his or her current level of mastery for the chapter's key terms and contents, while also identifying specific areas where they need to do additional study.

Additional Instructor Resources Availble with WileyPLUS with Orion

WileyPLUS with Orion provides reliable, customizable resources that reinforce course goals inside and outside of the classroom as well as instructor visibility into individual student progress.

Powerful multimedia resources for classroom presentations:

- **More than 50 Wiley Psychology Videos** are available, which connect key psychology concepts and themes to current issues in the news.
- **15 Wiley Psychology Animations** have been developed around key concepts and themes in psychology. The animations go beyond what is presented in the book, providing additional visual examples and descriptive narration.
- **More than 30 Tutorial Videos,** featuring author Karen Huffman and Katherine Dowdell of Des Moines Area Community College, provide students with explanations and examples of some of the most challenging concepts in psychology. These 3 to 5 minute videos reflect the richness and diversity of psychology, from the steps of the experimental method to the interaction of genes and our environment, to the sources of stress.
- **20 Virtual Field Trips** allow students to view psychology concepts in the real world as they've never seen them before. These 5 to 10 minute virtual field trips include visits to places such as a neuroimaging center, a film studio where 3-D movies are created, and a sleep laboratory, to name only a few.
- **More than 20 Visual Drag-and-Drop Exercises** that allow students a different, and more interactive, way to visualize and label key structures and important concepts.

Ready-to-go teaching materials and assessments help instructors optimize their time:

- The **Instructor's Manual,** prepared by Vicki Ritts, St. Louis Community College is carefully crafted to help instructors maximize student learning. It provides teaching suggestions for each chapter of the text, including lecture starters, lecture extensions, classroom discussions and activities, out of the classroom assignments, Internet and print resources, and more! Every chapter contains a **Lecture PowerPoint Presentation,** prepared by Katherine Williams, Tri-County Technical College, with a combination of key concepts, figures and tables, and examples from the textbook.

- **Media Enriched PowerPoint™ Presentations,** also prepared by Katherine Williams, are only available in *WileyPLUS*. They contain up-to-date, exciting embedded links to multimedia sources, both video and animation, and can be easily modified according to your needs.
- **Instructor's Test Bank,** prepared by Mike Majors, Delgado Community College, is available in Word document format or through Respondus. Instructors can easily alter or add new questions or answer options. They also can create multiple versions of the same test by quickly scrambling the order of all questions found in the Word version of the test bank. The test bank has over 2000 multiple choice questions, including approximately 10 essay questions for each chapter (with suggested answers). Each multiple-choice question has been linked to a specific, student learning outcome, coded as "Factual" or "Applied," and the correct answer is provided with section references to its source in the text.
- **Gradebook: WileyPLUS** provides instant access to reports on trends in class performance, student use of course materials, and progress toward learning objectives, helping inform decisions and drive classroom discussions.

For more information, visit **www.wileyplus.com**

Additional Student Resources Availble with WileyPLUS

A wide variety of personalized resources are readily available 24/7, including:

- **Digital Version of the Complete Textbook** with integrated videos, animations, and quizzes.
- **Chapter Exams**, prepared by Paulina Multhaupt, Macomb Community College, give students a way to easily test themselves on course material before exams. Each chapter exam contains page referenced fill-in-the-blank, application, and multiple-choice questions. The correct answer for each question is provided, which allows immediate feedback and increased understanding. All questions and answers are linked to a specific learning objective within the book to further aid a student's concept mastery.
- **Interactive Flashcards** allow students to easily test their knowledge of key vocabulary terms.
- **Handbook for Non-Native Speakers** clarifies idioms, special phrases, and difficult vocabulary, which has a documented history of significantly improving student performance—particularly for those who do not use English as their first language.

Create a Custom Text

Wiley Custom offers you an array of tools and services *designed to put content creation back in your hands*. Our suite of custom products empowers you to create high-quality, economical education solutions tailored to meet your individual classroom needs. Adapt or augment an existing text, combining individual chapters from across our extensive Wiley library to ensure content matches your syllabus.

Real World Psychology is ready for immediate customization with two supplementary chapters not part of the standard text: "Gender and Human Sexuality" and "Industrial/Organizational Psychology." Visit wiley.com/college/custom to review these chapters today.

Enhance Your Book

Add your personal, departmental, or institutional content. We can even deliver part of the proceeds of the custom title back to help fund content development, scholarship funds, student activities, or purchase supplies.

Ask your Wiley sales representative about customizing ***Real World Psychology*** to fit your course!

ACKNOWLEDGMENTS

Voices from the Classroom: We wish to thank the following professors who provided us with real-life examples they use in class to illustrate psychological concepts. These examples, found within each chapter, enrich the content, and we are very grateful for the contributions of these individuals.

David Baskind	Delta College, University Center, Michigan
Amy Beeman	San Diego Mesa College, San Diego, California
Charles Dufour	University of Maine, Orono, Maine
Brett Heintz	Delgado Community College, New Orleans, Louisiana
Jeffrey Henriques	University of Wisconsin, Madison, Wisconsin
Carmon Weaver Hicks	Ivy Tech Community College, Madison, Indiana
Barbara Kennedy	Brevard Community College, Palm Bay, Florida
R. D. Landis	Weatherford Community College, Weatherford, Texas
Mike Majors	Delgado Community College, New Orleans, Louisiana
Jan Mendoza	Golden West College, Huntington Beach, California
Paulina Multhaupt	Macomb Community College, Clinton Township, Michigan
Ronnie Naramore	Angelina College, Lufkin, Texas
Vicki Ritts	St. Louis Community College, Meramec, Missouri
David Steitz	Nazareth College, Rochester, New York
Keith W. Swain	Red Rocks Community College, Lakewood, Colorado
Kate Townsend-Merino	Palomar College, San Marcos, California
Rebekah Wanic	University of California, San Diego, California

Class Testers: A number of professors class tested chapters with their students and provided us with invaluable feedback and constructive recommendations. We benefitted greatly from this class testing and offer our sincere appreciation to these individuals for their helpful feedback.

Roxanna Anderson	Palm Beach State College
Christine Bachman	University of Houston-Downtown
Amy Beeman	San Diego Mesa College
Shannon Bentz	Northern Kentucky University
Vivian Bergamotto	Manhattan College
Jamie Borchardt	Tarleton State University
Amber Chenoweth	Hiram College
Jennifer Cohen	Metropolitan Community College of Omaha, Nebraska
Lisa Connolly	Ivy Tech Community College-Bloomington
Katrina Cooper	Bethany College
Kristi Cordell-McNulty	Angelo State University
Maureen Donegan	Delta College
Lauren Doninger	GateWay Community College
Denise Dunovant	Hudson County Community College
Daniella Errett	Pennsylvania Highlands Community College
Lenore Frigo	Shasta College
Kim Glackin	Metropolitan Community College-Blue River
Jonathan Golding	University of Kentucky
Justin Hackett	University of Houston-Downtown
Brett Heintz	Delgado Community College
Amy Houlihan	Texas A&M University–Corpus Christi
Mildred Huffman	Virginia Western Community College
Andrew Johnson	Park University
James Johnson	Illinois State University
Deana Julka	University of Portland
Marvin Lee	Tennessee State University
Wade Lueck	Mesa Community College
Claire Mann	Coastline Community College
Monica Marsee	University of New Orleans
Robert Martinez	University of the Incarnate Word
T. Darin Matthews	The Citadel, The Military College of South Carolina
Jason McCoy	Cape Fear Community College
Valerie Melburg	SUNY Onondaga Community College
Jan Mendoza	Golden West College
Dan Muhwezi	Butler Community College, Andover Campus
Paulina Multhaupt	Macomb Community College
Jennifer Ortiz-Garza	University of Houston–Victoria
Alexandr Petrou	CUNY Medgar Evers College
Sandra Prince-Madison	Delgado Community College
Sadhana Ray	Delgado Community College
Vicki Ritts	St. Louis Community College, Meramec
Brendan Rowlands	College of Southern Idaho
Spring Schafer	Delta College
Kelly Schuller	Bethany College
Randi Shedlosky-Shoemaker	York College of Pennsylvania
Barry Silber	Hillsborough Community College–Dale Mabry
Jonathan Sparks	Vance-Granville Community College
Laura Thornton	University of New Orleans
Virginia Tompkins	The Ohio State University at Lima
Rebekah Wanic	University of California, San Diego
Mark Watman	South Suburban College
Molly Wernli	College of Saint Mary
Khara Williams	University of Southern Indiana
Carl Wilson	Ranken Technical College
Stacy Wyllie	Delgado Community College
Gary Yarbrough	Arkansas Northeastern College

Reviewers: To the professors who reviewed material and who gave their time and constructive criticism, we offer our sincere appreciation. We are deeply indebted to the following individuals and trust that they will recognize their contributions throughout the text.

Kojo Allen	Metropolitan Community College of Omaha
Patrick Allen	College of Southern Maryland
Dennis Anderson	Butler Community College, Andover Campus
Roxanna Anderson	Palm Beach State College
Sheryl Attig	Tri-County Technical College
Pamela Auburn	University of Houston-Downtown
Christine Bachman	University of Houston-Downtown
Linda Bajdo	Macomb Community College
Michelle Bannoura	Hudson Valley Community College
Elizabeth Becker	Saint Joseph's University
Karen Bekker	Bergen Community College
Jamie Borchardt	Tarleton State University
Debi Brannan	Western Oregon University
Donald Busch	Bergen Community College
Elizabeth Casey	SUNY Onondaga Community College
April Cobb	Macomb Community College
Jennifer Cohen	Metropolitan Community College of Omaha
Lisa Connolly	Ivy Tech Community College - Bloomington
Katrina Cooper	Bethany College
Kristi Cordell-McNulty	Angelo State University
Kristen Couture	Manchester Community College
Denise Dunovant	Hudson County Community College
Judith Easton	Austin Community College
Betty Jane Fratzke	Indiana Wesleyan University
Lenore Frigo	Shasta College
Adia Garrett	University of Maryland, Baltimore County
Nichelle Gause	Clayton State University
Jeffrey Gibbons	Christopher Newport University
Cameron Gordon	University Of North Carolina, Wilmington
Peter Gram	Pensacola State College
Keith Happaney	CUNY Lehman College
Sidney Hardyway	Volunteer State Community College
Jaime Henning	Eastern Kentucky University
Sandra Holloway	Saint Joseph's University
Amy Houlihan	Texas A&M University Corpus Christi
Cory Howard	Tyler Junior College
Sayeedul Islam	Farmingdale State College
Nita Jackson	Butler Community College, Andover Campus
Michael James	Ivy Tech Community College - Bloomington
Judy Jankowski	Grand Rapids Community College
Margaret Jenkins	Seminole State College of Florida
Deana Julka	University of Portland
Kiesa Kelly	Tennessee State University
Robert Lawyer	Delgado Community College
Juliet Lee	Cape Fear Community College
Marvin Lee	Tennessee State University
Robin Lewis	California Polytechnic State University
Shayn Lloyd	Tallahassee Community College
Wade Lueck	Mesa Community College
Lisa Lynk-Smith	College of Southern Maryland
Mike Majors	Delgado Community College
Jason McCoy	Cape Fear Community College
Bradley McDowell	Madison Area Technical College of Florida
Valerie Melburg	SUNY Onondaga Community College
Jan Mendoza	Golden West College
Yesimi Milledge	Pensacola State College
Tal Millet	Bergen Community College
Brendan Morse	Bridgewater State University
Elizabeth Moseley	Pensacola State College
Ronald Mulson	Hudson Valley Community College
Bill Overman	University Of North Carolina, Wilmington
Andrea Phronebarger	York Technical College
Susan Pierce	Hillsborough Community College
Harvey Pines	Canisius College
Lydia Powell	Vance Granville Community College
Sandra Prince-Madison	Delgado Community College,
Sadhana Ray	Delgado Community College
Monica Schneider	SUNY Geneseo
John Schulte	Cape Fear Community College
Mary Shelton	Tennessee State University
Barry Silber	Hillsborough Community College
Deirdre Slavik	Northwest Arkansas Community College
Theodore Smith	University of Louisiana, Lafayette
Jonathan Sparks	Vance Granville Community College
Jessica Streit	Northern Kentucky University
William Suits	Seminole State College of Florida
Griffin Sutton	University of North Carolina, Wilmington
Mark Watman	South Suburban College
Keith Williams	Oakland University
Stacy Wyllie	Delgado Community College

Special Thanks

- We'd like to offer our very special thank you to the superb editorial and production teams at John Wiley and Sons. Like any cooperative effort, writing a book requires an immense support team, and we are deeply grateful to this remarkable group of people: Janet Foxman, Senior Production Editor; Micheline Frederick, Senior Content Manager; Mary Ann Price, Senior Photo Editor; Maureen Eide, Senior Designer; Beth Tripmacher, Product Designer; Kristen Mucci, Editorial Assistant; and a host of others. Each of these individuals helped enormously in the initial launch of this text and throughout its production. Without them, this book and its wide assortment of ancillaries would not have been possible.
- This first edition text particularly benefited from the incredible patience, wisdom, and insight of Elisa Adams and Helen McInnis who carefully guided us through the text's development and the tricky world of permissions. They made sure that every page was perfect and ready for print.

- Our deepest gratitude also goes out to Chris Johnson, Executive Editor. We're continually impressed by, and eternally grateful for, his invaluable feedback and suggestions, thoughtful guidance from beginning to end, and tremendous support for our vision of this new book. He's also a fun guy and delightful work partner!
- We're deeply indebted to Margaret Barrett, Senior Marketing Manager, who handles all the ins and outs of marketing. She was instrumental in the creative ideas for the cover design, and captured the "voice" of our book.
- ***Real World Psychology*** also could not exist without a great ancillary author team. We gratefully acknowledge the expertise and immense talents of our Video Tutorials director, Katherine Dowdell, and her teammates; Test Bank author, Mike Majors, Delagdo Community College; Instructor's Resource Guide author, Vicki Ritts of St. Louis Community College; PowerPoint author, Katherine Williams of Tri-County Technical College; and Practice Test author, Paulina Multhaupt of Macomb Community College.
- The staff at Furino Production deserves a special note of thanks. Their careful and professional approach was critical to the successful production of this book. Jeanine Furino, the Project Manager, should be particularly commended for her infinite patience, gracious handholding, and personal support. Even during the sad, personal loss of her father during one of the heaviest times in production, Jeanine maintained her professionalism and incredible work ethic—never missing a single date in the schedule!
- We'd also like to express our heartfelt appreciation to the hundreds of faculty across the country who contributed their constructive ideas to this first edition and to our many students over all the years. They've taught us what students want to know and inspired us to write this book.
- All the writing, producing, and marketing of this book would be wasted without an energetic and dedicated sales staff. We wish to sincerely thank all the publishing representatives for their tireless efforts and good humor. It's a true pleasure to work with such a remarkable group of people.

Personal Acknowledgments

- The writing of this text has been a group effort involving the input and support of all our wonderful families, friends, and colleagues. To each person we offer our sincere thanks: Haydn Davis, Tom Frangicetto, Mike Garza, Teresa Jacob, Jim Matiya, Lou Milstein, Kandis Mutter, Tyler Mutter, Roger Morrissette, Katie Townsend-Merino, Maria Pok, Fred Rose, and Kathy Young. They provided careful editing of this text, library research, and a unique sense of what should and should not go into an introduction to psychology text. A special note of appreciation goes to Taylor Penzel, who carefully checked and edited all the references for each chapter of the text.
- From Catherine Sanderson: Thank you to my husband, Bart Hollander, who supported me in taking on this immense challenge, even though he understood it would require considerable late night writing, a (very) messy study, and even more take-out dinners. I also want to express my appreciation to my children—Andrew, Robert, and Caroline—who sometimes allowed me peace and quiet with which to write.
- From Karen Huffman: A big hug and continuing appreciation to my family, friends, and students who supported and inspired me. I also want to offer my deepest gratitude to two very special people, Richard Hosey and Rita Jeffries. Their careful editing, constructive feedback, professional research skills, and shared authorship were essential to this revision. Having saved the truly best for last, I want to thank my dear friend and beloved husband, Bill Barnard—may the magic continue.

REAL WORLD PSYCHOLOGY

chapter one

Introduction and Research Methods

CHAPTER OUTLINE

realworldpsychology

THINGS YOU'LL LEARN IN CHAPTER 1

Q1 How does your culture influence what you look for in a romantic partner?

Q2 Can diet, preschool education, and parental behavior increase a child's intelligence?

Q3 Are older people happier than younger people?

Q4 Why do heavy drinkers misreport their alcohol use?

Q5 How do spreading your study sessions and practice testing improve test scores?

THROUGHOUT THE CHAPTER, MARGIN ICONS FOR Q1–Q5 INDICATE WHERE THE TEXT ADDRESSES THESE QUESTIONS.

A+ great work photo: © Olga Danylenko / iStockphoto; elderly man smiling happy: Kurhan / Shutterstock; schoolgirl with apple: © Ljupco / iStockphoto; empty beer bottles: © TokenPhoto / iStockphoto; indian couple in traditional clothing: Uniquely India / Getty Images

chapteroverview

Welcome to **Real World Psychology**! As our title suggests, we believe psychology's unique contributions to the scientific world are best shown through every day, real-life examples. Our innermost thoughts, our relationships, our politics, our "gut" feelings, and our deliberate decisions are all shaped by a complex psychological system that affects us at every level, from the cellular to the cultural. Psychology encompasses not only humankind but our nonhuman compatriots as well—from rats and pigeons to cats and chimps.

We invite you to let us know how your study of psychology (and this text) affects you and your life. You can reach us at khuffman@palomar.edu and casanderson@amherst.edu. We look forward to hearing from you.

Warmest regards,

courtesy of Karen Huffman

courtesy of Catherine Sanderson

INTRODUCING PSYCHOLOGY

LEARNING OBJECTIVES

RETRIEVAL PRACTICE While reading the upcoming sections, respond to each Learning Objective in your own words. Then compare your responses to those found at www.wiley.com/college/huffman.

1 **DEFINE** psychology.

2 **IDENTIFY** modern psychology's seven major perspectives.

3 **SUMMARIZE** psychology's major career options.

Psychology The scientific study of behavior and mental processes.

The term **psychology** derives from the roots *psyche*, meaning "mind," and *logos*, meaning "word." Modern psychology is most commonly defined as the *scientific study of behavior and mental processes. Scientific* is a key feature of the definition because psychologists follow strict scientific procedures to collect and analyze their data. *Behavior* (such as crying, hitting, and sleeping) can be directly observed. *Mental processes* are private, internal experiences that cannot be directly observed (like feelings, thoughts, and memories).

Critical thinking The process of objectively evaluating, comparing, analyzing, and synthesizing information.

For many psychologists, the most important part of the definition of psychology is the word *scientific*. Psychology places high value on *empirical evidence* that can be objectively tested and evaluated. Psychologists also emphasize **critical thinking**, *the process of objectively evaluating, comparing, analyzing, and synthesizing information* (Forshaw, 2013).

Be careful not to confuse psychology with *pseudopsychologies*, which are based on common beliefs, folk wisdom, or superstitions. (*Pseudo* means "false.") These sometimes give the appearance of science, but they do not follow the basics of the scientific method. Examples include purported psychic powers, horoscopes, mediums, and self-help and "pop psych" statements such as "I'm mostly right- brained" or "We use only 10% of our brain." Given the popularity of these misleading beliefs, be sure to test your own possible myths in the *Psychology and You* section.

TEST YOURSELF: PSYCHOLOGY VERSUS PSEUDOPSYCHOLOGY

psychology and you

TRUE OR FALSE?

____ 1. The best way to learn and remember information is to "cram," or study it intensively during one concentrated period.

____ 2. Advertisers and politicians often use subliminal persuasion to influence our behavior.

____ 3. Most brain activity stops when we're asleep.

____ 4. Punishment is the most effective way to permanently change behavior.

____ 5. Eyewitness testimony is often unreliable.

____ 6. Polygraph ("lie detector") tests can accurately and reliably reveal whether a person is lying.

____ 7. Behaviors that are unusual or that violate social norms may indicate a psychological disorder.

____ 8. People with schizophrenia have two or more distinct personalities.

____ 9. Similarity is one of the best predictors of long-term relationships.

____ 10. In an emergency, as the number of bystanders increases, your chance of getting help decreases.

Henry Groskinsky/Time Life Pictures/Getty Images

The magician James Randi has dedicated his life to educating the public about fraudulent pseudopsychologists. Along with the prestigious MacArthur Foundation, Randi has offered $1 million to "anyone who proves a genuine psychic power under proper observing conditions" (Randi, 1997; The Amazing Meeting, 2011). Even after many years, the money has never been collected.

Answers: 1. False (Chapter 1), 2. False (Chapter 4), 3. False (Chapter 5), 4. False (Chapter 6), 5. True (Chapter 7), 6. False (Chapter 10), 7. True (Chapter 12), 8. False (Chapter 12), 9. True (Chapter 14), 10. True (Chapter 14)

Before we go on, we'd like to introduce you to a special feature in this text. In addition to the *Real World* research and practical applications you'll encounter throughout the text, we invited psychology professors from around the country to contribute their best stories and anecdotes, called "Voices from the Classroom."

Voices from the Classroom

The Joys of Teaching Intro Psych One of the things I like most is teaching a freshman class of Introduction to Psychology. Why? Because I can still remember how powerful my first psychology class was to me. My childhood consisted mainly of going to school and to church, two places that basically told me what to think. When I started college, I really didn't know how to think for myself. My first psych professor began class one day with a simple question. "If there was a pill that could make you happy all the time, would you take it?" He had no interest in a "correct" answer; he just wanted us to *think*. Why? Because psychology is the science of thought and behavior. That day in class, I realized that psychology could help me answer questions I had about *my own thoughts* and about *my own behaviors*. I was hooked. So, with that in mind, let me see if I can hook you with a question. In 1637, French philosopher Renee Descartes stated, (in Latin), "*Cogito ergo sum*," or in English, "I think, therefore I am." Here's my question: If you were brain dead, and no longer capable of action or thought, have you ceased to exist? Cool question, huh? Welcome to psychology!

Professor Keith W. Swain
Red Rocks Community College
Lakewood, Colorado

FIGURE 1.1 WILLIAM JAMES (1842–1910)

William James broadened psychology to include animal behavior and biological processes. In the late 1870s, James established the first psychology laboratory in the United States, at Harvard University.

Psychology's Past

Although people have long been interested in human nature, it was not until the first psychological laboratory was founded in 1879 that psychology as a science officially began. As interest in the new field grew, psychologists adopted various perspectives on the "appropriate" topics for psychological research and the "proper" research methods. These diverse viewpoints and subsequent debates molded and shaped modern psychological science.

Psychology's history as a science began in 1879, when Wilhelm Wundt [VILL-helm Voont], generally acknowledged as the "father of psychology," established the first psychological laboratory in Leipzig, Germany. Wundt and his followers were primarily interested in how we form sensations, images, and feelings. Their chief methodology was termed "introspection," and it relied on self-monitoring and reporting on conscious experiences (Freedheim & Weiner, 2013; Goodwin, 2012).

A student of Wundt's, Edward Titchener, brought his ideas to the United States. Titchener's approach, now known as *structuralism*, sought to identify the basic building blocks, or structures, of mental life through introspection and then to determine how these elements combine to form the whole of experience. Because introspection could not be used to study animals, children, or more complex mental disorders, however, structuralism failed as a working psychological approach. Although short-lived, it did establish a model for studying mental processes scientifically.

Structuralism's intellectual successor, *functionalism*, studied the way the mind functions to enable humans and other animals to adapt to their environment. William James was the leading force in the functionalist school (**Figure 1.1**). Although functionalism also eventually declined, it expanded the scope of psychology to include research on emotions and observable behaviors, initiated the psychological testing movement, and influenced modern education and industry.

Psychoanalytic perspective An approach to understanding behavior and mental processes developed by Freud, which focuses on unconscious processes and unresolved conflicts.

During the late 1800s and early 1900s, while functionalism was prominent in the United States, the **psychoanalytic perspective** was forming in Europe. Its founder, Austrian physician Sigmund Freud, believed that a part of the human mind, the unconscious, contains thoughts, memories, and desires that lie outside personal awareness yet they still exert great influence. For example, according to Freud, a man who is cheating on his wife might slip up and say, "I wish you were her," when he consciously planned to say, "I wish you were here." Such seemingly meaningless, so-called Freudian slips supposedly reveal a person's true unconscious desires and motives.

Freud also believed many psychological problems are caused by unconscious sexual or aggressive motives and conflicts between "acceptable" and "unacceptable" behaviors (Chapter 11). His theory led to a system of therapy known as *psychoanalysis* (Chapter 13).

Modern Psychology

As summarized in **Table 1.1**, contemporary psychology reflects seven major perspectives: *psychodynamic*, *behavioral*, *humanistic*, *cognitive*, *biological*, *evolutionary*, and *sociocultural*. Although there are numerous differences between these seven perspectives, most psychologists recognize the value of each orientation and agree that no one view has all the answers.

Psychodynamic perspective An approach to understanding behavior and mental processes that emphasizes unconscious dynamics, internal motives, conflicts, and past experiences; actions are viewed as stemming from inherited instincts, biological drives, and attempts to resolve conflicts between personal needs and social requirements.

Behavioral perspective An approach to understanding behavior and mental processes that emphasizes objective, observable environmental influences on overt behavior.

Freud's nonscientific approach and emphasis on sexual and aggressive impulses have long been controversial, and today there are few strictly Freudian psychoanalysts left. However, the broad features of his theory remain in the modern **psychodynamic perspective**. The general goal of psychodynamic psychologists is to explore unconscious *dynamics*—internal motives, conflicts, and past experiences.

In the early 1900s, another major perspective appeared that dramatically shaped the course of modern psychology. Unlike earlier approaches, the **behavioral perspective** emphasizes objective, observable environmental influences on overt

TABLE 1.1 MODERN PSYCHOLOGY'S SEVEN MAJOR PERSPECTIVES

Perspectives	Major Emphases	Sample Research Questions	
Psychodynamic	Unconscious dynamics, motives, conflicts, and past experiences	How do adult personality traits or psychological problems reflect unconscious processes and early childhood experiences?	
Behavioral	Objective, observable, environmental influences on overt behavior; stimulus–response relationships and consequences for behavior	How do we learn both our good and bad habits? How can we increase desirable behaviors and decrease undesirable ones?	
Humanistic	Free will, self-actualization, and human nature as naturally positive and growth seeking	How can we promote a client's capacity for self-actualization and understanding of his or her own development? How can we promote international peace and reduce violence?	
Cognitive	Thinking, perceiving, problem solving, memory, language, and information processing	How do our thoughts and interpretations affect how we respond in certain situations? How can we improve how we process, store, and retrieve information?	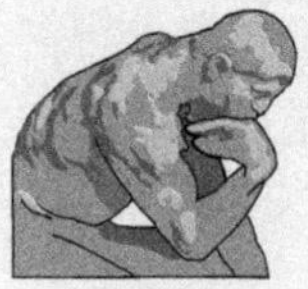
Biological	Genetic and biological processes in the brain and other parts of the nervous system	How might changes in neurotransmitters or damage to parts of the brain lead to psychological problems and changes in behavior and mental processes?	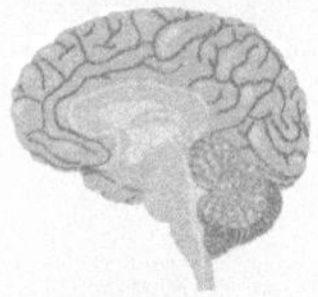
Evolutionary	Natural selection, adaptation, and evolution of behavior and mental processes	How does natural selection help explain why we love and help certain people and hurt others? Do we have specific genes for aggression and altruism?	
Sociocultural	Social interaction and the cultural determinants of behavior and mental processes	How do the values and beliefs transmitted from our social and cultural environments affect our everyday psychological processes?	

behavior. Behaviorism's founder, John B. Watson (1913), rejected the practice of introspection and the influence of unconscious forces. Instead, Watson adopted Russian physiologist Ivan Pavlov's concept of *conditioning* (Chapter 6) to explain behavior as a result of observable stimuli (in the environment) and observable responses (behavioral actions).

Most early behaviorist research was focused on learning; nonhuman animals were ideal subjects for this research. One of the best-known behaviorists, B. F. Skinner, was convinced that behaviorist approaches could be used to "shape" human behavior (**Figure 1.2**).

As you'll discover in Chapters 6 and 13, therapeutic techniques rooted in the behavioristic perspective have been most successful in treating observable behavioral problems, such as those related to phobias and alcoholism (Kiefer & Dinter, 2013; May et al., 2013; Sarafino, 2012).

FIGURE 1.2 B. F. SKINNER (1904–1990)

B. F. Skinner was one of the most influential psychologists of the twentieth century. Here he uses the so-called "Skinner box" to train a rat to press a lever for a reward.

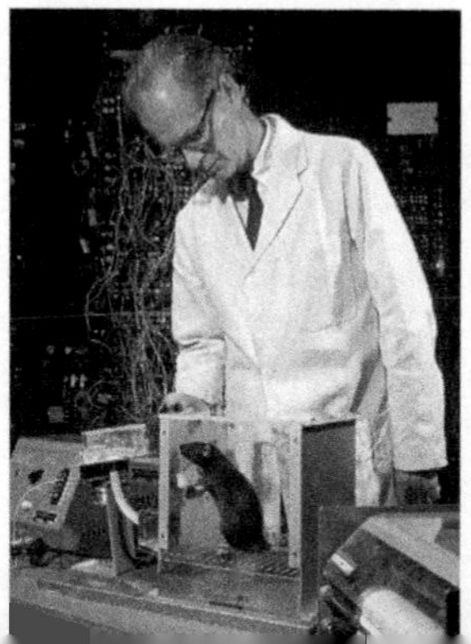

Nina Leen/Time Life Pictures/Getty Images

FIGURE 1.3 **WHAT MAKES US HAPPY?** | realworldpsychology

Research in positive psychology finds that our happiness increases when we give to others. When adults are given money and told to spend it on others, they experience higher levels of happiness than do those who are told to spend it on themselves (Dunn et al., 2008). Amazingly enough, even children as young as 2 years of age are happier when they give treats such as Goldfish crackers to other children than when they keep the treats for themselves (Aknin et al., 2012). Other research finds that those who experience more positive emotions also live longer than those with more negative emotions (Diener & Chan, 2011).

Humanistic perspective An approach to understanding behavior and mental processes that perceives human nature as naturally positive and growth seeking; it emphasizes free will and self-actualization.

Positive psychology The study of optimal human functioning; it emphasizes positive emotions, traits, and institutions.

Cognitive perspective An approach to understanding behavior and mental processes that focuses on thinking, perceiving, and information processing.

Biological perspective An approach to understanding behavior and mental processes that focuses on genetics and biological processes in the brain and other parts of the nervous system.

Evolutionary perspective An approach to understanding behavior and mental processes that stresses natural selection, adaptation, and evolution; it assumes that mental capabilities evolved over millions of years to serve particular adaptive purposes.

Although the psychoanalytic and behavioral perspectives dominated U.S. psychology for some time, in the 1950s a new approach emerged—the **humanistic perspective**, which stresses *free will* (voluntarily chosen behavior) and *self-actualization* (an inborn drive to develop all one's talents and capabilities). According to Carl Rogers and Abraham Maslow, two central humanist figures, all individuals naturally strive to develop and move toward self-actualization. Like psychoanalysis, humanist psychology developed an influential theory of personality and their own form of psychotherapy (Chapters 11 and 13). The humanistic approach also led the way to a contemporary research specialty known as **positive psychology**—the study of optimal human functioning (**Figure 1.3**) (Cummins, 2013; Diener, 2008; Seligman, 2003, 2011; Taylor & Sherman, 2008).

One of the most influential modern approaches, the **cognitive perspective**, recalls psychology's earliest days in that it emphasizes thoughts, perception, and information processing (Kellogg, 2011; Sternberg, 2012). Modern cognitive psychologists study the ways we gather, encode, and store information using a vast array of mental processes. These include perception, memory, imagery, concept formation, problem solving, reasoning, decision making, and language. Many cognitive psychologists also use an *information-processing approach*, likening the mind to a computer that sequentially takes in information, processes it, and then produces a response.

During the past few decades, scientists have explored the role of biological factors in almost every area of psychology. Using sophisticated tools and technologies, scientists who adopt this **biological perspective** examine behavior through the lens of genetics and biological processes in the brain and other parts of the nervous system. For example, research shows that genes influence many aspects of our behavior, including whether we finish high school and college, how kind we are to other people, and even whom we vote for in elections (Beaver et al., 2011; Hatemi & McDermott, 2012; Poulin et al., 2012).

The **evolutionary perspective** stresses natural selection, adaptation, and evolution of behavior and mental processes (Buss, 2011; Durrant & Ellis, 2013; Maner & Menzel, 2013). Its proponents argue that natural selection favors behaviors that enhance an organism's reproductive success. According to the evolutionary perspective, there's even an evolutionary explanation for the longevity of humans over other primates–it's grandmothers! Without them, a mother who has a two-year-old and then gives birth would have to devote her time and resources to the newborn at the expense of the older child. Grandmothers act as supplementary caregivers.

Finally, the **sociocultural perspective** emphasizes social interactions and cultural determinants of behavior and mental processes. Although we are often unaware of their influence, factors such as ethnicity, religion, occupation, and socioeconomic class have an enormous psychological impact on our mental processes and behavior (Berry et al., 2011; Boer & Fischer, 2013). For example, in countries with low levels of gender equality, women are more likely to be attracted by their partner's resources and men by physical attractiveness (Zentner & Mitura, 2012).

Sociocultural perspective An approach to understanding behavior and mental processes that emphasizes the social interaction and cultural determinants of behavior and mental processes.

Q1

Gender and Minority Influences

One of the first women to be recognized in the field of psychology was Mary Calkins. Her achievements are particularly noteworthy, considering the significant discrimination that she overcame. During the late 1800s and early 1900s, most colleges and universities provided little opportunity for women and ethnic minorities, either as students or as faculty members. In Mary Calkins' case, even after she completed all the requirements for a Ph.D. at Harvard University in 1895, and was described by William James as his brightest student, the university refused to grant the degree to a woman. Nevertheless, Calkins went on to perform valuable research on memory, and in 1905 served as the first female president of the American Psychological Association (APA). The first woman to receive her Ph.D. in psychology was Margaret Floy Washburn (Cornell, 1894), who wrote several influential books and served as the second female president of the APA.

Francis Cecil Sumner became the first African American to earn a Ph.D. in psychology. He earned it from Clark University in 1920 and later chaired one of the country's leading psychology departments, at Howard University. In 1971, one of Sumner's students, Kenneth B. Clark, became the first African American to be elected APA president. Clark's research with his wife, Mamie Clark, documented the harmful effects of prejudice and directly influenced the Supreme Court's landmark 1954 ruling against racial segregation in schools, Brown v. Board of Education (**Figure 1.4**).

Library of Congress Prints and Photographs Division

FIGURE 1.4 KENNETH CLARK (1914–2005) AND MAMIE PHIPPS CLARK (1917–1985)

Kenneth Clark and his wife, Mamie Phipps Clark, conducted experiments with black and white dolls to study children's attitudes about race. This research and their expert testimony contributed to the U.S. Supreme Court's ruling that racial segregation in public schools was unconstitutional.

Sumner, Clark, Calkins, and Washburn, along with other important minorities and women, made significant and lasting contributions to psychology's development. In recent times, people of color and women have been actively encouraged to pursue graduate degrees in psychology. Today, women earning doctoral degrees in psychology greatly outnumber men, but minorities are still underrepresented (New Ph.D.s and Employment Outcomes, 2011; Willyard, 2011).

Biopsychosocial Model

The seven major perspectives, as well as gender and minority influences, each make different contributions to modern psychology, which is why most contemporary psychologists do not adhere to one single intellectual perspective. Instead, a more integrative, unifying theme—the **biopsychosocial model**—has gained wide acceptance. This model views biological processes (genetics, neurotransmitters, evolution), psychological factors (learning, personality, motivation), and social forces (family, culture, ethnicity) as interrelated. It also sees all three factors as influences inseparable from the seven major perspectives (**Figure 1.5**).

Biopsychosocial model An integrative, unifying theme of modern psychology that sees biological, psychological, and social processes as interacting influences.

Why is the biopsychosocial model so important? As the old saying goes, "A fish doesn't know it's in water." Similarly, as individuals living alone inside our own heads, we're often unaware of the numerous, interacting factors that affect us—particularly cultural forces. For example, most North Americans and Western Europeans are raised to be very individualistic and are surprised to learn that over 70% of the world's population lives in collectivistic cultures. As you can see in **Table 1.2**, in *individualistic cultures*, the needs and goals of the individual are emphasized over the needs and goals of the group. When asked to complete the statement "I am . . . ,"

FIGURE 1.5 THE BIOPSYCHOSOCIAL MODEL | realworldpsychology

When we consider people as individuals (**Figure a**), we don't always get a complete picture of their emotions and motivations.

Stepping back to see the same individuals in a broader context (**Figure b**) can provide new insights. With this "bigger picture" (the child's immediate surroundings and his or her group's behavior) in mind, can you better understand why each child might be feeling and acting as he or she is? The biopsychosocial model recognizes that there is usually no single cause for our behavior or our mental states (**Figure c**). For example, our moods and feelings are often influenced by genetics and neurotransmitters (biological), our learned responses and patterns of thinking (psychological), and our socioeconomic status and cultural views of emotion (sociocultural).

A

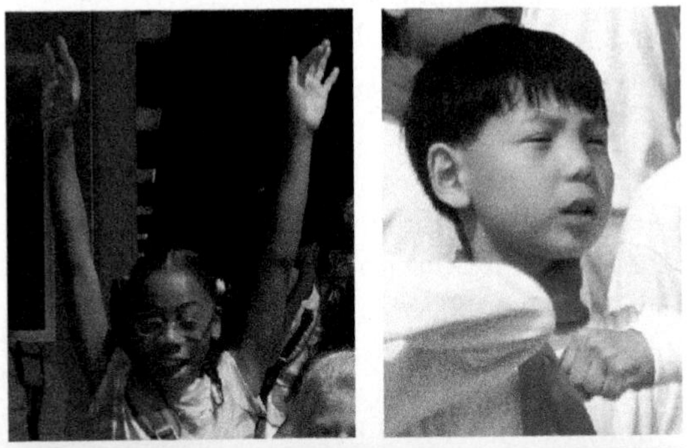

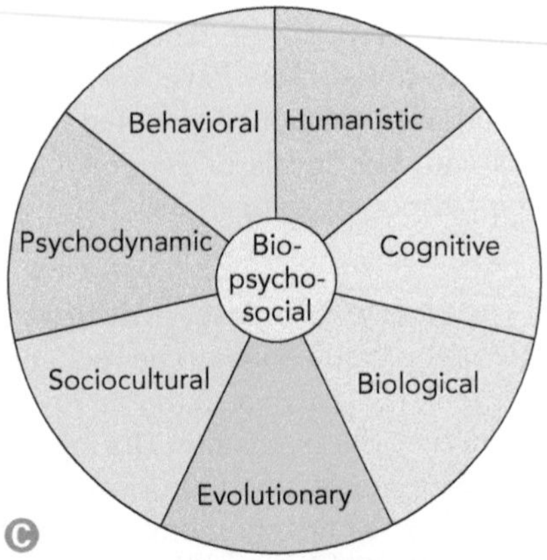

C

B

©Bonnie Jacobs/iStockphoto

©Jurgen Schulzki/Imagebroker/Age Fotostock America, Inc.

people from individualistic cultures tend to respond with personality traits ("I am shy"; "I am outgoing") or their occupation ("I am a teacher"; "I am a student").

In *collectivistic cultures*, however, the person is defined and understood primarily by looking at his or her place in the social unit (Berry et al., 2011; Dierdorff et al., 2011; Greenfield & Quiroz, 2013; McCrae, 2004, 2011). Relatedness, connectedness, and interdependence are valued, as opposed to separateness, independence, and individualism. When asked to complete the statement "I am . . . ," people from collectivistic cultures tend to mention their families or nationality ("I am a daughter"; "I am Chinese"). Keep in mind, however, that these sample countries and their sample values exist on a continuum, and that within each country there is a wide range of individual differences.

Looking back at the two photos from the two cultures in Figure 1.5, can you see how learning more about the biopsychosocial model offers increased understanding of ourselves, our friends, and our families, and how it may improve our understanding and sensitivity to other cultures? For example, North Americans generally define *sincerity* as behaving in accordance with our inner feelings, whereas people from collectivist cultures tend to see their equivalent word for sincerity as behavior that conforms to a person's role expectations and duties. (Yamada, 1997). This explains why collectivistic behaviors might appear insincere to a North American.

Careers in Psychology

Many people think of psychologists only as therapists, and it's true that the fields of clinical and counseling psychology do make up the largest specialty areas. However, many psychologists have no connection with therapy. Instead, they work as researchers, teachers, or consultants in academic, business, industry, and government

TABLE 1.2 A COMPARISON BETWEEN INDIVIDUALISTIC AND COLLECTIVISTIC CULTURES

Sample Individualistic Countries	**Sample Collectivistic Cultures**
United States	Hong Kong
Australia	China
Great Britain	India
Canada	Japan
The Netherlands	West Africa region
Germany	Thailand
New Zealand	Taiwan
Sample Individualistic Values	**Sample Collectivistic Values**
Independence	Interdependence
Individual rights	Obligations to others
Self-sufficiency	Reliance on group
Individual achievement	Group achievement
Independent living	Living with kin
Personal failure leads to shame and guilt	Failing the group leads to shame and guilt

settings, or in a combination of settings. As you can see in **Table 1.3**, there are several career paths and valuable life skills associated with a bachelor's degree in psychology. Of course, your options are even greater if you go beyond the bachelor's degree and earn your master's degree, Ph.D, or Psy.D—see **Table 1.4**. For more information about what psychologists do—and how to pursue a career in psychology—check out the websites of the American Psychological Association (APA) and the Association for Psychological Science (APS).

TABLE 1.3 WHAT CAN I DO WITH A BACHELOR'S DEGREE IN PSYCHOLOGY?
realworldpsychology

Top Careers with a Bachelor's Degree in Psychology
Management and administration
Sales
Social work
Labor-relations, personnel and training
Real estate, business services, insurance
Sample Skills Gained from a Psychology Major
Improved ability to predict and understand behavior
Better understanding of how to use and interpret data
Increased communication and interpersonal skills
Increased ability to manage difficult situations and high-stress environments
Enhanced insight into problem behavior
Note that the U.S. Department of Labor predicts only an average rate of growth for psychologists in the next decade. However, the good news is that a degree in our field, and this course in general psychology, will provide you with invaluable lifetime skills.

TABLE 1.4 SAMPLE CAREERS AND SPECIALTIES IN PSYCHOLOGY | real world psychology

Zigy Kaluzny/Getty Images, Inc.

Dolphin Inst./Photo Researchers

CAREER/SPECIALTY	DESCRIPTION
Biopsychologist/ neuroscientist	Investigates the relationship between biology, behavior, and mental processes, including how physical and chemical processes affect the structure and function of the brain and nervous system
Clinical psychologist	Specializes in the evaluation, diagnosis, and treatment of psychological disorders
Cognitive psychologist	Examines "higher" mental processes, including thought, memory, intelligence, creativity, and language
Comparative psychologist	Studies the behavior and mental processes of nonhuman animals; emphasizes evolution and cross-species comparisons
Counseling psychologist	Overlaps with clinical psychology, but generally works with less seriously disordered individuals and focuses more on social, educational, and career adjustment
Cross-cultural psychologist/ psychological anthropologist	Studies similarities and differences in and across various cultures and ethnic groups
Developmental psychologist	Studies the course of human growth and development from conception to death
Educational psychologist	Studies the processes of education and works to promote the academic, intellectual, social, and emotional development of children in the school environment
Environmental psychologist	Investigates how people affect and are affected by the physical environment
Experimental psychologist	Examines processes such as learning, conditioning, motivation, emotion, sensation, and perception in humans and other animals (Note that psychologists working in almost all other areas of specialization also conduct experiments.)
Forensic psychologist	Applies principles of psychology to the legal system, including jury selection, psychological profiling, assessment, and treatment of offenders
Gender and/or cultural psychologist	Investigates how men and women and different cultures vary from one another and how they are similar
Health psychologist	Studies how biological, psychological, and social factors affect health and illness
Industrial/ organizational psychologist	Applies principles of psychology to the workplace, including personnel selection and evaluation, leadership, job satisfaction, employee motivation, and group processes within the organization
Personality psychologist	Studies the unique and relatively stable patterns in a person's thoughts, feelings, and actions
Positive psychologist	Examines factors related to optimal human functioning
School psychologist	Collaborates with teachers, parents, and students within the educational system to help children with needs related to a disability and/or their academic and social progress; also provides evaluation and assessment of a student's functioning and eligibility for special services
Social psychologist	Investigates the role of social forces in interpersonal behavior, including aggression, prejudice, love, helping, conformity, and attitudes
Sports psychologist	Applies principles of psychology to enhance physical performance

RETRIEVAL PRACTICE: INTRODUCING PSYCHOLOGY

Self-Test

Completing this self-test and comparing your answers with those in Appendix B provides immediate feedback and helpful practice for exams. Additional interactive, self-tests are available at www.wiley.com/college/huffman.

1. Psychology is defined as the ________.

a. science of conscious and unconscious forces
b. empirical study of the mind and behavior
c. scientific study of the mind
d. scientific study of behavior and mental processes

2. ________ rely on common beliefs, folk wisdom, or even superstitions and do not follow the basics of the scientific method.

a. Pseudopsychologies
b. Sociologists
c. Astronomers
d. Counselors

3. ________ is generally acknowledged to be the father of psychology.

a. Sigmund Freud
b. B. F. Skinner
c. Wilhelm Wundt
d. William James

4. Which of the following terms do not belong together?

a. structuralism, unconscious behavior
b. behaviorism, observable behavior
c. psychoanalytic, unconscious conflict
d. humanism, free will

Think Critically

1 Psychologists are among the least likely to believe in psychics, palmistry, astrology, and other paranormal phenomena. Why might that be?

2 Which of the seven modern perspectives of psychology do you most agree with? Why?

3 How might the biopsychosocial model explain difficulties or achievements in your own life?

realworldpsychology

How does your culture influence what you look for in a romantic partner?

HINT: LOOK IN THE MARGIN FOR Q1

THE SCIENCE OF PSYCHOLOGY

RETRIEVAL PRACTICE While reading the upcoming sections, respond to each Learning Objective in your own words. Then compare your responses with those found at www.wiley.com/college/huffman.

1 **COMPARE** the fundamental goals of basic and applied research.
2 **DESCRIBE** the scientific method.
3 **IDENTIFY** psychology's four main goals.

LEARNING OBJECTIVES

In science, research strategies are generally categorized as either *basic* or *applied*. **Basic research** is most often conducted to advance core scientific knowledge, whereas **applied research** is designed to solve practical ("real world") problems (**Figure 1.6**). As you'll see in Chapter 6, classical and operant conditioning principles evolved from numerous *basic research* studies designed to advance the general understanding of how human and nonhuman animals learn. In Chapters 12 and 13, you'll also discover how *applied research* based on these principles has been used to successfully treat psychological disorders such as phobias. Similarly, in Chapter 7, you'll see how basic research on how we create, store, and retrieve our memories has led to practical applications in the legal field, such as a greater appreciation for the fallibility of eyewitness testimony.

Basic research Research that typically focuses on fundamental principles and theories; most often conducted in universities and research laboratories.

Applied research Research that is generally conducted outside the laboratory; its data are typically used for real world application.

FIGURE 1.6 APPLIED RESEARCH IN PSYCHOLOGY

Note how psychological research has helped design safe and more reliable appliances, machinery, and instrument controls (*Psychology Matters*, 2006).

A Spatial correspondence
Controls for stovetops should be arranged in a pattern that corresponds to the placement of the burners.

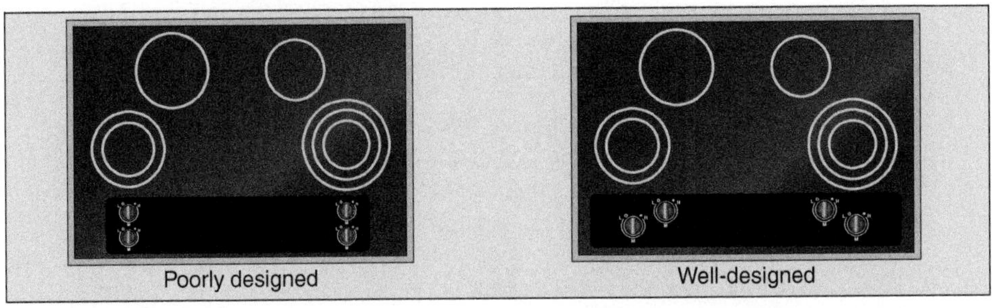

B Visibility
Automobile gauges for fuel, temperature, and speed should be easily visible to the driver.

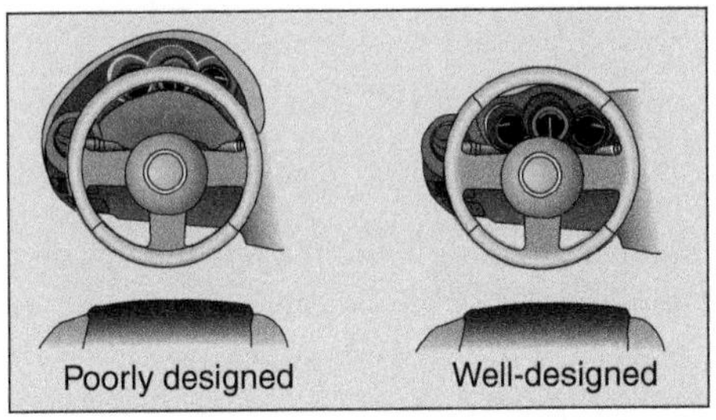

C Arrangement of numbers
A top-down arrangement of numbers on a cell phone is more efficient than the bottom-up arrangement on a computer's key board.

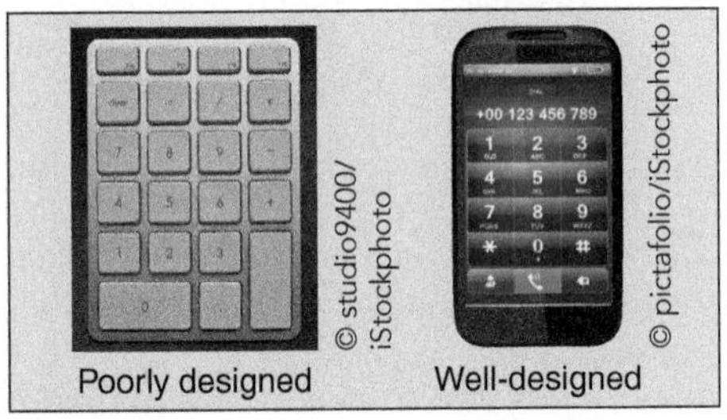

Keep in mind that basic and applied research approaches are not polar opposites. Instead, they frequently share similar goals, and their outcomes interact, with one building on the other.

The Scientific Method

Like scientists in any other field, psychologists follow strict, standardized procedures so that others can understand, interpret, and repeat or test their findings. Most scientific investigations consist of six basic steps, collectively based on the **scientific method** (**Figure 1.7**).

Scientific method The cyclical and cumulative research process used for gathering and interpreting objective information in a way that minimizes error and yields dependable results.

Hypothesis A tentative and testable explanation about the relationship between two or more variables; a testable prediction or question.

Operational definition A precise description of how the variables in a study will be observed, manipulated, and measured.

Have you wondered whether completing the Retrieval Practice exercises that follow the Learning Objectives, Self-Test, and Key Terms in each of the chapters of this text is worth your time? Have you thought, "Will I get a better grade on my exams if I do these exercises?" How would you use the scientific method to answer these general questions? Starting with Step 1, you could go to professional journals and read up on the research about retrieval practice that already exists on this topic. To complete Step 2, you would first form an educated guess based on your literature review in Step 1. You would then turn this guess into a statement, called a **hypothesis**, which provides predictions that can be tested in some way. You would then need to explicitly state how each of your variables in your hypothesis will be **operationally defined** (observed, manipulated, and measured). For example, a better grade on my exams might be operationally defined as earning one letter grade higher than the letter grade on my previous exam.

Using your initial question about the value of the Retrieval Practice exercises, your hypothesis and operational definitions might be: "Students who spend two hours studying Chapter 1 in this text and one hour completing the three Retrieval Practice exercises will earn higher scores on a standard academic exam than students who spend three hours using free-choice study techniques without completing the Retrieval Practice exercises."

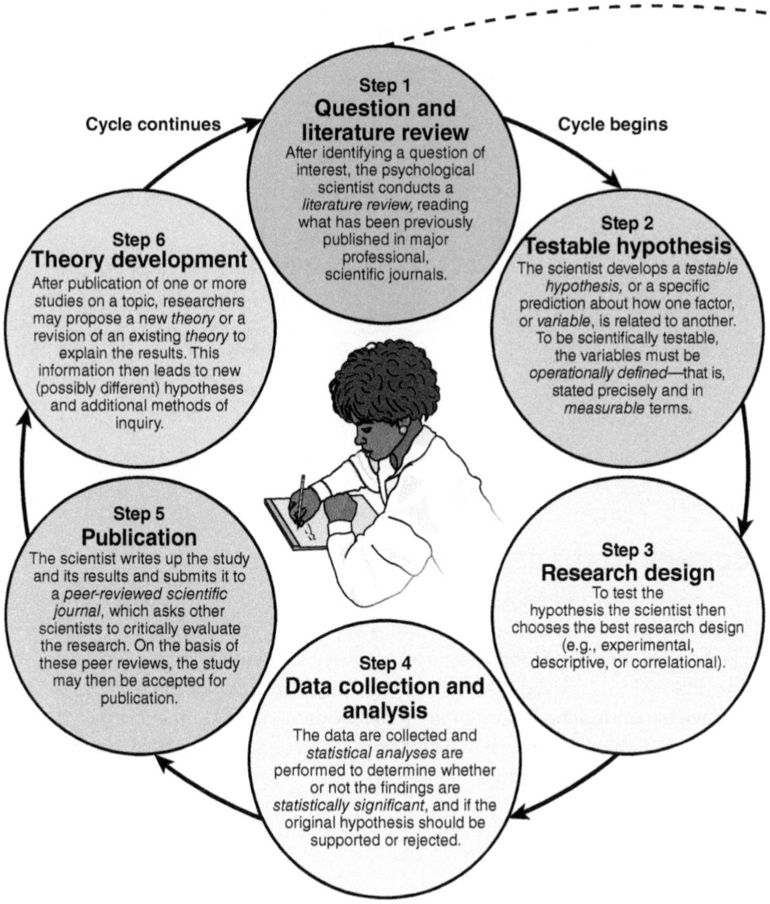
Cycle continues
Cycle begins
Step 1
Question and literature review
After identifying a question of interest, the psychological scientist conducts a *literature review,* reading what has been previously published in major professional, scientific journals.
Step 2
Testable hypothesis
The scientist develops a *testable hypothesis,* or a specific prediction about how one factor, or *variable,* is related to another. To be scientifically testable, the variables must be *operationally defined*—that is, stated precisely and in *measurable* terms.
Step 3
Research design
To test the hypothesis the scientist then chooses the best research design (e.g., experimental, descriptive, or correlational).
Step 4
Data collection and analysis
The data are collected and *statistical analyses* are performed to determine whether or not the findings are *statistically significant,* and if the original hypothesis should be supported or rejected.
Step 5
Publication
The scientist writes up the study and its results and submits it to a *peer-reviewed scientific journal,* which asks other scientists to critically evaluate the research. On the basis of these peer reviews, the study may then be accepted for publication.
Step 6
Theory development
After publication of one or more studies on a topic, researchers may propose a new *theory* or a revision of an existing *theory* to explain the results. This information then leads to new (possibly different) hypotheses and additional methods of inquiry.

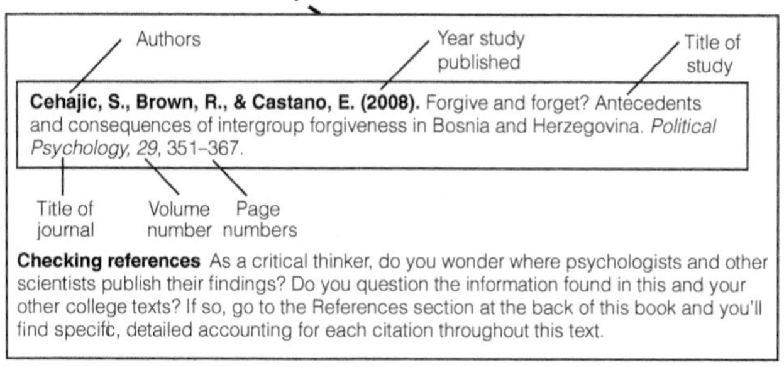

Title of study
Cehajic, S., Brown, R., & Castano, E. (2008). Forgive and forget? Antecedents and consequences of intergroup forgiveness in Bosnia and Herzegovina. *Political Psychology, 29,* 351–367.
Title of journal
Volume number

Checking references As a critical thinker, do you wonder where psychologists and other scientists publish their findings? Do you question the information found in this and your other college texts? If so, go to the References section at the back of this book and you'll find specific, detailed accounting for each citation throughout this text.

FIGURE 1.7 THE SCIENTIFIC METHOD

Scientific knowledge is constantly evolving and self-correcting through application of the scientific method. As soon as one research study is published, the cycle almost always begins again.

For Step 3, you would then most likely choose an experimental research design and solicit 100 volunteers from various classes, 50 of whom should be randomly assigned to Group 1 (Retrieval Practice) and the other 50 to Group 2 (no Retrieval Practice). After both groups study for three hours, you would present and score a 20-point quiz, followed by a statistical analysis (Step 4) to determine whether the difference in test scores between the two groups is **statistically significant**. To be statistically significant, the difference between the groups must be large enough that the result is probably not due to chance. In Step 5, you could publish your research, and then you go on to further investigate additional study techniques that might contribute to theory development on the most effective study methods, Step 6. [You'll be interested to know that research does exist on the superiority of retrieval practice on retention of material and improved exam scores (Agarwal et al., 2012; Karpicke & Smith, 2012), which is why they're emphasized in this text.]

Statistical significance A statistical statement of how likely it is that a study's result occurred merely by chance.

Meta-analysis A statistical technique for combining and analyzing data from many studies in order to determine overall trends.

Theory An organized, interrelated set of concepts that explain a phenomenon or body of data.

Note also in Figure 1.7 that the scientific method is cyclical and cumulative. Scientific progress comes from repeatedly challenging and revising existing theories and building new ones. If numerous scientists, using different procedures or participants in varied settings, can repeat, or *replicate,* a study's findings, there is increased scientific confidence in the findings. If the findings cannot be replicated, researchers look for other explanations and conduct further studies. When different studies report contradictory findings, researchers may average or combine the results of all such studies and reach conclusions about the overall weight of the evidence, a popular statistical technique called **meta-analysis**. For example, one recent meta-analysis found that a healthy diet, high-quality preschool, and interactive reading with parents can all lead to increases in children's intelligence (Protzko et al., 2013).

Q2

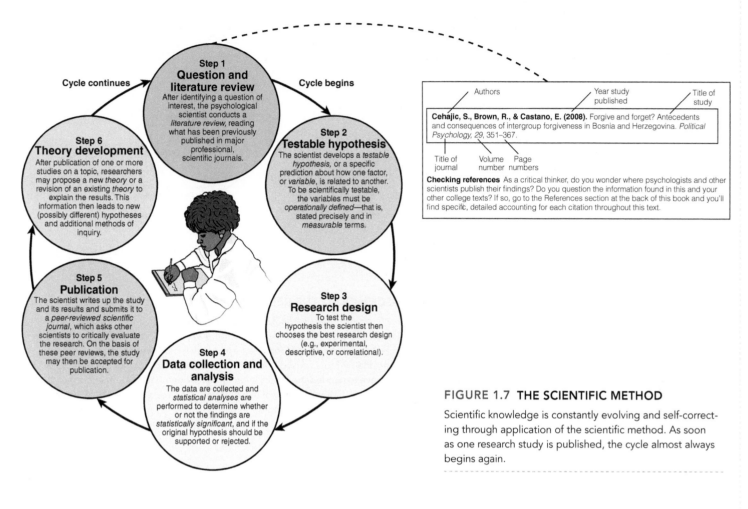

After many related findings have been collected and confirmed, scientists may generate a **theory** to explain the data through a systematic, interrelated set of

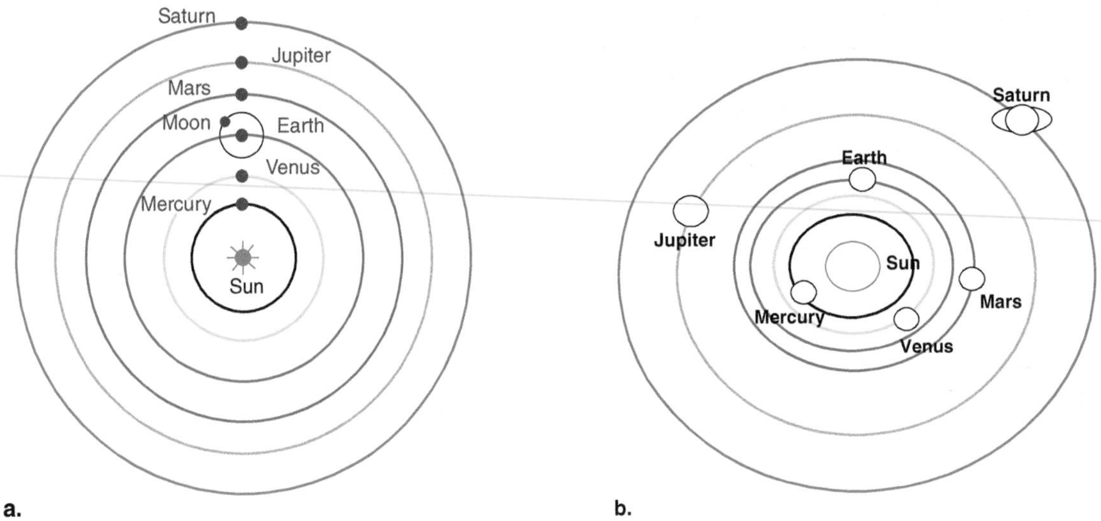

FIGURE 1.8 **OPINIONS VERSUS FACTS—SCIENCE TO THE RESCUE!**

Early experiments, conducted primarily by *Nicolaus Copernicus* (1473–1543), led to a collection of facts and the ultimate theory that the Earth was not the center of the universe (as generally assumed at the time) **(Figure a)**. Instead, it rotated around the sun with the other planets in concentric circles. Later scientists (astronomers Johannes Kepler and Tycho Brahe) built on this Copernican (heliocentric) theory with additional experiments that led to a revised theory, in which the orbits were not mere circles but rather elliptical orbits. **(Figure b)**. Today, researchers have expanded the theory even further by demonstrating that our sun is not the center of the universe, but only a part of a galaxy that in turn is only one of many billions. Can you see how these incremental changes illustrate the value of scientific theories and their self-correcting nature?

concepts. In common usage, the term *theory* is often assumed to mean something is only a hunch or someone's personal opinion. In reality, scientific theories are evidence based, rigorously tested, and self-correcting (**Figure 1.8**).

Psychology's Four Main Goals

In contrast to *pseudopsychologies*, which we discussed earlier and which rely on unsubstantiated beliefs and opinions, psychology is based on rigorous scientific methods. When conducting their research, psychologists have four major goals—to *describe*, *explain*, *predict*, and *change* behavior and mental processes:

1. **Description** Description tells what occurred. In some studies, psychologists attempt to *describe*, or name and classify, particular behaviors by making careful scientific observations. Description is usually the first step in understanding behavior. For example, if someone says, "Boys are more aggressive than girls," what does that mean? The speaker's definition of aggression may differ from yours. Science requires specificity.
2. **Explanation** An explanation tells why a behavior or mental process occurred. *Explaining* a behavior or mental process requires us to discover and understand its causes. One of the most enduring debates in science is the **nature–nurture controversy** (Gruber, 2013; Tyson et al., 2011). Are we controlled by biological and genetic factors (the nature side) or by the environment and learning (the nurture side)? As you will see throughout the text, psychology (like all other sciences) generally avoids "either or" positions and focuses instead on *interactions*. Today, almost all scientists agree that most psychological, and even physical, traits reflect an interaction between nature and nurture. For example, research suggests numerous interacting causes or explanations for aggression, including culture, learning, genes, brain damage, and high levels of testosterone (Garfield et al.; 2011; Longino, 2013; Pournaghash-Tehrani, 2011).

Nature–nurture controversy An ongoing dispute about the relative contributions of nature (heredity) and nurture (environment) in determining the development of behavior and mental processes.

3. **Prediction** Psychologists generally begin with description and explanation (answering the "whats" and "whys"). Then they move on to the higher-level goal

of *prediction*, identifying "when" and under what conditions a future behavior or mental process is likely to occur. For instance, knowing that alcohol leads to increased aggression (Ferguson, 2010; Parker & McCaffree, 2013), we can predict that more fights will erupt in places where alcohol is consumed than in places where it isn't.

4. **Change** For some people, change as a goal of psychology brings to mind evil politicians or cult leaders brainwashing unknowing victims. However, to psychologists, *change* means applying psychological knowledge to prevent unwanted outcomes or bring about desired goals. In almost all cases, change as a goal of psychology is positive. Psychologists help people improve their work environment, stop addictive behaviors, become less depressed, improve their family relationships, and so on. Furthermore, as you may know from personal experience, it is very difficult (if not impossible) to change someone against her or his will. (*Here is an old joke*: Do you know how many psychologists it takes to change a light bulb? *Answer*: None. The light bulb has to want to change.)

RETRIEVAL PRACTICE: THE SCIENCE OF PSYCHOLOGY

Self-Test

Completing this self-test and comparing your answers with those in Appendix B provides immediate feedback and helpful practice for exams. Additional interactive, self-tests are available at www.wiley.com/college/huffman.

1. If you conducted a study on areas of the brain most affected by drinking alcohol, it would be ________ research.

a. unethical
b. basic
c. pseudopsychology
d. applied

2. A(n) _____ provides a precise definition of how the variables in a study will be observed and measured.

a. meta-analysis
b. theory
c. independent observation
d. operational definition

3. The goal of ________ is to tell what occurred, whereas the goal of ________ is to tell when.

a. health psychologists; biological psychologists
b. description; prediction
c. psychologists; psychiatrists
d. pseudopsychologists; clinical psychologists

4. Label the six steps in the scientific method.

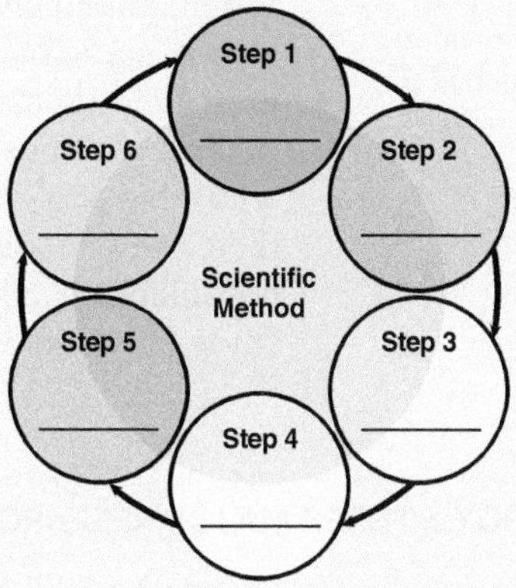

Think Critically

1. What is the difference between a scientific theory, an opinion, and a hunch?
2. Nonhuman animals are sometimes used in psychological research when it would be impractical or unethical to use human participants. What research questions might require the use of nonhuman animals?
3. Which side of the debate, nature or nurture, has had the most influence on your life?

realworldpsychology

Can diet, preschool education, and parental behavior increase a child's intelligence?

HINT: LOOK IN THE MARGIN FOR Q2

RESEARCH METHODS

LEARNING OBJECTIVES

RETRIEVAL PRACTICE While reading the upcoming sections, respond to each Learning Objective in your own words. Then compare your responses to those found at www.wiley.com/college/huffman.

1. **DESCRIBE** the four key types of descriptive research.
2. **EXPLAIN** how to interpret a correlation coefficient.
3. **IDENTIFY** the key components of experimental research.
4. **DESCRIBE** the ethical guidelines for psychological research.

Having studied the scientific method and psychology's four main goals, we can now examine how psychologists conduct their research. Psychologists generally draw on three major research methods—*descriptive*, *correlational*, and *experimental* (**Table 1.5**). Each of these approaches has advantages and disadvantages, and psychologists often use variations of all three methods to study a single problem. In fact, when multiple approaches lead to similar conclusions, scientists have an especially strong foundation for concluding that one variable does affect another in a particular way.

Descriptive Research

Descriptive research A research method in which the researcher observes and records behavior and mental processes without manipulating variables.

Naturalistic observation The process of observing and recording a research participant's behavior and mental processes in his or her natural setting, without interfering.

Almost everyone observes and describes others in an attempt to understand them, but in conducting **descriptive research**, psychologists do so systematically and scientifically. The key types of descriptive research are *naturalistic observation*, *survey/interview*, *case study*, and *archival research*.

Naturalistic Observation

When conducting **naturalistic observation**, researchers systematically observe and record participants' behavior in their natural setting, without interfering. Many settings lend themselves to naturalistic observation, from supermarkets to airports to outdoor settings. For example, Jane Goodall's classic naturalistic observations of wild chimpanzees provided invaluable insights into their everyday lives, such as their use of tools, acts of aggression, demonstrations of affection, and, sadly, even the killing of other chimps' babies (infantacide). In Chapter 5 you'll read about a study in which researchers used naturalistic observation to examine whether drivers

TABLE 1.5 PSYCHOLOGY'S THREE MAJOR RESEARCH METHODS

Method	Purpose	Advantages	Disadvantages
Descriptive (naturalistic observation, survey/interview, case study, archival research)	Observe, collect, and record data (meets psychology's goal of description)	Minimizes artificiality, makes data collection easier, allows description of behavior and mental processes as they occur	Little or no control over variables, researcher or participant biases, cannot identify cause and effect 
Correlational (statistical analyses of relationships between variables)	Identify relationships and assess how well one variable predicts another (meets psychology's goal of *prediction*)	Helps clarify relationships between variables that cannot be examined by other methods and allows prediction	Little or no control over variables, cannot identify cause and effect 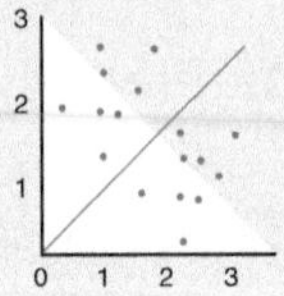
Experimental (manipulation and control of variables)	Identify cause and effect (meets psychology's goal of *explanation*)	Allows researchers to have precise control over variables, helps identify cause and effect	Ethical concerns, practical limitations, artificiality of lab conditions, uncontrolled variables may confound results, researcher and participant biases 

Note that the three methods are not mutually exclusive. Researchers may use one, two, or all three methods to explore the same topic.

talking on a cell phone were less likely to come to a complete stop at a stop sign (Strayer et al., 2011). Can you guess what they found?

The chief advantage of naturalistic observation is that researchers can obtain data about natural behavior rather than about behavior that is a reaction to an artificial experimental situation. But naturalistic observation can be difficult and time-consuming, and the lack of control by the researcher makes it difficult to conduct observations for behavior that occurs infrequently.

For a researcher who wants to observe behavior in a more controlled setting, *laboratory observation* has many of the advantages of naturalistic observation, but with greater control over the variables (**Figure 1.9**).

FIGURE 1.9 LABORATORY OBSERVATION

In this type of observation, the researcher brings participants into a specially prepared room in the laboratory, with one-way mirrors, or an inconspicuous camera, and microphones. While hidden from view, the researcher can observe school children at work, families interacting, or the like.

Survey/Interview

Psychologists use **surveys/interviews** to ask people to report their behaviors, opinions, and attitudes (Nestor & Schutt, 2012). In Chapter 6 you'll read about a study in which researchers interviewed 3- to 6-year-old girls about their preference for using game pieces depicting thinner or heavier women when playing Candy Land to measure preference for the thin ideal (Harriger et al., 2010). In Chapter 10, you'll read about the use of survey research to study how a person's first sexual experience may impact subsequent sexual relationships (Smith & Shaffer, 2013). One key advantage of this approach is that researchers can gather data from many more people than is generally possible with other research designs.

Survey/interview A research technique that questions a large sample of people to assess their behaviors and mental processes.

Unfortunately, most surveys/interviews rely on self-reported data, and not all participants are honest. As you might imagine, people are especially motivated to give less-than-truthful answers when asked about highly sensitive topics, such as infidelity, drug use, and pornography.

Case Studies

What if a researcher wants to investigate photophobia (fear of light)? In such a case, it would be difficult to find enough participants to conduct an experiment or to use surveys/interviews or naturalistic observation. For rare disorders or phenomena, researchers try to find someone who has the problem and study him or her intensively. This type of in-depth study of a single research participant, or a small group of individuals, is called a **case study** (Moore et al., 2012). In Chapter 9, we'll share a fascinating case study that examined the impact of severe neglect during childhood on language acquisition. This study obviously could not be conducted using another method, for ethical reasons, and because of the rarity of such severe deprivation.

Case study An in-depth study of a single research participant or a small group of individuals.

Archival research A descriptive research approach that studies existing data to find answers to research questions.

Archival Research

The fourth type of descriptive research is **archival research**, in which researchers study previously recorded data. For example, and as described in Chapter 14, using preexisting data from more than 50 years of Major League Baseball games, researchers revealed that more batters are deliberately hit by pitchers on hot days than on cooler days (Larrick et al., 2011). Interestingly, the new "digital democracy," based on spontaneous comments on Twitter or Facebook, may turn out to be an even better method of research than the traditional random sampling of adults. Researchers who used a massive archive of billions of stored data from Twitter found "tweet share" predicted the winner in 404 out of 435 competitive races in the U.S. House elections in 2010 (DiGrazia et al., 2013). Apparently, only the total amount of discussion—good or bad—is a very good predictor of votes.

"What I drink and what I tell the pollsters I drink are two different things."

Correlational Research

Correlational research Research that measures the degree of relationship (if any) between two or more variables in order to determine how well one variable predicts another.

Correlation coefficient A number from −1.00 to +1.00 that indicates the direction and strength of the relationship between two variables.

Data collected from descriptive research provides invaluable information on behavior and mental processes. However, when researchers are interested in examining more than one variable, they can take a further step and calculate the degree and type of relationship between the variables. As the name **correlational research** implies, when any two variables are co-related, a change in one is accompanied by a change in the other. For example, researchers in one study examined the link between happiness and age in a sample of more than 5,000 people across the United States (Sutin et al., 2013). This study revealed that, contrary to common stereotypes, happiness actually increases with age!

Q3

An important advantage of correlational studies is that they allow us to make predictions about one variable based on knowledge of another. For instance, suppose scientists notice a relationship between the use of cell phones and the number of traffic accidents, or between the hours of television viewing and performance on exams. First, they would carefully measure the two factors. Next, they would analyze their measurements using a statistical formula that gives a **correlation coefficient** (**Figure 1.10**).

FIGURE 1.10 INTERPRETING A CORRELATION COEFFICIENT

A correlation coefficient is a number from −1.00 to +1.00 that represents the direction and strength of a relationship between two variables. Understanding it is crucial to becoming an educated consumer of research.

- **Direction of the correlation** (left-hand column) The + or − sign in the correlation coefficient indicates the *direction* of the correlation, either positive or negative, which is often depicted in graphs called *scatterplots*. Each dot on these graphs represents one participant's score on both variables.
- **Strength of the correlation** (right-hand column) A correlation of +1.00 and a −1.00 magnitude both indicate the strongest possible relationship. As the number decreases and gets closer to 0.00, the relationship weakens. We interpret correlations close to zero as representing no relationship between the variables—like the "relationship" between broken mirrors and years of bad luck.

Chris Carroll/Corbis Images

Direction of the correlation

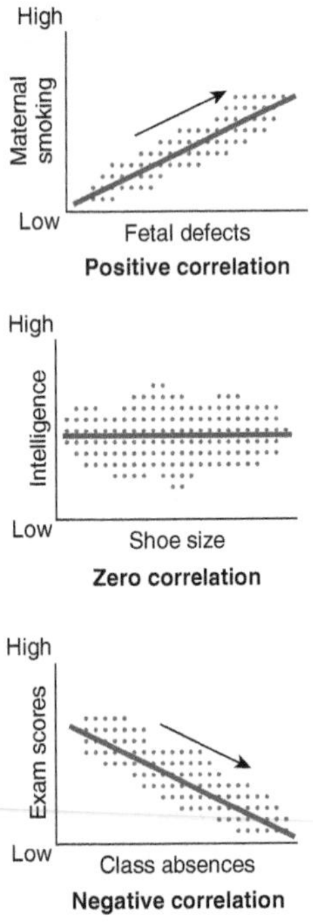

Strength of the Correlation

+1.00	Perfect positive relationship (100% of the variance)
+.80 to +.99	Very strong positive relationship (64–98% of the variance)
+.60 to +.79	Strong positive relationship (36–62% of the variance)
+.40 to +.59	Moderate positive relationship (16–35% of the variance)
+.20 to +.39	Weak positive relationship (4–15% of the variance)
0.00	No relationship (0% of the variance)
−.20 to −.39	Weak negative relationship (4–15% of the variance)
−.40 to −.59	Moderate negative relationship (16–35% of the variance)
−.60 to −.79	Strong negative relationship (36–62% of the variance)
−.80 to −.99	Very strong negative relationship (64–98% of the variance)
−1.00	Perfect negative relationship (100% of the variance)

Think Critically

Can you identify whether each of the following pairs most likely has a positive, negative, or zero correlation?

1. Health and exercise
2. Hours of TV viewing and student grades
3. Happiness and helpfulness
4. Hours of sleep and number of friends
5. Extraversion and loneliness

Answers: 1. positive, 2. negative, 3. positive, 4. zero, 5. negative

Looking closely at the right-hand side of the chart in Figure 1.10, you'll note that while the numbers in the first column (+1.00 to −1.00) describe the *strength* of the relationship between two variables, what's often overlooked is the second column, which shows the actual percentage of *variance* (or how widely individuals in a group vary). We calculate this variance by multiplying the correlation number by itself (in this example .5 × .5 = 25%). It's important to understand this because people often over-interpret popular examples such as the .5 correlation between IQ (intelligence quotient) and GPA (grade point average) or the .4 correlation between IQ and income. Now that you understand more about correlations, you can see that your GPA has only a weak relationship with your IQ (25%) and that there is an even lower relationship (16%) between your IQ and your eventual income. The good news is that many factors other than IQ explain both GPA and income—mainly hard work, motivation, and perseverance.

In addition to providing more accurate prediction, correlational studies often point to *possible* causation. For example, smoking cigarettes and drinking alcohol while pregnant are highly correlated with birth defects (Agopian et al., 2013; Pruett et al., 2013). This strong correlation led to a large number of animal experiments and other research methods that added supportive evidence, which has helped convince pregnant mothers to avoid these drugs while pregnant—thus preventing many infant birth defects.

In other cases, it's important to emphasize that a correlation between two variables does not *necessarily* mean that one variable *causes* another (**Figure 1.11**). When people read media reports about correlations between stress and cancer or between a full moon and increased crime, they often mistakenly infer that stress causes cancer or that a full moon causes crime. In fact, a wide variety of possible third factors may cause someone to have greater susceptibility to both the correlated phenomena. This point is so important and critical to becoming an educated consumer of scientific research that we offer another example (**Figure 1.12**).

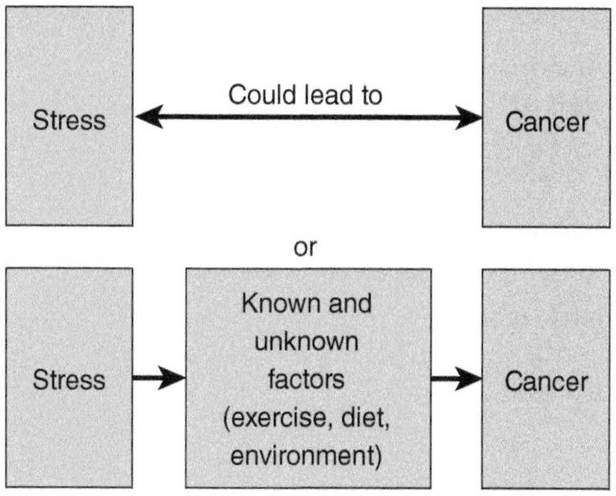

FIGURE 1.11 **CORRELATION VERSUS CAUSATION**

Research has found a strong correlation between stress and cancer (Chapter 3). However, this correlation does not tell us whether stress causes cancer, whether cancer causes stress, or whether other known and unknown factors, such as smoking, drinking, or pesticides could contribute to both stress and cancer. Can you think of a way to study the effects of stress on cancer that is not correlational?

FIGURE 1.12 **REVISITING CORRELATION VERSUS CAUSATION**

Ice cream consumption and drowning are highly correlated. Does this mean that eating ice cream causes people to drown? Of course not! A third factor, such as high temperatures, increases both ice cream consumption and participation in water-based activities.

Norbert Schwerin/
The Image Works

Chris Lowe/Photolibrary/
Getty Images

Experimental Research

As you've just seen, correlational studies are important because they reveal *associations* between variables. However, to determine *causation* (what causes what), we need **experimental research**. In Chapter 4, you'll discover how experiments were used to test the influence of pregnant women's food choices on taste preferences in their infants (Mennella et al., 2001). Similarly, in Chapter 13, you'll learn how experiments can help test the effectiveness of a particular psychotherapy approach at helping a spider-phobic person become comfortable enough to touch a tarantula (Hauner et al., 2012).

Experimental research A carefully controlled scientific procedure that involves the manipulation of variables to determine cause and effect.

Independent variable (IV) The variable that is manipulated to determine its causal effect on the dependent variable; also called the treatment variable.

Dependent variable (DV) The variable that is observed and measured for change; the factor that is affected by (or dependent on) the independent variable.

Experimental group The group that is manipulated (i.e., receives treatment) in an experiment.

Control group The group that is not manipulated (i.e., receives no treatment) during an experiment.

Experiments are considered the "gold standard" for scientific research because only through an experiment can researchers experimentally isolate and then examine a single factor's effect on a particular behavior (Goodwin, 2011). To accomplish this type of isolation and examination, an experiment has five critical components: a hypothesis (discussed earlier), an **independent variable (IV)**, a **dependent variable (DV)**, one or more **experimental group(s)**, and a **control group** (**Figure 1.13**).

How can we prevent bias and errors when creating and setting up our experiments? Sample bias may occur when a particular group of participants does not accurately reflect the composition of the larger population from which they are drawn. For example, critics suggest that much psychological literature is biased because it primarily uses college students as subjects. A way to minimize sample bias is to randomly select participants who constitute a representative sample of the entire population of interest.

Sample bias A bias that may occur when research participants are unrepresentative of the larger population.

Random assignment A research technique that involves using chance to assign participants to experimental or control conditions, thus minimizing the possibility of biases or preexisting differences in the group.

Confounding variable A stimulus, other than the variable an experimenter inadvertently introduces into a research setting, that may affect the outcome of the study and lead to erroneous conclusions.

Even if we avoid **sample bias** with representative sampling, we can still introduce bias into the experiment when we assign participates to the experimental or control group. As you can see in Step 2 of Figure 1.13, assigning participants to either group using a chance or random system, such as a coin toss, guaranties that each participant is equally likely to be assigned to any particular group, a technique called random assignment. **Random assignment** also helps control for extraneous, **confounding variables** (such as time of day, lighting conditions, and room temperature), which must be held constant across experimental and control groups so that they do not affect the different groups' results (**Figure 1.14**).

©terex/iStockphoto

realworldpsychology Do Aesthetics Affect Eating Behavior?

To answer this question, a group of researchers modified the environment in one section of a fast food restaurant by dimming the lights and adding relaxing music, plants, candles, and tablecloths. They then randomly assigned customers to sit in either the original section of the restaurant or this new section (Wansink & Van Ittersum, 2012). All participants freely ordered whatever food they preferred, but those in the more relaxing part of the restaurant took longer to eat their meal and ate 18% fewer calories.

Can you see how the *random assignment* of the customers controlled for any potential *confounding variables*? All participants freely entered the same restaurant, and each individual was equally likely to be assigned to either section in the restaurant. Thanks to these controls, the researchers can legitimately conclude that the *independent variable* (IV) (relaxing versus standard restaurant condition) caused the change in the *dependent variables* (DVs) (time spent eating and number of calories consumed).

In addition to the controls mentioned above, a good scientific experiment has other invaluable techniques for protecting against potential sources of error from

FIGURE 1.13 **EXPERIMENTAL RESEARCH DESIGN**

When designing an experiment, researchers must follow certain steps to ensure that their results are scientifically meaningful. In this example, researchers want to test whether watching violent television shows increases aggression in children.

1. The experimenter begins by identifying the hypothesis.
2. In order to avoid sample bias, the experimenter randomly assigns subjects to two different groups.
3. Having at least two groups allows the performance of one group to be compared to that of another.
4. The experimental group watches violent programs while the control group watches nonviolent programs. The amount of violent TV watched is the independent variable (IV).
5. The experimenter then counts how many times the child hits, kicks, or punches a large plastic doll. The number of aggressive acts is the dependent variable (DV).
6. The experimenter relates differences in aggressive behavior (DV) to the amount of violent television watched (IV).

To help you remember the independent and dependent variables (IV and DV), carefully study these drawings and create a visual picture in your own mind of how:

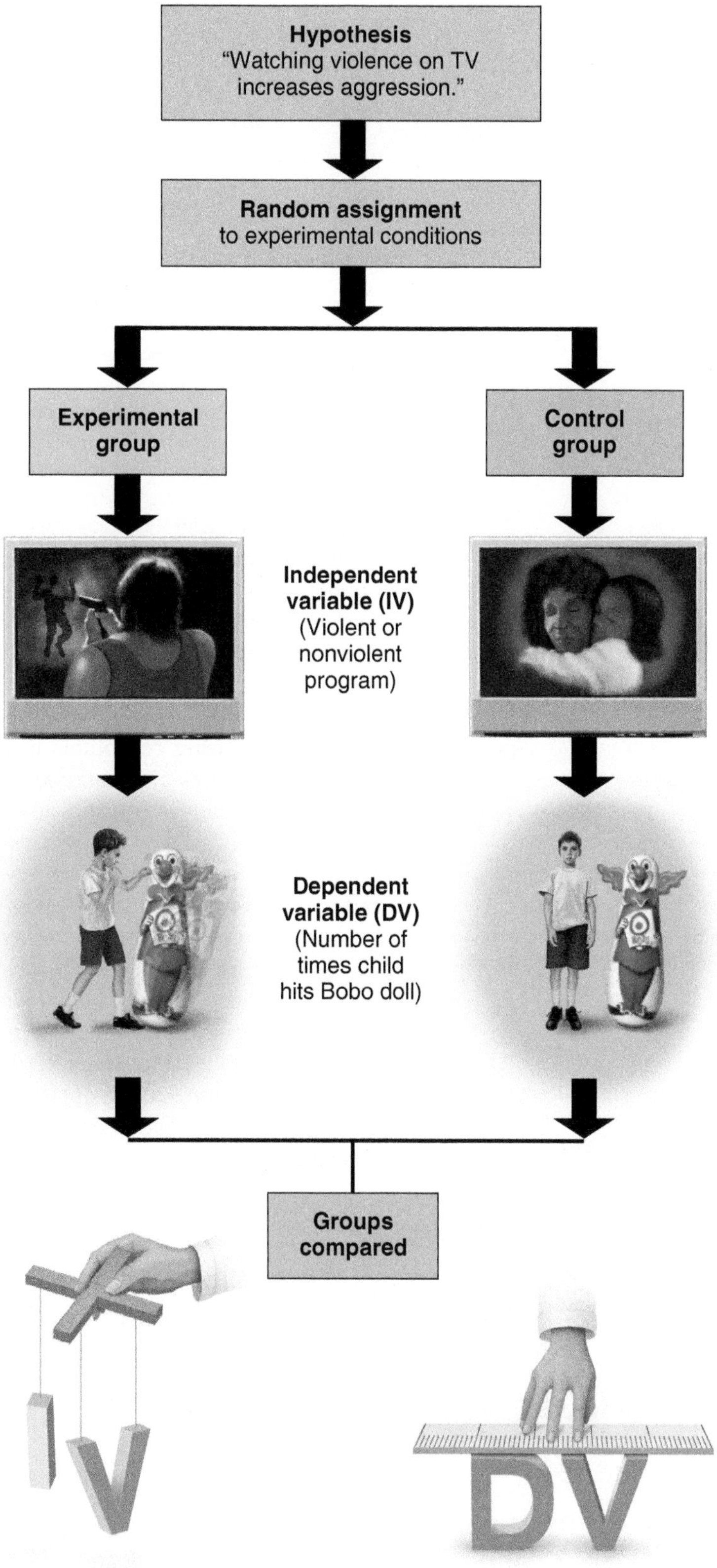

The experimenter "manipulates" the IV to determine its causal effect on the DV.

The experimenter "measures" the DV, which "depends" on the IV.

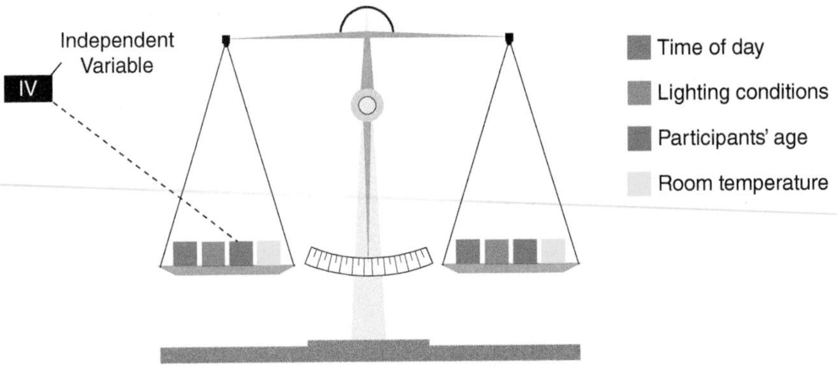

FIGURE 1.14 CONTROLLING FOR CONFOUNDING VARIABLES

Recognizing that certain, outside variables may affect their experiment, researchers strive for balance between the experimental and control groups, making sure the variables are the same for both. Once balance is achieved, and the independent variable (IV) is added to the experimental group, the experimenters check to see if the scale's balance is significantly disrupted. If so, they can then say that the IV *caused* the change. However, if the IV is not "heavy" enough to make a significant difference, then the experiment "failed," and experimenters go back to further refine their approach—or start over.

both the researcher and the participants. For example, if experimenters' beliefs and expectations are not controlled for, they can affect participants' responses, producing flawed results. Imagine what might happen if an experimenter breathed a sigh of relief when a participant gave a response that supported the researcher's hypothesis. One way to prevent such **experimenter bias** from destroying the validity of participants' responses is to establish objective methods for collecting and recording data, such as using computers to present stimuli and record responses.

Experimenters also can skew their results if they assume that behaviors typical in their own culture are typical in all cultures—a bias known as **ethnocentrism**. One way to avoid this problem is to have researchers from two cultures each conduct the same study twice, once with their own culture and once with at least one other culture. This kind of *cross-cultural sampling* isolates group differences in behavior that stem from researchers' ethnocentrism.

Just as researchers can inadvertently introduce error (the experimenter bias), participants also can produce a similar error, called **participant bias**. For example, research measuring accuracy of reports of alcohol consumption demonstrates that heavy drinkers tend to under-report how much alcohol they are consuming (Northcote & Livingston, 2011). In this case, participants may try to present themselves in a good light—called the *social desirability response*—or deliberately attempt to mislead the researcher. Q4

Experimenter bias Bias that occurs when a researcher influences research results in the expected direction.

Ethnocentrism The belief that one's culture is typical of all cultures; also, viewing one's own ethnic group (or culture) as central and "correct" and judging others according to this standard.

Participant bias Bias that can occur when experimental conditions influence the participant's behavior or mental processes.

Single-blind study An experiment where only the researcher, and not the participants, knows who is in either the experimental or control group.

Runzelkorn/Shutterstock

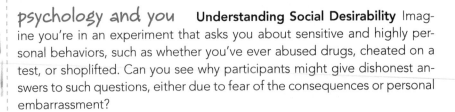

psychology and you **Understanding Social Desirability** Imagine you're in an experiment that asks you about sensitive and highly personal behaviors, such as whether you've ever abused drugs, cheated on a test, or shoplifted. Can you see why participants might give dishonest answers to such questions, either due to fear of the consequences or personal embarrassment?

Double-blind study An experimental technique in which both the researcher and the participants are unaware of (blind to) who is in the experimental or control groups.

Placebo An inactive substance or fake treatment used as a control technique, usually in drug research, or given by a medical practitioner to a patient.

Researchers attempt to control for this type of *participant bias* by offering anonymous participation and other guarantees of privacy and confidentiality. **Single-blind studies**, **double-blind studies**, and **placebos** offer additional safeguards (**Figure 1.15**).

Finally, one of the most effective (and controversial) ways of preventing participant bias is to temporarily deceive participants about the true nature of the research project. For example, in studies examining when and how people help others,

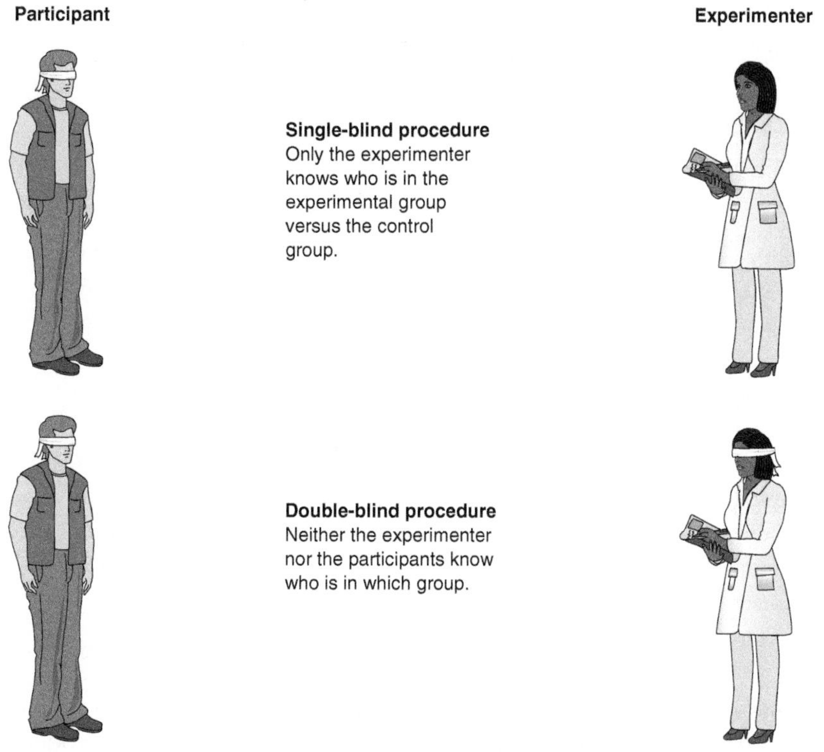

Participant
Experimenter
Single-blind procedure
Only the experimenter knows who is in the experimental group versus the control group.
Double-blind procedure
Neither the experimenter nor the participants know who is in which group.

FIGURE 1.15 A SINGLE- OR DOUBLE-BLIND EXPERIMENTAL DESIGN

To test a new drug, researchers administering the experimental drug and/or the participants taking the drug must be unaware of (or "blind" to) who is receiving a *placebo* (a fake pill or injection) and who is receiving the drug itself. Placebos are necessary because researchers know that the mere act of taking a pill or receiving an injection can change a participant's condition or responses, the so-called "placebo effect" (Barbui et al., 2011; Brown, 2013).

participants may not be told the true goal of the study because they might try to present themselves as more helpful than they actually would be in real life.

Recognizing that we've offered a large number of research problems and safeguards associated with the experimental method, we've gathered them all into **Figure 1.16**. Be sure to study it carefully. In addition, note that the problems and safeguards connected with descriptive and correlational research described earlier also apply to experimental research.

Before closing this section on research methods, we want to clarify that although experiments are considered the "gold standard" in research, descriptive and correlational methods also offer unique information that can help us live safer and more productive lives. For example, psychologists have repeatedly found high correlations between stress and disease (Chapter 3) and between cocaine use and heart attacks (Chapter 5). Can you see how we could never logistically or morally create human

FIGURE 1.16 POTENTIAL RESEARCH PROBLEMS AND SOLUTIONS

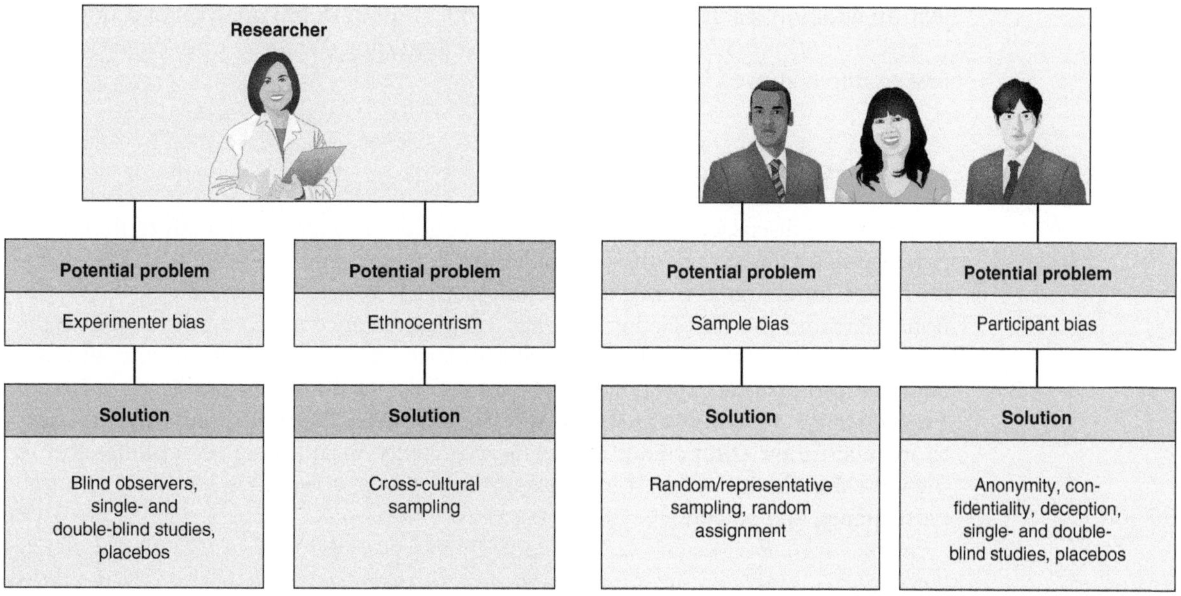

PSYCHSCIENCE

POLITICS AND DATING RELATIONSHIPS

Are you more likely to date a person if his or her political preference (conservative, moderate, liberal, or none) matches your own? To scientifically test this question, participants were brought into a research lab and shown profiles of fictional people, which were made to look like those on popular online dating websites and manipulated in several ways, including religion, education, and political preference (Huber & Malhotra, 2012).

The researchers were somewhat surprised that compatibility in political views significantly affected how much participants stated they would like to date someone. But they were even more surprised to find that participants also rated the fictional person as more physically attractive when they believed they shared similar political beliefs!

To see whether this artificial laboratory study would accurately predict behavior in a real-life situation, the researchers then conducted a second study, using data from an existing dating website called *OkCupid*. Given that online messages sent from one person and replied to by another generally indicate a shared interest in dating, the researchers reported that shared political views increased interest by 9.5%.

Why is this research important? *Similarity* is one of the best predictors of long-term relationships (Chapter 14). But what happens if we restrict our dating (and friendship) partners to those we already agree with? Aren't we more likely to fall victim to *groupthink* (Chapter 14) and *confirmation bias* (Chapter 8)?

RESEARCH CHALLENGE

1. Based on the information provided, did these two studies (Huber & Malhotra, 2012) use descriptive, correlational, and/or experimental research? (Tip: Be sure to look for two separate answers for the two different studies.)
2. If you chose:
    - descriptive research, is this a naturalistic observation, survey/interview, case study, or archival research?
    - correlational research, is this a positive, negative, or zero correlation?
    - experimental research, label the IV, DV, experimental group(s), and control group.

>> CHECK YOUR ANSWERS IN APPENDIX B.

NOTE: The information provided in this study is admittedly limited, but the level of detail is similar to what is presented in most textbooks and public reports of research findings. Answering these questions, and then comparing your answers to those in the Appendix, will help you become a better critical thinker and consumer of scientific research.

experiments that would prove true cause and effect in these situations? Instead, we often have to rely on the accumulating weight of the evidence from nonexperimental studies and nonhuman animal experiments. If you'd like additional information about research methods and statistical analyses, see Appendix A at the back of this text. In addition, each chapter of this text offers an in-depth analysis of a hot topic in research (*Psych Science*), along with a self-grading *Research Challenge* (see the first example above).

Ethical Guidelines

So far, we've discussed how psychologists conduct research and analyze their data. Now we need to examine the general ethics that guide their research. The two largest professional organizations of psychologists, the American Psychological Association (APA) and the Association for Psychological Science (APS), both recognize the importance of maintaining high ethical standards in research, therapy, and all other areas of professional psychology. The preamble to the APA's publication *Ethical Principles of Psychologists and Code of Conduct* (2002, 2010) requires psychologists to maintain their competence, to retain objectivity in applying their skills, and to preserve the dignity and best interests of their clients, colleagues, students, research participants, and society.

Respecting the Rights of Human Participants

The APA and APS have developed rigorous guidelines regulating research with human participants, including:

- **Informed consent** Researchers must obtain an **informed consent** agreement from all participants *before* initiating an experiment. Participants are made aware of the nature of the study, what to expect, and significant factors that might influence their willingness to participate, including all physical risks, discomfort, and possibly unpleasant emotional experiences.
- **Voluntary participation** Participants must be told that they're free to decline to participate or to withdraw from the research at any time.
- **Restricted use of deception and debriefing** If participants knew the true purpose behind certain studies, they might not respond naturally. In one of the most famous studies in social psychology, researchers ordered participants to give electric shocks to another participant (who was really a confederate of the researcher and was not actually receiving any shocks). Although this study was testing participants' willingness to follow orders, they were told that the study was examining the use of shocks to assist with learning. Obviously in this case, participants' behavior could not be accurately measured if they were told the real focus of the study (Milgram, 1963). Therefore, researchers occasionally need to temporarily deceive participants about the actual reason for the experiment.

  However, when deception is necessary, important guidelines and restrictions still apply. One of the most important is **debriefing**, which is conducted once the data collection has been completed. The researchers provide a full explanation of the research, including its design and purpose, any deceptions used, and then clarify participants' misconceptions, questions, or concerns.
- **Confidentiality** All information acquired about people during a study must be kept private and not published in such a way that an individual's rights to privacy are compromised.

Informed consent A participant's agreement to take part in a study after being told what to expect.

Debriefing A discussion procedure conducted at the end of an experiment or study; participants are informed of the study's design and purpose, possible misconceptions are clarified, questions answered, and explanations are provided for any possible deception.

Respecting the Rights of Nonhuman Animals

Although they are used in only 7 to 8% of psychological research (APA, 2009; ILAR, 2009; MORI, 2005), nonhuman animals—mostly rats and mice—have made significant contributions to almost every area of psychology. Without nonhuman animals in *medical research*, how would we test new drugs, surgical procedures, and methods for relieving pain? *Psychological research* with nonhuman animals has led to significant advances in virtually every area of psychology—the brain and nervous system, health and stress, sensation and perception, sleep, learning, memory, motivation, and emotion.

Nonhuman animal research has also produced significant gains for some animal populations, such as the development of more natural environments for zoo animals and more successful breeding techniques for endangered species.

Despite the advantages, using nonhuman animals in psychological research remains controversial (Akins & Panicker, 2012; Baker & Serdikoff, 2013). While debate continues about ethical issues in such research, psychologists take great care in handling research animals. Researchers also actively search for new and better ways to protect the animals (Guidelines for Ethical Conduct, 2008; Pope & Vasquez, 2011).

Respecting the Rights of Psychotherapy Clients

Professional organizations such as the APA and APS, as well as academic institutions and state and local agencies, all may require that therapists, like researchers, maintain the highest ethical standards. Therapists must also uphold their clients' trust. All personal information and therapy records must be kept confidential, and records can be made available only to authorized persons and with the client's permission. However, therapists are legally required to break confidentiality if a client threatens violence to him- or herself or to others, if a client is suspected of abusing a child or an elderly person, and in other limited situations (Fisher, 2013; Kress et al., 2013; Tyson et al., 2011).

RETRIEVAL PRACTICE: RESEARCH METHODS

Self-Test

Completing this self-test and comparing your answers with those in Appendix B provides immediate feedback and helpful practice for exams. Additional interactive, self-tests are available at www.wiley.com/college/huffman.

1. In a case study, a researcher is most likely to ________.

a. interview many research subjects who have a single problem or disorder
b. conduct an in-depth study of a single research participant
c. choose and investigate a single topic
d. use any of these options, which describe different types of case studies

2. When a researcher observes or measures two or more variables to find relationships between them, without directly manipulating them or implying a causal relationship, he or she is conducting ________.

a. experimental research
b. a correlational study
c. non-causal metrics
d. a meta-analysis

3. If researchers gave participants varying amounts of a new memory drug and then gave them a story to read and measured their scores on a quiz, the ________ would be the IV, and the ________ would be the DV.

a. response to the drug; amount of the drug
b. experimental group; control group
c. amount of the drug; quiz scores
d. researcher variables; extraneous variables

4. A participant's agreement to take part in a study after being told what to expect is known as ________.

a. unethical pre-briefing
b. an experimental contract
c. a participant contract
d. informed consent

5. Debriefing is ________.

a. interviewing subjects after a study to find out what they were thinking during their participation
b. explaining the design and purpose of the study when it is over and revealing any deception used
c. disclosing potential physical and emotional risks and the nature of the study before it begins
d. interviewing subjects after a study to determine whether any deception used was effective in preventing them from learning the true purpose of the study

Think Critically

1 What is meant by the axiom "correlation is not causation"?

2 Cigarette companies have suggested that there is no scientific evidence that smoking causes lung cancer. How would you refute this claim?

realworldpsychology

Are older people happier than younger people?

Why do heavy drinkers misreport their alcohol use?

HINT: LOOK IN THE MARGIN FOR Q3 AND Q4

STRATEGIES FOR STUDENT SUCCESS

LEARNING OBJECTIVES

RETRIEVAL PRACTICE While reading the upcoming sections, respond to each Learning Objective in your own words. Then compare your responses to those found at www.wiley.com/college/huffman.

1 **DESCRIBE** the steps you can take to improve your study habits.
2 **IDENTIFY** how you might improve your current time management habits.

In this section, you will find several well-researched study strategies and techniques guaranteed to make you a more successful college student. They are grouped together under *study habits* and *time management.*

Study Habits

Do you sometimes read a paragraph many times yet remember nothing from it? Here are four ways to successfully read (and remember) information in this and most other texts:

1. **Familiarization** The first step is to familiarize yourself with the general text so that you can take full advantage of its contents. In *Real World Psychology*, the Preface, Table of Contents, Glossary (both running through the text of each chapter and at the end of each chapter), References, Name Index, and Subject Index will help give you a bird's-eye view of the rest of the text. In addition, as you scan the book to familiarize yourself with its contents, you should also take note of the many tables, figures, photographs, and special feature boxes, all of which will enhance your understanding of the subject.
2. **Active Reading** The next step is to make a conscious decision to actively read and learn the material. Reading a text is *not* like reading a novel or fun articles on the Internet! You must tell your brain to slow down, focus on details, and save the material for future recall.
3. **Distributed practice** Spreading your study sessions out over time (distributed practice) is far more efficient than waiting until right before an exam and cramming in all the information at once (massed practice) (Chapter 7). If you were a basketball player, you wouldn't wait until the night before a big play-off game to practice. The same is true for exam preparation. Keep in mind that distributed practice is NOT simply rereading the chapter several times over a few days. As mentioned above, you need to actively focus and study what you're reading. Q5
4. **Practice test taking** For most people, taking tests is NOT one of our favorite activities. However, it's important to note that research has clearly shown that practice test taking and distributed practice are two of the most efficient ways to study and learn (Carpenter, 2012; Dunlosky et al., 2013). Just as you need to repeatedly practice throwing baskets to become a good basketball player, you need to repeatedly practice your test taking skills. The easiest way to practice this skill (and to improve your grades) is by completing the Self-Tests and Think Critically Questions found in each chapter of this book. You also can easily access the free flashcards and other forms of self-testing on the student companion website for this text at www.wiley.com/college/huffman.

For more tips on improving your study habits, see *Psychology and You.*

psychology and you **The Importance of Focus** Think about a time when you were trying to study for an important test, but you continued to find your mind wandering. Perhaps you started thinking about what you were going to eat for dinner, or what weekend plans you hoped to make. As you might imagine, this type of distracted studying isn't very effective! This book will give you strategies for active learning that will help you not only in your psychology class but in all your other classes!

©Zastavkin/iStockphoto

SQ4R method A study technique based on six steps: Survey, Question, Read, Recite, Review, and wRite.

One of the best ways to read actively is to use the **SQ4R method**, which was developed by Francis Robinson (1970). The initials stand for six steps in effective reading: **S**urvey, **Q**uestion, **R**ead, **R**ecite, **R**eview, and w**R**ite. As you might have guessed, *Real World Psychology* was designed to incorporate each of these steps (**Figure 1.17**).

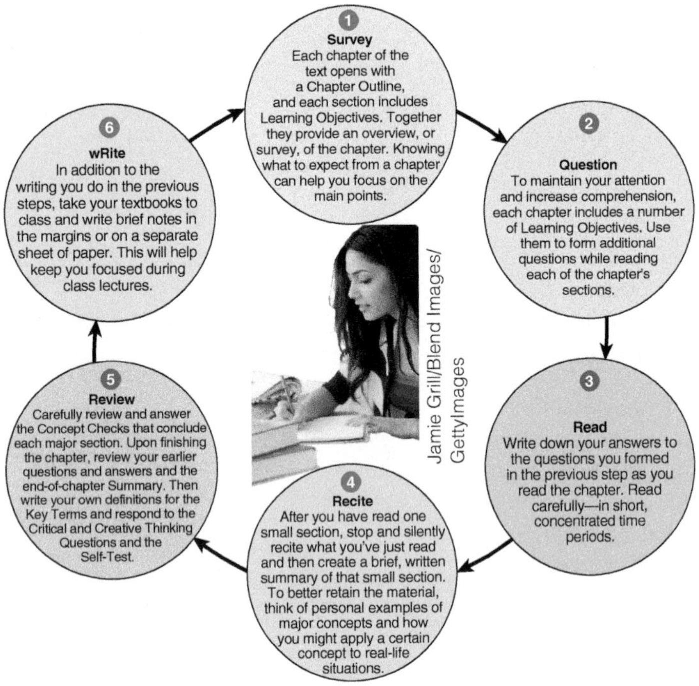
1
Survey
Each chapter of the text opens with a Chapter Outline, and each section includes Learning Objectives. Together they provide an overview, or survey, of the chapter. Knowing what to expect from a chapter can help you focus on the main points.
2
Question
To maintain your attention and increase comprehension, each chapter includes a number of Learning Objectives. Use them to form additional questions while reading each of the chapter's sections.
3
Read
Write down your answers to the questions you formed in the previous step as you read the chapter. Read carefully—in short, concentrated time periods.
4
Recite
After you have read one small section, stop and silently recite what you've just read and then create a brief, written summary of that small section. To better retain the material, think of personal examples of major concepts and how you might apply a certain concept to real-life situations.
5
Review
Carefully review and answer the Concept Checks that conclude each major section. Upon finishing the chapter, review your earlier questions and answers and the end-of-chapter Summary. Then write your own definitions for the Key Terms and respond to the Critical and Creative Thinking Questions and the Self-Test.
6
wRite
In addition to the writing you do in the previous steps, take your textbooks to class and write brief notes in the margins or on a separate sheet of paper. This will help keep you focused during class lectures.
Jamie Grill/Blend Images/
GettyImages

FIGURE 1.17 USING THE SQ4R METHOD

Follow these steps to improve your reading efficiency.

Time Management

If you find that you can't always strike a good balance between work, study, and social activities or that you aren't always good at budgeting your time, here are five basic time-management strategies:

- **Establish a baseline.** Before attempting any changes, simply record your day-to-day activities for one to two weeks. You may be surprised at how you spend your time.
- **Set up a realistic schedule.** Make a daily and weekly "to do" list, including all required activities, basic maintenance tasks (like laundry, cooking, child care, and eating), and a reasonable amount of down time. Then create a daily schedule of activities that includes time for each of these. To make permanent time-management changes, shape your behavior, starting with small changes and building on them.
- **Reward yourself.** Give yourself immediate, tangible rewards for sticking with your daily schedule.
- **Maximize your time.** To increase your efficiency, begin by paying close attention to the amount time you spend on true, focused studying versus the time you waste worrying, complaining, and/or fiddling around getting ready to study ("fretting and prepping"). Also be alert for hidden "time opportunities"—spare moments that normally go to waste that you might instead use productively.

psychology and you **Improving Your Grade** Here are five additional strategies for grade improvement and test taking that can further improve your success as a student:

- **Avoid highlighting and rereading** Marking with a yellow highlighter, or underlining potentially important portions of material, as well as rereading text material after initial reading, are common techniques students use while studying. Unfortunately, they are a waste of time! Research clearly shows that they are among the LEAST effective of all the major study techniques (Dunlosky et al., 2013). As previously discussed, you need to actively focus on your reading and these techniques encourage passive reading.
- **Take notes** While reading and listening to classroom lectures, ask yourself, "What is the main idea?" Write down key ideas and supporting details and examples. Effective note taking depends on active reading and active listening. Also, pay attention to the amount of pages and lecture time your text or instructors spend on various topics. It's generally a good indication of what is considered important for you to know.

©Chris Schmidt/iStockphoto

- **Improve your general test-taking skills** Expect a bit of stress but don't panic. Pace yourself but don't rush. Focus on what you know. Skip over questions when you don't know the answers, and then go back if time allows. On multiple-choice exams, carefully read each question and all the alternative answers before responding. Answer all questions and make sure you have recorded your answers correctly.
- **Overlearn** Many people tend to study new material just to the point where they can recite the information, but they do not attempt to understand it more deeply. For best results, however, you should overlearn. In other words, be sure to fully understand how key terms and concepts are related to one another and also be able to generate examples other than the ones in the text. In addition, you should repeatedly review the material (by visualizing the phenomena that are described and explained in the text and by rehearsing what you have learned) until the information is firmly locked in place. Overlearning is particularly important if you suffer from test anxiety.
- **Take study skills courses** Improve your reading speed and comprehension and your word-processing/typing skills by taking additional courses designed to develop these specific abilities. Also, don't overlook important human resources. Your instructors, roommates, classmates, friends, and family members often provide useful tips and encouragement.

Think Critically

1. What factors might prevent you from reading test questions carefully and responding accurately?
2. How could a friend or roommate help you improve your grades on tests?

RETRIEVAL PRACTICE: STRATEGIES FOR STUDENT SUCCESS

Self-Test

Completing this self-test and comparing your answers with those in Appendix B provides immediate feedback and helpful practice for exams. Additional interactive, self-tests are available at www.wiley.com/college/huffman.

1. List the six steps in the SQ4R method.

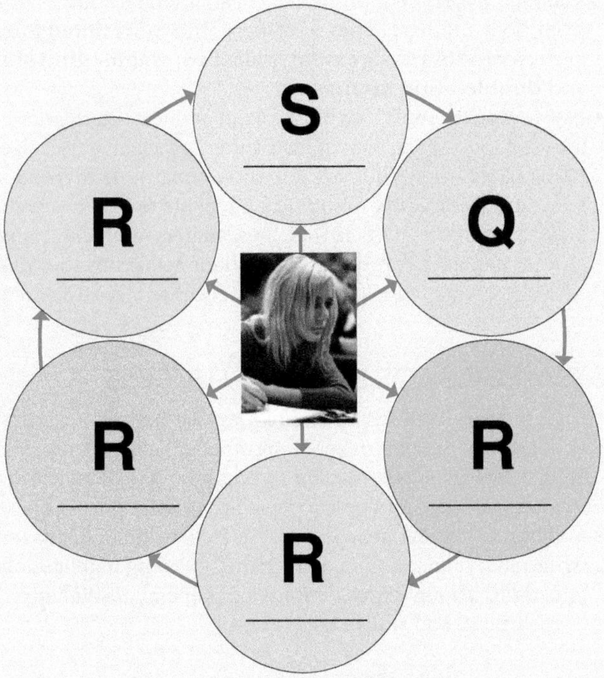

© Chris Schmidt/iStockphoto

2. One of the clearest findings in psychology is that ______ practice is a much more efficient way to study and learn than ______ practice.

a. spaced (distributed); massed
b. active; passive
c. applied; basic
d. none of these options

3. Research suggests that ______ might be two of the most important keys to improving grades.

a. highlighting and rereading
b. personal control and better time management
c. active studying and the SQ4R method
d. distributed practice and practice testing

4. ______ is particularly important if you suffer from test anxiety.

a. Overlearning
b. Hyper-soma control
c. Active studying
d. Passive listening

Think Critically

1 Identify how you might improve your current time management.

2 What do you think prevents you or the people you know from fully employing the strategies for student success presented in this chapter?

realworldpsychology

How do spreading your study sessions and practice testing improve test scores?

HINT: LOOK IN THE MARGIN FOR Q5

Summary

1 INTRODUCING PSYCHOLOGY 4

- **Psychology** is the scientific study of *behavior* and *mental processes.* The discipline places high value on *empirical evidence* and **critical thinking**. *Pseudopsychologies,* such as belief in psychic powers, are not based on scientific evidence.
- Wilhelm Wundt, considered the father of psychology, and his followers, including Edward Titchener, were interested in studying conscious experience. Their approach, *structuralism,* sought to identify the basic structures of mental life through introspection.
- The *functionalism* school, led by William James, studied the way the mind functions to enable humans and other animals to adapt to their environment.
- The **psychoanalytic perspective**, founded by Sigmund Freud, emphasized the influence of the unconscious mind, which lies outside personal awareness.
- Contemporary psychology reflects the ideas of seven major perspectives: **psychodynamic**, **behavioral**, **humanistic**, **cognitive**, **biological**, **evolutionary**, and **sociocultural**. Most contemporary psychologists embrace a unifying perspective known as the **biopsychosocial model**.
- Despite early societal limitations, women and minorities have made important contributions to psychology. Pioneers include Margaret Floy Washburn, Mary Calkins, Francis Cecil Sumner, and Kenneth and Mamie Clark.
- Psychologists work as therapists, researchers, teachers, and consultants, in a wide range of settings.

2 THE SCIENCE OF PSYCHOLOGY 13

- **Basic research** is aimed at advancing general scientific understanding, whereas **applied research** works to address real world problems.
- Most scientific investigations consist of six basic steps, collectively known as the **scientific method**. Scientific progress comes from repeatedly challenging and revising existing **theories** and building new ones.
- Psychology's four basic goals are to *describe, explain, predict,* and *change* behavior and mental processes through the use of scientific methods. One of the most enduring debates in science is the **nature–nurture controversy**.

3 RESEARCH METHODS 18

- **Descriptive research** systematically observes and records behavior and mental processes without manipulating variables. The four major types of descriptive research are **naturalistic observation**, **survey/interview**, **case study**, and **archival research**.
- **Correlational research** measures the relationship between two variables. Researchers analyze their results using a **correlation coefficient**. Correlations can be positive or negative. A correlation between two variables does not necessarily mean that one causes the other.
- **Experimental research** manipulates and controls variables to determine cause and effect. An experiment has five critical components: **hypothesis, independent** and **dependent variables** and **experimental** and **control groups**. A good scientific experiment protects against potential sources of error from both the researcher and the participants through means such as **random assignment, placebos**, **single-blind studies** and **double-blind studies.**
- Psychologists must maintain high ethical standards. This includes respecting the rights of therapy clients and research participants (both human and nonhuman). **Informed consent** and **debriefing** are critical elements of any research that includes human participants. Researchers and clinicians are held professionally responsible for their actions by the APA and APS, their research institutions, and local and state agencies.

4 STRATEGIES FOR STUDENT SUCCESS 29

- Several well-documented techniques will help you understand and absorb written material most completely. They include familiarization, active reading through the **SQ4R method**, distributed practice, and practice testing.
- Additional techniques include effective time management (while studying and during an exam), avoiding highlighting and rereading, taking notes, improving general test-taking skills, overlearning, and study skills courses.

applyingrealworldpsychology

We began this chapter with five intriguing Real World Psychology questions, and you were asked to revisit these questions at the end of each section. Questions like these have an important and lasting impact on all of our lives. See if you can answer these additional critical thinking questions related to real world examples.

Jonathan Selig/Getty Images

1. Nonhuman animals, like the mice in this photo, are sometimes used in psychological research when it would be impractical or unethical to use human participants. Do you believe nonhuman animal research is ethical? Why or why not?
2. What research questions might require the use of nonhuman animals? How would you ensure the proper treatment of these animals?
3. On p. 22, we discussed a potential experimental design to test whether watching violent TV might increase aggression in children. Assuming that we did find a significant increase, can you think of reasons the findings might not generalize to real world situations?
4. You may have heard that dog owners are healthier than cat owners, which leads some to believe that getting a dog would improve their health. Given this chapter's repeated warning that "correlation does not prove causation," can you think of an alternative explanation for why dog owners might be healthier?
5. People often confuse critical thinking with simply being critical and argumentative. How would you explain the true meaning and value of critical thinking?
6. How does psychology's emphasis on the scientific method contribute to critical thinking?

Key Terms

RETRIEVAL PRACTICE Write a definition for each term before turning back to the referenced page to check your answer.

- applied research 13
- archival research 19
- basic research 13
- behavioral perspective 6
- biological perspective 8
- biopsychosocial model 9
- case study 19
- cognitive perspective 8
- confounding variable 22
- control group 22
- correlational research 20
- correlation coefficient 20
- critical thinking 4
- debriefing 27
- dependent variable (DV) 22
- descriptive research 18
- double-blind study 24
- ethnocentrism 24
- evolutionary perspective 8
- experimental group 22
- experimental research 22
- experimenter bias 24
- humanistic perspective 8
- hypothesis 14
- independent variable (IV) 22
- informed consent 27
- meta-analysis 15
- naturalistic observation 18
- nature–nurture controversy 16
- operational definition 14
- participant bias 24
- placebo 24
- positive psychology 8
- psychoanalytic perspective 6
- psychodynamic perspective 6
- psychology 4
- random assignment 22
- sample bias 22
- scientific method 14
- single-blind study 24
- sociocultural perspective 9
- SQ4R method 30
- statistical significance 15
- survey/interview 19
- theory 15

chaptertwo

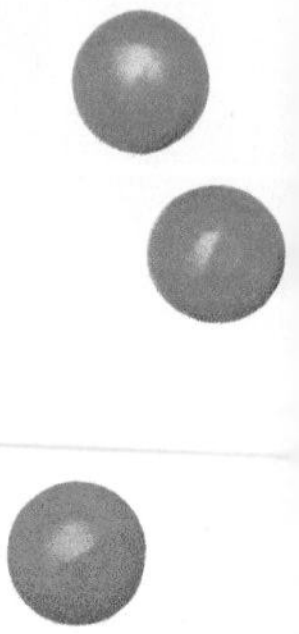

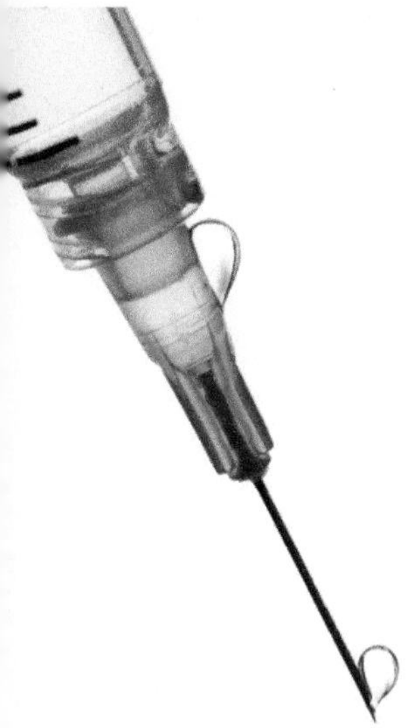

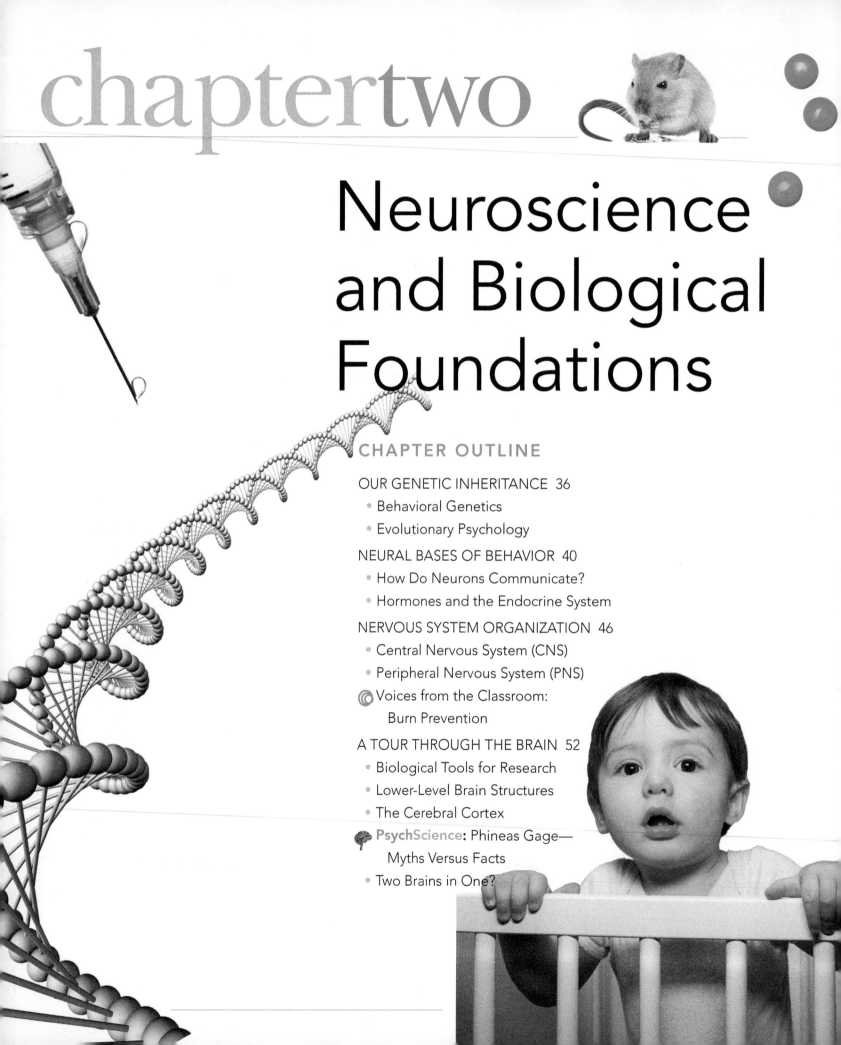

Neuroscience and Biological Foundations

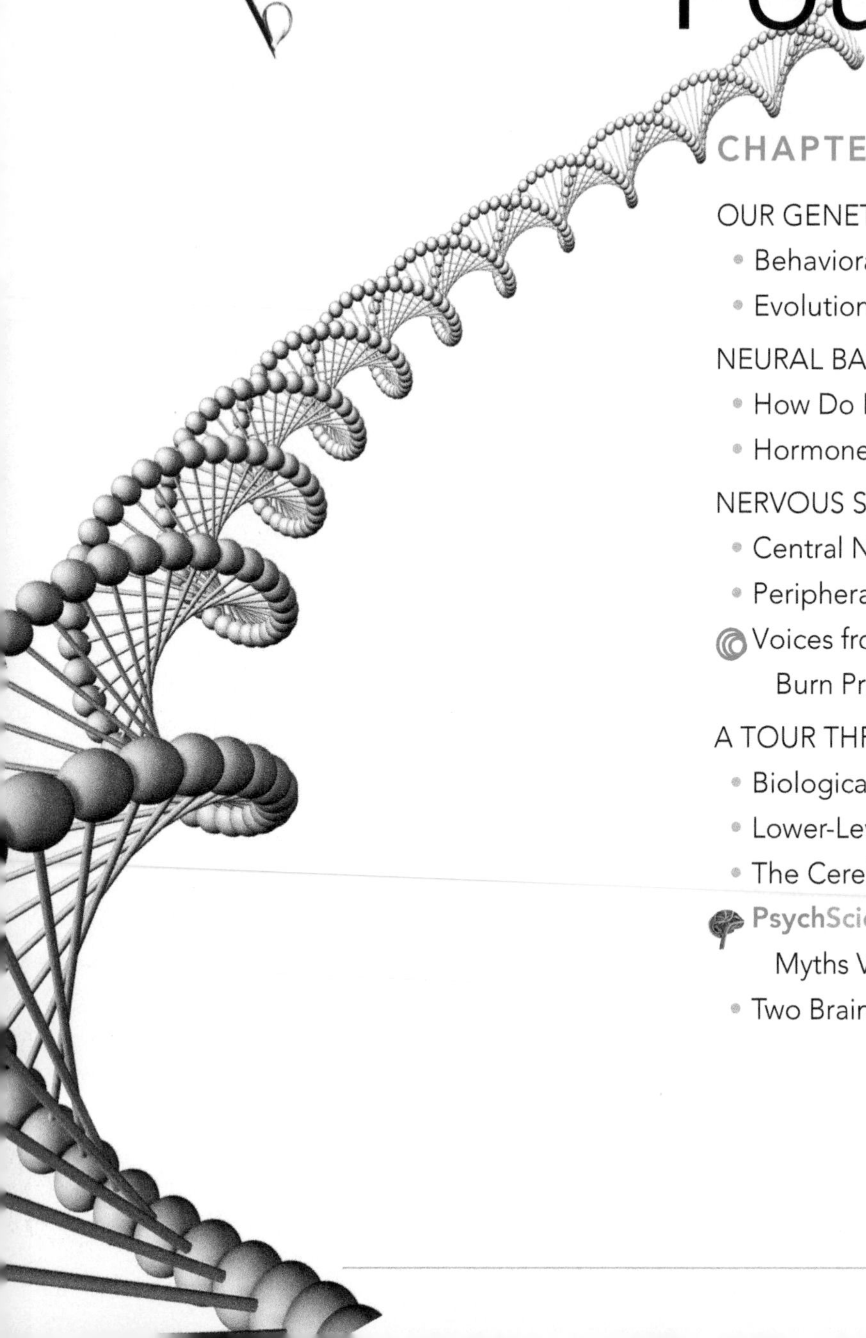

CHAPTER OUTLINE

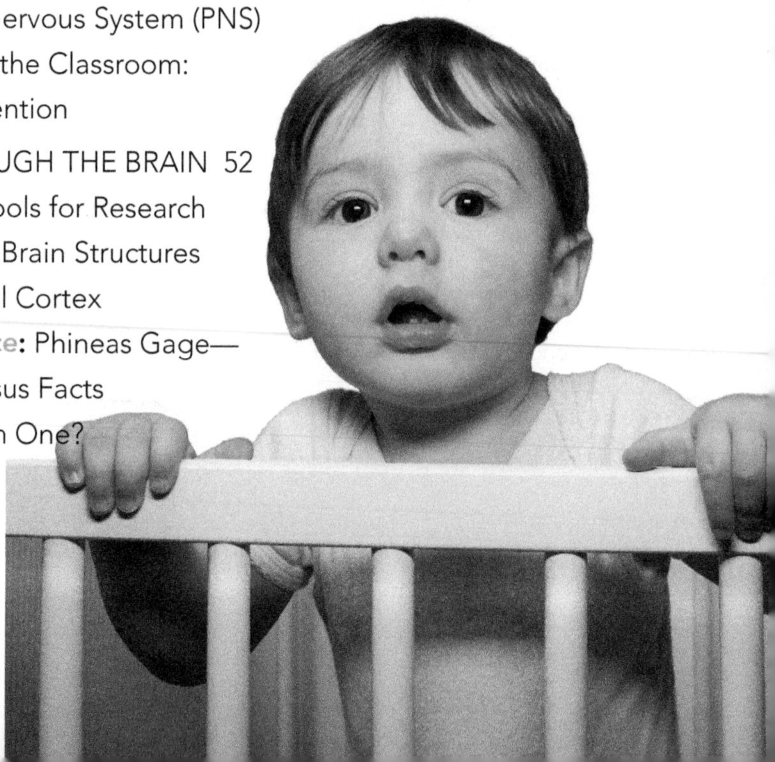

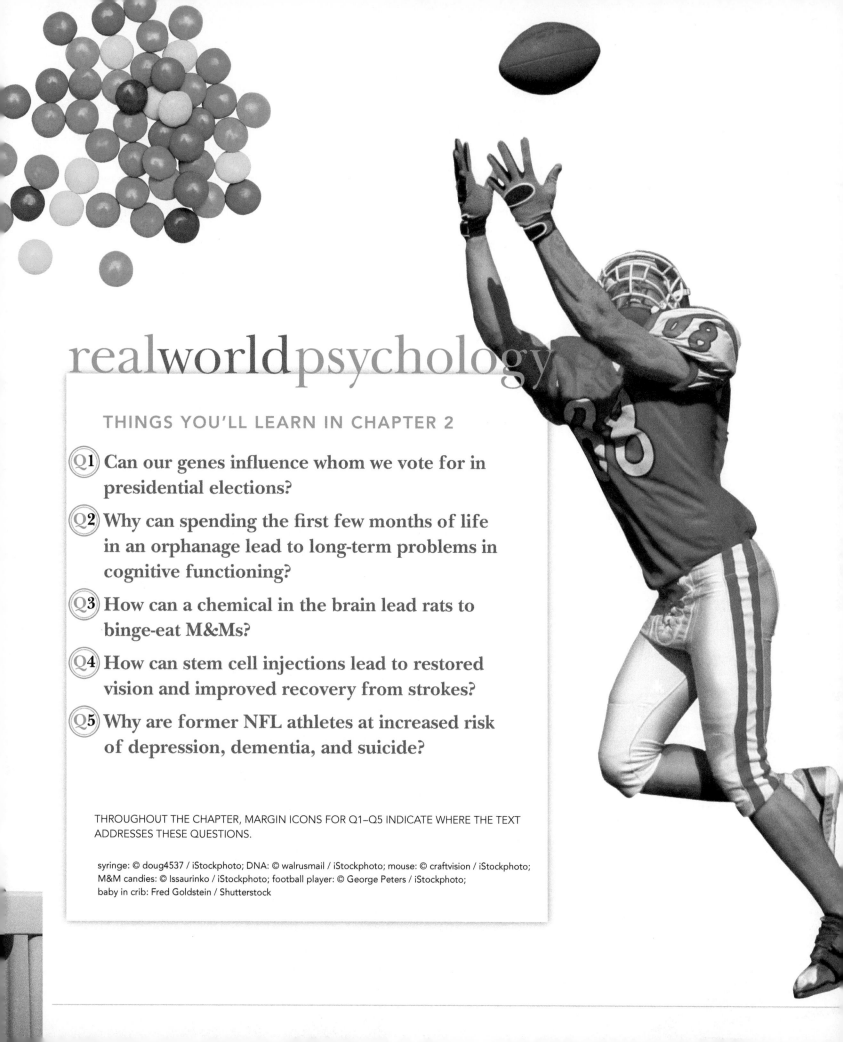

realworldpsychology

THINGS YOU'LL LEARN IN CHAPTER 2

Q1 **Can our genes influence whom we vote for in presidential elections?**

Q2 **Why can spending the first few months of life in an orphanage lead to long-term problems in cognitive functioning?**

Q3 **How can a chemical in the brain lead rats to binge-eat M&Ms?**

Q4 **How can stem cell injections lead to restored vision and improved recovery from strokes?**

Q5 **Why are former NFL athletes at increased risk of depression, dementia, and suicide?**

THROUGHOUT THE CHAPTER, MARGIN ICONS FOR Q1–Q5 INDICATE WHERE THE TEXT ADDRESSES THESE QUESTIONS.

chapteroverview

The brain is the last and grandest biological frontier, the most complex thing we have yet discovered in our universe. It contains hundreds of billions of cells interlinked through trillions of connections. The brain boggles the mind.

—James Watson
(Nobel Prize Winner)

Ancient cultures, including the Egyptian, Indian, and Chinese, believed the heart was the center of all thoughts and emotions. Today we know that the brain and the rest of the nervous system are the power behind our psychological life and much of our physical being. This chapter introduces you to the important and exciting field of *neuroscience* and *biopsychology*, the scientific study of the *biology* of behavior and mental processes, while also providing a foundation for understanding several fascinating discoveries and essential biological processes discussed throughout the text.

OUR GENETIC INHERITANCE

LEARNING OBJECTIVES

RETRIEVAL PRACTICE While reading the upcoming sections, respond to each Learning Objective in your own words. Then compare your responses with those found at www.wiley.com/college/huffman.

1 **DESCRIBE** how genetic material passes from one generation to the next.
2 **OUTLINE** the approaches scientists take to explore human genetic inheritance.
3 **EXPLAIN** the process of natural selection.

Behavioral genetics The study of the relative effects of heredity and the environment on behavior and mental processes.

Evolutionary psychology The branch of psychology that studies the application of the principles of evolution to explain behavior and mental processes.

Gene A segment of DNA (deoxyribonucleic acid) that occupies a specific place on a particular chromosome and carries the code for hereditary transmission.

Millions of years of evolution have contributed to what we are today. Our ancestors foraged for food, fought for survival, and passed on traits that were selected and transmitted down through the generations. How do these transmitted traits affect us today? For answers, psychologists often turn to **behavioral genetics**, the study of how heredity and environment affect us, and **evolutionary psychology**, the application of the principles of evolution to explain behavior and mental processes.

Behavioral Genetics

Genes are the most important and basic building blocks of our biological inheritance (Barnes, 2013) (**Figure 2.1**). Each of our human characteristics and behaviors is

FIGURE 2.1 HEREDITARY CODE

The genes we inherit from our biological parents help determine many of our physical traits (like height and hair color) and also are possible determinants of numerous behaviors (such as aggression, sensation-seeking, and sociability).

A Conception
At the moment of conception, a father's sperm and a mother's egg each contribute 23 chromosomes, for a total of 46.

B Cell nucleus
Each cell in the human body (except red blood cells) contains a nucleus.

C Chromosomes
Each cell nucleus contains 46 chromosomes, which are threadlike molecules of DNA (deoxyribonucleic acid).

D Genes
Each DNA molecule contains thousands of genes, which are the most basic units of heredity.

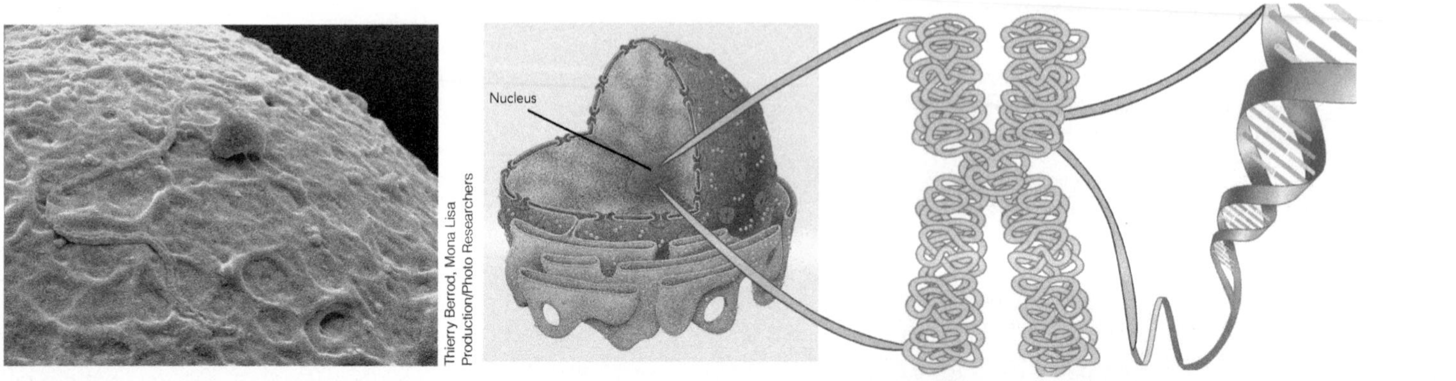

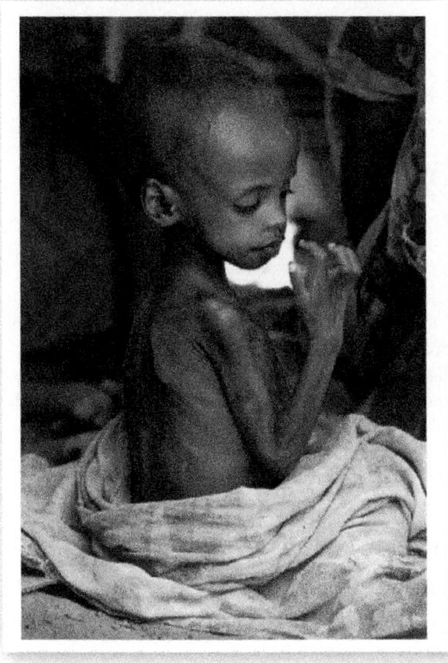

Per-Anders Pettersson/Getty Images

FIGURE 2.2 GENE–ENVIRONMENT INTERACTION

Children who are malnourished may not reach their full potential genetic height or maximum intelligence. Can you see how environmental factors interact with genetic factors to influence many traits?

related to the presence or absence of particular genes that control the transmission of traits. In some traits, such as blood type, a single pair of genes (one from each parent) determines what characteristics we will possess. When two genes for a given trait conflict, the outcome depends on whether the gene is *dominant* or *recessive*. A dominant gene reveals its trait whenever the gene is present. In contrast, the gene for a recessive trait is normally expressed only if the other gene in the pair is also recessive.

It was once assumed that characteristics such as eye color, hair color, and height were the result of either one dominant gene or two paired recessive genes. But modern geneticists believe that these characteristics are *polygenic*, meaning they are controlled by multiple genes. Most polygenic traits like height and intelligence also are affected by environmental and social factors (**Figure 2.2**). Fortunately, most serious genetic disorders are not transmitted through a dominant gene. Can you guess why?

Why do scientists study human inheritance? As you'll see throughout this text, researchers are finding increasing evidence that our personality traits, cognitive abilities, behavioral habits, sexual orientation, and psychological disorders are all determined, at least in part, by genetic factors. For example, genetic or chromosomal abnormalities have been found to be important factors in Alzheimer's disease and schizophrenia, as well as in diabetes, heart disease, and cancer (**Figure 2.3**). Surprisingly, researchers have even discovered that our genes can influence which particular political party we identify with, as well as our political views, including beliefs about the death penalty, unemployment, and abortion (Hatemi & McDermott, 2012). Q1

In addition to studying how genes affect us as individuals, behavioral geneticists also examine how and when they're transmitted from one generation to the next.

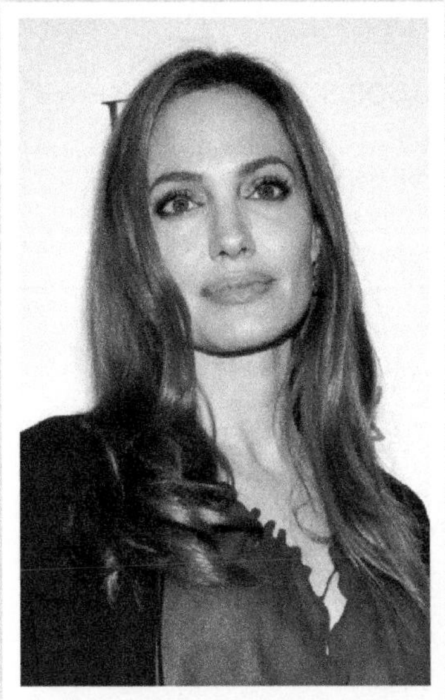

Daniel Zuchnik/Getty Images

FIGURE 2.3 SAVING HER OWN LIFE?

realworldpsychology

In May 2013, actor Angelina Jolie announced that she had undergone a preventive double mastectomy (the removal of both of her breasts) to reduce her personal risk of developing breast cancer. She made this decision after learning that she carries a mutation in her BRAC1 gene, which leads to a 65% lifetime risk of developing breast cancer.

FIGURE 2.4 **IDENTICAL VERSUS FRATERNAL TWINS**

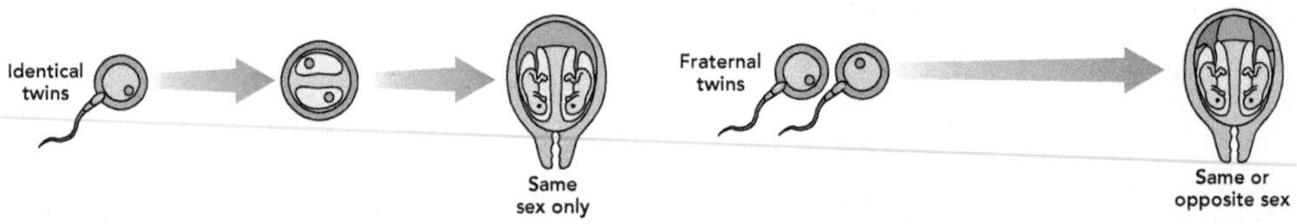

Ⓐ Identical (*monozygotic*—one egg) twins share 100% of the same genes because they develop from a single egg fertilized by a single sperm. They also share the same placenta and have the same sex and same genetic makeup.

Ⓑ Fraternal (*dizygotic*—two eggs) twins share, on average, 50% of their genes because they are formed when two separate sperm fertilize two separate eggs. Although they share the same general environment within the womb, they are no more genetically similar than nontwin siblings. They're simply nine-month "womb mates."

Can you see why this makes the study of identical and fraternal twins a top priority? Identical twins share all their genes, whereas fraternal twins share only about half of their genes (**Figure 2.4**). Also, both sets of twins share the same parents and develop in relatively the same environment, thereby providing an invaluable "natural experiment." If heredity influences a trait or behavior to some degree, identical twins should be more alike than fraternal twins. For example, studies of intelligence show that identical twins have more similar intelligence test scores than fraternal twins (Plomin & Spinath, 2004; Trzaskowski et al., 2013), which suggests a genetic influence on intelligence.

In addition to twin studies, researchers also study families with biological and adopted children to determine whether adopted children are more like their adoptive parents (who controlled the home environment) or their biological parents (who controlled the genetic inheritance) (**Figure 2.5**). Research using these family studies has found that many traits and mental disorders, such as intelligence, sociability, and depression, are most strongly influenced by genetics (Davies et al., 2011; Kang et al., 2012; Stein et al., 2012).

Findings from research studies like these have allowed behavioral geneticists to estimate the **heritability** of various traits, which is the percentage of variation in a population attributable to heredity. If genetics contributed nothing to a trait, it would have a heritability estimate of 0%. If a trait is completely due to genetics, it would have a heritability estimate of 100%.

Heritability A statistical formula that provides a percentage of variation in a population attributable to genetic factors rather than to differences in the environment.

Before going on, it's very important to emphasize that *heritability estimates do not apply to individuals*. Height has one of the highest heritability estimates—around 90% (Plomin, 1990). But, it's impossible to predict with certainty an individual's height from a heritability estimate (**Figure 2.6**). Furthermore, *heritability does not trump environment*. For example, if you inherited a gene known to increase your chances of developing emphysema from smoking, you should not overreact. Smoking is an environmental factor, and if you never smoke you have little or no chance of developing emphysema.

FIGURE 2.5 **ADOPTION STUDIES**

If adopted children are more like their biological family in some trait, then genetic factors probably had the greater influence. Conversely, if adopted children resemble their adopted family, even though they do not share similar genes, then environmental factors may predominate.

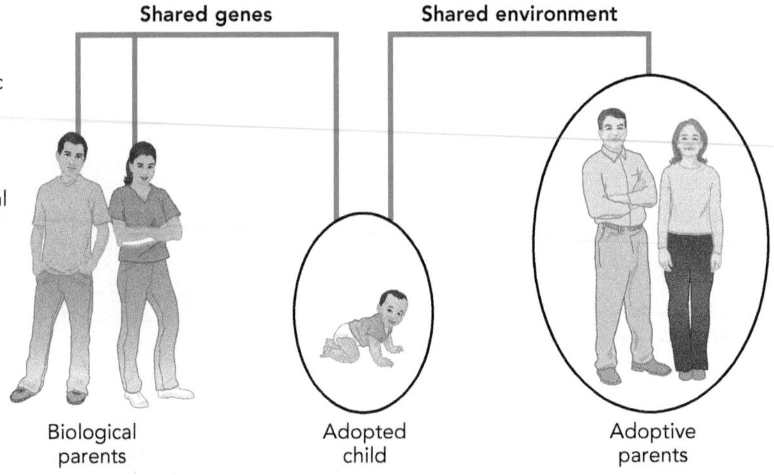

As we've seen, behavioral genetics studies help explain the role of heredity (nature) and the environment (nurture) in our individual behavior. To increase our understanding of genetic dispositions, we also need to look at universal behaviors transmitted from our evolutionary past.

Evolutionary Psychology

Evolutionary psychology suggests that many behavioral commonalities, from eating to fighting with our enemies, emerged and remain in human populations because they helped our ancestors (and ourselves) survive (Buss, 2011; Durrant & Ellis, 2013). This perspective stems from the writings of Charles Darwin (1859), who suggested that natural forces select traits that aid an organism's survival. This process of **natural selection** occurs when a particular genetic trait gives an organism a reproductive advantage over others. Because of natural selection, the fastest, strongest, smartest, or otherwise most fit organisms are most likely to live long enough to reproduce and thereby pass on their genes to the next generation.

Genetic mutations also help explain behavior. Everyone likely carries at least one gene that has mutated, or changed from the original. Very rarely, a mutated gene will be significant enough to change an individual's behavior. It might cause someone to be more or less social, risk taking, shy, or careful. If the gene then gives the person a reproductive advantage, he or she will be more likely to pass on the gene to future generations. However, this mutation doesn't guarantee long-term survival. Even a well-adapted population can perish if its environment changes too rapidly.

FIGURE 2.6 HEIGHT AND HERITABILITY

Imagine a small village, in which the average height of all adult women was 4 feet 5 inches. The heritability of height in this group could be quite high; women with short parents would be on average much shorter than women of tall parents. So how would you explain the difference in height between the parent and child in this photo?

Image Source/Getty Images

Natural selection The process by which heritable traits that increase an organism's chances of survival or reproduction are favored over less beneficial traits.

RETRIEVAL PRACTICE: OUR GENETIC INHERITANCE

Self-Test

Completing this self-test and comparing your answers with those in Appendix B provides immediate feedback and helpful practice for exams. Additional interactive, self-tests are available at www.wiley.com/college/huffman.

1. Behavioral genetics is the study of the relative effects of _____.

a. behavior and genetics on survival
b. heredity and environment on behavior and mental processes
c. genetics on natural selection
d. natural selection and adaptation

2. Evolutionary psychology studies the _____.

a. ways in which humans adapted their environment to survive and evolve
b. effects of genetics on humankind's behavior over the millennia
c. methods humans used to evolve and change behavior
d. application of evolutionary principles to explain behavior and mental processes.

3. _____ is a measure of the degree to which a characteristic is related to genetic versus environmental factors.

a. Heritability
b. Inheritance
c. Biological ratio
d. Genome biostatistics

4. The term _____ refers to a process by which heritable traits that increase an organism's chances of survival or reproduction are favored over less beneficial traits.

a. natural selection
b. devolution
c. survival of the fastest
d. reproductive success

Think Critically

1 Imagine that scientists were able to identify specific genes linked to serious criminal behavior. If it were possible to remove or redesign these genes, would you be in favor of this type of gene manipulation? Why or why not?

2 Using an evolutionary perspective, can you explain why people are more likely to help family members than to help strangers?

realworldpsychology

Can our genes influence whom we vote for in presidential elections?

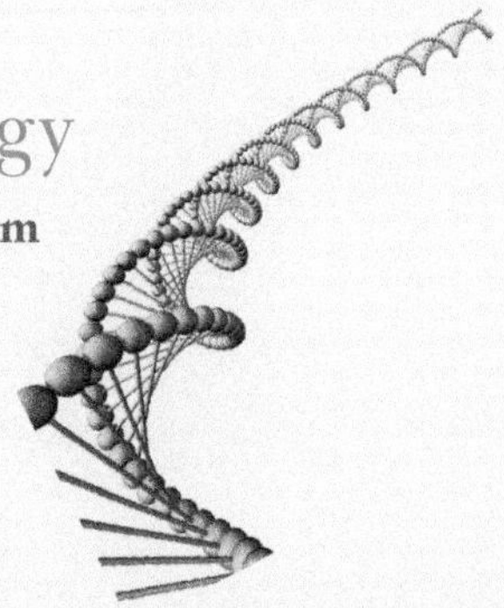

HINT: LOOK IN THE MARGIN FOR Q1

NEURAL BASES OF BEHAVIOR

LEARNING OBJECTIVES

RETRIEVAL PRACTICE While reading the upcoming sections, respond to each Learning Objective in your own words. Then compare your responses with those found at www.wiley.com/college/huffman.

1 **IDENTIFY** the key role and features of neurons.
2 **EXPLAIN** how neurons communicate throughout the body.
3 **DESCRIBE** the role of hormones and the endocrine system.

Neuron The basic building block (nerve cell) of the nervous system, responsible for receiving, processing, and transmitting electrochemical information.

Glial cells The cells that provide structural, nutritional, and other support for neurons, as well as communication within the nervous system; also called glia or neuroglia.

Dendrites The branching fibers of neurons that receive neural impulses from other neurons and convey impulses toward the cell body.

Cell body The part of a neuron that contains the cell nucleus and other structures that help the neuron carry out its functions; also known as the soma.

Axon A long, tube-like structure that conveys impulses away from a neuron's cell body toward other neurons or to muscles or glands.

Action potential A neural impulse, or brief electrical charge, that carries information along the axon of a neuron; movement is generated when positively charged ions move in and out through channels in the axon's membrane.

Our brain and the rest of our nervous system essentially consist of **neurons**. Each neuron is a tiny information-processing system with thousands of connections for receiving and sending electrochemical signals to other neurons. Each human body may have as many as 1 *trillion* neurons. (Note that a *neuron* is an individual cell, whereas a nerve is a group of neurons.)

Neurons are held in place and supported by **glial cells**, which make up about 90% of the brain's total cells. They also supply nutrients and oxygen, perform cleanup tasks, and insulate one neuron from another so that their neural messages are not scrambled. In addition, they play a direct role in nervous system communication (Burnstock, 2013; Thyssen et al., 2013; Weaver, 2012). However, the "star" of the communication show is still the neuron.

No two neurons are alike, but most share three basic features: **dendrites**, the **cell body**, and an **axon** (**Figure 2.7**). To remember how information travels through the neuron, think of these three in reverse alphabetical order: *D*endrite → *C*ell *B*ody → *A*xon.

How Do Neurons Communicate?

A neuron's basic function is to transmit information throughout the nervous system. Neurons "speak" in a type of electrical and chemical language. The process of neural communication begins within the neuron itself, when the dendrites and cell body receive electrical messages. These messages move along the axon in the form of a neural impulse, or **action potential** (**Figure 2.8**).

FIGURE 2.7 **KEY PARTS OF A NEURON**

Red arrows in the figure on the left indicate direction of information flow: dendrites → cell body → axon → terminal buttons of axon.

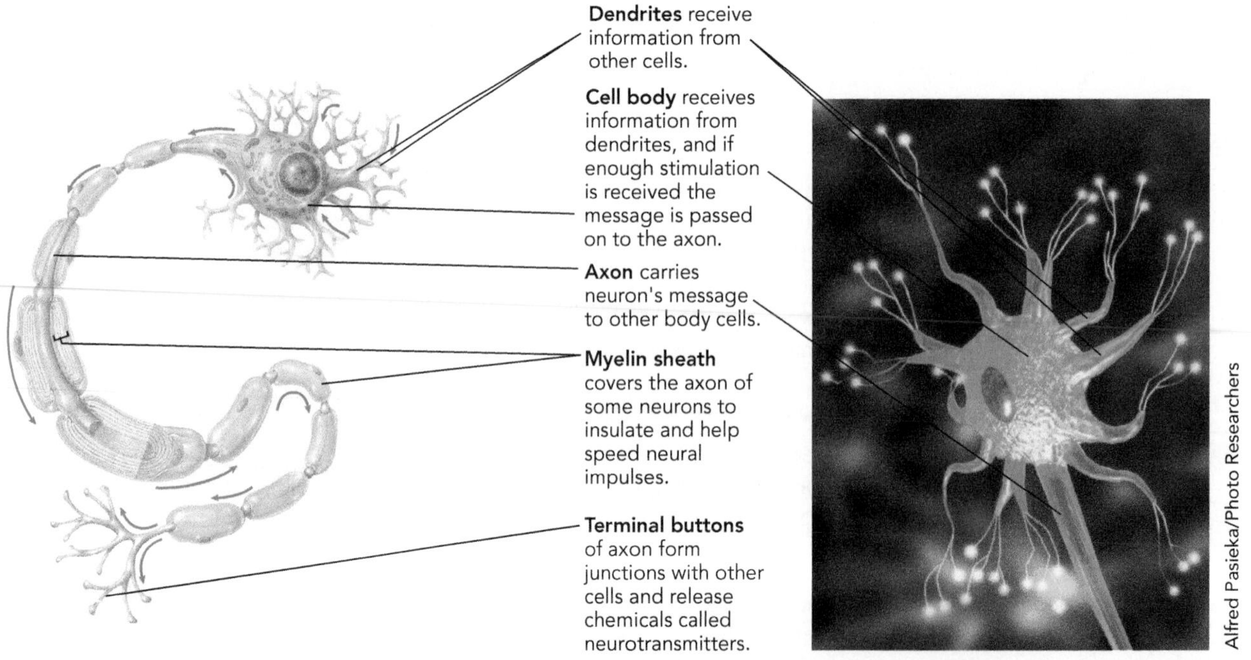
Dendrites receive information from other cells.
Cell body receives information from dendrites, and if enough stimulation is received the message is passed on to the axon.
Axon carries neuron's message to other body cells.
Myelin sheath covers the axon of some neurons to insulate and help speed neural impulses.
Terminal buttons of axon form junctions with other cells and release chemicals called neurotransmitters.
Alfred Pasieka/Photo Researchers

FIGURE 2.8 COMMUNICATION *WITHIN* THE NEURON

The process of neural communications begins within the neuron itself, when the dendrites and cell body receive information and conduct it toward the axon. From there, the information moves down the entire length of the axon via a brief traveling electrical charge called an *action potential*, which can be described in the following three steps:

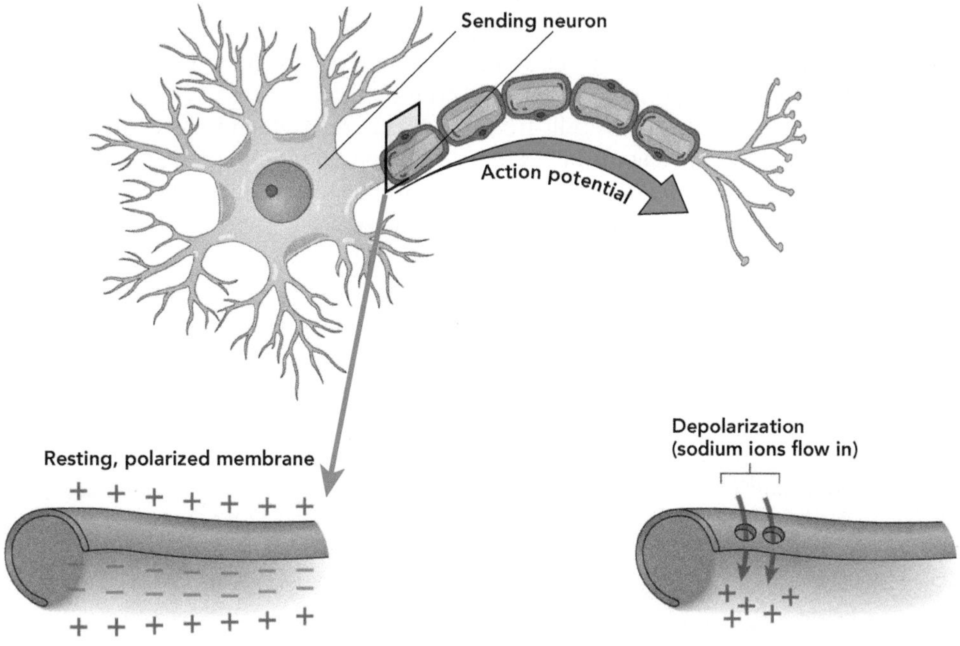

1 Resting potential
When an axon is not stimulated, it is in a polarized state, called the *resting potential*. "At rest," the fluid inside the axon has more negatively charged ions than the fluid outside. This results from the selective permeability of the axon membrane and a series of mechanisms, called *sodium-potassium pumps*, which pull potassium ions in and pump sodium ions out of the axon. The inside of the axon has a charge of about −70 millivolts relative to the outside.

2 Action potential initiation
When an "at rest" axon membrane is stimulated by a sufficiently strong signal, it produces an action potential (or depolarization). This action potential begins when the first part of the axon opens its "gates" and positively charged sodium ions rush through. The additional sodium ions change the previously negative charge inside the axon to a positive charge—thus depolarizing the axon.

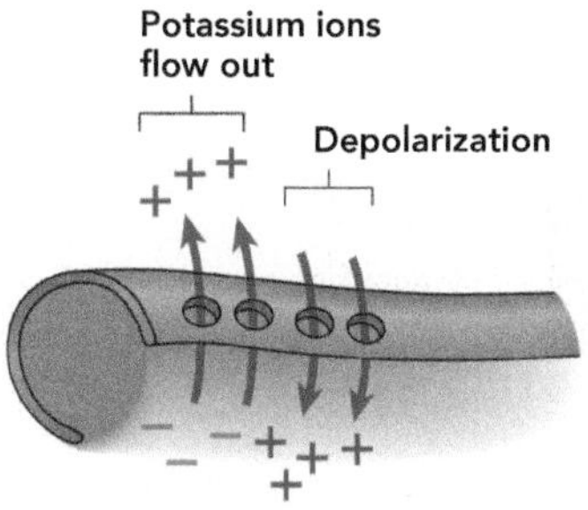

3 Spreading of action potential and repolarization
The initial depolarization (or action potential) of Step 2 produces a subsequent imbalance of ions in the adjacent axon membrane. This imbalance thus causes the action potential to spread to the next section. Meanwhile, "gates" in the axon membrane of the initially depolarized section open and potassium ions flow out, thus allowing the first section to repolarize and return to its resting potential.

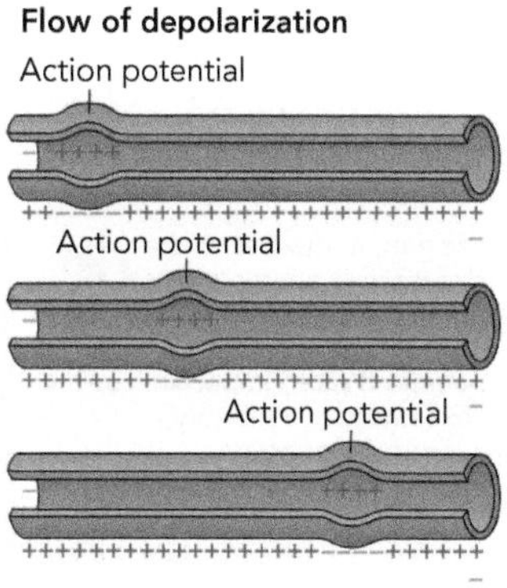

Overall summary
The sequential process of depolarization and repolarization moving the action potential from the cell body to the terminal buttons is similar to fans at an athletic event doing the "wave." One section of fans first stands up and waves their arms (action potential initiation), then sits down (resting potential), and then the "wave" spreads on. Note that this is an "all-or-none" event.

Myelin sheath The layer of fatty insulation wrapped around the axon of some neurons that increases the rate at which neural impulses travel along the axon.

Neural impulses move much more slowly than electricity moves through a wire. A neural impulse travels along a bare axon at only about 10 meters per second. (Electricity moves at 36 million meters per second.)

Some axons, however, are enveloped in fatty insulation, the **myelin sheath**. This sheath blankets the axon, with the exception of periodic *nodes*, points at which the myelin is very thin or absent. In a myelinated axon, the neural impulse moves about 10 times faster than in a bare axon because the action potential jumps from node to node rather than travel along the entire axon. Sadly, research shows that social isolation during the early weeks and months of life (as occurs for babies who are in orphanages) prevents cells from producing the right amount of myelin, which leads to long-term problems in cognitive functioning (Makinodan et al., 2012).

Communication *within* the neuron (Figure 2.8) is not the same as communication *between* neurons (**Figure 2.9**). Within the neuron, messages travel electrically,

FIGURE 2.9 **COMMUNICATION *BETWEEN* NEURONS**

Within the neuron (see Figure 2.8), messages travel electrically. Between neurons, messages are transmitted chemically. The three steps shown here summarize this chemical transmission.

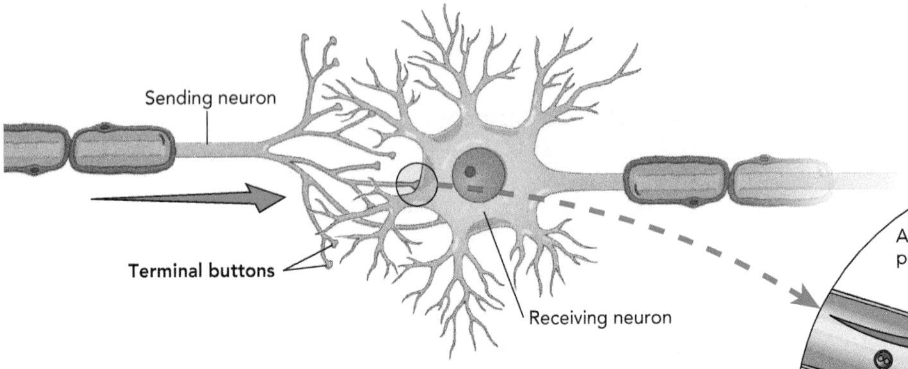

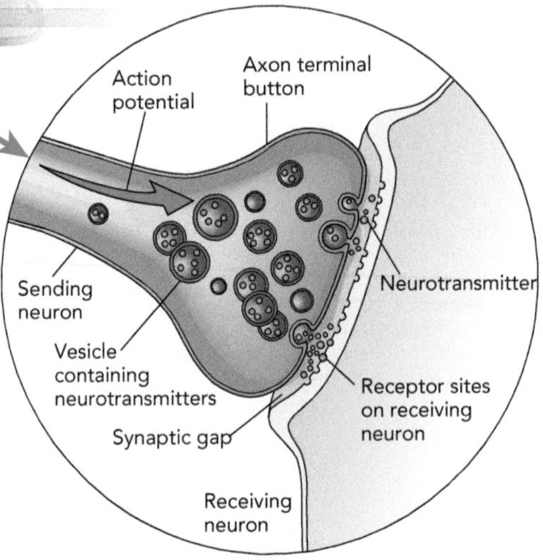

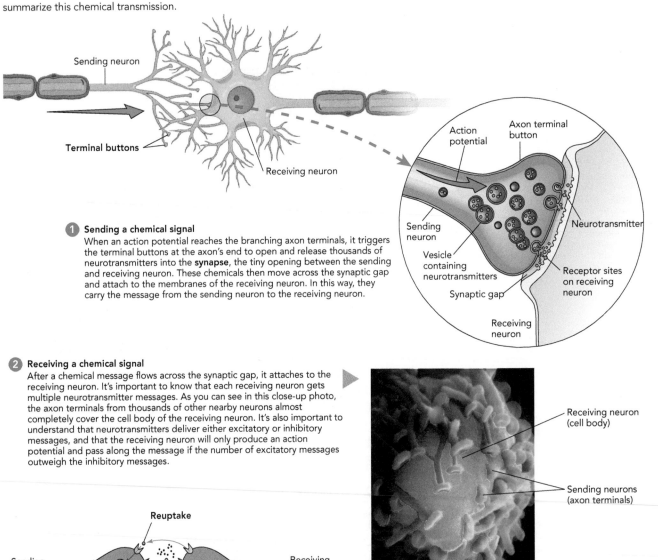

1 Sending a chemical signal
When an action potential reaches the branching axon terminals, it triggers the terminal buttons at the axon's end to open and release thousands of neurotransmitters into the **synapse**, the tiny opening between the sending and receiving neuron. These chemicals then move across the synaptic gap and attach to the membranes of the receiving neuron. In this way, they carry the message from the sending neuron to the receiving neuron.

2 Receiving a chemical signal
After a chemical message flows across the synaptic gap, it attaches to the receiving neuron. It's important to know that each receiving neuron gets multiple neurotransmitter messages. As you can see in this close-up photo, the axon terminals from thousands of other nearby neurons almost completely cover the cell body of the receiving neuron. It's also important to understand that neurotransmitters deliver either excitatory or inhibitory messages, and that the receiving neuron will only produce an action potential and pass along the message if the number of excitatory messages outweigh the inhibitory messages.

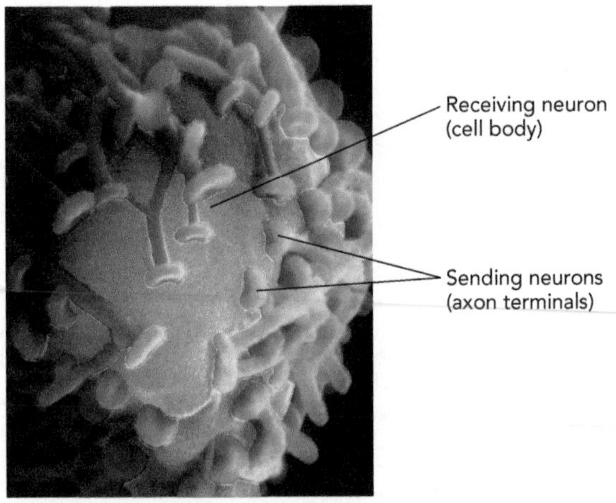

Science Source/Photo Researchers,Inc.

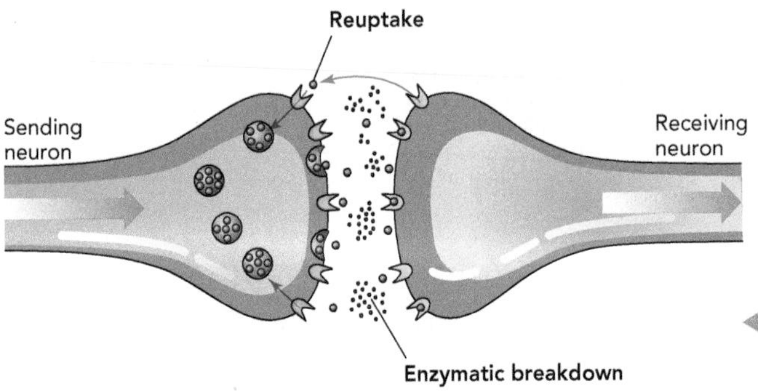

3 Dealing with leftovers
Given that some neurons have thousands of receptors, which are only responsive to specific neurotransmitters, what happens to excess neurotransmitters or to those that do not "fit" into the adjacent receptor sites? The sending neuron normally reabsorbs the excess (called "reuptake"), or they are broken down by special enzymes.

FIGURE 2.10 HOW POISONS AND DRUGS AFFECT OUR BRAINS | *psychology and you*

Foreign chemicals, like poisons and drugs, can mimic or block ongoing actions of neurotransmitters, thus interfering with normal functions.

altrendo images/Stockbyte/Getty Images, Inc.

Most snake venom and some poisons, like *botulinum* toxin (Botox®), seriously affect normal muscle contraction. Ironically, these same poisons are sometimes used to treat certain medical conditions involving abnormal muscle contraction—as well as for some cosmetic purposes.

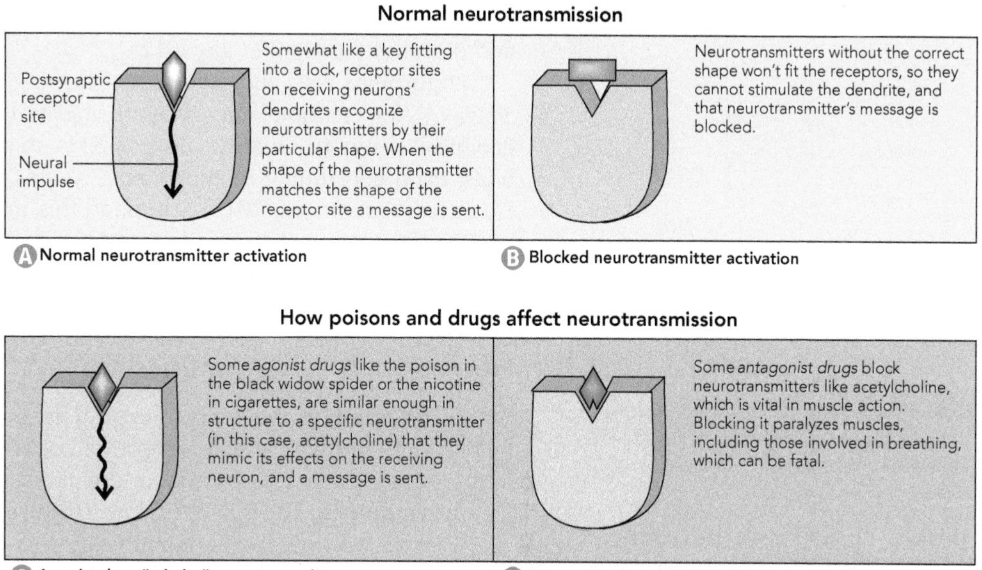
Normal neurotransmission
Postsynaptic receptor site
Neural impulse
Somewhat like a key fitting into a lock, receptor sites on receiving neurons' dendrites recognize neurotransmitters by their particular shape. When the shape of the neurotransmitter matches the shape of the receptor site a message is sent.
Neurotransmitters without the correct shape won't fit the receptors, so they cannot stimulate the dendrite, and that neurotransmitter's message is blocked.
How poisons and drugs affect neurotransmission
Some *agonist drugs* like the poison in the black widow spider or the nicotine in cigarettes, are similar enough in structure to a specific neurotransmitter (in this case, acetylcholine) that they mimic its effects on the receiving neuron, and a message is sent.
Some *antagonist drugs* block neurotransmitters like acetylcholine, which is vital in muscle action. Blocking it paralyzes muscles, including those involved in breathing, which can be fatal.

A Normal neurotransmitter activation

B Blocked neurotransmitter activation

C Agonist drug "mimics" neurotransmitter

D Antagonist drug fills receptor space and blocks neurotransmitter

whereas between neurons the messages are carried across the *synaptic gap* via chemicals called **neurotransmitters**.

Researchers have discovered hundreds of substances that function as neurotransmitters. For example, some **agonist drugs** enhance or "mimic" the action of particular neurotransmitters, whereas **antagonist drugs** block or inhibit the effects (**Figure 2.10**)

One benefit of studying the brain and its neurotransmitters is that it will help us understand some common medical problems. For example, we know that decreased levels of the neurotransmitter dopamine are associated with Parkinson's disease (PD), whereas excessively high levels of dopamine appear to contribute to some forms of schizophrenia. **Table 2.1** presents additional examples of the better-understood neurotransmitters.

Neurotransmitter A chemical messenger released by neurons that travels across the synapse and allows neurons to communicate with one another.

Agonist drug A substance that mimics and enhances a neurotransmitter's effect.

Antagonist drug A substance that blocks normal neurotransmitter functioning.

TABLE 2.1 HOW NEUROTRANSMITTERS AFFECT US

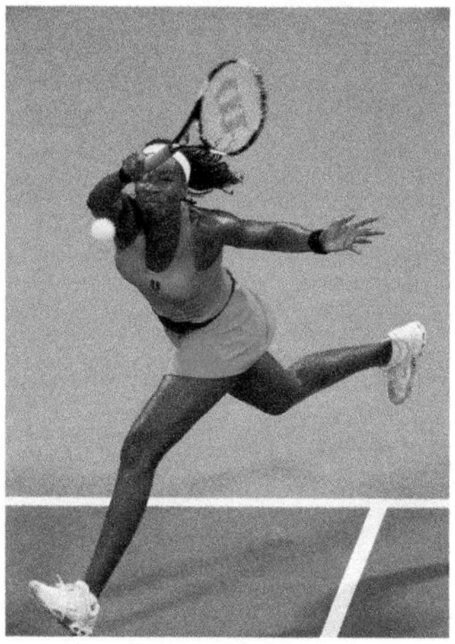

AP/Wide World Photos

Which neurotransmitters best explain this professional tennis player's exceptional skills?

Neurotransmitter	Known or Suspected Effects
Acetylcholine (ACh)	Muscle action, learning, memory, REM (rapid-eye-movement) sleep, emotion; decreased ACh plays a suspected role in Alzheimer's disease
Dopamine (DA)	Movement, attention, memory, learning, and emotion; excess DA associated with schizophrenia; too little DA linked with Parkinson's disease; also plays a role in addiction and the reward system
Endorphins	Mood, pain, memory, learning, blood pressure, appetite, and sexual activity
Epinephrine (or adrenaline)	Emotional arousal, memory storage, and metabolism of glucose necessary for energy release
GABA (gamma-aminobutyric acid)	Neural inhibition in the central nervous system; tranquilizing drugs, like Valium, increase GABA's inhibitory effects and thereby decrease anxiety
Norepinephrine (NE) [or noradrenaline (NA)]	Learning, memory, dreaming, emotion, waking from sleep, eating, alertness, wakefulness, reactions to stress; low levels of NE associated with depression; high levels of NE linked with agitated, manic states
Serotonin	Mood, sleep, appetite, sensory perception, arousal, temperature regulation, pain suppression, and impulsivity; low levels of serotonin associated with depression

Endorphin A chemical substance in the nervous system similar in structure and action to opiates; involved in pain control, pleasure, and memory.

Perhaps the best-known neurotransmitters are the endogenous opioid peptides, commonly known as **endorphins** (a contraction of *endogenous* [self-produced] and *morphine*). These chemicals mimic the effects of opium-based drugs such as morphine: They elevate mood and reduce pain. In fact, drinking alcohol causes endorphins to be released in parts of the brain that are responsible for feelings of reward and pleasure (Mitchell et al., 2012).

Q3

Endorphins also affect memory, learning, blood pressure, appetite, and sexual activity. For example, rats that are injected in the brain with an endorphin-like chemical eat considerably more M&Ms than they would under normal conditions, even consuming as much as 17 grams (more than 5% of their body weight; DiFeliceantonio et al., 2012). Although this may not seem like a lot of chocolate to you, it is the equivalent of a normal-sized adult eating 7.5 pounds of M&Ms in a single session!

Hormones and the Endocrine System

Endocrine system A network of glands located throughout the body that manufacture and secrete hormones into the bloodstream.

Hormone Chemical messengers manufactured and secreted by the endocrine glands, which circulate in the bloodstream to produce bodily changes or maintain normal bodily functions.

We've just seen how the nervous system uses neurotransmitters to transmit messages throughout the body. A second type of communication system also exists. This second system is made up of a network of glands, called the **endocrine system**, which uses **hormones** to carry its messages (**Figure 2.11**).

Why do we need two communication systems? Like e-mails we send to particular people, neurotransmitters deliver messages to specific receptors, which other neurons nearby probably don't "overhear." Hormones, in contrast, are like a global e-mail message that we send to everyone in our address book.

FIGURE 2.11 THE ENDOCRINE SYSTEM

This figure shows the major endocrine glands, along with some internal organs to help you locate the glands.

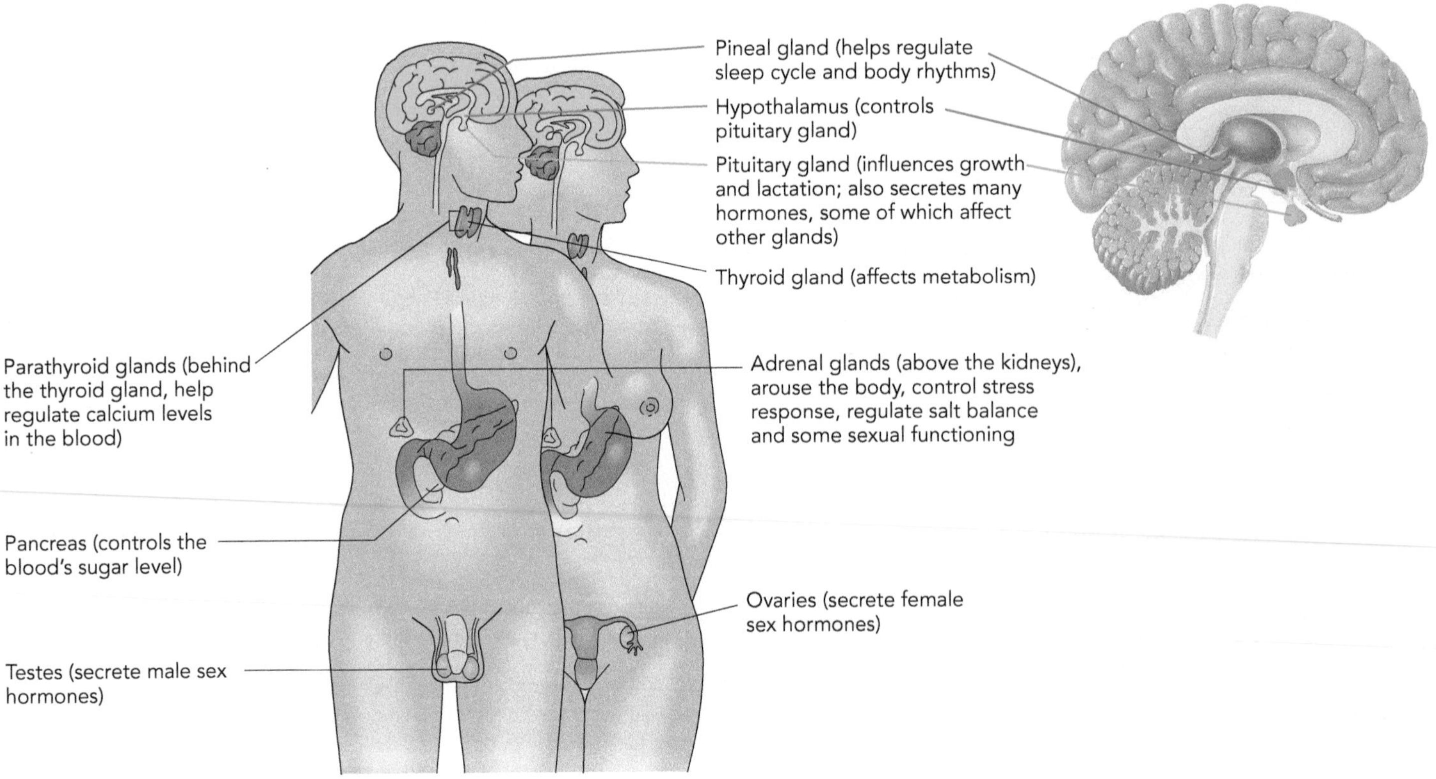

In addition, neurotransmitters are released from a neuron's terminal buttons into the **synapse**, a small open gap between neurons. In contrast, hormones are released from endocrine glands directly into our bloodstream. The messages are then carried by the blood throughout our bodies to any cell that will listen. Like our global e-mail recipients who may forward our message on to other people, messages from hormones are often forwarded on to other parts of the body. For example, a small part of the brain called the hypothalamus releases hormones that signal the pituitary (another small brain structure), which in turn stimulates or inhibits the release of other hormones.

Our hormone-releasing endocrine system has several important functions. It helps regulate long-term bodily processes, such as growth and sexual characteristics. It also maintains ongoing bodily processes, such as digestion and elimination. Finally, hormones control the body's response to emergencies. In times of crisis, the hypothalamus sends messages through two pathways—the neural system and the endocrine system (primarily the pituitary gland). The pituitary sends hormonal messages to the adrenal glands (located right above the kidneys). The adrenal glands then release *cortisol*, a stress hormone that boosts energy and blood sugar levels, *epinephrine* (commonly called adrenaline), and *norepinephrine* (or nonadrenaline). (Remember that these same chemicals also can serve as neurotransmitters.)

Synapse The gap between the axon tip of the sending neuron and the dendrite and/or cell body of the receiving neuron; during an action potential, neurotransmitters are released and flow across the synapse.

RETRIEVAL PRACTICE: NEURAL BASES OF BEHAVIOR

Self-Test

Completing this self-test and comparing your answers with those in Appendix B provides immediate feedback and helpful practice for exams. Additional interactive, self-tests are available at www.wiley.com/college/huffman.

1. An action potential is _____.

a. the likelihood that a neuron will take action when stimulated
b. the tendency for a neuron to be potentiated by neurotransmitters
c. a neural impulse that carries information along the axon of a neuron
d. the firing of a nerve, either toward or away from the brain

2. Too much of the neurotransmitter _____ may be related to schizophrenia, whereas too little may be related to Parkinson's disease.

a. acetylcholine
b. dopamine
c. norepinephrine
d. serotonin

3. Chemicals manufactured by endocrine glands and circulated in the bloodstream to change or maintain bodily functions are called _____.

a. vasopressors
b. gonadotropins
c. hormones
d. steroids

4. Chemical messengers that are released by axons and travel across the synapse are called _____.

a. chemical agonists
b. neurotransmitters
c. synaptic transmitters
d. neuroactivists

Think Critically

1 Why is it valuable for scientists to understand how neurotransmitters work at a molecular level?

2 What are some examples of how hormones affect your daily life?

realworldpsychology

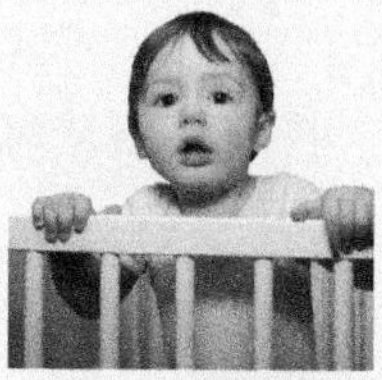

Why can spending the first few months of life in an orphanage lead to long-term problems in cognitive functioning?

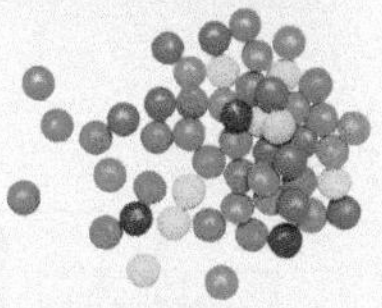

How can a chemical in the brain lead rats to binge-eat M&Ms?

HINT: LOOK IN THE MARGIN FOR Q2 AND Q3

NERVOUS SYSTEM ORGANIZATION

LEARNING OBJECTIVES

RETRIEVAL PRACTICE While reading the upcoming sections, respond to each Learning Objective in your own words. Then compare your responses with those found at www.wiley.com/college/huffman.

1 IDENTIFY the major elements of the nervous system.

2 EXPLAIN the role of the central nervous system (CNS).

3 DESCRIBE the components of the peripheral nervous system (PNS).

Have you heard the expression "Information is power"? Nowhere is this truer than in the human body. Without information, we could not survive. Neurons within our nervous system must take in sensory information from the outside world and then pass along this information to the entire human body. Just as the circulatory system handles blood, which conveys chemicals and oxygen, our nervous system uses chemicals and electrical processes to convey information.

The nervous system is divided and subdivided into several branches (**Figure 2.12**). The main branch includes the brain and a bundle of nerves that form the *spinal cord*. Because this system is located in the center of our body (within our skull and spine), it is called the **central nervous system (CNS)**. The CNS is primarily responsible for processing and organizing information.

Central nervous system (CNS) The part of the nervous system consisting of the brain and spinal cord.

The second major branch of our nervous system includes all the nerves outside the brain and spinal cord. This **peripheral nervous system (PNS)** carries messages (action potentials) to and from the central nervous system to the periphery of the body. Now, let's take a closer look at the CNS and the PNS.

Peripheral nervous system (PNS) The part of the nervous system composed of the nerves and neurons connecting the central nervous system (CNS) to the rest of the body.

FIGURE 2.12 **THE NERVOUS SYSTEM**

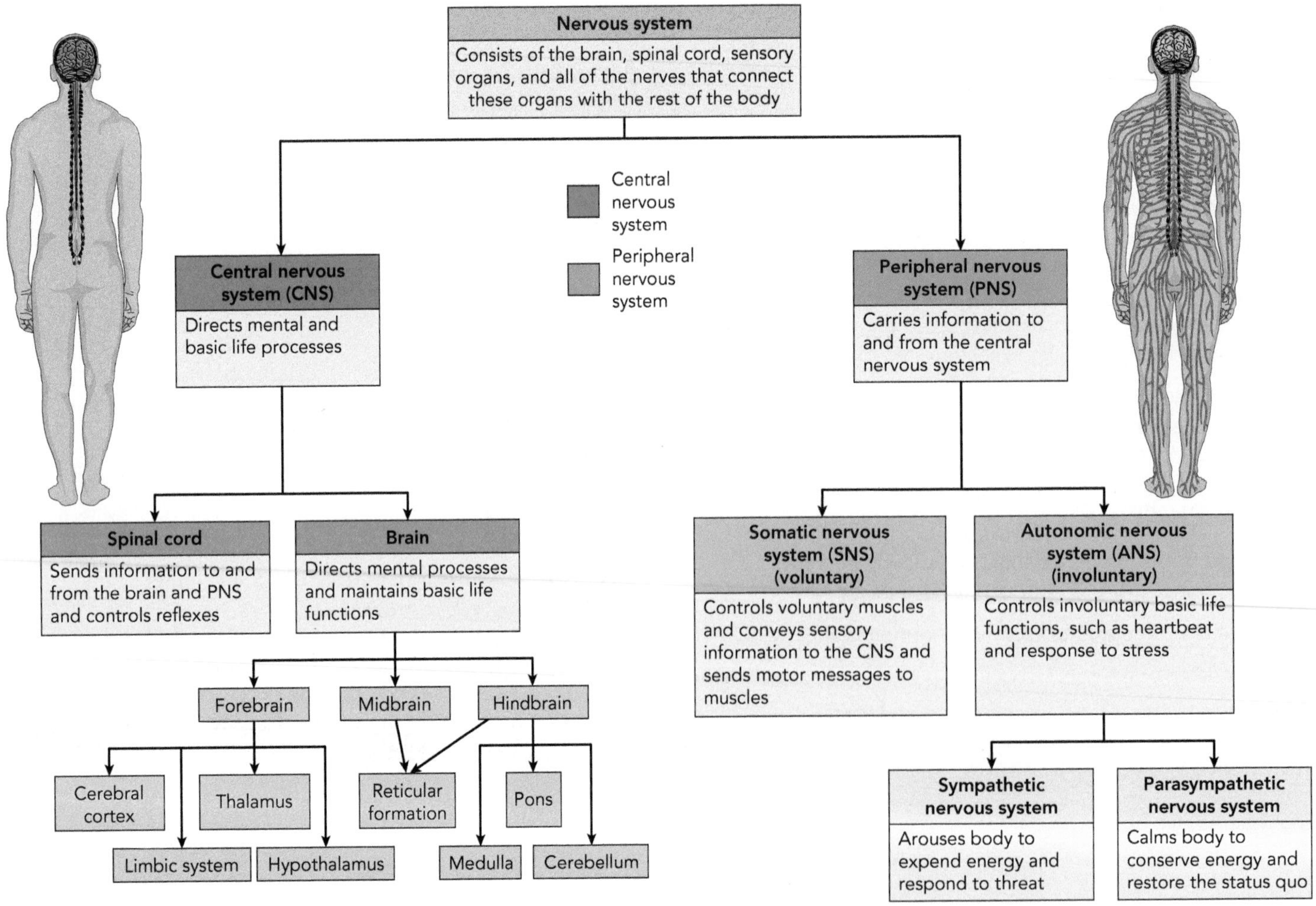

Central Nervous System (CNS)

The central nervous system (CNS) is the branch of the nervous system that makes us unique. Most other animals can smell, run, see, and hear far better than we can. But thanks to our CNS, we can process information and adapt to our environment in ways that no other animal can. Unfortunately, our CNS is also incredibly fragile. Unlike neurons in the PNS that can regenerate and require less protection, neurons in the CNS can suffer serious and permanent damage. However, the brain may not be as "hard wired" as we once thought.

Scientists long believed that after the first two or three years of life most animals, including humans, were unable to repair or replace damaged neurons in the brain or spinal cord. We now know that the brain is capable of lifelong **neuroplasticity** and **neurogenesis**.

Courtesy Taub Therapy Clinc/UAB Media Relations

FIGURE 2.13 A BREAKTHROUGH IN NEUROSCIENCE

By immobilizing the unaffected arm or leg and requiring rigorous and repetitive exercise of the affected limb, psychologist Edward Taub and colleagues "recruit" stroke patients' intact brain cells to take over for damaged cells. The therapy has restored function in some patients as long as 21 years after their strokes.

Neuroplasticity

Rather than being a fixed, solid organ, the brain is capable of changing its structure and function as a result of usage and experience (Bowden et al., 2013; Marcotte et al., 2013). This "rewiring" is what makes our brains so wonderfully adaptive. For example, it makes it possible for us to learn a new sport or a foreign language.

Remarkably, this rewiring has even helped "remodel" the brain following strokes. For example, psychologist Edward Taub and his colleagues (2004, 2012) have had success working with stroke patients (**Figure 2.13**).

Neuroplasticity The brain's ability to reorganize and change its structure and function throughout the life span.

Neurogenesis The process by which new neurons are generated.

Stem cells Immature (uncommitted) cells that have the potential to develop into almost any type of cell, depending on the chemical signals they receive.

Neurogenesis

Our brains continually replace lost cells with new cells that originate deep within the brain and migrate to become part of its circuitry. The source of these newly created cells is neural **stem cells**—rare, immature cells that can grow and develop into any type of cell. Their fate depends on the chemical signals they receive. Experiments and clinical trials on both human and nonhuman animals have used stem cells for bone marrow transplants, and to repopulate or replace cells devastated by injury or disease. This research offers hope to patients suffering from strokes, Alzheimer's, Parkinson's, epilepsy, stress, and depression (e.g., Austin & Rini, 2013; Inden et al., 2013; Kim et al., 2013; Yin et al., 2012). In addition, stem cell injections into the eyes of patients with untreatable eye diseases and severe visual problems have led to dramatic improvements in vision (Schwartz et al., 2012).

Q4

realworldpsychology **Stem Cell Therapy** Will stem cell transplants allow people paralyzed from spinal cord injuries to walk again? Scientists have had some success transplanting stem cells into spinal cord–injured nonhuman animals (Cusimano et al., 2012; Lee et al., 2011; Rossi, 2011; Sieber-Blum, 2010; Wang et al., 2013). When the damaged spinal cord was viewed several weeks later, the implanted cells had survived and spread throughout the injured area. More important, the transplant animals also showed some improvement in previously paralyzed parts of their bodies. Medical researchers have also recently begun testing the safety of embryonic stem cell therapy for human paralysis patients, and future trials may determine whether these cells will repair damaged spinal cords and/or improve sensation and movement in paralyzed areas (Conger, 2011; Curt et al., 2012; Robbins, 2013).

© 26ISO/iStockphoto

FIGURE 2.14 HOW THE SPINAL REFLEX OPERATES

In a simple reflex arc, a sensory receptor responds to stimulation and initiates a neural impulse that travels to the spinal cord. This signal then travels back to the appropriate muscle, which then contracts. The response is automatic and immediate in a reflex because the signal only travels as far as the spinal cord before action is initiated, not all the way to the brain. The brain is later "notified" of the action when the spinal cord sends along the message. What might be the evolutionary advantages of the reflex arc?

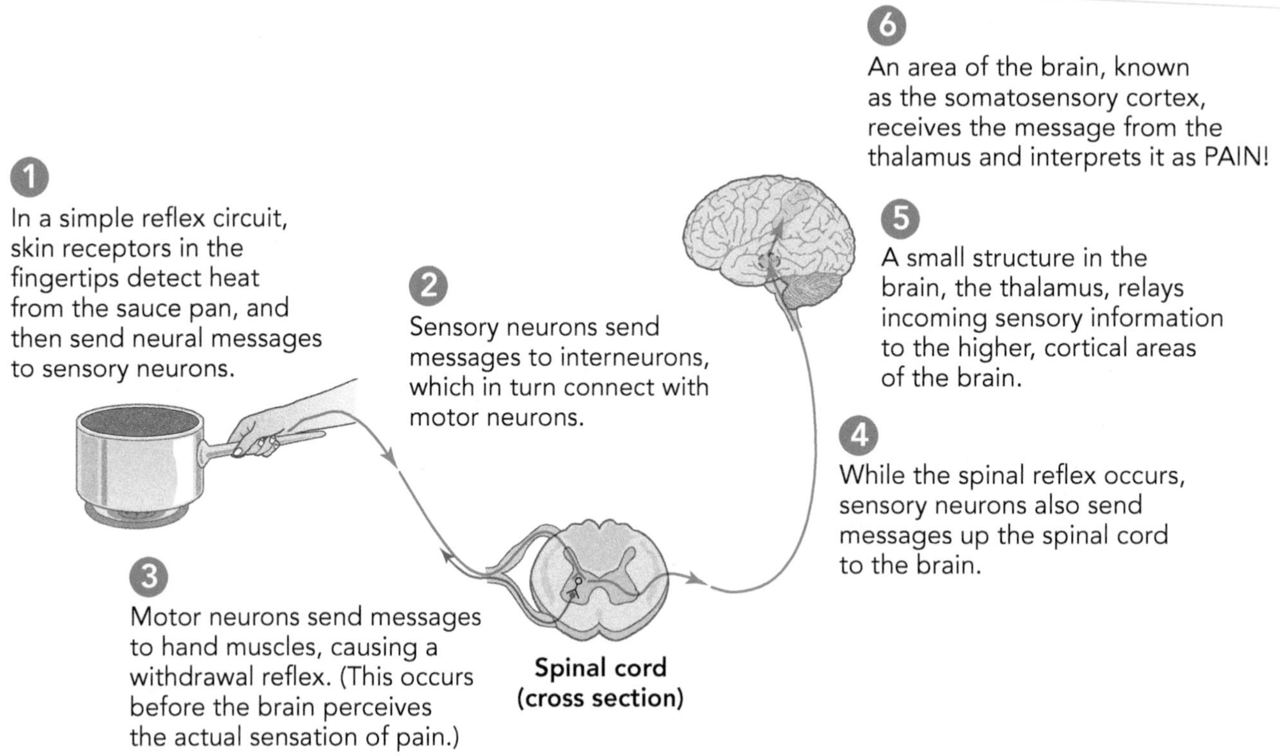
1
In a simple reflex circuit, skin receptors in the fingertips detect heat from the sauce pan, and then send neural messages to sensory neurons.
2
Sensory neurons send messages to interneurons, which in turn connect with motor neurons.
3
Motor neurons send messages to hand muscles, causing a withdrawal reflex. (This occurs before the brain perceives the actual sensation of pain.)
Spinal cord (cross section)
4
While the spinal reflex occurs, sensory neurons also send messages up the spinal cord to the brain.
5
A small structure in the brain, the thalamus, relays incoming sensory information to the higher, cortical areas of the brain.
6
An area of the brain, known as the somatosensory cortex, receives the message from the thalamus and interprets it as PAIN!

Now that we have discussed neuroplasticity and neurogenesis within the central nervous system (CNS), let's take a closer look at the spinal cord. Because of its central importance for psychology and behavior, we'll discuss the brain in detail in the next major section.

Spinal Cord

Beginning at the base of our brains and continuing down our backs, the spinal cord carries vital information from the rest of the body into and out of the brain. But the spinal cord doesn't simply relay messages. It can also initiate some automatic behaviors on its own. We call these involuntary, automatic behaviors **reflexes**, or *reflex arcs*, because the response to the incoming stimuli is automatically "reflected" back to the spinal cord, which allows an immediate action response without the delay of routing signals directly to the brain.

Reflex An innate, automatic response to a stimulus that has a biological relevance for an organism (for example, knee-jerk reflex).

As you can see in the simple reflex arc depicted in **Figure 2.14**, a sensory receptor first responds to stimulation and initiates a neural impulse that travels to the spinal cord. This signal then travels back to the appropriate muscle, which contracts. The response is automatic and immediate in a reflex because the signal travels only as far as the spinal cord before action is initiated, not all the way to the brain. The brain is later "notified" of the action when the spinal cord sends along the message. What might be the evolutionary advantages of the reflex arc?

We're all born with numerous reflexes, many of which fade over time (**Figure 2.15**). But even as adults, we still blink in response to a puff of air in our eyes, gag when something touches the back of the throat, and urinate and defecate in response to pressure in the bladder and rectum.

psychology and you **Sexual Response Reflexes** Reflexes even influence our sexual responses. Certain stimuli, such as the stroking of the genitals, can lead to arousal and the reflexive muscle contractions of orgasm in both men and women. However, in order for us to have the passion, thoughts, and emotion we normally associate with sex, the sensory information from the stroking and orgasm must be carried by the spinal cord to the appropriate areas of the brain that receive and interpret these specific sensory messages.

Kovalchynskyy Mykola/Shutterstock

Peripheral Nervous System (PNS)

The peripheral nervous system (PNS) is just what it sounds like—the part that involves nerves *peripheral* to (or outside) the brain and spinal cord. The chief function of the peripheral nervous system (PNS) is to carry information to and from the central nervous system (CNS). It links the brain and spinal cord to the body's sense receptors, muscles, and glands.

The PNS is subdivided into the somatic nervous system and the autonomic nervous system. The **somatic nervous system (SNS)** consists of all the nerves that connect to sensory receptors and skeletal muscles. The name comes from the term *soma*, which means "body," and the somatic nervous system plays a key role in communication throughout the entire body. In a kind of two-way street, the somatic nervous system (also called the skeletal nervous system) first carries sensory information to the brain and spinal cord (CNS) and then carries messages from the CNS to skeletal muscles.

Somatic nervous system (SNS) A subdivision of the peripheral nervous system (PNS) that connects the central nervous system (CNS) to sensory receptors and controls skeletal muscles.

Think Critically

1. What might happen if infants lacked these reflexes?
2. Can you explain why most infant reflexes disappear within the first year?

FIGURE 2.15 **TESTING FOR REFLEXES** psychology and you

If you have a newborn or young infant in your home, you can easily (and safely) test for these simple reflexes. (Most infant reflexes disappear within the first year of life. If they reappear in later life, it generally indicates damage to the central nervous system.)

Ⓐ **Rooting reflex**
Lightly stroke the cheek or side of the mouth, and watch how the infant automatically (reflexively) turns toward the stimulation and attempts to suck.

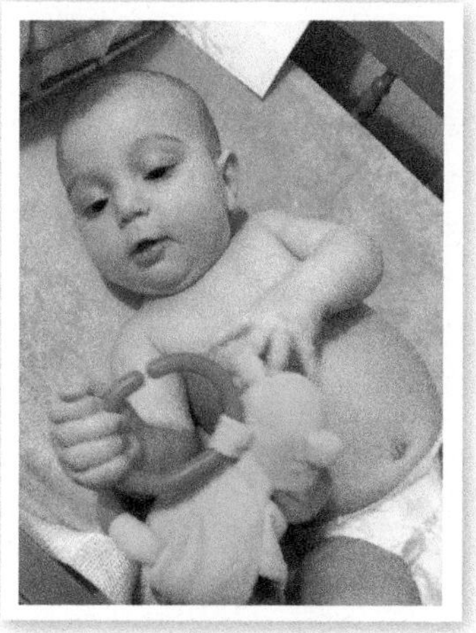

Ⓑ **Grasping reflex**
Place your finger or an object in the infant's palm and note the automatic grasp.

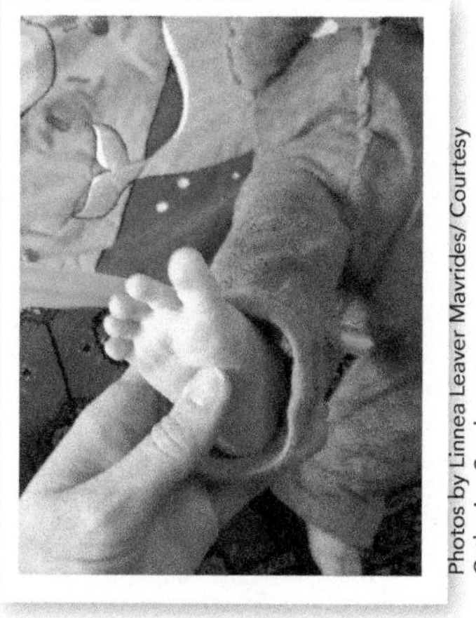

Photos by Linnea Leaver Mavrides/ Courtesy Catherine Sanderson

Ⓒ **Babinski reflex**
Lightly stroke the sole of the infant's foot, and the big toe will move toward the top of the foot, while the other toes fan out.

Autonomic nervous system (ANS) The subdivision of the peripheral nervous system (PNS) that controls the body's involuntary motor responses by connecting the sensory receptors to the central nervous system (CNS) and the CNS to the smooth muscle, cardiac muscle, and glands.

Sympathetic nervous system The subdivision of the autonomic nervous system (ANS) that is responsible for arousing the body and mobilizing its energy during times of stress; also called the "fight-or-flight" system.

Parasympathetic nervous system The subdivision of the autonomic nervous system (ANS) that is responsible for calming the body and conserving energy.

The other subdivision of the PNS is the **autonomic nervous system (ANS)**. The ANS is responsible for involuntary tasks, such as heart rate, digestion, pupil dilation, and breathing. Like an automatic pilot, the ANS can sometimes be consciously overridden. But as its name implies, the autonomic system normally operates on its own (autonomously).

The autonomic nervous system is further divided into two branches, the sympathetic and parasympathetic, which tend to work in opposition to each other to regulate the functioning of such target organs as the heart, the intestines, and the lungs. Like two children on a teeter-totter, one will be up while the other is down, but they essentially balance each other out. **Figure 2.16** illustrates a familiar example of the interaction between the sympathetic and parasympathetic nervous systems.

During stressful times, either mental or physical, the **sympathetic nervous system** mobilizes bodily resources to respond to the stressor. This emergency response is often called the "fight or flight" response. If you noticed a dangerous snake coiled and ready to strike, your sympathetic nervous system would increase your heart rate, respiration, and blood pressure; stop your digestive and eliminative processes; and release hormones, such as cortisol, into the bloodstream. The net result of sympathetic activation is to get more oxygenated blood and energy to the skeletal muscles, thus allowing you to cope with the stress—to either fight or flee.

In contrast to the sympathetic nervous system, the **parasympathetic nervous system** is responsible for calming our bodies and conserving energy. It returns our normal bodily functions by slowing our heart rate, lowering our blood pressure, and increasing our digestive and eliminative processes.

The sympathetic nervous system provides an adaptive, evolutionary advantage. At the beginning of human evolution, when we faced a dangerous bear or an aggressive human intruder, there were only two reasonable responses—fight or flight. The automatic mobilization of bodily resources can still be critical, even in modern times. However, less life-threatening events, such as traffic jams, also activate our sympathetic nervous system. As the next chapter discusses, ongoing sympathetic system response to such chronic, daily stress can become detrimental to our health. For a look at how the autonomic nervous system affects our sexual lives, see **Figure 2.17**.

FIGURE 2.16 ACTIONS OF THE AUTONOMIC NERVOUS SYSTEM (ANS)

The ANS is responsible for a variety of independent (autonomous) activities, such as salivation and digestion. It exercises this control through its two divisions—the sympathetic and parasympathetic branches.

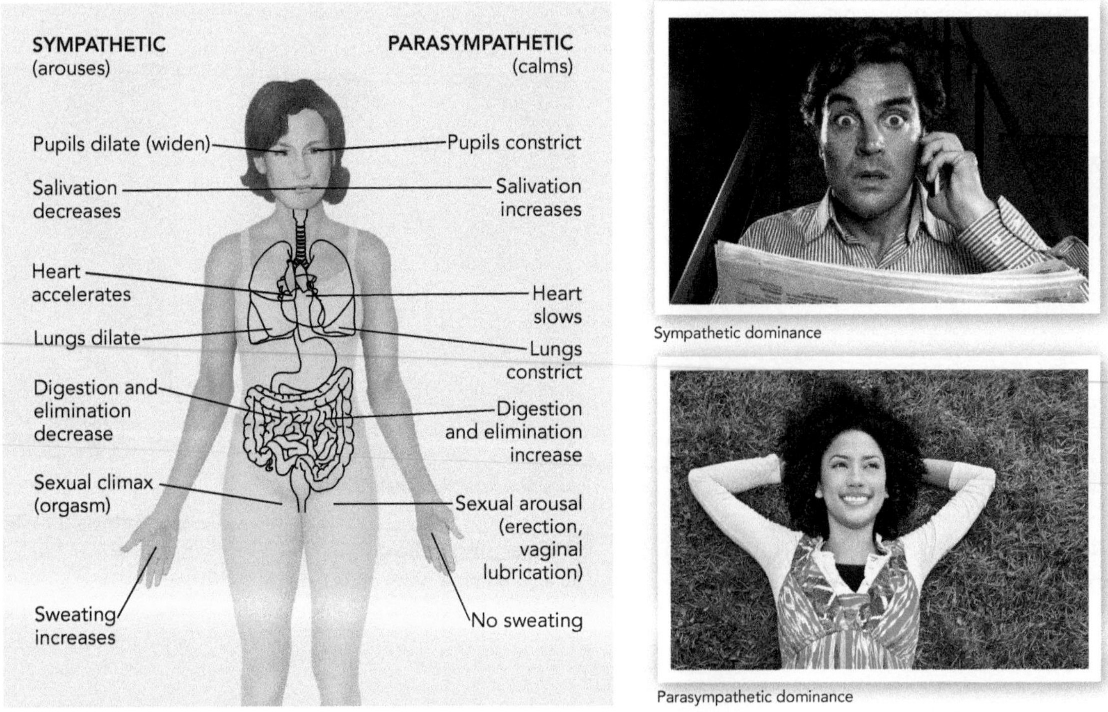

Sympathetic dominance

Beto Hacker/Getty Images, Inc.

Parasympathetic dominance

Geri Lavrov/Photographer's Choice/Getty Images, Inc.

FIGURE 2.17 AUTONOMIC NERVOUS SYSTEM AND SEXUAL AROUSAL | psychology and you

The complexities of sexual interaction—and, in particular, the difficulties couples sometimes have in achieving sexual arousal or orgasm—illustrate the balancing act between the sympathetic and parasympathetic nervous systems.

Piotr Marcinski/Shutterstock

A Parasympathetic dominance
Sexual arousal and excitement require that the body be relaxed enough to allow increased blood flow to the genitals—in other words, the nervous system must be in *parasympathetic dominance.* Parasympathetic nerves carry messages from the central nervous system directly to the sexual organs, allowing for a localized response (increased blood flow and genital arousal).

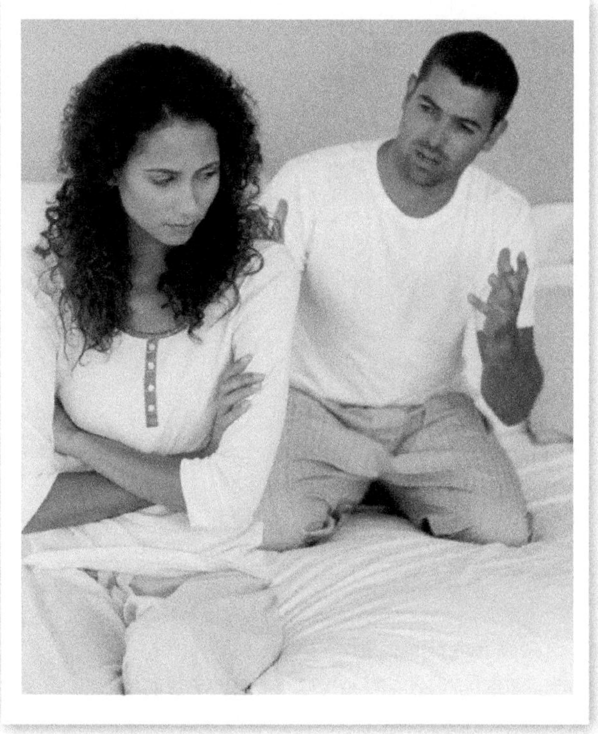

© 4774344sean/iStockphoto

B Sympathetic dominance
During strong emotions, such as anger, anxiety, or fear, the body shifts to *sympathetic dominance*, which causes blood flow to the genitals and other organs to decrease because the body is preparing for "fight or flight." As a result, the person is unable (or less likely) to become sexually aroused. Any number of circumstances—performance anxiety, fear of unwanted pregnancy or disease, or tensions between partners—can trigger sympathetic dominance.

Voices from the Classroom

Burn Prevention—Thanks to the CNS and PNS To explain the importance of how well the CNS and PNS communicate with one another, I often ask my students to raise their hands if they have ever have been burned. Every student, every single time raises his or her hand. But, hands quickly drop when I ask, "How many have been burned more than 20 times?" Ultimately, I'm left only with people who work in environments with hot stimuli (i.e., bakers, cooks, welders, etc.). I explain that during the process of being burned, our PNS does an excellent job of sending info about hot stimuli sensed from the five senses to the CNS. The CNS then quickly learns to associate and detect hot stimuli picked up by the PNS: from the sounds of boiling water, the feel the heat from a red hot stove surface, the smell of something burning, to recognizing the flicking shadows of a flame. Once we've learned these associations between "hot stimuli" and being burned, getting burned again is a rare experience–thanks to the excellent relay system between the CNS and PNS!

Professor R. D. Landis
Weatherford Community College
Weatherford, Texas

RETRIEVAL PRACTICE: NERVOUS SYSTEM ORGANIZATION

Self-Test

Completing this self-test and comparing your answers with those in Appendix B provides immediate feedback and helpful practice for exams. Additional interactive, self-tests are available at www.wiley.com/college/huffman.

1. The _____ nervous system is responsible for fight or flight, whereas the _____ nervous system is responsible for maintaining calm.

a. central; peripheral
b. parasympathetic; sympathetic
c. sympathetic; parasympathetic
d. autonomic; somatic

2. The peripheral nervous system is _____.

a. composed of the spinal cord and peripheral nerves
b. less important than the central nervous system
c. contained within the skull and spinal column
d. a combination of all the nerves and neurons outside the brain and spinal cord

3. If you are startled by the sound of a loud explosion, the _____ nervous system will become dominant.

a. semiautomatic
b. afferent
c. parasympathetic
d. sympathetic

4. The central nervous system _____.

a. consists of the brain and spinal cord
b. is the most important nervous system
c. includes the automatic and other nervous systems
d. all these options

Think Critically

1 Some stem cell research comes from tissue taken from aborted fetuses, which has led to great controversy and severe restrictions in some states. Do you believe this specific form of research should be limited? If so, how and why?

2 What are some everyday examples of neuroplasticity—that is, of the way the brain is changed and shaped by experience?

realworldpsychology

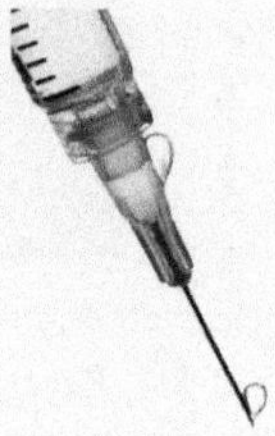

How can stem cell injections lead to restored vision and improved recovery from strokes?

HINT: LOOK IN THE MARGIN FOR Q4

A TOUR THROUGH THE BRAIN

LEARNING OBJECTIVES

RETRIEVAL PRACTICE While reading the upcoming sections, respond to each Learning Objective in your own words. Then compare your responses with those found at www.wiley.com/college/huffman.

1 **DESCRIBE** how neuroscientists study the brain and nervous system.
2 **IDENTIFY** the major structures of the hindbrain, midbrain, and forebrain.
3 **SUMMARIZE** the major roles of the lobes of the cerebral cortex.
4 **DESCRIBE** how the brain is divided into two specialized hemispheres.

We begin our exploration of the brain with a discussion of the tools that neuroscientists use to study it. Then we offer a quick tour of the brain, beginning at its lower end, where the spinal cord joins the base of the brain, and then move upward, all the way to the top of the skull. As we move from bottom to top, "lower," basic processes, such as breathing, generally give way to more complex mental processes (**Figure 2.18**).

Biological Tools for Research

How do we know how the brain and nervous system work? The earliest explorers of the brain *dissected* the brains of deceased humans and conducted experiments on other animals using *lesioning* techniques (systematically destroying brain tissue to study the effects on behavior and mental processes). By the mid-1800s, this research had produced a basic map of the nervous system, including some areas of the brain. Early researchers also relied on clinical observations and case studies of living people who had experienced injuries, diseases, and disorders that affected brain functioning.

Modern researchers still use such methods, but they also employ other techniques to examine biological processes that underlie our behavior (**Table 2.2**). For example, recent advances in brain science have led to various types of brain-imaging scans, which can be used in both clinical and laboratory settings. Most of these methods are relatively *noninvasive*—that is, their use does not involve breaking the skin or entering the body.

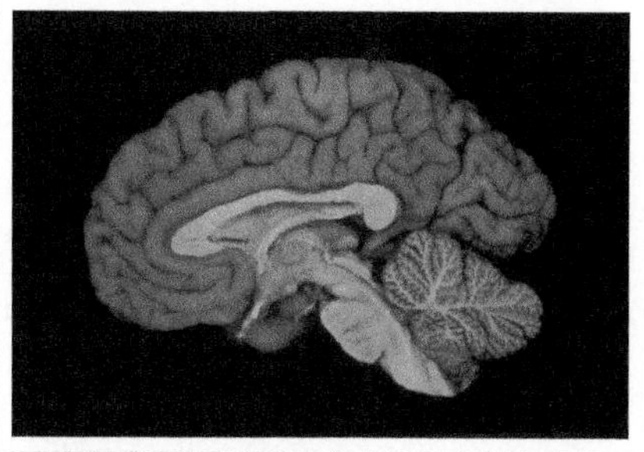

Science Pictures Limited/Photo Researchers

A photo of the human brain
This deceased human's brain is sliced down the center, split into right and left halves. Like the diagram below, only the right half of the brain is shown in this photo.

Lower-Level Brain Structures

Having studied the tools scientists use for exploring the brain, we can now begin our tour. Let's talk first about brain size and complexity, which vary significantly from species to species. For example, fish and reptiles have smaller, less complex brains than do cats and dogs. The most complex brains belong to whales, dolphins, and higher primates, such as chimps, gorillas, and humans. The billions of neurons that make up the human brain control much of what we think, feel, and do. Certain brain structures are specialized to perform certain tasks, a process known as *localization of function*. However, most parts of the brain perform integrating, overlapping functions.

FIGURE 2.18 THE HUMAN BRAIN

Note on the left side of this figure how the forebrain, midbrain, and hindbrain radically change in their size and placement during prenatal development. The profile drawing in the middle highlights key structures and functions of the right half of the adult brain. As you read about each of these structures, keep this drawing in mind and refer to it as necessary. (The diagram shows the brain structures as if the brain were split vertically down the center and the left hemisphere were removed.)

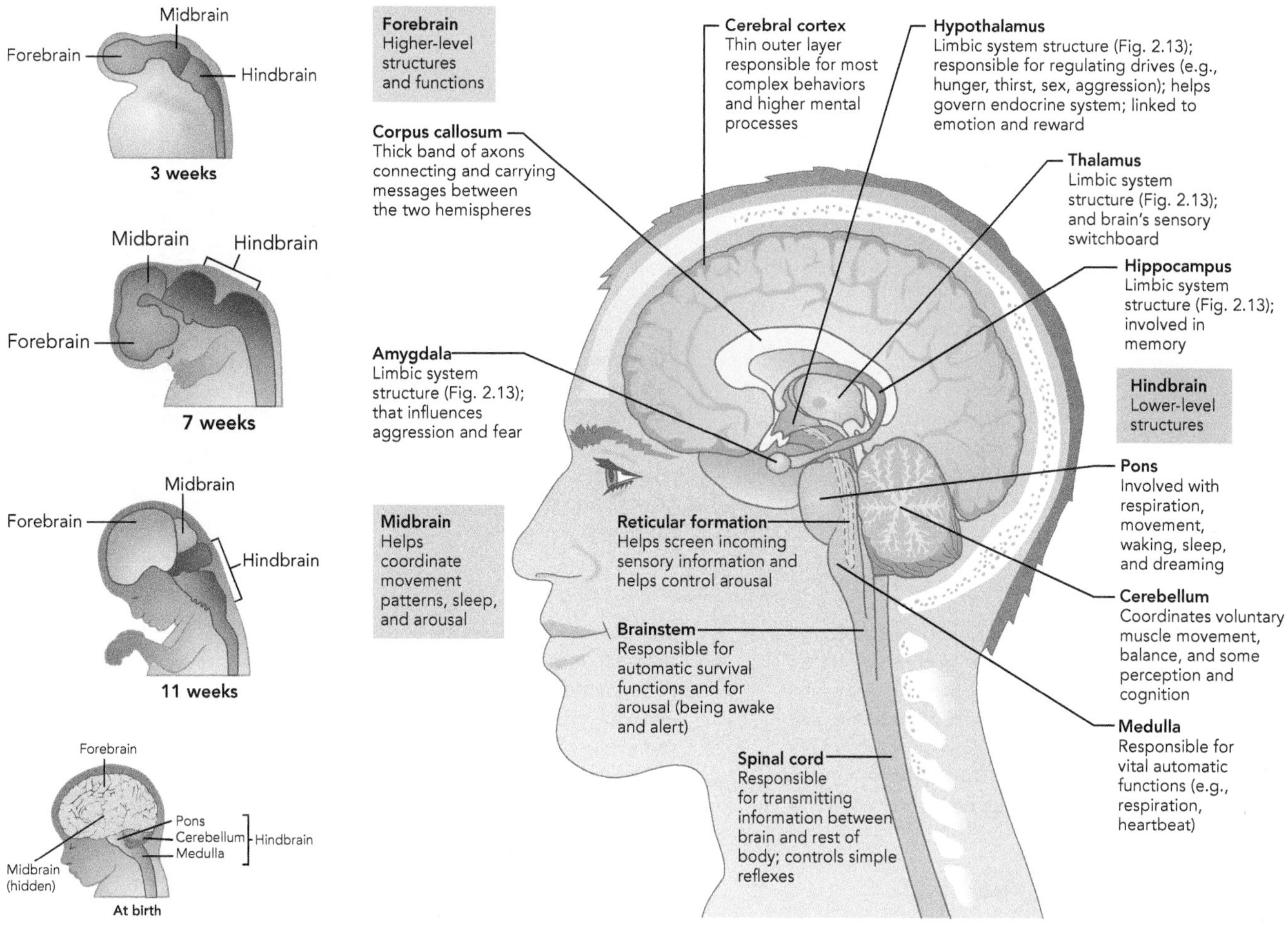

TABLE 2.2 SAMPLE TOOLS FOR BIOLOGICAL RESEARCH

Tool	Description	Purpose	
Electrical recordings Electrical activity throughout the brain sweeps in regular waves across its surface, and the electroencephalogram (EEG) is a read out of this activity.	Using electrodes attached to the skin or scalp, brain activity is detected and recorded on an EEG.	Reveals areas of the brain most active during particular tasks or mental states such as reading or sleeping; also traces abnormal brain waves caused by brain malfunctions, such as epilepsy or tumors.	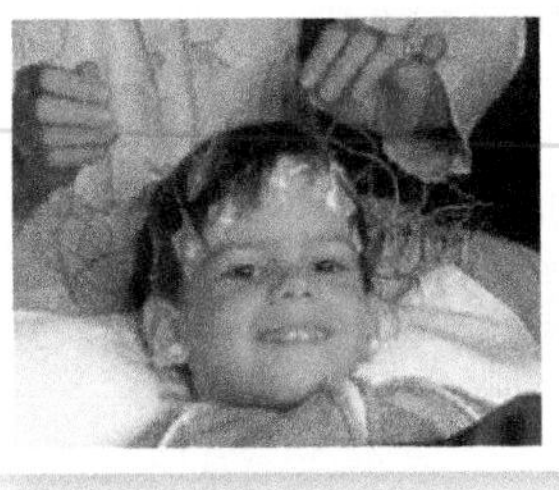 Larry Mulvehill/Photo Researchers, Inc.
CT (computed tomography) scan This CT scan used X-rays to locate a brain tumor, which is the deep purple mass at the top left.	Computer-created cross-sectional X-rays of the brain or other parts of the body produce 3-D images. Least expensive type of imaging and widely used in research.	Reveals the effects of strokes, injuries, tumors, and other brain disorders.	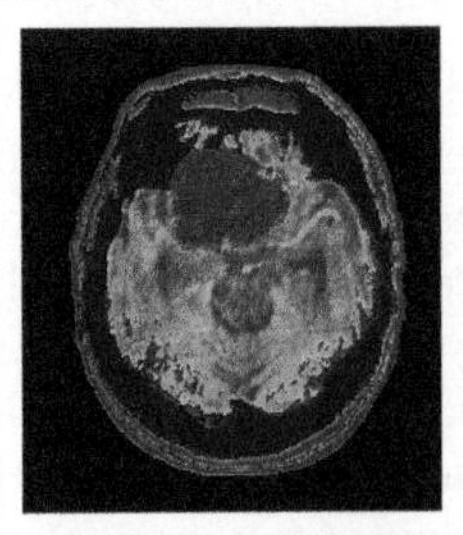 Mehau Kulyk/Photo Researchers, Inc.
PET (positron emission tomography) scan The left PET scan shows brain activity when the eyes are open, whereas the one on the right is with the eyes closed. Note the increased activity, red and yellow, in the left photo when the eyes are open.	A radioactive form of glucose is injected into the bloodstream; a scanner records the amount of glucose used in particularly active areas of the brain and produces a computer-constructed picture of the brain.	Originally designed to detect abnormalities, now used to identify brain areas active during ordinary activities (such as reading or singing).	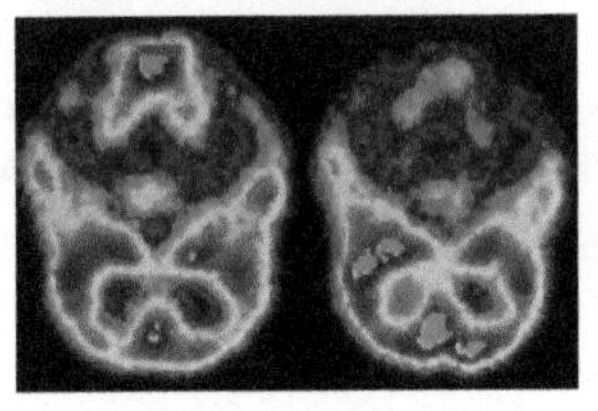 N.I. H/Photo Researchers, Inc.
MRI (magnetic resonance imaging) Note the fissures and internal structures of the brain. The throat, nasal airways, and fluid surrounding the brain are dark.	Powerful electromagnets produce a high-frequency magnetic field that is passed through the brain.	Produces high-resolution 3-D pictures of the brain useful for identifying abnormalities and mapping brain structures and function.	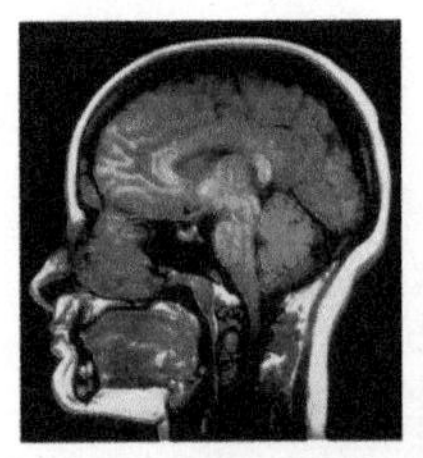 Scott Camazine/Photo Researchers, Inc.
fMRI (functional magnetic resonance imaging)	Newer, faster version of MRI that detects blood flow by picking up magnetic signals from blood, which has given up its oxygen to activate brain cells.	Measures blood flow, which indicates areas of the brain that are active and inactive during ordinary activities or responses (like reading or talking); also shows changes associated with various disorders.	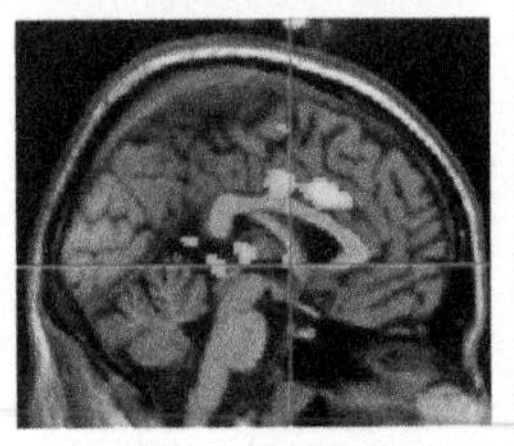 Science Photo Library/ Photo Researchers, Inc.
Other methods: (a) Cell body or tract (myelin) staining, (b) Microinjections, and (c) Intrabrain electrical recordings	(a) Colors/stains selected neurons or nerve fibers. (b) Injects chemicals into specific areas of the brain. (c) Records activity of one or a group of neurons inside the brain.	Increases overall information of structure and function through direct observation and measurement. Intrabrain wire probes allow scientists to "see" individual neuron activity.	

Hindbrain

You're asleep and in the middle of a frightening nightmare. Your heart is racing, your breathing is rapid, and you're attempting to run away but find you can't move! Suddenly, your nightmare is shattered by a buzzing alarm clock. All your automatic behaviors and survival responses in this scenario are controlled or influenced by parts of the hindbrain. The **hindbrain** includes the medulla, pons, and cerebellum.

The **medulla** is essentially an extension of the spinal cord, with many neural fibers passing through it carrying information to and from the brain. It also controls many essential automatic bodily functions, such as respiration and heart rate.

The **pons** is involved in respiration, movement, sleeping, waking, and dreaming (among other things). It also contains axons that cross from one side of the brain to the other (*pons* is Latin for "bridge").

The cauliflower-shaped **cerebellum** (Latin for "little brain") is, evolutionarily, a very old structure. It coordinates fine muscle movement and balance (**Figure 2.19**). Researchers using functional magnetic resonance imaging (fMRI) have shown that parts of the cerebellum also are important for memory, sensation, perception, cognition, language, learning, and even "multitasking" (e.g., Bellebaum & Daum, 2011; Eichenbaum, 2013; Manganelli et al., 2013; Thompson, 2005; Wu et al., 2013).

Hindbrain The lower or hind region of the brain; collection of structures including the medulla, pons, and cerebellum.

Medulla The hindbrain structure responsible for vital, automatic functions, such as respiration and heartbeat.

Pons The hindbrain structure involved in respiration, movement, waking, sleep, and dreaming.

Cerebellum The hindbrain structure responsible for coordinating fine muscle movement, balance, and some perception and cognition.

Midbrain

The **midbrain** helps us orient our eye and body movements to visual and auditory stimuli, and it works with the pons to help control sleep and level of arousal. It also contains a small structure, the *substantia nigra*, that secretes the neurotransmitter dopamine. Parkinson's disease, an age-related degenerative condition, is related to the deterioration of neurons in the substantia nigra and the subsequent loss of dopamine.

Running through the core of the hindbrain, midbrain, and brainstem is the **reticular formation (RF)**. This diffuse, finger-shaped network of neurons helps screen incoming sensory information and alerts the higher brain centers to important events. Without our reticular formation, we would not be alert or perhaps even conscious.

Midbrain The collection of structures in the middle of the brain responsible for coordinating movement patterns, sleep, and arousal.

Reticular formation (RF) The diffuse set of neurons that helps screen incoming information and controls arousal.

FIGURE 2.19 **WALK THE LINE**

Asking drivers to perform tasks like walking the white line is a common test for possible intoxication. Why? The cerebellum, responsible for smooth and precise movements, is one of the first areas of the brain to be affected by alcohol.

Bill Fritsch/Getty Images, Inc.

Forebrain

The **forebrain** is the largest and most prominent part of the human brain. It includes the cerebral cortex, hypothalamus, limbic system, and thalamus (**Figure 2.20**). The last three structures are located near the top of the brainstem. The cerebral cortex (discussed separately, in the next section) is wrapped above and around them. (*Cerebrum* is Latin for "brain," and *cortex* is Latin for "covering" or "bark.")

Forebrain The collection of upper-level brain structures including the thalamus, hypothalamus, limbic system, and cerebral cortex.

Thalamus The forebrain structure at the top of the brainstem that serves as the brain's switchboard, relaying sensory messages to the cerebral cortex.

The **thalamus** integrates input from the senses, and it may also function in learning and memory (Barnes, 2013). It receives input from nearly all sensory systems, except smell, and then directs the information to the appropriate cortical areas. The thalamus also transmits some higher brain information to the cerebellum and medulla. Think of the thalamus as the switchboard in an air traffic control center that receives information from all aircraft and directs them to landing or takeoff areas.

Because the thalamus is the brain's major sensory relay center to the cerebral cortex, damage or abnormalities in the thalamus might cause the cortex to misinterpret or not receive vital sensory information. Interestingly, brain-imaging research links thalamus abnormalities to schizophrenia, a serious psychological disorder characterized by problems with sensory filtering and perception (Bor et al., 2011; Hazlett et al., 2012; Kubota et al., 2013).

Hypothalamus The small brain structure beneath the thalamus that helps govern drives (hunger, thirst, sex, and aggression) and hormones.

Beneath the thalamus lies the kidney bean–sized **hypothalamus**. (*Hypo-* means "under.") This organ has been called the "master control center" for emotions and for many basic motives such as hunger, thirst, sex, and aggression (Feinstein, 2013; Hull, 2011; Moll et al., 2012). It regulates the body's internal environment, including temperature control, which it accomplishes by regulating the endocrine system.

FIGURE 2.20 **STRUCTURES OF THE FOREBRAIN**

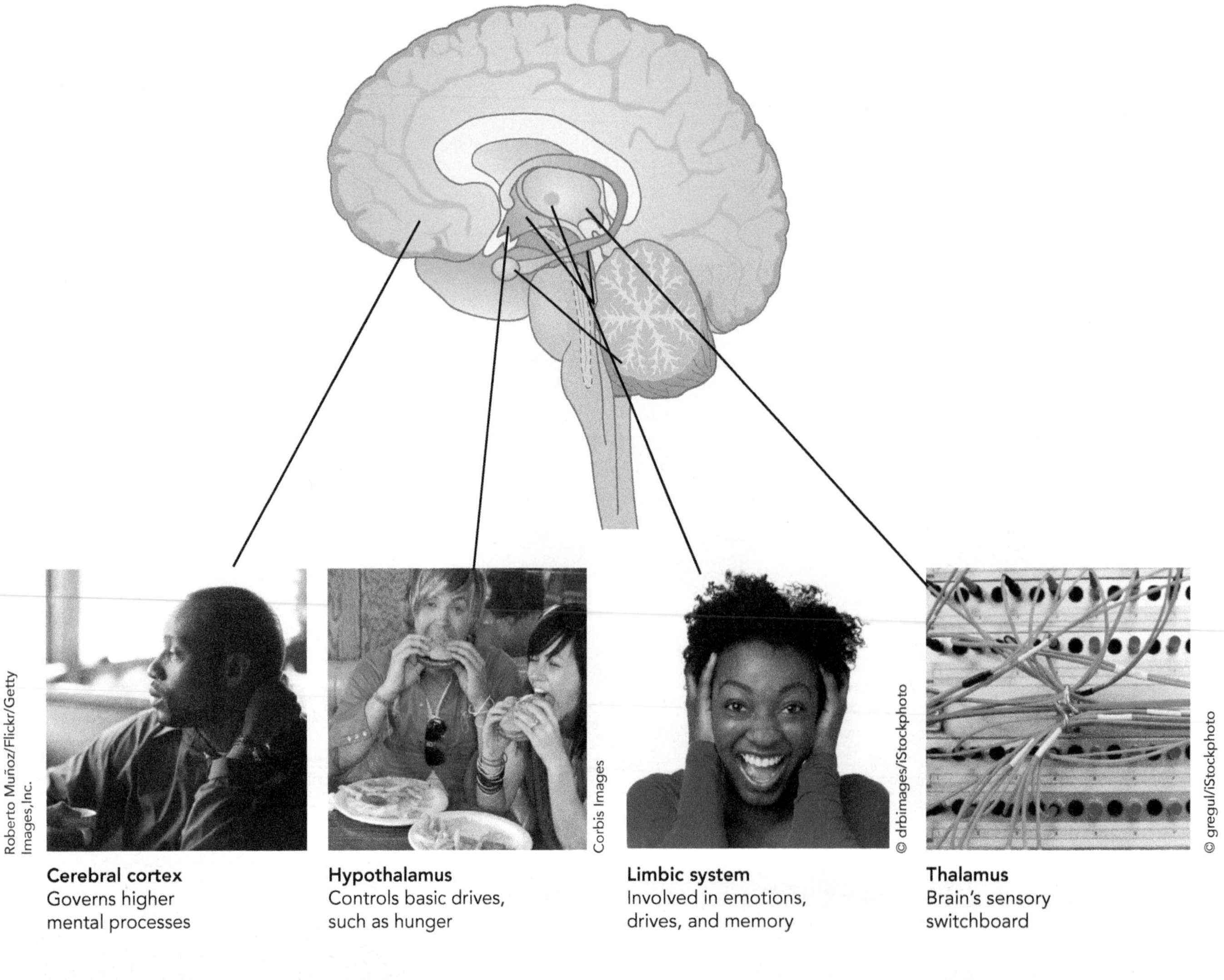

psychology and you **Diet and the Hypothalamus** Have you ever gone on a diet to try to lose weight or lost weight but then struggled to maintain your new weight? One of the reasons long-term weight loss is so hard for many people is that eating a high-fat diet can lead to long-term changes in the hypothalamus (Thaler et al., 2012). These changes make it harder for the body to regulate its weight, meaning that you will continue to feel hungry even when you have just eaten plenty of food. Sadly, this process makes it hard to stick to a diet and thereby increases the risk of obesity.

© donmedia/iStockphoto

Hanging down from the hypothalamus, the *pituitary gland* is usually considered the master endocrine gland because it releases hormones that activate the other endocrine glands. The hypothalamus influences the pituitary through direct neural connections and through release of its own hormones into the blood supply of the pituitary. The hypothalamus also directly influences some important aspects of behavior, such as eating and drinking patterns.

An interconnected group of forebrain structures, known as the **limbic system**, is located roughly along the border between the cerebral cortex and the lower-level brain structures (**Figure 2.21**). The limbic system is generally responsible for emotions, drives, and memory. In Chapter 7, you'll discover how the **hippocampus**, a key part of the limbic system, is involved in forming and retrieving our memories. However, the limbic system's major focus of interest is the **amygdala**, which is linked to the production and regulation of emotions–especially aggression and fear (Armony, 2013; LeDoux, 1998, 2002, 2007; Pinho et al., 2013; Whalen et al., 2013).

Another well-known function of the limbic system is its role as part of the so-called "pleasure center," a set of brain structures whose stimulation leads to highly enjoyable feelings (Bjork et al., 2012; Kolb, 2013; Olds & Milner, 1954). Even though limbic system structures and neurotransmitters are instrumental in emotions, the frontal lobes of the cerebral cortex also play an important role.

Limbic system The interconnected group of forebrain structures involved with emotions, drives, and memory, as well as major physiological functions.

Hippocampus The sea-horse shaped part of the limbic system involved in forming and retrieving memories.

Amygdala A part of the limbic system that controls emotions, like aggression and fear, and the formation of emotional memory.

Cerebral cortex The thin surface layer on the cerebral hemispheres that regulates most complex behavior, including sensations, motor control, and higher mental processes.

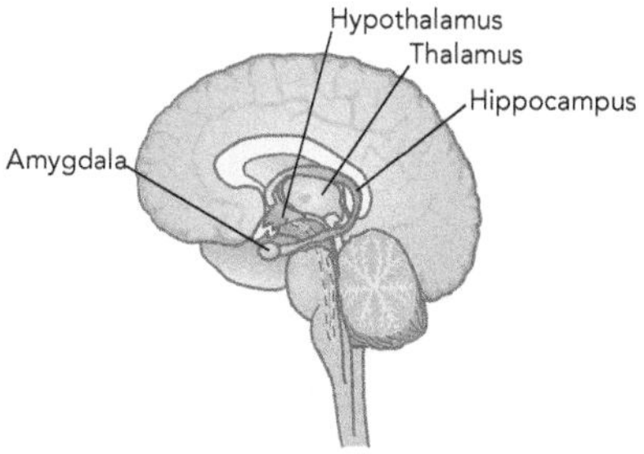

FIGURE 2.21 MAJOR BRAIN STRUCTURES COMMONLY ASSOCIATED WITH THE LIMBIC SYSTEM

The Cerebral Cortex

The gray, wrinkled **cerebral cortex**, the surface layer of the cerebral hemispheres, is responsible for most complex behaviors and higher mental processes. It plays such a vital role that many consider it the essence of life. In fact, physicians may declare a person legally dead when the cerebral cortex dies, even when the lower-level brain structures and the rest of the body are fully functioning.

Although the cerebral cortex is only about one-eighth of an inch thick, it's made up of approximately 30 billion neurons and nine times as many glial cells. Its numerous wrinkles, called *convolutions*, significantly increase its surface area. Q5 Damage to the cerebral cortex is linked to numerous problems, including suicide, substance abuse, and dementia (McKee et al., 2012). Evidence suggests that such trauma is particularly common in athletes who experience head injuries in sports like football, ice hockey, boxing, and soccer (**Figure 2.22**).

Drew Hallowell/Philadelphia Eagles/Getty Images

FIGURE 2.22 DAMAGE TO THE BRAIN

realworldpsychology

On March 20, 2013, the owners of the National Football League voted to ban runners from leading with their helmets when they hit other players. This so-called "crown rule" is designed to help reduce concussions, as might have occurred on September 9, 2012, when Cleveland Browns running back Trent Richardson ran into Philadelphia Eagles safety Kurt Coleman, knocking his helmet into the air.

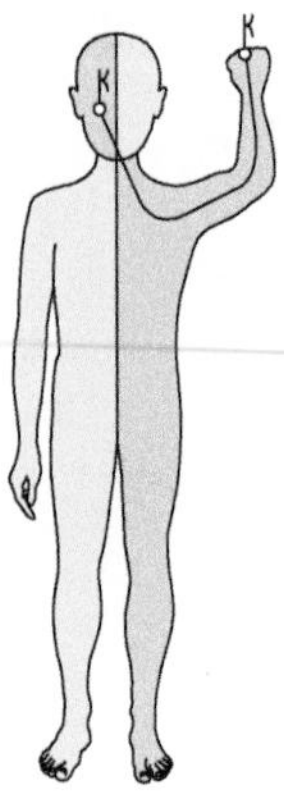

FIGURE 2.23 INFORMATION CROSSOVER

Our brain's right hemisphere controls the left side of our body, whereas the left hemisphere controls the right side.

Frontal lobes The two lobes at the front of the brain that govern motor control, speech production, and higher functions, such as thinking, personality, emotion, and memory.

The full cerebral cortex and the two cerebral hemispheres beneath it closely resemble an oversized walnut. The division, or *fissure*, down the center marks the separation between the left and right *hemispheres* of the brain, which make up about 80% of the brain's weight. The hemispheres are mostly filled with axon connections between the cortex and the other brain structures. Each hemisphere controls the opposite side of the body (**Figure 2.23**).

The cerebral hemispheres are each divided into four distinct areas, or lobes (**Figure 2.24**). Like the lower-level brain structures, each lobe specializes in somewhat different tasks, another example of localization of function. However, some functions overlap two or more lobes.

Frontal Lobes

Our two large **frontal lobes** coordinate messages received from all the other lobes. An area at the very back of these frontal lobes, known as the *motor cortex*, instigates all voluntary movement. In the lower-left frontal lobe lies *Broca's area*. In 1865, French physician Paul Broca discovered that damage to this area causes difficulty in speech, but not in language comprehension. This type of impaired language ability is known as *Broca's aphasia*.

Finally, the frontal lobes control most of our higher functions—the functions that distinguish humans from other animals, such as thinking, personality, emotion, and memory. Abnormalities in the frontal lobes are often observed in patients with schizophrenia (Chapter 13). For example, teenagers with schizophrenia often show loss of gray matter, as well as increases in cerebrospinal fluid in the frontal lobes (Arango et al., 2012). Research also shows that damage to the frontal lobes affects personality, motivation, drives, creativity, self-awareness, initiative, reasoning, and emotional behavior. But as you'll see in the *Psych Science* feature, updated information about the classic case of Phineas Gage indicates that our brains are remarkably flexible and

FIGURE 2.24 LOBES OF THE BRAIN

This is a view of the brain's left hemisphere showing its four lobes—*frontal, parietal, temporal*, and *occipital*. The right hemisphere has the same four lobes. Divisions between the lobes are marked by visibly prominent folds. Keep in mind that Broca's and Wernicke's areas occur only in the left hemisphere.

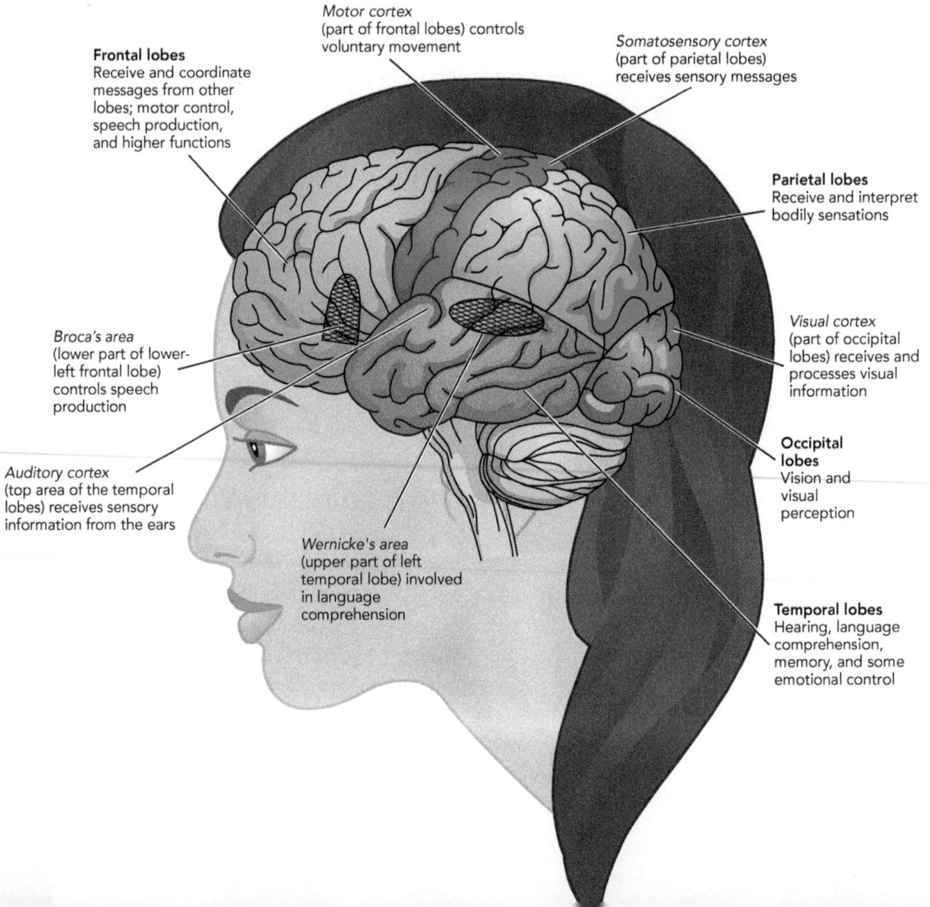

that damage to the frontal lobes (and other parts of the brain) may not be as permanent as we once thought—thanks to *neuroplasticity* and *neurogenesis*.

Temporal Lobes

The **temporal lobes** are responsible for hearing, language comprehension, memory, and some emotional control. The *auditory cortex*, which processes sound, is located at the top front of each temporal lobe. This area is responsible for receiving incoming sensory information and sending it on to the parietal lobes, where it is combined with other sensory information.

Temporal lobes The two lobes on each side of the brain above the ears that are involved in audition (hearing), language comprehension, memory, and some emotional control.

A part of the left temporal lobe called *Wernicke's area* aids in language comprehension. About a decade after Broca's discovery, German neurologist Carl Wernicke noted that patients with damage in this area could not understand what they read

PSYCHSCIENCE

PHINEAS GAGE—MYTHS VERSUS FACTS

In 1848, a 25-year-old railroad foreman named Phineas Gage had a metal rod (13½ pounds, 3 feet 7 inches long, and 1¼ inches in diameter) accidentally blown through the front of his face, destroying much of his brain's left frontal lobe. Amazingly, Gage was immediately able to sit up, speak, and move around, and he did not receive medical treatment until about 1½ hours later. After his wound healed, he tried to return to work, but was soon fired. The previously friendly, efficient, and capable foreman was now "fitful, impatient, and lacking in deference to his fellows" (Macmillan, 2000). In the words of his friends: "Gage was no longer Gage" (Harlow, 1868).

This so-called "American Crowbar Case" is often cited in current texts and academic papers as one of the earliest in-depth studies of an individual's survival after massive damage to the brain's frontal lobes. The evidence is clear that Gage did experience several dramatic changes in his behavior and personality after the accident, but the extent and permanence of these changes are in dispute. Most accounts of post-accident Gage report him as impulsive and unreliable until his death. However, more reliable evidence later showed that Gage spent many years driving stagecoaches–a job that required high motor, cognitive, and interpersonal skills (Macmillan, 2000, 2008; Macmillan & Lena, 2010).

So why bother reporting this controversy? As you'll note throughout this text, we discuss several popular misconceptions in psychology in order to clarify and correct them. Phineas Gage's story is particularly important because it highlights how a small set of reliable facts can be distorted and shaped to fit existing beliefs and scientific theories. For example, at the time of Gage's accident, little was known about how the brain functions, and damage to it was believed to be largely irreversible. Can you see how our current research techniques (e.g., Van Horn et al., 2012), along with our new understanding of *neurogenesis* and *neuroplasticity* might now explain the previously ignored evidence of Gage's significant recovery in later life?

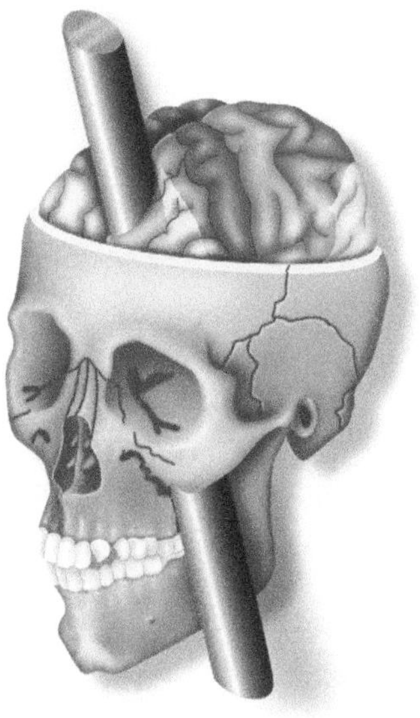

RESEARCH CHALLENGE

1. Based on the information provided, did the researchers in this study of Phineas Gage use descriptive, correlational, and/or experimental research?
2. If you chose:
   - descriptive research, is this a naturalistic observation, survey/interview, case study, or archival research?
   - correlational research, is this a positive, negative, or zero correlation?
   - experimental research, label the IV, DV, experimental group(s), and control group.

>>CHECK YOUR ANSWERS IN APPENDIX B.

NOTE: The information provided in this study is admittedly limited, but the level of detail is similar to what is presented in most textbooks and public reports of research findings. Answering these questions, and then comparing your answers to those in the Appendix, will help you become a better critical thinker and consumer of scientific research.

or heard, but they could speak quickly and easily. However, their speech was often unintelligible because it contained made-up words, sound substitutions, and word substitutions. This syndrome is now referred to as *Wernicke's aphasia*.

Occipital Lobes

Occipital lobes The two lobes at the back of the brain that are primarily responsible for vision and visual perception.

The **occipital lobes** are responsible for, among other things, vision and visual perception. Damage to the occipital lobes can produce blindness, even if the eyes and their neural connection to the brain are perfectly healthy.

Parietal Lobes

Parietal lobes The two lobes located at the top of the brain, in which bodily sensations are received and interpreted.

The **parietal lobes** receive and interpret bodily sensations including pressure, pain, touch, temperature, and location of body parts. A band of tissue on the front of the parietal lobes, called the *somatosensory cortex*, receives information about touch in different body areas. Areas of the body with more somatosensory and motor cortex devoted to them (such as the hands and face) are most sensitive to touch and have the most precise motor control (**Figure 2.25**).

Association Areas

Association areas The "quiet" areas in the cerebral cortex involved in interpreting, integrating, and acting on information processed by other parts of the brain.

One of the most popular myths in psychology is that we use only 10% of our brain. This myth might have begun with early research which showed that approximately three-fourths of the cortex is "quiet" (with no precise, specific function responsive to electrical brain stimulation). These areas are not dormant, however. They are clearly engaged in interpreting, integrating, and acting on information processed by other parts of the brain. They are called **association areas** because they associate, or connect, various areas and functions of the brain. The association areas in the frontal lobes, for example, help in decision making and planning. Similarly, the association area right in front of the motor cortex aids in the planning of voluntary movement.

FIGURE 2.25 BODY REPRESENTATION OF THE MOTOR CORTEX AND SOMATOSENSORY CORTEX

This drawing shows a vertical cross section taken from the left hemisphere's motor cortex and right hemisphere's somatosensory cortex. If body areas were truly proportional to the amount of tissue on the motor and somatosensory cortices that affect them, our bodies would look like the oddly shaped human figures draped around the outside edge of the cortex.

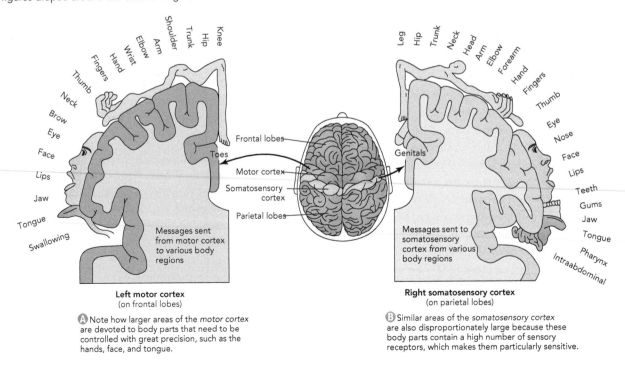

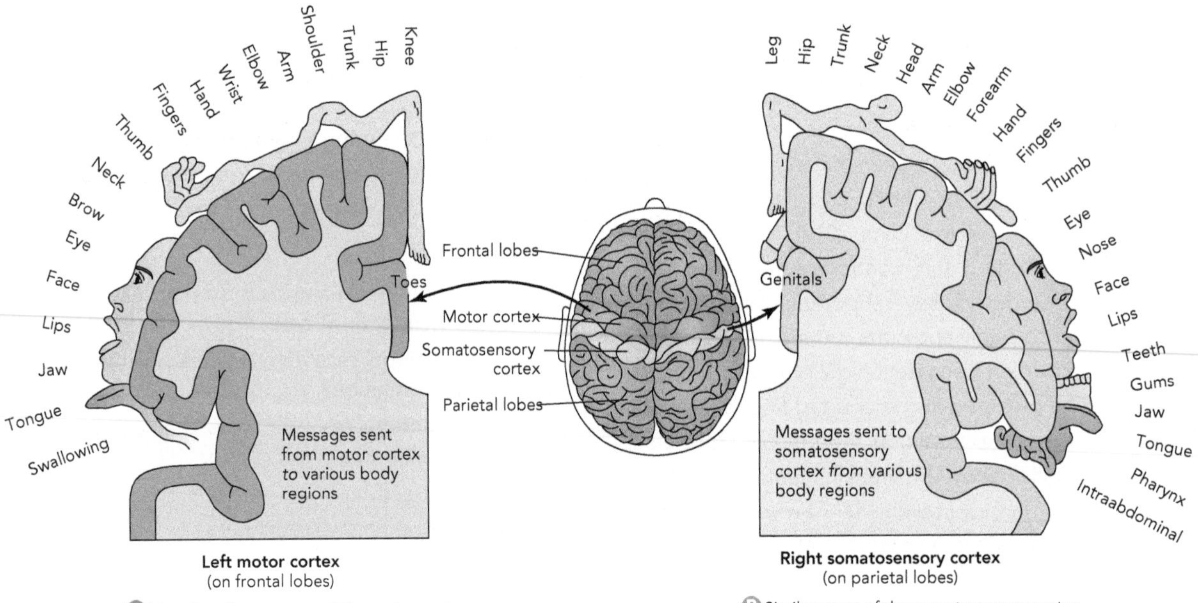

A Note how larger areas of the *motor cortex* are devoted to body parts that need to be controlled with great precision, such as the hands, face, and tongue.

B Similar areas of the *somatosensory cortex* are also disproportionately large because these body parts contain a high number of sensory receptors, which makes them particularly sensitive.

FIGURE 2.26 VIEWS OF THE CORPUS CALLOSUM

In the photo on the left, a human brain was sliced vertically from the top to the bottom to expose the corpus callosum, which conveys information between the two hemispheres of the cerebral cortex. In the illustration on the right, a brain was cut horizontally, which shows how fibers, or *axons*, of the corpus callosum link to both the right and left hemispheres. Note: The deep, extensive cuts shown in these photos are to reveal the corpus callosum. In split-brain surgeries on live patients, only fibers within the corpus callosum itself are cut.

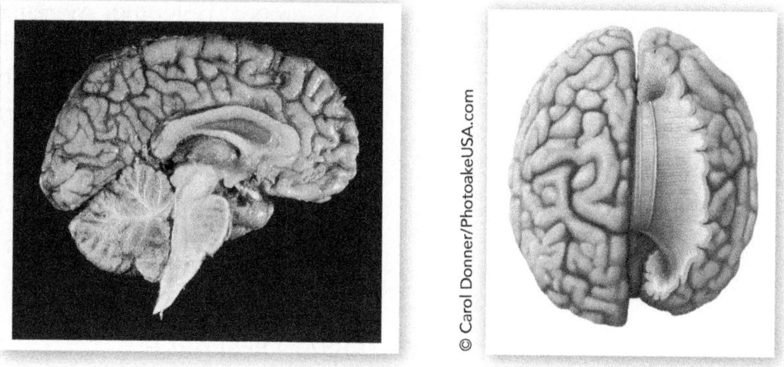

Martin M. Rotker/SPL/Photo Researchers, Inc.

© Carol Donner/PhotoakeUSA.com

Two Brains in One?

We mentioned earlier that the brain's left and right cerebral hemispheres control opposite sides of the body. Each hemisphere also has separate areas of specialization. This is another example of localization of function, technically referred to as *lateralization*.

Early researchers believed the right hemisphere was subordinate or nondominant to the left, with few special functions or abilities. In the 1960s, landmark **split-brain surgeries** began to change this view.

Split-brain surgery The cutting of the corpus callosum to separate the brain's two hemispheres; used medically to treat severe epilepsy; also provides information on the functions of the two hemispheres.

The primary connection between the two cerebral hemispheres is a thick, ribbon-like band of neural fibers under the cortex called the **corpus callosum** (**Figure 2.26**). In some rare cases of severe epilepsy, when other forms of treatment have failed, surgeons cut the corpus callosum to stop the spread of epileptic seizures from one hemisphere to the other. Because this operation cuts the only direct communication link between the two hemispheres, it reveals what each half of the brain can do in isolation from the other. The resulting research has profoundly improved our understanding of how the two halves of the brain function.

Corpus callosum A bundle of neural fibers that connects the brain's two hemispheres.

For example, when someone has a brain stroke and loses his or her ability to speak, we know this generally points to damage on the left hemisphere, because this is where *Broca's area*, which controls speech production, is located (refer back to Figure 2.24). However, we now know that when specific regions of the brain are injured or destroyed their functions can sometimes be picked up by a neighboring region—even the opposite hemisphere.

realworldpsychology **The Myth of the "Neglected Right Brain"** Popular accounts of split-brain research have led to some exaggerated claims and unwarranted conclusions about differences between the left and right hemispheres. For example, courses and books directed at "right-brain thinking" and "drawing on the right side of the brain" often promise to increase our intuition, creativity, and artistic abilities by waking up our neglected and underused right brain. Contrary to this myth, research has clearly shown that the two hemispheres work together in a coordinated, integrated way, each making important contributions (Barnes, 2013).

If you are a member of a soccer or basketball team, you can easily understand this principle. Just as you and your teammates often specialize in different jobs, such as offense and defense, the hemispheres also somewhat divide their workload. However, like good team players, each of the two hemispheres is generally aware of what the other is doing.

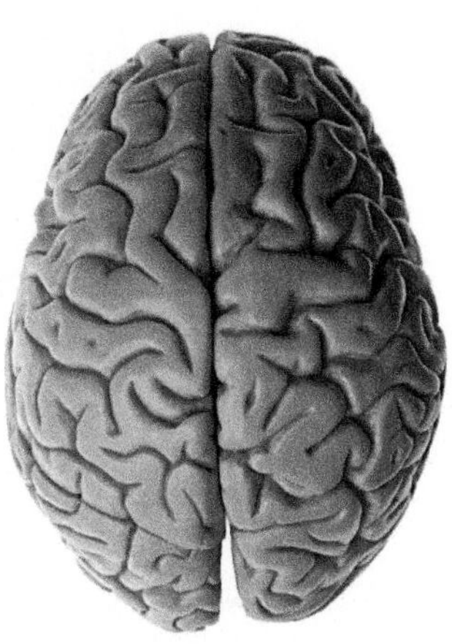

© Debbi Smirnoff/iStockphoto

Although most split-brain surgery patients generally show very few outward changes in their behavior, other than fewer epileptic seizures, the surgery does create a few unusual responses. For example, one split-brain patient reported that when he dressed himself, he sometimes pulled his pants down with his left hand and up with his right (Gazzaniga, 2009). The subtle changes in split-brain patients normally appear only with specialized testing. See **Figure 2.27** for an illustration and description of this type of specialized test. Keep in mind that in actual split-brain surgery on live patients, only some fibers within the corpus callosum are cut (*not* the lower brain structures), and this surgery is performed only in rare cases of intractable epilepsy.

In our tour of the nervous system, the principles of localization of function, lateralization, and specialization recur: Dendrites receive information, the occipital lobes specialize in vision, and so on. Keep in mind, however, that, like a great soccer or basketball team, all parts of the brain and nervous system also play overlapping and synchronized roles.

FIGURE 2.27 **SPLIT-BRAIN RESEARCH**

Experiments on split-brain patients often present visual information to only the patient's left or right hemisphere, which leads to some intriguing results.

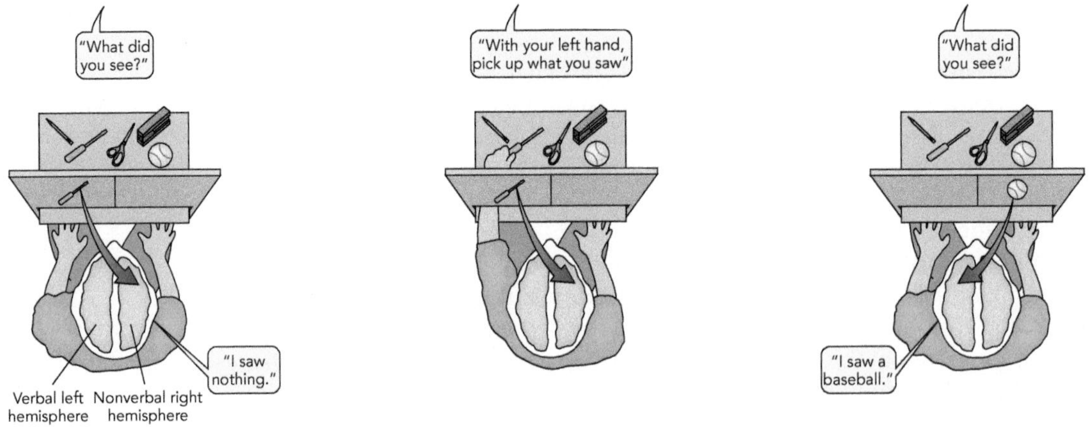

Ⓐ When a split-brain patient is asked to stare straight ahead while a photo of a screwdriver is flashed only to the right hemisphere, he will report that he "saw nothing."

Ⓑ However, when asked to pick up with his left hand what he saw, he can reach through and touch the items hidden behind the screen and easily pick up the screwdriver.

Ⓒ When the left hemisphere receives an image of a baseball, the split-brain patient can easily name it.

Assuming you have an intact, nonsevered corpus callosum, if the same photos were presented to you in the same way, you could easily name both the screwdriver and the baseball. Can you explain why? The answers lie in our somewhat confusing visual wiring system (as shown in drawings d and e below).

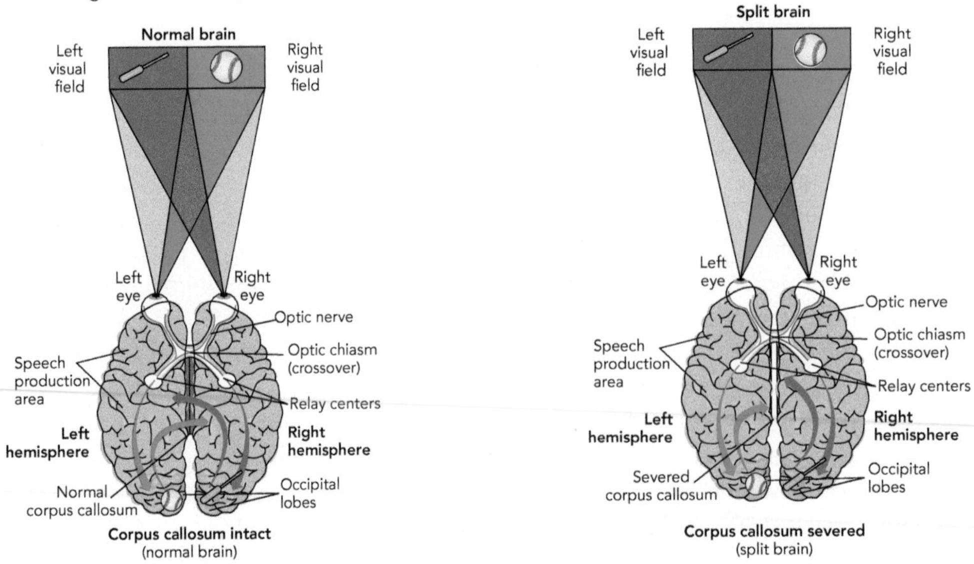

Ⓓ As you can see, our eyes normally connect to our brains in such a way that, when we look straight ahead, information from the left visual field travels to our right hemisphere (the blue line). In contrast, information from the right visual field travels to our left hemisphere (the red line). The messages received by either hemisphere are then quickly sent to the other across the corpus callosum (the red and blue arrows).

Ⓔ When the corpus callosum is severed (note the white line down the middle of the two hemispheres), a split-brain patient cannot verbalize what he sees. This is because in this particular task the visual information is presented only to the right hemisphere and the information cannot travel to the opposite (verbal) hemisphere.

RETRIEVAL PRACTICE: A TOUR THROUGH THE BRAIN

Self-Test

Completing this self-test and comparing your answers with those in Appendix B provides immediate feedback and helpful practice for exams. Additional interactive, self-tests are available at www.wiley.com/college/huffman.

1. Label the following structures/areas of the brain:

a. corpus callosum b. amygdala
c. cerebellum d. thalamus
e. hippocampus f. cerebral cortex

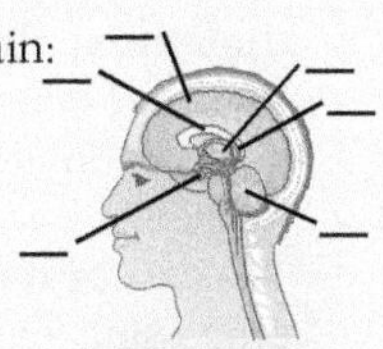

2. Label the four lobes of the brain:

a. frontal b. parietal
c. temporal d. occipital

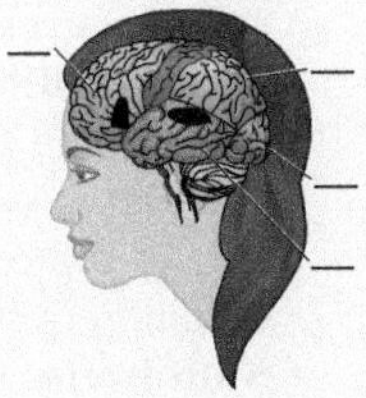

3. The _____ lobes are largely responsible for motor control, speech production, and higher functions, such as thinking, personality, and memory.

a. cortical b. frontal
c. parietal d. occipital

4. Although the left and right hemispheres sometimes perform different, specialized functions, they are normally in close communication and share functions, thanks to the _____.

a. thalamus b. sympathetic nervous system
c. cerebellum d. corpus callosum

Think Critically

1 Imagine that you are giving a speech. Name the cortical lobes involved in the following behaviors:

a. Seeing faces in the audience
b. Hearing questions from the audience
c. Remembering where your car is parked when you are ready to go home
d. Noticing that your new shoes are too tight and hurting your feet

2 What are some everyday examples of the different functions of the two hemispheres?

realworldpsychology

Why are former NFL athletes at increased risk of depression, dementia, and suicide?

HINT: LOOK IN THE MARGIN FOR Q5

Summary

1 OUR GENETIC INHERITANCE 36

- Neuroscience/biopsychology studies how biological processes relate to behavioral and mental processes.
- **Genes** (dominant or recessive) hold the code for inherited traits. **Behavioral geneticists** use studies of twins and families with biological and adopted children to help determine **heritability**, the relative influences of heredity and environment on various traits.
- **Evolutionary psychology** suggests that many behavioral commonalities emerged and remain in human populations through **natural selection** because they helped ensure our "genetic survival."

2 NEURAL BASES OF BEHAVIOR 40

- **Neurons**, supported by **glial cells**, receive and send electrochemical signals to other neurons and to the rest of the body. Their major components are **dendrites**, a **cell body**, and an **axon**.
- Within a neuron, a neural impulse, or **action potential**, moves along the axon. Neurons communicate with each other using **neurotransmitters**, which are released at the **synapse** and attach to the receiving neuron. Neurons receive input from many synapses. Hundreds of different neurotransmitters regulate a wide variety of physiological processes. Many **agonist** and **antagonist drugs** and poisons act by mimicking or interfering with neurotransmitters.
- The **endocrine system** uses **hormones** to broadcast messages throughout the body. The system regulates long-term bodily processes, maintains ongoing bodily processes, and controls the body's response to emergencies.

3 NERVOUS SYSTEM ORGANIZATION 46

- The **central nervous system (CNS)** includes the brain and spinal cord. The CNS allows us to process information and adapt to our environment in ways that no other animal can. The spinal cord transmits information between the brain and the rest of the body, and it initiates involuntary **reflexes**. Although the CNS is very fragile, recent research shows that the brain is capable of lifelong **neuroplasticity** and **neurogenesis**. Neurogenesis is made possible by **stem cells**.

- The **peripheral nervous system (PNS)** includes all the nerves outside the brain and spinal cord. It links the brain and spinal cord to the body's sense receptors, muscles, and glands. The PNS is subdivided into the **somatic nervous system (SNS)**, which controls voluntrary movement, and the **autonomic nervous system (ANS)**, which is responsible for automatic behavior.
- The ANS includes the **sympathetic nervous system** and the **parasympathetic nervous system**. The sympathetic nervous system mobilizes the body's "fight or flight" response. The parasympathetic nervous system returns the body to its normal functioning.

4 A TOUR THROUGH THE BRAIN 52

- Neuroscientists have developed several tools to explore the human brain and nervous system. Early researchers used dissection and other methods like clinical observation and case studies of living people. Recent scientific advances include newer brain imaging scans, which have improved scientists' ability to examine these processes and to do so noninvasively.
- The brain is divided into the **hindbrain**, the **midbrain**, and the **forebrain**. The brainstem includes parts of each of these. Certain brain structures are specialized to perform certain tasks thanks to *localization of function*.
- The hindbrain, including the **medulla**, **pons**, and **cerebellum**, controls automatic behaviors and survival responses.
- The midbrain helps us orient our eye and body movements, helps control sleep and arousal, and is involved with the neurotransmitter dopamine. The **reticular formation (RF)** runs through the core of the hindbrain, midbrain, and brainstem, and is responsible for screening information and managing our levels of alertness.
- Forebrain structures, including the **cerebral cortex**, **hypothalamus**, **limbic system**, and **thalamus**, integrate input from the senses, control basic motives, regulate the body's internal environment, and regulate emotions, learning, and memory.
- The **cerebral cortex**, part of the forebrain, governs most higher processing and complex behaviors. It is divided into two hemispheres, each controlling the opposite side of the body. The **corpus callosum** links the hemispheres. Each hemisphere is divided into **frontal**, **parietal**, **temporal**, and **occipital lobes**. Each lobe specializes in somewhat different tasks, but a large part of the cortex is devoted to integrating actions performed by different brain regions.
- **Split-brain** research shows that each hemisphere performs somewhat different functions, although they work in close communication.

applyingrealworldpsychology

We began this chapter with five intriguing Real World Psychology questions, and you were asked to revisit these questions at the end of each section. Questions like these have an important and lasting impact on all of our lives. See if you can answer these additional critical thinking questions related to real world examples.

1. Most traits are polygenic, meaning they are controlled by more than one gene. Given that tongue curling is one of the few traits that depends on only one dominant gene, can you explain why both of the parents of the three boys in this photo are "noncurlers"?
2. Why might humans and other animals have evolved to possess complex traits such as tongue curling?
3. If neuroscientists were able to use brain scans to determine what a person is thinking, what might be the ethical considerations of this type of research?
4. Imagine that your friend "John" has suffered a major automobile accident, and now has right-sided paralysis. Given that he has lost his ability to speak, can you identify the specific section of the brain and which hemisphere was most likely damaged in the accident?
5. Some research suggests that women are better than men at multitasking. What part(s) of the brain would explain this possible difference?

Courtesy Karen Huffman

Key Terms

RETRIEVAL PRACTICE Write a definition for each term before turning back to the referenced page to check your answer.

- action potential 40
- agonist drug 43
- amygdala 57
- antagonist drug 43
- association areas 60
- autonomic nervous system (ANS) 50
- axon 40
- behavioral genetics 36
- cell body 40
- central nervous system (CNS) 46
- cerebellum 55
- cerebral cortex 57
- corpus callosum 61
- dendrites 40
- endocrine system 44
- endorphin 44
- evolutionary psychology 36
- forebrain 56
- frontal lobes 58
- gene 36
- glial cells 40
- heritability 38
- hindbrain 55
- hippocampus 57
- hormone 44
- hypothalamus 56
- limbic system 57
- medulla 55
- midbrain 55
- myelin sheath 42
- natural selection 39
- neurogenesis 47
- neuron 40
- neuroplasticity 47
- neurotransmitter 43
- occipital lobes 60
- parasympathetic nervous system 50
- parietal lobes 60
- peripheral nervous system (PNS) 46
- pons 55
- reflex 48
- reticular formation (RF) 55
- somatic nervous system (SNS) 49
- split-brain surgery 61
- stem cells 47
- sympathetic nervous system 50
- synapse 45
- temporal lobes 59
- thalamus 56

chapterthree

Stress and Health Psychology

CHAPTER OUTLINE

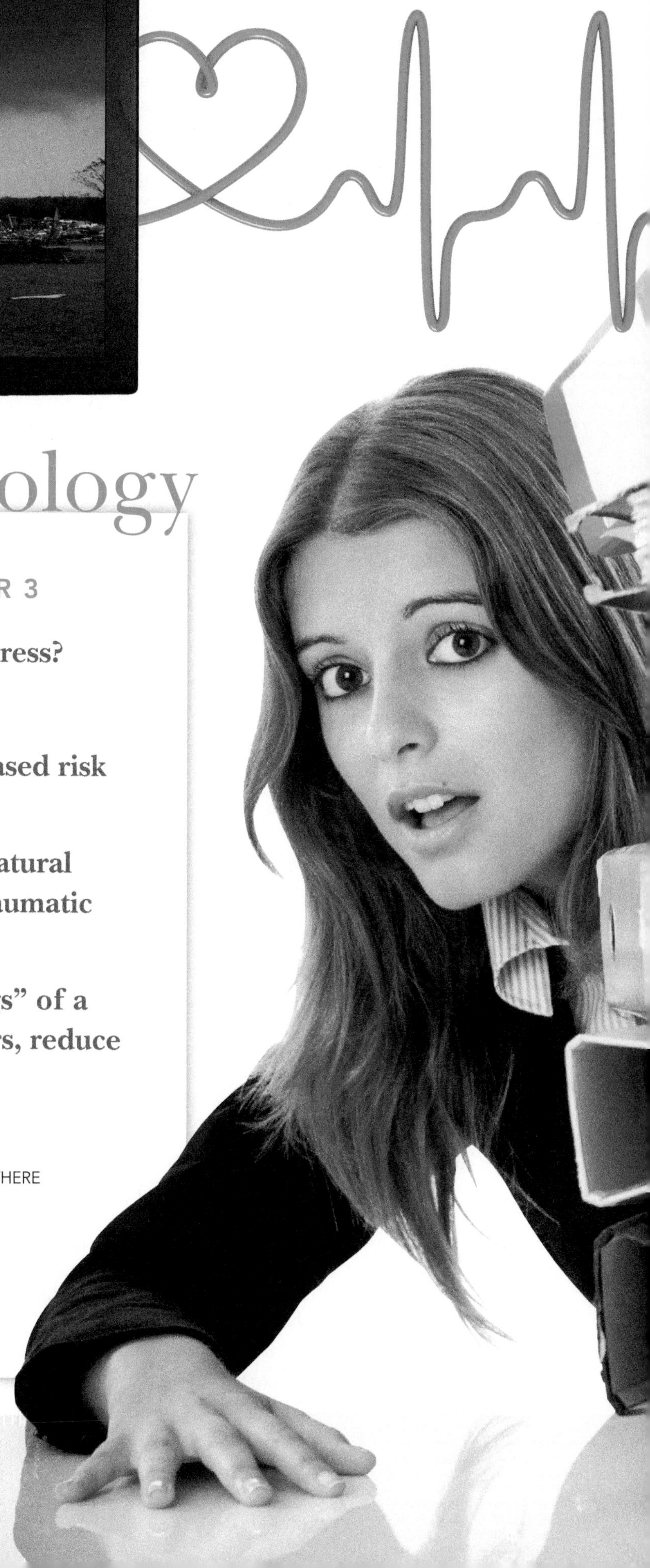

realworldpsychology

THINGS YOU'LL LEARN IN CHAPTER 3

Q1 **Does the use of social media lead to stress?**

Q2 **Can loneliness make you sick?**

Q3 **Are people with stressful jobs at increased risk of experiencing a heart attack?**

Q4 **Does watching televised coverage of natural disasters increase symptoms of posttraumatic stress disorder?**

Q5 **Could thinking about the "silver linings" of a stressful event, or sharing it with others, reduce depression?**

THROUGHOUT THE CHAPTER, MARGIN ICONS FOR Q1–Q5 INDICATE WHERE THE TEXT ADDRESSES THESE QUESTIONS.

chapteroverview

Do you recall the 2013 dramatic rescue of the three women held hostage in a suburban house in Cleveland, Ohio? Despite having been raped, beaten, and caged under horrific conditions for over a decade, these women apparently survived with their physical and emotional health relatively intact. As you might expect, stress exists on a continuum, and it's largely in the eye of the beholder. We would all agree that what these women endured was extreme, unimaginable stress. In comparison, if you've done poorly on previous exams and are only just now reading this chapter at the last minute before an exam, you may be experiencing personally high levels of stress. But, if you're a student who's generally well prepared and performs well on exams, you're probably experiencing little or no stress. In short, stress is largely dependent on our interpretations of events and our perceived resources for coping with them.

In this chapter, we'll focus on a general understanding of stress, its relationship with major illness, and healthy ways to manage it.

UNDERSTANDING STRESS

LEARNING OBJECTIVES

RETRIEVAL PRACTICE While reading the upcoming sections, respond to each Learning Objective in your own words. Then compare your responses with those found at www.wiley.com/college/huffman.

1. **IDENTIFY** the major sources of stress.
2. **REVIEW** the three phases of the general adaptation syndrome (GAS).
3. **DESCRIBE** the SAM system and the HPA axis.

Stress The interpretation of specific events, called *stressors*, as threatening or challenging; the physical and psychological reactions to stress, known as the *stress response*.

Stressor A trigger or stimulus that induces stress.

Everyone experiences **stress**, and we generally know what a person means when he or she say speaks of being "stressed." But scientists generally define stress as *the interpretation of specific events, called* **stressors**, *as threatening or challenging*. The resulting physical and psychological reactions to stressors are known as the *stress response* (Cardeña et al., 2013; Sanderson, 2013). Using these definitions, can you see how an upcoming exam on this material could be called a stressor, whereas your physical and psychological reactions are your stress response? In this following section, we'll discuss the key sources of stress and how it affects us.

Sources of Stress

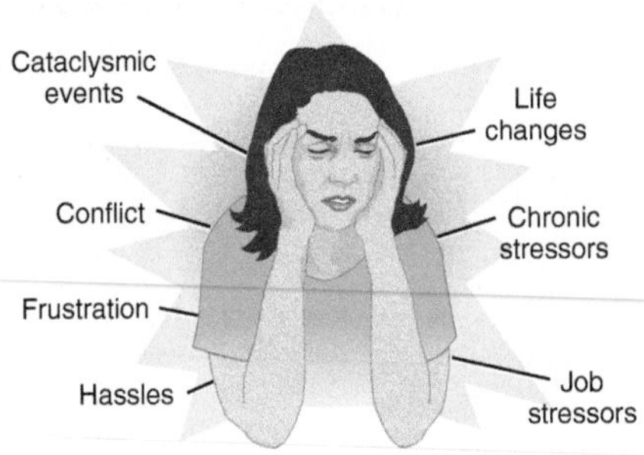

FIGURE 3.1 SEVEN MAJOR SOURCES OF STRESS

realworldpsychology

Although literally hundreds of things can cause stress in all our lives, psychological science has focused on seven major sources **(Figure 3.1)**. For example, early stress researchers Thomas Holmes and Richard Rahe (1967) believed that any *life change* that required some adjustment in behavior or lifestyle could cause some degree of stress. They also believed that exposure to numerous stressful events in a short period could have a direct detrimental effect on health.

To investigate the relationship between change and stress, Holmes and Rahe created the Social Readjustment Rating Scale (SRRS), which asks people to check off all the life events they have experienced in the previous year (see *Psychology and You*).

The SRRS is an easy and popular tool for measuring stress (e.g., Fabre et al., 2013), and cross-cultural studies have shown that most people also rank the magnitude of their stressful events similarly (Hashimoto et al., 2012; Thoits, 2010).

TEST YOURSELF: MEASURING LIFE CHANGES

psychology and you

To score yourself on the Social Readjustment Rating Scale (SRRS), add up the "life change units" for all life events you have experienced during the last year and compare your score with the following standards: 0–150 = No significant problems; 150–199 = Mild life crisis (33% chance of illness); 200–299 = Moderate life crisis (50% chance of illness); 300 and above = Major life crisis (80% chance of illness).

Life Events	Life Change Units
Death of spouse	100
Divorce	73
Marital separation	65
Jail term	63
Death of a close family member	63
Personal injury or illness	53
Marriage	50
Fired at work	47
Marital reconciliation	45
Retirement	45
Change in health of family member	44
Pregnancy	40
Sex difficulties	39
Gain of a new family member	39
Business readjustment	39
Change in financial state	38
Death of a close friend	37
Change to different line of work	36
Change in number of arguments with spouse	35
Mortgage or loan for major purchase	31
Foreclosure on mortgage or loan	30
Change in responsibilities at work	29
Son or daughter leaving home	29
Trouble with in-laws	29
Outstanding personal achievement	28
Spouse begins or stops work	26
Begin or end school	26
Change in living conditions	25
Revision of personal habits	24
Trouble with boss	23
Change in work hours or conditions	20
Change in residence	20
Change in schools	20
Change in recreation	19
Change in church activities	19
Change in social activities	18
Mortgage or loan for lesser purchase (car, major appliance)	17
Change in sleeping habits	16
Change in number of family get-togethers	15
Change in eating habits	15
Vacation	13
Christmas	12
Minor violations of the law	11

Source: Reprinted from the *Journal of Psychosomatic Research*, Vol. III; Holmes and Rahe: "The Social Readjustment Rating Scale," 213–218, 1967, with permission from Elsevier.

But the SRRS is not foolproof. For example, it only shows a correlation between stress and illness; it does not prove that stress actually causes illnesses. Moreover, not all stressful situations are **cataclysmic events**, such as a terrorist attack, or single events like a death or a birth. **Chronic stress**, such as war, a bad marriage, poor working conditions, or a repressive political climate, can be significant, too **(Figure 3.2)** (Cardeña et al., 2013; Enoch, 2011; Filipović et al., 2013). Even the stress of persistent environmental noise is associated with measurable hormonal and brain changes (Fooladi, 2012). Interestingly, women with high levels of emotional exhaustion become more sensitive to sound after an acute stress task (Hasson et al., 2013).

Cataclysmic event A stressful occurrence that occurs suddenly and generally affects many people simultaneously.

Chronic stress A continuous state of arousal in which demands are perceived as greater than the inner and outer resources available for dealing with them.

FIGURE 3.2 DISCRIMINATION AS A CHRONIC STRESSOR

One type of stressful event that some people experience is discrimination based on their race or social class, which can lead to higher levels of dangerous health-related behaviors, including substance abuse and risky sexual choices (Stock et al., 2013). Discrimination also is linked with negative health consequences, such as high blood pressure, cardiovascular disease, and diabetes (Bratter & Gorman, 2011; Fuller-Rowell et al., 2012; Szanton et al., 2011).

Our social lives can also be chronically stressful because making and maintaining friendships requires considerable thought and energy (Sias et al., 2004). For example, although people often use Facebook to maintain friendships, research suggests that your stress level increases the more Facebook "friends" you have and the more time you spend on the site. In addition, an online survey of college students' attitudes about Facebook revealed the following (Charles, 2011):

Q1

- 12% reported that Facebook made them feel anxious.
- 63% reported delaying responses to friend requests.
- 32% reported that rejecting friend requests made them feel guilty and uncomfortable.
- 10% reported disliking receiving friend requests (perhaps because they may lead to guilt and discomfort!).

What is stressful about Facebook? People may feel excluded from social events that are often described and photographed on Facebook, experience pressure to be entertaining when they post, and fear that they are missing important information if they don't check in repeatedly. These findings suggest that keeping in touch with friends through Facebook may have some disadvantages as well as some advantages.

Given the recent global economic downturn, one of our most pressing concerns is *job stress*, which can result from unemployment, job change, worries about job performance, and so on (Halbesleben et al., 2013; Hoppe, 2011; O'Neill & Davis, 2011). One study found that leaders—including military officers and government officials—experience lower levels of stress than nonleaders, presumably because they have higher levels of control in their work environment (Sherman et al., 2012). The most stressful jobs are those that make great demands on performance and concentration but allow little creativity or opportunity for advancement (Quick et al., 2013; Sanderson, 2013).

Stress at work can also cause serious stress at home, not only for the worker but for other family members as well. In our private lives, divorce, child and spousal abuse, alcoholism, and money problems can all place severe stress on a family (Aboa-Éboulé, 2008; Newman & Roberts, 2013; Rosenström et al., 2011).

Stress can also arise when we experience **conflict**—that is, when we are forced to make a choice between at least two incompatible alternatives. There are three basic types of conflict, **approach-approach**, **approach-avoidance**, and **avoidance-avoidance** **(Table 3.1)**.

Generally, approach–approach conflicts are the easiest to resolve and produce the least stress. Avoidance–avoidance conflicts, on the other hand, are usually the most difficult and take the longest because either choice leads to unpleasant results. Furthermore, the longer any conflict exists, or the more important the decision, the more stress a person will experience.

The minor **hassles** of daily living also can pile up and become a major source of stress. We all share many hassles, such as time pressures and financial concerns. But our reactions to them vary. Persistent hassles can lead to a form of physical,

Conflict A forced choice between two or more incompatible goals or impulses.

Approach–approach conflict The forced choice between two options, both of which have equally desirable characteristics.

Approach–avoidance conflict The forced choice within one option, which has equally desirable and undesirable characteristics.

Avoidance–avoidance conflict The forced choice between two options, both of which have equally undesirable characteristics.

Hassle Any small problem of daily living that accumulates and sometimes become a major source of stress.

TABLE 3.1 TYPES OF CONFLICT

Conflict	Description/Resolution	Example/Resolution	
Approach–approach + +	Forced choice between two options, both of which have equally desirable characteristics Generally easiest and least stressful conflict to resolve	Two equally desirable job offers, but you must choose one of them because you're broke You make a pro/con list and/or "flip a coin"	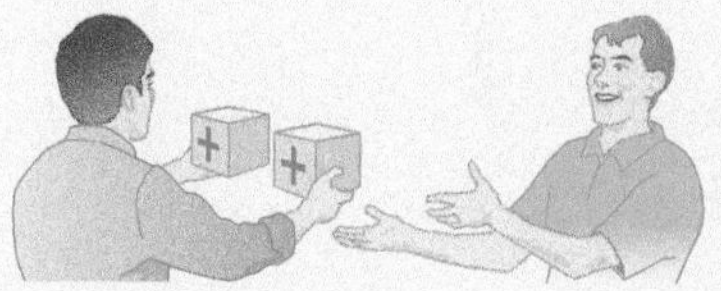
Avoidance–avoidance – –	Forced choice between two options, both of which have equally undesirable characteristics Difficult, stressful conflict, generally resolved with a long delay and considerable denial	Two equally undesirable job offers, but you must choose one of them because you're broke You make a pro/con list and/or "flip a coin" and then delay the decision, hoping for additional job offers	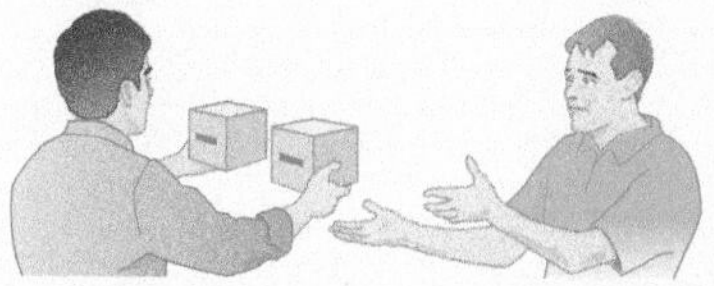
Approach–avoidance + –	Forced choice within one option, which has equally desirable and undesirable characteristics	One high-salary job offer that requires you to relocate to an undesirable location away from all your friends and family	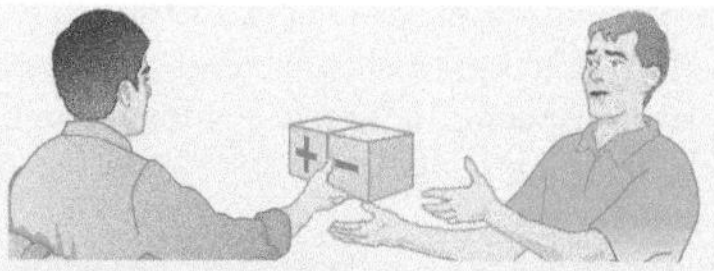

Think Critically

The expression on this man's face indicates that he's experiencing some form of conflict.

1. Can you explain how this could be both an avoidance–avoidance and/or an approach–avoidance conflict?
2. What might be the best way resolve this conflict?

Lisa Peardon/Taxi/Getty

Burnout A state of psychological and physical exhaustion that results from chronic exposure to high levels of stress, with little personal control.

Frustration Unpleasant tension, anxiety, and heightened sympathetic activity that results from a blocked goal.

mental, and emotional exhaustion known as **burnout** (Chen & Kao, 2013; Jung & Kim, 2012; Kumar & Mellsop, 2013). Over time, some people in chronically stressful professions, such as firefighters, police officers, doctors, and nurses, become emotionally drained. Burnout can cause more work absences, less productivity, and increased risk of illness.

Some authorities believe hassles can be more significant than major life events in creating stress (Kubiak et al., 2008; Stefanek et al., 2012). Divorce is extremely stressful, but it may be so because of the increased number of hassles it brings—changes in finances, child-care arrangements, longer working hours, and so on.

Like hassles, **frustration**, a negative emotional state resulting from a blocked goal, can cause stress. And the more motivated we are, the more frustrated we become when our goals are blocked.

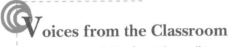

Voices from the Classroom

Frustration and Grades When talking about stress, arousal, and coping, I try to select real world events to which my students can relate, such as a frustrating bad exam score and how they responded and coped with it. I ask them, "Is stress in the eye of the beholder?" "Did you allow the low score to question your ability in the class—high and irrational stress?" "Or did you see it as an opportunity to reassess your studying habits and class participation—moderate, and most importantly, manageable stress?" I want my students to think about their own role in assessing stress and then become proactive about it. Not surprisingly, my office hours are significantly busier from this point of the semester forward!

Professor David W. Steitz,
Nazareth College
Rochester, New York

General adaptation syndrome (GAS) Selye's three-stage (alarm, resistance, exhaustion) reaction to chronic stress; a pattern of nonspecific, adaptational response to a continuing stressor.

Effects of Stress

When mentally or physically stressed, our bodies undergo several biological changes that can be detrimental to health. In 1936, Canadian physician Hans Selye (SELL-yay) described a generalized physiological reaction to stress that he called the **general adaptation syndrome (GAS)**. The GAS occurs in three phases—*alarm*, *resistance*, and *exhaustion*—activated by efforts to adapt to any stressor, whether physical or psychological **(Figure 3.3)**.

Most of Selye's ideas about the GAS pattern of stress response have proven to be correct, but we now know that different stressors evoke different responses and that people vary widely in their reactions to them. For example, one of the most interesting differences has to do with gender. Men more often choose "fight or flight." In contrast, women "tend and befriend," which means that they more often take care of themselves and their children (tending) and form strong social bonds with others (befriending) (Taylor, 2006, 2012; von Dawans et al., 2012).

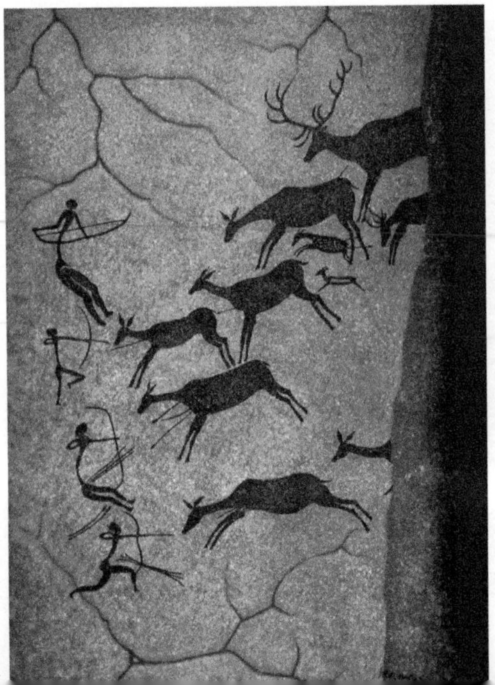

Art Resource

Stress in Ancient Times

As shown in these ancient cave drawings, the automatic fight-or-flight response was adaptive and necessary for early human survival. However, in modern society, it occurs as a response to ongoing situations where we often cannot fight or flee. This repeated arousal can be detrimental to our health.

FIGURE 3.3 GENERAL ADAPTATION SYNDROME (GAS)

The three phases of this syndrome (*alarm, resistance,* and *exhaustion*) focus on the biological response to stress—particularly the "wear and tear" on the body that results from prolonged stress.

1 Alarm phase
When surprised or threatened, your body enters an alarm phase during which your resistance to stress is temporarily suppressed, while your arousal is high (e.g., increased heart rate and blood pressure) and blood is diverted to your skeletal muscles to prepare for "fight-or-flight" (Chapter 2).

2. Resistance phase
If the stress continues, your body rebounds to a phase of increased resistance. Physiological arousal remains higher than normal, and there is an outpouring of stress hormones. During this resistance stage, people use a variety of coping methods. For example, if your job is threatened, you may work longer hours and give up your vacation days.

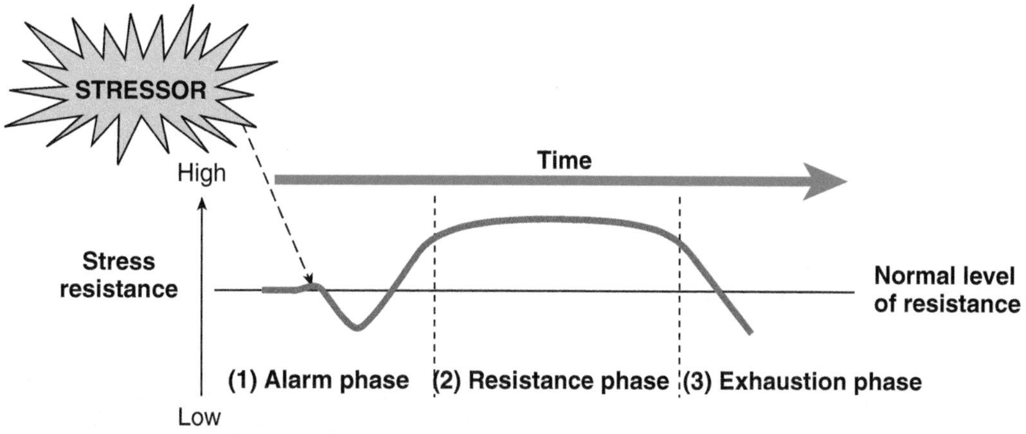

3. Exhaustion phase
Your body's resistance to stress can only last so long before exhaustion sets in. During this final phase, you become more susceptible to serious illnesses, and possibly irreversible damage to your body. Selye maintained that one outcome of this exhaustion phase for some people is the development of *diseases of adaptation*, including asthma, ulcers, and high blood pressure. Unless a way of relieving stress is found, the eventual result may be complete collapse and death.

Some researchers believe these differences are hormonal in nature. Although oxytocin is released during stress in both men and women, the female's higher level of estrogen tends to enhance oxytocin, which results in more calming and nurturing feelings. In contrast, the hormone testosterone, which men produce in higher levels during stress, reduces the effects of oxytocin.

What is Selye's most important take-home message? *Our bodies are relatively well designed for temporary stress but poorly equipped for prolonged stress.* The same biological processes that are adaptive in the short run, such as the fight-or-flight response, can be hazardous in the long run (e.g., Dougall et al., 2013; Viena et al., 2012).

To understand these dangers, we need to first describe how our bodies (ideally) respond to stress. As you can see in **Figure 3.4**, once our brains identify a stressor, our **SAM** (sympatho–adreno–medullary) **system** and **HPA** (hypothalamic–pituitary–adrenocortical) **axis** then work together to increase our arousal and energy levels to deal with the stress. Once the stress is resolved, these systems turn off, and our bodies return to normal, baseline functioning, known as **homeostasis**.

Unfortunately, given our increasingly stressful modern lifestyle, our bodies are far too often in a state of elevated, chronic arousal, which can wreak havoc on our health. Some of the most damaging effects of stress are on our *immune system* and our *cognitive functioning*.

SAM system Our body's initial, rapid-acting stress response, involving the sympathetic nervous system and the adrenal medulla; called the sympatho–adreno–medullary (SAM) system.

HPA axis Our body's delayed stress response, involving the hypothalamus, pituitary, and adrenal cortex; also called the hypothalamic–pituitary–adrenocortical (HPA) axis.

Homeostasis Our body's tendency to maintain a relatively balanced and stable internal state, such as a constant internal temperature.

Stress and the Immune System

The discovery of the relationship between stress and the immune system has been very important. When people are under stress, the immune system is less able to regulate the normal inflammation system, which makes us more susceptible to diseases, such as cancer, bursitis, colitis, Alzheimer's disease, rheumatoid arthritis,

FIGURE 3.4 **THE STRESS RESPONSE—AN INTERRELATED SYSTEM**

Faced with stress, our sympathetic nervous system prepares us for immediate action—to "fight or flee." Our slower-acting HPA axis maintains our arousal. Here's how it happens:

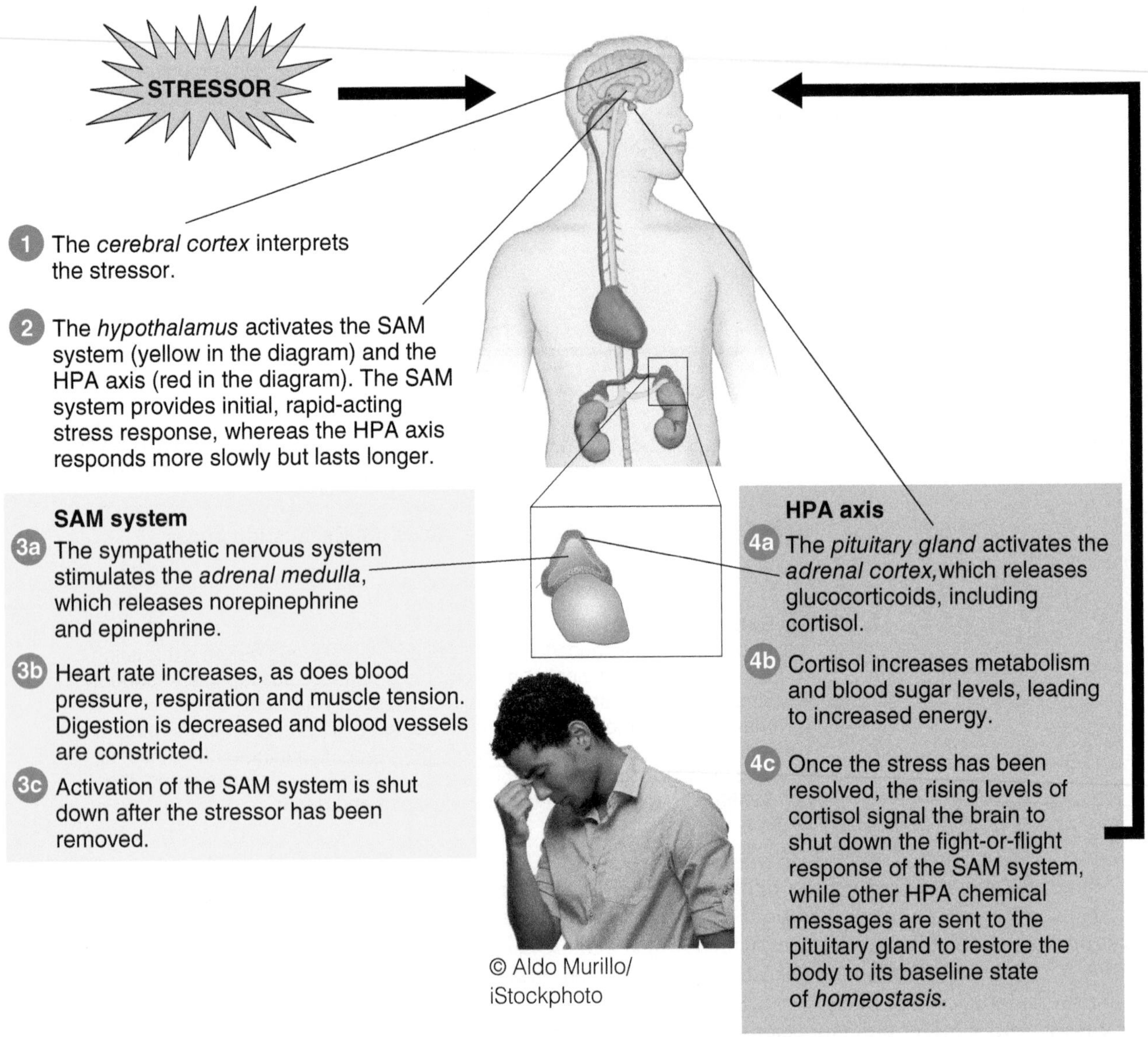
STRESSOR
1 The *cerebral cortex* interprets the stressor.
2 The *hypothalamus* activates the SAM system (yellow in the diagram) and the HPA axis (red in the diagram). The SAM system provides initial, rapid-acting stress response, whereas the HPA axis responds more slowly but lasts longer.
SAM system
3a The sympathetic nervous system stimulates the *adrenal medulla*, which releases norepinephrine and epinephrine.
3b Heart rate increases, as does blood pressure, respiration and muscle tension. Digestion is decreased and blood vessels are constricted.
3c Activation of the SAM system is shut down after the stressor has been removed.
HPA axis
4a The *pituitary gland* activates the *adrenal cortex*, which releases glucocorticoids, including cortisol.
4b Cortisol increases metabolism and blood sugar levels, leading to increased energy.
4c Once the stress has been resolved, the rising levels of cortisol signal the brain to shut down the fight-or-flight response of the SAM system, while other HPA chemical messages are sent to the pituitary gland to restore the body to its baseline state of *homeostasis*.
© Aldo Murillo/ iStockphoto

periodontal disease, and even the common cold (Carroll et al., 2011; Cohen et al., 2002, 2012; Cohen & Lemay, 2007; Dantzer et al., 2008; Gasser & Raulet, 2006; Segerstrom & Miller, 2004).

Prolonged, excessive, and/or chronic stress also contributes to hypertension, memory problems, depression, posttraumatic stress disorder (PTSD), drug and alcohol abuse, and even low birth weight (Bagley et al., 2011; Johnson et al., 2008; Stalder et al., 2010; Straub, 2011; Yuen et al., 2012).

Interestingly, the relationship between stress and depression has even been shown in rats. For example, researchers in one study caused stress in rats by restricting their food and play time, isolating them from other rats, and switching around their sleep and awake times for three weeks (Son et al., 2012). After experiencing this stress, the rats showed clear signs of depression, including having little interest in eating or drinking tasty sugar water and showing immobility instead of swimming when placed in water.

As if the long list of ill effects for both human and nonhuman animals weren't enough, severe or prolonged stress can also produce premature aging, faster growth of cancer cells, and even death (Ahola et al., 2012; Cohen et al., 2012; Russ et al., 2012; Wikgren et al., 2011).

How does this happen? *Cortisol*, a key element of the HPA axis, plays a critical role in the long-term negative effects of stress. Although increased cortisol levels initially help us fight stressors, if these levels stay high, which occurs when stress continues over time, the body's disease-fighting immune system is suppressed. For example, one study found that people who are lonely—which is another type of chronic stressor—have an impaired immune response, leaving their bodies vulnerable to infections, allergies, and many of the other illnesses cited above (Jaremka et al., 2013).

Q2

Knowledge that psychological factors have considerable control over infectious diseases has upset the long-held assumption in biology and medicine that these diseases are strictly physical. The clinical and theoretical implications are so important that a new interdisciplinary field, called **psychoneuroimmunology**, has emerged (Stowell et al., 2013). It studies the effects of psychological and other factors on the immune system.

Psychoneuroimmunology The interdisciplinary field that studies the effects of psychological and other factors on the immune system.

Stress and Cognitive Functioning

What happens to our brain and thought processes when we're under immediate stress? As we've just seen, cortisol helps us deal with immediate dangers by mobilizing our energy resources. It also helps us create memories for short-term, highly emotional events, which explains the so-called *flashbulb memories* discussed in Chapter 7. Can you see why scientists believe that our increased memories for emotional events may have evolved to help us remember what to avoid or protect in the future?

realworldpsychology **Short-Term Stress** Just as flashbulb memories affect our memories for highly emotional events, short-term stress can affect the retrieval of existing memories, the laying down of new memories, and general information processing (Almela et al., 2011; Guenzel et al., 2013; Pechtel & Pizzagalli, 2011; Schwabe & Wolf, 2013). This interference with cognitive functioning helps explain why you may forget important information during a big exam and why people may become dangerously confused during a fire and be unable to find the fire exit. The good news is that once the cortisol washes out, memory performance generally returns to normal levels.

Luis Alvarez/Getty Images

What happens during prolonged stress? Long-term exposure to cortisol can permanently damage cells in the hippocampus, a key part of the brain involved in memory (Chapter 7). Furthermore, once the hippocampus has been damaged, it cannot provide proper feedback to the hypothalamus, so cortisol continues to be secreted, and a vicious cycle can develop **(Figure 3.5)**.

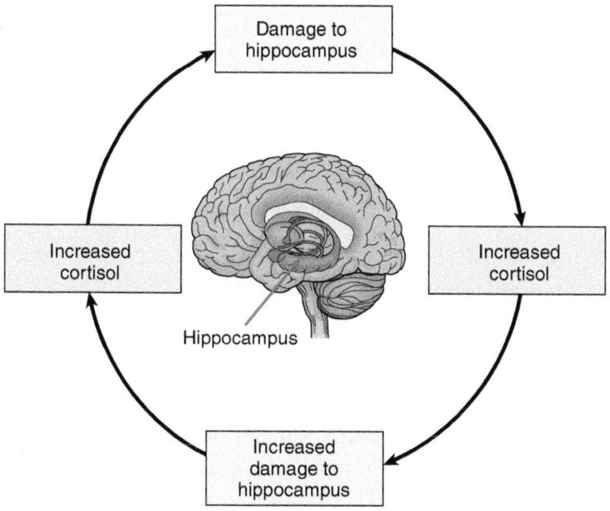

FIGURE 3.5 **STRESS AND THE BRAIN**

Cortisol released in response to stress damages the brain, triggering a vicious cycle.

RETRIEVAL PRACTICE: UNDERSTANDING STRESS

Self-Test

Completing this self-test and comparing your answers with those in Appendix B provides immediate feedback and helpful practice for exams. Additional interactive, self-tests are available at www.wiley.com/college/huffman.

1. When John saw his girlfriend kissing another man at a party, he became very upset. In this situation, watching someone you love kiss a potential competitor is ______, and becoming upset is ______.

a. a stressor; a biological imperative
b. distressing; a life change event
c. a cataclysmic event; evidence of a burnout
d. a stressor; a stress response

2. A state of physical, emotional, and mental exhaustion due to persistent emotionally demanding situations is called ______.

a. primary conflict
b. technostress
c. burnout
d. secondary conflict

3. In an approach–approach conflict, we must choose between two or more goals that will lead to ______, whereas in an avoidance–avoidance conflict, we must choose between two or more goals that will lead to ______.

a. less conflict; more conflict
b. frustration; hostility
c. a desirable result; an undesirable result
d. effective coping; ineffective coping

4. As Michael watches his instructor pass out papers, he suddenly realizes that this is the first major exam, and he is unprepared. Which phase of the GAS is he most likely experiencing?

a. resistance
b. alarm
c. exhaustion
d. phase out

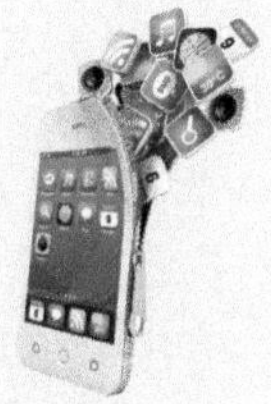

Think Critically

1 What are the major sources of stress in your life?

2 How does chronic stress threaten our immune system?

realworldpsychology

Does the use of social media lead to stress?

Can loneliness make you sick?

HINT: LOOK IN THE MARGIN FOR Q1 AND Q2

STRESS AND ILLNESS

LEARNING OBJECTIVES

RETRIEVAL PRACTICE While reading the upcoming sections, respond to each Learning Objective in your own words. Then compare your responses with those found at www.wiley.com/college/huffman.

1 **EXPLAIN** how biological and psychological factors can jointly influence the development of gastric ulcers.
2 **DESCRIBE** the relationship between stress and cancer.
3 **DEFINE** the personality patterns that can influence how we respond to stress.
4 **IDENTIFY** the cause and key symptoms of posttraumatic stress disorder (PTSD).

As we've just seen, stress has dramatic effects on our bodies. This section explores how stress is related to four serious illnesses—gastric ulcers, cancer, cardiovascular disorders, and posttraumatic stress disorder (PTSD).

Gastric Ulcers

Gastric ulcers are lesions to the lining of the stomach (and duodenum—the upper section of the small intestine) that can be quite painful. In extreme cases, they may even be life-threatening. Beginning in the 1950s, psychologists reported strong evidence that stress can lead to ulcers. Studies found that people who live in stressful situations have a higher incidence of ulcers than people who don't. And numerous experiments with laboratory animals have shown that stressors, such as shock or confinement to a very small space for a few hours, can produce ulcers in some laboratory animals (Andrade & Graeff, 2001; Bhattacharya & Muruganandam, 2003; Gabry et al., 2002; Takahashi et al., 2012).

The relationship between stress and ulcers seemed well established until researchers identified a bacterium (*Helicobacter pylori*, or *H. pylori*) that appears to be associated with ulcers. Later studies confirmed that this bacterium clearly damages the stomach wall, and that antibiotic treatment helps many patients. However, approximately 75% of normal control subjects' stomachs also have the bacterium. This suggests that the bacterium may cause the ulcer, but only in people who are compromised by stress. Furthermore, behavior modification and other psychological treatments, used alongside antibiotics, can help ease ulcers. In other words, although stress *by itself* does not cause ulcers, it is a contributing factor, along with biological factors (Fink, 2011).

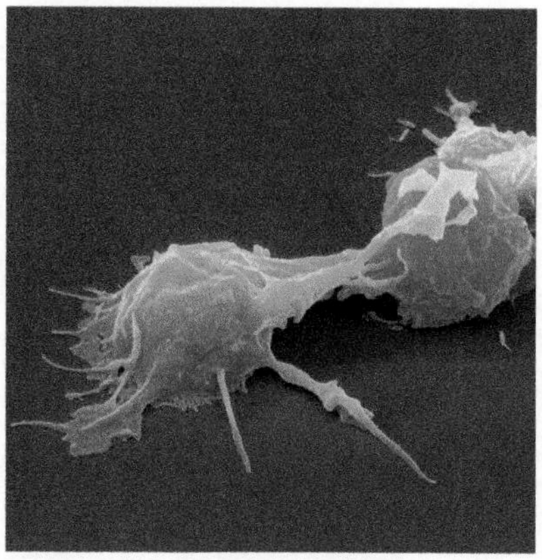

Rainbow/Photo Researchers, Inc.

FIGURE 3.6 THE IMMUNE SYSTEM IN ACTION

Stress can compromise the immune system, but the actions of a healthy immune system are shown here. The round red structures are leukemia cells. Note how the yellow killer cells are attacking and destroying the cancer cells.

Cancer

Cancer is among the leading causes of death for adults in the United States. It occurs when a particular type of primitive body cell begins rapidly dividing and then forms a tumor that invades healthy tissue. In a healthy person, whenever cancer cells start to multiply, the immune system checks the uncontrolled growth by attacking the abnormal cells **(Figure 3.6)**. Unless destroyed or removed, the tumor eventually damages organs and causes death. More than 100 types of cancer have been identified. They appear to be caused by an interaction between environmental factors (such as diet, smoking, and pollutants) and inherited predispositions. *Psych Science* describes how one type of environmental factor, child abuse, contributes to the development of cancer.

Note that research does *not* support the popular myths that stress *causes* cancer or that positive attitudes can fight it off (Coyne & Tennen, 2010; Lilienfeld et al., 2010; Surtees et al., 2009). However, stress does increase the spread of cancer cells to other organs, including the bones, which decreases the likelihood of survival (Campbell et al., 2012).

But this is not to say that developing a positive attitude and reducing our stress levels aren't worthy health goals (Dempster et al., 2011; O'Brien & Moorey, 2010; Quick et al., 2013). As you read earlier, prolonged stress causes the adrenal glands to release hormones that negatively affect the immune system, and a compromised immune system is less able to resist infection or to fight off cancer cells (Bernabé et al., 2011; Flint et al., 2013; Hassan et al., 2013; Krukowski et al., 2011). For example, when researchers disrupted the sleep of 21 healthy people over a period of six weeks, they found increases in blood sugar and decreases in metabolism, which may lead to obesity as well as diabetes (Buxton et al., 2012).

psychology and you **Stress and Illness** Think about a time when you were experiencing stress, such as studying for a difficult exam, having a fight with a loved one, or struggling to pay your bills. Both minor and major stressors can decrease the effectiveness of your immune system and thereby lead to both short- and long-term health problems.

© Keeweeboy/
iStockphoto

You'll be happy to know about all of the available resources for coping with stress, in addition to sleep, that are listed at the end of this chapter. Keep in mind that reducing stress can, at least in some cases, have a substantial impact on psychological as well as physical health. For example, some research suggests that women with breast cancer who receive a psychological intervention to teach them strategies for reducing stress show an increase in quality of life as well as length of survival

PSYCHSCIENCE

THE SAD AND LASTING IMPACT OF CHILD ABUSE ON HEALTH

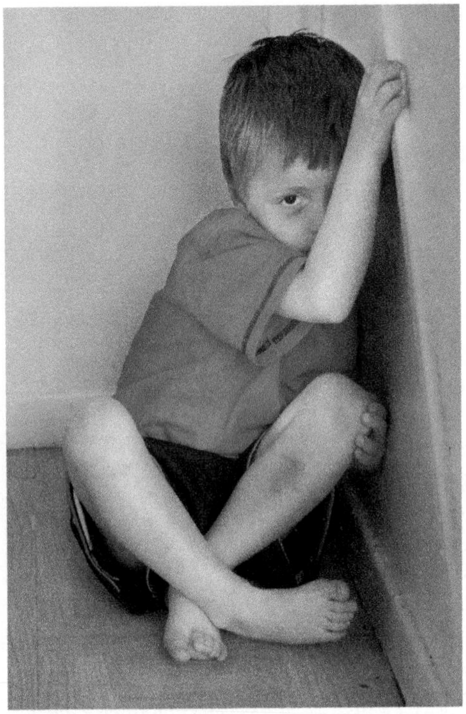

© Agostinosangel/iStockphoto

Researchers interested in examining the long-term consequences of childhood abuse on health surveyed 2,101 adults across the United States (Morton et al., 2012). Participants were questioned about their childhood experiences, including poverty, their parents' highest level of education, and how frequently their parents had exhibited behaviors, such as:

- Refusing to talk to them
- Threatening to hit them
- Pushing, grabbing, or shoving them
- Throwing something at them
- Kicking, biting, or hitting them with a fist
- Choking them
- Burning or scalding them

Sadly, children who experienced frequent emotional and/or physical abuse were found to be at much higher risk of developing cancer as adults than children who had not experienced such abuse. Boys who experienced both types of abuse were 6 times more likely to report developing cancer as adults, and girls who experienced both types of abuse were 15 times more likely to develop cancer. Given your new understanding of the link between stress and health outcomes, how would you explain these findings?

RESEARCH CHALLENGE

1. Based on the information provided, did the study (Morton et al., 2012) use descriptive, correlational, and/or experimental research?
2. If you chose:
   - descriptive research, is this a naturalistic observation, survey/interview, case study, or archival research?
   - correlational research, is this a positive, negative, or zero correlation?
   - experimental research, label the IV, DV, experimental group(s), and control group.

>>CHECK YOUR ANSWERS IN APPENDIX B.

NOTE: The information provided in this study is admittedly limited, but the level of detail is similar to what is presented in most textbooks and public reports of research findings. Answering these questions, and then comparing your answers to those in the Appendix, will help you become a better critical thinker and consumer of scientific research.

(Andersen et al., 2010). In fact, women who receive this intervention are 45% less likely to have a cancer recurrence than those without this training.

Cardiovascular Disorders

Cardiovascular disorders contribute to over half of all deaths in the United States (American Heart Association, 2012). Understandably, health psychologists are concerned because stress is a major contributor to these deaths (Emery et al., 2013; Landsbergis et al., 2011; Montoro-Garcia et al., 2011; Steptoe & Kivimäki, 2013).

Heart disease is a general term for all disorders that eventually affect the heart muscle and lead to heart failure. *Coronary heart disease* occurs when the walls of the coronary arteries thicken, reducing or blocking the blood supply to the heart.

Symptoms of such disease include *angina* (chest pain due to insufficient blood supply to the heart) and *heart attack* (death of heart muscle tissue).

When the body is stressed, the autonomic nervous system releases epinephrine (adrenaline) and cortisol into the bloodstream. These hormones increase heart rate and release fat and glucose from the body's stores to give muscles a readily available source of energy. If no physical fight-or-flight action is taken (and this is most likely the case in our modern lives), the fat that was released into the bloodstream is not burned as fuel. Instead, it may adhere to the walls of blood vessels. These fatty deposits are a major cause of blood-supply blockage, which causes heart attacks.

Type A and Type B Behavior Patterns

The effects of stress on heart disease may be amplified if a person tends to be hard driving, competitive, ambitious, impatient, and hostile—a **Type A** behavior pattern. The opposite of the Type A pattern is the **Type B** behavior pattern, which is characterized by a laid-back, relaxed attitude toward life.

Type A A pattern of behaviors and emotions that includes intense ambition, competition, exaggerated time urgency, and a cynical, hostile outlook; hostility increases the risk of coronary heart disease.

Type B A pattern of behaviors and emotions that is less competitive, less aggressive, more relaxed, and less hostile than a Type A.

Among Type A characteristics, hostility is the strongest predictor of heart disease (Allan, 2011; Buneviciute et al., 2013; Mommersteeg & Pouwer, 2012). In particular, the constant stress associated with cynical hostility—constantly being "on watch" for problems—translates physiologically into higher blood pressure, heart rates, and levels of stress-related hormones. People who are hostile, suspicious, argumentative, and competitive also tend to have more interpersonal conflicts. This can heighten autonomic activation, leading to increased risk of cardiovascular disease (Boyle et al., 2004; Bunde & Suls, 2006; Haukkala et al., 2010; Williams, 2010).

Health psychologists have developed two types of behavior modification for Type A people. The shotgun approach aims to eliminate or modify all Type A behaviors. The major criticism of this approach is that it eliminates not only undesirable Type A behaviors but also desirable traits, such as ambition. In contrast, the target behavior approach focuses on only Type A behaviors that are likely to cause heart disease—namely, cynical hostility.

Positive affect Demonstrating a sense of pleasure in the environment, including feelings of happiness, joy, enthusiasm, and contentment.

Positive Affect (Emotion)

Have you ever wondered why some people survive in the face of great stress (personal tragedies, demanding jobs, or an abusive home life) while others do not? One answer may be that these "survivors" have a unique trait called **positive affect**, meaning they have a sense of pleasure in their environment, including feelings of happiness, joy, enthusiasm, and contentment (**Figure 3.7**). Interestingly, people who are high in positive affect also experience fewer colds, strokes, and auto accidents (Kim & Park, 2012; Ostir et al., 2001; Pressman & Cohen, 2005).

Positive states are also associated with longer life expectancy. One study of more than 2,000 women found that those who are higher on extraversion and positive affect live on average 2 to 3 years longer than those who are low on these measures (Terracciano et al., 2008). Positive affect is even associated with a lower risk of mortality in patients with diabetes, which is a leading cause of death in the United States (Moskowitz et al., 2008).

Of course, having a Type A personality and lacking a positive affect are not the only risk factors associated with heart disease. Other factors include smoking, obesity, a high-fat diet, and lack of exercise (Go et al., 2013; Lim et al., 2013; Scarborough et al., 2012). In addition, a large, meta-analysis of the correlation between job strain and coronary heart disease found that people with stressful jobs are 23% more likely to experience a heart attack than those without stressful jobs (Kivimäki et al., 2012).

FIGURE 3.7 POSITIVE PSYCHOLOGY IN ACTION

Based on his smile and cheery wave, it looks like this patient may be one of those lucky people with a naturally positive outlook on life. Can you see how this approach might help him cope and recuperate from his serious injuries?

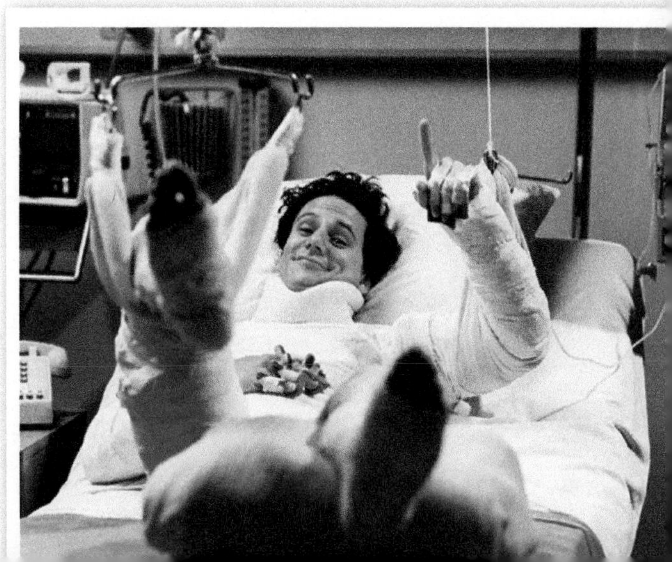

Stuart Hughes/Corbis

Posttraumatic Stress Disorder (PTSD)

Posttraumatic stress disorder (PTSD) A trauma- and stressor-related disorder that develops from directly or indirectly experiencing actual or threatened death, serious injury, or violence.

One of the most powerful examples of the effects of severe stress is **posttraumatic stress disorder (PTSD)** (American Psychiatric Association, 2013; Baker et al., 2011; Pace & Heim, 2011; Ruzek et al., 2011).

Research shows that approximately 40% of all children and teens will experience a traumatic stressor and that the lifetime prevalence for trauma is between 50 to 90% (Brown et al., 2013). However, the vast majority will not go on to develop PTSD, which is a long-lasting, trauma and stressor-related disorder occurring in both men and women, adults, and children.

PTSD's essential feature is the development of characteristic symptoms **(Table 3.2)** following exposure to one or more traumatic events (American Psychiatric Association, 2013). These symptoms may continue for months or even years after the event. Unfortunately, some victims of PTSD turn to alcohol and other drugs to cope, which generally compound the problem (Cougle et al., 2011; McCauley et al., 2012; Simpson et al., 2012).

Many people think PTSD results only from direct experiences in military combat, but victims of natural disasters, physical or sexual assault, terrorist attacks, and rescue workers facing overwhelming situations also may develop PTSD. Sadly, research shows that simply watching television coverage of major natural disasters, such as hurricanes, earthquakes and tornados, can increase the number of PTSD symptoms, especially in children who are already experiencing some symptoms (Weems et al., 2012). Q4

PTSD is not a new problem. During the Industrial Revolution, workers who survived horrific railroad accidents sometimes developed a condition very similar to PTSD. It was called "railway spine" because experts thought the problem resulted from a twisting or concussion of the spine. Later, doctors working with combat veterans referred to the disorder as "shell shock" because they believed it was a response to the physical concussion caused by exploding artillery. Today, we know that PTSD is caused by exposure to extraordinary stress **(Figure 3.8)**.

What can we do to help? Professionals have had success with various forms of therapy and medication for PTSD (Foa et al., 2013). They've also offered several constructive tips for the general public **(Table 3.3)**.

Boston Globe/Getty Images, Inc.

FIGURE 3.8 STRESS AND PTSD

People who experience traumatic events, such as the survivors of the bombing attack during the Boston Marathon on April 15, 2013, may develop symptoms of PTSD.

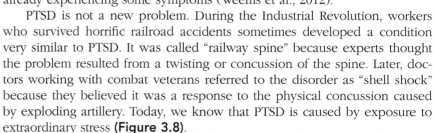

TABLE 3.2 KEY CHARACTERISTICS OF PTSD

1. Exposure to serious trauma by directly experiencing it, witnessing it happen to others, learning that it happened to close family or friends, recurring exposure to the event (e.g., police and other first responders).
2. Presence of trauma-related intrusive symptoms, such as recurrent memories and/or dreams, dissociative reactions (e.g., flashbacks), intense or prolonged psychological or physiological distress over cues associated with traumatic event.
3. Persistent avoidance of stimuli associated with traumatic event.
4. Negative and persistent changes in thoughts or moods, including forgetting important aspects of traumatic event, negative beliefs ("I'm bad," "The world is completely dangerous"), negative emotions (fear, anger, guilt), feeling detached from others, inability to experience positive emotions.
5. Marked changes in arousal and reactivity, such as irritability, angry outbursts, reckless or self-destructive behavior, exaggerated startle response, sleep disturbances.

Source: Adapted from American Psychiatric Association (2013), *Diagnostic and statistical manual of mental disorders* (DSM-5).

TABLE 3.3 FIVE IMPORTANT TIPS FOR COPING WITH CRISIS

1. If you have experienced a traumatic event, recognize your feelings about the situation and talk to others about your fears. Know that these feelings are a normal response to an abnormal situation.
2. If you know someone who has been traumatized, be willing to patiently listen to their account of the event, pay attention to their feelings, and encourage them to seek counseling, if necessary.
3. Be patient with people. Tempers are short in times of crisis, and others may be feeling as much stress as you.
4. Recognize normal crisis reactions, such as sleep disturbances and nightmares, withdrawal, reversion to childhood behaviors, and trouble focusing on work or school.
5. Take time with your children, spouse, life partner, friends, and coworkers to do something you enjoy.

Source: American Counseling Association, 2006, and adapted from Pomponio, 2002.

RETRIEVAL PRACTICE: STRESS AND ILLNESS

Self-Test

Completing this self-test and comparing your answers with those in Appendix B provides immediate feedback and helpful practice for exams. Additional interactive, self-tests are available at www.wiley.com/college/huffman.

1. Which of the following is true?

a. Stress is a leading cause of cancer.
b. Positive attitudes can prevent cancer.
c. Both of these options.
d. None of these options.

2. Stress may contribute to heart disease by releasing _____ and _____, which increase the level of fat in the blood.

a. angina; cortisol
b. hormones; GABA
c. cynical hostility; hormones
d. epinephrine (adrenaline); cortisol

3. Research suggests that one particular Type A characteristic is *most* associated with heart disease. What characteristic is this?

a. intense ambition
b. impatience
c. cynical hostility
d. time urgency

4. People who experience flashbacks, nightmares, and impaired functioning following a life-threatening or other horrifying event may be _____.

a. suffering from a psychosomatic illness
b. experiencing posttraumatic stress disorder
c. having a psychotic breakdown
d. weaker than people who take such events in stride

Think Critically

1. What does it mean to say that stress is a contributing factor to gastric ulcers?
2. At different times in your life, how has stress contributed to your own illnesses, and what can you do to avoid or decrease future illnesses?

realworldpsychology

Are people with stressful jobs at increased risk of experiencing a heart attack?

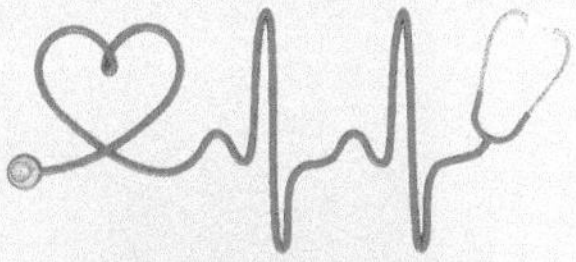

Does watching televised coverage of natural disasters increase symptoms of posttraumatic stress disorder?

HINT: LOOK IN THE MARGIN FOR Q3 AND Q4

HEALTH PSYCHOLOGY AND STRESS MANAGEMENT

LEARNING OBJECTIVES

RETRIEVAL PRACTICE While reading the upcoming sections, respond to each Learning Objective in your own words. Then compare your responses with those found at www.wiley.com/college/huffman.

1. **EXPLAIN** what health psychologists do.
2. **COMPARE** emotion-focused and problem-focused forms of coping.
3. **REVIEW** the major resources for stress management.

Health psychology A subfield of psychology that studies how people stay healthy, why they become ill, and how they respond when they become ill.

How people stay healthy, why they become ill, and how they respond when they become ill is the focus of **health psychology**. In this section, we will first discuss the work of health psychologists and then explore how we cognitively appraise potential stressors, cope with perceived threats, and make use of eight resources for stress management.

What Does a Health Psychologist Do?

Health psychologists are interested in how people's lifestyles and activities, emotional reactions, ways of interpreting events, and personality characteristics influence their physical health and well-being.

As researchers, health psychologists are particularly interested in how changes in behavior can improve health outcomes (Belar et al., 2013; Suls et al., 2010). They also emphasize the relationship between stress and the immune system. As we discovered earlier, a normally functioning immune system helps defend against disease. On the other hand, a suppressed immune system leaves the body susceptible to a number of illnesses.

As practitioners, health psychologists can work as independent clinicians or as consultants alongside physicians, physical and occupational therapists, and other health care workers. The goal of health psychologists is to reduce psychological distress or unhealthy behaviors. They also help patients and families make critical decisions and prepare psychologically for surgery or other treatment. Health psychologists have become so involved with health and illness that medical centers are one of their major employers (Considering a Career, 2011).

Health psychologists also educate the public about health *maintenance*. They provide information about the effects of stress, smoking, alcohol, lack of exercise, and other health issues. For example, tobacco use endangers both smokers and those who breathe secondhand smoke, so it's not surprising that health psychologists are concerned with preventing smoking and getting those who already smoke to stop.

The first puff on a cigarette is rarely pleasant. So why do people start smoking? The answer can be found in the biopsychosocial model **(Figure 3.9)**. From a biological perspective, nicotine is highly addictive. So once a person begins to smoke, there is a biological need to continue **(Figure 3.10)**. Nicotine addiction appears to be very similar to heroin, cocaine, and alcohol addiction (David et al., 2013; Wang et al., 2011).

From a psychological and social perspective, smokers learn to associate smoking with pleasant things, such as good food, friends, and sex. People also form such associations from seeing smoking in the movies, which is one reason researchers believe that requiring all movies with characters who smoke to be rated R would reduce smoking in teenagers by 20% (Sargent et al., 2012).

Warner Bros. Pictures/Photofest

HOLLYWOOD AND NICOTINE ADDICTION

Does watching movie stars smoke encourage others to follow suit?

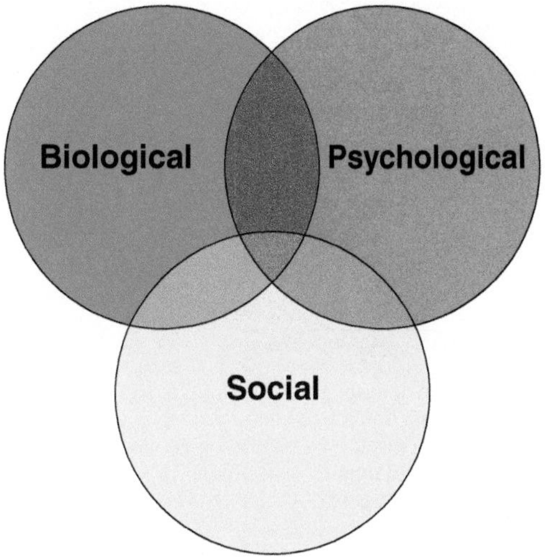

FIGURE 3.9 **NICOTINE AND THE BIOPSYCHOSOCIAL MODEL**

The three factors in the *biopsychosocial model* interact to help explain how smoking tobacco may lead to a serious, life-threatening addiction.

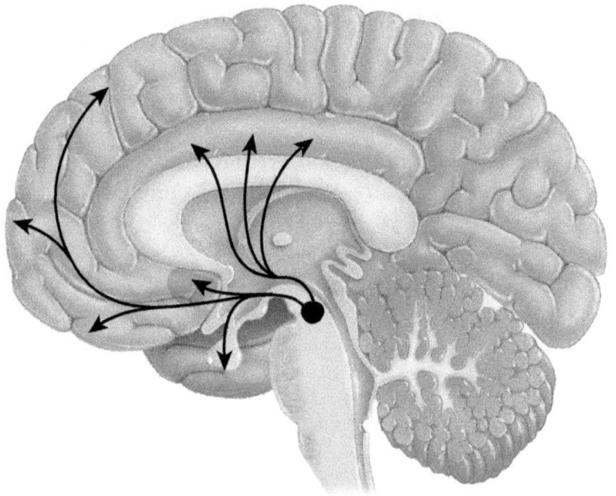

FIGURE 3.10 **THE BRAIN'S REWARD CENTER PATHWAYS**

Nicotine quickly increases the release of acetylcholine and norepinephrine in our brain, increasing alertness, concentration, memory, and feelings of pleasure. Nicotine also stimulates the release of dopamine, the neurotransmitter most closely related to reward centers in the brain (David et al., 2013; Lee & Messing, 2011; Marti et al., 2012).

In addition, to encouraging smokers to stop or to never start smoking, health psychologists also help people cope with conditions such as chronic pain, diabetes, and high blood pressure, as well as unhealthful behaviors such as inappropriate anger and/or lack of assertiveness. If you're interested in a career in this field, check with your college's counseling or career center, as well as the website www.wiley.com/college/huffman.

Coping with Stress

Because we can't escape stress, we need to learn how to effectively cope with it. Simply defined, *coping* is an attempt to manage stress in some effective way. It is not one single act but a process that allows us to deal with various stressors **(Figure 3.11)**.

One of the biggest challenges during the process of coping is deciding whether to try to change the stressor itself or our emotional reactions to it. **Problem-focused coping** strategies work to deal directly with a stressor in order to eventually decrease or eliminate it (Graven & Grant, 2013; Jopp & Schmitt, 2010; Peng et al., 2012). We tend to choose this approach, and find it most effective, when we have some control over a stressful situation.

Problem-focused coping The strategies we use to deal directly with a stressor to eventually decrease or eliminate it.

Many times, however, it seems that nothing can be done to alter the stressful situation, so we turn to **emotion-focused coping**, in which we attempt to relieve or regulate our emotional reactions. For example, suppose you were refused a highly desirable job. You might initially feel disappointed and/or rejected. But you could successfully cope with these feelings by reappraising the situation and deciding the job wasn't the right match for you or that you weren't really qualified or ready for it.

Emotion-focused coping The strategies we use to relieve or regulate the emotional impact of a stressful situation.

When faced with unavoidable stress, Freud believed that we often resort to **defense mechanisms**, in which we supposedly unconsciously distort reality to protect our egos and to avoid anxiety. Can you see how fantasizing about what you will do on your next vacation can help relieve stress? This shows how defense mechanisms can sometimes act as a beneficial type of emotion-focused coping. At other times, they can be destructive. For example, if we fail to get a highly coveted promotion at work, we may resort to elaborate excuses for our failure. This type of *rationalization* helps blunt the emotional impact of a stressful situation, but it also

Defense mechanisms Freud's description of the strategies the ego supposedly uses to protect itself from anxiety, which distorts reality and may increase self-deception.

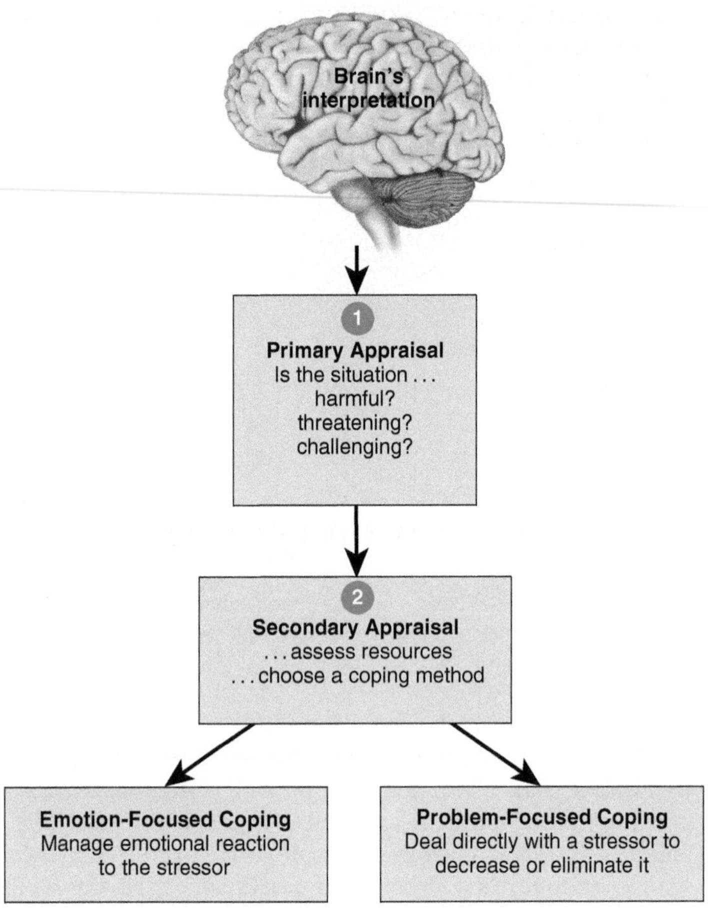

FIGURE 3.11 COGNITIVE APPRAISAL AND COPING

Research suggests that our emotional response to an event depends largely on how we interpret the event. First, we go through a *primary appraisal* process to evaluate the threat. Next, during the *secondary appraisal*, we assess our resources for coping with the stress. Then, we generally choose either *emotion-* or *problem-focused* methods of coping, or a combination of the two.

may block us from seeing a situation more clearly and realistically, which in turn can prevent us from developing valuable skills or qualities.

Note that emotion-focused forms of coping can't change the problem, but they do make us feel better about the stressful situation. For example, teenagers who are asked to think about the benefits of a recent stressful event—such as having a fight or losing a loved one—show increases in positive mood and decreases in negative mood (Rood et al., 2012). Interestingly, instant messaging (IM) also helps distressed teenagers share their emotions and receive immediate social support and advice (Dolev-Cohen & Barak, 2013).

Q5

Keep in mind that emotion-focused coping can be beneficial, as long it reflects fairly accurate reappraisals of stressful situations, is not overused, and does not distort reality (Giacobbi et al., 2004; Hoar et al., 2012; Völlink et al., 2013).

Resources for Healthy Living

A person's ability to cope effectively with stress depends in large part on his or her own personality and internal resources. Having a positive attitude with an optimistic outlook on life can be especially helpful (Seligman, 2007, 2011). For example, people who see stress as enhancing, not debilitating, show more adaptive – healthier - cortisol responses (Crum et al., 2013). Hope can sustain a person in the face of severe odds, as is often documented in news reports of people who have triumphed over seemingly unbeatable circumstances.

Similarly, having a good sense of humor is one of the best ways to reduce stress. The ability to laugh at oneself and at life's inevitable ups and downs allows us to relax and gain a broader perspective. In short: "Don't sweat the small stuff."

Perhaps one of the most important personal resources for stress management is a sense of personal control. People who believe they are the "masters of their own destiny" have what is known as an **internal locus of control**. Believing they control their own fate, they tend to make more effective decisions and healthier lifestyle changes, are more likely to follow treatment programs, and more often find ways to positively cope with a situation.

Internal locus of control The belief that we control our own fate.

Conversely, people with an **external locus of control** believe that chance or outside forces beyond our control determine our fate. Therefore, they tend to feel powerless to change their circumstances, are less likely to make effective and positive changes, and are more likely to experience higher levels of stress (e.g., Bennett et al., 2013; Cheng et al., 2013; Rotter, 1966, Wulandari et al., 2013).

External locus of control The belief that chance or outside forces beyond our control determine our fate.

In addition to the individual's personality and internal resources, effective coping also depends on the available external resources. For example, recent research shows that **mindfulness-based stress reduction (MBSR)** programs are particularly effective in stress management, and its practice has even been linked to positive, and perhaps, permanent brain changes (Hölzel et al., 2011; Hülsheger et al., 2013; Roeser et al., 2013). Based on developing a state of consciousness that attends to ongoing events in a receptive and non-judgmental way, therapists have found it useful for a variety of problems, most notably for anxiety- and stress-related disorders (Call et al., 2013). But it can be practiced by anyone.

Mindfulness-based stress reduction (MBSR) A stress reduction strategy based on developing a state of consciousness that attends to ongoing events in a receptive and non-judgmental way.

One of the most effective and frequently overlooked external resources for stress management is *social support*. Having the support of others helps offset the stressful effects of divorce, the loss of a loved one, chronic illness, pregnancy, physical abuse, job loss, and work overload. When we are faced with stressful circumstances, our friends and family often help us take care of our health, listen, hold our hands, make us feel important, and provide stability to offset the changes in our lives. People who have greater social support also experience better health outcomes, including greater psychological well-being, greater physical well-being, faster recovery from illness, and a longer life expectancy (Creaven et al., 2013; Giles et al., 2005; Gremore et al., 2011; Slater et al., 2013).

realworldpsychology **Surgery and Social Support** Did you know that individuals undergoing surgery who have high levels of social support experience less anxiety, receive lower doses of narcotics, and are released from the hospital 1.42 days faster than those with lower levels of support (Krohne & Slangen, 2005)? These findings help explain why married people live longer than unmarried people (Liu, 2009) and why people who experience a marital separation or divorce are at greater risk of an early death (Sbarra & Nietert, 2009). So what is the important take-home message from this emphasis on social support? *Don't be afraid to offer help and support to others and to ask for the same for yourself!*

Chris Schmidt/Getty Images

Six additional external resources for healthy living and stress management are exercise, social skills, behavior change, stressor control, material resources, and relaxation (Archer, 2011; Chou et al., 2011; Krypel & Henderson-King, 2010; Marks et al., 2011; McLoyd, 2011; Quick et al., 2013). These resources are summarized in **Table 3.4** and *Psychology and You*.

TABLE 3.4 SIX ADDITIONAL EXTERNAL STRESS RESOURCES

Exercise	Exercising and keeping fit helps minimize anxiety and depression, which are associated with stress. Exercise also helps relieve muscle tension; improves cardiovascular efficiency; and increases strength, flexibility, and stamina.	 © RichVintage/iStockphoto
Social skills	People who acquire social skills (such as knowing appropriate behaviors for certain situations, having conversation starters up their sleeves, and expressing themselves well) suffer less anxiety than people who do not. In fact, people who lack social skills are more at risk for developing illness than those who have them. Social skills not only help us interact with others but also communicate our needs and desires, enlist help when we need it, and decrease hostility in tense situations.	 NewsCom
Behavior change	When under stress, do you smoke, drink, overeat, zone out in front of the TV or computer, sleep too much, procrastinate, or take your stress out on others? If so, substitute these activities with healthier choices.	 © Hill Street Studios/ Blend Images/Corbis
Stressor control	While not all stress can be eliminated, it helps to recognize and avoid unnecessary stress by: analyzing your schedule and removing nonessential tasks, controlling your environment (avoiding people and topics that stress you, finding a less stressful job), and give yourself permission to say "no" to extra tasks and responsibilities.	 © PK-Photos/iStockphoto
Material resources	Money increases the number of options available for eliminating sources of stress or reducing the effects of stress. When faced with the minor hassles of everyday living, or when faced with chronic stressors or major catastrophes, people with money and the skills to effectively use it generally fare better and experience less stress than people without money.	 © Juanmonino/iStockphoto/
Relaxation	There are a variety of relaxation techniques. *Biofeedback* is often used in the treatment of chronic pain, but it is also useful in teaching people to relax and manage their stress. *Progressive relaxation* helps reduce or relieve the muscular tension commonly associated with stress (see *Psychology and You*).	 Dynamic Graphics Value/ SUPERSTOCK

TEST YOURSELF: PRACTICING PROGRESSIVE RELAXATION

psychology and you

You can use progressive relaxation techniques anytime and anywhere you feel stressed, such as before or during an exam. Here's how:

1. Sit in a comfortable position, with your head supported.
2. Start breathing slowly and deeply.
3. Let your entire body relax. Release all tension. Try to visualize your body getting progressively more relaxed with each breath.
4. Systematically tense and release each part of your body, beginning with your toes. Curl them tightly while counting to 10. Now, release them. Note the difference between the tense and relaxed states. Next, tense your feet to the count of 10. Then relax them and feel the difference. Continue upward with your calves, thighs, buttocks, abdomen, back muscles, shoulders, upper arms, forearms, hands and fingers, neck, jaw, facial muscles, and forehead. Try practicing progressive relaxation twice a day for about 15 minutes each time. You will be surprised at how quickly you can learn to relax—even in the most stressful situations.

RETRIEVAL PRACTICE: HEALTH PSYCHOLOGY AND STRESS MANAGEMENT

Self-Test

Completing this self-test and comparing your answers with those in Appendix B provides immediate feedback and helpful practice for exams. Additional interactive, self-tests are available at www.wiley.com/college/huffman.

1. Which of the following is *true* of health psychology?
   a. It studies the relationship between psychological behavior and physical health.
   b. It studies the relationship between social factors and illness.
   c. It emphasizes wellness and the prevention of illness.
   d. All these statements are true.

2. Emotion-focused forms of coping are based on relieving or regulating our______when faced with stressful situations.
   a. feelings
   b. behavior
   c. defense mechanisms
   d. all these options

3. Research suggests that people with a(n) ______ have less psychological stress than those with a______.
   a. external locus of control; internal locus of control
   b. internal locus of control; external locus of control
   c. attributional coping style; person-centered coping style
   d. none of these options

4. Which of the following is *not* one of the ways to cope with stress outlined in the chapter?
   a. exercise
   b. sense of humor
   c. social support
   d. stimulant drugs

Think Critically

1. Why is it so difficult for people to quit smoking?
2. Which do you generally prefer: an emotion-focused style of coping or a problem-focused style of coping when faced with a stressful situation? Why?

realworldpsychology

Could thinking about the "silver linings" of a stressful event, or sharing it with others, reduce depression?

HINT: LOOK IN THE MARGIN FOR Q5

Summary

1 UNDERSTANDING STRESS 68

- **Stress** is the interpretation of specific events, called **stressors**, as threatening or challenging. The resulting physical and psychological reactions to these stressors are known as the *stress response*. There are several sources of stress, and three basic types of conflict: **approach–approach**, **avoidance–avoidance**, and **approach–avoidance**.
- The **general adaptation syndrome (GAS)** is a pattern of nonspecific adaptational responses to a continuing stressor. It was first identified by Selye, and it includes three stages—alarm, resistance, and exhaustion.
- The **SAM system** and the **HPA axis** control significant physiological responses to stress. The SAM system prepares us for immediate action; the HPA axis responds more slowly but lasts longer. A new interdisciplinary field, called **psychoneuroimmunology**, studies the effects of psychological and other factors on the immune system.

2 STRESS AND ILLNESS 76

- Stress increases the risk of developing *gastric ulcers* among people who have the *H. pylori* bacterium in their stomachs.
- Stress makes the immune system less able to resist infection and cancer development.
- Stress hormones can cause fat to adhere to blood vessel walls, increasing the risk of heart attack. Having a **Type A** behavior pattern (hostile, aggressive) versus a **Type B** pattern (relaxed, easy-going) increases the risk of stress- related heart disease. People with a **positive affect** also tend to deal better with stress.
- Exposure to extraordinary stress can cause **posttraumatic stress disorder (PTSD)**, a type of trauma- and stressor-related disorder characterized by the persistent re-experiencing of traumatic events, which resulted from directly or indirectly experiencing actual or threatened death, serious injury, or violence.

3 HEALTH PSYCHOLOGY AND STRESS MANAGEMENT 82

- **Health psychology,** a subfield of psychology, studies how people stay healthy, why they become ill, and how they respond when they become ill.
- Our level of stress generally depends on both our interpretation of and our reaction to stressors. **Emotion-focused** forms of coping involve emotional or cognitive strategies that help us manage our reactions to a stressful situation. Some emotion-focused **defense mechanisms**, such as rationalization, can be destructive because they distort reality and prevent us from developing valuable skills or qualities. It is often more effective to use **problem-focused** forms of coping, which deal directly with a stressor to decrease or eliminate it.
- Positive beliefs, a good sense of humor, and having an **internal locus of control** (believing that we control our own fate), as opposed to having an **external locus of control** (believing that chance or outside forces beyond our control determine our fate) are all effective personal strategies for stress management. External resources include **mindfulness-based stress reduction (MBSR)**, as well as social support, exercise, social skills, behavior change, stressor control, material resources, and relaxation.

applyingrealworldpsychology

We began this chapter with five intriguing Real World Psychology questions, and you were asked to revisit these questions at the end of each section. Questions like these have an important and lasting impact on all of our lives. See if you can answer these additional critical thinking questions related to real world examples.

1. How might the child in this photo be affected biologically, psychologically, and socially (the biopsychosocial model) by her mother's drinking?
2. Are you more of a Type A or Type B person? What are the advantages and disadvantages to each type?
3. What could a health psychologist do to improve the well-being of the mother and child in this photo?
4. Health psychologists often advise us to make lifestyle changes to improve our health and longevity. Do you think this is important? If so, what do you plan to change in your own life?
5. Would you like to be a health psychologist? Why or why not?

Dennis MacDonald/PhotoEdit

Key Terms

RETRIEVAL PRACTICE Write a definition for each term before turning back to the referenced page to check your answer.

- approach–approach conflict 71
- approach–avoidance conflict 71
- avoidance–avoidance conflict 71
- burnout 72
- cataclysmic event 69
- chronic stress 69
- conflict 71
- defense mechanisms 83
- emotion-focused coping 83
- external locus of control 85
- frustration 72
- general adaptation syndrome (GAS) 72
- hassle 71
- health psychology 82
- homeostasis 73
- HPA axis 73
- internal locus of control 85
- mindfulness-based stress reduction (MBSR) 85
- positive affect 79
- posttraumatic stress disorder (PTSD) 80
- problem-focused coping 83
- psychoneuroimmunology 75
- SAM system 73
- stress 68
- stressor 68
- Type A behavior patterns 79
- Type B behavior patterns 79

chapterfour

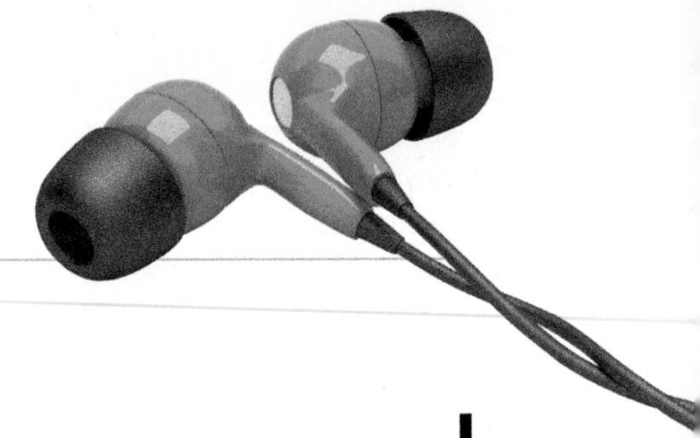

Sensation and Perception

CHAPTER OUTLINE

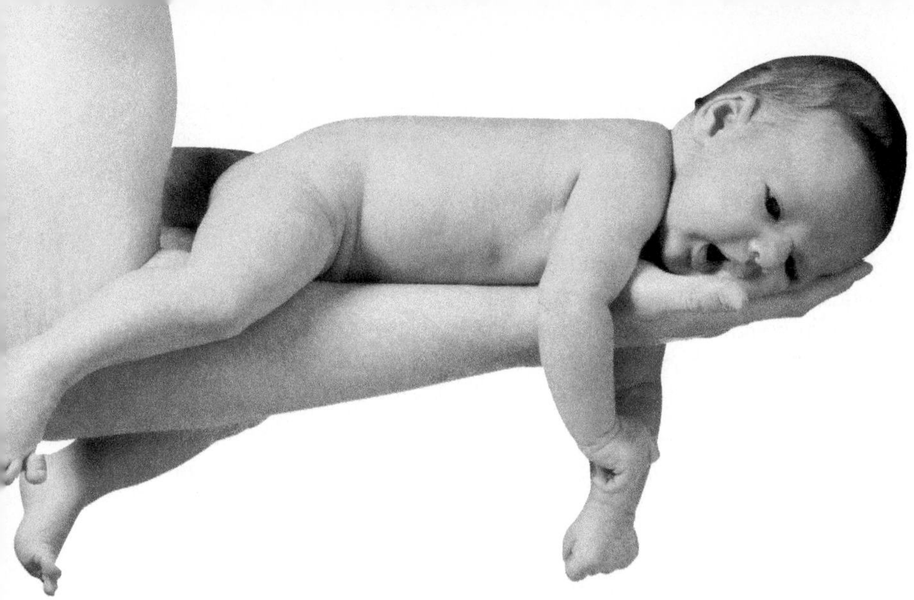

realworldpsychology

THINGS YOU'LL LEARN IN CHAPTER 4

Q1 Do athletes have a higher pain tolerance than non-athletes?

Q2 Can looking at a photograph of a loved one lead you to feel less pain?

Q3 How can listening to loud music on headphones damage your hearing?

Q4 Why do premature babies grow faster when they receive skin-to-skin contact?

Q5 Why do people rate themselves as more athletic if they compare themselves to the Pope than to a professional basketball player?

THROUGHOUT THE CHAPTER, MARGIN ICONS FOR Q1–Q5 INDICATE WHERE THE TEXT ADDRESSES THESE QUESTIONS.

Girl: Andersen Ross/Blend Images/Getty Images, headphones: © maxuser/iStockphoto, Photogragh album: © Alina Vincent Photography, LLC/iStockphoto, Baby: © carenas1/iStockphoto, basketball player: © Yuri/iStockphoto, hat: © Floortje/iStockphoto

chapteroverview

Imagine that your visual field has been suddenly inverted and reversed. Things you normally expect to be on your right are now on your left, and those above your head are now below. How would you ride a bike, read a book, or even walk through your home? Do you think you could ever adapt to this upside-down world?

To answer that question, psychologist George Stratton (1896) invented, and for eight days wore, special prism goggles that flipped his view of the world from up to down and right to left. For the first few days, Stratton had a great deal of difficulty navigating in this environment and coping with everyday tasks. But by the third day, he noted:

Walking through the narrow spaces between pieces of furniture required much less care than hitherto. I could watch my hands as they wrote, without hesitating or becoming embarrassed thereby.

By the fifth day, Stratton had almost completely adjusted to his strange perceptual environment, and when he later removed the headgear, he quickly readapted.

What does this experiment have to do with everyday life? At this very moment, our bodies are being bombarded with stimuli from the outside world—light, sound, heat, pressure, texture, and so on—while our brains are floating in complete silence and utter darkness within our skulls. Stratton's experiment shows us that sensing the world is not enough. Our brains must receive, convert, and constantly adapt the information from our sense organs into useful mental representations of the world. How we get the outside world inside to our brains, and what our brains do with this information, are the key topics of this chapter.

UNDERSTANDING SENSATION

LEARNING OBJECTIVES

RETRIEVAL PRACTICE While reading the upcoming sections, respond to each Learning Objective in your own words. Then compare your responses with those found at www.wiley.com/college/huffman.

1. **DESCRIBE** how raw sensory stimuli are processed and converted to signals in the brain.
2. **EXPLAIN** how our experience of stimuli can be measured.
3. **SUMMARIZE** the factors involved in sensory adaptation.

Psychologists are keenly interested in our senses because they are our mind's window to the outside world. We're equally interested in how our mind perceives and interprets the information it receives from the senses.

Sensation begins with specialized receptor cells located in our sense organs (eyes, ears, nose, tongue, skin, and internal body tissues). When sense organs detect an appropriate stimulus (light, mechanical pressure, chemical molecules), they convert it into neural impulses (action potentials) that are transmitted to our brain. Through the process of **perception**, the brain then assigns meaning to this sensory information **(Table 4.1)**.

Sensation The process of detecting, converting, and transmitting raw sensory information from the external and internal environments to the brain.

Perception The processes of selecting, organizing, and interpreting sensory information into meaningful patterns; interpreting sensory images as having been produced by stimuli from the external, three-dimensional world.

Transduction The process whereby sensory receptors convert stimuli into neural impulses to be sent to the brain (for example, transforming light waves into neural impulses).

Coding The process in which neural impulses travel by different routes to different parts of the brain; it allows us to detect various physical stimuli as distinct sensations.

Processing

Our eyes, ears, skin, and other sense organs all contain special cells called receptors, which receive and process sensory information from the environment. For each sense, these specialized cells respond to a distinct stimulus, such as sound waves or odor molecules. Next, during the process of **transduction**, the receptors convert the energy from the specific sensory stimulus into neural impulses, which are sent to the brain. For example, in hearing, tiny receptor cells in the inner ear convert mechanical vibrations from sound waves into electrochemical signals. Neurons then carry these signals to the brain, where specific sensory receptors detect and interpret the information.

How does our brain differentiate between sensations, such as sounds and smells? Through a process known as **coding**, the brain interprets different physical

TABLE 4.1 SENSATION AND PERCEPTION

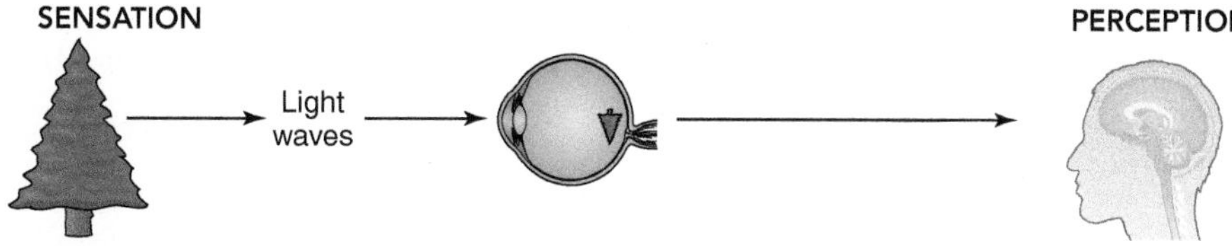

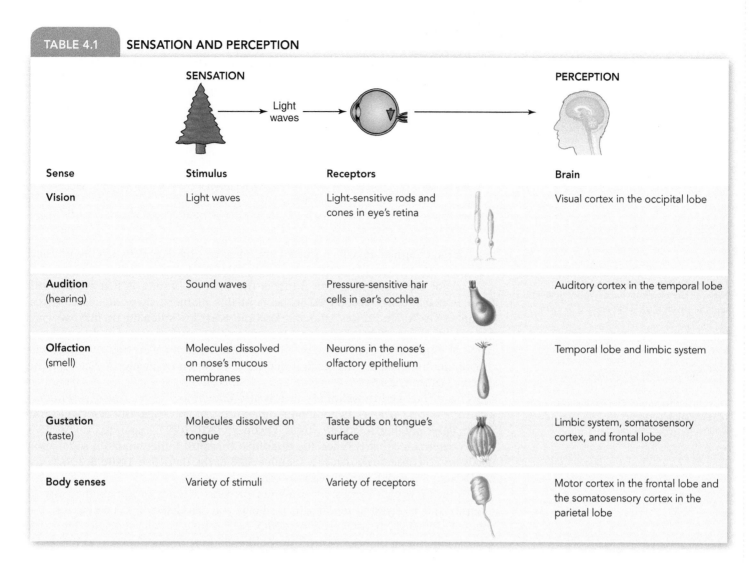

Sense	Stimulus	Receptors		Brain
Vision	Light waves	Light-sensitive rods and cones in eye's retina		Visual cortex in the occipital lobe
Audition (hearing)	Sound waves	Pressure-sensitive hair cells in ear's cochlea		Auditory cortex in the temporal lobe
Olfaction (smell)	Molecules dissolved on nose's mucous membranes	Neurons in the nose's olfactory epithelium		Temporal lobe and limbic system
Gustation (taste)	Molecules dissolved on tongue	Taste buds on tongue's surface		Limbic system, somatosensory cortex, and frontal lobe
Body senses	Variety of stimuli	Variety of receptors		Motor cortex in the frontal lobe and the somatosensory cortex in the parietal lobe

stimuli as distinct sensations because their neural impulses travel by different routes and arrive at different parts of the brain **(Figure 4.1)**.

We also have structures that purposefully reduce the amount of sensory information we receive. In this process of *sensory reduction*, we analyze and then filter incoming sensations before sending neural impulses on for further processing in other parts of our brain. Without this natural filtering of stimuli, we would constantly hear blood rushing through our veins and feel our clothes brushing against our skin. Some level of filtering is needed to prevent our brain from being overwhelmed with unnecessary information.

All species have evolved selective receptors that suppress or amplify information for survival. Humans, for example, cannot sense ultraviolet light, electric or magnetic fields, the ultrasonic sound of a dog whistle, or infrared heat patterns from warm-blooded animals, as some other animals can.

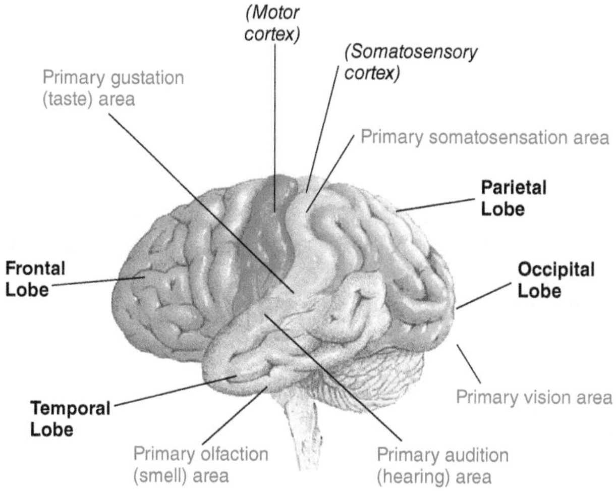

FIGURE 4.1 SENSORY PROCESSING WITHIN THE BRAIN

Neural messages from the various sense organs must travel to the brain in order for us to see, hear, smell, and so on. Shown here in the red-colored labels are the primary locations in the cerebral cortex for vision, hearing, taste, smell, and somatosensation (which includes touch, pain, and temperature sensitivity).

Psychophysics

How can scientists measure the exact amount of stimulus energy it takes to trigger a conscious experience? The answer come from the

TABLE 4.2 EXAMPLES OF HUMAN ABSOLUTE THRESHOLDS

Sense	Absolute Threshold
Vision	A candle flame seen from 30 miles away on a clear, dark night
Audition (hearing)	The tick of an old-fashioned watch at 20 feet
Olfaction (smell)	One drop of perfume spread throughout a six-room apartment
Gustation (taste)	One teaspoon of sugar in 2 gallons of water
Body senses	A bee's wing falling on your cheek from a height of about half an inch

field of **psychophysics**, which studies and measures the link between the physical characteristics of stimuli and the sensory experience of them.

Psychophysics The study of the link between the physical characteristics of stimuli and the psychological experience of them.

Difference threshold The smallest physical difference between two stimuli that is consciously detectable 50% of the time; also called the *just noticeable difference (JND)*.

Absolute threshold The minimum amount of stimulation necessary to consciously detect a stimulus 50% of the time.

One of the most interesting insights from psychophysics is that what is out there is not directly reproduced in here. At this moment, there are light waves, sound waves, odors, tastes, and microscopic particles touching us that we cannot see, hear, smell, taste, or feel. We are consciously aware of only a narrow range of stimuli in our environment. German scientist Ernst Weber (1795–1878) was one of the first to study the smallest difference between two weights that could be detected (Coren, 2013).

This **difference threshold**, which is also known as *Weber's Law of just noticeable differences (JND)*, is the minimum difference that is consciously detectable 50% of the time. Another scientist, Gustav Fechner (1801–1887), expanded on Weber's law to determine what is called the **absolute threshold**, the minimum stimulation necessary to consciously detect a stimulus 50% of the time. See **Table 4.2** for a list of absolute thresholds for our various senses.

To measure your senses, an examiner presents a series of signals that vary in intensity and asks you to report which signals you can detect. In a hearing test, the softest level at which you can consistently hear a tone is your absolute threshold. The examiner then compares your threshold with those of people with normal hearing to determine whether you have hearing loss **(Figure 4.2)**.

Interestingly, many nonhuman animals have higher and lower thresholds than humans. For example, a dog's absolute and difference thresholds for smell are far more sensitive than those of a human. For this reason, specially trained dogs provide invaluable help in sniffing out dangerous plants, animals, drugs, and explosives; tracking criminals; and assisting in search-and-rescue operations **(Figure 4.3)**. Some researchers believe dogs can even detect chemical signs of certain illnesses, such as diabetes or cancer, and possibly even predict seizures in humans (Akers & Denbow, 2008; Buszewski et al., 2012; McCulloch et al., 2012).

FIGURE 4.2 MEASURING THE ABSOLUTE AND DIFFERENCE THRESHOLDS FOR HEARING

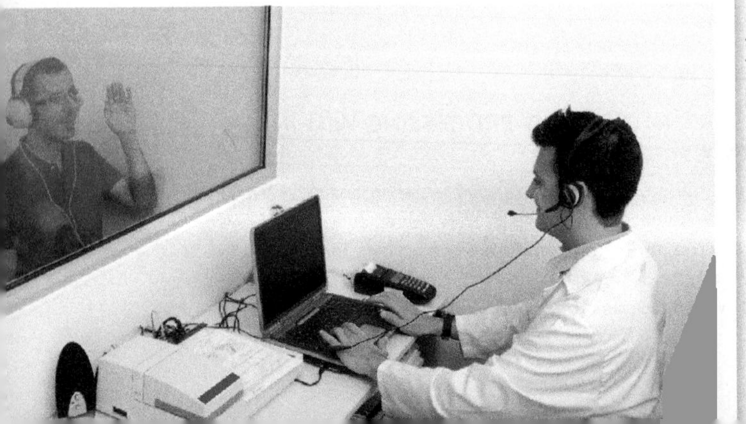

Subliminal Stimuli

Have you heard some of the wild rumors about subliminal messages? During the 1970s, it was said that rock songs contained demonic messages, which could only be heard when the songs were played backwards! Similarly, in the 1990s many suggested that some Disney films contained obscene subliminal messages. For example, in the film *Aladdin*, the lead character supposedly whispers, "all good teenagers take off your clothes," and *The Lion King* reportedly showed close ups of the dust with a secret spelling out of the word "sex." In addition, at one time movie theaters were reportedly flashing messages like "Eat popcorn" and "Drink Cola-Cola" on the screen. Even though the messages were so brief that viewers weren't aware of seeing them, it was believed they increased consumption of these products (Blecha, 2004; Vokey & Read, 1985).

Can unconscious stimuli affect our behavior? As you've just discovered about *absolute thresholds*, it's clearly possible to perceive something without conscious awareness (Brooks et al., 2012; Irvine,

2013; Smith, 2012). Experimental studies on **subliminal perception** commonly use an instrument, called a *tachistoscope,* to flash images too quickly for conscious recognition but slowly enough to be registered by the brain.

For example, in one study, experimenters subliminally presented photographs to two groups of participants who were receiving either a painful or a not-so-painful heat shock (Jensen et al., 2012). A photo of one man was presented every time the painful heat shock was delivered, whereas a different man's photo was presented every time the not-so-painful shock was delivered.

Next, the experimenters subliminally presented all participants with these same photos before they received a moderate shock. As predicted, participants from the group who saw the photo previously associated with the painful heat shock rated the moderate shock as more severe than those in the group who saw the photo associated with the not-so-painful shock.

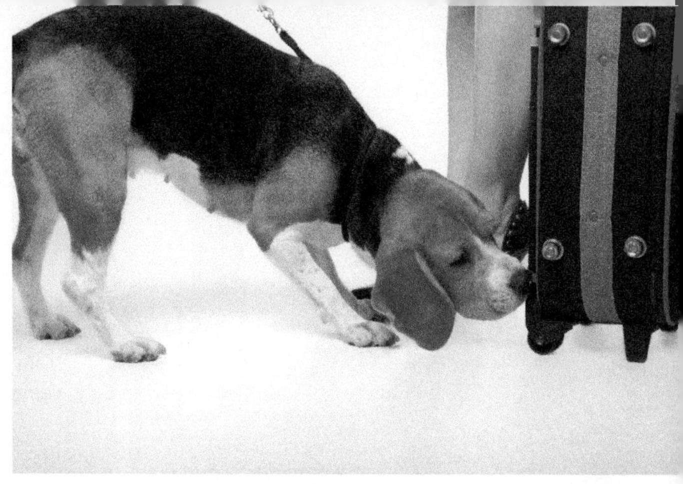

FIGURE 4.3 PUTTING ANIMALS' HIGHER SENSORY RECEPTORS TO WORK

Subliminal perception The perception of stimuli presented below conscious awareness.

realworldpsychology **The Limits of Subliminal Perception** Evidence that subliminal perception occurs doesn't necessarily mean that such processes lead to *subliminal persuasion*. Subliminal stimuli are basically weak stimuli. At best, they have a modest (if any) effect on consumer behavior, and they have absolutely no effect on the attitudes of youth listening to rock music or on citizens' voting behavior (Bermeritinger et al., 2009; Fennis & Stroebe, 2010; Salpeter & Swirsky, 2012). As for subliminal tapes promising to help you lose weight or relieve stress, save your money! Blank "placebo" tapes appear to be just as effective.

Sensory Adaptation

Imagine that friends have invited you to come visit their beautiful new baby. As they greet you at the door, you are overwhelmed by the odor of a wet diaper. Why don't your friends do something about that smell? The answer lies in the previously mentioned sensory reduction, as well as **sensory adaptation**. When a constant stimulus is presented for a length of time, sensation often fades or disappears. Receptors in our sensory system become less sensitive. They get "tired" and actually fire less frequently.

Sensory adaptation The process by which receptor cells become less sensitive due to constant stimulation.

Sensory adaptation can be understood from an evolutionary perspective. We can't afford to waste attention and time on unchanging, normally unimportant stimuli. "Turning down the volume" on repetitive information helps the brain cope with an overwhelming amount of sensory stimuli and enables us to pay attention to change. Sometimes, however, adaptation can be dangerous, as when people stop paying attention to a small gas leak in the kitchen.

Although some senses, like smell and touch, adapt quickly, we never completely adapt to visual stimuli or to extremely intense stimuli, such as the odor of ammonia or the pain of a bad burn. From an evolutionary perspective, these limitations on sensory adaptation aid survival by reminding us, for example, to keep a watch out for dangerous predators, avoid strong odors and heat, and to take care of that burn.

If we don't adapt to pain, how do athletes keep playing despite painful injuries? In certain situations, including times of physical exertion, the body releases natural painkillers called *endorphins* (Chapter 2), which inhibit pain perception. This is the so-called "runner's high," which may help explain why athletes have been found to have a higher pain tolerance than nonathletes (Tesarz et al., 2012). (As a critical thinker, is it possible that individuals with a naturally high pain tolerance are just more attracted to athletics? Or does the experience of playing sports change your pain tolerance?) Q1

In addition to endorphin release, one of the most widely accepted explanations of pain perception is the **gate-control theory of pain**, first proposed by Ronald

Gate-control theory of pain The theory that pain sensations are processed and altered by certain cells in the spinal cord, which act as gates to interrupt and block some pain signals while sending others on to the brain.

Ian MacNicol/Getty Images

FIGURE 4.4 **OVERCOMING EXCRUCIATING PAIN!**

realworldpsychology

Our body's ability to inhibit pain perception sometimes makes it possible for athletes to "play through" painful injuries. For example, Manteo Mitchell broke his left leg in the qualifying heats of the 4 × 400-meter relay race in the 2012 Olympics. Recalling the moment of the accident, Manteo said, "I felt it break . . . it hurt so bad . . . it felt like somebody literally just snapped my leg in half" (Moore, 2013). However, he continued running so that the American team could get into the finals. Many people admired his courage and determination, while others thought the potential for lasting damage was too high a price to pay for a medal or trophy. What do you think?

Melzack and Patrick Wall (1965). According to this theory, the experience of pain depends partly on whether or not the neural message gets past a "gatekeeper" in the spinal cord. Normally, the gate is kept shut, either by impulses coming down from the brain or by messages coming from large-diameter nerve fibers that conduct most sensory signals, such as touch and pressure. However, when body tissue is damaged, impulses from smaller pain fibers open the gate (Goldstein, 2014; Moayedi & Davis, 2013).

Can you see how this gate-control theory helps explain why massaging an injury or scratching an itch can temporarily relieve discomfort? It's because pressure on large-diameter neurons interferes with pain signals.

Messages from our brain also can control the pain gate, which explains how athletes and soldiers can carry on despite excruciating pain. When we're soothed by endorphins or distracted by competition or fear, our experience of pain can be greatly diminished **(Figure 4.4)**. Holding the hand of a loved one—or even just looking at a photograph of him or her—can also help reduce pain during a medical procedure (Master et al., 2009). Similarly, actively listening to music—meaning concentrating on specific musical cues in songs people know well, such as "Mary Had a Little Lamb"—can help reduce pain, especially among those who are very anxious (Bradshaw et al., 2012).

Q2

Research also suggests that the pain gate may be chemically controlled, that a neurotransmitter called *substance P* opens the pain gate, and that endorphins close it (Bianchi et al., 2008; Lin et al., 2012; Papathanassoglou et al., 2010). Other research finds that when normal sensory input is disrupted, the brain can generate pain and other sensations on its own (Melzack, 1999; Moayedi & Davis, 2013; Snijders et al., 2010).

For example, amputees sometimes continue to feel pain (and itching or tickling) long after a limb has been amputated. This *phantom limb pain* occurs because nerve cells send conflicting messages to the brain. The brain interprets this "static" as pain since the message arises in the area of the spinal cord responsible for pain signaling. When amputees are fitted with prosthetic limbs and begin using them, and sometimes when *mirror visual therapy* is used, phantom pain often disappears because the brain is somehow tricked into believing that there is no longer a missing limb (Foell & Flor, 2012; Giummarra & Moseley, 2011; Gracely et al., 2002; Plumbe et al., 2013).

(Mirror therapy involves a box with two mirrors—one facing each way. The amputee patient places his or her good limb into one side of the box and the amputated limb in the other. He or she then concentrates on looking into the mirror on the side that reflects the good limb, while making movements with both the good and amputated limbs. Thanks to the artificial feedback provided by the two mirrors, the patient sees only the reflected image of the good limb moving and interprets this as the phantom limb also moving.)

Now that we've studied how we perceive pain and how we might ignore or "play through" it, it's important to point out that other research finds that when we get anxious or dwell on our pain, we can intensify it (Lin et al., 2013; Ruscheweyh et al., 2013; Sullivan et al., 1998). Interestingly, social and cultural factors, such as well-meaning friends who ask chronic pain sufferers about their pain, may unintentionally reinforce and increase it (Flor, 2013; Jolliffe & Nicholas, 2004).

The following *Psychology and You* offers an assessment and strategies for managing your personal pain.

TEST YOURSELF: HOW WELL DO YOU MANAGE YOUR PAIN?

psychology and you

Score yourself on how often you use one or more of these strategies, using the following scale:
0 = never, 2 = seldom, 3 = occasionally, 4 = often, 5 = almost always, 6 = always.

_____**1.** I do something I enjoy, such as watching TV or listening to music.

_____**2.** I try to be around other people.

_____**3.** I do something active, like household chores or projects.

_____**4.** I try to feel distant from the pain, almost as if the pain were in somebody else's body.

_____**5.** I try to think about something pleasant.

_____**6.** I replay in my mind pleasant experiences from the past.

_____**7.** I tell myself that I can overcome the pain.

_____**8.** I don't think about the pain.

These questions are based on effective pain management techniques, such as distraction, ignoring pain, and reinterpreting it. Review those items that you checked as "never" or "seldom" and consider adding them to your pain management skills.

RETRIEVAL PRACTICE: UNDERSTANDING SENSATION

Self-Test

Completing this self-test and comparing your answers with those in Appendix B provides immediate feedback and helpful practice for exams. Additional interactive, self-tests are available at www.wiley.com/college/huffman.

1. Transduction is the process of converting ______.

a. sensory stimuli into neural impulses that are sent along to the brain
b. receptors into transmitters
c. a particular sensory stimulus into a specific sensation
d. receptors into neural impulses

2. Sensory reduction refers to the process of ______.

a. reducing your dependence on a single sensory system
b. decreasing the number of sensory receptors that are stimulated
c. filtering and analyzing incoming sensations before sending a neural message on for further processing
d. reducing environmental sensations by physically preventing your sensory organs from seeing, hearing, and so on

3. Experiments on subliminal perception have ______.

a. supported its existence, but shown that it has little or no effect on persuasion
b. shown that subliminal perception occurs only among children and some adolescents
c. shown that subliminal messages affect only people who are highly suggestible
d. failed to support the phenomenon

4. The _____ theory of pain helps explain why it sometimes helps to rub or massage an injured area.

a. sensory adaptation
b. gate-control
c. just noticeable difference
d. Lamaze

Think Critically

1 Sensation and perception are closely linked. What is the central distinction between the two?

2 If we sensed and attended equally to each stimulus in the world, the amount of information would be overwhelming. What sensory and perceptual processes help us lessen the din?

3 If we don't adapt to pain, why is it that people can sometimes "tune out" painful injuries?

realworldpsychology

Do athletes have a higher pain tolerance than non-athletes?

Can looking at a photograph of a loved one lead you to feel less pain?

HINT: LOOK IN THE MARGIN FOR Q1 AND Q2

HOW WE SEE AND HEAR

LEARNING OBJECTIVES

RETRIEVAL PRACTICE While reading the upcoming sections, respond to each Learning Objective in your own words. Then compare your responses with those found at www.wiley.com/college/huffman.

1. **IDENTIFY** the three major characteristics of light and sound waves.
2. **EXPLAIN** how the eye captures and focuses light energy and how it converts it into neural signals.
3. **DESCRIBE** the path that sound waves take in the ear.
4. **SUMMARIZE** the two theories that explain how we distinguish among different pitches.

Many people mistakenly believe that what they see and hear is a copy of the outside world. In fact, vision and hearing are the result of what our brains create in response to light and sound waves. What we see and hear is based on wave phenomena, similar to ocean waves **(Figure 4.5)**.

In addition to wavelength/frequency shown in Figure 4.5, waves also vary in height (technically called *amplitude*). This wave height/amplitude determines the intensity of sights and sounds. Finally, waves also vary in range, or complexity, which mixes together waves of various wavelength/frequency and wave height/amplitude **(Figure 4.6)**.

Vision

Did you know that Major League batters can routinely hit a 90-miles-per-hour fastball four-tenths of a second after it leaves the pitcher's hand? How can the human eye receive and process information that fast? To understand the marvels of vision, we need to start with the basics—that light waves are a form of electromagnetic energy and only a small part of the full *electromagnetic spectrum* **(Figure 4.7)**.

To fully appreciate how our eyes turn these light waves into the experience we call *vision*, we need to first examine the various structures in our eyes that capture and focus the light waves. Then, we need to understand how these waves are transformed (transduced) into neural messages (action potentials) that our brain can process into images we consciously see. (Be sure to carefully study this step-by-step process in **Figure 4.8**.)

FIGURE 4.5 WAVES OF LIGHT AND SOUND

Ocean waves have a certain distance between them (the *wavelength*), and they pass by you at intervals. If you counted the number of passing waves in a set amount of time (for example, 5 waves in 60 seconds), you could calculate the *frequency* (the number of complete wavelengths that pass a point in a given time). Longer wavelength means lower frequency and vice versa.

© S. Greg Panosian/iStockphoto

FIGURE 4.6 PROPERTIES OF LIGHT AND SOUND

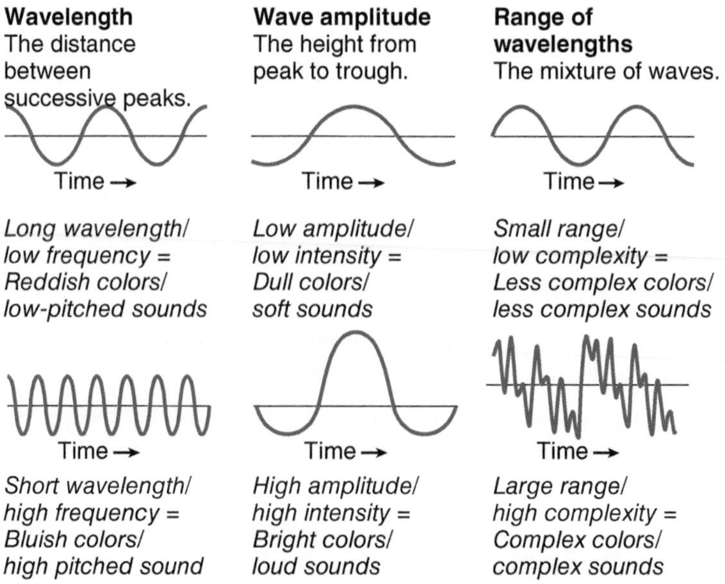

FIGURE 4.7 THE ELECTROMAGNETIC SPECTRUM FOR VISION

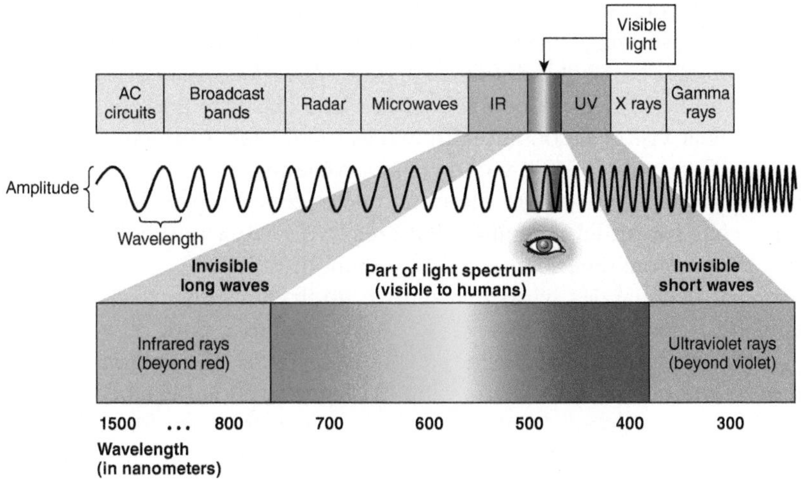

The full spectrum of electromagnetic waves contains very long wavelength AC circuits and radio waves at one end, and relatively short gamma ray waves at the other.

Only the light waves, in the middle of the electromagnetic spectrum can be seen by the human eye. Note how the longer visible wavelengths are the light waves that we see as red, and the shortest are those we perceive as blue. In between are the rest of the colors.

FIGURE 4.8 HOW OUR EYES SEE

Various structures of your eye work together to capture and focus the light waves from the outside world. Receptor cells in your retina (rods and cones) then convert these waves into messages that are sent along the optic nerve to be interpreted by your brain.

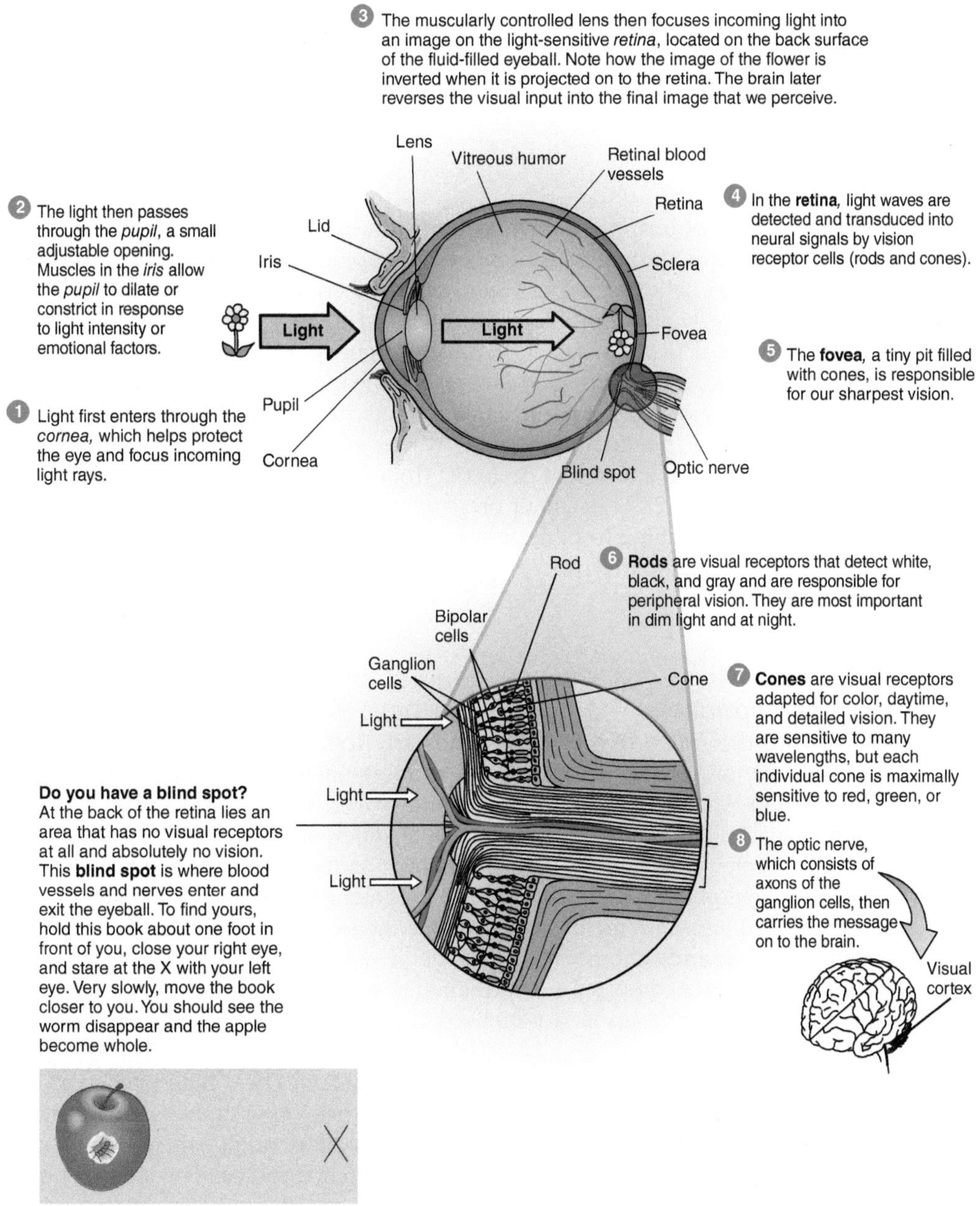
3 The muscularly controlled lens then focuses incoming light into an image on the light-sensitive *retina*, located on the back surface of the fluid-filled eyeball. Note how the image of the flower is inverted when it is projected on to the retina. The brain later reverses the visual input into the final image that we perceive.
Lens
Vitreous humor
Retinal blood vessels
Retina
Lid
Iris
Sclera
Light
Light
Fovea
Pupil
Cornea
Blind spot
Optic nerve
2 The light then passes through the *pupil*, a small adjustable opening. Muscles in the *iris* allow the *pupil* to dilate or constrict in response to light intensity or emotional factors.
1 Light first enters through the *cornea*, which helps protect the eye and focus incoming light rays.
4 In the **retina**, light waves are detected and transduced into neural signals by vision receptor cells (rods and cones).
5 The **fovea**, a tiny pit filled with cones, is responsible for our sharpest vision.
Rod
6 **Rods** are visual receptors that detect white, black, and gray and are responsible for peripheral vision. They are most important in dim light and at night.
Bipolar cells
Ganglion cells
Cone
Light
Light
Light
7 **Cones** are visual receptors adapted for color, daytime, and detailed vision. They are sensitive to many wavelengths, but each individual cone is maximally sensitive to red, green, or blue.
8 The optic nerve, which consists of axons of the ganglion cells, then carries the message on to the brain.
Visual cortex
Do you have a blind spot?
At the back of the retina lies an area that has no visual receptors at all and absolutely no vision. This **blind spot** is where blood vessels and nerves enter and exit the eyeball. To find yours, hold this book about one foot in front of you, close your right eye, and stare at the X with your left eye. Very slowly, move the book closer to you. You should see the worm disappear and the apple become whole.
X

Vision Problems and Peculiarities

Thoroughly understanding the processes detailed in Figure 4.8 offers clues that help us understand several visual peculiarities. For example, small abnormalities in the eye sometimes cause images to be focused in front of the **retina** in the case of *nearsightedness (myopia)*, or behind it in the case of *farsightedness (hyperopia)*. In addition, during middle age, most people's lenses lose elasticity and the ability to accommodate for near vision, a condition known as *presbyopia*. Corrective lenses or laser surgery can often correct these visual acuity problems.

Retina The light-sensitive inner surface of the back of the eye, which contains the receptor cells for vision (rods and cones).

Blind spot The point at which the optic nerve leaves the eye, which contains no receptor cells for vision—thus creating a "blind spot."

Rods Photoreceptors concentrated in the periphery of the retina that are most active in dim illumination; rods do not produce sensation of color.

Cones Visual receptor cells that are concentrated near the center of the retina and are responsible for color vision and fine detail; they are most sensitive in brightly lit conditions.

Fovea A tiny pit in the center of the retina that is densely filled with cones; it is responsible for sharp vision.

Audition The sense or act of hearing.

A visual peculiarity occurs where the optic nerve exits the eye. Because there are no receptor cells for visual stimuli in that area, we have a tiny hole, or **blind spot**, in our field of vision. (See Figure 4.8 for a demonstration.)

Two additional peculiarities happen when we go from a bright to dark setting and vice versa. Have you noticed that when you walk into a dark movie theater on a sunny afternoon, you're almost blind for a few seconds? The reason is that in bright light, the pigment inside the **rods** (refer to Figure 4.8) is bleached, making them temporarily nonfunctional. It takes a second or two for the rods to become functional enough again for you to see. This process of *dark adaptation* continues for 20 to 30 minutes.

In contrast, *light adaptation*, the adjustment that takes place when you go from darkness to a bright setting, takes about 7 to 10 minutes and is the work of the **cones**. Interestingly, a region in the center of the retina, called the **fovea**, has the greatest density of cones, which are most sensitive in brightly lit conditions. They're also responsible for color vision and fine detail.

Hearing

The sense or act of hearing, known as **audition**, has a number of important functions, ranging from alerting us to dangers to helping us communicate with others. In this section we talk first about sound waves, then about the ear's anatomy and function, and finally about problems with hearing.

Like the visual process, which transforms light waves into vision, the auditory system is designed to convert sound waves into hearing. Sound waves are produced by air molecules moving in a particular wave pattern. For example, vibrating objects like vocal cords or guitar strings create waves of compressed and expanded air resembling ripples on a lake that circle out from a tossed stone. Our ears detect and respond to these waves of small air pressure changes, our brain then interprets the neural messages resulting from these waves, and we hear!

To fully understand this process, pay close attention to the step-by-step diagram in **Figure 4.9**.

Pitch perception

Place theory for hearing The theory that pitch perception is linked to the particular spot on the cochlea's basilar membrane that is most stimulated; pitch is coded by the place at which activation occurs.

Frequency theory for hearing The theory that pitch perception occurs when a tone produces a rate of vibration in the basilar membrane equal to its frequency, with the result that pitch can be coded by the frequency of the neural response.

How do we determine that certain sounds are from a child's voice and not from an adult's? We distinguish between high- and low-pitched sounds by the *frequency* of the sound waves. High-frequency sound waves, which produce high-pitched sounds, maximally stimulate the hair cells at different locations along the basilar membrane (refer to Figure 4.9). This is known as the **place theory for hearing**. Conversely, low-pitched sounds cause hair cells along the basilar membrane to bend and fire neural messages (action potentials) at the same rate as the frequency of that sound, the **frequency theory for hearing**.

In short, place theory best explains how we hear high-pitched sounds, whereas frequency theory is a better explanation for how we hear low-pitched sounds **(Table 4.3)**.

Interestingly, as we age, we tend to lose our ability to hear high-pitched sounds but are still able to hear low-pitched sounds. Given that young students can hear a cell phone ringtone that sounds at 17 kilohertz—too high for adult ears to detect—they can take advantage of this age-related hearing difference and call one another during

FIGURE 4.9 **HOW OUR EARS HEAR**

The **outer ear** captures and funnels sound waves into the eardrum. Next, three tiny bones in the **middle ear** pick up the eardrum's vibrations, and transmit them to the **inner ear**. Finally, the snail-shaped **cochlea** in the inner ear transforms (transduces) the sound waves into neural messages (action potentials) that our brain processes into what we consciously hear.

1. The **outer ear** captures and funnels sound waves onto the tympanic membrane (ear drum).
2. Vibrations of the tympanic membrane strike the **middle ear's** ossicles (hammer, anvil, and stirrup). Then the stirrup hits the oval window.
3. Vibrations of the oval window create waves in the **inner ear's** cochlear fluid which deflects the basilar membrane. This movement bends the hair cells.
4. The hair cells communicate with the auditory nerve, which sends neural impulses to the brain.

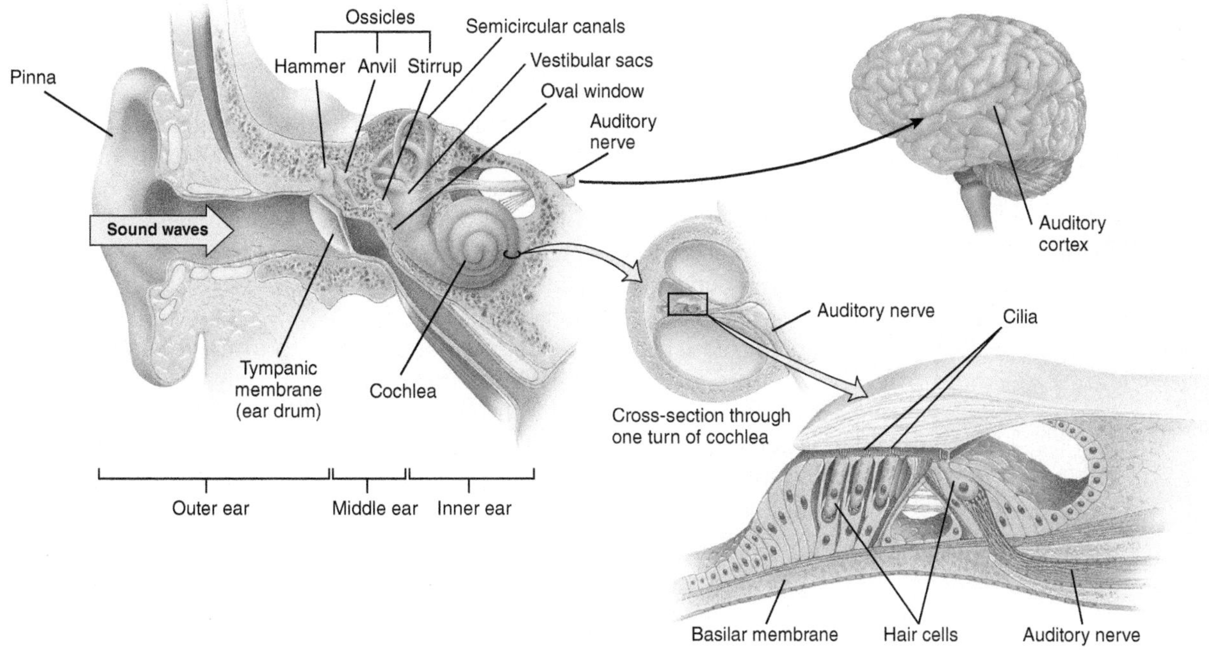

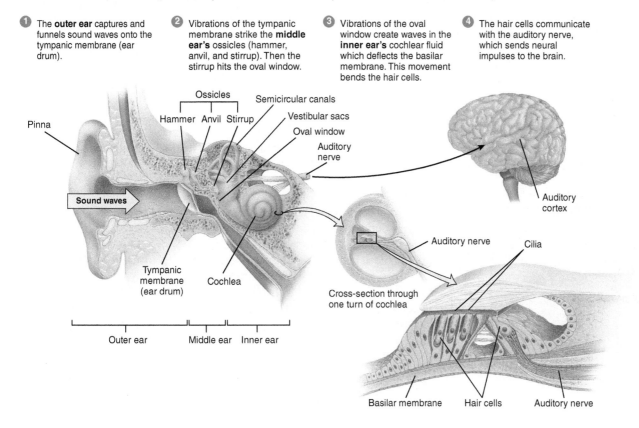

class **(Figure 4.10).** Ironically, the cell phone's ringtone that teachers can't hear is an offshoot of another device, called the Mosquito, which was originally designed to help shopkeepers annoy and drive away loitering teens!

Softness versus Loudness

How we detect a sound as being soft or loud depends on its amplitude (or wave height). Waves with high peaks and low valleys produce loud sounds; waves with relatively low peaks and shallow valleys produce soft sounds. The

Outer ear The pinna, auditory canal, and eardrum structures which funnel sound waves to the middle ear.

Middle ear The hammer, anvil, and stirrup structures of the ear, which concentrate eardrum vibrations onto the cochlea's oval window.

Inner ear The semicircular canals, vestibular sacs, and cochlea, which generate neural signals that are sent to the brain.

Cochlea [KOK-lee-uh] The fluid-filled, coiled tube in the inner ear that contains the receptors for hearing.

TABLE 4.3 **HOW WE DISTINGUISH AMONG SOUNDS OF DIFFERENT PITCH**

Theory	Frequency	Pitch	Example
Place theory Hair cells are stimulated at different locations on basilar membrane.	High frequency	High-pitched sounds	A squeal or a child's voice
Frequency theory Hair cells fire at the same rate as the frequency for the sound.	Low frequency	Low-pitched sounds	A growl or an adult's voice

FIGURE 4.10 **STUDENTS EXPLOITING AGE-RELATED HEARING LOSS**

realworldpsychology

© Monkey Business Images/iStockphoto

relative loudness or softness of sounds is measured on a scale of *decibels* (**Figure 4.11**).

Hearing Problems

What are the types, causes, and treatments of hearing loss? **Conduction hearing loss**, also called conduction deafness, results from problems with the mechanical system that conducts sound waves to the cochlea. Hearing aids that amplify the incoming sound waves, and some forms of surgery, can help with this type of hearing loss.

In contrast, **sensorineural hearing loss**, also known as nerve deafness, results from damage to the cochlea's receptor (hair) cells or to the auditory nerve. Disease and biological changes associated with aging can result in sensorineural hearing loss. But its most common (and preventable) cause is continuous exposure to loud noise, which can damage hair cells and lead to permanent hearing loss. Even brief exposure to really loud sounds, like a stereo or headphones at full blast, a jackhammer, or a jet airplane engine, can cause permanent nerve deafness (refer to Figure 4.11). In fact, a high volume on earphones can reach the same noise level as a jet engine! All forms of high volume noise can damage the coating on nerve cells, making it harder for the nerve cells to send information from the ears to the brain (Pilati et al., 2012). Q3

Although most hearing loss is temporary, damage to the auditory nerve or receptor cells is generally considered irreversible. The only treatment for auditory nerve damage is a small electronic device called a *cochlear implant*. If the auditory nerve is intact, the implant bypasses hair cells to stimulate the nerve. Currently, cochlear implants produce only a crude approximation of hearing, but the technology is improving.

Conduction hearing loss A type of hearing loss that results from damage to the mechanical system that conducts sound waves to the cochlea; also called conduction deafness.

Sensorineural hearing loss A type of hearing loss resulting from damage to cochlea's receptor (hair) hearing cells or to the auditory nerve; also called nerve deafness.

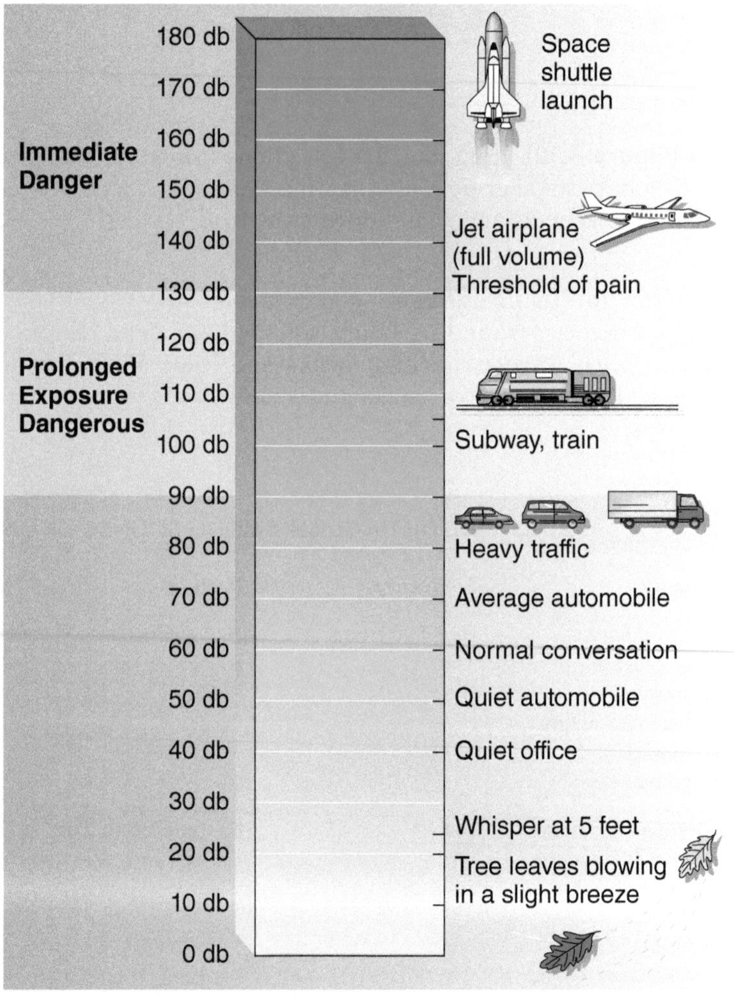

FIGURE 4.11 **BEWARE OF LOUD SOUNDS**

The higher a sound's decibel reading, the more damaging it is to the ear.

psychology and you **Strategies for Protecting Hearing**
Given the limited benefits of medicine or technology to help improve hearing following damage, it's important to protect our sense of hearing. We can do this by avoiding exceptionally loud noises, wearing earplugs when we cannot avoid such stimuli, and paying attention to bodily warnings of possible hearing loss, including a change in our normal hearing threshold and *tinnitus*, a whistling or ringing sensation in the ears. These relatively small changes can have lifelong benefits!

Bernd Leitner Fotodesign/Shutterstock

RETRIEVAL PRACTICE: HOW WE SEE AND HEAR

Self-Test

Completing this self-test and comparing your answers with those in Appendix B provides immediate feedback and helpful practice for exams. Additional interactive, self-tests are available at www.wiley.com/college/huffman.

1. Identify the parts of the eye, placing the appropriate label on the figure to the right.

cornea	rod
iris	cone
pupil	fovea
lens	blind spot
retina	optic nerve

2. A visual acuity problem that occurs when the cornea and lens focus an image in front of the retina is called ______.

a. farsightedness
b. hyperopia
c. myopia
d. presbyopia

3. Identify the parts of the ear, placing the appropriate label on the figure to the right.

tympanic membrane	hammer
anvil	oval window
stirrup	cochlea

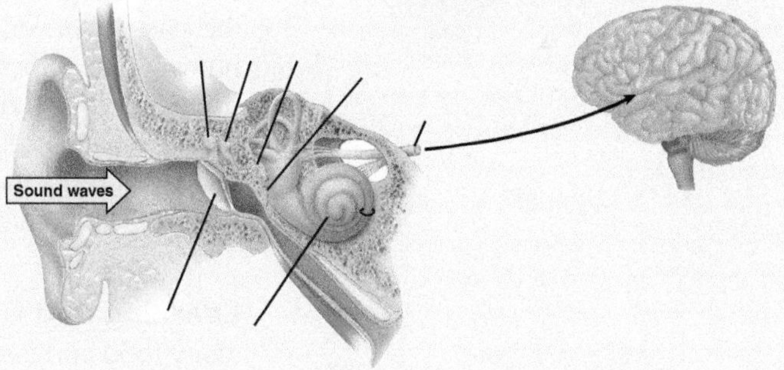

4. Chronic exposure to loud noise can cause permanent ______.

a. auditory illusions
b. auditory hallucinations
c. nerve deafness
d. conduction deafness

Think Critically

1 Which of your sensations, vision or hearing, would you most and least like to lose? Why?

2 Many people believe that blind people have supernatural hearing. How would you use terms like brain plasticity to explain that enhanced hearing might result from greater reliance on hearing or from just using auditory information more effectively?

3 Using what you've learned about pitch, how would you explain why an older person often has an easier time of hearing a man's voice than a woman's voice?

realworldpsychology

How can listening to loud music on headphones damage your hearing?

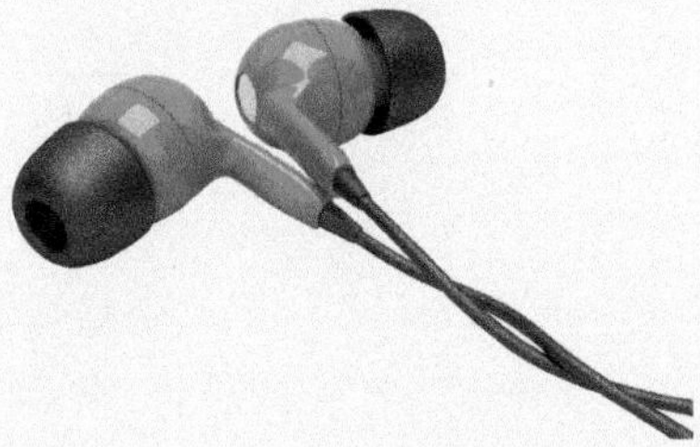

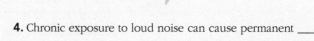

HINT: LOOK IN THE MARGIN FOR Q3

OUR OTHER IMPORTANT SENSES

LEARNING OBJECTIVES

RETRIEVAL PRACTICE While reading the upcoming sections, respond to each Learning Objective in your own words. Then compare your responses with those found at www.wiley.com/college/huffman.

1 **DESCRIBE** how the information contained in odor molecules reaches the brain.
2 **EXPLAIN** how the information contained in food molecules reaches the brain.
3 **IDENTIFY** the body senses.

Vision and audition may be the most prominent of our senses, but the others—smell, taste, and the body senses—are also important for gathering information about our environment.

Smell and Taste

Smell and taste are sometimes referred as the *chemical senses* because they both rely on chemoreceptors that are sensitive to certain chemical molecules. Have you wondered why we have trouble we separating the two sensations? Smell and taste receptors are located near each other and closely interact **(Figure 4.12)**.

Our sense of smell, **olfaction**, is remarkably useful and sensitive. We possess more than 1,000 types of olfactory receptors, which allow us to detect more than 10,000 distinct smells. The nose is more sensitive to smoke than any electronic detector, and—through practice—blind people can quickly recognize others by their unique odors.

Olfaction The sense or act of smelling.

Pheromones [FARE-oh-mones] Chemical signals released by organisms to communicate with other; they may affect behavior, including recognition of family members, aggression, territorial marking, and sexual mating.

Gustation The sense or act of taste.

Some research on **pheromones**—chemicals found in natural body scents that affect various behaviors—supports the idea that certain chemical odors increase sexual behaviors—even in humans (Derntl et al., 2013; Kohl, 2012; Marazziti et al., 2010; Pause, 2012). However, others suggest that human sexuality is far more complex than that of other animals—and more so than perfume advertisements would have you believe.

Today, the sense of taste, **gustation**, may be the least critical of our senses. In the past, however, it probably contributed significantly to our survival. For example, humans and other animals have a preference for sweet foods, which are generally nonpoisonous and are good sources of energy. However, the major function of taste, aided by smell, is to help us avoid eating or drinking harmful substances. Because many plants that taste bitter contain toxic chemicals, an animal is more likely to survive if it avoids bitter-tasting plants (Cooper et al., 2002; Goldstein, 2014; Negri et al., 2012).

Learning and Culture

Many food and taste preferences also are learned from personal learning experiences (Liem et al., 2012; Yantis, 2013). For example, adults who are told a bottle of wine costs $90 rather than its real price of $10 report that it tastes better than the supposedly cheaper brand. Ironically, these false expectations actually trigger areas of the brain that respond to pleasant experiences (Plassmann et al., 2008). This means that in a neurochemical sense the wine we believe is better does in fact taste better!

The culture we live in also affects our taste preferences. Many Japanese children eat raw fish, and some Chinese children eat chicken feet as part of their normal diet. Although most U.S. children might consider these foods "yucky," they tend to love cheese, which children in many other cultures find repulsive. The upcoming *Psych Science* section describes how these tastes preferences are created very early in life.

Before going on, we need to update you on recent research findings on taste perception. It was long believed that we had only four distinct tastes: sweet, sour, salty, and bitter. However, we now know that we also have a fifth taste sense, *umami*, a word that means "delicious" or "savory" and refers to sensitivity to an amino acid called glutamate (Jinap & Hajeb, 2010; Lanfer et al., 2013). Glutamate is found in meats, meat broths, and monosodium glutamate (MSG).

Scientists also once believed that specific areas of the tongue were dedicated to detecting bitter, sweet, salty, and other tastes. Today, we know that taste receptors, like smell receptors, respond differentially to the varying shapes of food

FIGURE 4.12 WHY WE ENJOY EATING PIZZA: OLFACTION PLUS GUSTATION

realworldpsychology

What happens when we eat pizza? Taste receptor cells, as well as sensory cells that respond to touch and temperature, are activated on our tongues. Smell receptor cells in our nose are activated by odors from the pizza. This combined sensory information is then sent to the brain, where it is processed in various association regions of the cerebral cortex. These circuits, together with those that store memories related to our previous pizza experiences, work together to produce our perceptions of each pizza experience.

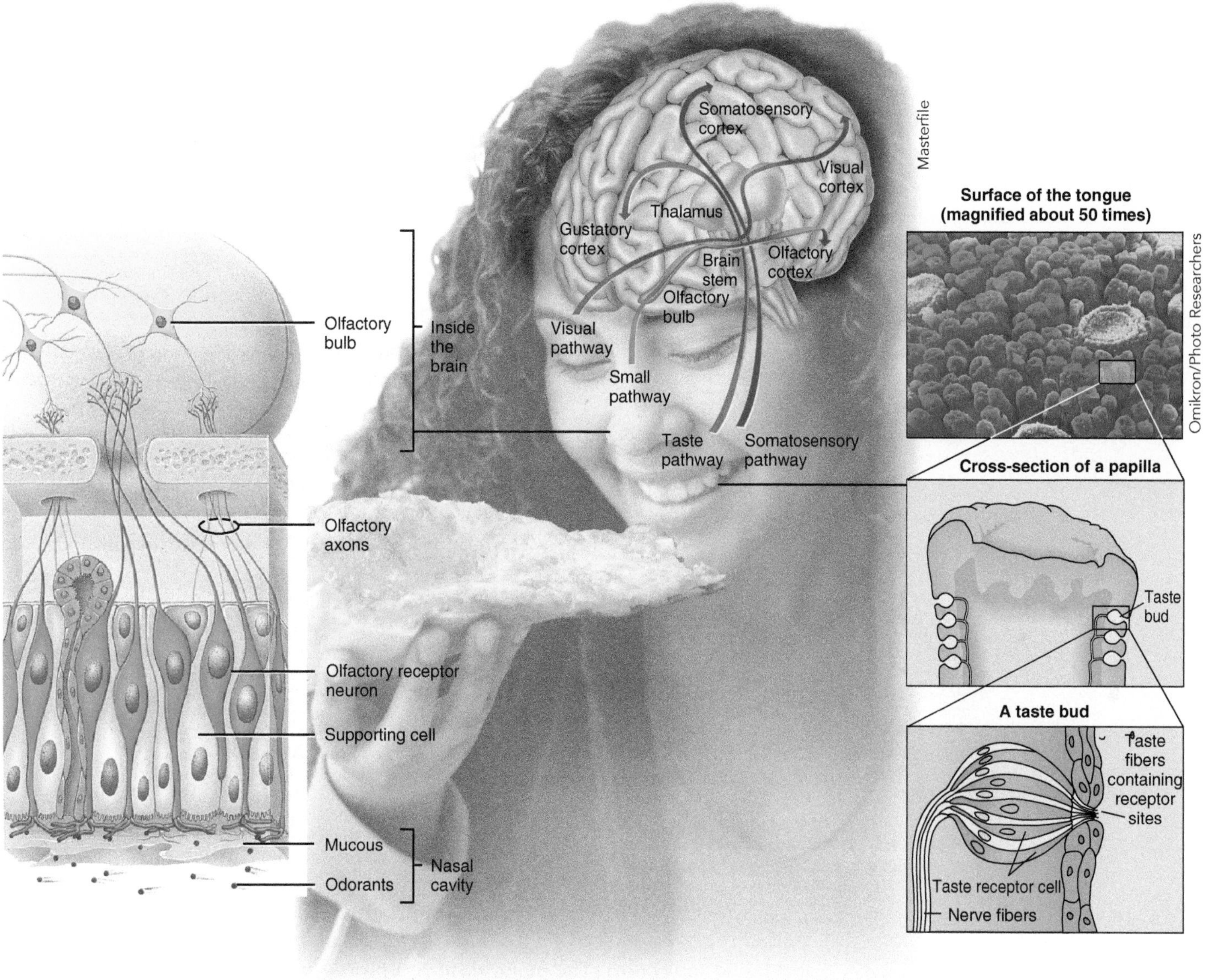

A The smell pathway
Olfactory receptor neurons (shown here in blue) transduce information from odorant molecules that enter the nose. The olfactory nerve carries this information into the olfactory bulb, where most information related to smell is processed before being sent on to other parts of the brain. (Note that olfaction is the only sensory system that is NOT routed through the thalamus.)

B The taste pathway
When we eat and drink, liquids and dissolved foods flow over papillae (the lavender circular areas) and into their pores to the taste buds, which contain the receptors for taste. These nerves carry information into the brain stem, thalamus, gustatory cortex, and somatosensory cortex.

PSYCHSCIENCE

CAN INFANTS LOVE CARROTS?

Would you believe that our taste preferences are shaped even before we are born? Researchers have conducted very clever studies to examine how the foods that pregnant women eat influence the types of tastes their babies prefer after birth. In one study, pregnant women who were planning to breastfeed were randomly assigned to one of three groups (Mennella et al., 2001):

- Women in one group drank carrot juice four times a week for three weeks during pregnancy.
- Women in another group drank carrot juice four times a week for three weeks after the baby was born.
- Women in the third group did not drink carrot juice.

© Cindy Charles/PhotoEdit

The researchers then asked the mothers to rate their babies' facial reactions to different types of foods and to measure how much of a carrot-flavored cereal the babies ate. Babies who were exposed to the taste of carrots either during pregnancy or through breast milk ate more of the carrot-flavored cereal than babies who had no exposure to this taste. Thus showing that taste preferences may be established very early in life—in fact, even before birth.

RESEARCH CHALLENGE

1. Based on the information provided, did the study (Menella et al., 2001) use descriptive, correlational, and/or experimental research?
2. If you chose:
   - descriptive research, is this a naturalistic observation, survey/interview, case study, or archival research?
   - correlational research, is this a positive, negative, or zero correlation?
   - experimental research, label the IV, DV, experimental group(s), and control group.

>> CHECK YOUR ANSWERS IN APPENDIX B.

NOTE: The information provided in this study is admittedly limited, but the level of detail is similar to what is presented in most textbooks and public reports of research findings. Answering these questions, and then comparing your answers to those in the Appendix, will help you become a better critical thinker and consumer of scientific research.

and liquid molecules. The major taste receptors—taste buds—are distributed all over our tongues within little bumps called papillae (refer to Figure 4.12).

The Body Senses

In addition to smell and taste, we have three important body senses that help us navigate our world—skin, vestibular, and kinesthesis **(Figure 4.13)**.

Skin Senses

Our skin is uniquely designed for the detection of touch (or pressure), temperature, and pain **(Figure 4.13a)**. The concentration and depth of the receptors for each of these stimuli vary (Fitzpatrick & Mooney, 2012; Hsiao & Gomez-Ramirez, 2013). For example, touch receptors are most concentrated on the face and fingers and least concentrated in the back and legs. Getting a paper cut can feel so painful

FIGURE 4.13 **OUR BODY SENSES—SKIN, VESTIBULAR, AND KINESTHESIS**

A Skin senses
The tactile senses rely on a variety of receptors located in different parts of the skin. Both humans and nonhuman animals are highly responsive to touch.

© Philip Dyer/iStockphoto

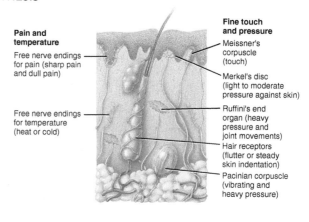

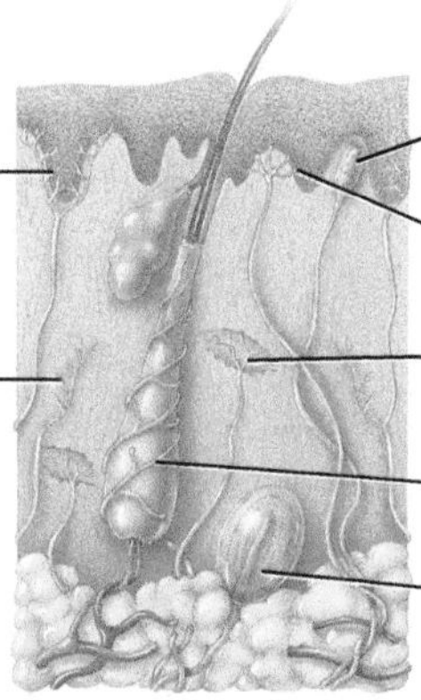

B Vestibular sense
Part of the "thrill" of amusement park rides comes from our vestibular sense becoming confused. The vestibular sense is used by the eye muscles to maintain visual fixation and sometimes by the body to change body orientation. We can become dizzy or nauseated if the vestibular sense becomes "confused" by boat, airplane, or automobile motion. Children between ages 2 and 12 years have the greatest susceptibility to motion sickness.

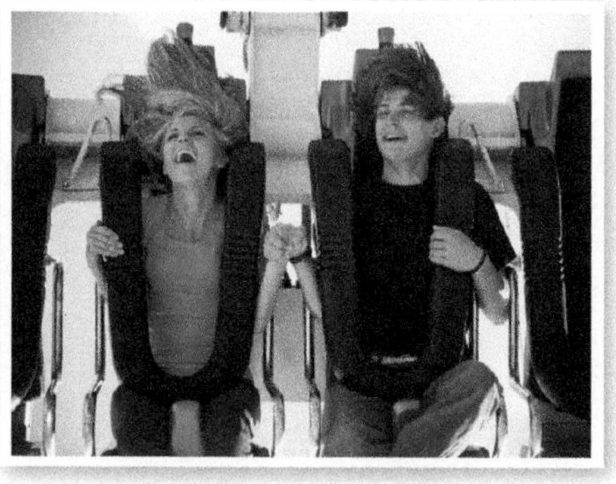

© RubberBall/Alamy Limited

© Mike Blake/Reuters/Corbis

C Kinesthesis
This athlete's finely-tuned behaviors are the result of information provided by receptors in her muscles, joints, and tendons that detect bodily position and movement.

because we have many receptors on our fingertips. Some receptors respond to more than one type of stimulation. For example, itching, tickling, and vibrating sensations seem to be produced by light stimulation of both pressure and pain receptors.

The benefits of touch are so significant for human growth and development that the American Academy of Pediatrics recommends that all mothers and babies have skin-to-skin contact in the first hours after birth. This type of contact, which is called *kangaroo care*, is especially beneficial for preterm and low-birth-weight infants, who then experience greater weight gain, fewer infections, and improved cognitive and motor development.

How does kangaroo care lead to these improvements in infant health? This type of skin-to-skin touch helps babies in several ways, including providing warmth (babies don't have to expend so much energy themselves to stay warm), reducing pain (babies have lower levels of stress and arousal, which improves immune functioning), and improving sleep quality (babies have more time and energy to devote to growth) (Johnston et al., 2011). Q4

Vestibular Sense

Our sense of balance, the **vestibular sense**, informs our brain of how our body, and particularly our head, are oriented with respect to gravity and three-dimensional space **(Figure 4.13b)**. When our head moves, liquid in the *semicircular canals*,

Vestibular sense The sense, located in the inner ear, that detects body movement and position with respect to gravity; also called the sense of balance.

located in our inner ear, moves and bends hair cell receptors. At the end of the semicircular canals are the *vestibular sacs*, which contain hair cells sensitive to our bodily movement relative to gravity (see again Figure 4.9). Information from the semicircular canals and the *vestibular sacs* is converted to neural impulses that are then carried to our brain.

Kinesthesis

Kinesthesis The sense, located in muscles, joints, and tendons, that detects bodily posture, orientation, and movement of body parts relative to each other.

The sense that provides the brain with information about bodily posture, orientation, and movement of individual body parts is called **kinesthesis (Figure 4.13c)**. Kinesthetic receptors are found throughout the muscles, joints, and tendons of our body. They tell our brain which muscles are being contracted or relaxed, how our body weight is distributed, where our arms and legs are in relation to the rest of our body, and so on.

RETRIEVAL PRACTICE: OUR OTHER IMPORTANT SENSES

Self-Test

Completing this self-test and comparing your answers with those in Appendix B provides immediate feedback and helpful practice for exams. Additional interactive, self-tests are available at www.wiley.com/college/huffman.

1. Most information related to smell is processed in the ______.

a. nasal cavity
b. temporal lobe
c. olfactory bulb
d. parietal lobe

2. Most of our taste receptors are found on the ______.

a. olfactory bulb
b. gustatory cells
c. taste buds
d. frenulum

3. The skin senses include ______.

a. pressure
b. pain
c. warmth and cold
d. all these

4. The weightlessness experienced by space travelers from zero gravity has its greatest effect on the _____ senses.

a. visceral
b. reticular
c. somasthetic
d. vestibular

Think Critically

1 From an evolutionary perspective, which is more important—smell or taste?

2 From a personal perspective, which sense is most important to you—your sense of smell, taste, skin senses, vestibular, or kinesthetic?

realworldpsychology

Why do premature babies grow faster when they receive skin-to-skin contact?

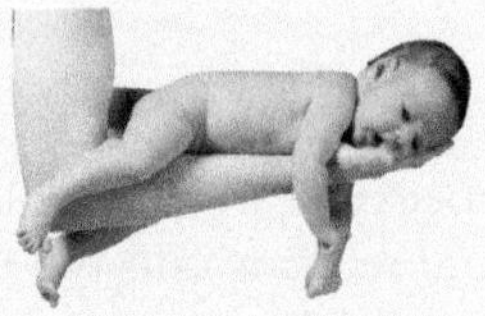

HINT: LOOK IN THE MARGIN FOR Q4

UNDERSTANDING PERCEPTION

LEARNING OBJECTIVES

RETRIEVAL PRACTICE While reading the upcoming sections, respond to each Learning Objective in your own words. Then compare your responses with those found at www.wiley.com/college/huffman.

1 **DOCUMENT** the relationship between selective attention, feature detectors, and habituation.

2 **DESCRIBE** the four ways we organize sensory data.

3 **SUMMARIZE** the factors in perceptual interpretation.

We are ready to move from *sensation* and the major senses to *perception*, the process of selecting, organizing, and interpreting incoming sensations into useful mental representations of the world.

Normally, our perceptions agree with our sensations. When they do not, the result is called an **illusion**, a false or misleading impression produced by errors in the perceptual process or by actual physical distortions, as in desert mirages. Illusions provide psychologists with a tool for studying the normal process of perception **(Figure 4.14)**.

Illusion A false or misleading perception shared by others in the same perceptual environment.

Note that illusions are NOT the same as hallucinations or delusions. *Hallucinations* are false sensory experiences that occur without external stimuli, such as hearing voices during a psychotic episode or seeing particular images after using some type of hallucinogenic drug, such as LSD or hallucinogenic mushrooms. *Delusions* refer to false beliefs, often of persecution or grandeur, that may accompany drug or psychotic experiences.

Selection

In almost every situation, we confront more sensory information than we can reasonably pay attention to. Three major factors help us focus on some stimuli and ignore others: *selective attention*, *feature detectors*, and *habituation*.

Certain basic mechanisms for perceptual selection are built into the brain. For example, through the process of **selective attention (Figure 4.15)**, the brain picks out the information that is important to us and discards the rest (Haab et al., 2011; Kar, 2013; Lamy et al., 2013).

Selective attention The process of filtering out and attending only to important sensory messages.

FIGURE 4.14 UNDERSTANDING PERCEPTUAL ILLUSIONS

realworldpsychology

As you may have noticed, this text highlights numerous popular *myths* about psychology because it's important to understand and correct our misperceptions. For similar reasons, you need to know how illusions mislead out normal information processing and recognize that "seeing is believing, but seeing isn't always believe correctly" (Lilienfeld et al., 2010, p.7).

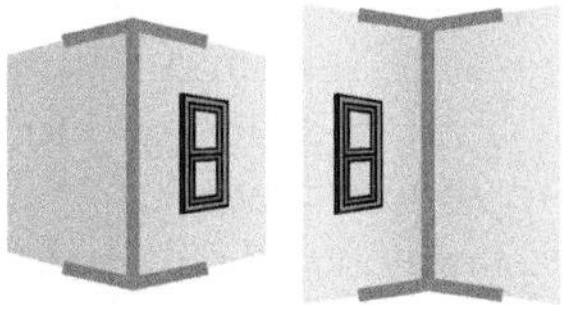

A Müller-Lyer illusion
Which vertical line is longer? In fact, the two vertical lines are the same length, but psychologists have learned that people who live in urban environments normally see the one on the right as longer. This is because they have learned to make size and distance judgments from perspective cues created by right angles and horizontal and vertical lines of buildings and streets.

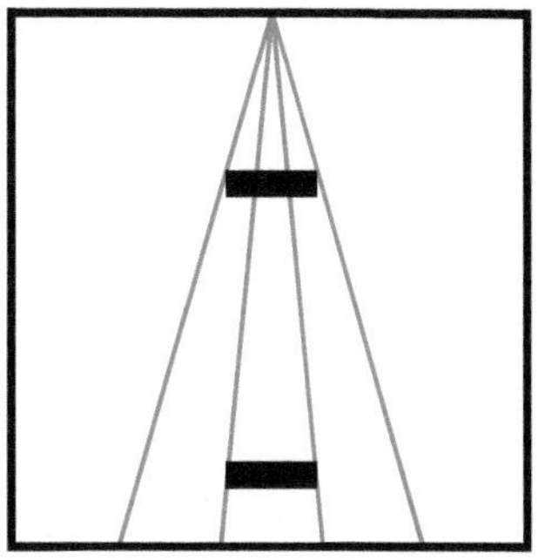

B Ponzo illusion
Which of the two horizontal lines is longer? In fact, both lines are the exact same size, but the converging lines provide depth cues telling you that the top dark, horizontal, line is farther away than the bottom line and therefore much larger.

Think Critically

1. What do you think causes "errors" in the perceptual process, such as the optical illusions described here?
2. When you watch films of moving cars, the wheels appear to go backward. Can you explain this common visual illusion?

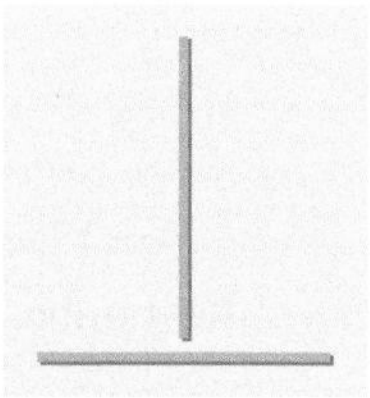

C The horizontal-vertical illusion
Which is longer, the horizontal (flat) or the vertical (standing) line? People living in areas where they regularly see long straight lines, such as roads and train tracks, perceive the horizontal line as shorter because of their environmental experiences.

D Shepard's tables
Do these two table tops have the same dimensions? Get a ruler and check it for yourself.

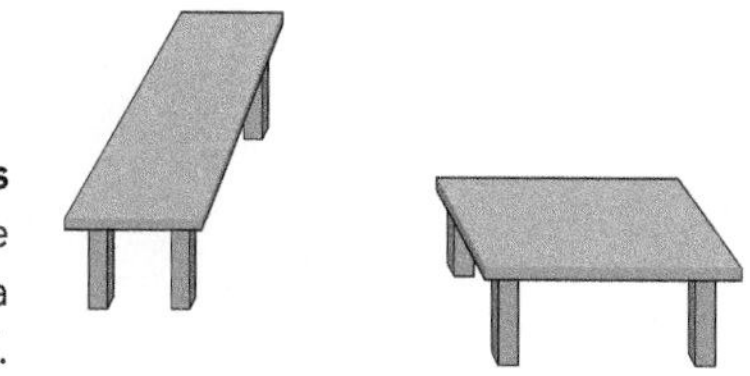

FIGURE 4.15 **SELECTIVE ATTENTION**

Have you noticed that when you're at a noisy party, you can still select and attend to the voices of people you find interesting, or that you can suddenly pick up on another group's conversation if someone in that group mentions your name? These are prime examples of *selective attention*, also called the "cocktail party phenomenon."

© Greg Hinsdale/Corbis

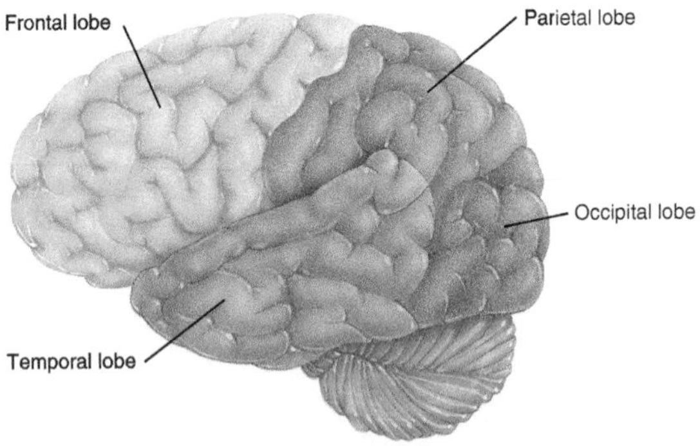

FIGURE 4.16 **LOCATION OF FEATURE DETECTORS IN THE BRAIN**

Feature detectors Specialized neurons that respond only to certain sensory information.

Habituation The brain's reduced responsiveness due to repeated stimulation of the same receptors.

In addition to selective attention, the brains of humans and other animals contain specialized cells, called **feature detectors**, which respond only to certain stimuli. For example, studies with humans have found feature detectors in the temporal and occipital lobes that respond maximally to faces **(Figure 4.16)**. Problems in these areas can produce a condition called *prosopagnosia* (*prosopon* means "face," and *agnosia* means "failure to know"). Interestingly, people with prosopagnosia can recognize that they are looking at a face. But they cannot say whose face is reflected in a mirror, even if it is their own or that of a friend or relative (Avidan et al., 2013; Stollhoff et al., 2011; Susilo & Duchaine, 2013).

Other examples of the brain's ability to filter experience are evidenced by **habituation**, a decrease in responding due to repeated stimulation of the same stimulus. Apparently, the brain is "prewired" to pay more attention to changes in the environment than to stimuli that remain constant. Developmental psychologists often use measurements of habituation to tell when a stimulus can be detected and discriminated by infants who are too young to speak. When presented with a new stimulus, infants pay attention, but with repetition their responses weaken.

Habituation also can help explain why attention and compliments from a stranger are generally more exciting than those from a long-term romantic partner. Unfortunately, some people (who haven't taken psychology courses or read this text) may misinterpret and overvalue this new attention. They may even leave good relationships, not realizing that they will also soon habituate to the new person!

©Yuri_Arcurs/iStockphoto

realworldpsychology **Using Selective Attention, Feature Detectors, and Habituation in Advertising** As advertisers and political operatives well know, people tend to automatically select stimuli that are intense, novel, moving, contrasting, and repetitious. For sheer volume of sales (or votes), if an ad gets your attention, that's all that matters. Whether you like the ad or not is irrelevant. This phenomenon also helps explain why sometimes you don't like a song when you first hear it on the radio or at a club, but after you've heard it hundreds of times, you actually might find it kind of catchy!

Organization

Raw sensory data are like the parts of a watch—the parts must be assembled in a meaningful way before they are useful. We organize sensory data in terms of form, constancy, depth, and color.

Form perception Gestalt psychologists were among the first to study how the brain organizes sensory impressions into a *gestalt*—a German word meaning "form" or "whole." They emphasized the importance of organization and patterning in enabling us to perceive the whole stimulus rather than perceive its discrete parts as separate entities. The Gestaltists proposed several laws of organization that specify how people perceive form **(Figure 4.17)**.

The most fundamental Gestalt principle of organization is our tendency to distinguish between the *figure* (our main focus of attention) and *ground* (the background or surroundings).

Your sense of figure and ground is at work in what you are doing right now—reading. Your brain is receiving sensations of black lines and white paper, but your brain is organizing these sensations into black letters and words on a white background. You perceive the letters as the figure and the white as the ground. If you make a great effort, you might be able to force yourself to see the page reversed, as though a black

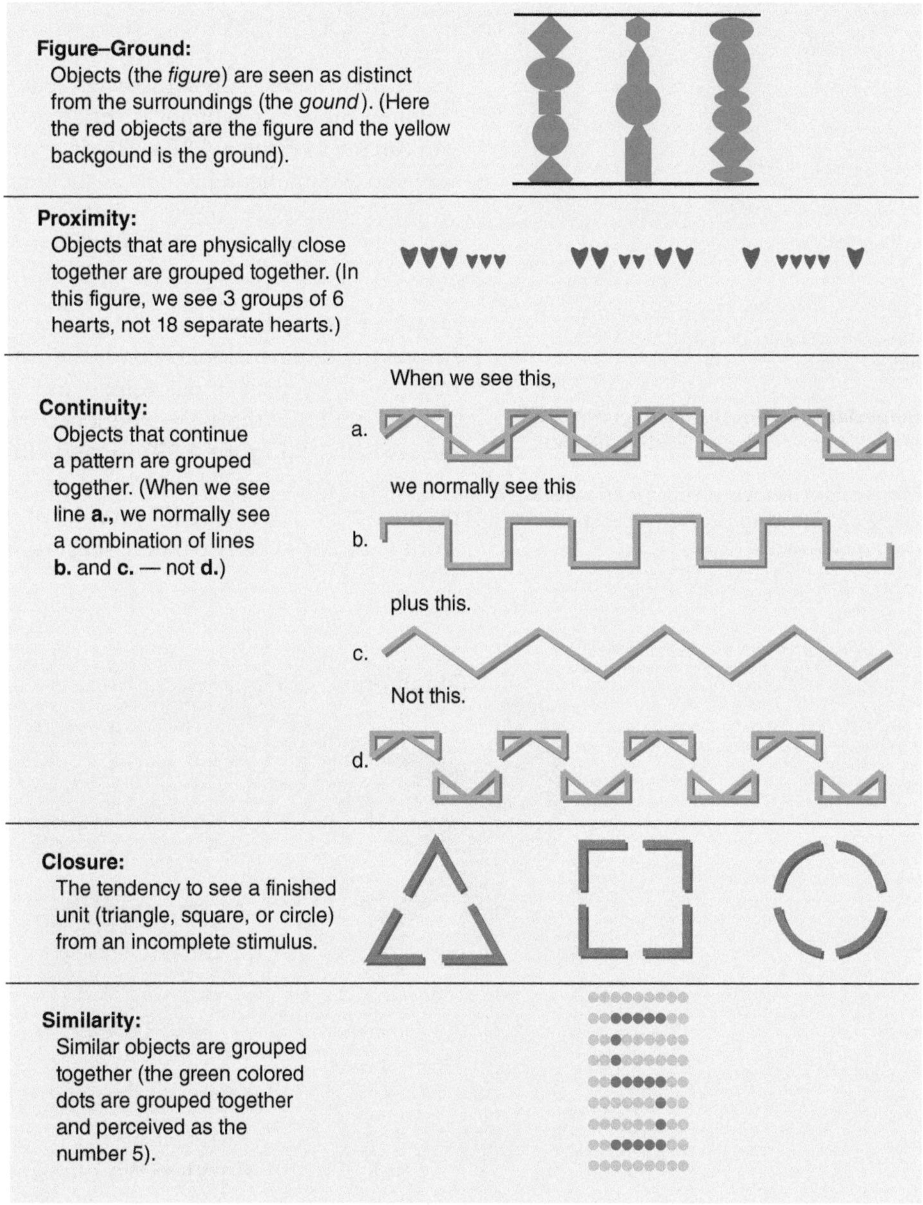
Figure–Ground:
Objects (the *figure*) are seen as distinct from the surroundings (the *gound*). (Here the red objects are the figure and the yellow backgound is the ground).
Proximity:
Objects that are physically close together are grouped together. (In this figure, we see 3 groups of 6 hearts, not 18 separate hearts.)
Continuity:
Objects that continue a pattern are grouped together. (When we see line **a.**, we normally see a combination of lines **b.** and **c.** — not **d.**)
When we see this,
a.
we normally see this
b.
plus this.
c.
Not this.
d.
Closure:
The tendency to see a finished unit (triangle, square, or circle) from an incomplete stimulus.
Similarity:
Similar objects are grouped together (the green colored dots are grouped together and perceived as the number 5).

FIGURE 4.17 UNDERSTANDING GESTALT PRINCIPLES OF ORGANIZATION

Gestalt principles are based on the notion that we all share a natural tendency to force patterns onto whatever we see. Although the examples of the Gestalt principles in this figure are all visual, each principle applies to other modes of perception as well. For example, the Gestalt principle of *contiguity* cannot be shown because it involves nearness in time, not visual nearness. Similarly, the aural (hearing) effects of figure and ground aren't shown in this figure, but you've undoubtedly experienced them in a movie theater. Despite nearby conversations in the audience, you can still listen to the voices on the film because you make them your focus (the figure) versus the ground.

FIGURE 4.18 UNDERSTANDING REVERSIBLE AND IMPOSSIBLE FIGURES

Ⓐ This so-called *reversible figure* demonstrates alternating figure–ground relations. It can be seen as a woman looking in a mirror or as a skull, depending on what you see as figure or ground.

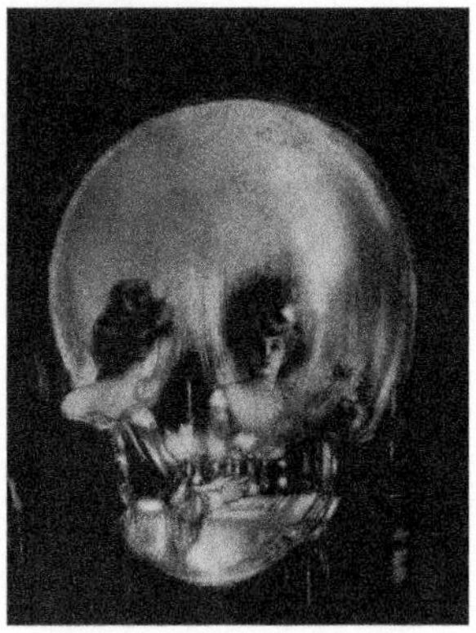

Rykoff Collection/Corbis

Ⓑ When you first glance at this famous painting by the Dutch artist M.C. Escher, you detect specific features of the stimuli and judge them as sensible figures. But as you try to sort and organize the different elements into a stable, well-organized whole, you realize they don't add up—they're impossible. There is no one-to-one correspondence between your actual sensory input and your final perception.

background were showing through letter-shaped-holes in a white foreground. There are times, however, when it is very hard to distinguish the figure from the ground, as you can see in **Figure 4.18a**. This is known as a *reversible figure*. Your brain alternates between seeing the light areas as the figure and seeing them as the ground.

Like reversible figures, *impossible figures* help us understand perceptual principles—in this case, the principle of form organization **(Figure 4.18b)**.

Depth perception The ability to perceive three-dimensional space and to accurately judge distance.

Binocular cues Visual input from two eyes that allows perception of depth or distance.

Monocular cues Visual input from a single eye alone that contributes to perception of depth or distance.

Depth Perception

In our three-dimensional world, the ability to perceive the depth and distance of objects—as well as their height and width—is essential. **Depth perception** is learned primarily through experience. However, research using an apparatus called the *visual cliff* **(Figure 4.19)** suggests that some depth perception is inborn.

One mechanism by which we perceive depth is the interaction of both eyes to produce **binocular cues (Figure 4.20)**. The other relies on **monocular cues**, which work with each eye separately **(Figure 4.21)**.

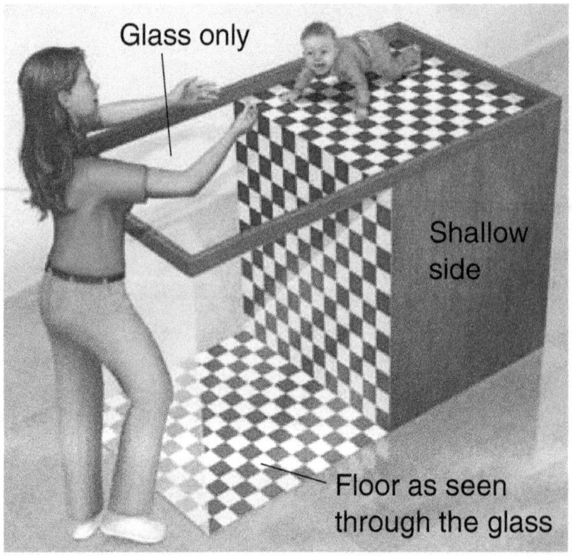

FIGURE 4.19 VISUAL CLIFF

realworldpsychology

Crawling infants hesitate or refuse to move to the "deep end" of the visual cliff indicating that they perceive the difference in depth. The same is true for baby animals that walk almost immediately after birth. Even 2-month-old human infants show a change in heart rate when placed on the deep versus shallow side of the visual cliff (Adolph & Kretch, 2012; Banks & Salapatek, 1983; Gibson & Walk, 1960; Ueno et al., 2012).

FIGURE 4.20 **BINOCULAR DEPTH CUES**

How do we perceive a three-dimensional world with a two-dimensional receptor system? One mechanism is the interaction of both eyes to produce binocular cues.

Ⓐ Retinal disparity

Stare at your two index fingers a few inches in front of your eyes with their tips half an inch apart. Do you see the "floating finger"? Move it farther away and the "finger" will shrink. Move it closer and it will enlarge. Because our eyes are about 2½ inches apart, objects at different distances (such as the "floating finger") project their images on different parts of the retina, an effect called **retinal disparity**. Far objects project on the retinal area near the nose, whereas near objects project farther out, closer to the ears.

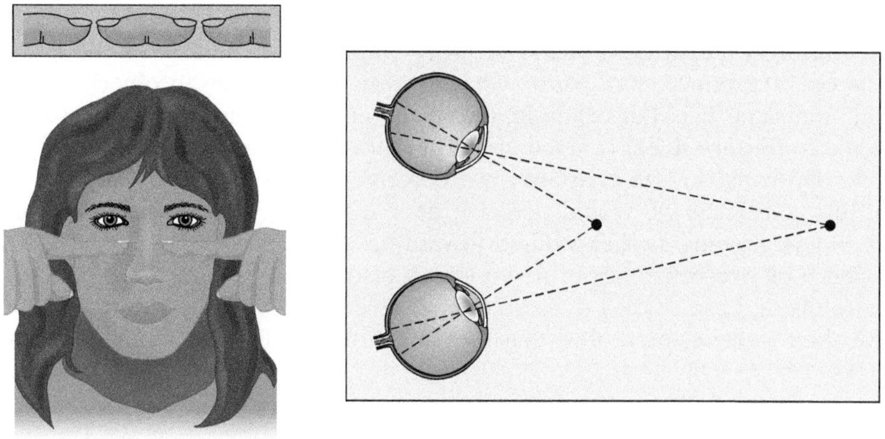

Ⓑ Convergence

Hold your index finger at arm's length in front of you and watch it as you bring it closer until it is right in front of your nose. The amount of strain in your eye muscles created by the **convergence**, or turning inward of the eyes, is used as a cue by your brain to interpret distance.

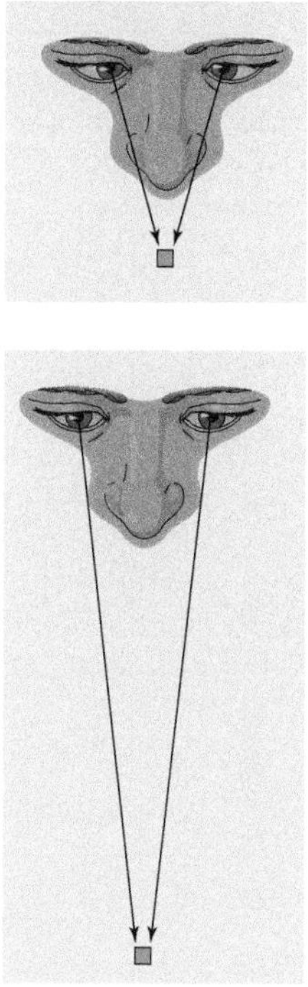

The binocular (two eyes) cues of **retinal disparity** and **convergence** are inadequate in judging distances longer than the length of a football field. Luckily, we have several monocular (one-eye) cues available separately to each eye. Imagine yourself as an artist and see whether you can identify each of the following cues in this beautiful photo of the Taj Mahal, a famous mausoleum in India (Figure 4.21):

- **Linear perspective** Parallel lines converge, or angle toward one another, as they recede into the distance.
- **Interposition** Objects that obscure or overlap other objects are perceived as closer.
- **Relative size** Close objects cast a larger retinal image than distant objects.
- **Texture gradient** Nearby objects have a coarser and more distinct texture than distant ones.
- **Aerial perspective** Distant objects appear hazy and blurred compared to close objects because of intervening atmospheric dust or haze.
- **Light and shadow** Brighter objects are perceived as being closer than darker objects.
- **Relative height** Objects positioned higher in our field of vision are perceived as farther away.

Two additional monocular cues for depth perception, **accommodation** of the lens of the eye and *motion parallax*, cannot be used by artists and are not shown in Figure 4.21. In *accommodation*, muscles that adjust the shape of the lens as it focuses on an object send neural messages to the brain, which interprets the signal to perceive distance. For near objects, the lens bulges; for

Retinal disparity The binocular cue of distance in which the separation of the eyes causes different images to fall on each retina.

Convergence A binocular depth cue in which the eyes turn inward (or converge) to fixate on an object.

Accommodation The process by which the eye's ciliary muscles change the shape (thickness) of the lens so that light is focused on the retina; adjustment of the eye's lens permitting focusing on near and distant objects.

FIGURE 4.21 **MONOCULAR DEPTH CUES AND THE TAJ MAHAL**

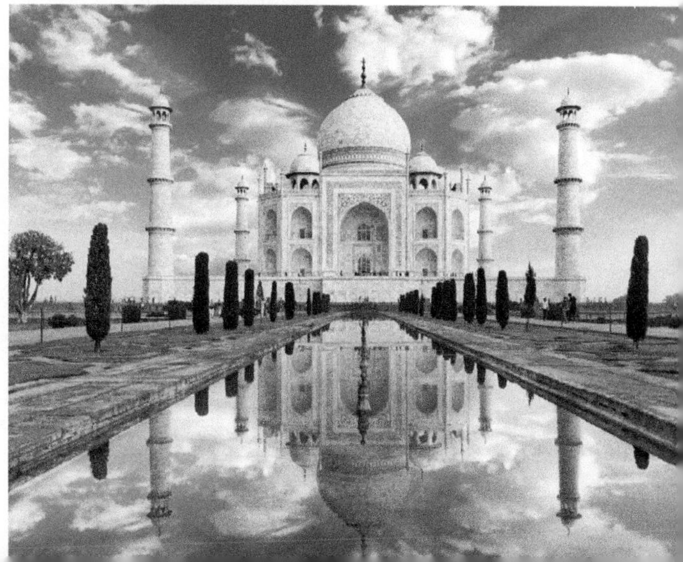

far objects, it flattens. *Motion parallax* (also known as *relative motion*) refers to the fact that when we are moving, close objects appear to whiz by, whereas farther objects seem to move more slowly or remain stationary. This effect can easily be seen when traveling by car or train.

Constancies Perception

Perceptual constancy The ability to retain an unchanging perception of an object despite changes in the sensory input.

To organize our sensations into meaningful patterns, we develop **perceptual constancies**, the learned tendency to perceive the environment as stable, despite changes in an object's *size*, *shape*, *color*, and *brightness*. Without perceptual constancy, things would seem to grow as we get closer to them, change shape as our viewing angle changes, and change color as light levels change (Durgin et al., 2012; Goldstein, 2014; Granrud, 2012).

Size constancy Regardless of the distance from us (or the size of the image it casts on our retina), *size constancy* allows us to interpret an object as always being the same size. For example, the image of the couple in the foreground of the photo **(Figure 4.22)** is much larger on our retina than the trees behind them. However, thanks to size constancy, we perceive them to be of normal size. Without this constancy, we would perceive people walking away from us as shrinking and as growing as they walked toward us. Although researchers have found evidence of size constancy in newborns, it also develops from learning and the environment. Case studies of people who have been blind since birth, and then have their sight restored, find that they initially have little or no size constancy (Sacks, 1995).

Color and brightness constancies Our perception of color and brightness remain the same even when the light conditions change. Look at the two dogs' fur in this photo **(Figure 4.23)**. We perceive the color and brightness as constant

FIGURE 4.22 **SIZE CONSTANCY**

courtesy Karen Huffman

FIGURE 4.23 **COLOR AND BRIGHTNESS CONSTANCIES**

GK Hart/Vikki Hart/Getty Images, Inc.

FIGURE 4.24 **SHAPE CONSTANCY**

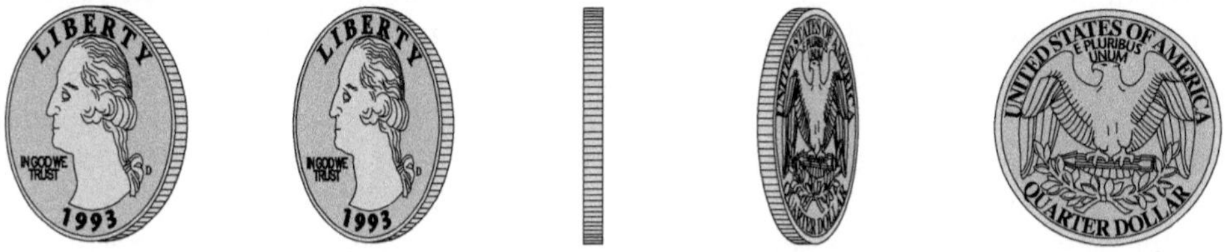

Note how as the coin is rotated, it changes shape, but we still perceive it as the same coin—thanks to shape constancy.

The so-called Ames room illusion (shown in this diagram) also illustrates size and shape constancy. To a viewer peering through the peephole, the Ames room appears to be a normal cubic-shaped room. But the true shape is trapezoidal. In addition, the walls are slanted and the floor and ceiling are at an incline. Because our brains mistakenly assume that the two people are the same distance away, we compensate for the apparent size difference by making the person on the left appear much smaller.

despite the fact that the wavelength of light reaching our retina may vary as the light changes.

Shape constancy One additional perceptual constancy is the tendency to perceive an object's shape as staying constant even when the angle of our view changes **(Figure 4.24)**.

Color perception

Our ability to perceive color is at least as remarkable and useful as depth perception. Humans may be able to discriminate among 7 million different hues, and research conducted in many cultures suggests that we all seem to see essentially the same colored world (Davies, 1998; Ozturk et al., 2013). Furthermore, studies of infants old enough to focus and move their eyes show that they are able to see color nearly as well as adults and have color preferences similar to those of adults (Franklin et al., 2010).

Although we know color is produced by different wavelengths of light, the actual way in which we perceive color is a matter of scientific debate. Traditionally, there have been two theories of color vision: the trichromatic (three-color) theory and the opponent-process theory. The **trichromatic theory of color** (from the Greek word *tri*, meaning "three," and *chroma*, meaning "color") suggests that we have three "color systems," each of which is maximally sensitive to red, green, or blue (Young, 1802). The proponents of this theory demonstrated that mixing lights of these three colors could yield the full spectrum of colors we perceive.

Trichromatic theory of color The theory that color perception results from three types of cones in the retina, each most sensitive to either red, green, or blue; other colors result from a mixture of these three.

Opponent-process theory of color The theory that all color perception is based on three systems, each of which contains two color opposites (red versus green, blue versus yellow, and black versus white).

However, trichromatic theory doesn't fully explain color vision, and other researchers have proposed alternative theories. For example, the **opponent-process theory of color** agrees that we have three color systems, but it says that each system is sensitive to two opposing colors—blue and yellow, red and green, black and white—in an "on/off" fashion. In other words, each color receptor responds either to blue or yellow, or to red or green, with the black-or-white systems responding to differences in brightness levels. This theory makes a lot of sense because when different-colored lights are combined, people are unable to see reddish greens and bluish yellows. In fact, when red and green lights or blue and yellow lights are mixed in equal amounts, we see white. This opponent-process theory also explains *color afterimages*, a fun type of optical illusion in which an image briefly remains after the original image has faded (see *Test Yourself*).

TEST YOURSELF: UNDERSTANDING AND TESTING YOURSELF FOR COLOR AFTERIMAGES

psychology and you

Try staring at the dot in the middle of this color-distorted U.S. flag for 60 seconds. Then stare at a plain sheet of white paper. You should get interesting color aftereffects—red in place of green, blue in place of yellow, and white in place of black: a "genuine" U.S. flag. (If you don't see the afterimage, blink once or twice and try again.)

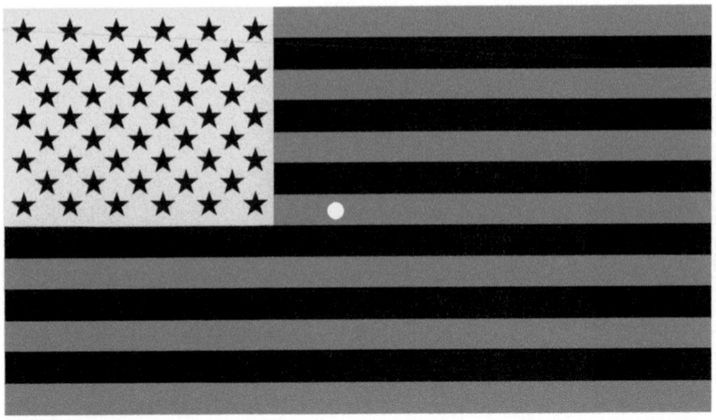

What happened? As you stared at the green, black, and yellow colors, the neural systems that process those colors became fatigued. Then when you looked at the plain white paper, which reflects all wavelengths, a reverse opponent process occurred: Each fatigued receptor responded with its opposing red, white, and blue colors! This is a good example of color afterimages—and further support for the opponent-process theory.

Think Critically

1. In what kinds of situations do you think color afterimages are likely to occur?
2. Other than learning that our eyes can play tricks on our brain, why might illusions like this afterimage be important?

Today we know that both trichromatic and opponent-process theories are correct—they just operate at different levels in visual processing. Color vision is processed in a trichromatic fashion in the retina. In contrast, color vision during opponent processing involves the retina, optic nerve, and brain.

Color-Deficient Vision

Most people perceive three different colors—red, green, and blue—and are called *trichromats*. However, a small percentage of the population has a genetic deficiency in the red–green system, the blue–yellow system, or both. Those who perceive only two colors are called *dichromats*. People who are sensitive to only the black–white system are called *monochromats*, and they are totally color blind. If you'd like to test yourself for red–green color blindness, see *Test Yourself*.

TEST YOURSELF: UNDERSTANDING COLOR BLINDNESS

psychology and you

Are you color blind? People who suffer red–green deficiency have trouble perceiving the number in this design. Although we commonly use the term *color blindness*, most problems are color confusion rather than color blindness. Furthermore, most people who have some color blindness are not even aware of it.

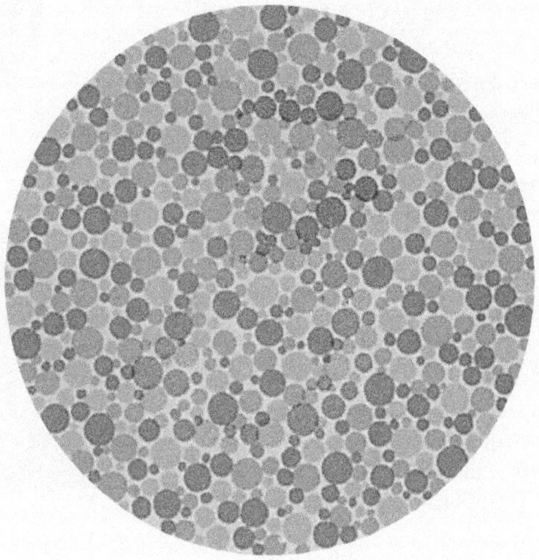

Interpretation

After selectively sorting through incoming sensory information and organizing it, the brain uses this information to explain and make judgments about the external world. This final stage of perception—*interpretation*—is influenced by several factors, including sensory adaptation, perceptual set, frame of reference, and bottom-up or top-down processing.

Stratton's experiment with the inverting goggles, discussed in the chapter overview, illustrates the critical role that sensory adaptation plays in the way we interpret the information that our brains gather. Without his ability to adapt his perceptions to a skewed environment, Stratton would not have been able to function. His brain's ability to retrain itself to interpret his new surroundings allowed him to create coherence from what would otherwise have been chaos.

As you can see in the *Real World Psychology* example below, our previous experiences, assumptions, and expectations also affect how we interpret and perceive the world, by creating a **perceptual set**, or a readiness to perceive in a particular manner, based on expectations (Dunning & Balcetis, 2013). In other words, we largely see what we expect to see!

Perceptual set The readiness to perceive in a particular manner, based on expectations.

realworldpsychology

Crime and Perceptual Sets In some cases, our *perceptual sets*, or expectations, can have hazardous effects. For example, researchers asked both white and black participants to play a videogame in which they were told to shoot targets who were carrying a gun but not those who were unarmed (Correll et al., 2002).

Participants of both races made the decision to shoot an armed target more quickly if the target was black than white. They also chose NOT to shoot an unarmed target more quickly if the target was white than black.

This study points to the influence of our expectations on real-life situations in which police officers must decide almost instantly whether to shoot a potential suspect—and may partially explain why blacks are at greater risk than whites of being accidentally shot by police officers.

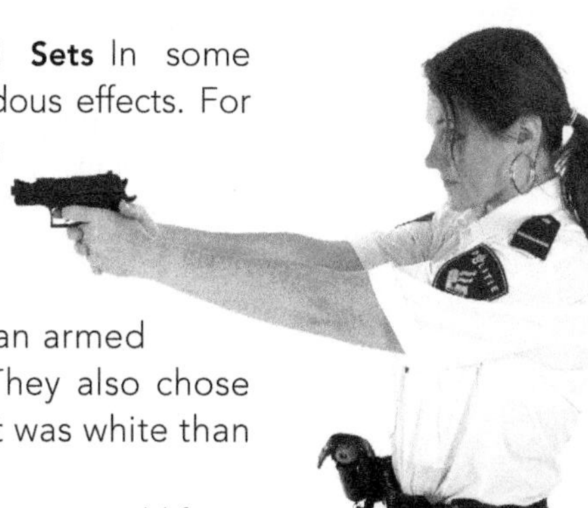

Foto Bouten/Shutterstock

FIGURE 4.25 PERCEPTUAL SET?
When you look at this drawing, do you see a young woman looking back over her shoulder or an older woman with her chin buried in a fur collar? It may depend on your age. Younger students tend to first see a young woman, and older students first see an older woman. Although the basic sensory input stays the same, your brain's attempt to interpret ambiguous stimuli creates a type of perceptual dance, shifting from one interpretation to another (Gaetz et al., 1998).

Bottom-up processing Perceptual analysis that begins "at the bottom," with raw sensory data being sent "up" to the brain for higher-level analysis; it is data-driven processing that moves from the parts to the whole.

Top-down processing Perceptual analysis that starts "at the top," with higher-level cognitive processes (such as expectations and knowledge), and then works down; it is conceptually driven processing that moves from the whole to the parts.

In addition to possible problems with *perceptual set* **(Figure 4.25)**, the way we perceive people, objects, or situations is also affected by the *frame of reference*, or context. An elephant is perceived as much larger when it is next to a mouse than when it stands next to a giraffe. This is the reason professional athletes who make huge amounts of money sometimes feel underpaid: They're comparing what they make to the pay of those around them, who also make huge sums, and not to the average person in the United States! The influence of frame of reference on perception also helps explain why people rate themselves as more athletic if they compare themselves to the Pope than to a professional basketball player (Mussweiler et al., 2004)! Q5

Finally, recall that we began this chapter by discussing how we receive sensory information (sensation) and work our way upward to the top levels of perceptual processing (perception), **bottom-up processing**. In contrast, **top-down processing** begins with "higher," "top"-level processing of thoughts, previous experiences, expectations, language, and cultural background and works down to the sensory level (Antúnez et al., 2013; Chica et al., 2013; Freeman & Ambady, 2011; Zhaoping & Guyader, 2007) (see *Psychology and You*).

Jose Luis Pelaez/Iconica/Getty Images, Inc.

psychology and you **Reading and Processing** When first learning to read, you used bottom-up processing. You initially learned that certain arrangements of line and "squiggles" represented specific letters. You later realized that these letters make up words.

Now, yuor aiblity to raed uisng top-dwon prcessoing mkaes it psosible to unedrstnad thsi sntenece desipte its mnay mssipllengis.

Science and ESP

Extrasensory perception (ESP) The perceptual, so-called "psychic," abilities that supposedly go beyond the known senses (for example, telepathy, clairvoyance, precognition, and psychokinesis).

So far in this chapter, we have talked about sensations provided by our eyes, ears, nose, mouth, and skin. What about a so-called sixth sense? Can some people perceive things that cannot be perceived with the usual sensory channels, by using **extrasensory perception (ESP)**? Those who claim to have ESP profess to be able to read other people's minds (*telepathy*), perceive objects or events that are inaccessible to their normal senses (*clairvoyance*), predict the future (*precognition*), or move or affect objects without touching them (psychokinesis).

As we discussed in Chapter 1, each of these claims falls under the name *pseudopsychology,* including Daryl Bem's highly publicized research (Bem, 2011). Furthermore, virtually all reports and so-called studies of ESP have been successfully debunked (Alcock, 2011; Bones, 2012; Galak et al., 2012; Irwin, 2008; Shaffer & Jadwiszczok, 2010). Findings in ESP are notoriously "fragile" in that they do not hold up to intense scrutiny.

Perhaps the most serious weakness of ESP is its failure of replication by rivals in independent laboratories, which is a core requirement for scientific acceptance (Francis, 2012; Hyman, 1996; Rouder et al., 2013). (Recall also from Chapter 1 that magician James Randi and the MacArthur Foundation has offered $1 million to "anyone who proves a genuine psychic power under proper observing conditions." But even after many years, the money has never been collected!)

So why do so many people believe in ESP? One reason is that, as mentioned earlier in the chapter, our motivations and interests often influence our perceptions, driving us to selectively attend to things we want to see or hear. In addition, the subject of extrasensory perception often generates strong emotional responses. When individuals feel strongly about an issue, they sometimes fail to recognize the faulty reasoning underlying their beliefs.

Belief in ESP is particularly associated with illogical or noncritical thinking. For example, people often fall victim to the *fallacy of positive instances*, or the *confirmation bias*, noting and remembering events that confirm personal expectations and beliefs (the "hits") and ignoring nonsupportive evidence (the "misses"). Other times, people fail to recognize chance occurrences for what they are. Finally, human information processing often biases us to notice and remember the most vivid information. Rather than relying on scientific research based on analyzing numerous data points, we prefer colorful anecdotes and heartfelt personal testimonials.

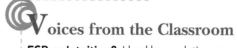

Voices from the Classroom

ESP or Intuition? I had been dating my girlfriend for nearly three years when a job offer caused me to move to another state. Soon after moving, I realized that I needed to propose to her to show her how serious I was about our relationship. When she came in town to visit me, I proposed to her the day after we had been dating for four years. I told no one in advance of this proposal. I was very excited to share this news with my mother; my mom and I have always been close. Even though we lived far from each other, we talked at least once or twice a week. So, I called my mom to share the big news with her. I said, "Hi mom." The first thing my mother said was, "Are you engaged?" Was this ESP or just mother's intuition? What do you believe?

Professor David Baskind
Delta College
University Center, Michigan

RETRIEVAL PRACTICE: UNDERSTANDING PERCEPTION

Self-Test

Completing this self-test and comparing your answers with those in Appendix B provides immediate feedback and helpful practice for exams. Additional interactive, self-tests are available at www.wiley.com/college/huffman.

1. When our brain is sorting out and attending only to the most important messages from the senses, it is engaged in the process of ______.

a. sensory adaptation
b. sensory habituation
c. selective attention
d. selective sorting

2. In the ______ shown below, the discrepancy between figure and ground is too vague, and we may have difficulty perceiving which is figure and which is ground.

a. illusion
b. reversible figure
c. optical illusion
d. hallucination

3. The tendency for the environment to be perceived as remaining the same even with changes in sensory input is called ______.

a. perceptual constancy
b. the constancy of expectation
c. an illusory correlation
d. Gestalt's primary principle

4. The ______ of color vision says that color perception results from three types of cones in the retina.

a. tricolor theory
b. trichromatic theory
c. tripigment theory
d. opponent-process theory

5. A readiness to perceive in a particular manner is known as ______.

a. sensory adaptation
b. perceptual set
c. habituation
d. frame of reference

Think Critically

1. Can you explain how your own perceptual sets might create prejudice or discrimination?
2. How has reading this chapter's information about ESP influenced your beliefs about this topic?
3. Why do you think no one has ever received the $1 million dollar award that was offered for a provable case of ESP?

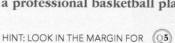

realworldpsychology

Why do people rate themselves as more athletic if they compare themselves to the Pope than to a professional basketball player?

HINT: LOOK IN THE MARGIN FOR Q5

Summary

1 UNDERSTANDING SENSATION 92

- **Sensation** is the process by which we detect stimuli and convert them into neural signals (**transduction**). During **coding**, the neural impulses generated by different physical stimuli travel by separate routes and arrive at different parts of the brain. In sensory reduction, we filter and analyze incoming sensations.
- In **sensory adaptation**, sensory receptors fire less frequently with repeated stimulation so that sensation decreases over time.
- **Psychophysics** measures our experience of sensory stimuli. The **absolute threshold** is the minimum stimulation necessary to consciously detect a stimulus 50% of the time. The **difference threshold**, or just noticeable difference (JND), is the smallest difference between two stimuli that is consciously detectable 50% of the time.
- Subliminal stimuli, though perceivable, have a modest effect on behavior.
- According to the **gate-control theory**, our experience of pain depends partly on whether the neural message gets past a "gatekeeper" in the spinal cord, which researchers believe is chemically controlled.

2 HOW WE SEE AND HEAR 98

- Light and sound move in waves. Light waves are a form of electromagnetic energy, and sound waves are produced when air molecules move in a particular wave pattern. Both light waves and sound waves vary in wavelength/frequency, wave height/amplitude, and wave range/complexity.
- Light enters the eye at the front of the eyeball. The cornea protects the eye and helps focus light rays. The lens further focuses light, adjusting to allow focusing on objects at different distances. At the back of the eye, incoming light waves reach the **retina**, which contains light-sensitive **rods** and **cones**. A network of neurons in the retina transmits neural information to the brain.
- The **outer ear** gathers sound waves, the **middle ear** amplifies and concentrates the sounds, and the **inner ear** changes the mechanical energy of sounds into neural impulses. The frequency and intensity of sounds determine how we distinguish among sounds of different pitches and loudness, respectively.

3 OUR OTHER IMPORTANT SENSES 104

- Smell and taste, sometimes called the chemical senses, involve chemoreceptors that are sensitive to certain chemical molecules. In **olfaction**, odor molecules stimulate receptors in the olfactory epithelium, in the nose. The resulting neural impulse travels to the olfactory bulb, where the information is processed before being sent elsewhere in the brain. Our sense of taste (**gustation**) involves five tastes: sweet, sour, salty, bitter, and umami (umami means "savory" or "delicious"). The taste buds are clustered on our tongues within the papillae.
- The body senses— the skin senses, the **vestibular sense**, and **kinesthesis**—tell the brain what it's touching or being touched by, how the body is oriented, and where and how it is moving.

4 UNDERSTANDING PERCEPTION 108

- **Perception** is the process of selecting, organizing, and interpreting incoming sensations into useful mental representations of the world. **Selective attention** allows us to filter out unimportant sensory messages. **Feature detectors** are specialized cells that respond only to certain sensory information. **Habituation** is a decrease in responsiveness due to repeated stimulation of the same stimulus.
- To be useful, sensory data must be assembled in a meaningful way. We organize sensory data in terms of form, constancy, depth, and color. Size and shape constancy are demonstrated in the Ames room. Traditionally there have been two theories of color vision: the **trichromatic theory** and the **opponent-process theory**.
- **Perceptual adaptation**, **perceptual set**, frame of reference, and **bottom-up processing** versus **top-down processing** affect our interpretation of what we sense and perceive.

applyingrealworldpsychology

Lindsey Hebberd/Corbis

We began this chapter with five intriguing Real World Psychology questions, and you were asked to revisit these questions at the end of each section. Questions like these have an important and lasting impact on all of our lives. See if you can answer these additional critical thinking questions related to real world examples.

1. The man in this photo willingly endures what would normally be excruciating pain. What information did you gain from this chapter that would help explain this man's behavior?
2. How has sensory adaptation been both advantageous and disadvantageous in your own life?
3. Why is it important to test all young children's vision and hearing capabilities?
4. If scientists could improve your sensory capabilities (for example, vision and hearing) far beyond the normal range, would you volunteer for this treatment? What might be the advantages and disadvantages?
5. Imagine yourself as a hiker who happens upon an unusual structure in the middle of the desert. How might information from this chapter help you capture this structure in a painting?

Disruptions in circadian rhythms are not just a problem for teenagers. We all are at risk of serious health issues and personal concerns, including increased risk of cancer, heart disease, autoimmune disorders, obesity, sleep disorders, and accidents, as well as decreased concentration and productivity (Dawson et al., 2011; Eckel-Mahan & Sassone-Corsi, 2013; Halvig et al., 2013; Jackson et al., 2013; Karatsoreos et al., 2011; Kyriacou & Hastings, 2010; Narasimamurthy et al., 2012; Menegaux et al., 2013; Pilcher et al., 2013; Wyse, 2012; Zhu & Zee, 2012). The most serious disruptions and ill effects tend to be with physicians, nurses, police, and others—about 20% of employees in the United States—whose occupations require rotating "shift work" schedules. Typically divided into a first shift (8 a.m. to 4 p.m), second shift (4 p.m. to midnight) and a third shift (midnight to 8 a.m.), these work shifts often change from week to week, and clearly disrupt the workers' circadian rhythms. Some research suggests that shifting from days to evenings to nights may make it easier to adjust to rotating shift schedules—probably because it's easier to go to bed later than to get up earlier. Workers' health, productivity, and safety are also believed to increase when shifts are rotated every three weeks instead of every week and napping is allowed (Asaoka et al., 2013; Landy & Conte, 2013; Roth, 2012).

Image Source/Getty Images

Coping with disrupted circadian rhythms?

Although you might assume that only babies and small children need to nap, napping is actually very common among professional athletes. This extra sleep is important because they often play their games at night and in varying time zones, which disrupts their regular night-time sleep cycle (Abrams, 2011).

psychology and you **Understanding Jet Lag** Like shift work, flying across several time zones can also cause fatigue and irritability, decreased alertness and mental agility, as well as exacerbation of psychiatric disorders (Jones & Benca, 2013; Paul et al., 2011; Sack, 2010). Jet lag tends to be worse when we fly eastward because our bodies adjust more easily to going to bed later than to going to sleep earlier than normal.

© Pierivb/iStockphoto

Sleep Deprivation

One of the biggest problems with disrupted circadian rhythms is the corresponding disruptions in the amount and quality of our sleep, which poses its own set of hazards. Sleep deprivation is clearly associated with reduced cognitive and motor performance, irritability and other mood alterations, and increased cortisol levels, which are all signs of stress (Doane et al., 2010; Gupta & Gupta, 2013; Martella et al., 2011; Orzel-Gryglewska, 2010). Sleep deprivation also leads to impairment in the immune system, which is one reason adults who get fewer than seven hours of sleep a night are three times as likely to develop a cold as those who sleep at least eight hours a night (Ackerman et al., 2012; Cohen et al., 2009). In addition, sleep-deprived adults are more likely to become obese. This may be because getting inadequate amounts of sleep interferes with the production of hormones that control appetite (Knutson, 2012).

Perhaps the most frightening danger is that lapses in attention among sleep-deprived pilots, physicians, truck drivers, and other workers cause serious accidents and cost thousands of lives each year (Chiang et al., 2012; Hallvig et al., 2013; Jackson et al., 2013; Mansukhani et al., 2012; Williamson et al., 2011). Are you wondering if you're sleep-deprived? Take the two-part test in the following *Psychology and You* to find out.

Suzanne DeChillo/The New York Times/Redux

Sleep deprivation can be fatal!

At 5:30 a.m. on March 12, 2011, a bus crashed on the outskirts of New York City, killing 15 people and injuring 14 others. In the three days prior to the crash, the bus driver had slept only during a few brief naps (McGeehan, 2012). The National Transportation Safety Board attributed the cause of this accident to driver fatigue.

TEST YOURSELF: SLEEP DEPRIVATION

psychology and you

Take the following test to determine whether you are sleep deprived.

Part 1 Set up a small mirror next to this text and trace the black star pictured here, using your nondominant hand, while watching your hand in the mirror. The task is difficult, and sleep-deprived people typically make many errors. If you are not sleep deprived, it still may be difficult to trace the star, but you'll probably do it accurately.

Part 2 Give yourself one point each time you answer yes to the following:

_____ **1.** I generally need an alarm clock or my cell phone alarm to wake up in the morning.

_____ **2.** I have a hard time getting out of bed in the morning.

_____ **3.** I try to only take late morning or early afternoon college classes because it's so hard to wake up early.

_____ **4.** People often tell me that I look tired and sleepy.

_____ **5.** I often struggle to stay awake during class, especially in warm rooms.

_____ **6.** I find it hard to concentrate and often nod off while I'm studying.

_____ **7.** I often feel sluggish and sleepy in the afternoon.

_____ **8.** I need several cups of coffee or other energy drinks to make it through the day.

_____ **9.** My friends often tell me I'm less moody and irritable when I've had enough sleep.

_____ **10.** I tend to get colds and infections, especially around final exams.

_____ **11.** When I get in bed at night, I generally fall asleep within four minutes.

_____ **12.** I try to catch up on my sleep debt by sleeping as long as possible on the weekends.

Pixtal/Age Fotostock America, Inc.

Effects of Sleep Deprivation
Insufficient sleep can seriously affect your college grades, as well as your physical health, motor skills, and overall mood.

The average student score is between 4 and 6. The higher your number, the greater your level of sleep deprivation.

Sources: Kaida et al., 2008; Mathis & Hess, 2009; National Sleep Foundation, 2012; Smith et al., 2012; Winerman, 2004.

Stages of Sleep

Having discussed our 24- to 25 hour circadian cycle, and the problems associated with its disruption, we now turn our attention to our cyclic patterns of sleep, which consist of five different stages. We begin with an exploration of how scientists study sleep. Surveys and interviews can provide general information, but for more detailed and precise data researchers in sleep laboratories use a number of sophisticated instruments **(Figure 5.2)**.

Imagine that you are a participant in a sleep experiment. When you arrive at the sleep lab, you are assigned one of several bedrooms. The researcher hooks you up to various physiological recording devices **(Figure 5.2a)**. You will probably need a night or two to adapt to the equipment before the researchers can begin to monitor your typical night's sleep. At first, you enter a relaxed, *presleep* state. As you continue relaxing, your brain's electrical activity slows even further. In the course of about an hour, you progress through several distinct stages of sleep, each progressively deeper **(Figure 5.2b)**. Then the sequence begins to reverse. Note that we don't necessarily go through all sleep stages in this exact sequence. But during the course of a night, people usually complete four to five cycles of light to deep sleep and back, each lasting about 90 minutes **(Figure 5.2c)**.

Figure 5.2b also shows an interesting phenomenon that occurs at the end of the first sleep cycle (and subsequent cycles). You reverse back through Stages 3, 2, and 1. At the end of Stage 1, you enter a very different phase noted by the characteristic rapid eye movements occurring under your closed eyelids. Researchers call this stage **rapid-eye-movement (REM) sleep**. During REM sleep, your scalp recordings display a pattern of small-amplitude, fast-wave activity, similar to an awake, vigilant person's brain waves. Your breathing and pulse rates become fast and irregular, and your genitals likely show signs of arousal. Yet your musculature is deeply relaxed and unresponsive. Because of these contradictory qualities, this REM stage is also sometimes referred to as *paradoxical sleep*.

Rapid-eye-movement (REM) sleep The fifth stage of sleep marked by rapid eye movements, high-frequency brain waves, paralysis of large muscles, and often dreaming.

FIGURE 5.2 SCIENTIFIC STUDY OF SLEEP AND DREAMING

Data collected in sleep labs has helped scientists understand the stages of sleep.

Ⓐ Participants in sleep research labs wear electrodes on their heads and bodies to measure brain and bodily responses during the sleep cycle. An electroencephalogram (EEG) detects and records brain-wave changes by means of small electrodes on the scalp. Other electrodes measure muscle activity and eye movements.

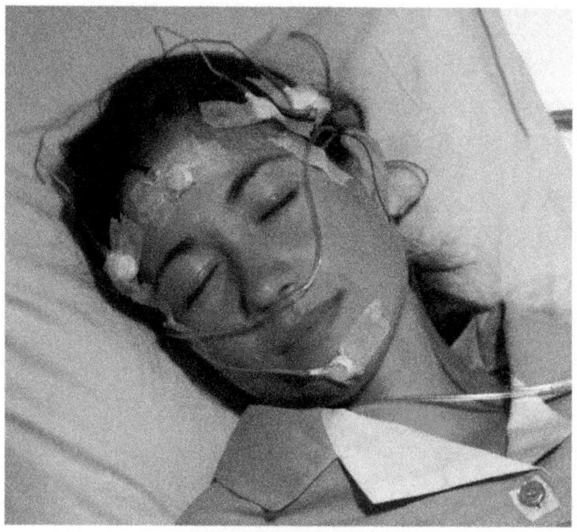

Philippe Garo/Photo Researchers

Ⓑ The stages of sleep, defined by telltale changes in brain waves, are indicated by the jagged lines. The compact brain waves of alertness gradually lengthen as we drift into Stages 1–4. Then we enter a fifth stage, called REM sleep, which has a different set of compact, faster brain waves.

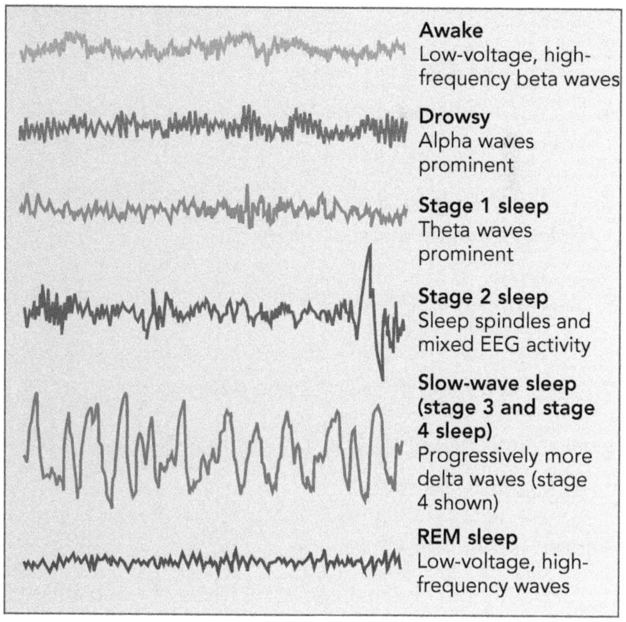

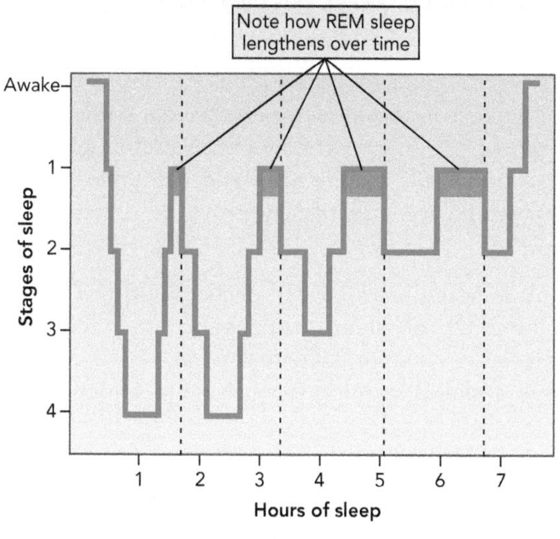

Ⓒ Your first sleep cycle generally lasts about 90 minutes from awake and alert, downward through Stages 1–4, and then back up through Stages 3, 2, and REM. If you sleep 8 hours, you'll typically go through approximately four or five sleep cycles (as shown by the vertical dotted lines). Note how the overall amount of REM sleep increases as the night progresses, while the amount of deep sleep (Stages 3 and 4) decreases.

Non-rapid-eye-movement (NREM) sleep Stages 1 through 4 of sleep during which a sleeper does not show rapid eye movements.

When awakened from REM sleep, people almost always report dreaming. Because REM sleep is so different from the other periods of sleep, Stages 1 through 4 are often collectively referred to as **non-rapid-eye-movement (NREM) sleep**. Dreams very similar to those from REM sleep also occur during NREM sleep, but less frequently (Chellappa et al., 2011; Wamsley et al., 2007).

Why Do We Sleep and Dream?

There are many myths and misconceptions about why we sleep and dream (see *Psychology and You*). Fortunately, scientists have carefully studied what sleep and dreaming do for us and why we spend approximately 25 years of our life in these alternate states of consciousness (ASCs).

TEST YOURSELF: HAVE YOU HEARD THESE COMMON MYTHS?

psychology and you

Before reading the facts about each myth, place a check by any statement that you currently believe to be true.

1. _____ *Everyone needs 8 hours of sleep a night to maintain sound mental and physical health.*
2. _____ *Dreams have special or symbolic meaning.*
3. _____ *Some people never dream.*
4. _____ *Dreams last only a few seconds and occur only in REM sleep.*
5. _____ *When genital arousal occurs during sleep, it means the sleeper is having a sexual dream.*
6. _____ *Most people dream only in black and white, and blind people don't dream.*
7. _____ *Dreaming of dying can be fatal.*
8. _____ *It's easy to learn new, complicated things, like a foreign language, while asleep.*

Facts:

1. *Fact:* Although the average is 7.6 hours of sleep a night, some people get by on an incredible 15 to 30 minutes. Others may need as much as 11 hours (Colrain, 2011; Daan, 2011; Doghramji, 2000; Maas et al., 1999).
2. *Fact:* Many people mistakenly believe that dreams can foretell the future, reflect unconscious desires, have secret meaning, reveal the truth, or contain special messages, but scientific research finds little or no support for these beliefs (Blum, 2011; Domhoff, 2010; Hobson et al., 2011; Lilienfeld et al., 2010; Montangero, 2012).
3. *Fact:* In rare cases, adults with certain brain injuries or disorders do not dream (Solms, 1997). But otherwise, virtually all adults regularly dream, but many don't remember doing so. Even people who firmly believe they never dream report dreams if they are repeatedly awakened during an overnight study in a sleep laboratory. Children also dream regularly. For example, between ages 3 and 8, they dream during approximately 25% of their sleep time (Foulkes, 1993, 1999).
4. *Fact:* Research shows that most dreams occur in real time. For example, a dream that seemed to last 20 minutes probably did last approximately 20 minutes (Dement & Wolpert, 1958). Dreams also occur in NREM sleep (Jones & Benca, 2013; Oudiette et al., 2012).
5. *Fact:* When sleepers are awakened during this time, they are no more likely to report sexual dreams than at other times.
6. *Fact:* People frequently report seeing color in their dreams. Those who are blind do dream, but they report visual images only if they lost their sight after approximately age 7 (Lilienfeld et al., 2010).
7. *Fact:* This is a good opportunity to exercise your critical thinking skills. Where did this myth come from? Although many people have personally experienced and recounted a fatal dream, how would we scientifically prove or disprove this belief?
8. *Fact:* Although some learning can occur doing the lighter stages (1 and 2) of sleep, processing and retention of this material is minimal (Lilienfeld et al., 2010; Ogilvie et al., 1989). Wakeful learning is much more effective and efficient.

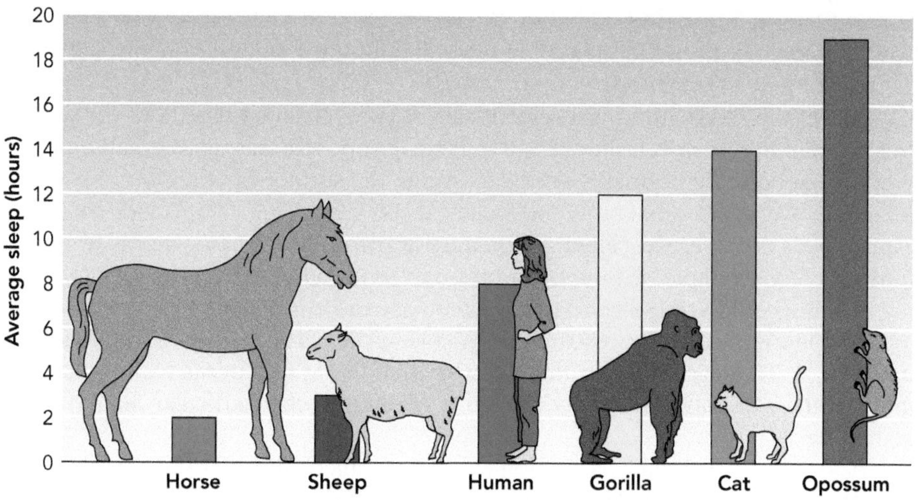

FIGURE 5.3 **AVERAGE DAILY HOURS OF SLEEP FOR DIFFERENT MAMMALS**

According to the adaptation/protection theory, differences in diet and number of predators affect different species' sleep habits. For example, opossums sleep many hours each day because they are relatively safe in their environment and are able to easily find food and shelter. In comparison, sheep and horses sleep very little because their diets require almost constant foraging for food in more dangerous open grasslands.

Four Sleep Theories

How do scientists explain our shared need for sleep? There are four key theories:

1. **Adaptation/protection theory** Sleep evolved because animals need to conserve energy and protect themselves from predators that are more active at night (Acerbi & Nunn, 2011; Drew, 2013; Siegel, 2008; Tsoukalas, 2012). As you can see in **Figure 5.3**, animals with the highest need to feed themselves and the lowest ability to hide tend to sleep the least.
2. **Repair/restoration theory** Sleep helps us recuperate from the depleting effects of daily waking activities. Essential chemicals and bodily tissues are repaired or replenished while we sleep. We recover not only from physical fatigue but also from emotional and intellectual demands (Colrain, 2011). When deprived of REM sleep, most people "catch up" later by spending more time than usual in this state (the so-called REM rebound), which further supports this theory.
3. **Growth/development theory** The percentage of deepest sleep (Stage 4) changes over the life span and coincides with changes in the structure and organization of the brain, as well as the release of growth hormones from the pituitary gland—particularly in children. As we age, our brains change less, and we release fewer of these hormones, grow less, and sleep less.
4. **Learning/memory theory** Sleep is important for learning and the consolidation, storage, and maintenance of memories (Fenn & Hambrick, 2012; Inostroza et al., 2013; Payne et al., 2012; Sara, 2010). This is particularly true for REM sleep, which increases after periods of stress or intense learning. For example, fetuses, infants, and young children, who generally are learning more than adults, spend far more of their sleep time in REM sleep **(Figure 5.4)**.

Adaptation/protection theory of sleep The theory that sleep evolved to conserve energy and provide protection from predators.

Repair/restoration theory of sleep The theory that sleep allows organisms to repair or recuperate from depleting daily waking activities.

Growth/development theory of sleep The theory that deep sleep (Stage 4) is correlated with physical development, including changes in the structure and organization of the brain; infants spend far more time in Stage 4 sleep than adults.

Learning/memory theory of sleep The theory that sleep is important for learning and for the consolidation, storage, and maintenance of memories.

FIGURE 5.4 **AGING AND THE SLEEP CYCLE**

Our biological need for sleep changes throughout our life span. The pie charts in this figure show the relative amounts of REM sleep, NREM sleep, and awake time the average person experiences as an infant, an adult, and an elderly person.

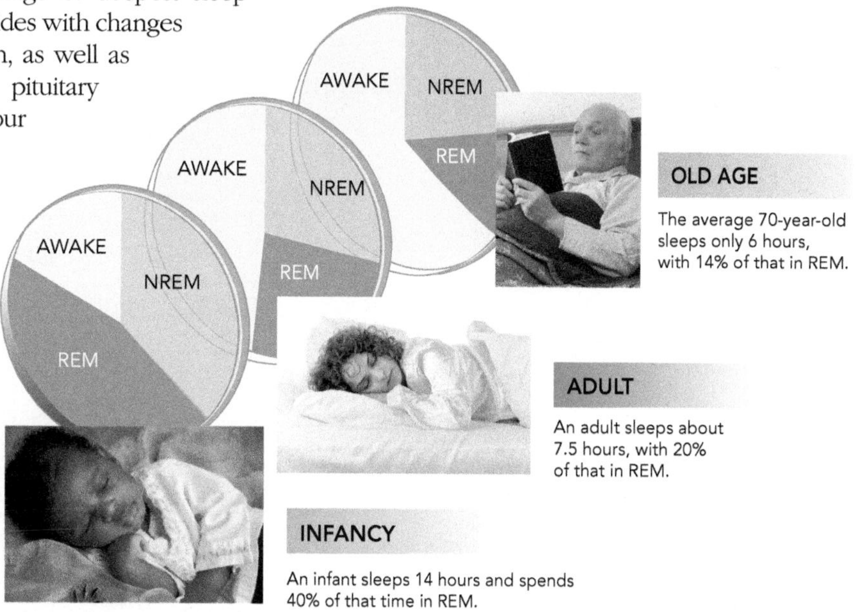

Wish-fulfillment view of dreams The Freudian belief that dreams provide an outlet for unacceptable desires.

Latent content of dreams According to Freud, a dream's unconscious, hidden meaning transformed into symbols within the dream's manifest content (story line).

Manifest content of dreams In Freudian dream analysis, the "surface," or remembered, story line, which contains symbols that mask the dream's latent content (the true meaning).

Activation–synthesis hypothesis of dreams The perspective that dreams are by-products of random stimulation of brain cells, which the brain attempts to combine (or synthesize) into coherent patterns, known as dreams.

Cognitive view of dreams The perspective that dreams are a type of information processing that help interpret daily experiences and organize them into memories.

Three Dream Theories

Now let's look at three theories of why we dream—and whether dreams carry special meaning or information.

One of the oldest and most scientifically controversial explanations for why we dream is Freud's **wish-fulfillment view**. Freud proposed that unacceptable desires, which are reportedly normally repressed, rise to the surface of consciousness during dreaming. We avoid anxiety, Freud believed, by disguising our forbidden unconscious needs (what Freud called the dream's **latent content**) as symbols (**manifest content**). For example, a journey supposedly symbolizes death; horseback riding and dancing could symbolize sexual intercourse; and a gun might represent a penis.

Most modern scientific research does not support Freud's view (Domhoff, 2004; Dufresne, 2007; Siegel, 2010). Critics also say that Freud's theory is highly subjective and that the symbols can be interpreted according to the particular analyst's view or training.

In contrast to Freud, a biological view called the **activation–synthesis hypothesis** suggests that dreams are a by-product of random stimulation of brain cells during REM sleep (Hobson, 1999, 2005; Wamsley & Stickgold, 2010). Alan Hobson and Robert McCarley (1977) proposed that specific neurons in the brain stem fire spontaneously during REM sleep and that the cortex struggles to "synthesize," or make sense of, this random stimulation by manufacturing dreams. This is *not* to say that dreams are totally meaningless. Hobson (1999, 2005) suggests that even if our dreams begin with essentially random brain activity, our individual personalities, motivations, memories, and life experiences guide how our brains construct the dream.

Finally, some researchers support the **cognitive view of dreams**, which suggests that dreams are simply another type of information processing. That is, our dreams help us organize and interpret our everyday, waking experiences and thoughts into memories. For example, some research reports strong similarities between dream content and waking thoughts, fears, and concerns (Domhoff, 2005, 2007, 2010; Erlacher & Schredl, 2004).

Gender Differences and Similarities

Men and women tend to share many of the common dream themes shown in **Table 5.1.** But women are more likely to report dreams of children, family members and other familiar people, household objects, and indoor events. In contrast, men tend to report dreams about strangers, violence, weapons, sexual activity, achievement, and outdoor events (Blume-Marcovici, 2010; Domhoff, 2003, 2007, 2010; Schredl, 2012). (As a critical thinker, can you see how attitudes toward "proper" male and female gender roles, like caring for children, sex, weapons, and violence, might have affected what the participants were willing to report?)

TABLE 5.1 TOP TEN COMMON DREAM THEMES

1. Being attacked or pursued
2. Falling
3. Sexual experiences
4. Being lost
5. Being paralyzed
6. Flying
7. Being naked in public
8. School, teachers, studying
9. Arriving too late
10. Death of close people or dead people as alive

Best View Stock /Getty Images, Inc.

Sources: Griffith, Miyagi, & Tago, 1958/2009; Nielsen et al., 2003; Schredl, 2010; Yu, 2012.

Culture and Dreams

Dreams about basic human needs and fears (like sex, aggression, and death) seem to be found in all cultures. Children around the world often dream about large, threatening monsters or wild animals. In addition, dreams around the world typically include more misfortune than good fortune, and the dreamer is more often the victim of aggression than the cause of it (Chang, 2012; Domhoff, 2003, 2007, 2010; Honig & Nealis, 2012; Yu, 2012).

Sleep–Wake Disorders

In any given year, an estimated 40 million Americans suffer from chronic sleep disorders, and another 30 million experience occasional sleep disorders serious enough to disrupt their daily activity (Purves & Piatt, 2012).

Judging by these statistics, and your own experiences, it's not surprising to learn that almost everyone has difficulty sleeping at some point in his or her lifetime. The most common or serious of these disorders are summarized in **Table 5.2**.

Although it's normal to have trouble sleeping before an exciting event, as many as 1 person in 10 may suffer from **insomnia**, and they experience persistent difficulty falling asleep or staying asleep or wakes up too early. Nearly everybody has insomnia at some time (Bastien, 2011; Colrain, 2011; Morin et al., 2013); a telltale sign is feeling poorly rested the next day. Most people with serious insomnia have other medical or psychological disorders as well (American Psychiatric Association, 2013; Boland & Alloy, 2013; Van Der Kloet, 2013).

Insomnia A sleep disorder characterized by persistent problems falling asleep, staying asleep, or awakening too early.

TABLE 5.2 SLEEP-WAKE DISORDERS

Label	Characteristics
Insomnia	Persistent difficulty falling asleep, maintaining sleep, or waking up too early
Narcolepsy	Sudden, irresistible onset of sleep during waking hours, characterized by sudden sleep attacks while standing, talking, or even driving
Breathing-Related Sleep Disorder (Sleep apnea)	Repeated interruption of breathing during sleep, causing loud snoring or poor-quality sleep and excessive daytime sleepiness
Nightmare	Bad dream that significantly disrupts REM sleep
NREM Sleep Arousal Disorder (Sleep terror)	Abrupt awakening with feelings of panic that significantly disrupts NREM sleep

realworldpsychology **The Hazards of Sleep Medication** To cope with insomnia, many people turn to nonprescription, over-the-counter sleeping pills, which generally don't work. In contrast, prescription tranquilizers and barbiturates do help people sleep, but they decrease Stage 4 and REM sleep, seriously affecting sleep quality. In the short term, limited use of drugs such as Ambien, Dalmane, Xanax, Halcion, and Lunesta may be helpful in treating sleep problems related to anxiety and acute, stressful situations. However, chronic users run the risk of psychological and physical drug dependence (Abadinsky, 2014; Farber & Banks, 2013). The hormone *melatonin* may provide a safer alternative. Some research suggests that taking even a relatively small dose (just .3 to .4 milligrams) can help people fall asleep and stay asleep (Brzezinski et al., 2005; Gooneratne et al., 2012).

Africa Studio/Shutterstock

Fortunately, there are many effective strategies for alleviating sleep problems without medication. For example, did you know that using a computer right before you try to fall asleep can make it harder to sleep (Wood et al., 2012)? Exposure to light from the electronic screens of a computer or an iPad reduces the level of melatonin in the body by about 22%, which makes it more difficult to fall asleep (especially for teenagers). See the following *Psychology and You* section for other recommendations about getting and staying asleep. Q2

NATURAL SLEEP AIDS

psychology and you

Are you wondering what research recommends for sleep problems? Behavior therapy offers consistent benefits that you can apply in your own life (Constantino et al., 2007; Smith et al., 2005). For example, when you're having a hard time going to sleep, don't keep checking the clock and worrying about your loss of sleep. Instead, remove all TVs, stereos, and books and limit the use of your bedroom to sleep rather than to reading, watching movies, checking e-mail, and the like. If you need additional help, try some of the following suggestions.

During the Day

Exercise. Daily physical activity works away tension. But don't exercise vigorously late in the day, or you'll get fired up instead.

Keep regular hours. An erratic schedule can disrupt biological rhythms. Get up at the same time each day.

Avoid stimulants. Coffee, tea, soft drinks, chocolate, and some medications contain caffeine. Nicotine may be an even more potent sleep disrupter.

Avoid late meals and heavy drinking. Overindulgence can interfere with your normal sleep pattern.

Stop worrying. Focus on your problems at a set time earlier in the day.

Use presleep rituals. Follow the same routine every evening: listen to music, write in a diary, meditate.

Practice yoga. These gentle exercises help you relax.

In Bed

Use progressive muscle relaxation. Alternately tense and relax various muscle groups.

Use fantasies. Imagine yourself in a tranquil setting. Feel yourself relax.

Use deep breathing. Take deep breaths, telling yourself you're falling asleep.

Try a warm bath. This can induce drowsiness because it sends blood away from the brain to the skin surface.

Narcolepsy The sudden and irresistible compulsion to sleep during the daytime. (*Narco* means "numbness," and *lepsy* means "seizure.")

Narcolepsy, a sleep disorder characterized by sudden and irresistible onsets of sleep during normal waking hours, afflicts about 1 person in 2,000 and generally runs in families (Kotagal & Kumar, 2013; Pedrazzoli et al., 2007; Raggi et al., 2011). During an attack, REM-like sleep suddenly intrudes into the waking state of consciousness. Victims may experience sudden, incapacitating attacks of muscle weakness or paralysis (known as cataplexy). They may even fall asleep while walking, talking, or driving a car. Although long naps each day and stimulant or antidepressant drugs can help reduce the frequency of attacks, both the causes and cure of narcolepsy are still unknown **(Figure 5.5)**.

Sleep apnea A sleep disorder of the upper respiratory system that causes a repeated interruption of breathing during sleep; it also leads to loud snoring or poor-quality sleep and excessive daytime sleepiness.

Perhaps the most serious sleep disorder is **sleep apnea**. People with sleep apnea may fail to breathe for a minute or longer and then wake up gasping for breath. When they do breathe during their sleep, they often snore. Sleep apnea seems to result from blocked upper airway passages or from the brain's ceasing to send signals to the diaphragm, thus causing breathing to stop.

Unfortunately, people with sleep apnea are often unaware they have this disorder, and fail to understand how their repeated awakenings during the night leave them feeling tired and sleepy during the day. More importantly, they should know that sleep apnea can lead to high blood pressure, stroke, cancer, depression, and heart attack

© Juniors/SuperStock

FIGURE 5.5 **NARCOLEPSY**

Research on specially bred narcoleptic dogs has found degenerated neurons in certain areas of the brain (Siegel, 2000). Whether human narcolepsy results from similar degeneration is a question for future research. Note how this hungry puppy has lapsed suddenly from alert wakefulness to deep sleep even when offered his preferred food.

(Culebras, 2012; Emdin et al., 2013; Furukawa et al., 2010; Nieto et al., 2012; Nikolaou et al., 2011; Vitulano et al., 2013; Wheaton et al., 2012).

Treatment for sleep apnea depends partly on its severity. If the problem occurs only when you're sleeping on your back, sewing tennis balls to the back of your pajama top may help remind you to sleep on your side. Because obstruction of the breathing passages is related to obesity and heavy alcohol use (Roehrs & Roth, 2012; Sarkhosh et al., 2013), dieting and alcohol restriction are often recommended. For other sleepers, surgery, dental appliances that reposition the tongue, or machines that provide a stream of air to keep the airway open may provide help.

Recent findings suggest that even "simple" snoring (without the breathing stoppage characteristic of sleep apnea) can lead to heart disease and possible death (Jones & Benca, 2013; Li et al., 2012). Although occasional mild snoring is fairly normal, chronic snoring is a possible warning sign that should prompt people to seek help.

Two additional abnormal sleep disturbances are **nightmares** and **sleep terrors** **(Figure 5.6)**. *Sleepwalking*, which sometimes accompanies sleep terrors, usually occurs during NREM sleep. (Recall that large muscles are paralyzed during REM sleep, which explains why sleepwalking normally occurs during NREM sleep.) An estimated 4% of U.S. adults—meaning over 8 million people—have at least one episode of sleepwalking each year (Ohayon et al., 2012). *Sleeptalking* can occur during any stage of sleep, but it appears to arise most commonly during NREM sleep. It can consist of single indistinct words or long, articulate sentences. It is even possible to engage some sleep talkers in a limited conversation.

Nightmares Anxiety-arousing dreams that generally occur near the end of the sleep cycle, during REM sleep.

Sleep terrors Abrupt awakenings from NREM (non-rapid-eye-movement) sleep accompanied by intense physiological arousal and feelings of panic.

Nightmares, sleep terrors, sleepwalking, and sleeptalking are all more common among young children, but they can also occur in adults, usually during times of stress or major life events (Hiscock & Darvey, 2013; Hobson & Silvestri, 1999). Patience and soothing reassurance at the time of the sleep disruption are usually the only treatment recommended for both children and adults.

Zigy Kaluzny/Getty Images, Inc.

FIGURE 5.6 **NIGHTMARE OR SLEEP TERROR?**

Nightmares, or bad dreams, occur toward the end of the sleep cycle, during REM sleep. Less common but more frightening are sleep terrors, which occur early in the cycle, during Stage 3 or Stage 4 of NREM sleep. Like the child in this photo, the sleeper may sit bolt upright, screaming and sweating, walk around, and talk incoherently and may be almost impossible to awaken.

RETRIEVAL PRACTICE: CONSCIOUSNESS, SLEEP, AND DREAMING

Self-Test

Completing this self-test and comparing your answers with those in Appendix B provides immediate feedback and helpful practice for exams. Additional interactive, self-tests are available at www.wiley.com/college/huffman.

1. *Consciousness* is defined as _____.

a. ordinary and extraordinary wakefulness
b. an organism's awareness of internal events and of the external environment
c. mental representations of the world in the here and now
d. any mental state that requires thinking and processing of sensory stimuli

2. *Circadian rhythms* are _____.

a. patterns that repeat themselves on a twice-daily schedule
b. physical and mental changes associated with the cycle of the moon
c. rhythmical processes in your brain
d. biological changes that occur on a 24- to 25-hour cycle

3. The sleep stage marked by irregular breathing, eye movements, high-frequency brain waves, and dreaming is called _____ sleep.

a. beta
b. hypnologic
c. REM
d. transitional

4. The _____ theory says that sleep allows us to replenish what was depleted during daytime activities.

a. repair/restoration
b. evolutionary/circadian
c. supply-demand
d. conservation of energy

Think Critically

1. How are you affected by sleep deprivation and disruption of your circadian rhythms?
2. Which of the major theories of dreaming best explains your own dreams?

realworldpsychology

Can getting too little sleep increase your risk of getting a cold?

Can using a computer or an iPad late at night make it harder to fall asleep?

HINT: LOOK IN THE MARGIN FOR Q1 AND Q2

PSYCHOACTIVE DRUGS

LEARNING OBJECTIVES

RETRIEVAL PRACTICE While reading the upcoming sections, respond to each Learning Objective in your own words. Then compare your responses with those found at www.wiley.com/college/huffman.

1. **EXPLAIN** how psychoactive drugs affect nervous system functioning.
2. **COMPARE** the four major categories of psychoactive drugs.
3. **DESCRIBE** the effects of club drugs on the nervous system.

Psychoactive drug A chemical that changes mental processes and conscious awareness, mood, and/or perception.

Agonist drug A drug that binds to a receptor and triggers a response in the cell, which mimics or enhances a neurotransmitter's effect.

Antagonist drug A drug that binds to a receptor and triggers a response in the cell, which blocks a neurotransmitter's effect.

Have you noticed how difficult it is to have a logical, nonemotional discussion about drugs? In our society, where the most popular **psychoactive drugs** are caffeine, tobacco, and ethyl alcohol, people often become defensive when these drugs are grouped with illicit drugs such as marijuana and cocaine. Similarly, marijuana users are disturbed that their drug of choice is grouped with "hard" drugs like heroin. Most scientists believe that there are good and bad uses of all drugs. The way drug use differs from drug abuse and how chemical alterations in consciousness affect a person, psychologically and physically, are important topics in psychology.

Alcohol, for example, has a diffuse effect on neural membranes throughout the nervous system. Most psychoactive drugs, however, act in a more specific way: by either enhancing a particular neurotransmitter's effect, as does an **agonist drug**, or inhibiting it, as does an **antagonist drug** **(Figure 5.7)**.

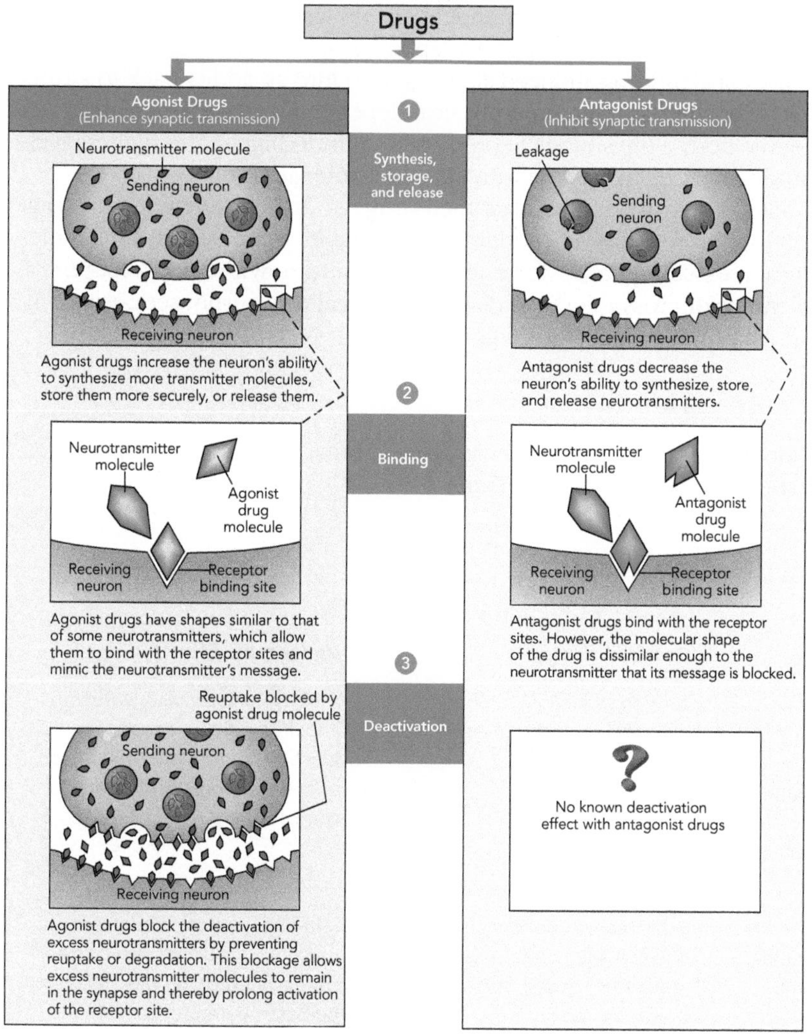

Drugs
Agonist Drugs (Enhance synaptic transmission)
Antagonist Drugs (Inhibit synaptic transmission)
1
Synthesis, storage, and release
Neurotransmitter molecule
Sending neuron
Receiving neuron
Agonist drugs increase the neuron's ability to synthesize more transmitter molecules, store them more securely, or release them.
Leakage
Sending neuron
Receiving neuron
Antagonist drugs decrease the neuron's ability to synthesize, store, and release neurotransmitters.
2
Binding
Neurotransmitter molecule
Agonist drug molecule
Receiving neuron
Receptor binding site
Agonist drugs have shapes similar to that of some neurotransmitters, which allow them to bind with the receptor sites and mimic the neurotransmitter's message.
Neurotransmitter molecule
Antagonist drug molecule
Receiving neuron
Receptor binding site
Antagonist drugs bind with the receptor sites. However, the molecular shape of the drug is dissimilar enough to the neurotransmitter that its message is blocked.
3
Deactivation
Reuptake blocked by agonist drug molecule
Sending neuron
Receiving neuron
Agonist drugs block the deactivation of excess neurotransmitters by preventing reuptake or degradation. This blockage allows excess neurotransmitter molecules to remain in the synapse and thereby prolong activation of the receptor site.
?
No known deactivation effect with antagonist drugs

FIGURE 5.7 HOW DO AGONIST AND ANTAGONIST DRUGS PRODUCE THEIR PSYCHOACTIVE EFFECTS?

Most psychoactive drugs produce their mood, energy, and perception-altering effects by changing the body's supply of neurotransmitters. Note how they can alter the synthesis, storage, or release of neurotransmitters ❶. They also can change the neurotransmitters' effects on the receiving site of the receptor neuron ❷. After neurotransmitters carry their messages across the synapse, the sending neuron normally deactivates the excess, or leftover, neurotransmitter ❸. However, when agonist drugs block this process, excess neurotransmitters remain in the synapse, which prolongs the effect of the psychoactive drug.

Is drug abuse the same as drug addiction? The term **drug abuse** generally refers to drug taking that causes emotional or physical harm to oneself or others. Drug consumption among abusers is also typically compulsive, frequent, and intense. **Addiction** is a broad term that refers to a condition in which a person feels compelled to use a specific drug or almost any type of compulsive activity, from working to surfing the Internet (Potenza, 2013; Ross et al., 2010). In fact, the latest version of the *Diagnostic and Statistical Manual (DSM-5)*, which officially classifies mental disorders, now includes *gambling disorders* as part of their substance-related and addictive disorders category. But other disorders, like "sex addiction" or "exercise addiction" were not included due to insufficient evidence at this time (American Psychiatric Association, 2013).

Interestingly, some evidence shows that we can become addicted to Facebook and that risky trading in financial markets can create a high indistinguishable from that experienced in drug addiction (Andreassen et al., 2012; Zweig, 2007). Researchers in one study prompted people with a series of statements, such as "You feel an urge to use Facebook more and more," and "You become restless or troubled if you are prohibited from using Facebook" (Andreassen et al., 2012). The degree to which you agree with items like these may indicate that you are addicted, meaning that you feel unreasonably compelled to check and use Facebook throughout the day.

Q3

In addition to distinguishing between drug abuse and addiction, many researchers use the term **psychological dependence** to refer to the mental desire or craving to achieve a drug's effects, whereas **physical dependence** describes changes in bodily processes that make a drug necessary for minimum daily functioning. Physical dependence appears most clearly when the drug is withheld and the user undergoes **withdrawal** reactions, including physical pain and intense cravings.

Drug abuse Drug taking that causes emotional or physical harm to the drug user or others.

Addiction A broad term that describes a condition in which the body requires a drug (or specific activity) in order to function without physical and psychological reactions to its absence; it is often the outcome of tolerance and dependence.

Psychological dependence The psychological desire or craving to achieve a drug's effect.

Physical dependence The changes in bodily processes that make a drug necessary for minimal functioning.

Withdrawal The discomfort and distress, including physical pain and intense cravings, experienced after stopping the use of an addictive drug.

Tolerance The bodily adjustment to continued use of a drug in which the drug user requires greater dosages to achieve the same effect.

Keep in mind that psychological dependence is no less damaging than physical dependence. The craving in psychological dependence can be strong enough to keep the user in a constant drug-induced state—and to lure an addict back to a drug habit long after he or she has overcome physical dependence. After repeated use of a drug, many of the body's physiological processes adjust to higher and higher levels of the drug, producing a decreased sensitivity called **tolerance**.

Tolerance leads many users to escalate their drug use and experiment with other drugs in an attempt to re-create the original pleasurable altered state. Sometimes using one drug increases tolerance for another, a result known as *cross-tolerance*. Developing tolerance or cross-tolerance does not prevent drugs from seriously damaging the brain, heart, liver, and other organs.

Four Drug Categories

Psychologists divide psychoactive drugs into four broad categories: depressants, stimulants, opiates, and hallucinogens **(Table 5.3)**.

TABLE 5.3 **EFFECTS OF THE MAJOR PSYCHOACTIVE DRUGS**

	Category	Desired Effects	Undesirable Effects
 RICHARD NOWITZ/NG Image Collection	**Depressants (sedatives)** Alcohol, barbiturates, anxiolytics, also known as anti-anxiety drugs or tranquilizers (Xanax), Rohypnol (roofies), Ketamine (Special K), Gamma-hydroxybutyrate (GHB)	Tension reduction, euphoria, disinhibition, drowsiness, muscle relaxation	Anxiety, nausea, disorientation, impaired reflexes and motor functioning, amnesia, loss of consciousness, shallow respiration, convulsions, coma, death
 TAYLOR S. KENNEDY/NG Image Collection	**Stimulants** Cocaine, amphetamine, methamphetamine (crystal meth), MDMA (Ecstasy)	Exhilaration, euphoria, high physical and mental energy, reduced appetite, perceptions of power, sociability	Irritability, anxiety, sleeplessness, paranoia, hallucinations, psychosis, elevated blood pressure and body temperature, convulsions, death
	Caffeine	Increased alertness	Insomnia, restlessness, increased pulse rate, mild delirium, ringing in the ears, rapid heartbeat
 SAM ABELL/NG Image Collection	Nicotine	Relaxation, increased alertness, sociability	Irritability, increased blood pressure, stomach pains, vomiting, dizziness, cancer, heart disease, emphysema
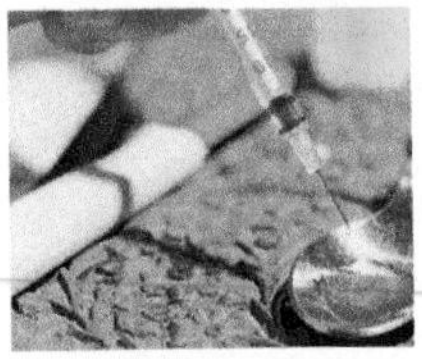 Uwe Schmid/OKAPIA/ Photo Researchers	**Opiates (Narcotics)** Morphine, heroin, codeine, oxycodone	Euphoria, "rush" of pleasure, pain relief, prevention of withdrawal discomfort, sleep	Nausea, vomiting, constipation, painful withdrawal, shallow respiration, convulsions, coma, death
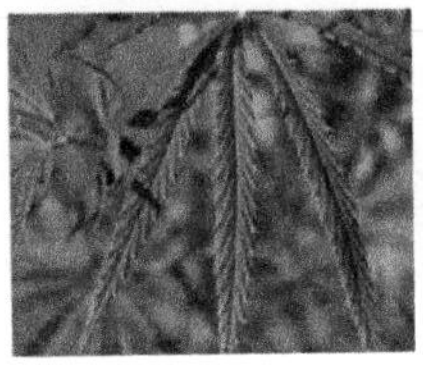 JOEL SARTORE/NG Image Collection	**Hallucinogens (Psychedelics)** Lysergic acid diethylamide (LSD), mescaline (extract from the peyote cactus), psilocybin (extract from mushrooms)	Heightened aesthetic responses, euphoria, mild delusions, hallucinations, distorted perceptions and sensation	Panic, nausea, longer and more extreme delusions, hallucinations, perceptual distortions ("bad trips"), psychosis
	Marijuana	Relaxation, mild euphoria, nausea relief	Perceptual and sensory distortions, hallucinations, fatigue, increased appetite, lack of motivation, paranoia, possible psychosis

TABLE 5.4 ALCOHOL'S EFFECT ON THE BODY AND BEHAVIOR

Number of drinks[a] in two hours	Blood alcohol (content (%)[b]	Effect
(2)	0.05	Relaxed state; increased sociability
(3)	0.08	Everyday stress lessened
(4)	0.10	Movements and speech become clumsy
(7)	0.20	Very drunk; loud and difficult to understand; emotions unstable
(12)	0.40	Difficult to wake up; incapable of voluntary action
(15)	0.50	Coma and/or death

[a]A drink refers to one 12-ounce beer, a 4-ounce glass of wine, or a 1.25-ounce shot of hard liquor.

[b]In America, the legal blood alcohol level for "drunk driving" varies from 0.05 to 0.12.

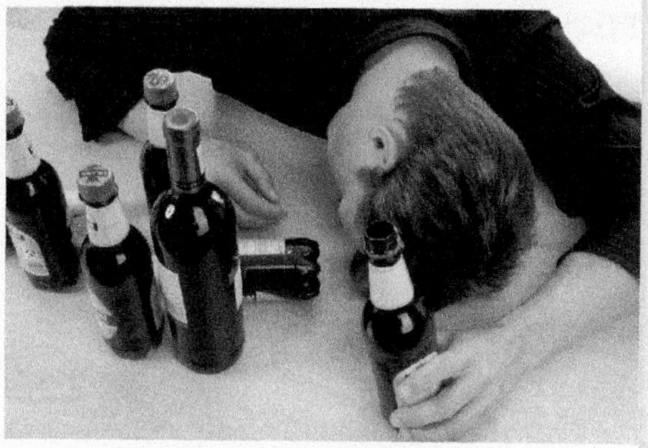

McPHOTO/Blickwinkel/Age Fotostock America, Inc.

Depressant A drug that decreases bodily processes and overall responsiveness.

Depressants, sometimes called "downers," act on the central nervous system to suppress or slow bodily processes and to reduce overall responsiveness. Because tolerance and both physical and psychological dependence are rapidly acquired with these drugs, there is strong potential for abuse.

Although alcohol is primarily a depressant, at low doses it has stimulating effects, thus explaining its reputation as a "party drug." As consumption increases, symptoms of drunkenness appear. Alcohol's effects are determined primarily by the amount that reaches the brain **(Table 5.4)**. Because the liver breaks down alcohol at the rate of about 1 ounce per hour, the number of drinks and the speed of consumption are both very important. People can die after drinking large amounts of alcohol in a short period of time **(Figure 5.8)**. In addition, men's bodies are more efficient than women's at breaking down alcohol. Even after accounting for differences in size and muscle-to-fat ratio, women have a higher blood-alcohol level than men following equal doses of alcohol.

Alcohol should not be combined with any other drug; combining alcohol and barbiturates—both depressants—is particularly dangerous. Together, they can relax the diaphragm muscles to such a degree that the person suffocates.

Does this information surprise you? Take the quiz in *Psychology and You* to discover if some of your other ideas about alcohol are really misconceptions.

Kyle Bursaw/Daily Chronicle/AP

FIGURE 5.8 ALCOHOL IS FAR TOO OFTEN FATAL

On November 2, 2012, 19-year-old David Bogenberger, a finance major at Northern Illinois University, died of alcohol poisoning following hazing activities at his fraternity, Pi Kappa Alpha. His blood alcohol concentration was .35, which is five times the legal limit for driving in Illinois. Twenty-two members of his fraternity have been charged in his death.

TEST YOURSELF: WHAT'S YOUR ALCOHOL IQ?

psychology and you

TRUE OR FALSE?

___ **1.** Alcohol increases sexual desire.

___ **2.** Alcohol helps you sleep.

___ **3.** Alcohol kills brain cells.

___ **4.** It's easier to get drunk at high altitudes.

___ **5.** Switching among different types of alcohol is more likely to lead to drunkenness.

___ **6.** Drinking coffee and taking a cold shower are great ways to sober up after heavy drinking.

___ **7.** Alcohol warms the body.

___ **8.** You can't become an alcoholic if you drink only beer.

___ **9.** Alcohol's primary effect is as a stimulant.

___ **10.** People experience impaired judgment after drinking only if they show obvious signs of intoxication.

Answers: All these statements are false. Detailed answers are provided in this chapter and in Lilienfeld et al., 2010.

Stimulant A drug that increases overall activity and general responsiveness.

Depressants suppress central nervous system activity, whereas **stimulants**, or "uppers," increase the overall activity and responsiveness of the central nervous system.

Cocaine is a powerful central nervous system stimulant extracted from the leaves of the coca plant. It produces feelings of alertness, euphoria, well-being, power, energy, and pleasure. But it also acts as an *agonist drug* to block the reuptake of our body's natural neurotransmitters that produce these same effects **(Figure 5.9)**.

Although cocaine was once considered a relatively harmless "recreational drug," even small initial doses can be fatal because cocaine interferes with the electrical system of the heart, causing irregular heartbeats and, in some cases, heart failure. It also can produce heart attacks, hypertension, and strokes by temporarily constricting blood vessels (Abadinsky, 2014; Kontak & Vongpatanasin, 2013; NIDA, 2010; Vidal et al., 2012), as well as cognitive declines and brain atrophy (Ersche et al., 2012). The most dangerous form of cocaine is the smokable, concentrated version known as "crack," or "rock." Its lower price makes it affordable and attractive to a large audience. And its greater potency makes it more highly addictive.

FIGURE 5.9 COCAINE: AN AGONIST DRUG IN ACTION

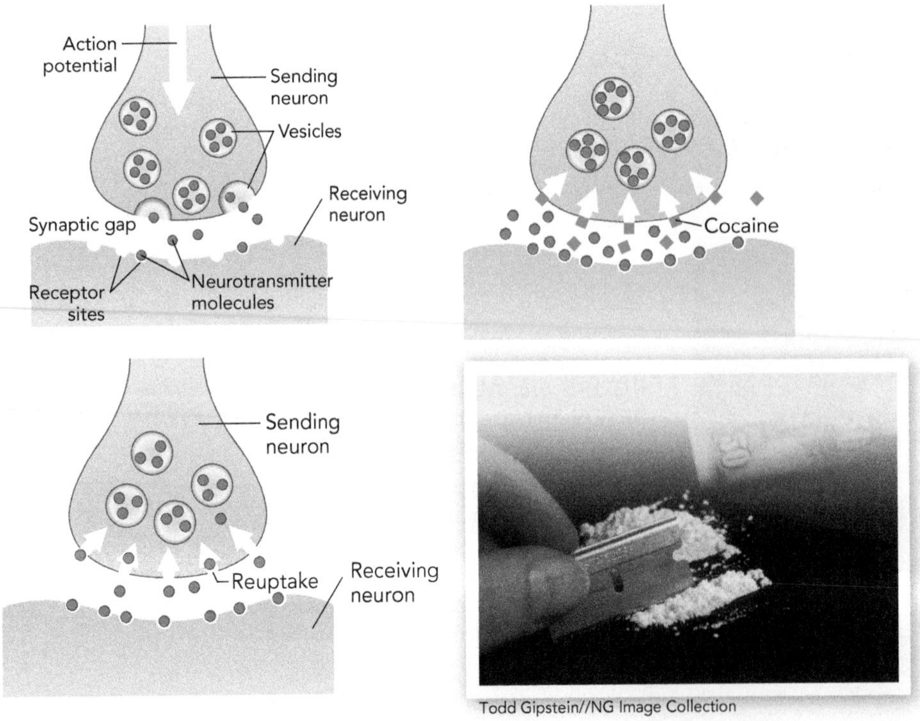

Todd Gipstein//NG Image Collection

A The two figures depict how after releasing neurotransmitter into the synapse, the sending neuron normally reabsorbs (or reuptakes) excess neurotransmitter back into the terminal buttons.

B This figure shows that when cocaine is present in the synapse, it will block the reuptake of dopamine, serotonin, and norepinephrine, and levels of these substances will increase. The result is overstimulation and a brief euphoric high. When the drug wears off, the depletion of neurotransmitters may cause the drug user to "crash."

Even legal stimulants can lead to serious problems. For example, the U.S. Public Health Service considers cigarette smoking the single most preventable cause of death and disease in the United States (Pearson et al., 2013). Researchers have found that nicotine activates the same brain areas as cocaine (Dandekar et al., 2011; David et al., 2013; Tronci & Balfour, 2011). Nicotine's effects—relaxation, increased alertness, and diminished pain and appetite—are so powerfully reinforcing that some people continue to smoke even after having a cancerous lung removed.

Opiates, or narcotics, which are derived from the opium poppy, are used medically to relieve pain (Connolly et al., 2013; Dalal & Bruera, 2013) because they mimic the brain's natural endorphins (Chapter 2), which numb pain and elevate mood. This creates a dangerous pathway to drug abuse, however. After repeated flooding with artificial opiates, the brain eventually reduces or stops the production of its own opiates. If the user later attempts to stop, the brain lacks both the artificial and normal level of painkilling chemicals, and withdrawal becomes excruciatingly painful **(Figure 5.10)**.

So far, we have discussed three of the four types of psychoactive drugs: depressants, stimulants, and opiates. One of the most intriguing alterations of consciousness comes from **hallucinogens**, drugs that produce sensory or perceptual distortions, including visual, auditory, and kinesthetic hallucinations. Some cultures have used hallucinogens for religious purposes, as a way to experience "other realities" or to communicate with the supernatural. In Western societies, most people use hallucinogens for their reported "mind-expanding" potential.

Hallucinogens are commonly referred to as *psychedelics* (from the Greek for "mind manifesting"). They include mescaline (derived from the peyote cactus), psilocybin (derived from mushrooms), phencyclidine (chemically derived), and LSD (lysergic acid diethylamide, derived from ergot, a rye mold).

LSD, or "acid," produces dramatic alterations in sensation and perception, including an altered sense of time, synesthesia (blending of the senses), and spiritual experiences. Perhaps because the LSD experience is so powerful, few people "drop acid" on a regular basis. Nevertheless, LSD can be an extremely dangerous drug. Bad LSD "trips" can be terrifying and may lead to accidents, deaths, or suicide. One 32-year-old man, with no known psychiatric disorder, intentionally removed his own testes after the first and single use of LSD combined with alcohol (Blacha et al., 2013)!

Marijuana, also called cannabis, is classified as a hallucinogen even though it has some properties of a depressant—it induces drowsiness and lethargy—and some of a narcotic—it acts as a weak painkiller. In low doses, marijuana produces mild euphoria; moderate doses lead to an intensification of sensory experiences and the illusion that time is passing slowly. High doses may produce hallucinations, delusions, and distortions of body image (Abadinsky, 2014; Gorelick et al., 2013; Hart & Ksir, 2013). The active ingredient in marijuana is THC, or tetrahydrocannabinol, which attaches to receptors that are abundant throughout the brain.

Kevin Winter/Getty Images

The High Cost of Drug Abuse

In July 2013, Cory Monteith, a 31-year-old actor who starred in the television show "Glee," died of an accidental overdose of heroin and alcohol. He struggled with addiction for years, and had recently undergone treatment for substance abuse addiction.

Opiate A drug derived from opium that numbs the senses and relieves pain.

Hallucinogen A drug that produces sensory or perceptual distortions.

FIGURE 5.10 HOW OPIATES CREATE PHYSICAL DEPENDENCE

Psychoactive drugs such as opiates affect the brain and body in a variety of ways.

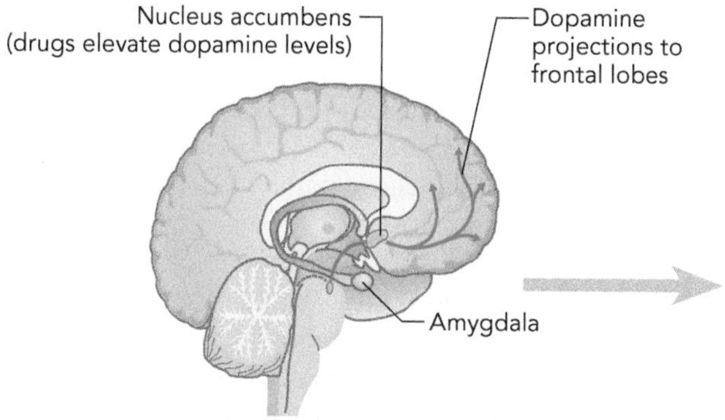

Ⓐ Most researchers believe that increased dopamine activity in this so-called *reward pathway* of the brain accounts for the reinforcing effects of most addictive drugs.

Jim Varney/Science Photo Library/Photo Researchers, Inc.

Ⓑ Absence of the drug triggers withdrawal symptoms (e.g., intense pain and cravings).

Voices from the Classroom

Exercise, Marijuana, and Chocolate When discussing the benefits of exercise for stress relief, and the role of endorphins, I ask my students if they've heard the term "anandamide." Almost everyone say no. They're surprised to learn that it's a naturally produced neurotransmitter, like endorphins, which is released during exercise. And I tell them about a recent study that found male athletes who warmed up and cooled down and exercised for 45 minutes at 70% effort increased their anandamide release by 80%. They're even more surprised when I explain that anandamides bind to the same brain receptors as do the cannabinoid (THC/ marijuana) molecules. In that dark chocolate also has been found to promote anandamide release, I conclude the discussion by providing dark chocolate for the entire class.

Professor Jan Mendoza
Golden West College
Huntington Beach, California

Some research has found marijuana to be therapeutic in treating glaucoma (an eye disease), alleviating the nausea and vomiting associated with chemotherapy, and dealing with other health problems (Borgelt et al., 2013; Green & De-Vries, 2010; Hart & Ksir, 2013).

Chronic marijuana use, however, can lead to throat and respiratory disorders, impaired lung functioning and immune response, declines in testosterone levels, reduced sperm count, and disruption of the menstrual cycle and ovulation (Hall & Degenhardt, 2010; Karavolos et al., 2013; Rooke et al., 2013; Skinner et al., 2011).

Marijuana use can also lead to decreases in IQ. Researchers in one study examined IQ in a sample of more than 1,000 13-year-olds and then retested their IQs 25 years later (Meier et al., 2012). Findings revealed that teenagers who started smoking marijuana before age 18 and were addicted to this drug by age 38 showed decreases in IQ points, including drops of as much as 8 points for those who reported the heaviest use. Although some research supports the popular belief that marijuana serves as a "gateway" to other illegal drugs, other studies find little or no connection (Hart & Ksir, 2013; Kirisci et al., 2013; Panlilio et al., 2013).

Marijuana also can be habit forming, but few users experience the intense cravings associated with cocaine or opiates. Withdrawal symptoms are mild because the drug dissolves in the body's fat and leaves the body very slowly, which explains why a marijuana user can test positive for days or weeks after the last use. Q4

Club Drugs

As you can see in **Figure 5.11**, and may know from television or newspapers, psychoactive drugs like Rohypnol (the "date rape drug," also called "roofies") and MDMA (3,4-methylenedioxymethylamphetamine, or "ecstasy") are among our nation's most popular drugs of abuse. Other "club" drugs, like GHB (gamma-hydroxybutyrate), Ketamine ("special K"), methamphetamine ("ice" or "crystal meth"), and LSD, are also gaining in popularity (DeMaria, 2012; Hopfer, 2011; Shimane et al., 2013; van Laar, 2012). However, these drugs can have very serious consequences. For example, recreational use of "ecstasy" is associated with a reduction in the neurotransmitter serotonin in the brain, which can lead to problems regulating mood, appetite, sleep, learning, memory, and even death (Di Iorio et al., 2012).

One of the most threatening recent trends in club drugs is the swallowing, injecting, or snorting of synthetic stimulants, called "bath salts," which are currently legally sold in small packets. Although marked "not for human ingestion," they are increasingly popular among those associated with the dance music scene. Widely available on the Internet and marketed with enticing names such as"White Lightning" or "Lovey Dovey," these bath salts produce cocaine or ecstasy-like effects. But they're far more toxic. Following reports of cases like Neil Brown, who slit his face and stomach repeatedly with a skinning knife, and numerous overdoses or deaths, several states now ban their sale (Baumann et al., 2013; Oz, 2011; Winder et al., 2013).

In addition, club drugs, like all illicit drugs, are particularly dangerous because there are no truth-in-packaging laws to protect buyers from unscrupulous practices. Sellers often substitute unknown cheaper, and possibly even more dangerous, substances for the ones they claim to be selling. Also, club drugs (like most psychoactive drugs) affect the motor coordination, perceptual skills, and reaction time necessary for safe driving.

Impaired decision making is a serious problem as well. Just as "drinking and driving don't mix," club drug use may lead to risky sexual behaviors and increased risk of sexually transmitted infections. Add in the fact that some drugs, like Rohypnol, are odorless, colorless, tasteless, and can easily be added to beverages by individuals who want to intoxicate or sedate others, and you can see that the dangers of club drug use go far beyond the drug itself.

FIGURE 5.11 BEWARE OF CLUB DRUGS

Although club drugs can produce initially desirable effects, such as MDMA's reported feelings of great empathy and connectedness with others, almost all psychoactive drugs can cause serious health problems—in some cases, even death (Chamberlin & Saper, 2009; Jaehne et al., 2011; National Institute on Drug Abuse, 2012).

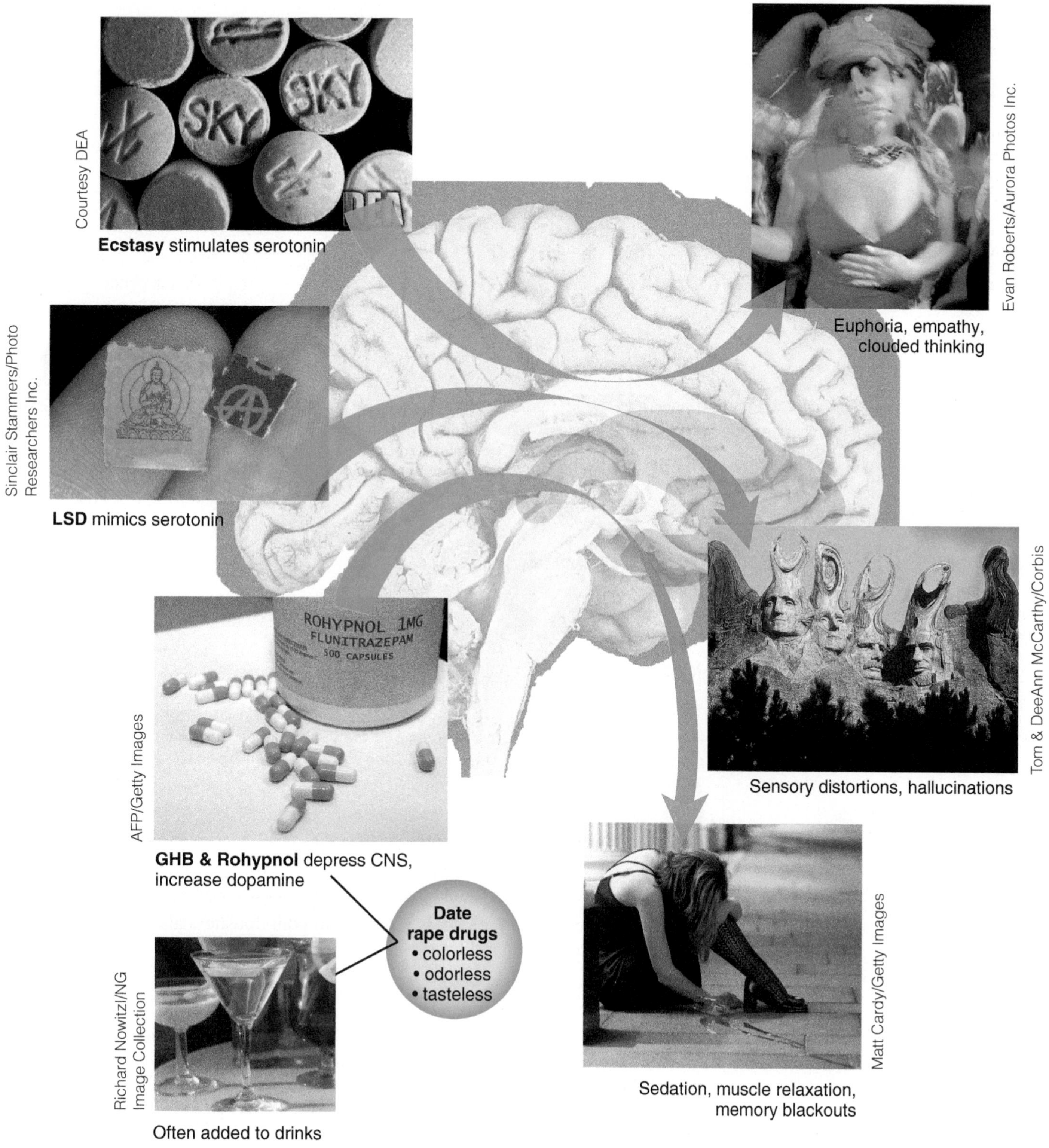

RETRIEVAL PRACTICE: PSYCHOACTIVE DRUGS

Self-Test

Completing this self-test and comparing your answers with those in Appendix B provides immediate feedback and helpful practice for exams. Additional interactive, self-tests are available at www.wiley.com/college/huffman.

1. Psychoactive drugs ______.

a. change conscious awareness, mood, or perception
b. are addictive, mind altering, and dangerous to your health
c. are illegal unless prescribed by a medical doctor
d. all these options

2. Depressants include all the following *except* ______.

a. antianxiety drugs
b. alcohol
c. tobacco
d. Rohypnol

3. ______ drugs inhibit normal synaptic transmission, whereas ______ drugs enhance synaptic transmission.

a. Antagonist; agonist
b. Agonist; antagonist
c. Protagonist; agonist
d. Protagonist; co-agonist

4. Drug taking that causes emotional or physical harm to the drug user or others is known as ______.

a. addiction
b. physical dependence
c. psychological dependence
d. drug abuse

Think Critically

1 Which is more important in creating addiction—physical dependence or psychological dependence?

2 Do you think marijuana use should be legal? Why or why not?

realworldpsychology

Are you addicted to Facebook?

Can using marijuana decrease your IQ?

HINT: LOOK IN THE MARGIN FOR Q3 AND Q4

MEDITATION AND HYPNOSIS

LEARNING OBJECTIVES

RETRIEVAL PRACTICE While reading the upcoming sections, respond to each Learning Objective in your own words. Then compare your responses with those found at www.wiley.com/college/huffman.

1 **DESCRIBE** the effect of meditation on the nervous system.

2 **EXPLAIN** the features of the hypnotic state.

As we have seen, factors such as sleep, dreaming, and psychoactive drug use can create altered states of consciousness. Changes in consciousness also can be achieved by means of meditation and hypnosis.

Meditation

"Suddenly, with a roar like that of a waterfall, I felt a stream of liquid light entering my brain through the spinal cord . . . I experienced a rocking sensation and then felt myself slipping out of my body, entirely enveloped in a halo of light. I felt the point of consciousness that was myself growing wider, surrounded by waves of light" (Krishna, 1999, pp. 4–5).

This is how spiritual leader Gopi Krishna described his experience with **meditation**, a group of techniques designed to focus attention, block out distractions, and produce an altered state of awareness **(Figure 5.12)**. Although most people in the beginning stages of meditation report a simpler, mellow type of relaxation followed by a mild euphoria and a sense of timelessness. Some advanced meditators report experiences of profound rapture, joy, and/or strong hallucinations.

Meditation A group of techniques designed to alter consciousness; it's believed to enhance self-knowledge and well-being through reduced self-awareness.

FIGURE 5.12 BENEFITS OF MEDITATION | *psychology and you*

Ⓐ Some meditation techniques, such as tai chi and hatha yoga, include body movements and postures, while in other techniques, the meditator remains motionless, chanting or focusing on a single point, like a candle flame.

Dan Dalton/Getty Images

Ⓑ During meditation, the hypothalamus diminishes the sympathetic response and increases the parasympathetic response. Shutting down the so-called fight-or-flight response in this way allows for deep rest, slower respiration, and overall relaxation.

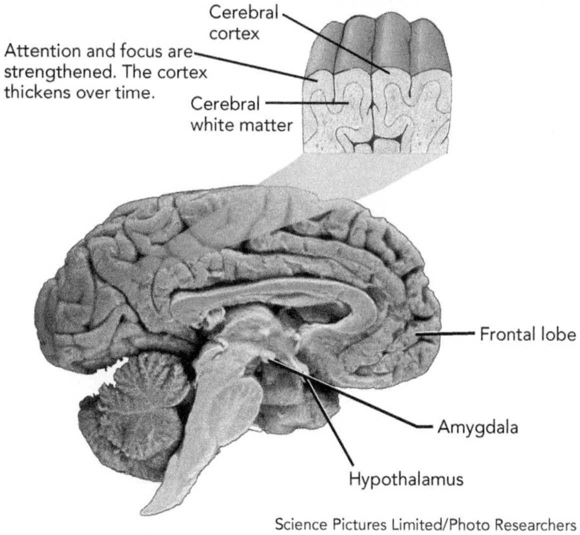

Science Pictures Limited/Photo Researchers

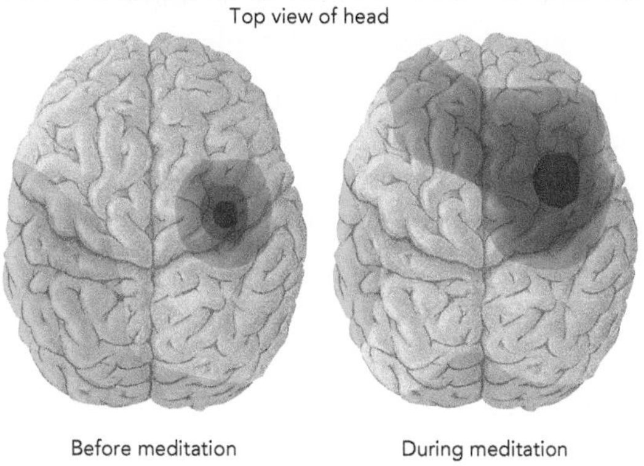

Ⓒ Researchers have found that an increased area of the brain responds to sensory stimuli during meditation, suggesting that meditation enhances the coordination between the brain hemispheres (Kilpatrick et al., 2011; Lyubimov, 1992). Note how much the blue-colored areas enlarged and spread from the right to the left hemisphere during meditation.

How can we explain these effects? Brain imaging studies suggest that meditation's requirement to focus attention, block out distractions, and focus on a single object, emotion, or word, reduces the number of brain cells that must be devoted to the multiple, competing tasks normally going on within the brain's frontal lobes. This narrowed focus thus explains the feelings of timelessness and mild euphoria (Cvetkovic & Cosic, 2011; Wachholtz & Austin, 2013).

Research has also verified that meditation can produce dramatic changes in basic physiological processes, including heart rate, oxygen consumption, sweat gland responses, and brain activity. In addition, it's been somewhat successful in reducing pain, anxiety, and stress; lowering blood pressure; increasing creativity, and improving overall mental health (Colzato et al., 2012; Gans et al., 2013; Gordon et al., 2013; Grant et al., 2011). As you can see in **Figures 5.12b and c**, studies have also found that meditation can change the body's sympathetic and parasympathetic responses, and increase structural support for the sensory, decision-making, emotion regulation, and attention-processing centers of the brain (Libby et al., 2012; Lo & Chang, 2013; Malinowski, 2013; Tang & Posner, 2013; Urry et al., 2012).

Interestingly, one study provided participants with eight weeks of training in meditation and examined brain activation in response to upsetting images both before and after the training (Desbordes et al., 2012). Results indicated that after training participants showed lower levels of activation in the amygdala (a part of the brain that responds to emotion), even if they were not meditating at the time.

Hypnosis

Relax . . . your eyelids are so very heavy . . . your muscles are becoming more and more relaxed . . . your breathing is becoming deeper and deeper . . . relax . . . your eyes are closing . . . let go . . . relax.

Hypnosis An alternate state of consciousness characterized by deep relaxation and a trancelike state of heightened suggestibility and intense focus.

Hypnotists use suggestions like these to begin **hypnosis**, a trance-like state of heightened suggestibility, deep relaxation, and intense focus. Once hypnotized, some people can be convinced that they are standing at the edge of the ocean, listening to the sound of the waves and feeling the ocean mist on their faces. Invited to eat a "delicious apple" that is actually an onion, the hypnotized person may relish the flavor. Told they are watching a very funny or sad movie, hypnotized people may begin to laugh or cry at their self-created visions.

From the 1700s to modern times, entertainers and quacks have used (and abused) hypnosis **(Table 5.5)**, but physicians, dentists, and therapists also have long employed it as a respected clinical tool. Modern scientific research has removed much of the mystery surrounding hypnosis. A number of features characterize the hypnotic state (Jamieson & Hasegawa, 2007; Jensen et al., 2008; Robertson, 2013):

- Narrowed, highly focused attention (ability to "tune out" competing sensory stimuli)
- Increased use of imagination and hallucinations
- A passive and receptive attitude
- Decreased responsiveness to pain
- Heightened suggestibility, or a greater willingness to respond to proposed changes in perception ("This onion is an apple")

Today, even with available anesthetics, hypnosis is occasionally used in surgery and for the treatment of cancer, chronic pain and severe burns (Jensen et al., 2008, 2011; Montgomery et al., 2013; Nusbaum et al., 2011; Smith, 2011). It has found its best use in medical areas such as dentistry and childbirth, where patients have a high

TABLE 5.5 HYPNOSIS MYTHS AND FACTS

Myth	Fact
Faking Hypnosis participants are "faking it" and playing along with the hypnotist.	There are conflicting research positions about hypnosis. Although most participants are not consciously faking hypnosis, some researchers believe the effects result from a blend of conformity, relaxation, obedience, suggestion, and role playing. Other theorists believe that hypnotic effects result from a special altered state of consciousness. A group of "unified" theorists suggests that hypnosis is a combination of both relaxation/role playing and a unique alternate state or consciousness.
Forced hypnosis People can be hypnotized against their will or hypnotically "brainwashed."	Hypnosis requires a willing, conscious choice to relinquish control of one's consciousness to someone else. The best potential subjects are those who are able to focus attention, are open to new experiences, and are capable of imaginative involvement or fantasy.
Unethical behavior Hypnosis can make people behave immorally or take dangerous risks against their will.	Hypnotized people retain awareness and control of their behavior, and they can refuse to comply with the hypnotist's suggestions.
Superhuman strength Under hypnosis, people can perform acts of special superhuman strength.	When nonhypnotized people are simply asked to try their hardest on tests of physical strength, they generally can do anything a hypnotized person can do.
Exceptional memory Under hypnosis, people can recall things they otherwise could not.	Although the heightened relaxation and focus that hypnosis engenders improves recall for some information, it adds little if anything to regular memory, and hypnotized people also are more willing to guess. Because memory is normally filled with fabrication and distortion (Chapter 7), hypnosis generally increases the potential for error.

Sources: Hilgard, 1978, 1992; Lilienfeld et al., 2010; Lynn et al., 2010; Montgomery et al., 2013; Orne, 2006; Terhune et al., 2011; Wickramasekera, 2008.

degree of anxiety, fear, and misinformation. For example, some studies have found that women who use hypnosis in labor and childbirth experience lower levels of pain and a shorter duration of labor (Madden et al., 2012). Because tension and anxiety strongly affect pain, any technique that helps the patient relax is medically useful. Q5

In psychotherapy, hypnosis can help patients relax, recall painful memories, and reduce anxiety. Despite the many myths about hypnosis, it has been used with modest success in the treatment of phobias and in helping people to lose weight, stop smoking, and improve study habits (Amundson & Nuttgens, 2008; Robertson, 2013; Smith, 2011).

One final note

Before going on to the next chapter, we'd like to take an unusual step for authors. We'd like to offer you, our reader, a piece of caring, personal and professional advice about alternate states of consciousness (ASCs). The core problem while you're in any ASC is that you're less aware of external reality, which places you at high risk. This applies to both men and women. Interestingly, we all recognize these dangers while sleeping and dreaming, and we've developed standard ways to protect ourselves. For example, when we're driving on a long trip and start to feel sleepy, we stop for coffee, walk around, and/or rent a hotel room before allowing ourselves to fall asleep.

Our simple advice to you is to follow this same "sleepy driver" logic and standards. If you decide to use drugs, meditate, undergo hypnosis, or engage in any other form of altered consciousness, research the effects and risks of your ASC and plan ahead for the best options for dealing with it—just like you set up a designated driver before drinking. Take care and best wishes,

RETRIEVAL PRACTICE: MEDITATION AND HYPNOSIS

Self-Test

Completing this self-test and comparing your answers with those in Appendix B provides immediate feedback and helpful practice for exams. Additional interactive, self-tests are available at www.wiley.com/college/huffman.

1. Alternate states of consciousness (ASCs) can be achieved in which of the following ways?

a. during sleep and dreaming
b. via chemical channels
c. through hypnosis and meditation
d. all these options

2. ______ is a group of techniques designed to focus attention, block out all distractions, and produce an alternate state of consciousness (ASC).

a. Hypnosis
b. MDMA
c. Parapsychology
d. Meditation

3. ______ is occasionally used in surgery and for the treatment of chronic pain and severe burns.

a. Parasomnia
b. Meditation
c. Hypnosis
d. Parapsychology

4. ______ is an alternate state of heightened suggestibility characterized by deep relaxation and a trancelike state.

a. Meditation
b. Amphetamine psychosis
c. Hypnosis
d. Daydreaming

Think Critically

1 Why is it almost impossible to hypnotize an unwilling participant?

2 Describe the possible health benefits of hypnosis and meditation.

realworldpsychology

Can hypnosis decrease the pain of childbirth?

HINT: LOOK IN THE MARGIN FOR Q5

Summary

1 CONSCIOUSNESS, SLEEP, AND DREAMING 124

- **Consciousness**, an organism's awareness of internal events and the external environment, varies in its depth and exists along a continuum. We spend most of our time in waking consciousness, but also in various **alternate states of consciousness (ASCs)**, such as sleep and dreaming.
- Many physiological functions follow 24-hour **circadian rhythms**. Disruptions in these rhythms, as well as long-term sleep deprivation, lead to increased fatigue, cognitive and mood disruptions, and other health problems.
- During a normal night's sleep, we progress through four distinct stages of **non-rapid-eye-movement (NREM) sleep**, with periods of **rapid-eye-movement (REM) sleep** generally occurring at the end of each sleep cycle. Both REM and NREM sleep are important for our biological functioning.
- There are four major theories about why we sleep. **Adaptation/protection theory** proposes that sleep evolved to conserve energy and to provide protection from predators. The **repair/restoration theory** suggests that sleep helps us recuperate from the day's events. The **growth/development theory** argues that we use sleep for growth. The **learning/memory theory** says that we use sleep for consolidation, storage, and maintenance of memories.
- Three major theories about why we dream are Freud's **wish-fulfillment view**, the **activation–synthesis hypothesis**, and the **cognitive view**.
- Sleep–wake disorders include **insomnia**, **narcolepsy**, **sleep apnea**, **nightmares**, and **sleep terrors**. Natural sleep aids, based on behavior therapy, are helpful ways to treat sleep-wake disorders and avoid problems associated with medication.

2 PSYCHOACTIVE DRUGS 136

- **Psychoactive drugs** influence the nervous system in a variety of ways. Alcohol affects neural membranes throughout the entire nervous system. Most psychoactive drugs act in a more specific way, by either enhancing a particular neurotransmitter's effect—an **agonist drug**—or inhibiting it—an **antagonist drug**.
- The term **drug abuse** refers to drug-taking behavior that causes emotional or physical harm to oneself or others. **Addiction** refers to a condition in which a person feels compelled to use a specific drug. **Psychological dependence** refers to the mental desire or craving to achieve a drug's effects. **Physical dependence** refers to biological changes that make a drug necessary for minimum daily functioning, and **withdrawal** symptoms. Repeated use of a drug can produce decreased sensitivity, or **tolerance**. Sometimes, using one drug increases tolerance for another (**cross-tolerance**).
- Psychologists divide psychoactive drugs into four categories: **depressants** (such as alcohol, barbiturates, Rohypnol, and Ketamine), **stimulants** (such as caffeine, nicotine, cocaine, and amphetamines), **opiates** (such as morphine, heroin, and codeine), and **hallucinogens** (such as marijuana and LSD). Almost all psychoactive drugs may cause serious health problems and, in some cases, even death.

3 MEDITATION AND HYPNOSIS 144

- **Meditation** refers to techniques designed to focus attention, block out distractions, and produce an alternate state of consciousness. Researchers have verified that it can produce dramatic changes in basic physiological processes.
- Modern research has removed the mystery surrounding **hypnosis**, a trancelike state of heightened suggestibility, deep relaxation, and intense focus. It is used in psychotherapy and medicine, and it is especially useful for those with a high degree of anxiety, fear, and misinformation.

Dorling Kindersley/Getty Images, Inc.

Neo Vision/Getty Images, Inc.

applyingrealworldpsychology

We began this chapter with five intriguing Real World Psychology questions, and you were asked to revisit these questions at the end of each section. Questions like these have an important and lasting impact on all of our lives. See if you can answer these additional critical thinking questions related to real world examples.

1. In which stage of sleep is the kitten in each photo, and how do you know?
2. Why might REM sleep serve an important adaptive function for cats?
3. Imagine that someone marketed a drug that allowed you to get complete rest and recuperation from only one hour of sleep, but it stopped you from dreaming. Would you take the drug? Why or why not?
4. Why do you think Freud's dream theory remains so popular, despite serious scientific questions and alternative modern theories?
5. Why do you think alcohol is more popular and culturally acceptable than the other drugs discussed in this chapter?
6. What are some possible ethical considerations of using hypnosis?

Key Terms

RETRIEVAL PRACTICE Write a definition for each term before turning back to the referenced page to check your answer.

- activation–synthesis hypothesis of dreams 132
- adaptation/protection theory of sleep 131
- addiction 137
- agonist drug 136
- alternate state of consciousness (ASC) 124
- antagonist drug 136
- circadian rhythm 126
- cognitive view of dreams 132
- consciousness 124
- depressant 139
- drug abuse 137
- growth/development theory of sleep 131
- hallucinogen 141
- hypnosis 146
- insomnia 133
- latent content of dreams 132
- learning/memory theory of sleep 131
- manifest content of dreams 132
- meditation 144
- narcolepsy 134
- nightmares 135
- non-rapid-eye-movement (NREM) sleep 130
- opiate 141
- physical dependence 137
- psychoactive drug 136
- psychological dependence 137
- rapid-eye-movement (REM) sleep 129
- repair/restoration theory of sleep 131
- sleep apnea 134
- sleep terrors 135
- stimulant 140
- tolerance 138
- wish-fulfillment view of dreams 132
- withdrawal 137

chaptersix

Learning

CHAPTER OUTLINE

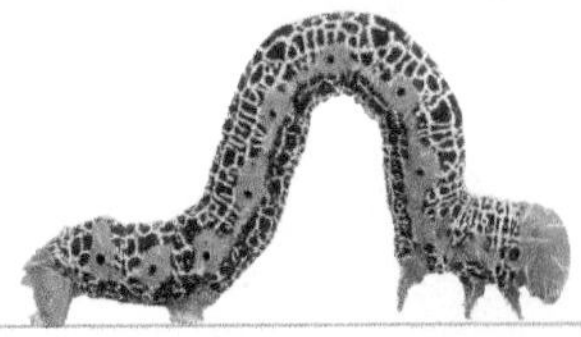

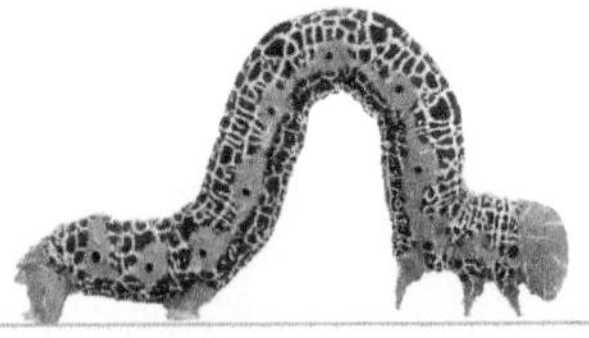

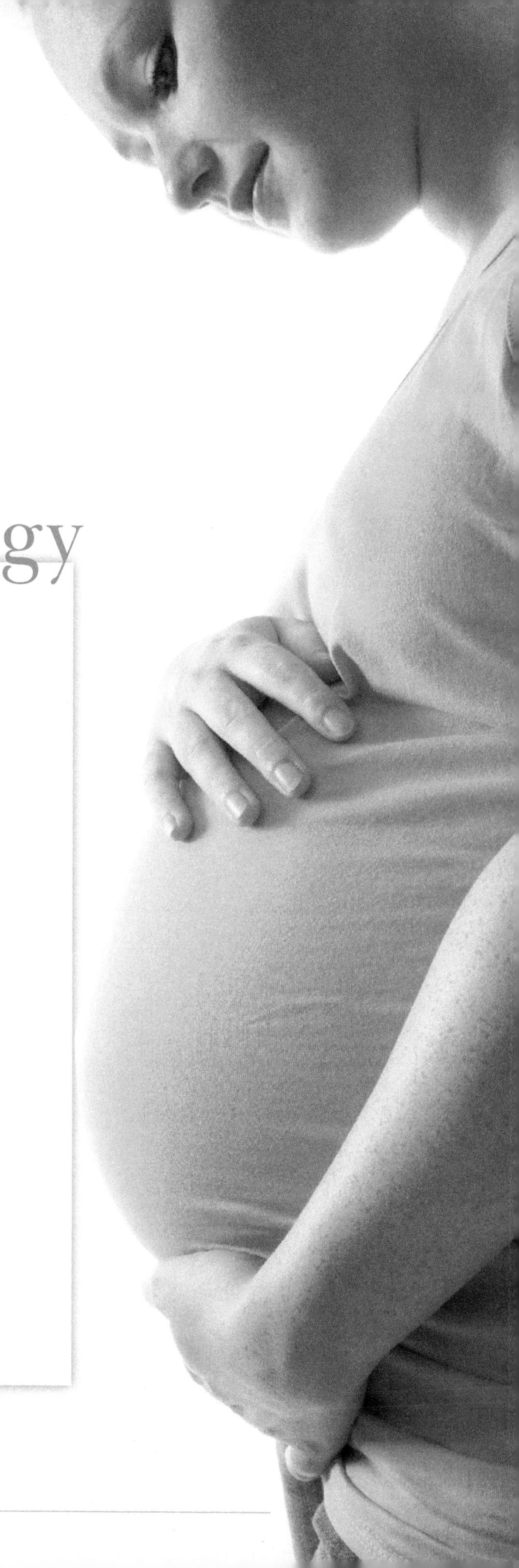

realworldpsychology

THINGS YOU'LL LEARN IN CHAPTER 6

Q1 Why can simply hearing the drill in a dentist's office—even if that drill is nowhere near you—make you feel anxious?

Q2 How can decreasing the cost of fruit and vegetables lead to healthier eating?

Q3 Why do gamblers have such trouble quitting, even when they continue to lose money?

Q4 Does watching sex on TV increase the risk of teen pregnancies?

Q5 Why can even young children recognize a picture of a snake much faster than a picture of a frog or caterpillar?

THROUGHOUT THE CHAPTER, MARGIN ICONS FOR Q1–Q5 INDICATE WHERE THE TEXT ADDRESSES THESE QUESTIONS.

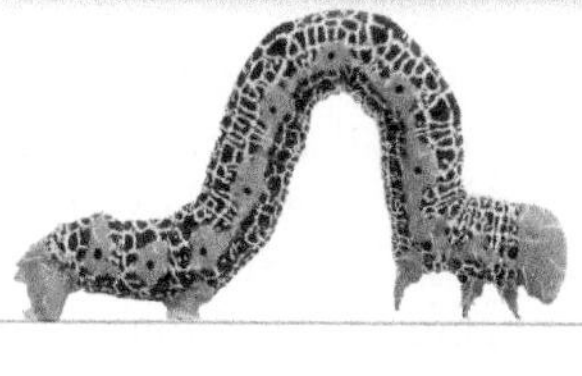

chapteroverview

Imagine yourself in the following situations:

On your way to campus, you note a bad traffic jam up ahead and quickly decide to try a new shortcut someone mentioned several weeks ago.

Later, in your general psychology class, you watch a video on service dogs for the blind, and are amazed by these dogs opening and closing doors, helping their owners dress and undress, carrying items in a backpack, and even differentiating between classrooms, bathrooms, escalators, and elevators.

While leaving campus, you note that the pitcher on your college's baseball team ritualistically kicks the dirt twice with each foot, then spits in his glove, and finally taps the top of his ball cap three times before throwing each pitch.

Now ask yourself, how did you manage that new shortcut to campus? How did those guide dogs perform such amazing acts? Why did the baseball pitcher engage in such strange, superstitious rituals? All three of these sets of behavior are clearly not genetic or present at the moment of birth. Instead, they result from *learning*.

We usually think of learning as classroom activities, such as math and reading, or as motor skills, like riding a bike or playing the piano. But for psychologists, learning is an all-encompassing process allowing us to adapt to our ever-changing environment. We learn that certain objects or events, such as food or pain, are associated with our survival (classical conditioning). We also learn to avoid punishing situations, and to repeat acts that bring rewards (operant conditioning). Finally, we learn through personal insights and from watching others (cognitive-social learning). Without the ability to learn, we simply could not exist.

In this chapter, we will study these three forms of learning, followed by the biology of learning, which explains how our brain and nervous system change when we learn.

CLASSICAL CONDITIONING

LEARNING OBJECTIVES

RETRIEVAL PRACTICE While reading the upcoming sections, respond to each Learning Objective in your own words. Then compare your responses with those found at www.wiley.com/college/huffman.

1. **DESCRIBE** Pavlov and Watson's contributions to our understanding of learning.
2. **EXPLAIN** the three steps in classical conditioning.
3. **SUMMARIZE** the six principles of classical conditioning.

Learning A relatively permanent change in behavior or mental processes caused by experience.

Before we go on, we need to operationally define **learning** *as a relatively permanent change in behavior or mental processes caused by experience.* This relative permanence applies not only to bad habits, like texting while driving or procrastinating, but also to useful behaviors and emotions, such as training guide dogs for the blind or falling in love.

We begin this chapter with a study of one of the earliest forms of learning, *classical conditioning*, made famous by Pavlov's salivating dogs.

FIGURE 6.1 PAVLOV'S EXPERIMENTAL SETUP

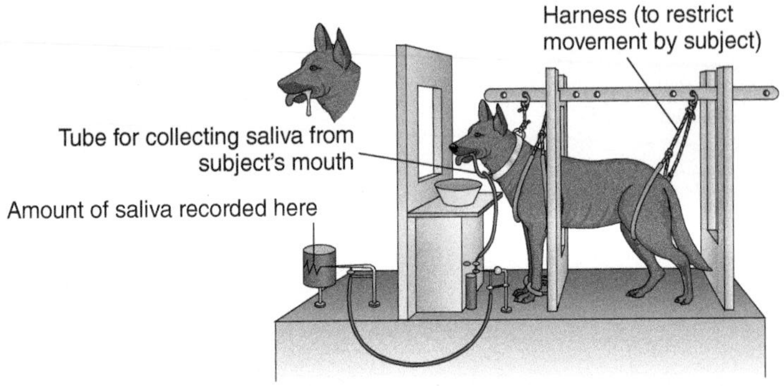

Beginnings of Classical Conditioning

Why does your mouth water when you stare at a large slice of delicious cake or a juicy steak? The answer to this question was accidentally discovered in the laboratory of Russian physiologist Ivan Pavlov (1849–1936). Pavlov's initial plan was to study the role of saliva in digestion by using a tube attached to dogs' salivary glands **(Figure 6.1)**.

Ironically, during these experiments, one of Pavlov's students noticed that even before receiving the actual food, many dogs began salivating at the mere sight of the food, the food dish, the smell of the food, or even just the sight of the person who customarily delivered the food! Pavlov's genius was in recognizing the importance of this "unscheduled" salivation. He realized that the dogs were not only responding on the basis of hunger (a biological need), but also as a result of experience or learning.

Excited by this accidental discovery, Pavlov and his students conducted several experiments, including sounding a tone on a tuning fork just before food was placed in the dogs' mouths. After several pairings of the tone and food, dogs in the laboratory began to salivate on hearing the tone alone.

Pavlov and later researchers found that many things can become conditioned stimuli for salivation if they are paired with food—a bell, a buzzer, a light, and even the sight of a circle or triangle drawn on a card. This type of learning, in which a neutral stimulus (such as the tone on a tuning fork) comes to elicit a response after repeated pairings with a naturally occurring stimulus (like food), is now known as **classical conditioning**.

To fully understand classical conditioning, and how it applies to our everyday life, the first step is to recognize that **conditioning** is simply another word for learning. Next, we need to explain that classical conditioning is a three-step process—*before*, *during*, and *after conditioning*. A process that is explained in detail below and visually summarized in **Figure 6.2**.

Classical conditioning A type of learning that develops through involuntarily paired associations; a previously neutral stimulus (NS) is paired (associated) with an unconditioned stimulus (US) to elicit a conditioned response (CR).

Conditioning The process of learning associations between stimuli and behavioral responses.

FIGURE 6.2 **THE BEGINNINGS AND A MODERN APPLICATION OF CLASSICAL CONDITIONING**

Although Pavlov's initial experiment used a metronome, a ticking instrument designed to mark exact time, his best-known method (depicted here) involved a tone from a tuning fork. As you can see, the basic process of classical conditioning is simple. Just as you've been classically conditioned to respond to your cell phone's tones, or possibly to just the sight of a pizza box, Pavlov's dogs learned to respond to the tuning fork's tone. Unfortunately, many students get confused by these technical terms. So here's a tip that might help: The actual stimuli (tone and meat) remain the same—only their names change from neutral to conditioned or from unconditioned to conditioned. A similar name change happens for the response (salivation)—from unconditioned to conditioned.

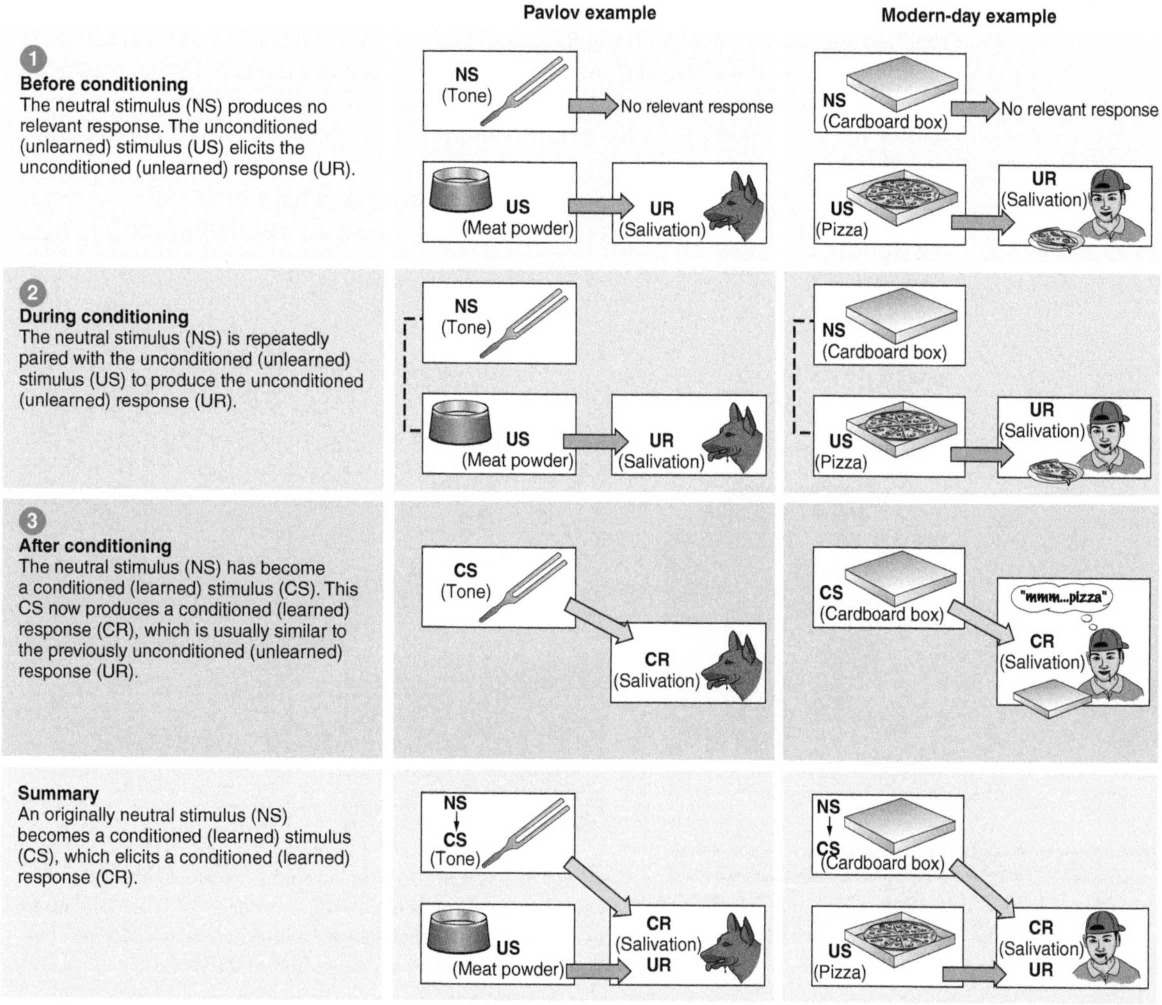

Neutral stimulus (NS) A stimulus that, before conditioning, does not naturally bring about the response of interest.

Unconditioned stimulus (US) In classical conditioning, a stimulus that elicits an unconditioned response (UR) without previous conditioning.

Unconditioned response (UR) In classical conditioning, a learned reaction to an unconditioned stimulus (US) that occurs without previous conditioning.

Conditioned stimulus (CS) In classical conditioning, a previously neutral stimulus (NS) becomes conditioned through repeated pairings with an unconditioned stimulus (US), and it now elicits a conditioned response (CR).

Conditioned response (CR) In classical conditioning, a learned reaction to a conditioned stimulus (CS) that occurs because of previous repeated pairings with an unconditioned stimulus (US).

Conditioned emotional response (CER) Through classical conditioning, an emotion, such as fear, becomes a conditioned response to a previously neutral stimulus (NS).

STEP 1 Before conditioning, the sound of the tone does NOT lead to salivation, which makes the tone a **neutral stimulus (NS)**. Conversely, food naturally brings about salivation, which makes food an *unlearned*, **unconditioned stimulus (US)**. The initial, salivary reflex of salivation also is *unlearned*, so it is called an **unconditioned response (UR)**.

STEP 2 During conditioning, the tuning fork (NS) is repeatedly sounded right before the presentation of the meat (US).

STEP 3 After conditioning, the tone alone will bring about salivation. At this point, we can say that the dog is *classically conditioned*. The previously neutral stimulus (NS) (the tone) has now become a *learned*, **conditioned stimulus (CS)**, that produced a *learned*, **conditioned response (CR)** (the dog's salivation). (Note that the "R" in UR in Step 1 and the CR in this Step 3 refers to both "reflex" and "response.")

In sum, the overall goal of Pavlov's classical conditioning was for the dog to learn to associate the tone with the unconditioned stimulus (meat), and then to show the same response (salivation) to the tone as to the meat.

So what does a salivating dog have to do with your everyday life? Classical conditioning is a fundamental way that all animals, including humans, learn. The human feelings of excitement and/or compulsion to gamble, your love for your parents (or significant other), drooling at the sight of chocolate cake or pizza, and the almost universal fear of public speaking all largely result from classical conditioning.

How do we learn to be afraid of public speaking or of typically harmless things like mice and elevators? In a now-famous experiment, John Watson and Rosalie Rayner (1920) demonstrated how a fear of rats could be classically conditioned.

In this study, a healthy 11-month-old child, later known as "Little Albert," was first allowed to play with a white laboratory rat **(Figure 6.3)**. Like most other infants, Albert was curious and reached for the rat, showing no fear. Knowing that infants are naturally frightened by loud noises, Watson stood behind Albert and when he reached for the rat, Watson banged a steel bar with a hammer. The loud noise obviously frightened the child and made him cry. The rat was paired with the loud noise only seven times before Albert became classically conditioned and demonstrated fear of the rat even without the noise. The rat had become a CS that brought about the CR (fear).

Although this deliberate experimental creation of what's now called a **conditioned emotional response (CER)** remains a classic in psychology, it has been heavily criticized and would never be allowed under today's experimental guidelines

FIGURE 6.3 **LITTLE ALBERT'S FEARS**

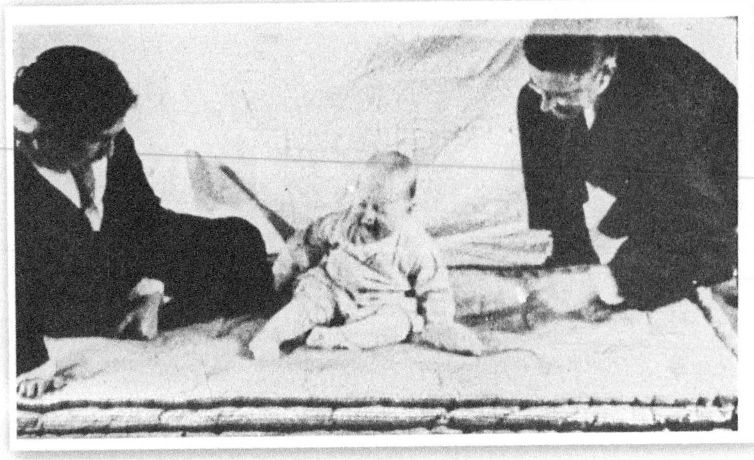

Benjamin Harris

Ⓐ Watson and Rayner's famous "Little Albert" study demonstrated how some fears can originate through conditioning.

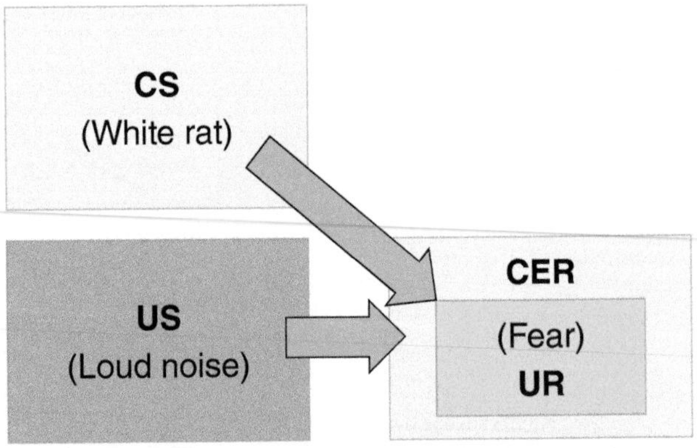

Ⓑ Using classical conditioning terms, we would say that the white rat (a neutral stimulus/NS) was paired with the loud noise (an unconditioned stimulus/US) to produce a conditioned emotional response (CER) in Albert, fear of the rat.

(Ethical Principles of Psychologists, 2010; Fridlund et al., 2012; Ollendick et al., 2012; Paul & Blumenthal, 1989). The research procedures used by Watson and Rayner violated several ethical guidelines for scientific research (Chapter 1). They not only deliberately created a serious fear in a child, but they also ended their experiment without *extinguishing* (removing) it. In addition, the researchers have been criticized because they did not measure Albert's fear objectively. Their subjective evaluation raises doubt about the degree of fear conditioned.

Despite such criticisms, this study of Little Albert showed us that many of our likes, dislikes, prejudices, and fears are examples of *conditioned emotional responses (CERs)*. For example, if your romantic partner always uses the same shampoo, simply the smell of that shampoo may soon elicit a positive response. In Chapter 13, you'll discover how Watson's research later led to powerful clinical tools for eliminating exaggerated and irrational fears of a specific object or situation, known as *phobias* (Cal et al., 2006; Field, 2006; Schachtman & Reilly, 2011; Schweckendiek et al., 2011). For more examples of how classical conditioning impacts everyday life, see **Figure 6.4**.

FIGURE 6.4 CLASSICAL CONDITIONING IN EVERYDAY LIFE

realworldpsychology

Have you ever wondered why people are prejudiced and discriminate against others? These behaviors, as well as advertising and medicine, are all heavily influenced by classical conditioning.

Ⓐ Prejudice
How do children, like the one holding the KKK sign in this photo, develop prejudice at such an early age? As shown in the diagram, children are naturally upset and become afraid (UR) when they see that their parents are upset and afraid (US). Over time, they may learn to associate their parents' reaction with all members of a disliked group (CS), thus becoming prejudiced like their parents.

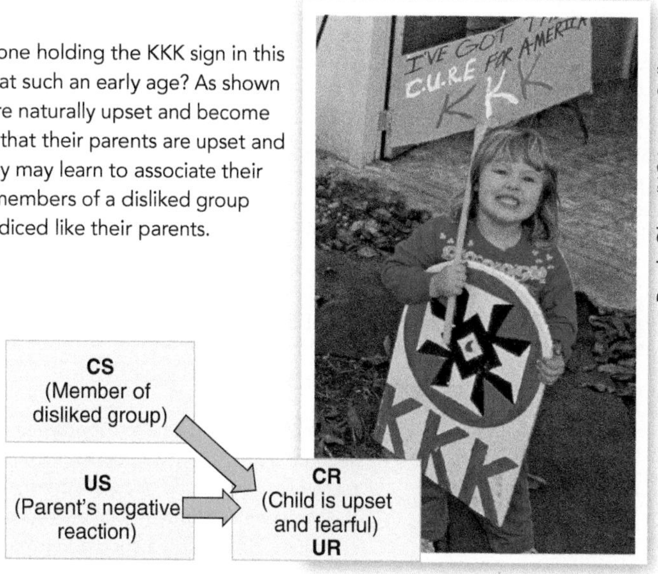

Randy Olsen/NG Image Collection

Ⓑ Advertising
Magazine ads, TV commercials, and business promotions often use higher-order classical conditioning to pair their products or company logo, the neutral stimulus (NS), with previously conditioned pleasant images, like attractive models and celebrities, the conditioned stimulus (CS). These attractive models then trigger desired behaviors, the conditioned response (CR), such as purchasing their products (Krugman, 2013; Miller & Allen, 2012; Sweldens et al., 2010).

Bill Aron/PhotoEdit

Ⓒ Medicine
Classical conditioning also is used in the medical field. For example, a treatment designed for alcohol-addicted patients pairs alcohol with a nausea-producing drug. Afterward, just the smell or taste of alcohol makes the person sick. Some, but not all, patients have found this treatment helpful.

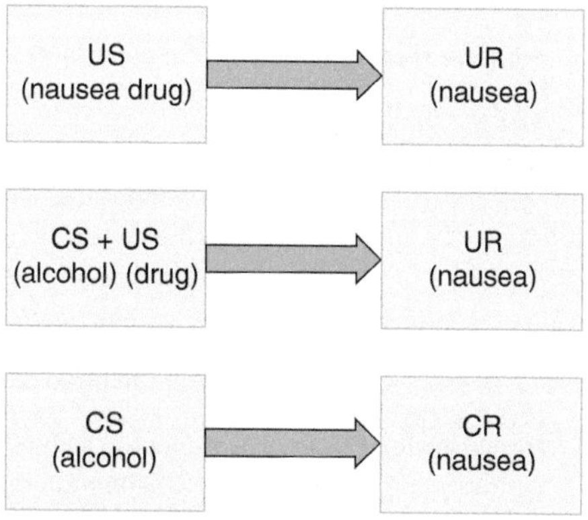

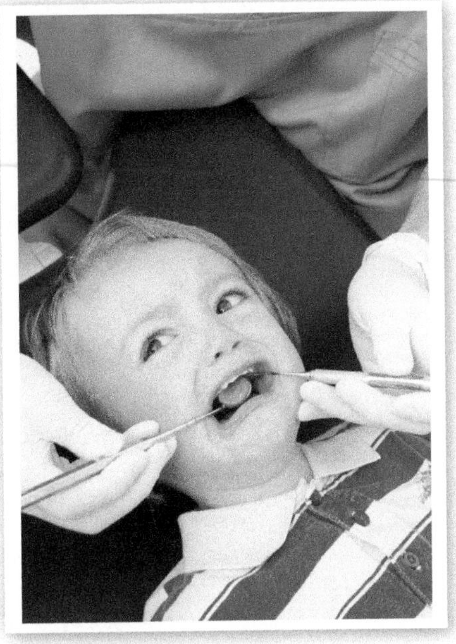

© oneblink-cj/iStockphoto

Are you afraid of dentists?

Acquisition The final step in a classical conditioning experiment during which the conditioned stimulus (CS) elicits the conditioned response (CR).

Stimulus generalization The conditioned response (CR) is elicited not only by the conditioned stimulus (CS) but also by stimuli similar to the conditioned stimulus (CS).

Stimulus discrimination A conditioning process in which an organism learns to respond differently to stimuli that differ from the conditioned stimulus on some dimension.

Principles of Classical Conditioning

Fear and avoidance of dental work is very common. How did it develop? Imagine being seated in a dental chair, and, even though the drill is nowhere near you, its sound can make you feel anxious. Your anxiety is obviously not innate. Little babies don't cringe at the sound of a dental drill. Your fear of the drill, and maybe dentistry in general, involves one or more of the six principles shown in **Table 6.1**. As you'll discover in Chapters 12 and 13, the good news is that even people with serious dental phobias can learn to overcome them (Elsesser et al., 2013). Q1

Acquisition, Stimulus Generalization, and Stimulus Discrimination

After Pavlov's original (accidental) discovery of classical conditioning, he conducted numerous experiments beyond the basic **acquisition** phase, a general term for the third step in classical conditioning in which the conditioned response (CR) is first elicited by the conditioned stimulus (CS).

One of his most interesting findings was that stimuli similar to the original conditioned stimulus (CS) also can elicit the conditioned response (CR). For example, after first conditioning dogs to salivate to the sound of low-pitched tones, Pavlov later demonstrated that the dogs would also salivate in response to higher-pitched tones. Similarly, after conditioning, the infant in Watson and Rayner's experiment ("Little Albert") feared not only rats but also a rabbit, a dog, and a bearded Santa Claus mask. This spreading or *generalizing* of the CR to similar stimuli, even though they have never been paired with the US, is called **stimulus generalization**.

In contrast, just as Pavlov's dogs learned to generalize and respond to similar stimuli, they also learned how to *discriminate* between similar stimuli. For example, when he gave the dogs food following a high-pitched tone, but not when he used a low-pitched tone, he found that they learned the difference between the two tones and only salivated to the high-pitched one. Likewise, Albert learned to recognize differences between rats and other stimuli, and presumably overcame his fear of Santa Claus. This ability to distinguish or discriminate between stimuli is known as **stimulus discrimination**.

TABLE 6.1 SIX PRINCIPLES AND APPLICATIONS OF CLASSICAL CONDITIONING | psychology and you

Process	Description	Example
Acquisition of basic classical conditioning	Process of learning a new response, in which the neutral stimulus (NS) and unconditioned stimulus (US) are first paired to produce the unconditioned response (UR); then the neutral stimulus (NS) becomes a conditioned stimulus (CS), eliciting a conditioned response (CR)	You learn to fear (CR) a dentist's drill (CS) because you associate it with the pain of your tooth extraction (US).
Stimulus generalization	Conditioned response (CR) is elicited not only by the conditioned stimulus (CS) but also by stimuli similar to the conditioned stimulus (CS)	You generalize your fear of the dentist's drill to your dentist's office and other dentists' offices.
Stimulus discrimination	Stimuli similar to the conditioned stimulus (CS) do not elicit the conditioned response (CR)	You are not afraid of your physician's office because you've learned to differentiate it from your dentist's office.
Extinction	Conditioned stimulus (CS) is presented alone, without the unconditioned stimulus (US); eventually the conditioned stimulus (CS) no longer elicits the conditioned response (CR)	You return several times to your dentist's office for routine checkups, with no dental drill; your fear (CR) gradually diminishes.
Spontaneous recovery	Sudden reappearance of a previously extinguished conditioned response (CR)	While watching a movie depicting dental drilling, your previous fear (CR) suddenly returns.
Higher-order conditioning	Neutral stimulus (NS) becomes a conditioned stimulus (CS) through repeated pairing with a previously conditioned stimulus (CS)	You fear just the sight of the sign outside your dentist's office, an originally neutral stimulus (NS). Why? It has become a conditioned stimulus (CS), associated with the previous conditioned stimulus (CS) of the dental drill.

Voices from the Classroom

Stimulus Discrimination in Childhood Growing up, there was a park at the end of the street where I lived. After finishing my homework, I would join the neighborhood kids down at the park to play until dinner time. Our dads would all whistle to signal when it was time for us to come home for dinner. At first, I ran home when I heard any whistle (stimulus generalization). Then, I learned the sound of MY dad's whistle (stimulus discrimination). This enabled me to be able to play longer as my dinner time was often a half hour later than some of my friends.

Professor Amy Beeman
San Diego Mesa College
San Diego, California

Extinction, Spontaneous Recovery, and Higher-Order Conditioning

What do you think happened when Pavlov repeatedly sounded the tone without presenting food? The answer is that the dogs' salivation gradually declined, a process Pavlov called **extinction**—the gradual weakening of a conditioned response (CR).

Once extinguished, is a conditioned response (CR) gone for good? Extinction is not unlearning—it does not "erase" the learned connection between the stimulus and the response (Bouton et al., 2012; Storsve et al., 2012). Pavlov found that sometimes, after a conditioned response had apparently been extinguished, if he sounded the tone once again the dogs would salivate. This reemergence of a previously extinguished conditioned response (CR) after a period of rest is called **spontaneous recovery** (see *Psychology and You*).

Extinction The gradual disappearance of a conditioned response (CR); it occurs when an unconditioned stimulus (US) is withheld whenever the conditioned stimulus (CS) is presented.

Spontaneous recovery The sudden, reappearance of a previously extinguished conditioned response (CR) after a rest period.

psychology and you **Spontaneous Recovery** Have you ever felt renewed excitement at the sight of a former girlfriend or boyfriend, even though years have passed, you have a new partner, and extinction has occurred? This may be an example of spontaneous recovery. It also may help explain why people might misinterpret a sudden flare-up of feelings and be tempted to return to unhappy relationships. To make matters worse, when a conditioned stimulus is reintroduced after extinction, the conditioning occurs much faster the second time around—a phenomenon known as *reconditioning*.

The good news is that those who have taken general psychology (or read this book) are far less likely to make this mistake. Looking at **Figure 6.5**, you can see that even if you experience spontaneous recovery, your sudden peak of feelings for the old love partner will gradually return to their previously extinguished state. So don't overreact.

GoodMood Photo/Shutterstock

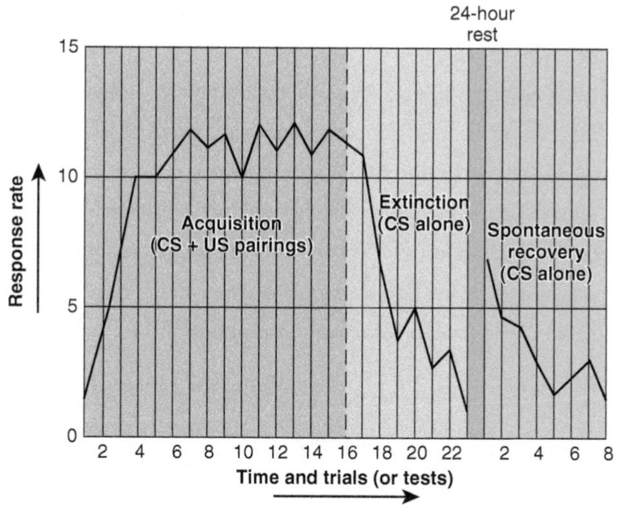

FIGURE 6.5 THREE KEY PRINCIPLES OF CLASSICAL CONDITIONING

During acquisition, the strength of the conditioned response (CR) rapidly increases and then levels off near its maximum. During extinction, the CR declines erratically until it is extinguished. After a "rest" period in which the organism is not exposed to the conditioned stimulus (CS), spontaneous recovery may occur, and the CS will once again elicit a (weakened) CR.

Higher-order conditioning A process in which a neutral stimulus (NS) becomes a conditioned stimulus (CS) through repeated pairings with a previously conditioned stimulus (CS).

Both spontaneous recovery and reconditioning help underscore why it can be so difficult for us to break bad habits (such as eating too much chocolate cake) or internalize new beliefs (such as egalitarian gender or racial beliefs). The phenomenon of **higher-order conditioning (Figure 6.6)** further expands our understanding of complex learned habits and associations.

FIGURE 6.6 THE POWER OF HIGHER-ORDER CONDITIONING | realworldpsychology

Children are not born salivating to the sight of McDonald's golden arches. So why do they beg adults to take them to "Mickey D's" after simply seeing an ad showing the golden arches? It's because of higher-order conditioning, which occurs when a neutral stimulus (NS) becomes a conditioned stimulus (CS) through repeated pairings with a previously conditioned stimulus (CS).

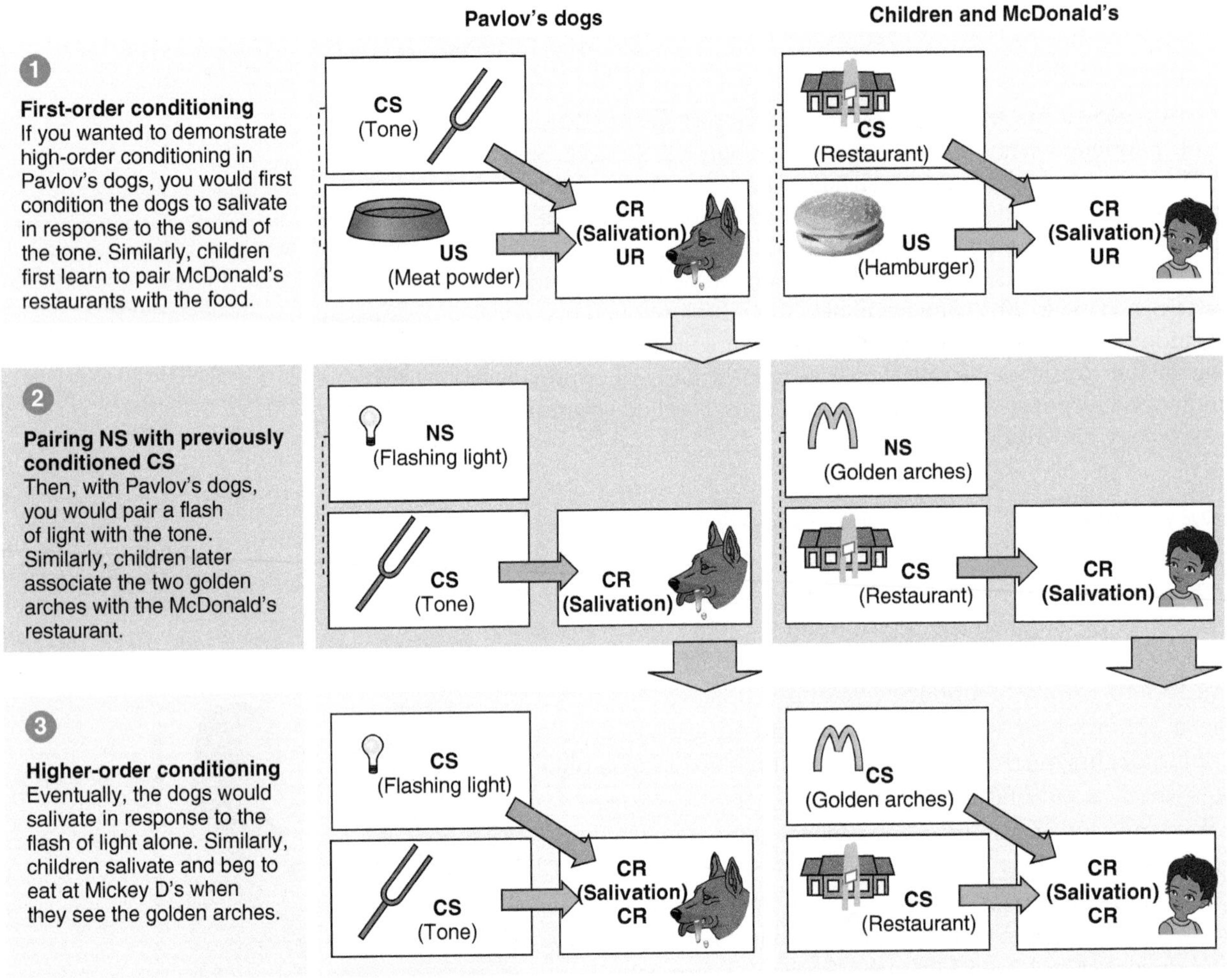
Pavlov's dogs
Children and McDonald's
1
First-order conditioning
If you wanted to demonstrate high-order conditioning in Pavlov's dogs, you would first condition the dogs to salivate in response to the sound of the tone. Similarly, children first learn to pair McDonald's restaurants with the food.
CS (Tone)
US (Meat powder)
CR (Salivation) UR
CS (Restaurant)
US (Hamburger)
CR (Salivation) UR
2
Pairing NS with previously conditioned CS
Then, with Pavlov's dogs, you would pair a flash of light with the tone. Similarly, children later associate the two golden arches with the McDonald's restaurant.
NS (Flashing light)
CS (Tone)
CR (Salivation)
NS (Golden arches)
CS (Restaurant)
CR (Salivation)
3
Higher-order conditioning
Eventually, the dogs would salivate in response to the flash of light alone. Similarly, children salivate and beg to eat at Mickey D's when they see the golden arches.
CS (Flashing light)
CS (Tone)
CR (Salivation) CR
CS (Golden arches)
CS (Restaurant)
CR (Salivation) CR

Voices from the Classroom

Cats and Classical Conditioning To review the major principles of classical conditioning, I use several examples based on a cat's eating behavior. *Basic, initial classical conditioning* = cat meows to the sound of a spoon banging on the side of a food bowl. *Higher-order conditioning* = meowing occurs when the spoon drawer is opened. *Generalization* = meowing occurs when any kitchen drawer is opened. *Discrimination* = meowing occurs when just the spoon drawer is opened. *Extinction* = cat slowly stops meowing because canned cat food is banned due to cat's health issues. *Spontaneous recovery* = one day cat suddenly meows after hearing a spoon bang the side of the food bowl or when the spoon drawer is opened.

Professor Jeffrey Henriques
University of Wisconsin
Madison, Wisconsin

RETRIEVAL PRACTICE: CLASSICAL CONDITIONING

Self-Test

Completing this self-test and comparing your answers with those in Appendix B provides immediate feedback and helpful practice for exams. Additional interactive, self-tests are available at www.wiley.com/college/huffman.

1. _____ conditioning occurs when a neutral stimulus becomes associated with an unconditioned stimulus to elicit a conditioned response.

a. Reflex   b. Instinctive
c. Classical   d. Basic

2. The process of learning associations between environmental stimuli and behavioral responses is known as _____.

a. maturation   b. contiguity learning
c. conditioning   d. latent learning

3. In John Watson's demonstration of classical conditioning with Little Albert, the unconditioned stimulus was _____.

a. symptoms of fear   b. a rat
c. a bath towel   d. a loud noise

4. A baby is bitten by a small dog and then is afraid of all small animals. This is an example of _____.

a. stimulus discrimination   b. extinction
c. reinforcement   d. stimulus generalization

Think Critically

1. How might Watson and Rayner, who conducted the famous "Little Albert" study, have designed a more ethical study of conditioned emotional responses (CERs)?
2. Most classical conditioning is involuntary. Considering this, is it ethical for politicians and advertisers to use classical conditioning to influence our thoughts and behavior? Why or why not?

realworldpsychology

Why can simply hearing the drill in a dentist's office—even if that drill is nowhere near you—make you feel anxious?

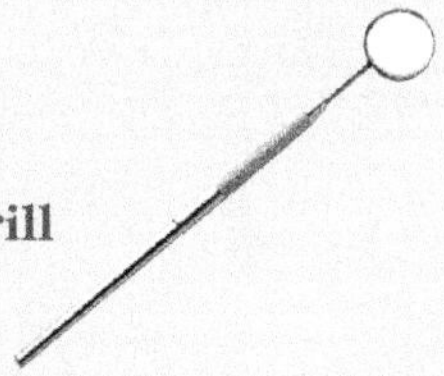

HINT: LOOK IN THE MARGIN FOR Q1

OPERANT CONDITIONING

RETRIEVAL PRACTICE While reading the upcoming sections, respond to each Learning Objective in your own words. Then compare your responses with those found at www.wiley.com/college/huffman.

LEARNING OBJECTIVES

1. **DESCRIBE** Thorndike's and Skinner's contributions to operant conditioning research.
2. **EXPLAIN** how reinforcement and punishment influence behavior.
3. **SUMMARIZE** how shaping and schedules of reinforcement affect behavior.

As we've just seen, classical conditioning is based on what happens *before* we *involuntarily* respond: Something happens to us, and we learn a new response. In contrast, **operant conditioning** is based on what happens *after* we *voluntarily* perform a behavior: We do something and learn from the consequences **(Figure 6.7)**.

Note that *consequences* are the heart of operant conditioning. In classical conditioning, consequences are irrelevant—Pavlov's dogs still got to eat whether they salivated or not. But in operant conditioning, the organism voluntarily performs a behavior (an *operant*) that produces a consequence—either reinforcement or punishment. **Reinforcement** strengthens the response, making it more likely to recur. **Punishment** weakens the response, making it less likely to recur.

Operant conditioning Learning through voluntary behavior and its subsequent consequences; reinforcement increases behavioral tendencies, whereas punishment decreases them.

Reinforcement The adding or taking away of a stimulus following a response, which increases the likelihood of that response being repeated.

Punishment The adding or taking away of a stimulus following a response, which decreases the likelihood of that response being repeated.

FIGURE 6.7 **CLASSICAL VERSUS OPERANT CONDITIONING**

Classical conditioning is based on involuntary behavior, whereas operant conditioning is based on voluntary behavior.

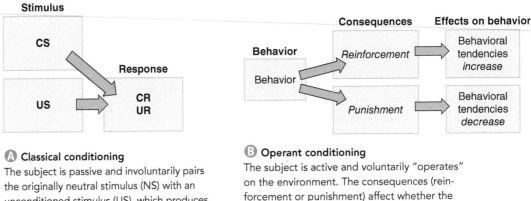

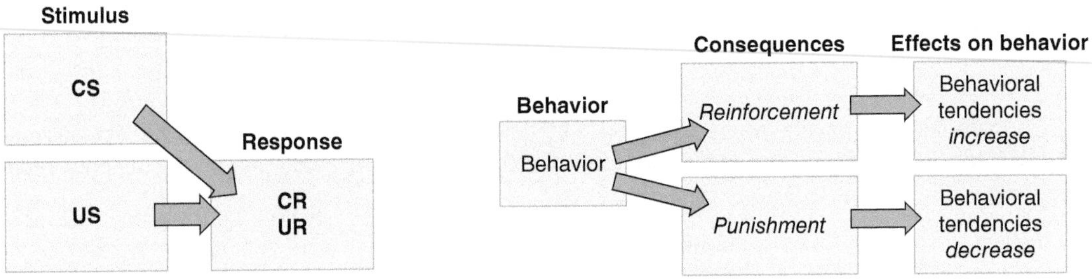

Ⓐ Classical conditioning
The subject is passive and involuntarily pairs the originally neutral stimulus (NS) with an unconditioned stimulus (US), which produces a conditioned stimulus (CS) that leads to a learned, conditioned response (CR).

Ⓑ Operant conditioning
The subject is active and voluntarily "operates" on the environment. The consequences (reinforcement or punishment) affect whether the behavior will increase or decrease.

Q2

Thankfully, operant conditioning principles can be used to change our negative health-related behaviors by reinforcing healthy choices and punishing unhealthy ones. For example, only allowing yourself to watch TV while exercising will improve your general physical health. And, several studies have shown that decreasing the cost of fruits and vegetables, while increasing the price of soda, can lead people to make healthier food and drink choices (Eyles et al., 2012). Similarly, increasing the cost of smoking—often by increasing taxes on cigarettes—reduces smoking rates (Cavazos-Rehg et al., 2012; Wilson et al., 2012). The effect of increased taxes on cigarettes is particularly true for heavy smokers, who pay considerably more due to their higher consumption, and for teenagers, who tend to have less discretionary income.

Beginnings of Operant Conditioning

Law of effect Thorndike's rule that responses that produce a satisfying effect are more likely to occur again, whereas those that produce a discomforting effect become less likely to occur again.

Edward Thorndike (1874–1949), a pioneer of operant conditioning, determined that the frequency of a behavior is modified by its consequences (Thorndike, 1911). Thorndike's **law of effect** was an important first step in understanding how consequences can modify active, voluntary behaviors **(Figure 6.8)**.

FIGURE 6.8 **THORNDIKE'S LAW OF EFFECT**

In his most famous experiment, Thorndike put a cat inside a specially built puzzle box. When the cat stepped on a pedal inside the box (at first, through trial and error), the door opened, and the cat could get out and eat. With each additional success, the cat's actions became more purposeful, and it soon learned to open the door immediately (from Thorndike, 1898).

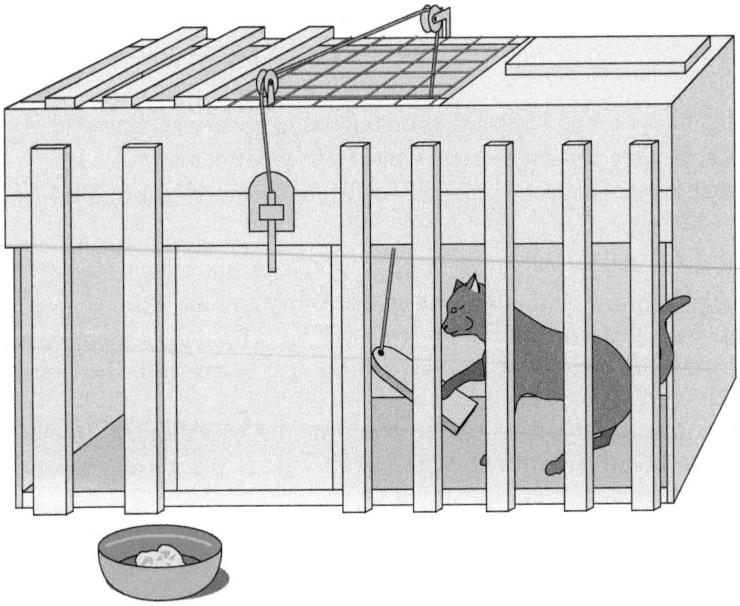

B. F. Skinner (1904–1990) extended Thorndike's law of effect to more complex behaviors. He also emphasized that reinforcement and punishment should always be presented *after* the behavior of interest has occurred. This was because Skinner believed that the only way to know how we have influenced someone's behavior is to check whether it increases or decreases. As he pointed out, we too often think we're reinforcing or punishing behavior when we're actually doing the opposite (see *Psychology and You*).

psychology and you **The Challenge of Reinforcement** A professor may think she is encouraging shy students to talk by repeatedly praising them each time they speak up in class. But what if you are one of those shy students and are embarrassed by this extra attention? If so, you may actually decrease the number of times you talk in class. Can you see why it's important to always remember that what is reinforcing or punishing for one person may not be so for another?

Michele Cozzolino/Shutterstock

Reinforcement and Punishment

Reinforcers, which strengthen a response, can be a powerful tool in all parts of our lives. Psychologists group them into two types, primary and secondary. **Primary reinforcers** satisfy an intrinsic, unlearned biological need (like food, water, and sex). **Secondary reinforcers** are not intrinsic; the value of this reinforcer is learned (like money, praise, and attention). Each type of reinforcer can produce **positive reinforcement** or **negative reinforcement**, depending on whether certain stimuli are added or taken away **(Table 6.2)**.

Primary reinforcers Any stimuli that increase the probability of a response because of their innate, biological value, such as food and water.

Secondary reinforcers Any stimuli that increase the probability of a response because of their learned value, such as money and material possessions.

Positive reinforcement The adding (or presenting) of a stimulus, thereby strengthening a response and making it more likely to recur.

Negative reinforcement The taking away (or removing) of a stimulus, thereby strengthening a response and making it more likely to recur.

TABLE 6.2 HOW REINFORCEMENT INCREASES (OR STRENGTHENS) BEHAVIOR psychology and you

	POSITIVE REINFORCEMENT Stimulus added (+) and behavior increases	NEGATIVE REINFORCEMENT Stimulus taken away (–) and behavior increases
PRIMARY REINFORCERS *Satisfy biological needs*	You hug your baby and he smiles at you. The "addition" of his smile increases the likelihood that you will hug him again. You do a favor for a friend and she buys you lunch in return, which makes it more likely that you'll do more favors for your friend in the future.	You baby is crying, so you hug him and he stops crying. The "removal" of crying increases the likelihood that you will hug him again when he cries. You take an aspirin for your headache, which takes away the pain, and makes it more likely that you'll take an aspirin again when you have future pains.
SECONDARY REINFORCERS *Satisfy learned needs*	You increase profits and receive $200 as a bonus. The "addition" of the bonus increases the likelihood that you'll work hard in the future to increase profits. You study hard and receive a good grade on your psychology exam, which makes it more likely that you'll study hard in the future.	After high sales, your boss says you won't have to work on weekends. The "removal" of having to work on weekends makes it more likely that you'll work harder for high sales in the future. You're allowed to skip the final exam because you did so well on your unit exams, which makes it more likely that you'll work hard to do well on unit exams in the future.

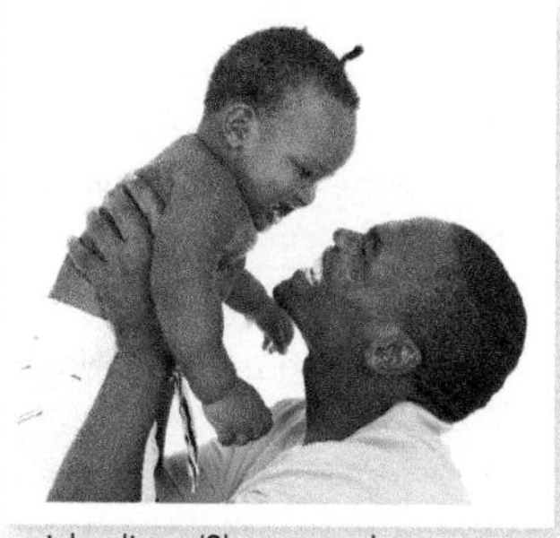
michaeljung/Shutterstock

© diego_cervo/iStockphoto

Premack principle The use of a naturally occurring high-frequency response to reinforce and increase low-frequency responses.

Primary punishers Any stimuli that decrease the probability of a response because of their innate, biological value, such as hunger and thirst.

Secondary punishers Any stimuli that decrease the probability of a response because of their learned value, such as poor grades or a parking ticket.

Positive punishment The addition (or presenting) of a stimulus, thereby weakening a response and making it less likely to recur.

Negative punishment The taking away (or removing) of a stimulus, thereby weakening a response and making it less likely to recur.

Interestingly, when you make yourself do some necessary but tedious task—say, paying bills—before letting yourself go to the movies, you are not only using positive reinforcement, you're also using the **Premack principle**. This principle is named after psychologist David Premack, who found that any naturally occurring, high-frequency response can be used to reinforce and increase low-frequency responses (Goldfield, 2012; Poling, 2010). Recognizing that you love to go to movies, you intuitively tie your less desirable low-frequency activity (paying bills) to your high-frequency or highly desirable behavior (going to the movies).

It's very important to note that negative reinforcement is NOT punishment. The two concepts are actually completely opposite. Reinforcement (both positive and negative) *strengthens* a behavior, whereas punishment (both positive and negative) *weakens* a behavior. Knowing that this terminology is confusing, we encourage you to think of positive and negative in a *mathematical* sense. Instead of automatically assuming that positive means something "good" and negative means something "bad," recognize that in mathematics positive is adding something [+], and negative is taking something away [–].

As with reinforcement, there are two kinds of punishers—primary and secondary, and two kinds of punishment—positive and negative.

Primary punishers are unmet innate, biological needs (e.g., hunger, thirst, discomfort). **Secondary punishers** are unmet learned needs (e.g., poor grades, bad hair day, loss of an election). In turn, **positive punishment** is the addition (+) of a stimulus that decreases (or weakens) the likelihood of the response occurring again. **Negative punishment** is the taking away (–) of a reinforcing stimulus, which decreases (or weakens) the likelihood of the response occurring again **(Table 6.3)**. (To check your understanding of the principles of reinforcement and punishment, see **Figure 6.9**.)

Keep in mind that punishment is a difficult, and tricky, concept that's difficult to use appropriately and effectively. We often think we're punishing yet the behaviors continue. Similarly, we too often mistakenly think we're reinforcing when we're actually punishing. The key thing to remember is that punishment, by definition, is a process that adds or takes away something and causes a behavior to decrease. If

TABLE 6.3 HOW PUNISHMENT DECREASES (OR WEAKENS) BEHAVIOR psychology and you

	POSITIVE PUNISHMENT **Stimulus added (+) and behavior decreases (or weakens)**	NEGATIVE PUNISHMENT **Stimulus taken away (–) and behavior decreases (or weakens)**	
PRIMARY PUNISHERS Unlearned, *biological needs are not met*	A rat receives an electric shock when it crosses an electric grid. The "addition" of the shock decreases the likelihood that the rat will cross the electric grid in the future. You must run four extra laps on a hot day because you were late to your gym class. Adding the four extra laps makes it less likely that you'll be late for gym class in the future.	A hungry child is denied dessert because she refused to eat her dinner. The "removal" of the dessert option decreases the likelihood of the child refusing to eat her dinner in the future. You lose sleep for several nights because you didn't study ahead of time in order to prepare for your final exams. The loss of sleep makes it less likely that you'll be unprepared for future final exams.	 © jtyler/iStockphoto
SECONDARY PUNISHERS *Learned needs are not met*	A parent adds extra chores following a child's bad report card. The "addition" of the extra chores decreases the likelihood that the child will get a bad report card in the future. You study hard and still receive a low grade on your psychology exam. The "addition" of the low grade after studying hard decreases the likelihood that you will study hard the future.	A child's favorite toy is taken away because he/she disobeyed. The "removal" of the toy decreases the likelihood that the child will disobey in the future. Your bonus is taken away because of poor performance on your job. Removing the bonus makes it less likely that you'll turn in a poor performance in the future.	 © ajkkafe/iStockphoto

FIGURE 6.9 **USING THE "SKINNER BOX" FOR BOTH REINFORCEMENT AND PUNISHMENT**

To test his behavioral theories, Skinner used an animal, usually a pigeon or a rat, and an apparatus that has come to be called a *Skinner Box*.

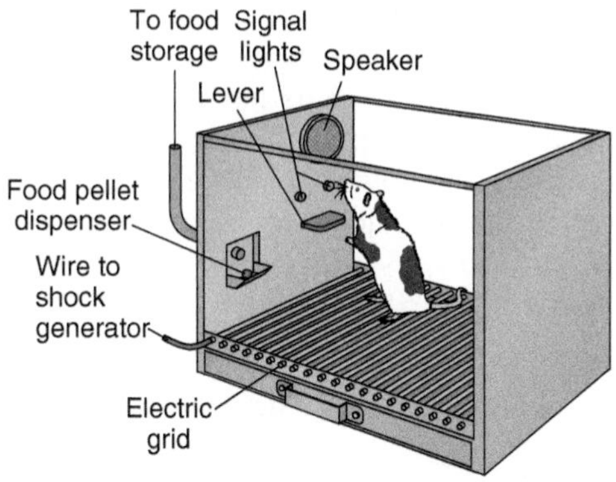

Ⓐ In Skinner's basic experimental design, an animal (such as a rat) could press a lever and food pellets or shocks (administered through an electric grid on the cage floor) could be used to give the animal reinforcement or punishment.

Ⓑ Are these examples of positive reinforcement, negative reinforcement, positive punishment, or negative punishment? Fill in the appropriate learning principle in the space provided.

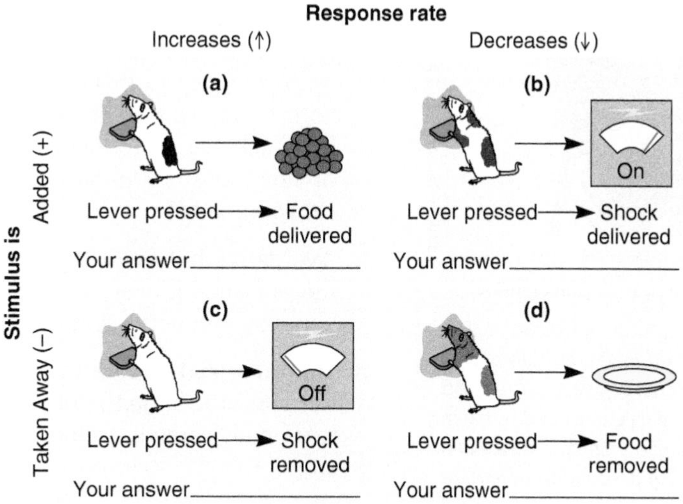

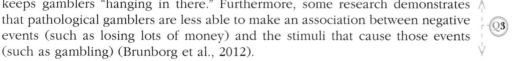

Answers: (a) positive reinforcement, (b) positive punishment, (c) negative reinforcement, (d) negative punishment

the behavior does not decrease it's NOT punishment! So it's always important to watch the actual behavior and not what you think should happen. Thus, if parents ignore all the A's on their child's report card ("taking away" encouraging comments) and ask repeated questions about the B's and C's, they may unintentionally be punishing the child's excellent grade achievement and weakening the likelihood of future A's. Similarly, dog owners who yell at or spank their dogs for finally coming to them ("adding" verbal or physical aggression) after being called several times are actually punishing the desired behavior—coming when called.

In addition to these problems with punishment, to be effective it should always be *clear*, *direct*, *immediate*, and *consistent*. However, in the real world, this is extremely hard to do. Police officers cannot stop every driver each and every time they speed. To make matters worse, when punishment is not immediate, during the delay, the behavior is likely to be reinforced on a partial schedule, which makes it highly resistant to extinction.

Voices from the Classroom

Operant Conditioning and Driving with Kids I have two children, who used to fight like cats and dogs, especially in the confined area of the car. Rather than punish them, I decided to ignore their bickering (as long as no arms or legs flew out the window). If we made it all the way to the shopping mall without an argument, I immediately praised them highly, showed excitement, and told them how great I felt. Another time when they made it to the mall without bickering, I stopped and we had ice cream on the way home. (Trips with bickering were ignored; no reinforcement.) Happily, within about five or six trips to the mall, there was virtually no bickering. It was awesome!

Professor Barbara Kennedy
Brevard Community College
Palm Bay, Florida

Think about gambling. It should be a punishing situation; gamblers usually lose far more than they win. However, the fact that they occasionally win keeps gamblers "hanging in there." Furthermore, some research demonstrates that pathological gamblers are less able to make an association between negative events (such as losing lots of money) and the stimuli that cause those events (such as gambling) (Brunborg et al., 2012). Q3

Even if punishment immediately follows the misbehavior, the recipient may only learn what *not* to do, but not necessarily what he or she *should* do. It's much more efficient to teach someone by giving him or her clear examples of correct behavior than to simply punish the incorrect behavior.

Photo Researchers, Inc.

Is this positive or negative punishment?

Answer: It depends. If the child's behavior decreases, it would be punishment. Forcing him or her to sit in a chair away from other people and activities removes, or takes away (−), the opportunity to be near and interact with caregivers and/or playmates.

In sum, reinforcement and punishment can change behavior in laboratory settings, but evidence from real life suggests that these two approaches are not equal in their ease of application or effectiveness. Also, reinforcement is generally more ethical than punishment. However, punishment is sometimes necessary. If you decide to use it in cases of serious and potentially dangerous situations, keep in mind that punishment has at least seven important drawbacks:

1. **Passive aggressiveness** For the recipient, punishment often leads to frustration, anger, and possible aggression. But most of us have learned from experience that retaliatory aggression toward a punisher (especially one who is bigger and more powerful) is usually followed by more punishment. So instead, we may resort to subtle techniques, called *passive aggressiveness*, in which we deliberately show up late, "forget" to do an assigned chore, or complete the chore in a half-hearted way (Hopwood & Wright, 2012; Johnson, 2008).
2. **Avoidance behavior** No one likes to be punished, so we naturally try to avoid the punisher. If every time you come home a parent or spouse starts yelling at you, you will delay coming home—or will find another place to go.
3. **Inappropriate modeling** Have you ever seen a parent spank or hit his or her child for hitting another child? Ironically, the punishing parent may unintentionally serve as a "model" for the same behavior he or she is attempting to stop.
4. **Temporary suppression versus elimination** Punishment generally suppresses the behavior only temporarily, while the punisher is nearby.
5. **Learned helplessness** Research shows that nonhuman animals will fail to learn an escape response after experiencing inescapable aversive events (Jones et al., 2013; Maier, 1970; Seligman & Maier, 1967). Can you see how this phenomenon, known as *learned helplessness*, might explain, in part, why some people stay in abusive relationships (Miller et al., 2012)? Or why some students, who've experienced many failures in academic settings, might passively accept punishingly low grades, and/or engage in self-defeating behaviors, such as procrastination or minimal effort responses?
6. **Rewarded aggression** Because punishment often produces a decrease in undesired behavior, at least for the moment, the punisher is in effect rewarded for applying punishment.
7. **Perpetuated aggression** A vicious cycle may be established in which both the punisher and recipient are reinforced for inappropriate behavior—the punisher for punishing and the recipient for being fearful and submissive. This side effect partially explains the escalation of violence in family abuse and bullying (Anderson et al., 2008; Hamby & Grych, 2013; Miller et al., 2012).

Using this list of punishment's seven drawbacks, see if you can explain the following questions: Why do you think roommates, children, and spouses refuse to load the dishwasher despite repeated nagging? Why do drivers quickly slow down when they see a police car following behind and then quickly resume speeding once the police officer is out of sight? Given all the problems associated with punishment, why is it so often used?

The best answer to the dishwasher question may be item number 1—*passive aggressiveness*. The driver speeding up after the police officer leaves may be an example of number 4—*temporary suppression*. And the continued use of punishment, despite its drawbacks, may be best explained by the sixth and seventh points—*rewarded and perpetuated aggression*!

Shaping and Maintaining Behavior

It's easy to see how reinforcement is better than punishment for teaching and learning of most things, but how would you teach someone complex things like how to play the piano or to speak a foreign language? How do seals in zoos and amusement parks learn how to balance beach balls on their noses, or how to clap their flippers together on command from the trainers?

For new and complex behaviors such as these, which aren't likely to occur naturally, **shaping** is the key. Skinner believed that shaping, or *rewarding successive approximations*, explains a variety of abilities that each of us possesses, from eating with a fork to playing a musical instrument, to driving a car. Parents, athletic coaches, teachers, therapists, and animal trainers all use shaping techniques (Heinicke et al., 2013; Lefrancois, 2012; McDougall, 2013).

For example, Momoko, a female monkey, is famous in Japan for her water-skiing, deep-sea diving, and other amazing abilities **(Figure 6.10)**. Her animal trainers used the successive steps of shaping to teach her these skills. First, they reinforced Momoko (with a small food treat) for standing or sitting on the water ski. Then they reinforced her each time she accomplished a successive step in learning to water-ski.

Kaku Kurita/Getty Images, Inc.

FIGURE 6.10 **CAN SHAPING TEACH A MONKEY TO WATERSKI?**

Now that we've discussed how we learn complex behaviors through shaping, you may want to know how to maintain it. When Skinner was training his animals, he found that learning was most rapid if the response was reinforced every time it occurred—a pattern called **continuous reinforcement**.

As you have probably noticed, however, real life seldom provides continuous reinforcement. Instead, most of our responses are reinforced only sometimes—a pattern called **partial (or intermittent) reinforcement**. Think of how parents or spouses keep nagging one another even when they're only occasionally reinforced, how telemarketers keep calling even when most people hang up on them, and how children keep whining even when parents only occasionally give in! The fact that these behaviors are only intermittently reinforced explains why they're so persistent—and so resistant to extinction! On a happier note, partial (intermittent) reinforcement also encourages productive, desirable behaviors like business owners who keep revising their product and students who keep plugging away at their college classes until they graduate. For better or worse, persistence pays off!

Keep in mind that a continuous schedule is best used in the initial stages of learning. However, once a task is well learned, you'll want to move on to a partial (intermittent) schedule—thanks to its strong resistance to extinction.

When using partial reinforcement, it's also important to note that some partial **schedules of reinforcement** are better suited for maintaining or changing behavior than others. As you can see in **Table 6.4**, there are four schedules—**fixed ratio (FR)**, **variable ratio (VR)**, **fixed interval (FI)**, and **variable interval (VI)**.

Before going on, **Figure 6.11** offers even more examples of how operant conditioning applies to everyday life. In addition, if you're feeling a bit overwhelmed with all the terms and concepts for both classical and operant condtioning, carefully study the summary provided in **Table 6.5**. Also, note that while it's convenient to divide classical and operant conditioning into separate categories, almost all behaviors result from a combination of both forms of conditioning.

Shaping A training method where reinforcement is delivered for successive approximations of the desired response.

Continuous reinforcement A reinforcement pattern in which every correct response is reinforced.

Partial (intermittent) reinforcement A reinforcement pattern in which some, but not all, correct responses are reinforced.

Schedules of reinforcement Specific patterns of reinforcement (either fixed or variable) that determine when a behavior will be reinforced.

Fixed ratio (FR) schedule A schedule of reinforcement in which a reinforcer is delivered for the first response made after a fixed number of responses.

Variable ratio (VR) schedule A schedule of reinforcement in which a reinforcer is delivered for the first response made after a variable number of responses whose average is predetermined.

Fixed interval (FI) schedule A schedule of reinforcement in which a reinforcer is delivered for the first response made after a fixed period of time.

Variable interval (VI) schedule A schedule of reinforcement in which a reinforcer is delivered for the first response made after a variable period of time whose average is predetermined.

TABLE 6.4 FOUR SCHEDULES OF PARTIAL (INTERMITTENT) REINFORCEMENT | realworldpsychology

		Definitions	Response rates	Example
Ratio schedules (response based)	**Fixed ratio (FR)**	Reinforcement occurs after a predetermined number of responses	High rate of response, but a brief drop-off just after reinforcement	You receive a free flight from your frequent flyer program after accumulating a given number of flight miles. 
	Variable ratio (VR)	Reinforcement occurs after a varying number of responses	High response rate, no pause after reinforcement, and very resistant to extinction	Slot machines are designed to pay out after an average number of responses (maybe every 10 times), but any one machine may pay out on the first responses, then seventh, then the twentieth. 
Interval schedules (time based)	**Fixed Interval (FI)**	Rainforcement occurs after a fixed period of time	Responses tend to increase as the time for the next reinforcement is near, but drop off after reinforcement and during interval	You receive a monthly paycheck. Rat's behavior is reinforced with a food pellet when (or if) it presses a bar after 20 seconds have elapsed. 
	Variable interval (VI)	Reinforcement occurs after varying periods of time	Relatively low, but steady, response rates because respondents cannot predict when reward will come	Your professor gives pop quizzes at random times throughout the course. Rat's behavior is reinforced with a food pellet after a response and a variable unpredictable interval of time. 

FIGURE 6.11 OPERANT CONDITIONING IN EVERYDAY LIFE | realworldpsychology

Reinforcement and punishment shape behavior in many aspects of our lives.

A Prejudice and discrimination
Although prejudice and discrimination show up early in life, children are not born believing others are inferior. What reinforcement might these boys receive for teasing this boy? Can you see how operant conditioning, beginning at an early age, can promote prejudice and discrimination?

B Superstition
Like prejudice and discrimination, we are not born being superstitious, these attitudes are learned—partly through operant conditioning. Knocking on wood for good fortune, a bride wearing "something old" at her wedding, or this baseball player placing gum on his helmet are all superstitious behaviors that generally develop from accidental reinforcement. For example, the baseball player might have once placed his gum on his helmet and then hit a home run. He then associated the gum with winning and continued the practice for all later games.

C Biofeedback
Biofeedback relies on operant conditioning to treat ailments such as anxiety and chronic pain. For example, chronic pain patients are sometimes connected to electrodes and watch a monitor screen with a series of flashing lights, or listen to different beeps, which display changes in their internal bodily functions. The patients then use the machine's "feedback," flashing lights or beeps, to gauge their progress as they try various relaxation strategies to receive corresponding relief from the pain of muscle tension.

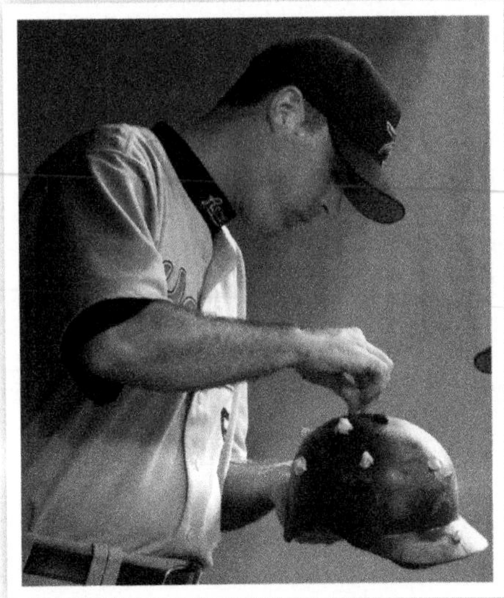

TABLE 6.5 COMPARING CLASSICAL AND OPERANT CONDITIONING

	Classical Conditioning	Operant Conditioning
Example	Cringing at the sound of a dentist's drill	A baby cries and you pick it up
Pioneers	Ivan Pavlov	Edward Thorndike
	John B. Watson	B. F. Skinner
Key Terms	Neutral stimulus (NS)	Reinforcers and punishers (primary/secondary)
	Unconditioned stimulus (US)	Reinforcement (positive/negative)
	Conditioned stimulus (CS)	Punishment (positive/negative)
	Unconditioned response (UR)	Superstition
	Conditioned response (CR)	Shaping
	Conditioned emotional response (CER)	Schedules of reinforcement (continuous/partial)
Major Similarities	Acquisition	Acquisition
	Generalization	Generalization
	Discrimination	Discrimination
	Extinction	Extinction
	Spontaneous recovery	Spontaneous recovery
	Higher-order conditioning	Higher-order conditioning
Major Differences	Subject is passive; learning based on involuntary responses and pairing of NS with US	Subject is active; learning based on voluntary responses and their consequences
	Order of effects (most effective when NS comes *before* US)	Order of effects (most effective when reinforcement or punishment come *after* behavior)

RETRIEVAL PRACTICE: OPERANT CONDITIONING

Self-Test

Completing this self-test and comparing your answers with those in Appendix B provides immediate feedback and helpful practice for exams. Additional interactive, self-tests are available at www.wiley.com/college/huffman.

1. Learning in which voluntary responses are controlled by their consequences is called _____.

a. self-efficacy
b. operant conditioning
c. classical conditioning
d. shaping

2. An employer who gives his or her employees a cash bonus after they've done a good job is an example of _____.

a. positive reinforcement
b. incremental conditioning
c. classical conditioning
d. bribery

3. _____ reinforcers normally satisfy an unlearned biological need.

a. Positive
b. Negative
c. Primary
d. none of these options

4. The most effective way to decrease the probability of your teenager engaging in undesired behaviors is to use _____.

a. punishment and negative reinforcement
b. modeling and extinction
c. extinction and negative reinforcement
d. all of these options

Think Critically

1. You observe a parent yelling "No!" to his or her child who is screaming for candy in a supermarket. Given what you've learned about operant conditioning, can you predict how both the parent and the child will respond in similar future situations?

2. Can you think of a better alternative to yelling "No!"?

realworldpsychology

How can decreasing the cost of fruit and vegetables lead to healthier eating?

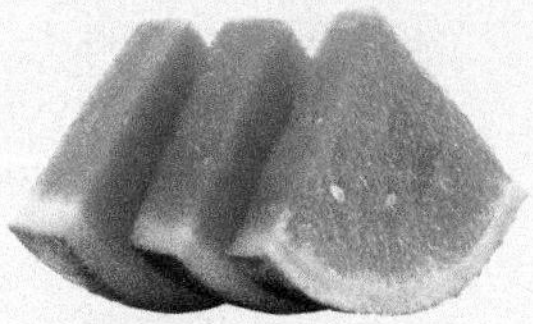

Why do gamblers have such trouble quitting, even when they continue to lose money?

HINT: LOOK IN THE MARGIN FOR Q2 AND Q3

COGNITIVE-SOCIAL LEARNING

LEARNING OBJECTIVES

RETRIEVAL PRACTICE While reading the upcoming sections, respond to each Learning Objective in your own words. Then compare your responses with those found at www.wiley.com/college/huffman.

1. **SUMMARIZE** the cognitive-social theory of learning.
2. **DESCRIBE** insight learning and latent learning.
3. **EXPLAIN** the principles of observational learning.

So far, we have examined learning processes that involve associations between a stimulus and an observable behavior. Although some behaviorists believe that almost all learning can be explained in such stimulus–response terms, other psychologists feel that all of learning can not be explained solely by operant and classical conditioning. **Cognitive-social learning theory** (also called cognitive-social learning or cognitive-behavioral theory) incorporates the general concepts of conditioning, but rather than relying on a simple S–R (stimulus and response) model, this theory emphasizes the interpretation or thinking that occurs within the organism: S–O–R (stimulus–organism–response).

Cognitive-social learning theory A theory that emphasizes the roles of thinking and social learning.

According to this view, humans have attitudes, beliefs, expectations, motivations, and emotions that affect learning. Furthermore, humans and many nonhuman animals also are social creatures that are capable of learning new behaviors through the observation and imitation of others. For example, children who perceive that at least one of their parents is physically active are much more likely to be physically active themselves (Voss & Sandercock, 2013).

Insight and Latent Learning

Early behaviorists likened the mind to a "black box" whose workings could not be observed directly. German psychologist Wolfgang Köhler (1887-1967) wanted to look inside the box. He believed that there was more to learning—especially learning to solve a complex problem—than responding to stimuli in a trial-and-error fashion.

In one of a series of experiments, Köhler placed a banana just outside the reach of a caged chimpanzee. To reach the banana, the chimp had to use a stick placed near the cage to extend its reach. Köhler noticed that the chimp did not solve the problem in a random trial-and-error fashion. Instead, he seemed to sit and think about the situation for a while. Then, in a flash of **insight**, the chimp

Insight A sudden understanding or realization of how a problem can be solved.

picked up the stick and maneuvered the banana to within its grasp (Köhler, 1925). Köhler called this *insight learning* because some internal mental event, which he could only describe as "insight," went on between the presentation of the banana and the use of the stick to retrieve it. (See **Figure 6.12** for another example of how Köhler's chimps solved a different version of the same problem.)

Like Köhler, Edward C. Tolman (1898–1956) believed that previous researchers underestimated human and nonhuman animals' cognitive processes and cognitive learning. He noted that, when allowed to roam aimlessly in an experimental maze with no food reward at the end, rats seemed to develop a **cognitive map**, or mental representation of the maze.

To further test the idea of cognitive learning, Tolman allowed one group of rats to aimlessly explore a maze, with no reinforcement. A second group was reinforced with food whenever they reached the end of the maze. The third group was not rewarded during the first 10 days of the trial, but starting on day 11, they found food at the end of the maze.

As expected from simple operant conditioning, the first and third groups were slow to learn the maze, whereas the second group, which had reinforcement, showed fast, steady improvement. However, when the third group started receiving reinforcement (on the 11th day), their learning quickly caught up to the group that had been reinforced every time (Tolman & Honzik, 1930). This showed that the nonreinforced rats had been thinking and building cognitive maps of the area during their aimless wandering and that their **latent learning** only showed up when there was a reason to display it (the food reward).

Cognitive maps and latent learning are not limited to rats. For example, a chipmunk will pay little attention to a new log in its territory (after initially checking it for food). When a predator comes along, however, the chipmunk heads directly for and hides beneath the log. Recent experiments provide additional clear evidence of latent learning and the existence of internal, cognitive maps in both human and nonhuman animals (Lew, 2011; Nadel, 2013; Redish & Ekstrom, 2013) **(Figure 6.13)**.

FIGURE 6.12 COGNITIVE-SOCIAL LEARNING

In a second Köhler experiment, chimpanzees were placed in a room with several scattered boxes, none of which was high enough to enable them to reach the banana. They initially ran around and unproductively jumped for the banana. Then, all of a sudden, they saw the solution—they stacked the boxes and then used them to climb up and grab the banana! (Also, note how the chimp in the background is engaged in observational learning, our next topic.)

Cognitive map A mental image of a three-dimensional space that an organism has navigated.

Latent learning Hidden learning that exists without behavioral signs.

Observational learning The learning of new behaviors or information by watching and imitating others (also known as social learning or modeling).

Observational Learning

In addition to classical and operant conditioning and cognitive processes (such as insight and latent learning), we also learn many things through **observational learning**. From birth to death, observational learning is very important to our

Ty Milford/Masterfile

FIGURE 6.13 COGNITIVE MAPS IN HUMANS

This young woman rides through her neighborhood for fun, without a specific destination. However, she is developing her own internal cognitive maps, and she could probably easily return to the local park even though she might not be able to give specific directions. Can you think of examples of similar cognitive maps from your own life?

Albert Bandura

Albert Bandura

FIGURE 6.14 **BANDURA'S BOBO DOLL STUDY**

biological, psychological, and social survival (the *biopsychosocial model*). Watching others helps us avoid dangerous stimuli in our environment, teaches us how to think and feel, and shows us how to act and interact socially (Hora & Klassen, 2012; Kalat, 2013).

Q4 Unfortunately, watching others also may lead to negative outcomes. For example, one correlational study found that teenagers who watched high levels of televised sexual content were twice as likely to become pregnant or get a partner pregnant within the next three years compared to teens who watched low levels (Chandra et al., 2008). Further research suggests that these unintended pregnancies may reflect the fact that mainstream media focuses on glamorized, casual sex, while ignoring the risks and consequences (Strasburger, 2010).

Much of our knowledge about the power of observational learning initially came from the work of Albert Bandura and his colleagues (Bandura, 2007; Bandura, Ross, & Ross, 1961; Bandura & Walters, 1963). Wanting to know whether children learn to be aggressive by watching others be aggressive, Bandura and his colleagues set up several experiments. They allowed children to watch a live or televised adult model punch, throw, and hit a large inflated Bobo doll **(Figure 6.14 top)**. Later, the children were allowed to play in the same room with the same toys. As Bandura hypothesized, children who had seen the live or televised aggressive model were much more aggressive with the Bobo doll than children who had not seen the modeled aggression **(Figure 6.14 bottom)**. In other words, "Monkey see, monkey do."

Thanks to the Bobo doll studies and his other experiments, Bandura established that observational learning requires at least four separate processes: *attention*, *retention*, *reproduction*, and *motivation* **(Figure 6.15)**.

FIGURE 6.15 **BANDURA'S FOUR KEY FACTORS IN OBSERVATIONAL LEARNING**

A child wanting to become a premier ballerina would need to incorporate these four factors to maximize learning.

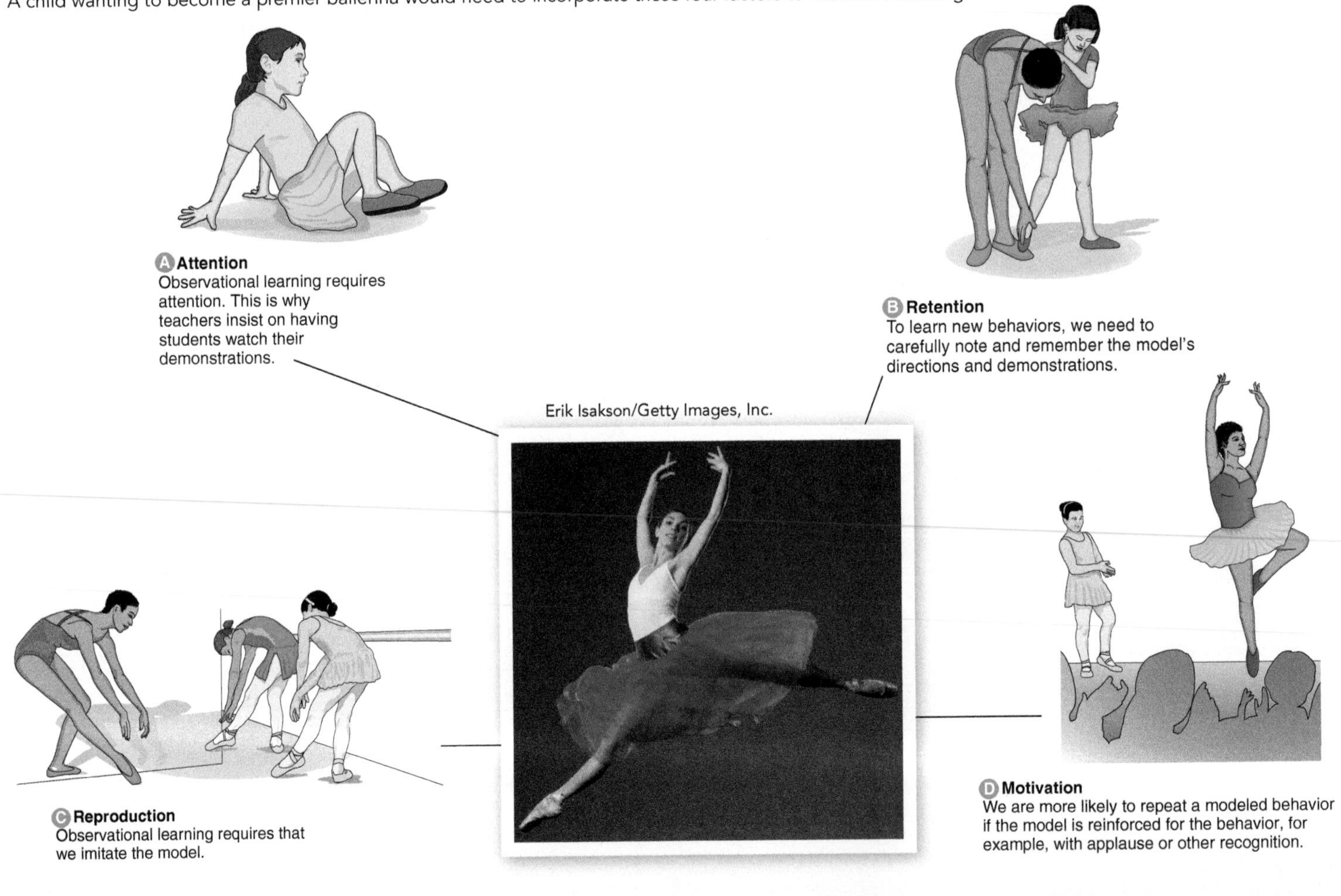
A Attention
Observational learning requires attention. This is why teachers insist on having students watch their demonstrations.
B Retention
To learn new behaviors, we need to carefully note and remember the model's directions and demonstrations.
Erik Isakson/Getty Images, Inc.
C Reproduction
Observational learning requires that we imitate the model.
D Motivation
We are more likely to repeat a modeled behavior if the model is reinforced for the behavior, for example, with applause or other recognition.

PSYCHSCIENCE

THE (SCARY) POWER OF OBSERVATIONAL LEARNING

Karl Prouse/Catwalking/Getty Images

© aldomurillo/iStockphoto

© chrisgramly/iStockphoto

What do we learn from images like these? Researchers in one study wanted to know whether the preference for the thin ideal is seen even in very young children, who should have little exposure to this type of media image of women (Harriger et al., 2010). To examine this question, these researchers asked preschool girls (ages 3 to 5) to play a game of either Candy Land or Chutes and Ladders with them. The girls were told they could select which of three game piece characters they wanted to be. Unlike the women in the photos above, these game piece characters were exactly the same, except in terms of their body size (one character was thin, one was average, one was fat).

If the girls had no preference for a particular body type, then about 33% of the girls should have randomly chosen one of the three figures. However, the researchers found that the girls showed an overwhelming preference for the character with the thin figure:

- 69% chose the thin figure.
- 20% chose the average figure.
- Only 11% chose the fat figure.

When asked to explain why they chose a particular figure, many of the girls expressed negative attitudes about the fat figure. For example, one girl said, "I hate her because she has a fat stomach." Another girl said, "I don't want to be her; she's fat and ugly." This research sadly suggests that this preference for the thinness norm emerges very early in life.

RESEARCH CHALLENGE

1. Based on the information provided, did this study (Harriger et al., 2010) use descriptive, correlational, and/or experimental research?
2. If you chose:
   - descriptive research, is this a naturalistic observation, survey/interview, case study, or archival research?
   - correlational research, is this a positive, negative, or zero correlation?
   - experimental research, label the IV, DV, experimental group(s), and control group.

>> CHECK YOUR ANSWERS IN APPENDIX B.

NOTE: The information provided in this study is admittedly limited, but the level of detail is similar to what is presented in most textbooks and public reports of research findings. Answering these questions, and then comparing your answers to those in the Appendix, will help you become a better critical thinker and consumer of scientific research.

RETRIEVAL PRACTICE: COGNITIVE-SOCIAL LEARNING

Self-Test

Completing this self-test and comparing your answers with those in Appendix B provides immediate feedback and helpful practice for exams. Additional interactive, self-tests are available at www.wiley.com/college/huffman.

1. Insight is _____.

a. based on unconscious classical conditioning
b. an innate human reflex
c. a sudden flash of understanding
d. an artifact of operant conditioning

2. When walking to your psychology class, you note that the path you normally take is blocked for construction, so you quickly choose an alternate route. This demonstrates that you've developed _____ of your campus.

a. a hidden, latent mastery
b. insight into the layout
c. a cognitive map
d. none of these options

3. Latent learning occurs without being rewarded and _____.

a. remains hidden until a future time when it is needed
b. is easily extinguished
c. serves as a discriminative stimuli
d. has been found only in nonhuman species

4. Bandura's observational learning studies focused on how _____.

a. rats learn cognitive maps through exploration
b. children learn aggressive behaviors by observing aggressive models
c. cats learn problem solving through trial and error
d. chimpanzees learn problem solving through reasoning

Think Critically

1 What are some examples of how insight learning has benefited you in your life?

2 Are there instances in which observational learning has worked to your advantage?

realworldpsychology

Does watching sex on TV increase the risk of teen pregnancies?

HINT: LOOK IN THE MARGIN FOR Q4

BIOLOGY OF LEARNING

LEARNING OBJECTIVES

RETRIEVAL PRACTICE While reading the upcoming sections, respond to each Learning Objective in your own words. Then compare your responses with those found at www.wiley.com/college/huffman.

1 **EXPLAIN** how learning changes the brain.
2 **DESCRIBE** the biological foundation for empathy.
3 **SUMMARIZE** the role of evolution in learning.

So far in this chapter, we have considered how external forces—from reinforcing events to our observations of others—affect learning. But we also know that for changes in behavior to persist over time, lasting biological changes must occur within the organism. In this section, we will examine neurological and evolutionary influences on learning.

Neuroscience and Learning

Each time we learn something, either consciously or unconsciously, that experience creates new synaptic connections and alterations in a wide network of our brain

FIGURE 6.16 ENVIRONMENTAL ENRICHMENT AND THE BRAIN | realworldpsychology

For humans and nonhuman animals alike, environmental conditions play an important role in enabling learning. How might a classroom rich with stimulating toys, games, and books foster intellectual development in young children?

PhotoDisc Green/Getty Images

Top-Pet-Pics/Alamy

structures, including the cortex, cerebellum, hippocampus, hypothalamus, thalamus, and amygdala.

Evidence that learning changes brain structure first emerged in the 1960s, from studies of animals raised in enriched versus deprived environments. Compared with rats raised in a stimulus-poor environment, those raised in a colorful, stimulating "rat Disneyland" had a thicker cortex, increased nerve growth factor (NGF), more fully developed synapses, more dendritic branching, and improved performance on many tests of learning and memory (Hamilton et al., 2012; Harati et al., 2011; Lorez-Arnaiz et al., 2007; Speisman et al., 2013).

Admittedly, it is a big leap from rats to humans, but research suggests that the human brain also responds to environmental conditions **(Figure 6.16)**. For example, older adults who are exposed to stimulating environments generally perform better on intellectual and perceptual tasks than those who are in restricted environments (Daffner, 2010; Petrosini et al., 2013; Schaie, 1994, 2008).

Similarly, babies who spend their early weeks and months of life in an orphanage, and receive little or no one-on-one care or attention, show deficits in the cortex of the brain, indicating that early environmental conditions may have a lasting impact on cognitive development (Almas et al., 2012; Sheridan et al., 2012). The good news, however, is that children who are initially placed in an orphanage but later move on to foster care—where they receive more individual attention—show some improvements in brain development.

Mirror Neurons and Imitation

Recent research has identified another neurological influence on learning processes, particularly imitation. When an adult models a facial expression, even very young infants will respond with a similar expression **(Figure 6.17)**. At 9 months, infants will imitate facial actions a full day after first seeing them (Heimann & Meltzoff, 1996).

How can newborn infants so easily imitate the facial expressions of others? Using fMRIs and other brain-imaging techniques,

FIGURE 6.17 INFANT IMITATION—EVIDENCE OF MIRROR NEURONS?

In a series of well-known studies, Andrew Meltzoff and M. Keith Moore (1977, 1985, 1994) found that newborns could imitate such facial movements as tongue protrusion, mouth opening, and lip pursing.

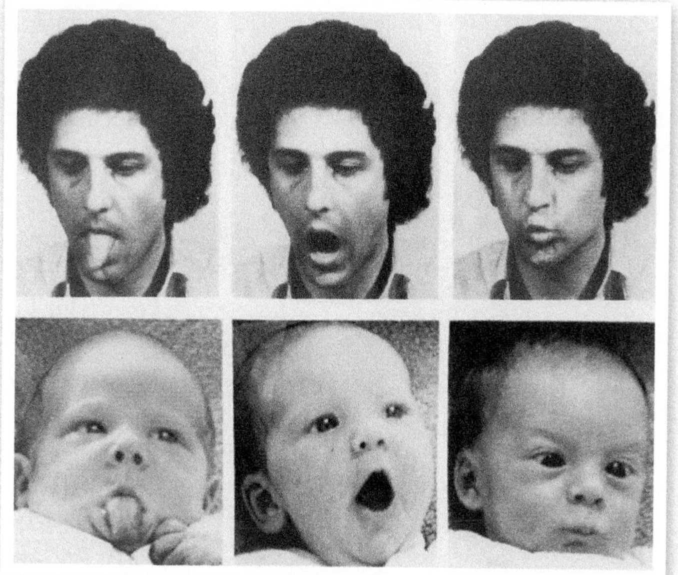

From: A.N. Meltzoff & M.K. Moore, "Imitation of facial and manual gestures by human neonates." Science, 1977, 198, 75–78.

Mirror neuron A type of neuron that fires (or activates) when an action is performed, as well as when observing the actions or emotions of another; believed to be responsible for empathy, imitation, language, and the deficits of some mental disorders.

researchers have identified specific **mirror neurons** believed to be responsible for human empathy and imitation (Ahlsén, 2008; Baird et al., 2011; Caggiano et al., 2011; Haker et al., 2013). These neurons are found in several key areas of the brain, and are believed to be responsible for how we identify with what others are feeling and imitate their actions. When we see another person in pain, one reason we empathize and "share their pain" may be that our mirror neurons are firing. Similarly, if we watch others who are smiling, our mirror neurons make it harder for us to frown.

Mirror neurons were first discovered by neuroscientists who implanted wires in the brains of monkeys to monitor areas involved in planning and carrying out movement (Ferrari et al., 2005; Rizzolatti et al., 2002, 2006). When these monkeys moved and grasped an object, specific neurons fired, but they also fired when the monkeys simply observed another monkey performing the same or similar tasks.

Carlos E. Santa Maria/Shutterstock

realworldpsychology **Mirror Neurons** Have you noticed how spectators at an athletic event sometimes slightly move their arms or legs in synchrony with the athletes? Mirror neurons may be the underlying biological mechanism for this imitation. Deficiencies in these neurons also might help explain the emotional deficits of children and adults with autism or schizophrenia, who often misunderstand the verbal and nonverbal cues of others (Enticott et al., 2012; Kana et al., 2011; Rizzolatti, 2012).

Although scientists are excited about the promising links between mirror neurons and human emotions, imitation, language, learning, and learning disabilities, we do not yet know how they develop. In addition, other researchers have suggested that more research is needed to justify the claims for the role of mirror neurons (Baird et al., 2011; Thomas, 2012). Stay tuned.

Evolution and Learning

Humans and other animals are born with various innate reflexes and instincts. Although these biological tendencies help ensure evolutionary survival, they are inherently inflexible. Learning allows us to more flexibly respond to complex environmental cues, such as spoken words and written symbols, which in turn enables us to survive and prosper in a constantly changing world.

Because animals can be classically conditioned to salivate to tones and operantly conditioned to perform a variety of novel behaviors, such as a seal balancing a ball on its nose, learning theorists initially believed that the fundamental laws of conditioning would apply to almost all species and all behaviors. However, researchers have discovered that some associations are much more readily learned than others.

Taste-aversion A classically conditioned dislike for, and avoidance of, a specific food whose ingestion is followed by illness.

For example, when a food or drink is associated with nausea or vomiting, that particular food or drink more readily becomes a conditioned stimulus (CS) that triggers a conditioned **taste aversion**. Like other classically conditioned responses, taste aversions develop involuntarily.

© robtek/iStockphoto

psychology and you **Taste Aversion** Years ago, a young woman named Rebecca unsuspectingly bit into a Butterfinger candy bar filled with small, wiggling maggots. Horrified, she ran gagging and screaming to the bathroom. Many years later, Rebecca still feels nauseated when she sees a Butterfinger candy bar. Can you see how stimulus discrimination explains why she doesn't feel similarly nauseated by the sight of her boyfriend, who bought her the candy?

Rebecca's graphic (and true!) story illustrates an important evolutionary process. Being biologically prepared to quickly associate nausea with food or drink is obviously adaptive because it helps us avoid that or similar food or drink in the future (Domjan, 2005; Garcia, 2003; Lotem & Halpern, 2012; Swami, 2011).

Further evidence comes from John Garcia and his colleague Robert Koelling (1966) who produced a taste aversion in lab rats by pairing sweetened water (NS) and a shock (US), which produced nausea (UR). After being conditioned and then recovering from the illness, the rats refused to drink the sweetened water (CS) because of the conditioned taste aversion. Remarkably, however, Garcia also discovered that only certain neutral stimuli could produce the nausea. Pairings of a noise (NS) with the shock (US) produced no taste aversion.

Similarly, perhaps because of the more "primitive" evolutionary threat posed by snakes, darkness, spiders, and heights, people tend to more easily develop phobias of these stimuli and situations far more easily than of guns, knives, and electrical outlets. Research also shows that both adults and very young children have an innate ability to very quickly identify the presence of a snake, whereas they are less able to quickly identify other (non-life-threatening) objects, including a caterpillar, flower, or toad (LoBue & DeLoache, 2008; Young et al., 2012). We apparently inherit a built-in (innate) readiness to form associations between certain stimuli and responses—but not others. This is known as **biological preparedness**. Q5

Biological preparedness The built-in (innate) readiness to form associations between certain stimuli and responses.

Just as Garcia couldn't produce classically conditioned noise–nausea associations, other researchers have found that an animal's natural behavior pattern can interfere with operant conditioning. For example, early researchers tried to teach a chicken to play baseball (Breland & Breland, 1961). Through shaping and reinforcement, the chicken first learned to pull a loop that activated a swinging bat and then learned to actually hit the ball. But instead of running to first base, it would chase the ball as if it were food. Regardless of the lack of reinforcement for chasing the ball, the chicken's natural behavior took precedence. This type of biological behavior, is known as **instinctive drift**, along with taste aversions and the variability in phobic responses, are all examples of biological preparedness.

Instinctive drift The tendency for conditioned responses to revert (drift back) to innate response patterns.

In this chapter, we've discussed three general types of learning, classical, operant, and cognitive-social. We've also examined the biological effect on learning. As humans, we also have the capacity to learn and change thanks to our ability to remember, think, and to use language, as well as our individual forms of intelligence. Each of these exciting topics are discussed in the next two chapters.

RETRIEVAL PRACTICE: BIOLOGY OF LEARNING

Self-Test

Completing this self-test and comparing your answers with those in Appendix B provides immediate feedback and helpful practice for exams. Additional interactive, self-tests are available at www.wiley.com/college/huffman.

1. _____ neurons may be responsible for human empathy and imitation.

   a. Motor b. Sensitivity
   c. Empathy d. Mirror

2. Rebecca's story of becoming nauseated and vomiting after eating a spoiled candy bar is a good example of _____.

   a. a biological imperative b. a taste aversion
   c. learned empathy d. negative reinforcement

3. Being innately predisposed to form associations between certain stimuli and responses is called _____.

   a. prejudice b. vicarious learning
   c. superstitious priming d. biological preparedness

4. A biological constraint where an animal's conditioned responses tend to shift toward innate response patterns is called _____.

   a. biological preparedness b. reflexes
   c. instinctive drift d. taste aversion

Think Critically

1 If mirror neurons explain human empathy, could they also explain why first responders (like police and firefighters) are more vulnerable to job burnout? Why or why not?

2 Do you have any taste aversions? If so, how would you use information in this chapter to remove them?

realworldpsychology

Why can even young children recognize a picture of a snake much faster than a picture of a frog or caterpillar?

HINT: LOOK IN THE MARGIN FOR Q5

Summary

1 CLASSICAL CONDITIONING 152

- **Learning** is a relatively permanent change in behavior or mental processes caused by experience. Pavlov discovered a fundamental form of **conditioning** (learning) called **classical conditioning**, a type of learning that develops through involuntarily paired associations. A previously **neutral stimulus (NS)** becomes associated with an **unconditioned stimulus (US)** to elicit a **conditioned response (CR)**.
- In the "Little Albert" study, Watson and Rayner demonstrated how many of our likes, dislikes, prejudices, and fears are examples of a **conditioned emotional response (CER)**, which develops in response to a previously neutral stimulus (NS).
- **Acquisition**, the first of six key principles of classical conditioning, occurs when the **conditioned stimulus (CS)** leads to a CR. **Stimulus generalization** occurs when an event similar to the originally conditioned stimulus triggers the same conditioned response. With experience, animals learn to distinguish between an original conditioned stimulus and similar stimuli—**stimulus discrimination**. **Extinction** is a gradual weakening or suppression of a previously conditioned response. However, if a conditioned stimulus is reintroduced after extinction, an extinguished response may **spontaneously recover**. **Higher-order conditioning** occurs when the NS becomes a CS through repeated pairings with a previous CS.

2 OPERANT CONDITIONING 159

- In **operant conditioning**, an organism learns as a result of voluntary behavior and its subsequent consequences. **Reinforcement** strengthens the response, while **punishment** weakens the response.
- Thorndike developed the **law of effect**, in which responses that produce a satisfying effect are more likely to recur, whereas those that produce a discomforting effect become less likely to recur. Skinner extended Thorndike's law of effect to more complex behaviors.
- **Primary reinforcers** and **primary punishers** are innate, whereas **secondary reinforcers** and **secondary punishers** are learned. Each type of reinforcer can produce **positive reinforcement** or **negative reinforcement,** and both of these forms of reinforcement strengthen the response they follow. Negative reinforcement is NOT punishment. Both **positive punishment** and **negative punishment** weaken a response.
- Punishment can have serious side effects: passive aggressiveness, avoidance behavior, inappropriate modeling, temporary suppression, learned helplessness, rewarded aggression, and perpetuated aggression.
- Organisms learn complex behaviors through **shaping**, in which reinforcement is delivered for successive approximations of the desired response.
- **Schedules of reinforcement** refers to the rate or interval at which responses are reinforced. Most behavior is rewarded and maintained through one of four partial schedules of reinforcement: **fixed ratio (FR)**, **variable ratio (VR)**, **fixed interval (FI)**, or **variable interval (VI)**.

3 COGNITIVE-SOCIAL LEARNING 168

- **Cognitive-social learning theory** emphasizes cognitive and social aspects of learning. Köhler discovered that animals sometimes learn through sudden **insight**, rather than through trial and error. Tolman provided evidence of hidden, **latent learning** and internal **cognitive maps**.
- Bandura's research found that children who watched an adult behave aggressively toward an inflated Bobo doll were later more aggressive than those who had not seen the aggression. According to Bandura, **observational learning** requires attention, retention, reproduction, and motivation.

4 BIOLOGY OF LEARNING 172

- Learning creates structural changes in the brain. Early evidence for such changes came from research on animals raised in enriched environments versus deprived environments.
- **Mirror neurons** fire when an action is performed, as well as when observing the actions or emotions of another.
- Learning is an evolutionary adaptation that enables organisms to survive and prosper in a constantly changing world. Researchers have identified biological constraints that limit the generality of conditioning principles: **biological preparedness** and **instinctive drift**.

Chris Fitzgerald/CandidatePhotos/NewsCom

applyingrealworldpsychology

We began this chapter with five intriguing Real World Psychology questions, and you were asked to revisit these questions at the end of each section. Questions like these have an important and lasting impact on all of our lives. See if you can answer these additional critical thinking questions related to real world examples.

1. What principles of learning best explain why politicians kiss babies?
2. What other stimuli or symbols do politicians use in their campaigns that are based on learning principles?
3. Have you ever used learning principles to get others to do what you want? Was it ethical?
4. How could the media be used to promote desirable traits and behaviors in the viewing public?
5. Imagine if someone developed a secret pill that could make alcohol, tobacco, and fatty foods an immediate taste aversion for everyone. Would that be a good or bad thing? Assuming that it was safe, would you take the pill? Why or why not?

Key Terms

RETRIEVAL PRACTICE Write a definition for each term before turning back to the referenced page to check your answer.

chapterseven

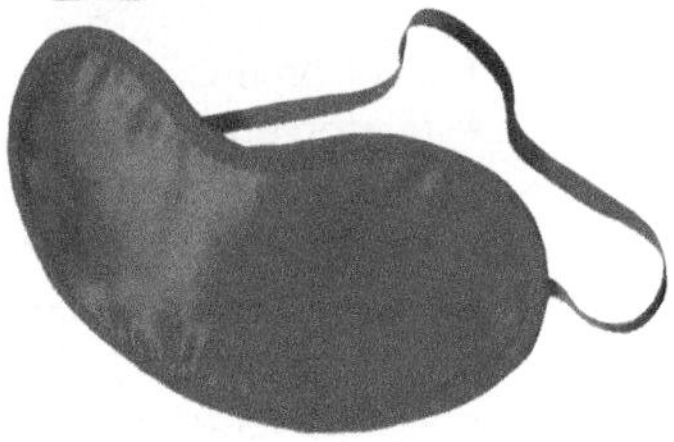

Memory

CHAPTER OUTLINE

realworldpsychology

THINGS YOU'LL LEARN IN CHAPTER 7

Q1 **Do daydreamers actually have better working-memory skills than people who don't daydream?**

Q2 **How can taking a nap improve your memory?**

Q3 **Can merely imagining engaging in a behavior create a false memory of actually performing that behavior?**

Q4 **Why might exposure to pornography interfere with memory?**

Q5 **Does accuracy increase when eyewitnesses have only a few seconds to make an identification?**

THROUGHOUT THE CHAPTER, MARGIN ICONS FOR Q1–Q5 INDICATE WHERE THE TEXT ADDRESSES THESE QUESTIONS.

chapteroverview

When H.M. was 27, he underwent brain surgery to correct his severe epileptic seizures. Although the surgery improved his medical problem, now something was clearly wrong with H.M.'s long-term memory. When his uncle died, he grieved in a normal way. But soon after, he began to ask why his uncle never visited him. H.M. had to be repeatedly reminded of his uncle's death, and each reminder would begin a new mourning process.

H.M. lived another 55 years not recognizing the people who cared for him daily. Each time he met his caregivers, read a book, or ate a meal, it was as if for the first time (Barbeau, Puel, & Pariente, 2010; Carey, 2008; Corkin, 2002). Sadly, H.M. died in 2008—never having regained his long-term memory.

What should we make of this true, real-life example? What would it be like to be H.M.—existing only in the present moment, unable to learn and form new memories? How can we remember our second-grade teacher's name, but forget the name of someone we just met? In this chapter, you'll discover answers to these and other fascinating questions about memory.

THE NATURE OF MEMORY

LEARNING OBJECTIVES

RETRIEVAL PRACTICE While reading the upcoming sections, respond to each Learning Objective in your own words. Then compare your responses with those found at www.wiley.com/college/huffman.

1. **REVIEW** the core principles of the major memory models.
2. **DESCRIBE** the purpose of sensory memory.
3. **EXPLAIN** the function of short-term memory (STM) and how it operates as our working memory.
4. **DESCRIBE** the functions and various types of long-term memory (LTM).
5. **EXPLAIN** how organization, elaborative rehearsal, and retrieval cues improve long-term memory.

Memory The internal record or representation of some prior event or experience; the mental capacity to encode, store, and retrieve information.

Constructive process The process of organizing and shaping information during processing, storage, and retrieval of memories.

Memory allows us to learn from our experiences and to adapt to ever-changing environments. Without it, we would have no past or future. Yet our memories are also highly fallible. Although some people think of **memory** as a gigantic library or an automatic video recorder, our memories are not exact recordings of events. Instead, memory is a **constructive process** through which we actively organize and shape information as it is being processed, stored, and retrieved. As expected, this construction often leads to serious errors and biases, which we'll discuss throughout the chapter.

Memory Models

To understand memory (and its constructive nature), you need a model of how it operates. Over the years, psychologists have developed numerous models for memory, and we'll focus on the two most important ones.

Encoding, Storage, and Retrieval (ESR) Model

Encoding, storage, and retrieval (ESR) model A memory model which suggests that memory is formed through three processes: *encoding* (getting information in), *storage* (retaining information for future use), and *retrieval* (recovering information).

Encoding The process by which a mental representation is formed in memory.

Storage The retention of encoded information over time.

According to the **encoding, storage,** and **retrieval (ESR) model**, the barrage of information that we encounter every day goes through three basic operations: *encoding, storage*, and *retrieval*. Each of these processes represents a different function that is closely analogous to the parts and functions of a computer **(Figure 7.1)**.

To input data into a computer, you begin by typing letters and numbers on the keyboard. The computer then translates these keystrokes into its own electronic language. In a roughly similar fashion, your brain **encodes** sensory information (sound, visual images, and other senses) into a neural code (language) it can understand and use.

Once information is *encoded*, it must be **stored**. Computer information is normally stored on a flash drive or hard drive, whereas human information is stored in the brain.

FIGURE 7.1 **ENCODING, STORAGE, AND RETRIEVAL**

The encoding, storage, and retrieval model of memory can be compared to a computer's information processing system.

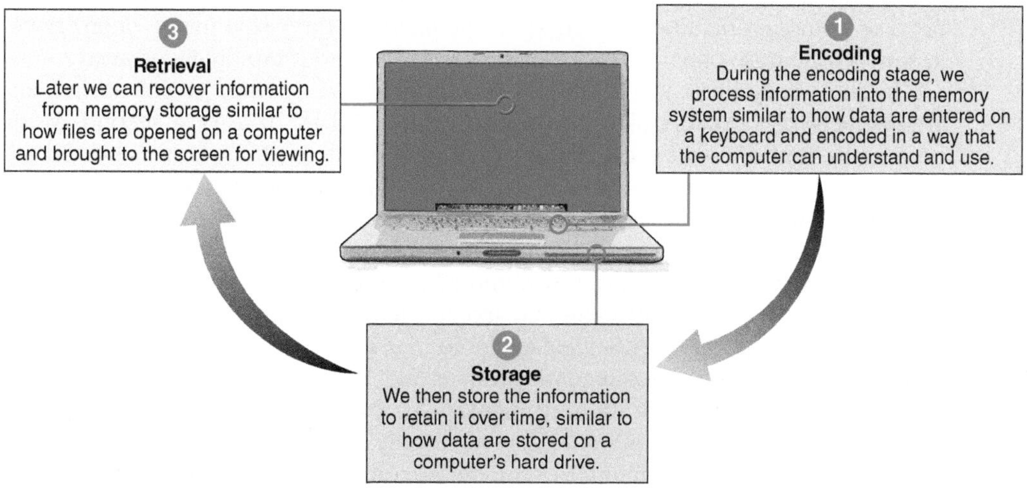
3
Retrieval
Later we can recover information from memory storage similar to how files are opened on a computer and brought to the screen for viewing.
1
Encoding
During the encoding stage, we process information into the memory system similar to how data are entered on a keyboard and encoded in a way that the computer can understand and use.
2
Storage
We then store the information to retain it over time, similar to how data are stored on a computer's hard drive.

Finally, information must be **retrieved**, or taken out of storage. We retrieve stored information by going to files on our computer or to "files" in our brain. Keep this model in mind. To do well in college, or almost any other pursuit, you must successfully encode, store and retrieve a large amount of facts and concepts. Throughout this chapter, we'll discuss ways to improve your memory during each of these processes.

Retrieval The recovery of information from memory storage.

Three-Stage Memory Model

Since the late 1960s, the most highly researched and widely used memory model has been the **three-stage memory model** (Atkinson & Shiffrin, 1968; Eichenbaum, 2013; Nairne & Neath, 2013). It remains the leading paradigm in memory research because it offers a convenient way to organize the major findings. According to this model, three different storage "boxes," or memory stages, hold and process information. Each stage has a different purpose, duration, and capacity **(Figure 7.2)**. Let's discuss each stage in more detail.

Three-stage memory model A memory model which suggests that memory storage requires passage of information through three stages (sensory, short-term, and long-term memory).

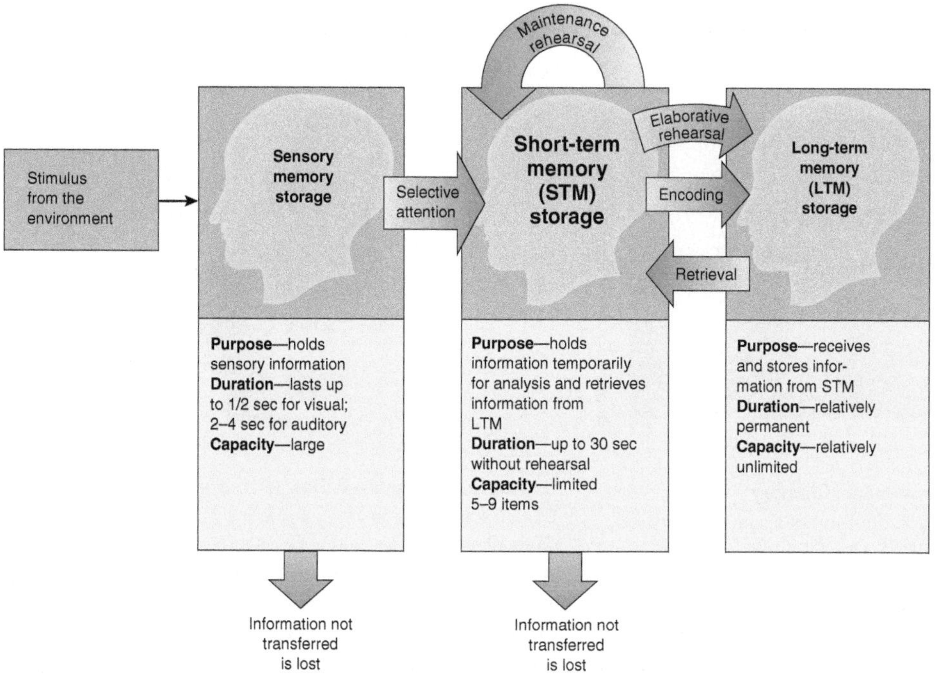

FIGURE 7.2 **THE TRADITIONAL THREE-STAGE MEMORY MODEL**

Each "box" represents a separate memory system that differs in purpose, duration, and capacity. When information is not transferred from sensory memory or short-term memory, it is assumed to be lost. Information stored in long-term memory can be retrieved and sent back to short-term memory for use.

Sensory Memory

Sensory memory The initial memory stage, which holds sensory information; it has relatively large capacity but the duration is only a few seconds.

Everything we see, hear, touch, taste, and smell must first enter our **sensory memory**. Once it's entered, the information remains in sensory memory just long enough for our brain to locate relevant bits of data and transfer it on to the next stage of memory. For visual information, known as *iconic memory*, the visual image (icon) stays in sensory memory only about one-half a second before it rapidly fades away.

In an early study of iconic sensory memory, George Sperling (1960) flashed an arrangement of 12 letters like the ones in **Figure 7.3** for 1/20 of a second. Most people, he found, could recall only 4 or 5 of the letters. But when instructed to report just the top, middle, or bottom row, depending on whether they heard a high, medium, or low tone, they reported almost all the letters correctly. Apparently, all 12 letters are held in sensory memory right after they are viewed, but only those that are immediately attended to are noted and processed.

K	Z	R	A
Q	B	T	P
S	G	N	Y

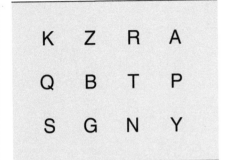

FIGURE 7.3 SPERLING'S TEST FOR ICONIC MEMORY

Like the fleeting visual images in iconic memory, auditory stimuli (what we hear) is also temporary but a weaker "echo," or *echoic memory*, of this auditory input lingers for up to four seconds (Inui et al., 2010; Neisser, 1967; Radvansky, 2011). Why are iconic and auditory memories so fleeting? We cannot process all incoming stimuli, so lower brain centers need only a few seconds to "decide" if the information is important enough to promote to conscious awareness **(Figure 7.4).**

Early researchers believed that sensory memory had an unlimited capacity. However, later research suggests that sensory memory does have limits and that stored images are fuzzier than once thought (Franconeri et al., 2013; Goldstein, 2010; Moulin, 2011).

Short-Term Memory (STM)

Short-term memory (STM) The second memory stage, which temporarily stores sensory information and decides whether to send it on to long-term memory (LTM); its capacity is limited to five to nine items and it has a duration of about 30 seconds.

Chunking The process of grouping separate pieces of information into a single unit (or chunk) on the basis of similarity or some other organizing principle.

The second stage of memory processing, **short-term memory (STM)**, temporarily stores and processes sensory stimuli. If the information is important, STM organizes and sends this information along to long-term (LTM)—otherwise, information decays and is lost. STM also retrieves stored memories from LTM. Otherwise, information decays and is lost.

The capacity and duration of STM are limited (Bankó & Vidnyánsky, 2010; Nairne & Neath, 2013). To extend the *capacity* of STM, you can use a technique called **chunking** (Glicksohn & Cohen, 2011; Miller, 1956; Oberauer et al., 2013; Thornton & Conway, 2013). Have you noticed that your credit card, Social Security, and telephone numbers are almost always grouped into three or four units separated

FIGURE 7.4 DEMONSTRATING ICONIC AND ECHOIC MEMORIES *psychology and you*

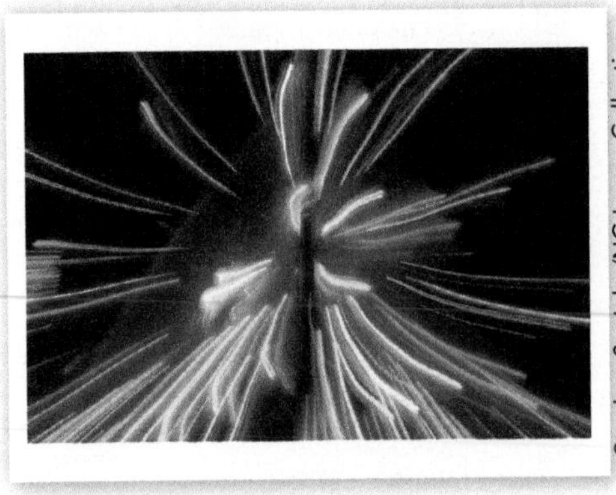

Stephen St. John/NG Image Collection

A Visual Images—Iconic Memory
To demonstrate the duration of visual memory, or *iconic memory*, swing a flashlight in a dark room. Because the image, or icon, lingers for a fraction of a second after the flashlight is moved, you see the light as a continuous stream, as in this photo, rather than as a succession of individual points.

Blue Jean Images/Getty Images

B Auditory Stimuli—Echoic Memory
Think back to a time when someone asked you a question while you were deeply absorbed in a task. Did you ask "What?" and then immediately find you could answer them without hearing their repeated response? Now you know why. A weaker "echo" (echoic memory) of auditory information is available for up to four seconds.

by hyphens? The reason is that it's easier to remember numbers in chunks rather than as a string of single digits.

Chunking also helps in football. What do you see when you observe this arrangement of players from a page of a football playbook **(Figure 7.5)**? To the inexpert eye, it looks like a random assembly of lines and arrows, and a naive person generally would have little or no understanding or appreciation of the skills required in football. But experienced players and seasoned fans generally recognize many or all of the standard plays. To them, the scattered lines form meaningful patterns—classic arrangements that recur often. Just as you group the letters of this sentence into meaningful words and remember them long enough to understand the meaning of the sentence, expert football players group the different football plays into easily recalled patterns (or chunks).

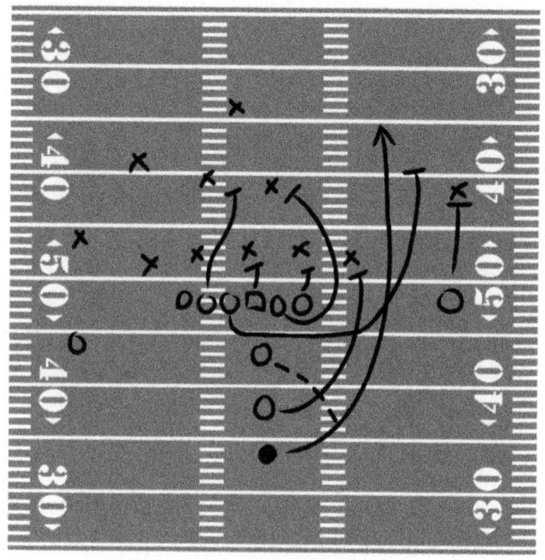

FIGURE 7.5 CHUNKING IN FOOTBALL

You can also extend the *duration* of your STM almost indefinitely by consciously "juggling" the information—a process called **maintenance rehearsal**. You are using maintenance rehearsal when you look up a phone number and repeat it over and over until you key in the number.

Maintenance rehearsal The memory-improvement technique of repeating information over and over to maintain it in short-term memory (STM).

People who are good at remembering names also know to take advantage of maintenance rehearsal. They repeat the name of each person they meet, aloud or silently, to keep it active in STM. They also make sure that other thoughts (such as their plans for what to say next) don't intrude.

As you can see in **Figure 7.6**, short-term memory is more than just a passive, temporary "holding area." Given that active processing of information also occurs in STM, many researchers prefer the term **working memory** (Baddeley, 1992, 2007; Barrouillet & Camos, 2012; Brady & Tenenbaum, 2013; Thornton & Conway, 2013). All our conscious thinking occurs in this "working memory," and the manipulation of information that occurs here helps explain some of the memory errors and false constructions described in this chapter.

Working memory An alternate term for short-term memory (STM), which emphasizes the active processing of information.

Interestingly, people who daydream while completing simple tasks may show even higher working-memory capabilities (Levinson et al., 2012). Researchers in one study first tested participants on their level of working memory, meaning how much information they could hold in their minds at one time. The participants then completed relatively mindless tasks, such as pressing a button each time a certain letter appeared on a computer screen. Participants were asked periodically whether their minds were focused on the assigned task or were wandering to other thoughts. People with higher working-memory scores reported more mind wandering during the mindless task, presumably because they needed to spend less attention on the simple task. These findings suggest that having better working-memory skills may allow for more daydreaming!

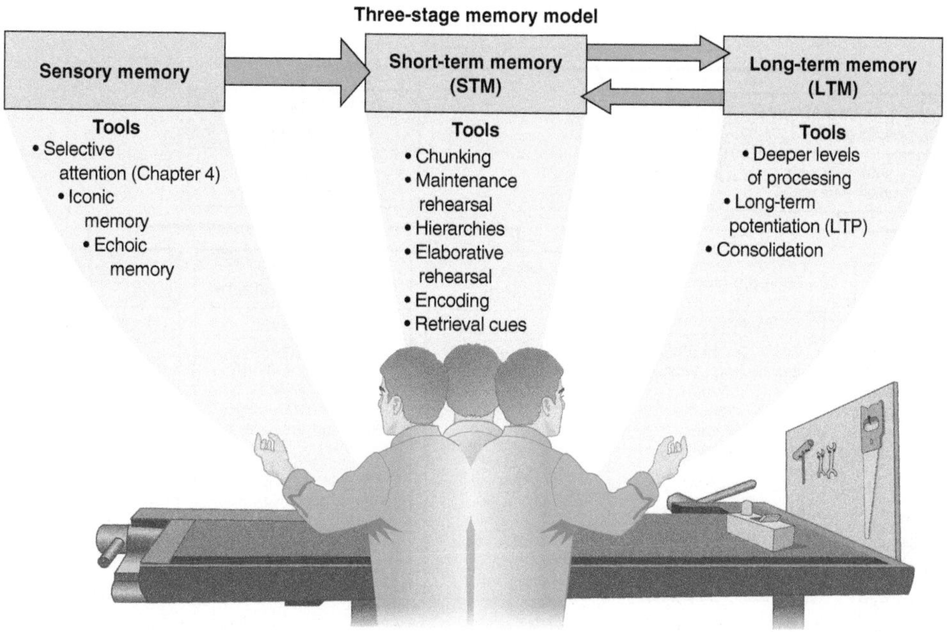

FIGURE 7.6 HOW WORKING MEMORY MIGHT WORK

Given that short-term memory (STM) is active, or *working*, It helps to visually picture STM as a "workbench," with a "worker" at the bench who selectively attends to certain sensory information and also sends and retrieves it from long-term memory (LTM). The worker also manipulates the incoming, transferred, and retrieved information. Note the "tools" the "worker" uses during the three stages of processing.

Long-Term Memory (LTM)

Long-term memory (LTM) The third stage of memory, which stores information for long periods of time; the capacity is virtually limitless, and the duration is relatively permanent.

Explicit/declarative memory A subsystem within long-term memory (LTM) that consciously stores facts, information, and personal life experiences.

Semantic memory A subsystem of long-term memory (LTM) that stores general knowledge; a mental encyclopedia or dictionary.

Episodic memory A subsystem of long-term memory (LTM) that stores autobiographical events and the contexts in which they occurred; a mental diary of a person's life.

Implicit/nondeclarative memory A subsystem within long-term memory (LTM) that unconsciously stores procedural skills and simple classically conditioned responses.

Once information has been transferred from STM, it is organized and integrated with other information in **long-term memory (LTM)**. LTM serves as a storehouse for information that must be kept for long periods. When we need the information, it is sent back to STM for our conscious use. Compared with sensory memory and short-term memory, long-term memory has relatively unlimited *capacity* and *duration* (Eichenbaum, 2013). But, just as with any other possession, the better we label and arrange our memories, the more readily we'll be able to retrieve them.

How do we store the vast amount of information we collect over a lifetime? Several types of LTM exist **(Figure 7.7)**.

Explicit/declarative memory refers to intentional learning or conscious knowledge. If asked to remember your phone number or your mother's name, you can easily state (*declare*) the answers directly (*explicitly*).

Explicit/declarative memory can be further subdivided into two parts. **Semantic memory** is memory for general knowledge, rules, events, facts, and specific information. It is our mental encyclopedia. In contrast, **episodic memory** is like a mental diary. It records the major events (*episodes*) in our lives. Some of our episodic memories are short-lived, whereas others can last a lifetime.

Have you ever wondered why most adults can recall almost nothing of the years before they reached age 3? Research suggests that a concept of self, sufficient language development, and growth of the frontal lobes of the cortex (along with other structures) may be necessary for us to encode and retrieve early events many years later (Bauer & Lukowski, 2010; Pathman & Bauer, 2013; Rose et al., 2011).

Implicit/nondeclarative memory refers to unintentional learning or unconscious knowledge. Try telling someone else how you tie your shoelaces without demonstrating the actual behavior. Because your memory of this skill is unconscious and hard to describe (*declare*) in words, this type of memory is sometimes referred to as *nondeclarative.*

Implicit/nondeclarative memory consists of *procedural* motor skills, like tying your shoes or riding a bike, as well as *classically conditioned memory* responses, such as fears or taste aversions.

FIGURE 7.7 TYPES OF LONG-TERM MEMORY (LTM)

LTM is divided and subdivided into various types.

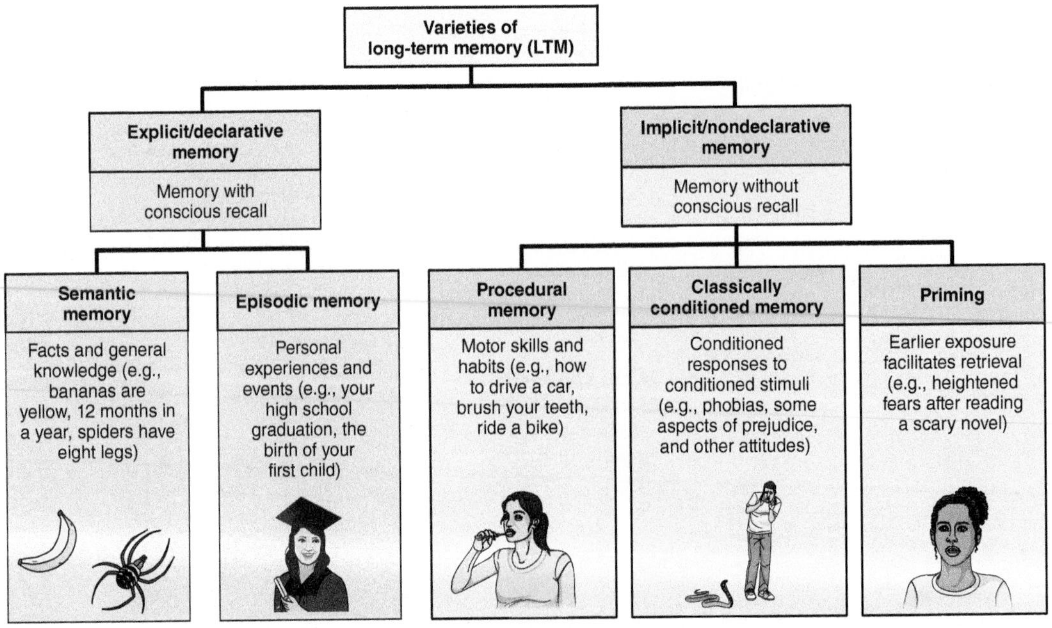

Implicit/nondeclarative memory also includes **priming**, in which prior exposure to a stimulus (*prime*) facilitates or inhibits the processing of new information (McKoon & Ratcliff, 2012; Northup & Mulligan, 2013; Schmitz & Wentura, 2012). Priming often occurs even when we do not consciously remember being exposed to the prime.

Priming A process in which a prior exposure to a stimulus (or prime) facilitates or inhibits the processing of new information, even when one has no conscious memory of the initial learning and storage.

psychology and you **How Our Moods Are Primed** Have you ever felt nervous being home alone while reading a Stephen King novel, experienced sadness after hearing about a tragic event in the news, or developed amorous feelings while watching a romantic movie? These are all examples of how the situation we are in may influence our mood, in conscious or unconscious ways. Given this new insight into how priming can "set you up" for certain emotions, can you see how others who haven't studied psychology might be more likely to mislabel or overreact to their emotions?

© CBW/Alamy Inc.

Improving Long-Term Memory

There are several ways we can improve long-term memory. These include *organization*, *rehearsal* (or *repetition*), and *retrieval*.

One additional trick for giving your memory a boost is to use **mnemonic** devices to encode items in a special way (see *Improving Your Memory Using Mnemonic Devices* on the next page). However, these devices take practice and time, and some students find that they get better results using the other well-researched principles discussed throughout this chapter.

Mnemonic A strategy or device that uses familiar information during the encoding of new information to enhance subsequent access to the information in memory.

Organization

To successfully encode information for LTM, we need to *organize* material into hierarchies. This means arranging a number of related items into broad categories that we further divide and subdivide. (This organizational strategy for LTM is similar to the strategy of chunking material in STM.) For instance, by grouping small subsets of ideas together (as subheadings under larger, main headings and within diagrams, tables, and so on), we hope to make the material in this book more understandable and *memorable*.

Admittedly, organization takes time and work. But you'll be happy to know that some memory organization and filing is done automatically while you sleep (Groch et al., 2013; Payne et al., 2012; Stickgold & Walker, 2013; Verleger et al., 2011). In fact, research shows that people who rest and close their eyes for as little as 10 minutes show greater memory for details of a story they've just heard (Dewar et al., 2012). Unfortunately, despite claims to the contrary, research shows that we can't recruit our sleeping hours to memorize new material, such as a foreign language.

Q2

Rehearsal

Like organization, *rehearsal* also improves encoding for both STM and LTM. If you need to hold information in STM for longer than 30 seconds, you can simply keep repeating it (maintenance rehearsal). But storage in LTM requires *deeper levels of processing*, called **elaborative rehearsal**.

The immediate goal of elaborative rehearsal is to *understand*—not to memorize. Fortunately, this attempt to understand is one of the best ways to encode new information into long-term memory.

Elaborative rehearsal A technique for improving memory by linking new information to previously stored material; also known as deeper levels of processing.

IMPROVING YOUR MEMORY USING MNEMONIC DEVICES

psychology and you

These three mnemonics improve memory by tagging information to physical locations (*method of loci*), organizing information into main and subsidiary topics (an *outline*), and using familiar information to remember the unfamiliar (*acronyms*).

Ⓐ Method of loci

Greek and Roman orators developed the *method of loci* to keep track of the many parts of their long speeches. Orators would imagine the parts of their speeches attached to places in a courtyard. For example, if an opening point in a speech was the concept of *justice*, they might visualize a courthouse placed in the first corner of their garden. Continuing this imaginary garden walk, the second point the orator might make would be about the prison system, and the third would be the need for balance in government.

Ⓑ Outline organization

When listening to lectures and/or reading the text, draw a vertical line approximately 3 inches from the left margin of your notebook paper. Write main headings from the chapter outline to the left of the line and add specific details and examples from the lecture or text on the right, as in this example:

Outline	Details and Examples from Lecture and Text
1. Nature of Memory	______________
a. Memory Models	______________
b. Sensory Memory	______________
c. Short-Term Memory (STM)	______________

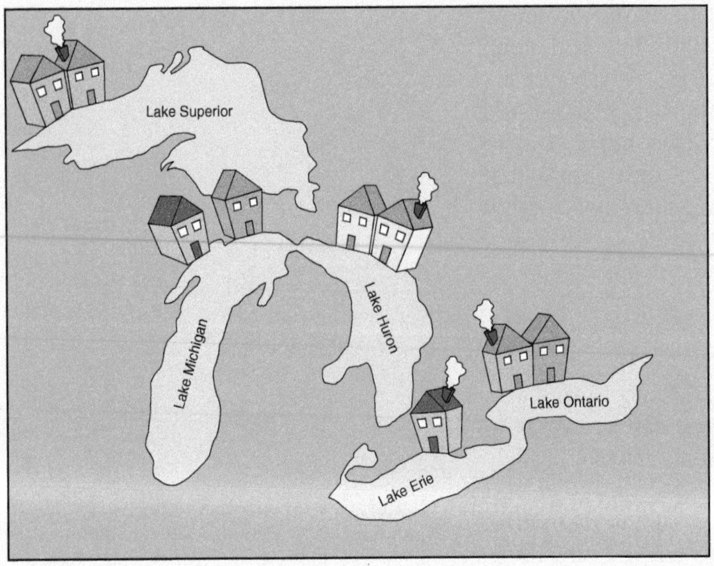

Ⓒ Acronyms

To use the *acronym method*, create a new code word from the first letters of the items you want to remember. For example, to recall the names of the Great Lakes, think of *HOMES* on a *great lake* (*H*uron, *O*ntario, *M*ichigan, *E*rie, *S*uperior). Visualizing homes on each lake also helps you remember your code word *homes*.

Think Critically

1. How could you use the method of loci to remember several items on your grocery shopping list?
2. How would you use the acronym method to remember the names of the last seven presidents of the United States?

Retrieval

Finally, effective *retrieval* is critical to improving long-term memory. There are two types of **retrieval cues (Figure 7.8)**. *Specific* cues require you only to *recognize* the correct response. *General* cues require you to *recall* previously learned material by searching through all possible matches in LTM—a much more difficult task.

Retrieval cue A prompt or stimulus that aids recall or retrieval of a stored piece of information from long-term memory (LTM).

psychology and you **The Power of Retrieval Cues** Whether cues require recall or only recognition is not all that matters. Imagine that while house hunting, you walk into a stranger's kitchen and are greeted with the unmistakable smell of freshly baked bread. Instantly, the aroma transports you to your grandmother's kitchen, where you spent many childhood afternoons doing your homework. You find yourself suddenly thinking of the mental shortcuts your grandmother taught you to help you learn your multiplication tables. You hadn't thought about these little tricks for years, but somehow a whiff of baking bread brought them back to you. Why?

© M Studio/iStockphoto

In this imagined baking bread episode, you have stumbled upon the **encoding-specificity principle** (Tulving & Thompson, 1973). In most cases, we're able to remember better when we attempt to recall information in the *same* context in which we learned it (Lin et al., 2013; Unsworth et al., 2012). Have you noticed that you tend to do better on exams when you take them in the same seat and classroom in which you originally studied the material? This happens because the matching location acts as a retrieval cue for the information.

Encoding-specificity principle The principle that retrieval of information is improved if cues received at the time of recall are consistent with those present at the time of encoding.

People also remember information better if their moods during learning and retrieval match (Forgas & Eich, 2013; Howe & Malone, 2011). This phenomenon, called *mood congruence*, occurs because a given mood tends to evoke memories that are consistent with that mood. When you're sad (or happy or angry), you're

FIGURE 7.8 RECALL VERSUS RECOGNITION

Can you *recall*, in order, the names of the planets in our solar system? If not, it's probably because recall, like questions on an essay exam, requires retrieval using only general, nonspecific cues—like naming the planets. In contrast, a recognition task only requires you to identify the correct response, like a multiple-choice exam. Note how much easier it is to *recognize* the names of the planets when you're provided a specific retrieval cue, in this case the first three letters of each planet: Mer-, Ven-, Ear-, Mar-, Jup-, Sat-, Ura-, Nep-, Plu-. (Note that in 2006, Pluto was officially declassified as a planet and is now considered a "dwarf planet.")

Antonio M. Rosario/Photographer's Choice/Getty Images

more likely to remember events and circumstances from other times when you were sad (or happy or angry).

Finally, memory retrieval is most effective when we are in the same state of consciousness as we were in when the memory was formed. For example, people who are intoxicated will better remember events that happened in a previous drunken state, compared to when they are sober (Nasehi et al., 2010; Sanday et al., 2013). This is called *state-dependent retrieval.*

RETRIEVAL PRACTICE: THE NATURE OF MEMORY

Self-Test

Completing this self-test and comparing your answers with those in Appendix B provides immediate feedback and helpful practice for exams. Additional interactive, self-tests are available at www.wiley.com/college/huffman.

1. Information in _____ lasts only a few seconds or less and has a relatively large (but not unlimited) storage capacity.

a. perceptual processes
b. working memory
c. short-term storage
d. sensory memory

2. _____ is the process of grouping separate pieces of information into a single unit.

a. Chunking
b. Collecting
c. Conflation
d. Dual-coding

3. In answering this question, the correct multiple-choice option may serve as a _____ for recalling accurate information from your long-term memory.

a. specificity code
b. retrieval cue
c. priming pump
d. flashbulb stimulus

4. The encoding-specificity principle says that information retrieval is improved when _____.

a. both maintenance and elaborative rehearsal are used
b. reverberating circuits consolidate information
c. conditions of recovery are similar to encoding conditions
d. long-term potentiation is accessed

Think Critically

1 What are some of the possible advantages and disadvantages of the fact that memory is a constructive process?

2 If you were forced to lose one type of memory—sensory, short-term, or long-term—which would you select? Why?

realworldpsychology

Do daydreamers actually have better working-memory skills than people who don't daydream?

How can taking a nap improve your memory?

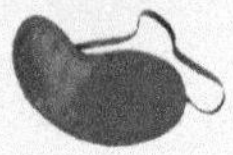

HINT: LOOK IN THE MARGIN FOR Q1 AND Q2

FORGETTING

LEARNING OBJECTIVES

RETRIEVAL PRACTICE While reading the upcoming sections, respond to each Learning Objective in your own words. Then compare your responses with those found at www.wiley.com/college/huffman.

1 **DESCRIBE** Ebbinghaus's research on learning and forgetting.
2 **REVIEW** the five key theories about why we forget.
3 **EXPLAIN** the six most important factors that contribute to forgetting.

Psychologists have long been interested in how and why we forget. Hermann Ebbinghaus first introduced the experimental study of learning and forgetting in 1885 **(Figure 7.9)**.

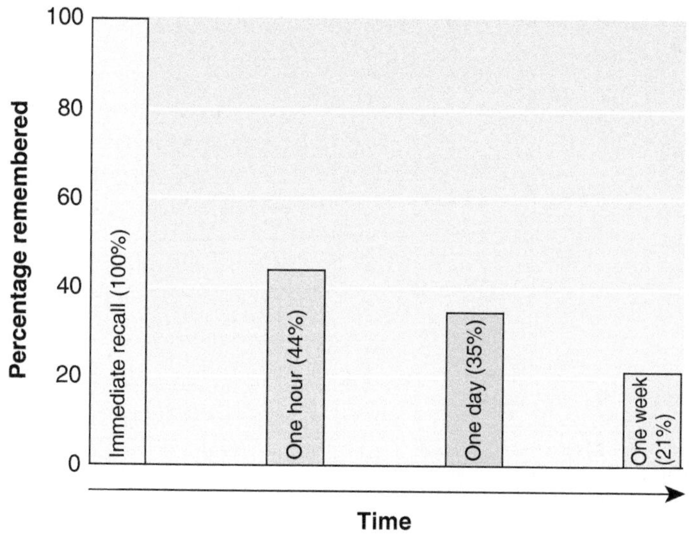

FIGURE 7.9 HOW QUICKLY WE FORGET

Using himself as a subject, Ebbinghaus calculated how long it took to learn a list of three-letter *nonsense syllables*, such as *SIB* and *RAL*. He found that one hour after he knew a list perfectly, he remembered only 44% of the syllables. A day later he recalled 35%, and a week later only 21%.

Although Ebbinghaus's research showed a dramatic drop in his previously learned material, keep in mind that meaningful material is much more memorable than nonsense syllables. Furthermore, after some time had passed and Ebbinghaus thought he had completely forgotten the list, he discovered that *relearning* it took less time than the initial learning took. Similarly, if your college requires you to repeat some of the math or foreign language courses you took in high school, you'll be happily surprised by how much you recall and how much easier it is to relearn the information the second time around.

More recent research based on Ebbinghaus's discoveries has identified an ideal time to practice something you have just learned. Practicing too soon is a waste of time, but if you practice too late, you will already have forgotten what you learned. The ideal time to practice is when you are about to forget.

Polish psychologist Piotr Wozniak used Ebbinghaus's insight regarding the ideal practice time to create a software program called SuperMemo. The program can be used to predict the future state of an individual's memory and help the person schedule reviews of learned information at the optimal time. So far the program has been applied mainly to language learning, helping users retain huge amounts of vocabulary. But Wozniak hopes that someday programs like SuperMemo will tell people when to wake and when to exercise, help them remember what they have read and whom they have met, and remind them of their goals (Wolf, 2008).

Theories of Forgetting

Although we all sometimes wish we had complete recall of everything we've learned, if we truly couldn't forget, our minds would be filled with meaningless data, such as what we ate for breakfast every morning and every conversation we've ever had. Similarly, think of the pain we'd continuously endure if we couldn't distance ourselves from tragedy through forgetting. The ability to forget is essential to the proper functioning of memory, and psychologists have developed several theories to explain why forgetting occurs **(Figure 7.10)**: *decay*, *interference*, *motivated forgetting*, *encoding failure*, and *retrieval failure*. Each theory focuses on a different stage of the memory process or a particular type of problem in processing information.

In *decay theory*, memory is processed and stored in a physical form—for example, in a network of neurons. Connections between neurons probably deteriorate over time, leading to forgetting. This theory explains why skills and memory degrade if they go unused ("use it or lose it").

In *interference theory*, forgetting is caused by two competing memories, particularly memories with similar qualities. At least two types of interference exist: *retroactive* and *proactive* **(Figure 7.11).** When new information leads to forgetting old material, it is called **retroactive interference** (acting backward in time). Learning your new phone number may cause you to forget your old phone number (old,

Retroactive interference A memory error in which new information interferes with remembering old information; it is backward-acting interference.

FIGURE 7.10 **WHY WE FORGET: FIVE KEY THEORIES**

Which of the five theories of forgetting best applies to this cartoon?

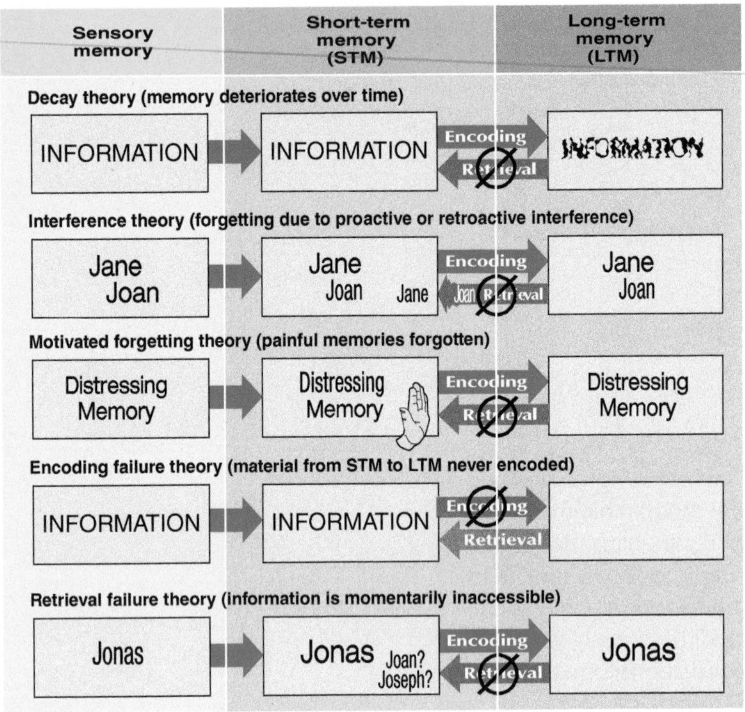

Mick Stevens/The New Yorker Collection/www.cartoonbank.com

Proactive interference A memory error in which old information interferes with remembering new information; it is forward-acting interference.

"retro," information is forgotten). Conversely, when old information leads to forgetting of new information, it is called **proactive interference** (acting forward in time). Old information (like the Spanish you learned in high school) may interfere with your ability to learn and remember your new college course in French.

Motivated forgetting theory is based on the idea that we forget some information for a reason. According to Freudian theory, people forget unpleasant or anxiety-producing information, either consciously or unconsciously.

In *encoding failure theory*, our sensory memory receives the information and passes it to STM. But during STM, we may overlook precise details, and may not fully encode it, which would result in a failure to pass along a complete memory for proper storage in LTM.

FIGURE 7.11 **RETROACTIVE INTERFERENCE AND PROACTIVE INTERFERENCE**

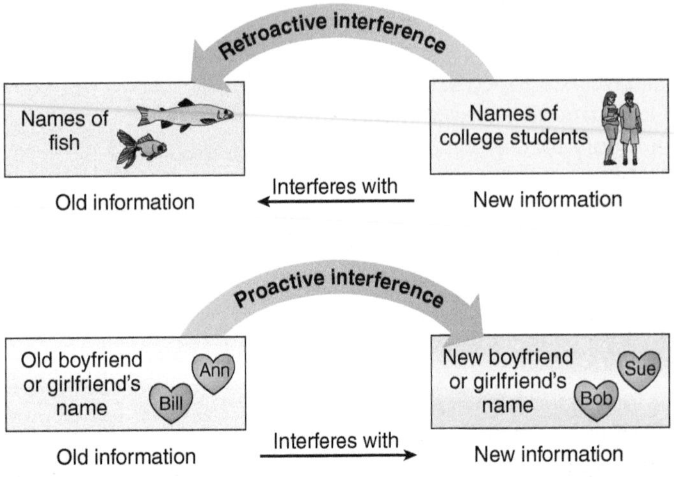

Ⓐ **Retroactive** (backward-acting) **interference** occurs when new information interferes with old information. This example comes from a story about an absent-minded ichthyology professor (fish specialist) who refused to learn the name of his college students. Asked why, he said, "Every time I learn a student's name, I forget the name of a fish!"

Ⓑ **Proactive** (forward-acting) **interference** occurs when old information interferes with new information. Have you ever been in trouble because you used an old partner's name to refer to your new partner? You now have a guilt-free explanation—proactive interference.

TEST YOURSELF: WHICH IS THE REAL PENNY?

psychology and you

If you want a simple (but fascinating) example of *encoding failure*, try to identify the correct penny among this sample of 10. Despite having seen a real penny thousands of times in our lives, most of us have difficulty recognizing the details. The U.S. penny has eight easily distinguishing characteristics (Lincoln's head, the date it was minted, which way Lincoln is facing, and so on). However, the average person can only remember three characteristics (Nickerson & Adams, 1979). Because we can easily recognize pennies by their size and color, we don't encode the fine details and pass them on for storage in LTM. Can you see how this applies to reading a textbook? You can't read a text the way you read a novel. You need to pay close attention to details in order to "recognize" the correct answers on exams!

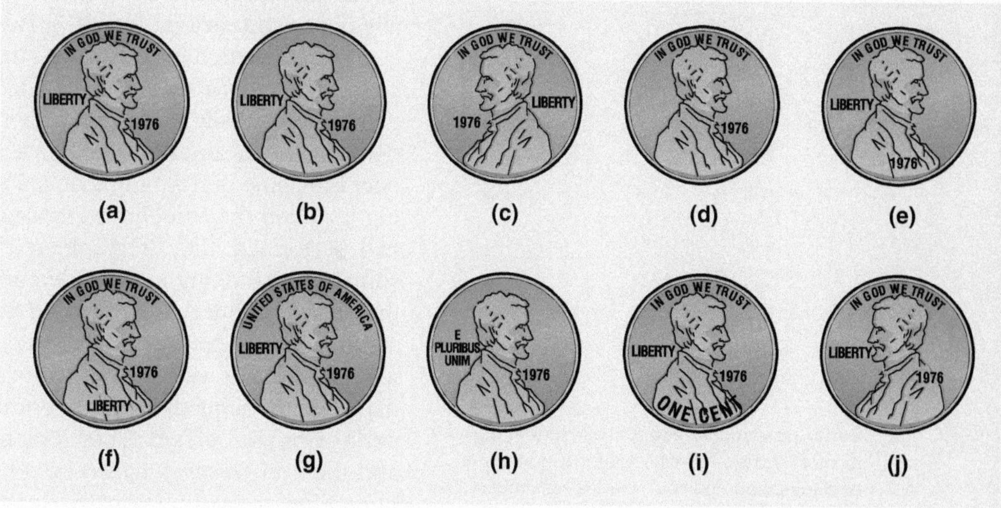

According to *retrieval failure theory*, memories stored in LTM aren't forgotten. They're just momentarily inaccessible. For example, the **tip-of-the-tongue (TOT) phenomenon**—the feeling that a word or an event you are trying to remember will pop out at any second—is known to result from interference, faulty cues, and high emotional arousal.

Tip-of-the-tongue (TOT) phenomenon Feeling that specific information is stored in your long-term memory but being temporarily unable to retrieve it.

Factors Involved in Forgetting

Misinformation effect A memory distortion that results from misleading post-event information.

Since Ebbinghaus's original research, scientists have discovered numerous factors that contribute to forgetting. Six of the most important are the *misinformation effect*, the *serial- position effect*, *source amnesia*, the *sleeper effect*, *spacing of practice*, and *culture*.

Many people (who haven't studied this chapter or taken a psychology course) believe that when they're recalling an event, they're remembering it as if it were a kind of instant replay. However, as you know, our memories are highly fallible and filled with personal constructions that we create during encoding and storage. Research on the **misinformation effect** shows that information that occurs *after an event* may further alter and revise those constructions.

For example, in one study, participants completed an interview in one room and then answered questions about it in another room (Morgan et al., 2012). Participants who received neutral questions like "Was there a telephone in the room?" answered accurately for the most part, making errors on only 10% of the questions. However, other participants were asked questions such as "What color was the telephone?" which falsely implied that there had been a telephone in the room. Of these respondents, 98% "remembered" a telephone. Other

Voices from the Classroom

"False Daughter" Memories One of the co-authors of this book, Karen Huffman, is a dear friend of mine and we've co-taught intro psych for many years. During our times together in the classroom, we've often told stories about our own children to provide real-life examples of various psychological principles. Ironically, in the chapter on memory, we suddenly realized that some of the stories we were currently telling our students about our respective daughters were becoming blended in our own minds. We couldn't remember whether certain events happened to one of my three daughters or to Karen's only daughter! For us, this became a perfect, personal example of both the *constructive* nature of memory, as well as *source amnesia*!

Professor Katie Townsend-Merino
Palomar College
San Marcos, CA

experiments have created false memories, by showing subjects doctored photos of themselves taking a completely fictitious hot-air balloon ride or by asking subjects to simply imagine an event, such as having a nurse remove a skin sample from their finger. In these and similar cases, a large number of subjects later believed that the misleading information was correct and that the fictitious or imagined events actually occurred (Fazio et al., 2013; Hess et al., 2012; Wright et al., 2013).

Q3

Some research even suggests that watching someone else engage in a behavior, or merely *imagining* ourselves doing that behavior, can lead us to (falsely) believe that we've actually done that activity ourselves. For example, one study asked students to read a series of statements, such as "shake the bottle," and were then told to either imagine performing that action or to watch a video of someone else performing it. When the students were asked two weeks later to recall which actions they had performed, they "remembered" performing 23% of the actions they had seen someone else doing in the video and "remembered" performing 33% of the actions they had imagined doing themselves (Lindner et al., 2010)!

Serial-position effect A characteristic of memory retrieval in which information at the beginning and end of a series is remembered better than material in the middle.

In addition to having problems with the misinformation effect, study participants who are asked to memorize lists of words remember some words better than others, depending on where they occurred in the list, a result known as the **serial-position effect**. They remember the words at the beginning (*primacy effect*) and the end (*recency effect*) better than those in the middle of the list, which are quite often forgotten (Bonk & Healy, 2010; Overstreet & Healy, 2011).

The reasons for the serial-position effect are complex, but they have interesting real-life implications. For example, a potential employer's memory of you might be enhanced if you are either the first or the last candidate interviewed.

Source amnesia A memory error caused by forgetting the true source of a memory (also called source confusion or source misattribution).

Sleeper effect A memory error in which information from an unreliable source that was initially discounted later gains credibility because the source is forgotten.

Each day we read, hear, and process an enormous amount of information, and it's easy to get confused about who said what to whom and in what context. Forgetting the true source of a memory is known as **source amnesia** (Kleider et al., 2008; Leichtman, 2006; Paterson et al., 2011).

When we first hear something from an unreliable source, we tend to disregard that information in favor of a more reliable source. However, as the source of the information is forgotten (source amnesia), the unreliable information is no longer discounted. This is called the **sleeper effect** (see *Real World Psychology*) (Appel & Richter, 2007; Ecker et al., 2011; Nabi & Moyer-Gusé, 2013).

© Tampa Bay Times/ZUMAPRESS/Alamy Inc.

realworldpsychology **The Power of Negative Political Campaigns**

Think back to a recent heated political election. What type of television advertisements most readily come to mind? People are most likely to recall ads that rely on creating negative feelings about one of the candidates. These negative advertisement work because they stick with us, even if we initially have negative feelings about them (Lariscy & Tinkham, 1999). Over time, the "facts" stay in our memory, and we forget the source, illustrating both source amnesia and the sleeper effect!

Distributed practice A study technique in which practice (or study) sessions are interspersed with rest periods.

Massed practice A study technique in which time spent learning is grouped (or massed) into long, unbroken intervals; also known as cramming.

If we try to memorize too much information at once (as when students "cram" before an exam), we're not likely to learn and remember as much as we would with more distributed study (Dunn et al., 2013; Fulton et al., 2013; Karpicke & Bauernschmidt, 2011). **Distributed practice** refers to spacing your learning periods, with rest periods between sessions. Cramming is called **massed practice** because the time spent learning is massed into long, unbroken intervals. For example, researchers in one study asked musicians to practice a note sequence in three practice sessions that were separated by either 5 minutes, 6 hours, or 24 hours (Simmons, 2012). Those whose practice sessions were separated by 24 hours showed significantly greater memory of the notes than those with shorter times between practice sessions.

Finally, as illustrated in **Figure 7.12**, cultural factors can play a role in how well people remember what they have learned.

(c) Ferdinando Scianna/MagnumPhotos, Inc.

FIGURE 7.12 CULTURE AND MEMORY

In many societies, tribal leaders pass down vital information through orally related stories. As a result, children living in these cultures have better memories for information that is related through stories than do other children. Can you think of other ways in which culture might influence memory?

RETRIEVAL PRACTICE: FORGETTING

Self-Test

Completing this self-test and comparing your answers with those in Appendix B provides immediate feedback and helpful practice for exams. Additional interactive, self-tests are available at www.wiley.com/college/huffman.

1. According to the ______ theory of forgetting, memory is processed and stored in a physical form, and connections between neurons deteriorate over time.

a. decay
b. interference
c. motivated forgetting
d. retrieval failure

2. The ______ theory suggests that forgetting is caused by two competing memories, particularly memories with similar qualities.

a. decay
b. interference
c. motivated forgetting
d. encoding failure

3. Which of the following is *not* one of the six factors that contribute to forgetting outlined in the text?

a. misinformation effect
b. serial-position effect
c. race and/or ethnicity
d. source amnesia

4. Distributed practice is a learning technique in which ______.

a. students are distributed (spaced) equally throughout the room
b. learning periods alternate with nonlearning rest periods
c. learning decays faster than it can be distributed
d. several students study together, distributing various subjects according to their individual strengths

Think Critically

1. Briefly describe an example from your own life of source amnesia and the sleeper effect.
2. Why might advertisers of shoddy services or products benefit from channel surfing if the television viewer is skipping from news programs to cable talk shows to infomercials?

realworldpsychology

Can merely imagining engaging in a behavior create a false memory of actually performing that behavior?

HINT: LOOK IN THE MARGIN FOR Q3

BIOLOGICAL BASES OF MEMORY

LEARNING OBJECTIVES

RETRIEVAL PRACTICE While reading the upcoming sections, respond to each Learning Objective in your own words. Then compare your responses with those found at www.wiley.com/college/huffman.

1. **DESCRIBE** two kinds of biological changes that occur when we learn something new.
2. **EXPLAIN** the effect of hormones on memory.
3. **IDENTIFY** some brain areas involved in memory.
4. **EXPLAIN** how injury and disease can affect memory.

A number of biological changes occur when we learn something new. Among them are neuronal and synaptic changes and hormonal changes. We discuss these changes in this section, along with the questions of where memories are located and what causes memory loss.

Neuronal and Synaptic Changes

We know that learning modifies the brain's neural networks (Chapters 2 and 6). As you learn to play tennis, for example, repeated practice builds specific neural pathways that make it easier and easier for you to get the ball over the net. This **long-term potentiation (LTP)** happens in at least two ways.

Long-term potentiation (LTP) A long-lasting increase in neural excitability, which may be a biological mechanism for learning and memory.

First, as early research with rats raised in enriched environments showed (Rosenzweig et al., 1972), repeated stimulation of a synapse can strengthen the synapse by causing the dendrites to grow more spines (Chapter 6). This results in more synapses, more receptor sites, and more sensitivity.

Second, when learning and memory occur, there is a measurable change in the amount of neurotransmitter released, which thereby increases the neuron's efficiency in message transmission. Research with *Aplysia* (sea slugs) clearly demonstrates this effect **(Figure 7.13)**.

FIGURE 7.13 **HOW DOES A SEA SLUG LEARN AND REMEMBER?**

After repeated squirting with water, followed by a mild shock, the sea slug, *Aplysia*, releases more neurotransmitters at certain synapses. These synapses then become more efficient at transmitting signals that allow the slug to withdraw its gills when squirted. As a critical thinker, can you explain why this ability might provide an evolutionary advantage?

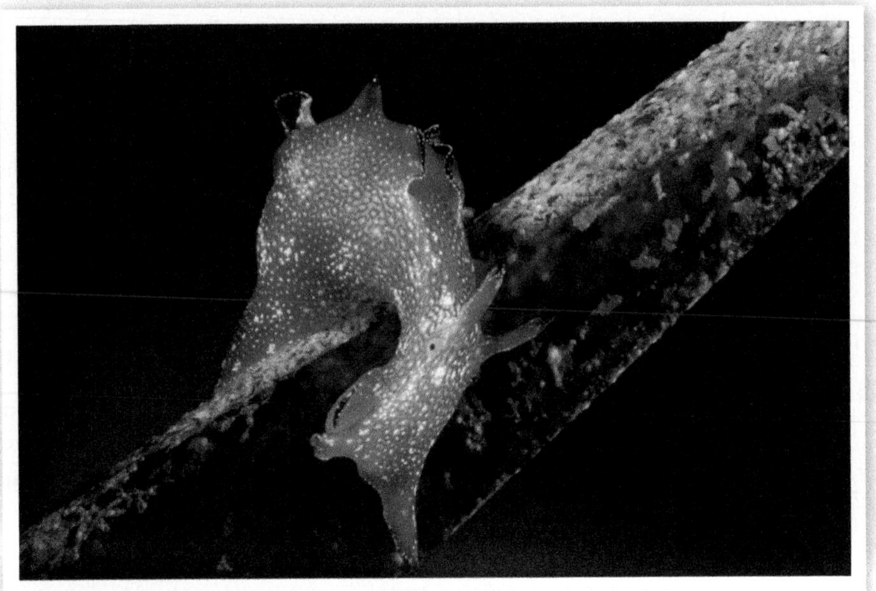

Further evidence comes from research with genetically engineered "smart mice," which have extra receptors for a neurotransmitter named NMDA (N-methyl-d-aspartate). These mice performed significantly better on memory tasks than did normal mice (Brim et al., 2013; Mohamad et al., 2013; Tang et al., 2001; Tsien, 2000).

Although it is difficult to generalize from sea slugs and mice, research on long-term potentiation (LTP) in humans also supports the idea that LTP is one of the major biological mechanisms underlying learning and memory (Berger et al., 2008; Kullmann & Lamsa, 2011; Shin et al., 2010).

Hormonal Changes and Emotional Arousal

When stressed or excited, we naturally produce hormones that arouse the body, such as *epinephrine* and *cortisol* (Chapter 3). These hormones in turn affect the amygdala (a brain structure involved in emotion), which then stimulates the hippocampus and cerebral cortex (parts of the brain that are important for memory storage). Research has shown that epinephrine or cortisol, or electrical stimulation of the amygdala, increase the encoding and storage of new information (Hupbach & Fieman, 2012; Jurado-Berbel et al., 2010; McIntyre et al., 2012). However, prolonged or excessive stress and emotional arousal can increase, as well as interfere with, memory (Baucom et al., 2012; Guenzel et al., 2013; Morgan et al., 2012; Schilling et al., 2013).

Interestingly, some research suggests that exposure to pornography can disrupt memory. Researchers in one study (Laier et al., 2013) asked men to view a series of both pornographic and nonpornographic images and judge whether they had previously seen each image. Men who saw the nonsexual images gave 80% correct answers, whereas men who saw the pornographic images gave only 67% correct answers. Can you see how sexual arousal interferes with working memory and how it may help explain these findings? Q4

The powerful effect of hormones on memory also can be seen in what are known as **flashbulb memories (FBMs)**—vivid, detailed, and near-permanent images associated with surprising or strongly emotional events (Brown & Kulik, 1977). In such situations, we secrete a flood of hormones when we initially experience or learn of the event, and then we replay the event in our minds again and again, actions that both make for stronger memories. In addition to widely shared public events, such as the Boston Marathon bombings on April 15, 2013, your personal flashbulb memories might include your first kiss, the birth of your first child, or the loss of a loved one.

Flashbulb memory (FBM) A recall of vivid, detailed, and near-permanent images associated with surprising or strongly emotional events; it may or may not be accurate.

Despite their intensity, flashbulb memories may not be as accurate as you might think (Kvavilashvili et al., 2010; Lanciano et al., 2010; Schmidt, 2012). For example, when asked how he heard the news of the September 11, 2001, attacks, President George W. Bush's answers contained several errors (Greenberg, 2004). Our flashbulb memories for specific details (particularly the time and place the emotional event occurred) are fairly accurate (Rimmele et al., 2012). But, overall, flashbulb memories, like all other memories, are not perfect recordings of events. What separates them from ordinary, everyday memories is their vividness and our subjective confidence in their accuracy. Keep in mind that confidence is not the same as accuracy—an important point we'll return to in the last part of this chapter.

Where Are Memories Located?

Early memory researchers believed that memory was *localized*, or stored in a particular brain area. Later research suggests that, in fact, memory tends to be localized not in a single area but in many separate areas throughout the brain **(Figure 7.14)**.

FIGURE 7.14 **THE BRAIN AND MEMORY**

Damage to any one of these areas can affect encoding, storage, and retrieval of memories.

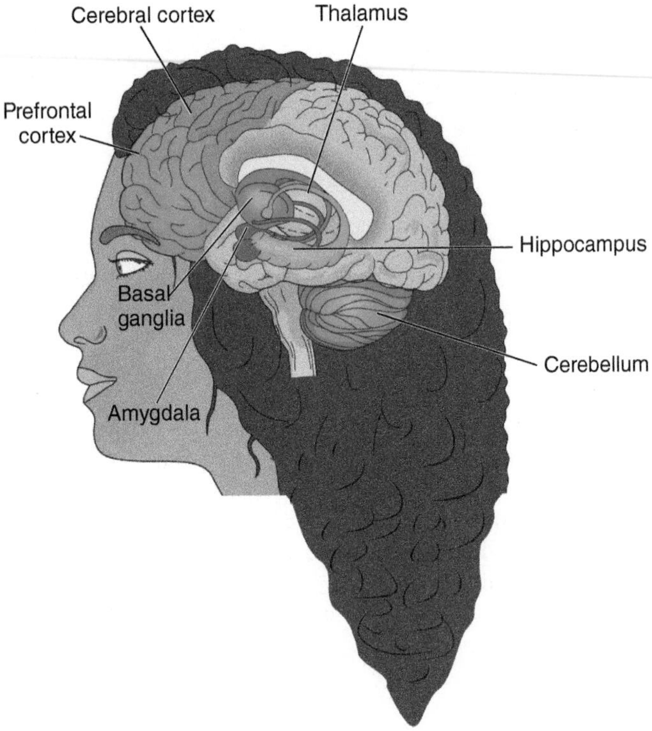

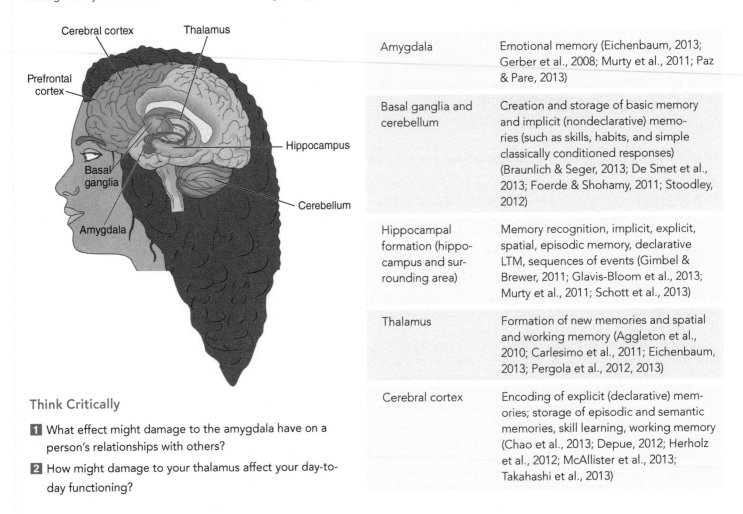

Amygdala	Emotional memory (Eichenbaum, 2013; Gerber et al., 2008; Murty et al., 2011; Paz & Pare, 2013)
Basal ganglia and cerebellum	Creation and storage of basic memory and implicit (nondeclarative) memories (such as skills, habits, and simple classically conditioned responses) (Braunlich & Seger, 2013; De Smet et al., 2013; Foerde & Shohamy, 2011; Stoodley, 2012)
Hippocampal formation (hippocampus and surrounding area)	Memory recognition, implicit, explicit, spatial, episodic memory, declarative LTM, sequences of events (Gimbel & Brewer, 2011; Glavis-Bloom et al., 2013; Murty et al., 2011; Schott et al., 2013)
Thalamus	Formation of new memories and spatial and working memory (Aggleton et al., 2010; Carlesimo et al., 2011; Eichenbaum, 2013; Pergola et al., 2012, 2013)
Cerebral cortex	Encoding of explicit (declarative) memories; storage of episodic and semantic memories, skill learning, working memory (Chao et al., 2013; Depue, 2012; Herholz et al., 2012; McAllister et al., 2013; Takahashi et al., 2013)

Think Critically

1. What effect might damage to the amygdala have on a person's relationships with others?
2. How might damage to your thalamus affect your day-to-day functioning?

Today, research techniques are so advanced that we can experimentally induce and measure memory-related brain changes as they occur—on-the-spot reporting! For example, James Brewer and his colleagues (1998) used functional magnetic resonance imaging (fMRI) to locate areas of the brain responsible for encoding memories of pictures. They showed 96 pictures of indoor and outdoor scenes to participants while scanning their brains, and then they later tested participants' ability to recall the pictures. Brewer and his colleagues identified the *right prefrontal cortex* and the *parahippocampal cortex* as being the most active during the encoding of the pictures. These are only two of several brain regions involved in memory storage.

Biological Causes of Memory Loss

The leading cause of neurological disorders—including memory loss—among young U.S. men and women between the ages of 15 and 25 is *traumatic brain injury*. These injuries most commonly result from car accidents, falls, blows, and gunshot wounds.

Traumatic brain injury happens when the skull suddenly collides with another object. Compression, twisting, and distortion of the brain inside the skull all cause serious and sometimes permanent damage to the brain. The frontal and temporal

FIGURE 7.15 **TWO TYPES OF AMNESIA**

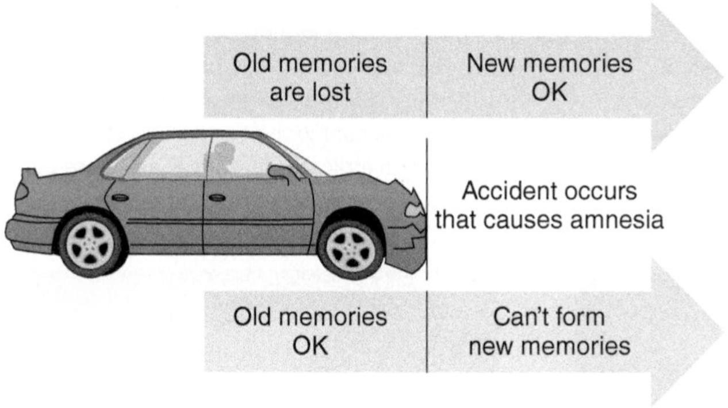

A Retrograde amnesia
The person loses memories of events that occurred *before* the accident, yet has no trouble remembering things that happened afterward (old, "retro" memories are lost).

B Anterograde amnesia
The person cannot form new memories for events that occur *after* the accident. Anterograde amnesia also may result from a surgical injury or from diseases such as chronic alcoholism.

lobes often take the heaviest hit because they directly collide with the bony ridges inside the skull.

Loss of memory as a result of brain injury or trauma is called *amnesia*, and there are two major types—*retrograde* and *anterograde* **(Figure 7.15)**. In **retrograde amnesia** (acting backward in time), the person loses memory (is amnesic) for events that occurred *before* the brain injury. However, the same person has no trouble remembering things that happened after the injury. As the name implies, only the old, "retro," memories are lost.

Retrograde amnesia The loss of memory for events before a brain injury; backward-acting amnesia.

Consolidation The process by which neural changes associated with recent learning become durable and stable.

Anterograde amnesia The inability to form new memories after a brain injury; forward-acting amnesia.

What causes retrograde amnesia? In cases where the individual is only amnesic for the events right before the brain injury, the cause may be a failure of consolidation. We learned earlier that during long-term potentiation (LTP), our neurons change to accommodate new learning. We also know that it takes a certain amount of time for these neural changes to become fixed and stable in long-term memory, a process known as **consolidation**. Like heavy rain on wet cement, the brain injury "wipes away" unstable memories because the cement has not had time to harden (*retrograde amnesia*).

In contrast to retrograde amnesia, in which people lose memories for events *before* a brain injury, some people lose memory for events that occur *after* a brain injury, which is called **anterograde amnesia** (acting forward in time). This type of amnesia generally results from a surgical injury or from diseases such as chronic alcoholism. Continuing our analogy with wet cement, anterograde amnesia would be like having permanently hardened cement. You can't lay down new long-term memories because the cement is hardened.

Keep in mind that retrograde amnesia is normally temporary. Unfortunately, anterograde amnesia is most often permanent, but patients show surprising abilities to learn and remember implicit/nondeclarative tasks (such as procedural motor skills like mowing a lawn).

Another way to understand these two forms of amnesia is to compare them to the functions of a computer. Experiencing retrograde amnesia would be like having your latest stored data (memories) erased from your hard drive. In contrast, having anterograde amnesia would be similar to disconnecting your hard drive from the computer—no new data (memories) could be stored.

Amnesia at work
Fifty-five-year-old Kay Delaney slipped and hit her head at work, which led to severe memory loss. Sadly, she now believes she's only 34 and has no memory of the past 21 years, including raising her three children. Is this an example of retrograde or anterograde amnesia?

Casey Gutteridge/SWNS

FIGURE 7.16 **THE EFFECT OF ALZHEIMER'S DISEASE ON THE BRAIN**

Ⓐ **Normal brain**
Note the high amount of red and yellow color (signs of brain activity) in the positron emission tomography scans of the normal brain.

Ⓑ **Brain of an Alzheimer's disease patient**
The reduced activity in the brain of the Alzheimer's disease patient is evident. The loss is most significant in the temporal and parietal lobes, which indicates that these areas are particularly important for storing memories.

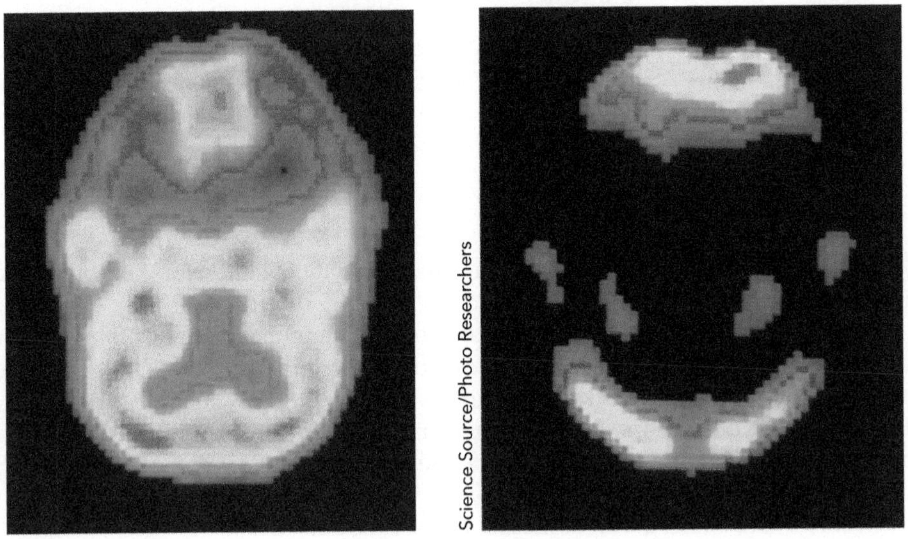

Science Source/Photo Researchers

Science Source/Photo Researchers

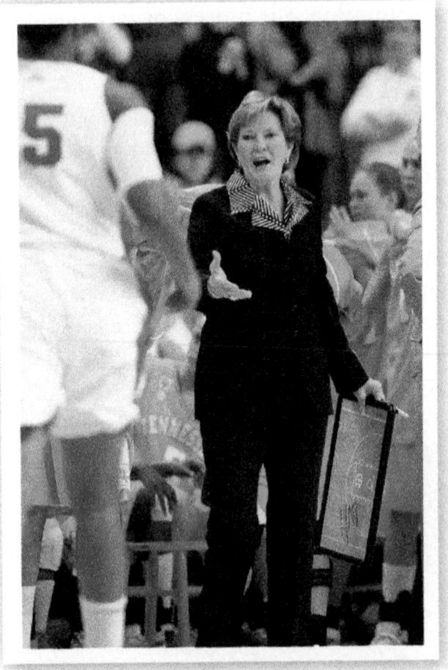

© Duncan Williams/Icon SMI/Corbis

Pat Summit, coach of the Tennessee Lady Vols basketball team from 1974 until 2012 and the winningest college basketball coach of all time, announced in 2011 that she had early-stage Alzheimer's disease.

Alzheimer's disease (AD) A chronic organic brain syndrome characterized by gradual loss of memory, decline in intellectual ability, and deterioration of personality.

Like traumatic brain injuries, disease can alter the physiology of the brain and nervous system, affecting memory processes. For example, **Alzheimer's disease (AD)** is a progressive mental deterioration that occurs most commonly in old age **(Figure 7.16)**. The most noticeable early symptoms are disturbances in memory, which become progressively worse until, in the final stages, the person fails to recognize loved ones, needs total nursing care, and ultimately dies.

Alzheimer's does not attack all types of memory equally. A hallmark of the disease is an extreme decrease in *explicit/declarative memory* (Irish et al., 2011; Libon et al., 2007; Satler et al., 2007). Alzheimer's patients fail to recall facts, information, and personal life experiences, yet they still retain some *implicit/nondeclarative* memories, such as simple classically conditioned responses and procedural tasks like brushing their teeth.

Brain autopsies of people with Alzheimer's show unusual *tangles* (structures formed from degenerating cell bodies) and *plaques* (structures formed from degenerating axons and dendrites). Hereditary Alzheimer's generally strikes its victims between the ages of 45 and 55. Some experts believe the cause of Alzheimer's is primarily genetic, but others think instead that genetic makeup may make some people more susceptible to environmental triggers (Bettens et al., 2013; Sillén et al., 2011; Yu et al., 2013).

© Alexsi/iStockphoto

realworldpsychology **A New Treatment for Alzheimer's Disease?**
Researchers have recently experimented with electrical brain stimulation for patients with severe epilepsy (Suthana et al., 2012). Those who received stimulation to a particular part of the cortex, which is one of the first parts of the brain to be damaged in patients with Alzheimer's disease, showed improvement in memory. This technique also may be useful in treating patients with Alzheimer's and other forms of severe memory loss.

RETRIEVAL PRACTICE: BIOLOGICAL BASES OF MEMORY

Self-Test

Completing this self-test and comparing your answers with those in Appendix B provides immediate feedback and helpful practice for exams. Additional interactive, self-tests are available at www.wiley.com/college/huffman.

1. The long-lasting increase in neural excitability believed to be a biological mechanism for learning and memory is called _____.

   a. maintenance rehearsal b. adrenaline activation
   c. long-term potentiation d. the reverberating response

2. Your vivid memory of what you were doing when you were first informed about your parents' impending divorce is an example of _____.

   a. encoding specificity b. long-term potentiation
   c. latent learning d. a flashbulb memory

3. Ralph can't remember anything that happened to him before he fell through the floor of his tree house. His lack of memory of events before his fall is called _____ amnesia.

   a. retroactive b. proactive
   c. anterograde d. retrograde

4. A progressive mental deterioration characterized by severe memory loss that occurs most commonly in elderly people is called _____.

   a. retrieval loss syndrome deterioration b. prefrontal cortex
   c. Alzheimer's disease d. age-related amnesia

Think Critically

1 What might be the evolutionary benefit of flashbulb memories?

2 How might Alzheimer's disease affect a person's relationships with others?

realworldpsychology

Why might exposure to pornography interfere with memory?

HINT: LOOK IN THE MARGIN FOR Q4

MEMORY DISTORTIONS

RETRIEVAL PRACTICE While reading the upcoming sections, respond to each Learning Objective in your own words. Then compare your responses with those found at www.wiley.com/college/huffman.

LEARNING OBJECTIVES

1 **EXPLAIN** why our memories sometimes become distorted.
2 **DESCRIBE** problems with using eyewitnesses in the criminal justice system.
3 **DISTINGUISH** between false and repressed memories.

At this point in your life, you've undoubtedly experienced a painful breakup of a serious love relationship and/or witnessed similar breakups among your close friends. During these breakups, did you wonder how the reported experiences of two people in the same partnership could be so different? Why would each partner reconstruct his or her own personal memory of the relationship?

There are several reasons we shape, rearrange, and distort our memories. One of the most common is our need for *logic* and *consistency*. When we're initially forming new memories or sorting through old ones, we fill in missing pieces, make "corrections," and rearrange information to make it logical and consistent with our previous experiences or personal desires. For example, if you left a relationship because you found a new partner, you might rearrange your memories to suit your belief that you are just a weak-willed person who can't stay faithful or that you were mismatched from the beginning. However, if you were the one left behind, you might reconstruct your memories and now believe that you're doomed to lose people you love or that your partner was a manipulative "player" from the beginning. Of course, not all memory reconstructions are so dramatic. However, it's important that we recognize and remember the fallibility of our memory processes during initial encoding, current storage, and future retrieval. To experience first-hand the constructive nature of memory, try the memory test below.

We also shape and construct our memories for the sake of *efficiency*. We summarize, augment, and tie new information in with related memories in LTM. Similarly, when we need to retrieve the stored information, we leave out seemingly unimportant elements or misremember the details.

Despite all their problems and biases, our memories are normally fairly accurate and serve us well in most situations. They have evolved to encode, store, and retrieve general and/or vital information, such as the location of various buildings on our college campus or looking both ways when we cross the street. However, when faced with tasks that require encoding, storing, and retrieving precise details like those in a scholarly text, remembering names and faces of

TEST YOURSELF: A PERSONAL MEMORY TEST

psychology and you

Carefully read through all the words in the following list.

Sour	Chocolate	Pie	Bitter	Soda
Nice	Heart	Honey	Good	Honey
Honey	Cake	Candy	Taste	
Artichoke	Tart	Sugar	Tooth	

Now cover the list and write down all the words you remember.

Number of correctly recalled words:

15 to 18 words = excellent memory

10 to 14 words = average

5 to 9 words = below average

4 or fewer words = you might need a nap

How did you do? Do you have a good or excellent memory? Did you recall seeing the words *sleep* and *doctor*? Did you recall seeing the words "sour" and "honey"? Most students do, and it's a good example of the *serial-position effect*—the first and last words in the list (p. 00). Did you remember the word "artichoke" and "honey"? If you recalled "artichoke," it illustrates the power of *distinctiveness*, whereas if you remembered seeing "honey" it's because it was repeated three times. Both of these examples demonstrate how distinctive and/or repeated material are more easily encoded, stored, and recalled. Finally, did you see the word "*sweet*"? Look back over the list. That word is not there, yet most students commonly report seeing it. Why? As mentioned in the introduction to this chapter, memory is not a faithful duplicate of an event; it is a *constructive process*. We actively shape and build on information as it is encoded and retrieved.

Think Critically

1. Other than this example of seeing the word "sweet," can you think of another example in which you created a false memory?
2. How might constructive memories create misunderstandings at work and in our everyday relationships?

potential clients, or recalling where we left our house keys, our brains are not as well-equipped.

Memory and the Criminal Justice System

When our memory errors come into play in the criminal justice system, they may lead to wrongful judgments of guilt or innocence with possible life or death consequences!

In the past, one of the best forms of trial evidence a lawyer could have was an *eyewitness*—"I was there; I saw it with my own eyes." Unfortunately, research has identified several problems with eyewitness testimony (Cutler & Kovera, 2013; Herve et al., 2013; Loftus, 2000, 2001, 2007, 2011). One of the most serious is that it's relatively easy to create false memories (Fazio et al., 2013; Frenda et al., 2011; Loftus & Cahill, 2007; Strange et al., 2011; Wright et al., 2013).

Even more troubling are the findings that once false memories have been formed, they can multiply over time and last for years. Researchers in one study showed participants pictures of an event, such as a girl's wallet being stolen (Zhu et al., 2012). Participants then read a series of statements about the event, which included both accurate information (for instance, the person who took the girl's wallet was a man) and false information (the person who took the girl's wallet put it in his pants pocket, when in reality the picture showed him hiding the wallet in his jacket). Initially, after reading these statements, participants identified only 31% of the false events as having occurred. However, when participants were asked 1½ years later which events had occurred, they identified 39% of the false statements as true, indicating that false memories not only last but can even multiply over time. What might be the implications of this research for eyewitness testimony in court?

Recall our earlier discussion of the misinformation effect and how experimenters created a false memory of seeing a telephone in a room (page 191). Participants who were asked neutral questions, such as "Was there a telephone in the room?" made errors on only 10% of the queries (Morgan et al., 2013). In contrast, when participants were asked "What color was the telephone?" falsely implying that a telephone had been in the room, 98% "remembered" it being there. The *Psych Science* box further describes how our biases can influence our "memory" of an event.

Problems with eyewitness recollections are so well established and important that judges now allow expert testimony on the unreliability of eyewitness testimony and routinely instruct jurors on its limits (Cutler & Kovea, 2013; Pezdek, 2012). If you serve as a member of a jury or listen to accounts of crimes in the news, remind yourself of these problems. Also, keep in mind that research participants in eyewitness studies generally report their inaccurate memories with great self-assurance and strong conviction (Douglass & Pavletic, 2012; Goodwin et al., 2013; Jaeger et al., 2012). Eyewitnesses to an actual crime may similarly identify an innocent person as the perpetrator with equally high confidence **(Figure 7.17)**. In one experiment, participants watched people committing a staged crime. Only an hour later, 20% of the eyewitnesses identified innocent

FIGURE 7.17 THE DANGERS OF EYEWITNESS TESTIMONY

realworldpsychology

Damon Thibodeaux served 15 years in prison for killing his step-cousin before being released on September 28, 2012, after he was officially cleared via DNA testing. He was convicted at age 22 based in part on testimony by two eyewitnesses.

© Michael DeMocker/TheTimes Picayune/Landov

PSYCHSCIENCE

DO WE "REMEMBER" WHAT WE WANT TO REMEMBER?

Photo left and right: Reprinted from Journal of Experimental Social Psychology Volume 49, Issue 2, Steven J. Frenda et al. False memories of fabricated political events. Copyright 2013, with permission from Elsevier

To study how false memories are formed, researchers in one recent study asked more than 5,000 participants about their memories of several political events (Frenda et al., 2013). Some of these political events had actually occurred, such as George W. Bush's winning the 2000 presidential election. However, other political events had been deliberately created by the experimenters to appear as if they had occurred when in fact they had not. Each fabricated story included a photograph supposedly showing the event. Participants were then asked whether they remembered the event occurring and how they felt about it at the time.

Can you predict what these researchers found? In line with prior research on the ease with which false memories are created, approximately half the participants "remembered" that the false event happened, and about 27% "remembered" seeing it reported on the news. Interestingly, participants' political orientation influenced the formation of false memories.

For example, participants who were politically liberal were significantly more likely to create a false memory of President George W. Bush supposedly socializing with a famous baseball star during the Hurricane Katrina disaster (see the fabricated photo on the left). In contrast, participants who were politically conservative were more likely to falsely remember seeing President Barack Obama supposedly shaking hands with the President of Iran (note the fabricated photo on the right). These findings indicate that we are particularly likely to form false memories of events that fit with, and reinforce, our preexisting attitudes.

RESEARCH CHALLENGE

1. Based on the information provided, did this study (Frenda et al., 2013) use descriptive, correlational, and/or experimental research?
2. If you chose:
   - descriptive research, is this a naturalistic observation, survey/interview, case study, or archival research?
   - correlational research, is this a positive, negative, or zero correlation?
   - experimental research, label the IV, DV, experimental group(s), and control group.

>> CHECK YOUR ANSWERS IN APPENDIX B.

NOTE: The information provided in this study is admittedly limited, but the level of detail is similar to what is presented in most textbooks and public reports of research findings. Answering these questions, and then comparing your answers to those in the Appendix, will help you become a better critical thinker and consumer of scientific research.

people from mug shots, and a week later, 8% identified innocent people in a lineup (Brown et al., 1977).

Q5 Ironically, research now suggests that the accuracy of eyewitness testimony can be improved if people are asked to make very fast judgments (Brewer et al., 2012). In fact, giving people only a few seconds to identify the culprit in a lineup increases the accuracy of such identifications by 20 to 30%, compared to allowing people to take as long as they want to make a decision. **Figure 7.18** offers further tips for improving eyewitness testimony.

"Thank you, gentlemen—you may all leave except for No. 3."

FIGURE 7.18 EYEWITNESSES AND POLICE LINEUPS

As humorously depicted in this cartoon, officials now recommend that suspects should never "stand out" from the others in a lineup. Witnesses also are cautioned to not assume that the real criminal is in the lineup, and they should never "guess" when asked to make an identification.

False Versus Repressed Memories

Like eyewitness testimony, false memories can have serious legal, personal, and social implications. Consider this true story of psychologist Elizabeth Loftus, one of modern psychology's most famous memory scientists.

When Elizabeth was 14, her mother drowned in the family's pool. Decades later, a relative told Elizabeth that she, Elizabeth, had been the one to find her mother's body. Despite her initial shock, Elizabeth's memories slowly started coming back. Her recovery of these gruesome childhood memories, although painful, initially brought great relief. It also seemed to explain why she had always been fascinated by the topic of memory.

Then her brother called to say there had been a mistake! The relative who told Elizabeth that she had been the one to discover her mother's body later remembered—and other relatives confirmed—that it had actually been Aunt Pearl, not Elizabeth. Loftus, an expert on memory distortions, had unknowingly created her own *false memory*.

Creating false memories may be somewhat common, but can we recover true memories that are buried in childhood? *Repression* is the supposed unconscious coping mechanism by which we prevent anxiety-provoking thoughts from reaching consciousness. According to some research, repressed memories are *actively* and *consciously* "forgotten" in an effort to avoid the pain of their retrieval (Anderson et al., 2004; Boag, 2012). Others suggest that some memories are so painful that they exist only in an *unconscious* corner of the brain, making them inaccessible to the individual (Haaken, 2010; Mancia & Baggott, 2008). In these cases, therapy supposedly would be necessary to unlock the hidden memories.

Repression is a complex and controversial topic in psychology. No one doubts that some memories are forgotten and later recovered. What some question is the idea that *repressed memories* of painful experiences (especially childhood sexual abuse) are stored in the unconscious mind (Klein, 2012; Lambert et al., 2010; Loftus & Cahill, 2007).

Critics suggest that most people who have witnessed or experienced a violent crime or are adult survivors of childhood sexual abuse have intense, persistent memories. They have trouble *forgetting*, not remembering. Some critics also wonder whether therapists sometimes inadvertently create false memories in their clients during therapy. Some worry that if a clinician even suggests the possibility of abuse, the client's own *constructive processes* may lead him or her to create a false memory. The client might start to incorporate portrayals of abuse from movies and books into his or her own memory, forgetting their original sources and eventually coming to see them as reliable.

This is not to say that all psychotherapy clients who recover memories of sexual abuse (or other painful incidents) have invented those memories. For example, some research suggests that children may remember experiencing sexual abuse but not understand or recognize those behaviors as abuse until adulthood (McNally, 2012).

Unfortunately, the repressed memory debate has grown increasingly bitter, and research on both sides is hotly contested. The stakes are high because lawsuits and criminal prosecutions of sexual abuse are sometimes based on recovered memories of childhood sexual abuse. As researchers continue exploring the mechanisms underlying delayed remembering, we must be careful not to ridicule or condemn people who recover true memories of abuse. In the same spirit, we must protect innocent people from wrongful accusations that come from false memories. Hopefully, with continued research (and perhaps new technology) we may someday better protect the interests of both the victim and the accused.

RETRIEVAL PRACTICE: MEMORY DISTORTIONS

Self-Test

Completing this self-test and comparing your answers with those in Appendix B provides immediate feedback and helpful practice for exams. Additional interactive, self-tests are available at www.wiley.com/college/huffman.

1. Problems with eyewitness recollections are so well established and important that judges now _____.

a. allow expert testimony on the unreliability of eyewitness testimony
b. routinely instruct jurors on the limits and unreliability of eyewitness recollections
c. both the above
d. none of the above

2. Researchers have demonstrated that it is _____ to create false memories.

a. relatively easy
b. rarely possible
c. moderately difficult
d. never possible

3. Dave was told the same childhood story of his father saving his neighbor from a fire so many times that he is now sure it is true, but all the evidence proves it never happened. This is an example of _____.

a. a repressed memory
b. deluded childhood fantasies
c. a false memory
d. early-onset juvenile dementia

4. _____ memories are related to anxiety-provoking thoughts or events that are supposedly prevented from reaching consciousness.

a. Suppressed
b. Flashbulb
c. Flashback
d. Repressed

Think Critically

1 As an eyewitness to a crime, how could you use information in this chapter to improve your memory for specific details?

2 If you were a juror, what would you say to the other jurors about the reliability of eyewitness testimony?

realworldpsychology

Does accuracy increase when eyewitnesses have only a few seconds to make an identification?

HINT: LOOK IN THE MARGIN FOR Q5

Summary

1 THE NATURE OF MEMORY 180

- **Memory** is an internal representation of some prior event or experience. It's also a **constructive process** that organizes and shapes information. Major perspectives on memory include the **encoding, storage,** and **retrieval (ESR) model** and the **three-stage memory model**.
- Information enters memory in three stages: **encoding**, **storage**, and **retrieval**. In contrast, the **three-stage memory model** proposes that information is stored and processed in **sensory memory**, **short-term memory (STM)**, and **long-term memory (LTM)**; these differ in purpose, duration, and capacity.
- **Chunking** and **maintenance rehearsal** improve STM's duration and capacity. Researchers think of STM as our **working memory**.
- **LTM** is an almost unlimited storehouse for information that must be kept for long periods. The two major types of LTM are **explicit/declarative memory** and **implicit/nondeclarative memory**. Organization and **elaborative rehearsal** improve encoding. **Retrieval cues** help stimulate retrieval of information from LTM. According to the **encoding-specificity principle**, retrieval is improved when conditions of recovery are similar to encoding conditions.

2 FORGETTING 188

- Researchers have proposed that we forget information through decay, **retroactive** and **proactive interference**, motivated forgetting, encoding failure, and retrieval failure.
- Early research by Ebbinghaus showed that we tend to forget newly learned information quickly, but we relearn the information more readily the second time.

TABLE 8.4 **GARDNER'S MULTIPLE INTELLIGENCES**

Type of Intelligence	Possible Careers
Linguistic Language, such as speaking, reading a book, writing a story	Novelist, journalist, teacher
Spatial Mental maps, such as figuring out how to pack multiple presents in a box or how to draw a floor plan	Engineer, architect, pilot
Bodily/kinesthetic Body movement, such as dancing, soccer, and football	Athlete, dancer, ski instructor
Intrapersonal Understanding oneself, such as setting achievable goals or recognizing self-defeating emotions	Increased success in almost all careers
Logical/mathematical Problem solving or scientific analysis, such as following a logical proof or solving a mathematical problem	Mathematician, scientist, engineer
Musical Musical skills, such as singing or playing a musical instrument	Singer, musician, composer
Interpersonal Social skills, such as managing diverse groups of people	Salesperson, manager, therapist, teacher
Naturalistic Being attuned to nature, such as noticing seasonal patterns or using environmentally safe products	Biologist, naturalist
Spiritual/existential Attunement to meaning of life and death and other conditions of life	Philosopher, theologian

Source: Adapted from Gardner, 1983, 1999, 2008, 2011.

Bloomberg/Getty Images

Oli Scarff/Getty Images

Elisa Estrada/Real Madrid/ Getty Images

TABLE 8.5 **STERNBERG'S TRIARCHIC THEORY OF SUCCESSFUL INTELLIGENCE**

	Analytical Intelligence	Creative Intelligence	Practical Intelligence
Sample skills	Good at analysis, evaluation, judgment, and comparison skills	Good at invention, coping with novelty, and imagination skills	Good at application, implementation, execution, and utilization skills
Methods of assessment	Intelligence tests assess the meaning of words based on context, and how to solve number-series problems	Open-ended tasks, writing a short story, drawing a piece of art, solving a scientific problem requiring insight	Tasks requiring solutions to practical, personal problems

Emotional intelligence (EI) is generally defined as *the ability to perceive, appraise, express, and regulate emotions accurately and appropriately*. In other words, an emotionally intelligent person successfully combines the three components of emotions (cognitive, physiological, and behavioral). Proponents of EI have suggested ways in which the close collaboration between emotion and reason may promote personal well-being and growth (Salovey et al., 2000) **(Figure 8.11)**.

FIGURE 8.11 HOW DO WE DEVELOP EMOTIONAL INTELLIGENCE?

The mother in this photo appears to be empathizing with her young daughter and helping her to recognize and manage her own emotions. According to Goleman, this type of modeling and instruction is vital to the development of emotional intelligence.

Digital Vision/Getty Images

© Michaeljung/iStockphoto

realworldpsychology **Should We Teach EI in Schools?** Popular accounts such as Goleman's have suggested that traditional measures of human intelligence ignore a crucial range of abilities that characterize people who excel in real life: self-awareness, impulse control, persistence, zeal and self-motivation, empathy, and social deftness. Goleman also proposes that many societal problems, such as domestic abuse and youth violence, can be attributed to low EI. Therefore, he argues, EI should be fostered and taught to everyone. In line with this, researchers in one study found that elementary schools in which emotional intelligence is taught show higher levels of warmth between students and teachers, more leadership among students, and teachers with a greater focus on students' interests and motivations (Rivers et al., 2012).

Critics fear that a handy term like EI invites misuse, but their strongest reaction is to Goleman's proposals for teaching EI. For example, Paul McHugh, director of psychiatry at Johns Hopkins University, suggests that Goleman is "presuming that someone has the key to the right emotions to be taught to children. We don't even know the right emotions to be taught to adults" (cited in Gibbs, 1995, p. 68).

Measuring Intelligence

Different IQ tests approach the measurement of intelligence from different perspectives. However, most are designed to predict grades in school. Let's look at the most commonly used IQ tests.

The *Stanford-Binet Intelligence Scale* is loosely based on the first IQ tests developed in France around the turn of the twentieth century by Alfred Binet. In the United States, Lewis Terman (1916) developed the Stanford-Binet (at Stanford University) to test the intellectual ability of U.S.-born children ages 3 to 16. The test is revised periodically—most recently in 2003. The test is administered individually and consists of such tasks as copying geometric designs, identifying similarities, and repeating number sequences.

In the original version of the Stanford-Binet, results were expressed in terms of a mental age. For example, if a 7-year-old's score equaled that of an average 8-year-old, the child was considered to have a mental age of 8. To determine the child's

FIGURE 8.12 ITEMS SIMILAR TO THOSE ON THE WECHSLER ADULT INTELLIGENCE SCALE (WAIS)

These are sample, simulated items resembling those found in the Wechsler Adult Intelligence Scale, Fourth Edition (WAIS-IV). Previous editions of the WAIS included sections, such as Picture Arrangement, Block Design, and Object Assembly, which were dropped to increase reliability, and user friendliness. WAIS-IV also takes less time to administer and the results show smaller differences based on level of education or racial/ethnic group membership. *Source*: Based on simulated items from the Wechsler Adult Intelligence Scale, Fourth Edition (WAIS-IV).

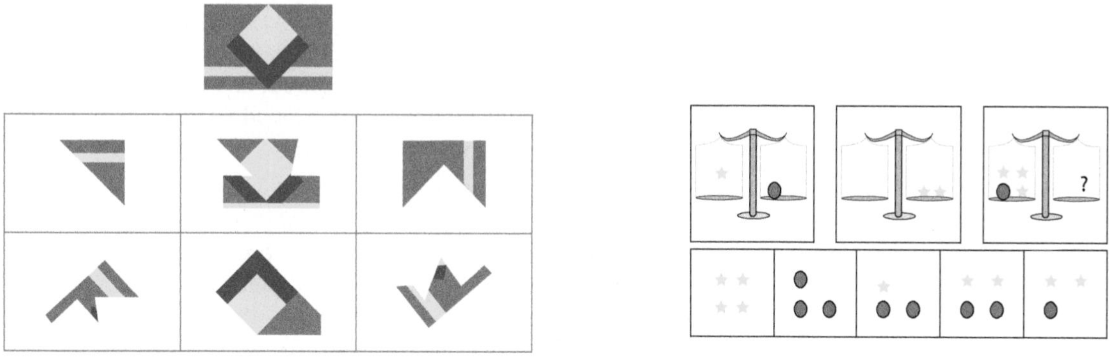

A Visual Puzzles
The test administrator asks: "Which three pieces go together to make this puzzle?"

B Figure Weights
The test administrator asks: "Which one of these works to balance the scale?"

intelligence quotient (IQ), mental age was divided by the child's chronological age (actual age in years) and multiplied by 100.

The most widely used intelligence test today, the *Wechsler Adult Intelligence Scale (WAIS)*, was developed by David Wechsler in the early 1900s. He later created a similar test for school-aged children. Like the Stanford-Binet, Wechsler's tests yield an overall intelligence score, but there are separate scores for verbal intelligence (such as vocabulary comprehension, and knowledge of general information) and performance (such as arranging blocks to match a given pattern) **(Figure 8.12)**. The advantages of Wechsler's test are that different abilities can be evaluated either separately or together, and the test can be used with non-English speakers (in which case the verbal portion is omitted).

Today, most intelligence test scores are expressed as a comparison of a single person's score to a national sample of similar-aged people **(Figure 8.13)**. Even though the actual IQ is no longer calculated using the original formula comparing mental and chronological ages, the term *IQ* remains as a shorthand expression for intelligence test scores.

What makes a good test? How are the tests developed by Binet and Wechsler any better than those published in popular magazines and presented on television programs? To be scientifically acceptable, all psychological tests must fulfill three basic requirements:

- **Standardization** Intelligence tests (as well as personality, aptitude, and most other tests) must be **standardized** in two senses (Gregory, 2011; Kolen & Hendrickson, 2013; Plucker & Esping, 2013). First, every test must have *norms*,

Intelligence quotient (IQ) An index of intelligence initially derived from standardized tests and by dividing mental age by chronological age and then multiplying by 100; now derived by comparing individual scores with the scores of others of the same age.

Standardization A set of uniform procedures for treating each participant in a test, interview, or experiment or for recording data.

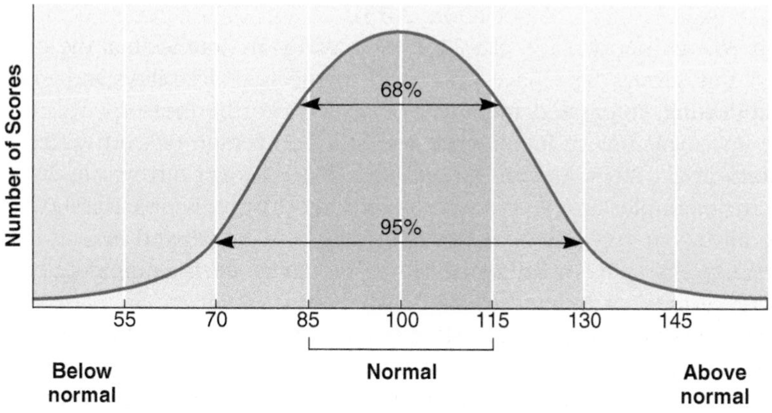

FIGURE 8.13 THE DISTRIBUTION OF SCORES ON THE STANFORD-BINET INTELLIGENCE TEST

Sixty-eight percent of children score within one standard deviation (16 points) above or below the national average, which is 100 points. About 16% score above 116, and about 16% score below 84.

or average scores, developed by giving the test to a representative sample of people (a diverse group of people who resemble those for whom the test is intended). Second, testing procedures must be standardized. All test takers must be given the same instructions, questions, and time limits, and all test administrators must follow the same objective score standards.

Reliability The degree to which a test produces similar scores each time it is used; stability or consistency of the scores produced by an instrument.

Validity The degree to which a test measures what it is intended to measure.

- **Reliability** is usually determined by retesting subjects to see whether their test scores change significantly (Geisinger, 2013; Gregory, 2011). Retesting can be done via the *test–retest method*, in which participants' scores on two separate administrations of the same test are compared, or via the *split-half method*, which splits a test into two equivalent parts (such as odd and even questions) and determines the degree of similarity between the two halves.
- **Validity** is the ability of a test to measure what it is designed to measure. The most important type of validity is *criterion-related validity*, or the accuracy with which test scores can be used to predict another variable of interest (known as the criterion). Criterion-related validity is expressed as the *correlation* (Chapter 1) between the test score and the criterion. If two variables are highly correlated, then one can be used to predict the other. Thus, if a test is valid, its scores will be useful in predicting an individual's behavior in some other specified situation. One example is using intelligence test scores to predict grades in college.

Can you see why a test that is standardized and reliable but not valid is worthless? For example, a test for skin sensitivity may be easy to standardize (the instructions specify exactly how to apply the test agent), and it may be reliable (similar results are obtained on each retest). But it certainly would not be valid for predicting college grades.

Voices from the Classroom

The Value of IQ Testing Intelligence tests, given under the appropriate circumstances, can be very valuable. If a student is struggling in school and the reasons are not obvious, an intelligence test can offer insight into that student's struggle. If the test results indicate a learning disability, such as dyslexia, then that student has a right to accommodations in school, which can ultimately help that student succeed.

Another example of the usefulness of intelligence tests is a personal one. My youngest son has significant facial paralysis and speech articulation difficulties due to a rare genetic condition. His school thought it best to place him in a special education classroom. I vehemently disagreed and had a psychologist test his intellectual level. When the results came back that his intelligence was completely normal, the school had no choice but to place him in a general education classroom, right where I knew he belonged all along!

Professor Paulina Multhaupt
Macomb Community College
Clinton Township, Michigan

Extremes in Intelligence

One of the best methods for judging the validity of a test is to compare people who score at the extremes. Despite the uncertainties discussed in the previous section, intelligence tests provide one of the major criteria for assessing mental ability at the extremes—specifically, for diagnosing *intellectual disability* and *mental giftedness*.

The clinical label *intellectually disabled* (previously referred to as *mentally retarded*) is applied when someone has significant deficits in general mental abilities, such as reasoning, problem solving, and academic learning. And these deficits result in impairments of adaptive functioning including communication, social participation, and personal independence (American Psychiatric Association, 2013).

Fewer than 3% of people are classified as having an intellectual disability **(Table 8.6)**. Of this group, 85% have only mild intellectual disability, and many become self-supporting, integrated members of society. Furthermore, people can score low on some measures of intelligence and still be average or even gifted in others (Armstrong et al., 2013; Meyer, 2011; Olson, 2010; Kreger Silverman, 2013). The most dramatic examples are people with **savant syndrome**. People with savant syndrome generally score very low on IQ tests (usually between 40 and 70), yet they demonstrate exceptional skills or brilliance in specific areas, such as rapid calculation, art, memory, or musical ability **(Figure 8.14)**.

Savant syndrome A condition in which a person with generally limited mental abilities exhibits exceptional skill or brilliance in some limited field.

Some forms of intellectual disability stem from genetic abnormalities, such as Down syndrome, fragile-X syndrome, and phenylketonuria (PKU). Other causes are environmental, including prenatal exposure to alcohol and other drugs, extreme

TABLE 8.6 DEGREES OF INTELLECTUAL DISABILITY

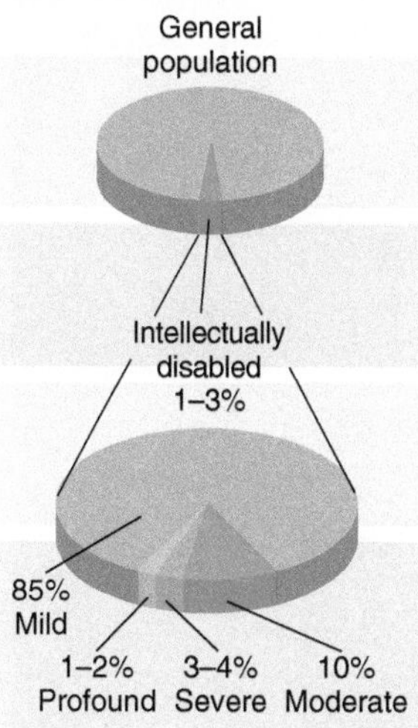

Level of Disability	IQ Scores	Characteristics
Mild (85%)	50–70	Usually able to become self-sufficient; may marry, have families, and secure full-time jobs in unskilled occupations
Moderate (10%)	35–49	Generally able to perform simple unskilled tasks; may contribute to a certain extent to their livelihood
Severe (3–4%)	20–34	Generally able to follow daily routines, but with continual supervision; with training, may learn basic communication skills
Profound (1–2%)	below 20	Generally able to perform only the most rudimentary behaviors, such as walking, feeding themselves, and saying a few phrases

deprivation or neglect in early life, and brain damage from physical trauma, such as auto accidents or sports injuries. However, in many cases, there is no known cause of the intellectual disability. At the other end of the intelligence spectrum are people with especially high IQs (typically defined as being in the top 1 or 2%).

In 1921, Lewis Terman identified 1,500 gifted children—affectionately nicknamed the "Termites"—with IQs of 140 or higher and tracked their progress through adulthood. The number who became highly successful professionals was many times the number a random group would have provided (Kreger Silverman, 2013; Leslie, 2000; Terman, 1954). Those who were most successful tended to have extraordinary motivation, and they also had someone at home or school who was especially encouraging (Goleman, 1980). Unfortunately, some "Termites" also became alcoholics, got divorced, and committed suicide at close to the national rate (Campbell & Feng, 2011; Leslie, 2000; Terman, 1954). In sum, a high IQ is no guarantee of success in every endeavor; it only offers more intellectual opportunities.

FIGURE 8.14 SAVANT SYNDROME—AN UNUSUAL FORM OF INTELLIGENCE

Derek Paravicini, a musical savant, pictured here, was born premature, blind, and with a severe learning disability. In spite of all these challenges, he plays the concert piano entirely by ear and has a repertoire of thousands of memorized pieces.

Nature, Nurture, and IQ

Psychologists have long debated several important questions related to intelligence: How is brain functioning related to intelligence? What factors—environmental or hereditary—influence an individual's intelligence? Are IQ tests culturally biased? These questions, and the controversies surrounding them, are discussed in this section.

The Brain's Influence on Intelligence

A basic tenet of neuroscience is that all mental activity (including intelligence) results from neural activity in the brain. Most recent research on the biology of intelligence has focused on brain functioning. For example, neuroscientists have found that people who score highest on intelligence tests also respond more quickly on tasks requiring perceptual judgments (Bowling & Mackenzie, 1996; Posthuma et al., 2001; Sternberg, 2013).

In addition to a faster response time, research using positron emission tomography (PET) scans to measure brain activity (Chapter 2) suggests that intelligent brains work smarter, or more efficiently, than less-intelligent brains (Jung & Haier, 2007; Neubauer et al., 2004; Posthuma et al., 2001) **(Figure 8.15)**.

FIGURE 8.15 **DO INTELLIGENT BRAINS WORK MORE EFFICIENTLY?**

In PET scan images red and yellow indicate more activity in relevant brain areas. Note how during problem-solving tasks, low-IQ brains (left) show more activity than high-IQ brains (right). This research suggests that lower-IQ brains actually work harder, although less efficiently, than higher-IQ brains.

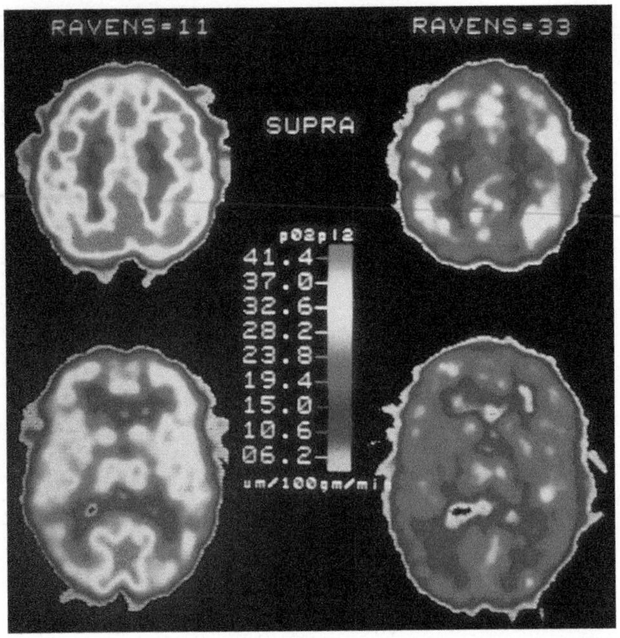

Courtesy Richard J. Haier, University of California-Irvine

Does size matter? It makes logical sense that bigger brains would be smarter; after all, humans have larger brains than less intelligent species, such as dogs. (Some animals, such as whales and dolphins, have larger brains than humans, but our brains are larger relative to our body size.) In fact, brain-imaging studies have found a significant correlation between brain size (adjusted for body size) and intelligence (Christensen et al., 2008; Colom et al., 2013; Deary et al., 2007). On Q4 the other hand, Albert Einstein's brain was no larger than normal (Witelson et al., 1999). In fact, some of Einstein's brain areas were actually smaller than average, but the area responsible for processing mathematical and spatial information was 15% larger than average.

Genetic and Environmental Influences on Intelligence

Similarities in intelligence between family members are due to a combination of hereditary (shared genetic material) and environmental factors (similar living arrangements and experiences). Researchers who are interested in the role of heredity in intelligence often focus on identical (monozygotic) twins because they share 100% of their genetic material, as shown in **Figure 8.16**.

Why are some people intellectually gifted, whereas others struggle? As identical twin studies demonstrate, genetics play an important role. In Figure 8.15, note the

FIGURE 8.16 **GENETIC AND ENVIRONMENTAL INFLUENCES ON IQ**

Note the higher correlations between identical twins' IQ test scores compared to correlations between all other pairs. Genes no doubt play a significant role in intelligence, but these effects are difficult to separate from environmental influences. (Based on Bouchard & McGue, 1981; Bouchard et al., 1998; Molenaar et al., 2013).

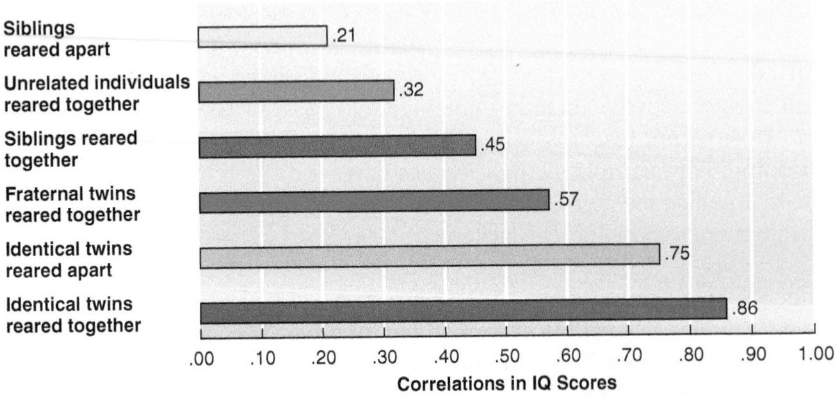

PhotoDisc, Inc./Getty Images

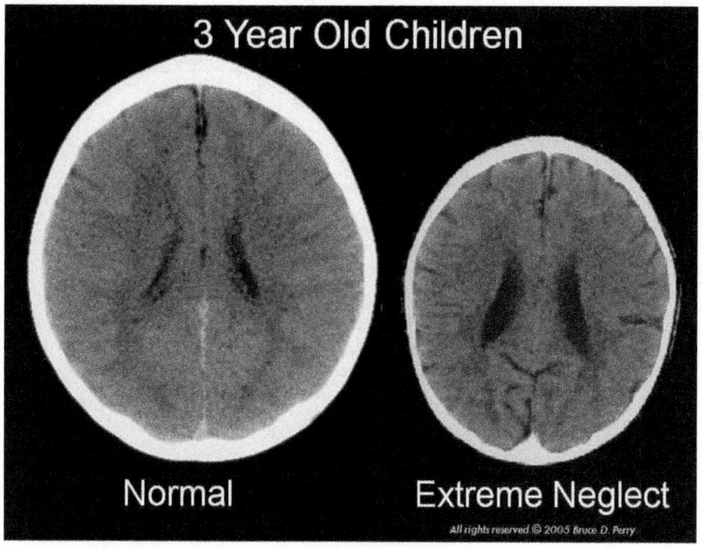

FIGURE 8.17 **NEGLECT AND IQ**

These images illustrate the negative impact of neglect on the developing brain. The CT scans on the left are from healthy three-year-old children with an average head size (50th percentile). The image on the right is from a series of three, three-year-old children following severe sensory-deprivation neglect in early childhood.

Each child's brain is significantly smaller than average and each has abnormal development of cortex (cortical atrophy) and other abnormalities suggesting abnormal development of the brain.

With kind permission from Springer Science+Business Media: Perry, B.D. Childhood experience and the expression of genetic potential: what childhood neglect tells us about nature and nurture Brain and Mind 3: 79-100, 2002.

Q5

higher correlations between identical twins' IQ scores compared to the correlations between all other pairs (Bouchard & McGue, 1981; Bouchard et al., 1998; McGue et al., 1993; Trzaskowski et al., 2013). Although heredity equips each of us with innate intellectual capabilities, the environment significantly influences whether a person will reach his or her full intellectual potential (Dickens & Flynn, 2001; Sangwan, 2001). For example, early malnutrition can retard a child's brain development, which in turn affects the child's curiosity, responsiveness to the environment, and motivation for learning—all of which can lower the child's IQ. The reverse is also true: An enriching early environment can set the stage for intellectual growth.

The long-running Minnesota Study of Twins, an investigation of identical twins raised in different homes and reunited only as adults (Bouchard, 1994, 1999; Bouchard et al., 1998; Johnson et al., 2007), found that genetic factors appear to play a surprisingly large role in the IQ scores of identical twins.

However, such results are not conclusive. Adoption agencies tend to look for similar criteria in their choice of adoptive parents. Therefore, the homes of these "reared apart" twins were actually quite similar. In addition, these twins shared the same nine-month prenatal environment, which also might have influenced their brain development and intelligence (White et al., 2002). Further evidence of the way the environment may affect intelligence comes from brain scans of children who are seriously neglected **(Figure 8.17)**.

realworldpsychology **Multiple Sad Effects of Neglect and Abuse** In addition to permanent brain changes, children who lack reliable care and stable attachment or who experience deliberate abuse in the first few years of life show not only lower intelligence but also less empathy for others and a greater vulnerability to later substance abuse and addiction (Luby et al., 2012). In contrast, children who are enrolled in high-quality preschool programs and are regularly read to by their parents show increases in IQ. These studies provide further evidence that the environment, for better or worse, has a major impact (Protzko et al., 2013).

Twin Design/Shutterstock

Between Versus Within Group Differences

One of the most controversial issues in psychology is historic group differences in average IQ scores between black and white people in the United States. As we've just seen, intelligence in general does show a high degree of heritability. However, it's VERY important to recognize that heritability cannot explain *between*-group differences! Note the overall difference between the average height of plants on the left and

FIGURE 8.18 GENETICS VERSUS ENVIRONMENT

Note that even when you begin with the same package of seeds (genetic inheritance), the average height of corn plants in the fertile soil will be greater than the average height of corn plants in the poor soil (environmental influences). Therefore, no valid or logical conclusions can be drawn about the overall genetic differences between the two groups of plants because the two environments (soil) are so different. Similar logic must be applied to intelligence scores between ethnic groups.

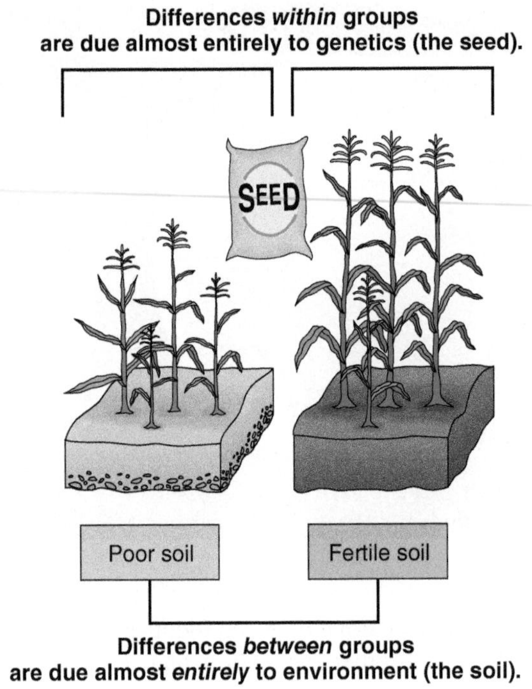
Differences *within* groups
are due almost entirely to genetics (the seed).
SEED
Poor soil
Fertile soil
Differences *between* groups
are due almost *entirely* to environment (the soil).

those on the right in **Figure 8.18**. Just as we cannot say that the difference *between* these two groups of plants is due to heredity, we similarly cannot say that differences in IQ *between* any two ethnic groups are due to heredity.

Note also the considerable variation in height *within* the group of plants on the left and those *within* the group on the right. Just as some plants are taller than others, there are blacks who score high on IQ tests and whites who score low, while the reverse is equally true. Always remember that the greatest differences in IQ scores occur when we compare individuals *within* groups—not *between* groups.

Why are we calling such attention to this *between*- and *within*-group distinction? In 1969, Arthur Jensen sparked a heated debate when he argued that genetic factors are "strongly implicated" as the cause of ethnic differences in intelligence. A book by Richard J. Herrnstein and Charles Murray titled *The Bell Curve: Intelligence and Class Structure in American Life* reignited this debate in 1994, when the authors claimed that African Americans score below average in IQ because of their "genetic heritage."

Although there is no clear resolution to this ongoing debate, some of the strongest proponents of the "heritability of intelligence" argument seem to ignore the "fertile soil" background of the groups who score highest on IQ tests. As an open-minded, critical thinker, carefully consider these important research findings:

- Environmental and cultural factors may override genetic potential and later affect IQ test scores. Like plants that come from similar seeds, but are placed in poor versus enriched soil, minority children are more likely to grow up in lower socioeconomic conditions, which may hamper their true intellectual potential. Also, in some ethnic groups and economic classes, a child who excels in school may be ridiculed for trying to be different from his or her classmates. Moreover, if children's own language and dialect do not match their education system or the IQ tests they take, they are obviously at a disadvantage (Cathers-Schiffman & Thompson, 2007; García & Náñez, 2011; Johnson et al., 2010; Sidhu et al., 2010; Sternberg & Grigorenko, 2008). Furthermore, environmental stress can also lead to short-term decreases in test scores (see *Psych Science*).

- Traditional IQ tests may be culturally biased. If standardized IQ tests contain items that reflect white, middle-class culture, they will discriminate against minority-group members whose language, knowledge and values differ from those of the white majority (Abedi, 2013; Suzuki et al., 2013). Researchers have attempted to create a *culture-fair* or *culture-free* IQ test, but they have found it

PSYCHSCIENCE

THE IMPACT OF EXPOSURE TO HOMICIDE ON INTELLIGENCE

Researchers in one study were interested in examining whether exposure to violence, and in particular to homicides, in their local community could have an impact on children's test scores (Sharkey, 2010). To test this question, researchers reviewed scores on both vocabulary and reading tests for African American children (ages 5 to 17) in a local public school. They then compared the test scores of children who were tested in the week after a homicide in their neighborhood to those of other children in the same neighborhood who were tested at different times. Sadly, their findings reveal that exposure to a nearby homicide in the week before the testing led to lower scores on both vocabulary and reading scores than scores achieved by peers in the same neighborhood who were tested at different times. Can you understand how and why children who are exposed to violence in their environment may therefore suffer short-term decreases in their cognitive abilities? How might this exposure to violence also affect their social and emotional well being?

RESEARCH CHALLENGE

1. Based on the information provided, did this study (Sharkey, 2010) use descriptive, correlational, and/or experimental research?
2. If you chose:
   - descriptive research, is this a naturalistic observation, survey/interview, case study, or archival research?
   - correlational research, is this a positive, negative, or zero correlation?
   - experimental research, label the IV, DV, experimental group(s), and control group.

>> CHECK YOUR ANSWERS IN APPENDIX B.

NOTE: The information provided in this study is admittedly limited, but the level of detail is similar to what is presented in most textbooks and public reports of research findings. Answering these questions, and then comparing your answers to those in the Appendix, will help you become a better critical thinker and consumer of scientific research.

virtually impossible to do. Past experiences, motivation, test-taking abilities, and previous experiences with tests are powerful influences on IQ scores.

- Intelligence (as measured by IQ tests) is not a fixed trait. Around the world, IQ scores have increased over the past half century. This well-established phenomenon, known as the *Flynn effect*, may be due to improved nutrition, better public education, more proficient test-taking skills, and rising levels of education for a greater percentage of the world's population (Flynn, 1987, 2007, 2010; Huang & Hauser, 1998; Pietschnig et al., 2011; Watkins & Smith, 2013).
- Selectively highlighting IQ scores from one group (African American) is deceptive because race and ethnicity, like intelligence itself, are almost impossible to define. Depending on the definition we use, there are between 3 and 300 races, and no race is pure in a biological sense (Fujimura et al., 2010; Kite, 2013; Sternberg & Grigorenko, 2008). Furthermore, like President Barack Obama, Tiger Woods, and Mariah Carey, many people today self-identify as multiracial.
- Negative stereotypes about minority groups can cause some group members to doubt their abilities. This phenomenon, called **stereotype threat** may, in turn, reduce their intelligence test scores (Owens & Massey, 2011; Ryan & Sackett, 2013; Tomasetto & Appoloni, 2013).

Stereotype threat Awareness of a negative stereotype that affects oneself and may lead to impairment in performance.

In the first study of stereotype threat, Claude Steele and Joshua Aronson (1995) recruited Black and White University students (with similar ability levels) to complete a difficult verbal exam. In the group of students who were told that the exam was diagnostic of their intellectual abilities, Blacks underperformed in relation to Whites. However, in the non-diagnostic group taking the same exam, there were no differences between the two group scores.

This and other research suggests that stereotype threat occurs because members of stereotyped groups are anxious that they will fulfill their group's negative stereotype. This anxiety in turn hinders their performance on tests. Some people cope with stereotype threat by *disidentifying*, telling themselves they don't care about the

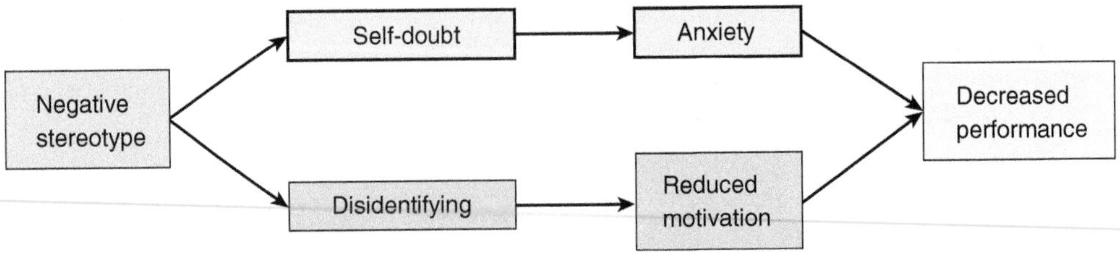

FIGURE 8.19 HOW STEREOTYPE THREAT LEADS TO DECREASED PERFORMANCE

test scores (Major et al., 1998). Unfortunately, this attitude reduces motivation and also leads to decreased performance **(Figure 8.19)**.

Stereotype threat affects many social groups, including African Americans, women, Native Americans, Latinos, low-income people, elderly people, and white male athletes (Joanisse et al., 2013; Keller & Bless, 2008; Owens & Massey, 2011). This research helps explain some group differences in intelligence and achievement tests. As such, it underscores why relying solely on such tests to make critical decisions affecting individual lives—for example, in hiring, college admissions, or clinical application—is unwarranted and possibly even unethical.

What's the good news? First, some early research suggested that having Barack Obama as a positive role model improved academic performance by African Americans—thus offsetting the stereotype threat (Marx et al., 2009) **(Figure 8.20)**. Second, people who have the opportunity to self-affirm, or validate, their identities in some type of meaningful way do not show the negative effects of stereotype threat. For example, African American first-year college students who receive information about how to feel more connected to their college or university show higher

FIGURE 8.20 "OBAMA EFFECT" VERSUS STEREOTYPE THREAT | realworldpsychology

Preliminary research found a so-called "Obama effect," which promised to offset problems related to the stereotype threat (Dillon, 2009). However, later studies found either no relationship between test performance and positive thoughts about Obama or mixed results (Aronson et al., 2009; Smith, 2012).

Reuters/Larry Downing/Landov

GPAs as well as better health three years later (Walten & Cohen, 2011). Similarly, African American adults with hypertension, or high blood pressure, who self-affirm by focusing on positive moments in their lives show higher levels of adherence to their blood pressure medication (Ogedegbe et al., 2011).

So what's the most important take-away message? In this chapter, we've explored three cognitive processes (*thinking, language*, and *intelligence*), each of which is greatly affected by numerous interacting factors. To solve problems, be creative, communicate with others, and adapt to our environment requires various mental abilities, most of which are not genetic and can be easily learned (see *Psychology and You*).

psychology and you **Optimizing Your Well-Being** In Chapter 1, we introduced you to the field of *positive psychology*—the scientific study of optimal human functioning. One of the key researchers in this area, Martin Seligman, believes optimal well-being results from five core factors: *Positive emotion, Engagement, Relationships, Meaning*, and *Accomplishment* (PERMA). To learn more about positive psychology and these five factors, while also gaining invaluable personal insights, visit Dr. Seligman's home page. While there, be sure to complete one or more of the free, scientifically validated surveys: www.authentichappiness.sas.upenn.edu.

© Yuri/iStockphoto

RETRIEVAL PRACTICE: INTELLIGENCE

Self-Test

Completing this self-test and comparing your answers with those in Appendix B provides immediate feedback and helpful practice for exams. Additional interactive, self-tests are available at www.wiley.com/college/huffman.

1. The definition of intelligence in this book stresses the global capacity to ______.

a. successfully perform within relationships, in school, and on the job
b. read, write, and do computations at home and at work
c. perform verbally and physically within the environment
d. think rationally, act purposefully, profit from experience, and deal effectively with the environment

2. Which is the most widely used intelligence test?

a. Wechsler Intelligence Scale for Children
b. Wechsler Adult Intelligence Scale
c. Stanford-Binet Intelligence Scale
d. Binet-Terman Intelligence Scale

3. The development of uniform procedures for administering and scoring a test is called ______.

a. norming
b. procedural protocol
c. standardization
d. normalization

4. ______ suggested that people differ in their "profiles of intelligence" and that each person shows a unique pattern of strengths and weaknesses.

a. Spearman
b. Binet
c. Wechsler
d. Gardner

Think Critically

1 How would someone with exceptionally low or high emotional intelligence behave?

2 Do you believe IQ test are culturally biased? Why or why not?

realworldpsychology

Do bigger brains indicate greater intelligence?

Does caregiving in the first years of life have a lasting impact on brain size and development?

HINT: LOOK IN THE MARGIN FOR Q4 AND Q5

Summary

1 THINKING 208

- Thinking is a central aspect of **cognition**. Thought processes are distributed throughout the brain in neural networks. **Mental images** and **concepts** aid our thought processes. There are three major building blocks for concepts—**prototypes**, **artificial concepts**, and hierarchies.
- **Problem solving** usually has three steps: *preparation*, *production*, and *evaluation*. **Algorithms** and **heuristics** help us produce solutions.
- Barriers to problem solving include **mental sets**, **functional fixedness**, **confirmation bias**, **availability heuristic**, and the **representativeness heuristic.**
- **Creativity** is the ability to produce valued outcomes in a novel way. Tests of creativity usually focus on **divergent thinking**.

2 LANGUAGE 215

- **Language** supports thinking and enables us to communicate. To produce language, we use **phonemes**, **morphemes**, and **grammar** (syntax and semantics). Several different parts of our brain are involved in producing and listening to language.
- According to Whorf's **linguistic relativity hypothesis**, language determines thought. Generally, Whorf's hypothesis is not supported. However, language does strongly influence thought.
- Children communicate nonverbally from birth. Their verbal communication proceeds in stages: *prelinguistic*, which includes crying, **cooing**, and **babbling**, and *linguistic*, which includes single utterances, **telegraphic speech**, and acquisition of rules of grammar.
- According to Chomsky, humans are "prewired" with a **language acquisition device (LAD)** that enables language development. Nurturists hold that children learn language through rewards, punishments, and imitation. Most psychologists hold an intermediate view.
- Research with chimpanzees, gorillas, and dolphins suggests that these animals can learn and use basic rules of language. However, critics suggest nonhuman animal language is less complex, less creative, and not as rule-laden as human language.

3 INTELLIGENCE 221

- There is considerable debate over the meaning of **intelligence**. Here it is defined as the global capacity to think rationally, act purposefully, and deal effectively with the environment.
- Spearman proposed that intelligence is a single factor, which he termed **general intelligence (g)**. Thurstone and Guilford argued that intelligence included numerous distinct abilities. Cattell proposed two subtypes of *g*: **fluid intelligence (gf)** and **crystallized intelligence (gc)**. Many contemporary cognitive theorists, including Gardner and Sternberg, believe that intelligence is a collection of many separate specific abilities. Goleman believes that **emotional intelligence (EI)**, the ability to empathize and manage our emotions and relationships, is just as important as any other kind of intelligence.
- Early intelligence tests computed a person's mental age to arrive at an **intelligence quotient (IQ)**. Today, two of the most widely used intelligence tests are the *Stanford-Binet Intelligence Scale* and the *Wechsler Adult Intelligence Scale (WAIS)*. Intelligence tests commonly compare the performance of an individual with other individuals of the same age. To be scientifically acceptable, all psychological tests must fulfill three basic requirements: **standardization**, **reliability**, and **validity**.
- Intelligence tests provide one of the major criteria for assessing **intellectual disability** and **mental giftedness**, both of which exist on a continuum. Studies of people who are intellectually gifted found that they had more intellectual opportunities and tended to excel professionally. However, a high IQ does not guarantee success in every endeavor.
- Most recent research on the biology of intelligence has focused on brain functioning, not size. Research indicates that intelligent people's brains respond especially quickly and efficiently.
- In answer to the question of how race affects IQ, heredity and intelligence are interacting, inseparable factors.

applyingrealworldpsychology

We began this chapter with five intriguing Real World Psychology questions, and you were asked to revisit these questions at the end of each section. Questions like these have an important and lasting impact on all of our lives. See if you can answer these additional critical thinking questions related to real world examples.

T K Wanstal/The Image Works

1. Jerry Levy and Mark Newman, the two men shown in this photo, are identical twins who were separated at birth and first met as adults at a firefighter's convention. Research shows that IQ tends to be highly correlated for identical twins, but do you believe identical twins share a special connectedness? Why or why not?
2. Does the brothers' choosing the same uncommon profession seem like a case of special "twin-telepathy"? If so, how might *confirmation bias* contribute to the perception of twin-telepathy?
3. What is the role of emotional intelligence (EI) in business? Should it be a factor in hiring and promotions? What might be the advantages and drawbacks if it did?
4. Should preschools and elementary schools be required to teach children multiple languages? Why or why not?
5. Which of the barriers to problem solving described in this chapter are the biggest problems for you? How will you work to overcome them?

Key Terms

RETRIEVAL PRACTICE Write a definition for each term before turning back to the referenced page to check your answer.

- algorithm 210
- artificial concept 209
- availability heuristic 212
- babbling 218
- cognition 208
- concept 208
- confirmation bias 211
- cooing 218
- creativity 213
- crystallized intelligence (*gc*) 222
- divergent thinking 214
- emotional intelligence (EI) 222
- fluid intelligence (*gf*) 222
- functional fixedness 211
- general intelligence (*g*) 222
- grammar 215
- heuristic 210
- intelligence 221
- intelligence quotient (IQ) 225
- language 215
- language acquisition device (LAD) 219
- mental image 208
- mental set 211
- morpheme 215
- overextension 218
- overgeneralization 218
- phoneme 215
- prototype 209
- reliability 226
- representativeness heuristic 212
- savant syndrome 226
- standardization 225
- stereotype threat 231
- telegraphic speech 218
- validity 226

Solutions

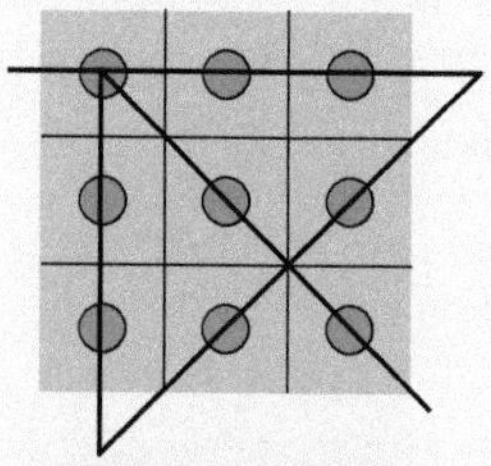

Nine-dot problem solution (page 211)

People find this puzzle difficult because they see the arrangement of dots as a square—a mental set that limits its possible solutions.

Candle problem solution (page 211)

Use the tacks to mount the matchbox tray to the wall. Light the candle and use some melted wax to mount the candle to the matchbox.

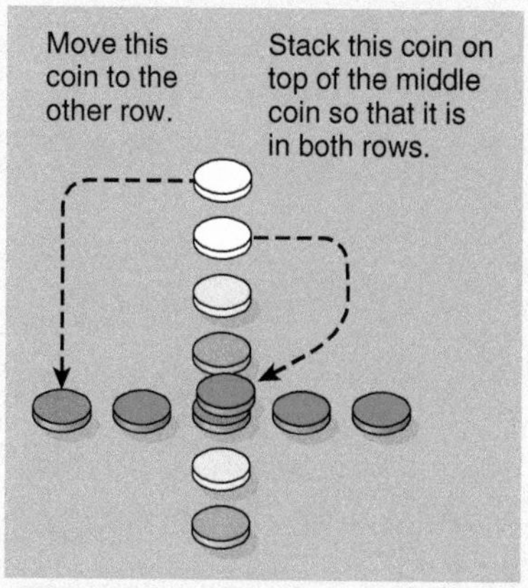

Move this coin to the other row.
Stack this coin on top of the middle coin so that it is in both rows.

Coin problem solution (page 214)

Ⓐ "Which three pieces go together to make this puzzle?"

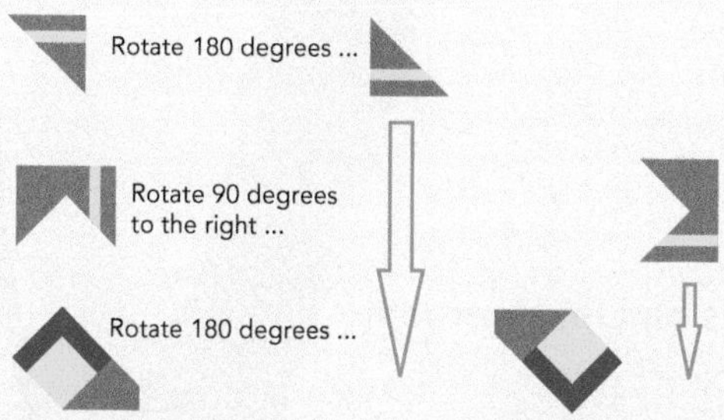

Wechsler Adult Intelligence Scale solution (page 225)

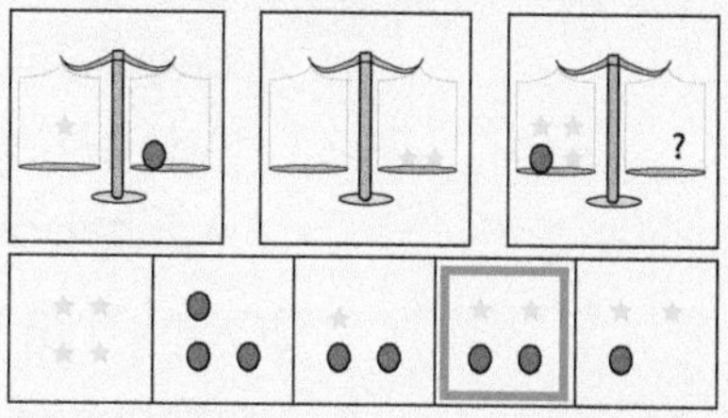

Ⓑ "Which one of these works to balance the scale?"

From the middle image, we deduce an empty scale would be out of balance, since we need two stars added to the right just to be in balance.

From the first image, since we know that the scale is two stars heavy on the left, if adding one star to the already heavier left side balances with one ball, a ball must equal three stars!

The final image shows three stars and one ball on the left. To balance on the right, we match what is shown on the left AND ADD two stars since we know the scale, by itself, is two stars heavy on the left.

Therefore we need one ball and five stars to balance. But that is NOT one of the answers! But we know one ball equals three stars. Looking at the possible answers, we see that two stars and two balls (1+1+3+3=8 stars) is the same as one ball and five stars (3+1+1+1+1+1=8 stars)—and that is the answer!

chapternine

Life Span Development

CHAPTER OUTLINE

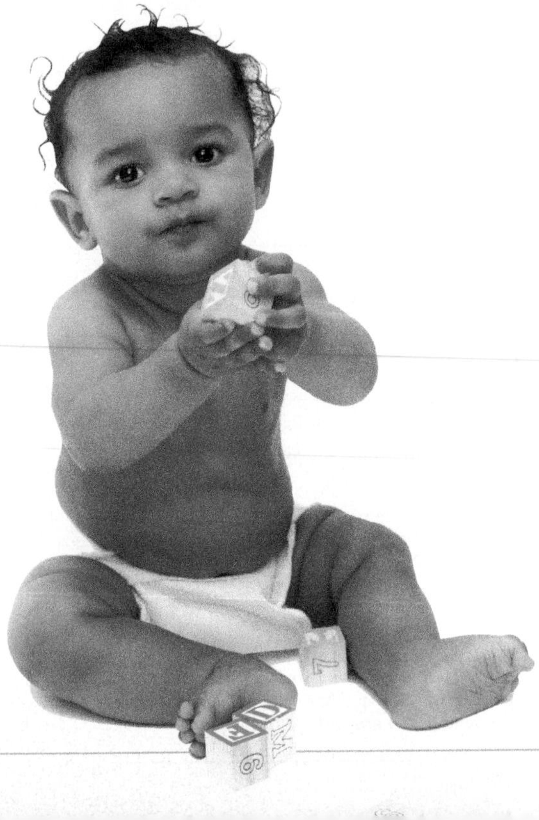

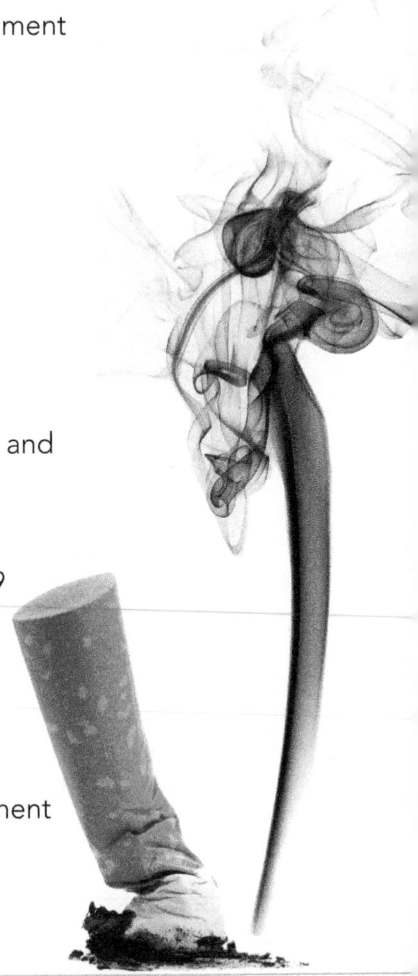

realworldpsychology

THINGS YOU'LL LEARN IN CHAPTER 9

Q1 **Are our childhood friends' predictions of our adult personality better than our own self-ratings?**

Q2 **Does prenatal exposure to smoke increase the risk of obesity later in life?**

Q3 **Why do teenagers seem to sleep so much?**

Q4 **Do babies learn faster when they're sitting up than when they're lying down?**

Q5 **Do today's college students want women to propose marriage?**

THROUGHOUT THE CHAPTER, MARGIN ICONS FOR Q1–Q5 INDICATE WHERE THE TEXT ADDRESSES THESE QUESTIONS.

pillows: © karammiri/iStockphoto; baby: © jfairone/iStockphoto; cigarette: © milosluz/iStockphoto; smoke: © Nocturnus/iStockphoto; three students: londoneye/Getty Images; woman proposing: © Pojoslaw/Shutterstock

chapteroverview

Are you one of the lucky ones who grew up with loving parents who documented every stage of your development with photos, videos, and/or journals—starting with your birth, first smile, first day of school, and all the way to your high school graduation? If so, you have a head start on the material in this chapter. As you might expect, studying development across the entire life span is a monumental task, so we've organized this chapter into three major sections—*physical, cognitive,* and *social-emotional development.* Before we begin, we need to briefly examine the research issues and methods psychologists use to study development.

STUDYING DEVELOPMENT

LEARNING OBJECTIVES

RETRIEVAL PRACTICE While reading the upcoming sections, respond to each Learning Objective in your own words. Then compare your responses with those found at www.wiley.com/college/huffman.

1 **SUMMARIZE** the three most important debates or questions in developmental psychology.

2 **CONTRAST** the cross-sectional research design with the longitudinal research design.

Developmental psychology The study of age-related changes in behavior, mental processes, and stages of growth, from conception to death.

Maturation The continuing influence of heredity throughout development; age-related physical and behavioral changes characteristic of a species.

Critical period A time of special sensitivity to specific types of learning, which shapes the capacity for future development.

Imprinting An inherited, primitive form of rapid learning (within a critical period) in which some infant animals physically follow and form an attachment to the first moving object they see and/or hear.

Just as some parents carefully document their child's progress throughout his or her life span, the field of **developmental psychology** studies growth and change throughout the eight major stages of life—from conception to death, or "womb to tomb" **(Table 9.1)**. Their studies have led to three key theoretical issues.

Theoretical Issues

Almost every area of research in human development frames questions around three major issues:

1. **Nature or nurture?** How do both genetics (nature) and life experiences (nurture) influence development? According to the *nature position,* development is largely governed by automatic, genetically predetermined signals in a process known as **maturation**. Just as a flower unfolds in accord with its genetic blueprint, humans crawl before we walk and walk before we run.

   In addition, naturists believe there are **critical periods**, or windows of opportunity, that occur early in life when exposure to certain stimuli or experiences is necessary for proper development. For example, many newborn animals form rigid attachments to particular stimuli shortly after birth, a process called **imprinting (Figure 9.1)**.

TABLE 9.1 LIFE SPAN DEVELOPMENT

Stage	Approximate Age
Prenatal	Conception to birth
Infancy	Birth to 18 months
Early childhood	18 months to 6 years
Middle childhood	6 to 12 years
Adolescence	12 to 20 years
Young adulthood	20 to 45 years
Middle adulthood	45 to 60 years
Later adulthood	60 years to death

Human children also may have critical periods for normal development. Research has shown that appropriate social interaction in the first few weeks of life is essential for creating normal cognitive and social development (Ekas et al., 2013; Feldman, 2014). Sadly, a study of both Israeli and Palestinian children also found that exposure to serious military/political violence at age 8 is associated with more aggressive behavior later on, whereas witnessing such violence at later ages doesn't lead to such aggression (Boxer et al., 2013). These and other similar studies provide further evidence for critical periods—at least in the early years (see *Psych Science*).

2. **Stages or continuity?** Some developmental psychologists suggest that development generally occurs in *stages* that are discrete and qualitatively different from one to another, whereas others believe it follows a *continuous pattern*, with gradual but steady and quantitative (measurable) changes **(Figure 9.2)**.

Nina Leen/Time Life Pictures/Getty Images

FIGURE 9.1 CRITICAL PERIODS AND IMPRINTING

Konrad Lorenz's (1937) early studies of *imprinting* found that baby geese will attach to (or imprint on) the first suitable moving stimulus they see within a certain *critical period*—normally the first 36 hours of their lives. While baby geese normally imprint on their mother, Lorenz discovered that if he was the first moving creature the geese observed, they would imprint and follow him everywhere.

PSYCHSCIENCE

DEPRIVATION AND DEVELOPMENT

What happens if a child is deprived of appropriate stimulation during a critical period of development? Consider the story of Genie, the so-called "wild child." From the time she was 20 months old until authorities rescued her at age 13, Genie was locked alone in a tiny, windowless room. By day, she sat naked and tied to a child's toilet with nothing to do and no one to talk to. At night, she was immobilized in a kind of straitjacket and "caged" in a covered crib. Genie's abusive father forbade anyone to speak to her for those 13 years. If Genie made noise, her father beat her while he barked and growled like a dog.

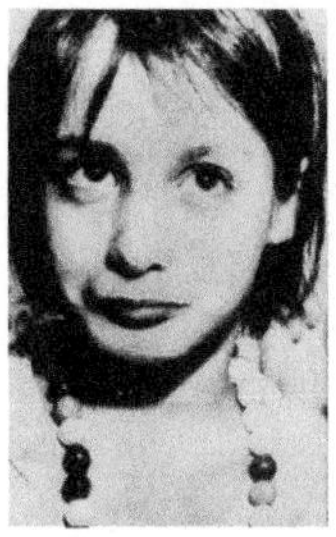

AP/Wide World Photos

Genie's tale is a heartbreaking account of the lasting scars from a disastrous childhood. In the years after her rescue, Genie spent thousands of hours receiving special training, and by age 19 she could use public transportation and was adapting well to special classes at school. Genie was far from normal, however. Her intelligence scores were still close to the cutoff for intellectual disability. And although linguists and psychologists worked with her for many years, she was never able to master grammatical structure, and was limited to sentences like "Genie go." This suggests that because of her extreme childhood isolation and abuse, Genie, like other seriously neglected or environmentally isolated children, missed a necessary critical period for language development (Baird, 2010; Curtiss, 1977; LaPointe, 2005; Raaska et al., 2013; Rymer, 1993; Saxton, 2010; Sylvestre & Mérette, 2010). To make matters worse, she was also subjected to a series of foster home placements, some of which were emotionally and physically abusive. According to the latest information, Genie now lives in a privately run facility for mentally underdeveloped adults (James, 2008).

RESEARCH CHALLENGE

1. Based on the information provided, did this study (Rymer, 1993) use descriptive, correlational, and/or experimental research?
2. If you chose:
   - descriptive research, is this a naturalistic observation, survey/interview, case study, or archival research?
   - correlational research, is this a positive, negative, or zero correlation?
   - experimental research, label the IV, DV, experimental group(s), and control group.

>> CHECK YOUR ANSWERS IN APPENDIX B.

NOTE: The information provided in this study is admittedly limited, but the level of detail is similar to what is presented in most textbooks and public reports of research findings. Answering these questions, and then comparing your answers to those in the Appendix, will help you become a better critical thinker and consumer of scientific research.

FIGURE 9.2 STAGES VERSUS CONTINUITY IN DEVELOPMENT

There is an ongoing debate about whether development is better characterized by discrete stages or by gradual, continuous development.

Ⓐ Stage theorists think development results from discrete, qualitative changes.

Ⓑ Continuity theorists believe development results from gradual, quantitative (incremental) changes.

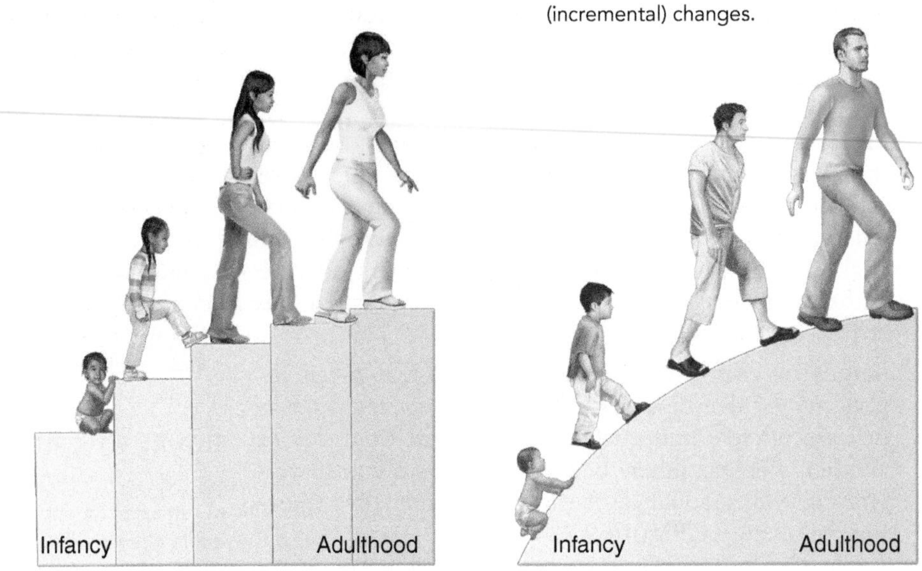

3. **Stability or change?** Which of our traits are stable and present throughout our life span, and what aspects will change? Psychologists who emphasize *stability* hold that measurements of personality taken during childhood are important predictors of adult personality; those who emphasize *change* disagree.

Research Approaches

To answer these three controversies and other questions, developmental psychologists typically use all the research methods discussed in Chapter 1. To study the entire human life span, they also need two additional techniques—*cross sectional* and *longitudinal* **(Figure 9.3)**.

Cross-sectional design A research technique that measures individuals of various ages at one point in time and provides information about age differences.

The **cross-sectional design** examines people of various ages (such as 20, 40, 60, and 80) all at the same time to see how each age differs at that one specific time of measurement. For example, one cross-sectional study examined women in

FIGURE 9.3 CROSS-SECTIONAL VERSUS LONGITUDINAL RESEARCH

To study development, psychologists may use either a cross-sectional or longitudinal design for their research.

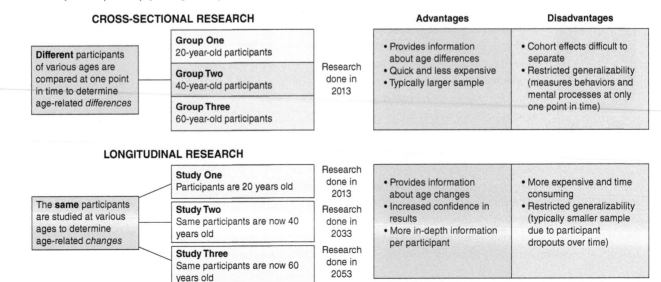

CROSS-SECTIONAL RESEARCH

	Groups	Research done	Advantages	Disadvantages
Different participants of various ages are compared at one point in time to determine age-related *differences*	**Group One** 20-year-old participants **Group Two** 40-year-old participants **Group Three** 60-year-old participants	Research done in 2013	• Provides information about age differences • Quick and less expensive • Typically larger sample	• Cohort effects difficult to separate • Restricted generalizability (measures behaviors and mental processes at only one point in time)

LONGITUDINAL RESEARCH

	Studies	Research done	Advantages	Disadvantages
The **same** participants are studied at various ages to determine age-related *changes*	**Study One** Participants are 20 years old	Research done in 2013	• Provides information about age changes • Increased confidence in results • More in-depth information per participant	• More expensive and time consuming • Restricted generalizability (typically smaller sample due to participant dropouts over time)
	Study Two Same participants are now 40 years old	Research done in 2033		
	Study Three Same participants are now 60 years old	Research done in 2053		

three different age groups (ages 22–34, 35–49, and 50–65) to examine whether body weight dissatisfaction changes with age (Siegel, 2010). Unfortunately, female body dissatisfaction appears to be quite stable—and relatively high—across the life span.

In contrast, a **longitudinal design** takes repeated measures of one person or a group of same-aged people over a long period of time to see how the individual or the group changes over time. For example, a group of developmental researchers wondered if peer ratings of personality taken during childhood might be better predictors of later adult personality than self-ratings (Martin-Storey et al., 2012)? They first asked grade school children in 1976-1978 to rate themselves and their peers on several personality factors, such as likeability, aggression, and social withdrawal. In 1999-2003, the researchers returned and asked the same participants, now in mid-adulthood, to complete a second series of personality tests. As hypothesized, the peer ratings were better than self-ratings in predicting adult personality. Does this finding surprise you? If so, try contacting some of your childhood peers and then compare notes on how you remember one another's personality as children and now as adults.

Q1

Longitudinal design A research design that measures a single individual or group of individuals over an extended period and gives information about age changes.

Now that you have a better idea of these two types of research, if you were a developmental psychologist interested in studying intelligence in adults, which design would you choose—cross-sectional or longitudinal? Before you decide, note the different research results shown in **Figure 9.4**.

Why do the two methods show such different results? Cross-sectional studies sometimes confuse genuine age differences with *cohort effects*—differences that result from specific histories of the age group studied. As shown in the top line in Figure 9.4, the 81-year-olds measured by the cross-sectional design have dramatically lower scores than the 25-year-olds. But is this due to aging, or perhaps to broad environmental differences, such as less formal education or poor nutrition? Because the different age groups, called *cohorts*, grew up in different historical periods, the results may not apply to people growing up at other times. With the cross-sectional design, age effects and cohort effects are sometimes inextricably tangled.

Longitudinal studies also have limits. They are expensive in terms of time and money, and it is difficult for us to generalize their results. Because participants often drop out or move away during the extended test period, the experimenter may end up with a self-selected sample that differs from the general population in important ways. Each method of research has strengths and weaknesses (as you recall from the right-hand side of Figure 9.3). Keep these differences in mind when you read the findings of developmental research.

Before we go on, it's important to point out that modern researchers sometimes combine both cross-sectional and longitudinal designs into one study. For example, in Chapter 1, we discussed a study that examined whether well-being decreases with age (Sutin et al., 2013). When these researchers examined their combined cross-sectional and longitudinal data from two independent samples taken over 30 years, they initially found that well-being *declined* with age. However, when they then controlled for the fact that older cohorts started out with lower levels of well-being, they found that all the cohorts *increased* rather than decreased in well-being with age. The reversal in findings was explained by the fact that the older group of people had experienced instances of major turmoil in their younger years, including the Great Depression. This means that this group started out with lower levels of well-being than those who grew up during more prosperous times.

Can you see why this combination of two research designs is important? It offers a more accurate and positive view of well-being in old age than what was indicated in either the cross-sectional design or the longitudinal design. It also suggests some troubling possibilities for today's young adults who are entering a stagnant workforce and high unemployment. As the study's authors say, this "economic turmoil may impede [their] psychological, as well as financial, growth even decades after times get better" (Sutin et al., 2013, p. 384).

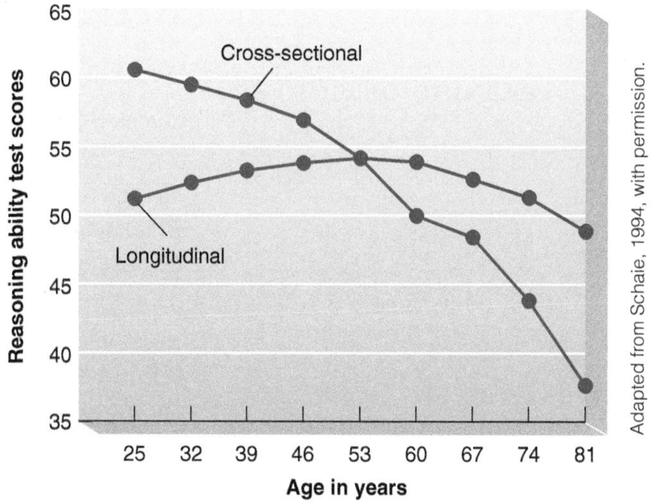

FIGURE 9.4 **WHICH RESULTS ARE "TRUE"?**

Cross-sectional studies have shown that reasoning and intelligence reach their peak in early adulthood and then gradually decline. In contrast, longitudinal studies have found that a marked decline does not begin until about age 60.

RETRIEVAL PRACTICE: STUDYING DEVELOPMENT

Self-Test

Completing this self-test and comparing your answers with those in Appendix B provides immediate feedback and helpful practice for exams. Additional interactive, self-tests are available at www.wiley.com/college/huffman.

1. _______ studies age-related changes in behavior and mental processes from conception to death.
   a. Thanatology b. Teratogenology
   c. Human development d. Developmental psychology

2. _______ is governed by automatic, genetically predetermined signals.
   a. The cohort effect b. Secondary aging
   c. Thanatology d. Maturation

3. What three major questions are studied in developmental psychology?
   a. nature versus nurture, stages versus continuity, and stability versus change
   b. nature versus nurture, "chunking" versus continuity, and instability versus change
   c. nature versus nurture, stages versus continuity, and stagnation versus instability
   d. none of these

4. _______ studies are the most time-efficient method, whereas _______ studies provide the most in-depth information per participant.
   a. Latitudinal; longitudinal b. Neo-gerontology; longitudinal
   c. Cross-sectional; longitudinal d. Class-racial; longitudinal

Think Critically

1. Which of the three important debates or questions in developmental psychology do you find most valuable? Why?
2. Based on what you have learned about critical periods, can you think of a circumstance in your own development, or that of your friends, when a critical period might have been disrupted or lost?

realworldpsychology

Are our childhood friends' predictions of our adult personality better than our own self-ratings?

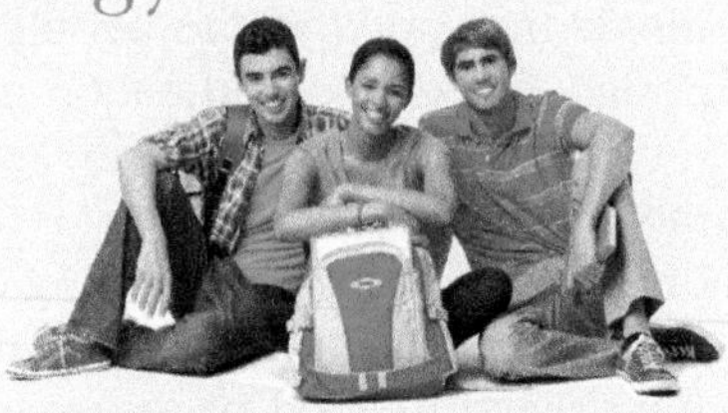

HINT: LOOK IN THE MARGIN FOR Q1

PHYSICAL DEVELOPMENT

LEARNING OBJECTIVES

RETRIEVAL PRACTICE While reading the upcoming sections, respond to each Learning Objective in your own words. Then compare your responses with those found at www.wiley.com/college/huffman.

1. **IDENTIFY** the three phases of prenatal physical development.
2. **SUMMARIZE** physical development during early childhood.
3. **DESCRIBE** the physical changes that occur during adolescence and adulthood.

After studying the photos of your two authors as they've aged over the life span **(Figure 9.5)** (or after reviewing your own similar photos), you may be amused and surprised by all the dramatic changes in physical appearance. But have you stopped to appreciate the incredible underlying process that transforms all of us from birth to death? In this section, we will explore the fascinating processes of physical development from conception through childhood, adolescence, and adulthood.

Prenatal Development

Your prenatal development began at conception, when your mother's egg, or ovum, united with your father's sperm cell **(Figure 9.6)**. At that time, you were

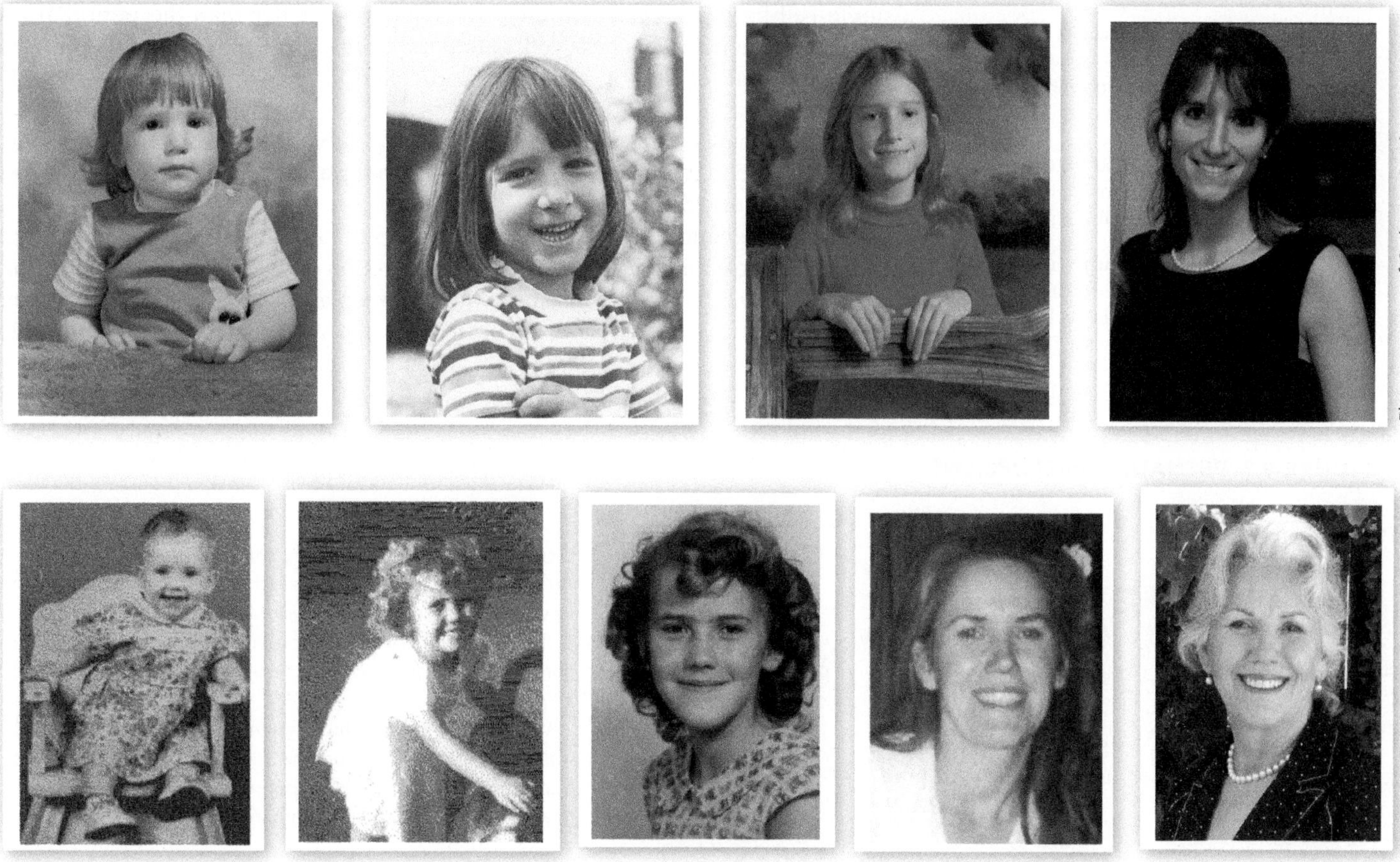

Photos courtesy of Catherine Sanderson

Photos courtesy of Karen Huffman

FIGURE 9.5 CHANGES IN PHYSICAL DEVELOPMENT OVER THE LIFE SPAN

As this series of photos of your two textbook authors show, physical changes occur throughout our lives. Our cognitive, social, and emotional processes, as well as our personalities also are continually changing, but the changes aren't as visible. (The top row is Catherine Sanderson at ages 1, 5, 10, 30, and the bottom row is Karen Huffman at ages 1, 4, 10, 30 and 60.)

FIGURE 9.6 CONCEPTION

Millions of sperm are released when a man ejaculates into a woman's vagina.

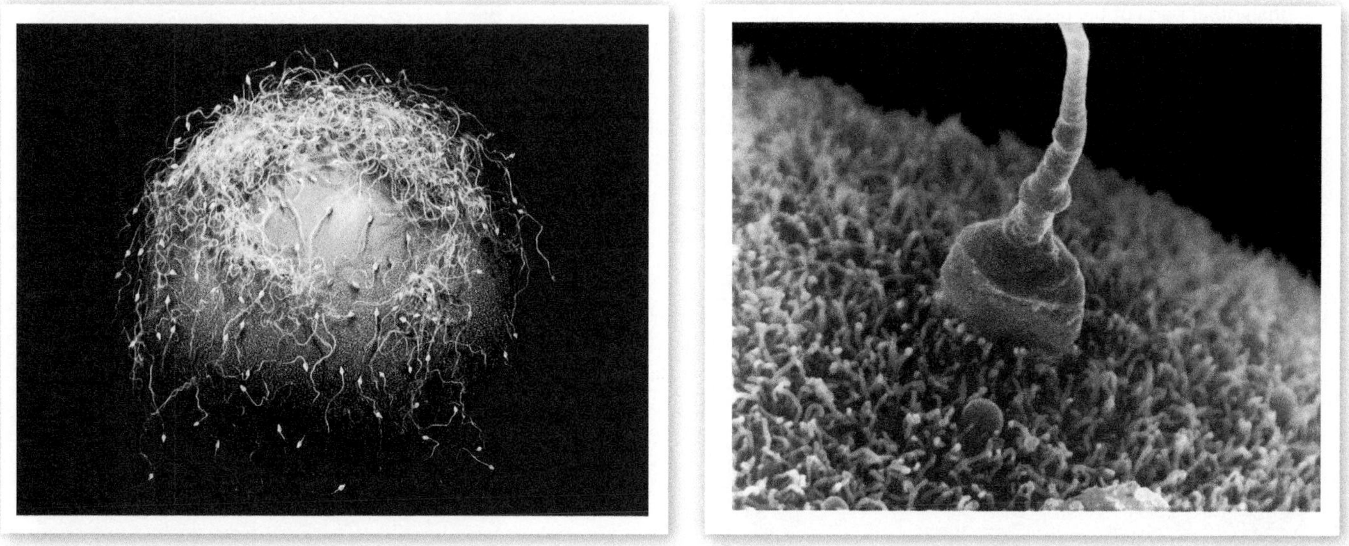

Francis Leroy, Biocosmos/Photo Researchers

David M. Phillips/Photo Researchers

Ⓐ Only a few hundred sperm survive the arduous trip up to the egg.

Ⓑ Although a joint effort is required to break through the outer coating, only one sperm will actually fertilize the egg.

Germinal period The first stage of prenatal development, beginning with ovulation and followed by conception and implantation in the uterus; the first two weeks of pregnancy.

Embryonic period The second stage of prenatal development, which begins after uterine implantation and lasts through the eighth week.

Fetal period The third, and final, stage of prenatal development (eight weeks to birth); characterized by rapid weight gain in the fetus and the fine detailing of bodily organs and systems.

a single cell barely 1/175 of an inch in diameter—smaller than the period at the end of this sentence. This new cell, called a *zygote*, then began a process of rapid cell division that resulted in a multimillion-celled infant (you) some nine months later.

The vast changes that occur during the nine months of a full-term pregnancy are usually divided into three stages: the **germinal period**, the **embryonic period**, and the **fetal period** **(Figure 9.7)**.

During pregnancy, the *placenta* connects the fetus to the mother's uterus and serves as the link for delivery of food and excretion of wastes. It also screens out some, but not all, harmful substances. Environmental hazards such as X-rays and toxic waste, drugs, and diseases can still cross the placental barrier **(Table 9.2)**.

FIGURE 9.7 PRENATAL DEVELOPMENT

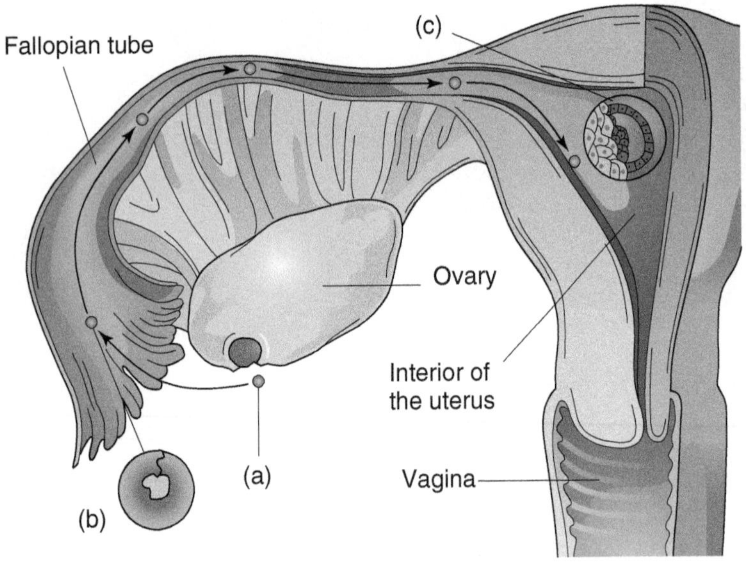

1 Germinal period: From conception to implantation
After discharge from either the left or right ovary (a), the ovum travels to the opening of the fallopian tube.

If fertilization occurs (b), it normally takes place in the first third of the fallopian tube. The fertilized ovum is referred to as a zygote.

When the zygote reaches the uterus, it implants itself in the wall of the uterus (c) and begins to grow tendril-like structures that intertwine with the rich supply of blood vessels located there. After implantation, the organism is known as an embryo.

2 Embryonic period: From implantation to eight weeks
At eight weeks, the major organ systems have become well differentiated. Note that at this stage, the head grows at a faster rate than other parts of the body.

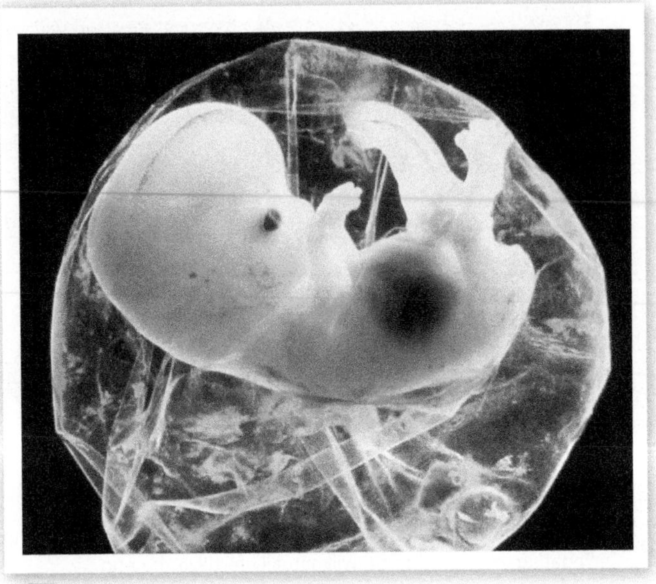

Biophoto Associates/Photo Researchers

3 Fetal period: From the end of the second month to birth
At four months, all the actual body parts and organs are established. The fetal stage is primarily a time for increased growth and "fine detailing."

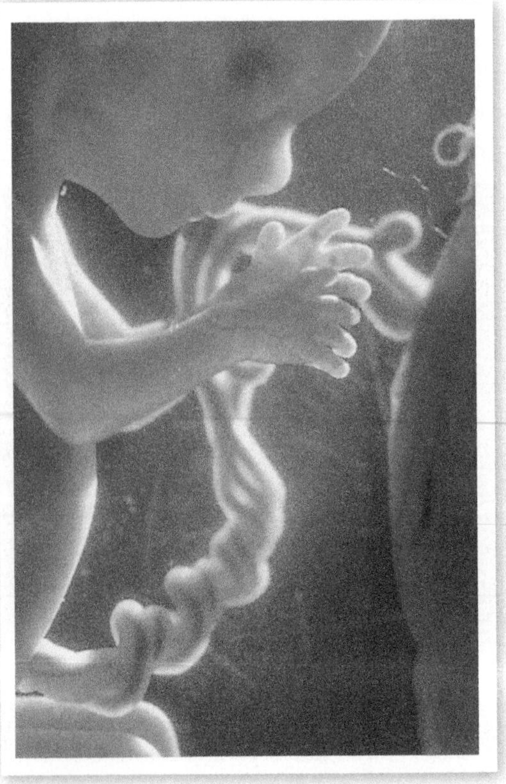

Petit Format/Nestle/Photo Researchers

TABLE 9.2 SAMPLE PRENATAL ENVIRONMENTAL CONDITIONS THAT ENDANGER A CHILD

Maternal Factors	Possible Effects on Embryo, Fetus, Newborn, or Young Child
Malnutrition	Low birth weight, malformations, less developed brain, greater vulnerability to disease
Stress exposure	Low birth weight, hyperactivity, irritability, feeding difficulties
Exposure to X-rays	Malformations, cancer
Legal and illegal drugs: Alcohol, nicotine, cocaine, methamphetamine	Inhibition of bone growth, hearing loss, low birth weight, fetal alcohol syndrome (FAS), intellectual disability, attention deficits in childhood, death
Diseases: German measles (rubella), herpes, HIV/AIDS, toxoplasmosis	Blindness, deafness, intellectual disability, heart and other malformations, brain infection, spontaneous abortion, premature birth, low birth weight, death

Sources: Abadinsky, 2014; Levinthal, 2011; Maisto et al., 2014; Whitbourne, 2011.

These influences generally have the most devastating effects during the first three months of pregnancy, making this a *critical period* in development.

What about the father's role? Environmentally, a father's smoking may pollute the air the mother breathes, and genetically, he may transmit heritable diseases. In addition, research suggests that alcohol, opiates, cocaine, various gases, lead, pesticides, and industrial chemicals can damage his sperm (Baker & Nieuwenhuijsen, 2008; Ji et al., 2013; Levy et al., 2011; Miranda-Contreras et al., 2013).

Perhaps the most important—and generally avoidable—danger to a fetus comes from drugs, both legal and illegal. Nicotine and alcohol are major **teratogens**, environmental agents that cause damage during prenatal development. Mothers who smoke tobacco or drink alcohol during pregnancy have significantly higher rates of premature births, low-birth-weight infants, and fetal deaths. Their children also show increased behavior and cognitive problems **(Figure 9.8)** (Brady et al., 2013; Espy et al., 2011; Larkby et al., 2011; Pruett et al., 2013). Research also has shown that children whose mothers smoked during pregnancy are more likely to be obese as adolescents, perhaps because in-utero exposure to nicotine changes a part of the brain that increases a preference for fatty foods (Haghighi et al., 2013). Q2

Teratogen An environmental agent that causes damage during prenatal development; comes from the Greek word *teras*, meaning "malformation."

Andy Levin/Science Source

FIGURE 9.8 FETAL ALCOHOL SYNDROME

Prenatal exposure to alcohol can result in a neurotoxic syndrome called **fetal alcohol syndrome (FAS)**, including facial abnormalities and stunted growth. But the most disabling features of FAS are brain damage and neurobehavioral problems, ranging from hyperactivity and learning disabilities to intellectual disability, depression, and psychoses (National Organization on Fetal Alcohol Syndrome, 2012; Pruett et al., 2013; Shaffer & Kipp, 2013; Sowell et al., 2008; Warren & Murray, 2013).

Fetal alcohol syndrome (FAS) A combination of birth defects, including organ deformities and mental, motor, and/or growth retardation, that result from maternal alcohol abuse.

Early Childhood Development

Like the prenatal period, early childhood is also a time of rapid physical development. Let's explore three key areas of change in early childhood: *brain*, *motor*, and *sensory/perceptual development*.

Brain Development

Our brain and other parts of the nervous system grow faster than any other part of the body during both prenatal development and the first two years of life, as illustrated in **Figure 9.9**. This brain development and learning occur primarily because neurons grow in size and because the number of axons and dendrites, as well as the extent of their connections, increases (DiPietro, 2000; Gilles & Nelson, 2012).

Motor Development

Compared to the hidden, internal changes in brain development, the orderly emergence of active movement skills, known as *motor development*, is easily observed and measured. A newborn's first motor abilities are limited to *reflexes*, or involuntary responses to stimulation. For example, the rooting reflex occurs when something touches a baby's cheek: The infant will automatically turn its head, open its mouth, and root for a nipple.

In addition to simple reflexes, the infant soon begins to show voluntary control over the movement of various body parts **(Figure 9.10)**. Thus, a helpless newborn, who cannot even lift her head, is soon transformed into an active toddler capable of crawling, walking, and climbing. In fact, babies are highly motivated to begin walking because they can move faster than when crawling, and they get better with practice (Adolph et al., 2012). Keep in mind that motor development is largely due to natural maturation, but, like brain development, it can also be affected by environmental influences such as disease and neglect.

Sensory and Perceptual Development

At birth, and during the final trimester of pregnancy, the developing child's senses are quite advanced (Colombo et al., 2013; Shaffer & Kipp, 2013). For example, research shows that a newborn infant prefers his or her mother's voice, providing evidence that the developing fetus can hear sounds outside the mother's body (Von Hofsten, 2013). In addition, a newborn can smell most odors and distinguish between sweet, salty, and bitter tastes. Breast-fed newborns also recognize the odor of their mother's milk compared to other mother's milk, formula, and other substances (Allam et al., 2010; Aoyama et al., 2010; Nishitani et al., 2009). Similarly, the newborn's sense of touch and pain is highly developed, as evidenced by reactions to circumcision and to heel pricks for blood testing, and by the fact that their pain reactions are lessened by the smell of their own mother's milk (Nishitani et al., 2009; Rodkey & Riddell, 2013; Williamson, 1997).

The newborn's sense of vision, however, is poorly developed. At birth, an infant is estimated to have vision between 20/200 and 20/600 (Haith & Benson, 1998). Imagine what the infant's visual life is like: The level of detail you see at 200 or 600 feet (if you have 20/20 vision) is what an infant sees at 20 feet. Within the first few months, vision quickly improves, and by 6 months it is 20/100 or better. At 2 years, visual acuity is nearly at the adult level of 20/20 (Courage & Adams, 1990).

One of the most interesting findings in infant sensory and perceptual research concerns hearing. Not only can the newborn hear quite well at birth, but also, during the last few months in the womb, the fetus can hear sounds outside the mother's body. This raises the interesting possibility of fetal learning, and some have advocated special stimulation for the fetus as a way of increasing intelligence, creativity, and general alertness (Muenssinger et al, 2013, Partanen et al., 2013; Van de Carr & Lehrer, 1997).

FIGURE 9.9 BRAIN DEVELOPMENT

The brain undergoes dramatic changes from conception through the first few years of life. Keep in mind, however, that our brains continue to change and develop throughout our life span.

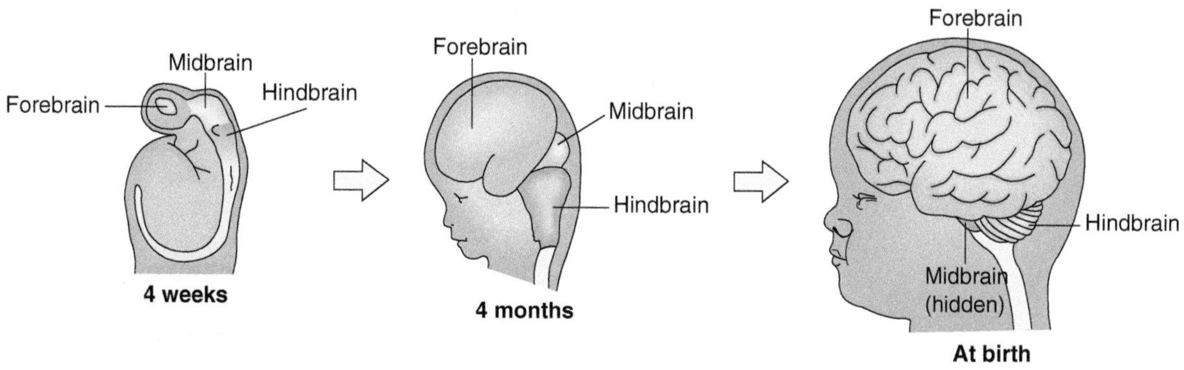

A Prenatal brain development

Recall from Chapter 2 that the human brain is divided into three major sections—the hindbrain, midbrain, and forebrain. Note how at three weeks after conception these three brain sections are one long neural tube, which later becomes the brain and spinal cord.

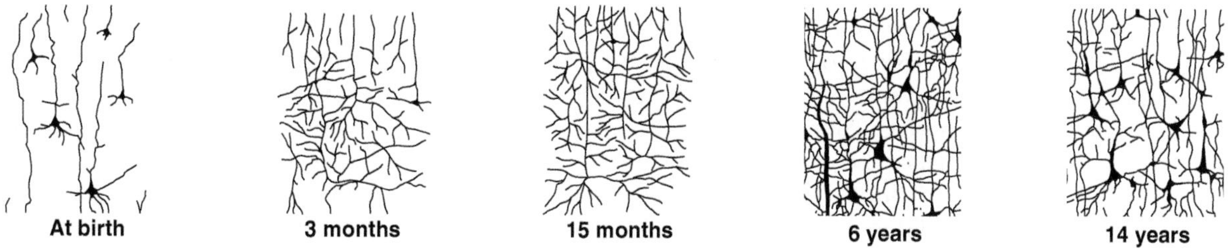

B Brain growth in the first two years

As infants learn and develop, synaptic connections between active neurons strengthen, and dendritic connections become more elaborate. Synaptic pruning (reduction of unused synapses) helps support this process. Myelination, the accumulation of fatty tissue coating the axons of nerve cells, continues until early adulthood.

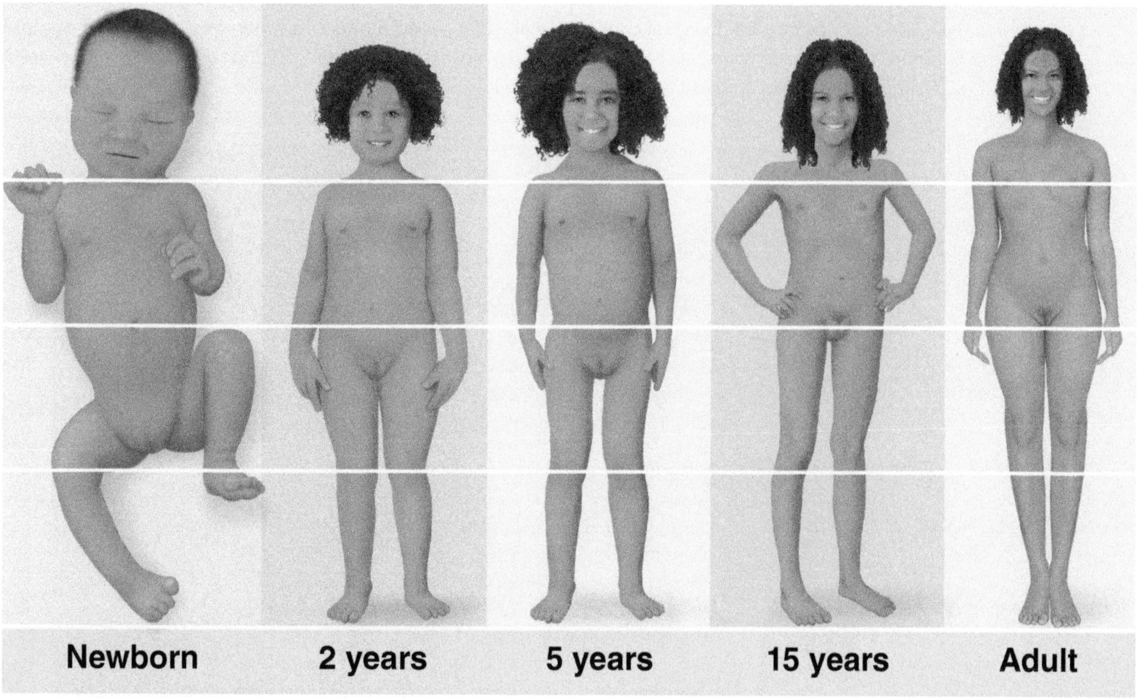

C Brain and body changes over our life span

There are dramatic changes in our brain and body proportions as we grow older. At birth, our heads were one-fourth our total body's size, whereas in adulthood, our head is one-eighth.

FIGURE 9.10 **MILESTONES IN MOTOR DEVELOPMENT**

The acquisition and progression of motor skills, from chin up to walking up steps, is generally the same for all children, but each child will follow his or her own personal timetable (Adolph & Berger, 2012; Atun-Einy et al., 2012; Benjamin Neelon et al., 2012; Mitchell & Ziegler, 2013).

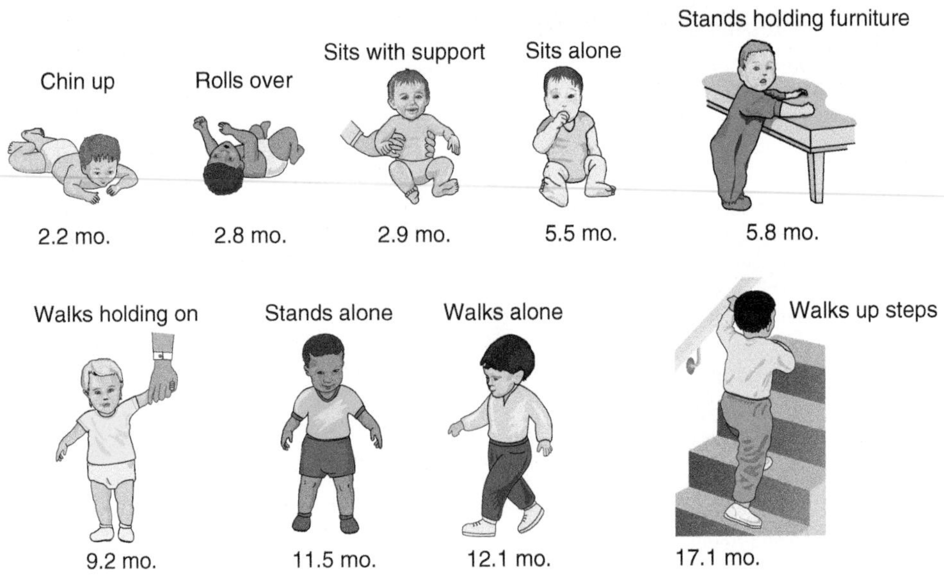

Adolescence

Changes in height and weight, breast development and menstruation for girls, and a deepening voice and beard growth for boys are important milestones for adolescents. **Puberty**, the period of adolescence when a person becomes capable of reproduction, is a major physical milestone for everyone. It is a clear biological signal of the end of childhood.

Puberty The biological changes during adolescence that lead to an adult-sized body and sexual maturity.

Adolescence is the loosely defined psychological period of development between childhood and adulthood, commonly associated with puberty. In the United States, it roughly corresponds to the teenage years. However, the concept of adolescence and its meaning vary greatly across cultures **(Figure 9.11)**.

FIGURE 9.11 **READY FOR RESPONSIBILITY?** realworldpsychology

Adolescence is not a universal concept. Unlike the United States and other Western nations, some non-industrialized countries have no need for a slow transition from childhood to adulthood; children simply assume adult responsibilities as soon as possible.

John Miles/The Image Bank /Getty Images, Inc.

The clearest and most dramatic physical sign of puberty is the *growth spurt*, which is characterized by rapid increases in height, weight, and skeletal growth **(Figure 9.12)** and by significant changes in reproductive structures and sexual characteristics. Maturation and hormone secretion cause rapid development of the ovaries, uterus, and vagina and the onset of menstruation (*menarche*) in the adolescent female. In the adolescent male, the testes, scrotum, and penis develop, and he experiences his first ejaculation (*spermarche*). The testes and ovaries in turn produce hormones that lead to the development of secondary sex characteristics, such as the growth of pubic hair, deepening of the voice and growth of facial hair in men, and growth of breasts in women **(Figure 9.13)**.

Q3 Have you ever wondered why teenagers seem to sleep so much? Researchers have found that puberty is triggered by changes in the brain, including the release of certain hormones, which occur only during periods of *deep sleep* (Shaw et al., 2012). This finding suggests that getting adequate, deep (slow-wave) sleep (see Chapter 5) during adolescence is an essential part of activating the reproductive system. Can you see why the increasing number of sleep problems in adolescents is a cause for concern, and why parents should actually be encouraging "oversleeping" in their teenagers?

Sergey Novikov/Shutterstock

FIGURE 9.12 ADOLESCENT GROWTH SPURT

Note the gender differences in height gain during puberty. Most girls are about two years ahead of boys in their growth spurt and are therefore taller than most boys between the ages of 10 and 14.

Adulthood

Age-related physical changes that occur after the obvious pubertal changes are less dramatic. Other than some modest increases in height and muscular development during the late teens and early twenties, most individuals experience only minor physical changes until middle age.

For women, *menopause*, the cessation of the menstrual cycle, which occurs somewhere between the ages of 45 and 55, is the second most important life milestone in physical development. The decreased production of estrogen (the dominant female hormone) produces certain physical changes, including decreases in some types of cognitive and memory skills (Weber et al., 2013). However, the popular belief that menopause (or "the change of life") causes serious psychological mood swings, loss of sexual interest, and depression is not supported by current research (Matlin, 2012; Moilanen et al., 2010). In fact, most studies find that postmenopausal women report relief, increased libido, and other positive reactions to the end of their menstrual cycles (Chrisler, 2008; Strauss, 2010).

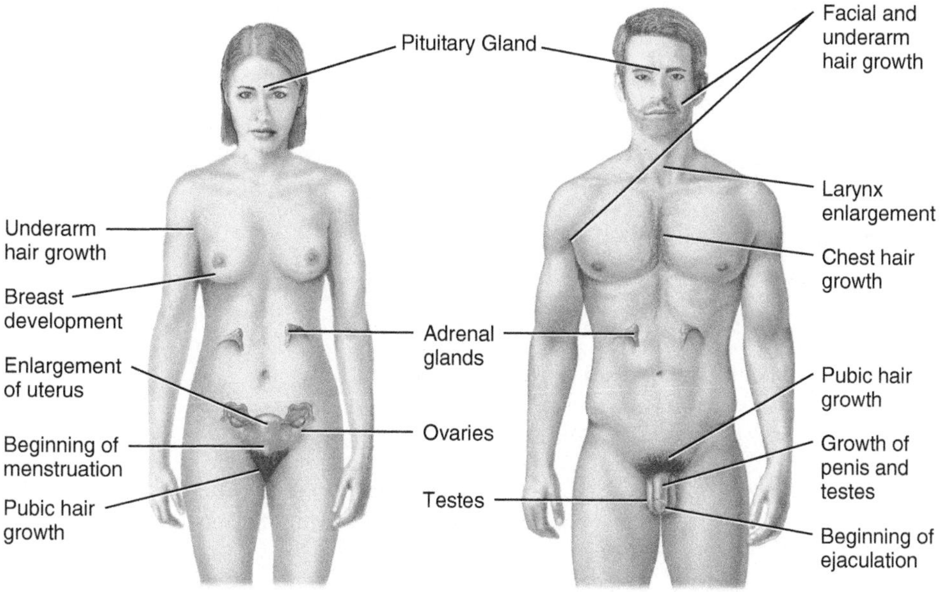

FIGURE 9.13 SECONDARY SEX CHARACTERISTICS

Complex physical changes in puberty primarily result from hormones secreted from the ovaries and testes, the pituitary gland in the brain, and the adrenal glands near the kidneys.

In contrast to women, men experience a more gradual decline in hormone levels, and most men can father children until their seventies or eighties. Physical changes such as unexpected weight gain, decline in sexual responsiveness, loss of muscle strength, and graying or loss of hair may lead some men (and women as well) to feel depressed and to question their life progress. They often see these alterations as a biological signal of aging and mortality. Such physical and psychological changes in some men are generally referred to as the *male climacteric* (or *andropause*). However, the popular belief that almost all men (and some women) go through a deeply disruptive midlife crisis, experiencing serious dissatisfaction with their work and personal relationships, is largely a myth.

After middle age, most physical changes in development are gradual and occur in the heart and arteries and in the sensory receptors. For example, cardiac output (the volume of blood pumped by the heart each minute) decreases, whereas blood pressure increases due to the thickening and stiffening of arterial walls. Visual acuity and depth perception decline, hearing acuity lessens (especially for high-frequency sounds), smell sensitivity decreases, and there is some decline in cognitive and memory skills (Baldwin & Ash, 2011; Edelstein et al., 2013; Fletcher & Rapp, 2013; Heinrich & Schneider, 2011; Siegler et al., 2013).

Ageism Prejudice or discrimination based on physical age; similar to racism and sexism in its negative stereotypes.

Sadly, television, magazines, movies, and advertisements too often present aging as a time for endless attempts at hiding gray hair, preventing or hiding wrinkles, avoiding or restoring thin or balding hair, and recovering lost sexual potency. Such negative portrayals contribute to our society's widespread **ageism**—prejudice or discrimination based on physical age. However, a recent survey of more than 1,000 older adults revealed an increase in well-being with age, contrary to what negative stereotypes about aging might predict (Jeste et al., 2012). Furthermore, as advertising companies consider the huge number of aging baby boomers, there has been a recent shift toward more positive and accurate portrayals of aging as a time of vigor, interest, and productivity.

Mark Wilson/Getty Images

realworldpsychology **Achievement in Later Years** Our cognitive abilities generally grow and improve throughout our life span, as demonstrated by the achievements of people like Ruth Bader Ginsburg. Justice Ginsburg worked tirelessly as a staunch courtroom advocate for many years, and now in her eighties continues to serve as a Supreme Court Justice for the United States—only the second of four woman to be appointed to this high honor.

RETRIEVAL PRACTICE: PHYSICAL DEVELOPMENT

Self-Test

Completing this self-test and comparing your answers with those in Appendix B provides immediate feedback and helpful practice for exams. Additional interactive, self-tests are available at www.wiley.com/college/huffman.

1. Teratogens are ______

a. maternal defects that cause damage during neo-natal development.
b. environmental agents that cause damage during prenatal development.
c. popular children's toys that studies have shown cause damage during early childhood development.
d. environmental diseases that cause damage during early childhood development.

2. The ______ is the first stage of prenatal development, which begins with ovulation and ends with implantation in the uterus (the first two weeks).

a. embryonic period
b. zygote stage
c. critical period
d. germinal period

3. Which of the following is *not* true regarding infant sensory and perceptual development?

a. A newborn's vision is almost 20/20 at birth.
b. A newborn's sense of pain is highly developed at birth.
c. An infant can recognize, and prefers, its own mother's breast milk by smell.
d. An infant can recognize, and prefers, its own mother's breast milk by taste.

4. The clearest and most physical sign of puberty is the ______, characterized by rapid increases in height, weight, and skeletal growth.

a. menses
b. spermarche
c. growth spurt
d. age of fertility

5. Some employers are reluctant to hire older workers (50 years of age and older) because of a generalized belief that they are sickly and will take too much time off. This is an example of ______.

a. discrimination
b. prejudice
c. ageism
d. all the above

Think Critically

1 If a mother knowingly ingests a quantity of alcohol, which causes her child to develop fetal alcohol syndrome (FAS), is she guilty of child abuse? Why or why not?

2 Based on what you have learned about development during late adulthood, do you think this period is inevitably a time of physical and mental decline? Why or why not?

realworldpsychology

Does prenatal exposure to smoke increase the risk of obesity later in life?

Why do teenagers seem to sleep so much?

HINT: LOOK IN THE MARGIN FOR Q2 AND Q3

COGNITIVE DEVELOPMENT

RETRIEVAL PRACTICE While reading the upcoming sections, respond to each Learning Objective in your own words. Then compare your responses with those found at www.wiley.com/college/huffman.

LEARNING OBJECTIVES

1 **EXPLAIN** the role of schemas, assimilation, and accommodation in cognitive development.

2 **DESCRIBE** the major characteristics of Piaget's four stages of cognitive development.

3 **COMPARE** Piaget's theory of cognitive development to Vygotsky's.

Just as a child's body and physical abilities change, his or her way of knowing and perceiving the world also grows and changes. Jean Piaget [pee-ah-ZHAY] provided some of the first great demonstrations of how children develop thinking and reasoning abilities. He showed that an infant begins at a cognitively "primitive" level and that intellectual growth progresses in distinct stages, motivated by an innate need to know.

To appreciate Piaget's contributions, we need to consider three major concepts: schemas, assimilation, and accommodation. **Schemas** are the most basic units of intellect. They act as patterns that organize our interactions with the environment, like an architect's drawings or a builder's blueprints (see *Test Yourself*).

Schema The cognitive structures, framework, or "blueprints" of knowledge, regarding objects, people, and situations, which grow and differentiate with experience.

TEST YOURSELF: DO YOU HAVE AN ARTISTIC SCHEMA?

psychology and you

Study the "impossible figure" to the right, and then try drawing this figure without tracing it. Students with artistic training generally find it relatively easy to reproduce, whereas the rest of us find it very hard or "impossible." This is because we lack the necessary artistic schema and cannot assimilate what we see. With practice and training, we could accommodate the new information and easily draw the figure.

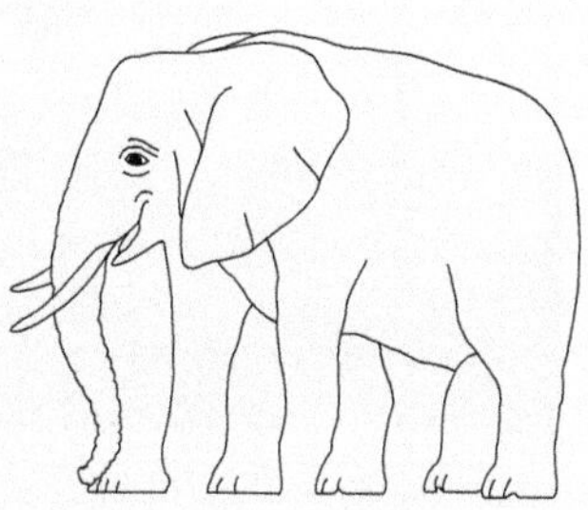

© amana images inc./Alamy

FIGURE 9.14 ACCOMMODATION

An infant uses accommodation to make the transition from milk to solid foods.

In the first few weeks of life, for example, the infant apparently has several *schemas* based on the innate reflexes of sucking, grasping, and so on. These schemas are primarily motor and may be little more than stimulus-and-response mechanisms (for example, the nipple is presented, and the baby sucks). Soon, other schemas emerge. The infant develops a more detailed schema for eating solid food, a different schema for the concepts of "mother" and "father," and so on.

Assimilation and *accommodation* are the two major processes by which schemas grow and change over time. **Assimilation** is the process of absorbing new information into existing schemas. For instance, infants use their sucking schema not only in sucking nipples but also in sucking blankets and fingers. In **accommodation**, existing ideas are modified to fit new information. Accommodation generally occurs when new information or stimuli cannot be assimilated. New schemas are developed or old schemas are changed to better fit with the new information. An infant's first attempt to eat solid food with a spoon is a good example of accommodation **(Figure 9.14)**.

Interestingly, researchers in one study found that babies who sat upright in infant seats while they explored different objects were much better at distinguishing between those objects than babies who were lying down while they explored (Woods & Wilcox, 2013). Although the researchers weren't exactly sure why sitting up helped babies learn more about different objects, it may be that a sitting position allows babies to better reach for, hold, and manipulate objects. Q4

Assimilation In Piaget's theory, applying existing mental patterns (schemas) to new information; new information is incorporated (assimilated) into existing schemas; works in tandem with accommodation.

Accommodation According to Piaget, the process of adjusting (accommodating) existing mental patterns (schemas) or developing new ones to better fit with new information; works in tandem with assimilation.

Stages of Cognitive Development

According to Piaget, all children go through approximately the same four stages of cognitive development, regardless of the culture in which they live **(Table 9.3)**. Piaget also believed that these stages cannot be skipped because skills acquired at earlier stages are essential to mastery at later stages.

Sensorimotor Stage

The **sensorimotor stage** lasts from birth until "significant" language acquisition (about age 2). During this time, children explore the world and develop their schemas primarily through their senses and motor activities—hence the term *sensorimotor*. One important concept that infants lack at the beginning of the sensorimotor stage is **object permanence**—an understanding that objects continue to exist even when they cannot be seen, heard, or touched **(Figure 9.15)**. The attainment of object permanence generally signals a transition from the sensorimotor to the preoperational stage.

Sensorimotor stage Piaget's first stage of cognitive development (birth to approximately age 2), in which schemas are developed through sensory and motor activities.

Object permanence The Piagetian term for an infant's recognition that objects (or people) continue to exist even when they cannot be seen, heard, or touched directly.

FIGURE 9.15 OBJECT PERMANENCE

Prior to about 8 months of age, infants tend to lack object permanence, as shown by the child in the first two photos, who apparently believes the toy no longer exists once it is blocked from sight. In contrast, the older child in the third photo knows that the object still exists even if it is hidden—as shown by her attempt to seek out the toy that is hidden under the sofa. Thus demonstrating that she has formed a mental representation (a schema) of the object and has acquired a recognition of object permanence.

Doug Goodman/Photo Researchers/Getty Images

Doug Goodman/Photo Researchers/Getty Images

Heleen Sitter/The Image Bank/Getty Images

TABLE 9.3 PIAGET'S FOUR STAGES OF COGNITIVE DEVELOPMENT

Sensorimotor stage (birth to age 2)	**Limits** • Beginning of stage lacks object permanence (understanding that things continue to exist even when not seen, heard, or felt) **Abilities** • Uses senses and motor skills to explore and develop cognitively **Example** • Children at this stage like to play with their food.	 Jeff R Clow/Flickr/Getty Images
Preoperational stage (ages 2 to 7)	**Limits** • Cannot perform "operations" (lacks reversibility) • Intuitive thinking versus logical reasoning • Egocentric thinking (inability to consider another's point of view) • Animistic thinking (believing all things are living) **Abilities** • Has significant language and thinks symbolically **Example** • Children at this stage often believe the moon follows them.	 © Igor Demchenkov/iStockphoto
Concrete operational stage (ages 7 to 11)	**Limits** • Cannot think abstractly and hypothetically • Thinking tied to concrete, tangible objects and events **Abilities** • Can perform "operations" on concrete objects • Understands conservation (realizing that changes in shape or appearance can be reversed) • Less egocentric • Can think logically about concrete objects and events **Example** • Children at this stage begin to question the existence of Santa.	 Hill Street Studios/Blend Images/Getty Images, Inc.
Formal operational stage (age 11 and over)	**Limits** • Adolescent egocentrism at the beginning of this stage, with related problems of the personal fable and imaginary audience **Abilities** • Can think abstractly and hypothetically **Example** • Children at this stage show great concern for physical appearance.	 © Adrian Burke/Corbis Images

Preoperational stage Piaget's second stage of cognitive development (roughly age 2 to 7), characterized by the ability to employ significant language and to think symbolically, but the child lacks operations (reversible mental processes), and thinking is egocentric and animistic.

Egocentrism In cognitive development, the inability to take the perspective of another person; a hallmark of Piaget's preoperational stage.

Preoperational Stage

During the **preoperational stage** (roughly ages 2 to 7), language advances significantly, and the child begins to think symbolically—using symbols, such as words, to represent concepts. Three other qualities characterize this stage: *lack of operations*, *egocentrism*, and *animism*.

Piaget labeled this period "preoperational" because the child *lacks operations*, or reversible mental processes. For instance, if a preoperational boy who has a brother is asked, "Do you have a brother?" he will easily respond, "Yes." However, when asked, "Does your brother have a brother?" he will answer, "No!" To understand that his brother has a brother, he must be able to reverse the concept of "having a brother."

Children at this stage have difficulty understanding that there are points of view other than their own, which is known as **egocentrism**. The preschooler who moves in front of you to get a better view of the TV or repeatedly asks questions while you are talking to someone else on the telephone is demonstrating egocentrism. Children of this age assume that others see, hear, feel, and think exactly as they do.

Voices from the Classroom

Egocentrism and a Dump Truck! It was getting close to my brother's birthday, and I called him up. After we chatted, he put his 4-year-old son Josh on the phone. I asked Josh, "What do you think we should get your dad for his birthday?" It took him very little time to blurt out, "A dump truck!" Being aware of Josh's personal love of bulldozers and dump trucks, which obviously wouldn't be my brother's choice for a birthday present, I realized that my nephew was in Piaget's preoperational stage and demonstrating egocentrism.

Professor David Baskind
Delta College
University Center, Michigan

Children in the preoperational stage also believe that objects such as the sun, trees, clouds, and bars of soap have motives, feelings, and intentions (for example, "dark clouds are angry" and "soap sinks because it is tired"). *Animism* refers to the belief that all things are living (or animated).

Concrete operational stage Piaget's third stage of cognitive development (roughly age 7 to 11), in which the child can perform mental operations on concrete objects and understand reversibility and conservation, but thinking is tied to concrete, tangible objects and events.

Conservation According to Piaget, the understanding that certain physical characteristics (such as volume) remain unchanged, even though appearances may change.

Concrete Operational Stage

At approximately age 7, children enter the **concrete operational stage**. During this time, many important thinking skills emerge. However, as the name implies, thinking tends to be limited to *concrete*, tangible objects and events. Unlike preoperational children, children in this stage are less egocentric in their thinking and become capable of true logical thought. As most parents know, children now stop believing in Santa Claus because they logically conclude that one man can't deliver presents to everyone in one night.

Because they understand the concept of *reversibility*, concrete operational children also can now successfully perform "operations." They recognize that certain physical attributes (such as volume) remain unchanged, although the outward appearance is altered, in a process known as **conservation**. Tests for conservation can identify whether a child is in the preoperational or the concrete operational stage (see *Putting Piaget to the Test*).

PUTTING PIAGET TO THE TEST

psychology and you

If you have access to children in the preoperational or concrete operational stages, try some of the following experiments, which researchers use to test Piaget's various forms of conservation. The equipment is easily obtained, and you will find their responses fascinating. Keep in mind that this should be done as a game. The child should not feel that he or she is failing a test or making a mistake.

Type of conservation task (average age at which concept is fully grasped)	**Your task as experimenter . . .**	**Child is asked . . .**
Length (ages 6–7)	**Step 1** Center two sticks of equal length. Child agrees that they are of equal length. **Step 2** Move one stick. 	**Step 3** "Which stick is longer?" Preoperational child will say that one of the sticks is longer. Child in concrete stage will say that they are both the same length.
Substance amount (ages 6–7)	**Step 1** Center two identical clay balls. Child acknowledges that the two have equal amounts of clay. **Step 2** Flatten one of the balls. 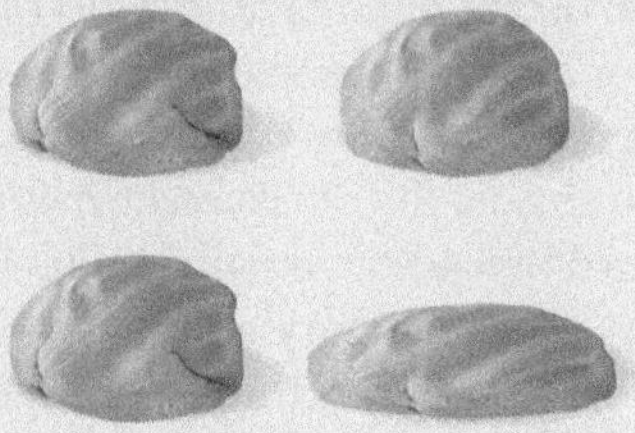	**Step 3** "Do the two pieces have the same amount of clay?" Preoperational child will say that the flat piece has more clay. Child in concrete stage will say that the two pieces have the same amount of clay.
Liquid volume (ages 7–8)	**Step 1** Present two identical glasses with liquid at the same level. Child agrees that liquid is at the same height in both glasses. **Step 2** Pour the liquid from one of the short, wide glasses into the tall, thin one. 	**Step 3** "Do the two glasses have the same amount of liquid?" Preoperational child will say that the tall, thin glass has more liquid. Child in concrete stage will say that the two glasses have the same amount of liquid.
Area (ages 8–10)	**Step 1** Center two identical pieces of cardboard with wooden blocks placed on them in identical positions. Child acknowledges that the same amount of space is left open on each piece of cardboard. **Step 2** Scatter the blocks on one piece of the cardboard. 	**Step 3** "Do the two pieces of cardboard have the same amount of open space?" Preoperational child will say that the cardboard with scattered blocks has less open space. Child in concrete stage will say that both pieces have the same amount of open space.

Think Critically

1. Based on their responses, are the children you tested in the preoperational or concrete stage?
2. If you repeat the same tests with each child, do their answers change? Why or why not?

Formal Operational Stage

The final period in Piaget's theory, the **formal operational stage**, typically begins around age 11. In this stage, children begin to apply their operations to abstract concepts in addition to concrete objects. They also become capable of hypothetical thinking ("What if?"), which allows systematic formulation and testing of concepts.

Formal operational stage Piaget's fourth stage of cognitive development (around age 11 and beyond), characterized by abstract and hypothetical thinking.

For example, before filling out applications for part-time jobs, adolescents may think about possible conflicts with school and friends, the number of hours they want to work, and the kind of work for which they are qualified. Formal operational thinking also allows the adolescent to construct a well-reasoned argument based on hypothetical concepts and logical processes. Consider the following argument:

1. If you hit a glass with a feather, the glass will break.
2. You hit the glass with a feather.

What is the logical conclusion? The correct answer, "The glass will break," is contrary to fact and direct experience. Therefore, the child in the concrete operational stage would have difficulty with this task, whereas the formal operational thinker understands that this problem is about abstractions that need not correspond to the real world.

Along with the benefits of this cognitive style come several problems. Adolescents in the early stages of the formal operational period demonstrate a type of egocentrism different from that of the preoperational child. Adolescents certainly recognize that others have unique thoughts and perspectives. However, they may fail to differentiate between what they are thinking and what others are thinking. For example, if they get a new haircut or fail to make the sports team, they may be overly concerned about how others will react. Instead of considering that everyone is equally wrapped up in his or her own appearance, concerns, and plans, they tend to believe that they are the center of others' thoughts and attentions. David Elkind (1967, 2000, 2007) referred to this as the *imaginary audience*.

In sharp, ironic contrast to believing that others are always watching and evaluating them (the imaginary audience), Piaget believed that adolescents also often feel that they are special and unique. They alone are having insights or difficulties that no one else understands or experiences. Elkind described this as the *personal fable*.

In sum, the imaginary audience apparently results from an inability to differentiate the self from others, whereas the personal fable may be a product of differentiating too much. Thankfully, these two forms of adolescent egocentrism tend to decrease during later stages of the formal operational period.

© fstop123/iStockphoto

psychology and you **Understanding Your Own Adolescent Egocentrism** Do these descriptions of the imaginary audience and personal fable ring true for you? If so, do you now understand how these beliefs might help explain some of the problems and challenges you faced in adolescence? For example, many teens have difficulty accepting comfort and support from parents due to their belief that no one has ever felt or experienced what they have. One young woman remembered being very upset in middle school when her mother tried to comfort her over the loss of an important relationship. "I felt like she couldn't possibly know how it felt—no one could. I couldn't believe that anyone had ever suffered like this or that things would ever get better."

The most important danger of adolescent egocentrism is undoubtedly the fact that several forms of risk taking, such as engaging in sexual intercourse without protection, driving dangerously, and experimenting with drugs, seem to arise from the personal fable (Alberts et al., 2007; Flavell et al., 2002; Hill & Lapsley, 2011; Moshman, 2011). Adolescents have a sense of uniqueness, invulnerability, and immortality. They do recognize the dangers of risky activities, but given their adolescent egocentrism and personal fable, they believe the rules and statistical dangers just don't apply to them.

As a critical thinker, can you see how these Piagetian concepts of the imaginary audience and personal fable meet psychology's goal of *description* (Chapter 1)? If so, you'll also note how **Figure 9.16** and the following *Real World Psychology* offer biological insights toward the goal of *explanation*.

FIGURE 9.16 **BIOLOGY AND TEEN RISK TAKING**

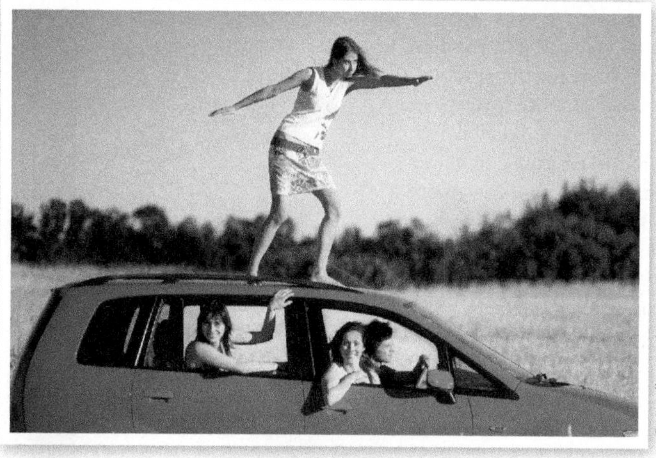

© Radka Linkova/Alamy Inc.

Ⓐ Can you see how this type of risk-taking behavior may reflect the personal fable—adolescents' tendency to believe they are unique and special and that dangers don't apply to them?

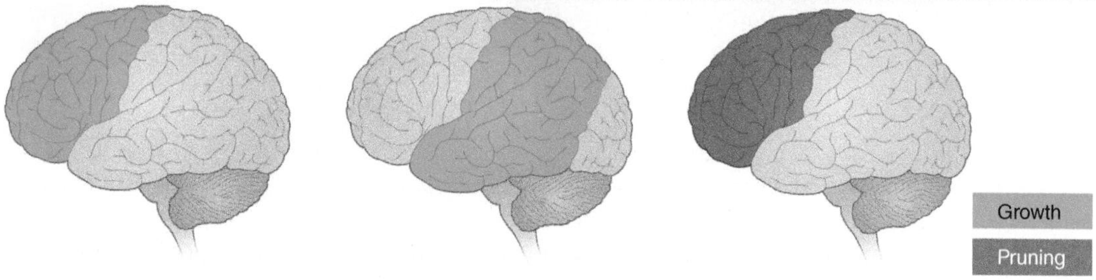

Ⓑ During early childhood (ages 3–6), the frontal lobes experience a significant increase in the connections between neurons, which helps explain a child's rapid cognitive growth.

Ⓒ This rapid synaptic growth shifts to the temporal and parietal lobes during the ages of 7 to 15, which corresponds to their significant increases in language and motor skills.

Ⓓ During the teen years (ages 16–20), synaptic pruning is widespread in the frontal lobes.

realworldpsychology **Brain and Behavior in Adolescence**
Adolescents are often criticized for their exaggerated, self-conscious concern for what others think, as well as for their extreme mood swings, poor decisions, and risky behaviors **(Figure 9.16)**. Rather than simply describing and labeling these as the imaginary audience and personal fable, psychologists now believe these effects may be largely due to their less-developed frontal lobes (Bunge & Toga, 2013; Christakou et al., 2011; Moshman, 2011; Pokhrel et al., 2013). In contrast to the rapid synaptic growth experienced in the earlier years **(Figures 9.16b** and **c)**, the adolescent's brain actively destroys (prunes) unneeded connections **(Figure 9.16d)**. Although it may seem counterintuitive, this pruning actually improves brain functioning by making the remaining neurons more efficient. Full maturity of the frontal lobes occurs around the mid-twenties. Recall from Chapter 2 that our frontal lobes are largely responsible for higher-level cognitive functioning, such as emotional regulation, planning ahead, and avoiding reckless behavior.

Vygotsky Versus Piaget

As influential as Piaget's account of cognitive development has been, there are other important theories, and criticisms of Piaget, to consider. For example, Russian psychologist Lev Vygotsky emphasized the sociocultural influences on a child's cognitive development, rather than Piaget's internal schemas. According to Vygotsky, children construct knowledge through their culture, language, and collaborative social interactions with more experienced thinkers (Mahn & John-Steiner, 2013; Trawick-Smith & Dziurgot, 2011). Unlike Piaget, Vygotsky believed that adults play an important

FIGURE 9.17 VYGOTSKY'S ZONE OF PROXIMAL DEVELOPMENT (ZPD)

Have you heard of "instructional scaffolding"? This term refers to providing support during the learning process that is tailored to the needs of the student. Vygotsky was one of the first to apply the general idea of scaffolding to early cognitive development. He proposed that the most effective teaching focuses on tasks between those a learner can do without help (the lower limit) and those he or she cannot do even with help (the upper limit). In this *zone of proximal development (ZPD)*, tasks and skills can be "stretched" to higher levels with the guidance and encouragement of a more knowledgeable person.

Zone of proximal development (ZPD) In Vygotsky's theory of cognitive development, the area between what children can accomplish on their own and what they can accomplish with the help of others who are more competent.

instructor role in development and that this instruction is particularly helpful when it falls within a child's **zone of proximal development (ZPD) (Figure 9.17)**.

Having briefly discussed Vygotsky's alternative theory, let's consider two major criticisms of Piaget—*underestimated abilities* and *underestimated genetic and cultural influences*. Research shows that Piaget may have underestimated young children's cognitive development. As you've just seen, Piaget believed that infancy and early childhood were a time of extreme egocentrism, in which children have little or no understanding of the perspective of others. However, later research finds that empathy develops at a relatively young age **(Figure 9.18)**. Furthermore, even newborn babies tend to cry in response to the cry of another baby (Diego & Jones, 2007; Geangu et al., 2010). Also, preschoolers will adapt their speech by using shorter, simpler expressions when talking to 2-year-olds as compared to talking with adults.

Piaget's model, like other stage theories, has also been criticized for not sufficiently taking into account genetic and cultural differences (Cole & Gajdamaschko, 2007; Shweder, 2011; Zelazo et al., 2010). Despite criticisms, however, Piaget's contributions to psychology are enormous. As one scholar put it, "assessing the impact of Piaget on developmental psychology is like assessing the impact of Shakespeare on English literature or Aristotle on philosophy—impossible" (Beilin, 1992, p. 191).

FIGURE 9.18 ARE PREOPERATIONAL CHILDREN ALWAYS EGOCENTRIC?

Some toddlers and preschoolers clearly demonstrate empathy for other people. How does this ability to take another's perspective contradict Piaget's beliefs about egocentrism in very young children?

RETRIEVAL PRACTICE: COGNITIVE DEVELOPMENT

Self-Test

Completing this self-test and comparing your answers with those in Appendix B provides immediate feedback and helpful practice for exams. Additional interactive, self-tests are available at www.wiley.com/college/huffman.

1. ______ was one of the first scientists to demonstrate that a child's intellect is fundamentally different from an adult's.

a. Baumrind b. Beck
c. Piaget d. Elkind

2. ______ occurs when existing schemas are used to absorb new information, whereas ______ makes changes and modifications to the schemas.

a. Adaptation; accommodation b. Adaptation; reversibility
c. Egocentrism; postschematization d. Assimilation; accommodation

3. A child's belief that the moon follows him as he travels in a car is an example of ______.

a. sensorimotor delusions b. formal operational thinking
c. wet concrete thinking d. animism

4. The ability to think abstractly and hypothetically occurs in Piaget's ______ stage.

a. egocentric b. postoperational
c. formal operational d. concrete operational

Think Critically

1 Piaget's theory states that all children progress through all the discrete stages of cognitive development in order and without skipping any. Do you agree with this theory? Do you know any children who seem to contradict this theory?

2 Based on what you've learned about schemas, what are some new schemas you've developed as part of your transition from high school to college?

realworldpsychology

Do babies learn faster when they're sitting up than when they're lying down

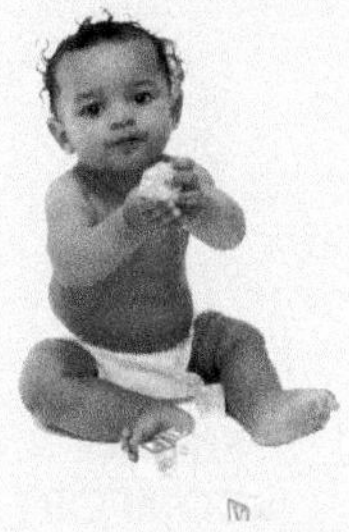

HINT: LOOK IN THE MARGIN FOR Q4

SOCIAL-EMOTIONAL DEVELOPMENT

RETRIEVAL PRACTICE While reading the upcoming sections, respond to each Learning Objective in your own words. Then compare your responses with those found at www.wiley.com/college/huffman.

LEARNING OBJECTIVES

1 **DESCRIBE** how attachment and parenting styles influence social-emotional development.
2 **SUMMARIZE** the central characteristics of Kohlberg's theory of moral development.
3 **REVIEW** Erikson's eight stages of psychosocial development.
4 **DESCRIBE** how sex and gender affect development.

In addition to physical and cognitive development, developmental psychologists study the way social and emotional factors affect development over the life span. In this section, we focus on *attachment*, *parenting styles*, *moral reasoning*, *personality*, *sex*, and *gender*.

Attachment

An infant arrives in the world with a multitude of behaviors that encourage a strong bond of **attachment** with primary caregivers. Returning to our earlier discussion of the nature–nurture controversy, researchers who advocate the nativist, or innate, position suggest that newborn infants are biologically equipped with verbal and

Attachment A strong emotional bond with special others that endures over time.

nonverbal behaviors (such as crying, clinging, and smiling) and imprinting ("following") behaviors (such as crawling and walking after the caregiver) that elicit instinctive nurturing responses from the caregiver (Bowlby, 1969, 1989, 2000).

Touch

Harry Harlow and his colleagues (1950, 1966, 1971) also investigated the variables that might affect attachment. They created two types of wire-framed surrogate (substitute) "mother" monkeys: one covered by soft terry cloth and one left uncovered **(Figure 9.19)**. The infant monkeys were fed by either the cloth or the wire mother, but they otherwise had access to both mothers. The researchers found that monkeys "reared" by a cloth mother clung frequently to the soft material of their surrogate mother and developed greater emotional security and curiosity than did monkeys assigned to the wire mother.

Thanks in part to Harlow's research, psychologists discovered that *contact comfort*, the pleasurable tactile sensations provided by a soft and cuddly "parent," is a powerful contributor to attachment **(Figure 9.20)**. Further support comes from a study described in Chapter 4 which shows that touch is an essential part of normal human infant development. This is why hospitals now encourage premature babies to receive "kangaroo care," in which babies have skin-to-skin contact with a parent (Schneider et al., 2012).

Although physical contact between caregiver and child appears to be an innate, biological part of attachment, Mary Ainsworth and her colleagues (1967, 1978) discovered several interesting differences in the type and levels of human attachment **(Figure 9.21)**. Note, however, that while Ainsworth studied

FIGURE 9.19 HARLOW'S STUDY AND CONTACT COMFORT

Although Harlow's studies of attachment in infant monkeys would be considered unethical today, it did clearly demonstrate that *touch*, and not *feeding*, is crucial to an infant's attachment.

Nina Leen/Time Life Pictures/Getty Images

FIGURE 9.20 THE POWER OF TOUCH

Parents around the world tend to kiss, nuzzle, comfort, and respond to their children with lots of physical contact, which points out its vital role in infant development. It also provides support for the biological, nature argument for attachment.

Marili Forastieri/Digital Vision/ Getty Images

FIGURE 9.21 RESEARCH ON INFANT ATTACHMENT

For most children, parents are the earliest and most important factor in social development, and the attachment between parent and child is of particular interest to developmental psychologists. In fact, research shows that strong levels of social connectedness, meaning social attachments to friends and parents, have a stronger impact on well-being in adulthood than does academic achievement in adolescence (Olsson et al., 2012).

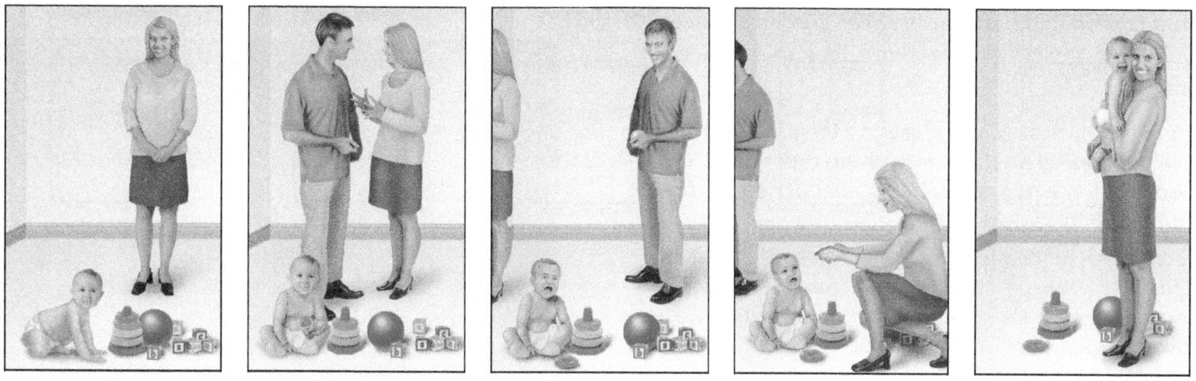

1. The baby plays while the mother is nearby.
2. A stranger enters the room, speaks to the mother, and approaches the child.
3. The mother leaves and the stranger stays in the room with an unhappy baby.
4. The mother returns and the stranger leaves.
5. The baby is reunited with the mother.

Ⓐ Strange situation procedure

Mary Ainsworth and her colleagues (1967, 1978, 2010) found significant differences in the typical levels of attachment between infants and their mothers using a technique called the strange situation procedure, in which they observed how infants responded to the presence or absence of their mother and a stranger.

Banana Stock/AgeFotostock

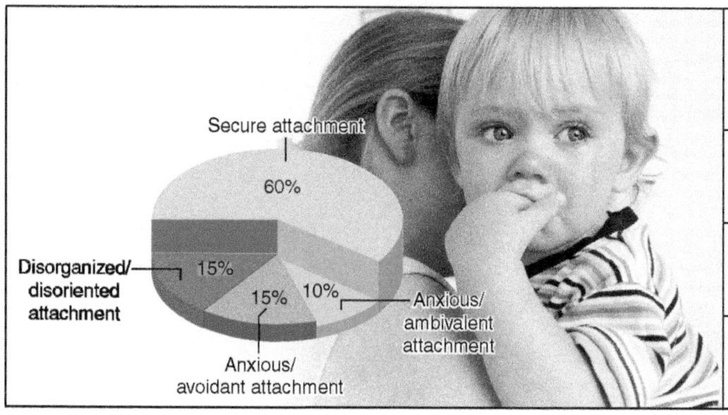

Secure
Seeks closeness with mother when stranger enters. Uses her as a safe base from which to explore, shows moderate distress on separation from her, and is happy when she returns.

Anxious/ambivalent
Infant becomes very upset when mother leaves the room and shows mixed emotions when she returns.

Anxious/avoidant
Infant does not seek closeness or contact with the mother and shows little emotion when the mother departs or returns.

Disorganized/disoriented
Infant exhibits avoidant or ambivalent attachment, often seeming either confused or apprehensive in the presence of the mother.

Ⓑ Degrees of attachment

Using the strange situation procedure, Ainsworth found that children could be divided into three groups: *Secure, anxious/avoidant, and anxious/ambivalent.* A later psychologist, Mary Main, added a fourth category, *disorganized/disoriented* (Main & Solomon, 1986, 1990).

attachment between mothers and infants, later research demonstrated that *both* mothers and fathers have a lasting impact on development (Khaleque & Rohner, 2011).

In addition to finding varying levels of infant attachment to parents, researchers also have observed that these early patterns of attachment tend to be related to our later adult styles of romantic love (Fraley et al., 2013; Graham, 2011; Hatfield & Rapson, 2010; Kilmann et al., 2013; Sprecher & Fehr, 2011; Tatkin, 2011). If we developed a secure, anxious/ambivalent, anxious/avoidant, or disorganized/disoriented style as infants, we tend to follow these same patterns in our adult approach to intimacy and affection. For example, young adults who experienced either unresponsive or overintrusive parenting during childhood are more likely to avoid committed romantic relationships as adults (Dekel & Farber, 2012). You can check your own romantic attachment style in *Test Yourself.* However, keep in mind that it's always risky to infer causation from correlation (see Chapter 1). Even if early attachment experiences are correlated with our later relationships, they do not determine them. Throughout life, we can learn new social skills and different approaches to all our relationships.

TEST YOURSELF: WHAT'S YOUR ROMANTIC ATTACHMENT STYLE?

psychology and you

Thinking of your current and past romantic relationships, place a check next to the statement that best describes your feelings about relationships.

____**1.** *I find it relatively easy to get close to others and am comfortable depending on them and having them depend on me. I don't often worry about being abandoned or about someone getting too close.*

____**2.** *I am somewhat uncomfortable being close. I find it difficult to trust partners completely or to allow myself to depend on them. I am nervous when anyone gets close, and love partners often want me to be more intimate than is comfortable for me.*

____**3.** *I find that others are reluctant to get as close as I would like. I often worry that my partner doesn't really love me or won't stay with me. I want to merge completely with another person, and this desire sometimes scares people away.*

According to research, 55% of adults agree with item 1 (secure attachment), 25% choose number 2 (anxious/avoidant attachment), and 20% choose item 3 (anxious/ambivalent attachment) (adapted from Fraley & Shaver, 1997; Hazan & Shaver, 1987). Note that the percentages for these adult attachment styles do not perfectly match those in Figure 9.21, partly because the disorganized/disoriented attachment pattern was not included in this measurement of adult romantic attachments.

Think Critically

1 Do your responses as an adult match your childhood attachment experiences?

2 Does your romantic attachment style negatively affect your present relationship? If so, how might you use this new information to make positive changes?

© GlobalStock / iStockphoto

Parenting Styles

How much of our personality comes from the way our parents treat us as we're growing up? Researchers since the 1920s have studied the effects of different methods of childrearing on children's behavior, development, and mental health. For example, when researchers did follow-up studies of children with the various levels of attachment we just discussed, they found that infants with a secure attachment style had caregivers who were sensitive and responsive to their signals of distress, happiness, and fatigue (Ainsworth, 1967; Ainsworth et al., 1978; Gini et al., 2007; Higley, 2008; Völker, 2007). Anxious/avoidant infants had caregivers who were aloof and distant, and anxious/ambivalent infants had inconsistent caregivers who alternated between strong affection and indifference. Follow-up studies found that, over time, securely attached children were the most sociable, emotionally aware, enthusiastic, cooperative, persistent, curious, and competent (Flaherty & Sadler, 2011; Friedman et al., 2013; Johnson et al., 2007).

Other studies by Diana Baumrind (1980, 1995, 2013) found that parenting styles could be reliably divided into four broad patterns—*permissive-neglectful,*

TABLE 9.4 PARENTING STYLES | realworldpsychology

Parenting style	Description	Example	Effect on children
Permissive-neglectful (permissive-indifferent) (low C, low W)	Parents make few demands, with little structure or monitoring, and show little interest or emotional support; may be actively rejecting.	"I don't care about you—or what you do."	Children tend to have poor social skills and little self-control (being overly demanding and disobedient).
Permissive-indulgent (low C, high W)	Parents set few limits or demands, but are highly involved and emotionally connected.	"I care about you—and you're free to do what you like!"	Children often fail to learn respect for others and tend to be impulsive, immature, and out of control.
Authoritarian (high C, low W)	Parents are rigid and punitive, while also being low on warmth and responsiveness.	"I don't care what you want. Just do it my way, or else!"	Children tend to be easily upset, moody, aggressive, and often fail to learn good communication skills.
Authoritative (high C, high W)	Parents generally set and enforce firm limits, while also being highly involved, tender, and emotionally supportive.	"I really care about you, but there are rules and you need to be responsible."	Children become self-reliant, self-controlled, high achieving, and emotionally welladjusted; also seem more content, goal oriented. friendly, and socially competent.

Sources: Baumrind, 1991, 1995, 2013; Celada, 2011; Driscoll et al., 2008; Martin & Fabes, 2009; McKinney et al., 2008; Topham et al., 2011.

permissive-indulgent, *authoritarian*, and *authoritative*—which can be differentiated by their degree of *control/demandingness* (*C*) and *warmth/responsiveness* (*W*) **(Table 9.4)**.

Moral Development

Developing a sense of right and wrong, or morality, is a part of psychological development. Consider what you would do in the following situation:

> In Europe, a cancer-ridden woman was near death, but an expensive drug existed that might save her. The woman's husband, Heinz, begged the druggist to sell the drug cheaper or to let him pay later. But he refused. Heinz became desperate and broke into his store and stole it. (Adapted from Kohlberg, 1964, pp. 18–19)

Was Heinz right to steal the drug? What do you consider moral behavior? Is morality "in the eye of the beholder," or are there universal moral truths and principles? Whatever your answer, your ability to think, reason, and respond to Heinz's dilemma may demonstrate your current level of moral development.

One of the most influential researchers in moral development was Lawrence Kohlberg (1927–1987). He presented what he called "moral stories" like the Heinz dilemma to people of all ages, not to see whether they judged Heinz right or wrong but to examine the reasons they gave for their decisions. On the basis of his findings, Kohlberg (1964, 1984) developed a model of moral development with three broad levels in the evolution of moral reasoning, and each of the three levels composed of two distinct stages **(Figure 9.22)**. Individuals at each stage and level may or may not support Heinz's stealing of the drug, but their reasoning changes from level to level.

Preconventional level The first level of Kohlberg's theory of moral development, where morality is based on rewards, punishment, and exchange of favors.

Conventional level The second level of Kohlberg's theory of moral development, where moral judgments are based on compliance with the rules and values of society.

Postconventional level The highest level of Kohlberg's theory of moral development, where individuals develop personal standards for right and wrong and define morality in terms of abstract principles and values that apply to all situations and societies.

FIGURE 9.22 **KOHLBERG'S STAGES OF MORAL DEVELOPMENT**

Lawrence Kohlberg believed that individuals progress through three levels and six stages of moral development.

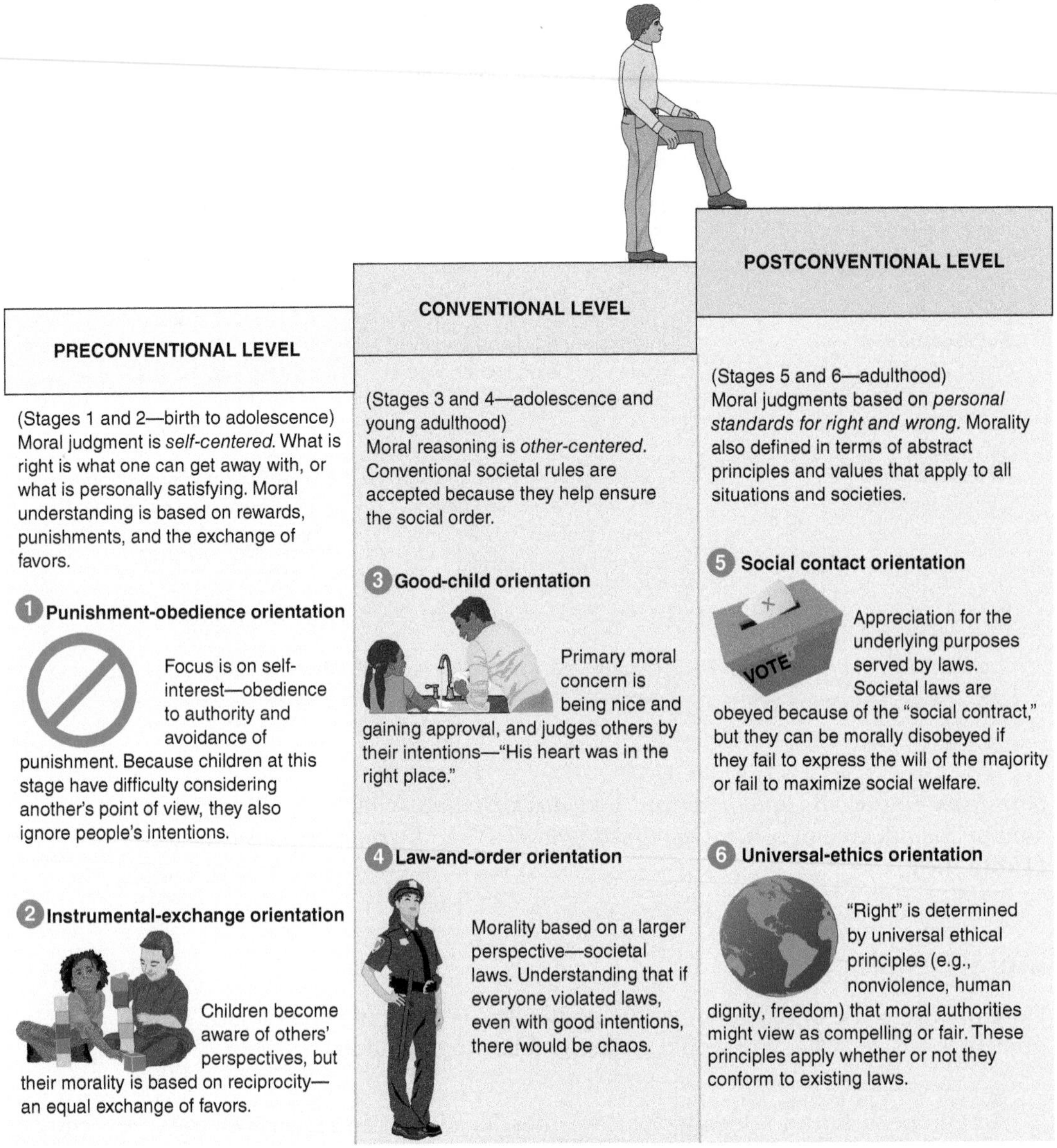
PRECONVENTIONAL LEVEL
(Stages 1 and 2—birth to adolescence) Moral judgment is *self-centered.* What is right is what one can get away with, or what is personally satisfying. Moral understanding is based on rewards, punishments, and the exchange of favors.
1 Punishment-obedience orientation
Focus is on self-interest—obedience to authority and avoidance of punishment. Because children at this stage have difficulty considering another's point of view, they also ignore people's intentions.
2 Instrumental-exchange orientation
Children become aware of others' perspectives, but their morality is based on reciprocity—an equal exchange of favors.
CONVENTIONAL LEVEL
(Stages 3 and 4—adolescence and young adulthood) Moral reasoning is *other-centered.* Conventional societal rules are accepted because they help ensure the social order.
3 Good-child orientation
Primary moral concern is being nice and gaining approval, and judges others by their intentions—"His heart was in the right place."
4 Law-and-order orientation
Morality based on a larger perspective—societal laws. Understanding that if everyone violated laws, even with good intentions, there would be chaos.
POSTCONVENTIONAL LEVEL
(Stages 5 and 6—adulthood) Moral judgments based on *personal standards for right and wrong.* Morality also defined in terms of abstract principles and values that apply to all situations and societies.
5 Social contact orientation
VOTE
Appreciation for the underlying purposes served by laws. Societal laws are obeyed because of the "social contract," but they can be morally disobeyed if they fail to express the will of the majority or fail to maximize social welfare.
6 Universal-ethics orientation
"Right" is determined by universal ethical principles (e.g., nonviolence, human dignity, freedom) that moral authorities might view as compelling or fair. These principles apply whether or not they conform to existing laws.

Sources: Based on Kohlberg, L. "Stage and Sequence: The Cognitive Developmental Approach to Socialization," in D. A. Goslin, *The handbook of socialization theory and research*. Chicago: Rand McNally, 1969, p. 376 (Table 6.2).

Assessing Kohlberg's Theory

Kohlberg's ideas have led to considerable research on how we think about moral issues (Carlo et al., 2013; Krettenauer et al., 2013; Malti, 2013; Mitchell & Ziegler, 2013; Paciello et al., 2013). But his theories have also been the focus of three major areas of criticism:

1. *Moral reasoning versus behavior* Are people who achieve higher stages on Kohlberg's scale really more moral than others? Or do they just "talk a good game"?

   Some researchers have shown that a person's sense of moral identity, meaning the use of moral principles to define oneself, is often a good predictor of his or her behavior in real-world situations (Johnston et al., 2013; Stets & Carter, 2012). But others have found that situational factors are better predictors of moral behavior (Bandura, 1986, 1991, 2008; Minnameier & Schmidt, 2013; van

Ijizendoorn et al., 2013). For example, research participants are more likely to steal when they are told the money comes from a large company rather than from individuals (Greenberg, 2002). And both men and women will tell more sexual lies during casual relationships than during close relationships (Williams, 2001).

2. *Cultural differences* Cross-cultural studies confirm that children from a variety of cultures generally follow Kohlberg's model and progress sequentially from his first level, the *preconventional*, to his second, the *conventional* (Rest et al., 1999; Snarey, 1995). However, other studies find differences among cultures (Jensen, 2011; LePage et al., 2011; Rai & Fiske, 2011). For example, cross-cultural comparisons of responses to Heinz's moral dilemma show that Europeans and Americans tend to consider whether they like or identify with the victim in questions of morality. In contrast, Hindu Indians consider social responsibility and personal concerns two separate issues (Miller & Bersoff, 1998). Researchers suggest that the difference reflects the Indians' broader sense of social responsibility.

   Furthermore, in India, Papua New Guinea, and China, as well as in Israeli kibbutzim, people don't choose between the rights of the individual and the rights of society (as the top levels of Kohlberg's model require). Instead, most people seek a compromise solution that accommodates both interests (Killen & Hart, 1999; Miller & Bersoff, 1998). Thus, Kohlberg's standard for judging the highest level of morality (the postconventional) may be more applicable to cultures that value individualism over community and interpersonal relationships.

3. *Possible gender bias* Researcher Carol Gilligan criticized Kohlberg's model because on his scale women often tend to be classified at a lower level of moral reasoning than men. She suggested that this difference occurred because Kohlberg's theory emphasizes values more often held by men, such as rationality and independence, while de-emphasizing common female values, such as concern for others and belonging (Gilligan, 1977, 1990, 1993; Kracher & Marble, 2008). However, most follow-up studies of Gilligan's specific theory, have found few, if any, gender differences (Bateman & Valentine, 2010; Fumagalli et al., 2010; Mercadillo et al., 2011; Smith, 2007).

realworldpsychology **Morality—Personal Trait or the Situation?** Which do you believe is the better predictor of moral behavior—the person or the situation? You've undoubtedly seen this dilemma when students are faced with a choice to cheat on an exam or shoplift. How about the case of Lance Armstrong, who chose to use performance-enhancing drugs in sports competition? Was it the situation or his personal morality that most influenced his behavior?

Ragnar Singsaas /Getty Images, Inc.

Personality Development

Like Piaget and Kohlberg, Erik Erikson (1902–1994) developed a stage theory of development. He identified eight **psychosocial stages** of social development **(Figure 9.23)**, each marked by a psychosocial crisis or conflict related to a specific developmental task. Erikson believed that the more successfully we overcome each psychosocial crisis, the better chance we have to develop in a healthy manner (Erikson, 1950).

Psychosocial stages Erikson's theory that individuals pass through eight developmental stages, each involving a specific crisis that must be successfully resolved; each stage incorporates both the sexual and social aspects of an individual's development.

Also like Piaget and Kohlberg, Erikson's insights and theory have stimulated considerable research (Conzen, 2010; Fukase & Okamoto, 2010; Marcia & Josselson, 2013; Zhang & He, 2011). However, Erikson also has critics (Beyers & Seiffge-Krenke, 2010; Spano et al., 2010). First, Erikson's psychosocial stages are difficult to test scientifically.

FIGURE 9.23 **ERIKSON'S EIGHT STAGES OF PSYCHOSOCIAL DEVELOPMENT**

Erikson identified eight stages of development, each of which is associated with its own unique psychosocial crisis.

Steve Raymer/NG Image Collection

1 Trust versus mistrust (birth–age 1)

Infants learn to *trust* or *mistrust* their caregivers and the world based on whether or not their needs—such as food, affection, safety—are met.

Prof. Karen Huffman

2 Autonomy versus shame and doubt (ages 1–3)

Toddlers start to assert their sense of independence (*autonomy*). If caregivers encourage this self-sufficiency, the toddler will learn to be independent versus feelings of *shame* and *doubt*.

Dynamic Graphics, Inc./Creatas

3 Initiative versus guilt (ages 3–6)

Preschoolers learn to *initiate* activities and develop self-confidence and a sense of social responsibility. If not, they feel irresponsible, anxious, and *guilty*.

PhotoDisc/Getty Images, Inc.

4 Industry versus inferiority (ages 6–12)

Elementary school-aged children who succeed in learning new, productive life skills, develop a sense of pride and competence (industry). Those who fail to develop these skills feel inadequate and unproductive (*inferior*).

Randy Olson/NG Image Collection

5 Identity versus role confusion (ages 12–20)

Adolescents develop a coherent and stable self-definition (identity) by exploring many roles and deciding who or what they want to be in terms of career, attitudes, and so on. Failure to resolve this *identity crisis* may lead to apathy, withdrawal, and/or *role confusion*.

Pablo Corral Vega/NG Image Collection

6 Intimacy versus isolation (early adulthood)

Young adults form lasting, meaningful relationships, which help them develop a sense of connectedness and *intimacy* with others. If not, they become psychologically *isolated*.

IT Stock

7 Generativity versus stagnation (middle adulthood)

The challenge for middle-aged adults is to be nurturant of the younger generation. Failing to meet this challenge leads to self-indulgence and a sense of *stagnation*.

Richard Olsenius/NG Image Collection

8 Ego integrity versus despair (late adulthood)

During this stage, older adults reflect on their past. If this reflection reveals a life well-spent, the person experiences self-acceptance and satisfaction (*ego integrity*). If not, he or she experiences regret and deep dissatisfaction

Second, the labels he used to describe the eight stages may not be entirely appropriate cross-culturally. For example, in individualistic cultures, *autonomy* is highly preferable to *shame and doubt*. But in collectivist cultures, the preferred resolution might be *dependence* or *merging relations* (Berry et al., 2011). Despite their limits, Erikson's stages have greatly contributed to the study of development throughout the life span. And, like Piaget and Kohlberg, Erikson remains a major figure in developmental psychology.

Voices from the Classroom

Erikson and a 90% Pay Cut! When discussing Erikson, I tell my classes about a previous student, who said that Erikson's stage of *generativity versus stagnation* really described him well. At age 18, he was hired at a computer development corporation, and over the years his salary reached the mid six figures, and he had two homes, children in private schools, and money to spare. Then, at age 45, he realized that if he were to die, the company would just hire a new 18-year-old to replace him. So he retired and started school at Delgado, with plans to earn a degree in teaching. When I pointed out that he was taking a 90% pay cut, he replied that if he could help shape one child to better himself/herself, then leaving his job was worth it! I asked him if I could use his story every semester, and he agreed.

Professor Brett Heintz
Delgado College
New Orleans, Louisiana

Sex and Gender Influences on Development

Imagine for a moment what your life would be like if you were a member of the other sex. Would you think differently? Would you be more or less sociable and outgoing? Would your career plans or friendship patterns change? In this section, we will explore how our development is affected by *sex* (a biological characteristic determined at the moment of conception), **gender** (psychological and sociocultural meanings added to biological maleness or femaleness), **gender roles** (societal expectations for "appropriate" male and female attitudes and behaviors), and *cultural differences*.

Gender A psychological and sociocultural phenomenon referring to learned sex-related behaviors and attitudes of males and females.

Gender roles The societal expectations for "appropriate" male and female attitudes and behavior and expressed publicly by the individual.

Sex and Gender Differences

Physical anatomy is the most obvious biological sex difference between men and women. In addition to biological sex differences, scientists have also noted numerous gender differences that affect our cognitive and personality development **(Table 9.5)**. Keep in mind that these variations are statistically small, however, and represent few meaningful differences.

Gender-Role Development

By age 2, children are well aware of gender roles. They recognize that boys "should" be strong, independent, aggressive, dominant, and achieving, whereas girls "should" be soft, dependent, passive, emotional, and "naturally" interested in children (Collins, 2011; Endendijk et al., 2013; King, 2012; Leaper, 2013; Matlin, 2012; Wood, 2013). For example, one large-scale study of more than 10,000 U.S. adults found that compared to men, women have higher levels of sensitivity and warmth, whereas men score higher on dominance and vigilance (Del Giudice et al., 2012). The existence of similar gender roles in many cultures suggests that evolution and biology may play a role in their formation. However, most research emphasizes two major theories of gender-role development: *social learning* and *cognitive developmental* **(Figure 9.24)**.

Social-learning theorists emphasize the power of the immediate situation and observable behaviors on gender-role development. Girls learn how to be "feminine," and boys learn how to be "masculine" in two major ways: (1) They receive rewards or punishments for specific gender-role behaviors, and (2) they watch and imitate the behavior of others, particularly the same-sex parent (Bandura, 1989, 2008; Collins, 2011; Fulcher, 2011; Risman & Davis, 2013). A boy who puts on his father's tie or baseball cap wins big, indulgent smiles from his parents. But what would happen if he put on his mother's nightgown or lipstick? Parents, teachers, and friends generally reward or punish behaviors according to traditional gender-role expectations. Thus, a child "socially learns" what it means to be male or female.

According to the *cognitive-developmental theory*, social learning is part of gender-role development, but it's much more than a passive process of receiving rewards or punishments and modeling others. Instead, cognitive developmentalists argue that children actively observe, interpret, and judge the world around them

TABLE 9.5 RESEARCH-SUPPORTED SEX AND GENDER DIFFERENCES

Behavior	More Often Shown by Men	More Often Shown by Women
Sexual	• Begin masturbating sooner in life cycle and higher overall occurrence rates • Start sexual life earlier and have first orgasm through masturbation • More likely to recognize their own sexual arousal • More orgasm consistency with sexual partner	• Begin masturbating later in life cycle and lower overall occurrence rates • Start sexual life later and have first orgasm from partner stimulation • Less likely to recognize their own sexual arousal • Less orgasm consistency with sexual partner
Touching	• Touched, kissed, and cuddled less by parents • Less physical contact with other men and respond more negatively to being touched • More likely to initiate both casual and intimate touch with sexual partner	• Touched, kissed, and cuddled more by parents • More physical contact with other women and respond more positively to being touched • Less likely to initiate either casual or intimate touch with sexual partner
Friendship	• Larger number of friends and express friendship by shared activities	• Smaller number of friends and express friendship by shared communication about self
Personality	• More aggressive from a very early age • More self-confident of future success • Attribute success to internal factors and failures to external factors • Achievement more task oriented; motives are mastery and competition • More self-validating • Higher self-esteem	• Less aggressive from a very early age • Less self-confident of future success • Attribute success to external factors and failures to internal factors • Achievement more socially directed, with emphasis on self-improvement; higher work motives • More dependent on others for validation • Lower self-esteem
Cognitive abilities	• Slightly superior in math and visuospatial skills	• Slightly superior in verbal skills

Sources: Blair & Lee, 2013; Bull et al., 2013; Casey, 2013; Crooks & Baur, 2013; King, 2012; Leaper, 2013; Masters & Johnson, 1961, 1966, 1970; Shibley Hyde & DeLamater, 2014; Wood, 2013.

(Bem, 1981, 1993; Hollander et al., 2011; Leaper, 2013). As children process information about the world, they also create internal rules governing correct behaviors for boys and for girls. On the basis of these rules, they form *gender schemas* (mental images) of how they should act.

Maartje van Caspel/Getty Images

realworldpsychology **Gender Roles and Teenagers** How do gender roles affect older children? Researchers in one study asked teenagers (ages 13 to 16) to describe two positive and two negative stories about themselves (Fivush et al., 2012). When the researchers examined the stories, they found striking differences. The stories told by girls were generally longer, more coherent, more detailed, and more descriptive of their own feelings and emotions. The boys' stories, in contrast, were more matter-of-fact and less self-reflective. What causes such differences? One factor may be that parents talk to boys and girls about emotions in different ways.

Androgyny

Androgyny [an-DRAH-juh-nee] Exhibiting both masculine and feminine traits; from the Greek *andro* for "male" and *gyn* for "female."

One way to overcome rigid or destructive gender-role stereotypes is to express both the "masculine" and "feminine" traits found in each individual—for example, being assertive and aggressive when necessary but also gentle and nurturing. Combining characteristics in this way is known as **androgyny [an-DRAH-juh-nee]**. Researchers

FIGURE 9.24 GENDER-ROLE DEVELOPMENT

Social-learning theory focuses on a child's passive process of learning about gender through observation, rewards, and punishments, whereas cognitive-developmental theory emphasizes a child's active role in building a gender schema.

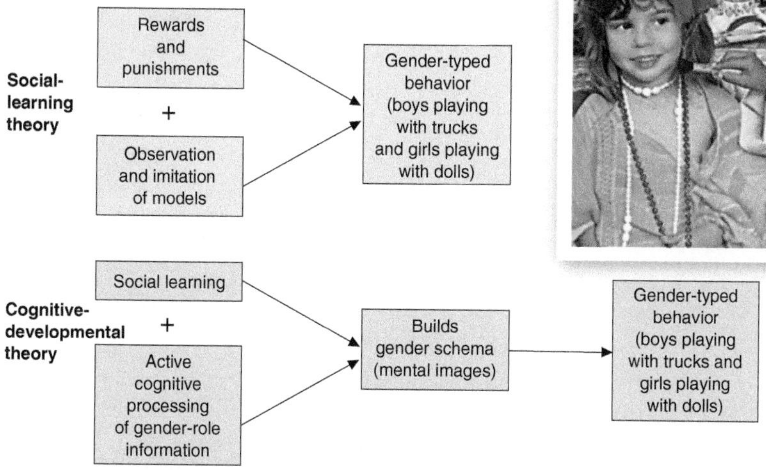

Elizabeth Crews/The Image Works

have found that this blending of traits leads to higher self-esteem and more success and adjustment in today's complex society because it allows us to display whatever behaviors and traits are most appropriate in a given situation (Bem, 1981, 1993; Huang et al., 2012; Kark et al., 2012; Stoltzfus et al., 2011; Wood, 2013).

Recent studies also show that gender roles are becoming less rigidly defined (Cotter et al., 2011; Hollander et al., 2011; Signorielli, 2013). Asian American and Mexican American groups show some of the largest changes toward androgyny, and African Americans remain among the most androgynous of all ethnic groups (Denmark et al., 2005; Duval, 2006; Renzetti et al., 2006).

Ironically, a recent survey of college students at a comparatively liberal university in California found that more than two-thirds of both women and men strongly prefer traditional gender roles when it comes to marriage proposals. In fact, the title of the published research article is: "Girls don't propose! Ew." (Robnett & Leaper, 2013). Furthermore, over 60% of the women surveyed were either "very willing" or "somewhat willing" to take their husband's surname. Q5

Rachael Robnett, the lead author on this research, suggested that this type of "benevolent sexism" looks positive on the surface, but it contributes to power differentials between men and women and does a disservice to women (Lasnier, 2013). What do you think? Would relationships be better if both men and women were free to propose, and if they both kept their own names when they married?

RETRIEVAL PRACTICE: SOCIAL-EMOTIONAL DEVELOPMENT

Self-Test

Completing this self-test and comparing your answers with those in Appendix B provides immediate feedback and helpful practice for exams. Additional interactive, self-tests are available at www.wiley.com/college/huffman.

1. According to Harlow's research with cloth and wire surrogate mother monkeys, ________ is the most important variable for attachment.

   a. contact comfort
   b. "comfort food"
   c. neonatal breast feeding
   d. age group peer contact ("free play" periods)

2. According to Kohlberg, moral judgment is self-centered and based on obtaining rewards and avoiding punishment during the ________ level of moral development.

   a. trust versus mistrust
   b. industry versus inferiority
   c. conventional
   d. preconventional

3. Calvin would like to wear baggy, torn jeans and a nose ring, but he is concerned that others will disapprove. Calvin is at Kohlberg's ________ level of morality.

a. conformity
b. approval seeking
c. conventional
d. preconventional

4. According to Erikson, industry is the result of the successful completion of the ________ stage of development.

a. infancy and toddlerhood
b. ages 6 through 12
c. young adulthood
d. middle adulthood

Think Critically

1 Describe how attachment has influenced your social development. Which of Ainsworth's attachment styles best describes you?

2 What stage of moral development do you think you would qualify for, according to Kohlberg? Do you agree or disagree with this categorization?

3 How have your sex and gender affected your social development?

realworldpsychology

Do today's college students want women to propose marriage?

HINT: LOOK IN THE MARGIN FOR Q5

Summary

1 STUDYING DEVELOPMENT 238

- **Developmental psychology** is the study of age-related changes in behavior and mental processes from conception to death. Development is an ongoing, lifelong process.
- The three most important debates or questions in human development are about *nature versus nurture* (including studies of **maturation** and **critical periods**), *stages versus continuity*, and *stability versus change.*
- Developmental psychologists use two special techniques in their research: **cross-sectional design** and **longitudinal design**. Although both have valuable attributes, each also has disadvantages. Cross-sectional studies can confuse genuine age differences with *cohort effects.* On the other hand, longitudinal studies are expensive and time-consuming, and their results are restricted in generalizability.

2 PHYSICAL DEVELOPMENT 242

- Prenatal development begins at conception and is divided into three stages: the **germinal period**, the **embryonic period**, and the **fetal period**. During pregnancy, the *placenta* serves as the link for food and the excretion of wastes, and it screens out some harmful substances—but not **teratogens**, such as alcohol and nicotine.
- Early childhood is a time of rapid physical development, including brain, motor, and sensory/perceptual development. During *adolescence*, both boys and girls undergo dramatic changes in appearance and physical capacity. **Puberty** is the period of adolescence when a person becomes capable of reproduction. During adulthood, most individuals experience only minor physical changes until middle age. Around age 45–55, women experience *menopause*, the cessation of the menstrual cycle. At the same time, men experience a gradual decline in the production of sperm and testosterone, as well as other physical changes, known as the *male climacteric*.
- After middle age, most physical changes in development are gradual and occur in the heart and arteries and in the sensory receptors. One of the greatest problems for the elderly is the various negative stereotypes that contribute to our society's widespread **ageism**.

3 COGNITIVE DEVELOPMENT 251

- Three major concepts are central to Piaget's theory: **schemas**, **assimilation**, and **accommodation**. According to Piaget, all children progress through four stages of cognitive development: the **sensorimotor stage**, the **preoperational stage**, the **concrete operational stage**, and the **formal operational stage**. As they move through these stages, children acquire progressively more sophisticated ways of thinking.
- Piaget's account of cognitive development has been enormously influential, but it has also received significant criticisms. For example, Vygotsky emphasized the sociocultural influences on a child's cognitive development, rather than Piaget's internal schemas. He also believed that adults play an important instructor role in development and that this instruction is particularly helpful when it falls within a child's **zone of proximal development (ZPD)**. Piaget has also been criticized for underestimating children's abilities, as well as the genetic and cultural influences on cognitive development.

4 SOCIAL-EMOTIONAL DEVELOPMENT 259

- Harlow's and his colleagues' research with monkeys raised by cloth or wire "mothers" found that *contact comfort* might be the most important factor in **attachment**.
- Using the strange situation procedure, Ainsworth found that children could be divided into three groups: Secure, anxious/avoidant, and anxious/ambivalent. Mary Main, later added a fourth category, disorganized/disoriented.
- In addition to attachment patterns, Baumrind's four parenting styles—*permissive-neglectful, permissive-indulgent, authoritarian*, and *authoritative*—also affect a child's social development.
- Kohlberg proposed three levels in the evolution of moral reasoning: the **preconventional level** (Stages 1 and 2), the **conventional level** (Stages 3 and 4), and the **postconventional level** (Stages 5 and 6).

© imaginary_nl/iStockphoto

FIGURE 10.1 **INSTINCTS**

Ⓐ Instinctual behaviors are obvious in many animals. Birds build nests, bears hibernate, and salmon swim upstream to spawn.

Ⓑ Sociobiologists such as Edward O. Wilson (1975, 1978) believe that humans also have instincts, like competition or aggression, that are genetically transmitted from one generation to another.

© asiseeit /iStockphoto

Biological Theories

Many theories of **motivation** focus on inborn biological processes that control behavior. Among these biologically oriented theories are *instinct*, *drive-reduction*, and *arousal* theories.

One of the earliest researchers, William McDougall (1908), proposed that humans had numerous instincts, such as repulsion, curiosity, and self-assertiveness. Other researchers later added their favorite instincts, and by the 1920s, the list of recognized instincts had become impossibly long. One researcher found listings for more than 10,000 human instincts (Bernard, 1924).

In addition, the label *instinct* led to unscientific, circular explanations—"men are aggressive because they are instinctively aggressive" or "women are maternal because they have a natural maternal instinct." However, in recent years, a branch of biology called sociobiology has revived the case for **instincts** when strictly defined as a *fixed, unlearned response patterns found in almost all members of a species* **(Figure 10.1)**.

In the 1930s, the concepts of drive and drive reduction began to replace the theory of instincts. According to **drive-reduction theory** (Hull, 1952), when biological needs such as for food, water, and oxygen are unmet, a state of tension known as a *drive* is created. The organism is then motivated to reduce that drive. Drive-reduction theory is based largely on the biological concept of **homeostasis**, a term that literally means "standing still" and describes the body's natural tendency to maintain a state of internal balance **(Figure 10.2)**.

Motivation A set of factors that activate, direct, and maintain behavior, usually toward some goal.

Instinct Fixed, unlearned response patterns found in almost all members of a species.

Drive-reduction theory The theory that motivation begins with a physiological need (a lack or deficiency) that elicits a drive toward behavior that will satisfy the original need; once the need is met, a state of balance (homeostasis) is restored, and motivation decreases.

Homeostasis The body's tendency to maintain a relatively balanced and stable internal state, such as a constant internal temperature.

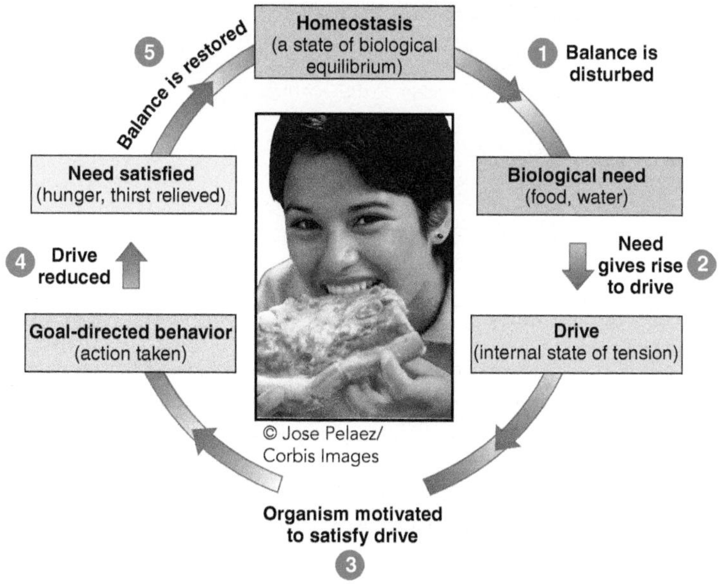

FIGURE 10.2 **DRIVE-REDUCTION THEORY**

realworldpsychology

When we are hungry or thirsty, the disruption of our normal state of equilibrium creates a drive that motivates us to search for food or water. Once action is taken and the need is satisfied, homeostasis is restored, and our motivation decreases.

Optimal-arousal theory The theory that organisms are motivated to achieve and maintain an optimal level of arousal.

In addition to having obvious biological needs, humans and other animals are innately curious and require a certain amount of novelty and complexity from the environment.

According to **optimal-arousal theory**, organisms are motivated to achieve and maintain an optimal level of arousal that maximizes their performance. Both too much and too little arousal diminish performance **(Figure 10.3)**. The desired amount of arousal also may vary from person to person (see *Test Yourself*).

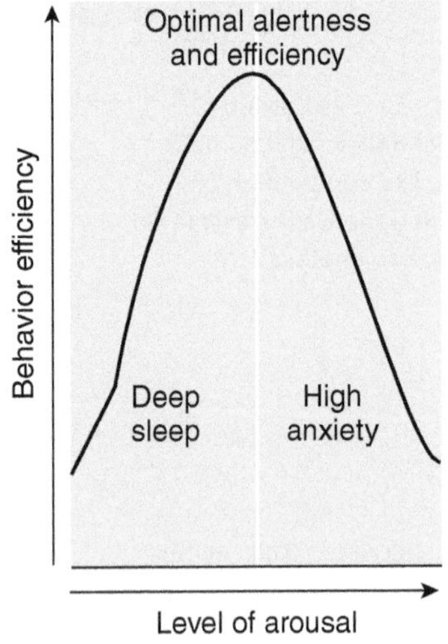

FIGURE 10.3 **OPTIMAL LEVEL OF AROUSAL**
realworldpsychology

Our need for stimulation (the arousal motive) suggests that behavior efficiency increases as we move from deep sleep to increased alertness. However, once we pass the maximum level of arousal, our performance declines.

TEST YOURSELF: SENSATION SEEKING

psychology and you

What motivates people to bungee jump over deep canyons or white-water raft down dangerous rivers? According to research, these "high-sensation seekers" may be biologically "prewired" to need a higher-than-usual level of stimulation (Zuckerman, 1979, 1994, 2013).

To sample the kinds of questions asked on tests of levels of sensation seeking, circle the choice (a or b) that best describes you:

1. a. I would like a job that requires a lot of traveling.
   b. I would prefer a job in one location.
2. a. I get bored seeing the same old faces.
   b. I like the comfortable familiarity of everyday friends.
3. a. The most important goal of life is to live it to the fullest and experience as much as possible.
   b. The most important goal of life is to find peace and happiness.
4. a. I would like to try parachute jumping.
   b. I would never want to try jumping out of a plane, with or without a parachute.
5. a. I prefer people who are emotionally expressive even if they are a bit unstable.
   b. I prefer people who are calm and even-tempered.

Source: Zuckerman, M. (1978, February). The search for high sensation, *Psychology Today*, pp. 38–46.

Imagemore/Getty Images

Think Critically

1 If your answers to the brief quiz above indicate that you are a high-sensation seeker, what do you do to satisfy that urge, and what can you do to make sure it doesn't get out of control?

2 If you are low in sensation seeking, has this trait interfered with some aspect of your life? If so, what could you do to improve your functioning in this area?

How did you score on the sensation-seeking scale? Research suggests that four distinct factors characterize sensation seeking (Legrand et al., 2007; Manna et al., 2013; Peer & Rosenbloom, 2013; Zuckerman, 2004, 2008, 2013).

1. Thrill and adventure seeking (skydiving, driving fast, or trying to beat a train)
2. Experience seeking (travel, unusual friends, drug experimentation)
3. Disinhibition ("letting loose")
4. Susceptibility to boredom (lower tolerance for repetition and sameness)

Can you see how being very high or very low in sensation seeking might cause problems in relationships with two individuals who score toward opposite extremes? This is true not just between partners or spouses but also between parent and child and therapist and patient. There also might be job difficulties for high-sensation seekers in routine clerical or assembly-line jobs and for low-sensation seekers in highly challenging and variable occupations.

Psychological Theories

Instinct and drive-reduction theories explain some motivations, but why do we continue to eat after our biological need has been completely satisfied? Why do some of us work overtime when our salary is sufficient to meet all basic biological needs? These questions are best answered by psychosocial theories that emphasize incentives and cognition.

Unlike drive-reduction theory, which states that internal factors *push* people in certain directions, **incentive theory** maintains that external stimuli *pull* people toward desirable goals or away from undesirable ones. Most of us initially eat because our hunger "pushes" us (drive-reduction theory). But the sight of apple pie or ice cream too often "pulls" us toward continued eating (incentive theory).

Incentive theory The theory that motivation results from external stimuli that "pull" an organism in certain directions.

Researchers interested in increasing good grades, adherence to school rules, and regular school attendance found that paying middle-school students $2.00 daily for each goal met was enough incentive to produce higher reading test scores, especially for boys, and those with disciplinary problems in the past (Fryer, 2010). But as you'll discover later in this chapter, this type of *extrinsic reward* (paying students for achieved goals) may create problems of its own. Q1

According to *cognitive theories*, motivation is directly affected by *attributions*, or the ways in which we interpret or think about our own and others' actions (see *Psychology and You*).

psychology and you **Using Attributions to Explain Grades**

Imagine that you receive a high grade on a test in your psychology course. You can interpret that grade in several ways: You earned it because you really studied, you "lucked out" because the test was easy, or the textbook was exceptionally interesting and helpful (our preference!). People who attribute their successes to personal ability and effort tend to work harder toward their goals than people who attribute their successes to luck (Beacham et al., 2011; Martinko et al., 2011; Weiner, 1972, 1982; Zhou & Urhahne, 2013).

© Maridav/iStockphoto

Expectancies, or what we believe or assume will happen, are also important to motivation (Reinhard & Dickhäuser, 2011; Schmidt et al., 2013; Senko & Hulleman, 2013) **(Figure 10.4)**. If you anticipate that you will receive a promotion at work, you're more likely to work overtime for no pay than if you do not expect a promotion.

Don Smetzer/PhotoEdit

FIGURE 10.4 EXPECTANCIES AS PSYCHOLOGICAL MOTIVATORS

What expectations might these students have that would motivate them to master a new language?

Hierarchy of needs Maslow's view that basic human motives form a hierarchy; the lower motives (such as physiological and safety needs) must be met before advancing to higher needs (such as belonging and self-actualization).

Self-actualization The humanistic term for the inborn drive to develop all one's talents and capabilities.

Biopsychosocial Theories

Research in psychology generally emphasizes either biological or psychosocial factors (nature or nurture). But biopsychosocial factors almost always provide the best explanation, and theories of motivation are no exception. One researcher who recognized this was Abraham Maslow (1954, 1970, 1999). Maslow believed we all have numerous needs that compete for fulfillment but that some needs are more important than others. For example, your need for food and shelter is generally more important than your need for good grades.

Maslow's **hierarchy of needs** prioritizes human needs, starting with survival needs (which must be met before others) at the bottom and social, spiritual needs at the top **(Figure 10.5)**.

Maslow's hierarchy of needs seems intuitively correct: A starving person would first look for food, then love and friendship, and then self-esteem. This prioritizing and the concept of **self-actualization**, the inborn drive to develop all our talents and capabilities, are important factors in motivation, and Maslow's work has had a major impact on psychology, economics, and other related fields (Brink & van Bronswijk, 2013; Serlin, 2011; Stoll & Ha-Brookshire, 2012). For example, standard marketing texts often use Maslow's hierarchy of needs to imply that brand consumption is a natural, driving force in shopping behaviors. Ironically, Maslow's work and humanistic ideals would emphasize less, not more, consumption (Hackley, 2007).

Maslow's critics argue that parts of Maslow's theory are poorly researched and biased toward Western preferences for individualism. Furthermore, his theory presupposes that the lower needs must be satisfied before someone can achieve self-actualization, but people sometimes seek to satisfy higher-level needs even when their lower-level needs have not been met (Cullen & Gotell, 2002; Kress et al., 2011; Neher, 1991). For example, protestors all over the world have used starvation as a way to protest unfair laws and political situations.

FIGURE 10.5 MASLOW'S HIERARCHY OF NEEDS

Maslow's theory of motivation suggests that we all share a compelling need to "move up"—to grow, improve ourselves, and ultimately become "self-actualized."

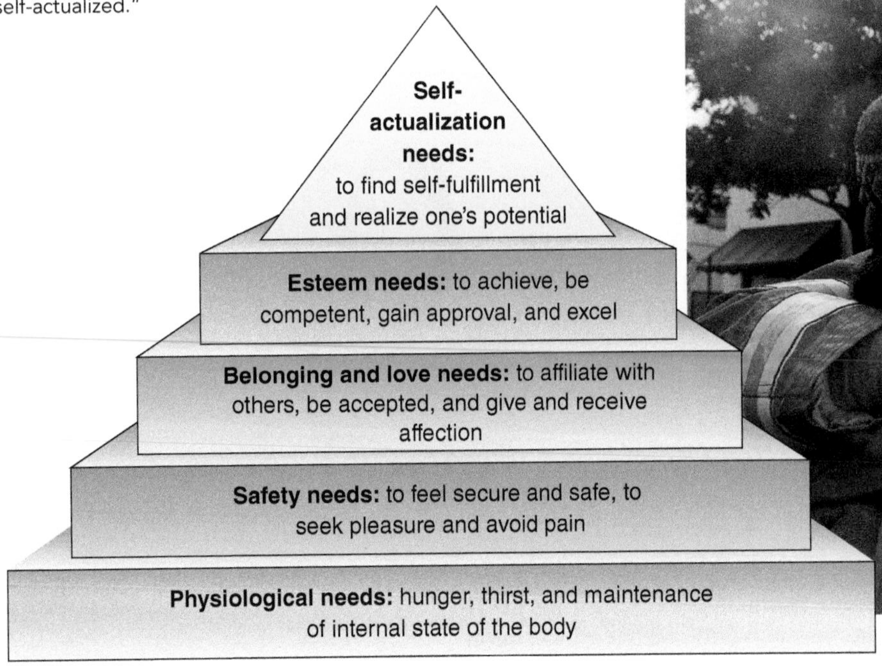

Nam Y Huh/©AP/Wide World Photos

Which of Maslow's five levels of need are on display in this photo? Can you see how the needs of the rescuer clearly differ from those of the person who is being rescued?

RETRIEVAL PRACTICE: THEORIES OF MOTIVATION

Self-Test

Completing this self-test and comparing your answers with those in Appendix B provides immediate feedback and helpful practice for exams. Additional interactive, self-tests are available at www.wiley.com/college/huffman.

1. Motivation is best defined as _____.

a. a set of factors that activate, direct, and maintain behavior, usually toward a goal
b. the physiological and psychological arousal that occurs when a person really wants to achieve a goal
c. what makes you do what you do
d. goal-directed unconscious thoughts

2. This diagram illustrates the _____ theory, in which motivation decreases once homeostasis occurs.

a. cognitive
b. hierarchy of needs
c. incentive
d. drive-reduction theory

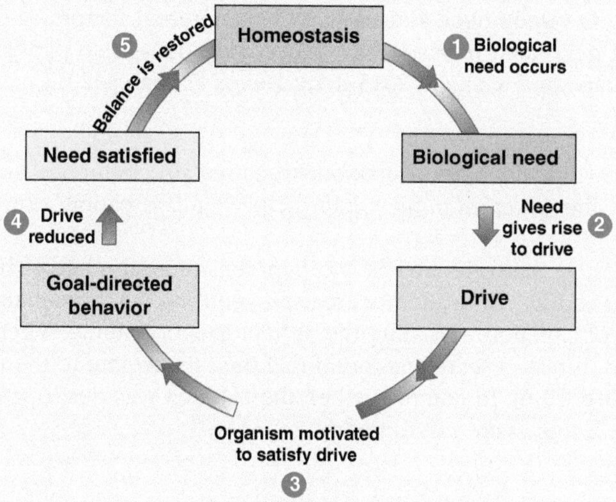

3. _____ says people are "pulled" by external stimuli to act a certain way.

a. Cognitive theory
b. Incentive theory
c. Maslow's hierarchy of needs
d. Drive reduction theory

4. According to Maslow's _____, some motives have to be satisfied before a person can advance to fulfilling higher motives.

a. psychosexual stages of development
b. moral stages of development
c. psychosocial stages of development
d. hierarchy of needs

Think Critically

1 Why are modern sociobiological theories of instincts more scientifically useful than older instinct theories?

2 At what level would you rank yourself on Maslow's hierarchy of needs? What can you do to advance to a higher level?

realworldpsychology

Why might paying students to get good grades be a good idea?

HINT: LOOK IN THE MARGIN FOR Q1

MOTIVATION AND BEHAVIOR

LEARNING OBJECTIVES

RETRIEVAL PRACTICE While reading the upcoming sections, respond to each Learning Objective in your own words. Then compare your responses with those found at www.wiley.com/college/huffman.

1 **DESCRIBE** how internal (biological) and external (psychosocial) factors direct hunger and eating as well as how they are involved in serious eating disorders.

2 **IDENTIFY** the traits of high achievers and explain why they are more motivated than others.

3 **SUMMARIZE** the major factors in human sexuality.

4 **COMPARE** intrinsic and extrinsic motivation.

Why do people put themselves in dangerous situations? Why do salmon swim upstream to spawn? Behavior results from many motives. For example, we discuss the need for sleep in Chapter 5, and we look at aggression, altruism, and interpersonal attraction in Chapter 14. Here, we focus on three basic motives: hunger, achievement, and sexuality. Then we turn to a discussion of how different kinds of motivation affect our intrinsic interests and performance.

Hunger and Eating

What motivates hunger? Is it your growling stomach? Or is it the sight of a juicy hamburger or the smell of a freshly baked cinnamon roll?

The Stomach

Early hunger researchers believed that the stomach controlled hunger, contracting to send hunger signals when it was empty. Today, we know it's more complicated. As dieters who drink lots of water to keep their stomachs feeling full have been disappointed to discover, sensory input from an empty stomach is not essential for feeling hungry. In fact, humans and nonhuman animals without stomachs continue to experience hunger.

However, there is a connection between the stomach and feeling hungry. Receptors in the stomach and intestines detect levels of nutrients, and specialized pressure receptors in the stomach walls signal feelings of either emptiness or *satiety* (fullness). The stomach and other parts of the gastrointestinal tract also release chemical signals that play a role in hunger (Hellström, 2013; Moran & Daily, 2011; Nicolaidis, 2011).

Biochemistry

Like the stomach, the brain and other parts of the body produce numerous neurotransmitters, hormones, enzymes, and other chemicals that affect hunger and satiety (Arumugam et al., 2008; Cooper et al., 2011; Hellström, 2013; Stadlbauer et al., 2013). Research in this area is complex because of the large number of known (and unknown) bodily chemicals and the interactions among them. It's unlikely that any one chemical controls our hunger and eating. Other internal factors, such as *thermogenesis*—the heat generated in response to food ingestion—also play a role (Acheson et al., 2011; Drapeau & Gallant, 2013; Ping-Delfos & Soares, 2011).

The Brain

In addition to its chemical signals, particular brain structures also influence hunger and eating. Let's look at the *hypothalamus*, which helps regulate eating, drinking, and body temperature.

Early research suggested that one area of the hypothalamus, the lateral hypothalamus (LH), stimulates eating, while another area, the ventromedial hypothalamus (VMH), creates feelings of satiation, signaling the animal to stop eating. When the VMH area was destroyed in rats, researchers found that the rats overate to the point of extreme obesity **(Figure 10.6)**. In contrast, when the LH area was destroyed, the animals starved to death if they were not force-fed.

FIGURE 10.6 HOW THE BRAIN AFFECTS EATING

Several areas of the brain are active in the regulation of hunger.

Ⓐ This diagram shows a section of the human brain, including the ventromedial hypothalamus (VMH) and the lateral hypothalamus (LH), which are involved in the regulation of hunger.

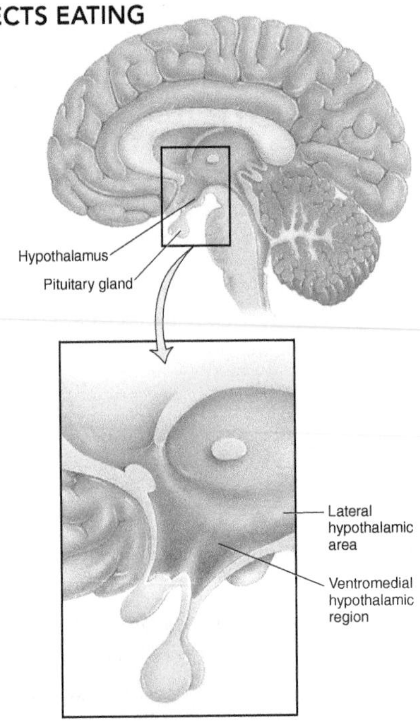

Ⓑ After the ventromedial area of the hypothalamus of the rat on the left was destroyed, its body weight tripled. A rat of normal weight is shown on the right for comparison.

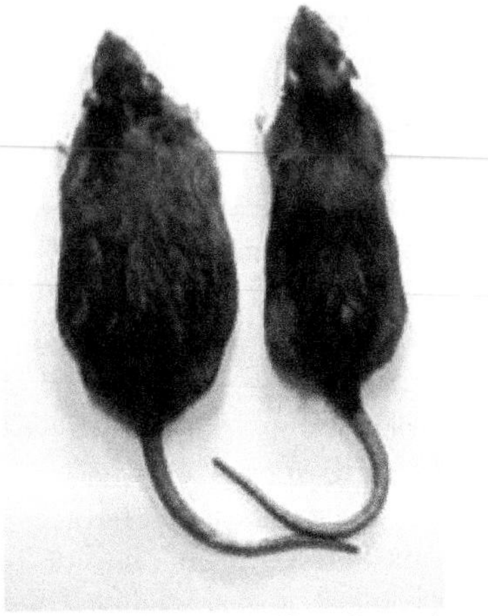

Olivier Voisin/Photo Researchers

Later research, however, showed that the LH and VMH areas are not simple on–off switches for eating. For example, lesions (damage) to the VMH make animals picky eaters that reject a wide variety of foods. The lesions also increase insulin secretion, which may cause overeating (Challem et al., 2000; Figlewicz & Sipols, 2010). Today, researchers know that the hypothalamus plays an important role in hunger and eating, but it is not the brain's "eating center." In fact, hunger and eating, like virtually all other behaviors, are influenced by numerous neural circuits that run throughout the brain (Berman et al., 2013; Nolan-Poupart et al., 2013; van der Laan et al., 2011).

Psychosocial Factors

The internal motivations for hunger we've discussed (the stomach, biochemistry, and the brain) are powerful. But *psychosocial factors*—for example, spying a luscious dessert or a McDonald's billboard, or even simply noticing that it's almost lunchtime—can be equally important stimulus cues for hunger and eating. In fact, researchers in one study found that simply looking at pictures of high-fat foods, such as hamburgers, cookies, and cake, can stimulate parts of the brain in charge of appetite, thereby increasing feelings of hunger and cravings for sweet and salty foods (Luo et al., 2013). Q2

Another important psychosocial influence on when, what, where, and why we eat is cultural conditioning. North Americans, for example, tend to eat dinner at around 6 p.m., whereas people in Spain and South America tend to eat around 10 p.m. When it comes to *what* we eat, have you ever eaten rat, dog, or horse meat? If you are a typical North American, this might sound repulsive to you, yet most Hindus in India would feel a similar revulsion at the thought of eating meat from cows.

In sum, numerous biological and psychosocial factors operate in the regulation of hunger and eating **(Figure 10.7)**, and researchers are still struggling to discover and explain how all these processes work together.

FIGURE 10.7 **KEY MECHANISMS IN HUNGER REGULATION**

Different parts of your body communicate with your brain to trigger feelings of hunger.

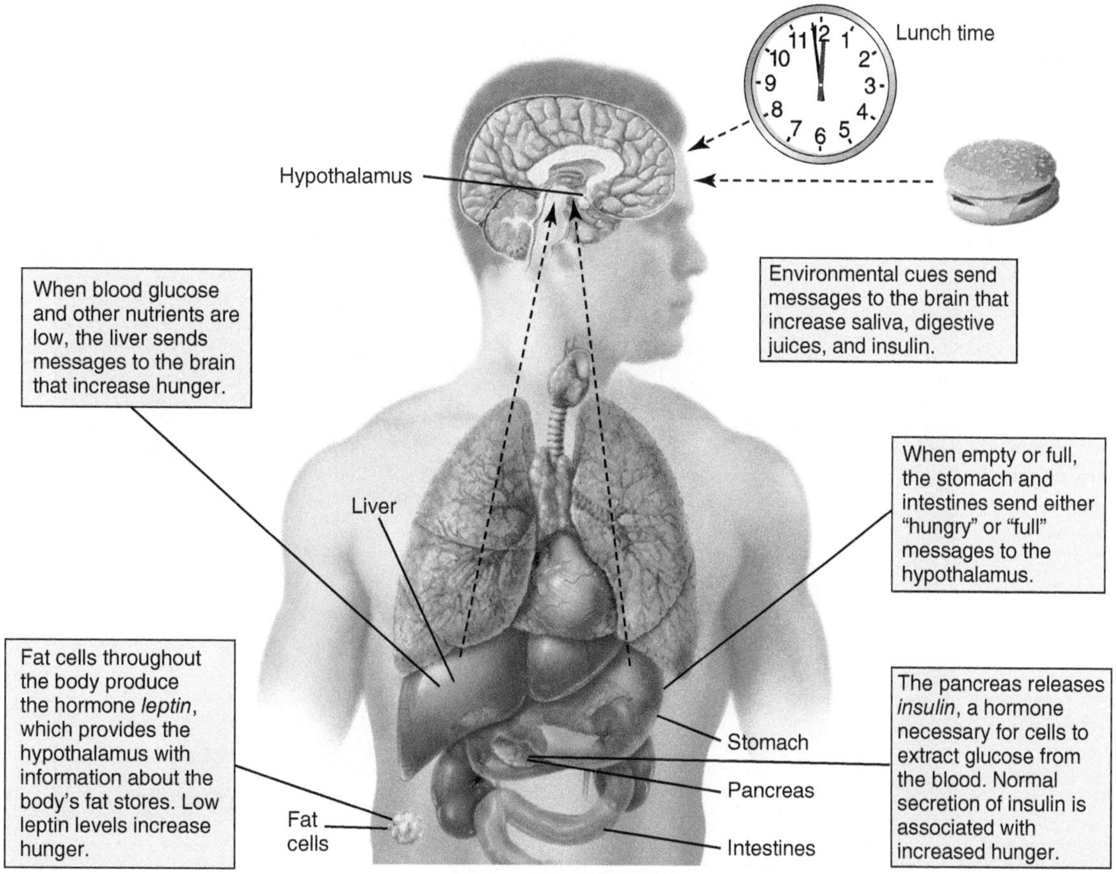

Eating Disorders

The same biopsychosocial forces that explain hunger and eating also play a role in four serious eating disorders: *obesity*, *anorexia nervosa*, *bulimia nervosa*, and *binge-eating disorder*.

Obesity

Imagine yourself being born and living your life on another planet, but you could receive all the Earth's normal television channels. Given that almost all the television stars, newscasters, and commercial spokespeople you've ever seen are very thin, would you wonder why there are so many ads promoting weight loss? How would you explain the recent news that obesity has reached epidemic proportions in the United States and other developed nations?

Obviously, there is large gap between the select few appearing on television and the real world. In fact, according to the latest 2013 data, more than one-third of adults in the United States are considered to be overweight, and another third are considered to be medically obese (American Heart Association, 2013; Corsica & Perri, 2013; Gallup Well-Being, 2013). In 2013, obesity was officially classified as a disease in the DSM-5 (American Psychiatric Association, 2013). (See Chapter 12 for a discussion of the DSM-5.)

Obesity Having a body mass index of 30 or above, based on height and weight.

What is **obesity**? The most widely used measure of weight status is *body mass index (BMI)*, which is a single numerical value that calculates height in relation to weight (see *Psychology and You*). Sadly, obesity is one of our greatest health threats because of its significant contribution to serious illnesses like heart disease, diabetes, stroke and certain cancers (American Heart Association, 2013; Corsica & Perri, 2013). In addition, each year, billions of dollars are spent treating serious and life-threatening medical problems related to obesity, with consumers spending billions more on largely ineffective weight-loss products and services.

Controlling weight is a particularly difficult task for people in the United States. We are among the most sedentary people of all, and we've become accustomed to "supersized" cheeseburgers, "Big Gulp" drinks, and huge servings of dessert (Duffey & Popkin, 2013; Fisher et al., 2013; Herman & Polivy, 2008). We've also learned that we should eat three meals a day, whether we're hungry or not; that "tasty" food requires lots of salt, sugar, and fat; and that food is an essential part of the workplace and all social gatherings **(Figure 10.8)**.

FIGURE 10.8 A FATTENING ENVIRONMENT | realworldpsychology

One of the most popular television programs, *The Biggest Loser*, shows how difficult it is for contestants to lose weight. Even more difficult, and seldom shown, is how hard it is to maintain weight loss. To make it permanent, we need to make permanent lifestyle changes regarding exercise and the amount and types of foods we eat and when we eat them. Can you see how our everyday environments, such as in the workplace shown here, might prevent a person from making healthy lifestyle changes?

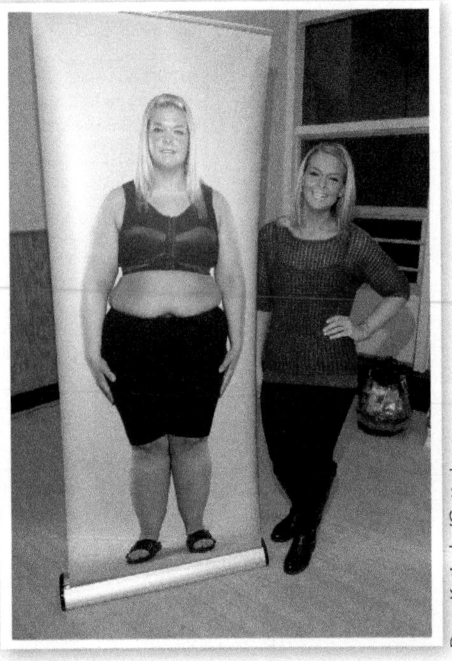

Dave Kotinsky/Getty Images

Christian Thomas/Getty Images

psychology and you **Calculating Your Own BMI** To determine your BMI, use the *Adult BMI Calculator* at the Centers for Disease Control and Prevention site: http://www.cdc.gov/healthyweight/assessing/bmi/adult_bmi/

Or follow these three steps:

1. Multiply your weight in pounds by 703.
2. Multiply your height in inches by itself (e.g., If you are 63 inches in height, you would multiply 63 x 63).
3. Divide step 1 by step 2.

If your BMI is:	You are:
18.5 and below	Underweight
18.5 to 24.9	Normal weight
25.0 to 29.9	Overweight
30.0 and above	Obese

Note: If your BMI is due to muscle or bone, rather than fat, it's possible to have a high BMI and still be healthy.

Source: Centers for Disease Control and Prevention, 2011.

However, we all know some people who can seemingly eat anything they want and still not add pounds. This may be a result of their ability to burn calories more effectively in the process of thermogenesis, a higher metabolic rate, or other factors. Adoption and twin studies indicate that genetics also plays a role (Andersson & Walley, 2011; Bernhard et al., 2013; Xia & Grant, 2013). Unfortunately, identifying the genes for obesity is difficult. Researchers have isolated a large number of genes that contribute to normal and abnormal weight (Camarena et al., 2004; Warrington et al., 2013; Xia & Grant, 2013).

The good news is that one of these identified genes may provide a potential genetic explanation for why some people overeat and run a greater risk for obesity. Recent research finds that people who carry variants of the FTO gene don't feel full after eating and overeat because they have higher blood levels of ghrelin—a known hunger-producing hormone (Karra et al., 2013). But the researchers cautioned that more research is needed, and that human appetite and obesity are undoubtedly more complex than a single hormone. In addition, this focus on genes should not encourage people to feel helpless against obesity. Ghrelin also can be reduced by exercise and a high-protein diet (Thompson, 2013; Williams, 2013).

Other Eating Disorders

Like obesity, the other major eating disorders—*anorexia nervosa, bulimia nervosa,* and *binge-eating disorder*—are widespread. They're also found in all cultures, ethnicities, and socioeconomic classes, but are more common in women (American Psychiatric Association, 2013; Insel, 2012; Mond & Arrighi, 2011; Smink et al., 2012). **Anorexia nervosa** is characterized by an overwhelming fear of becoming obese, a need for control, the use of dangerous weight-loss measures, and a body image that is so distorted that even a skeletal, emaciated body is perceived as fat. The resulting extreme malnutrition often leads to emaciation, osteoporosis, bone fractures, interruption of menstruation, and loss of brain tissue. A significant percentage of individuals with anorexia nervosa ultimately die of the disorder (Akey et al., 2013; Kaye et al., 2013; Reel, 2013).

Anorexia nervosa An eating disorder characterized by severe loss of weight resulting from self-imposed starvation and an obsessive fear of obesity.

Occasionally, a person suffering from anorexia nervosa succumbs to the desire to eat and gorges on food, then vomits or takes laxatives. However, this type of bingeing and purging is more characteristic of **bulimia nervosa**. Individuals with bulimia go on recurrent eating binges and then purge by self-induced vomiting or the use of laxatives. They often show impulsivity in other areas, sometimes engaging in excessive shopping, alcohol abuse, or petty shoplifting (Claes et al., 2011;

Bulimia nervosa An eating disorder characterized by recurrent episodes of consuming large quantities of food (bingeing), followed by self-induced vomiting (purging), extreme exercise, laxative use, and other medications.

Binge-eating disorder An eating disorder characterized by recurrent episodes of consuming large amounts of food in a discrete period of time, while feeling a lack of control, but not followed by purge behaviors.

Fischer et al., 2013; Vaz-Leal et al., 2011). The vomiting associated with bulimia nervosa causes severe damage to the teeth, throat, and stomach. It also leads to cardiac arrhythmia, metabolic deficiencies, and serious digestive disorders.

Note that bulimia is similar to but not the same as **binge-eating disorder**. This disorder involves recurrent episodes of consuming large amounts of food in a discrete period of time, while feeling a lack of control over eating. However, the individual does not try to purge (American Psychiatric Association, 2013). Individuals with binge-eating disorder generally eat more rapidly than normal, eat until they are uncomfortably full and eat when not feeling physically hungry. They also tend to eat alone because of embarrassment at the large quantities they are consuming, and they feel disgusted, depressed, or very guilty after bingeing.

There are many suspected causes of anorexia nervosa, bulimia nervosa, and binge-eating disorder. Some theories focus on physical causes, such as hypothalamic disorders, low levels of various neurotransmitters, and genetic or hormonal disorders. Other theories emphasize psychosocial factors, such as a need for perfection, a perceived loss of control, teasing about body weight, destructive thought patterns, depression, dysfunctional families, distorted body image, and emotional or sexual abuse (e.g., American Psychiatric Association, 2013; Caqueo-Urizar et al., 2011; Friederich et al., 2013; Heaner & Walsh, 2013; Jenkins et al., 2013; Kaye et al., 2013; Kreipe et al., 2012; Steiger et al., 2013).

Culture and ethnicity also play important roles in eating disorders (George & Franko, 2010; Pilecki et al., 2012; Swanson et al., 2012). For instance, African Americans report fewer eating and dieting disorders and greater body satisfaction than do Caucasian and European Americans (Taylor et al., 2013; Watson et al., 2013; Whaley et al., 2011). Interestingly, binge-eating disorder appears to be equally represented across racial/ethnic minority groups in the United States (Franko et al., 2013; Taylor et al., 2013). This research suggests that both culture and biology help explain eating disorders. Regardless of the causes, it is important to recognize the symptoms of anorexia, bulimia, and binge-eating disorder **(Table 10.2)** and to seek therapy if the symptoms apply to you.

TABLE 10.2 DSM-5 SYMPTOMS OF ANOREXIA NERVOSA, BULIMIA NERVOSA, AND BINGE-EATING DISORDER

Anorexia Nervosa	Bulimia Nervosa	Binge-Eating Disorder
• Body mass index equal to or below 17 • Intense fear of becoming fat or gaining weight, or persistent behavior that interferes with weight gain, even though underweight • Disturbance in one's body image or perceived weight • Denial of seriousness of abnormally low body weight • Self-evaluation unduly influenced by body shape or weight	• Recurrent episodes of binge eating • During the episode of binge eating, consuming, in a discrete period of time, an amount of food that is much larger than most people would consume • Feeling a lack of control over eating during the episode of binge eating • Purging behavior (self-induced vomiting; misuse of laxatives, diuretics, or other medications) • Fasting and/or excessive exercise to prevent weight gain • Self-evaluation unduly influenced by body shape or weight	• Recurrent episodes of binge eating • During the episode of binge eating, consuming, in a discrete period of time, an amount of food that is much larger than most people would consume • Feeling a lack of control over eating during the episode of binge eating • No compensatory purging behavior (self-induced vomiting; misuse of laxatives, diuretics, or other medications) • During the episode of binge eating, eating more rapidly than normal, eating until uncomfortably full and when not feeling physically hungry, eating alone because of embarrassment, feeling disgusted, depressed, or very guilty after bingeing

Chris Wolf/Getty Images

Many celebrities, like Lady Gaga, have publicly shared their battles with eating disorders. But does this type of publicity increase or decrease the chance that their fans will suffer similar problems?

Source: American Psychiatric Association, 2013.

The key point to remember is that all eating disorders are serious and chronic conditions that require treatment. In fact, some studies find that they have the highest mortality rates of all mental illnesses (Akey et al., 2013; Friederich et al., 2013; Insel, 2012; Reel, 2013)!

Achievement

Do you wonder what motivates Olympic athletes to work so hard for a gold medal? What about someone like Oprah Winfrey, famous television star, thriving businesswoman, and generous philanthropist? Or Mark Zuckerberg, cofounder of Facebook? What drives some people to high achievement?

The key to understanding what motivates high-achieving individuals lies in what psychologist Henry Murray (1938) identified as a high need for achievement (nAch), or **achievement motivation**. Several traits distinguish people who have this high nAch (Deaner, 2013; McClelland, 1958, 1987, 1993; Mokrova et al., 2013; Schunk & Zimmerman, 2013; Senko et al., 2008; Sheard, 2013):

Achievement motivation The desire to excel, especially in competition with others.

- **Preference for moderately difficult tasks** People high in nAch (need for achievement) avoid tasks that are too easy because they offer little challenge or satisfaction. They also avoid extremely difficult tasks because the probability of success is too low.
- **Competitiveness** High-achievement-oriented people are more attracted to careers and tasks that involve competition and an opportunity to excel.
- **Preference for clear goals with competent feedback** High-achievement-oriented people tend to prefer tasks with clear outcomes and situations in which they can receive feedback on their performance. They also prefer criticism from a harsh but competent evaluator to criticism from one who is friendlier but less competent.
- **Self-regulation and personal responsibility** High-achievement-oriented people purposefully control their thoughts and behaviors to attain their goals. In addition, they prefer being personally responsible for a project so that they can feel satisfied when the task is well done.
- **Mental toughness and persistence** High-achievement-oriented people have a mindset that allows them to persevere through difficult circumstances. It includes attributes like sacrifice and self-denial, which overcome obstacles while also maintaining concentration and motivation when things are going well. In one study, 47% of high nAch individuals persisted on an "unsolvable task" until time was called, compared with only 2% of people with low nAch.
- **More accomplished** People who have high nAch scores do better than others on exams, earn better grades in school, and excel in their chosen professions.

Achievement orientation appears to be largely learned in early childhood, primarily through interactions with parents (**Figure 10.9**). Highly motivated children tend to have parents who encourage independence and frequently reward successes (Aunola et al., 2013; Katz et al., 2011; Pomerantz & Kempner, 2013). In fact, children's motivation for academic success—along with their study skills—are better predictors of long-term math achievement than IQ (Murayama et al., 2012). Our cultural values also affect achievement needs (Chi, 2013; Greenfield & Quiroz, 2013; Xu & Barnes, 2011).

Q3

FIGURE 10.9 FUTURE ACHIEVER

A study by Richard de Charms and Gerald Moeller (1962) found a significant correlation between the achievement themes in children's literature and the industrial accomplishments of various countries.

Dave & Les Jacobs/Blend/Getty Images

Sexuality

Obviously, there is strong motivation to engage in sexual behavior: It's essential for the survival of our species, and it's also pleasurable. But *sexuality* includes much more than reproduction. For most humans (and some other animals), a sexual relationship fulfills many needs, including the need for connection, intimacy, pleasure, and the release of sexual tension. Given the large role sex plays throughout our lives, can you predict how the quality of the first sexual experience might affect later relationships? See the *Psych Science* box.

PSYCHSCIENCE

DO INITIAL SEXUAL EXPERIENCES HAVE A LASTING IMPACT?

To study this question, researchers asked 331 young men and women to anonymously complete a questionnaire measuring degree of anxiety, regret, and contentment surrounding their first sexual act, as well as rating their current sex life (Smith & Shaffer, 2013).

As you might expect, those who reported more positive first-time experiences also reported higher levels of physical and emotional satisfaction in their subsequent and current relationships. Specifically, those who felt loved and respected by their partner during their first sexual experience found later encounters more emotionally satisfying. Sadly, people who described feelings of anxiety and negativity during their first sexual experience reported lower sexual satisfaction with their current sex lives.

Why is this research important? Some people may believe that the first sexual experience is "no big deal" or something you just have to get out of the way. However, this research reveals that it may have a lasting impact.

RESEARCH CHALLENGE

1. Based on the information provided, did this study (Smith & Shaffer, 2013) use descriptive, correlational, and/or experimental research?
2. If you chose:
   - descriptive research, is this a naturalistic observation, survey/interview, case study, or archival research?
   - correlational research, is this a positive, negative, or zero correlation?
   - experimental research, label the IV, DV, experimental group(s), and control group.

>> CHECK YOUR ANSWERS IN APPENDIX B.

Note: The information provided in this study is admittedly limited, but the level of detail is similar to what is presented in most textbooks and public reports of research findings. Answering these questions, and then comparing your answers to those in the Appendix, will help you become a better critical thinker and consumer of scientific research.

Sexual response cycle Masters and Johnson's description of the four-stage bodily response to sexual arousal, which consists of excitement, plateau, orgasm, and resolution.

William Masters and Virginia Johnson (1966) were the first to conduct laboratory studies on what happens to the human body during sexual activity. They attached recording devices to male and female volunteers and monitored or filmed their physical responses as they moved from nonarousal to orgasm and back to nonarousal. They labeled the bodily changes during this series of events a **sexual response cycle (Figure 10.10)**. Researchers have further characterized differences between sexual response patterns in men and women **(Figure 10.11)**.

Sexual Orientation

Sexual orientation A primary erotic attraction toward members of the same sex (homosexual, gay, lesbian), both sexes (bisexual), or the other sex (heterosexual).

Of course, an important part of people's sexuality is the question of to whom they are sexually attracted. What leads some people to be sexually interested in members of their own sex, the opposite sex, or both sexes? The roots of human **sexual orientation** are poorly understood. However, most studies suggest that genetics and biology play the dominant role (Ashley, 2013; Bao & Swaab, 2011; Hines, 2013; LeVay, 2011; Segal, 2013). For example, studies on identical twins found that if one identical twin was gay, the second twin was also gay 48 to 65% of the time, whereas

FIGURE 10.10 **MASTERS AND JOHNSON'S VIEW OF THE SEXUAL RESPONSE CYCLE**

Masters and Johnson identified a typical four-stage pattern of sexual response. Note that this simplified description does not account for individual variation and should not be used to judge what's "normal."

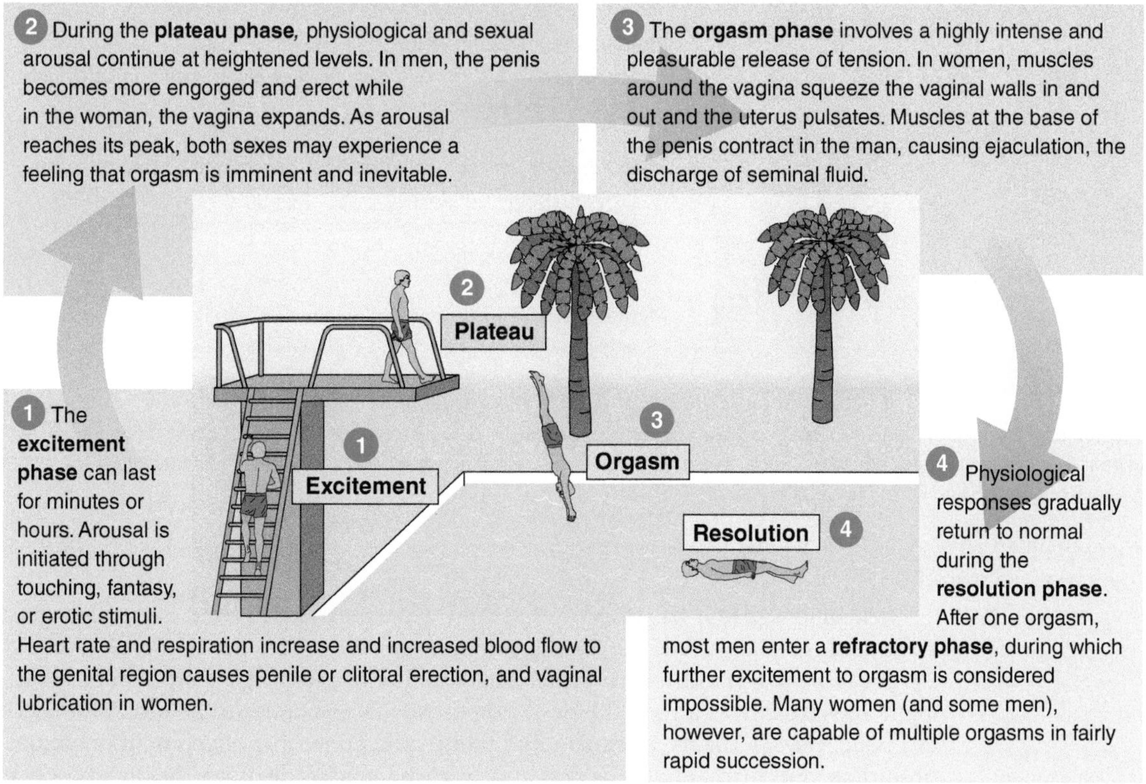
2 During the **plateau phase**, physiological and sexual arousal continue at heightened levels. In men, the penis becomes more engorged and erect while in the woman, the vagina expands. As arousal reaches its peak, both sexes may experience a feeling that orgasm is imminent and inevitable.
3 The **orgasm phase** involves a highly intense and pleasurable release of tension. In women, muscles around the vagina squeeze the vaginal walls in and out and the uterus pulsates. Muscles at the base of the penis contract in the man, causing ejaculation, the discharge of seminal fluid.
2 Plateau
1 Excitement
3 Orgasm
Resolution 4
1 The **excitement phase** can last for minutes or hours. Arousal is initiated through touching, fantasy, or erotic stimuli. Heart rate and respiration increase and increased blood flow to the genital region causes penile or clitoral erection, and vaginal lubrication in women.
4 Physiological responses gradually return to normal during the **resolution phase**. After one orgasm, most men enter a **refractory phase**, during which further excitement to orgasm is considered impossible. Many women (and some men), however, are capable of multiple orgasms in fairly rapid succession.

the rate for fraternal twins was 26 to 30% (Ando et al., 2013; Hyde, 2005; Långstrom et al., 2010; Moutinho et al., 2011).

Research with rats and sheep hints that prenatal hormone levels may also affect fetal brain development and sexual orientation (Bagermihl, 1999; Hines, 2013; Roselli et al., 2011). However, the effects of hormones on human sexual orientation are unknown. Furthermore, no well-controlled study has ever found a difference in adult hormone levels between heterosexuals and gays and lesbians (Hall & Schaeff, 2008; Hines, 2013; LeVay, 2003, 2011).

FIGURE 10.11 **DIFFERENCES BETWEEN MALE AND FEMALE SEXUAL RESPONSE PATTERNS**

Although the overall pattern of sexual response is similar in the two sexes, there is more variation in specific patterns among women.

A Immediately after orgasm, men generally enter a refractory period, which lasts from several minutes to up to a day.

B Female sexual responses generally follow one or more of three basic patterns.

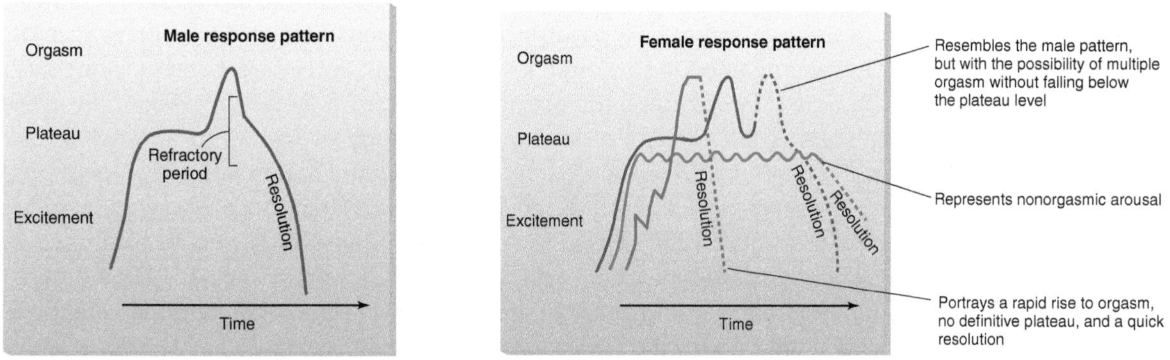

TABLE 10.3 SEXUAL ORIENTATION MYTHS

Patsy Lynch/Retna Ltd/Corbis

Myth #1: Seduction theory: Gays and lesbians were seduced as children by adults of their own sex.

Myth #2: "By default" theory: Gays and lesbians were unable to attract partners of the other sex or have experienced unhappy heterosexual experiences.

Myth #3: Poor parenting theory: Sons become gay because of domineering mothers and weak fathers. Daughters become lesbians because their mothers were weak or absent or their fathers were their primary role model.

Myth #4: Modeling theory: Children raised by gay and lesbian parents usually end up adopting their parents' sexual orientation.

On June 26, 2013, the U.S. Supreme Court ruled the federal Defense of Marriage Act (DOMA), which defined marriage as a union between one man and one woman, unconstitutional. This decision, along with other judicial and legislative action and changing societal views surrounding gay marriage, has brought attitudes about sexual orientation into full public debate.

Scientific research has disproved several widespread myths and misconceptions about homosexuality (Asley, 2013; Bergstrom-Lynch, 2008; Drucker, 2010; LeVay, 2003, 2011) **(Table 10.3)**. Although mental health authorities long ago discontinued labeling homosexuality as a mental illness, homosexuality continues to be a divisive societal issue. Gays, lesbians, bisexuals, and transgendered people often confront **sexual prejudice**, and many endure verbal and physical attacks, disrupted family and peer relationships, and high rates of anxiety, depression, and suicide (Johns et al., 2013; Nadal, 2013; Plöderl et al., 2013; Rivers, 2011). Sexual prejudice is a socially reinforced phenomenon, not an individual pathology (as the older term *homophobia* implies).

Sexual prejudice A negative attitude toward an individual because of her or his sexual orientation.

Extrinsic Versus Intrinsic Motivation

Should parents reward children for getting good grades? There is an ongoing controversy within psychological research over whether giving external, or extrinsic, rewards increases or decreases motivation (e.g., Anderman & Dawson, 2011; Anik et al., 2011; Babula, 2013; Deci & Moller, 2005; Deci & Ryan, 2012; Gunderman & Kamer, 2011; Kerr et al., 2013). Some researchers are concerned that providing such **extrinsic motivation** will seriously affect the individual's internal, **intrinsic motivation**. When we perform a task for no ulterior purpose, we are intrinsically motivated ("because I like it" or "because it's fun"). In contrast, when we perform a task for a reward, we are extrinsically motivated.

Extrinsic motivation Motivation based on external rewards or threats of punishment.

Intrinsic motivation Motivation resulting from internal, personal satisfaction from a task or activity.

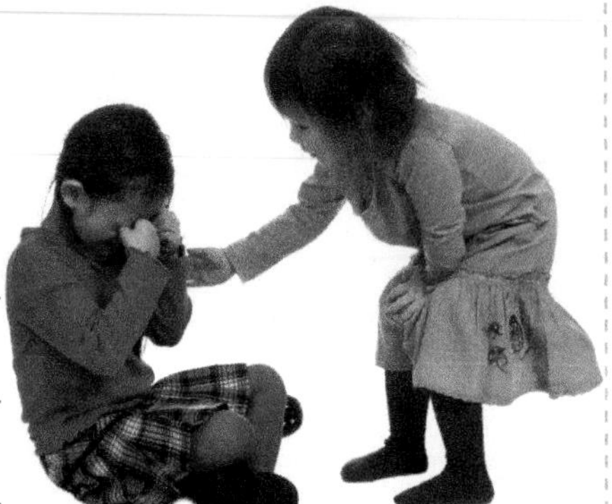

© perkmeup /iStockphoto

realworldpsychology **Problems with Extrinsic Rewards** Some research has shown that people who are given extrinsic rewards like money or praise for an intrinsically satisfying activity, such as watching TV, playing cards, or even engaging in sex, often lose enjoyment and interest and may decrease the time they spend on the activity (Hennessey & Amabile, 1998; Kohn, 2000; Moneta & Siu, 2002). For example, one study of visitors to a national park found that those who were intrinsically motivated had measurably higher positive feelings and higher life-satisfaction levels than those who were extrinsically motivated (Cini et al., 2013). Similarly, 2-year-olds who receive rewards for helping someone else—which, like going to a national park, should be an intrinsically rewarding activity—are later less likely to offer help than are those who receive no reward (Warneken & Tomasello, 2008).

FIGURE 10.12 **WHEN EXTRINSIC REWARDS ARE MOTIVATING**

Extrinsic rewards used to control or gain approval inhibit intrinsic motivation (**a**). But when they inform or provide valuable feedback, they tend to increase motivation and enjoyment (**b**).

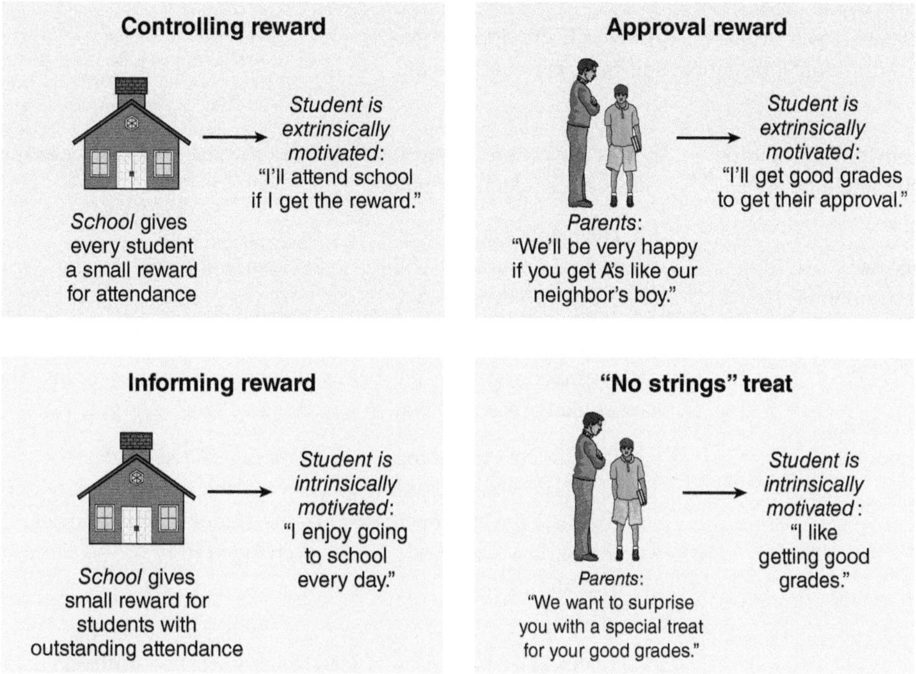

Controlling reward
Student is extrinsically motivated: "I'll attend school if I get the reward."
School gives every student a small reward for attendance
Approval reward
Student is extrinsically motivated: "I'll get good grades to get their approval."
Parents: "We'll be very happy if you get A's like our neighbor's boy."
Informing reward
Student is intrinsically motivated: "I enjoy going to school every day."
School gives small reward for students with outstanding attendance
"No strings" treat
Student is intrinsically motivated: "I like getting good grades."
Parents: "We want to surprise you with a special treat for your good grades."

Ⓐ If extrinsic rewards are used to control or gain approval—for example, when schools pay all students for simple attendence or when parents give children approval or privileges for achieving good grades—they often decrease motivation (Eisenberger & Armeli, 1997; Eisenberger & Rhoades, 2002; Houlfort, 2006).

Ⓑ Extrinsic rewards can be motivating if they are used to produce intrinsic motivation. For example, when superior perfor mance is recognized with an award or a special "no strings attached" treat (Deci, 1995), it may increase enjoyment.

As it turns out, not all extrinsic motivation is bad. As you can see in **Figure 10.12a**, it depends on how extrinsic rewards are used. When they are used to control or gain approval, as when schools pay all students for simple attendance or parents give children approval or privileges for good grades, they often decrease motivation (Eisenberger & Armeli, 1997; Eisenberger & Rhoades, 2002; Houlfort, 2006). On the other hand, extrinsic rewards can be motivating if they are used to inform a person of improved or superior performance or as a special "no strings attached" treat (Deci, 1995; Emmett & McGee, 2013; Panagopoulos, 2013). (See **Figure 10.12b**.) In fact, they may intensify the desire to do well again.

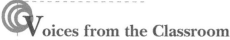

Voices from the Classroom

When Extrinsic Motivation Becomes Intrinsic When I discuss the topic of motivation, I always tell my students a piece of my life story. I am a first-generation college student. Neither of my parents had a high school diploma. Their goal was to have their children graduate from high school. After graduation, I was working in a local grocery store and realized that that I didn't want to do that for my entire life. Wanting more in life, I began attending the local community college when I was 23 years old, where I soon met with academic success. Boy, did it feel good! I enjoyed succeeding in my classes. Maybe I could do this college thing! I put together a plan to finish community college, get a B.S. degree in psychology, and eventually a Ph.D. What began as *extrinsic motivation* turned into *intrinsic motivation*. These are not just esoteric concepts; they apply to real life!

Professor Vicki Ritts
St. Louis Community College, Meramec Campus
St. Louis, Missouri

RETRIEVAL PRACTICE: MOTIVATION AND BEHAVIOR

Self-Test

Completing this self-test and comparing your answers with those in Appendix B provides immediate feedback and helpful practice for exams. Additional interactive, self-tests are available at www.wiley.com/college/huffman.

1. Maria appears to be starving herself and has obviously lost a lot of weight in just a few months. You suspect she might be suffering from _____.

a. anorexia nervosa
b. bulimia nervosa
c. obesity phobia
d. none of these options

2. The desire to excel, especially in competition with others, is known as _____.

a. drive-reduction theory
b. intrinsic motivation
c. achievement motivation
d. all these options

3. _____ is a term for negative attitudes toward someone based on his or her sexual orientation.

a. Heterophobia
b. Heterosexism
c. Sexual prejudice
d. Sexual phobia

4. A high school began paying students $5 for each day they attended school. Overall rates of attendance increased in the first few weeks and then fell below the original starting point. The most likely reason is that _____.

a. the students felt going to school wasn't worth $5
b. money is a secondary reinforcer, not a primary one
c. extrinsic rewards decreased the intrinsic value of attending school
d. the students' expectancies changed to fit the situation

Think Critically

1. Most adults (and many children) find it difficult to control their weight. Using information from this chapter, can you identify the factors or motives that best explain your experience?
2. How can you restructure elements of your personal, work, or school life to increase intrinsic motivation over extrinsic?

realworldpsychology

How can just looking at pictures of high-fat foods make you feel hungry?

Is motivation a better predictor of math success in children than IQ?

HINT: LOOK IN THE MARGIN FOR Q2 AND Q3

COMPONENTS AND THEORIES OF EMOTION

LEARNING OBJECTIVES

RETRIEVAL PRACTICE While reading the upcoming sections, respond to each Learning Objective in your own words. Then compare your responses with those found at www.wiley.com/college/huffman.

1. **DESCRIBE** the biological, cognitive, and behavioral components of emotion.
2. **COMPARE** the three major theories of emotion.
3. **EXPLAIN** cultural similarities and differences in emotion.
4. **REVIEW** the problems with relying on polygraph testing as a lie detector.

Emotion A complex pattern of feelings that includes arousal (heart pounding), cognitions (thoughts, values, and expectations), and expressive behaviors (smiles, frowns, and gestures).

Emotions play an important role in our lives. They color our dreams, memories, and perceptions. When they are disordered, they contribute significantly to psychological problems (Christenfeld & Mandler, 2013; Whalen et al., 2013). But what do we really mean by the term **emotion**? In everyday usage, we use it to describe feeling states; we feel "thrilled" when our political candidate wins an election, "dejected" when our candidate loses, and "miserable" when our loved ones reject us. Obviously, what you and I mean by these terms, or what we individually experience with different emotions, can vary greatly among individuals.

Three Components of Emotion

Psychologists define and study emotion according to three basic components—*biological*, *cognitive*, and *behavioral*.

Biological (Arousal) Component

Internal physical changes occur in our bodies whenever we experience an emotion. Imagine walking alone on a dark street and having someone jump from behind a stack of boxes and start running toward you. How would you respond? Like most other people, you would probably interpret the situation as threatening and would run. Your predominant emotion, fear, would inspire several physiological reactions, such as increased heart rate and blood pressure, perspiration, and goose bumps (piloerection). Such biological reactions are controlled by certain brain structures and by the autonomic branch of the nervous system (ANS).

Our emotional experiences appear to result from important interactions between several areas of the brain, particularly the *cerebral cortex* and *limbic system* (Feinstein, 2013; Langenecker et al., 2005; Panksepp, 2005; Whalen et al., 2013). As we discuss in Chapter 2, the cerebral cortex, the outermost layer of the brain, serves as our body's ultimate control and information-processing center, including our ability to recognize and regulate our emotions.

Studies of the limbic system, located in the innermost part of the brain, have shown that one area, the **amygdala**, plays a key role in emotion—especially fear **(Figure 10.13)**. It sends signals to the other areas of the brain, causing increased heart rate and all the other physiological reactions related to fear.

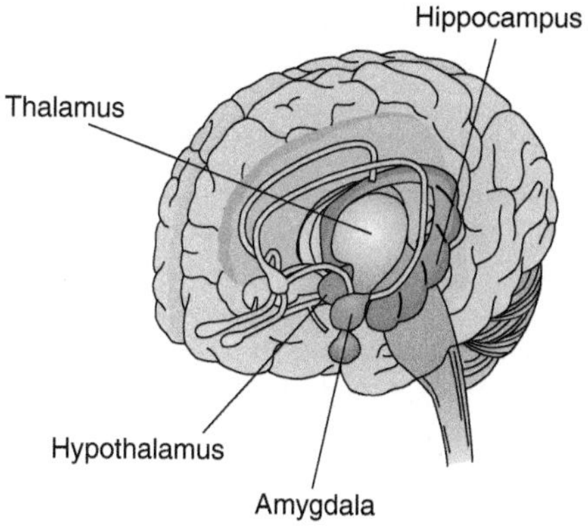

FIGURE 10.13 THE LIMBIC SYSTEM'S ROLE IN EMOTION

In addition to being involved in drive regulation, memory, and other functions, the limbic system is very important in emotions. It consists of several subcortical structures that form a border (or limbus) around the brain stem.

Amygdala A part of the limbic system structure linked to the production and regulation of emotions.

Emotional arousal sometimes occurs without our conscious awareness. According to psychologist Joseph LeDoux (1996, 2002, 2007), when the *thalamus* (our brain's sensory switchboard) receives sensory inputs, it sends separate messages up to the cortex, which "thinks" about the stimulus, and to the amygdala, which immediately activates the body's alarm system. Although this dual pathway occasionally leads to "false alarms," such as when we mistake a stick for a snake, LeDoux believes it is a highly adaptive warning system essential to our survival. He states that "the time saved by the amygdala in acting on the thalamic interpretation, rather than waiting for the cortical input, may be the difference between life and death" (LeDoux, 1996, p. 166).

As important as the brain is to emotion, it is the *autonomic nervous system* (Chapter 2) that produces the obvious signs of arousal. These largely automatic responses result from interconnections between the ANS and various glands and muscles **(Figure 10.14)**.

Sympathetic		Parasympathetic
Pupils dilated	Eyes	Pupils constricted
Decreased saliva	Mouth	Increased saliva
Vessels constricted (skin cold and clammy)	Skin	Vessels dilated (normal blood flow)
Respiration increased	Lungs	Respiration normal
Increased heart rate	Heart	Decreased heart rate
Increased epinephrine and norepinephrine	Adrenal glands	Decreased epinephrine and norepinephrine
Decreased motility	Digestion	Increased motility

FIGURE 10.14 EMOTION AND THE AUTONOMIC NERVOUS SYSTEM

During emotional arousal, the sympathetic branch of the autonomic nervous system prepares the body for fight or flight. (The hormones epinephrine and norepinephrine keep the system under sympathetic control until the emergency is over.) The parasympathetic branch returns the body to a more relaxed state (homeostasis).

Cognitive (Thinking) Component

Emotional reactions are very individual: What you experience as intensely pleasurable may be boring or aversive to another. To study the cognitive (thought) component of emotions, psychologists typically use self-report techniques, such as paper-and-pencil tests, surveys, and interviews. However, people are sometimes unable or unwilling to accurately remember or describe their emotional states. For these reasons, our cognitions about our own and others' emotions are difficult to measure scientifically. This is why many researchers supplement participants' reports on their emotional experiences with methods that assess emotional experience indirectly (e.g., measuring physiological responses such as heart rate, pupil dilation, blood flow).

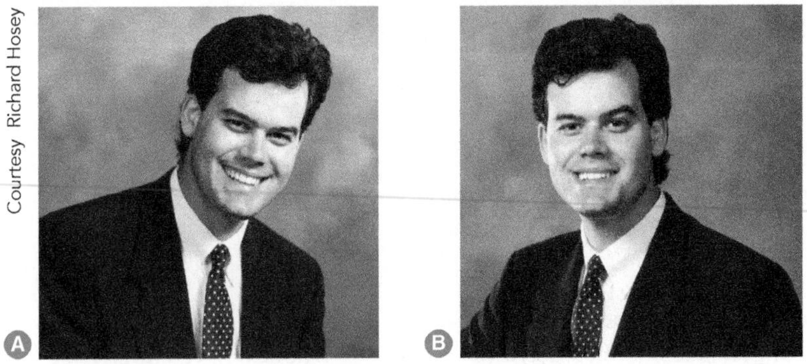

Courtesy Richard Hosey

FIGURE 10.15 DUCHENNE SMILE

People who show a Duchenne, or real, smile (**a**) and laughter elicit more positive responses from strangers and enjoy better interpersonal relationships and personal adjustment than those who use a social smile (**b**) (Keltner et al., 1999; Platt et al., 2013; Prkachin & Silverman, 2002).

Behavioral (Expressive) Component

Emotional expression is a powerful form of communication, and facial expressions may be our most important form of emotional communication. Researchers have developed sensitive techniques to measure subtleties of feeling and to differentiate honest expressions from fake ones. Perhaps most interesting is the difference between the *social smile* and the *Duchenne smile* (named after French anatomist Duchenne de Boulogne, who first described it in 1862) **(Figure 10.15)**. In a false, social smile, our voluntary cheek muscles are pulled back, but our eyes are unsmiling. Smiles of real pleasure, on the other hand, use the muscles not only around the cheeks but also around the eyes.

The Duchenne smile illustrates the importance of nonverbal means of communicating emotion. We all know that people communicate in ways other than speaking or writing. However, few people recognize the full importance of nonverbal signals.

© Ocean/Corbis

psychology and you **The Power of Nonverbal Cues** Imagine yourself as a job interviewer. Your first applicant greets you with a big smile, full eye contact, a firm handshake, and an erect, open posture. The second applicant doesn't smile, looks down, offers a weak handshake, and slouches. Whom do you think you will hire?

Psychologist Albert Mehrabian would say that you're much less likely to hire the second applicant due to his or her "mixed messages." Mehrabian's research suggests that when we're communicating feelings or attitudes and our verbal and nonverbal dimensions don't match, the receiver trusts the predominant form of communication, which is about 93% nonverbal and consists of the way the words are said and the facial expression rather than the literal meaning of the words (Mehrabian, 1968, 1971, 2007).

Unfortunately, Mehrabian's research is often overgeneralized, and many people misquote him as saying that "over 90% of communication is nonverbal." Clearly, if a police officer says, "Put your hands up," his or her verbal words might carry 100% of the meaning. However, when we're confronted with a mismatch between verbal and nonverbal communication, it is safe to say that we pay far more attention to the nonverbal because we believe it more often tells us what someone is really thinking or feeling. The importance of nonverbal communication, particularly facial expressions, is further illustrated by the popularity of smileys and other emoticons in our everyday e-mail and text messages.

Three Major Theories of Emotion

Researchers generally agree that emotion has biological, cognitive, and behavioral components, but there is less agreement about *how* we become emotional (Christenfeld & Mandler, 2013). The major competing theories are the *James-Lange*, *Cannon-Bard*, and *Schachter and Singer's two-factor theories* **(Figure 10.16)**.

FIGURE 10.16 **COMPARING THREE MAJOR THEORIES OF EMOTION**

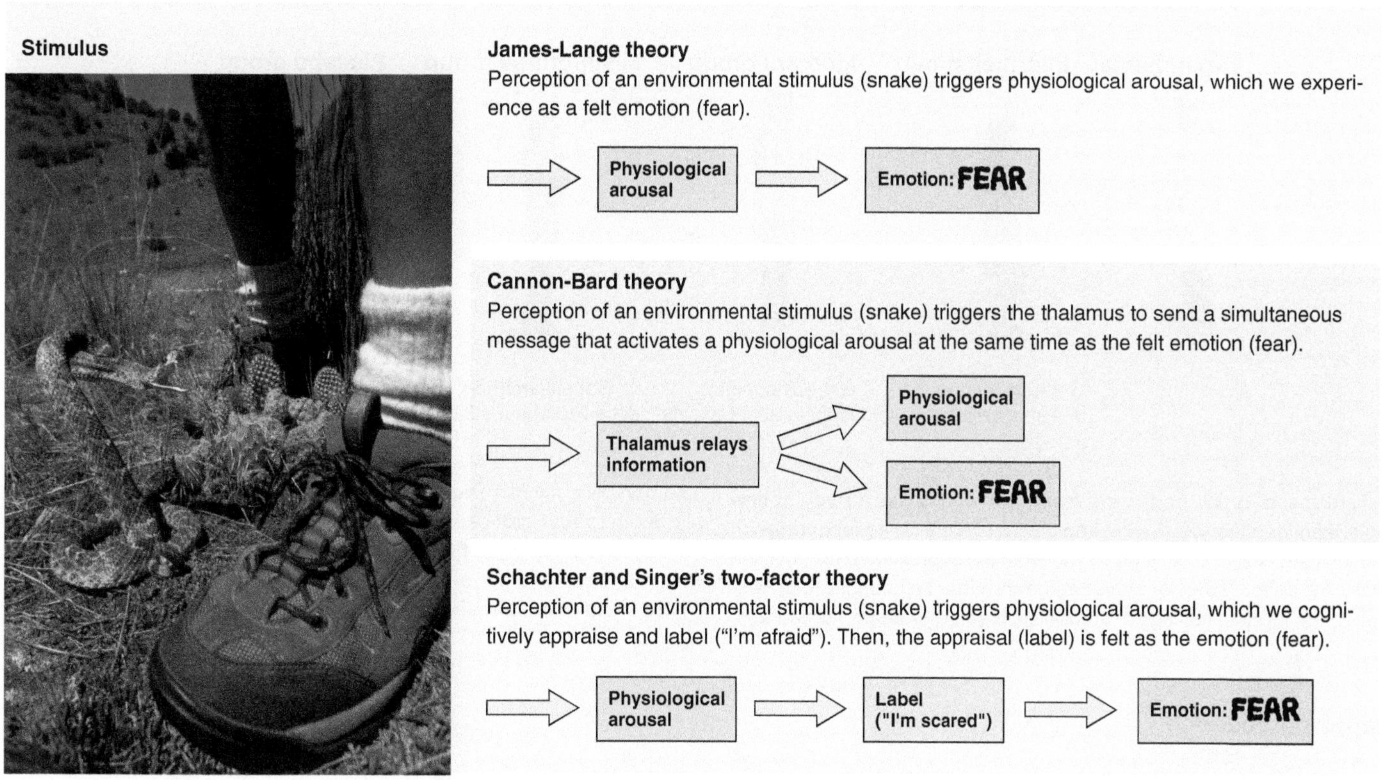

Stimulus
James-Lange theory
Perception of an environmental stimulus (snake) triggers physiological arousal, which we experience as a felt emotion (fear).
Physiological arousal
Emotion: FEAR
Cannon-Bard theory
Perception of an environmental stimulus (snake) triggers the thalamus to send a simultaneous message that activates a physiological arousal at the same time as the felt emotion (fear).
Thalamus relays information
Physiological arousal
Emotion: FEAR
Schachter and Singer's two-factor theory
Perception of an environmental stimulus (snake) triggers physiological arousal, which we cognitively appraise and label ("I'm afraid"). Then, the appraisal (label) is felt as the emotion (fear).
Physiological arousal
Label ("I'm scared")
Emotion: FEAR

Gordon Wiltsie/National Geographic/Getty Images

Imagine that you're walking in the desert and suddenly see a coiled snake on the path next to you. What emotion would you experience? Most people would say they would be very afraid. But why? Common sense tells us that our hearts pound and we tremble when we're afraid or that we cry when we're sad. But according to the **James-Lange theory**, felt emotions begin with physiological arousal of the ANS (Chapter 2). This arousal (a pounding heart, breathlessness, trembling all over) then causes us to experience the emotion we call "fear." Contrary to popular opinion, James wrote: "We feel sorry because we cry, angry because we strike, afraid because we tremble" (James, 1890).

In contrast, the **Cannon-Bard theory** proposes that arousal and emotion occur separately but simultaneously. Following perception of an emotion-provoking stimulus, the thalamus (a subcortical brain structure) sends two simultaneous messages: one to the ANS, which causes physiological arousal, and one to the brain's cortex, which causes awareness of the felt emotion.

Finally, Schachter and Singer's **two-factor theory** suggests that our emotions start with physiological arousal followed by a conscious, cognitive appraisal. We then look to external cues from the environment and to others around us to find a label and explanation for the arousal. Therefore, if we cry at a wedding, we label our emotion as joy or happiness. If we cry at a funeral, we label the emotion as sadness.

In their classic study demonstrating this effect, Schachter and Singer (1962) gave research participants injections of epinephrine (adrenaline), a hormone/neurotransmitter that produces feelings of arousal, or saline shots (a placebo) and then exposed the participants to either a happy or angry confederate **(Figure 10.17)**. The way participants responded suggested that arousal could be labeled happiness or anger, depending on the context. Thus, Schachter and Singer's research demonstrated that emotion is determined by two factors: physiological arousal and cognitive appraisal (labeling).

Schachter and Singer's two-factor theory may have important practical implications. Depending on the cues present in our environment, we apparently can interpret exactly the same feelings of arousal in very different ways. For example, if

James-Lange theory A theory of emotion which suggests that the subjective experience of emotion results from physiological changes rather than being their cause ("I feel sad because I'm crying"); in this view, each emotion is physiologically distinct.

Cannon-Bard theory A theory which states that emotions and physiological changes occur simultaneously ("I'm crying and feeling sad at the same time"); in this view, all emotions are physiologically similar.

Two-factor theory Schachter and Singer's theory that emotion depends upon two factors—physiological arousal and cognitive labeling of that arousal.

FIGURE 10.17 **SCHACHTER AND SINGER'S CLASSIC STUDY**

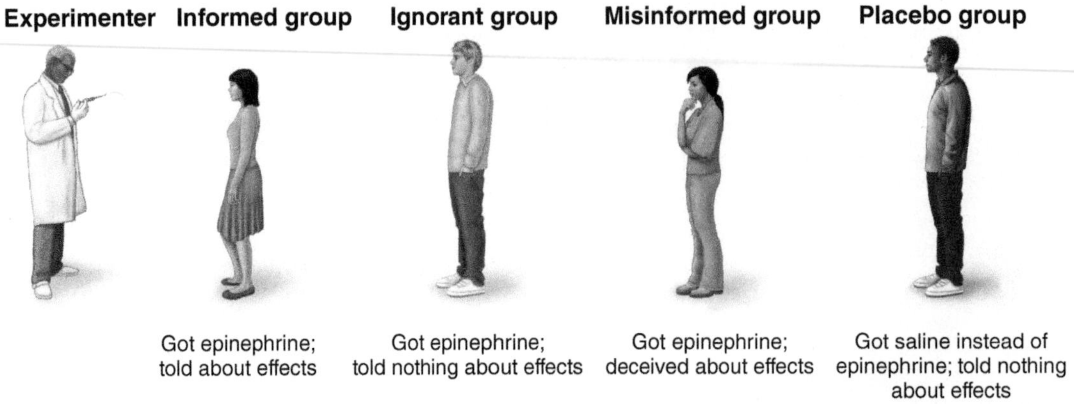

A Participants in this study were first told that this was a study of how certain vitamins affect visual skills, and then they were asked for permission to be injected with a small shot of the vitamin "Suproxin." (This injection actually was a shot of the hormone/neurotransmitter epinephrine [or adrenaline], which triggers feelings of arousal such as racing heart, flushed skin, and trembling hands.) Those participants who gave permission were then divided into four groups and given injections. Those in the three groups who received the shot of epinephrine were correctly informed about the drug's effects, ignorant of the effects, or misinformed about the effects. Those in the fourth placebo group received a neutral, saline solution.

Happy confederate
I feel strange, it must be the injection
I feel strange, sort of "happy" like that fella
I feel strange. I guess I feel very happy like that guy over there
I feel strange, sort of happy like that fella

B Each participant was then placed in a room with either a "happy" or an "angry" trained confederate (who was actually an accomplice of the experimenter). Both the participants and confederate were told that before they could take the supposed vision test, they needed to complete a questionnaire and allow time for the drug to take effect. The confederate was instructed in each condition to behave in line with his supposed emotion: He acted joyously in the happy condition—flying paper airplanes, bouncing a ball, etc.—and acted irate in the angry condition—complaining about the experiment, refusing to answer some items on the questionnaire, etc. As predicted, when participants were placed in a room with the happy confederate, they rated themselves as happy. They also behaved in a more joyous way, engaging in more "happy" acts, just like the confederate had modeled. When placed with the angry, irritated confederate, they reported feeling angry and behaved more irately. Although the subjects were feeling similar effects of the epinephrine, they labeled those effects differently (happy or angry), depending on the external cues in their environment, and acted accordingly.

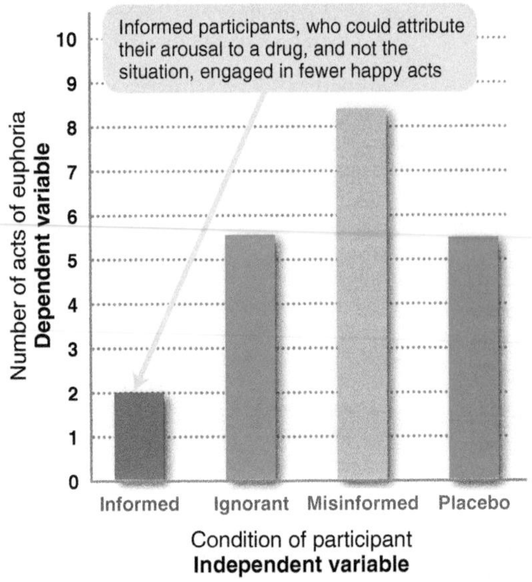

C This effect on emotions was most apparent in the groups that were misinformed about the true effects of the injections. Why? Those in the informed group correctly attributed their arousal to the drug rather than to the environment.

you're shy or afraid of public speaking, try interpreting your feelings of nervousness as the result of too much coffee or the heating in the room. Some research on this type of *misattribution of arousal* has had positive outcomes (Chafin et al., 2008; Inzlicht & Al-Khindi, 2012; Thornton & Tizard, 2010).

Later research on emotion has supported or discounted parts of all three of these major theories and added some new ideas. For example, as we saw earlier in discussing the behavioral component of emotion, facial expressions like the Duchenne smile help us express our emotions. And, according to the **facial-feedback hypothesis**, movements of our facial muscles produce and/or intensify our subjective experience of emotion (see *Psychology and You*). More specifically, sensory input (such as seeing a snake) is first routed to subcortical areas of the brain that activate facial movements. These facial changes then initiate and intensify emotions (Adelmann & Zajonc, 1989; Ceschi & Scherer, 2001; Dimberg & Söderkvist, 2011; Neal & Chartrand, 2011; Sander, 2013; Vrticka et al., 2013). Researchers in one study asked participants to maintain a smile while they were engaging in a stress-inducing task, such as keeping their hand in a bucket of very cold ice water (Kraft & Pressman, 2012). Compared to participants who held their face in a neutral position, those who smiled had lower heart rates, showing that smiling can help reduce the experience of stress—thus supporting the facial-feedback hypothesis.

Q4

Voices from the Classroom

Two-Factor Theory and "No Fear" Skiing This is an example I give for Schachter and Singer's two-factor theory of emotion, involving physiological arousal and a "label" based on a cognitive appraisal of the environment/situation. Once while snow skiing, I allowed myself to ski faster and faster, trying to keep up with my friend, Pete, who had suddenly zoomed passed me from behind. Because Pete was skiing that fast, I must be able to also, so I was "exhilarated" instead of "afraid" to be skiing that fast.

Then I fell. When I looked up, Pete kept skiing without waiting for me. That was odd. Then I turned to look behind and I saw Pete! The fast skier was in fact a different skier wearing the same style ski jacket as Pete's. Had I known he was not Pete, I would never have skied that fast without labeling my experience as "fear" instead of "exhilaration."

Professor Charles Dufour
University of Maine
Orono, Maine

Facial-feedback hypothesis The hypothesis that movements of the facial muscles produce and/or intensify our subjective experience of emotion.

psychology and you **Testing the Facial-Feedback Hypothesis** Hold a pen or pencil between your teeth with your mouth open. Spend about 30 seconds in this position. How do you feel? According to research, pleasant feelings are more likely when teeth are showing than when they are not.

Source: Adapted from Strack et al., 1988.

Mark Owens/John Wiley & Sons, Inc.

Other research emphasizes specific pathways between the *thalamus*, *amygdala*, and *cerebral cortex* to help explain different emotional responses, such as the almost instantaneous emotional response to some stimuli versus our slower-developing responses (Armony, 2013; Lazarus, 1991, 1998; LeDoux, 1996, 2003, 2007; Paz & Pare, 2013; Somerville et al., 2013; Zajonc, 1984).

Applying this specific pathway idea to our earlier example of hiking in the woods and noticing a large snake near your foot, your first response would most likely be to freeze in fear or jump away to safety. Only later would you be able to logically evaluate the danger this particular snake posed. This type of two-phase fear response is a result of two different pathways for sensory data in the brain **(Figure 10.18)**.

Evolution, Culture, and Emotion

Early research indicated that people in all cultures express, recognize, and experience several basic emotions, such as happiness, surprise, anger, sadness, fear, and disgust, in essentially the same way (Darwin, 1872; Ekman & Friesen, 1971; Izard, 1971; Plutchik, 1980; Tomkins, 1962). In other words, across cultures, a frown is recognized as a sign of displeasure and a smile as a sign of pleasure.

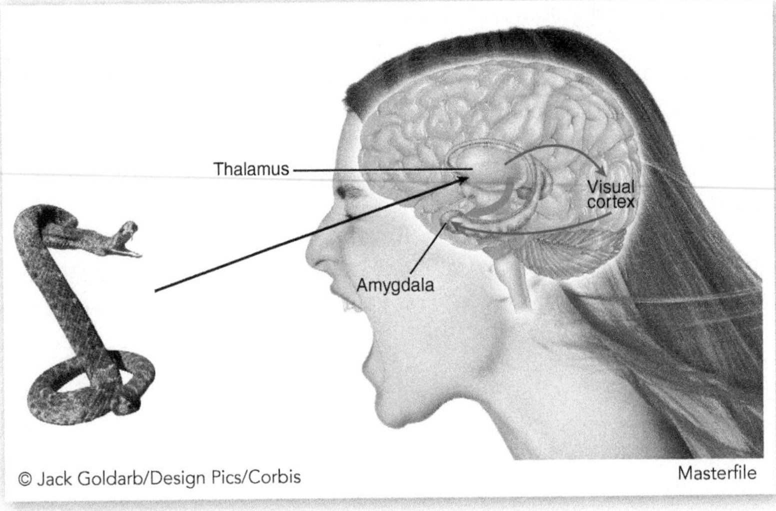

© Jack Goldarb/Design Pics/Corbis Masterfile

FIGURE 10.18 FAST AND SLOW PATHWAYS FOR FEAR

When sensory input arrives at the thalamus, the thalamus sends it along a fast route directly to the amygdala (the red arrow), as well as along a slower, more indirect route to the visual cortex (the blue arrow). This speedy, direct route allows us to quickly respond to a feared stimulus (like the snake) even before we're consciously aware of our emotions or behaviors. In contrast, the indirect route, engaging the visual cortex, provides more detailed information that allows us to consciously evaluate the danger of this particular snake and our most appropriate response.

© Ocean/Corbis

© Kevork Djansezian/AP Photo

FIGURE 10.19 CAN YOU IDENTIFY THESE EMOTIONS?

Most people easily recognize the emotional expression of happiness, such as the man in the photo on the top. However, on occasion, our facial expressions don't seem to match our presumed emotions, as is the case in the photo on the bottom. In this case, Halle Berry was the first black actress to win the highly-coveted Best Actress award, yet she looks sad rather than happy.

Interestingly, researchers in one study asked participants from both the United States and South Korea to select from a list of options the emotions portrayed by Olympic athletes who had just won a medal (Matsumoto & Hwang, 2012). Across both countries, participants rated faces that showed grimaces or yelling, clenched fists, and arms raised above the shoulders as indicating "triumph." Similarly, participants in both cultures rated faces with a small smile and heads tilted back, and arms sticking out away from the body with hands open as showing "pride." Q5

From an evolutionary perspective, the idea of universal facial expressions makes adaptive sense because such expressions signal others about our current emotional state (Ekman & Keltner, 1997). Charles Darwin first advanced the evolutionary theory of emotion in 1872. He proposed that expression of emotions evolved in different species as a part of survival and natural selection. For example, fear helps animals avoid danger, whereas expressions of anger and aggression are useful when fighting for mates or resources. Modern evolutionary theory suggests that basic emotions originate in the *limbic system*. Given that higher brain areas like the cortex developed later than the subcortical limbic system, evolutionary theory proposes that basic emotions evolved before thought.

Studies with infants provide further support for an evolutionary basis for emotions. For example, infants only a few hours old show distinct expressions of emotion that closely match adult facial expressions, and by the age of 7 months they can reliably interpret and recognize emotional information across both face and voice (Field et al., 1982; Grossman, 2013; Meltzoff & Moore, 1977, 1985, 1994). And all infants, even those who are born deaf and blind, show similar facial expressions in similar situations (Field et al., 1982; Gelder et al., 2006). In addition, a recent study showed that families may have characteristic facial expressions, shared even by family members who have been blind from birth (Peleg et al., 2006). This collective evidence points to a strong biological, evolutionary basis for emotional expression and decoding.

In contrast to the evolutionary approach, other researchers suggest that emotions are much more complex than originally thought (Fernández-Dols, 2013; Mead, 1928; Miyamoto & Ryaff, 2011; Nelson & Russell, 2013; Ortony & Turner, 1990). For example, although we may all share similar facial expressions for some emotions, each culture has its own *display rules* governing how, when, and where to express them (De Leersnyder et al., 2013; Ekman, 1993, 2004; Fok et al., 2008; Glikson & Erez, 2013; Koopmann-Holm & Matsumoto, 2011; Matsumoto & Hwang, 2011). In addition to culture, gender, family background, norms, and individual differences also affect our emotions and their expression **(Figure 10.19)**.

realworldpsychology **Understanding Display Rules for Emotions**

How do we learn our culture's display rules? Parents and other adults pass along their culture's specific display rules to children by responding negatively or ignoring some emotions and being supportive and sympathetic to others. Public physical contact is also governed by display rules. North Americans and Asians are less likely than people in other cultures to touch each other; only the closest family members and friends might hug in greeting or farewell. In contrast, Latin Americans and Middle Easterners often kiss, embrace, and hold hands as a sign of casual friendship (Axtell, 2007). Some Middle Eastern men commonly greet one another with a kiss. Can you imagine this same behavior among men in North America, who generally shake hands or pat one another's shoulders?

Behrouz Mehri/AFP/Getty Images

The Polygraph as a Lie Detector

We've discussed the three major theories of emotion, and the way emotions are affected by culture and evolution. Now we turn our attention to one of the hottest, and most controversial, topics in emotion research—the **polygraph**.

Polygraph An instrument that measures sympathetic arousal (heart rate, respiration rate, blood pressure, and skin conductivity) to detect emotional arousal, which in turn supposedly reflects lying versus truthfulness.

Traditional polygraph tests are based on the theory that when people lie, they feel guilty and anxious. Special sensors supposedly detect these testable emotions by measuring sympathetic and parasympathetic nervous system responses (Grubin, 2010; Tomash & Reed, 2013) **(Figure 10.20)**.

The problem is that lying is only loosely related to anxiety and guilt. Some people become nervous even when telling the truth, whereas others remain calm when deliberately lying. A polygraph cannot tell which emotion is being felt (nervousness, excitement, sexual arousal, and so on) or whether a response is due to emotional arousal or something else. One study found that people could affect the level of arousal shown on the polygraph by about 50% simply by pressing their toes against the floor or biting their tongues (Honts & Kircher, 1994). In fact, although proponents claim that polygraph tests are 90% accurate or better, actual tests show error rates ranging between 25 and 75% (DeClue, 2003; Handler et al., 2009; Iacono, 2008). Countless millions of dollars have been spent on new and improved lie-detection

FIGURE 10.20 POLYGRAPH TESTING | realworldpsychology

Polygraph testing is based on the assumption that when we lie, we feel guilty, fearful, or anxious.

A During a standard polygraph test, a band around the person's chest measures breathing rate, a cuff monitors blood pressure, and finger electrodes measure sweating, or galvanic skin response (GSR).

© Mark Burnett/Alamy

B Note how the GSR rises sharply in response to the question "Have you ever taken money from this bank?"

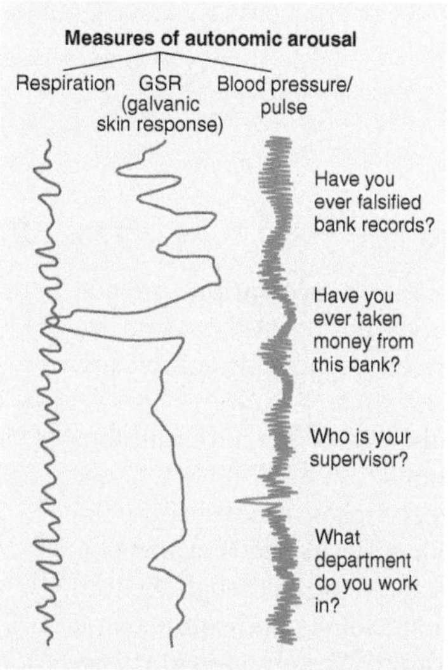
Measures of autonomic arousal
Respiration
GSR (galvanic skin response)
Blood pressure/ pulse
Have you ever falsified bank records?
Have you ever taken money from this bank?
Who is your supervisor?
What department do you work in?

techniques (Kluger & Masters, 2006). Perhaps the most promising is the use of brain scans like the *functional magnetic resonance imaging (fMRI)*. Unfortunately, each of these new lie-detection techniques has potential problems and researchers have questioned their reliability and validity, while civil libertarians and judicial scholars question their ethics and legality (Ganis et al., 2011; Gómez-Restrepo, 2007; Roskies et al., 2013; Schweitzer & Saks, 2011).

For these reasons, legal and scientific research suggests caution in using the polygraph as a lie detector (DeClue, 2003; Handler et al., 2013; Tomash & Reed, 2013; Van Iddekinge et al., 2012).

RETRIEVAL PRACTICE: COMPONENTS AND THEORIES OF EMOTION

Self-Test

Completing this self-test and comparing your answers with those in Appendix B provides immediate feedback and helpful practice for exams. Additional interactive, self-tests are available at www.wiley.com/college/huffman.

1. The three components of emotion are _____.

a. cognitive, biological, and behavioral
b. perceiving, thinking, and acting
c. positive, negative, and neutral
d. active/passive, positive/negative, and direct/indirect

2. According to the _____, emotions and physiological changes occur simultaneously

a. Cannon-Bard theory
b. James-Lange theory
c. facial-feedback hypothesis
d. two-factor theory

3. The _____ suggests that we look to external rather than internal cues to understand emotions.

a. Cannon-Bard theory
b. James-Lange theory
c. facial feedback hypothesis
d. two-factor theory

4. The polygraph, or lie detector, measures primarily the _____ component of emotions.

a. physiological
b. articulatory
c. cognitive
d. subjective

Think Critically

1 If you were going on a date with someone or applying for an important job, how might you use the three key theories of emotion to increase the chances that things will go well?

2 Why do you think people around the world experience and express the same basic emotions, and what evolutionary advantages might help explain these similarities?

3 After reading the section on polygraph tests, would you be willing to take a "lie detector" test if you were accused of a crime? Why or why not?

realworldpsychology

How can a simple smile reduce stress?

Why do emotional expressions of Olympic athletes appear the same across all cultures?

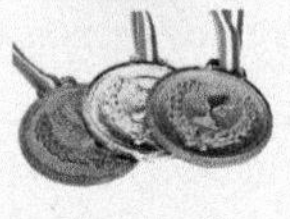

HINT: LOOK IN THE MARGIN FOR Q4 AND Q5

Summary

1 THEORIES OF MOTIVATION 274

- The three major biological theories of **motivation** provide roles for **instincts**, drives (produced by the body's need for **homeostasis**), and arousal (the need for novelty, complexity, and stimulation).
- Psychological theories emphasize the role of incentives, attributions, and expectancies in cognition.
- Maslow's **hierarchy of needs** theory takes a biopsychosocial approach. It prioritizes needs, with survival needs at the bottom and social and spiritual needs at the top. Although the theory has made important contributions, some critics argue that it is poorly researched and biased toward Western individualism.

2 MOTIVATION AND BEHAVIOR 279

- Hunger is one of the strongest motivational drives, and both biological factors (the stomach, biochemistry, the brain) and psychosocial factors (stimulus cues and cultural conditioning) affect hunger and eating. These factors play a similar role in **obesity**, **anorexia nervosa**, **bulimia nervosa**, and **binge-eating disorder**.
- A high need for achievement (nAch), or **achievement motivation**, is generally learned in early childhood primarily through interactions with parents.
- The human motivation for sex is extremely strong. Masters and Johnson first studied and described the **sexual response cycle**,

the series of physiological and sexual responses that occurs during sexual activity. Other sex research has focused on the roots of **sexual orientation**, and most studies suggest that genetics and biology play the dominant role. Sexual orientation remains a divisive issue, and gays, lesbians, bisexuals, and transgendered people often confront **sexual prejudice**.

- Providing **extrinsic motivation** like money or praise for an intrinsically satisfying activity can undermine people's enjoyment and interest—their **intrinsic motivation**—for the activity.

3 COMPONENTS AND THEORIES OF EMOTION 290

- **Emotion** has biological components (brain and autonomic nervous system), cognitive components (thoughts), and behavioral components (expressive).
- The major theories about how the components of emotion interact are the **James-Lange theory**, **Cannon-Bard theory**, and Schachter and Singer's **two-factor theory**. Each emphasizes different sequences or aspects of the three elements. Other research emphasizes how different pathways in the brain trigger faster and slower emotional responses.
- Some researchers believe there are basic, universal emotions shared by people of all cultures, who also express and recognize the basic emotions in essentially the same way. These findings and studies with infants support this evolutionary theory of emotion. However, other researchers question the existence of basic emotions. *Display rules* for emotional expressions vary across cultures.
- **Polygraph** tests attempt to detect lying by measuring physiological signs of guilt and anxiety. However, because lying is only loosely related to these emotions, most judges and scientists have serious reservations about using polygraphs as accurate lie detectors.

applyingrealworldpsychology

We began this chapter with five intriguing Real World Psychology questions, and you were asked to revisit these questions at the end of each section. Questions like these have an important and lasting impact on all of our lives. See if you can answer these additional critical thinking questions related to real world examples.

Tetra Images/SuperStock, Inc.

1. Nonhuman animals, like the kitten in this photo, sometimes display what we humans would label "curiosity." How might this trait be important for the survival and achievement of both human and nonhuman animals?
2. How do you think nonhuman animal motivation, like this kitten's, might differ from that of humans?
3. Think about your favorite hobbies or recreational activities (for example, riding your bike, watching TV, playing videogames). How would you explain these activities using the six theories of motivation (see Table 10.1, p. 274)?
4. Imagine yourself in a career as a health psychologist (Chapter 3). What type of public health efforts would you recommend to treat the rising epidemic and dangers associate with eating disorders?
5. Think back to a time when you felt very angry and upset over a misunderstanding with a special friend. Which of the three key components of emotion (biological, cognitive, or behavioral) best accounted for the intensity of your feelings? Which of the three major theories (the James-Lange, Cannon-Bard, or two-factor theory) best explains your overall emotional experience?
6. Do you believe people can (and should) control their emotions? Why or why not?

Key Terms

RETRIEVAL PRACTICE Write a definition for each term before turning back to the referenced page to check your answer.

- achievement motivation 285
- amygdala 291
- anorexia nervosa 283
- binge-eating disorder 284
- bulimia nervosa 283
- Cannon-Bard theory 293
- drive-reduction theory 275
- emotion 290
- extrinsic motivation 288
- facial-feedback hypothesis 295
- hierarchy of needs 278
- homeostasis 275
- incentive theory 277
- instinct 275
- intrinsic motivation 288
- James-Lange theory 293
- motivation 275
- obesity 282
- optimal-arousal theory 276
- polygraph 297
- self-actualization 278
- sexual orientation 286
- sexual prejudice 288
- sexual response cycle 286
- two-factor theory 293

chapter eleven

Personality

CHAPTER OUTLINE

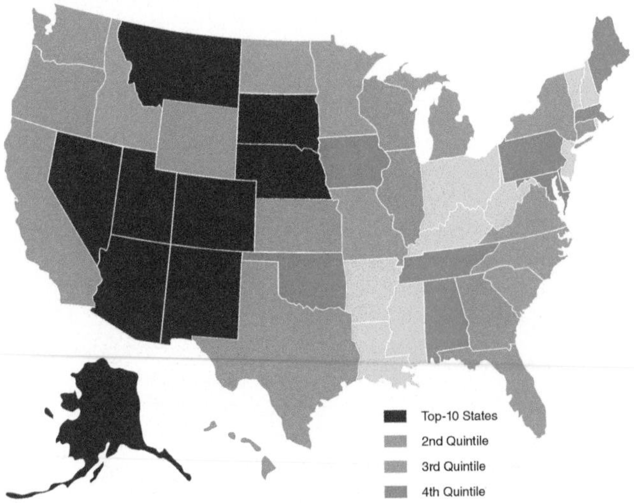

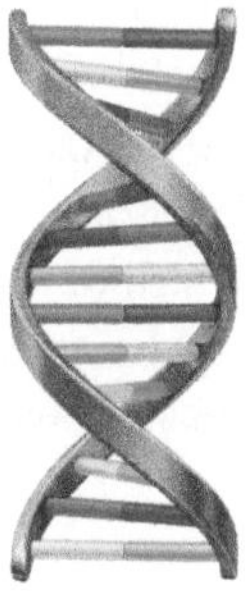

realworldpsychology

THINGS YOU'LL LEARN IN CHAPTER 11

Q1 Are some people with highly negative attitudes toward gay people repressing their own sexual desires?

Q2 Can personality traits predict the type of music we like?

Q3 What parenting skills are also associated with increased marital satisfaction?

Q4 Does helping parents prepare a meal increase a child's preference for healthy foods?

Q5 Can our genes predict how much we will give to charity?

Q6 Why do people from different states vary in their entrepreneurial spirit?

THROUGHOUT THE CHAPTER, MARGIN ICONS FOR Q1–Q6 INDICATE WHERE THE TEXT ADDRESSES THESE QUESTIONS.

chapteroverview

You have a strong need for other people to like and admire you. You tend to be critical of yourself. Although you have some personality weaknesses, you are generally able to compensate for them. At times, you have serious doubts about whether you have made the right decision or done the right thing.

—Adapted from Ulrich et al., 1963

Does this sound like you? A high percentage of research participants who read a similar personality description reported that the description was "very accurate"—even after they were informed that it was a *phony* horoscope (Hyman, 1981). Other research shows that about three-quarters of adults read newspaper horoscopes and that many of them believe astrological horoscopes were written especially for them (Sugarman et al., 2011; Wyman & Vyse, 2008).

Why are such spurious personality assessments so popular? One reason is that they seem to tap into our unique selves. Supporters of these horoscopes, however, ignore the fact that the traits they supposedly reveal are characteristics that almost everyone shares. Do you know anyone who doesn't "have a strong need for other people to like and admire" them? The traits in horoscopes are also generally flattering, or at least neutral.

Unlike the pseudopsychologies such as these newspaper horoscopes and Chinese fortune cookies, the descriptions presented by personality researchers are based on empirical studies. In this chapter, we examine the most prominent theories and up-to-date findings in personality research. We also explore professional techniques that psychologists use to assess personality.

Voices from the Classroom

Personality in the Dating World I once went on a date with someone who had the personality of an annoyed Chihuahua. What's weird about that statement is you know *exactly* what I mean. That's right, she was the woman with the high-pitched voice, angrily barking at the waiter, and shivering because she didn't wear enough clothes, right? And then there's me, the golden retriever sitting across the table from her, smiling away at the waiter, reassuring him that he's doing a great job, nervously drinking from everyone's water glasses, and despite not liking her very much, deeply hoping she still liked me. Of course, the key word here is *personality.* One's personality is that impression we give ourselves, (and others), of who we are: a unique pattern created from a combination of our typical thoughts, feelings, and behaviors. But I don't want to leave you with the wrong impression. While I may think that it would feel good to have strangers scratch my head in public, I tend to not do that.

Professor Keith W. Swain
Red Rocks Community College
Arvada, Colorado

PSYCHOANALYTIC/PSYCHODYNAMIC THEORIES

LEARNING OBJECTIVES

RETRIEVAL PRACTICE While reading the upcoming sections, respond to each Learning Objective in your own words. Then compare your responses with those found at www.wiley.com/college/huffman.

1. **DISCUSS** the major concepts of psychoanalytic/psychodynamic theories of personality.
2. **EXPLAIN** how Adler's, Jung's, and Horney's theories differ from Freud's thinking.
3. **EXPLORE** the major contributions and criticisms of Freud's psychoanalytic theories.

Before discussing the following psychoanalytic/psychodynamic theories, we need to provide a basic definition of **personality** as *a unique and relatively stable pattern of thoughts, feelings, and actions*. In other words, it describes how we are different from other people and what patterns of behavior are typical of us. We might qualify as an "extrovert," for example, if we're talkative and outgoing most of the time. Or we may be described as "conscientious" if we're responsible and self-disciplined most of the time. (Keep in mind that *personality* is not the same as *character*, which refers to our ethics, morals, values, and integrity.)

Personality A unique and relatively stable pattern of thoughts, feelings, and actions.

Freud's Psychoanalytic Theory

One of the earliest theories of personality was Sigmund Freud's psychoanalytic perspective, which emphasized unconscious processes and unresolved past conflicts. Working from about 1890 until he died in 1939, Freud developed a theory of personality that has been one of the most influential—and controversial—theories in all of science (Barenbaum & Winter, 2013; Bornstein et al., 2013; Cautin, 2011; Cordón, 2012). Let's examine some of Freud's most basic and debatable concepts.

Freud called the mind the "psyche" and asserted that it contains three *levels of consciousness*, or awareness: the **conscious**, the **preconscious**, and the **unconscious (Figure 11.1)**. For Freud, the unconscious is all-important because it reportedly stores our most primitive, instinctual motives, plus anxiety-laden thoughts and memories, which are normally blocked from our personal awareness. However, it supposedly still has an enormous impact on our behavior—like the hidden part of the iceberg that sunk the ocean liner *Titanic*.

Interestingly, because many of our unconscious thoughts and motives are unacceptable and threatening, Freud believed that they are normally *repressed* (held out of awareness)—unless they are unintentionally revealed by dreams or slips of the tongue, later called *Freudian slips* **(Figure 11.2)**.

Freud believed that most psychological disorders originate from repressed memories or sexual and aggressive instincts hidden in the unconscious. To treat these disorders, he developed a form of therapy called *psychoanalysis* (Chapter 13).

Conscious In Freudian terms, thoughts or motives that a person is currently aware of or is remembering.

Preconscious Freud's term for thoughts, motives, or memories that exist just beneath the surface of awareness and can be called to consciousness when necessary.

Unconscious Freud's term for a part of the psyche that stores repressed urges and primitive impulses.

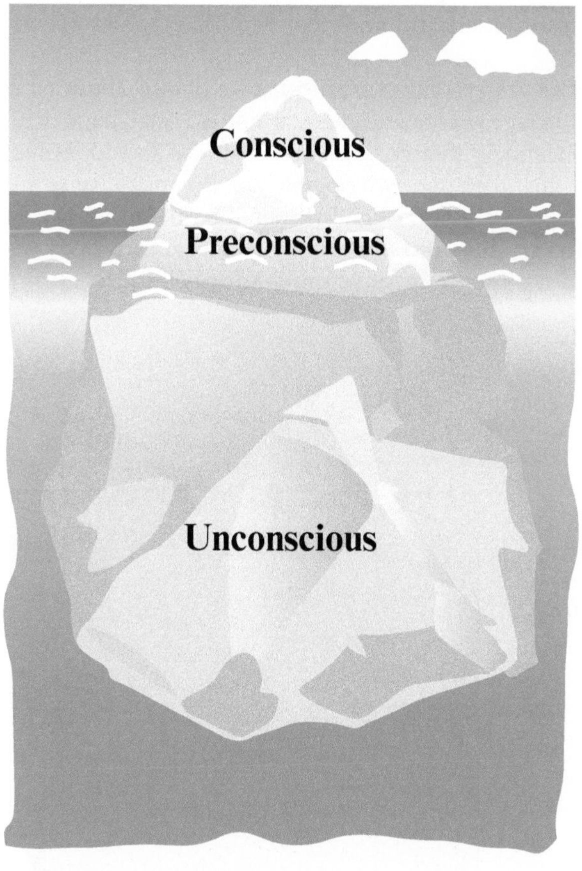

FIGURE 11.1 FREUD'S THREE LEVELS OF CONSCIOUSNESS

Although Freud never used the analogy himself, his levels of awareness are often compared to an iceberg:

- The tip of the iceberg would be analogous to the *conscious* mind, which is above the water and open to easy inspection.
- The *preconscious* mind (the area only shallowly submerged) contains information that can be viewed with a little extra effort.
- The large base of the iceberg is somewhat like the *unconscious*, completely hidden from personal inspection.

FIGURE 11.2 **FREUDIAN SLIPS**

Freud believed that a small slip of the tongue (now known as a *Freudian slip*) can reflect unconscious feelings that we normally keep hidden.

"Good morning, beheaded—uh, I mean beloved."

Id According to Freud, the primitive, unconscious component of personality that operates irrationally and acts on the pleasure principle.

Pleasure principle In Freud's theory, the principle on which the id operates—seeking immediate gratification.

Ego In Freud's theory, the rational, decision-making component of personality that operates according to the reality principle; from the Latin term *ego*, meaning "I."

Reality principle According to Freud, the principle on which the conscious ego operates as it seeks to delay gratification of the id's impulses until appropriate outlets and situations can be found.

Superego In Freud's theory, the aspect of personality that operates on the morality principle; the "conscience" that internalizes society's values, standards, and morals.

Morality principle In Freudian terms, the principle on which the superego operates; feelings of guilt result if its rules are violated.

Defense mechanisms In Freudian theory, the ego's protective method of reducing anxiety by self-deception and distorting reality.

In addition to proposing that the mind functions at three levels of consciousness, Freud also believed personality was composed of three mental structures: *id*, *ego*, and *superego* **(Figure 11.3)**.

According to Freud, the **id** is made up of innate biological instincts and urges. It is immature, impulsive, and irrational. The id is also totally unconscious and serves as the reservoir of mental energy. When its primitive drives build up, the id seeks immediate gratification to relieve the tension—a concept known as the **pleasure principle**. In other words, the id is like a newborn baby. It wants what it wants when it wants it!

Freud further believed that the second part of the psyche, the **ego**, is responsible for planning, problem solving, reasoning, and controlling the potentially destructive energy of the id. In Freud's system, the ego corresponds to the *self*—our conscious identity of ourselves as persons.

One of the ego's tasks is to channel and release the id's energy in ways that are compatible with the external world. Thus, the ego is responsible for delaying gratification when necessary. Contrary to the id's pleasure principle, the ego operates on the **reality principle** because it can understand and deal with objects and events in the real world.

The final part of the psyche to develop is the **superego**, a set of ethical rules for behavior. The superego develops from internalized parental and societal standards. It constantly strives for perfection and is therefore as unrealistic as the id. Some Freudian followers have suggested that the superego operates on the **morality principle** because violating its rules results in feelings of guilt. When the ego fails to satisfy both the id and the superego, anxiety slips into our conscious awareness. Because anxiety is uncomfortable, we avoid it through **defense mechanisms (Figure 11.4)**.

FIGURE 11.3 **FREUD'S PERSONALITY STRUCTURE**

According to Freud, personality is composed of three structures—the id, ego, and superego. Note how the ego is primarily conscious and preconscious, whereas the id is entirely unconscious.

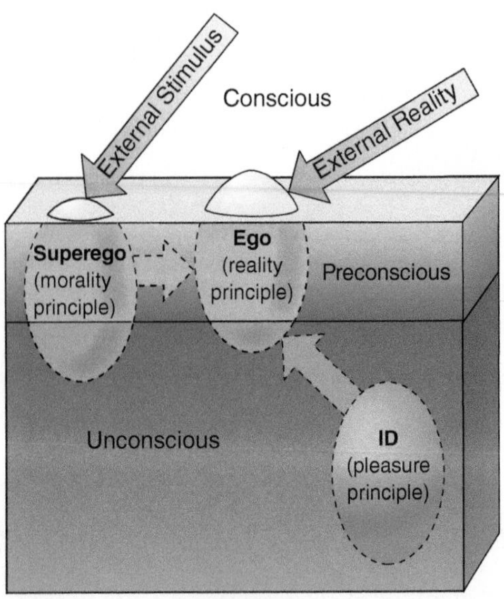

FIGURE 11.4 WHY DO WE USE DEFENSE MECHANISMS? | realworldpsychology

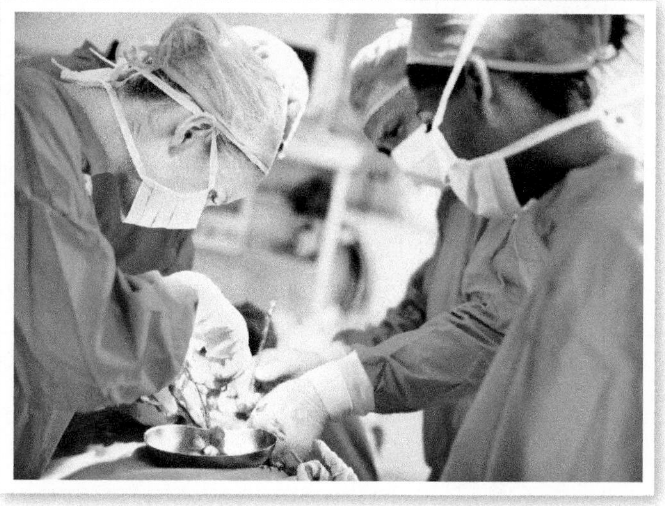

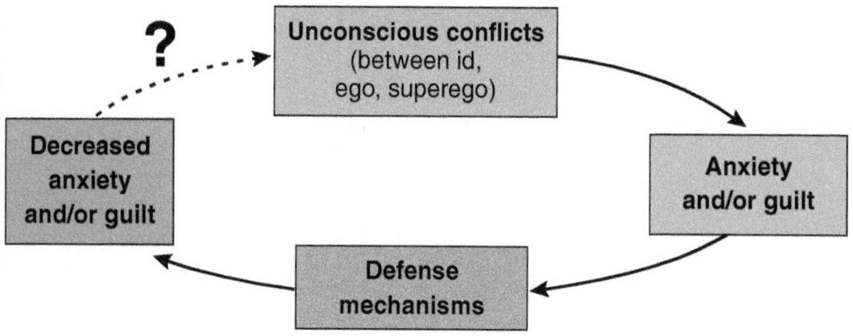

Ⓐ Freud believed defense mechanisms help us deal with unconscious conflicts, explaining why these physicians may *intellectualize* and distance themselves from the gruesome aspects of their work to avoid personal anxieties. Defense mechanisms can be healthy and helpful if we use them in moderation or on a temporary basis.

Ⓑ Unfortunately, defense mechanisms almost always distort reality, and they create some of our most dangerous habits through a vicious self-reinforcing cycle. For example, an alcoholic who uses his paycheck to buy drinks may feel very guilty, but he can easily reduce this conflict by *rationalizing* that he deserves to relax and unwind with alcohol because he works so hard.

In addition to intellectualization and rationalization (shown in Figure 11.4), Freud identified several other defense mechanisms **(Table 11.1)**.

Although defense mechanisms are now an accepted part of modern psychology, other Freudian ideas are more controversial. For example, according to Freud, strong biological urges residing within the id push all children through five universal **psychosexual stages (Figure 11.5)**. The term *psychosexual* reflects Freud's belief that children experience sexual feelings from birth (in different forms from those experienced by adolescents or adults).

Psychosexual stages In Freudian theory, five developmental periods (oral, anal, phallic, latency, and genital) during which particular kinds of pleasures must be gratified if personality development is to proceed normally.

TABLE 11.1 SAMPLE PSYCHOLOGICAL DEFENSE MECHANISMS

Defense Mechanism	Description	Example
Repression	Preventing painful or unacceptable thoughts from entering consciousness	Forgetting the details of a tragic accident
Sublimation	Redirecting socially unacceptable impulses into acceptable activities	Redirecting aggressive impulses by becoming a professional fighter
Denial	Refusing to accept an unpleasant reality	Alcoholics refusing to admit their addiction
Rationalization	Creating a socially acceptable excuse to justify unacceptable behavior	Justifying cheating on an exam by saying "everyone else does it"
Intellectualization	Ignoring the emotional aspects of a painful experience by focusing on abstract thoughts, words, or ideas	Discussing your divorce without emotion while ignoring underlying pain
Projection	Transferring unacceptable thoughts, motives, or impulses to others	Becoming unreasonably jealous of your mate while denying your own attraction to others
Reaction formation	Not acknowledging unacceptable impulses and overemphasizing their opposite	Promoting a petition against adult bookstores even though you are secretly fascinated by pornography
Regression	Reverting to immature ways of responding	Throwing a temper tantrum when a friend doesn't want to do what you'd like
Displacement	Redirecting impulses from the original source toward a less threatening person or object	Yelling at a coworker after being criticized by your boss

FIGURE 11.5 FREUD'S FIVE PSYCHOSEXUAL STAGES OF DEVELOPMENT

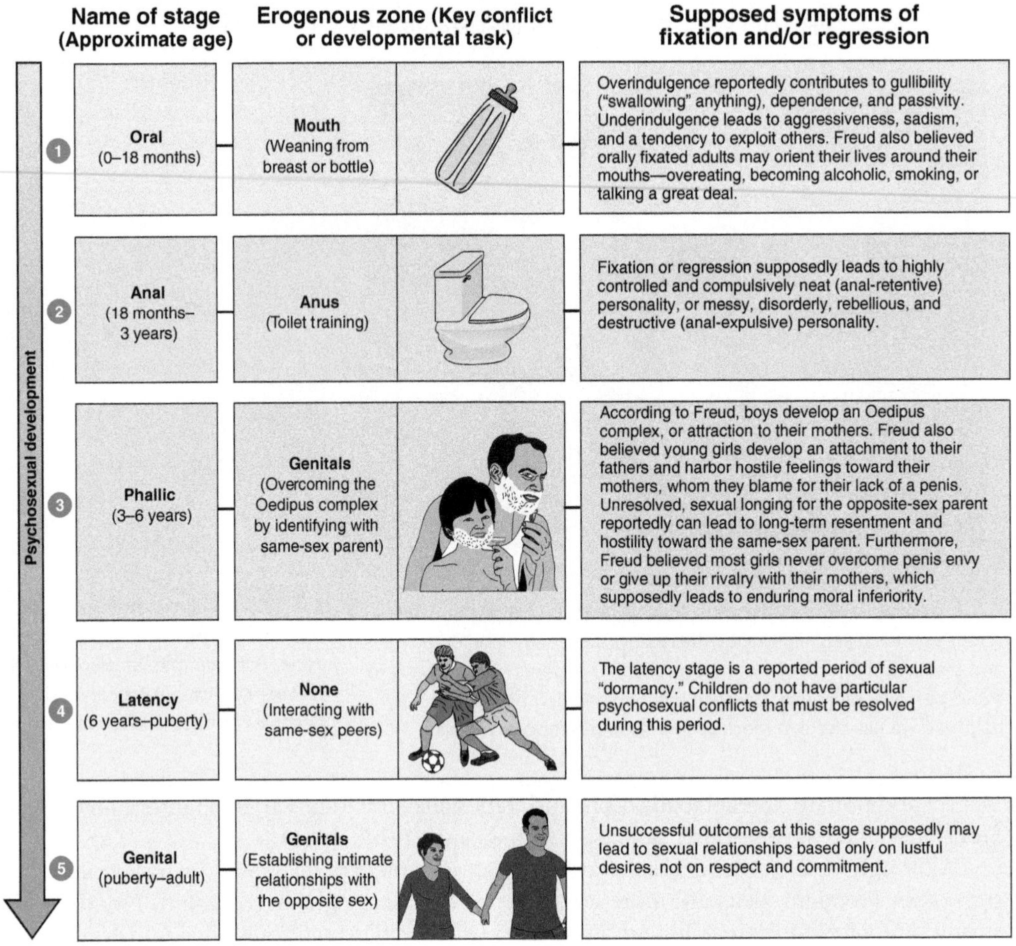
Name of stage (Approximate age)
Erogenous zone (Key conflict or developmental task)
Supposed symptoms of fixation and/or regression
Psychosexual development
1 Oral (0–18 months)
Mouth (Weaning from breast or bottle)
Overindulgence reportedly contributes to gullibility ("swallowing" anything), dependence, and passivity. Underindulgence leads to aggressiveness, sadism, and a tendency to exploit others. Freud also believed orally fixated adults may orient their lives around their mouths—overeating, becoming alcoholic, smoking, or talking a great deal.
2 Anal (18 months–3 years)
Anus (Toilet training)
Fixation or regression supposedly leads to highly controlled and compulsively neat (anal-retentive) personality, or messy, disorderly, rebellious, and destructive (anal-expulsive) personality.
3 Phallic (3–6 years)
Genitals (Overcoming the Oedipus complex by identifying with same-sex parent)
According to Freud, boys develop an Oedipus complex, or attraction to their mothers. Freud also believed young girls develop an attachment to their fathers and harbor hostile feelings toward their mothers, whom they blame for their lack of a penis. Unresolved, sexual longing for the opposite-sex parent reportedly can lead to long-term resentment and hostility toward the same-sex parent. Furthermore, Freud believed most girls never overcome penis envy or give up their rivalry with their mothers, which supposedly leads to enduring moral inferiority.
4 Latency (6 years–puberty)
None (Interacting with same-sex peers)
The latency stage is a reported period of sexual "dormancy." Children do not have particular psychosexual conflicts that must be resolved during this period.
5 Genital (puberty–adult)
Genitals (Establishing intimate relationships with the opposite sex)
Unsuccessful outcomes at this stage supposedly may lead to sexual relationships based only on lustful desires, not on respect and commitment.

Inferiority complex Adler's idea that feelings of inferiority develop from early childhood experiences of helplessness and incompetence.

Freud held that if a child's needs are not met or are overindulged at one particular psychosexual stage, the child may become *fixated*, and a part of his or her personality will remain stuck at that stage. Furthermore, under stress, individuals supposedly may return, or *regress*, to a stage at which earlier needs were frustrated or overly gratified. Obviously, Freud's theory does not imply that children should engage in sexual activity with each other, or with adults; such activity is clearly abuse and can have lasting consequences.

FIGURE 11.6 AN UPSIDE TO FEELINGS OF INFERIORITY?

Adler suggested that the will-to-power could be positively expressed through social interest—by identifying with others and cooperating with them for the social good. Can you explain how these volunteers might be fulfilling their will-to-power interest?

© Hero Images/Corbis

Psychodynamic/Neo-Freudian Theories

Some initial followers of Freud later rebelled and proposed theories of their own; they became known as *neo-Freudians*.

Alfred Adler (1870–1937) was the first to leave Freud's inner circle. Instead of seeing behavior as motivated by unconscious forces, Adler believed it is purposeful and goal directed. According to his *individual psychology*, we are motivated by our goals in life—especially our goals of obtaining security and overcoming feelings of inferiority (Carlson & Englar-Carlson, 2013).

Adler believed that almost everyone suffers from an **inferiority complex**, or deep feelings of inadequacy and incompetence that arise from our feelings of helplessness as infants. According to Adler, these early feelings result in a "will-to-power" that can take one of two paths. It can lead children to strive to develop superiority over others through dominance, aggression, or expressions of envy. Or, on a more positive note, it can encourage them to develop their full potential and creativity and to gain mastery and control in their lives (Adler, 1964, 1998) **(Figure 11.6)**.

Another early Freud follower turned dissenter, Carl Jung [Yoong], developed *analytical psychology*. Like Freud, Jung (1875–1961) emphasized unconscious processes, but he believed that the unconscious contains positive and spiritual motives as well as sexual and aggressive forces.

Jung also thought that we have two forms of unconscious mind: the personal unconscious and the collective unconscious. The *personal unconscious* is created from our individual experiences, whereas the **collective unconscious** is identical in each person and is inherited (Jung, 1946, 1959, 1969). The collective unconscious consists of primitive images and patterns of thought, feeling, and behavior that Jung called **archetypes (Figure 11.7)**.

Collective unconscious Jung's concept of the part of an individual's unconscious that is inherited, evolutionarily developed, and common to all members of the species.

Archetypes According to Jung, the universal, inherited, primitive, and symbolic representations of a particular experience or object, which reside in the collective unconscious.

Because of archetypal patterns in the collective unconscious, we perceive and react in certain predictable ways. One set of archetypes refers to gender roles (Chapter 9). Jung claimed that both males and females have patterns for feminine aspects of personality—*anima*—and masculine aspects of personality—*animus*—which allow us to express both masculine and feminine personality traits and to understand the opposite sex.

Like Adler and Jung, psychoanalyst Karen Horney [HORN-eye] was an influential follower of Freud who later came to reject major aspects of Freudian theory. She is credited with having developed a creative blend of Freudian, Adlerian, and Jungian theory, along with the first feminist critique of Freud's theory (Horney, 1939, 1945). Horney emphasized women's positive traits and suggested that most of Freud's ideas about female personality reflected male bias and misunderstanding. For example, she proposed that women's everyday experience with social inferiority led to power envy, not to Freud's idea of biological *penis envy*.

Horney also emphasized that personality development depends largely on social relationships—particularly on the relationship between parent and child. She believed that when a child's needs are not met by nurturing parents, the child may develop lasting feelings of helplessness and insecurity. The way people respond to this so-called **basic anxiety**, in Horney's view, sets the stage for later adult psychological health. She believed that everyone copes with this basic anxiety in one of

Basic anxiety According to Horney, feelings of helplessness and insecurity that adults experience because as children they felt alone and isolated in a hostile environment.

Roger Wood/Corbis

FIGURE 11.7 ARCHETYPES IN THE COLLECTIVE UNCONSCIOUS?

According to Jung, the collective unconscious is the ancestral memory of the human race and explains similarities in religion, art, symbolism, and dream imagery across cultures, such as the repeated symbol of the snake in ancient Egyptian tomb painting. Can you think of other explanations, such as the fact that snakes pose an evolutionary danger across time and cultures?

three ways—we move toward, away from, or against other people—and that psychological health requires a balance among these three styles.

In sum, Horney proposed that our adult personalities are shaped by our childhood relationship with our parents—not by fixation or regression at some stage of psychosexual development, as Freud argued.

FIGURE 11.8 ORAL FIXATION OR SIMPLE SELF-SOOTHING?

Is this an example of Freud's earliest stage of psychosexual development, or just a part of all infants' normal sucking behaviors?

© PonyWang/iStockphoto

Evaluating Psychoanalytic Theories

Before going on, let's consider the major criticisms of Freud's psychoanalytic theories:

- **Inadequate empirical support** Many psychoanalytic concepts—such as the psychosexual stages—cannot be empirically tested.
- **Overemphasis on sexuality, biology, and unconscious forces** Modern psychologists believe Freud underestimated the role of learning and culture in shaping personality **(Figure 11.8)**.
- **Sexism** Many psychologists, beginning with Karen Horney, reject Freud's theories as derogatory toward women.

In contrast to the claim of inadequate empirical support, numerous modern studies have supported certain Freudian concepts like the defense mechanisms and the belief that a lot of our information processing occurs outside our conscious awareness (*automatic processing*, Chapter 5, and *implicit memories*, Chapter 7). In addition, a recent study found that people who identify as having a heterosexual orientation but show a strong sexual attraction to same-sex people in psychological tests tend to have more homophobic attitudes and higher levels of hostility toward gay people (Weinstein et al., 2012). Can you see how Freud's theory might suggest that these negative attitudes and beliefs spring from unconscious repression of same-sex desires? Moreover, many contemporary clinicians still value Freud's insights about childhood experiences and unconscious influences on personality development (Bornstein et al., 2013; Celes, 2010; De Sousa, 2011; Kring et al., 2012; Siegel, 2010). Q1

Today there are few Freudian purists. Instead, modern psychodynamic theorists and psychoanalysts tend to place less emphasis on sexual instincts and more on sociocultural influences on personality development.

RETRIEVAL PRACTICE: PSYCHOANALYTIC/PSYCHODYNAMIC THEORIES

Self-Test

Completing this self-test and comparing your answers with those in Appendix B provides immediate feedback and helpful practice for exams. Additional interactive, self-tests are available at www.wiley.com/college/huffman.

1. _____ is defined as a unique and relatively stable pattern of thoughts, feelings, and actions.

a. Character
b. Trait
c. Temperament
d. Personality

2. In Freudian terms, the _____ operates on the pleasure principle, seeking immediate gratification. The _____ operates on the reality principle, and the _____ contains the conscience and operates on the morality principle.

a. psyche; ego; id
b. id; ego; superego
c. conscious; preconscious; unconscious
d. oral stage; anal stage; phallic stage

3. According to Freud, when anxiety slips into our conscious awareness, we tend to avoid it through the use of _____.

a. latency overcompensation
b. the Oedipus complex
c. regression to the oral stage
d. defense mechanisms

4. Used excessively, defense mechanisms can be dangerous because they _____.

a. block intellectualization
b. become ineffective
c. distort reality
d. become fixated

5. Three of the most influential neo-Freudians were _____.

a. Plato, Aristotle, and Descartes
b. Dr. Laura, Dr. Phil, and Dr. Ruth
c. Adler, Jung, and Horney
d. None of these options

Think Critically

1. If scientists have so many problems with Freud, why do you think his theories are still popular with the public? Should psychologists continue to discuss his theories (and include them in textbooks)?
2. What is a possible example of sexism in Freud's psychoanalytic theory?

realworldpsychology

Are some people with highly negative attitudes toward gay people repressing their own sexual desires?

HINT: LOOK IN THE MARGIN FOR Q1

TRAIT THEORIES

RETRIEVAL PRACTICE While reading the upcoming sections, respond to each Learning Objective in your own words. Then compare your responses with those found at www.wiley.com/college/huffman.

LEARNING OBJECTIVES

1. **EXPLAIN** how early trait theorists approached the study of personality.
2. **IDENTIFY** the Big Five personality traits.
3. **SUMMARIZE** the major contributions and criticisms of trait theory.

Think for a moment about the key personality characteristics of your best friend. For example, you might say: *He's a great guy who's a lot of fun to be with. But I sometimes get tired of his constant jokes and pranks. On the other hand, he does listen well and will be serious when I need him to be.*

When describing another's personality, we generally use terms that refer to that person's most frequent and typical characteristics ("fun," "constant jokes and pranks," "listens well"). These unique and defining characteristics are the foundation for the *trait approach*, which seeks to discover what characteristics form the core of human personality.

Early Trait Theorists

An early study of dictionary terms found almost 4,500 words that described personality **traits** (Allport & Odbert, 1936). Faced with this enormous list, Gordon Allport (1937) believed that the best way to understand personality was to arrange a person's unique personality traits into a hierarchy, with the most pervasive or important traits at the top.

Trait A relatively stable personality characteristic that can be used to describe someone.

Later psychologists reduced the list of possible personality traits using a statistical technique called *factor analysis*, in which large arrays of data are grouped into more basic units (factors). Raymond Cattell (1950, 1965, 1990) condensed the list of traits to 16 source traits. Hans Eysenck (1967, 1982, 1990) reduced the list even further. He described personality as a relationship among three basic types of traits: *extroversion–introversion*, *neuroticism* (the tendency toward insecurity, anxiety, guilt, and moodiness), and *psychoticism* (being out of touch with reality).

Modern Trait Theory

Five-factor model (FFM) A comprehensive descriptive personality system that includes openness, conscientiousness, extroversion, agreeableness, and neuroticism; informally called the Big Five.

Factor analysis was also used to develop the most promising modern trait theory, the **five-factor model (FFM)** (Costa & McCrae, 2011; McCrae & Costa, 2013; Soto et al., 2011). A handy way to remember this model is to note that the first letters of the five words spell *ocean* **(Figure 11.9)**.

Combining previous research findings and the long list of possible personality traits, researchers discovered that these five traits came up repeatedly, even when different tests were used:

O Openness People who rate high in this factor are original, imaginative, curious, open to new ideas, artistic, and interested in cultural pursuits. Low scorers tend to be conventional, down-to-earth, narrower in their interests, and not artistic. Interestingly, critical thinkers tend to score higher than others on this factor (Clifford et al., 2004).

C Conscientiousness This factor ranges from responsible, self-disciplined, organized, and achieving at the high end to irresponsible, careless, impulsive, lazy, and undependable at the other.

E Extroversion This factor contrasts people who are sociable, outgoing, talkative, fun loving, and affectionate at the high end with introverted individuals who tend to be withdrawn, quiet, passive, and reserved at the low end.

A Agreeableness Individuals who score high in this factor are good-natured, warm, gentle, cooperative, trusting, and helpful, whereas low scorers are irritable, argumentative, ruthless, suspicious, uncooperative, and vindictive.

N Neuroticism (*or emotional stability*) People who score high in neuroticism are emotionally unstable and prone to insecurity, anxiety, guilt, worry, and moodiness. People at the other end are emotionally stable, calm, even-tempered, easygoing, and relaxed.

FIGURE 11.9 **THE FIVE-FACTOR MODEL (FFM)**

Different adjectives may describe your personality, depending on whether you score high or low in each of the "Big Five" traits. Note that the lines on the right, below each of the five factors, indicate that scores on each factor exist on a continuum from low scorers to high scorers.

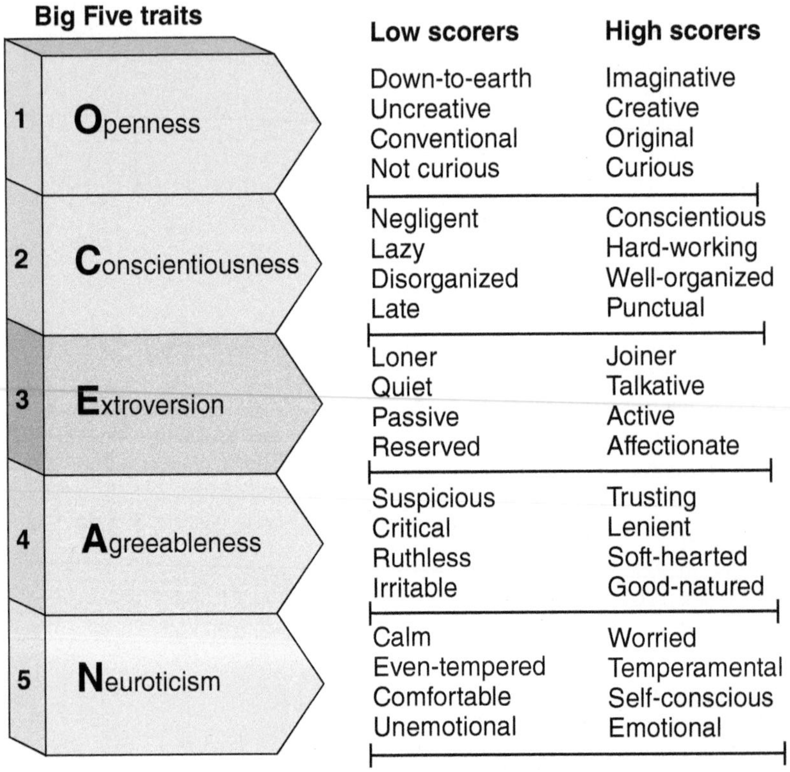

Big Five traits
1 Openness
2 Conscientiousness
3 Extroversion
4 Agreeableness
5 Neuroticism
Low scorers
High scorers
Down-to-earth
Uncreative
Conventional
Not curious
Imaginative
Creative
Original
Curious
Negligent
Lazy
Disorganized
Late
Conscientious
Hard-working
Well-organized
Punctual
Loner
Quiet
Passive
Reserved
Joiner
Talkative
Active
Affectionate
Suspicious
Critical
Ruthless
Irritable
Trusting
Lenient
Soft-hearted
Good-natured
Calm
Even-tempered
Comfortable
Unemotional
Worried
Temperamental
Self-conscious
Emotional

This five-factor model (FFM) has led to numerous research follow-ups and intriguing insights about personality. For example, researchers who examined personality traits in 243 people age 95 and older discovered that these older adults were more likely to show particular traits, such as optimism, extraversion, and conscientiousness. They also were less likely to show other traits, such as negative affect (Kato et al., 2012). Can you see how these findings indicate that personality traits may help predict how long we live?

What about nonhuman animals? Do you think they have distinct personalities? If so, do they also have specific personality traits that might be associated with a longer life span? (See *Psych Science*.)

Evaluating Trait Theories

The five-factor model (FFM) is the first model to achieve the major goal of trait theory—to describe and organize personality characteristics using the smallest number of traits. There also is strong cross-cultural research support for the FFM. Psychologist David Buss and his colleagues (1989, 1990, 2003) surveyed more than 10,000 men and women from 37

PSYCHSCIENCE

DO ANIMALS HAVE UNIQUE PERSONALITIES?

Martin Harvey/Digital Vision/Getty Images

Pet owners have long believed that their dogs and cats have unique personalities, and a growing body of research tends to agree with them (Brodin et al., 2013; Gosling & John, 1999; Zuckerman, 2013). Moreover, the use of personality ratings has become a common tool for managing farm and zoo animals (Grand et al., 2012).

Dog lovers might be interested in knowing that when 78 dogs of all shapes and sizes were rated by both owners and strangers, a strong correlation was found on traits such as affection versus aggression, anxiety versus calmness, and intelligence versus stupidity. Researchers also found that personalities vary widely within a breed, which means that not all pit bulls are aggressive and not all Labrador retrievers are affectionate (Gosling et al., 2004).

To discover whether particular personality traits were associated with a longer life expectancy in nonhuman animals, researchers studied 298 gorillas in zoos and sanctuaries across North America. Using standardized measures similar to the FFM, they asked zoo keepers, volunteers, researchers, and caretakers who knew the gorillas well to score each gorilla's personality. With these scorings, they reliably identified four distinct personality traits: *dominance*, *extroversion*, *neuroticism*, and *agreeableness* (Weiss et al., 2013).

Next, the researchers examined the association between levels of each of these personality traits and life expectancy. They found that gorillas scoring high on extroversion, which included behaviors such as sociability, activity, play, and curiosity, lived longer lives. This link was found in both male and female gorillas and across all the different types of environments in which this research was conducted.

What might explain this link? One possibility is that extroverted ape—just like extroverted people—develop stronger social networks, which helps increase survival and reduce stress. Can you think of other possible explanations?

RESEARCH CHALLENGE

1. Based on the information provided, did this study (Weiss et al., 2013) use descriptive, correlational, and/or experimental research?
2. If you chose:
   - descriptive research, is this a naturalistic observation, survey/interview, case study, or archival research?
   - correlational research, is this a positive, negative, or zero correlation?
   - experimental research, label the IV, DV, experimental group(s), and control group.

>>CHECK YOUR ANSWERS IN APPENDIX B.

NOTE: The information provided in this study is admittedly limited, but the level of detail is similar to what is presented in most textbooks and public reports of research findings. Answering these questions, and then comparing your answers to those in the Appendix, will help you become a better critical thinker and consumer of scientific research.

countries and found a surprising level of agreement in the characteristics that men and women value in a mate **(Table 11.2)**. Note that both sexes tend to prefer mates with traits that closely match the FFM—dependability (conscientiousness), emotional stability (low neuroticism), pleasing disposition (agreeableness), and sociability (extroversion) to the alternatives.

Why is there such a high degree of shared preferences for certain personality traits? Scientists suggest that these traits may provide an evolutionary advantage to people who are more conscientious, extroverted, and agreeable—and less neurotic. The evolutionary advantage also is confirmed by other cross-cultural studies (Brumbaugh & Wood, 2013; Figueredo et al., 2011; McCrae, 2011; Rushton & Irwing, 2011) and comparative studies with dogs, chimpanzees, and other species (Adams, 2011; Gosling, 2008; Mehta & Gosling, 2006; Weiss et al., 2013).

TABLE 11.2 MATE PREFERENCES AND THE FIVE-FACTOR MODEL (FFM) | realworldpsychology

What Men Want in a Mate	What Women Want in a Mate
1. Mutual attraction—love	1. Mutual attraction—love
2. Dependable character	2. Dependable character
3. Emotional stability and maturity	3. Emotional stability and maturity
4. Pleasing disposition	4. Pleasing disposition
5. Good health	5. Education and intelligence
6. Education and intelligence	6. Sociability
7. Sociability	7. Good health
8. Desire for home and children	8. Desire for home and children
9. Refinement, neatness	9. Ambition and industriousness
10. Good looks	10. Refinement, neatness

Source: Based on Buss et al., 1990.

© Michelle Marsan/Shutterstock

Q2

In addition to having strong cross-cultural support, trait theories, like the FFM, allow us to predict real-life preferences and behaviors. For example, using the FFM, people who are extraverted have been found to prefer upbeat, energetic, and rhythmic types of music, such as rap and hip-hop. People who are open to experience prefer complex, intense, and rebellious music, such as classical and rock (Langemeyer et al., 2012). As you might expect, personality may also affect your career choice and job satisfaction (see *Test Yourself*).

TEST YOURSELF: MATCHING YOUR PERSONALITY WITH YOUR CAREER

psychology and you

Are some people better suited for certain jobs than others? According to psychologist John Holland's *personality-job-fit theory*, a match (or "good fit") between our individual personality and our career choice is a major factor in determining job satisfaction (Holland, 1985, 1994). Research shows that a good fit between personality and occupation helps increase subjective well-being, job success, and job satisfaction. In other words, people tend to be happier and like their work when they're well matched to their jobs (Joeng et al., 2013; Perkmen & Sahin, 2013; Williamson & Lounsbury, 2013). Check this table to see what job would be a good match for your personality.

Personality Characteristics	Holland Personality Type	Matching/Congruent Occupations
Shy, genuine, persistent, stable, conforming, practical	1. *Realistic:* Prefers physical activities that require skill, strength, and coordination	Mechanic, drill press operator, assembly-line worker, farmer
Analytical, original, curious, independent	2. *Investigative:* Prefers activities that involve thinking, organizing, and understanding	Biologist, economist, mathematician, news reporter
Sociable, friendly, cooperative, understanding	3. *Social:* Prefers activities that involve helping and developing others	Social worker, counselor, teacher, clinical psychologist
Conforming, efficient, practical, unimaginative, inflexible	4. *Conventional:* Prefers rule-regulated, orderly, and unambiguous activities	Accountant, bank teller, file clerk, manager
Imaginative, disorderly, idealistic, emotional, impractical	5. *Artistic:* Prefers ambiguous and unsystematic activities that allow creative expression	Painter, musician, writer, interior decorator
Self-confident, ambitious, energetic, domineering	6. *Enterprising:* Prefers verbal activities with opportunities to influence others and attain power	Lawyer, real estate agent, public relations specialist, small business manager

Source: Adapted and reproduced with special permission of the publisher, Psychological Assessment Resources, Inc., 16204 North Florida Avenue, Lutz, Florida 33549, from the *Dictionary of Holland Occupational Codes*, 3rd edition, by Gary D. Gottfredson, Ph.D., and John L. Holland, Ph.D., Copyright 1982, 1989, 1996. Further reproduction is prohibited without permission from PAR, Inc.

Trait theories, particularly the FFM, have proven to be successful at *describing* personality and predicting certain behaviors and preferences. However, critics argue that they fail to consider situational determinants of personality or to offer sufficient *explanations* for why people develop specific traits (Chamorro-Premuzic, 2011; Cheung et al., 2011; Furguson et al., 2011). And although trait theories have documented fairly high levels of personality stability over the life span, they have failed to identify which characteristics last a lifetime and which are most likely to change (Allemand et al., 2013; Boyce et al., 2013; Kandler et al., 2012; McCrae, 2011).

realworldpsychology **Can Personality Change?** Prior to serving jail time for dog fighting, NFL quarterback Michael Vick relied almost exclusively on his natural athletic ability. Out of jail, he became a great teammate—the first to the field and the last to leave, and in 2010, he was named NFL's "Comeback Player of the Year" (Wilner, 2011). Do you think this change is permanent? Why or why not?

Jonathan Ernst/Getty Images, Inc.

RETRIEVAL PRACTICE: TRAIT THEORIES

Self-Test

Completing this self-test and comparing your answers with those in Appendix B provides immediate feedback and helpful practice for exams. Additional interactive, self-tests are available at www.wiley.com/college/huffman.

1. _____ is a statistical technique that groups large arrays of data into more basic units.

a. MMPI
b. FFM
c. Factor analysis
d. Regression analysis

2. What are the "Big Five" personality traits in the five-factor model?

a. conscientiousness, openness, extroversion, agreeableness, and neuroticism
b. openness, conscientiousness, introversion, agreeableness, and neuroticism
c. shyness, conscientiousness, extroversion, agreeableness, and neuroticism
d. shyness, conscientiousness, introversion, agreeableness, and neuroticism

3. People who score high in _____ are emotionally unstable and prone to insecurity, anxiety, guilt, worry, and moodiness.

a. openness
b. conscientiousness
c. extroversion
d. neuroticism

4. Trait theories of personality have been criticized for _____.

a. failing to explain why people develop specific traits
b. not including a large number of central traits
c. failing to identify which traits last and which are transient
d. not considering situational determinants of personality
e. all but one of these options

Think Critically

1 After reading the descriptions for each of the Big Five personality dimensions, how well do you think they describe your key traits? Thinking of someone you know very well, can you predict how he or she might score on each of these traits?

2 What limitations do you believe trait theory has when we are looking at human development over the life span?

realworldpsychology

Can personality traits predict the type of music we like?

HINT: LOOK IN THE MARGIN FOR Q2

HUMANISTIC THEORIES

LEARNING OBJECTIVES

RETRIEVAL PRACTICE While reading the upcoming sections, respond to each Learning Objective in your own words. Then compare your responses with those found at www.wiley.com/college/Huffman.

1. **EXPLAIN** the importance of the self in Rogers's theory of personality.
2. **DESCRIBE** how Maslow's hierarchy of needs affects personality.
3. **IDENTIFY** the pros and cons of humanistic theories.

Humanistic theories of personality emphasize each person's internal feelings, thoughts, and sense of basic worth. In contrast to Freud's generally negative view of human nature, humanists believe that people are naturally good (or, at worst, neutral) and that they possess a natural tendency toward **self-actualization**, the inborn drive to develop all their talents and capabilities.

Self-actualization The humanistic term for the inborn drive to realize one's full potential and to develop all one's inherent talents and capabilities.

According to this view, our personality and behavior depend on how we perceive and interpret the world, not on traits, unconscious impulses, or rewards and punishments. Humanistic psychology was developed largely by Carl Rogers and Abraham Maslow.

Rogers's Theory

To psychologist Carl Rogers (1902–1987), the most important component of personality is our **self-concept**, the way we see and feel about ourselves. Rogers emphasized that mental health and adjustment reflect the degree of overlap (congruence) between our perceived real and ideal selves (see *Test Yourself*). This self-perception is relatively stable over time and develops from our life experiences, particularly the feedback and perception of others.

Self-concept A person's relatively stable self-perception, or mental model, based on life experiences, particularly the feedback and perception of others.

TEST YOURSELF: MEASURING YOUR PERSONAL SELF-CONCEPT

psychology and you

Stop for a moment and briefly describe yourself as you'd *ideally* like to be and as how you *actually* are. Now draw two circles, labeled "real self" and "ideal self," depicting how much your two perceived selves overlap. According to Carl Rogers, if your *real* self and *ideal* self are nearly the same, with considerable overlap in the two circles, you have congruence between your two "selves" and a positive self-concept. Unfortunately, many people have experienced negative life events and feedback from others that have led to negative self-concepts. In Rogers's view, poor mental health and personality maladjustment develop from a mismatch, or *incongruence*, between our ideal and real selves.

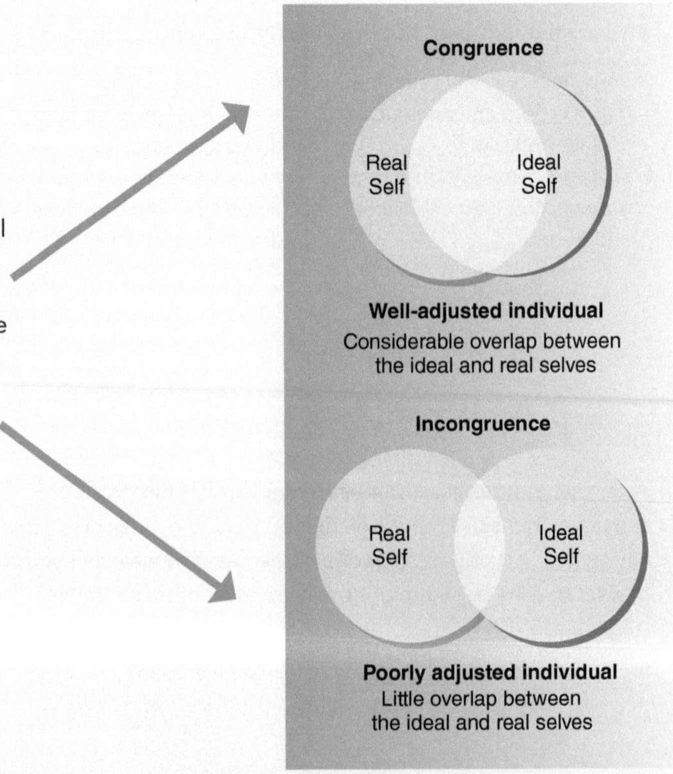

Why do some people develop negative self-concepts and poor mental health? Rogers believed that such outcomes generally result from early childhood experiences with parents and other adults who make their love and acceptance *conditional* and contingent on behaving in certain ways and expressing only certain feelings. Imagine being a child who is repeatedly told that your naturally occurring negative feelings and behaviors (which we all have) are totally unacceptable and unlovable. Can you see how your self-concept may become distorted? And why as an adult you might develop a shy, avoidant personality, always doubting the love and approval of others because they don't know "the real person hiding inside"?

To help children develop their fullest personality and life potential, Rogers cautioned that adults need to create an atmosphere of **unconditional positive regard**—a warm and caring environment in which a child is never disapproved of as a person. Interestingly, parents who engage in responsive caregiving, a form of unconditional positive regard, also tend to show this same pattern of behavior toward their spouses, which in turn leads to higher levels of relationship satisfaction (Millings et al., 2013). This suggests that unconditional positive regard is important in all types of relationships.

Q3

This is *not* to say that adults must approve of everything a child does. Rogers emphasizes that we must separate the value of the person from his or her behaviors—encouraging the person's innate positive nature, while discouraging destructive or hostile behaviors. Humanistic psychologists in general suggest that both children and adults must control their behavior so they can develop a healthy self-concept and satisfying relationships with others **(Figure 11.10)**.

Unconditional positive regard Rogers's term for love and acceptance with no contingencies attached.

Maslow's Theory

Like Rogers, Abraham Maslow believed there is a basic goodness to human nature and a natural tendency toward *self-actualization*. Maslow saw personality development as a natural progression from lower to higher levels—a basic *hierarchy of needs*. As newborns, we focus on physiological needs like hunger and thirst, and then as we grow

David Laurens/PhotoAlto/Corbis

FIGURE 11.10 UNCONDITIONAL POSITIVE REGARD

In response to a child who is angry and hits his younger sister, the parent acknowledges that it is the behavior that is unacceptable, and not the child: "I know you're angry with your sister, but we don't hit. And you won't be able to play with her for a while unless you control your anger."

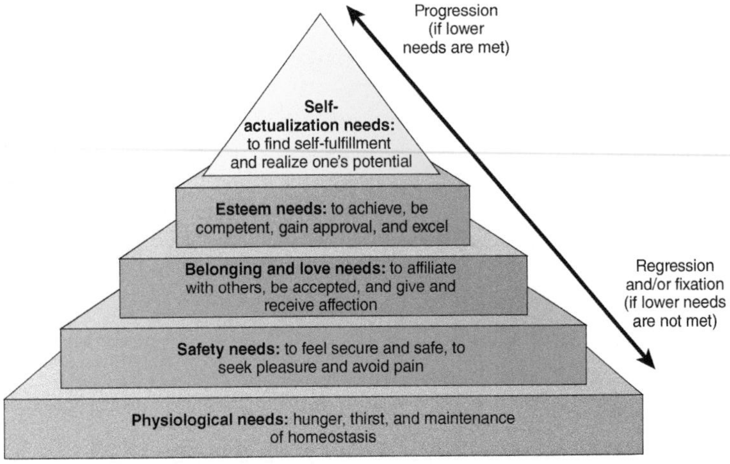

Timothy A Clary/AFP/Getty Images

FIGURE 11.11 MASLOW'S HIERARCHY OF NEEDS

Although our natural movement is upward from physical needs toward the highest level, *self-actualization*, Maslow also believed we sometimes "regress" toward a lower level—especially under stressful conditions. For example, during national disasters, people first rush to stockpile food and water (physiological needs) and then often clamor for a strong leader to take over, enforce the rules, and make things right (safety needs).

and develop, we move on through four higher levels **(Figure 11.11)**. Cross-cultural support for Maslow's theory comes from recent surveys of people from 123 countries, which found that people from around the world do share a focus on the same basic needs, and when those needs are met, they report higher levels of happiness.

According to Maslow, self-actualization is the inborn drive to develop all our talents and capacities. It requires understanding our own potential, accepting ourselves and others as unique individuals, and taking a problem-centered approach to life (Maslow, 1970). Self-actualization is an ongoing process of growth rather than an end product or accomplishment.

Maslow believed that only a few, rare individuals, such as Albert Einstein, Mohandas Gandhi, and Eleanor Roosevelt, become fully self-actualized. However, he saw self-actualization as part of every person's basic hierarchy of needs. (See Chapter 10 for more information about Maslow's theory.)

Evaluating Humanistic Theories

Humanistic psychology was extremely popular during the 1960s and 1970s. It was seen as a refreshing new perspective on personality after the negative determinism of the psychoanalytic approach and the mechanical nature of learning theories (Chapter 6). Although this early popularity has declined, humanistic theories have provided valuable insights that are useful for personal growth and self-understanding. They also play a major role in contemporary counseling and psychotherapy, as well as in modern childrearing, education, and managerial practices (DeRobertis, 2013; Greenberg et al., 2013; Tennen et al., 2013).

However, humanistic theories have also been criticized (Cervone & Pervin, 2010; Chamorro-Premuzic, 2011; Funder, 2000; Schmid, 2013) for the following:

1. **Naïve assumptions** Some critics suggest that humanistic theories are unduly optimistic and overlook the negative aspects of human nature. For example, how would humanists explain immoral politicians, the spread of terrorism, and humankind's ongoing history of war and murder?
2. **Poor testability and inadequate evidence** Like many psychoanalytic terms and concepts, humanistic concepts such as unconditional positive regard and self-actualization are difficult to define operationally and to test scientifically.
3. **Narrowness** Like trait theories, humanistic theories have been criticized for merely describing personality rather than explaining it. For example, where does the motivation for self-actualization come from? To say that it is an "inborn drive" doesn't satisfy those who favor using experimental research and hard data to learn about personality.

RETRIEVAL PRACTICE: HUMANISTIC THEORIES

Self-Test

Completing this self-test and comparing your answers with those in Appendix B provides immediate feedback and helpful practice for exams. Additional interactive, self-tests are available at www.wiley.com/college/huffman.

1. The _____ approach emphasizes internal experiences, like feelings, thoughts, and the basic worth of the individual.

a. humanistic b. psychodynamic
c. personalistic d. motivational

2. Rogers suggested that _____ is necessary for a child to develop his or her fullest personality and life potential.

a. authoritative parenting b. a challenging environment
c. unconditional positive regard d. a friendly neighborhood

3. _____ believed in the basic goodness of individuals and their natural tendency toward self-actualization.

a. Karen Horney b. Alfred Adler
c. Abraham Maslow d. Carl Jung

4. A major criticism of humanistic psychology is that most of its concepts and assumptions _____.

a. are invalid b. are unreliable
c. cannot be tested scientifically d. lack a theoretical foundation

Think Critically

1. Do you agree with Rogers that unconditional positive regard from parents is key to healthy personality development? Why or why not?
2. Thinking of the traits of a fully self-actualized person, can you identify someone who exhibits all or most of these qualities? What criticism of humanistic theories is also a weakness of trait theories?

realworldpsychology

What parenting skills are also associated with increased marital satisfaction?

HINT: LOOK IN THE MARGIN FOR Q3

SOCIAL-COGNITIVE THEORIES

RETRIEVAL PRACTICE While reading the upcoming sections, respond to each Learning Objective in your own words. Then compare your responses with those found at www.wiley.com/college/Huffman.

LEARNING OBJECTIVES

1. **EXPLAIN** Bandura's concept of self-efficacy and Rotter's concept of locus of control.
2. **SUMMARIZE** the attractions and criticisms of the social-cognitive perspective on personality.

As you've just seen, psychoanalytic/psychodynamic, trait, and humanistic theories all tend to focus on internal, personal factors in personality development. In contrast, today's *social-cognitive* theories emphasize the influence of our *social* interpersonal interactions with the environment, along with our *cognitions*—our thoughts, feelings, expectations, and values.

Bandura's and Rotter's Approaches

Albert Bandura (also discussed in Chapter 6) has played a major role in reintroducing thought processes into personality theory. Cognition, or thought, is central to his concept of **self-efficacy**, which is very similar to our everyday notion of self-confidence (Bandura, 1997, 2011, 2012).

Self-efficacy Bandura's term for a person's learned expectation of success in a given situation; also, another term for self-confidence.

According to Bandura, if you have a strong sense of self-efficacy, you believe you can generally succeed and reach your goals, regardless of past failures and current obstacles. Your self-efficacy will in turn affect which challenges you choose to accept and the effort you expend in reaching goals. For example, one study found that children who assisted their parents with meal preparation reported higher self-efficacy for selecting and eating healthy foods (Chu et al., 2013).

Q4

psychology and you **Self-efficacy in Daily Life** The classic children's story *The Little Engine That Could* illustrates how we learn self-efficacy through our personal experiences with success. The little engine starts up a steep hill, saying, "I think I can, I think I can." After lots of hard work and perseverance, he ends up at the top of the hill and says, "I know I can, I know I can."

Bandura emphasized that self-efficacy is a *learned* expectation of success, but only in a given situation. It doesn't necessarily transfer to other circumstances. Bandura would suggest that the little engine's new-found self-efficacy will help him climb future hills. However, it wouldn't necessarily improve his overall speed or his ability to turn sharp corners. Similarly, self-defense training significantly affects a woman's belief that she can improve her odds of escaping from or disabling a potential assailant or rapist. But it does not lead her to feel more capable in all areas of her life (Weitlauf et al., 2001).

How then can we transfer self-efficacy to other parts of our everyday life? If you've experienced success as an athlete, a parent, or even a videogame player, consider how the skills you've demonstrated in these areas can be transferred to your academic life. Instead of saying, "I just can't find time to study" or "I never do well on tests," remind yourself of how your ongoing success in athletics, parenting, or videogames has resulted from good time management, hours of practice, patience, hard work, and perseverance. Applying skills that are the same as or similar to skills you've successfully used before will help move you from "I can't" to "I think I can." And then when you get your first high grade in a difficult course, you can move on to "I know I can, I know I can!"

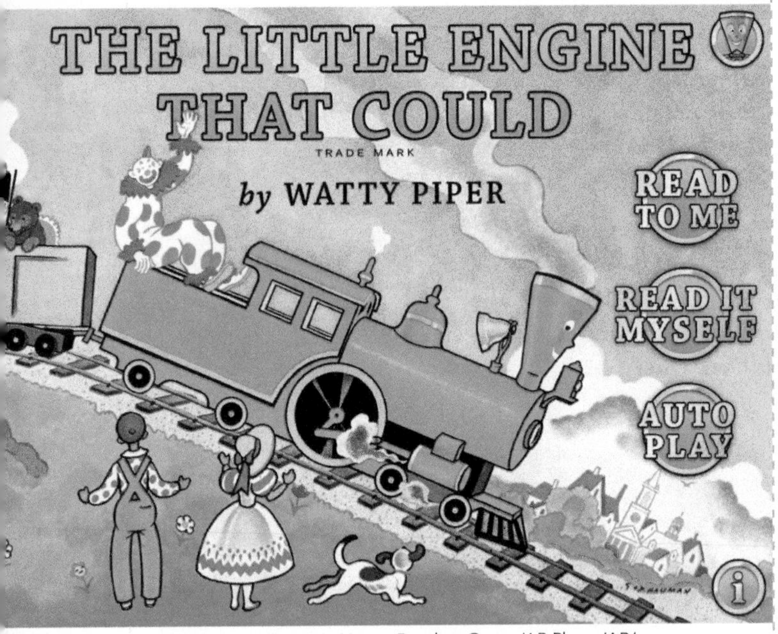

PRNewsFoto/Penguin Young Readers Group/AP Photo/AP/Wide World Photos

Reciprocal determinism Bandura's belief that a complex reciprocal interaction exists among the individual, his or her behavior, and environmental stimuli.

How does self-efficacy affect personality? Bandura sees personality as being shaped by **reciprocal determinism**, how the *person* (his or her personality, thoughts, expectations, etc.), *environment*, and *behavior* interact and influence one another **(Figure 11.12)**. Using Bandura's concept of self-efficacy, can you see how your own beliefs will affect how others respond to you and thereby influence your chance for success? Your belief ("I can succeed") will affect behaviors ("I'll work hard and ask for a promotion"), which in turn will affect the environment ("My employer recognized my efforts and promoted me").

Julian Rotter's theory is similar to Bandura's in that it suggests that learning experiences create *cognitive expectancies* that guide behavior and influence the environment (Rotter, 1954, 1990). According to Rotter, your behavior or personality is determined by (1) what you expect to happen following a specific action and (2) the reinforcement value attached to specific outcomes.

To understand your personality and behavior, Rotter would use personality tests that measure your internal versus external *locus of control* (Chapter 3). Rotter's tests ask subjects to respond to statements such as, "People get ahead in this world primarily by luck and connections rather than by hard work and perseverance" and "When someone doesn't like you, there is little you can do about it." As you may suspect, people with an external locus of control think the environment and external

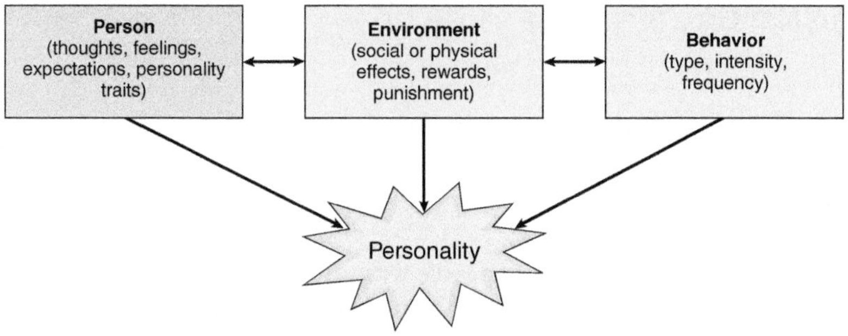

FIGURE 11.12 BANDURA'S THEORY OF RECIPROCAL DETERMINISM

According to Albert Bandura, personality is determined by a three-way, reciprocal interaction of the internal characteristics of the person, the external environment, and the person's behavior.

forces have primary control over their lives, whereas people with an *internal locus of control* think they can personally control events in their lives through their own efforts **(Figure 11.13)**.

Evaluating Social-Cognitive Theories

The social-cognitive perspective holds several attractions. First, it offers testable, objective hypotheses and operationally defined terms, and it relies on empirical data. Second, social-cognitive theories emphasize how the environment affects, and is affected by, individuals. Walter Mischel, a social-cognitive theorist, ignited the classic *person–situation debate* when he suggested that our personalities change according to a given situation (Mischel, 1968, 1984, 2004; Mischel & Shoda, 2008). Most of us behave differently in different situations—a shy person who never speaks up in large crowds may be very talkative at home or with friends.

Recognizing this flexibility, Mischel initially argued that personality traits are relatively poor predictors of actual behavior. He later softened his position, and said that behavior emerges from the interplay between personality characteristics and situational forces.

While this person versus situation debate continues, critics argue that social-cognitive theories focus too much on situational influences. They also suggest that this approach fails to adequately acknowledge the stability of personality, as well as unconscious, emotional, and biological influences (Ahmetoglu & Chamorro-Premuzic, 2013; Cook, 2013; Westen, 1998, 2007).

"We're encouraging people to become involved in their own rescue."

FIGURE 11.13 LOCUS OF CONTROL AND ACHIEVEMENT

Despite this cartoon's humorous message, research does link a perception of control with higher achievement, greater life satisfaction, and better overall mental health (Fitzgerald & Clark, 2013; Greene & Murdock, 2013; Herbert et al., 2013; You et al., 2011; Zampieri & Pedrosa de Souza, 2011).

RETRIEVAL PRACTICE: SOCIAL-COGNITIVE THEORIES

Self-Test

Completing this self-test and comparing your answers with those in Appendix B provides immediate feedback and helpful practice for exams. Additional interactive, self-tests are available at www.wiley.com/college/huffman.

1. According to Bandura, _____ relies on a person's belief about whether he or she can successfully engage in behaviors related to personal goals.

a. self-actualization
b. self-esteem
c. self-efficacy
d. self-congruence

2. Bandura's theory of _____ suggests that the person, behavior, and environment all interact to produce personality.

a. self-actualization
b. self-esteem maximization
c. self-efficacy
d. reciprocal determinism

3. According to Rotter, people with a(n) _____ believe the environment and external forces control events, whereas those with a(n) _____ believe in personal control.

a. self-actualized personality; efficacy personality
b. external locus of control; internal locus of control
c. fatalistic view; humanistic opinion
d. global locus of control; selfish locus of control

4. Walter Mischel, a social-cognitive theorist, ignited the classic person–situation debate when he suggested that _____.

a. our personalities change according to a given situation
b. our personalities change according to prenatal nutrition
c. our personalities seldom change over our lifetimes
d. our personalities change according to our horoscope

Think Critically

1 How would Bandura's social-cognitive concept of self-efficacy explain why bright students sometimes don't do well in college?

2 Do you have an internal or external locus of control? How might this affect your academic and lifetime achievement?

realworldpsychology

Does helping parents prepare a meal increase a child's preference for healthy foods?

HINT: LOOK IN THE MARGIN FOR Q4

BIOLOGICAL THEORIES

LEARNING OBJECTIVES

RETRIEVAL PRACTICE While reading the upcoming sections, respond to each Learning Objective in your own words. Then compare your responses with found at www.wiley.com/college/Huffman.

1 **SUMMARIZE** the roles that brain structures, neurochemistry, and genetics play in personality.

2 **EXPLAIN** the contributions and limitations of biological theories.

3 **DESCRIBE** how the biopsychosocial model integrates different theories of personality.

In this section, we explore how biological factors influence our personalities. We conclude with a discussion of how all theories of personality ultimately interact in the *biopsychosocial model.*

Three Major Contributors to Personality

Hans Eysenck, the trait theorist mentioned earlier in the chapter, was one of the first to propose that personality traits are biologically based—at least in part. And modern research agrees that certain brain structures, neurochemistry, and genetics all may contribute to some personality characteristics. For example, how do we decide in the real world which risks are worth taking and which are not? Modern research using functional magnetic resonance imaging (fMRI) and other brain mapping techniques documents specific areas of the brain that correlate with trait impulsiveness and areas that differ between people with risk-averse and those with risk-seeking personalities (Cox et al., 2010; Schilling et al., 2013).

Earlier research also found that increased electroencephalographic (EEG) activity in the left frontal lobes of the brain is associated with sociability (or extroversion), whereas greater EEG activity in the right frontal lobes is associated with shyness or introversion versus extroversion (Fishman & Ng, 2013; Tellegen, 1985).

A major limitation of research on brain structures and personality is the difficulty of identifying which structures are uniquely connected with particular personality traits. Neurochemistry seems to offer more precise data on how biology influences personality. For example, sensation seeking (Chapter 11) has consistently been linked with levels of monoamine oxidase (MAO), an enzyme that regulates levels of neurotransmitters such as dopamine (Lee, 2011; Zuckerman, 1994, 2004). Dopamine also seems to be correlated with addictive personality traits, novelty seeking, and extroversion (Blum et al., 2013; Camperio et al., 2013; Marusich et al., 2011; Nemoda et al., 2011; Thomson et al., 2013).

realworldpsychology **Biology's Impact on Personality** How can neurochemistry have such effects? Studies suggest that high-sensation seekers and extroverts tend to experience less physical arousal than introverts from the same stimulus (Figueredo et al., 2011; Fishman & Ng, 2013; Munoz & Anastassiou-Hadjicharalambous, 2011). Extroverts' low arousal apparently motivates them to seek out situations that will elevate their arousal. Moreover, it is believed that a higher arousal threshold is genetically transmitted. In other words, personality traits like sensation seeking and extroversion may be inherited.

© FurmanAnna/iStockphoto

This recognition that genetic factors have an important influence on personality has contributed to the relatively new field called *behavioral genetics* (Lessov-Schlaggar et al., 2013; Maxson, 2013), which attempts to determine the extent to which behavioral differences among people are due to genetics as opposed to the environment (Chapter 2). One interesting study found that when participants' saliva was genetically tested, those who had a "niceness gene" were more likely to report engaging in various types of prosocial behaviors, such as giving blood and engaging in volunteer work and making charitable contributions (Poulin et al., 2012). This finding suggests that even how nice we are may be at least partially based on our biology! Q5

One way to measure genetic influences is to compare similarities in personality between identical twins and fraternal twins. For example, studies of the five-factor model (FFM) personality traits suggest that genetic factors contribute about 40 to 50% of personality (Bouchard, 1997, 2004; Eysenck, 1967, 1990; Kan et al., 2013; McCrae et al., 2004; Plomin, 1990; Slutske et al., 2013; Veselka et al., 2011).

In addition to conducting twin studies, researchers compare the personalities of parents with those of their biological children and their adopted children. Studies of extroversion and neuroticism have found that parents' traits correlate moderately with those of their biological children and hardly at all with those of their adopted children (Bouchard, 1997; McCrae et al., 2000).

Evaluating Biological Theories

Modern research in biological theories has provided exciting insights, and it has established clear links between some personality traits and various brain areas, neurotransmitters, and/or genetics. However, it's important to keep in mind that personality traits are never the result of a single biological process. For example, studies do show a strong inherited basis for personality, but researchers are careful not to overemphasize genetics (Ahmetoglu & Chamorro-Premuzic, 2013; Beauchamp et al., 2011; Chadwick, 2011; Cook, 2013). Some believe the importance of the unshared environment—aspects of the environment that differ from one individual to another, even within a family—has been overlooked. Others fear that research on "genetic determinism" could be misused to "prove" that an ethnic or a racial group is inferior, that male dominance is natural, or that social progress is impossible.

In sum, there is no doubt that biological studies have produced valuable results. However, as is true for all the theories discussed in this chapter, no single personality theory explains everything we need to know about personality. Each theory offers different insights into how a person develops the distinctive set of characteristics we call "personality." That's why instead of adhering to any one theory, many psychologists believe in the *biopsychosocial approach*, or the idea that several factors—biological, psychological, and social—overlap in their contributions to personality **(Figure 11.14)**.

FIGURE 11.14 MULTIPLE INFLUENCES ON PERSONALITY

Research indicates that three major factors influence personality: genetic (inherited) factors, nonshared environmental factors (the way each individual's genetic factors react and adjust to his or her environment), and shared environmental factors (parental and family experiences).

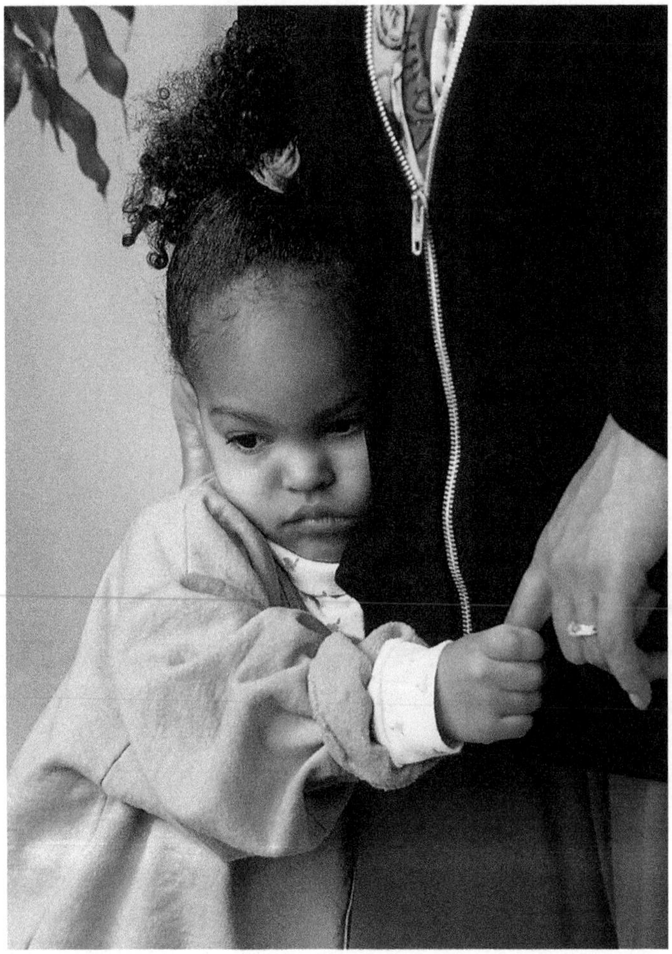

Rosanne Olson/Stone/Getty Images

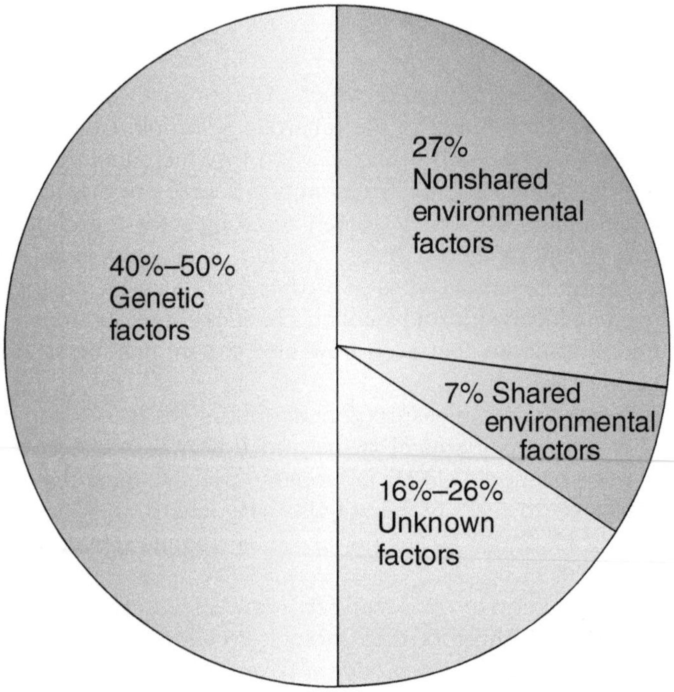

Source: Bouchard, 1997, 2004; Eysenck, 1967, 1990; Jang et al., 2006; McCrae et al., 2004; Plomin, 1990; Weiss et al., 2008

RETRIEVAL PRACTICE: BIOLOGICAL THEORIES

Self-Test

Completing this self-test and comparing your answers with those in Appendix B provides immediate feedback and helpful practice for exams. Additional interactive, self-tests are available at www.wiley.com/college/huffman.

1. _____ was one of the earliest theorists to suggest that personality traits are biologically based—at least in part.

a. Albert Bandura
b. Hans Eysenck
c. Abraham Maslow
d. Karen Horney

2. Dopamine is reportedly involved in the personality trait(s) _____.

a. conscientiousness, extroversion, and altruism
b. extroversion and neuroticism
c. impulsivity, aggression and altruism
d. novelty seeking, extroversion, and sensation seeking

3. _____ theories emphasize the importance of genetics in the development of personality.

a. Behavioral genetics
b. Behavioral metrics
c. Social/personal genetics
d. Biometrical engineering

4. The _____ approach represents a blending of several theories of personality.

a. inherited basis
b. biopsychosocial
c. social/overlap
d. none of these options

Think Critically

1 If biological factors explain certain personality traits, what advice would you give to someone who is painfully shy and wants to become more outgoing?

2 Given that many of the same brain structures most closely associated with personality are also linked with emotions, what does this suggest about the role of emotions in our personalities?

realworldpsychology

Can our genes predict how much we will give to charity?

HINT: LOOK IN THE MARGIN FOR Q5

PERSONALITY ASSESSMENT

RETRIEVAL PRACTICE While reading the upcoming sections, respond to each Learning Objective in your own words. Then compare your responses with those found at www.wiley.com/college/Huffman.

LEARNING OBJECTIVES

1 **SUMMARIZE** the four major methods psychologists use to measure personality.
2 **DESCRIBE** the benefits and limitations of each method of personality assessment.
3 **DISCUSS** the three logical fallacies associated with pseudo-personality tests.

Numerous unscientific methods have been used over the decades to assess personality **(Figure 11.15)**. As we saw in the opening paragraphs of this chapter, even today, some people consult fortune-tellers, horoscope columns in the newspaper, tarot cards, and even fortune cookies in Chinese restaurants. But scientific research has provided much more reliable and valid methods for measuring personality. Clinical and counseling psychologists, psychiatrists, and other helping professionals use these modern methods to help with the diagnosis of patients and to assess their progress in therapy. Personality assessments can be grouped into a few broad categories: *interviews*, *observations*, *objective tests*, and *projective tests*.

Interviews and Observation

We all use informal "interviews" to get to know other people. When first meeting someone, we usually ask about his or her job, academic interests, family, or hobbies. Psychologists also use interviews. In an unstructured format, interviewers get

FIGURE 11.15 PERSONALITY AND BUMPS ON THE HEAD?

In the 1800s, if you wanted to have your personality assessed, you would go to a phrenologist, who would determine your personality by measuring the bumps on your skull and comparing the measurements with a chart that associated different areas of the skull with particular traits, such as *sublimity* (ability to squelch natural impulses, especially sexual) and *ideality* (ability to live by high ideals). What traits might be measured if we still believed in phrenology today?

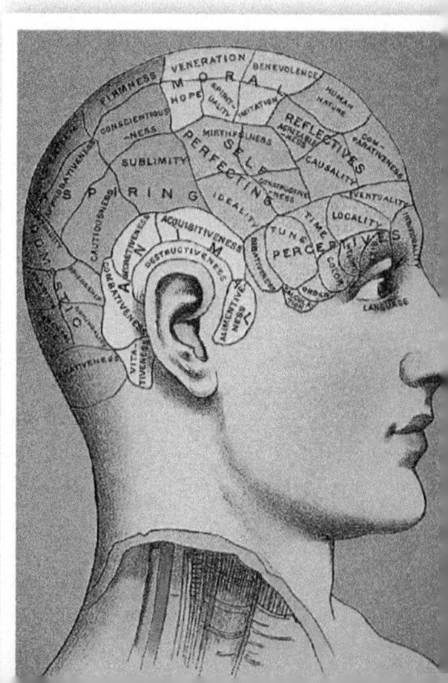

© Bettmann/CORBIS

impressions and pursue hunches or let the interviewee expand on information that promises to disclose personality characteristics. In structured interviews, the interviewer asks specific questions in order to evaluate the interviewee's responses more objectively and compare them with others' responses.

In addition to conducting interviews, psychologists also assess personality by directly and methodically observing behavior. They look for examples of specific behaviors and follow a careful set of evaluation guidelines. For instance, a psychologist might arrange to observe a troubled client's interactions with his or her family. Does the client become agitated by the presence of certain family members and not others? Does he or she become passive and withdrawn when asked a direct question? Through careful observation, the psychologist gains valuable insights into the client's personality as well as family dynamics **(Figure 11.16)**.

Objective Tests

Objective personality tests, or inventories, are the most widely used method of assessing personality, for two reasons: They can be administered to a large number of people relatively quickly, and they can be evaluated in a standardized fashion. Some objective tests measure one specific personality trait, such as sensation seeking (Chapter 10) or locus of control. However, psychologists in clinical, counseling, and industrial settings often wish to assess a range of personality traits. To do so, they generally use multitrait, or *multiphasic*, inventories.

Minnesota Multiphasic Personality Inventory (MMPI) The most widely researched and clinically used self-report personality test. (MMPI-2 is the revised version.)

The most widely studied and clinically used multitrait test is the **Minnesota Multiphasic Personality Inventory (MMPI)**—or its revision, the MMPI-2 (Butcher, 2000, 2011; Butcher & Perry, 2008; Silverstein, 2013; Tennen et al., 2013). This test consists of more than 500 statements to which participants respond with *True*, *False*, or *Cannot Say*. The following are examples of the kinds of statements found on the MMPI:

My stomach frequently bothers me.

I have enemies who really wish to harm me.

I sometimes hear things that other people can't hear.

I would like to be a mechanic.

I have never indulged in any unusual sex practices.

FIGURE 11.16 BEHAVIORAL OBSERVATION

How might careful observation help a psychologist better understand a troubled client's personality and family dynamics?

David De Lossy/Getty Images

TABLE 11.3 SUBSCALES OF THE MMPI-2

Clinical Scales	Typical Interpretations of High Scores
1. Hypochondriasis	Numerous physical complaints
2. Depression	Seriously depressed and pessimistic
3. Hysteria	Suggestible, immature, self-centered, demanding
4. Psychopathic deviate	Rebellious, nonconformist
5. Masculinity–femininity	Interests like those of the other sex
6. Paranoia	Suspicious and resentful of others
7. Psychasthenia	Fearful, agitated, brooding
8. Schizophrenia	Withdrawn, reclusive, bizarre thinking
9. Hypomania	Distractible, impulsive, dramatic
10. Social introversion	Shy, introverted, self-effacing
Validity Scales	**Typical Interpretations of High Scores**
1. L (lie)	Denies common problems, projects a "saintly" or false picture
2. F (confusion)	Answers are contradictory
3. K (defensiveness)	Minimizes social and emotional complaints Many items left unanswered
4. ? (cannot say)	

Did you notice that some of these questions are about very unusual, abnormal behavior? Although there are many "normal" questions on the full MMPI, the test is designed primarily to help clinical and counseling psychologists diagnose psychological disorders. MMPI test items are grouped into 10 clinical scales, each measuring a different disorder **(Table 11.3)**. There are also a number of validity scales designed to reflect the extent to which respondents (1) distort their answers in an attempt to fake psychological disturbances or to appear more psychologically healthy than they really are, (2) do not understand the items, (3) are being uncooperative, and/or (4) genuinely cannot answer the questions.

Other objective personality measures are less focused on psychological disorders. A good example is the NEO Personality Inventory–Revised, which assesses the dimensions of the five-factor model.

Note that personality tests like the MMPI are often confused with *career inventories*, or vocational interest tests. Career counselors use these latter tests (along with aptitude and achievement tests) to help people identify occupations and careers that match their unique traits, values, and interests.

Projective Tests

Unlike objective tests, **projective tests** use unstructured stimuli that subjects can perceive in many ways. When you listen to a piece of music or look at a picture, you might say that the music is sad or that the people in the picture look happy—but not everyone would have the same interpretation. Some psychologists believe that these different interpretations reveal important things about each individual's personality.

As the name implies, projective tests are meant to allow each person to project his or her own unconscious conflicts, psychological defenses, motives, and personality traits onto the test materials. Because respondents may be unable or unwilling to express their true feelings if asked directly, the ambiguous stimuli reportedly provide an indirect "psychological X-ray" of important unconscious processes (Hogan, 2006). Two of the most widely used projective tests are the **Rorschach Inkblot Test** and the **Thematic Apperception Test (TAT)** (Choca, 2013; Silverstein, 2013) **(Figure 11.17)**.

Projective test A method of personality assessment in which an individual is presented with a standardized set of ambiguous stimuli, such as inkblots or abstract drawings, which allow the test taker to project his or her unconscious onto the test material; the individual's responses are assumed to reveal inner feelings, motives, and conflicts.

Rorschach Inkblot Test A projective test based on 10 cards with symmetrical abstract patterns, known as inkblots, which asks respondents to describe what they "see" in the image; the subject's response is thought to be a projection of unconscious processes.

Thematic Apperception Test (TAT) A projective test in which pictures of ambiguous scenes are presented to an individual, who is encouraged to generate stories about them; the responses supposedly reflect a projection of the respondent's unconscious processes.

FIGURE 11.17 SAMPLE PROJECTIVE TESTS

The verbal or written responses participants make to projective tests reportedly reflect unconscious, hidden parts of their personalities that they unintentionally "project" onto the stimuli.

Ⓐ The *Rorschach Inkblot Test* was introduced in 1921 by Swiss psychiatrist Hermann Rorschach. With this technique, individuals are shown 10 inkblots like the one shown here, one at a time, and are asked to report what figures or objects they see in each of them.

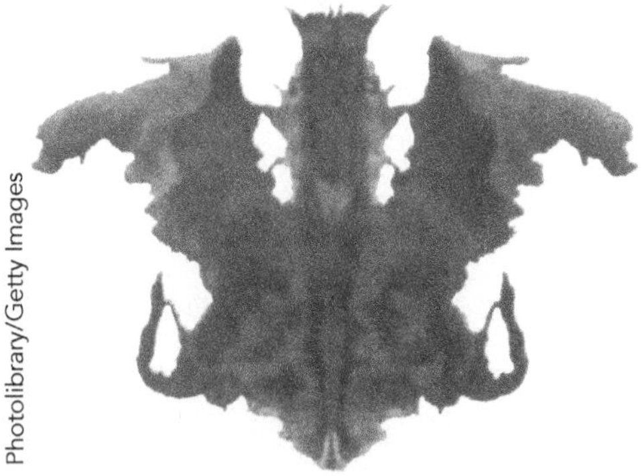

Photolibrary/Getty Images

Ⓑ Created by personality researcher Henry Murray in 1938, the *Thematic Apperception Test (TAT)* consists of a series of ambiguous black-and-white pictures that are shown to the test taker, who is asked to create a story related to each one.

Are Personality Measurements Accurate?

Let's evaluate the strengths and the challenges of each of the four methods of personality assessment: *interviews*, *observation*, *objective tests*, and *projective tests*.

Interviews and Observations

Both interviews and observations can provide valuable insights into personality, but they are time-consuming and expensive. Furthermore, raters of personality tests frequently disagree in their evaluations of the same individuals. Interviews and observations also take place in unnatural settings, and, in fact, the very presence of an observer can alter a subject's behavior.

Objective Tests

Tests like the MMPI-2 provide specific, objective information about a broad range of personality traits in a relatively short period. However, they are also subject to at least three major criticisms:

1. **Deliberate deception and social desirability bias** Some items on personality inventories are easy to see through, so respondents may intentionally, or unintentionally, fake particular personality traits. In addition, some respondents want to look good and will answer questions in ways that they perceive are socially desirable.To avoid these problems, the MMPI-2 has built-in validity scales described earlier. In addition, personality researchers and some businesses avoid self-reports. Instead, they rely on other people, such as friends or coworkers, to rate an individual's personality, as well as how their personality influences their work performance (Connelly & Hülsheger, 2012). Given that most personality tests are based on self-report measures, and that three meta-analyses involving over 44,000 participants found that ratings from others were better predictors of actual behavior, academic achievement, and job performance (Connelly & Ones, 2010), can you see why other-ratings are so important?
2. **Diagnostic difficulties** In addition to the problems with all self-report inventories, when they are used for diagnosis, overlapping items sometimes make it difficult to pinpoint a disorder (Ben-Porath, 2013; Graham, 1991). Clients with severe disorders also sometimes score within the normal range, and normal clients sometimes score within the elevated range (Borghans et al., 2011; Morey, 2013).

3. **Cultural bias and inappropriate use** Some critics think the standards for "normalcy" on objective tests fail to recognize the impact of culture (Hill et al., 2012). For example, Latinos generally score higher on the masculine end of the masculinity–femininity scale of the MMPI-2 than respondents from North American and Western European cultures (Dana, 2005; Ketterer, 2011; Mundia, 2011). However, this tendency probably reflects traditional gender roles and cultural training more than any individual personality traits. Similarly, some recent research examining personality traits in members of the Tsimané culture, a community of foragers and farmers in Bolivia with relatively little contact with the outside world, reveals two distinct dimensions of personality—prosociality and industriousness—instead of the more widely accepted five personality traits (Gurven et al., 2012).

Differences in personality may also be seen in different parts of a single country. For example, one study of over half a million people in the United States revealed regional differences in personality traits linked with entrepreneurial activity, defined as business-creation and self-employment rates (Obschonka et al., 2013). As you can see in **Figure 11.18**, certain regions are much more entrepreneurial than others. Why? The authors of the study suggested that the higher scores in the West, for example, might be a reflection of America's historical migration patterns of people moving from the East into the West (or from outside of America). They cite other research (e.g., Rentfrow et al., 2008) that suggests this selective migration may have had a lasting effect on personality due to the heritability of personality traits and the passing on of norms and values within the regions.

What do you think? How would you explain the differences? Can you see the overall value of expanding our study of personality from just looking at differences between individuals to examining regional differences, and how this expansion might increase our understanding of how personality is formed and its potential applications?

Q6

Projective Tests

Although projective tests are extremely time-consuming to administer and interpret, their proponents suggest that because the method is unstructured, respondents may be more willing to talk honestly about sensitive topics. Critics point out, however, that the *reliability* and *validity* (Chapter 8) of projective tests is among the lowest of all tests of personality (Gacono et al., 2008; Krug, 2013; Wood et al., 2011). (Recall from Chapter 8 that reliability—the consistency of test results—and reliability—whether the test actually measures what it was designed to measure—are the two most important measures of a good test.)

As you can see, each of these methods has limits, which is why psychologists typically combine the results from various scientific methods to create a fuller picture of any individual's personality. However, you're unlikely to have access to this type of professional analysis, so what's the most important take-home message? Beware of pop-psych books and pop-culture personality quizzes in magazines and websites! They may be entertaining, but they're rarely based on standardized testing or scientific research of any kind, and you should never base important decisions on their input.

Finally, throughout this text, we have emphasized the value of critical thinking, which also is useful in evaluating personality tests (see *What's Wrong With Pseudo-Personality Quizzes?*).

FIGURE 11.18 **ENTREPRENEURSHIP IN THE UNITED STATES**

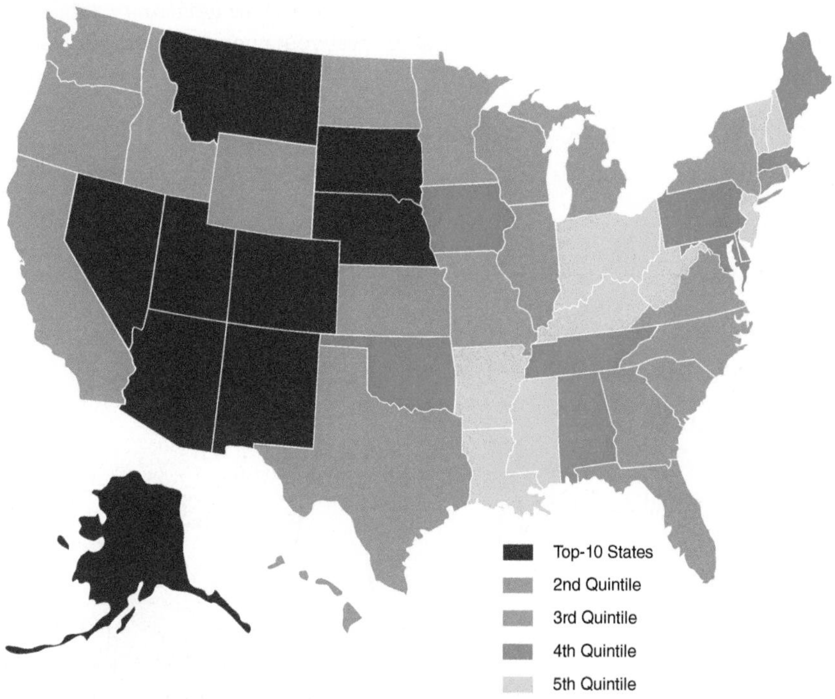

 Obschonka, et al. The regional distribution and correlates of an entrepreneurship-prone personality profile in the United States, Germany, and the United Kingdom: A socioecological perspective. Journal of Personality and Social Psychology, Vol 105(1), Jul 2013, 104-122. The use of APA information does not imply endorsement by APA.

WHAT'S WRONG WITH PSEUDO-PERSONALITY QUIZZES?

psychology and you

The personality horoscope presented in the chapter opener (p. 302) contains several logical fallacies. Using your critical thinking skills, can you see how the following three factors help explain why so many people believe in phony personality descriptions and predictions?

BARNUM EFFECT

We often accept pseudo-personality descriptions and horoscope predictions because we think they are accurate. We tend to believe these tests have somehow tapped into our unique selves. In fact, they are ambiguous, broad statements that fit just about anyone (e.g., "You have a strong need for other people to like and admire you"). The existence of such generalities led to the term the *Barnum effect*, named for the legendary circus promoter P.T. Barnum, who said, "Always have a little something for everyone" (Wyman & Vyse, 2008).

FALLACY OF POSITIVE INSTANCES

Look again at the introductory personality profile and count the number of times you agree with the statements. According to the *confirmation bias* (Chapter 8), we tend to notice and remember events that confirm our expectations and ignore those that are nonconfirming. If we see ourselves as independent thinkers, for example, we ignore the "needing to be liked by others" part and vice versa.

SELF-SERVING BIAS

Now check the overall tone of the bogus personality profile. Can you see how the traits are generally positive and flattering—or at least neutral? According to the *self-serving bias*, we tend to prefer information that maintains our positive self-image (Krusemark et al., 2008; Shepperd et al., 2008). In fact, research shows that the more favorable a personality description is, the more people believe it, and the more likely they are to believe it is personally unique (Guastello et al., 1989).

Taken together, these three logical fallacies help explain the common support for pop-psych personality tests and newspaper horoscopes. They offer something for everyone (*Barnum effect*). We pay attention only to what confirms our expectations (*confirmation bias*). And we like flattering descriptions (*self-serving bias*). You can test your understanding of these three biases in the following:

TESTING YOUR CRITICAL THINKING

Using the information in this *Psychology and You* section, can you identify the two major fallacies in this cartoon?

Answer: The self-serving bias and the Barnum effect.

RETRIEVAL PRACTICE: PERSONALITY ASSESSMENT

Self-Test

Completing this self-test and comparing your answers with those in Appendix B provides immediate feedback and helpful practice for exams. Additional interactive, self-tests are available at www.wiley.com/college/huffman.

1. In the 1800s, if you wanted to have your personality assessed, you would go to a phrenologist, who would determine your personality by studying/measuring _____.

a. projective tests
b. ambiguous stimuli results
c. inkblot stain responses
d. bumps on your head

2. The most widely researched and clinically used self-report personality test is the _____.

a. MMPI
b. Rorschach Inkblot Test
c. TAT
d. SVII

3. The Rorschach Inkblot Test is an example of a(n) _____ test.

a. projective
b. ambiguous stimuli
c. inkblot
d. all these options

4. Two important criteria for evaluating the usefulness of tests used to assess personality are _____.

a. concurrence and prediction
b. reliability and validity
c. consistency and correlation
d. diagnosis and prognosis

Think Critically

1 Which method of personality assessment (interviews, behavioral observation, objective testing, or projective testing) do you think is likely to be most informative? Can you think of circumstances in which one kind of assessment might be more effective than the others?

2 Why do you think objective personality tests like the MMPI are so popular and so widely used?

realworldpsychology

Why do people from different states vary in their entrepreneurial spirit?

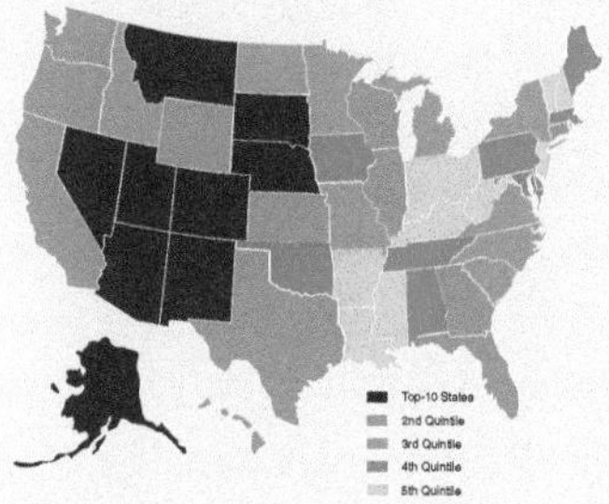

HINT: LOOK IN THE MARGIN FOR Q6

Summary

1 PSYCHOANALYTIC/PSYCHODYNAMIC THEORIES 302

- Freud, the founder of psychodynamic theory, believed that the mind contained three *levels of consciousness*: **conscious**, **preconscious**, and **unconscious**. He believed that most psychological disorders originated from unconscious memories and instincts. Freud also asserted that personality was composed of the **id**, the **ego**, and the **superego**. When the ego fails to satisfy both the id and the superego, anxiety slips into conscious awareness, which triggers **defense mechanisms**. In addition, Freud believed that all children go through five **psychosexual stages**, which affect personality development.
- *Neo-Freudians* such as Adler, Jung, and Horney were influential followers of Freud who later rejected major aspects of Freudian theory.

2 TRAIT THEORIES 309

- Allport believed that the best way to understand personality was to arrange a person's unique personality **traits** into a hierarchy. Cattell and Eysenck later reduced the list of possible personality traits using *factor analysis*.
- The **five-factor model (FFM)** identifies major dimensions of personality, or the *Big Five*.

3 HUMANISTIC THEORIES 314

- According to Rogers, mental health and self-esteem are related to the degree of congruence between our **self-concept** and life experiences. Rogers argued that poor mental health results when young children do not receive **unconditional positive regard** from caregivers.

- Maslow saw personality as the quest to fulfill basic physiological needs and to move toward the highest level of **self-actualization**.

4 SOCIAL-COGNITIVE THEORIES 317

- Cognition is central to Bandura's concept of **self-efficacy**. According to Bandura, self-efficacy affects which challenges we choose to accept and the effort we expend in reaching goals. His concept of **reciprocal determinism** states that self-efficacy beliefs will also affect others' responses to us.
- Rotter's theory says that learning experiences create *cognitive expectancies* that guide behavior and influence the environment. Rotter believed that having an internal versus external *locus of control* affects personality and achievement.

5 BIOLOGICAL THEORIES 320

- Certain brain areas may contribute to personality. However, neurochemistry seems to offer more precise data on how biology influences personality. Research in *behavioral genetics* indicates that genetic factors also strongly influence personality.
- Instead of adhering to any one theory of personality, many psychologists believe in the biopsychosocial approach—the idea that several factors overlap in their contributions to personality.

6 PERSONALITY ASSESSMENT 323

- In an unstructured interview format, interviewers get impressions and pursue hunches or let the interviewee expand on information that promises to disclose personality characteristics. In structured interviews, interviewers ask specific predetermined questions so they can evaluate and compare multiple interviewee's responses more objectively. Psychologists also assess personality by directly observing behavior.
- **Objective personality tests** are widely used because we can administer them broadly and relatively quickly and evaluate them in a standardized fashion. To assess a range of personality traits, psychologists use multitrait inventories, such as the **MMPI**.
- **Projective tests** use unstructured stimuli that can be perceived in many ways. Projective tests, such as the **Rorschach Inkblot Test**, supposedly allow each person to project his or her own unconscious conflicts, psychological defenses, motives, and personality traits onto the test materials.

Cameron/Corbis Images

applyingrealworldpsychology

We began this chapter with six intriguing Real World Psychology questions, and you were asked to revisit these questions at the end of each section. Questions like these have an important and lasting impact on all of our lives. See if you can answer these additional critical thinking questions related to real world examples.

1. As first discussed in Chapter 9 and throughout this chapter, early childhood relationships, particularly between parent and child, are very important to our personality development and overall psychological health. According to the five psychosexual stages of development, how might Freud interpret this woman and her son's obvious attachment to one another? Can you think of an alternative, more logical, explanation for their attachment?
2. How would Rogers's emphasis on unconditional positive regard and Bandura's social-cognitive concept of self-efficacy relate to this mother's display of pleasure at her son's attempt to dry her hair?
3. Can you identify one or more defense mechanisms that you use in your life? If you find them to be unhealthy, what can you do to change them?
4. If you agree that self-actualization is a worthy goal, what are you doing to move in that direction?
5. Which theory of personality discussed in this chapter do you find most useful in understanding yourself and others? Why?

Key Terms

RETRIEVAL PRACTICE Write a definition for each term before turning back to the referenced page to check your answer.

- archetypes 307
- basic anxiety 307
- collective unconscious 307
- conscious 303
- defense mechanisms 304
- ego 304
- five-factor model (FFM) 310
- id 304
- inferiority complex 306
- Minnesota Multiphasic Personality Inventory (MMPI) 324
- morality principle 304
- personality 303
- pleasure principle 304
- preconscious 303
- projective test 325
- psychosexual stages 305
- reality principle 304
- reciprocal determinism 318
- Rorschach Inkblot Test 325
- self-actualization 314
- self-concept 314
- self-efficacy 317
- superego 304
- Thematic Apperception Test (TAT) 325
- trait 309
- unconditional positive regard 315
- unconscious 303

chaptertwelve

Psychological Disorders

CHAPTER OUTLINE

realworldpsychology

THINGS YOU'LL LEARN IN CHAPTER 12

Q1 How can media coverage of mass shootings create negative misperceptions about people with mental illness?

Q2 Do people with a phobia see the object that frightens them as larger than it really is?

Q3 Can eating fast food lead to depression later on?

Q4 Why might children who experience trauma be at increased risk of developing schizophrenia later in life?

Q5 How do changes in the brain help explain severe antisocial personality disorder?

Q6 Are symptoms of depression in women more distressing, deserving of sympathy, and difficult to treat than the same signs in men?

THROUGHOUT THE CHAPTER, MARGIN ICONS FOR Q1–Q6 INDICATE WHERE THE TEXT ADDRESSES THESE QUESTIONS.

chapteroverview

Are you excited? Throughout history, psychological disorders have been the subject of intense fascination. Now, you finally get to read and study the part of psychology you've probably been waiting for from the very beginning! Hopefully, while reading this chapter, you'll recognize how the earlier chapters have prepared you for a better understanding and appreciation of the complex issues surrounding abnormal behavior. We begin with a discussion of how psychological disorders are identified, explained, and classified. Then we explore six major categories of psychological disorders: anxiety disorders, depressive and bipolar disorders, schizophrenia, obsessive-compulsive disorder (OCD), and personality disorders. We close with a look at gender and cultural factors related to mental disorders.

STUDYING PSYCHOLOGICAL DISORDERS

LEARNING OBJECTIVES

RETRIEVAL PRACTICE While reading the upcoming sections, respond to each Learning Objective in your own words. Then compare your responses with those found at www.wiley.com/college/huffman.

1. **DESCRIBE** abnormal behavior and the four criteria for identifying psychological disorders.
2. **EXPLAIN** how perspectives on the causes of psychological disorders have changed throughout history.
3. **DISCUSS** the purposes and criticisms of the *Diagnostic and Statistical Manual of Mental Disorders* (*DSM*).

Most people agree that neither the artist who stays awake for 72 hours finishing a painting nor the shooter who kills 20 young school children is behaving normally. But what exactly is "normal"? How do we distinguish between eccentricity in the first case and abnormal behavior in the second?

Identifying and Explaining Psychological Disorders

Abnormal behavior Patterns of behaviors, thoughts, or emotions considered pathological (diseased or disordered) for one or more of these four reasons: deviance, dysfunction, distress, or danger.

Mental health professionals generally agree on four criteria for identifying **abnormal behavior** (or psychopathology). Often called the four *D*'s, these signs are *deviance*, *dysfunction*, *distress*, and *danger* **(Figure 12.1)**. Keep in mind that abnormal behavior, like intelligence or creativity, exists on a continuum.

As you consider these criteria, remember that no single criterion is adequate for identifying all forms of abnormal behavior. Furthermore, when considering the two criteria *deviance* and *danger*, note that judgments of what is deviant vary historically and cross-culturally and that the public generally overestimates the danger posed by the mentally ill. (See **Table 12.1** for more about this and other myths of mental illness.)

What causes abnormal behavior? Historically, evil spirits and witchcraft have been blamed (Amin & Noggle, 2013; Goodwin, 2012; Millon, 2004; Petry, 2011; Riva et al., 2011). Stone Age people, for example, believed that abnormal behavior stemmed from demonic possession; the "therapy" was to bore a hole in the skull so the evil spirit could escape, a process we call *trephining*. During the European Middle Ages, a troubled person was sometimes treated with *exorcism*, an effort to drive the Devil out by praying, fasting, making noise, and beating the sufferer and administering terrible-tasting brews. During the fifteenth century, as the Renaissance got under way, many believed that some individuals chose to consort with the Devil. These supposed witches were often tortured, imprisoned for life, or executed.

As the Middle Ages ended, special mental hospitals called *asylums* began to appear in Europe. Initially designed to provide quiet retreats from the world and to protect society (Barlow & Durand, 2012; Coleborne & Mackinnon, 2011; Hamlett & Hoskins, 2013; Millon, 2004), the asylums unfortunately became overcrowded, inhumane prisons.

FIGURE 12.1 FOUR CRITERIA FOR IDENTIFYING ABNORMAL BEHAVIOR

Behavior may be considered abnormal if it meets one or more of these four criteria.

Corbis Flirt/Alamy

A Deviance
Behaviors, thoughts, or emotions may be considered abnormal when they deviate from a society or culture's norms or values. For example, it's normal to be a bit concerned if friends are whispering, but abnormal if you're equally concerned when total strangers are whispering.

Ian West/Alamy

B Dysfunction
When someone's dysfunction interferes with his or her daily functioning, such as drinking to the point that you cannot hold a job, stay in school, or maintain relationships, it would be considered abnormal behavior.

Peter Dazeley /Photographer'sChoice/Getty Image, Inc.

C Distress
Behaviors, thoughts, or emotions that cause significant personal distress may qualify as abnormal. Self-abuse relationship problems, and suicidal thoughts all indicate serious personal\distress and unhappiness.

D Danger
If someone's thoughts, emotions, or behaviors present a danger to self or others, such as engaging in road rage to the point of physical confrontation, it would be considered abnormal.

Digital Vision/Getty Images

TABLE 12.1 COMMON MYTHS ABOUT MENTAL ILLNESS realworldpsychology

- ***Myth: Mentally ill people are often dangerous and unpredictable***.

  Fact: Only a few disorders, such as some psychotic and antisocial personality disorders, are associated with violence. The stereotype that connects mental illness and violence persists because of prejudice, selective media attention, and negative portrayals in movies and on television.

- ***Myth: People with psychological disorders act in bizarre ways and are very different from normal people.***

  Fact: This is true for only a small minority of individuals and during a relatively brief portion of their lives. In fact, sometimes even mental health professionals find it difficult to distinguish normal from abnormal behaviors without formal screening.

- ***Myth: Mental disorders are a sign of personal weakness***.

  Fact: Psychological disorders are a function of many factors, such as exposure to stress, genetic predispositions, and a host of personal and sociocultural experiences., and family background. Mentally disturbed individuals can't be blamed for their illness any more than we blame people who develop cancer or other illnesses.

- ***Myth: A mentally ill person is only suited for low-level jobs and never fully recovers.***

  Fact: Like all other illnesses, mental disorders are complex, and their symptoms, severity, and prognoses differ for each individual. With therapy, the vast majority of those who are diagnosed as mentally ill eventually improve and lead normal, productive lives. Moreover, the extreme symptoms of some mental disorders are generally only temporary. For example, U.S. President Abraham Lincoln, British Prime Minister Winston Churchill, scientist Isaac Newton, and other high achieving people all suffered from serious mental disorders at various times throughout their careers.

Boris Roessler//AFP/Getty Images

Is this behavior abnormal? Eccentric? Yes. Mentally disordered? Probably not.

Sources: Barnow & Balkin, 2013; Famous people with mental illness, 2011; Famous people with schizophrenia, 2011; Hooley et al., 2013; Lilienfeld et al., 2010.

FIGURE 12.2 SEVEN PSYCHOLOGICAL PERSPECTIVES

As you can see in this diagram, the seven major perspectives differ in their various explanations for the general causes of psychological disorders, but there is still considerable overlap.

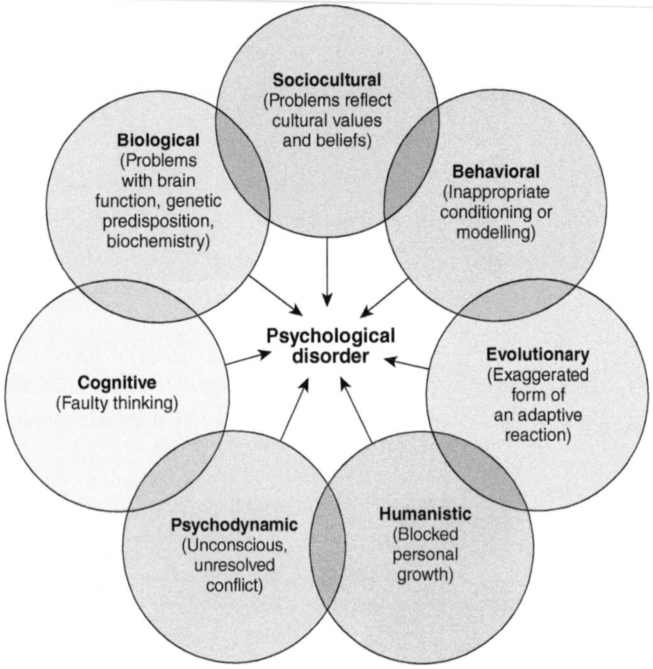

Improvement came in 1792, when Philippe Pinel, a French physician, was placed in charge of a Parisian asylum. Believing that inmates' behavior was caused by underlying physical illness, he insisted that they be unshackled and removed from their unlighted, unheated cells. Many inmates improved so dramatically that they could be released. Pinel's **medical model** eventually gave rise to the modern specialty of **psychiatry**.

Unfortunately, when we label people "mentally ill," we may create new problems. One of the most outspoken critics of the medical model, psychiatrist Thomas Szasz (1960, 2004, 2012), believed it encourages people to believe they have no responsibility for their actions. Furthermore, he contended that mental illness is a myth used to label individuals who are peculiar or offensive to others and that these labels can become self-perpetuating. In other words, a person may begin to behave according to his or her diagnosed disorder.

In addition to potential problems for the identified person, the public also may develop negative attitudes about those labeled as mentally ill and about mental illness in general. This is particularly common following intensive media coverage of mass shootings committed by someone with such a disorder, despite the fact that most people with mental illness are not violent (McGinty et al., 2013). Q1

Despite these potential dangers, the medical model—and the concept of mental illness—remains a founding principle of psychiatry. Psychology, in contrast, offers a multifaceted approach to explaining abnormal behavior, as shown in **Figure 12.2**.

Medical model The diagnostic perspective which assumes that diseases (including mental illness) have physical causes that can be diagnosed, treated, and possibly cured.

Psychiatry The branch of medicine that deals with the diagnosis, treatment, and prevention of mental disorders.

Voices from the Classroom

Dangerous and Painful Labels Our society seems to have a fascination with labeling people, especially people who struggle with psychiatric disorders. I wonder why that is. Should we really be calling someone a schizophrenic? An anorexic? An autistic? We don't refer to people by their illness in other fields, so why do we in psychology? I have a close friend, who happens to be a brilliant physician and an amazing mother of four, who has struggled with a handful of severe episodes of major depressive disorder. Thankfully, she has always recovered from these episodes. That said, they seem to creep up on her and have the power to really throw her life off kilter. Knowing that her depression easily spirals into terrifying suicidal thoughts and urges, she admits herself to the hospital for treatment. While she is under care from the hospital staff, she doesn't want to be called the depressive or the mental patient. It is dehumanizing and offensive. Undergoing treatment for any psychiatric disorder is challenging enough. Our society doesn't need to make it any harder by labeling people and chipping away at their self-esteem. If we really want to label people, perhaps we should use their legal label . . . their actual name.

Professor Paulina Multhaupt
Macomb Community College
Clinton Township, Michigan

Classifying Psychological Disorders

Without a clear, reliable system for classifying the wide range of psychological disorders, scientific research on them would be almost impossible, and communication among mental health professionals would be seriously impaired. Fortunately,

FIGURE 12.3 THE INSANITY PLEA—GUILTY OF A CRIME OR MENTALLY ILL?

On March 27, 2012, JetBlue Airways captain Clayton Osbon dangerously disrupted a cross-country flight by running through the cabin, screaming about terrorists and religion. He was later charged with interference with a flight crew and was found not guilty by reason of insanity after a neuropsychologist testified that he had a "brief psychotic disorder" brought on by lack of sleep. Osbon was allowed to go free but with several restrictions, including not being allowed to fly or board any commercial or private planes. The insanity plea is used in fewer than 1% of all cases that reach trial and is successful in only a fraction of those (Claydon, 2012; Dirks-Linhorst, 2013; Goldstein et al., 2013).

© STRINGER/Reuter/ Corbis

mental health specialists share a uniform classification system, the ***Diagnostic and Statistical Manual of Mental Disorders (DSM)*** (American Psychiatric Association, 2013). This manual has been updated and revised several times, and the latest, fifth edition, was published in 2013.

Each revision of the *DSM* has expanded the list of disorders and changed the descriptions and categories to reflect both the latest in scientific research and any changes in the way abnormal behaviors are viewed within our social context (Hauser & Johnston, 2013; Widiger, 2013). For example, take the terms **neurosis** and **psychosis**. In previous editions of the *DSM*, the term *neurosis* reflected Freud's belief that all neurotic conditions arise from unconscious conflicts (Chapter 11). Now, conditions that were previously grouped under the heading *neurosis* have been formally studied and redistributed as separate categories. Unlike neurosis, the term *psychosis* is still listed in the current edition of the *DSM* because it remains useful for distinguishing the most severe mental disorders, such as schizophrenia.

What about the term *insanity*? Where does it fit in? **Insanity** is a legal term indicating that a person cannot be held responsible for his or her actions or is incompetent to manage his or her own affairs because of mental illness. In the law, the definition of mental illness rests primarily on a person's inability to tell right from wrong **(Figure 12.3)**.

Diagnostic and Statistical Manual of Mental Disorders (DSM) A classification system developed by the American Psychiatric Association that is used to describe abnormal behaviors.

Neurosis An outmoded term and category dropped from *DSM*-111, in which a person does not have signs of brain abnormalities and does not display grossly irrational thinking or violate basic norms but does experience subjective distress.

Psychosis A serious mental disorder characterized by extreme mental disruption and defective or lost contact with reality.

Insanity The legal (not clinical) designation for the state of an individual judged to be legally irresponsible or incompetent to manage his or her own affairs because of mental illness.

Comorbidity The co-occurrence of two or more disorders in the same person at the same time, as when a person suffers from both depression and alcoholism.

Understanding and Evaluating the *DSM*

To understand a disorder, we must first name and describe it. The *DSM* identifies and describes the symptoms of approximately 400 disorders, which are grouped into 22 categories **(Table 12.2)**. Note that we focus on only the first 7 in this chapter (categories 8–11 are discussed in other chapters; 12–21 are beyond the scope of this book). Also, keep in mind that people may be diagnosed with more than one disorder at a time, a condition referred to as **comorbidity**.

Classification and diagnosis of mental disorders are essential to scientific study. Without a system such as the *DSM*, we could not effectively identify and diagnose the wide variety of disorders, predict their future courses, or suggest appropriate treatment. The *DSM* also facilitates communication among professionals and patients, and it serves as a valuable educational tool.

Unfortunately, the *DSM* does have limitations and potential problems. For example, critics suggest that it may be casting too wide a net and *overdiagnosing*. Given that insurance companies compensate physicians and psychologists only if each client is assigned a specific *DSM* code number, can you see how compilers of the *DSM* may be encouraged to add more diagnoses?

In addition, the *DSM* has been criticized for a potential *cultural bias*. It does provide a culture-specific section and a glossary of culture-bound syndromes, such as *amok* (Indonesia), *genital retraction syndrome* (Asia), and *windigo psychosis* (First Nations' cultures), which we discuss later in this chapter. However, the overall classification still reflects a Western European and U.S. perspective (Gellerman & Lu, 2011; Malhi, 2013; Sachdev, 2013).

Perhaps the most troubling criticism of the *DSM* is its possible overreliance on the medical model and the way it may unfairly label people. Consider the classic study conducted by David Rosenhan (1973) in which he and his seven colleagues presented themselves at several hospital admissions offices complaining of hearing voices (a classic symptom of schizophrenia). Aside from making this single false complaint

TABLE 12.2 SUBCATEGORIES OF MENTAL DISORDERS IN THE *DSM*

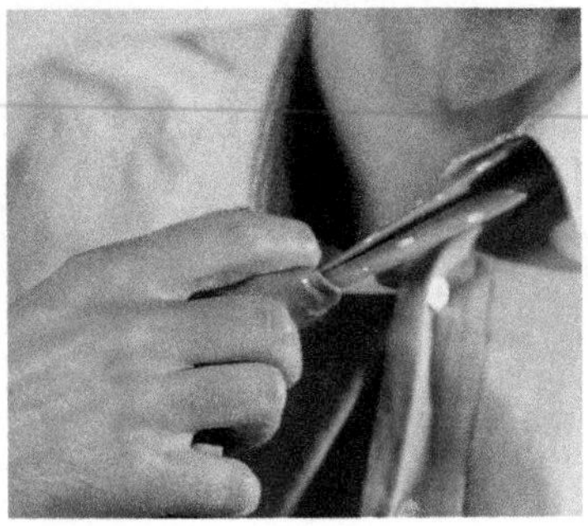
© Image Source/Corbis

© Aldo Murillo/iStockphoto

© gabyjalbert/iStockphoto

1. ***Anxiety disorders*** Problems associated with excessive fear and anxiety and related behavioral disturbances.
2. ***Depressive disorders*** Problems characterized by the presence of sad, empty, or irritable mood.
3. ***Bipolar and related disorders*** Problems associated with alternating episodes of depression and mania.
4. ***Schizophrenia spectrum and other psychotic disorders*** Group of disorders characterized by delusions, hallucinations, disorganized thinking or motor behavior, and negative symptoms, such as diminished emotional expression.
5. ***Obsessive-compulsive and related disorders*** Group of disorders characterized by the presence of obsessions, compulsions, preoccupations, and/or repetitive behaviors or mental acts.
6. ***Dissociative disorders*** Group of disorders characterized by the disruption and/or discontinuity in the normal integration of consciousness, memory, identity, emotion, perception, body representation, motor control, and behavior.
7. ***Personality disorders*** Problems related to an enduring pattern of experience and behavior that deviates markedly from the expectations of an individual's culture, and leads to distress or impairment.
8. ***Trauma- and stressor-related disorders*** Problems associated with exposure to a traumatic or stressful event (see Chapter 3).
9. ***Sleep–wake disorders*** Dissatisfaction regarding the quality, timing, and amount of sleep (see Chapter 5).
10. ***Substance-related and addictive disorders*** A cluster of cognitive, behavioral, and physiological symptoms related to alcohol, tobacco, other drugs, and gambling (see Chapter 5).
11. ***Feeding and eating disorders*** Problems related to persistent disturbance of eating or eating-related behavior (see Chapter 10).
12. ***Paraphilic disorders*** Problems involving an intense and persistent sexual interest causing distress or impairment to the person or whose satisfaction has entailed personal harm, or risk of harm, to others (see optional Chapter 15).
13. ***Sexual dysfunctions*** A significant disturbance in a person's ability to respond sexually or to experience sexual pleasure (see optional Chapter 15).
14. ***Gender dysphoria*** Distress that may accompany the incongruence between a person's experienced or expressed gender and one's assigned gender (see optional Chapter 15).
15. ***Neurodevelopmental disorders*** Developmental deficits that typically manifest early in development, often before the child enters grade school, and produce impairments of personal, social, academic, or occupational functioning.
16. ***Somatic symptom and related disorders*** Problems related to unusual preoccupation with physical health or physical symptoms producing significant distress and impairment.
17. ***Elimination disorders*** Problems related to the inappropriate elimination of urine or feces, usually first diagnosed in childhood or adolescence.
18. ***Disruptive, impulse-control, and conduct disorders*** Problems related to kleptomania (impulsive stealing), pyromania (setting of fires), and other disorders characterized by inability to resist impulses, drives, or temptations to perform certain acts harmful to self or others.
19. ***Neurocognitive disorders*** A group of disorders involving cognitive function, including Alzheimer's disease, Huntington's disease, and physical trauma to the brain.
20. ***Other mental disorders*** Residual category of mental disorders causing significant distress or impairment but do not meet the full criteria for any other disorder in DSM-5.
21. ***Medication-induced movement disorders and other adverse effects of medication*** These are not mental disorders but are included because of their importance in the management by medication and differential diagnosis of mental disorders.
22. ***Other conditions that may be a focus of clinical attention*** These are not mental disorders but are included to draw attention to and document issues that may be encountered in routine clinical practice.

Sources: American Psychiatric Association, 2013; American Psychiatric Association, NICHY, 2012.

and providing false names and occupations, the researchers answered all questions truthfully. Not surprisingly, given their reported symptom, they were all diagnosed with mental disorders and admitted to the hospital. Once there, the "patients" stopped reporting any symptoms and behaved as they normally would, yet none were ever recognized by hospital staff as phony. Note that all of them were eventually released, after an average stay of 19 days, but only with a label on their permanent record of "schizophrenia in remission." Can you see the inherent dangers and "stickiness" of all forms of labels? Once the label "nerd," "jock," "criminal," or "mental patient" is applied, they may become self-fulfilling, and in the case of "criminal" or "mentally ill" they involve serious legal and employment issues.

Having noted the real and potential dangers of the label of mental illness, we need to explore a very common *Psych Science* question before going on: Are creative people at increased risk of suffering from mental illness?

PSYCHSCIENCE

CREATIVITY AND MENTAL DISORDERS

© Fox Searchlight Pictures/Photofest

What do you picture when you think of a creative genius? Thanks to movies, television, and novels, many people share the stereotypical image of an eccentric inventor or deranged artist, like the lead ballerina in the film *Black Swan*.

Is there an actual link between creativity and mental disorders? Researchers interested in this question collected data from more than 1 million people, including their specific professions, whether they had ever been diagnosed and treated for a mental disorder, and if so what type (Kyaga et al., 2012). Kyaga and his colleagues found that individuals in generally creative professions (scientific or artistic) were no more likely to suffer from investigated psychiatric disorders than control subjects. However, bipolar disorder was significantly more common in artists and scientists, and particularly in authors.

What do you think? How would you explain this intriguing association between certain creative professions and bipolar disorder? Does the manic phase of bipolar disorder increase the energy levels of artists, scientists, and authors, giving them greater access to creative ideas than they would otherwise have? Or does it interfere with their overall output? Can you see how variables like choice of occupation might confound these results (Patra & Balhara, 2012)? As you'll discover later in this chapter, there is a strong genetic component in bipolar disorders. And, just as you are much more likely to enter a profession similar to that of your parents because of familiarity, access, and modeling, children of artists, scientists, and authors are more likely to choose similar professions—thus possibly explaining the link between creativity and mental illness.

If you find these questions fascinating and the lack of answers frustrating, you may be the perfect candidate for a career as a research psychologist. Recall from Chapter 1 that the scientific method is circular and never-ending—but guaranteed to excite!

RESEARCH CHALLENGE

1. Based on the information provided, did this study (Kyaga et al., 2012) use descriptive, correlational, and/or experimental research?
2. If you chose:
   - descriptive research, is this a naturalistic observation, survey/interview, case study, or archival research?
   - correlational research, is this a positive, negative, or zero correlation?
   - experimental research, label the IV, DV, experimental group(s), and control group.

>>CHECK YOUR ANSWERS IN APPENDIX B.

NOTE: The information provided in this study is admittedly limited, but the level of detail is similar to what is presented in most textbooks and public reports of research findings. Answering these questions, and then comparing your answers to those in the Appendix, will help you become a better critical thinker and consumer of scientific research.

RETRIEVAL PRACTICE: STUDYING PSYCHOLOGICAL DISORDERS

Self-Test

Completing this self-test and comparing your answers with those in Appendix B provides immediate feedback and helpful practice for exams. Additional interactive, self-tests are available at www.wiley.com/college/huffman.

1. *Abnormal behavior* is defined as __________.

a. statistically infrequent patterns of pathological emotion, thought, or action
b. patterns of emotion, thought, and action that are considered disordered
c. patterns of behaviors, thoughts, or emotions considered pathological for one or more of four reasons: deviance, dysfunction, distress, or danger
d. all these options

2. __________ is the branch of medicine that deals with the diagnosis, treatment, and prevention of mental disorders.

a. Psychology
b. Psychiatry
c. Psychobiology
d. Psychodiagnostics

3. In the early treatment of psychological disorders, __________ was used to allow evil spirits to escape, whereas __________ was designed to drive the Devil out through prayer, fasting, and so on.

a. trephining; exorcism
b. demonology; hydrotherapy
c. the medical model; the dunking test
d. none of these options

4. Label the seven psychological perspectives on psychological disorders.

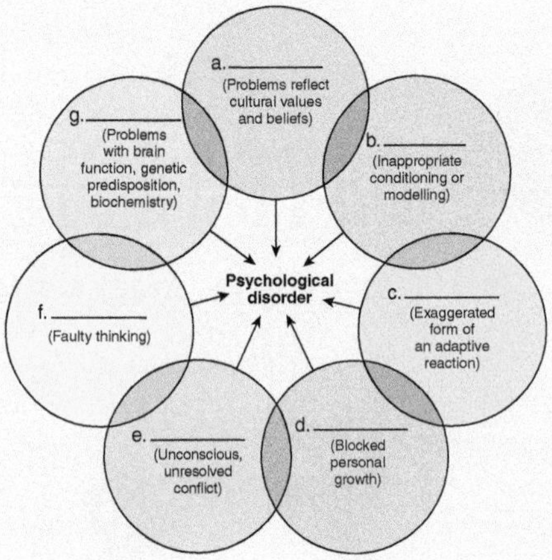

Think Critically

1 Can you think of cases in which someone might have a psychological disorder not described by the four criteria deviance, dysfunction, distress, and/or danger?

2 Do you think the insanity plea, as it is currently structured, should be abolished? Why or why not?

realworldpsychology

How can media coverage of mass shootings create negative misperceptions about people with mental illness?

HINT: LOOK IN THE MARGIN FOR Q1

ANXIETY DISORDERS

LEARNING OBJECTIVES

RETRIEVAL PRACTICE While reading the upcoming sections, respond to each Learning Objective in your own words. Then compare your responses with those found at www.wiley.com/college/huffman.

1 **DESCRIBE** anxiety disorders and the symptoms of generalized anxiety disorder (GAD), panic disorder, and phobias.

2 **SUMMARIZE** how psychological, biological, and sociocultural factors contribute to anxiety disorders.

Anxiety disorder A mental disorder characterized by overwhelming tension and irrational fear accompanied by physiological arousal.

Have you ever faced a very important exam, job interview, or first date and broken out in a cold sweat, felt your heart pounding, and had trouble breathing? If so, you have some understanding of anxiety, but the experiences and symptoms of those who suffer from **anxiety disorders** are much more intense and life disrupting. Fortunately, anxiety disorders are also among the easiest to treat and offer some of the best chances for recovery (Chapter 13).

realworldpsychology **Coping with Anxiety Disorders** What would you do if you were a promising new professional basketball player expected to fly all over the country with your team but suffered from an intense fear of flying? This is just one of the many challenges facing NBA rookie player Royce White, who speaks openly about his illness and personal experiences, hoping to boost public awareness of mental illness. Although twice as many women as men are diagnosed with anxiety disorders, men like White also suffer from this widespread disease. In fact, anxiety disorders are the most frequently occurring mental disorders in the general population (Essau & Petermann, 2013; National Institute of Mental Health, 2011; Zerr et al., 2011).

Albert Pena/Cal Sport Media/NewsCom

Describing Anxiety Disorders

In this section, we discuss three anxiety disorders: *generalized anxiety disorder* (GAD), *panic disorder*, and *phobias* **(Figure 12.4)**. Although we cover these disorders separately, two or more often occur together (Corr, 2011; Johnston et al., 2013; Leyfer et al., 2013).

Generalized Anxiety Disorder

Sufferers of **generalized anxiety disorder (GAD)** experience fear and worries that are not focused on any one specific threat, which is why it's referred to as *generalized* (Hooley et al., 2013; Robichaud, 2013; Zink et al., 2013). Their anxiety also is chronic and uncontrollable and lasts at least six months. Because of persistent muscle tension and autonomic fear reactions, people with this disorder may develop headaches, heart palpitations, dizziness, and insomnia, making it even harder to cope with normal daily activities. The disorder affects twice as many women as men (Horwath & Gould, 2011).

Generalized anxiety disorder (GAD) An anxiety disorder characterized by persistent, uncontrollable, and free-floating, nonspecified anxiety.

Panic Disorder

Sudden but brief attacks of intense apprehension that cause trembling, dizziness, and difficulty breathing are symptoms of **panic disorder**. *Panic attacks* generally happen after frightening experiences or prolonged stress (and sometimes even after exercise). Panic disorder is diagnosed when several apparently spontaneous panic

Panic disorder An anxiety disorder in which sufferers experience sudden and inexplicable panic attacks; symptoms include difficulty breathing, heart palpitations, dizziness, trembling, terror, and feelings of impending doom.

FIGURE 12.4 ANXIETY DISORDERS

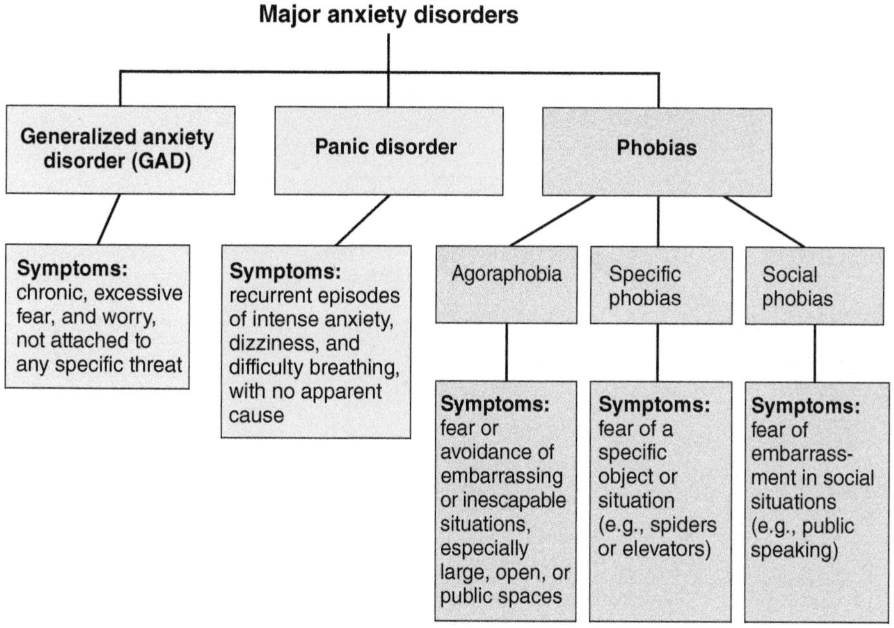

attacks lead to a persistent concern about future attacks. A common complication of panic disorder is agoraphobia, discussed in the next section (Horwath & Gould, 2011; Kircher et al., 2013).

FIGURE 12.5 SPIDER PHOBIA

Can you imagine being so frightened by a spider that you would try to jump out of a speeding car to get away from it? This is how a person suffering from a phobia might feel.

Phobia A persistent and intense, irrational fear and avoidance of a specific object or situation.

Phobias

Phobias include a strong, irrational fear and avoidance of objects or situations that are usually considered harmless (elevators or the dentist, for example). Although the person recognizes that the fear is irrational, the experience is still one of overwhelming anxiety, and a full-blown panic attack may follow. The fifth edition of the *DSM* divides phobias into separate categories: agoraphobia, specific phobias, and social anxiety disorder (social phobia).

People with *agoraphobia* restrict their normal activities because they fear having a panic attack in crowded, enclosed, or wide-open places where they would be unable to receive help in an emergency. In severe cases, people with agoraphobia may refuse to leave the safety of their homes.

A *specific phobia* is a fear of a specific object or situation, such as needles, rats, spiders, or heights. Claustrophobia (fear of closed spaces) and acrophobia (fear of heights) are the specific phobias most often treated by therapists. People with specific phobias generally recognize that their fears are excessive and unreasonable, but they are unable to control their anxiety and will go to great lengths to avoid the feared stimulus **(Figure 12.5)**.

Q2

One factor that helps explain why people with phobias have such extreme reactions is that they perceive the feared objects as larger than they actually are. Researchers in one study asked people with spider phobias to stand beside a glass tank and observe five different tarantulas (Vasey et al., 2012). They were then asked to estimate the size of each tarantula by drawing a line on an index card to illustrate its length. Those who reported experiencing the highest levels of fear while standing beside the tank drew the longest lines.

People with *social anxiety disorder* (or *social phobia*) are irrationally fearful of embarrassing themselves in social situations. Fear of public speaking and of eating in public are the two most common social phobias. The fear of public scrutiny and potential humiliation may become so pervasive that normal life is impossible (Kariuki & Stein, 2013; Moitra et al., 2011; Stopa et al., 2013).

Explaining Anxiety Disorders

Why do people develop anxiety disorders? Research has focused on the roles of psychological, biological, and sociocultural processes (the *biopsychosocial model*) **(Figure 12.6)**.

FIGURE 12.6 ANXIETY DISORDERS AND THE BIOPSYCHOSOCIAL MODEL

The biopsychosocial model takes into account the wide variety of factors than can contribute to anxiety disorders.

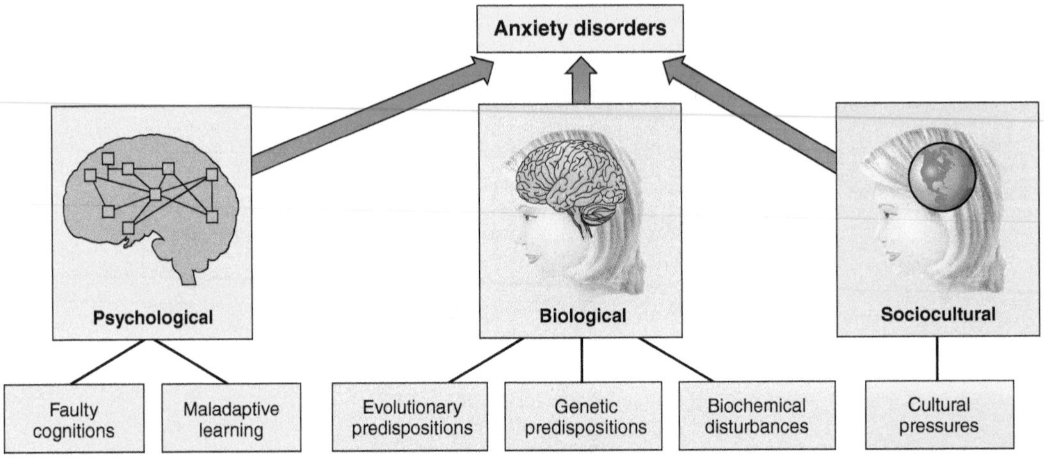

Psychological Factors

Researchers generally agree on the two major psychological contributions to anxiety disorders: *faulty cognitive processes* and *maladaptive learning*.

People with anxiety disorders tend to have habits of thinking, or cognitive processes, that make them prone to fear. These faulty cognitions tend to make them hypervigilant—meaning they constantly scan their environment for signs of danger and ignore signs of safety. They also tend to magnify ordinary threats and failures and to be hypersensitive to others' opinions of them.

In contrast to this cognitive explanation, learning theorists suggest that anxiety disorders result from maladaptive learning, such as inadvertent and improper conditioning and social learning (Chapter 6) (Gazendam et al., 2013; Grills-Taquechel & Ollendick, 2013; Lovibond, 2011). During classical conditioning, for example, a stimulus that is originally neutral (say a harmless spider) becomes paired with a frightening event (a sudden panic attack) so that it becomes a conditioned stimulus that elicits anxiety. The person then begins to avoid spiders in order to reduce anxiety (an operant conditioning process known as negative reinforcement) (Chapter 6) **(Figure 12.7)**.

Some researchers contend that because most people with phobias cannot remember a specific instance that led to their fear, and because frightening experiences do not always trigger phobias, conditioning may not be the only explanation. Social learning theorists propose that some phobias result from modeling and imitation. For example, children whose parents, especially fathers, are afraid of going to the dentist are much more likely to also have such a fear themselves (Lara-Sacido et al., 2012).

Biological Factors

Some researchers believe phobias reflect an evolutionary predisposition to fear things that were dangerous to our ancestors (Beckers et al., 2013; Glover, 2011; Mineka & Oehlberg, 2008; Noggle & Dean, 2013; Soares & Esteves, 2013). Some people with panic disorder also seem genetically predisposed toward an overreaction of the autonomic nervous system, further supporting the argument for a biological

FIGURE 12.7 **CONDITIONING AND PHOBIAS**

Classical conditioning combined with operant conditioning can lead to phobias. Consider the example of Little Albert's classically conditioned fear of rats, discussed in Chapter 6.

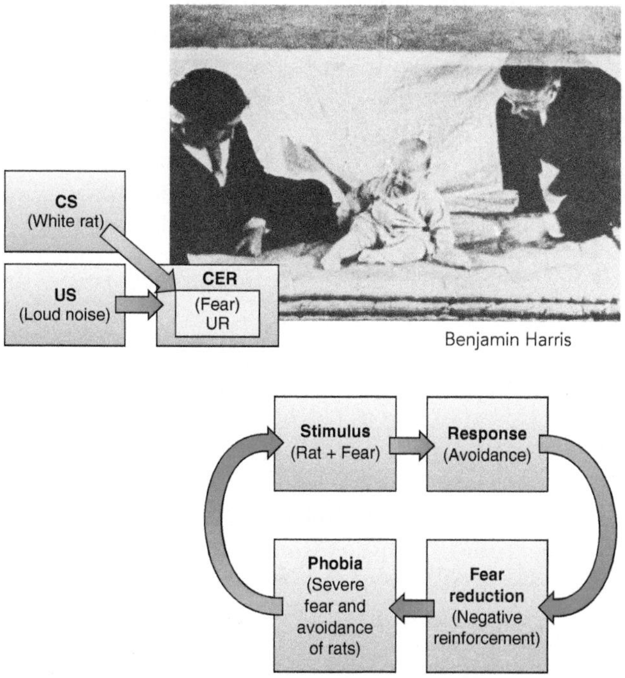

Ⓐ **Classical conditioning**
By pairing the white rat with a loud noise, experimenters used classical conditioning to teach Little Albert to fear rats.

Ⓑ **Operant conditioning**
Later Albert might have learned to avoid rats through operant conditioning. Avoiding rats would reduce Albert's fear, giving unintended reinforcement to his fearful behavior.

Ⓒ **Phobia**
Over time, this cycle of fear and avoidance could produce an even more severe fear, or phobia.

component. In addition, stress and arousal seem to play a role in panic attacks, and drugs such as caffeine or nicotine and even hyperventilation can trigger an attack, all suggesting a biochemical disturbance.

Sociocultural Factors

In addition to psychological and biological components, sociocultural factors can contribute to anxiety. There has been a sharp rise in anxiety disorders in the past 50 years, particularly in Western industrialized countries. Can you see how our fast-paced lives—along with our increased mobility, decreased job security, and decreased family support—might contribute to anxiety? Unlike the dangers early humans faced in our evolutionary history, today's threats are less identifiable and less immediate. This may in turn lead some people to become hypervigilant and predisposed to anxiety disorders.

Further support for sociocultural influences on anxiety disorders is our recognition that they can have dramatically different forms in other cultures. For example, in a collectivist twist on anxiety, some Japanese experience a type of social phobia called *taijin kyofusho* (*TKS*), a morbid dread of doing something to embarrass *others*. This disorder is quite different from the Western version of social phobia, which centers on a fear of criticism.

RETRIEVAL PRACTICE: ANXIETY DISORDERS

Self-Test

Completing this self-test and comparing your answers with those in Appendix B provides immediate feedback and helpful practice for exams. Additional interactive, self-tests are available at www.wiley.com/college/huffman.

1. Label the three key anxiety disorders.

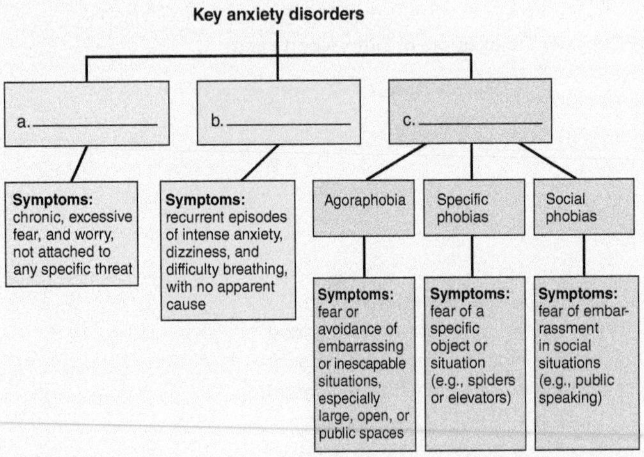

2. Anxiety disorders are ____________.

a. characterized by overwhelming tension, irrational fear, and physiological arousal
b. the least frequent of the mental disorders
c. twice as common in men as in women
d. all these options

3. Persistent, uncontrollable, and free-floating, non-specified anxiety might be diagnosed as a ____________.

a. generalized anxiety disorder
b. panic disorder
c. phobia
d. all these options

4. In the Japanese social phobia called TKS, people fear that they will ____________.

a. evaluate others negatively
b. embarrass themselves
c. embarrass others
d. be embarrassed by others

Think Critically

1 Why do you suppose anxiety disorders are among the easiest disorders to treat?

2 How would you explain the high number of anxiety disorders in the United States?

realworldpsychology

Do people with a phobia see the object that frightens them as larger than it really is?

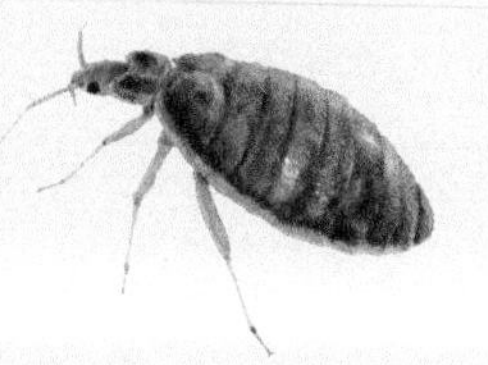

HINT: LOOK IN THE MARGIN FOR Q2

DEPRESSIVE AND BIPOLAR DISORDERS

LEARNING OBJECTIVES

RETRIEVAL PRACTICE While reading the upcoming sections, respond to each Learning Objective in your own words. Then compare your responses with those found at www.wiley.com/college/huffman.

1 **EXPLAIN** how depressive disorders and bipolar disorders differ.

2 **SUMMARIZE** research on the biological and psychological factors that contribute to depressive and bipolar disorders.

3 **DISCUSS** what to do if someone is suicidal.

Both depressive disorders and bipolar disorders are characterized by extreme disturbances in emotional states.

Describing Depressive and Bipolar Disorders

We all feel "blue" sometimes—especially following the loss of a job, end of a relationship, or death of a loved one. People suffering from **depressive disorders**, however, are so deeply sad and discouraged that they often have trouble sleeping, are likely to lose (or gain) significant weight, and may feel so fatigued that they cannot go to work or school or even comb their hair and brush their teeth. They may sleep constantly, have problems concentrating, and feel so profoundly sad and guilty that they consider suicide. Seriously depressed individuals have a hard time thinking clearly or recognizing their own problems (Hammen & Keenan-Miller, 2013; Wyrobeck et al., 2013).

Depressive disorders A group of mental disorders, including disruptive mood dysregulation disorder and major depressive disorder, characterized by sad, empty, or irritable moods that interfere with the ability to function.

realworldpsychology **Hollywood's Depiction of Bipolar Disorder**

Did you know that the Oscar nominated film *Silver Linings Playbook* was originally a gift from the director to his son, Matthew, who suffers from *bipolar disorder*? Viewers and mental health professionals, however, all agree that it's a gift for all because it casts a sensitive subject in a warmer light and helps offset the stigma so commonly associated with mental illness (Lopez, 2013).

YOU SEEM TO BE DEPRESSED
The DAWN of PSYCHIATRY

Bipolar disorder A mental disorder characterized by repeated episodes of mania (unreasonable elation, often with hyperactivity) alternating with depression.

When depression is *unipolar*, and the depressive episode ends, the person generally returns to a normal emotional level. People with **bipolar disorders**, however, rebound to the opposite state, known as *mania* **(Figure 12.8)**.

During a manic episode, the bipolar person is overly excited, extremely active, and easily distracted. In addition, he or she exhibits unrealistically high self-esteem, an inflated sense of importance, and poor judgment—giving away valuable possessions or going on wild spending sprees. The person also is often hyperactive and may not sleep for days at a time yet does not become fatigued. Thinking is faster than normal and can change abruptly to new topics, showing "rapid flight of ideas." Speech is also rapid ("pressured speech"), making it difficult for others to get a word in edgewise. A manic episode may last a few days or a few months, and it generally ends abruptly. The ensuing depressive episode generally lasts three times as long.

The lifetime risk for bipolar disorder is low—between 0.5 and 1.6%—but it can be one of the most debilitating and lethal disorders, with a suicide rate between 10 and 20% among sufferers (Bender & Alloy, 2011; Hammen & Keenan-Miller, 2013; Thaler et al., 2013). Suicide also is a serious risk for anyone suffering from several other mental health issues, particularly depressive disorders. See *Test Yourself: Danger Signs for Suicide* to first test your own level of depression and then to learn more about common suicide myths.

Explaining Depressive and Bipolar Disorders

Biological factors appear to play a significant role in both depressive disorders and bipolar disorders. For example, both disorders are sometimes treated with antidepressants, which affect the amount or functioning of norepinephrine, dopamine, and/or serotonin in the brain. In addition, recent research suggests that structural brain changes may contribute to these mood disorders. Sadly, NFL players are at greater risk of developing depression as they age, possibly due to brain damage caused by repeated concussions. One recent study on former NFL players revealed that 41% show cognitive problems and 24% show clinical depression, which may result from neurological changes caused by concussions (Hart et al., 2013). Their brain scans also revealed changes in blood flow within the brain and

FIGURE 12.8 DEPRESSIVE VERSUS BIPOLAR DISORDERS

If depressive disorders and bipolar disorders were depicted on a graph, they might look something like this. Note that only in bipolar disorders do people experience manic episodes.

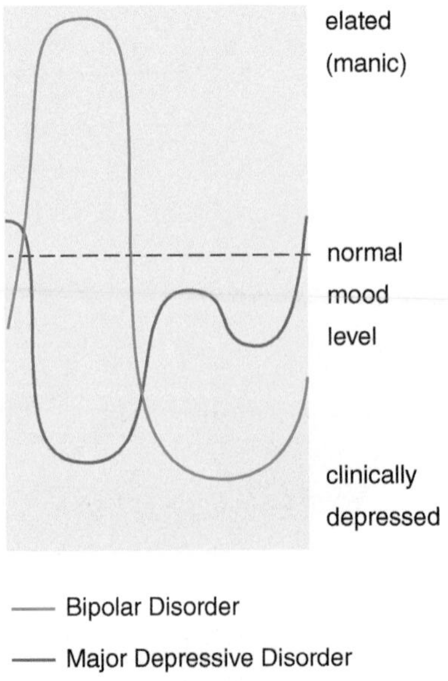

TEST YOURSELF: DANGER SIGNS FOR SUICIDE

psychology and you

Let's begin with a measure of your own symptoms of depression. Answer the following questions, based on how you have been feeling over the past two weeks. Use a scale of 1 = at no time to 6 = all the time.

© Bubbles Photolibrary/Alamy

Have you felt low in spirits or sad?

Have you lost interest in your daily activities?

Have you felt lacking in energy and strength?

Have you felt less self-confident?

Have you had a bad conscience or feelings of guilt?

Have you felt that life wasn't worth living?

Have you had difficulty concentrating?

Have you felt very restless?

Have you felt subdued or slowed down?

Have you had trouble sleeping at night?

Have you suffered from reduced appetite?

Have you suffered from increased appetite?

Higher numbers on this scale indicate higher levels of depression (Bech et al., 2011; Olsen et al., 2003). If you're currently feeling suicidal, seek help immediately! If not, read on about some misconceptions and stereotypes surrounding suicide. Can you correctly identify which of the following is true or false?

1. People who talk about suicide are less likely to commit suicide.
2. Suicide usually takes place with little or no warning.
3. Suicidal people are fully intent on dying.
4. Children of parents who attempt suicide are at greater risk of committing suicide.
5. Suicidal people remain so forever.
6. Men are more likely than women to actually kill themselves by suicide.
7. When a suicidal person has been severely depressed and seems to be "snapping out of it," the danger of suicide decreases substantially.
8. Only depressed people commit suicide.
9. Thinking about suicide is rare.
10. Asking a depressed person about suicide will push him or her over the edge and cause a suicidal act that would not otherwise have occurred.

Now, compare your responses to the experts' answers and explanations (Bailey et al., 2011; Baldessarini & Tondo, 2008; Callanan & Davis, 2012; Lilienfeld et al., 2010; Schneidman, 1981; Stricker et al., 2013; Taub & Thompson, 2013; Walsh et al., 2013).

1. and **2. False**. Up to three-quarters of those who take their own lives talk about it and give warnings about their intentions beforehand. They may say, "If something happens to me, I want you to . . . " or "Life just isn't worth living." They also provide behavioral clues, such as giving away valued possessions, withdrawing from family and friends, and losing interest in favorite activities.

3. False. Only about 3 to 5% of suicidal people truly intend to die. Most are just unsure about how to go on living. They cannot see their problems objectively enough to realize that they have alternative courses of action. They often gamble with death, arranging it so that fate or others will save them. Moreover, once the suicidal crisis passes, they are generally grateful to be alive.

4. True. Children of parents who attempt or commit suicide are at much greater risk of following in their footsteps. As Schneidman (1969) puts it, "The person who commits suicide puts his psychological skeleton in the survivor's emotional closet" (p. 225).

5. False. People who want to kill themselves are usually suicidal only for a limited period.

6. True. Although women are much more likely to attempt suicide, men are far more likely to actually commit suicide. Men are also more likely to use stronger methods, such as guns instead of pills.

7. **False**. When people are first coming out of a depression, they are in fact at greater risk because they now have the energy to actually commit suicide.

8. **False**. Suicide rates are highest among people with major depressive disorders. However, suicide is also the leading cause of premature death in people who suffer from schizophrenia, and a major cause of death in people with anxiety disorders and alcohol and other substance-related disorders. Furthermore, suicide is not limited to people with depression. Poor physical health, serious illness, substance abuse (particularly of alcohol), loneliness, unemployment, and even natural disasters may push many over the edge.

9. **False**. Estimates from various studies are that 40 to 80% of the general public have thought about committing suicide at least once in their lives.

10. **False**. Because society often considers suicide a terrible, shameful act, asking directly about it can give the person permission to talk. In fact, not asking might lead to further isolation and depression.

abnormalities in various parts of the brain. Sadly, these changes may contribute to serious depression and increased risk of suicide **(Figure 12.9)**.

Other research points to imbalances of the neurotransmitters serotonin, norepinephrine, and dopamine as possible causes of mood disorders (Barton et al., 2008; Lopez-Munoz & Alamo, 2011; Pu et al., 2011; Wiste et al., 2008). Drugs that alter the activity of these neurotransmitters also decrease the symptoms of depression (and are therefore called antidepressants) (Chuang, 1998). Interestingly, researchers in one study found that people who regularly ate fast food and commercially produced baked goods (such as croissants and doughnuts) were 51% more likely to develop depression later on. This may be the result of the chemicals in such foods leading to physiological changes in the brain and body (Sanchez-Villegas et al., 2011).

Q3

Some biological research indicates that both depressive and bipolar disorders may be inherited (Boardman et al., 2011; Gonzales et al., 2013; McGue & Christensen, 2013; Melas et al., 2013). In contrast, research that takes an evolutionary perspective suggests that moderate depression may be a normal and healthy adaptive response to a very real loss, such as the death of a loved one, which helps us to step back and reassess our goals (Baddeley, 2013; Carvalho et al., 2013; Nettle, 2011; Raison & Miller, 2013). And clinical, severe depression may just be an extreme version of this generally adaptive response.

FIGURE 12.9 **BRAIN DAMAGE AND PROFESSIONAL SPORTS**

Junior Seau, who played in the NFL for 20 years, committed suicide with a gunshot wound to his chest in 2012 at the age of 43. Later studies concluded that he suffered from *chronic traumatic encephalopathy* (CTE), a form of concussion-related brain damage that has also been found in other NFL players.

Kent C. Horner/Getty Images

Psychosocial theories of depression focus on environmental stressors, disturbances in the person's interpersonal relationships or self-concept, and on any history of abuse or assault (Betancourt et al., 2011; Herrenkohl et al., 2013; Jewkes, 2013; Mendelson et al., 2011; Mota et al., 2012; Neri et al., 2012). The psychoanalytic explanation sees depression as the result of experiencing a real or imagined loss, which in internalized as guilt, shame, self-hatred and ultimately self-blame. The cognitive perspective explains depression as caused, at least in part, by negative thinking patterns, including a tendency to ruminate, or obsess, about problems (Brinker et al., 2013; Demeyer et al., 2012; Gibb et al., 2012). The humanistic school says that depression results when a person demands perfection of him- or herself or when positive growth is blocked (Keen, 2011; O'Connell, 2008; Stricker et al., 2013).

According to the **learned helplessness** theory (Seligman, 1975, 2007), depression occurs when people (and other animals) become resigned to the idea that they are helpless to escape from something painful. Learned helplessness may be particularly likely to trigger depression if the person attributes failure to causes that are internal ("my own weakness"), stable ("this weakness is long-standing and unchanging"), and global ("this weakness is a problem in lots of settings") (Alloy et al., 2011; Barnum et al., 2013; Newby & Moulds, 2011; Reivich et al., 2013).

Learned helplessness Seligman's term for a state of helplessness or resignation, in which human or nonhuman animals learn that escape from something painful is impossible; the organism stops responding and may become depressed.

Keep in mind that suicide is a major danger associated with both depressive disorder and bipolar disorder. Given that some people who suffer with these disorders are so disturbed that they lose contact with reality, they may fail to recognize the danger signs or to seek help. *What To Do If You Think Someone Is Suicidal* offers important information for both the sufferers and their family and friends.

WHAT TO DO IF YOU THINK SOMEONE IS SUICIDAL

psychology and you

If you believe someone is contemplating suicide, act on your beliefs. Stay with the person if there is any immediate danger. Encourage him or her to talk to you rather than withdraw. Show the person that you care but do not give false reassurances that "everything will be okay." This type of response may make the suicidal person feel *more* alienated. Instead, openly ask whether the person is feeling hopeless and suicidal. Do not be afraid to discuss suicide with people who feel depressed or hopeless, fearing that you will put ideas into their heads. The reality is that people who are left alone or who are told they can't be serious about suicide often attempt it.

If you suspect that someone is imminently suicidal, it is vitally important that you help the person obtain counseling. Get help immediately! Consider calling the police for emergency intervention, the person's therapist, and/or the toll-free 24/7 hotline 1-800-SUICIDE (784-2433). Most cities also have walk-in centers that provide emergency counseling.

In addition, share your suspicions with parents, friends, or others who can help in a suicidal crisis. To save a life, you may have to betray a secret when someone confides in you. If you feel you can't do this alone, get another person to help you.

Mirek Towski/DMI/Time LifePictures/Getty Images

Even people who enjoy fame and success may be at risk for suicide. Famous musicians like Mindy McCready (pictured here) and Kurt Cobain; professional athletes such as Olympic medalist Jeret Peterson, or football player Junior Seau; and well known writers and artists like Hunter S. Thompson, Virginia Woolf, Ernest Hemingway, and Vincent van Gogh have all died as a result of suicide.

RETRIEVAL PRACTICE: DEPRESSIVE AND BIPOLAR DISORDERS

Self-Test

Completing this self-test and comparing your answers with those in Appendix B provides immediate feedback and helpful practice for exams. Additional interactive, self-tests are available at www.wiley.com/college/huffman.

1. A major difference between depressive disorder and bipolar disorder is that only in bipolar disorder do people have ________.
   a. hallucinations or delusions b. depression
   c. manic episodes d. a biochemical imbalance

2. Depressive and bipolar disorders are sometimes treated by ________ drugs, which affect the amount or functioning of norepinephrine, dopamine, and serotonin in the brain.
   a. antidepressant b. antipsychotics
   c. mood congruence d. none of the above

3. Which of the following is a myth about suicide?
   a. People who talk about it are less likely to actually do it
   b. Suicide usually occurs with little or no warning
   c. Most people have never thought about suicide
   d. all of these options

4. According to the theory known as ________, when faced with a painful situation from which there is no escape, animals and people enter a state of helplessness and resignation.
   a. autonomic resignation b. helpless resignation
   c. resigned helplessness d. learned helplessness

Think Critically

1. Have you ever felt seriously depressed? How would you distinguish between "normal" depression and a serious depressive disorder?
2. Can you think of a personal example of how major depression served as a possible evolutionary advantage?

realworldpsychology

Can eating fast food lead to depression later on?

HINT: LOOK IN THE MARGIN FOR Q3

SCHIZOPHRENIA

LEARNING OBJECTIVES

RETRIEVAL PRACTICE While reading the upcoming sections, respond to each Learning Objective in your own words. Then compare your responses with those found at www.wiley.com/college/huffman.

1. **IDENTIFY** schizophrenia and its common symptoms.
2. **COMPARE** the traditional five-subtype system for classifying different types of schizophrenia with the two-group system that has recently emerged.
3. **SUMMARIZE** the biological and psychosocial factors that contribute to schizophrenia.

Imagine that your 17-year-old son's behavior has changed dramatically over the past few months, and he has gone from being actively involved in sports and clubs to suddenly quitting all activities and refusing to go to school. He now also talks to himself—mumbling and yelling out at times—and no longer regularly showers or washes his hair. Recently he announced, "The voices are telling me to jump out the window" (Kotowski, 2012).

Schizophrenia A group of severe disorders involving major disturbances in perception, language, thought, emotion, and behavior.

This description is taken from the true case history of a patient who suffers from **schizophrenia**. People with schizophrenia have serious problems caring for themselves, relating to others, and holding a job. In extreme cases, the illness is considered a *psychosis*, meaning the person is out of touch with reality, and treatment often requires institutional or custodial care.

Schizophrenia is one of the most widespread and devastating mental disorders. Approximately 1 of every 100 people will develop it in his or her lifetime, and approximately half of all people who are admitted to mental hospitals are diagnosed with this disorder (Gottesman, 1991; Harvey & Bowie, 2013; Kessler et al., 1994; Regier et al., 1993). Schizophrenia usually emerges between the late teens and the mid-30s and only rarely prior to adolescence or after age 45. It seems to be equally prevalent in men and women, but it's generally more severe and strikes earlier in men (Chang et al., 2011; Goldstein et al., 2013; Gottesman, 1991; Harvey & Bowie, 2013; Lee et al., 2011).

Many people confuse schizophrenia with dissociative identity disorder, which is sometimes referred to as *split* or *multiple personality disorder* (see *Real World Psychology*). *Schizophrenia* means "split mind," but when Eugen Bleuler coined the term in 1911, he was referring to the fragmenting of thought processes and emotions, not of personalities (Neale et al., 1983). As we discuss later in this chapter, dissociative identity disorder is popularly referred to as having a "split personality"—the rare and controversial condition of having more than one distinct personality.

realworldpsychology **Do People with Schizophrenia Have Multiple Personalities?** As shown in this cartoon and in popular movies and television shows, schizophrenia is commonly confused with *multiple personality disorder* (now known as *dissociative identity disorder*, p. 357). This widespread error persists in part because of confusing terminology. Literally translated, *schizophrenia* means "split mind," referring to a split from reality that shows itself in disturbed perceptions, language, thought, emotions, and/or behavior.

In contrast, dissociative identity disorder (DID) refers to the condition in which two or more distinct personalities exist within the same person at different times. People with schizophrenia have only one personality.

Why does this matter? Confusing schizophrenia with multiple personalities is not only technically incorrect, it also trivializes the devastating effects of both disorders, which may include severe anxiety, social isolation, unemployment, homelessness, substance abuse, clinical depression, and even suicide (Lilienfeld et al., 2010; Preventing Suicide, 2009; Smith et al., 2011; Stricker et al., 2013).

Dave Parker/CartoonStock

"THANKS FOR CURING MY SCHIZOPHRENIA—WE'RE BOTH FINE NOW!"

Symptoms of Schizophrenia

Schizophrenia is a group of disorders characterized by a disturbance in one or more of the following areas: *perception*, *language*, *thought*, *affect* (emotions), and *behavior*.

Perception

The senses of people with schizophrenia may be either enhanced or blunted. The filtering and selection processes that allow most people to concentrate on whatever they choose are impaired, and sensory stimulation is jumbled and distorted. People with schizophrenia may also experience **hallucinations**, false, imaginary sensory perceptions that occur without external stimuli. Auditory hallucinations (hearing voices and sounds) is one of the most commonly noted and reported symptoms of schizophrenia.

Hallucination A false, imaginary sensory perception that occurs without an external, objective source.

On rare occasions, people with schizophrenia hurt others in response to their distorted perceptions. But a person with schizophrenia is more likely to be self-destructive and suicidal than violent toward others.

Language and Thought

For people with schizophrenia, words lose their usual meanings and associations, logic is impaired, and thoughts are disorganized and bizarre. When language and thought disturbances are mild, the individual jumps from topic to topic. With more severe disturbances, the person jumbles phrases and words together (into a "word salad") or creates artificial words. The most common—and frightening—thought disturbance experienced by people with schizophrenia is lack of contact with reality (psychosis).

Delusion A false or irrational belief maintained despite clear evidence to the contrary.

Delusions, false beliefs or opinions despite invalidating evidence, are also common in people with schizophrenia. We all experience exaggerated thoughts from time to time, such as thinking a friend is trying to avoid us, but the delusions of schizophrenia are much more extreme. For example, if someone falsely believed that the postman who routinely delivered mail to his house every afternoon was a co-conspirator in a plot to kill him, it would likely qualify as a *delusion of persecution*. In *delusions of grandeur*, people believe that they are someone very important, perhaps Jesus Christ or the queen of England. In *delusions of reference*, unrelated events are given special significance, as when a person believes a radio program is sending him or her special messages.

A recent trend among individuals suffering from various mental disorders is to join Internet groups where they can share their experiences with others. For example, people with schizophrenia and other psychotic disorders can now share with fellow sufferers their belief that they are being stalked or that their minds are being controlled by technology. Some experts consider Internet groups that offer peer support to be helpful to mentally ill individuals, but others believe they may reinforce troubled thinking and impede treatment. Those who use the sites report feeling relieved by the sense that they are not alone in their suffering, but the groups are not moderated by professionals and pose the danger of amplifying the symptoms of mentally ill individuals (Kershaw, 2008).

"That's the doctor who is treating me for paranoia. I don't trust him."

Emotion

Changes in emotion usually occur in people with schizophrenia. In some cases, emotions are exaggerated and fluctuate rapidly. At other times, they become blunted. Some people with schizophrenia have *flattened affect*—almost no emotional response of any kind.

Behavior

Disturbances in behavior may take the form of unusual actions that have special meaning to the sufferer. For example, one patient massaged his head repeatedly to "clear it" of unwanted thoughts. People with schizophrenia also may become *cataleptic* and assume a nearly immobile stance for an extended period.

Types of Schizophrenia

For many years, researchers divided schizophrenia into five subtypes: *paranoid, catatonic, disorganized, undifferentiated*, and *residual*. Critics suggested that this system does not differentiate in terms of prognosis, cause, or response to treatment and that the undifferentiated type was merely a catchall for cases that are difficult to diagnose (American Psychiatric Association, 2013). For these reasons, researchers have proposed an alternative classification system:

1. **Positive schizophrenia symptoms** are additions to or exaggerations of normal thought processes and behaviors, including bizarre delusions and hallucinations.
2. **Negative schizophrenia symptoms** include the loss or absence of normal thought processes and behaviors and appear as impaired attention, limited or toneless speech, flat or blunted affect, and social withdrawal.

Positive symptoms are more common when schizophrenia develops rapidly, whereas negative symptoms are more often found in slow-developing schizophrenia. Positive symptoms are associated with better adjustment before the onset and a better prognosis for recovery.

Explaining Schizophrenia

Because schizophrenia comes in many different forms, it probably has multiple biological and psychosocial bases. Let's look at biological contributions first.

Prenatal stress and viral infections, birth complications, immune responses, maternal malnutrition, and advanced paternal age all may contribute to the development of schizophrenia (Kneeland & Fatemi, 2013; Miller et al., 2013; Noggle & Dean, 2013; Weinberger & Harrison, 2011). However, most biological theories of schizophrenia focus on genetics, neurotransmitters, and brain abnormalities:

- **Genetics** Although researchers are beginning to identify specific genes related to schizophrenia, most genetic studies have focused on twins and adoptions (Drew et al., 2011; Gilman et al., 2012; Owens et al., 2011; Svrakic et al., 2013; Wiener et al., 2013). This research indicates that the risk for schizophrenia increases with genetic similarity; that is, people who share more genes with a person who has schizophrenia are more likely to develop the disorder **(Figure 12.10)**.
- **Neurotransmitters** Precisely how genetic inheritance produces schizophrenia is unclear. According to the *dopamine hypothesis*, overactivity of certain dopamine neurons in the brain causes some forms of schizophrenia (Fusar-Poli & Meyer-Lindenberg, 2013; Madras, 2013; Nord & Farde, 2011; Sokoloff et al., 2013). This hypothesis is based on two observations. First, administering amphetamines increases the amount of dopamine and can produce (or worsen) some symptoms of schizophrenia, especially in people with a genetic predisposition to the disorder. Second, drugs that reduce dopamine activity in the brain reduce or eliminate some symptoms of schizophrenia.
- **Brain abnormalities** A third major biological theory for schizophrenia looks at abnormalities in brain function and structure. Researchers have found larger cerebral ventricles (fluid-filled spaces in the brain) in some people with schizophrenia (Agartz et al., 2011; Fusar-Poli et al., 2011; Pepe et al., 2013).

Also, some people with chronic schizophrenia have a lower level of activity in their frontal and temporal lobes—areas we use in language, attention, and memory **(Figure 12.11)**. Damage in

FIGURE 12.10 GENETICS AND SCHIZOPHRENIA

Biological relatives of people with schizophrenia have a higher risk than the general population of developing the disorder during their lifetimes. Closer relatives (who have a more similar genetic makeup) have a greater risk than more distant relatives (Gottesman, 1991).

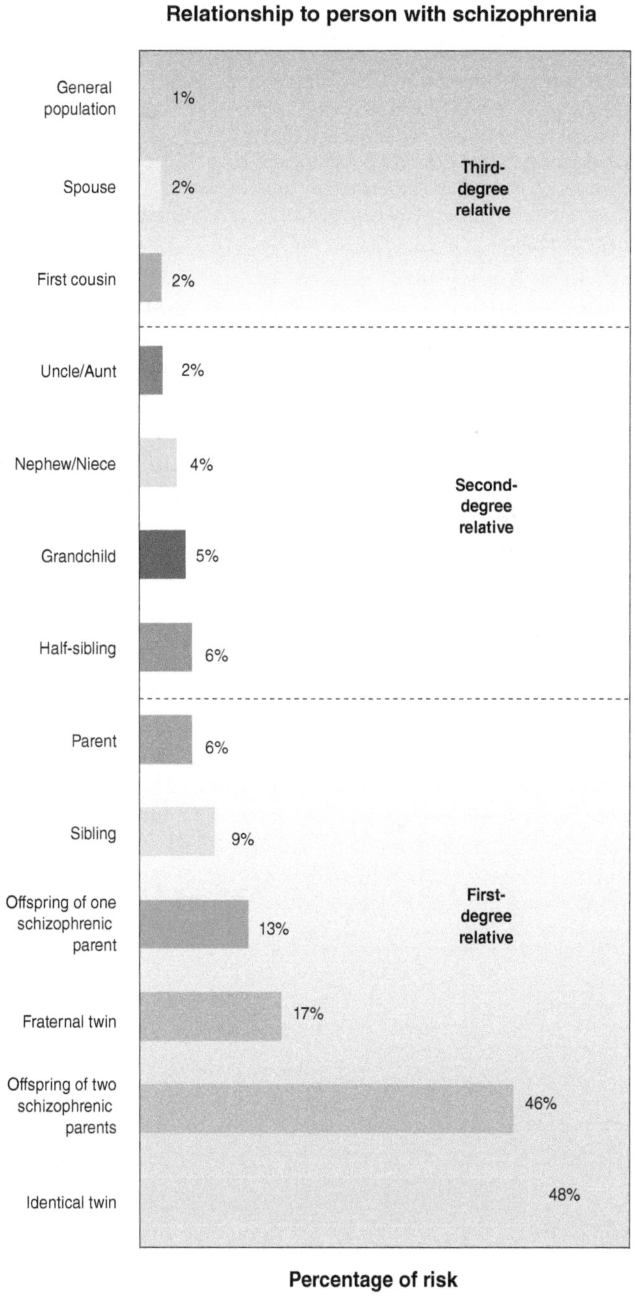

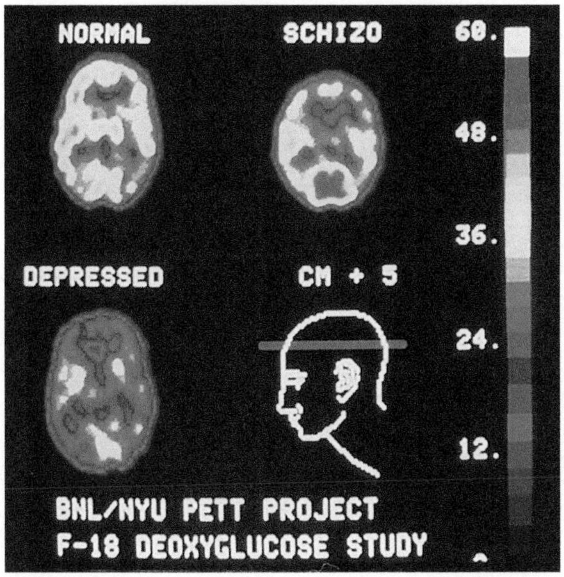

Science Source/Photo Researchers, Inc.

FIGURE 12.11 BRAIN ACTIVITY IN SCHIZOPHRENIA

Using these positron emission tomography (PET) scans, compare the normal levels of brain activity (upper left) with those of a person with schizophrenia (upper right), and then with those of a person with depression (lower left). Warmer colors (reds, yellows) indicate increased brain activity, whereas cooler colors (blues and greens) indicate decreased activity.

these regions might explain the thought and language disturbances that characterize schizophrenia. This lower level of brain activity, and schizophrenia itself, may also result from an overall loss of gray matter (neurons in the cerebral cortex) (Salgado-Pineda et al., 2011; Trost et al., 2013; Williams et al., 2013).

Clearly, biological factors play a key role in schizophrenia. But the fact that the heritability of schizophrenia is only 48% even in identical twins—who share identical genes—tells us that nongenetic factors must contribute the remaining percentage. Most psychologists believe there are at least two possible psychosocial contributors.

According to the **diathesis-stress model** of schizophrenia, stress plays an essential role in triggering schizophrenic episodes in people with an inherited predisposition (or diathesis) toward the disease (Arnsten, 2011; Beaton & Simon, 2011; Gallagher & Jones, 2013). In line with this model, children who experience severe trauma before age 16 are three times more likely than other people to develop schizophrenia (Bentall et al., 2012). People who experience stressful living environments, including poverty, unemployment, and crowding, are also at increased risk (Burns, 2013; Kirkbride et al., 2013). Q4

Diathesis-stress model A hypothesis about the cause of certain disorders, such as schizophrenia, which suggests that people inherit a predisposition (or "diathesis") that increases their risk for mental disorders if they are exposed to certain extremely stressful life experiences.

Some investigators suggest that communication disorders in family members may also be a predisposing factor for schizophrenia. Such disorders include unintelligible speech, fragmented communication, and parents' frequently sending severely contradictory messages to children. Several studies have also shown greater rates of relapse and worsening of symptoms among hospitalized patients who went home to families that were critical and hostile toward them or overly involved in their lives emotionally (McFarlane, 2011; Roisko et al., 2011; Wasserman et al., 2013).

How should we evaluate the different theories about the causes of schizophrenia? Critics of the dopamine hypothesis and the brain damage theory argue that those theories fit only some cases of schizophrenia. Moreover, with both theories, it is difficult to determine cause and effect. The disturbed-communication theories are also hotly debated, and research is inconclusive. Like almost all forms of mental illness, schizophrenia is probably the result of a combination of known and unknown interacting factors **(Figure 12.12)**.

FIGURE 12.12 **THE BIOPSYCHOSOCIAL MODEL AND SCHIZOPHRENIA**

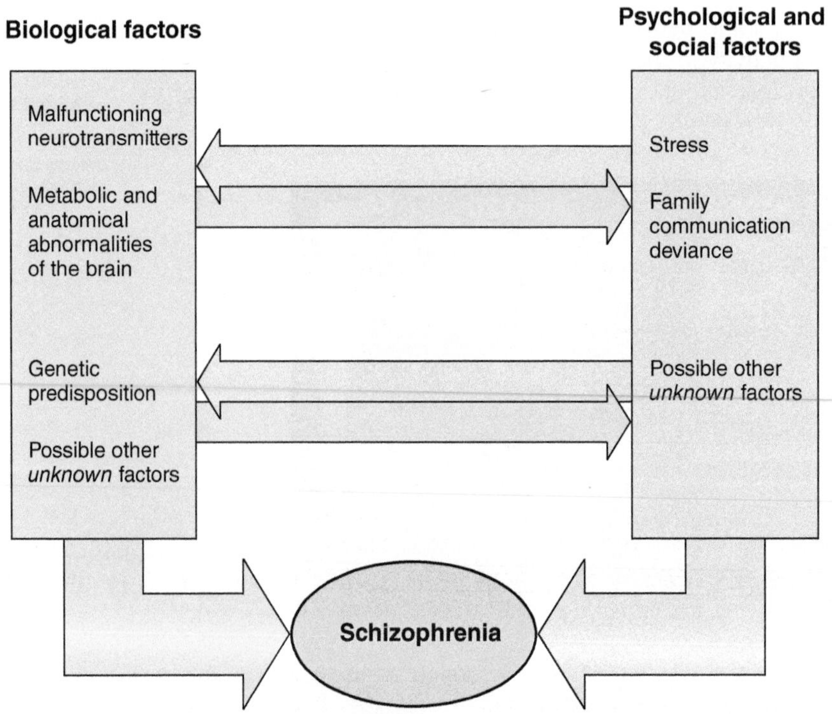

RETRIEVAL PRACTICE: SCHIZOPHRENIA

Self-Test

Completing this self-test and comparing your answers with those in Appendix B provides immediate feedback and helpful practice for exams. Additional interactive, self-tests are available at www.wiley.com/college/huffman.

1. Major disturbances in perception, language, thought, emotion, and behavior may be diagnosed as ________.

a. schizophrenia b. multiple dissociative disorder
c. borderline psychosis d. neurotic psychosis

2. ________ refers to "split mind," whereas refers to "split personality."

a. Psychosis; neurosis b. Insanity; multiple personalities
c. Schizophrenia; dissociative identity disorder (DID) d. Paranoia; borderline

3. In extreme cases, schizophrenia is also a form of ________, a term describing general lack of contact with reality.

a. multiple personality disorder b. psychosis
c. borderline polar psychosis d. all the above

4. Perceptions for which there are no appropriate external stimuli are called ________, and the most common type among people suffering from schizophrenia is ________.

a. hallucinations; auditory b. hallucinations; visual
c. delusions; auditory d. delusions; visual

Think Critically

1 Most of the disorders discussed in this chapter have some evidence for a genetic predisposition. What would you tell a friend who has a family member with one of these disorders and fears that he or she might develop the same disorder?

2 What do you think are the most important biological and psychosocial factors that contribute to schizophrenia?

realworldpsychology

Why might children who experience trauma be at increased risk of developing schizophrenia later in life?

HINT: LOOK IN THE MARGIN FOR Q4

OTHER DISORDERS

RETRIEVAL PRACTICE While reading the upcoming sections, respond to each Learning Objective in your own words. Then compare your responses with those found at www.wiley.com/college/huffman.

LEARNING OBJECTIVES

1 **SUMMARIZE** the major features of obsessive-compulsive disorder.
2 **DESCRIBE** dissociative disorders.
3 **IDENTIFY** the major characteristics of personality disorders.

Having discussed anxiety disorders, mood disorders, and schizophrenia, we now explore three additional disorders: obsessive-compulsive, dissociative, and personality disorders.

Obsessive-Compulsive Disorder (OCD)

OCD involves persistent, unwanted, fearful thoughts (obsessions) and/or irresistible urges to perform an act or repeated rituals (compulsions) to help relieve the anxiety created by the obsession. In adults, women are affected at a slightly higher rate than men, whereas men are more commonly affected in childhood (American Psychiatric Association, 2013).

Common examples of obsessions are fear of germs, fear of being hurt or of hurting others, and troubling religious or sexual thoughts. Examples of compulsions are repeatedly checking, counting, cleaning, washing all or specific body parts, or putting things in a certain order. While everyone worries and sometimes double-checks, people with OCD have these thoughts and do these rituals for at least an hour or more each day, often longer (Chang et al., 2013; Roth et al., 2013).

Imagine what it would be like to worry so obsessively about germs that you compulsively wash your hands hundreds of times a day, until they are raw and bleeding. Most sufferers of **obsessive compulsive disorder (OCD)** realize that their actions are senseless. But when they try to stop the behavior, they experience mounting anxiety, which is relieved only by giving in to the compulsions. Given that numerous biological and psychological factors contribute to OCD, it is most often treated with a combination of drugs and cognitive-behavior therapy (CBT) **(Figure 12.13)** (Amin & Noggle, 2013; Roth et al., 2013) (Chapter 13).

Obsessive-compulsive disorder (OCD) A mental disorder characterized by persistent, anxiety-provoking thoughts that will not go away (obsessions) and/or irresistible urges to perform repetitive behaviors (compulsions) performed according to certain rules or in a ritualized manner; compulsive behaviors persist because they help relieve the anxiety created by the obsessions.

Voices from the Classroom

OCD and Counting Stairs When we discuss *obsessive-compulsive disorder* in my class, I explain that everyone has some obsessive-compulsive behaviors, but it's not considered a disorder unless it becomes disruptive to your life. Some people count stairs as they go up or down (you know who you are)—not out loud but just silently.

After making this same statement in class one day, a student replied: "But you HAVE to count them. And if you get to the top or bottom and they're an odd number, you have to go back and start over. This time you have to continue counting with the number you stopped with so that they come out even." Counting the stairs to yourself is just a little obsessive-compulsive behavior, but having to go back and do it again so that they come out even is disruptive.

Professor Mike Majors
Delgado Community College
New Orleans, Louisiana

FIGURE 12.13 MANAGING OCD

Many celebrities suffer from OCD, including soccer star David Beckham, actors Megan Fox (pictured here) and Leonardo DiCaprio, and singer/actor Justin Timberlake. Fortunately, people can learn to manage the symptoms of OCD, through therapy and/or medication, and lead highly productive and fulfilling lives.

Kevin Winter/Getty Images

Image Source/Getty Images

FIGURE 12.14 DISSOCIATION AS AN ESCAPE

The major force behind all dissociative disorders is the need to escape from anxiety. Imagine witnessing a loved one's death in a horrible car accident. Can you see how your mind might cope by blocking out all memory of the event?

Dissociative Disorders

The most dramatic psychological disorders are **dissociative disorders**, psychological dysfunctions characterized by a major loss of memory without a clear physical cause. There are several types, but all are characterized by a splitting apart (a *dis-association*) of significant aspects of experience from memory or consciousness **(Figure 12.14)**. Unlike most other psychological disorders, dissociative disorders appear to be primarily caused by environmental variables, with little or no genetic influence (Hulette et al., 2011; Sinason, 2011; Waller & Ross, 1997).

Dissociative disorder A psychological disorder marked by a disturbance in the integration of consciousness, identity, memory, and other features.

The most severe dissociative disorder is **dissociative identity disorder (DID)**—previously known as multiple personality disorder (MPD)—in which at least two separate and distinct personalities exist within a person at the same time **(Figure 12.15)**. Each personality has unique memories, behaviors, and social relationships. Transition from one personality to another occurs suddenly and is often triggered by psychological stress. Usually, the original personality has no knowledge or awareness of the alternate personalities, but all the personalities may be aware of lost periods of time. The disorder is diagnosed about equally among men and women (American Psychiatric Association, 2013).

Dissociative identity disorder (DID) A mental disorder characterized by the presence of two or more distinct personality systems in the same individual at different times; previously known as multiple personality disorder (MPD).

DID is a controversial diagnosis. Some experts suggest that many cases are faked or result from false memories and an unconscious need to please the therapist (Boysen & VanBergen, 2013; Kihlstrom, 2005; Ost et al., 2013; Stafford & Lynn, 2002). On the other side of the debate are psychologists who accept the validity of DID and provide treatment guidelines (Brown, 2011; Chu, 2011; Dalenberg et al., 2007; Lipsanen et al., 2004; Moline, 2013).

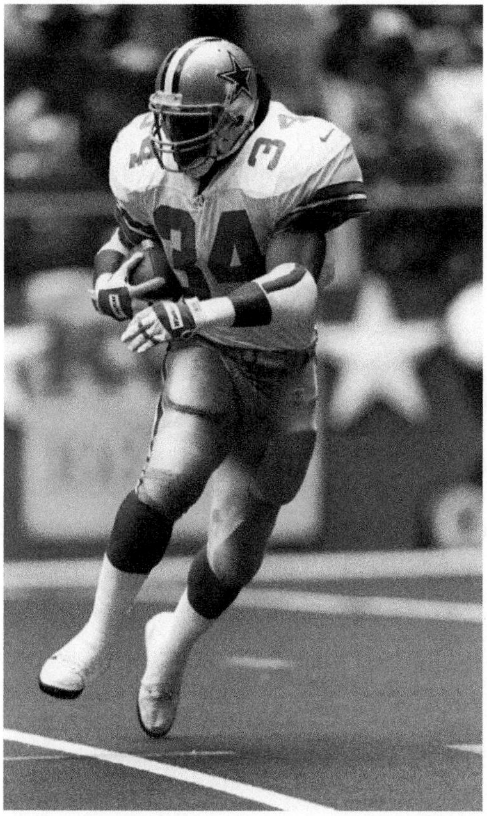

Stephen Dunn /Allsport / GettyImages.

FIGURE 12.15 A PERSONAL ACCOUNT OF DID

Herschel Walker, professional football player, pro bowler, Olympic bobsledder, and business and family man, now suggests that none of the people who played these roles were really he. They were his "alters," or alternate personalities. He has been diagnosed with the controversial diagnosis of *dissociative identity disorder* (*DID*). Although some have suggested that the disorder helped him succeed as a professional athlete, it played havoc with his personal life. He's now in treatment and has written a book, *Breaking Free*, hoping to change the public's image of DID.

Personality Disorders

Personality disorder A mental disorder characterized by chronic, inflexible, maladaptive personality traits, which cause significant impairment of social and occupational functioning.

What would happen if the characteristics of a personality were so inflexible and maladaptive that they significantly impaired someone's ability to function? This is what occurs with **personality disorders**. Several types of personality disorders are included in this category in the fifth edition of the *DSM*, but here we will focus on antisocial personality disorder and borderline personality disorder (American Psychiatric Association, 2013).

Antisocial Personality Disorder

Antisocial personality disorder The pervasive pattern of disregard for, and violation of, the rights of others beginning in childhood or early adolescence and continuing into adulthood; includes traits like unlawful behaviors, deceitful and manipulative behaviors, impulsivity, irritability and aggressiveness, consistent irresponsibility, reckless disregard for self and others, and lack of remorse.

People with **antisocial personality disorder**—also sometimes referred to as *psychopathy, sociopathy*, or *dissocial personality disorder*—show a pattern of disregard for, and violation of, the rights of others. These labels describe behavior so far outside the ethical and legal standards of society that many consider it the most serious of all mental disorders. Unlike people with anxiety, mood disorders, and schizophrenia, those with this diagnosis feel little personal distress (and may not be motivated to change). Yet their maladaptive traits generally bring considerable harm and suffering to others (Hervé et al., 2004; Noggle et al., 2013; Trull et al., 2013). Although serial killers are often seen as classic examples of people with antisocial personality disorder, most people who have this disorder generally harm others in less dramatic ways—for example, as ruthless businesspeople and crooked politicians.

RJ Samgostirj Sangostl /AFP /NewsCom

realworldpsychology **The Media and Mental Illness** The world was shocked and deeply saddened on July 20, 2012, when 25-year-old James Holmes went on a horrific shooting spree, killing 12 people and wounding or injuring 58 in a movie theater in Aurora, Colorado. The shootings prompted intense debate over gun control and violence in the media. Perhaps because he had been seeing a psychiatrist prior to the shooting, it also heightened attention to the detection and treatment of mental illness. But few questions were asked about the intensive media coverage. Given what you've learned in this chapter, how might news and social media discussions of tragic shooting events like these increase myths and misconceptions about people with a mental illness?

Unlike most other adults, individuals with antisocial personality disorder act impulsively, without giving thought to the consequences. They are usually poised when confronted with their destructive behavior and feel contempt for anyone they are able to manipulate. They also change jobs and relationships suddenly, and they often have a history of truancy from school and of being expelled for destructive behavior. People with antisocial personalities can be charming and persuasive, and they have remarkably good insight into the needs and weaknesses of other people.

Twin and adoption studies suggest a possible genetic predisposition to antisocial personality disorder (Beaver et al., 2011; Kendler & Prescott, 2006). Biological contributions are also suggested by studies that have found abnormally low autonomic activity during stress, right hemisphere abnormalities, and reduced gray matter in the frontal lobes and biochemical disturbances (Anderson et al., 2011; Bertsch et al., 2013; Portnoy et al., 2013; Schiffer et al., 2011; Sundram et al., 2011). For example, MRI brain scans of criminals currently in prison for violent crimes, such as rape, murder, or attempted murder, and showing little empathy and remorse for their crimes, revealed reduced gray matter volume in the prefrontal cortex (Gregory et al., 2012). (Recall from Chapter 2 that this is the area of the brain responsible for emotions, such as fear, empathy, and/or guilt.) Q5

Evidence also exists for environmental or psychological causes. People with antisocial personality disorder often come from homes characterized by abusive parenting styles, emotional deprivation, harsh and inconsistent disciplinary practices, and antisocial parental behavior (Calkins & Keane, 2009; Noggle et al., 2013; Torry & Billick, 2011; Wachlarowicz et al., 2012). Still other studies show a strong interaction between both heredity and environment (Douglas et al., 2011; Hudziak, 2008; Philibert et al., 2011; Trull et al., 2013).

Borderline Personality Disorder

Borderline personality disorder (BPD) is among the most commonly diagnosed and most functionally disabling of all mental disorders (Ansell & Grilo, 2007; Chanen & McCutcheon, 2013; Gunderson, 2011; Rizvi & Salters-Pedneault, 2013).

Borderline personality disorder (BPD) A mental disorder characterized by severe instability in emotion and self-concept, along with impulsive and self-destructive behaviors.

The core features of this disorder are impulsivity and instability in mood, relationships, and self-image. Originally, the term implied that the person was on the borderline between neurosis and schizophrenia (Schroeder et al., 2013). The modern conceptualization no longer has this connotation, but BPD remains one of the most complex and debilitating of all the personality disorders.

People with BPD experience extreme difficulties in relationships. Subject to chronic feelings of depression, emptiness, and intense fear of abandonment, they also engage in destructive, impulsive behaviors, such as sexual promiscuity, drinking, gambling, and eating sprees. In addition, they may attempt suicide and sometimes engage in self-mutilating behavior (Chapman et al., 2008; Lynam et al., 2011; Muehlenkamp et al., 2011; Turnbull et al., 2013).

Those with BPD also tend to see themselves and everyone else in absolute terms—as either perfect or worthless (Mak & Lam, 2013; Rizvi & Salters-Pedneault, 2013; Scott et al., 2011). Constantly seeking reassurance from others, they may quickly erupt in anger at the slightest sign of disapproval. The disorder is also typically marked by a long history of broken friendships, divorces, and lost jobs.

In short, people with this disorder appear to have a deep well of intense loneliness and a chronic fear of abandonment and they often seek therapy. Unfortunately, given their troublesome personality traits, friends, lovers, and even family members and therapists often do "abandon" them—thus creating a tragic self-fulfilling prophecy. The good news is that BPD can be reliably diagnosed and it does respond to professional intervention—particularly in young people (Chanen & McCutcheon, 2013; Fleischhaker et al., 2011; Leichsenring et al., 2011; Rizvi & Salters-Pedneault, 2013).

What causes BPD? Some research points to environmental factors, such as a childhood history of neglect, emotional deprivation, and physical, sexual, or emotional abuse (Chanen & McCutcheon, 2013; Distel et al., 2011). From a biological perspective, BPD also tends to run in families, and some data suggest that it is a result of impaired functioning of the brain's frontal lobes and limbic system, areas that control impulsive behaviors (Leichsenring et al., 2011; Mak & Lam, 2013; Schulze et al., 2011). For example, research using neuroimaging reveals that people with BPD show more activity in parts of the brain associated with the experience of negative emotions, coupled with less activity in parts of the brain that help suppress negative emotion (Ruocco et al., 2013). As in many cases, most researchers agree that BPD results from an interaction between the environment and biology (Carpenter et al., 2013; Ripoll et al., 2013).

RETRIEVAL PRACTICE: OTHER DISORDERS

Self-Test

Completing this self-test and comparing your answers with those in Appendix B provides immediate feedback and helpful practice for exams. Additional interactive, self-tests are available at www.wiley.com/college/huffman.

1. Repetitive, ritualistic behaviors, such as hand washing, counting, or putting things in order, are called a(n) __________.

a. obsessions
b. compulsions
c. ruminations
d. phobias

2. A disorder characterized by disturbances in consciousness, identity, memory, and other features is known as a(n) __________.

a. dissociative disorder
b. disoriented disorder
c. displacement disorder
d. identity disorder

3. A serial killer would likely be diagnosed as a(n) ________ personality in the *Diagnostic and Statistical Manual (DSM).*

a. dissociative disorder
b. antisocial personality disorder
c. multiple personality disorder
d. borderline psychosis

4. One possible biological contributor to BPD is a(n) ________.

a. childhood history of neglect
b. emotional deprivation
c. impaired functioning of the frontal lobes
d. all these options

Think Critically

1 How would you explain to others that schizophrenia is not the same as dissociative identity disorder (DID) (formerly called multiple personality disorder [MPD])?

2 Does the fact that research shows a genetic component to antisocial personality disorder change your opinion regarding the degree of guilt and responsibility someone like Adam Lanza has for the Sandy Hook shooting spree?

realworldpsychology

How do changes in the brain help explain severe antisocial personality disorder?

HINT: LOOK IN THE MARGIN FOR Q5

GENDER AND CULTURAL EFFECTS

LEARNING OBJECTIVES

RETRIEVAL PRACTICE While reading the upcoming sections, respond to each Learning Objective in your own words. Then compare your responses with those found at www.wiley.com/college/huffman.

1 **DISCUSS** the possible gender differences in psychological disorders.
2 **EXPLAIN** why it is difficult to directly compare mental disorders across cultures.
3 **OUTLINE** strategies for avoiding ethnocentrism in psychological disorders.

Among the Chippewa, Cree, and Montagnais-Naskapi Indians in Canada, there is a disorder called *windigo*—or *wiitiko—psychosis*, characterized by delusions and cannibalistic impulses. Believing they have been possessed by the spirit of a windigo, a cannibal giant with a heart and entrails of ice, victims become severely depressed (Faddiman, 1997). As the malady begins, the individual typically experiences loss of appetite, diarrhea, vomiting, and insomnia, and he or she may see people turning into beavers and other edible animals. In later stages, the victim becomes obsessed with cannibalistic thoughts and may even attack and kill loved ones in order to devour their flesh (Berreman, 1971).

If you were a therapist, how would you treat this disorder? Does it fit neatly into any of the categories of psychological disorders that you have learned about? We began this chapter by discussing the complexities and problems with defining, identifying, and classifying abnormal behavior. Before we close, we need to add two additional confounding factors: gender and culture. In this section, we explore a few of the many ways in which men and women differ in their experience of abnormal behavior. We also look at cultural variations in abnormal behavior.

Gender Differences

When you picture someone suffering from depression, anxiety, alcoholism, or antisocial personality disorder, what is the gender of each person? Most people tend to visualize a woman for the first two and a man for the last two. There is some truth to these stereotypes.

Research has found many gender differences in the prevalence rates of various mental disorders. Let's start with the well-established fact that around the world, the rate of severe depression for women is about double that for men (Dillard et al., 2012; Luppa et al., 2012; Sonnenberg et al., 2013; World Health Organization, 2011). Why is there such a striking gender difference?

Certain risk factors for depression (such as genetic predisposition, marital problems, pain, and medical illness) are common to both men and women. However, poverty is a well-known contributor to many psychological disorders, and women are far more likely than men to fall into the lowest socioeconomic groups. Women also experience more sexual trauma, partner abuse, and chronic stress in their daily lives, and these are all well-known contributing factors in depression (Doornbos et al., 2013; Harkness et al., 2010; Mapayi et al., 2013; Mota et al., 2012; Neri et al., 2012; Oram et al., 2013).

Recent research also suggests that some gender differences in depression may relate to the way women and men tend to internalize or externalize their emotions. Using structured interview techniques, researchers found that women ruminate more frequently than men, which means they are more likely to focus repetitively on their *internal* negative emotions and problems rather than engage in more external problem-solving strategies. In contrast, men tend to be more disinhibited and more likely to *externalize* their emotions and problems (Dawson et al., 2010; Schirmer, 2013; Tarter et al., 2003; Tompkins et al., 2011; Xu et al., 2012).

On the other hand, gender differences may result from misapplied gender role stereotypes. For example, the most common symptoms of depression, such as crying, low energy, dejected facial expressions, and withdrawal from social activities, are more socially acceptable for women than for men. And the fact that gender differences in depression are more pronounced in cultures with traditional gender roles (e.g., Seedat et al., 2009) suggests that male depression may be underdiagnosed because men are raised to be better at hiding and redirecting their emotions (Fields & Cochran, 2011). In U.S. society, men are typically socialized to suppress their emotions and to show their distress by acting out (showing aggression), acting impulsively (driving recklessly and committing petty crimes), or engaging in substance abuse.

To examine different expectations about depression as a function of gender, researchers in one study asked participants to read a story about a fictitious person (Kate in one version, Jack in the other). The story was exactly the same in both conditions and included the following information: "For the past two weeks, Kate/Jack has been feeling really down. S/he wakes up in the morning with a flat, heavy feeling that stick with her/him all day. S/he isn't enjoying things the way s/he normally would. S/he finds it hard to concentrate on anything." Although all participants read the same story, those who read about Kate rated her symptoms as more distressing, deserving of sympathy, and difficult to treat (Swami et al., 2012). Q6

psychology and you **Strategies for Managing Depression** Do you, or does someone you know, suffer from depression? Fortunately, many strategies can help both men and women cope with depression. For example, in order to prevent or reduce depression, women may benefit from learning better coping and cognitive skills to reduce the likelihood of rumination and just wallowing in sad feelings. On the other hand, if it's true that men more often express their depression through impulsive, acting-out behaviors, then rewarding deliberate, planned behaviors over unintentional, spur-of-the moment ones may be helpful for treating some forms of male depression (Eaton et al., 2012).

© Piotr Marcinski / Shutterstock

Understanding the importance of genetic predispositions, external environmental factors (like poverty), and cognitive factors (like internalizing versus externalizing emotions and problems) may help mental health professionals better understand individual and gender-related differences in depression.

Culture and Schizophrenia

Peoples of different cultures experience mental disorders in a variety of ways. For example, the reported incidence of schizophrenia varies in different cultures around the world. It is unclear whether these differences result from actual differences in prevalence of the disorder or from differences in definition, diagnosis, or reporting (Berry et al., 2011; Butler et al., 2011; Zandi, 2013). The symptoms of schizophrenia also vary across cultures (Barnow & Balkir, 2013; Burns, 2013), as do the particular stressors that may trigger its onset **(Figure 12.16)**.

Finally, despite the advanced treatment facilities and methods in industrialized nations, the prognosis for people with schizophrenia is actually better in nonindustrialized societies. The reason may be that the core symptoms of schizophrenia (poor rapport with others, incoherent speech, and so on) make it more difficult to survive in highly industrialized countries. In addition, in most industrialized nations, families and other support groups are less likely to feel responsible for relatives and friends who have schizophrenia (Barnow & Balkir, 2013; Eaton et al., 2011).

Avoiding Ethnocentrism

Most research on psychological disorders originates and is conducted primarily in Western cultures. Such a restricted sampling can limit our understanding of disorders in general and can lead to an ethnocentric view of mental disorders.

Fortunately, cross-cultural researchers have devised ways to overcome these difficulties (Matsumoto & Juang, 2013; Triandis, 2007). For example, Robert Nishimoto (1988) has found several *culture-general symptoms* that are useful in diagnosing disorders across cultures **(Table 12.3)**.

In addition, Nishimoto found several *culture-bound symptoms*. For example, Vietnamese Chinese respondents reported "fullness in head," Mexican respondents had "problems with [their] memory," and Anglo-American respondents reported "shortness of breath" and "headaches." Apparently, people learn to express their problems in ways that are acceptable to others in the same culture (Brislin, 1997, 2000; Butler et al., 2011; Dhikav et al., 2008; Iwata et al., 2011; Kanayama & Pope, 2011; Marques et al., 2011).

FIGURE 12.16 **WHAT IS STRESSFUL?**

David Alan Harvey/Magnum Photos,Inc.

Ⓐ Some stressors are culturally specific, such as feeling possessed by evil forces or being the victim of witchcraft.

Benelux/Zefa/Corbis

Ⓑ Other stressors are shared by many cultures, such as the unexpected death of a loved one or loss of a job (Al-Issa, 2000; Cechnicki et al., 2011; Neria et al., 2002; Ramsay et al., 2012).

TABLE 12.3 CULTURE-GENERAL SYMPTOMS OF MENTAL HEALTH DIFFICULTIES

Nervous	Trouble sleeping	Low spirits
Weak all over	Personal worries	Restless
Feel apart, alone	Can't get along	Hot all over
Worry all the time	Can't do anything worthwhile	Nothing turns out right

Source: Brislin, 2000.

This division between culture-general and culture-bound symptoms also helps us better understand depression. Certain symptoms of depression (such as intense sadness, poor concentration, and low energy) seem to exist across all cultures (Walsh & Cross, 2013; World Health Organization, 2011). But there is also evidence of some culture-bound symptoms. For example, feelings of guilt are found more often in North America and Europe than in other parts of the world. And in China, *somatization* (the conversion of depression into bodily complaints) occurs more frequently than it does in other parts of the world (Helms & Cook, 1999; Lawrence et al., 2011; Lim et al., 2011).

Just as there are culture-bound and culture-general symptoms, researchers have found that mental disorders are themselves sometimes culturally bound and generally only appear in one population group **(Figure 12.17)**. The earlier example of windigo psychosis, a disorder limited to a small group of Canadian Indians, illustrates just such a case.

As you can see, culture has a strong effect on mental disorders. Studying the similarities and differences across cultures can lead to better diagnosis and understanding. It also helps mental health professionals who work with culturally diverse populations understand both culturally general and culturally bound symptoms.

FIGURE 12.17 CULTURE-BOUND DISORDERS

Some disorders are fading as remote areas become more Westernized, whereas other disorders (such as anorexia nervosa) are spreading as other countries adopt Western values.

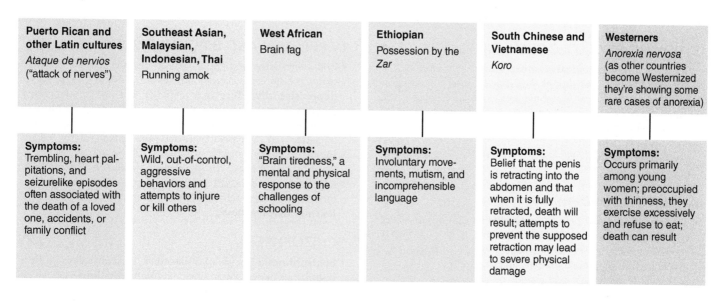

Puerto Rican and other Latin cultures	**Southeast Asian, Malaysian, Indonesian, Thai**	**West African**	**Ethiopian**	**South Chinese and Vietnamese**	**Westerners**
Ataque de nervios ("attack of nerves")	Running amok	Brain fag	Possession by the *Zar*	*Koro*	*Anorexia nervosa* (as other countries become Westernized they're showing some rare cases of anorexia)
Symptoms: Trembling, heart palpitations, and seizurelike episodes often associated with the death of a loved one, accidents, or family conflict	**Symptoms:** Wild, out-of-control, aggressive behaviors and attempts to injure or kill others	**Symptoms:** "Brain tiredness," a mental and physical response to the challenges of schooling	**Symptoms:** Involuntary movements, mutism, and incomprehensible language	**Symptoms:** Belief that the penis is retracting into the abdomen and that when it is fully retracted, death will result; attempts to prevent the supposed retraction may lead to severe physical damage	**Symptoms:** Occurs primarily among young women; preoccupied with thinness, they exercise excessively and refuse to eat; death can result

RETRIEVAL PRACTICE: GENDER AND CULTURAL EFFECTS

Self-Test

Completing this self-test and comparing your answers with those in Appendix B provides immediate feedback and helpful practice for exams. Additional interactive, self-tests are available at www.wiley.com/college/huffman.

1. When studying gender differences in mental health, researchers found that __________.

a. women ruminate more frequently than men
b. men tend to be more disinhibited and more likely to externalize their emotions and problems
c. men are typically socialized to suppress their emotions
d. all these options

2. Which of the following are examples of culture-general symptoms of mental health difficulties that are useful in diagnosing disorders across cultures?

a. trouble sleeping
b. worry all the time
c. can't get along
d. all the above

3. Symptoms of mental illness that generally only appear in one population group are known as ______.

a. culture-bound symptoms
b. group specific disorders
c. group-think syndrome
d. none of these

4. What disorder has the following symptoms: wild, out-of-control, aggressive behaviors and attempts to injure or kill others?

a. *Ataque de nervios* ("attack of nerves")
b. Running amok
c. Possession by the Zar
d. Koro

Think Critically

1 Culture clearly has strong effects on mental disorders. How does this influence what you think about what is normal or abnormal?

2 Some research suggests that depression in men is often overlooked because men are socialized to suppress their emotions and encouraged to express their distress by acting out, being impulsive, or engaging in substance abuse. Does this ring true with your own experiences and/or observations of others? If so, how might we change this situation?

realworldpsychology

Are symptoms of depression in women more distressing, deserving of sympathy, and difficult to treat than the same signs in men?

HINT: LOOK IN THE MARGIN FOR Q6

Summary

1 STUDYING PSYCHOLOGICAL DISORDERS 334

- Criteria for **psychological disorders** include *deviance, dysfunction, distress,* and *danger.* None of these criteria alone is adequate for classifying abnormal behavior.
- Superstitious explanations for abnormal behavior were replaced by the **medical model**, which eventually gave rise to the modern specialty of **psychiatry**. In contrast to the medical model, psychology offers a multifaceted approach to explaining abnormal behavior.

2 ANXIETY DISORDERS 340

- **Anxiety disorders** include **generalized anxiety disorder (GAD)**, **panic disorder**, and **phobias** (including agoraphobia, specific phobias, and social phobias).
- Psychological (faulty cognitions and maladaptive learning), biological (evolutionary and genetic predispositions, biochemical disturbances), and sociocultural (cultural pressures toward hypervigilance) factors likely all contribute to anxiety. Classical and operant conditioning also can contribute to phobias.

3 DEPRESSIVE AND BIPOLAR DISORDERS 345

- Both depressive and bipolar disorders are characterized by extreme disturbances in emotional states. People suffering from **depressive disorders** may experience a lasting depressed mood without a clear trigger. In contrast, people with **bipolar disorder** alternate between periods of depression and mania (characterized by hyperactivity and poor judgment).
- Biological factors play a significant role in mood disorders. Psychosocial theories of depression focus on environmental stressors and disturbances in interpersonal relationships, thought processes, self-concept, and learning history, including **learned helplessness**.

4 SCHIZOPHRENIA 350

- **Schizophrenia** is a group of disorders, each characterized by a disturbance in perception (including **hallucinations**), language, thought (including **delusions**), emotions, and/or behavior.
- In the past, researchers divided schizophrenia into multiple subtypes. More recently, researchers have proposed focusing

instead on **positive schizophrenia symptoms** versus **negative schizophrenia symptoms**.

- Most biological theories of schizophrenia focus on genetics, neurotransmitters, and brain abnormalities. Psychologists believe that there are also at least two possible psychosocial contributors: stress and communication disorders in families.

5 OTHER DISORDERS 355

- **Obsessive-compulsive disorder (OCD)** involves persistent, unwanted, fearful thoughts (obsessions) and/or irresistible urges to perform an act or repeated rituals (compulsions), which help relieve the anxiety created by the obsession. Given that numerous biological and psychological factors contribute to OCD, its most often treated with a combination of drugs and cognitive-behavior therapy (CBT).
- **Dissociative disorders** are characterized by a major loss of memory without a clear physical cause, and a subtype of these disorders, **dissociative identity disorder (DID)**, involves the presence of two or more distinct personality systems in the same individual at different times. Environmental variables appear to be the primary cause of dissociative disorders. Dissociation can be a form of escape from a past trauma.
- **Personality disorders** occur when inflexible, maladaptive personality traits cause significant impairment of social and occupational functioning. **Antisocial personality disorder** is a pattern of disregard for, and violation of, the rights of others. The most common personality disorder is **borderline personality disorder (BPD)**. Its core features are impulsivity and instability in mood, relationships, and self-image. Although some therapists have success with drug therapy and behavior therapy, the prognosis is not favorable.

6 GENDER AND CULTURAL EFFECTS 360

- Men and women differ in their rates and experiences of abnormal behavior. For instance, in the case of depression, modern research suggests that the gender-ratio differences may reflect an underlying predisposition toward internalizing or externalizing emotions and problems.
- Peoples of different cultures experience mental disorders in a variety of ways. For example, the reported incidence of schizophrenia varies in different cultures around the world, as do the disorder's symptoms, triggers, and prognosis.
- Some symptoms of psychological disorders, as well as some disorders themselves, are *culture general*, whereas others are *culture bound*.

applyingrealworldpsychology

We began this chapter with five intriguing Real World Psychology questions, and you were asked to revisit these questions at the end of each section. Questions like these have an important and lasting impact on all of our lives. See if you can answer these additional critical thinking questions related to real world examples.

Jodi Cobb/NG Image Collection

1. Is this man's behavior abnormal? Which criteria for psychological disorders do his piercings and tattoos meet? Which do they not?
2. Can you think of any behavior *you* exhibit that might be considered abnormal if your own cultural norms were not taken into account?
3. We've all experienced anxiety. Which of the explanations described in this section do you feel best describes your personal experiences with it? Why?
4. Recall an experience you've had with depression. How was it similar to or different from what was discussed in the section on major depressive disorders?
5. In the section on schizophrenia, we pointed out that if one identical twin develops schizophrenia, there is a 48% chance that the other twin will do so as well. How does this high correlation support the diathesis-stress model?
6. Think about someone you know—a friend, a family member, or yourself—who suffers from one of the disorders described in this chapter. How does the information we've provided differ from or match what you've discovered from your own or others' experiences?

Key Terms

RETRIEVAL PRACTICE Write a definition for each term before turning back to the referenced page to check your answer.

- abnormal behavior 334
- antisocial personality disorder 358
- anxiety disorder 340
- bipolar disorder 346
- borderline personality disorder (BPD) 359
- comorbidity 337
- delusion 352
- depressive disorders 345
- *Diagnostic and Statistical Manual of Mental Disorders* (*DSM*) 337
- diathesis-stress model 354
- dissociative disorder 357
- dissociative identity disorder (DID) 357
- generalized anxiety disorder (GAD) 341
- hallucination 351
- insanity 337
- learned helplessness 349
- medical model 336
- neurosis 337
- obsessive-compulsive disorder (OCD) 356
- panic disorder 341
- personality disorder 358
- phobia 342
- psychiatry 336
- psychosis 337
- schizophrenia 350

chapterthirteen

Therapy

CHAPTER OUTLINE

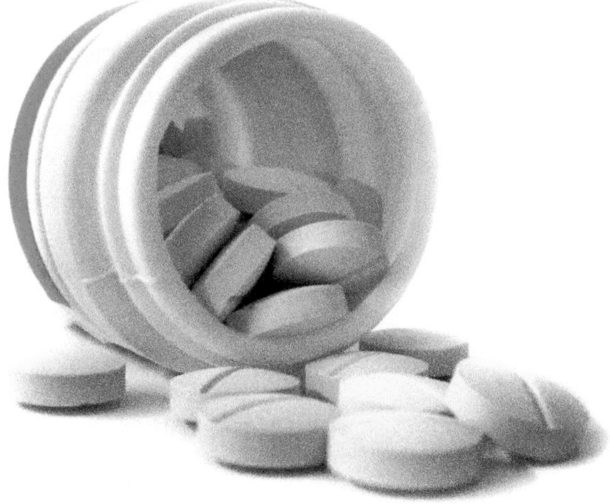

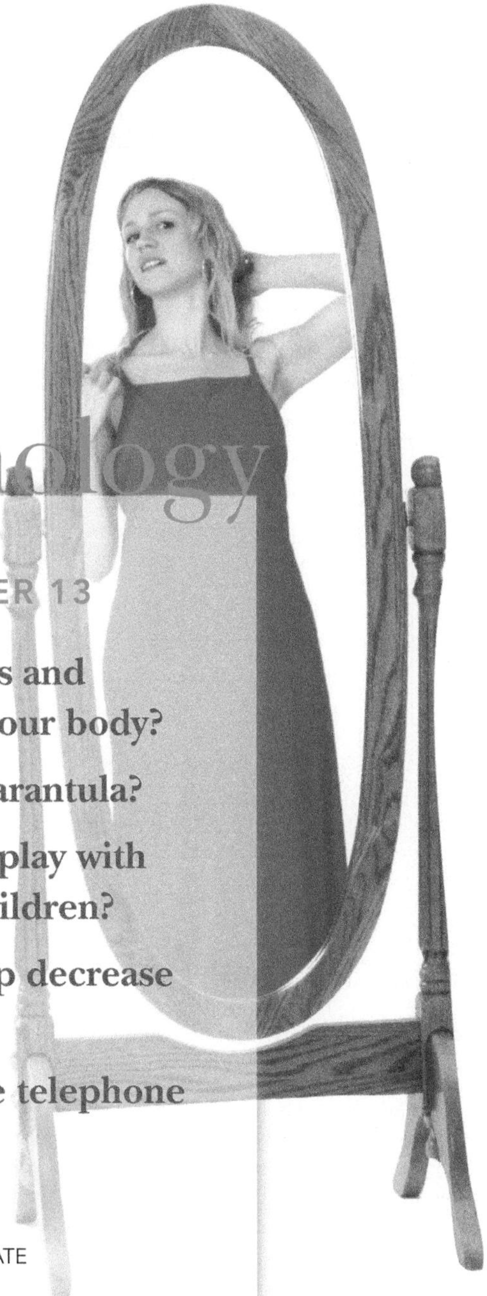

realworldpsychology

THINGS YOU'LL LEARN IN CHAPTER 13

Q1 Can changing your irrational thoughts and self-talk make you feel better about your body?

Q2 How might therapy help you hold a tarantula?

Q3 Does simply watching other children play with dogs reduce dog phobias in young children?

Q4 How do psychotherapeutic drugs help decrease thoughts of suicide?

Q5 Can therapy that is delivered over the telephone lead to lower levels of depression?

THROUGHOUT THE CHAPTER, MARGIN ICONS FOR Q1–Q5 INDICATE WHERE THE TEXT ADDRESSES THESE QUESTIONS.

chapteroverview

Throughout this text, we have emphasized the *science* of psychology, and this chapter is no exception. However, psychology is also a *practice*, in which psychologists conduct research and apply psychological principles to help people suffering from psychological disorders (Chapter 12). In this chapter, we'll discuss the three major approaches to psychotherapy **(Figure 13.1)**, its general goals and effectiveness, and other important issues and topics in the field. Along the way, we'll work to demystify and destigmatize its practice and dispel some common myths **(Table 13.1)**.

FIGURE 13.1 **AN OVERVIEW OF THE THREE MAJOR APPROACHES TO THERAPY**

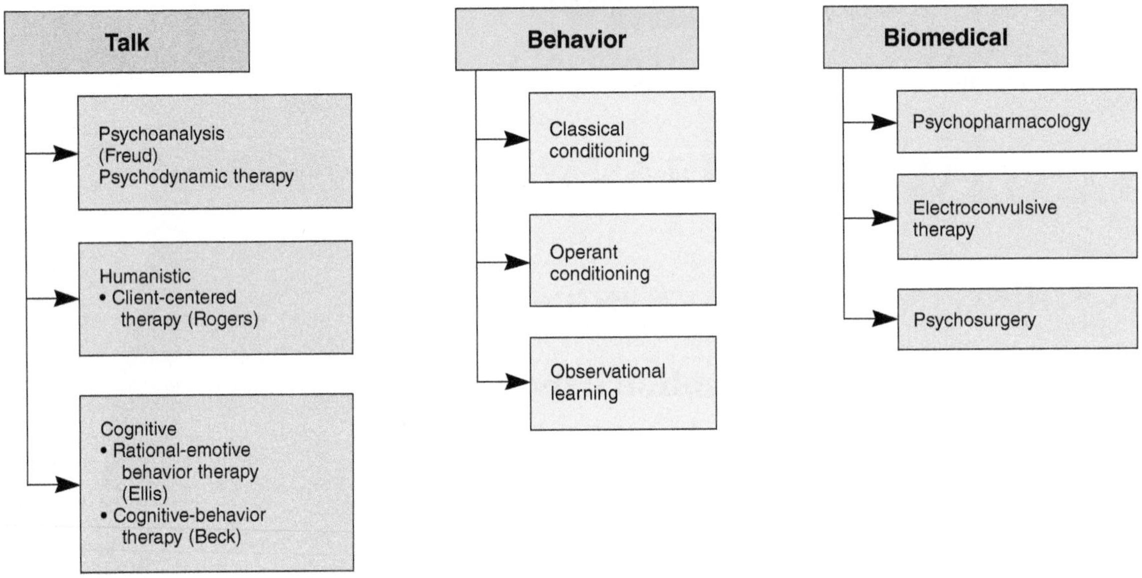

TABLE 13.1 **MYTHS ABOUT THERAPY** | realworldpsychology

- ***Myth: There is one best therapy.***
  Fact: Many problems can be treated equally well with many different forms of therapy.
- ***Myth: Therapists can read your mind.***
  Fact: Good therapists often seem to have an uncanny ability to understand how their clients are feeling and to know when someone is trying to avoid certain topics. This is not due to any special mind-reading ability; it simply reflects their specialized training and daily experience working with troubled people.
- ***Myth: People who go to therapists are crazy or weak.***
  Fact: Most people seek counseling because of stress in their lives or because they realize that therapy can improve their level of functioning. It is difficult to be objective about our own problems. Seeking therapy is a sign of wisdom and personal strength.
- ***Myth: Only the rich can afford therapy.***
  Fact: Therapy can be expensive. But many clinics and therapists charge on a sliding scale, based on the client's income. Some insurance plans also cover psychological services.
- ***Myth: If I am taking meds, I don't need therapy.***
  Fact: Medications, such as antidepressants, are only one form of therapy. They can change brain chemistry, but they can't teach us to think, feel, or behave differently. Research suggests that a combination of drugs and psychotherapy may be best for some situations, whereas in other cases, psychotherapy or drug therapy alone may be most effective.

© Mark Bowden/iStockphoto

TALK THERAPIES

RETRIEVAL PRACTICE While reading the upcoming sections, respond to each Learning Objective in your own words. Then compare your responses with those found at www.wiley.com/college/huffman.

LEARNING OBJECTIVES

1 **DESCRIBE** the core treatment techniques in psychoanalysis and modern psychodynamic therapies.
2 **SUMMARIZE** the key characteristics of humanistic therapies.
3 **EXPLAIN** the principles underlying cognitive therapies.

We begin our discussion of professional **psychotherapy** with traditional psychoanalysis and its modern counterpart, psychodynamic therapies. Then we explore humanistic and cognitive therapies. Although these therapies differ significantly, they're often grouped together as "talk therapies" because they emphasize communication between the therapist and client, as opposed to the behavioral and biomedical therapies we discuss later.

Psychotherapy Any of a group of therapies used to treat psychological disorders and to improve psychological functioning and adjustment to life.

Psychoanalysis/Psychodynamic Therapies

In **psychoanalysis**, a person's *psyche* (or mind) is *analyzed*. Traditional psychoanalysis is based on Sigmund Freud's central belief that abnormal behavior is caused by unconscious conflicts among the three parts of the psyche—the id, the ego, and the superego (Chapter 11).

During psychoanalysis, these conflicts are brought to consciousness. The patient comes to understand the reasons for his or her dysfunction and realizes that the childhood conditions under which the conflicts developed no longer exist. Once this realization or insight occurs, the conflicts can be resolved, and the patient can develop more adaptive behavior patterns (Altman, 2013; Cordón, 2012; Johnson, 2011).

Psychoanalysis A type of psychodynamic therapy developed by Freud; an intensive and prolonged technique for bringing unconscious conflicts into conscious awareness.

Free association In psychoanalysis, reporting whatever comes to mind without monitoring its contents.

Unfortunately, according to Freud, the ego has strong *defense mechanisms* that block unconscious thoughts from coming to light. Thus, to gain insight into the unconscious, the ego must be "tricked" into relaxing its guard. To meet that goal, psychoanalysts employ five major methods: *free association*, *dream analysis*, *analyzing resistance*, *analyzing transference*, and *interpretation*.

© Hulton-Deutsch Collection/©Corbis

Sigmund Freud (1856–1939)
Freud believed that during psychoanalysis, the therapist's (or psychoanalyst's) major goal was to bring unconscious conflicts into consciousness.

Free Association

According to Freud, when you let your mind wander and remove conscious censorship over thoughts—a process called **free association**—interesting and even bizarre connections seem to spring into awareness. Freud believed that the first thing to come to a patient's mind is often an important clue to what the person's unconscious wants to conceal. Having the patient recline on a couch, with only the ceiling to look at, is believed to encourage free association **(Figure 13.2)**.

Dream Analysis

Recall from Chapter 5 that, according to Freud, our psychological defenses are lowered during sleep. Therefore, our forbidden desires and unconscious conflicts are supposedly more freely expressed during dreams. Even while dreaming, however, we recognize these feelings and conflicts as unacceptable and must disguise them as

"The way this works is that you say the first thing that comes to your mind..."

© Joseph Farris/CartoonStock

FIGURE 13.2 **FREUD'S FREE ASSOCIATION**

Psychoanalysis is often portrayed as a patient lying on a couch engaging in free association. Freud believed that this arrangement—with the patient relaxed and the therapist out of his or her view—helps the patient let down his or her defenses, making the unconscious more accessible.

Dream analysis In psychoanalysis, interpretation of the underlying true meaning of dreams to reveal unconscious processes.

images that have deeper symbolic meaning. Thus, using Freudian **dream analysis**, a therapist might interpret a dream of riding a horse or driving a car—the surface description, or *manifest content*—as a desire for, or concern about, sexual intercourse—the hidden, underlying meaning, or *latent content*.

Analysis of Resistance

Resistance In psychoanalysis, the inability or unwillingness of a patient to discuss or reveal certain memories, thoughts, motives, or experiences.

During free association or dream analysis, Freud found that patients often show an inability or unwillingness to discuss or reveal certain memories, thoughts, motives, or experiences. For example, if the patient suddenly "forgets" what he or she was saying or completely changes the subject, it is the therapist's job to identify these possible cases of **resistance** and then help the patient face his or her problems and learn to deal with them more realistically.

Analysis of Transference

Transference In psychoanalysis, the process by which a client attaches (transfers) to a therapist feelings formerly held toward some significant person who figured in a past emotional conflict.

Freud believed that during psychoanalysis, patients disclose intimate feelings and memories, and the relationship between the therapist and patient may become complex and emotionally charged. As a result, patients often apply, or *transfer*, some of their unresolved emotions and attitudes from past relationships onto the therapist. The therapist uses this process of **transference** to help the patient "relive" painful past relationships in a safe, therapeutic setting so that he or she can move on to healthier relationships.

Interpretation

Interpretation A psychoanalyst's explanation of a patient's free associations, dreams, resistance, and transference; more generally, any statement by a therapist that presents a patient's problem in a new way.

The core of all psychoanalytic therapy is **interpretation**. During free association, dream analysis, resistance, and transference, the analyst listens closely and tries to find patterns and hidden conflicts. At the right time, the therapist explains or interprets the underlying meanings to the client.

Evaluating Psychoanalysis

As you can see, psychoanalysis is largely rooted in the assumption that repressed memories and unconscious conflicts actually exist. But, as we noted in Chapters 7 and 11, this assumption is the subject of heated, ongoing debate. Critics also point to two other problems with psychoanalysis (Messer & Gurman, 2011; Miltenberger, 2011; Siegel, 2010):

- **Limited applicability** Psychoanalysis is time-consuming (often lasting several years with four to five sessions a week) and expensive. In addition, critics suggest that it applies only to a select group of highly motivated, articulate patients with less severe disorders and not to more complex disorders, such as schizophrenia.
- **Lack of scientific credibility** According to critics, it is difficult, if not impossible, to scientifically document the major tenets of psychoanalysis. How do we prove or disprove the importance or meaning of unconscious conflicts or symbolic dream images?

Stockbyte/SUPERSTOCK

FIGURE 13.3 **INTERPERSONAL THERAPY (IPT)**

IPT, a variation of psychodynamic therapy, focuses on current relationships, with the goal of relieving immediate symptoms and teaching better ways to solve interpersonal problems. Research shows that it's effective for a variety of disorders, including depression, marital conflict, eating disorders, and drug addiction (Aldenhoff, 2011; Cuijpers et al., 2011; Hardy, 2011; Stricker et al., 2013).

Despite these criticisms, research shows that traditional psychoanalysis can be effective for those who have the time and money (Altman, 2013; Barratt, 2013; Lambert, 2013; Spurling, 2011).

Psychodynamic Therapy

A modern derivative of Freudian psychoanalysis, **psychodynamic therapy**, includes both Freud's theories and those of his major followers—Jung, Adler, and Erikson. In contrast to psychoanalysis, psychodynamic therapy is shorter and less intensive (one or twice a week vs. several times a week and only a few weeks or months vs. years). In addition, the patient is treated face-to-face rather than reclining on a couch, and the therapist takes a more directive approach rather than waiting for unconscious memories and desires to slowly be uncovered.

Also, contemporary psychodynamic therapists focus less on unconscious, early-childhood roots of problems and more on conscious processes and current problems (Frew & Spiegler, 2013; Hunsley & Lee, 2010; Zuckerman, 2011). Such refinements have helped make treatments shorter, more available, and more effective for an increasing number of people. See **Figure 13.3** for one of the most popular modern forms of psychodynamic therapy.

Psychodynamic therapy A type of therapy that focuses on conscious processes and current problems; a briefer, more directive, and more modern form of psychoanalysis.

Humanistic therapy A type of therapy that emphasizes maximizing a client's inherent capacity for self-actualization by providing a non-judgmental, accepting atmosphere.

Humanistic Therapies

In contrast to the rather aloof doctor-to-patient approach of the psychoanalytic and psychodynamic therapies, the humanistic approach emphasizes the *human* characteristics of a person's potential, free will, and self-awareness.

Humanistic therapy assumes that people with problems are suffering from a disruption of their normal growth potential and, hence, their self-concept. When obstacles are removed, the individual is free to become the self-accepting, genuine person everyone is capable of being.

One of the best-known humanistic therapists is Carl Rogers (Rogers, 1961, 1980), who developed an approach that encouraged people to actualize their potential and to relate to others in genuine ways. His approach is referred to as

Michael Rougier/Time & Life Pictures/Getty Images

Carl Rogers (1902–1987)

Comstock/SUPERSTOCK

FIGURE 13.4 **NURTURING GROWTH**

Recall how you've felt when you've been with someone who believes that you are a good person with unlimited potential, a person who believes that your "real self" is unique and valuable. These are the feelings that are nurtured in humanistic therapy.

client-centered therapy (Figure 13.4). (Rogers used the term *client* because he believed the label *patient* implied that someone was sick or mentally ill rather than responsible and competent.)

Client-centered therapy, like psychoanalysis and psychodynamic therapies, explores thoughts and feelings as a way to obtain insight into the causes for behaviors. For Rogerian therapists, however, the focus is on providing an accepting atmosphere and encouraging healthy emotional experiences. Clients are responsible for discovering their own maladaptive patterns.

Rogerian therapists create a therapeutic relationship by focusing on four important qualities of communication: *empathy*, *unconditional positive regard*, *genuineness*, and *active listening*.

Empathy

Using the technique of **empathy**, a sensitive understanding and sharing of another person's inner experience, therapists pay attention to body language and listen for subtle cues to help them understand the emotional experiences of clients. To further help clients explore their feelings, the therapist uses open-ended statements such as "You found that upsetting" or "You haven't been able to decide what to do about this" rather than asking questions or offering explanations.

Client-centered therapy Rogers's humanistic approach to therapy, which emphasizes the client's natural tendency to become healthy and productive; techniques include empathy, unconditional positive regard, genuineness, and active listening.

Empathy In Rogerian terms, an insightful awareness and ability to share another's inner experience.

Unconditional positive regard Rogers's term for complete love and acceptance of another, such as a parent for a child, with no conditions attached.

Genuineness In Rogerian terms, authenticity or congruence; the awareness of one's true inner thoughts and feelings and being able to share them honestly with others.

Active listening Listening with total attention to what another is saying; it includes reflecting, paraphrasing, and clarifying what the person says and means.

Unconditional Positive Regard

Regardless of the clients' problems or behaviors, humanistic therapists offer them **unconditional positive regard**, a genuine caring and nonjudgmental attitude toward people based on their innate value as individuals. They avoid evaluative statements such as "That's good" and "You did the right thing" because such comments imply that the therapist is judging the client. Rogers believed that most of us receive conditional acceptance from our parents, teachers, and others, which leads to poor self-concepts and psychological disorders **(Figure 13.5)**.

Genuineness

Humanists believe that when therapists use **genuineness** and honestly share their thoughts and feelings with their clients, the clients will in turn develop self-trust and honest self-expression.

Active Listening

Using **active listening**, which includes reflecting, paraphrasing, and clarifying what the client is saying, the clinician communicates that he or she is genuinely interested and paying close attention (see *Psychology and You*).

Pat Byrnes/The Cartoon Bank, Inc.

"Just remember, son, it doesn't matter whether you win or lose—unless you want Daddy's love."

FIGURE 13.5 **UNCONDITIONAL VERSUS CONDITIONAL POSITIVE REGARD**

According to Rogers, clients need to feel unconditionally accepted by their therapists in order to recognize and value their own emotions, thoughts, and behaviors. As this cartoon implies, some parents withhold their love and acceptance unless the child lives up to their expectations.

psychology and you **Using Active Listening Personally and Professionally** If you want to try active listening in your personal life, note that to *reflect* is to hold a mirror in front of the person, enabling that person to see him- or herself. To *paraphrase* is to summarize in different words what the other person is saying. To *clarify* is to check that both the speaker and listener are on the same wavelength.

When a professional uses active listening, he or she might notice a client's furrowed brow and downcast eyes while he is discussing his military experiences and then might respond, "It sounds like you're angry with your situation and feeling pretty miserable right now." Can you see how this statement reflects the client's anger, paraphrases his complaint, and gives feedback to clarify the communication? This type of attentive, active listening is a relatively simple and well-documented technique that you can use to improve your communication with virtually anyone—professors, employers, friends, family, and especially your love partner.

© Mark Bowden/iStockphoto

Evaluating Humanistic Theories

Supporters say that there is empirical evidence for the efficacy of client-centered therapy (Benjamin, 2011; Cain, 2013; Hazler, 2011; Messer & Gurman, 2011). However, critics argue that outcomes such as self-actualization and self-awareness are difficult to test scientifically, and research on specific humanistic techniques has had mixed results (Decker et al., 2013; Hodges & Biswas-Diener, 2007; Norcross & Wampold, 2011; Stiles, 2013).

Cognitive Therapies

Cognitive therapy assumes that faulty thought processes—beliefs that are irrational or overly demanding or that fail to match reality—create problem behaviors and emotions (Friedberg & Belsford, 2011; Palmer & Williams, 2013; Pomerantz, 2013).

Cognitive therapy A type of therapy that treats problem behaviors and mental processes by focusing on faulty thought processes and beliefs.

Like psychoanalysts, cognitive therapists believe that exploring unexamined beliefs can produce insight into the reasons for disturbed thoughts, feelings, and behaviors. However, instead of believing that a change occurs because of insight, cognitive therapists suggest that negative *self-talk*, the unrealistic things a person tells himself or herself, is most important. For example, research with women suffering from eating disorders found that changing a patient's irrational thoughts and self-talk, such as "If I eat that cake, I will become fat instantly" or "I'll never have a dating relationship if I don't lose 20 pounds," resulted in their having fewer negative thoughts about their bodies (Bhatnagar et al., 2013).

Q1

Through a process called **cognitive restructuring**, clients are taught to identify and then challenge this type of negative self-talk, as well as change the way they interpret events and modify their maladaptive behaviors **(Figure 13.6)**.

Cognitive restructuring A process in cognitive therapy that is designed to change destructive thoughts or inappropriate interpretations.

FIGURE 13.6 USING COGNITIVE RESTRUCTURING TO IMPROVE SALES | realworldpsychology

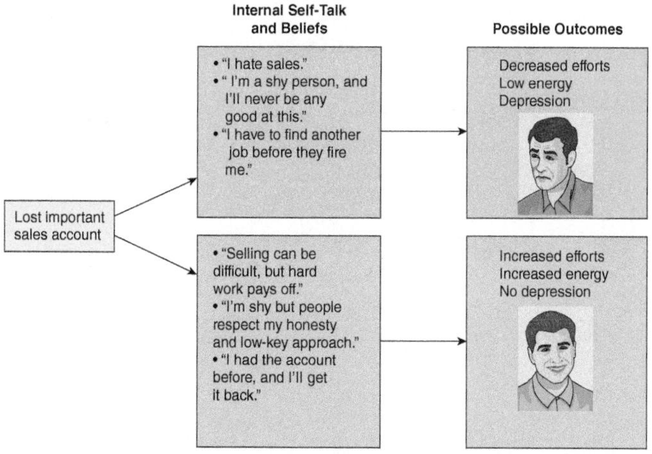

Internal Self-Talk and Beliefs
Possible Outcomes
Lost important sales account
• "I hate sales."
• "I'm a shy person, and I'll never be any good at this."
• "I have to find another job before they fire me."
Decreased efforts
Low energy
Depression
• "Selling can be difficult, but hard work pays off."
• "I'm shy but people respect my honesty and low-key approach."
• "I had the account before, and I'll get it back."
Increased efforts
Increased energy
No depression

Ⓐ Note how the negative interpretation and destructive self-talk leads to destructive and self-defeating outcomes.

Ⓑ Cognitive therapy teaches clients to challenge and change their negative beliefs and negative self-talk into positive ones, which, in turn, leads to more positive outcomes. Can you think of other situations in which such reinterpretation could be helpful?

Albert Ellis (1913–2007) © Bettman/Corbis

Rational-emotive behavior therapy (REBT) Ellis's cognitive therapy that focuses on eliminating emotional reactions through logic, confrontation, and examination of irrational beliefs.

Ellis's REBT

One of the best-known cognitive therapists, Albert Ellis, suggested that irrational beliefs are the primary culprit in problem emotions and behaviors. He proposed that most people mistakenly believe they are unhappy or upset because of external, outside events, such as receiving a bad grade on an exam. Ellis suggested that, in reality, these negative emotions result from faulty interpretations and irrational beliefs (such as interpreting the bad grade as a sign of your incompetence and an indication that you'll never qualify for graduate school or a good job).

To deal with these irrational beliefs, Ellis developed **rational-emotive behavior therapy (REBT)** (Ellis, 2008; Ellis & Ellis, 2011; Vernon, 2011). (See below.)

ELLIS'S RATIONAL-EMOTIVE BEHAVIOR THERAPY (REBT)

psychology and you

If you receive a poor performance evaluation at work, you might directly attribute your bad mood to the negative feedback. Psychologist Albert Ellis would argue that your self-talk ("I always mess up") between the event and the feeling is what actually upsets you. Furthermore, ruminating on all the other bad things in your life maintains your negative emotional state and may even lead to anxiety disorders, depression, and other psychological disorders.

To treat these problems, Ellis developed an A–B–C–D approach: **A** stands for *activating event*, **B** the person's *belief system*, **C** the emotional and behavioral *consequences*, and **D** the act of *disputing* erroneous beliefs. During therapy, Ellis helped his clients identify the A, B, C's underlying their irrational beliefs by actively arguing with, cajoling, and teasing them—sometimes in very blunt, confrontational language. Once clients recognized their self-defeating thoughts, he worked with them on how to *dispute* those beliefs and create and test out new, rational ones. These new beliefs then changed the maladaptive emotions—thus breaking the vicious cycle.

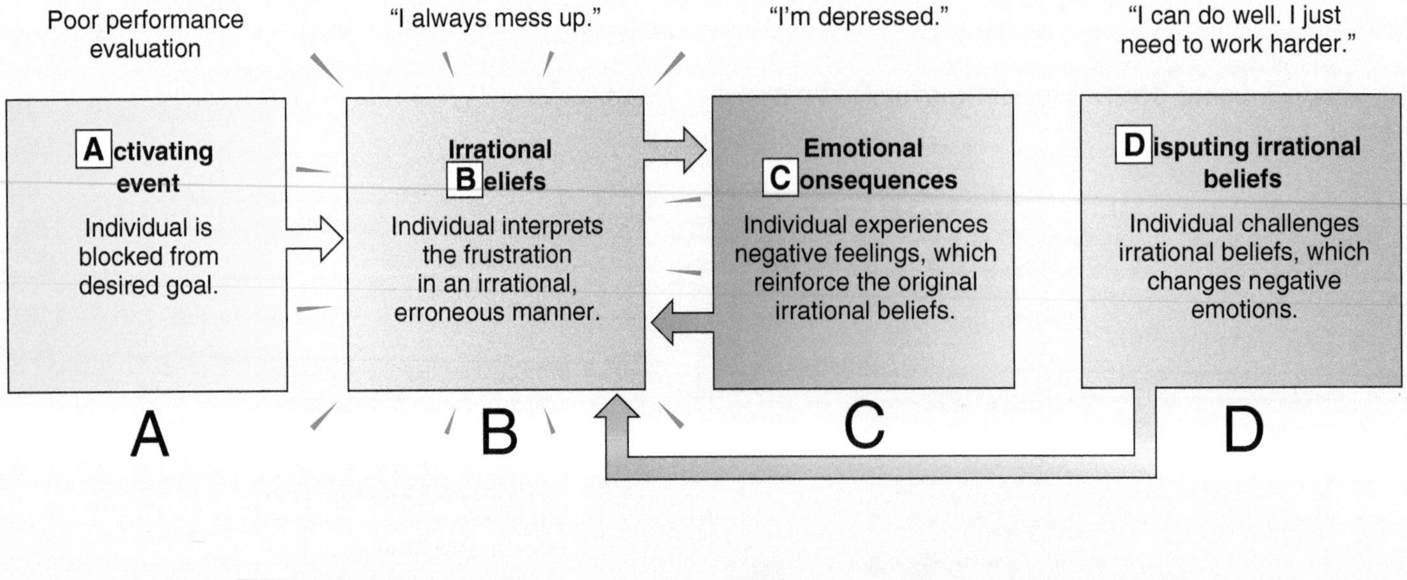

Voices from the Classroom

REBT and Your Grades Students put lots of pressure on themselves by thinking "I *must* do well on this test" or "I *have to* get a good test grade." We discuss this in terms of Ellis's REBT. First, this kind of pressure may hinder their performance. Second, I ask students, "Do you really *have to* get a good grade? What is the worst thing that would happen if you didn't?" They might fail the class, which might lower their GPA and/or cause them to retake the class, but plenty of people retake classes. Plus, a low grade probably won't cause them to fail the class. They are more likely to just get a lower class grade than desired. I encourage students to think more positively ("I hope to do well") or to come up with a success plan ("I will study nightly for at least one hour to get a good test score").

Professor David Baskind
Delta College
University Center, Michigan

Beck's Cognitive-Behavior Therapy (CBT)

Another well-known cognitive therapist, Aaron Beck, also believes psychological problems result from illogical thinking and destructive self-talk (Beck, 1976, 2000; Beck & Grant, 2008). But Beck seeks to directly confront and change the behaviors associated with destructive cognitions. Beck's **cognitive-behavior therapy (CBT)** is designed to reduce *both* self-destructive thoughts *and* self-destructive behaviors.

Cognitive-behavior therapy (CBT) A type of therapy that combines cognitive therapy (changing faulty thinking) with behavior therapy (changing maladaptive behaviors).

Using cognitive-behavior therapy, clients are first taught to recognize and keep track of their thoughts. Next, the therapist trains the client to develop ways to test these automatic thoughts against reality. This approach helps depressed people discover that negative attitudes are largely a product of faulty thought processes.

At this point, Beck introduces the second phase of therapy—persuading the client to actively pursue pleasurable activities. Depressed individuals often lose motivation, even for experiences they used to find enjoyable. Simultaneously taking an active rather than a passive role and reconnecting with enjoyable experiences can help in recovering from depression (see *A Cognitive Approach to Lifting Depression*).

A COGNITIVE APPROACH TO LIFTING DEPRESSION

realworldpsychology

As we've just seen, one of the most successful applications of Beck's CBT is in the treatment of depression (Beck, 1976, 2000; Beck et al., 2012; Hollon, 2011; Roelofs et al., 2013). Beck identified several thinking patterns believed to be common among depression-prone people. Recognizing these patterns in our own thought processes may help prevent or improve the occasional bad moods we all experience. To fully benefit from this approach, use what therapists call the "three C's"—*catch the faulty thought*, *challenge it*, and then *change it*. Here we provide an example of the three C's for the first thought pattern, and then you should try to do the same for the other three:

- **Selective perception** Focusing selectively on negative events while ignoring positive events. (*Catch the thought* ="Why am I the only person alone at this party?"; *Challenge it* = "I notice four other single people at this party"; *Change it* = "Being single has several advantages. I'll bet some of the couples are actually envying my freedom.")
- **Overgeneralization** Overgeneralizing and drawing negative conclusions about our own self-worth. ("I'm worthless because I failed that exam.")
- **Magnification** Exaggerating the importance of undesirable events or personal shortcomings and seeing them as catastrophic and unchangeable. ("She left me, and I'll never find anyone like her again!")
- **All-or-nothing thinking** Seeing things as black-or-white categories—where everything is either totally good or bad, right or wrong, a success or a failure. ("If I don't get straight A's, I'll never get a good job.")

Clem Murray/MCT/NewsCom

Aaron Beck

Evaluating Cognitive Therapies

Cognitive therapies are highly effective treatments for depression, as well as anxiety disorders, bulimia nervosa, anger management, addiction, and even some symptoms of schizophrenia and insomnia (Craighead et al., 2013; Grave, 2013; Thomas et al., 2011; Turner & Barker, 2013; Young et al., 2011). However, both Beck and Ellis have been criticized for ignoring or denying the client's unconscious dynamics, overemphasizing rationality, and minimizing the importance of the client's past (Granillo et al., 2013; Hammack, 2003).

Other critics suggest that cognitive therapies are successful because they employ behavior techniques, not because they change the underlying cognitive structure (Bandura, 1969, 1997, 2006, 2008; Corey, 2013; Frew & Spiegler, 2013; Pomerantz, 2013). Imagine that you sought treatment for depression and learned to construe events more positively and to curb your all-or-nothing thinking. Further imagine that your therapist also helped you identify activities and behaviors that lessened your depression. Obviously, it's difficult to identify whether changing your cognitions or changing your behavior was the most significant therapeutic factor. But for our everyday use, it doesn't matter. CBT combines both, and it has a proven track record for lifting depression!

RETRIEVAL PRACTICE: TALK THERAPIES

Self-Test

Completing this self-test and comparing your answers with those in Appendix B provides immediate feedback and helpful practice for exams. Additional interactive, self-tests are available at www.wiley.com/college/huffman.

1. Psychoanalysis/psychodynamic, humanistic, and cognitive therapies are often grouped together as _____.

a. talk therapies
b. behavior therapies
c. analytic therapies
d. cognitive restructuring

2. The system of psychotherapy developed by Freud that seeks to bring unconscious conflicts into conscious awareness is known as _____.

a. transference
b. cognitive restructuring
c. psychoanalysis
d. the "hot seat" technique

3. _____ therapy emphasizes conscious processes and current problems.

a. Self-talk
b. Belief-behavior
c. Psychodynamic
d. Thought analysis

4. Aaron Beck practices _____ therapy, which attempts to change not only destructive thoughts and beliefs but the associated behaviors as well.

a. psycho-behavior
b. cognitive-behavior
c. thinking-acting
d. belief-behavior

Think Critically

1 Would you rather go to a therapist who uses modern psychodynamic therapy or one who practices traditional psychoanalysis? Why?

2 What is the significance of the term *client-centered therapy*?

realworldpsychology

Can changing your irrational thoughts and self-talk make you feel better about your body?

HINT: LOOK IN THE MARGIN FOR Q1

BEHAVIOR THERAPIES

RETRIEVAL PRACTICE While reading the upcoming sections, respond to each Learning Objective in your own words. Then compare your responses with those found at www.wiley.com/college/huffman.

LEARNING OBJECTIVES

1. **DESCRIBE** how classical conditioning is used in therapy.
2. **EXPLORE** how operant conditioning can be used in therapy.
3. **SUMMARIZE** how observational learning is used in therapy.
4. **DESCRIBE** two major criticisms of behavior therapies.

Sometimes having insight into a problem does not automatically solve it. In **behavior therapy**, the focus is on the problem behavior itself rather than on any underlying causes. Although the person's feelings and interpretations are not disregarded, they are also not emphasized. The therapist diagnoses the problem by listing maladaptive behaviors that occur and adaptive behaviors that are absent. The therapist then attempts to shift the balance of the two, drawing on the learning principles of classical conditioning, operant conditioning, and observational learning (Chapter 6).

SidneyHarris/Science CartoonsPlus.com

Classical Conditioning

Behavior therapists use the principles of classical conditioning to decrease maladaptive behaviors by creating new associations to replace the faulty ones. We will explore two techniques based on these principles: *systematic desensitization* and *aversion therapy*.

Recall from Chapter 6 that classical conditioning occurs when a neutral stimulus (NS) becomes associated with an unconditioned stimulus (US) to elicit a conditioned response (CR). Sometimes a classically conditioned fear response becomes so extreme that we call it a "phobia." To treat phobias, behavior therapists often use **systematic desensitization**, which begins with relaxation training, followed by imagining or directly experiencing various versions of a feared object or situation while remaining deeply relaxed (Wolpe & Plaud, 1997). See **Figure 13.7** for a description of systematic desensitization useful for overcoming a driving phobia.

Behavior therapy A group of techniques based on learning principles to change maladaptive behaviors.

Systematic desensitization A behavioral therapy technique in which a client learns to prevent the arousal of anxiety by gradually confronting the feared stimulus while relaxed.

FIGURE 13.7 SYSTEMATIC DESENSITIZATION

In systematic desensitization, the therapist and client together construct a *fear hierarchy*, a ranked listing of 10 or so related anxiety-arousing images. While in a state of relaxation, the client mentally visualizes or physically experiences mildly anxiety-producing items at the lowest level of the hierarchy and then works his or her way up to the most anxiety-producing items at the top. Each progressive step on the fear hierarchy is repeatedly paired with relaxation, until the fear response or phobia is extinguished.

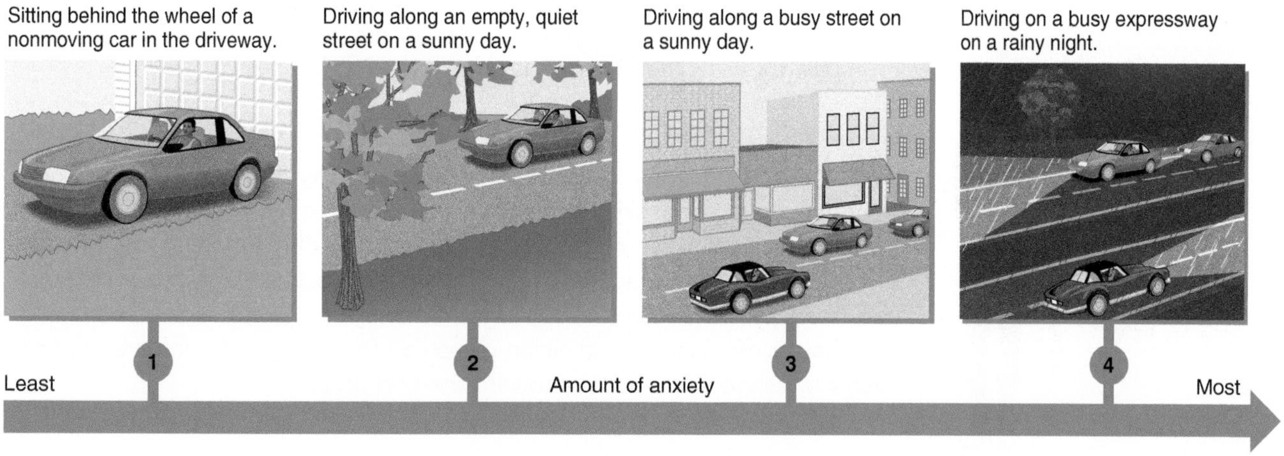

Sitting behind the wheel of a nonmoving car in the driveway.
Driving along an empty, quiet street on a sunny day.
Driving along a busy street on a sunny day.
Driving on a busy expressway on a rainy night.
1
2
3
4
Least
Amount of anxiety
Most

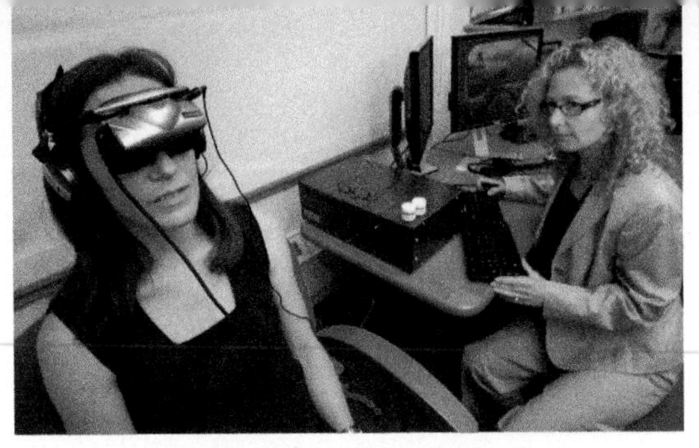

FIGURE 13.8 VIRTUAL REALITY THERAPY

Rather than use mental imaging or actual physical experiences of a fearful situation, virtual-reality headsets and data gloves allow a client with a fear of heights, for example, to have experiences ranging from climbing a stepladder all the way to standing on the edge of a tall building.

Similarly, if you or a friend suffers from a spider phobia, you may be amazed to know that after just two or three hours of therapy, starting with simply looking at photos of spiders and then moving next to a tarantula in a glass aquarium, patients are able to eventually pet and hold the spider with their bare hands (Hauner et al., 2012)! Q2

How does relaxation training desensitize someone? Recall from Chapter 2 that the parasympathetic nerves control autonomic functions when we are relaxed. Because the opposing sympathetic nerves are dominant when we are anxious, it is physiologically impossible to be both relaxed and anxious at the same time. The key to success is teaching the client how to replace his or her fear response with relaxation when *exposed* to the fearful stimulus, which explains why these and related approaches are often referred to as *exposure therapies*. Modern virtual reality technology also uses systematic desensitization to expose clients to feared situations right in a therapist's office **(Figure 13.8)**.

In contrast to systematic desensitization, **aversion therapy** uses classical conditioning techniques to create anxiety rather than extinguish it. People who engage in excessive drinking, for example, build up a number of pleasurable associations with alcohol. These pleasurable associations cannot always be prevented. However, aversion therapy provides *negative associations* to compete with the pleasurable ones **(Figure 13.9)**.

Aversion therapy A type of behavioral therapy characterized by the pairing of an aversive (unpleasant) stimulus with a maladaptive behavior in order to elicit a negative reaction to the target stimulus.

FIGURE 13.9 AVERSION THERAPY

The goal of aversion therapy is to create an undesirable, or *aversive*, response to a stimulus a person would like to avoid, such as alcohol.

1 During conditioning Someone who wants to stop drinking, for example, could take a drug called Antabuse that causes vomiting whenever alcohol enters the system.

2 After conditioning When the new connection between alcohol and nausea has been classically conditioned, engaging in the once desirable habit will cause an immediate aversive response.

Operant Conditioning

Shaping is a common operant conditioning technique used for bringing about a desired or target behavior. Recall from Chapter 6 that shaping provides immediate rewards for successive approximations of the target behavior. Therapists have found this technique particularly successful in developing language skills in children with autism. First, the child is rewarded for connecting pictures or other devices with words; later, rewards are given only for using the pictures to communicate with others.

psychology and you **Overcoming Shyness** Shaping can help people acquire social skills and greater assertiveness. If you are painfully shy, for example, a clinician might first ask you to role-play simply saying hello to someone you find attractive. Then you might practice behaviors that gradually lead you to suggest a get-together or date. During such role-playing, or behavior rehearsal, the clinician gives you feedback and reinforcement for each successive step you take toward the end goal.

Digital Vision/Getty Images

FIGURE 13.10 OBSERVATIONAL LEARNING

During modeling therapy, a client might learn how to interview for a job by first watching the therapist role-play the part of the interviewee. The client then imitates the therapist's behavior and plays the same role. Over the course of several sessions, the client becomes gradually desensitized to the anxiety of interviews.

Adaptive behaviors can also be taught or increased with techniques that provide immediate reinforcement in the form of tokens (Craighead et al., 2013; Reed & Martens, 2011; Spiegler, 2013). For example, patients in an inpatient treatment facility might at first be given tokens (to be exchanged for primary rewards, such as food, treats, TV time, a private room, or outings) for merely attending group therapy sessions. Later they will be rewarded only for actually participating in the sessions. Eventually, the tokens can be discontinued when the patient receives the reinforcement of being helped by participation in the therapy sessions.

Observational Learning

Q3

We all learn many things by observing others. Therapists use this principle in **modeling therapy**, in which clients are asked to observe and imitate appropriate models as they perform desired behaviors. For example, researchers successfully treated 4- and 5-year-old children with severe dog phobias by asking them first to watch other children play with dogs and then to gradually approach and get physically closer to the dogs themselves (May et al., 2012). When this type of therapy combines live modeling with direct and gradual practice, it is called *participant modeling*. This type of modeling is also effective in social skills training and assertiveness training **(Figure 13.10)**.

Modeling therapy A type of therapy characterized by watching and imitating models that demonstrate desirable behaviors.

Evaluating Behavior Therapies

Criticisms of behavior therapy fall into two major categories:

- **Generalizability** Critics argue that in the real world, patients are not consistently reinforced, and their newly acquired behaviors may disappear. To deal with this possibility, behavior therapists work to encourage clients to better recognize existing external real world rewards and to generate their own internal reinforcements, which they can then apply at their own discretion.
- **Ethics** Critics contend that it is unethical for one person to control another's behavior. Behaviorists, however, argue that rewards and punishments already control our behaviors. Behavior therapy actually increases our freedom by making these controls overt and by teaching people how to change their own behavior.

Despite these criticisms, behavior therapy is generally recognized as one of the most effective treatments for numerous problems, including phobias, obsessive-compulsive disorder, eating disorders, sexual dysfunctions, autism, intellectual disabilities, and delinquency (Ahearn & Tiger, 2013; Bergman, 2013; Haynes et al., 2011; Spiegler, 2013). For an immediate practical application of behavior therapy to your college life, see *Do You Have Test Anxiety?*

TEST YOURSELF: DO YOU HAVE TEST ANXIETY?

psychology and you

Stockbyte/Getty Images

Nearly everyone is somewhat anxious before an important exam. If you find this anxiety helpful and invigorating, skip ahead to the next section. However, if the days and evenings before a major exam are ruined by your anxiety and you sometimes "freeze up" while taking a test, try these tips, based on the three major forms of behavior therapy.

1. Classical Conditioning

This informal type of systematic desensitization will help decrease your feelings of anxiety:

Step 1: Review and practice the relaxation technique taught in Chapter 3 (p. 87).

Step 2: Create a 10-step "test-taking" hierarchy—starting with the least anxiety-arousing image (perhaps the day your instructor first mentions an upcoming exam) and ending with actually taking the exam.

Step 3: Beginning with the least-arousing image—say, hearing about the exam—picture yourself at each stage. While maintaining a calm, relaxed state, mentally work your way through all 10 steps. If you become anxious at any stage, stay there, repeating your relaxation technique until the anxiety diminishes.

Step 4: If you start to feel anxious the night before the exam, or even during the exam itself, remind yourself to relax. Take a few moments to shut your eyes and review how you worked through your hierarchy.

2. Operant Conditioning

One of the best ways to avoid "freezing up" or "blanking out" on a test is to be fully prepared. To maximize your preparation, "shape" your behavior! Start small by answering the multiple-choice questions at the end of each major section of each chapter and comparing your answers with those in Appendix B. Then move on to the longer self-grading quizzes that are available on our website, www.wiley.com/college/huffman. Following each of these "successive approximations," be sure to reward yourself in some way—call a friend, play with your children or pets, watch a video, or maybe check your Facebook page.

3. Observational Learning

Talk with your classmates who are getting good grades. Ask them for tips on how they prepare for exams and how they handle their own test anxieties. This type of modeling and observational learning can be very helpful—and it's a nice way to make friends.

RETRIEVAL PRACTICE: BEHAVIOR THERAPIES

Self-Test

Completing this self-test and comparing your answers with those in Appendix B provides immediate feedback and helpful practice for exams. Additional interactive, self-tests are available at www.wiley.com/college/huffman.

1. The main focus in behavior therapy is to increase _____ and decrease _____.

a. positive thoughts and feelings; negative thoughts and feelings
b. adaptive behaviors; maladaptive behaviors
c. coping resources; coping deficits
d. all these options

2. The three steps in systematic desensitization include all *except* _____.

a. learning to become deeply relaxed
b. arranging anxiety-arousing stimuli into a hierarchy from least to most arousing
c. practicing relaxation in response to anxiety-arousing stimuli, starting with the most arousing
d. all these options

3. In behavior therapy, _____ techniques use shaping and reinforcement to increase adaptive behaviors.

a. classical conditioning
b. modeling
c. operant conditioning
d. social learning

4. In contrast to systematic desensitization, _____ uses classical conditioning techniques to create anxiety rather than prevent its arousal.

a. anxiety-modeling therapy
b. aversion therapy
c. anxiety therapy
d. subversion therapy

Think Critically

1. Imagine that you were going to use the principles of cognitive-behavioral therapy to change some aspect of your own thinking and behavior. If you'd like to quit smoking, or be more organized, how would you identify the faulty thinking perpetuating these behaviors and fears?
2. Once you've identified your faulty thinking patterns, what could you do to change your behavior?
3. Under what circumstances might behavior therapy be unethical?

realworldpsychology

How might therapy help you hold a tarantula?

Does simply watching other children play with dogs reduce dog phobias in young children?

HINT: LOOK IN THE MARGIN FOR Q2 AND Q3

BIOMEDICAL THERAPIES

LEARNING OBJECTIVES

RETRIEVAL PRACTICE While reading the upcoming sections, respond to each Learning Objective in your own words. Then compare your responses with those found at www.wiley.com/college/huffman.

1. **DESCRIBE** biomedical therapies.
2. **IDENTIFY** the major types of drugs used to treat psychological disorders.
3. **EXPLAIN** what happens in electroconvulsive therapy and psychosurgery.
4. **DESCRIBE** the risks and benefits associated with biomedical therapies.

Some problem behaviors seem to be caused, at least in part, by chemical imbalances or disturbed nervous system functioning, and, as such, they can treated with **biomedical therapies**. Psychiatrists or other medical personnel are generally the only ones who use biomedical therapies. However, in some states, licensed psychologists can prescribe certain medications, and they often work with patients receiving biomedical therapies. In this section, we will discuss three aspects of biomedical therapies: *psychopharmacology*, *electroconvulsive therapy (ECT)*, and *psychosurgery*.

Biomedical therapy A treatment for psychological disorders that alters brain functioning with biological or physical interventions (for example, drugs, electroconvulsive therapy, psychosurgery).

Psychopharmacology

Since the 1950s, drug companies and **psychopharmacology** have helped correct chemical imbalances that underly some abnormal behaviors. In these instances, using a psychotherapeutic drug is similar to administering insulin to people with diabetes, whose own bodies fail to manufacture enough. In other cases, drugs have been used to relieve or suppress the symptoms of psychological disturbances even when the underlying cause was not thought to be biological. As shown in **Table 13.2**, psychotherapeutic drugs are classified into four major categories: *anti-anxiety*, *antipsychotic*, *mood stabilizer*, and *antidepressant*.

Psychopharmacology The study of the effect of drugs on behavior and mental processes.

How do drug treatments such as antidepressants actually work? Although we don't fully understand all the mechanisms at play, some studies suggest that antidepressants increase *neurogenesis*, the production of new neurons, or *synaptogenesis*, the production of new synapses, and/or stimulate activity in various areas of the brain (Anacker et al., 2011; Castrén & Hen, 2013; Ferreira et al., 2012; Li et al., 2012; Surget et al., 2011). The best-understood action of the drugs is to correct an imbalance in the levels of neurotransmitters in the brain

TABLE 13.2 PSYCHOTHERAPEUTIC DRUG TREATMENTS FOR PSYCHOLOGICAL DISORDERS

	Description	Examples (trade names)
Antianxiety drugs Medications used to reduce anxiety and decrease overarousal in the brain.	**Antianxiety drugs**, also known as *anxiolytics* and "minor tranquilizers," lower the sympathetic activity of the brain—the crisis mode of operation—so that anxiety is diminished and the person is calmer and less tense. However, they are potentially dangerous because they can reduce alertness, coordination, and reaction time. They also can have a synergistic (intensifying) effect with other drugs, which may lead to severe drug reactions and even death.	Ativan Halcion Librium Restoril Valium Xanax
Antipsychotic drugs Medications used to diminish or eliminate hallucinations, delusions, withdrawal, and other symptoms of psychosis; also known as neuroleptics or major tranquilizers.	**Antipsychotic drugs**, or *neuroleptics*, reduce the agitated behaviors, hallucinations, delusions, and other symptoms associated with psychotic disorders, such as schizophrenia. Traditional antipsychotics work by decreasing activity at the dopamine receptors in the brain. A large majority of patients markedly improve when treated with antipsychotic drugs.	Clozaril Haldol Mellaril Navane Prolixin Risperdal Seroquel Thorazine
Mood-stabilizer drugs Medications used to treat the combination of manic episodes and depression characteristic of bipolar disorders.	**Mood-stabilizer drugs** help steady mood swings, particularly for those suffering from bipolar disorder, a condition marked by extremes of both mania and depression. Because lithium acts relatively slowly—requiring up to three or four weeks to take effect—its primary use is in preventing future episodes and helping to break the manic-depressive cycle.	Eskalith CR Lithium Tegretol
Antidepressant drugs Medications used to treat depression, some anxiety disorders, and certain eating disorders (such as bulimia).	**Antidepressant drugs** are used primarily to treat people with depression, but they are also effective for some anxiety disorders and eating disorders. There are five types of antidepressant drugs: *tricyclics, monoamine oxidase inhibitors* (*MAOIs*), *selective serotonin reuptake inhibitors* (*SSRIs*), *serotonin and norepinephrine reuptake inhibitors* (*SNRIs*), and *atypical antidepressants*. Each class of drugs affects neurochemical pathways in the brain in a slightly different way, increasing or decreasing the availability of certain chemicals. SSRIs (such as *Paxil* and *Prozac*) are by far the most commonly prescribed antidepressants. The atypical antidepressants are prescribed for patients who fail to respond to or experience undesirable side effects from other antidepressants.	Anafranil Celexa Cymbalta Effexor Elavil Nardil Norpramin Parnate Paxil Prozac Tofranil Wellbutrin Zoloft

"Before Prozac, she loathed company."

(Figure 13.11). For example, researchers know that the drug ketamine works for bipolar disorders because it changes the levels of brain neurotransmitters, but another study found that 79% of those who received even a single dose of ketamine also showed lower rates of depression, including thoughts of suicide (Zarate et al., 2012). The next time you hear someone say that mental illness isn't real or that "it's all in your head," you can describe to them how changing the levels of brain chemicals has been successful for both bipolar disorder and major depression.

Q4

FIGURE 13.11 HOW ANTIDEPRESSANTS AFFECT THE BRAIN

Antidepressants work at the neural transmission level by increasing the availability of serotonin or norepinephrine, neurotransmitters that normally elevate mood and arousal. Shown here is the action of some of the most popular antidepressants—Prozac, Paxil, and other selective serotonin reuptake inhibitors (SSRIs).

A Serotonin's effect on the brain

People with depression are known to have lower levels of serotonin. Serotonin works in the prefrontal cortex, the hippocampus, and other parts of the brain to regulate mood, sleep, and appetite, among other things.

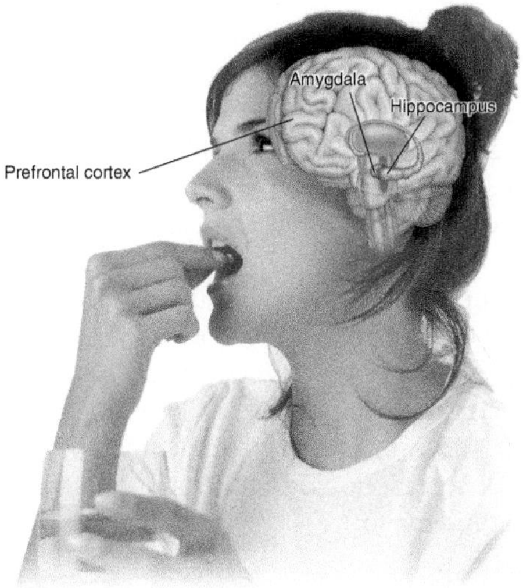

MedioImages/Photodisc/Getty Images, Inc.

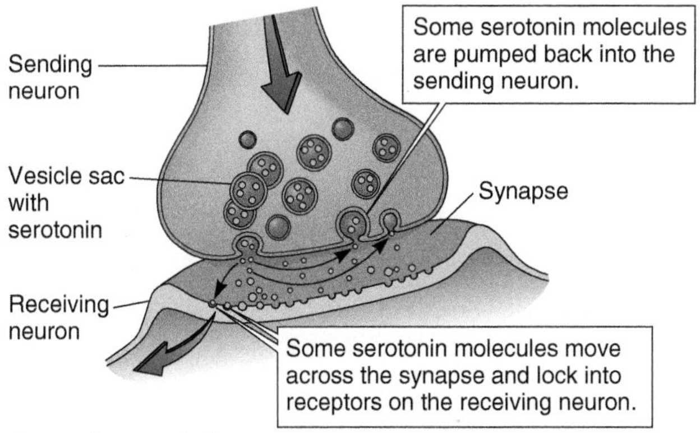

B Normal neural transmission

The sending neuron releases an excess of neurotransmitters, including serotonin. Some of the serotonin locks into receptors on the receiving neuron, but excess serotonin is pumped back into the sending neuron (called *reuptake*) for storage and reuse. If serotonin is reabsorbed too quickly, there is less available to the brain, which may result in depression.

C Partial blockage of reuptake by SSRIs

SSRIs, like Prozac, partially block the normal reuptake of excess serotonin, which leaves more serotonin molecules free to stimulate receptors on the receiving neuron. This increased neural transmission restores the normal balance of serotonin in the brain.

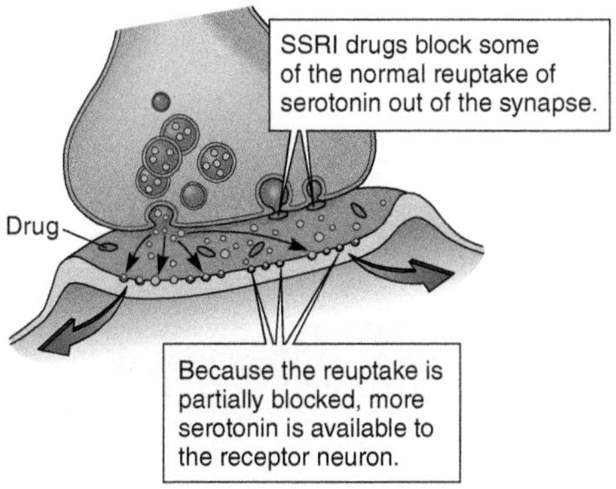

Electroconvulsive Therapy and Psychosurgery

There is a long history of using electrical stimulation to treat psychological disorders. In **electroconvulsive therapy (ECT)**, also known as electroshock therapy (EST), a moderate electrical current is passed through the brain between two electrodes placed on the outside of the head. The current triggers a widespread firing of neurons, or brief seizures. ECT can quickly reverse symptoms of certain mental illnesses and often works when other treatments have been unsuccessful. The electric current produces many changes in the central and peripheral nervous systems, including activation of the autonomic nervous system, increased secretion of various hormones and neurotransmitters, and changes in the blood–brain barrier **(Figure 13.12)**.

Electroconvulsive therapy (ECT) A biomedical therapy based on passing electrical current through the brain; it is used almost exclusively to treat serious depression when drug therapy fails.

Despite not knowing exactly how ECT works, or that it may cause some short-term memory loss immediately after treatment, and possible long-term memory

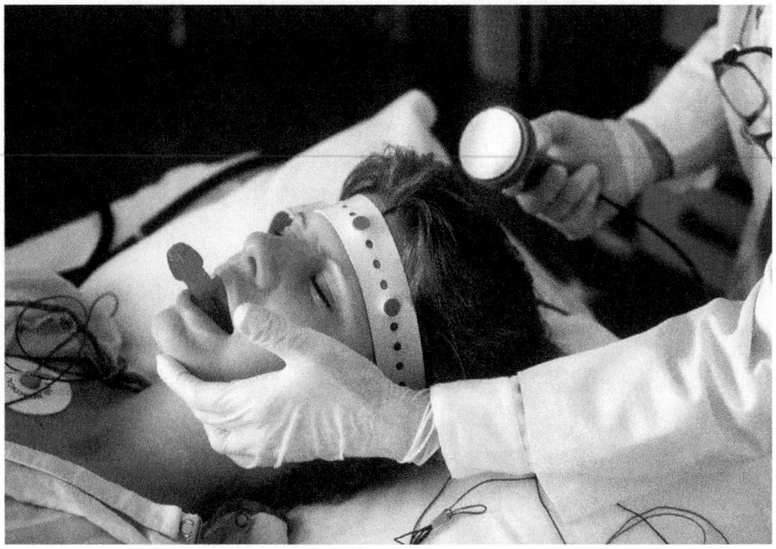

FIGURE 13.12 ELECTROCONVULSIVE THERAPY (ECT)

Modern ECT treatments are conducted with considerable safety precautions, including muscle-relaxant drugs that dramatically reduce muscle contractions and medication to help patients sleep through the procedure. ECT is used less often today and generally only when other treatments have failed, despite a 70% improvement rate for depression (Case et al., 2013; Perugi et al., 2012).

Will McIntyre/Photo Researchers, Inc.

problems, the risks of untreated, severe depression are generally considered greater than the risks of ECT. It is used primarily on patients who have not responded to drugs and psychotherapy, and on suicidal patients, because it works faster than antidepressant drugs (Kobeissi et al., 2011; Loo et al., 2011; Pfeiffer et al., 2011).

The most extreme, and least used, biomedical therapy is **psychosurgery**—brain surgery performed to reduce serious debilitating psychological problems. Attempts to change disturbed thoughts, feelings, and behavior by altering the brain have a long history. In Roman times, for example, it was believed that a sword wound to the head could relieve insanity. In 1936, Portuguese neurologist Egaz Moniz first treated uncontrollable psychoses with a form of *psychosurgery* called a **lobotomy**, in which he cut the nerve fibers between the frontal lobes (where association areas for monitoring and planning behavior are found) and the thalamus and hypothalamus. Although these surgeries did reduce emotional outbursts and aggressiveness, patients were left with permanent brain damage.

Psychosurgery A neurosurgical alteration of the brain to bring about desirable behavioral, cognitive, or emotional changes, which is generally used when patients have not responded to other forms of treatment; also called neurosurgery for mental disorder (NMD).

Lobotomy An outmoded neurosurgical procedure for mental disorders, which involved cutting nerve pathways between the frontal lobes and the thalamus and hypothalamus.

realworldpsychology **A Modern Alternative to Lobotomies** Two of the most notable examples of the damage from early lobotomies are Rosemary Kennedy, the sister of President John F. Kennedy, and Rose Williams, sister of American playwright Tennessee Williams. Both women were permanently incapacitated from lobotomies performed in the early 1940s. Thankfully, in the mid-1950s, when antipsychotic drugs came into use, psychosurgery virtually stopped.

Recently, however, psychiatrists have been experimenting with a much more limited and precise neurosurgical procedure called *deep brain stimulation* (*DBS*). The surgeon drills two tiny holes into the patient's skull and implants electrodes in the area of the brain believed to be associated with a specific disorder. These electrodes are then connected to a "pacemaker" implanted in the chest or stomach that sends low-voltage electricity to the problem areas in the brain.

Over time, this repeated stimulation can bring about significant improvement in Parkinson's disease, epilepsy, major depression and other disorders (Campbell et al., 2012; Chopra et al., 2012; Kennedy et al., 2011; Lageman et al., 2013; Spindler et al., 2013). In addition, research has shown that patients who receive this type of DBS along with antidepressants show lower rates of depression than those who receive either treatment alone (Brunoni et al., 2013).

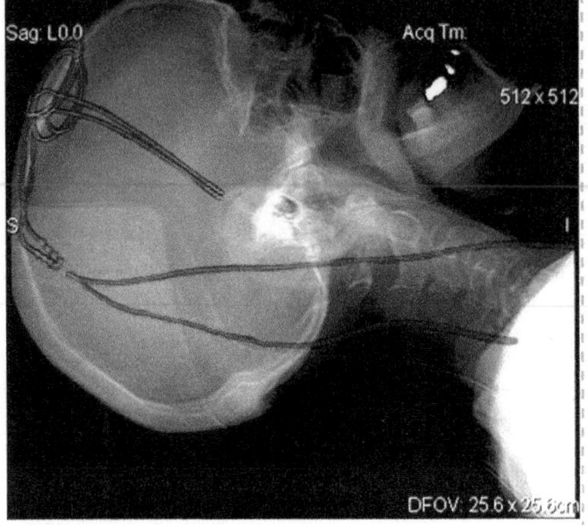

Photo Researchers/Getty Images

Evaluating Biomedical Therapies

Like all other forms of therapy, biomedical therapies have both proponents and critics.

Pitfalls of Psychopharmacology

Drug therapy poses several potential problems. First, although drugs may relieve symptoms for some people, they seldom provide cures. In addition, some patients become physically dependent on the drugs. Also, researchers are still learning about the drugs' long-term effects and potential interactions. Furthermore, psychiatric medications can cause a variety of side effects, ranging from mild fatigue to severe impairments in memory and movement. A final potential problem with drug treatment is that its relatively low cost and generally fast results have led to its overuse in some cases. Despite the problems associated with them, psychotherapeutic drugs have led to revolutionary changes in mental health. Before the use of drugs, some patients were destined to spend a lifetime in psychiatric institutions. Today, most improve enough to return to their homes and live successful lives if they continue to take their medications to prevent relapse.

Challenges to ECT and Psychosurgery

ECT currently serves as a valuable last-resort treatment for severe depression. However, similar benefits may be available through the latest advances in **repetitive transcranial magnetic stimulation (rTMS)**, which uses an electromagnet placed on the scalp that generates magnetic field pulses roughly the strength of an MRI scan **(Figure 13.13)**. To treat depression, the coil is usually placed over the prefrontal cortex, a region linked to deeper parts of the brain that regulate mood. Currently, rTMS's advantages over ECT are still unclear, but studies have shown marked improvement in depression, and patients experience fewer side effects (Berlim et al., 2013; Guse et al., 2013; Husain & Lisanby, 2011; Polley et al., 2011).

Repetitive transcranial magnetic stimulation (rTMS) A biomedical treatment that uses repeated magnetic field pulses targeted at specific areas of the brain.

Because all forms of psychosurgery are potentially dangerous and have serious or even fatal side effects, some critics say that it should be banned altogether. Furthermore, the consequences are generally irreversible. For these reasons, psychosurgery is considered experimental and remains a highly controversial treatment.

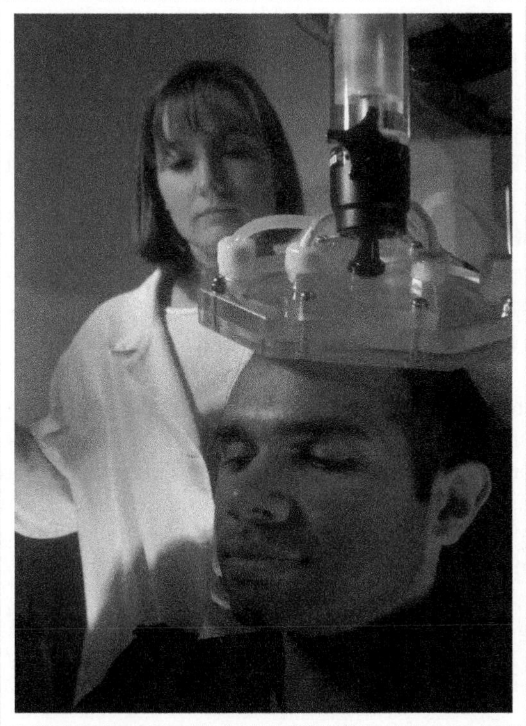

FIGURE 13.13 REPETITIVE TRANSCRANIAL MAGNETIC STIMULATION (rTMS)

Powerful electromagnets generate pulsed magnetic fields that are targeted at specific areas of the brain to treat depression.

RETRIEVAL PRACTICE: BIOMEDICAL THERAPIES

Self-Test

Completing this self-test and comparing your answers with those in Appendix B provides immediate feedback and helpful practice for exams. Additional interactive, self-tests are available at www.wiley.com/college/huffman.

1. The study of the effects of drugs on behavior and mental processes is known as _____.

a. psychiatry
b. psychoanalysis
c. psychosurgery
d. psychopharmacology

2. The effectiveness of antipsychotic drugs is thought to result primarily from decreasing activity at the _____ receptors.

a. serotonin
b. dopamine
c. epinephrine
d. all these options

3. In electroconvulsive therapy (ECT), _____.

a. current is never applied to the left hemisphere
b. seizures activate the central and peripheral nervous systems, stimulate hormone and neurotransmitter release, and change the blood–brain barrier
c. convulsions are extremely painful and long lasting
d. most patients receive hundreds of treatments because it is safer than in the past

4. ECT is used primarily to treat _____.

a. phobias
b. conduct disorders
c. severe depression
d. schizophrenia

Think Critically

1. Are the potential benefits of psychopharmacology worth the risks? Is it ever ethical to force someone to take drugs to treat his or her mental illness?
2. If you, or someone you loved, were seriously depressed would you be in favor of ECT? Why or why not?

realworldpsychology

How do psychotherapeutic drugs help decrease thoughts of suicide?

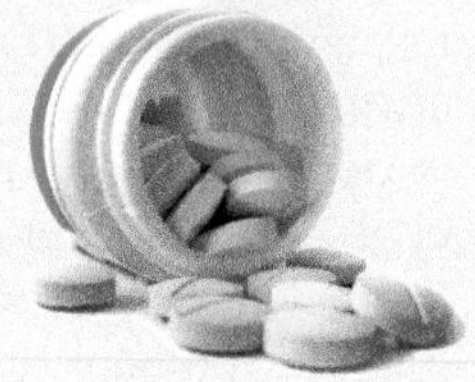

HINT: LOOK IN THE MARGIN FOR Q4

PSYCHOTHERAPY IN PERSPECTIVE

LEARNING OBJECTIVES

RETRIEVAL PRACTICE While reading the upcoming sections, respond to each Learning Objective in your own words. Then compare your responses with those found at www.wiley.com/college/huffman.

1. **SUMMARIZE** the goals and overall effectiveness of psychotherapy.
2. **DESCRIBE** group, marital, family, and telehealth/electronic therapies.
3. **IDENTIFY** the key cultural and gender issues important in therapy.
4. **SUMMARIZE** the major career options for someone interested in being a therapist.

Given that it's currently estimated that there are more than 400 forms of therapy, how would you choose one for yourself or someone you know? In the first part of this section, we discuss five goals common to all psychotherapies. Then we explore specific formats for therapy as well as considerations about culture and gender. Our aim is to help you synthesize the material in this chapter and put what you have learned about each of the major forms of therapy into a broader context.

Therapy Goals and Effectiveness

All major forms of therapy are designed to help the client in five specific areas **(Figure 13.14)**.

FIGURE 13.14 **THE FIVE MOST COMMON GOALS OF THERAPY**

Most therapies focus on one or more of these five goals. Can you identify which would be of most interest to psychodynamic, humanistic, cognitive, and behavioristic therapists?

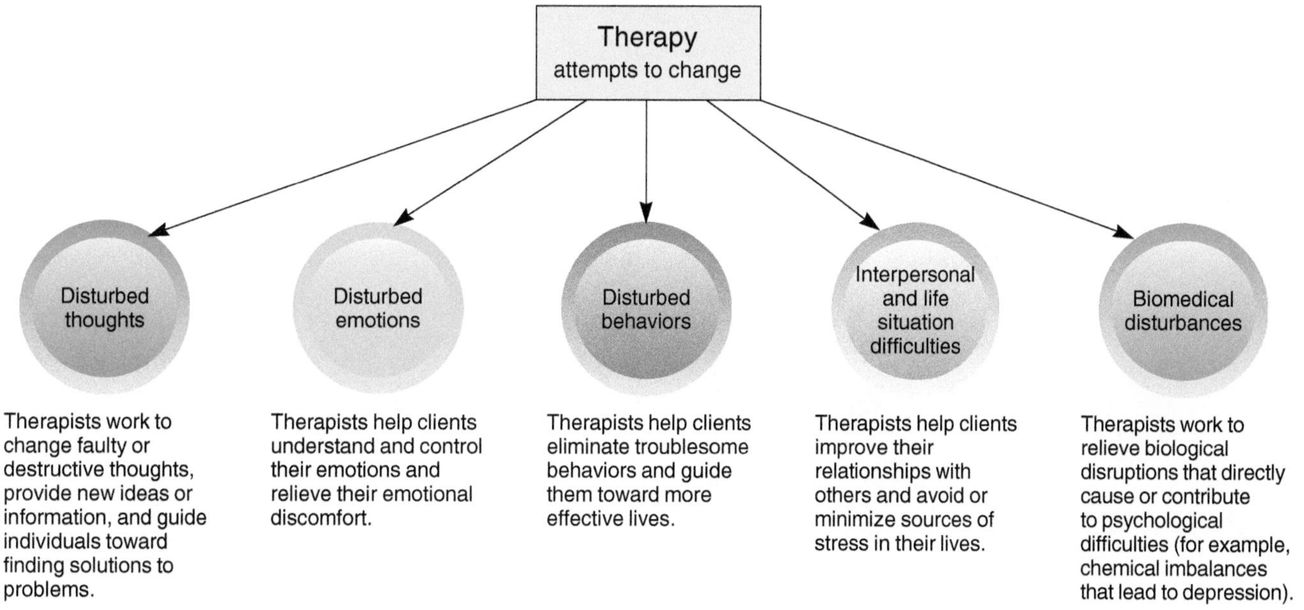

Therapy
attempts to change
Disturbed thoughts
Disturbed emotions
Disturbed behaviors
Interpersonal and life situation difficulties
Biomedical disturbances
Therapists work to change faulty or destructive thoughts, provide new ideas or information, and guide individuals toward finding solutions to problems.
Therapists help clients understand and control their emotions and relieve their emotional discomfort.
Therapists help clients eliminate troublesome behaviors and guide them toward more effective lives.
Therapists help clients improve their relationships with others and avoid or minimize sources of stress in their lives.
Therapists work to relieve biological disruptions that directly cause or contribute to psychological difficulties (for example, chemical imbalances that lead to depression).

Although most therapists work with clients in several of these areas, the emphasis varies according to the therapist's training and whether it is psychodynamic, cognitive, humanistic, behaviorist, or biomedical. Clinicians who regularly borrow freely from various theories are said to take an **eclectic approach**.

Eclectic approach A perspective on therapy that combines techniques from various theories to find the most appropriate treatment.

Does therapy work? After years of controlled studies and *meta-analysis*—a method of statistically combining and analyzing data from many studies—researchers have fairly clear evidence that it does. For example, one early meta-analytic review combined studies of almost 25,000 people and found that the average person who received treatment was better off than 75% of the untreated control clients **(Figure 13.15)**.

Studies also show that short-term treatments can be as effective as long-term treatments and that most therapies are equally effective for various disorders (Dewan et al., 2011; Gillies et al., 2012; Messer et al., 2013; Wachtel, 2011). Even informal therapy techniques, like simple writing exercises, have led to increased marital satisfaction (see *Psych Science*).

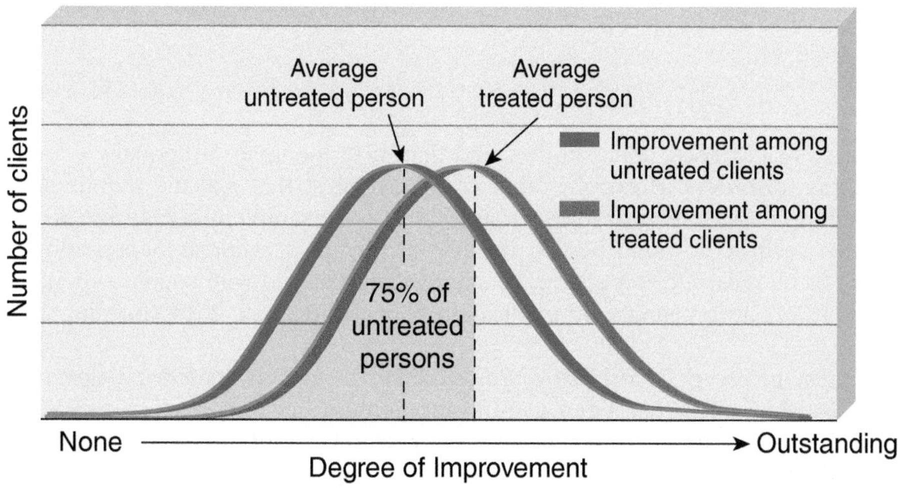

FIGURE 13.15 **IS THERAPY GENERALLY EFFECTIVE?**

The average person who receives therapy is better off after it than a similar person who does not get treatment (Campbell et al., 2013; Corey, 2013; Miller et al., 2013; Shedler, 2010; Smith et al., 1980). An analysis of more than 435 studies on the effectiveness of therapy for treating psychological disorders in children and adolescents revealed that therapy can lead to improvements in many different types of psychological disorders, including anxiety, autism, depression, disruptive behavior, eating problems, substance use, and traumatic stress (Chorpita et al., 2011).

PSYCHSCIENCE

CAN WRITING SAVE YOUR MARRIAGE?

© asiseeit/iStockphoto

Self-reflection and journaling are proven successful therapy techniques, so researchers in one study asked 120 volunteer married couples to describe the most significant disagreement they had experienced with their spouse during the past four months (Finkel et al., 2013). Half of the couples were then asked to complete a series of three seven-minute writing exercises. These writing exercises asked both spouses to reflect on the disagreement while taking the perspective of a neutral third party who wants the best for all involved. The researchers then contacted the couples every four months for the next two years. During these follow-up contacts, couples also were asked to provide a similar neutral summary of their most significant marital disagreement in the past four months and to report their level of relationship satisfaction, love, intimacy, trust, passion, and commitment.

Couples in both groups showed decreased marital satisfaction over the first year (a typical finding in married couples), but those that completed the writing exercises by taking the perspective of a neutral third party showed no additional decline in marital satisfaction in the second year. In contrast, couples that did not take this neutral perspective continued to show even greater declines in satisfaction.

Can you see how taking the perspective of a neutral third party might have indirectly trained the couples to use more *empathy* and *unconditional positive regard with one another*—two terms we discussed earlier in this chapter? Similarly, can you understand how this writing exercise might have helped these couples avoid Beck's negative thinking patterns of *selective perception*, *overgeneralization*, *magnification*, and *all-or-nothing thinking*? Most importantly, can you apply the results of this research, and the terms we've just identified, to improving your own relationships with love partners, family members, and friends?

RESEARCH CHALLENGE

1. **Based on the information provided, did this study (Finkel et al., 2013) use descriptive, correlational, and/or experimental research?**
2. **If you chose:**
   - **descriptive research, is this a naturalistic observation, survey/interview, case study, or archival research?**
   - **correlational research, is this a positive, negative, or zero correlation?**
   - **experimental research, label the IV, DV, experimental group(s), and control group.**

>>CHECK YOUR ANSWERS IN APPENDIX B.

NOTE: The information provided in this study is admittedly limited, but the level of detail is similar to what is presented in most textbooks and public reports of research findings. Answering these questions, and then comparing your answers to those in the Appendix, will help you become a better critical thinker and consumer of scientific research.

As we've just seen, some studies find that most therapies are equally effective for various disorders. However, other studies suggest that specific therapies are more effective for certain problems than others. For example, phobias and marital problems seem to respond best to behavioral therapies, whereas depression and obsessive-compulsive disorders can be significantly relieved with cognitive-behavior therapy (CBT) accompanied by medication (Craighead et al., 2013; Spiegler, 2013; Wilson, 2011).

Finally, in recent years, the *empirically supported*, or *evidence-based practice (EBP), movement* has been gaining momentum because it seeks to identify which therapies have received the clearest research support for particular disorders (Biegel et al., 2013; Duncan & Reese, 2013; Sharf, 2012; Thyer & Myers, 2011).

Like all other movements, it has been criticized, but this type of empirically based research promises to be helpful for therapists and clients alike in their treatment decisions. For specific tips on finding therapy for yourself or a loved one, see *Choosing a Therapist*.

CHOOSING A THERAPIST | psychology and you

How do you find a good therapist for your specific needs? If you have the time (and money) to explore options, there are several steps you can take to find a therapist best suited to your specific goals. First, you might consult your psychology instructor, college counseling system, or family physician for specific referrals. In addition, most HMOs and health insurers provide lists of qualified professionals. Next, call the referred therapists and ask for an opportunity to discuss some questions. You could ask what their training was like, what approach they use, what their fees are, and whether they participate in your insurance plan.

Finding a therapist takes time and energy. If you need immediate help—you're having suicidal thoughts or are the victim of abuse—you should see if your community is one of the many that have medical hospital emergency services and telephone hotlines that provide counseling services on a 24-hour basis. In addition, most colleges and universities have counseling centers that provide immediate, short-term therapy to students free of charge.

Finally, if you're concerned about a friend or family member who might need therapy, you can follow the tips above to help locate a therapist and then possibly offer to go with him or her on their first appointment. If the individual refuses help and the problem affects you, it is often a good idea to seek therapy yourself. You will gain insights and skills that will help you deal with the situation more effectively.

For general help in locating a skilled therapist, identifying what types of initial questions to ask, learning how to gain the most benefits during therapy, and so on, consult the American Psychological Association (APA) website.

Think Critically

1. If you were looking for a therapist, would you want the therapist's gender to be the same as yours? Why or why not?
2. Do you think all insurance companies should be required to offer mental health coverage? Why or why not?

Therapy Formats

The therapies described earlier in this chapter are conducted primarily in a face-to-face, therapist-to-client format. In this section, we focus on several major alternatives: *group*, *family*, and *marital therapies*, which treat multiple individuals simultaneously, and *telehealth/electronic therapy*, which treats individuals via the Internet, e-mail, and/or smart phones.

Group Therapy

In **group therapy**, multiple people meet together to work toward therapeutic goals. Typically, a group of 8 to 10 people meet with a therapist on a regular basis to talk about problems in their lives.

A variation on group therapy is the **self-help group**. Unlike other group approaches, self-help groups are not guided by a professional. They are simply circles of people who share a common problem, such as alcoholism, obesity, or breast cancer, and who meet to give and receive support. Faith-based Twelve-Step programs such as Alcoholics Anonymous, Narcotics Anonymous, and Spenders

Group therapy A form of therapy in which a number of people meet together to work toward therapeutic goals.

Self-help group A leaderless or nonprofessionally guided group in which members assist each other with a specific problem, as in Alcoholics Anonymous.

Anonymous are examples of self-help groups. Although group members don't get the same level of individual attention found in one-on-one therapies, group and self-help therapies provide their own unique advantages (Corey, 2011; Jaffe & Kelly, 2011; Kivlighan et al., 2012; Messer & Gurman, 2011; Piper & Hernandez, 2013). They are far less expensive than one-on-one therapies and provide a broader base of social support. Group members also can learn from each other's experiences, share insights and coping strategies, and role-play social interactions together.

Therapists often refer their patients to group therapy and to self-help groups in order to supplement individual therapy. For example, recovering alcoholics who choose to help others in Alcoholics Anonymous group sessions actually show lower levels of alcohol use themselves as long as 10 years later (Pagano et al., 2013). In sum, research on self-help groups for alcoholism, obesity, and other disorders suggests that they can be very effective, either alone or in addition to individual psychotherapy (Donovan et al., 2013; Jaffe & Kelly, 2011; Majer et al., 2013; Pomerantz, 2013).

Marital and Family Therapies

Given that a family or marriage is a system of interdependent parts, the problem of any one individual inevitably affects everyone, and therefore all members are potential beneficiaries of therapy (Dattilio & Nichols, 2011; Friedlander et al., 2011; Hills, 2013; Lebow & Stroud, 2013). The line between family and marital or couples therapy is often blurred. Here, our discussion will focus on *family therapy*, in which the primary aim is to change maladaptive family interaction patterns **(Figure 13.16)**. All members of the family attend therapy sessions, though at times the therapist may see family members individually or in twos or threes.

Family therapy is also useful in treating a number of disorders and clinical problems. As we discussed in Chapter 12, schizophrenic patients are at increased risk of relapsing if their family members express emotions, attitudes, and behaviors that suggest criticism, hostility, or emotional overinvolvement (Lobban et al., 2013; Pharoah et al., 2010; Quinn et al., 2003). Family therapy can help family members modify their behavior toward the patient. It can also be the most favorable setting for the treatment of adolescent drug abuse (Alexander et al., 2013; Mead, 2012; Morgan et al., 2013; O'Farrell, 2011).

Telehealth/Electronic Therapy

Today millions of people are receiving advice and professional therapy in newer, electronic formats, such as the Internet, e-mail, virtual reality (VR), and interactive web-based conference systems such as Skype. This latest form of electronic therapy,

FIGURE 13.16 FAMILY THERAPY

Many families initially come into therapy believing that one member is the cause of all their problems. However, family therapists generally find that this "identified patient" is a scapegoat for deeper disturbances. How could changing ways of interacting within the family system promote the health of individual family members and the family as a whole?

often referred to as *telehealth*, allows clinicians to reach more clients and provide them with greater access to information regarding their specific problems (see *Real World Psychology* feature).

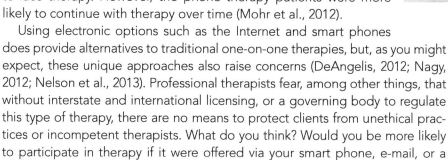

realworldpsychology **Therapy—Is There an App for That?** Studies have long shown that therapy outcomes improve with increased client contact, and the electronic/telehealth format may be the easiest and most cost-effective way to increase this contact (Campbell et al., 2013; DeAngelis, 2012; Myers & Turvey, 2013). For example, a recent study compared the effectiveness of cognitive behavioral therapy delivered over the telephone with the effectiveness of in-person visits for patients with major depressive disorder. The researchers found that those who received phone therapy showed improvement, but not as much as those who received face-to-face therapy. However, the phone therapy patients were more likely to continue with therapy over time (Mohr et al., 2012).

Q5

© David Ahn/iStockphoto

Using electronic options such as the Internet and smart phones does provide alternatives to traditional one-on-one therapies, but, as you might expect, these unique approaches also raise concerns (DeAngelis, 2012; Nagy, 2012; Nelson et al., 2013). Professional therapists fear, among other things, that without interstate and international licensing, or a governing body to regulate this type of therapy, there are no means to protect clients from unethical practices or incompetent therapists. What do you think? Would you be more likely to participate in therapy if it were offered via your smart phone, e-mail, or a website? Or is this too impersonal and high tech for you?

Cultural Issues in Therapy

The therapies described in this chapter are based on Western European and North American culture. Does this mean they are unique? Or do these psychotherapists accomplish some of the same things that, say, a native healer or shaman does? Are there similarities in therapies across cultures? Conversely, are there fundamental therapeutic differences among cultures?

When we look at therapies in all cultures, we find that they have certain key features in common (Barnow & Balkir, 2013; Berry et al., 2011; Buss 2011; Markus & Kitayama, 2010; Matsumoto & Juang, 2013):

- **Naming the problem** People often feel better just knowing that others experience the same problem and that the therapist has had experience with it.
- **Demonstrating the right qualities** Clients must feel that the therapist is caring, competent, approachable, and concerned with finding solutions to their problems.
- **Establishing credibility** Word-of-mouth testimonials and status symbols, such as diplomas on the wall, establish a therapist's credibility. A native healer may earn credibility by serving as an apprentice to a revered healer.
- **Placing the problem in a familiar framework** Some cultures believe evil spirits cause psychological disorders, so therapy is directed toward eliminating these spirits. Similarly, in cultures that emphasize the importance of early childhood experiences and the unconscious mind as the cause of mental disorders, therapy will be framed around these familiar issues.
- **Applying techniques to bring relief** In all cultures, therapy includes action. Either the client or the therapist must do something. Moreover, what therapists do must fit the client's expectations—whether it is performing a ceremony to expel demons or talking with the client about his or her thoughts and feelings.
- **Meeting at a special time and place** The fact that therapy occurs outside the client's everyday experiences seems to be an important feature of all therapies.

Although there are basic similarities in therapies across cultures, there are also important differences. In the traditional Western European and North American model, the emphasis is on the patient's self and on his or her having independence and control over his or her life—qualities that are highly valued in individualistic cultures. In collectivist cultures, however, the focus of therapy is on interdependence and the patient's accepting the realities of his or her life (Ross, 2013).

Sky Bonillo/PhotoEdit

realworldpsychology **Emphasizing Interdependence** In Japanese Naikan therapy, patients sit quietly from 5:30 a.m. to 9:00 p.m. for seven days and are visited by an interviewer every 90 minutes. During this time, they reflect on their relationships with others in order to discover personal guilt for having been ungrateful and troublesome and to develop gratitude toward those who have helped them (Moodley & Sutherland, 2010; Nakamura, 2006; Ozawa-de Silva, 2007; Shinfuku & Kitanishi, 2010).

Not only does culture affect the types of therapy that are developed, it also influences the perceptions of the therapist. What one culture considers abnormal behavior may be quite common—and even healthy—in others. For this reason, recognizing cultural differences is very important for building trust between therapists and clients and for effecting behavioral change (Barnow & Balkir, 2013; Frew & Spiegler, 2013; Moodley, 2012).

Gender and Therapy

In our individualistic Western culture, men and women present different needs and problems to therapists. Research has identified five unique concerns related to gender and psychotherapy (Bruns & Kaschak, 2011; Geller et al., 2013; Jordan, 2011; Remer, 2013):

1. **Rates of diagnosis and treatment of mental disorders** Women are diagnosed and treated for mental illness at a much higher rate than men. Are women "sicker" than men as a group, or are they just more willing to admit their problems? Or are the categories of illness biased against women? More research is needed to answer these questions.
2. **Stresses of poverty** Women are disproportionately likely to be poor. Poverty contributes to stress, which is directly related to many psychological disorders.
3. **Violence against women** Rape, incest, and sexual harassment—which are much more likely to happen to women than to men—may lead to depression, insomnia, posttraumatic stress disorders, eating disorders, and other problems.
4. **Stresses of multiple roles** Women today are mothers, wives, homemakers, wage earners, students, and more. The conflicting demands of their multiple roles often create special stresses.

Therapists must be sensitive to possible connections between clients' problems and their gender. Rather than prescribing drugs to relieve depression in women, for example, it may be more appropriate for therapists to explore ways to relieve the stresses of multiple roles or poverty. Can you see how helping a single mother identify parenting resources, such as play groups, parent support groups, and high-quality child care, might be just as effective at relieving depression as prescribing drugs? In the case of men, how might relieving loneliness or depression help decrease their greater problems with substance abuse and aggression?

If you've enjoyed this section on cultural and gender issues in therapy, as well as the earlier description of the various forms and formats of psychotherapy, you may be considering a possible career as a therapist. If so, see *Careers in Mental Health* below.

CAREERS IN MENTAL HEALTH | psychology and you

Most colleges have counseling or career centers with numerous resources and trained staff to help you with your career choices. However, to get you started and give you an overview of the general field of psychotherapy, we've included a brief summary of the major types of mental health professionals, their degrees, years of required education beyond the bachelor's degree, and type of training.

MAJOR TYPES OF MENTAL HEALTH PROFESSIONALS

Occupational Title	Degree	Nature of Training
Clinical psychologists	Ph.D. (doctor of philosophy), Psy.D. (doctor of psychology)	Most clinical psychologists have a doctoral degree with training in research and clinical practice and a supervised one-year internship in a psychiatric hospital or mental health facility. As clinicians, they work with patients suffering from mental disorders, but many also work in colleges and universities as teachers and researchers in addition to having their own private practice.
Counseling psychologists	Ph.D. (doctor of philosophy), Psy.D. (doctor of psychology), Ed.D. (doctor of education	Counseling psychologists have a doctoral degree with training that focuses on less severe mental disorders, such as emotional, social, vocational, educational, and health-related concerns. In addition to providing psychotherapy, other career paths are open, such as teaching, research, and vocational counseling.
Psychiatrists	M.D. (doctor of medicine)	After four years of medical school, an internship and residency in psychiatry are required, which includes supervised practice in psychotherapy techniques and biomedical therapies. In most states in the United States, psychiatrists, because they are M.D.s, are the only mental health specialists who can regularly prescribe drugs.
Psychiatric nurses	R.N. (registered nurse), M.A. (master of arts), Ph.D. (doctor of philosophy)	Psychiatric nurses usually have a bachelor's or master's degree in nursing, followed by advanced training in the care of mental patients in hospital settings and mental health facilities.
Psychiatric social workers	M.S.W. (master's in social work), D.S.W. (doctorate in social work), Ph.D. (doctor of philosophy)	Psychiatric social workers usually have a master's degree in social work, followed by advanced training and experience in hospitals or outpatient settings working with people who have psychological problems.
School psychologists	M.A. (master of arts), Ph.D. (doctor of philosophy), Psy.D. (doctor of psychology), Ed.D. (doctor of education)	School psychologists generally begin with a bachelor's degree in psychology, followed by graduate training in psychological assessment and counseling for school-related issues and problems.

RETRIEVAL PRACTICE: PSYCHOTHERAPY IN PERSPECTIVE

Self-Test

Completing this self-test and comparing your answers with those in Appendix B provides immediate feedback and helpful practice for exams. Additional interactive, self-tests are available at www.wiley.com/college/huffman.

1. Which of the following is *not* a culturally universal feature of therapy?

a. Naming the problem
b. Demonstrating the right qualities
c. Establishing rapport among family members
d. Placing the problem in a familiar framework

2. A Japanese therapy designed to help clients discover personal guilt for having been ungrateful and troublesome to others and to develop gratitude toward those who have helped them is known as _____.

a. Kyoto therapy
b. Okado therapy
c. Naikan therapy
d. Nissan therapy

3. A(n) _____ group does not have a professional leader, and members assist each other in coping with a specific problem.

a. self-help
b. encounter
c. peer
d. behavior

4. _____ treats the family as a unit, and members work together to solve problems.

a. Aversion therapy
b. An encounter group
c. A self-help group
d. Family therapy

Think Critically

1 Which of the universal characteristics of therapists do you believe is the most important? Why?

2 If a friend were having marital problems, how would you convince him or her to go to a marriage or family therapist, using information you've gained in this chapter?

realworldpsychology

Can therapy that is delivered over the telephone lead to lower levels of depression?

HINT: LOOK IN THE MARGIN FOR Q5

Summary

1 TALK THERAPIES 369

- Talk therapies are forms of **psychotherapy** that seek to increase insight into clients' difficulties.
- In **psychoanalysis**, the therapist seeks to identify the patient's unconscious conflicts and to help the patient resolve them. In modern **psychodynamic therapy**, treatment is briefer, and the therapist takes a more directive approach (and puts less emphasis on unconscious childhood memories) than in traditional psychoanalysis.
- **Humanistic therapy**, such as Rogers's **client-centered therapy**, seeks to maximize personal growth, encouraging people to actualize their potential and relate to others in genuine ways.
- **Cognitive therapy** seeks to help clients challenge faulty thought processes and adjust maladaptive behaviors. Ellis's **rational-emotive behavior therapy (REBT)** and Beck's **cognitive-behavior therapy (CBT)** are important examples of cognitive therapy.

2 BEHAVIOR THERAPIES 377

- In **behavior therapy**, the focus is on the problem behavior itself rather than on any underlying causes. The therapist uses learning principles to change behavior.
- Classical conditioning techniques include **systematic desensitization** and **aversion therapy**.
- Operant conditioning techniques used to increase adaptive behaviors include *shaping* and *reinforcement*.
- In **modeling therapy**, clients observe and imitate others who are performing the desired behaviors.

3 BIOMEDICAL THERAPIES 381

- **Biomedical therapies** are based on the premise that chemical imbalances or disturbed nervous system functioning contributes to problem behaviors.
- **Psychopharmacology** is the most common form of biomedical therapy. Major classes of drugs used to treat psychological disorders are **antianxiety drugs**, **antipsychotic drugs**, **mood stabilizer drugs**, and **antidepressant drugs**.

- In **electroconvulsive therapy (ECT)**, an electrical current is passed through the brain, stimulating convulsions that produce changes in the central and peripheral nervous systems. ECT is used primarily in cases of severe depression that do not respond to other treatments.
- In **repetitive transcranial magnetic stimulation (rTMS)**, powerful electromagnets generate pulsed magnetic fields that are targeted at specific areas of the brain to treat depression.
- The most extreme biomedical therapy is **psychosurgery**. **Lobotomy**, an older form of psychosurgery, is now outmoded. Recently, psychiatrists have been experimenting with a more limited and precise surgical procedure called *deep brain stimulation* (DBS).

4 PSYCHOTHERAPY IN PERSPECTIVE 386

- All major forms of therapy are designed to address disturbed thoughts, disturbed emotions, disturbed behaviors, interpersonal and life situation difficulties, and biomedical disturbances. Research indicates that, overall, therapy does work.
- In **group therapy**, multiple people meet together to work toward therapeutic goals. A variation is the **self-help group**, which is not guided by a professional. Therapists often refer their patients to group therapy and self-help groups in order to supplement individual therapy.
- In family therapy, the aim is to change maladaptive family interaction patterns. All members of the family attend therapy sessions, though at times the therapist may see family members individually or in twos or threes.
- Therapies in all cultures have certain key features in common; however, there are also important differences among cultures. Therapists must recognize cultural differences in order to build trust with clients and effect behavioral change. Therapists must also be sensitive to possible gender issues in therapy.

applyingrealworldpsychology

We began this chapter with five intriguing Real World Psychology questions, and you were asked to revisit these questions at the end of each section. Questions like these have an important and lasting impact on all of our lives. See if you can answer these additional critical thinking questions related to real world examples.

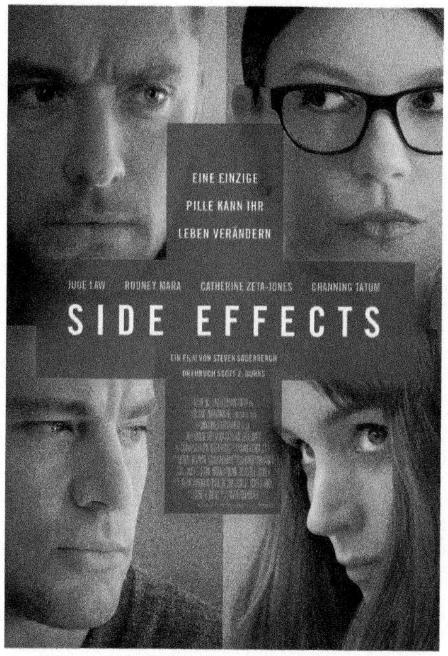

Snap Stills/Rex Features/AP Photos

1. In the 2013 movie *Side Effects*, Rooney Mara and Channing Tatum portray a successful young couple, Emily and Martin, whose entire world falls apart when Emily's psychiatrist prescribes a new (fictional) psychoactive drug called Ablixa to treat her anxiety. The true *side effects* of the drug, as well as the underlying motivations and mental health of the main characters, are revealed only during the film's final scenes. How might this film contribute to negative stereotypes of psychotherapy and psychopharmacology?
2. Given that advertising for the fictional drug in this *Side Effects* movie closely matches the ads for actual psychoactive drugs, what special dangers and applications does widespread advertising for psychotherapeutic drugs pose for the real world?
3. Can you think of a Hollywood film that offers a positive portrayal of psychotherapy and/or psychopharmacology?
4. You undoubtedly had certain beliefs and ideas about therapy before reading this chapter. Has studying this chapter changed any of those beliefs and ideas?
5. Which form of therapy described in this chapter do you personally find most appealing? Why?

Key Terms

RETRIEVAL PRACTICE Write a definition for each term before turning back to the referenced page to check your answer.

- active listening 372
- antianxiety drugs 382
- antidepressant drugs 382
- antipsychotic drugs 382
- aversion therapy 378
- behavior therapy 377
- biomedical therapy 381
- client-centered therapy 372
- cognitive restructuring 373
- cognitive therapy 373
- cognitive-behavior therapy (CBT) 375
- dream analysis 370
- eclectic approach 387
- electroconvulsive therapy (ECT) 383
- empathy 372
- free association 369
- genuineness 372
- group therapy 389
- humanistic therapy 371
- interpretation 370
- lobotomy 384
- modeling therapy 379
- mood-stabilizer drugs 382
- psychoanalysis 369
- psychodynamic therapy 371
- psychopharmacology 381
- psychosurgery 384
- psychotherapy 369
- rational-emotive behavior therapy (REBT) 374
- repetitive transcranial magnetic stimulation (rTMS) 385
- resistance 370
- self-help group 389
- systematic desensitization 377
- transference 370
- unconditional positive regard 372

chapter fourteen

Social Psychology

CHAPTER OUTLINE

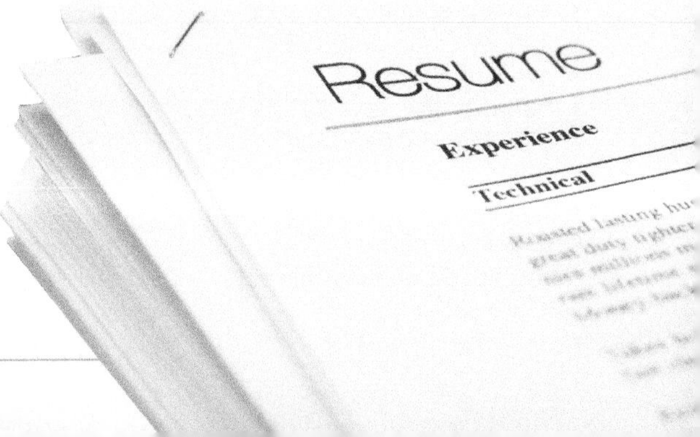

realworldpsychology

THINGS YOU'LL LEARN IN CHAPTER 14

Q1 Why do athletes often blame their losses on bad officiating?

Q2 If popular high-school students are anti-drinking, does that reduce underage drinking among their peers?

Q3 Are women less likely than men to share their opinions in a group?

Q4 Are men still more likely to get hired than equally qualified women?

Q5 How does simple nearness (proximity) influence attraction?

THROUGHOUT THE CHAPTER, MARGIN ICONS FOR Q1–Q5 INDICATE WHERE THE TEXT ADDRESSES THESE QUESTIONS.

chapteroverview

For many students and psychologists, your authors included, *social psychology* is the most exciting of all fields because it's about you and me and because almost everything we do is *social*! Unlike earlier chapters that focused on individual processes, like sensation and perception, memory, or personality, this chapter studies how large social forces, such as groups, social roles, and norms, bring out the best and worst in all of us. It is organized around three central themes: *social cognition*, *social influence*, and *social relations*. Before reading on, check the misconceptions you may have about these topics in *How Much Do You Know About the Social World?*

TEST YOURSELF: HOW MUCH DO YOU KNOW ABOUT THE SOCIAL WORLD?

psychology and you

TRUE OR FALSE?

____1. Most people judge others more harshly than they judge themselves.

____2. Persuasion is the most effective way to change attitudes.

____3. Groups generally make riskier or more conservative decisions than a single individual does.

____4. People wearing masks are more likely than unmasked individuals to engage in aggressive acts.

____5. Emphasizing gender differences may create and perpetuate prejudice.

____6. Substance abuse (particularly alcohol abuse) is a major factor in aggression.

____7. When people are alone, they are more likely to help another individual than when they are in a group.

____8. Looks are the primary factor in our initial feelings of attraction, liking, and love.

____9. Opposites attract.

____10. Romantic love generally starts to fade after 6 to 30 months.

Answers: Two of these statements are false. You'll find the answers within this chapter.

Jason Stitt/Shutterstock

SOCIAL COGNITION

RETRIEVAL PRACTICE While reading the upcoming sections, respond to each Learning Objective in your own words. Then compare your responses with those found at www.wiley.com/college/huffman.

LEARNING OBJECTIVES

1 **DESCRIBE** the field of social psychology.
2 **EXPLAIN** how attributions and their errors affect the way we perceive and judge others.
3 **IDENTIFY** attitudes and their three components.
4 **SUMMARIZE** how attitudes are formed and changed.
5 **DISCUSS** how culture affects cognitive dissonance.

Social psychology, one of the largest branches in the field of psychology, focuses on how others influence our thoughts, feelings, and actions. In turn, one of its largest and most important subfields, **social cognition**, examines the way we think about and interpret ourselves and others. In this section, we will look at two of the most important topics in social cognition—*attributions* and *attitudes*.

Social psychology The branch of psychology that studies how others influence our thoughts, feelings, and actions; it also studies group and intergroup phenomena.

Social cognition How we think about and interpret ourselves and others.

Attributions

Have you ever been in a serious verbal fight with a loved one—perhaps a parent, close friend, or romantic partner? If so, how did you react? Were you overwhelmed with feelings of anger? Did you attribute the fight to the other person's ugly, mean temper and consider ending the relationship? Or did you calm yourself with thoughts of how he or she is normally a rational person and therefore must be unusually upset by something that happened at work or college?

Can you see how these two alternative explanations for the causes of behavior or events (or **attributions**) can either destroy or maintain relationships? The study of attributions is a major topic in *social cognition and social psychology*. Everyone wants to understand and explain why people behave as they do and why events occur as they do. Humans are known to be the only reason-seeking animals! But social psychologists have discovered another explanation: Developing logical attributions for people's behavior makes us feel safer and more in control (Bodenhausen & Morales, 2013; Cushman & Greene, 2012; Ferrucci et al., 2011; Heider, 1958). In addition, they've found that the key to making correct attributions begins with the decision of whether a given action stems mainly from the person's internal disposition or from the external situation. Unfortunately, our attributions are frequently marred by two major errors: the *fundamental attribution error* (*FAE*) and the *self-serving bias*. Let's explore each of these.

Attribution The principles we follow when making judgments about the causes of events, others' behavior, and our own behavior.

Fundamental Attribution Error (FAE)

Think back to the example above. Do you recognize that attributing the fight to the bad character of the other person without considering possible situational factors, like pressures at work, may be the result of your own misguided bias in thinking? Suppose a new student joins your class and seems distant, cold, and uninterested in interaction. It's easy to conclude that she's unfriendly, and maybe even "stuck-up"—a dispositional (personality) attribution. If you later saw her in a one-to-one interaction with close friends, you might be surprised to find that she is very warm and friendly. In other words, her behavior depends on the situation. This bias toward personal, dispositional factors rather than situational factors in our explanations for others' behavior is so common that it is called the **fundamental attribution error (FAE)** (Arkes & Kajdasz, 2011; Coleman, 2013; Ross, 1977).

One reason for the FAE is that human personalities and behaviors are more salient or noticeable than situational factors. The **saliency bias** helps explain why people sometimes suggest that homeless people begging for money "should just go out and get a job"—a phenomenon also called "blaming the victim."

Keep in mind that when we focus on possible *situational* influences on behavior, we're more likely to make better and more accurate judgments of the causes of events and other people's behavior. Unfortunately, given people's enduring personality traits (Chapter 11), our shared tendency to take cognitive shortcuts (Chapter 8), and the saliency bias, we more often focus on dispositional (personality) factors—thus leading us to commit the FAE.

Fundamental attribution error (FAE) The tendency of observers to overestimate the influence of internal, dispositional factors on a person's behavior, while underestimating the impact of external, situational factors.

Saliency bias A type of attributional bias in which people tend to focus on the most noticeable (salient) factors when explaining the causes of behavior.

Self-Serving Bias

Self-serving bias A type of attributional bias in which people tend to take credit for their successes and externalize or deny responsibility for their failures.

Unlike the FAE, which commonly occurs when we're explaining others' behaviors, the **self-serving bias** more often happens when we explain our own behavior. In this case, we tend to favor internal (personality) attributions for our successes and external (situational) attributions for our failures. This bias is motivated by our desire to maintain positive self-esteem and a good public image (Martin & Carron, 2012; Sanjuán & Magallares, 2013; Vaillancourt, 2013). For example, students often take personal credit for doing well on an exam. If they fail a test, however, they tend to blame the instructor, the textbook, or the "tricky" questions. Similarly, elite Olympic athletes more often attribute their wins to internal (personal) causes, such as their skill and effort, while attributing their losses to external (situational) causes, such as bad equipment or poor officiating (Aldridge & Islam, 2012). (Q1)

Actor–observer effect The tendency to attribute one's own actions to external (situational) factors while attributing others' actions to internal (dispositional) causes.

How do we explain the discrepancy between the attributions we make for ourselves and those we make for others? According to the **actor–observer effect** (Jones & Nisbett, 1971), when examining our own behaviors, we are the *actors* in the situation and know more about our own intentions and behaviors and naturally look to the environment for explanations: "I didn't tip the waiter because I got really bad service." In contrast, when explaining the behavior of others, we are *observing* the actors and therefore tend to blame the person, using a personality attribution: "She didn't tip the waiter because she's cheap" **(Figure 14.1)**.

FIGURE 14.1 THE ACTOR–OBSERVER EFFECT

We tend to explain our own behavior in terms of external factors (situational attributions) and others' behavior in terms of their internal characteristics (dispositional attributions).

Actor

Situational attribution

Focuses attention on external factors

"I don't even like drinking beer, but it's the best way to meet women."

Christine Schneider/© Corbis

Observer

Dispositional attribution

Focuses on the personality of the actor

"He seems to always have a beer in his hand; he must have a drinking problem."

Culture and Attributional Biases

Interestingly, both the fundamental attribution error and the self-serving bias may depend in part on cultural factors (Han et al., 2011; Imada & Ellsworth, 2011; Lien et al., 2006; Sanjuán & de Lopez, 2013; Wirtz & Chiu, 2008). In highly individualistic cultures, like the United States, people are defined and understood as individual selves, largely responsible for their own successes and failures.

In contrast, people in collectivistic cultures, like China and Japan, are primarily defined as members of their social network, responsible for doing as others expect. Accordingly, they tend to be more aware of situational constraints on behavior, making the FAE less likely (Leung et al., 2012; Matsumoto & Juang, 2013; McClure et al., 2011).

The self-serving bias is also much less common in collectivistic cultures because self-esteem is related not to doing better than others but to fitting in with the group (Berry et al., 2011; Markus & Kitayama, 2003; Smith, 2011). In Japan, for instance, the ideal person is aware of his or her shortcomings and continually works to overcome them—rather than thinking highly of himself or herself (Heine & Renshaw, 2002; Shand, 2013).

Attitudes

When we observe and respond to the world around us, we are seldom completely neutral. Rather, our responses toward subjects as diverse as pizza, AIDS, and abortion

FIGURE 14.2 **ATTITUDE FORMATION**

When social psychologists study attitudes, they measure each of the three ABC components: Affective, Behavioal, and Cognitive.

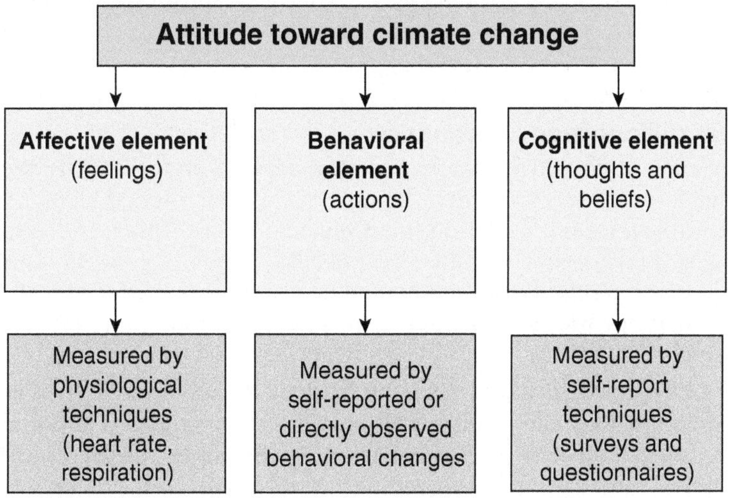

reflect our **attitudes**, which are *learned* predispositions to respond to a particular object in a particular way. Social psychologists generally agree that most attitudes have three ABC components: *affect*, or feelings; *behavior*, or actions; and *cognitions*, or thoughts and beliefs **(Figure 14.2)**.

Attitude The learned predisposition to respond cognitively, affectively, and behaviorally to a particular object, person, place, thing, or event in an evaluative way.

Attitude Formation

As mentioned, we tend to learn our attitudes—generally from direct instruction, through personal experiences, and by watching others. In some cases, these sources may differ, depending on our gender. For example, researchers have found that teenage boys are more likely to learn sexual attitudes from media representations of sexual behavior, whereas teenage girls tend to learn their sexual attitudes from their mothers, as long as they feel close to their mothers (Vanderbosch & Eggermont, 2011).

HEALTH AND SELF-IMAGE realworldpsychology

Given the high prevalence of very thin women and lean, "ripped" men displayed on magazines, TV, and movies, it's easy to see why many people in our Western culture develop a shared preference for a certain, limited body type. Thankfully, research finds that just showing 100 women photographs of plus-size models (with a minimum clothing size of 16 and a BMI between 36 and 42) caused them to change their initial attitudes, which had been to prefer the thin ideal (Boothroyd et al., 2012). Can you see how ads that offer more realistic images, as well as the devastating effects of anorexia (like the two photos on the right), might improve the overall health and self-image of both men and women? Sadly, the model in the photo on the far right, Isabel Caro, died of anorexia in 2010 at age 28.

JM5 WENN Photos/NewsCom

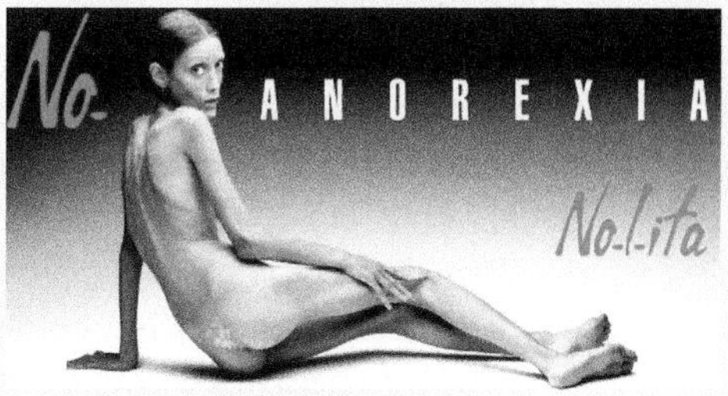

Agencia el Universal/El Universal de Mexico/NewsCom

Attitude Change

Although attitudes begin to form in early childhood, they're obviously not permanent, a fact that advertisers and politicians know and exploit. As we've just seen in the study described above, we can sometimes change attitudes through experiments. However, a much more common method is to make direct, persuasive appeals, such as in ads that say, "Friends Don't Let Friends Drive Drunk!" Interestingly, psychologists have identified an even more efficient strategy, which is to create contradictions between our attitudes, or between our attitudes and our behaviors, that lead to

Cognitive dissonance The unpleasant tension and anxiety caused by a discrepancy between two or more conflicting attitudes or between attitudes and behaviors.

feelings of discomfort, known as **cognitive dissonance** (Baumeister & Bushman, 2014; Moghaddam, 2013; Samnani et al., 2012; Sanderson, 2010; Sharpe et al., 2013). (See *Psych Science.*)

Once we've created or experienced cognitive dissonance, how can we reduce it **(Figure 14.3)**?

Culture and Cognitive Dissonance

The experience of cognitive dissonance may depend on a distinctly Western way of thinking about and evaluating the self. As we mentioned earlier, people in Eastern cultures tend not to define themselves in terms of their individual accomplishments. For this reason, making a bad decision may not pose the same threat to self-esteem that it would in more individualistic cultures, such as the United States (Dessalles, 2011; Imada & Kitayama, 2010; Kokkoris & Kühnen, 2013; Stephens & Swartz, 2013).

In sum, psychologists have long been particularly interested in how attitudes are formed—and how they can change. This emphasis on attitudes is important because they often, but not always, predict behavior. For example, research has found that teenage drivers' attitudes about speeding are a strong predictor of whether they actually speed—and receive speeding tickets—later on (Rowe et al., 2013).

PSYCHSCIENCE

WOULD YOU LIE FOR $1.00?

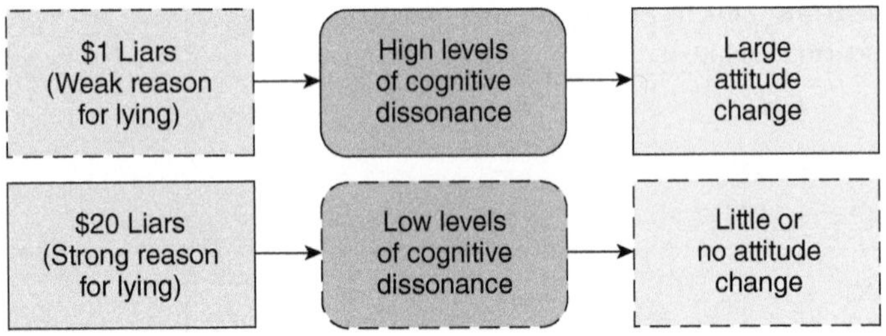

In one of the best-known tests of cognitive dissonance theory, Leon Festinger and J. Merrill Carlsmith (1959) paid participants either $1 or $20 to lie to fellow research participants by telling them that a boring experimental task in which they had just participated was actually very enjoyable and fun. Surprisingly, those who were paid just $1 to lie subsequently changed their minds about the task and actually reported more positive attitudes toward it than those who were paid $20.

Why was there more attitude change among those who were paid only $1? All participants who lied to other participants presumably recognized the discrepancy between their initial attitude (the task was boring) and their behavior (telling others it was enjoyable and fun). However, as you can see in the figure above, the participants who were given insufficient monetary justification for lying (the $1 liars) apparently experienced greater *cognitive dissonance*. Therefore, they expressed more liking for the dull task than those who received sufficient monetary justification (the $20 liars). This second group had little or no motivation to change their attitude—they lied for the money! (Note that in 1959, when the experiment was done, $20 would be worth about $200 today.)

RESEARCH CHALLENGE

1 Based on the information provided, did this study (Festinger & Carlsmith, 1959) use descriptive, correlational, and/or experimental research?

2 If you chose:

- descriptive research, is this a naturalistic observation, survey/interview, case study, or archival research?
- correlational research, is this a positive, negative, or zero correlation?
- experimental research, label the IV, DV, experimental group(s), and control group.

>> CHECK YOUR ANSWERS IN APPENDIX B.

NOTE: The information provided in this study is admittedly limited, but the level of detail is similar to what is presented in most textbooks and public reports of research findings. Answering these questions, and then comparing your answers to those in the Appendix, will help you become a better critical thinker and consumer of scientific research.

FIGURE 14.3 REDUCING COGNITIVE DISSONANCE

Why do some health professionals, who obviously know the dangers of smoking, continue to smoke?

1 When inconsistencies or conflicts exist between our thoughts, feelings, and actions, they can lead to strong tension and discomfort (*cognitive dissonance*).

Spencer Grant/Photo Edit

2 To reduce this cognitive dissonance, we are motivated to change our behavior or our attitude.

Change behavior

Change attitude

3a Changing behavior, such as quitting smoking, can be hard to do. → "I don't smoke cigarettes any more."

3b If unable or unwilling to change their behavior, individuals can use one or more of the four methods shown here to change their attitude.

- **Change perceived importance of one of the conflicting cognitions:** "Experiments showing that smoking causes cancer have only been done on animals."
- **Modify one or both of the conflicting cognitions:** "I don't smoke that much."
- **Add additional cognitions:** "I only eat healthy foods, so I'm better protected from cancer."
- **Deny conflicting cognitions are related:** "There's no real evidence linking cigarettes and cancer."

RETRIEVAL PRACTICE: SOCIAL COGNITION

Self-Test

Completing this self-test and comparing your answers with those in Appendix B provides immediate feedback and helpful practice for exams. Additional interactive, self-tests are available at www.wiley.com/college/huffman.

1. The study of how other people influence our thoughts, feelings, and actions is called _____.

a. social cognition
b. social science
c. social psychology
d. social influence

2. The principles we follow in making judgments about the causes of events, others' behavior, and our own behavior are known as _____.

a. impression management
b. stereotaxic determination
c. attributions
d. person perception

3. The two major attribution mistakes we make are the _____ and the _____.

a. fundamental attribution error; self-serving bias
b. situational attributions; dispositional attributions
c. actor bias; observer bias
d. stereotypes; biases

4. Label the three components of attitudes.

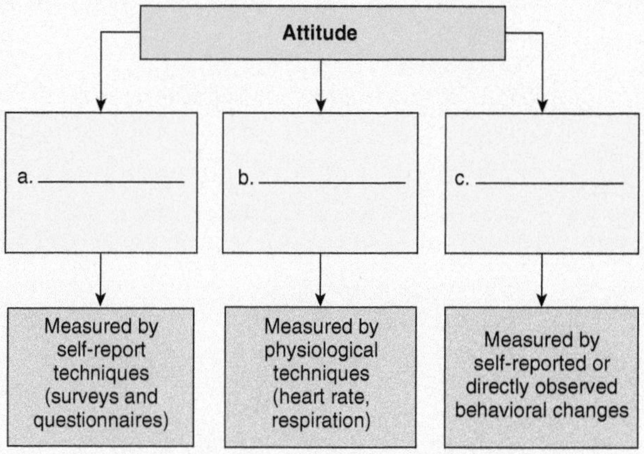

5. According to _____ theory, we're motivated to change our attitudes because of tension created by a mismatch between two or more competing attitudes or between our attitudes and behavior.

a. social learning
b. cognitive dissonance
c. defense mechanisms
d. power of inconsistencies

Think Critically

1. Why do we tend to blame others for their misfortunes but deny responsibility for our own failures?
2. Have you ever changed a strongly held attitude? What caused you to do so?
3. Can you think of an example of cognitive dissonance from your own life?

realworldpsychology

Why do athletes often blame their losses on bad officiating?

HINT: LOOK IN THE MARGIN FOR Q1

SOCIAL INFLUENCE

LEARNING OBJECTIVES

RETRIEVAL PRACTICE While reading the upcoming sections, respond to each Learning Objective in your own words. Then compare your responses with those found at www.wiley.com/college/huffman.

1. **IDENTIFY** conformity and the factors that contribute to it.
2. **DESCRIBE** obedience and the factors that contribute to it.
3. **EXPLAIN** how groups affect behavior and decision making.

Social influence How situational factors and other people affect us.

In the previous section, we explored the way we think about and interpret ourselves and others through *social cognition*. We now focus on **social influence**: how situational factors and other people affect us. In this section, we explore three key topics—*conformity*, *obedience*, and *group processes*.

Conformity

Imagine that you have volunteered for a psychology experiment on visual perception. All participants are shown two cards. The first card has only a single vertical line on it, while the second card has three vertical lines of varying lengths. Your task is to determine which of the three lines on the second card (marked A, B, or C) is the same length as the single line on the first card (marked X).

You are seated around a table with six other people, and everyone is called on in order. Because you are seated to the left of the seventh participant, you are always next to last to provide your answers. On the first two trials, everyone agrees on the correct line. However, on the third trial, your group is shown two cards like those in **Figure 14.4**. The first participant chooses line A as the closest in length to line

FIGURE 14.4 SOLOMON ASCH'S STUDY OF CONFORMITY

Which line (A, B, or C) is most like line X? Could anyone convince you otherwise?

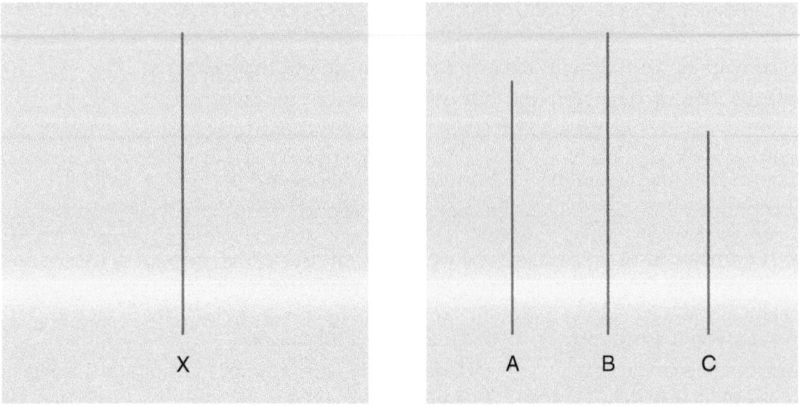

X, an obvious wrong answer! When the second, third, fourth, and fifth participants also say line A, you really start to wonder: "What's going on here? Are they wrong, or am I?"

What do you think you would do at this point in the experiment? Would you stick with your convictions and say line B, regardless of what the others have answered? Or would you go along with the group? In the original version of this experiment, conducted by Solomon Asch (1951), six of the seven participants were actually *confederates* of the experimenter (that is, they were working with the experimenter and purposely gave wrong answers). Their incorrect responses were designed to test the participant's degree of **conformity**.

Conformity Changes in behavior, attitudes, or values because of real or imagined group pressure.

More than one-third of Asch's participants conformed—they agreed with the group's obviously incorrect choice. (Participants in a control group experienced no group pressure and almost always chose correctly.) Asch's study has been conducted dozens of times, in at least 17 countries, and always with similar results (Mori & Arai, 2010; Tennen et al., 2013).

Why would so many people conform? To the onlooker, conformity is often difficult to understand. Even the conformer sometimes has a hard time explaining his or her behavior. Let's look at three factors that drive conformity:

- **Normative social influence** One of the first reasons we conform is that we want to go along with group *norms*, which are expected behaviors generally adhered to by members of a group. Most often norms are quite subtle and only implied (see *Psychology and You* and *Cultural Norms for Personal Space*).

Normative social influence Conformance to group pressure out of a need to be liked, accepted, and approved of by others.

psychology and you **Norms in Everyday Life** Have you ever asked what others are wearing to a party or copied your neighbor at a dinner party to make sure you picked up the right fork? We generally submit to normative social influence out of our need for approval and acceptance by the group and because conforming to group norms makes us feel good (Irwin & Simpson, 2013).

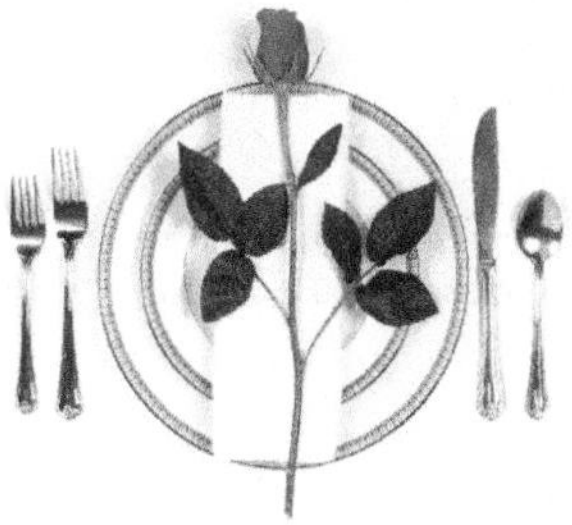
© cstar55/iStockphoto

CULTURAL NORMS FOR PERSONAL SPACE
realworldpsychology

Culture and socialization have a lot to do with shaping norms for personal space. If someone invades the invisible "personal bubble" around our bodies, we generally feel very uncomfortable. This may help explain why some people from the United States feel awkward when traveling to Mediterranean and Latin American countries where people generally maintain smaller interpersonal distances (Axtell, 2007; Steinhart, 1986). As you can see in this photo, these Middle Eastern men are apparently comfortable with a small personal space and with showing male-to-male affection.

Interestingly, children in our own Western culture also tend to stand very close to others until they are socialized to recognize and maintain greater personal distance. Furthermore, friends stand closer than strangers, women tend to stand closer than men, and violent prisoners prefer approximately three times as much personal space as nonviolent prisoners (Axtell, 2007; Gilmour & Walkey, 1981; Lawrence & Andrews, 2004).

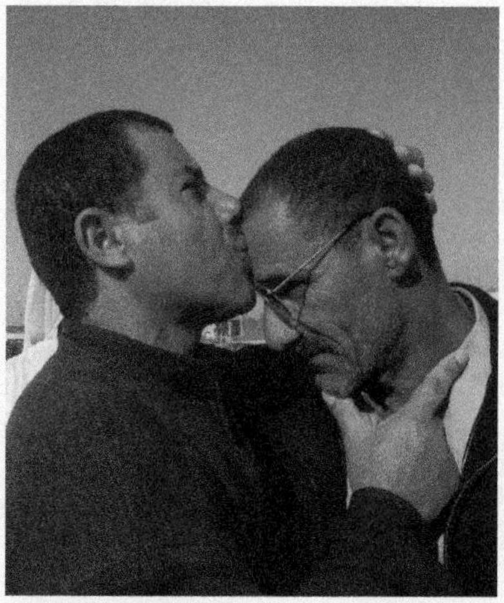
AFP/Getty Images, Inc.

Think Critically

1. How might cultural differences in personal space help explain why U.S. travelers abroad are sometimes seen as being "too loud and brassy"?
2. Given that men and women have different norms for personal space, what effect might this have on their relationships?

Informational social influence Conformance to a group out of a need for information and direction.

- **Informational social influence** Have you ever bought a specific product simply because of a friend's recommendation? In this case, you probably conformed not to gain your friend's approval, a case of normative social influence, but because you assumed that he or she had more information than you did, a case of informational social influence. Given that participants in Asch's experiment observed all the other participants giving unanimous decisions on the length of the lines, can you see how they may have conformed because they believed the others had more information than they did?

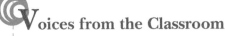

Voices from the Classroom

Santa and Informational Social Influence Conformity is a fun and pertinent topic because there is always a good, recent example to which students can relate. For example, when discussing *informational social influence*, I talk about kids lining up to meet Santa. It's a relatively novel experience for them, and they are often unsure of how to act, so they look to others for information. When one child becomes frightened by Santa or an elf and screams or cries, there's a ripple effect throughout the line. Soon all the other kids also are scared and crying.

Professor Rebekah Wanic
University of California, San Diego
La Jolla, California

Reference groups The people we conform to, or go along with, because we like, admire, and want to be like them.

Obedience Following direct commands, usually from an authority figure.

- **Reference groups** The third major factor in conformity is the power of *reference groups*—people we most admire, like, and want to resemble. Attractive actors and popular sports stars are paid millions of dollars to endorse products because advertisers know that we want to be as cool as LeBron James or as beautiful as Natalie Portman. Of course, we also have more important reference groups in our lives—parents, friends, family members, teachers, religious leaders, and classmates—all of whom affect our willingness to conform. For example, popular high school students' attitudes about alcohol use have been shown to have a substantial influence on alcohol consumption by other students in their high school (Teunissen et al., 2012). Surprisingly, popular peers who had *negative* attitudes toward alcohol use were even more influential in determining rates of teenage drinking than those with positive attitudes! This finding suggests that capitalizing on popular peers who have negative drinking attitudes might be a very effective strategy for reducing underage drinking. Q2

FIGURE 14.5 GOOD REASONS FOR CONFORMING AND OBEYING

These people willingly obey the firefighters who order them to evacuate a building, and many lives are saved. What would happen to our everyday functioning if most people did not go along with the crowd or generally did not obey orders?

David McNew/Getty Images

Obedience

As we've seen, conformity means going along with the group. A second form of social influence, **obedience**, involves going along with direct commands, usually from someone in a position of authority. From very early childhood, we're socialized to respect and obey our parents, teachers, and other authority figures.

Conformity and obedience aren't always bad **(Figure 14.5)**. In fact, we generally conform and obey most of the time because it's in our own best interests (and everyone else's) to do so. Like most other North Americans, we stand in line at a movie theatre instead of pushing ahead of others. This allows an orderly purchasing of tickets. Conformity and obedience allow social life to proceed with safety, order, and predictability.

However, on some occasions, it is important not to conform or obey. We don't want teenagers (or adults) engaging in risky sex or drug use just to be part of the crowd. And we don't want soldiers (or anyone else) mindlessly following orders just because they were told to do so by an authority figure. Recognizing and resisting destructive forms of obedience are particularly important to our society—and to social psychology. Let's start with an examination of a classic series of studies on obedience by Stanley Milgram (1963, 1974).

Imagine that you have responded to a newspaper ad seeking volunteers for a study on memory. At the Yale University laboratory, an experimenter explains to you and another participant that he is studying the effects of punishment on learning and memory. You are selected to play the role of the "teacher." The experimenter leads you into a room where he straps the other participant—the "learner"—into a chair. He applies electrode paste to the learner's wrist "to avoid blisters and burns" and attaches an electrode that is connected to a shock generator.

Next, you're led into an adjacent room and told to sit in front of this same shock generator, which is wired through the wall to the chair of the learner. (The setup for the experiment is illustrated in **Figure 14.6***.) The shock machine consists of 30 switches representing successively higher levels of shock, from 15 volts to 450 volts. Written labels appear below each group of switches, ranging from "Slight Shock" to "Danger: Severe Shock," all the way to "XXX." The experimenter explains that it is your job to teach the learner a list of word pairs and to punish any errors by administering a shock. With each wrong answer, you are to increase the shock by one level.*

You begin teaching the word pairs, but the learner's responses are often wrong. Before long, you are inflicting shocks that you can only assume must be extremely painful. After you administer 150 volts, the learner begins to protest: "Get me out of here . . . I refuse to go on."

You hesitate, and the experimenter tells you to continue. He insists that even if the learner refuses to answer, you must keep increasing the shock levels. But the other person is obviously in pain. What will you do?

FIGURE 14.6 MILGRAM'S STUDY ON OBEDIENCE

Under orders from an experimenter, would you, as "teacher," use this shock generator to shock a man (the "learner") who is screaming and begging to be released? Few people believe they would, but research shows otherwise.

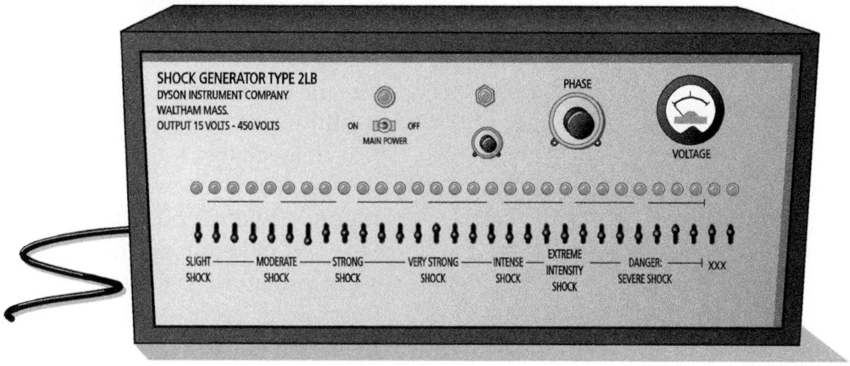

Milgram's Shock Generator

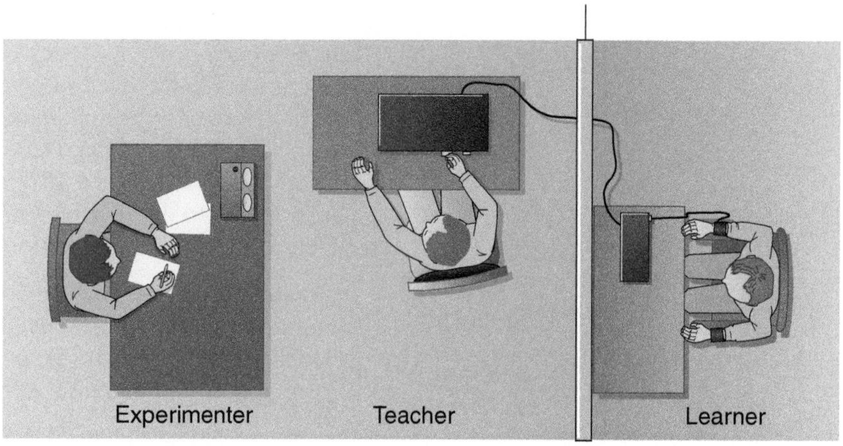

Experimental Set Up

It's important to note that the "learners" were confederates, who helped with the experiment and never received actual shocks. They only pretended to be in pain. However, the real subjects, the "teachers," believed they were delivering shocks to a person in obvious pain. Although the "teachers" sweated, trembled, stuttered, laughed nervously, and repeatedly protested that they did not want to hurt the learner, they still obeyed!

The psychologist who designed this study, Stanley Milgram, was actually investigating not punishment and learning but obedience to authority: Would participants obey the experimenter's prompts and commands to shock another human being? In Milgram's public survey, fewer than 25% thought they would go beyond 150 volts. And no respondents predicted that they would go past the 300-volt level. Yet 65% of the teacher-participants in this series of studies obeyed completely—going all the way to the end of the scale (450 volts), even beyond the point when the "learner" (Milgram's confederate) stopped responding altogether.

Even Milgram was surprised by his results. Before the study began, he polled a group of psychiatrists, and they predicted that most people would refuse to go beyond 150 volts and that fewer than 1% of those tested would "go all the way." But, as Milgram discovered, 65% of his participants—men and women of all ages and from all walks of life—administered the highest voltage. The study was replicated many times and in many other countries, with similarly high levels of obedience.

Although there have been some recent partial replications of Milgram's study (e.g., Burger, 2009), his full, original setup could never be undertaken today due to ethical and moral considerations. Deception is a necessary part of some research, but the degree of it in Milgram's research and the discomfort of the participants would never be allowed under today's research standards. Keep in mind, however, that immediately following the study, Milgram carefully debriefed each subject and then followed up with the participants for several months. Most of his "teachers" reported finding the experience personally informative and valuable.

One final, important reminder: The *"learner" was an accomplice of the experimenter and only pretended to be shocked.* Milgram provided specific scripts that they followed at every stage of the experiment. In contrast, the "teachers" were true volunteers who believed they were administering real shocks. Although they suffered and protested, in the final analysis, they still obeyed.

Why did the teachers in Milgram's study obey the orders to shock a fellow subject, despite their moral objections? Are there specific circumstances that increase or decrease obedience? In a series of follow-up studies, Milgram found several important factors that influenced obedience: *legitimacy and closeness of the authority figure*, *remoteness of the victim*, *assignment of responsibility*, and *modeling or imitation of others* (Blass, 1991, 2000; De Vos, 2010; Forsyth, 2013; Moghaddam, 2013; Pina e Cunha et al., 2010) **(Figure 14.7)**.

In addition to the four factors that Milgram identified, other social psychologists have emphasized several additional influences, including the following:

- **Socialization** Can you see how socialization might help explain many instances of mindless and sometimes destructive obedience? From an early age, we're all taught to listen to and respect people in positions of authority. In this case, participants in Milgram's study came into the research lab with a lifetime of

FIGURE 14.7 **FOUR FACTORS THAT AFFECT WHY WE OBEY**

As you can see in the first bar on the graph, 65% of the participants in Milgram's early studies gave the learner the full 450-volt level of shocks. Note also how the color coding on the other bars on the graph (dark pink, yellow, green, and blue) corresponds to the four major conditions that either increased or decreased obedience to authority.

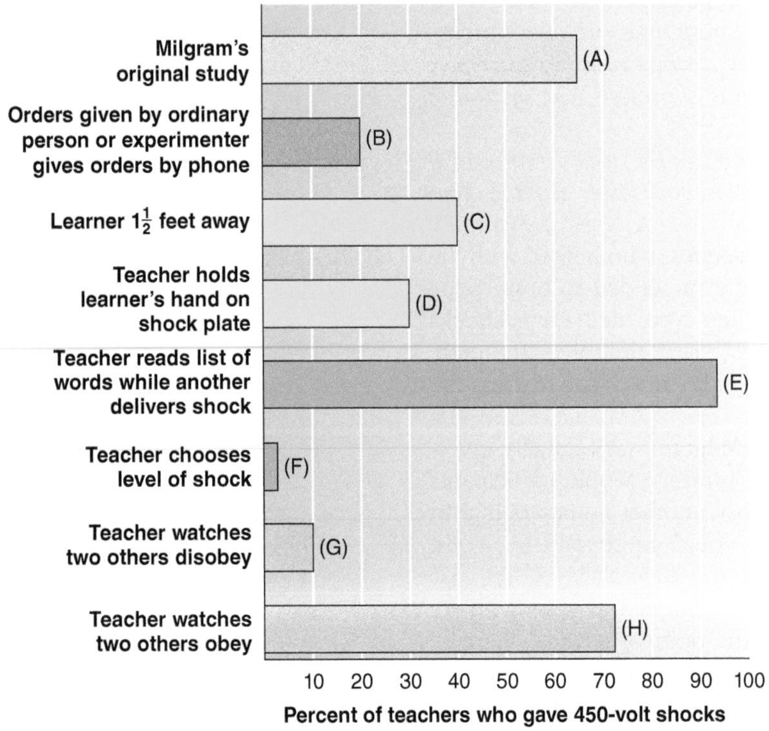

1. Legitimacy and closeness of the authority figure
When orders came from an ordinary person, and when the experimenter left the room and gave orders by phone, 20% of the teachers gave the full 450-volt shocks. (Bar B on graph.)

2. Remoteness of the victim
When the learner was only $1\frac{1}{2}$ feet away from the teacher, 40% of the teachers gave the highest level of shocks. However, when the teacher had to actually hold the learner's hand on the shock plate, obedience was only 30%. (Bars C and D on graph.)

3. Assignment of responsibility
When the teacher simply read the list of words, while another delivered the shock, obedience jumped to almost 94%. However, when the teacher was responsible for choosing the level of shock, only 3% obeyed. (Bars E and F on graph.)

4. Modeling or imitating others
When teachers watched two other teachers refuse to shock the learner, only 10% gave the full 450-volt shocks. However, when they watched two other teachers obey, their obedience jumped to over 70% (Milgram, 1963, 1974). (Bars G and Hon graph.)

socialization toward the value of scientific research and respect for the experimenter's authority. They couldn't suddenly step outside themselves and question the morality of this particular experimenter and his orders.

- **The foot-in-the-door technique** The step-wise actions in many obedience situations may also help explain why so many people were willing to give the maximum shocks in Milgram's study. The initial mild level of shocks may have worked as a **foot-in-the-door technique**, in which a first, small request is used as a setup for later, larger requests. Once Milgram's participants complied with the initial request, they might have felt obligated to continue.

Foot-in-the-door technique An initial, small request is used as a setup for a later, larger request.

- **Relaxed moral guard** One common intellectual illusion that hinders critical thinking about obedience is the belief that only evil people do evil things, or that evil announces itself. The experimenter in Milgram's study looked and acted like a reasonable person who was simply carrying out a research project. Because he was not seen as personally corrupt and evil, the participants' normal moral guard was down, which can maximize obedience. As philosopher Hannah Arendt has suggested, the horrifying thing about the Nazis was not that they were so deviant but that they were so "terrifyingly normal."

realworldpsychology **A Model of Civil Disobedience** Although the forces underlying obedience can be loud and powerful, even one quiet, courageous, dissenting voice can make a difference. Perhaps the most beautiful and historically important example of just this type of bravery occurred in Alabama in 1955. Rosa Parks boarded a bus and, as expected in those times, obediently sat in the back section marked "Negroes." When the bus became crowded, the driver told her to give up her seat to a white man. Surprisingly for those days, Parks quietly but firmly refused and was eventually forced off the bus by police and arrested. This single act of disobedience was the catalyst for the civil rights movement and the later repeal of Jim Crow laws in the South. Today, Rosa Parks's courageous stand also inspires the rest of us to carefully consider when it is appropriate and good to obey authorities and when we must resist unethical or dangerous demands.

Group Processes

Although we seldom recognize the power of group membership, social psychologists have identified several important ways that groups affect us.

Group Membership

How do the roles that we play within groups affect our behavior? This question fascinated social psychologist Philip Zimbardo. In his famous study at Stanford University, 24 carefully screened, well-adjusted young college men were paid $15 a day for participating in a two-week simulation of prison life (Haney et al., 1978; Zimbardo, 1993).

The students were randomly assigned to the role of either prisoner or guard. Prisoners were "arrested," frisked, photographed, fingerprinted, and booked at the police station. They were then blindfolded and driven to the "Stanford Prison." There, they were given ID numbers, deloused, issued prison clothing (tight nylon caps, shapeless gowns, and no underwear), and locked in cells. Participants assigned to be guards were outfitted with official-looking uniforms, official police nightsticks ("billy clubs"), and whistles, and they were given complete control.

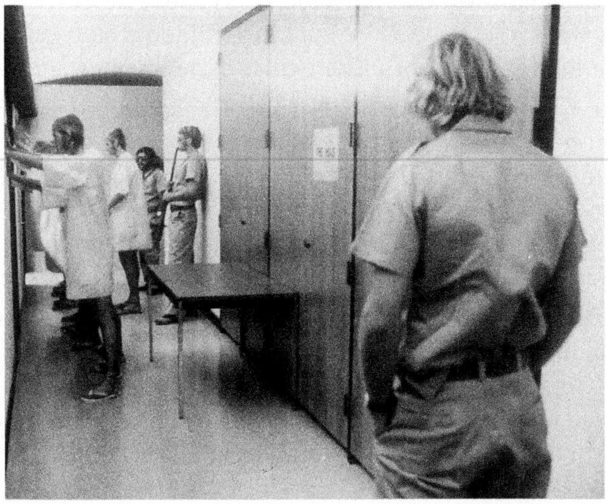

The Stanford Prison Experiment/Philip G. Zimbardo Professor Emeritus Stanford Unviersity

FIGURE 14.8 POWER CORRUPTS

Zimbardo's prison study showed how the demands of roles and situations could produce dramatic changes in behavior in just a few days. Can you imagine what happens to prisoners during life imprisonment, six-year sentences, or even a few nights in jail?

Not even Zimbardo foresaw how the study would turn out. Although some guards were nicer to the prisoners than others, they all engaged in some abuse of power. The slightest disobedience was punished with degrading tasks or the loss of "privileges" (such as eating, sleeping, and washing). As demands increased and abuses began, the prisoners became passive and depressed. Only one prisoner fought back with a hunger strike, which ended with a forced feeding by the guards.

Four prisoners had to be released within the first four days because of severe psychological reactions. The study was stopped after only six days because of the alarming psychological changes in the participants.

Note that this was not a true experiment in that it lacked control groups and clear measurements of the dependent variable (Chapter 1). However, it did provide valuable insights into the potential effects of roles on individual behavior **(Figure 14.8)**. According to interviews conducted after the study, the students became so absorbed in their roles that they forgot they were participants in a university study (Zimbardo et al., 1977).

Deindividuation The reduced self-consciousness, inhibition, and personal responsibility that sometimes occurs in a group, particularly when the members feel anonymous.

Zimbardo's study also demonstrates **deindividuation**. To be deindividuated means that we feel less self-conscious, less inhibited, and less personally responsible as a member of a group than when we're alone **(Figure 14.9)**. Groups sometimes actively promote deindividuation by requiring members to wear uniforms, for example, as a way to increase allegiance and conformity.

Group Decision Making

We've just seen how group membership affects the way we think about ourselves, but how do groups affect our decisions? Are two heads truly better than one?

Most people assume that group decisions are more conservative, cautious, and middle-of-the-road than individual decisions. But is this true? Initial investigations indicated that after discussing an issue, groups actually supported riskier decisions than decisions they made as individuals before the discussion (Stoner, 1961).

Subsequent research on this *risky-shift phenomenon*, however, shows that some groups support riskier decisions while others support conservative decisions (Liu & Latané, 1998; Tindale et al., 2013). How can we tell whether a given group's decision will be risky or conservative? A group's final decision depends primarily on its dominant *preexisting* tendencies. If the dominant initial position is risky, the final decision will be even riskier, and the reverse is true if the initial position is conservative—a process called **group polarization** (Baumeister & Bushman, 2014; Sanderson, 2010; Tindale & Posavac, 2011; Zhu, 2013).

Group polarization The tendency for groups to make decisions that are more extreme (either riskier or more conservative), depending on the members' initial dominant tendency.

Why? It appears that as individuals interact and share their opinions, they pick up new and more persuasive information that supports their original opinions, which may help explain why American politics has become so polarized in recent years (Miller, 2013). Can you see how if we only interact and work with like-minded people, or only talk politics with those who agree with us, we're likely to become even more polarized? An interesting study in Washington, DC found that interns

Don Emmert/AFP/Getty Images

FIGURE 14.9 **LOST IN THE CROWD**

One of the most compelling explanations for deindividuation is the fact that the presence of others tends to increase arousal and feelings of anonymity, which is a powerful disinhibitor. As you can see in this photo, deindividuation can be healthy and positive when we're part of a happy, celebratory crowd. However, it also helps explain why vandalism seems to increase on Halloween (when people commonly wear masks) and why most crimes and riots occur at night—under the cover of darkness (Haines & Mann, 2011; Lammers & Stapel, 2011; Rodrigues et al., 2005; Spears, 2011; Zimbardo, 2007). Can you imagine your own behavior changing under such conditions?

who worked in a partisan workplace became more polarized in their opinions than those who worked in less partisan environments (Jones, 2013).

Group polarization is also important within the legal system. Imagine yourself as a member of a jury **(Figure 14.10)**. In an ideal world, attorneys from both sides would present the essential facts of the case. Then, after careful deliberation, each individual juror would move from his or her initially neutral position toward the defendant to a more extreme position—either conviction or acquittal. In a not-so-ideal world, the quality of legal arguments from opposing sides may not be equal, you and the other members of the jury may not be neutral at the start, and group polarization may cause most jurors to make riskier or more conservative judgments than they would have on their own.

A related phenomenon is **groupthink** **(Figure 14.11)**. When a group is highly cohesive (a couple, a family, a panel of military advisers, an athletic team), the members' desire for agreement may lead them to ignore important information or points of view held by outsiders or critics (Hergovich & Olbrich, 2003; Hogg, 2013; Vaughn, 1996). To make matters worse, women are especially likely to refrain from speaking up in a group setting, so their opinions are less likely to be heard than men's (Karpowitz et al., 2012).

Groupthink The faulty decision making that occurs when a highly cohesive group strives for agreement, especially if it is in line with the leader's viewpoint, and avoids inconsistent information.

Q3

Many highly-publicized tragedies—from Franklin Roosevelt's failure to anticipate the attack on Pearl Harbor in 1941 to the Jerry Sandusky Penn State sex scandal in 2012—have been blamed on groupthink. In addition, groupthink may have contributed to the losses of the space shuttles *Challenger* and *Columbia*, the terrorist attack of September 11, 2001, the war in Iraq, and other important decisions (Barlow, 2008; Burnette et al., 2011; Ehrenreich, 2004; Janis, 1972, 1989; Post, 2011; Redd & Mintz, 2013; Strozier, 2011).

Exactostock/SuperStock

FIGURE 14.10 **JURIES AND GROUP POLARIZATION**

When might group polarization be both a desirable and an undesirable part of jury deliberation?

FIGURE 14.11 **HOW GROUPTHINK OCCURS** | realworldpsychology

A The process of groupthink begins when group members feel a strong sense of cohesiveness and isolation from the judgments of qualified outsiders. Add a directive leader and little chance for debate, and we have the recipe for a potentially dangerous decision.

Vstock LLC/Getty Images

B Few people realize that the decision to marry can be a form of groupthink. (Remember that a "group" can have as few as two members.) When planning a marriage, a couple may show symptoms of groupthink such as an illusion of invulnerability ("We're different—we won't ever get divorced"), collective rationalizations ("Two can live more cheaply than one"), shared stereotypes of the outgroup ("Couples with problems just don't know how to communicate"), and pressure on dissenters ("If you don't support our decision to marry, we don't want you at the wedding").

Groupthink

Antecedent Conditions

1 A highly cohesive group of decision makers
2 Insulation of the group from outside influences
3 A directive leader
4 Lack of procedures to ensure careful consideration of the pros and cons of alternative actions
5 High stress from external threats with little hope of finding a better solution than that favored by the leader

↓

Strong desire for group consensus—the groupthink tendency

↓

Symptoms of Groupthink

1 Illusion of invulnerability
2 Belief in the morality of the group
3 Collective rationalizations
4 Stereotypes of outgroups
5 Self-censorship of doubts and dissenting opinions
6 Illusion of unanimity
7 Direct pressure on dissenters

↓

Symptoms of Poor Decision Making

1 An incomplete survey of alternative courses of action
2 An incomplete survey of group objectives
3 Failure to examine risks of the preferred choice
4 Failure to reappraise rejected alternatives
5 Poor search for relevant information
6 Selective bias in processing information
7 Failure to develop contingency plans

↓

Low probability of successful outcome

RETRIEVAL PRACTICE: SOCIAL INFLUENCE

Self-Test

Completing this self-test and comparing your answers with those in Appendix B provides immediate feedback and helpful practice for exams. Additional interactive, self-tests are available at www.wiley.com/college/huffman.

1. The act of changing behavior as a result of real or imagined group pressure is called _____.

a. norm compliance b. obedience
c. conformity d. mob rule

2. What percentage of people in Milgram's original study were willing to give the highest level of shock (450 volts)?

a. 45 percent b. 90 percent
c. 65 percent d. 10 percent

3. Which of the following factors may contribute to destructive obedience?

a. remoteness of the victim b. foot-in-the-door
c. socialization d. All these options.

4. One of the most critical factors in deindividuation is _____.

a. loss of self-esteem b. anonymity
c. identity diffusion d. group cohesiveness

5. Faulty decision making resulting from a highly cohesive group striving for agreement to the point of avoiding inconsistent information is known as _____.

a. the risky-shift b. group polarization
c. groupthink d. destructive conformity

Think Critically

1. Explain how group membership has affected your own behavior and decision making.
2. How might Milgram's results relate to some aspects of modern warfare?
3. Have you ever done something wrong in a group that you would not have done if you were alone? What have you learned from this chapter that might help you avoid this behavior in the future?

realworldpsychology

If popular high-school students are anti-drinking, does that reduce underage drinking among their peers?

Are women less likely than men to share their opinions in a group?

HINT: LOOK IN THE MARGIN FOR Q2 AND Q3

SOCIAL RELATIONS

RETRIEVAL PRACTICE While reading the upcoming sections, respond to each Learning Objective in your own words. Then compare your responses with those found at www.wiley.com/college/huffman.

LEARNING OBJECTIVES

1. **EXPLAIN** the difference between prejudice and discrimination.
2. **IDENTIFY** the factors that contribute to, and those that combat, prejudice and discrimination.
3. **DISCUSS** aggression and the factors that increase and decrease it.
4. **DESCRIBE** altruism and the factors that increase and decrease it.
5. **SUMMARIZE** the factors that influence interpersonal attraction and love.

Kurt Lewin (1890–1947), often considered the "father of social psychology," was among the first person to suggest that all behavior results from interactions between the individual and the environment. In this final section, on **social relations**, we explore how we develop and are affected by interpersonal relations, including prejudice, aggression, altruism, and interpersonal attraction.

Social relations How we develop and are affected by interpersonal relationships.

Prejudice and Discrimination

Prejudice, which literally means prejudgment, creates enormous problems for its victims and also limits a perpetrator's ability to accurately judge others and to process information.

Like all other attitudes, prejudice is composed of three ABC elements: *affective* (emotions about the group), *behavioral* (predispositions and negative actions toward members of the group), and *cognitive* (**stereotypes** about group members). Although the terms *prejudice* and *discrimination* are often used interchangeably, they are not the same. Prejudice refers to an attitude, whereas **discrimination** refers to action (Fiske, 1998). The two often coincide, but not always **(Figure 14.12)**.

Prejudice A learned, generally negative, attitude toward members of a group; it includes thoughts (stereotypes), feelings, and behavioral tendencies (possible discrimination).

Stereotypes Generalizations about a group of people in which the same characteristics are assigned to all members of the group; also, the cognitive component of prejudice.

Discrimination Negative behaviors directed at others because of their membership in a particular group.

Discrimination	Prejudice: Yes	Prejudice: No
Yes	A minority person is *denied* a job because the owner of a business is prejudiced.	A minority person is *denied* a job because the owner of a business fears white customers won't buy from a minority salesperson.
No	A minority person is *given* a job because the owner of a business hopes to attract minority customers.	A minority person is *given* a job because he or she is the best suited for it.

FIGURE 14.12 PREJUDICE AND DISCRIMINATION

Prejudice and discrimination are closely related, but either condition can exist without the other. The only situation without prejudice or discrimination in this example occurs when someone is given a job simply because he or she is the best candidate.

How do prejudice and discrimination originate? Why do they persist? Five commonly cited sources of prejudice are *learning*, *personal experience*, *limited resources*, *displaced aggression*, and *mental shortcuts*.

Learning

People learn prejudice the same way they learn other attitudes—primarily through *classical* and *operant conditioning* and *social learning* (Chapter 6). For example, repeated exposure to stereotypical portrayals of minorities and women in movies, online, magazines, and TV teach children that such images are correct. Similarly, hearing parents, friends, and teachers express their prejudices also reinforces prejudice (Amodio & Hamilton, 2013; Biernat & Danaher, 2013; Conger et al., 2013; Ferguson & Porter, 2013). *Ethnocentrism*, believing our own culture represents the norm or is superior to others, is also a form of a learned prejudice.

Voices from the Classroom

Learning and Gender Role Stereotypes My friends were working outside with their 2 ½-year-old son nearby, when a heavy hammer fell on one parent's foot, followed by a very "colorful" exclamation of intense pain. Both parents quickly distracted their child, hoping to prevent him from learning and repeating the word. Disaster seemed to have been averted until the next day at church, when the boy dropped a Bible on his own foot and loudly repeated the same "colorful" word! Knowing that the parents were very embarrassed, the minister reassured the couple after the service by joking to the dad about thinking twice before using "colorful" language again. To his surprise, the father responded that he was not the one who used the word. It was his wife!

Like the minister, students in my class are equally surprised by this story. I use it as an example of gender-role stereotypes and how societal expectations and assumptions may not always be accurate.

Professor Ronnie Naramore
Angelina College
Lufkin, Texas

Personal Experience

We also develop prejudice through direct experience. For example, when people make prejudicial remarks or "jokes," they often gain attention and even approval from others. Sadly, denigrating others also seems to boost some people's self-esteem (Fein & Spencer, 1997; Hodson et al., 2010; Nelson, 2013). Also, once someone has one or more negative interactions or experiences with members of a specific group, he or she may generalize the resulting bad feelings and prejudice to all members of that group.

Limited Resources

Most of us understand that prejudice and discrimination exact a high price on their victims, but few appreciate the significant economic and political advantages they offer to the dominant group (Costello & Hodson, 2011; Danso & Lum, 2013; Kteily et al., 2011; Schaefer, 2008). For example, the stereotype that African Americans and Mexicans are inferior to European Americans helps justify and perpetuate a social order in the United States in which European Americans hold disproportionate power and resources.

Displaced Aggression

As we discuss in the next section, frustration sometimes leads people to attack the perceived cause of that frustration. But, as history has shown, when the source is ambiguous, or too powerful and capable of retaliation, people often redirect their aggression toward an alternative, innocent target, known as a *scapegoat*. There is strong historical evidence of the dangers of scapegoating. Jewish people were blamed for economic troubles in Germany before World War II. In the United States beginning in the 1980s, gay men were blamed for the AIDS epidemic, and Hispanic immigrant groups are now being blamed for the nation's recent economic troubles **(Figure 14.13)**.

Mental Shortcuts

Prejudice is also believed to develop from everyday *mental shortcuts* that we create to simplify our complex social world (Ambady & Adams, 2011; Dotsch et al., 2011; Ferguson & Porter, 2013; Sternberg, 2007, 2009). Stereotypes allow quick judgments about others, thereby freeing up mental resources for other activities. Note, however, that these mental shortcuts too often lead to negative outcomes. For example, when science faculty were sent identical résumés from a male and a female student applying for a job as a laboratory manager, both male and female faculty members rated the male applicant as more competent and hirable than the female (Moss-Racusin et al., 2012). Can you see how such stereotypes might have serious real-world consequences for women in the work force—especially for those trying to enter careers in stereotypically male fields? Q4

People use stereotypes as mental shortcuts when they classify others in terms of their membership in a group. Given that people generally classify themselves as part of the preferred group, they also create ingroups and outgroups. An *ingroup* is any category to which people see themselves as belonging; an *outgroup* is any other category.

Compared with the way they judge members of the outgroup, people tend to judge ingroup members as being more attractive, having better personalities, and so on—a phenomenon known as **ingroup favoritism** (DiDonato et al., 2011; Jackson & Rose, 2013; Reyes-Jaquez & Echols, 2013). People also tend to recognize greater diversity among members of their ingroup than they do among members of outgroups (Bendle, 2011; Kang & Lau, 2013; Ratner & Amodio, 2013). A danger of this **outgroup homogeneity effect** is that when members of minority groups are not recognized as varied and complex individuals, it is easier to treat them in discriminatory ways.

Ingroup favoritism Viewing members of the ingroup more positively than members of an outgroup.

Outgroup homogeneity effect Judging members of an outgroup as more alike and less diverse than members of the ingroup.

A good example is war. Viewing people on the other side as simply faceless enemies makes it easier to kill large numbers of soldiers and civilians. This dehumanization and facelessness also help perpetuate our current high levels of fear and anxiety associated with terrorism (Buckels & Trapnell, 2013; Dunham, 2011; Hutchison & Rosenthal, 2011; Savage, 2013).

FIGURE 14.13 PREJUDICE AND IMMIGRATION

Can you identify which of the five sources of prejudice best explains this behavior?

Implicit bias A hidden, automatic attitude that may guide behaviors independent of a person's awareness or control.

Unfortunately, stereotypes and prejudice can operate even without a person's conscious awareness or control. This process is known as automatic bias, or **implicit bias** (Cattaneo et al., 2011; Chapman et al., 2013; Columb & Plant, 2011; Soderberg & Sherman, 2013). The most prominent method for measuring implicit bias, the *Implicit Association Test (IAT)*, measures how quickly people sort stimuli into particular categories.

Overcoming Prejudice and Discrimination

What can we do to reduce and combat prejudice and discrimination? Four major approaches have been suggested: *cooperation and common goals*, *intergroup contact*, *cognitive retraining*, and *cognitive dissonance* **(Figure 14.14)**.

Cooperation and common goals Research shows that one of the best ways to combat prejudice and discrimination is to encourage *cooperation* rather than *competition* (Kuchenbrandt et al., 2013; Price et al., 2013). Muzafer Sherif and his colleagues (1966, 1998) conducted an ingenious study to show the role of competition in promoting prejudice. The researchers artificially created strong feelings of ingroup and outgroup identification in a group of 11- and 12-year-old boys at a summer camp. They did this by physically separating the boys into different cabins and assigning different projects to each group, such as building a diving board or cooking out in the woods.

Once each group developed strong feelings of group identity and allegiance, the researchers set up a series of competitive games, including tug-of-war and touch football. They awarded desirable prizes to the winning teams. Because of this treatment, the groups began to pick fights, call each other names, and raid each other's camps. Researchers pointed to these behaviors as evidence of the experimentally produced prejudice.

The good news is that after using competition to create prejudice between the two groups, the researchers created "mini-crises" and tasks that required expertise, labor, and cooperation from both groups. Prizes were awarded to all and prejudice between the groups slowly began to dissipate. By the end of the camp, the earlier hostilities and *ingroup favoritism* had vanished. Sherif's study showed not only the importance of cooperation as opposed to competition but also the importance of *superordinate goals* (the "mini-crises") in reducing prejudice.

Intergroup Contact A second approach to reducing prejudice is to increase contact and positive experiences between groups (Butz & Plant, 2011; Cameron et al., 2007;

© Kali Nine LLC/iStockphoto

FIGURE 14.14 **HOW CAN WE REDUCE PREJUDICE?**

realworldpsychology

Can you see how the four approaches to combatting prejudice are at work in this simple game of tug-of-war? Similarly, how might large changes in social policy, such as school busing, integrated housing, and increased civil rights legislation gradually change attitudes and eventually lead to decreased prejudice and discrimination?

& Harris, 2012). Cultures also show consistency in what they want in a mate. Women are valued more for looks and youth, whereas men are valued more for maturity, ambitiousness, and financial resources (Bryan et al., 2011; Buss, 1989, 2008, 2011; Chang et al., 2011; Li et al., 2011; Swami, 2011).

Why? Evolutionary psychologists would suggest that men prefer attractive women because youth and good looks generally indicate better health, sound genes, and high fertility. Similarly, women prefer men with maturity and resources because the responsibility of rearing and nurturing children has historically fallen primarily on women's shoulders.

So how do those of us who are not "superstar beautiful" manage to find mates? The good news is that people usually do not hold out for partners who are ideally attractive. Instead, both men and women tend to select partners whose physical attractiveness approximately matches their own (Regan, 1998, 2011; Sprecher & Regan, 2002; Taylor et al., 2011). Also, people use nonverbal flirting behavior to increase their attractiveness and signal interest to a potential romantic partner. Note that in heterosexual couples, the generally accepted norms are for the woman to first signal her interest and for the man to make the first approach (Lott, 2000, Moore, 1998).

Proximity

Attraction also depends on the two persons' being in the same place at the same time. Thus, *proximity*, or geographic nearness, is another major factor in attraction. One examination of over 300,000 Facebook users found that even though people can have relationships with people throughout the world, the likelihood of a friendship decreases as distance between people increases (Nguyen & Szymanski, 2012). If you're wondering if this is a case of correlation being confused with causation, that's great! You're becoming an educated consumer of research and a good critical thinker.

In fact, there is experimental evidence supporting a causative link between proximity and attraction. For example, oxytocin, a naturally occurring bodily chemical, is known to be a key facilitator of interpersonal attraction and parental attachment (Goodson, 2013; Weisman et al., 2012). In one very interesting experiment, the intranasal administration of oxytocin stimulated men in monogamous relationships, but not single ones, to keep a much greater distance between themselves and an attractive woman during a first encounter (Scheele et al., 2012). The researchers concluded that oxytocin may help maintain monogamous relationships by making men avoid close personal proximity to other women.

Q5

Why is proximity so important? It's largely due to the **mere-exposure effect**. Just as familiar people become more physically attractive over time, repeated exposure also increases overall liking (Monin, 2003; Rhodes et al., 2001). This makes sense from an evolutionary point of view. Things we have seen before are less likely to pose a threat than novel stimuli. It also explains why modern advertisers tend to run highly redundant ad campaigns with familiar faces and jingles. In short, repeated exposure increases liking! (See **Figure 14.17**.)

Mere-exposure effect A developed preference for people or things simply because they are familiar.

Bernhard Kuhmsted/Retna

FIGURE 14.17 THE FACE IN THE MIRROR

As a result of the mere-exposure effect, we generally prefer a reversed image of ourselves (the one on the left, in this case) because it is the familiar face we're accustomed to seeing in the mirror. However, when presented with reversed and nonreversed photos, close friends prefer the nonreversed images (Mita et al., 1977).

Similarity

The major cementing factor for long-term relationships, whether liking or loving, is *similarity*. We tend to prefer, and stay with, people who are most like us—those who share our ethnic background, social class, interests, and attitudes (Böhm et al., 2010; Caprara et al., 2007; Morry et al., 2011; Sanbonmatsu et al., 2011). In other words, "Birds of a feather flock together."

What about the old saying "opposites attract"? The term *opposites* here probably refers to personality traits rather than to social background or values. An attraction to a seemingly opposite person is more often based on the recognition that in one or two important personality traits, that person offers something we lack. In sum, lovers can enjoy some differences, but the more alike people are, the more both their loving and their liking endure.

The following *Psychology and You* feature offers a fun test of your understanding of the three factors in interpersonal attraction. Try it!

TEST YOURSELF: UNDERSTANDING INTERPERSONAL ATTRACTION

psychology and you

Based on your reading of this section, can you explain Kvack's love for the wooden dummy?

Answers: Research shows that similarity is the best predictor of long-term relationships. As shown here, however, many people ignore dissimilarities and hope that their chosen partner will change over time.

Loving Others

It's easy to see why interpersonal attraction is a fundamental building block of our feelings about others. But how do we make sense of love? Why do we love some people and not others? Many people find the subject to be alternately mysterious, exhilarating, comforting—and even maddening. In this section, we explore four perspectives on love—*Sternberg's triarchic theory*, *consummate love*, *romantic love*, and *companionate love*.

Triarchic theory of love Sternberg's theory that different stages and types of love result from three basic components—*intimacy*, *passion*, and *commitment*.

Robert Sternberg, a well-known researcher on creativity and intelligence (Chapter 8), produced a **triarchic** (triangular) **theory of love** (Sternberg, 1986, 1988, 2006) **(Figure 14.18)**, which suggests that different types and stages of love result from three basic components:

- **Intimacy**—emotional closeness and connectedness, mutual trust, friendship, warmth, private sharing of self-disclosure, and forming of "love maps."
- **Passion**—sexual attraction and desirability, physical excitement, a state of intense longing to be with the other.
- **Commitment**—permanence and stability, the decision to stay in the relationship for the long haul, and the feelings of security that go with this intention.

FIGURE 14.18 STERNBERG'S TRIARCHIC THEORY OF LOVE

According to Sternberg, we all experience various forms and stages of love, six of which are seen as being on the outside of the triangle. Only true *consummate love* is inside the triangle because it includes a healthy balance of intimacy, passion, and commitment. The balance among these three components naturally shifts and changes over the course of a relationship, but relationships based on only one or two of these elements are generally less fulfilling and less likely to survive.

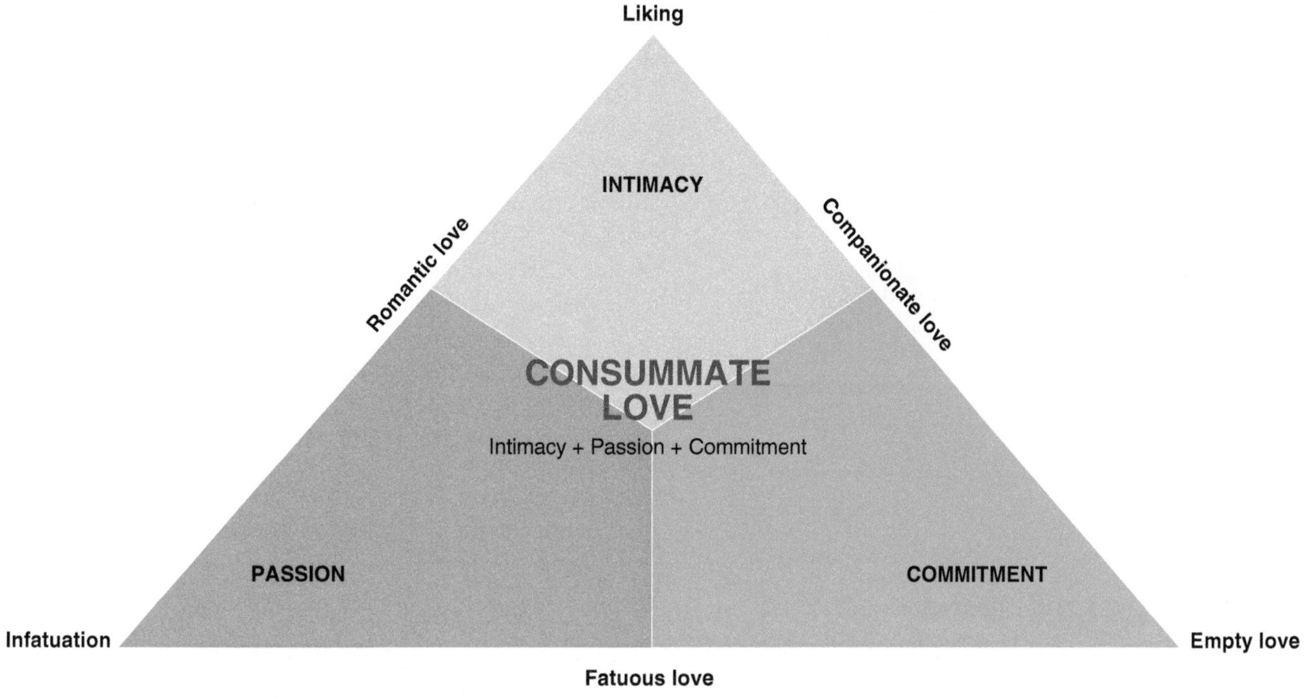

For Sternberg, a healthy degree of all three components in both partners characterizes the fullest form of love, **consummate love**. Trouble occurs when one of the partners has a higher or lower need for one or more of the components. For example, if one partner has a much higher need for intimacy and the other partner has a stronger interest in passion, this lack of compatibility can be fatal to the relationship—unless the partners are willing to compromise and strike a mutually satisfying balance (Sternberg, 1988).

Consummate love Sternberg's strongest and most enduring type of love, based on a balanced combination of intimacy, passion, and commitment.

Romantic Love

When you think of romantic love, do you imagine falling in love, a magical experience that puts you on cloud nine? **Romantic love** has intrigued people throughout history. Its intense joys and sorrows also have inspired countless poems, novels, movies, and songs around the world. A cross-cultural study by anthropologists William Jankowiak and Edward Fischer found romantic love in 147 of the 166 societies they studied. They concluded that "romantic love constitutes a human universal or, at the least, a near universal" (1992, p. 154).

Romantic love An intense feeling of attraction to another in an erotic context.

Romantic love may be almost universal, but even in the most devoted couples, the intense attraction and excitement of romantic love generally begin to fade 6 to 30 months after the relationship begins, whereas companionate love grows and evolves **(Figure 14.19)** (Hatfield & Rapson, 1996; Livingston, 1999). Why? Further research explains that **companionate love** is based on deep and lasting trust, caring, tolerance, and friendship, which slowly develops as couples grow and spend more time together. In contrast, romantic love is largely based on mystery and fantasy. People often fall in love with what they want another person to be—and these illusions usually fade with the realities of everyday living (Fletcher & Simpson, 2000; Levine, 2001).

Companionate love Strong and lasting attraction characterized by deep and lasting trust, caring, tolerance, and friendship.

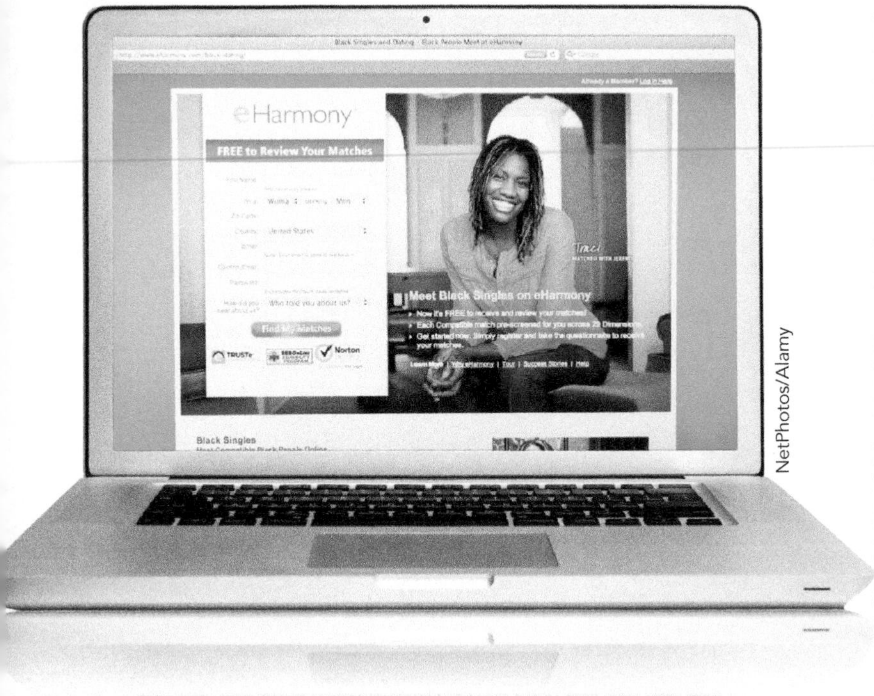

NetPhotos/Alamy

realworldpsychology Can You Find Lasting Love Via On-Line Dating? To test this question, researchers conducted an on-line survey of over 19,000 Americans (Cacioppo et al., 2013). Participants were asked if they were currently married, if they had ever been divorced, and/or if they met their current or former spouse on-line. Those who were married also completed a measure of relationship satisfaction.

Researchers then compared divorce rates and marital satisfaction for those who met their spouse on-line versus not on-line. Interestingly, they found a higher level of marital satisfaction and a significantly lower divorce rate for those whose marriages started on-line versus those that started off-line. Can you think of topics from this or any other chapter in this text, or from your own life experiences, that might explain why relationships which start on-line may in fact be longer lasting and more satisfying than those that start in more traditional ways?

FIGURE 14.19 LOVE OVER THE LIFESPAN

How can we keep romantic love alive? One of the most constructive ways is to recognize its fragile nature and nurture it with carefully planned surprises, flirting, flattery, and special dinners and celebrations. In the long run, however, romantic love's most important function might be to keep us attached long enough to move on to the deeper and more enduring companionate love.

As you can see in the figure, romantic love is high in the beginning of a relationship, but it tends to diminish over time, with periodic resurgences, or "spikes." In contrast, companionate love usually steadily increases over time. One reason may be that satisfaction grows as we come to recognize the lasting value of companionship and intimacy (Gottman, 2012; Jacobs Bao & Lyubomirsky, 2013; Regan, 2011). One tip for maximizing companionate love is to overlook each other's faults. People are more satisfied with relationships when they have a somewhat idealized perception of their partner (Barelds & Dijkstra, 2011; Campbell et al., 2001; Fletcher & Simpson, 2000; Regan, 2011). This makes sense in light of research on cognitive dissonance (discussed earlier). Idealizing our mates allows us to believe we have a good deal—and thereby avoid any cognitive dissonance that might arise when we see an attractive alternative. As Benjamin Franklin wisely said, "Keep your eyes wide open before marriage, and half shut afterwards."

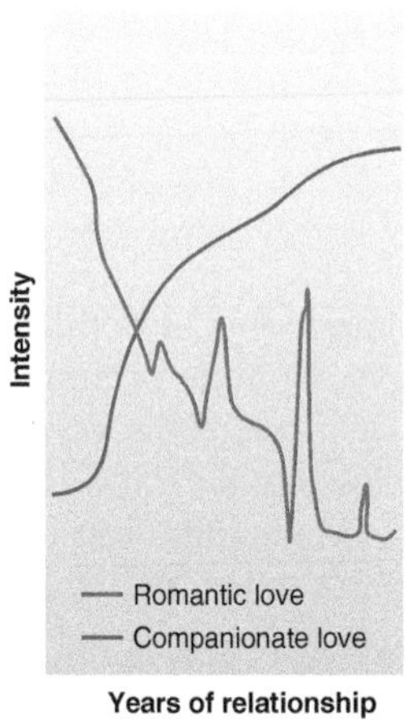

Sisse Brimberg & Cotton Coulson/NG Image Collection

Annie Griffiths Belt/NG Image Collection

Alaska Stock Images/NG Image Collection

RETRIEVAL PRACTICE: SOCIAL RELATIONS

Self-Test

Completing this self-test and comparing your answers with those in Appendix B provides immediate feedback and helpful practice for exams. Additional interactive, self-tests are available at www.wiley.com/college/huffman.

1. _____ is a learned, generally negative, attitude toward specific people solely because of their membership in an identified group.

a. Discrimination
b. Stereotyping
c. Cognitive biasing
d. Prejudice

2. Research suggests that one of the best ways to decrease prejudice is to encourage _____.

a. cooperation
b. friendly competition
c. reciprocity of liking
d. conformity

3. Onlookers to crimes sometimes fail to respond to cries for help because of the _____ phenomenon.

a. empathy–altruism
b. egoistic model
c. inhumanity of large cities
d. diffusion of responsibility

4. The positive feelings we have toward others is called _____.

a. affective relations
b. interpersonal attraction
c. interpersonal attitudes
d. affective connections

5. A strong and lasting attraction characterized by deep and lasting trust, caring, tolerance, and friendship called _____.

a. companionate love
b. intimate love
c. passionate love
d. all these options

Think Critically

1 Do you believe you are free of prejudice? After reading this chapter, which of the many factors that cause prejudice do you think is most important to change?

2 Which of the three major theories of helping do you find best explains why you tend to help others?

realworldpsychology

Are men still more likely to get hired than equally qualified women?

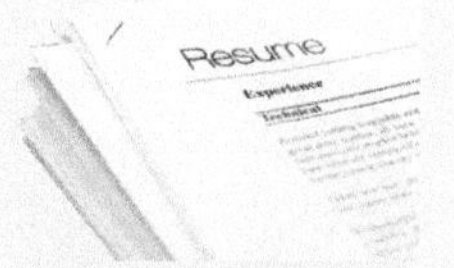

How does simple nearness (proximity) influence attraction?

HINT: LOOK IN THE MARGIN FOR Q4 AND Q5

Summary

1 SOCIAL COGNITION 399

- **Social psychology** is the study of the way other people influence our thoughts, feelings, and actions. **Social cognition**, the way we think about and interpret ourselves and others, relies on **attributions**, which help us explain behaviors and events. However, these attributions are frequently marred by the **fundamental attribution error (FAE)** and the **self-serving bias**. Both biases may depend in part on cultural factors.
- **Attitudes** have three ABC components: *affective*, *behavioral*, and *cognitive*. An efficient strategy for changing attitudes is to create **cognitive dissonance**. Like the tendency toward attributional biases, our experience of cognitive dissonance may depend on culture.

2 SOCIAL INFLUENCE 404

- Three factors drive conformity: *normative social influence*, *informational social influence*, and the role of *reference groups*. **Conformity** means going along with a group, while **obedience** means going along with a direct command, usually from someone in a position of authority. Milgram's research demonstrated the startling power of social situations to create obedience. The degree of deception and discomfort to which Milgram's participants were subjected raises serious ethical questions, and the same study would never be done today.
- The roles we play within groups strongly affect our behavior, as Zimbardo's Stanford Prison experiment showed. Zimbardo's study also demonstrated **deindividuation**. In addition, as we interact with others and discuss our opinions, **group**

polarization—a group's movement toward more extreme decisions—and **groupthink**—a group's tendency to strive for agreement and to avoid inconsistent information—tend to occur. Both processes may hinder effective decision making.

3 SOCIAL RELATIONS 413

- Like all other attitudes, **prejudice** includes three ABC components: *affective*, *behavioral*, and *cognitive*. Although the terms prejudice and **discrimination** are often used interchangeably, they are not the same. Five commonly cited sources of prejudice are *learning*, *personal experience*, *limited resources*, *displaced aggression*, and *mental shortcuts*.
- Several biological factors may help explain **aggression**, including genetic predisposition, aggression circuits in the brain, hormones, and neurotransmitters. Psychosocial explanations for aggression include substance abuse, aversive stimuli, media violence, and social learning.
- Evolutionary theory suggests that **altruism** is an evolved, instinctual behavior. Other research suggests that helping may actually be self-interest in disguise—the **egoistic model**. The **empathy–altruism hypothesis** proposes that although altruism is occasionally based on selfish motivations, it is sometimes truly selfless and motivated by empathy or concern for others. Latané and Darley found that in order for helping to occur, the potential helper must notice what is happening, interpret the event as an emergency, take personal responsibility for helping, decide how to help, and then actually initiate the helping behavior.
- Psychologists have found three compelling factors in **interpersonal attraction:** physical attractiveness, proximity, and similarity. Sternberg suggests that **consummate love** depends on a healthy degree of intimacy, passion, and commitment. **Romantic love** is an intense but generally short-lived attraction based on mystery and fantasy, whereas **companionate love** is a strong, lasting attraction based on trust, caring, tolerance, and friendship.

William Philpott/Reuters/© Corbis

applyingrealworldpsychology

We began this chapter with five intriguing Real World Psychology questions, and you were asked to revisit these questions at the end of each section. Questions like these have an important and lasting impact on all of our lives. See if you can answer these additional critical thinking questions related to real world examples.

1. What were the major social factors that contributed to Rosa Parks, pictured here, being willing to stand up against the bus driver who ordered her to give her seat to a white man? Does her model of disobedience encourage you to follow her example? Why or why not?
2. Can you think of an example from your own life, or from the life of one of your friends, in which attitudes did not match behavior? How might strong attitudes be a better predictor of actual behavior than weak ones?
3. In both Asch's conformity experiment and Milgram's study of obedience, the presence of another person greatly affected the behaviors of the research participants. How would you explain this?
4. Thinking about the most important romantic relationship in your life, explain how each of the major factors in interpersonal attraction—physical attractiveness, proximity, and similarity—affect this relationship.
5. Imagine yourself with a career as a social psychologist. Which of the key factors discussed in this chapter would you be most and least interested in studying? Why?

Key Terms

RETRIEVAL PRACTICE Write a definition for each term before turning back to the referenced page to check your answer.

- actor–observer effect 400
- aggression 417
- altruism 418
- attitude 401
- attribution 399
- bystander effect 420
- cognitive dissonance 402
- companionate love 423
- conformity 405
- consummate love 423
- deindividuation 410
- discrimination 413
- egoistic model of helping 418
- empathy–altruism hypothesis 419
- evolutionary theory of helping 418
- foot-in-the-door technique 409
- frustration–aggression hypothesis 417
- fundamental attribution error (FAE) 399
- group polarization 410
- groupthink 411
- implicit bias 416
- Informational social influence 406
- ingroup favoritism 415
- interpersonal attraction 420
- mere-exposure effect 421
- normative social influence 405
- obedience 406
- outgroup homogeneity effect 415
- prejudice 413
- reference groups 406
- romantic love 423
- saliency bias 399
- self-serving bias 400
- social cognition 399
- social influence 404
- social psychology 399
- social relations 413
- stereotype 413
- triarchic theory of love 422

Appendix A

STATISTICS AND PSYCHOLOGY

We are constantly bombarded by numbers: "On sale for 30 percent off," "70 percent chance of rain," "9 out of 10 doctors recommend," "Your scores on the SAT were in the 75th percentile." Business and advertisers use numbers to convince us to buy their products. College admission officers use SAT percentile scores to help them decide who to admit to their programs. And, as you've seen throughout this text, psychologists use numbers to support or refute psychological theories and demonstrate that certain behaviors are indeed results of specific causal factors.

When we use numbers in these ways, we're all using statistics. **Statistics** is a branch of applied mathematics that uses numbers to describe and analyze information on a subject.

Statistics The branch of applied mathematics that deals with the collection, calculation, analysis, interpretation, and presentation of numerical facts or data.

If you're considering a major in psychology, you may be surprised to learn that a full course in statistics is generally required for this major. Why? Statistics make it possible for psychologists to quantify the information we obtain in our studies. We can then critically analyze and evaluate this information. Statistical analysis is imperative for researchers to describe, predict, or explain behavior. For instance, Albert Bandura (1973) proposed that watching violence on television causes aggressive behavior in children. In carefully controlled experiments, he gathered numerical information and analyzed it according to specific statistical methods. The statistical analysis helped him substantiate that the aggression of his participants and the aggressive acts they had seen on television were related, and that the relationship was not mere coincidence.

Although statistics is a branch of applied mathematics, you don't have to be a math whiz. Simple arithmetic is all we need for most of the calculations. For more complex statistics involving more complicated mathematics, computer programs are readily available. What is more important than learning the mathematical computations, however, is developing an understanding of when and why each type of statistic is used. The purpose of this appendix is to help you develop this understanding and to become a better consumer of the statistics that bombard us each day. In addition, we hope to increase your appreciation for the important role this form of math plays in the science of psychology.

GATHERING AND ORGANIZING DATA

Psychologists design their studies to facilitate gathering information about the factors they want to study. The information they obtain is known as *data* (data is plural; its singular is datum). When the data are gathered, they are generally in the form of numbers; if they aren't, they are converted to numbers. After they are gathered, the data must be organized in such a way that statistical analysis is possible. In the following section, we will examine the methods used to gather and organize information.

Variables

When studying a behavior, psychologists normally focus on one particular factor to determine whether it has an effect on the behavior. This factor is known as a *variable,* which is in effect anything that can assume more than one value (see Chapter 1). Height, weight, sex, eye color, and scores on an IQ test or a video game are all factors that can assume more than one value and are therefore variables. Some will vary between people, such as sex (you are either male *or* female but not both at the same time). Some may even vary within one person, such as scores on a video game (the same person might get 10,000 points on one try and only 800 on another). Opposed to a variable, anything that remains the same and does not vary is called a *constant*. If researchers use only women in their research, then sex is a constant, not a variable.

In nonexperimental studies, variables can be factors that are merely observed through naturalistic observation or case studies, or they can be factors about which people are questioned in a test or survey. In experimental studies, the two major types of variables are independent and dependent variables.

Independent variables are those that are manipulated by the experimenter. For example, suppose we were to conduct a study to determine whether the sex of the debater influences the outcome of a debate. In this study, one group of participants watches a videotape of a debate between a man arguing the "pro" side and a woman arguing the "con"; another group watches the same debate, but with the pro and con roles reversed. In such a study, the form of the presentation viewed by each group (whether "pro" is argued by a man or a woman) is the independent variable because the experimenter manipulates the form of presentation seen by each group. Another example might be a study to determine whether a particular drug has any effect on a manual dexterity task. To study this question, we would administer the drug to one group and no drug to another. The independent variable would be the amount of drug given (some or none). The independent variable is particularly important when using *inferential statistics*, which we will discuss later.

The *dependent variable* is a factor that results from, or depends on, the independent variable. It is a measure of some outcome or, most commonly, a measure of the participants' behavior. In the debate example, each subject's choice of the winner of the debate would be the dependent variable. In the drug experiment, the dependent variable would be each subject's score on the manual dexterity task.

Frequency Distributions

After conducting a study and obtaining measures of the variable(s) being studied, psychologists need to organize the data in a meaningful way. **Table A.1** presents test scores from a Math Aptitude Test collected from 50 college students. This information is called *raw data* because there is no order to the numbers. They are presented as they were collected and are therefore "raw."

The lack of order in raw data makes them difficult to study. Thus, the first step in understanding the results of an experiment is to impose some order on the raw data. There are several ways to do this. One of the simplest is to create a *frequency distribution*, which shows the number of times a score or event occurs. Although frequency distributions are helpful in several ways, the major advantages are that

TABLE A.1 MATH APTITUDE TEST SCORES FOR 50 COLLEGE STUDENTS

73	57	63	59	50
72	66	50	67	51
63	59	65	62	65
62	72	64	73	66
61	68	62	68	63
59	61	72	63	52
59	58	57	68	57
64	56	65	59	60
50	62	68	54	63
52	62	70	60	68

they allow us to see the data in an organized manner and they make it easier to represent the data on a graph.

The simplest way to make a frequency distribution is to list all the possible test scores, then tally the number of people *(N)* who received those scores. **Table A.2** presents a frequency distribution using the raw data from Table A.1. As you can see, the data are now easier to read. Note how most of the test scores lie in the middle with only a few at the very high or very low end. This was not at all evident from looking at the raw data.

TABLE A.2 FREQUENCY DISTRIBUTION OF 50 STUDENTS ON MATH APTITUDE TEST

Score	Frequency	Score	Frequency
73	2	61	2
72	3	60	2
71	0	59	5
70	1	58	1
69	0	57	3
68	5	56	1
67	1	55	0
66	2	54	1
65	3	53	0
64	2	52	2
63	5	51	1
62	5	50	3
Total			50

This type of frequency distribution is practical when the number of possible scores is 20 or fewer. However, when there are more than 20 possible scores it can be even harder to make sense out of the frequency distribution than the raw data. This can be seen in **Table A.3**, which presents the hypothetical Psychology Aptitude Test scores for 50 students. Even though there are only 50 actual scores in this table, the number of possible scores ranges from a high of 1390 to a low of 400. If we included zero frequencies there would be 100 entries in a frequency distribution of

TABLE A.3 PSYCHOLOGY APTITUDE TEST SCORES FOR 50 COLLEGE STUDENTS

1350	750	530	540	750
1120	410	780	1020	430
720	1080	1110	770	610
1130	620	510	1160	630
640	1220	920	650	870
930	660	480	940	670
1070	950	680	450	990
690	1010	800	660	500
860	520	540	880	1090
580	730	570	560	740

this data, making the frequency distribution much more difficult to understand than the raw data. If there are more than 20 possible scores, therefore, a *group frequency distribution* is normally used.

In a *group frequency distribution*, individual scores are represented as members of a group of scores or as a range of scores (see **Table A.4**). These groups are called *class intervals*. Grouping these scores makes it much easier to make sense out of the distribution, as you can see from the relative ease in understanding Table A.4 as compared to Table A.3. Group frequency distributions are easier to represent on a graph.

TABLE A.4 GROUP FREQUENCY DISTRIBUTION OF PSYCHOLOGY APTITUDE TEST SCORES FOR 50 COLLEGE STUDENTS

Class Interval	Frequency
1300–1390	1
1200–1290	1
1100–1190	4
1000–1090	5
900–990	5
800–890	4
700–790	7
600–690	10
500–590	9
400–490	4
Total	50

When graphing data from frequency distributions, the class intervals are represented along the *abscissa* (the horizontal or x axis). The frequency is represented along the *ordinate* (the vertical or y axis). Information can be graphed in the form of a bar graph, called a *histogram*, or in the form of a point or line graph, called a *polygon*. **Figure A.1** shows a histogram presenting the data from Table A.4. Note that the class intervals are represented along the bottom line of the graph (the x axis) and the height of the bars indicates the frequency in each class interval. Now look at **Figure A.2**. The information presented here is exactly the same as that in Figure A.1 but is represented in the form of a polygon rather than a histogram. Can you see how both graphs illustrate the same information? Even though graphs like these are quite common today, we have found that many students have never been formally taught how to read graphs, which is the topic of our next section.

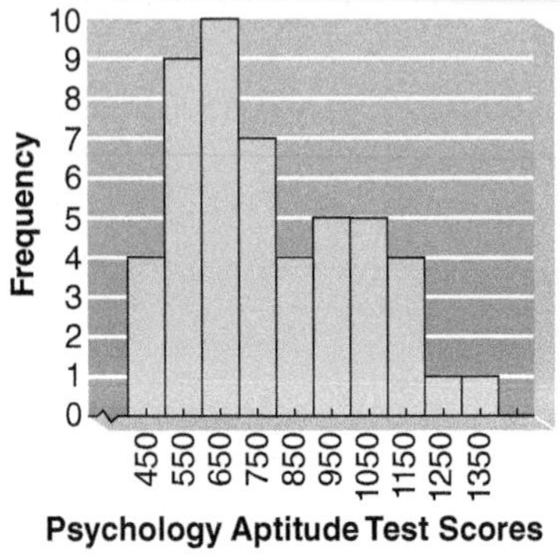

FIGURE A.1 A HISTOGRAM ILLUSTRATING THE INFORMATION FOUND IN TABLE A4

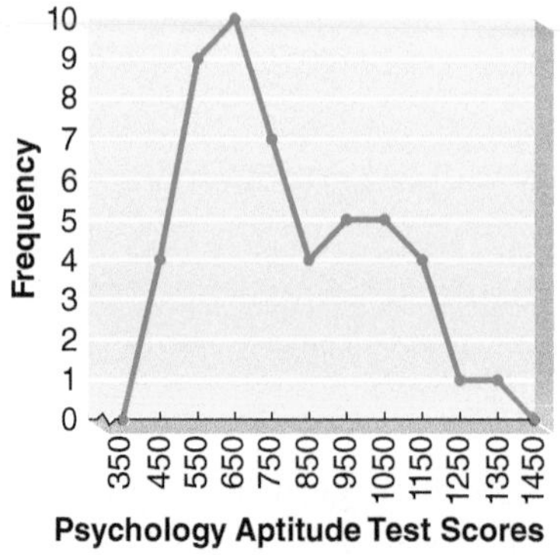

FIGURE A.2 A POLYGON ILLUSTRATING THE INFORMATION FOUND IN TABLE A4

How to Read a Graph

Every graph has several major parts. The most important are the labels, the axes (the vertical and horizontal lines), and the points, lines, or bars. Find these parts in Figure A.1.

The first thing we should all notice when reading a graph are the labels because they tell what data are portrayed. Usually the data consist of the descriptive statistics, or the numbers used to measure the dependent variables. For example, in Figure A.1 the horizontal axis is labeled "Psychology Aptitude Test Scores," which is the dependent variable measure; the vertical axis is labeled "Frequency," which means the number of occurrences. If a graph is not labeled, as we sometimes see in TV commercials or magazine ads, it is useless and should be ignored. Even when a graph *is* labeled, the labels can be misleading. For example, if graph designers want to distort the information, they can elongate one of the axes. Thus, it is important to pay careful attention to the numbers as well as the words in graph labels.

Next, we need to focus on the bars, points, or lines on the graph. In the case of histograms like the one in Figure A.1, each bar represents the class interval. The width of the bar stands for the width of the class interval, whereas the height of the bar stands for the frequency in that interval. Look at the third bar from the left in Figure A.1. This bar represents the interval "600 to 690 Psychology Aptitude Scores," which has a frequency of 10. Can you see how this directly corresponds to the same class interval in Table A.4? Graphs and tables are both merely alternate ways of illustrating information.

Reading point or line graphs is the same as reading a histogram. In a point graph, each point represents two numbers, one found along the horizontal axis and the other found along the vertical axis. A polygon is identical to a point graph except that it has lines connecting the points. Figure A.2 is an example of a polygon, where each point represents a class interval and is placed at the center of the interval and at the height corresponding to the frequency of that interval. To make the graph easier to read, the points are connected by straight lines.

Displaying the data in a frequency distribution or in a graph is much more useful than merely presenting raw data and can be especially helpful when researchers are trying to find relations between certain factors. However, as we explained earlier, if psychologists want to make precise predictions or explanations, we need to perform specific mathematical computations on the data. How we use these computations, or statistics, is the topic of our next section.

USES OF THE VARIOUS STATISTICS

The statistics psychologists use in a study depend on whether they are trying to describe and predict behavior or explain it. When they use statistics to describe behavior, as in reporting the average score on the hypothetical Psychology Aptitude Test, they are using **descriptive statistics**. When they use them to explain behavior, as Bandura did in his study of children modeling aggressive behavior seen on TV, they are using **inferential statistics**.

Descriptive statistics Mathematical methods used to describe and summarize sets of data in a meaningful way.

Inferential statistics Mathematical procedures that provide a measure of confidence about how likely it is that a certain result appeared by chance.

Descriptive Statistics

Descriptive statistics are the numbers used to describe the dependent variable. They can be used to describe characteristics of a *population* (an entire group, such as all people living in the United States) or a *sample* (a part of a group, such as a randomly selected group of 25 students from Cornell University). The major descriptive statistics include measures of central tendency (mean, median, and mode), measures of variation (variance and standard deviation), and correlation.

Mean The arithmetic average of a distribution, which is obtained by adding the values of all the scores and dividing by the number of scores (N).

Median The halfway point in a set of data; half the scores fall above the median, and half fall below it.

Mode The score that occurs most frequently in a data set.

Measures of Central Tendency

Statistics indicating the center of the distribution are called *measures of central tendency* and include the mean, median, and mode. They are all scores that are typical of the center of the distribution. The **mean** is the arithmetic average, and it is what most of us think of when we hear the word "average." The **median** is the middle score in a distribution—half the scores fall above it and half fall below it. The **mode** is the score that occurs most often.

Mean What is your average exam score in your psychology class? What is the average yearly rainfall in your part of the country? What is the average reading test score in your city? When these questions ask for the average, they are really asking for the "mean." The arithmetic *mean* is the weighted average of all the raw scores, which is computed by totaling all the raw scores and then dividing that total by the number of scores added together. In statistical computation, the mean is represented by an *"X"* with a bar above it ($\overline{X}$, pronounced *"X* bar"), each individual raw score by an "X," and the total number of scores by an *"N."* For example, if we wanted to compute the $\overline{X}$ of the raw statistics test scores in Table A.1, we would sum all the *X*'s (Σ, with Σ meaning sum) and divide by *N* (number of scores). In Table A.1, the sum of all the scores is equal to 3100 and there are 50 scores. Therefore, the mean of these scores is

$$\overline{X} = \frac{3100}{50} = 62$$

Table A.5 illustrates how to calculate the mean for 10 IQ scores.

TABLE A.5 COMPUTATION OF THE MEAN FOR 10 IQ SCORES

IQ Scores X
143
127
116
98
85
107
106
98
104
116
$\Sigma X = 1100$
$\text{Mean} = \overline{X} = \frac{\Sigma X}{N} = \frac{1{,}100}{10} = 110$

Median The *median* is the middle score in the distribution once all the scores have been arranged in rank order. If *N* (the number of scores) is odd, then there actually is a middle score and that middle score is the median. When *N* is even, there are two middle scores and the median is the mean of those two scores. **Table A.6** shows the computation of the median for two different sets of scores, one set with 15 scores and one with 10.

TABLE A.6 COMPUTATION OF MEDIAN FOR ODD AND EVEN NUMBERS OF IQ SCORES

IQ	IQ
139	137
130	135
121	121
116	116
107	108 ← middle score
101	106 ← middle score
98	105
96 ← middle score	101
84	98
83	97
82	N = 10
75	N is even
75	
68	
65	Median = $\frac{106 + 108}{2} = 107$
N = 15	
N is odd	

TABLE A.7 FINDING THE MODE FOR TWO DIFFERENT DISTRIBUTIONS

IQ	IQ
139	139
138	138
125	125
116 ←	116 ←
116 ←	116 ←
116 ←	116 ←
107	107
100	98 ←
98	98 ←
98	98 ←
Mode = most frequent score	Mode = 116 and 98
Mode = 116	

Mode Of all the measures of central tendency, the easiest to compute is the *mode*, which is merely the most frequent score. It is computed by finding the score that occurs most often. Whereas there is always only one mean and only one median for each distribution, there can be more than one mode. **Table A.7** shows how to find the mode in a distribution with one mode (unimodal) and in a distribution with two modes (bimodal).

There are several advantages to each of these measures of central tendency, but in psychological research the mean is used most often. A book solely covering psychological statistics will provide a more thorough discussion of the relative values of these measures.

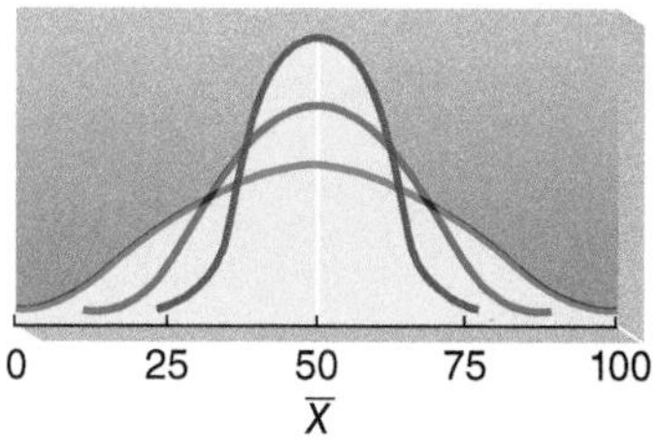

FIGURE A.3 **THREE DISTRIBUTIONS HAVING THE SAME MEAN BUT A DIFFERENT VARIABILITY**

Measures of Variation

When describing a distribution, it is not sufficient merely to give the central tendency; it is also necessary to give a *measure of variation*, which is a measure of the spread of the scores. By examining this **range**, or spread of scores, we can determine whether the scores are bunched around the middle or tend to extend away from the middle. **Figure A.3** shows three different distributions, all with the same mean but with different spreads of scores. You can see from this figure that, in order to describe these different distributions accurately, there must be some measures of the variation in their spread. The most widely used measure of variation is the **standard deviation**, which is represented by a lowercase s. The standard deviation is a standard measurement of how much the scores in a distribution deviate from the mean. The formula for the standard deviation is

$$s = \sqrt{\frac{\Sigma(X - \overline{X})^2}{N}}$$

Table A.8 illustrates how to compute the standard deviation.

Most distributions of psychological data are bell-shaped. That is, most of the scores are grouped around the mean, and the farther the scores are from the mean in either direction, the fewer the scores. Notice the bell shape of the distribution

Range A measure of the dispersion of scores between the highest and lowest scores.

Standard deviation A computed measure of how much scores in a sample differ from the mean of the sample.

TABLE A.8 COMPUTATION OF THE STANDARD DEVIATION FOR 10 IQ SCORES

IQ Scores X	$X - \bar{X}$	$(X - \bar{X})^2$
143	33	1089
127	17	289
116	6	36
98	−12	144
85	−25	625
107	−3	9
106	−4	16
98	−12	144
104	−6	36
116	6	36
$\Sigma X = 1100$		$\Sigma(X - \bar{X})^2 = 2424$

Standard Deviation = s

$$= \sqrt{\frac{\Sigma(X - \bar{X})^2}{N}} = \sqrt{\frac{2424}{10}}$$

$$= \sqrt{242.4} = 15.569$$

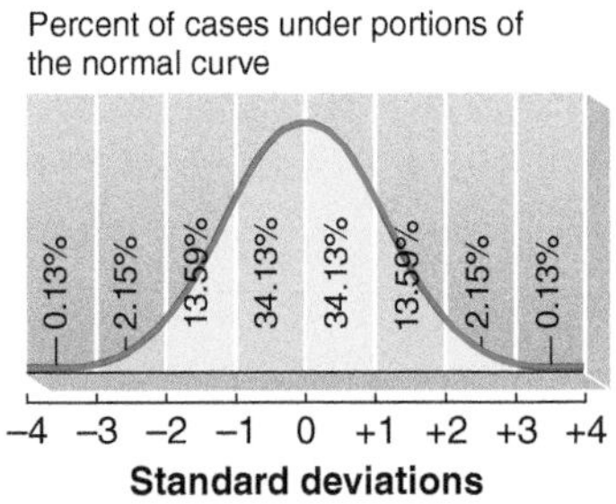

FIGURE A.4 **THE NORMAL DISTRIBUTION FORMS A BELL-SHAPED CURVE**

In a normal distribution, two-thirds of the scores lie between one standard deviation above and one standard deviation below the mean.

Normal distribution A symmetrical, bell-shaped curve that represents a set of data in which most scores occur in the middle of the possible range, with fewer and fewer scores near the extremes.

in **Figure A.4**. Distributions such as this are called **normal distributions**. In normal distributions, as shown in Figure A.4, approximately two-thirds of the scores fall within a range that is one standard deviation below the mean to one standard deviation above the mean. For example, the Wechsler IQ tests (see Chapter 7) have a mean of 100 and a standard deviation of 15. This means that approximately two-thirds of the people taking these tests will have scores between 85 and 115.

Correlation

Suppose for a moment that you are sitting in the student union with a friend. To pass the time, you and your friend decide to play a game in which you try to guess the height of the next man who enters the union. The winner, the one whose guess is closest to the person's actual height, gets a piece of pie paid for by the loser. When it is your turn, what do you guess? If you're like most people, you'll probably try to estimate the mean of all the men in the union and use that as your guess. The mean is almost always our best guess when we have no other information.

Now let's change the game a little and add a friend who stands outside the union and weighs the next man who enters the union. If your friend texts you with the information that this man weighs 125 pounds, without seeing him would you still predict that he's of average height? Probably not. You'd most likely guess that he's below the mean. Why? Because you intuitively understand that there is a *correlation* (Chapter 1), a relationship, between height and weight, with tall people usually weighing more than short people. Given that 125 pounds is less than the average weight for men, you'll probably guess a less-than-average height. The statistic used to measure this type of relationship between two variables is called a correlation coefficient.

Correlation Coefficient A *correlation coefficient* (Chapter 1), measures the relationship between two variables, such as height and weight or IQ and annual income. Given any two variables, there are three possible relationships between them: *positive, negative,* and *zero* (no relationship). A *positive relationship* exists when the two variables vary in the same direction (e.g., as height increases, weight normally also increases). A *negative relationship* occurs when the two variables vary in opposite directions (e.g., as temperatures go up, hot chocolate sales go down). There is a *zero*

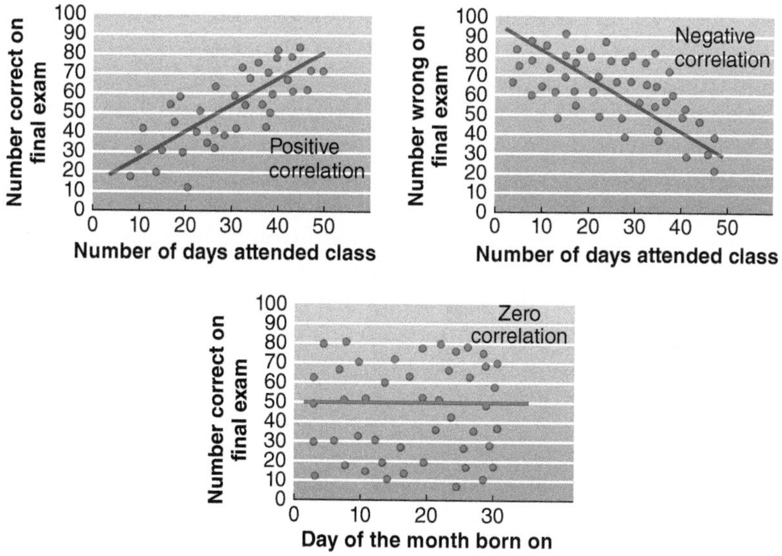

FIGURE A.5 THREE TYPES OF CORRELATION

Positive correlation (top left): as the number of days of class attendance increases, so does the number of correct exam items. Negative correlation (top right): as the number of days of class attendance increases, the number of incorrect exam items decreases. Zero correlation (bottom): the day of the month on which one is born has no relationship to the number of exam items correct.

(no) *relationship* when the two variables vary totally independently of one another (e.g., there is no relationship between your height and the color of your toothbrush). **Figure A.5** illustrates these three types of correlations.

The computation and the formula for a correlation coefficient (correlation coefficient is delineated by the letter *"r"*) are shown in **Table A.9**. The correlation coefficient *(r)* always has a value between +1 and −1 (it is never greater than +1 and it is never smaller than −1). When *r* is close to +1, it signifies a high positive relationship between the two variables (as one variable goes up, the other variable also goes up). When *r* is close to −1, it signifies a high negative relationship between the two variables (as one variable goes up, the other variable goes down). When *r* is 0, there is no linear relationship between the two variables being measured.

TABLE A.9 COMPUTATION OF CORRELATION COEFFICIENT BETWEEN HEIGHT AND WEIGHT FOR 10 MEN

Height (inches) X	X^2	Weight (pounds) Y	Y^2	XY
73	5,329	210	44,100	15,330
64	4,096	133	17,689	8,512
65	4,225	128	16,384	8,320
70	4,900	156	24,336	10,920
74	5,476	189	35,721	13,986
68	4,624	145	21,025	9,860
67	4,489	145	21,025	9,715
72	5,184	166	27,556	11,952
76	5,776	199	37,601	15,124
71	5,041	159	25,281	11,289
700	49,140	1,630	272,718	115,008

$$r = \frac{N \cdot \Sigma XY - \Sigma X \cdot \Sigma Y}{\sqrt{[N \cdot \Sigma X^2 - (\Sigma X)^2} \sqrt{[N \cdot \Sigma Y^2 - (\Sigma Y)^2]}}$$

$$r = \frac{10 \cdot 115{,}008 - 700 \cdot 1{,}630}{\sqrt{[10 \cdot 49{,}140 - 700^2]}\sqrt{[10 \cdot 272{,}718 - 1{,}630^2]}}$$

$$r = 0.92$$

Correlation coefficients can be quite helpful in making predictions. Bear in mind, however, that predictions are just that: *predictions*. They will have some error as long as the correlation coefficients on which they are based are not perfect (+1 or −1). Also, correlations cannot reveal any information regarding causation. Merely because two factors are correlated, it does not mean that one factor causes the other. Consider, for example, ice cream consumption and swimming pool use. These two variables are positively correlated with one another, in that as ice cream consumption increases, so does swimming pool use. But nobody would suggest that eating ice cream *causes* swimming, or vice versa. Similarly, just because LeBron James eats Wheaties and can do a slam dunk it does not mean that you will be able to do one if you eat the same breakfast. The only way to determine the *cause* of behavior is to conduct an experiment and analyze the results by using inferential statistics.

Inferential Statistics

Knowing the descriptive statistics associated with different distributions, such as the mean and standard deviation, can enable us to make comparisons between various distributions. By making these comparisons, we may be able to observe whether one variable is related to another or whether one variable has a causal effect on another. When we design an experiment specifically to measure causal effects between two or more variables, we use *inferential statistics* to analyze the data collected. Although there are many inferential statistics, the one we will discuss is the t-test, since it is the simplest.

t-*Test* Suppose we believe that drinking alcohol causes a person's reaction time to slow down. To test this hypothesis, we recruit 20 participants and separate them into two groups. We ask the participants in one group to drink a large glass of orange juice with one ounce of alcohol for every 100 pounds of body weight (e.g., a person weighing 150 pounds would get 1.5 ounces of alcohol). We ask the control group to drink an equivalent amount of orange juice with no alcohol added. Fifteen minutes after the drinks, we have each participant perform a reaction time test that consists of pushing a button as soon as a light is flashed. (The reaction time is the time between the onset of the light and the pressing of the button.) **Table A.10** shows the data from this hypothetical experiment. It is clear from the data that there is definitely a difference in the reaction times of the two groups: There is an obvious difference between the means. However, it is possible that this difference is due merely to chance. To determine whether the difference is real or due to chance, we can conduct a *t*-test. We have run a sample *t*-test in Table A.10.

The logic behind a *t*-test is relatively simple. In our experiment we have two samples. If each of these samples is from the *same* population (e.g., the population of all people, whether drunk or sober), then any difference between the samples will be due to chance. On the other hand, if the two samples are from *different* populations (e.g., the population of drunk individuals *and* the population of sober individuals), then the difference is a significant difference and not due to chance.

If there is a significant difference between the two samples, then the independent variable must have caused that difference. In our example, there is a significant difference between the alcohol and the no alcohol groups. We can tell this because p (the probability that this t value will occur by chance) is less than .05. To obtain the p, we need only look up the t value in a statistical table, which is found in any statistics book. In our example, because there is a significant difference between the groups, we can reasonably conclude that the alcohol did cause a slower reaction time.

TABLE A.10 REACTION TIMES IN MILLISECONDS (MSEC) FOR PARTICIPANTS IN ALCOHOL AND NO ALCOHOL CONDITIONS AND COMPUTATION OF t

RT (msec) Alcohol X_1	RT (msec) No Alcohol X_2
200	143
210	137
140	179
160	184
180	156
187	132
196	176
198	148
140	125
159	120
$SX_1 = 1{,}770$	$SX_2 = 1{,}500$
$N_1 = 10$	$N_2 = 10$
$\bar{X}_1 = 177$	$\bar{X}_2 = 150$
$s_1 = 24.25$	$s_2 = 21.86$
$\Sigma_{\bar{X}1} = \frac{s}{\sqrt{N_1 - 1}} = 8.08$	$\Sigma_{\bar{X}2} = \frac{s}{\sqrt{N_2 - 1}} = 7.29$

$$S_{\bar{X}_1 - \bar{X}_2} = \sqrt{S_{\bar{X}_1}^2 + S_{\bar{X}_2}^2} = \sqrt{8.08^2 + 7.29^2} = 10.88$$

$$t = \frac{\bar{X}_1 - \bar{X}_2}{S_{\bar{X}1 - \bar{X}2}} = \frac{177 - 150}{10.88} = 2.48$$

$t = 2.48, p < .05$

Appendix B

ANSWERS TO SELF-TEST RETRIEVAL PRACTICE QUESTIONS AND RESEARCH CHALLENGES

Chapter 1 Introduction and Research Methods

Self-Test—*Introducing Psychology* (p. 13) 1. d. 2. a. 3. c. 4. a. **Self-Test—*The Science of Psychology* (p. 17)** 1. c. 2. d. 3. b. 4. Step 1 = Observation and literature review, Step 2 = Testable hypothesis, Step 3 = Research design, Step 4 = Data collection and analysis, Step 5 = Publication, Step 6 = Theory development. **Self-Test—*Research Methods* (p. 27)** 1. b. 2. b. 3. c. 4. d. 5. b. **Self-Test—*Strategies for Student Success* (p. 30)** 1. Survey, Question, Read, Recite, Review, and wRite. 2. a. 3. d. 4. a. ***Research Challenge* (p. 25)**. Question 1: Study 1 = experimental; Study 2 = descriptive and correlational. As you'll discover in later psychology classes, descriptive and correlational studies often overlap. Question 2: Study 1: IV = political similarity; DV = interest in dating, ratings of physical attractiveness. Study 2: If you chose descriptive, the answer is archival research. If you chose correlational, this is a positive correlation.

Chapter 2 Neuroscience and Biological Foundations

Self-Test—*Our Genetic Inheritance* (pp. 36–37) 1. b. 2. d. 3. a. 4. a. **Self-Test—*Neural Bases of Behavior* (p. 42)** 1. c. 2. b. 3. c. 4. b. **Self-Test—*Nervous System Organization* (p. 48)** 1. c. 2. d. 3. d. 4. a. **Self-Test—*A Tour Through the Brain* (pp. 57–58)** 1. Compare your answers to Figure 2.19 (p. 49). 2. Compare your answers to Figure 2.24 (p. 53). 3. b. 4. d. ***Research Challenge* (p. 54)**. Question 1: Descriptive. Question 2: Case study.

Chapter 3 Stress and Health Psychology

Self-Test—*Understanding Stress* (pp. 68–69) 1. d. 2. c. 3. c. 4. b. **Self-Test—*Stress and Illness* (p. 74)** 1. d. 2. d. 3. c. 4. b. **Self-Test—*Health Psychology and Stress Management* (p. 79)** 1. d. 2. a. 3. b. 4. d. ***Research Challenge* (p. 70)**. Question 1: Descriptive and correlational. As you'll discover in later psychology classes, descriptive and correlational studies often overlap. Question 2: If you chose descriptive, the answer is survey/interview. If you chose correlational, this is a positive correlation.

Chapter 4 Sensation and Perception

Self-Test—*Understanding Sensation* (p. 89) 1. a. 2. c. 3. a. 4. b. **Self-Test—*How We See and Hear* (pp. 94–95)** 1. Compare your answers to Figure 4.8 (p. 91). 2. c. 3. Compare your answers to Figure 4.9 (p. 93). 4. c. **Self-Test—*Our Other Important Senses* (p. 99)** 1. c. 2. c. 3. d. 4. d. **Self-Test—*Understanding Perception* (p. 108–109)** 1. c. 2. b. 3. a. 4. b. 5. b. ***Research Challenge* (p. 97)**. Question 1: Experimental. Question 2: IV = whether and when drank carrot juice. DV = liking of carrot-flavored cereal, amount of cereal eaten. Note that experiments, like this one, often contain more than one level (or treatment) for the independent variable (IV), as well as multiple measures for the dependent variable (DV).

Chapter 5 States of Consciousness

Self-Test—*Consciousness, Sleep, and Dreaming* (pp. 125–126) 1. b. 2. d. 3. c. 4. a. **Self-Test—*Psychoactive Drugs* (pp. 132–133)** 1. a. 2. c. 3. a. 4. d. **Self-Test—*Meditation and Hypnosis* (p. 136)** 1. d. 2. d. 3. c. 4. c. ***Research Challenge* (p. 116)**. Question 1: Study 1 = Descriptive. Study 2 = Experimental. Question 2: Study 1 = Naturalistic observation. Study 2: IV = condition (no cell phone, cell phone, intoxicated). DV = number of accidents, brake reaction time, speed. Note that experiments, like this one, often contain more than one level (or treatment) for the independent variable (IV), as well as multiple measures for the dependent variable (DV).

Chapter 6 Learning

Self-Test—*Classical Conditioning* (p. 159) 1. c. 2. c. 3. d. 4. d. **Self-Test—*Operant Conditioning* (pp. 167–168)** 1. b. 2. a. 3. c. 4. c. **Self-Test—*Cognitive-Social Learning* (p. 172)** 1. c. 2. c. 3. a. 4. b. **Self-Test—*Biology of Learning* (p. 175)** 1. d. 2. b. 3. d. 4. c. ***Research Challenge* (p. 171)**. Question 1: Descriptive. Question 2: Survey/interview.

Chapter 7 Memory

Self-Test—*The Nature of Memory* (p. 188) 1. d. 2. a. 3. b. 4. c. **Self-Test—*Forgetting* (p. 193)** 1. a. 2. b. 3. c. 4. b. **Self-Test—*Biological Bases of Memory* (p. 199)** 1. c. 2. d. 3. d. 4. c. **Self-Test—*Memory Distortions* (p. 204)** 1. c. 2. a. 3. c. 4. d. ***Research Challenge* (p. 202)**. Question 1: Descriptive. Question 2: Survey/interview.

Chapter 8 Thinking, Language, and Intelligence

Self-Test—*Thinking* (p. 215) 1. c. 2. b. 3. a. 4. d. **Self-Test—*Language* (p. 221)** 1. d. 2. a. 3. b. 4. d. **Self-Test—*Intelligence* (p. 233)** 1. d. 2. b. 3. c. 4. d. ***Research Challenge* (p. 231)**. Question 1: Descriptive. Question 2: Archival research.

Chapter 9 Lifespan Development

Self-Test—*Studying Development* (p. 242) 1. d. 2. d. 3. a. 4. c. **Self-Test—*Physical Development* (pp. 250–251)** 1. b. 2. d. 3. a. 4. c. 5. d. **Self-Test—*Cognitive Development* (p. 259)** 1. c. 2. d. 3. d. 4. c. **Self-Test—*Social-Emotional Development* (pp. 269–270)** 1. a. 2. d. 3. c. 4. b. ***Research Challenge* (p. 239)**. Question 1: Descriptive. Question 2: Case study.

Chapter 10 Motivation and Emotion

Self-Test—*Theories of Motivation* (p. 279) 1. a 2. d. 3. b. 4. d. **Self-Test—*Motivation and Behavior* (p. 290)** 1. a. 2. c. 3. c. 4. c. **Self-Test—*Components and Theories of Emotion* (p. 298)** 1. a. 2. a. 3. d. 4. a. ***Research Challenge* (p. 286)**. Question 1: Descriptive. Question 2: Survey/interview.

Chapter 11 Personality

Self-Test—*Psychoanalytic/Psychodynamic Theories* (pp. 308–309) 1. d. 2. b. 3. d. 4. c. 5. c. **Self-Test—*Trait Theories* (p. 313)** 1. c. 2. a. 3. d. 4. e. **Self-Test—*Humanistic Theories* (p. 317)** 1. a. 2. c. 3. c. 4. c. **Self-Test—*Social-Cognitive Theories* (p. 320)** 1. c. 2. d. 3. b. 4. a. **Self-Test—*Biological Theories* (p. 323)** 1. b. 2. d. 3. a. 4. b. **Self-Test—*Personality Assessment* (p. 329)** 1. d. 2. a. 3. d. 4. b. ***Research Challenge* (p. 311)**. Question 1: Descriptive and correlational. As you'll discover in later psychology classes, descriptive and correlational studies often overlap. Question 2: If you chose descriptive, the answer is naturalistic observation. If you chose correlational, this is a positive correlation.

Chapter 12 Psychological Disorders

Self-Test—*Studying Psychological Disorders* (p. 340) 1. c. 2. b. 3. a. 4. Compare your answers with Figure 12.2 (p. 334). **Self-Test—*Anxiety Disorders* (p. 344)** 1. Compare your answers with Figure 12.4 (p. 341). 2. a. 3. a. 4. c. **Self-Test—*Depressive and Bipolar Disorders* (p. 350)** 1. c. 2. a. 3. d. 4. d. **Self-Test—*Schizophrenia* (p. 355)** 1. a. 2. c. 3. b. 4. a. **Self-Test—*Other Disorders* (pp. 359–360)** 1. b. 2. a. 3. b. 4. d. **Self-Test—*Gender and Cultural Effects* (p. 364)** 1. d. 2. d. 3. a. 4. b. ***Research Challenge*** (p. 337). Question 1: Descriptive. Question 2: Survey/interview.

Chapter 13 Therapy

Self-Test—*Talk Therapies* (p. 376) 1. a. 2. c. 3. c. 4. b. **Self-Test—*Behavior Therapies* (pp. 380–381)** 1. b. 2. c. 3. c. 4. b. **Self-Test—*Biomedical Therapies* (p. 386)** 1. d. 2. b. 3. b. 4. c. **Self-Test—*Psychotherapy in Perspective* (p. 394)** 1. c. 2. c. 3. a. 4. d. ***Research Challenge* (p. 388)**. Question 1: Experimental. Question 2: IV = condition (whether completed writing exercises or not). DV = change in marital satisfaction.

Chapter 14 Social Psychology

Self-Test—*Social Cognition* (pp. 403–404) 1. c. 2. c. 3. a. 4. a. cognitive, b. affective, c. behavioral. 5. b. **Self-Test—*Social Influence* (pp. 412–413)** 1. c. 2. c. 3. d. 4. b. 5. c. **Self-Test—*Social Relations* (p. 425)** 1. d. 2. a. 3. d. 4. b. 5. a. ***Research Challenge* (p. 402)**. Question 1: Experimental. Question 2: IV = amount paid ($1, $20). DV = attitudes towards the task.

Glossary

Abnormal behavior Patterns of behaviors, thoughts, or emotions considered pathological (diseased or disordered) for one or more of these four reasons: deviance, dysfunction, distress, or danger.

Absolute threshold The minimum amount of stimulation necessary to consciously detect a stimulus 50% of the time.

Accommodation According to Piaget, the process of adjusting (accommodating) existing mental patterns (schemas) or developing new ones to better fit with new information; works in tandem with assimilation (Chapter 9).

Accommodation The process by which the eye's ciliary muscles change the shape (thickness) of the lens so that light is focused on the retina; adjustment of the eye's lens permitting focusing on near and distant objects (Chapter 4).

Achievement motivation The desire to excel, especially in competition with others.

Acquisition The final step in a classical conditioning experiment during which the conditioned stimulus (CS) elicits the conditioned response (CR).

Action potential A neural impulse, or brief electrical charge, that carries information along the axon of a neuron; movement is generated when positively charged ions move in and out through channels in the axon's membrane.

Activation–synthesis hypothesis of dreams The perspective that dreams are by-products of random stimulation of brain cells, which the brain attempts to combine (or synthesize) into coherent patterns, known as dreams.

Active listening Listening with total attention to what another is saying; it includes reflecting, paraphrasing, and clarifying what the person says and means.

Actor–observer effect The tendency to attribute one's own actions to external (situational) factors while attributing others' actions to internal (dispositional) causes.

Adaptation/protection theory of sleep The theory that sleep evolved to conserve energy and provide protection from predators.

Addiction A broad term that describes a condition in which the body requires a drug (or specific activity) in order to function without physical and psychological reactions to its absence; it is often the outcome of tolerance and dependence.

Ageism Prejudice or discrimination based on physical age; similar to racism and sexism in its negative stereotypes.

Aggression Any behavior intended to cause psychological or physical harm to another individual.

Agonist drug A drug that binds to a receptor and triggers a response in the cell; a substance that mimics or enhances a neurotransmitter's effect.

AIDS (Acquired Immunodeficiency Syndrome) A disease in which human immunodeficiency virus (HIV) destroys the immune system's ability to fight other diseases, thus leaving the body vulnerable to a variety of opportunistic infections and cancers.

Algorithm A logical, step-by-step procedure that, if followed correctly, will always eventually solve the problem.

Alternate state of consciousness (ASC) A mental state, other than ordinary waking consciousness, that occurs during sleep, dreaming, psychoactive drug use, and hypnosis.

Altruism Prosocial behaviors designed to help others, with no obvious benefit to the helper.

Alzheimer's disease (AD) A chronic organic brain syndrome characterized by gradual loss of memory, decline in intellectual ability, and deterioration of personality.

Amygdala A part of the limbic system structure linked to the production and regulation of emotions; also responsible for the formation of emotional memory.

Androgyny [an-DRAH-juh-nee] Exhibiting both masculine and feminine traits; from the Greek *andro* for "male" and *gyn* for "female."

Anorexia nervosa An eating disorder characterized by severe loss of weight resulting from self-imposed starvation and an obsessive fear of obesity.

Antagonist drug A drug that binds to a receptor and triggers a response in the cell, which blocks a neurotransmitter's effect.

Anterograde amnesia The inability to form new memories after a brain injury; forward-acting amnesia.

Antianxiety drugs Medications used to reduce anxiety and decrease overarousal in the brain.

Antidepressant drugs Medications used to treat depression, some anxiety disorders, and certain eating disorders (such as bulimia).

Antipsychotic drugs Medications used to diminish or eliminate hallucinations, delusions, withdrawal, and other symptoms of psychosis; also known as neuroleptics or major tranquilizers.

Antisocial personality disorder The pervasive pattern of disregard for, and violation of, the rights of others beginning in childhood or early adolescence and continuing into adulthood; includes traits like unlawful behaviors, deceitful and manipulative behaviors, impulsivity, irritability and aggressiveness, consistent irresponsibility, reckless disregard for self and others, and lack of remorse.

Anxiety disorder A mental disorder characterized by overwhelming tension and irrational fear accompanied by physiological arousal.

Applied research Research that is generally conducted outside the laboratory; its data are typically used for real world application.

Approach–approach conflict The forced choice between two options, both of which have equally desirable characteristics.

Approach–avoidance conflict The forced choice within one option, which has equally desirable and undesirable characteristics.

Archetypes According to Jung, the universal, inherited, primitive, and symbolic representations of a particular experience or object, which reside in the collective unconscious.

Archival research A descriptive research approach that studies existing data to find answers to research questions.

Artificial concept A clearly defined concept based on a set of logical rules; also known as a formal concept.

Assertiveness The act of confidently and directly standing up for your rights, or putting forward your views, without infringing on the rights or views of others; striking a balance between passivity and aggression.

Assimilation In Piaget's theory, applying existing mental patterns (schemas) to new information; new information is incorporated (assimilated) into existing schemas; works in tandem with accommodation.

Association areas The "quiet" areas in the cerebral cortex involved in interpreting, integrating, and acting on information processed by other parts of the brain.

Attachment A strong emotional bond with special others that endures over time.

Attitude The learned predisposition to respond cognitively, affectively, and behaviorally to a particular object, person, place, thing, or event in an evaluative way.

Attribution The principles we follow when making judgments about the causes of events, others' behavior, and our own behavior.

Audition The sense or act of hearing.

Autocratic (authoritarian) leader A leader whose leadership style generally emerges during times of crisis; such a leader makes all major decisions, assigns tasks to members of the group, and demands full obedience.

Autonomic nervous system (ANS) The subdivision of the peripheral nervous system (PNS) that controls the body's involuntary motor responses by connecting the sensory receptors to the central nervous system (CNS) and the CNS to the smooth muscle, cardiac muscle, and glands.

Availability heuristic A cognitive strategy (or shortcut) that involves making judgments based on information that is readily available in memory.

Aversion therapy A type of behavioral therapy characterized by the pairing of an aversive (unpleasant) stimulus with a maladaptive behavior in order to elicit a negative reaction to the target stimulus.

Avoidance–avoidance conflict The forced choice between two options, both of which have equally undesirable characteristics.

Axon A long, tube-like structure that conveys impulses away from a neuron's cell body toward other neurons or to muscles or glands.

Babbling The vowel/consonant combinations that infants begin to produce at about 4 to 6 months of age.

Basic anxiety According to Horney, feelings of helplessness and insecurity that adults experience because as children they felt alone and isolated in a hostile environment.

Basic research Research that typically focuses on fundamental principles and theories; most often conducted in universities and research laboratories.

Behavior therapy A group of techniques based on learning principles to change maladaptive behaviors.

Behavioral genetics The study of the relative effects of heredity and the environment on behavior and mental processes.

Behavioral perspective An approach to understanding behavior and mental processes that emphasizes objective, observable environmental influences on overt behavior.

Binge-eating disorder An eating disorder characterized by recurrent episodes of consuming large amounts of food in a discrete period of time, while feeling a lack of control, but not followed by purge behaviors.

Binocular cues Visual input from two eyes that allows perception of depth or distance.

Biological perspective An approach to understanding behavior and mental processes that focuses on genetics and biological processes in the brain and other parts of the nervous system.

Biological preparedness The built-in (innate) readiness to form associations between certain stimuli and responses.

Biomedical therapy A treatment for psychological disorders that alters brain functioning with biological or physical interventions (for example, drugs, electroconvulsive therapy, psychosurgery).

Biopsychosocial model An integrative, unifying theme of modern psychology that sees biological, psychological, and social processes as interacting influences.

Bipolar disorder A mental disorder characterized by repeated episodes of mania (unreasonable elation, often with hyperactivity) alternating with depression.

Blind spot The point at which the optic nerve leaves the eye, which contains no receptor cells for vision—thus creating a "blind spot."

Borderline personality disorder (BPD) A mental disorder characterized by severe instability in emotion and self-concept, along with impulsive and self-destructive behaviors.

Bottom-up processing Perceptual analysis that begins "at the bottom," with raw sensory data being sent "up" to the brain for higher-level analysis; it is data-driven processing that moves from the parts to the whole.

Bulimia nervosa An eating disorder characterized by recurrent episodes of consuming large quantities of food (bingeing), followed by self-induced vomiting (purging), extreme exercise, laxative use, and other medications.

Burnout A state of psychological and physical exhaustion that results from chronic exposure to high levels of stress, with little personal control.

Bystander effect A phenomenon in which the greater the number of bystanders, the less likely it is that any one individual will feel responsible for seeking help or giving aid to someone who is in need of help.

Cannon-Bard theory A theory which states that emotions and physiological changes occur simultaneously ("I'm crying and feeling sad at the same time"); in this view, all emotions are physiologically similar.

Case study An in-depth study of a single research participant or a small group of individuals.

Cataclysmic event A stressful occurrence that occurs suddenly and generally affects many people simultaneously.

Cell body The part of a neuron that contains the cell nucleus and other structures that help the neuron carry out its functions; also known as the soma.

Central nervous system (CNS) The part of the nervous system consisting of the brain and spinal cord.

Cerebellum The hindbrain structure responsible for coordinating fine muscle movement, balance, and some perception and cognition.

Cerebral cortex The thin surface layer on the cerebral hemispheres that regulates most complex behavior, including sensations, motor control, and higher mental processes.

Child sexual abuse The unlawful sexual act involving a child that is intended to provide sexual gratification to a parent, caregiver, or other individual, including physical contact and non-contact exploitation.

Chronic stress A continuous state of arousal in which demands are perceived as greater than the inner and outer resources available for dealing with them.

Chunking The process of grouping separate pieces of information into a single unit (or chunk) on the basis of similarity or some other organizing principle.

Circadian rhythm A consistent pattern of cyclical bodily activities, governed by an internal biological clock, that generally occurs on a 24- to 25-hour cycle. (*Circa* means "about," and *dies* means "day.")

Classical conditioning A type of learning that develops through involuntarily paired associations; a previously neutral stimulus (NS) is paired (associated) with an unconditioned stimulus (US) to elicit a conditioned response (CR).

Client-centered therapy Rogers's humanistic approach to therapy, which emphasizes the client's natural tendency to become healthy and productive; techniques include empathy, unconditional positive regard, genuineness, and active listening.

Cochlea [KOK-lee-uh] The fluid-filled, coiled tube in the inner ear that contains the receptors for hearing.

Coding The process in which neural impulses travel by different routes to different parts of the brain; it allows us to detect various physical stimuli as distinct sensations.

Coercive power Authority based on the ability to use or threaten punishment.

Cognition The mental activities involved in acquiring, storing, retrieving, and using knowledge.

Cognitive dissonance The unpleasant tension and anxiety caused by a discrepancy between two or more conflicting attitudes or between attitudes and behaviors.

Cognitive map A mental image of a three-dimensional space that an organism has navigated.

Cognitive perspective An approach to understanding behavior and mental processes that focuses on thinking, perceiving, and information processing.

Cognitive restructuring A process in cognitive therapy that is designed to change destructive thoughts or inappropriate interpretations.

Cognitive therapy A type of therapy that treats problem behaviors and mental processes by focusing on faulty thought processes and beliefs.

Cognitive view of dreams The perspective that dreams are a type of information processing that help interpret daily experiences and organize them into memories.

Cognitive-behavior therapy (CBT) A type of therapy that combines cognitive therapy (changing faulty thinking) with behavior therapy (changing maladaptive behaviors).

Cognitive-social learning theory A theory that emphasizes the roles of thinking and social learning.

Collective unconscious Jung's concept of the part of an individual's unconscious that is inherited, evolutionarily developed, and common to all members of the species.

Communication The interdependent process of sending, receiving, and understanding messages.

Comorbidity The co-occurrence of two or more disorders in the same person at the same time, as when a person suffers from both depression and alcoholism.

Companionate love Strong and lasting attraction characterized by deep and lasting trust, caring, tolerance, and friendship.

Concept The mental representation of a group or category.

Concrete operational stage Piaget's third stage of cognitive development (roughly age 7 to 11), in which the child can perform mental operations on concrete objects and understand reversibility and conservation, but thinking is tied to concrete, tangible objects and events.

Conditioned emotional response (CER) Through classical conditioning, an emotion, such as fear, becomes a conditioned response to a previously neutral stimulus (NS).

Conditioned response (CR) In classical conditioning, a learned reaction to a conditioned stimulus (CS) that occurs because of previous repeated pairings with an unconditioned stimulus (US).

Conditioned stimulus (CS) In classical conditioning, a previously neutral stimulus (NS) becomes conditioned through repeated pairings with an unconditioned stimulus (US), and it now elicits a conditioned response (CR).

Conditioning The process of learning associations between stimuli and behavioral responses.

Conduction hearing loss A type of hearing loss that results from damage to the mechanical system that conducts sound waves to the cochlea; also called conduction deafness.

Cones Visual receptor cells that are concentrated near the center of the retina and are responsible for color vision and fine detail; they are most sensitive in brightly lit conditions.

Confirmation bias The bias of preferring information that confirms preexisting positions or beliefs, while ignoring or discounting contradictory evidence.

Conflict A forced choice between two or more incompatible goals or impulses.

Conformity Changes in behavior, attitudes, or values because of real or imagined group pressure.

Confounding variable A stimulus, other than the variable an experimenter inadvertently introduces into a research setting, that may affect the outcome of the study and lead to erroneous conclusions.

Conscious In Freudian terms, thoughts or motives that a person is currently aware of or is remembering.

Consciousness An organism's awareness of internal events and of the external environment.

Conservation According to Piaget, the understanding that certain physical characteristics (such as volume) remain unchanged, even though appearances may change.

Consolidation The process by which neural changes associated with recent learning become durable and stable.

Constructive process The process of organizing and shaping information during processing, storage, and retrieval of memories.

Consummate love Sternberg's strongest and most enduring type of love, based on a balanced combination of intimacy, passion, and commitment.

Continuous reinforcement A reinforcement pattern in which every correct response is reinforced.

Control group The group that is not manipulated (i.e., receives no treatment) during an experiment.

Conventional level The second level of Kohlberg's theory of moral development, where moral judgments are based on compliance with the rules and values of society.

Convergence A binocular depth cue in which the eyes turn inward (or converge) to fixate on an object.

Cooing The vowel-like sounds infants produce beginning around 2 to 3 months of age.

Corpus callosum A bundle of neural fibers that connects the brain's two hemispheres.

Correlation coefficient A number from −1.00 to +1.00 that indicates the direction and strength of the relationship between two variables.

Correlational research Research that measures the degree of relationship (if any) between two or more variables in order to determine how well one variable predicts another.

Creativity The ability to produce original, appropriate, and valued outcomes in a novel way; consists of three characteristics—originality, fluency, and flexibility.

Critical period A time of special sensitivity to specific types of learning, which shapes the capacity for future development.

Critical thinking The process of objectively evaluating, comparing, analyzing, and synthesizing information.

Cross-dressing The practice of wearing clothing and adopting gender role behaviors commonly associated with the other sex.

Cross-sectional design A research technique that measures individuals of various ages at one point in time and provides information about age differences.

Crystallized intelligence (*gc*) Knowledge and skills gained through experience and education and the ability to access that knowledge; intelligence that tends to increase over the life span.

Debriefing A discussion procedure conducted at the end of an experiment or study; participants are informed of the study's design and purpose, possible misconceptions are clarified, questions answered, and explanations are provided for any possible deception.

Defense mechanisms Freud's description of the strategies the ego supposedly uses to protect itself from anxiety, which distorts reality and may increase self-deception.

Deindividuation The reduced self- consciousness, inhibition, and personal responsibility that sometimes occurs in a group, particularly when the members feel anonymous.

Delusion A false or irrational belief maintained despite clear evidence to the contrary.

Democratic (participative) leader A leader whose leadership style is to encourage group discussion and decision making through consensus.

Dendrites The branching fibers of neurons that receive neural impulses from other neurons and convey impulses toward the cell body.

Dependent variable (DV) The variable that is observed and measured for change; the factor that is affected by (or dependent on) the independent variable.

Depressant A drug that decreases bodily processes and overall responsiveness.

Depressive disorders A group of mental disorders, including disruptive mood dysregulation disorder and major depressive disorder, characterized by sad, empty, or irritable moods that interfere with the ability to function.

Depth perception The ability to perceive three-dimensional space and to accurately judge distance.

Descriptive research A research method in which the researcher observes and records behavior and mental processes without manipulating variables.

Descriptive statistics Mathematical methods used to describe and summarize sets of data in a meaningful way.

Developmental psychology The study of age-related changes in behavior, mental processes, and stages of growth, from conception to death.

Diagnostic and Statistical Manual of Mental Disorders (DSM) A classification system developed by the American Psychiatric Association that is used to describe abnormal behaviors.

Diathesis-stress model A hypothesis about the cause of certain disorders, such as schizophrenia, which suggests that people inherit a predisposition (or "diathesis") that increases their risk for mental disorders if they are exposed to certain extremely stressful life experiences.

Difference threshold The smallest physical difference between two stimuli that is consciously detectable 50% of the time; also called the *just noticeable difference* (*JND*).

Discrimination Negative behaviors directed at others because of their membership in a particular group.

Dissociative disorder A psychological disorder marked by a disturbance in the integration of consciousness, identity, memory, and other features.

Dissociative identity disorder (DID) A mental disorder characterized by the presence of two or more distinct personality systems in the same individual at different times; previously known as multiple personality disorder (MPD).

Distributed practice A study technique in which practice (or study) sessions are interspersed with rest periods.

Divergent thinking An aspect of creativity characterized by an ability to produce unusual but appropriate alternatives from a single starting point.

Double-blind study An experimental technique in which both the researcher and the participants are unaware of (blind to) who is in the experimental or control groups.

Dream analysis In psychoanalysis, interpretation of the underlying true meaning of dreams to reveal unconscious processes.

Drive-reduction theory The theory that motivation begins with a physiological need (a lack or deficiency) that elicits a drive toward behavior that will satisfy the original need; once the need is met, a state of balance (homeostasis) is restored, and motivation decreases.

Drug abuse Drug taking that causes emotional or physical harm to the drug user or others.

Eclectic approach A perspective on therapy that combines techniques from various theories to find the most appropriate treatment.

Ego In Freud's theory, the rational, decision-making component of personality that operates according to the reality principle; from the Latin term *ego*, meaning "I."

Egocentrism In cognitive development, the inability to take the perspective of another person; a hallmark of Piaget's preoperational stage.

Egoistic model of helping A theory which states that altruism is motivated by anticipated gain—later reciprocation, increased self-esteem, or avoidance of distress and guilt.

Elaborative rehearsal A technique for improving memory by linking new information to previously stored material; also known as deeper levels of processing.

Electroconvulsive therapy (ECT) A biomedical therapy based on passing electrical current through the brain; it is used almost exclusively to treat serious depression when drug therapy fails.

Embryonic period The second stage of prenatal development, which begins after uterine implantation and lasts through the eighth week.

Emotion A complex pattern of feelings that includes arousal (heart pounding), cognitions (thoughts, values, and expectations), and expressive behaviors (smiles, frowns, and gestures).

Emotion-focused coping The strategies we use to relieve or regulate the emotional impact of a stressful situation.

Emotional intelligence (EI) The ability to perceive, appraise, express, and regulate emotions accurately and appropriately.

Empathy In Rogerian terms, an insightful awareness and ability to share another's inner experience.

Empathy–altruism hypothesis A theory which states that we help because of empathy for someone in need.

Encoding The process by which a mental representation is formed in memory.

Encoding, storage, and retrieval (ESR) model A memory model which suggests that memory is formed through three processes: *encoding* (getting information in), *storage* (retaining information for future use), and *retrieval* (recovering information).

Encoding-specificity principle The principle that retrieval of information is improved if cues received at the time of recall are consistent with those present at the time of encoding.

Endocrine system A network of glands located throughout the body that manufacture and secrete hormones into the bloodstream.

Endorphin A chemical substance in the nervous system similar in structure and action to opiates; involved in pain control, pleasure, and memory.

Episodic memory A subsystem of long-term memory (LTM) that stores autobiographical events and the contexts in which they occurred; a mental diary of a person's life.

Equity theory A cognitive theory of work motivation which proposes that workers are motivated by a need for a sense of balance between output and input.

Ethnocentrism The belief that one's culture is typical of all cultures; also, viewing one's own ethnic group (or culture) as central and "correct" and judging others according to this standard.

Evolutionary perspective An approach to understanding behavior and mental processes that stresses natural selection, adaptation, and evolution; it assumes that mental capabilities evolved over millions of years to serve particular adaptive purposes.

Evolutionary psychology The branch of psychology that studies the application of the principles of evolution to explain behavior and mental processes.

Evolutionary theory of helping A theory which states that altruism is an instinctual behavior that has evolved because it favors survival of one's genes.

Expectancy theory A cognitive theory of work motivation which proposes that workers are motivated by the expectancy of outcomes, their desirability, and the effort needed to achieve them.

Experimental group The group that is manipulated (i.e., receives treatment) in an experiment.

Experimental research A carefully controlled scientific procedure that involves the manipulation of variables to determine cause and effect.

Experimenter bias Bias that occurs when a researcher influences research results in the expected direction.

Expert power Authority based on experience and expertise (physician, lawyer).

Explicit/declarative memory A subsystem within long-term memory (LTM) that consciously stores facts, information, and personal life experiences.

External locus of control The belief that chance or outside forces beyond our control determine our fate.

Extinction The gradual disappearance of a conditioned response (CR); it occurs when an unconditioned stimulus (US) is withheld whenever the conditioned stimulus (CS) is presented.

Extrasensory perception (ESP) The perceptual, so-called "psychic," abilities that supposedly go beyond the known senses (for example, telepathy, clairvoyance, precognition, and psychokinesis).

Extrinsic motivation Motivation based on external rewards or threats of punishment.

Facial-feedback hypothesis The hypothesis that movements of the facial muscles produce and/or intensify our subjective experience of emotion.

Feature detectors Specialized neurons that respond only to certain sensory information.

Fetal alcohol syndrome (FAS) A combination of birth defects, including organ deformities and mental, motor, and/or growth retardation, that result from maternal alcohol abuse.

Fetal period The third, and final, stage of prenatal development (eight weeks to birth); characterized by rapid weight gain in the fetus and the fine detailing of bodily organs and systems.

Five-factor model (FFM) A comprehensive descriptive personality system that includes openness, conscientiousness, extroversion, agreeableness, and neuroticism; informally called the Big Five.

Fixed interval (FI) schedule A schedule of reinforcement in which a reinforcer is delivered for the first response made after a fixed period of time.

Fixed ratio (FR) schedule A schedule of reinforcement in which a reinforcer is delivered for the first response made after a fixed number of responses.

Flashbulb memory (FBM) A recall of vivid, detailed, and near-permanent images associated with surprising or strongly emotional events; it may or may not be accurate.

Fluid intelligence (*gf*) Aspects of innate intelligence, including reasoning abilities, memory, and speed of information processing; relatively independent of education and tends to decline as people age.

Foot-in-the-door technique An initial, small request is used as a setup for a later, larger request.

Forebrain The collection of upper-level brain structures including the thalamus, hypothalamus, limbic system, and cerebral cortex.

Formal operational stage Piaget's fourth stage of cognitive development (around age 11 and beyond), characterized by abstract and hypothetical thinking.

Fovea A tiny pit in the center of the retina that is densely filled with cones; it is responsible for sharp vision.

Free association In psychoanalysis, reporting whatever comes to mind without monitoring its contents.

Frequency theory for hearing The theory that pitch perception occurs when a tone produces a rate of vibration in the basilar membrane equal to its frequency, with the result that pitch can be coded by the frequency of the neural response.

Frontal lobes The two lobes at the front of the brain that govern motor control, speech production, and higher functions, such as thinking, personality, emotion, and memory.

Frustration Unpleasant tension, anxiety, and heightened sympathetic activity that results from a blocked goal.

Frustration–aggression hypothesis A hypothesis which states that the blocking of a desired goal (frustration) creates anger that may lead to aggression.

Functional fixedness The inability to think of an object functioning other than in its usual or customary way; adversely affects problem solving and creativity.

Fundamental attribution error (FAE) The tendency of observers to overestimate the influence of internal, dispositional factors on a person's behavior, while underestimating the impact of external, situational factors.

Gate-control theory of pain The theory that pain sensations are processed and altered by certain cells in the spinal cord, which act as gates to interrupt and block some pain signals while sending others on to the brain.

Gender A psychological and sociocultural phenomenon referring to learned sex-related behaviors and attitudes of males and females.

Gender identity Our self-identification as being a man or a woman or some transgendered position between the two; usually includes awareness and acceptance of our biological sex.

Gender role A set of learned societal expectations for behaviors and attitudes considered "appropriate" for men and women and expressed publicly by an individual.

Gene A segment of DNA (deoxyribonucleic acid) that occupies a specific place on a particular chromosome and carries the code for hereditary transmission.

General adaptation syndrome (GAS) Selye's three-stage (alarm, resistance, exhaustion) reaction to chronic stress; a pattern of nonspecific, adaptational response to a continuing stressor.

General intelligence (*g*) Spearman's term for overall, general intellectual ability.

Generalized anxiety disorder (GAD) An anxiety disorder characterized by persistent, uncontrollable, and free-floating, nonspecified anxiety.

Genuineness In Rogerian terms, authenticity or congruence; the awareness of one's true inner thoughts and feelings and being able to share them honestly with others.

Germinal period The first stage of prenatal development, beginning with ovulation and followed by conception and implantation in the uterus; the first two weeks of pregnancy.

Glial cells The cells that provide structural, nutritional, and other support for neurons, as well as communication within the nervous system; also called glia or neuroglia.

Goal-setting theory The theory that setting specific and difficult, but attainable, goals leads to higher performance.

Grammar The system of rules (syntax and semantics) used to create language and communication.

Great-person theory A theory that leadership results from specific, inherited personality traits.

Group polarization The tendency for groups to make decisions that are more extreme (either riskier or more conservative), depending on the members' initial dominant tendency.

Group therapy A form of therapy in which a number of people meet together to work toward therapeutic goals.

Groupthink The faulty decision making that occurs when a highly cohesive group strives for agreement, especially if it is in line with the leader's viewpoint, and avoids inconsistent information.

Growth/development theory of sleep The theory that deep sleep (Stage 4) is correlated with physical development, including changes in the structure and organization of the brain; infants spend far more time in Stage 4 sleep than adults.

Gustation The sense or act of taste.

Habituation The brain's reduced responsiveness due to repeated stimulation of the same receptors.

Hallucination A false, imaginary sensory perception that occurs without an external, objective source.

Hallucinogen A drug that produces sensory or perceptual distortions.

Halo error The tendency to rate individuals either too high or too low based on one outstanding trait.

Hassle Any small problem of daily living that accumulates and sometimes become a major source of stress.

Hawthorne effect A change in behavior resulting from the novelty of the research situation or from simply being observed.

Health psychology A subfield of psychology that studies how people stay healthy, why they become ill, and how they respond when they become ill.

Heritability A statistical formula that provides a percentage of variation in a population attributable to genetic factors rather than to differences in the environment.

Heuristic A cognitive strategy, or "rule of thumb," often used as a shortcut for problem solving; does not guarantee a solution to a problem but does narrow the alternatives.

Hierarchy of needs Maslow's view that basic human motives form a hierarchy; the lower motives (such as physiological and safety needs) must be met before advancing to higher needs (such as belonging and self-actualization).

Higher-order conditioning A process in which a neutral stimulus (NS) becomes a conditioned stimulus (CS) through repeated pairings with a previously conditioned stimulus (CS).

Hindbrain The lower or hind region of the brain; collection of structures including the medulla, pons, and cerebellum.

Hippocampus The sea-horse shaped part of the limbic system involved in forming and retrieving memories.

HIV positive The state of being infected by the human immunodeficiency virus (HIV).

Homeostasis Our body's tendency to maintain a relatively balanced and stable internal state, such as a constant internal temperature.

Hormone Chemical messengers manufactured and secreted by the endocrine glands, which circulate in the bloodstream to produce bodily changes or maintain normal bodily functions.

HPA axis Our body's delayed stress response, involving the hypothalamus, pituitary, and adrenal cortex; also called the hypothalamic–pituitary–adrenocortical (HPA) axis.

Humanistic perspective An approach to understanding behavior and mental processes that perceives human nature as naturally positive and growth seeking; it emphasizes free will and self-actualization.

Humanistic therapy A type of therapy that emphasizes maximizing a client's inherent capacity for self-actualization by providing a non-judgmental, accepting atmosphere.

Hypnosis An alternate state of consciousness characterized by deep relaxation and a trancelike state of heightened suggestibility and intense focus.

Hypothalamus The small brain structure beneath the thalamus that helps govern drives (hunger, thirst, sex, and aggression) and hormones.

Hypothesis A tentative and testable explanation about the relationship between two or more variables; a testable prediction or question.

Id According to Freud, the primitive, unconscious component of personality that operates irrationally and acts on the pleasure principle.

Illusion A false or misleading perception shared by others in the same perceptual environment.

Implicit bias A hidden, automatic attitude that may guide behaviors independent of a person's awareness or control.

Implicit/nondeclarative memory A subsystem within long-term memory (LTM) that unconsciously stores procedural skills and simple classically conditioned responses.

Imprinting An inherited, primitive form of rapid learning (within a critical period) in which some infant animals physically follow and form an attachment to the first moving object they see and/or hear.

Incentive theory The theory that motivation results from external stimuli that "pull" an organism in certain directions.

Independent variable (IV) The variable that is manipulated to determine its causal effect on the dependent variable; also called the treatment variable.

Industrial/organizational (I/O) psychology The field of psychology concerned with the development and application of scientific principles to the workplace.

Inferiority complex Adler's idea that feelings of inferiority develop from early childhood experiences of helplessness and incompetence.

Inferential statistics Mathematical procedures that provide a measure of confidence about how likely it is that a certain result appeared by chance.

Informational social influence Conformance to a group out of a need for information and direction.

Informed consent A participant's agreement to take part in a study after being told what to expect.

Ingroup favoritism Viewing members of the ingroup more positively than members of an outgroup.

Inner ear The semicircular canals, vestibular sacs, and cochlea, which generate neural signals that are sent to the brain.

Insanity The legal (not clinical) designation for the state of an individual judged to be legally irresponsible or incompetent to manage his or her own affairs because of mental illness.

Insight A sudden understanding or realization of how a problem can be solved.

Insomnia A sleep disorder characterized by persistent problems falling asleep, staying asleep, or awakening too early.

Instinct Fixed, unlearned response patterns found in almost all members of a species.

Instinctive drift The tendency for conditioned responses to revert (drift back) to innate response patterns.

Intelligence The global capacity to think rationally, act purposefully, profit from experience, and deal effectively with the environment.

Intelligence quotient (IQ) An index of intelligence initially derived from standardized tests and by dividing mental age by chronological age and then multiplying by 100; now derived by comparing individual scores with the scores of others of the same age.

Internal locus of control The belief that we control our own fate.

Interpersonal attraction Positive feelings toward another.

Interpretation A psychoanalyst's explanation of a patient's free associations, dreams, resistance, and transference; more generally, any statement by a therapist that presents a patient's problem in a new way.

Intrinsic motivation Motivation resulting from internal, personal satisfaction from a task or activity.

James-Lange theory A theory of emotion which suggests that the subjective experience of emotion results from physiological changes rather than being their cause ("I feel sad because I'm crying"); in this view, each emotion is physiologically distinct.

Job analysis A detailed description of the tasks involved in a job, as well as the knowledge, skills, abilities, and other personal characteristics (KSAOs) a successful employee must possess.

Kinesics A form of nonverbal communication using the body language and gestures of a particular culture.

Kinesthesis The sense, located in muscles, joints, and tendons, that detects bodily posture, orientation, and movement of body parts relative to each other.

Laissez-faire leader A leader whose leadership style features minimal involvement in the decision-making process; such a leader encourages worker to self-manage.

Language A form of communication using sounds and symbols combined according to specified rules.

Language acquisition device (LAD) According to Chomsky, an innate mechanism that enables a child to analyze language and extract the basic rules of grammar.

Latent content of dreams According to Freud, a dream's unconscious, hidden meaning transformed into symbols within the dream's manifest content (story line).

Latent learning Hidden learning that exists without behavioral signs.

Law of effect Thorndike's rule that responses that produce a satisfying effect are more likely to occur again, whereas those that produce a discomforting effect become less likely to occur again.

Leadership The process of using interpersonal influence to inspire or persuade others to support the goals and perform the tasks desired by the leader.

Learned helplessness Seligman's term for a state of helplessness or resignation, in which human or nonhuman animals learn that escape from something painful is impossible; the organism stops responding and may become depressed.

Learning A relatively permanent change in behavior or mental processes caused by experience.

Learning/memory theory of sleep The theory that sleep is important for learning and for the consolidation, storage, and maintenance of memories.

Legitimate power Authority based on a job title or position (president, police officer).

Limbic system The interconnected group of forebrain structures involved with emotions, drives, and memory, as well as major physiological functions.

Lobotomy An outmoded neurosurgical procedure for mental disorders, which involved cutting nerve pathways between the frontal lobes and the thalamus and hypothalamus.

Long-term memory (LTM) The third stage of memory, which stores information for long periods of time; the capacity is virtually limitless, and the duration is relatively permanent.

Long-term potentiation (LTP) A long-lasting increase in neural excitability, which may be a biological mechanism for learning and memory.

Longitudinal design A research design that measures a single individual or group of individuals over an extended period and gives information about age changes.

Maintenance rehearsal The memory-improvement technique of repeating information over and over to maintain it in short-term memory (STM).

Manifest content of dreams In Freudian dream analysis, the "surface," or remembered, story line, which contains symbols that mask the dream's latent content (the true meaning).

Massed practice A study technique in which time spent learning is grouped (or massed) into long, unbroken intervals; also known as cramming.

Maturation The continuing influence of heredity throughout development; age-related physical and behavioral changes characteristic of a species.

Mean The arithmetic average of a distribution, which is obtained by adding the values of all the scores and dividing by the number of scores (N).

Median The halfway point in a set of data; half the scores fall above the median, and half fall below it.

Medical model The diagnostic perspective which assumes that diseases (including mental illness) have physical causes that can be diagnosed, treated, and possibly cured.

Meditation A group of techniques designed to alter consciousness; it's believed to enhance self-knowledge and well-being through reduced self-awareness.

Medulla The hindbrain structure responsible for vital, automatic functions, such as respiration and heartbeat.

Memory The internal record or representation of some prior event or experience; the mental capacity to encode, store, and retrieve information.

Mental image The mental representation of a previously stored sensory experience, including visual, auditory, olfactory, tactile, motor, or gustatory imagery (for example, visualizing a train and hearing its horn).

Mental set A problem-solving strategy that has worked in the past, which we continue to use rather than try new strategies.

Mere-exposure effect A developed preference for people or things simply because they are familiar.

Meta-analysis A statistical technique for combining and analyzing data from many studies in order to determine overall trends.

Midbrain The collection of structures in the middle of the brain responsible for coordinating movement patterns, sleep, and arousal.

Middle ear The hammer, anvil, and stirrup structures of the ear, which concentrate eardrum vibrations onto the cochlea's oval window.

Mindfulness-based stress reduction (MBSR) A stress reduction strategy based on developing a state of consciousness that attends to ongoing events in a receptive and non-judgmental way.

Minnesota Multiphasic Personality Inventory (MMPI) The most widely researched and clinically used self-report personality test. (MMPI-2 is the revised version.)

Mirror neuron A type of neuron that fires (or activates) when an action is performed, as well as when observing the actions or emotions of another; believed to be responsible for empathy, imitation, language, and the deficits of some mental disorders.

Misinformation effect A memory distortion that results from misleading post-event information.

Mnemonic A strategy or device that uses familiar information during the encoding of new information to enhance subsequent access to the information in memory.

Mode The score that occurs most frequently in a data set.

Modeling therapy A type of therapy characterized by watching and imitating models that demonstrate desirable behaviors.

Monocular cues Visual input from a single eye alone that contributes to perception of depth or distance.

Mood-stabilizer drugs Medications used to treat the combination of manic episodes and depression characteristic of bipolar disorders.

Morality principle In Freudian terms, the principle on which the superego operates; feelings of guilt result if its rules are violated.

Morpheme The smallest meaningful unit of language; formed from a combination of phonemes.

Motivation A set of factors that activate, direct, and maintain behavior, usually toward some goal.

Myelin sheath The layer of fatty insulation wrapped around the axon of some neurons that increases the rate at which neural impulses travel along the axon.

Narcolepsy The sudden and irresistible compulsion to sleep during the daytime. (*Narco* means "numbness," and *lepsy* means "seizure.")

Natural selection The process by which heritable traits that increase an organism's chances of survival or reproduction are favored over less beneficial traits.

Naturalistic observation The process of observing and recording a research participant's behavior and mental processes in his or her natural setting, without interfering.

Nature–nurture controversy An ongoing dispute about the relative contributions of nature (heredity) and nurture (environment) in determining the development of behavior and mental processes.

Negative punishment The taking away (or removing) of a stimulus, thereby weakening a response and making it less likely to recur.

Negative reinforcement The taking away (or removing) of a stimulus, thereby strengthening a response and making it more likely to recur.

Neurogenesis The process by which new neurons are generated.

Neuron The basic building block (nerve cell) of the nervous system, responsible for receiving, processing, and transmitting electrochemical information.

Neuroplasticity The brain's ability to reorganize and change its structure and function throughout the life span.

Neurosis An outmoded term and category dropped from *DSM-*111, in which a person does not have signs of brain abnormalities and does not display grossly irrational thinking or violate basic norms but does experience subjective distress.

Neurotransmitter A chemical messenger released by neurons that travels across the synapse and allows neurons to communicate with one another.

Neutral stimulus (NS) A stimulus that, before conditioning, does not naturally bring about the response of interest.

Nightmares Anxiety-arousing dreams that generally occur near the end of the sleep cycle, during REM sleep.

Non-rapid-eye-movement (NREM) sleep Stages 1 through 4 of sleep during which a sleeper does not show rapid eye movements.

Nonverbal communication The process of sending and receiving messages through means other than words.

Normal distribution A symmetrical, bell-shaped curve that represents a set of data in which most scores occur in the middle of the possible range, with fewer and fewer scores near the extremes.

Normative social influence Conformance to group pressure out of a need to be liked, accepted, and approved of by others.

Obedience Following direct commands, usually from an authority figure.

Obesity Having a body mass index of 30 or above, based on height and weight.

Object permanence The Piagetian term for an infant's recognition that objects (or people) continue to exist even when they cannot be seen, heard, or touched directly.

Observational learning The learning of new behaviors or information by watching and imitating others (also known as social learning or modeling).

Obsessive-compulsive disorder (OCD) A mental disorder characterized by persistent, anxiety-provoking thoughts that will not go away (obsessions) and/or irresistible urges to perform repetitive behaviors (compulsions) performed according to certain rules or in a ritualized manner; compulsive behaviors persist because they help relieve the anxiety created by the obsessions.

Occipital lobes The two lobes at the back of the brain that are primarily responsible for vision and visual perception.

Olfaction The sense or act of smelling.

Operant conditioning Learning through voluntary behavior and its subsequent consequences; reinforcement increases behavioral tendencies, whereas punishment decreases them.

Operational definition A precise description of how the variables in a study will be observed, manipulated, and measured.

Opiate A drug derived from opium that numbs the senses and relieves pain.

Opponent-process theory of color The theory that all color perception is based on three systems, each of which contains two color opposites (red versus green, blue versus yellow, and black versus white).

Optimal-arousal theory The theory that organisms are motivated to achieve and maintain an optimal level of arousal.

Organizational citizenship behavior (OCB) Actions that go beyond formal job requirements and are beneficial to an organization.

Organizational culture A group's shared pattern of thought and action; common perception held by the organization's members.

Organizational psychology A branch of the I/O field of psychology that focuses on the employee within the social context of the workplace.

Outer ear The pinna, auditory canal, and eardrum structures which funnel sound waves to the middle ear.

Outgroup homogeneity effect Judging members of an outgroup as more alike and less diverse than members of the ingroup.

Overextension The overly broad use of a word to include objects that do not fit the word's meaning (or example, calling all men "Daddy").

Overgeneralization The grammatical error of applying the basic rules of grammar even to cases that are exceptions to the rule (for example, saying "mans" instead of "men"); also known as overregularization.

Panic disorder An anxiety disorder in which sufferers experience sudden and inexplicable panic attacks; symptoms include difficulty breathing, heart palpitations, dizziness, trembling, terror, and feelings of impending doom.

Paralanguage A form of nonverbal communication that includes pace, pitch, volume, tone of voice and inflection.

Paraphilic disorder Any of a group of psychosexual disorders characterized by distress about one's sexual interests, including disturbing and repetitive sexual fantasies, urges, or behaviors.

Parasympathetic nervous system The subdivision of the autonomic nervous system (ANS) that is responsible for calming the body and conserving energy.

Parietal lobes The two lobes located at the top of the brain, in which bodily sensations are received and interpreted.

Partial (intermittent) reinforcement A reinforcement pattern in which some, but not all, correct responses are reinforced.

Participant bias Bias that can occur when experimental conditions influence the participant's behavior or mental processes.

Perception The processes of selecting, organizing, and interpreting sensory information into meaningful patterns; interpreting sensory images as having been produced by stimuli from the external, three-dimensional world.

Perceptual constancy The ability to retain an unchanging perception of an object despite changes in the sensory input.

Perceptual set The readiness to perceive in a particular manner, based on expectations.

Performance anxiety The fear of being judged in connection with sexual activities.

Performance evaluation The formal procedure used to assess employee job performance.

Peripheral nervous system (PNS) The part of the nervous system composed of the nerves and neurons connecting the central nervous system (CNS) to the rest of the body.

Personality A unique and relatively stable pattern of thoughts, feelings, and actions.

Personality disorder A mental disorder characterized by chronic, inflexible, maladaptive personality traits, which cause significant impairment of social and occupational functioning.

Personality–job fit theory The theory that job satisfaction is determined by a "good fit" between personality type and occupation.

Pheromones [FARE-oh-mones] Chemical signals released by organisms to communicate with other; they may affect behavior, including recognition of family members, aggression, territorial marking, and sexual mating.

Phobia A persistent and intense, irrational fear and avoidance of a specific object or situation.

Phoneme The smallest basic unit of speech or sound in any given language that makes a meaningful difference in speech production and reception.

Physical dependence The changes in bodily processes that make a drug necessary for minimal functioning.

Place theory for hearing The theory that pitch perception is linked to the particular spot on the cochlea's basilar membrane that is most stimulated; pitch is coded by the place at which activation occurs.

Placebo An inactive substance or fake treatment used as a control technique, usually in drug research, or given by a medical practitioner to a patient.

Pleasure principle In Freud's theory, the principle on which the id operates—seeking immediate gratification.

Polygraph An instrument that measures sympathetic arousal (heart rate, respiration rate, blood pressure, and skin conductivity) to detect emotional arousal, which in turn supposedly reflects lying versus truthfulness.

Pons The hindbrain structure involved in respiration, movement, waking, sleep, and dreaming.

Positive affect Demonstrating a sense of pleasure in the environment, including feelings of happiness, joy, enthusiasm, and contentment.

Positive psychology The study of optimal human functioning; it emphasizes positive emotions, traits, and institutions.

Positive punishment The addition (or presenting) of a stimulus, thereby weakening a response and making it less likely to recur.

Positive reinforcement The adding (or presenting) of a stimulus, thereby strengthening a response and making it more likely to recur.

Postconventional level The highest level of Kohlberg's theory of moral development, where individuals develop personal standards for right and wrong and define morality in terms of abstract principles and values that apply to all situations and societies.

Posttraumatic stress disorder (PTSD) A trauma- and stressor-related disorder that develops from directly or indirectly experiencing actual or threatened death, serious injury, or violence.

Preconscious Freud's term for thoughts, motives, or memories that exist just beneath the surface of awareness and can be called to consciousness when necessary.

Preconventional level The first level of Kohlberg's theory of moral development, where morality is based on rewards, punishment, and exchange of favors.

Prejudice A learned, generally negative, attitude toward members of a group; it includes thoughts (stereotypes), feelings, and behavioral tendencies (possible discrimination).

Premack principle The use of a naturally occurring high-frequency response to reinforce and increase low-frequency responses.

Preoperational stage Piaget's second stage of cognitive development (roughly age 2 to 7), characterized by the ability to employ significant language and to think symbolically, but the child lacks operations (reversible mental processes), and thinking is egocentric and animistic.

Primary punishers Any stimuli that decrease the probability of a response because of their innate, biological value, such as hunger and thirst.

Primary reinforcers Any stimuli that increase the probability of a response because of their innate, biological value, such as food and water.

Priming A process in which a prior exposure to a stimulus (or prime) facilitates or inhibits the processing of new information, even when one has no conscious memory of the initial learning and storage.

Proactive interference A memory error in which old information interferes with remembering new information; it is forward-acting interference.

Problem-focused coping The strategies we use to deal directly with a stressor to eventually decrease or eliminate it.

Projective test A method of personality assessment in which an individual is presented with a standardized set of ambiguous stimuli, such as inkblots or abstract drawings, which allow the test taker to project his or her unconscious onto the test material; the individual's responses are assumed to reveal inner feelings, motives, and conflicts.

Prototype The example that embodies the "best" or most typical features of a concept or category.

Proxemics The form of nonverbal communication involving physical and personal space.

Psychiatry The branch of medicine that deals with the diagnosis, treatment, and prevention of mental disorders.

Psychoactive drug A chemical that changes mental processes and conscious awareness, mood, and/or perception.

Psychoanalysis A type of psychodynamic therapy developed by Freud; an intensive and prolonged technique for bringing unconscious conflicts into conscious awareness.

Psychoanalytic perspective An approach to understanding behavior and mental processes developed by Freud, which focuses on unconscious processes and unresolved conflicts.

Psychodynamic perspective An approach to understanding behavior and mental processes that emphasizes unconscious dynamics, internal motives, conflicts, and past experiences; actions are viewed as stemming from inherited instincts, biological drives, and attempts to resolve conflicts between personal needs and social requirements.

Psychodynamic therapy A type of therapy that focuses on conscious processes and current problems; a briefer, more directive, and more modern form of psychoanalysis.

Psychological dependence The psychological desire or craving to achieve a drug's effect.

Psychology The scientific study of behavior and mental processes.

Psychoneuroimmunology The interdisciplinary field that studies the effects of psychological and other factors on the immune system.

Psychopharmacology The study of the effect of drugs on behavior and mental processes.

Psychophysics The study of the link between the physical characteristics of stimuli and the psychological experience of them.

Psychosexual stages In Freudian theory, five developmental periods (oral, anal, phallic, latency, and genital) during which particular kinds of pleasures must be gratified if personality development is to proceed normally.

Psychosis A serious mental disorder characterized by extreme mental disruption and defective or lost contact with reality.

Psychosocial stages Erikson's theory that individuals pass through eight developmental stages, each involving a specific crisis that must be successfully resolved; each stage incorporates both the sexual and social aspects of an individual's development.

Psychosurgery A neurosurgical alteration of the brain to bring about desirable behavioral, cognitive, or emotional changes, which is generally used when patients have not responded to other forms of treatment; also called neurosurgery for mental disorder (NMD).

Psychotherapy Any of a group of therapies used to treat psychological disorders and to improve psychological functioning and adjustment to life.

Puberty The biological changes during adolescence that lead to an adult-sized body and sexual maturity.

Punishment The adding or taking away of a stimulus following a response, which decreases the likelihood of that response being repeated.

Random assignment A research technique that involves using chance to assign participants to experimental or control conditions, thus minimizing the possibility of biases or preexisting differences in the group.

Range A measure of the dispersion of scores between the highest and lowest scores.

Rape The unlawful act of coercing oral, anal, or vaginal penetration upon a person without consent, or upon someone incapable of giving consent (due to age or physical or mental incapacity).

Rapid-eye-movement (REM) sleep The fifth stage of sleep marked by rapid eye movements, high-frequency brain waves, paralysis of large muscles, and often dreaming.

Rational-emotive behavior therapy (REBT) Ellis's cognitive therapy that focuses on eliminating emotional reactions through logic, confrontation, and examination of irrational beliefs.

Reality principle According to Freud, the principle on which the conscious ego operates as it seeks to delay gratification of the id's impulses until appropriate outlets and situations can be found.

Reciprocal determinism Bandura's belief that a complex reciprocal interaction exists among the individual, his or her behavior, and environmental stimuli.

Reference groups The people we conform to, or go along with, because we like, admire, and want to be like them.

Referent power Authority derived from identification with another (movie stars, athletes, friends).

Reflex An innate, automatic response to a stimulus that has a biological relevance for an organism (for example, knee-jerk reflex).

Reinforcement The adding or taking away of a stimulus following a response, which increases the likelihood of that response being repeated.

Relationship-oriented leader A leader whose leadership style is to seek to maintain group morale, satisfaction, and motivation.

Reliability The degree to which a test produces similar scores each time it is used; stability or consistency of the scores produced by an instrument.

Repair/restoration theory of sleep The theory that sleep allows organisms to repair or recuperate from depleting daily waking activities.

Repetitive transcranial magnetic stimulation (rTMS) A biomedical treatment that uses repeated magnetic field pulses targeted at specific areas of the brain.

Representativeness heuristic A cognitive strategy (or shortcut) that involves making judgments based on how well an object or event matches (represents) an existing prototype in our minds.

Resistance In psychoanalysis, the inability or unwillingness of a patient to discuss or reveal certain memories, thoughts, motives, or experiences.

Reticular formation (RF) The diffuse set of neurons that helps screen incoming information and controls arousal.

Retina The light-sensitive inner surface of the back of the eye, which contains the receptor cells for vision (rods and cones).

Retinal disparity The binocular cue of distance in which the separation of the eyes causes different images to fall on each retina.

Retrieval The recovery of information from memory storage.

Retrieval cue A prompt or stimulus that aids recall or retrieval of a stored piece of information from long-term memory (LTM).

Retroactive interference A memory error in which new information interferes with remembering old information; it is backward-acting interference.

Retrograde amnesia The loss of memory for events before a brain injury; backward-acting amnesia.

Reward power Authority based on the ability to give or promise rewards.

Rods Photoreceptors concentrated in the periphery of the retina that are most active in dim illumination; rods do not produce sensation of color.

Romantic love An intense feeling of attraction to another in an erotic context.

Rorschach Inkblot Test A projective test based on 10 cards with symmetrical abstract patterns, known as inkblots, which asks respondents to describe what they "see" in the image; the participant's response is thought to be a projection of unconscious processes.

Saliency bias A type of attributional bias in which people tend to focus on the most noticeable (salient) factors when explaining the causes of behavior.

SAM system Our body's initial, rapid-acting stress response, involving the sympathetic nervous system and the adrenal medulla; called the sympatho–adreno–medullary (SAM) system.

Sample bias A bias that may occur when research participants are unrepresentative of the larger population.

Savant syndrome A condition in which a person with generally limited mental abilities exhibits exceptional skill or brilliance in some limited field.

Schedules of reinforcement Specific patterns of reinforcement (either fixed or variable) that determine when a behavior will be reinforced.

Schema The cognitive structures, framework, or "blueprints" of knowledge, regarding objects, people, and situations, which grow and differentiate with experience.

Schizophrenia A group of severe disorders involving major disturbances in perception, language, thought, emotion, and behavior.

Scientific method The cyclical and cumulative research process used for gathering and interpreting objective information in a way that minimizes error and yields dependable results.

Secondary punishers Any stimuli that decrease the probability of a response because of their learned value, such as poor grades or a parking ticket.

Secondary reinforcers Any stimuli that increase the probability of a response because of their learned value, such as money and material possessions.

Selective attention The process of filtering out and attending only to important sensory messages.

Self-actualization The humanistic term for the inborn drive to realize one's full potential and to develop all one's inherent talents and capabilities.

Self-concept A person's relatively stable self-perception, or mental model, based on life experiences, particularly the feedback and perception of others.

Self-efficacy Bandura's term for a person's learned expectation of success in a given situation; also, another term for self-confidence.

Self-help group A leaderless or nonprofessionally guided group in which members assist each other with a specific problem, as in Alcoholics Anonymous.

Self-serving bias A type of attributional bias in which people tend to take credit for their successes and externalize or deny responsibility for their failures.

Semantic memory A subsystem of long-term memory (LTM) that stores general knowledge; a mental encyclopedia or dictionary.

Sensation The process of detecting, converting, and transmitting raw sensory information from the external and internal environments to the brain.

Sensorimotor stage Piaget's first stage of cognitive development (birth to approximately age 2), in which schemas are developed through sensory and motor activities.

Sensorineural hearing loss A type of hearing loss resulting from damage to cochlea's receptor (hair) hearing cells or to the auditory nerve; also called nerve deafness.

Sensory adaptation The process by which receptor cells become less sensitive due to constant stimulation.

Sensory memory The initial memory stage, which holds sensory information; it has relatively large capacity but the duration is only a few seconds.

Serial-position effect A characteristic of memory retrieval in which information at the beginning and end of a series is remembered better than material in the middle.

Sex The biological differences between men and women, such as having a penis or vagina; also, physical activities, such as masturbation and intercourse.

Sexual dysfunction A problem that interferes with initiation of, consummation of, or satisfaction with sexual activities.

Sexual orientation Our emotional and erotic attraction, which can be primarily toward members of the same sex (homosexual, gay, lesbian), both sexes (bisexual), or the other sex (heterosexual).

Sexual prejudice A negative attitude toward an individual because of her or his sexual orientation.

Sexual response cycle Masters and Johnson's description of the four-stage bodily response to sexual arousal, which consists of excitement, plateau, orgasm, and resolution.

Sexual scripts The learned and socially constructed blueprint and guidelines for our sexual interactions.

Shaping A training method where reinforcement is delivered for successive approximations of the desired response.

Short-term memory (STM) The second memory stage, which temporarily stores sensory information and decides whether to send it on to long-term memory (LTM); its capacity is limited to five to nine items and it has a duration of about 30 seconds.

Single-blind study An experiment where only the researcher, and not the participants, knows who is in either the experimental or control group.

Sleep apnea A sleep disorder of the upper respiratory system that causes a repeated interruption of breathing during sleep; it also leads to loud snoring or poor-quality sleep and excessive daytime sleepiness.

Sleep terrors Abrupt awakenings from NREM (non-rapid-eye-movement) sleep accompanied by intense physiological arousal and feelings of panic.

Sleeper effect A memory error in which information from an unreliable source that was initially discounted later gains credibility because the source is forgotten.

Social cognition How we think about and interpret ourselves and others.

Social influence How situational factors and other people affect us.

Social psychology The branch of psychology that studies how others influence our thoughts, feelings, and actions; it also studies group and intergroup phenomena.

Social relations How we develop and are affected by interpersonal relationships.

Sociocultural perspective An approach to understanding behavior and mental processes that emphasizes the social interaction and cultural determinants of behavior and mental processes.

Somatic nervous system (SNS) A subdivision of the peripheral nervous system (PNS) that connects the central nervous system (CNS) to sensory receptors and controls skeletal muscles.

Source amnesia A memory error caused by forgetting the true source of a memory (also called source confusion or source misattribution).

Split-brain surgery The cutting of the corpus callosum to separate the brain's two hemispheres; used medically to treat severe epilepsy; also provides information on the functions of the two hemispheres.

Spontaneous recovery The sudden, reappearance of a previously extinguished conditioned response (CR) after a rest period.

SQ4R method A study technique based on six steps: Survey, Question, Read, Recite, Review, and wRite.

Standardization A set of uniform procedures for treating each participant in a test, interview, or experiment or for recording data.

Standard deviation A computed measure of how much scores in a sample differ from the mean of the sample.

Statistics The branch of applied mathematics that deals with the collection, calculation, analysis, interpretation, and presentation of numerical facts or data.

Statistical significance A statistical statement of how likely it is that a study's result occurred merely by chance.

Stem cells Immature (uncommitted) cells that have the potential to develop into almost any type of cell, depending on the chemical signals they receive.

Stereotype threat Awareness of a negative stereotype that affects oneself and may lead to impairment in performance.

Stereotypes Generalizations about a group of people in which the same characteristics are assigned to all members of the group; also, the cognitive component of prejudice.

Stimulant A drug that increases overall activity and general responsiveness.

Stimulus discrimination A conditioning process in which an organism learns to respond differently to stimuli that differ from the conditioned stimulus on some dimension.

Stimulus generalization The conditioned response (CR) is elicited not only by the conditioned stimulus (CS) but also by stimuli similar to the conditioned stimulus (CS).

Storage The retention of encoded information over time.

Stress The interpretation of specific events, called *stressors*, as threatening or challenging; the physical and psychological reactions to stress, known as the *stress response*.

Stressor A trigger or stimulus that induces stress.

Subliminal perception The perception of stimuli presented below conscious awareness.

Superego In Freud's theory, the aspect of personality that operates on the morality principle; the "conscience" that internalizes society's values, standards, and morals.

Survey/interview A research technique that questions a large sample of people to assess their behaviors and mental processes.

Sympathetic nervous system The subdivision of the autonomic nervous system (ANS) that is responsible for arousing the body and mobilizing its energy during times of stress; also called the "fight-or-flight" system.

Synapse The gap between the axon tip of the sending neuron and the dendrite and/or cell body of the receiving neuron; during an action potential, neurotransmitters are released and flow across the synapse.

Systematic desensitization A behavioral therapy technique in which a client learns to prevent the arousal of anxiety by gradually confronting the feared stimulus while relaxed.

Task-oriented leader A leader whose leadership style is characterized by direct assistance with group tasks to help reach a particular goal.

Taste-aversion A classically conditioned dislike for, and avoidance of, a specific food whose ingestion is followed by illness.

Telegraphic speech The two- or three-word sentences of young children that contain only the most necessary words.

Temporal lobes The two lobes on each side of the brain above the ears that are involved in audition (hearing), language comprehension, memory, and some emotional control.

Teratogen An environmental agent that causes damage during prenatal development; comes from the Greek word *teras*, meaning "malformation."

Thalamus The forebrain structure at the top of the brainstem that serves as the brain's switchboard, relaying sensory messages to the cerebral cortex.

Thematic Apperception Test (TAT) A projective test in which pictures of ambiguous scenes are presented to an individual, who is encouraged to generate stories about them; the responses supposedly reflect a projection of the respondent's unconscious processes.

Theory An organized, interrelated set of concepts that explain a phenomenon or body of data.

Three-stage memory model A memory model which suggests that memory storage requires passage of information through three stages (sensory, short-term, and long-term memory).

Tip-of-the-tongue (TOT) phenomenon Feeling that specific information is stored in your long-term memory but being temporarily unable to retrieve it.

Tolerance The bodily adjustment to continued use of a drug in which the drug user requires greater dosages to achieve the same effect.

Top-down processing Perceptual analysis that starts "at the top," with higher-level cognitive processes (such as expectations and knowledge), and then works down; it is conceptually driven processing that moves from the whole to the parts.

Trait A relatively stable personality characteristic that can be used to describe someone.

Transduction The process whereby sensory receptors convert stimuli into neural impulses to be sent to the brain (for example, transforming light waves into neural impulses).

Transference In psychoanalysis, the process by which a client attaches (transfers) to a therapist feelings formerly held toward some significant person who figured in a past emotional conflict.

Transgendered Being gender diverse and nonconforming to social expectations of masculinity and femininity; being between, beyond, or some combination of genders.

Transsexualism The state of being born with the biological characteristics of one sex but feeling psychologically as if belonging to the other gender; having a gender identity that does not match the biological sex.

Triarchic theory of love Sternberg's theory that different stages and types of love result from three basic components—*intimacy*, *passion*, and *commitment*.

Trichromatic theory of color The theory that color perception results from three types of cones in the retina, each most sensitive to either red, green, or blue; other colors result from a mixture of these three.

Two-factor theory Schachter and Singer's theory that emotion depends upon two factors—physiological arousal and cognitive labeling of that arousal.

Type A A pattern of behaviors and emotions that includes intense ambition, competition, exaggerated time urgency, and a cynical, hostile outlook; hostility increases the risk of coronary heart disease.

Type B A pattern of behaviors and emotions that is less competitive, less aggressive, more relaxed, and less hostile than a Type A.

Unconditional positive regard Rogers's term for complete love and acceptance of another, such as a parent for a child, with no conditions attached.

Unconditioned response (UR) In classical conditioning, a learned reaction to an unconditioned stimulus (US) that occurs without previous conditioning.

Unconditioned stimulus (US) In classical conditioning, a stimulus that elicits an unconditioned response (UR) without previous conditioning.

Unconscious Freud's term for a part of the psyche that stores repressed urges and primitive impulses.

Validity The degree to which a test measures what it is intended to measure.

Variable interval (VI) schedule A schedule of reinforcement in which a reinforcer is delivered for the first response made after a variable period of time whose average is predetermined.

Variable ratio (VR) schedule A schedule of reinforcement in which a reinforcer is delivered for the first response made after a variable number of responses whose average is predetermined.

Vestibular sense The sense, located in the inner ear, that detects body movement and position with respect to gravity; also called the sense of balance.

Wish-fulfillment view of dreams The Freudian belief that dreams provide an outlet for unacceptable desires.

Withdrawal The discomfort and distress, including physical pain and intense cravings, experienced after stopping the use of an addictive drug.

Working memory An alternate term for short-term memory (STM), which emphasizes the active processing of information.

Zone of proximal development (ZPD) In Vygotsky's theory of cognitive development, the area between what children can accomplish on their own and what they can accomplish with the help of others who are more competent.

References

Abadinsky, H. (2011). *Drug use and abuse: A comprehensive introduction* (7th ed.). Belmont, CA: Cengage.

Abadinsky, H. (2014). *Drug use and abuse: A comprehensive introduction* (8th ed.). Independence, KY: Cengage.

Abedi, J. (2013). Testing of English language learner students. In K. F. Geisinger, B. A. Bracken, J. F. Carlson, J.-I. C. Hansen, N. R. Kuncel, S. P. Reise, & M. C. Rodriguez (Eds.), *APA handbooks in psychology. APA handbook of testing and assessment in psychology, Vol. 3. Testing and assessment in school psychology and education* (pp. 355–368). Washington, DC: American Psychological Association.

Aboa-Éboulé, C. (2008). Job strain and recurrent coronary heart disease events—Reply. *Journal of the American Medical Association, 299*, 520–521.

Abrams, J. (2011). Napping is prevalent among N.B.A. players. *New York Times*, March 6. Retrieved from http://www.nytimes.com/2011/03/07/sports/basketball/07naps.html?pagewanted=all&_r=0&gwh=F4B759C38E8986D45D92E0A629B0EED2

Acerbi, A., & Nunn, C. L. (2011). Predation and the phasing of sleep: An evolutionary individual-based model. *Animal Behaviour, 81*, 801–811.

Acheson, K., Blondel-Lubrano, A., Oguey-Araymon, S., Beaumont, M., Emady-Azar, S., Ammon-Zufferey, C., . . . Bovetto, L. (2011). Protein choices targeting thermogenesis and metabolism. *The American Journal of Clinical Nutrition, 93*, 525–534.

Ackermann, K., Revell, V. L., Lao, O., Rombouts, E. J., Skene, D. J., & Kayser, M. (2012). Diurnal rhythms in blood cell populations and the effect of acute sleep deprivation in healthy young men. *Sleep, 35*, 933–940.

Adams, M. (2011). Evolutionary genetics of personality in nonhuman primates. In M. Inoue-Murayama, S. Kawamura, & A. Weiss (Eds.), *From genes to animal behavior* (pp. 137–164). Tokyo, Japan: Springer.

Adelmann, P. K., & Zajonc, R. B. (1989). Facial efference and the experience of emotion. *Annual Review of Psychology, 40*, 249–280.

Adler, A. (1964). The individual psychology of Alfred Adler. In H. L. Ansbacher & R. R. Ansbacher (Eds.), *The individual psychology of Alfred Adler*. New York: Harper & Row.

Adler, A. (1998). *Understanding human nature*. Center City, MN: Hazelden Information Education.

Adolph, K. E., & Berger, S. E. (2012). Physical and motor development. In M. H. Bornstein & M. E. Lamb (Eds.), *Cognitive development: An advanced textbook* (pp. 257–318). New York: Psychology Press.

Adolph, K. E., & Kretch, K. S. (2012). Infants on the edge. Developmental psychology: Revisiting the classic studies. Retrieved from http://www.psych.nyu.edu/adolph/publications/Adolph%20KE%20%20Kretch%20KS-Infants%20on%20the%20Edge%20Beyond%20the%20Visual%20Cliff.pdf

Adolph, K. E., Cole, W. G., Komati, M., Garciaguirre, J. S., Badaly, D., Lingeman, J. M., . . . Sotsky, R. B. (2012). How do you learn to walk? Thousands of steps and dozens of falls per day. *Psychological Science, 23*, 1387–1394.

Agartz, I., Brown, A., Rimol, L., Hartberg, C., Dale, A., Melle, I., . . . Andreassen, O. (2011). Common sequence variants in the major histocompatibility complex region associate with cerebral ventricular size in schizophrenia. *Biological Psychiatry*, 10, 696–698.

Agarwal, P. K., Bain, P. M., & Chamberlain, R. W. (2012). The value of applied research: Retrieval practice improves classroom learning and recommendations from a teacher, a principal, and a scientist. *Educational Psychology Review, 24*, 437–448.

Aggleton, J. P., O'Mara, S. M., Vann, S. D., Wright, N. F., Tsanov, M., & Erichsen, J. T. (2010). Hippocampal anterior thalamic pathways for memory: Uncovering a network of direct and indirect actions. *European Journal of Neuroscience, 31*, 2292–2307.

Agopian, A. J., Lupo, P. J., Herdt-Losavio, M. L., Langlois, P. H., Rocheleau, C. M., Mitchell, L. E., & National Birth Defects Prevention Study. (2012). Differences in folic acid use, prenatal care, smoking, and drinking in early pregnancy by occupation. *Preventive Medicine: An International Journal Devoted to Practice and Theory, 55*, 341–345.

Ahearn, W. H., & Tiger, J. H. (2013). Behavioral approaches to the treatment of autism. In G. J. Madden, W. V. Dube, T. D. Hackenberg, G. P. Hanley, & K. A. Lattal (Eds.), *APA handbook of behavior analysis, Vol. 2. Translating principles into practice* (pp. 301–327). Washington, DC: American Psychological Association.

Ahmetoglu, G., & Chamorro-Premuzic, T. (2013). *Psych 101. Personality 101*. New York: Springer.

Ahola, K., Sirén, I., Kivimäki, M., Ripatti, S., Aromaa, A., Lönnqvist, J., & Hovatta, I. (2012). Work-related exhaustion and telomere length: A population-based study. *PLoS ONE 7*: e40186.

Ainsworth, M. D. S. (1967). *Infancy in Uganda: Infant care and the growth of love*. Baltimore, MD: Johns Hopkins University Press.

Ainsworth, M. D. S. (2010). Security and attachment. In R. Volpe (Ed.), *The secure child: Timeless lessons in parenting and childhood education* (pp. 43–53). Charlotte, NC: IAP Information Age Publishing.

Ainsworth, M. D. S., Blehar, M., Waters, E., & Wall, S. (1978). *Patterns of attachment: Observations in the strange situation and at home*. Hillsdale, NJ: Erlbaum.

Akers, R. M., & Denbow, D. (2008). *Anatomy and physiology of domestic animals*. Hoboken, NJ: Wiley.

Akey, J. E., Rintamaki, L. S., & Kane, T. L. (2013). Health belief model deterrents of social support seeking among people coping with eating disorders. *Journal of Affective Disorders, 145*, 246–252.

Akins, C. K., & Panicker, S. (2012). Ethics and regulation of research with nonhuman animals. In H. Cooper, P. M. Camic, D. L. Long, A. T. Panter, D. Rindskopf, & K. J. Sher (Eds.), *APA handbook of research methods in psychology, Vol. 1. Foundations, planning, measures, and psychometrics* (pp. 75–82). Washington, DC: American Psychological Association.

Aknin, L. B., Hamlin, J. K., & Dunn, E. W. (2012). Giving leads to happiness in young children. *PLoS ONE 7*: e39211.

Alberts, A., Elkind, D., & Ginsberg, S. (2007). The personal fable and risk-taking in early adolescence. *Journal of Youth and Adolescence, 36*, 71–76.

Alcock, J. (2011). Back from the future: Parapsychology and the Bem affair. The

Committee for Skeptical Inquiry (CSI). Retrieved from http://www.csicop.org/specialarticles/show/back_from_the_future

Aldenhoff, J. (2011). Interpersonal therapy. *European Psychiatry, 26,* 1782.

Aldridge, L. J., & Islam, M. R. (2012). Cultural differences in athlete attributions for success and failure: The sports pages revisited. *International Journal of Psychology, 47,* 67–75.

Alexander, J. F., Waldron, H. B., Robbins, M. S., & Neeb, A. A. (2013). *Functional family therapy for adolescent behavior problems* (pp. 113–128). Washington, DC: American Psychological Association.

Al-Issa, I. (2000). Culture and mental illness in Algeria. In I. Al-Issa (Ed.), Al-Junun: *Mental illness in the Islamic world* (pp. 101–119). Madison, CT: International Universities Press.

Allan, R. F. J. (2011). Type A behavior pattern. In R. F. J. Allan (Ed.), *Heart and mind: The practice of cardiac psychology* (2nd ed., pp. 287–290). Washington, DC: American Psychological Association.

Allemand, M., Steiger, A. E., & Hill, P. L. (2013). Stability of personality traits in adulthood: Mechanisms and implications. *GeroPsych: The Journal of Gerontopsychology and Geriatric Psychiatry, 26,* 5–13.

Alloy, L. B., Wagner, C. A., Black, S. K., Gerstein, R. K., & Abramson, L. Y. (2011). The breakdown of self-enhancing and self-protecting cognitive biases in depression. In M. D. Alicke & C. Sedikides (Eds.), *Handbook of self-enhancement and self-protection* (pp. 358–379). New York: Guilford Press.

Allport, G. W., & Odbert, H. S. (1936). Trait-names: A psycho-lexical study. *Psychological Monographs: General and Applied, 47,* 1–21.

Almas, A. N., Degnan, K. A., Radulescu, A., Nelson, C. A., Zeanah, C. H., & Fox, N. A. (2012). Effects of early intervention and the moderating effects of brain activity on institutionalized children's social skills at age 8. *Proceedings of the National Academy of Sciences, 109,* 17228–17231.

Almela, M., Hidalgo, V., Villada, C., Espín, L., Gómez-Amor, J., & Salvador, A. (2011). The impact of cortisol reactivity to acute stress on memory: Sex differences in middle-aged people. *Stress: The International Journal on the Biology of Stress, 14,* 117–127.

Altman, N. (2013). Psychoanalytic therapy. In J. Frew & M. D. Spiegler (Eds.), *Contemporary psychotherapies for a diverse world (1st rev. ed.,* pp. 39–86). New York: Routledge/Taylor & Francis Group.

Ambady, N., & Adams, R. B., Jr. (2011). Us versus them: The social neuroscience of perceiving out-groups. In A. Todorov, S. T. Fiske, & D. A. Prentice (Eds.), *Oxford series in social cognition and social neuroscience. Social neuroscience: Toward understanding the underpinnings of the social mind* (pp. 135–143). New York: Oxford University Press.

American Heart Association (2013). *Statistical fact sheet: 2013 update.* Retrieved from: http://www.heart.org/idc/groups/heart-public/@wcm/@sop/@smd/documents/downloadable/ucm_319588.pdf

American Psychiatric Association (2013). *Diagnostic and statistical manual of mental disorders* (5th ed.). Washington, DC: American Psychiatric Association.

Amin, A. R., & Noggle, C. A. (2013). The neuropsychology of psychopathology: Historical shifts. In C. A. Noggle & R. S. Dean (Eds.), *Contemporary neuropsychology. The neuropsychology of psychopathology* (pp. 3–9). New York: Springer.

Amodio, D. M., & Hamilton, H. K. (2012). Intergroup anxiety effects on implicit racial evaluation and stereotyping. *Emotion, 12,* 1273–1280.

Amundson, J. K., & Nuttgens, S. A. (2008). Strategic eclecticism in hypnotherapy: Effectiveness research considerations. *American Journal of Clinical Hypnosis, 50,* 233–245.

Anacker, C., Zunszain, P. A., Cattaneo, A., Carvalho, L. A., Garabedian, M. J., Thuret, S., . . . Pariante, C. M. (2011). Antidepressants increase human hippocampal neurogenesis by activating the glucocorticoid receptor. *Molecular Psychiatry, 16,* 738–750.

Anderman, E., & Dawson, H. (2011). Learning with motivation. In R. Mayer & P. Alexander (Eds.), *Handbook of research on learning and instruction* (pp. 219–242). New York: Routledge.

Andersen, B. L., Thornton, L. M., Shapiro, C. L., Farrar, W. B., Mundy, B. L., Yang, H. C., & Carson, W. E. 3rd. (2010). Biobehavioral, immune, and health benefits following recurrence for psychological intervention participants. *Clinical Cancer Research, 16,* 3270–3278.

Anderson, C. A. (2001). Heat and violence. *Current Directions in Psychological Science, 10,* 33–38.

Anderson, C. A., Buckley, K. E., & Carnegey, N. L. (2008). Creating your own hostile environment: A laboratory examination of trait aggressiveness and the violence escalation cycle. *Personality and Social Psychology Bulletin, 34,* 462–473.

Anderson, J. R., Betts, S., Ferris, J. L., & Fincham, J. M. (2011). Cognitive and metacognitive activity in mathematical problem solving: Prefrontal and parietal patterns. *Cognitive, Affective and Behavioral Neuroscience, 11,* 52–67.

Anderson, M. C., Ochsner, K. N., Kuhl, B., Cooper, J., Robertson, E., Gabrieli, S. W., . . . Gabrieli, J. D. E. (2004). Neural systems underlying the suppression of unwanted memories. *Science, 303,* 232–235.

Andersson, J., & Walley, A. (2011). The contribution of heredity to clinical obesity. In R.H. Lustig (Ed.), *Obesity before birth* (pp. 25–52). New York: Springer.

Ando, J., Fujisawa, K. K., Shikishima, C., Hiraishi, K., Nozaki, M., Yamagata, S., . . . Ooki, S. (2013). Two cohort and three independent anonymous twin projects at the Keio Twin Research Center (KoTReC). *Twin Research & Human Genetics, 16,* 202–216.

Andrade, T. G., & Graeff, F. G. (2001). Effect of electrolytic and neurotoxic lesions of the median raphe nucleus on anxiety and stress. *Pharmacology, Biochemistry and Behavior, 70,* 1–14.

Andreassen, C. S., Torsheim, T., Brunborg, G. S., & Pallesen, S. (2012). Development of a Facebook addiction scale. *Psychological Reports, 110,* 501–517.

Anik, L., Aknin, L. B., Norton, M. L., & Dunn, E. W. (2011). Feeling good about giving: The benefits (and costs) of self-interested charitable behavior. In D. M. Oppenheimer & C. Y. Olivola (Eds.), *The science of giving: Experimental approaches to the study of charity. Society for Judgment and Decision Making series* (pp. 3–23). New York: Psychology Press.

Ansell, E. B., & Grilo, C. M. (2007). Personality disorders. In M. Hersen, S. M. Turner, & D. C. Beidel (Eds.), *Adult psychopathology and diagnosis* (5th ed., pp. 633–678). Hoboken, NJ: Wiley.

Antúnez, E., Palomino, A. J., Marfil, R., & Bandera, J. P. (2013). Perceptual organization and artificial attention for visual landmarks detection. *Cognitive Processing, 14,* 13 –18.

Aoyama, S., Toshima, T., Saito, Y., Konishi, N., Motoshige, K., Ishikawa, N., . . . Kobayashi, M. (2010). Maternal breast milk odour induces frontal lobe activation in neonates: A NIRS study. *Early Human Development, 86,* 541–545.

Appel, M., & Richter, T. (2007). Persuasive effects of fictional narratives increase over time. *Media Psychology, 10,* 113–134.

Arango, C., Rapado-Castro, M., Reig, S., Castro-Fornieles, J., Gonzalez-Pinto, A., Otero, S., . . . Desco, M. (2012). Progressive brain changes in children and adolescents with first-episode psychosis. *Archives of General Psychiatry,* 69, 16–26.

Archer, T. (2011). Physical exercise alleviates debilities of normal aging and Alzheimer's disease. *Acta Neurologica Scandinavica, 123,* 221–238.

Arkes, H., & Kajdasz, J. (2011). Intuitive theories of behavior. In National Research Council (Ed.), *Intelligence analysis: Behavioral and social scientific foundations* (pp. 143–168). Washington, DC: The National Academies Press.

Armony, J. L. (2013). Current emotion research in behavioral neuroscience: The role(s) of the amygdala. *Emotion Review, 5,* 104–115.

Armstrong, K., Hangauer, J., & Agazzi, H. (2013). Intellectual and developmental disabilities and other low-incidence disorders. In L. A. Reddy, A. S. Weissman, & J. B. Hale (Eds.), *Neuropsychological assessment and intervention for youth: An evidence-based approach to emotional and behavioral disorders* (pp. 227–246). Washington, DC: American Psychological Association.

Arnsten, A. F. T. (2011). Prefrontal cortical network connections: Key site of vulnerability in stress and schizophrenia. *International Journal of Developmental Neuroscience, 29,* 215–223.

Aronson, J., Jannone, S., McGlone, M., & Johnson-Campbell, T. (2009). The Obama effect: An experimental test. *Journal of Experimental Social Psychology, 45,* 957–960.

Arumugam, V., Lee, J-S., Nowak, J. K., Pohle, R. J., Nyrop, J. E., Leddy, J. J., & Pelkman, C. L. (2008). A high-glycemic meal pattern elicited increased subjective appetite sensations in overweight and obese women. *Appetite, 50,* 215–222.

Asaoka, S., Aritake, S., Komada, Y., Ozaki, A., Odagiri, Y., Inoue, S., . . . Inoue, Y. (2013). Factors associated with shift work disorder in nurses working with rapid-rotation schedules in Japan: The Nurses Sleep Health Project. *Chronobiology International, 30,* 628–636.

Asch, S. E. (1951). Effects of group pressure upon the modification and distortion of judgment. In H. Guetzkow (Ed.), *Groups, leadership, and men.* Pittsburgh, PA: Carnegie Press.

Ashley, K. B. (2013). The science on sexual orientation: A review of the recent literature. *Journal of Gay & Lesbian Mental Health, 17,* 175–182.

Åslund, C., Comasco, E., Nordquist, N., Leppert, J., Oreland, L., & Nilsson, K. W. (2013). Self-reported family socioeconomic status, the 5-HTTLPR genotype, and delinquent behavior in a community-based adolescent population. *Aggressive Behavior, 39,* 52–63.

Atkinson, R. C., & Shiffrin, R. M. (1968). Human memory: A proposed system and its control processes. In K. W. Spence & J. T. Spence (Eds.), *The psychology of learning and motivation* (Vol. 2, pp. 90–91). New York: Academic Press.

Atun-Einy, O., Berger, S. E., & Scher, A. (2012). Pulling to stand: Common trajectories and individual differences in development. *Developmental Psychobiology, 54,* 187–198.

Aunola, K., Viljaranta, J., Lehtinen, E., & Nurmi, J. E. (2013). The role of maternal support of competence, autonomy and relatedness in children's interests and mastery orientation. *Learning and Individual Differences, 25,* 171–177.

Austin, J. E., & Rini, C. (2013). Bone marrow and stem cell transplant. In A. R. Block & D. B. Sarwer (Eds.), *Presurgical psychological screening: Understanding patients, improving outcomes* (pp. 103–125). Washington, DC: American Psychological Association.

Avidan, G., Tanzer, M., Hadj-Bouziane, F., Liu, N., Ungerleider, L. G., & Behrmann, M. (2013). Selective dissociation between core and extended regions of the face processing network in congenital prosopagnosia. *Cerebral Cortex.* Retrieved from http://cercor.oxfordjournals.org/content/early/2013/01/31/cercor.bht007.full

Axtell, R. E. (2007). *Essential do's and taboos: The complete guide to international business and leisure travel.* Hoboken, NJ: Wiley.

Babula, M. W. (2013). The unlikely Samaritans. *Journal of Applied Social Psychology, 43,* 899–908.

Baddeley, A. D. (1992). Working memory. *Science, 255,* 556–559.

Baddeley, A. D. (2007). Working memory, thought, and action. *Oxford psychology series.* New York: Oxford University Press.

Baddeley, A. D. (2013). Working memory and emotion: Ruminations on a theory of depression. *Review of General Psychology, 17,* 20–27

Baer, J. (2013). Teaching for creativity: Domains and divergent thinking, intrinsic motivation, and evaluation. In M. Banks Gregerson, H. T. Snyder, & J. C. Kaufman (Eds.), *Teaching creatively and teaching creativity* (pp. 175–181). New York: Springer.

Bagermihl, B. (1999). *Biological exuberance: Animal homosexuality and natural diversity.* New York: St Martins Press.

Bagley, S. L., Weaver, T. L., & Buchanan, T. W. (2011). Sex differences in physiological and affective responses to stress in remitted depression. *Physiology and Behavior, 104,* 180–186.

Bailey, J. M., Dunne, M. P., & Martin, N. G. (2000). Genetic and environmental influences on sexual orientation and its correlates in an Australian twin sample. *Journal of Personality and Social Psychology, 78,* 524–536.

Baird, A. A. (2010). The terrible twelves. In P. D. Zelazo, M. Chandler, & E. Crone (Eds.), *Developmental social cognitive neuroscience. The Jean Piaget symposium series* (pp. 191–207). New York: Psychology Press.

Baker, D. G., Nievergelt, C. M., & O'Connor, D. T. (2011). Biomarkers of PTSD: Neuropeptides and immune signaling. *Neuropharmacology, 62,* 663–673.

Baker, D., & Nieuwenhuijsen, M. J. (Eds.) (2008). *Environmental epidemiology: Study methods and application.* New York: Oxford University Press.

Baker, S. C., & Serdikoff, S. L. (2013). Addressing the role of animal research in psychology. In D. S. Dunn, R. A. R. Gurung, K. Z. Naufel, & J. H. Wilson (Eds.), *Controversy in the psychology classroom: Using hot topics to foster critical thinking* (pp. 105–112). Washington, DC: American Psychological Association.

Baldessarini, R. J., & Tondo, L. (2008). Lithium and suicidal risk. *Bipolar Disorders, 10,* 114–115.

Bandura, A. (1969). *Principles of behavior modification.* New York: Holt, Rinehart & Winston.

Bandura, A. (1986). *Social foundations of thought and action: A social cognitive theory.* Englewood Cliffs, NJ: Prentice Hall.

Bandura, A. (1991). Human agency: The rhetoric and the reality. *American Psychologist, 46,* 157–162.

Bandura, A. (1997). *Self-efficacy: The exercise of control.* New York: Freeman.

Bandura, A. (2006). Going global with social cognitive theory: From prospect to paydirt. In D. E. Berger & K. Pezdek (Eds.), *The rise of applied psychology: New frontiers and rewarding careers* (pp. 53–79). Mahwah, NJ: Erlbaum.

Bandura, A. (2008). Reconstrual of "free will" from the agentic perspective of social cognitive theory. In J. Baer, J. C. Kaufman, & R. F. Baumeister (Eds.), *Are we free? Psychology and free will* (pp. 86–127). New York: Oxford University Press.

Bandura, A. (2012). On the functional properties of perceived self-efficacy revisited. *Journal of Management, 38,* 9–44.

Bandura, A. (2012). Social cognitive theory. In P. A. M. Van Lange, A. W. Kruglanski, &

E. T. Higgins (Eds.), *Handbook of theories of social psychology* (Vol. 1, pp. 349–373). Thousand Oaks, CA: Sage Publications.

Bankó, É. M., & Vidnyánszky, Z. (2010). Retention interval affects visual short-term memory encoding. *Journal of Neurophysiology, 103*, 1425–1430.

Banks, M. S., & Salapatek, P. (1983). Infant visual perception. In M. M. Haith & J. J. Campos (Eds.), *Handbook of child psychology*. Hoboken, NJ: Wiley.

Bao, A., & Swaab, D. (2011). Sexual differentiation of the human brain: Relation to gender identity, sexual orientation and neuropsychiatric disorders. *Frontiers in Neuroendocrinology, 32*, 214–226.

Barash, D. P., & Lipton, J. E. (2011). *Payback: Why we retaliate, redirect aggression, and take revenge*. New Yark: Oxford University Press.

Barbeau, E.-J., Puel, M., & Pariente, J. (2010). La mémoire déclarative antérograde et ses modèles [Anterograde declarative memory and its models]. *Revue Neurologique, 166,* 661–672.

Barbui, C., Cipriani, A., Patel, V., Ayuso-Mateos, J. L., & Ommeren, M. V. (2011). Efficacy of antidepressants and benzodiazepines in minor depression: Systematic review and meta-analysis. *The British Journal of Psychiatry, 198*, 11–16.

Barelds, D. P. H., & Dijkstra, P. (2011). Positive illusions about a partner's personality and relationship quality. *Journal of Research in Personality, 45*, 37–43.

Barenbaum, N. B., & Winter, D. G. (2013). Personality. In D. K. Freedheim & I. B. Weiner (Eds.), *Handbook of psychology, Vol. 1. History of psychology* (2nd ed., pp. 198–223). Hoboken, NJ: Wiley.

Barlow, D. H. (Ed.). (2008). *Clinical handbook of psychological disorders: A step-by-step treatment manual (4th ed.)*. New York: Guilford Press.

Barnes, J. (2013). *Essential biological psychology*. London, UK: Sage.

Barnow, S., & Balkir, N. (Eds.). (2013). *Cultural variations in psychopathology: From research to practice*. Cambridge, MA: Hogrefe Publishing.

Barnum, S. E., Woody, M. L., & Gibb, B. E. (2013). Predicting changes in depressive symptoms from pregnancy to postpartum: The role of brooding rumination and negative inferential styles. *Cognitive Therapy and Research, 37*, 71–77.

Barratt, B. B. (2013). *What is psychoanalysis? 100 years after Freud's 'secret committee.'* New York: Routledge/Taylor & Francis Group.

Barrouillet, P., & Camos, V. (2012). As time goes by: Temporal constraints in working memory. *Current Directions in Psychological Science, 21*, 413–419.

Bartlett, C. P., Harris, R. J., & Bruey, C. (2008). The effect of the amount of blood in a violent video game on aggression, hostility, and arousal. *Journal of Experimental Social Psychology, 44*, 539–546.

Barton, J. J. S. (2008). Prosopagnosia associated with a left occipitotemporal lesion. *Neuropsychologia, 46*, 2214–2224.

Bastien, C. H. (2011). Insomnia: Neurophysiological and neuropsychological approaches. *Neuropsychology Review, 21*, 22–40.

Bateman, C. R., & Valentine, S. R. (2010). Investigating the effects of gender on consumers' moral philosophies and ethical intentions. *Journal of Business Ethics, 95,* 393–414.

Batson, C. D. (1991). *The altruism question: Toward a social-psychological answer.* Hillsdale, NJ: Erlbaum.

Batson, C. D. (1998). Altruism and prosocial behavior. In D.T. Gilbert, S.T. Fiske, & G. Lindzey (Eds.), *The handbook of social psychology, Vol. 2* (4th ed., pp. 282–316). Boston, MA: McGraw-Hill.

Batson, C. D. (2006). "Not all self-interest after all": Economics of empathy-induced altruism. In D. De Cremer, M. Zeelenberg, & J. K. Murnighan (Eds.), *Social psychology and economics* (pp. 281–299). Mahwah, NJ: Erlbaum.

Batson, C. D. (2011). *Altruism in humans.* New York: Oxford University Press.

Baucom, B. R., Weusthoff, S., Atkins, D. C., & Hahlweg, K. (2012). Greater emotional arousal predicts poorer long-term memory of communication skills in couples. *Behaviour Research and Therapy, 50,* 442–447.

Bauer, P. J., & Lukowski, A. F. (2010). The memory is in the details: Relations between memory for the specific features of events and long-term recall during infancy. *Journal of Experimental Child Psychology, 107,* 1–14.

Baumann, M. H., Partilla, J. S., Lehner, K. R., Thorndike, E. B., Hoffman, A. F., Holy, M., . . . Schindler, C. W. (2013). Powerful cocaine-like actions of 3,4-methylenedioxpyrovalerone (MPDV), a principal constituent of psychoactive "bath salts" products. *Neuropsychopharmacology, 38,* 552–562.

Baumeister, R. F., & Bushman, B. J. (2014). *Social psychology and human nature* (3rd ed.). Belmont, CA: Thomson Wadsworth.

Baumrind, D. (2013). Authoritative parenting revisited: History and current status. In R. E. Larzelere, A. S. Morris, & A. W. Harrist (Eds.), *Authoritative parenting: Synthesizing nurturance and discipline for optimal child development* (pp. 11–34). Washington, DC: American Psychological Association.

Beacham, A., Stetson, B., Braekkan, K., Rothschild, C., Herbst, A., & Linfield, K. (2011). Causal attributions regarding personal exercise goal attainment in exerciser schematics and aschematics. *International Journal of Sport and Exercise Psychology, 9*, 48–63.

Beaton, E. A., & Simon, T. J. (2011). How might stress contribute to increased risk for schizophrenia in children with Chromosome 22q11.2 deletion syndrome? *Journal of Neurodevelopmental Disorders, 3*, 68–75.

Beauchamp, M. R., Rhodes, R. E., Kreutzer, C., & Rupert, J. L. (2011). Experiential versus genetic accounts of inactivity: Implications for inactive individuals' self-efficacy beliefs and intentions to exercise. *Behavioral Medicine, 37*, 8–14.

Beaver, K. M., Barnes, J. C., May, J. S., & Schwartz, J. A. (2011). Psychopathic personality traits, genetic risk, and gene-environment correlations. *Criminal Justice and Behavior, 38*, 896–912.

Bech, P., Fava, M., Trivedi, M. H., Wisniewski, S. R., & Rush, A. J. (2011). Factor structure and dimensionality of the two depression scales in STAR*D using level 1 datasets. *Journal of Affective Disorders, 132*, 396–400.

Beck, A. T., & Grant, P. M. (2008). Negative self-defeating attitudes: Factors that influence everyday impairment in individuals with schizophrenia. *American Journal of Psychiatry, 165,* 772.

Beck, A. T., Haigh, E. A. P., & Baber, K. F. (2012). Biological underpinnings of the cognitive model of depression: A prototype for psychoanalytic research. *Psychoanalytic Review, 99*, 515–537.

Beckers, T., Krypotos, A.-M., Boddez, Y., Effting, M., & Kindt, M. (2013). What's wrong with fear conditioning? *Biological Psychology, 92*, 90–96.

Beilin, H. (1992). Piaget's enduring contribution to developmental psychology. *Developmental Psychology, 28*, 191–204.

Belar, C. D., McIntyre, T. M., & Matarazzo, J. D. (2013). Health psychology. In D. K. Freedheim & I. B. Weiner (Eds.), *Handbook of psychology, Vol. 1. History of psychology* (2nd ed., pp. 488–506). Hoboken, NJ: Wiley.

Bellebaum, C., & Daum, I. (2011). Mechanisms of cerebellar involvement in associative learning. *Cortex: A Journal Devoted to* *the Study of the Nervous System and Behavior, 47,* 128–136.

Bem, D. J. (2011). Feeling the future: Experimental evidence for anomalous retroactive influences on cognition and affect. Journal of *Personality & Social Psychology, 100,* 407–425.

Bem, S. L. (1981). Gender schema theory: A cognitive account of sex typing. *Psychological Review, 88,* 354–364.

Bem, S. L. (1993). *The lenses of gender: Transforming the debate on sexual inequality.* New Haven, CT: Yale University Press.

Bender, R. E., & Alloy, L. B. (2011). Life stress and kindling in bipolar disorder: Review of the evidence and integration with emerging biopsychosocial theories. *Clinical Psychology Review, 31,* 383–398.

Bendle, N. T. (2011). Out-group homogeneity bias and strategic market entry. *Dissertation Abstracts International Section A: Humanities and Social Sciences, 71,* 3341.

Benjamin Neelon, S. E., Oken, E., Taveras, E. M., Rifas-Shiman, S. L., & Gillman, M. W. (2012). Age of achievement of gross motor milestones in infancy and adiposity at age 3 years. *Maternal and Child Health Journal, 16,* 1015–1020.

Benjamin, E. (2011). Humanistic psychology and the mental health worker. *Journal of Humanistic Psychology, 51,* 82–111.

Bennett, E., English, M. W., Rennoldson, M., & Starza-Smith, A. (2013). Predicting parenting stress in caregivers of children with brain tumours. *Psycho-Oncology, 22,* 629–636.

Ben-Porath, Y. S. (2013). Self-report inventories: Assessing personality and psychopathology. In J. R. Graham, J. A. Naglieri, & I. B. Weiner (Eds.), *Handbook of psychology, Vol. 10. Assessment psychology* (2nd ed., pp. 622–644). Hoboken, NJ: Wiley.

Bentall, R. P., Wickham, S., Shevlin, M., & Varese, F. (2012). Do specific early-life adversities lead to specific symptoms of psychosis? A study from the 2007 The Adult Psychiatric Morbidity Survey. *Schizophrenia Bulletin, 38,* 734–740.

Berger, M., Speckmann, E.-J., Pape, H. C., & Gorji, A. (2008). Spreading depression enhances human neocortical excitability in vitro. *Cephalalgia, 28,* 558–562.

Bergman, R. L. (2013). *Programs that work. Treatment for children with selective mutism: An integrative behavioral approach.* New York: Oxford University Press.

Bergstrom-Lynch, C. A. (2008). Becoming parents, remaining childfree: How same-sex couples are creating families and confronting social inequalities. *Dissertation Abstracts International Section A: Humanities and Social Sciences, 68,* 3608.

Berlim, M. T., Van den Eynde, F., & Daskalakis, Z. J. (2013). Clinically meaningful efficacy and acceptability of low-frequency repetitive transcranial magnetic stimulation (rTMS) for treating primary major depression: A meta-analysis of randomized, double-blind and sham-controlled trials. *Neuropsychopharmacology, 38,* 543–551.

Berman, S. M., Paz-Filho, G., Wong, M.-L., Kohno, M., Licinio, J., & London, E. D. (2013). Effects of leptin deficiency and replacement on cerebellar response to food-related cues. *The Cerebellum, 12,* 59–67.

Bermeitinger, C., Goelz, R., Johr, N., Neumann, M., Ecker, U. K. H., & Doerr, R. (2009). The hidden persuaders break into the tired brain. *Journal of Experimental Social Psychology, 45,* 320–326.

Bernabé, D. G., Tamae, A. C., Biasoli, É. R., & Oliveira, S. H.P. (2011). Stress hormones increase cell proliferation and regulates interleukin-6 secretion in human oral squamous cell carcinoma cells. *Brain, Behavior, and Immunity, 25,* 574–583.

Bernard, L. L. (1924). *Instinct.* New York: Holt.

Bernhard, F., Landgraf, K., Klöting, N., Berthold, A., Büttner, P., Friebe, D., . . . Körner, A. (2013). Functional relevance of genes implicated by obesity genome-wide association study signals for human adipocyte biology. *Diabetologia, 56,* 311–322.

Berreman, G. (1971). *Anthropology today.* Del Mar, CA: CRM Books.

Berry, J., Poortinga, Y., Breugelmans, S., Chasiotis, A., & Sam, D. (2011). *Cross-cultural psychology: Research and applications* (3rd ed.). Cambridge, UK: Cambridge University Press.

Bertsch, K., Grothe, M., Prehn, K., Vohs, K., Berger, C., Haunstein, K., . . . Herpetz, S. C. (2013). Brain volumes differ between diagnostic groups of violent criminal offenders. *European Archives of Psychiatry and Clinical Neuroscience, 263,* 593–606.

Betancourt, T. S., Borisova, I. I., de la Soudière, M., & Williamson, J. (2011). Sierra Leone's child soldiers: War exposures and mental health problems by gender. *Journal of Adolescent Health, 49,* 21–28.

Bettens, K., Sleegers, K., & Van Broeckhoven, C. (2013). Genetic insights in Alzheimer's disease. *The Lancet Neurology, 12,* 92–104.

Beutler, L. E. (2009). Making science matter in clinical practice: Redefining psychotherapy. *Clinical Psychology: Science and Practice, 16,* 301–317.

Beyers, W., & Seiffge-Krenke, I. (2010). Does identity precede intimacy? Testing Erikson's theory on romantic development in emerging adults of the 21st century. *Journal of Adolescent Research, 25,* 387–415.

Bhatnagar, K. A. C., Wisniewski, L., Solomon, M., & Heinberg, L. (2013). Effectiveness and feasibility of a cognitive-behavioral group intervention for body image disturbance in women with eating disorders. *Journal of Clinical Psychology, 69,* 1–13.

Bhattacharya, S. K., & Muruganandam, A. V. (2003). Adaptogenic activity of Withania somnifera: An experimental study using a rat model of chronic stress. *Pharmacology, Biochemistry and Behavior, 75,* 547–555.

Bianchi, M., Franchi, S., Ferrario, P., Sotgiu, M. L., & Sacerdote, P. (2008). Effects of the bisphosphonate ibandronate on hyperalgesia, substance P, and cytokine levels in a rat model of persistent inflammatory pain. *European Journal of Pain, 12,* 284–292.

Biegel, D. E., Kola, L. A., Ronis, R. J., & Kruszynski, R. (2013). Evidence-based treatment for adults with co-occurring mental and substance use disorders: Current practice and future directions. In J. Rosenberg & S. J. Rosenberg (Eds.), *Community mental health: Challenges for the 21st century* (2nd ed., pp. 215–237). New York: Routledge/Taylor & Francis Group.

Biernat, M., & Danaher, K. (2013). Prejudice. In H. Tennen, J. Suls, & I. B. Weiner (Eds.), *Handbook of psychology, Vol. 5. Personality and social psychology* (2nd ed., pp. 341–367). Hoboken, NJ: Wiley.

Bjork, J. M., Smith, A. R., Chen, G., & Hommer, D. W. (2012). Mesolimbic recruitment by nondrug rewards in detoxified alcoholics: Effort anticipation, reward anticipation, and reward delivery. *Human Brain Mapping, 33,* 2174–2188.

Blacha, C., Schmid, M. M., Gahr, M., Freudenmann, R. W., Plener, P. L., Finter, F., . . . Schönfeldt-Lecuona, C. (2013). Self-inflicted testicular amputation in first lysergic acid diethylamide use. *Journal of Addiction Medicine, 7,* 83–84.

Blair, R. J. R., & Lee, T. M. (2013). The social cognitive neuroscience of aggression, violence, and psychopathy. *Social Neuroscience, 8,* 108–111.

Blampied, N. M., & Bootzin, R. R. (2013). Sleep: A behavioral account. In G. J. Madden, W. V. Dube, T. D. Hackenberg, G. P. Hanley, & K. A. Lattal (Eds.), *APA handbook of behavior analysis, Vol. 2. Translating principles into practice* (pp. 425–453). Washington, DC: American Psychological Association.

Blass, T. (1991). Understanding behavior in the Milgram obedience experiment: The role of personality, situations, and their interactions. *Journal of Personality and Social Psychology, 60*, 398–413.

Blass, T. (2000). Stanley Milgram. In A. E. Kazdin (Ed.), *Encyclopedia of psychology* (Vol. 5, pp. 248–250). Washington, DC: American Psychological Association.

Blecha, P. (2004). *Taboo tunes: A history of banned bands and censored songs.* San Francisco, CA: Backbeat Books.

Blum, H. P. (2011). To what extent do you privilege dream interpretation in relation to other forms of mental representations? *The International Journal of Psychoanalysis, 92*, 275–277.

Blum, K., Oscar-Berman, M., Barh, D., Giordano, J., & Gold, M. S. (2013). Dopamine genetics and function in food and substance abuse. *Journal of Genetic Syndromes & Gene Therapy, 4*: 1000121.

Blume-Marcovici, A. (2010). Gender differences in dreams: Applications to dream work with male clients. *Dreaming, 20*, 199–210.

Boag, S. (2012). *Freudian repression, the unconscious, and the dynamics of inhibition.* London, England: Karnac Books.

Boardman, J., Alexander, K., & Stallings, M. (2011). Stressful life events and depression among adolescent twin pairs. *Biodemography and Social Biology, 57*, 53–66.

Bodenhausen, G. V., & Morales, J. R. (2013). Social cognition and perception. In H. Tennen, J. Suls, & I. B. Weiner (Eds.), *Handbook of psychology (Vol. 5). Personality and social psychology* (2nd ed., pp. 225–246). Hoboken, NJ: Wiley.

Boer, D., & Fischer, R. (2013). How and when do personal values guide our attitudes and sociality? Explaining cross-cultural variability in attitude–value linkages. *Psychological Bulletin, 139*, 1113–1147.

Boland, E. M., & Alloy, L. B. (2013). Sleep disturbance and cognitive deficits in bipolar disorder: Toward an integrated examination of disorder maintenance and functional impairment. *Clinical Psychology Review, 33*, 33–44.

Bones, A. K. (2012). We knew the future all along: Scientific hypothesizing is much more accurate than other forms of precognition—A satire in one part. *Perspectives on Psychological Science, 7*, 307–309.

Bonk, W. J., & Healy, A. F. (2010). Learning and memory for sequences of pictures, words, and spatial locations: An exploration of serial position effects. *The American Journal of Psychology, 123*, 137–168.

Boothroyd, L. G., Tovee, M. T., & Pollett, T. (2012). Mechanisms of change in body size preferences. *PLOS One, 7*: e48691.

Bor, J., Brunelin, J., Sappey-Marinier, D., Ibarrola, D., d'Amato, T., Suaud-Chagny, M.-F., & Saoud, M. (2011). Thalamus abnormalities during working memory in schizophrenia. An fMRI study. *Schizophrenia Research, 125*, 49–53.

Borgelt, L. M., Franson, K. L., Nussbaum, A. M., & Wang, G. S. (2013). The pharmacologic and clinical effects of medical cannabis. *Pharmacotherapy: The Journal of Human Pharmacology and Drug Therapy, 33*, 195–209.

Bornstein, R. F., Denckla, C. A., & Chung, W.-J. (2013). Psychodynamic models of personality. In H. Tennen, J. Suls, & I. B. Weiner (Eds.), *Handbook of psychology, Vol. 5. Personality and social psychology* (2nd ed., pp. 43–64). Hoboken, NJ: Wiley.

Borst, G., Kievit, R. A., Thompson, W. L., & Kosslyn, S. M. (2011). Mental rotation is not easily cognitively penetrable. *Journal of Cognitive Psychology, 23*, 60–75.

Bouchard, T. J., Jr. (1997). The genetics of personality. In K. Blum & E. P. Noble (Eds.), *Handbook of psychiatric genetics* (pp. 273–296). Boca Raton, FL: CRC Press.

Bouchard, T. J., Jr. (2004). Genetic influence on human psychological traits: A survey. *Current Directions in Psychological Science, 13*, 148–151.

Bouchard, T. J., Jr. & McGue, M. (1981). Familial studies of intelligence: A review. *Science, 212*, 1055–1059.

Bouchard, T. J., Jr., McGue, M., Hur, Y., & Horn, J. M. (1998). A genetic and environmental analysis of the California Psychological Inventory using adult twins reared apart and together. *European Journal of Personality, 12*, 307–320.

Bourne, L. E., Dominowski, R. L., & Loftus, E. F. (1979). *Cognitive processes.* Englewood Cliffs, NJ: Prentice Hall.

Bouton, M. E., Winterbauer, N. E., & Todd, T. P. (2012). Relapse processes after the extinction of instrumental learning: Renewal, resurgence, and reacquisition. *Behavioural Processes, 90*, 130–141.

Bowden, M. G., Woodbury, M. L., & Duncan, P. W. (2013). Promoting neuroplasticity and recovery after stroke: Future directions for rehabilitation clinical trials. *Current Opinion in Neurology, 26*, 37–42.

Bowlby, J. (1969). *Attachment and loss: Vol. 1. Attachment.* New York: Basic Books.

Bowlby, J. (1989). *Secure attachment.* New York: Basic Books.

Bowlby, J. (2000). *Attachment.* New York: Basic Books.

Bowling, A. C., & Mackenzie, B. D. (1996). The relationship between speed of information processing and cognitive ability. *Personality and Individual Differences, 20*, 775–800.

Boxer, P., Huesmann, L. R., Dubow, E. F., Landau, S. F., Gvirsman, S. D., Shikahi, K., & Ginges, J. (2013). Exposure to violence across the social ecosystem and the development of aggression: A test of ecological theory in the Israeli–Palestinian conflict. *Child Development, 84*, 163–177.

Boyce, C. J., Wood, A. M., & Powdthavee, N. (2013). Is personality fixed? Personality changes as much as "variable" economic factors and more strongly predicts changes to life satisfaction. *Social Indicators Research, 111*, 287–305.

Boyd, R., Richerson, P. J., & Henrich, J. (2011). Rapid cultural adaptation can facilitate the evolution of large-scale cooperation. *Behavioral Ecology and Sociobiology, 65*, 431–444.

Boyle, S. H., Williams, R. B., Mark, D. B., Brummett, B. H., Siegler, I. C., Helms, M. J., & Barefoot, J. C. (2004). Hostility as a predictor of survival in patients with coronary artery disease. *Psychosomatic Medicine, 66*, 629–632.

Boysen, G. A., & VanBergen, A. (2013). A review of published research on adult dissociative identity disorder: 2000–2010. *The Journal of Nervous and Mental Disease, 201*, 5–11.

Bradshaw, D. H., Chapman, C. R., Jacobson, R. C., & Donaldson, G. W. (2012). Effects of music engagement on responses to painful stimulation. Clinical *Journal of Pain, 28*, 418–427.

Brady, M. L., Diaz, M. R., Iuso, A., Everett, J. C., Valenzuela, C. F., & Caldwell, K. K. (2013). Moderate prenatal alcohol exposure reduces plasticity and alters NMDA receptor subunit composition in the dentate gyrus. *The Journal of Neuroscience, 33*, 1062–1067.

Brady, T. F., & Tenenbaum, J. B. (2013). A probabilistic model of visual working memory: Incorporating higher order regularities into working memory capacity estimates. *Psychological Review, 120*, 85–109.

Bratter, J., & Gorman, B. K. (2011). Does multiracial matter? A study of racial disparities in self-rated health. *Demography, 48,* 127–152.

Braunlich, K., & Seger, C. (2013). The basal ganglia. *Wiley Interdisciplinary Reviews: Cognitive Science, 4,* 135–148.

Brewer, J. B., Zhao, N., Desmond, J. E., Glover, G. H., & Gabriel, J. D. E. (1998). Making memories: Brain activity that predicts how well visual experience will be remembered. *Science, 281,* 1185–1187.

Brewer, N., Weber, N., Wootton, D., & Lindsay, D. (2012). Identifying the bad guy in a lineup using confidence judgments under deadline pressure. *Psychological Science, 23,* 1208–1214.

Brim, B. L., Haskell, R., Awedikian, R., Ellinwood, N. M., Jin, L., Kumar, A., . . . Magnusson, K. R. (2013). Memory in aged mice is rescued by enhanced expression of the GluN2B subunit of the NMDA receptor. *Behavioural Brain Research, 238,* 211–226.

Brink, M., & van Bronswijk, J. E. M. H. (2013). Addressing Maslow's deficiency needs in smart homes. *Gerontechnology, 11,* 445–451.

Brinker, J. K., Campisi, M., Gibbs, L., & Izzard, R. (2013). Rumination, mood and cognitive performance. *Psychology, 4,* 224–231.

Brislin, R. W. (1997). *Understanding culture's influence on behavior* (2nd ed.). San Diego, CA: Harcourt Brace.

Brislin, R. W. (2000). *Understanding culture's influence on behavior* (3rd ed.). Ft. Worth, TX: Harcourt.

Brodin, T., Lind, M., & Johansson, F. (2013). Personality trait differences between mainland and island populations in the common frog (*Rana temporaria*). *Behavioral Ecology and Sociobiology, 67,* 135–143.

Brooks, S. J., O'Daly, O. G., Uher, R., Schiöth, H. B., Treasure, J., & Campbell, I. C. (2012). Subliminal food images compromise superior working memory performance in women with restricting anorexia nervosa. *Consciousness & Cognition: An International Journal, 21,* 751–763.

Brown, L. M., Frahm, K. A., & Bongar, B. (2013). Crisis intervention. In G. Stricker, T. A. Widiger, & I. B. Weiner (Eds.), *Handbook of psychology, Vol. 8. Clinical psychology* (2nd ed., pp. 408–430). Hoboken, NJ: Wiley.

Brown, L. S. (2011). Guidelines for treating dissociative identity disorder in adults, third revision: A tour de force for the dissociation field. *Journal of Trauma and Dissociation, 12,* 113–114.

Brown, R., & Kulik, J. (1977). Flashbulb memories. *Cognition, 5,* 73–99.

Brown, W. A. (2013). *The placebo effect in clinical practice.* New York: Oxford University Press.

Brumbaugh, C. C., & Wood, D. (2013). Mate preferences across life and across the world. *Social Psychological and Personality Science, 4,* 100–107.

Brunoni, A. R., Valiengo, L., Baccaro, A., Zanão, T. A., de Oliveira, J. F., Goulart, A., . . . Fregni, F. (2013). The sertraline vs electrical current therapy for treating depression clinical study: Results from a factorial, randomized, controlled trial. *JAMA Psychiatry, 70,* 383–391.

Bruns, C. M., & Kaschak, E. (2011). Feminisms: Feminist therapies in the 21st century. *Women and Therapy, 34,* 1–5.

Bryan, A. D., Webster, G. D., & Mahaffey, A. L. (2011). The big, the rich, and the powerful: Physical, financial, and social dimensions of dominance in mating and attraction. *Personality and Social Psychology Bulletin, 37,* 365–382.

Brzezinski, A., Vangel, M. G., Wurtman, R. J., Norrie, G., Zhdanova, I., Ben-Shushan, A., & Ford, I. (2005). Effects of exogenous melatonin on sleep: A meta-analysis. *Sleep Medicine Reviews, 9,* 41–50.

Buckels, E. E., & Trapnell, P. D. (2013). Disgust facilitates outgroup dehumanization. *Group Processes & Intergroup Relations, 16,* 771–780.

Bull, R., Cleland, A. A., & Mitchell, T. (2013). Sex differences in the spatial representation of number. *Journal of Experimental Psychology: General, 142,* 181–192.

Bunde, J., & Suls, J. (2006). A quantitative analysis of the relationship between the Cook-Medley hostility scale and traditional coronary artery disease risk factors. *Health Psychology, 25,* 493–500.

Buneviciute, J., Staniute, M., Brozaitiene, J., Girdler, S. S., & Bunevicius, R. (2013). Mood symptoms and personality dimensions as determinants of health related quality of life in patients with coronary artery disease. *Journal of Health Psychology, 18,* 1493–1504.

Bunge, S. A., & Toga, A. W. (2013). Introduction to frontal lobe development. In D. Stuss & R. Knight (Eds.), *Oxford handbook of frontal lobe functions.* New York: Oxford University Press.

Burnette, J., Pollack, J., & Forsyth, D. (2011). Leadership in extreme contexts: A groupthink analysis of the May 1996 Mount Everest disaster. *Journal of Leadership Studies, 4,* 29–40.

Burns, J. K. (2013). The social determinants of schizophrenia: An African journey in social epidemiology. *Public Health Reviews, 34.* Retrieved from http://www.publichealthreviews.eu/upload/pdf_files/12/00_Burns.pdf

Burnstock, G. (2013). Introduction to purinergic signalling in the brain. *Glioma Signaling, 986,* 1–12.

Buss, D. M. (1989). Sex differences in human mate preferences: Evolutionary hypotheses tested in 37 cultures. *Behavioral and Brain Sciences, 12,* 1–49.

Buss, D. M. (1994). Mate preferences in 37 countries. In W. J. Lonner & R. Malpass (Eds.), *Psychology and culture.* Boston, MA: Allyn & Bacon.

Buss, D. M. (2003). *The evolution of desire: Strategies of human mating.* New York: Basic Books.

Buss, D. M. (2008). *Evolutionary psychology: The new science of the mind* (3rd ed.). Boston: Allyn & Bacon.

Buss, D. M. (2011). *Evolutionary psychology: The new science of the mind* (4th ed.). Upper Saddle River, NJ: Prentice-Hall.

Buss, D. M., Abbott, M., Angleitner, A., Asherian, A., Biaggio, A., Blanco-Villasenor, A., . . . Yang, K. -S. (1990). International preferences in selecting mates: A study of 37 cultures. *Journal of Cross-Cultural Psychology, 21,* 5–47.

Buszewski, B., Rudnicka, J., Ligor, T., Walczak, M., Jezierski, T., & Amann, A. (2012). Analytical and unconventional methods of cancer detection using odor. *Trends in Analytical Chemistry, 38,* 1–12.

Butcher, J. N. (2000). Revising psychological tests: Lessons learned from the revision of the MMPI. *Psychological Assessment, 12,* 263–271.

Butcher, J. N. (2011). *A beginner's guide to the MMPI-2* (3rd ed.). Washington, DC: American Psychological Association.

Butcher, J. N., & Perry, J. N. (2008). *Personality assessment in treatment planning: Use of the MMPI-2 and BTPI.* New York: Oxford University Press.

Butz, D. A., & Plant, E. A. (2011). Approaching versus avoiding intergroup contact: The role of expectancies and motivation. In L. R. Tropp & R. K. Mallett (Eds.), *Moving beyond prejudice reduction: Pathways to positive intergroup relations* (pp. 81–98). Washington, DC: American Psychological Association.

Buxton, O. M., Cain, S. W., O'Connor, S. P., Porter, J. H., Duffy, J. F., Wang, W. . . . Shea, S. A. (2012). Adverse metabolic consequences in humans of prolonged sleep restriction combined with circadian disruption. *Science Translational Medicine, 4,* 129ra43.

Cacioppo, J. T., Cacioppo, S., Gonzaga, G. C., Ogburn, E. L., & VanderWeele, T. J. (2013). Marial satisfaction and break-ups differ across on-line and off-line meeting venues. *Proceedings of the National Academy of Sciences, 110,* 10135–10140.

Cain, D. J. (2013). Person-centered therapy. In J. Frew & M. D. Spiegler (Eds.), *Contemporary psychotherapies for a diverse world* (1st rev. ed., pp. 165–213). New York: Routledge/Taylor & Francis Group.

Calkins, S. D., & Keane, S. P. (2009). Developmental origins of early antisocial behavior. *Development and Psychopathology, 21,* 1095–1109.

Call, D., Miron, L., & Orcutt, H. (2013). Effectiveness of brief mindfulness techniques in reducing symptoms of anxiety and stress. *Mindfulness.* Advance online publication. doi: 10.1007/s12671-013-0218-6.

Call, J. (2011). How artificial communication affects the communication and cognition of the great apes. *Mind and Language, 26,* 1–20.

Camarena, B., Santiago, H., Aguilar, A., Ruvinskis, E., González-Barranco, J., & Nicolini, H. (2004). Family-based association study between the monoamine oxidase A gene and obesity: Implications for psychopharmacogenetic studies. *Neuropsychobiology, 49,* 126–129.

Cameron, L., Rutland, A. & Brown, R. (2007). Promoting children's positive intergroup attitudes towards stigmatized groups: Extended contact and multiple classification skills training. *International Journal of Behavioral Development, 31,* 454–466.

Campbell, J. L., Britten, N., Green, C., Holt, T. A., Lattimer, V., Richards, S.H., . . . Fletcher, E. (2013). The effectiveness and cost-effectiveness of telephone triage of patients requesting same day consultations in general practice: study protocol for a cluster randomised controlled trial comparing nurse-led and GP-led management systems (ESTEEM). *Trials, 14,* 4.

Campbell, J. R., & Feng, A. X. (2011). Comparing adult productivity of American mathematics, physics, and chemistry Olympians with Terman's longitudinal study. *Roeper Review: A Journal on Gifted Education, 33,* 18–25.

Campbell, L. F., Norcross, J. C., Vasquez, M. J. T., & Kaslow, N. J. (2013). Recognition of psychotherapy effectiveness: The APA resolution. *Psychotherapy, 50,* 98–101.

Campbell, L., Simpson, J. A., Kashy, D. A., & Fletcher, G. J. O. (2001). Ideal standards, the self, and flexibility of ideals in close relationships. *Personality and Social Psychology Bulletin, 27,* 447–462.

Campbell, M. C., Black, K. J., Weaver, P. M., Lugar, H. M., Videen, T. O., Tabbal, S. D., . . . Hershey, T. (2012). Mood response to deep brain stimulation of the subthalamic nucleus in Parkinson's Disease. *Journal of Neuropsychiatry and Clinical Neurosciences, 24,* 28–36.

Camperio Ciani, A. S., Edelman, S., & Ebstein, R. P. (2013). The dopamine D4 receptor (DRD4) Exon 3 VNTR contributes to adaptive personality differences in an Italian small island population. *European Journal of Personality.* doi: 10.1002/per.1917

Cao, X. (2013). The effects of facial close-ups and viewers' sex on empathy and intentions to help people in need. *Mass Communication and Society, 16,* 161–178.

Caprara, G. V., Vecchione, M., Barbaranelli, C., & Fraley, R. C. (2007). When likeness goes with liking: The case of political preference. *Political Psychology, 28,* 609–632.

Caqueo-Urízar, A., Ferrer-García, M., Toro, J., Gutiérrez-Maldonado, J., Peñaloza, C., Cuadros-Sosa, Y., & Gálvez-Madrid, M. J. (2011). Associations between sociocultural pressures to be thin, body distress, and eating disorder symptomatology among Chilean adolescent girls. *Body Image, 8,* 78–81.

Cardeña, E., Butler, L. D., Reijman, S., & Spiegel, D. (2013). Disorders of extreme stress. In G. Stricker, T. A. Widiger, & I. B. Weiner (Eds.), *Handbook of psychology, Vol. 8. Clinical psychology (2nd ed.,* pp. 193–216). Hoboken, NJ: Wiley.

Carey, B. (2008, December 4). H. M., an unforgettable amnesiac, dies at 82. *The New York Times.* Retrieved from http://www.nytimes.com/2008/12/05/us/05hm.html

Carlesimo, G. A., Costa, A., Serra, L., Bozzali, M., Fadda, L., & Caltagirone, C. (2011). Prospective memory in thalamic amnesia. *Neuropsychologia, 49,* 2199–2208.

Carlo, G., Mestre, M. V., McGinley, M., Tur-Porcar, A., Samper, P., & Streit, C. (2013). The structure and correlates of a measure of prosocial moral reasoning in adolescents from Spain. *European Journal of Developmental Psychology, 10,* 174–189.

Carlson, J. D., & Englar-Carlson, M. (2013). Adlerian therapy. In J. Frew & M. D. Spiegler (Eds.), *Contemporary psychotherapies for a diverse world* (1st rev. ed., pp. 87–129). New York: Routledge/Taylor & Francis Group.

Carnagey, N. L., Anderson, C. A., & Bartholow, B. D. (2007). Media violence and social neuroscience: New questions and new opportunities. *Current Directions in Psychological Science, 16,* 178–182.

Carpenter, R. W., Tomko, R. L., Trull, T. J., & Boomsma, D. I. (2013). Gene-environment studies and borderline personality disorder: A review. *Current Psychiatry Reports, 15,* 1–7.

Carpenter, S. K. (2012). Testing enhances the transfer of learning. *Current Directions in Psychological Science, 21,* 279–283.

Carroll, J. E., Low, C. A., Prather, A. A., Cohen, S., Fury, J. M., Ross, D. C., & Marsland, A. L. (2011). Negative affective responses to a speech task predict changes in interleukin (IL)-6. *Brain, Behavior, and Immunity, 25,* 232–238.

Carskadon, M. A., Wolfson, A. R., Acebo, C., Tzischinsky, O., & Seifer, R. (1998). Adolescent sleep patterns, circadian timing, and sleepiness at a transition to early school days. *Sleep, 21,* 871–881.

Carvalho, S., Pinto-Gouveia, J., Pimentel, P., Maia, D., Gilbert, P., & Mota-Pereira, J. (2013). Entrapment and defeat perceptions in expressive symptomatology: Through an evolutionary approach. *Psychiatry: Interpersonal & Biological Processes, 76,* 53–67.

Case, B. G., Bertollo, D. N., Laska, E. M., Price, L. H., Siegel, C. E., Olfson, M., & Marcus, S. C. (2013). Declining use of electroconvulsive therapy in United States general hospitals. *Biological Psychiatry, 73,* 119–126.

Casey, B. M. (2013). Individual and group differences in spatial ability. In D. Waller & L. Nadel (Eds.), *Handbook of spatial cognition* (pp. 117–134). Washington, DC: American Psychological Association.

Castrén, E., & Hen, R. (2013). Neuronal plasticity and antidepressant actions. *Trends in Neurosciences,* 36, 259–267.

Cathers-Schiffman, T. A., & Thompson, M. S. (2007). Assessment of English-and Spanish-speaking students with the WISC-III and Leiter-R. *Journal of Psychoeducational Assessment, 25,* 41–52.

Cattaneo, Z., Mattavelli, G., Platania, E., & Papagno, C. (2011). The role of the prefrontal cortex in controlling gender-stereotypical associations: A TMS investigation. *NeuroImage, 56,* 1839–1846.

Cattell, R. B. (1950). *Personality: A systematic, theoretical, and factual study.* New York: McGraw-Hill.

Cattell, R. B. (1965). *The scientific analysis of personality.* Baltimore, MD: Penguin.

Cattell, R. B. (1990). Advances in Cattellian personality theory. In L. A. Pervin (Ed.), *Handbook of personality: Theory and research.* New York: Guilford Press.

Cautin, R. L. (2011). A century of psychotherapy, 1860–1960. In J. C. Norcross, G. R. VandenBos, & D. K. Freedheim (Eds.), *History of psychotherapy: Continuity and change* (2nd ed., pp. 3–38). Washington, DC: American Psychological Association.

Cavazos-Rehg, P. A., Krauss, M. J., Spitznagel, E. L., Chaloupka, F. J., Schootman, M., Grucza, R. A., & Bierut, L. J. (2012). Associations between selected state laws and teenagers' drinking and driving behaviors. *Alcoholism: Clinical and Experimental Research, 36,* 1647–1652.

Cechnicki, A., Helms, J. E., & Cook, D. A. (1999). *Using race and culture in counseling and psychotherapy: Theory and process.* Boston, MA: Allyn & Bacon.

Celes, L. A. M. (2010). Clinica psicanalitica: Aproximações histórico-conceituais e contemporâneas e perspectivas futuras [Psychoanalytic practice: Historical, conceptual and contemporary approaches and future perspectives]. *Psicologia: Teoria e Pesquisa, 26,* 65–80.

Centers for Disease Control and Prevention (2011). *Healthy weight—it's not a diet, it's a lifestyle!* Retrieved from: http://www.cdc.gov/healthyweight/assessing/bmi/adult_bmi/english_bmi_calculator/bmi_calcula tor.html

Cervone, D., & Pervin, L. A. (2010). *Personality theory and research* (11th ed.). Hoboken, NJ: Wiley.

Ceschi, G., & Scherer, K. R. (2001). Contrôler l'expression faciale et changer l'émotion: Une approche développementale. The role of facial expression in emotion: A developmental perspective. *Enfance, 53,* 257–269.

Chadwick, R. (2011). Personal genomes: No bad news? *Bioethics, 25,* 62–65.

Challem, J., Berkson, B., Smith, M. D., & Berkson, B. (2000). *Syndrome X: The complete program to prevent and reverse insulin resistance.* Hoboken, NJ: Wiley.

Chamberlin, N. L., & Saper, C. B. (2009). The agony of the ecstasy: Serotonin and obstructive sleep apnea. *Neurology, 73,* 1947–1948.

Chamorro-Premuzic, T. (2011). *Personality and individual differences.* Malden, MA: Blackwell.

Chanen, A. M., & McCutcheon, L. (2013). Prevention and early intervention for borderline personality disorder: current status and recent evidence. *The British Journal of Psychiatry, 202,* s24–s29.

Chang, C.-Y. (2012). The survey research of kindergarten children's dreams. *Chinese Journal of Guidance and Counseling, 33,* 1–23.

Chang, L., Wang, Y., Shackelford, T. K., & Buss, D. M. (2011). Chinese mate preferences: Cultural evolution and continuity across a quarter of a century. *Personality and Individual Differences, 50,* 678–683.

Chang, S. W., O'Neill, J., & Rosenberg, D. (2013). Obsessive-compulsive disorder. In L. A. Reddy, A. S. Weissman, & J. B. Hale (Eds.), *Neuropsychological assessment and intervention for youth: An evidence-based approach to emotional and behavioral disorders* (pp. 41–71). Washington, DC: American Psychological Association.

Chao, O. Y. H., Pum, M. E., & Huston, J. P. (2013). The interaction between the dopaminergic forebrain projections and the medial prefrontal cortex is critical for memory of objects: Implications for Parkinson's disease. *Experimental Neurology, 247,* 373–382.

Chapman, A. L., Leung, D. W., & Lynch, T. R. (2008). Impulsivity and emotion dysregulation in borderline personality disorder. *Journal of Personality Disorders, 22,* 148–164.

Chapman, E. N., Kaatz, A., & Carnes, M. (2013). Physicians and implicit bias: How doctors may unwittingly perpetuate health care disparities. *Journal of General Internal Medicine, 28,* 1504–1510.

Charles, K. (2011). Retrieved from www.napier.ac.uk/media/Pages/NewsDetails.aspx?NewsID=187.

Chellappa, S. L., Frey, S., Knoblauch, V., & Cajochen, C. (2011). Cortical activation patterns herald successful dream recall after NREM and REM sleep. *Biological Psychology, 87,* 251–256.

Chen, C-F., & Kao, Y-L. (2013). The connection between the hassles–burnout relationship, as moderated by coping, and aberrant behaviors and health problems among bus drivers. *Accident Analysis and Prevention, 53,* 105–111.

Cheng, C., Cheung, S-F., Chio, J. H., & Chan, M. S. (2013). Cultural meaning of perceived control: A meta-analysis of locus of control and psychological symptoms across 18 cultural regions. *Psychological Bulletin, 139,* 152–188.

Cheung, F., van de Vijver, F., & Leong, F. (2011). Toward a new approach to the study of personality in culture. *American Psychologist, 66,* 596–603.

Chi, L. (2013). Intergenerational transmission of educational attainment: Three levels of parent–child communication as mediators. *PsyCh Journal, 2,* 26–38.

Chiang, Y. Y., Tsai, P. Y., Chen, P. C., Yang, M. H., Li, C. Y., Sung, F. C., & Chen, K. B. (2012). Sleep disorders and traffic accidents. *Epidemiology, 23,* 643–644.

Chica, A. B., Bartolomeo, P., & Lupiáñez, J. (2013). Two cognitive and neural systems for endogenous and exogenous spatial attention. *Behavioural Brain Research, 237,* 107–123.

Choca, J. P. (2013). Interpretative basics. In J. P. Choca (Ed.), *The Rorschach inkblot test: An interpretive guide for clinicians* (pp. 27–33). Washington, DC: American Psychological Association.

Chopra, A., Tye, S. J., Lee, K. H., Sampson, S., Matsumoto, J., Adams, A., . . . Frye, M. A. (2012). Underlying neurobiology and clinical correlates of mania status after subthalamic nucleus deep brain stimulation in Parkinson's Disease: A review of the literature. *Journal of Neuropsychiatry and Clinical Neurosciences, 24,* 102–110.

Chorpita, B. F., Daleiden, E. L., Ebesutani, C., Young, J., Becker, K. D., Nakamura, B. J., . . . Starace, N. (2011). Evidence-based treatments for children and adolescents: An updated review of indicators of efficacy and effectiveness. *Clinical Psychology: Science and Practice, 18,* 154–172.

Chou, Y.-C., Chiao, C., & Fu, L.-Y. (2011). Health status, social support, and quality of life among family carers of adults with profound intellectual and multiple disabilities (PIMD) in Taiwan. *Journal of Intellectual and Developmental Disability, 36,* 73–79.

Chrisler, J. C. (2008). The menstrual cycle in a biopsychosocial context. In F. Denmark & M. A. Paludi (Eds.), *Psychology of women: A handbook of issues and theories* (2nd ed., pp. 400–439). *Women's psychology.* Westport, CT: Praeger/Greenwood.

Christakou, A., Brammer, M., & Rubia, K. (2011). Maturation of limbic corticostriatal activation and connectivity associated with developmental changes in temporal discounting. *NeuroImage, 54,* 1344–1354.

Christandl, F., Fetchenhauer, D., & Hoelzl, E. (2011). Price perception and confirmation bias in the context of a VAT increase. *Journal of Economic Psychology, 32,* 131–141.

Christenfeld, N. J. S., & Mandler, G. (2013). Emotion. In D. K. Freedheim & I. B. Weiner (Eds.), *Handbook of psychology, Vol. 1. History of psychology (2nd ed.,* pp. 177–197). Hoboken, NJ: Wiley.

Christensen, D. (2000). Is snoring a diZZZease? Nighttime noises may serve as a wake-up call for future illness. *Science News, 157,* 172–173.

Christensen, H., Anstey, K. J., Leach, L. S., & Mackinnon, A. J. (2008). Intelligence, education, and the brain reserve hypothesis. In F. I. M. Craik & T. A. Salthouse (Eds.), *The handbook of aging and cognition* (3rd ed., pp. 133–188). New York: Psychology Press.

Chu, J. (2011). *Rebuilding shattered lives: Treating complex PTSD and dissociative disorders* (2nd ed.). Hoboken, NJ: Wiley.

Chu, Y. L., Farmer, A., Fung, C., Kuhle, S., Storey, K. E., & Veugelers, P. J. (2013). Involvement in home meal preparation is associated with food preference and self-efficacy among Canadian children. *Public Health Nutrition, 16,* 108–112.

Chuang, D. (1998). Cited in J. Travis, Simulating clue hints how lithium works. *Science News, 153,* 165.

Cini, F., Kruger, S., & Ellis, S. (2013). A model of intrinsic and extrinsic motivations on subjective well-being: The experience of overnight visitors to a national park. *Applied Research in Quality of Life, 8,* 45–61.

Claes, L., Bijttebier, P., Mitchell, J. E., de Zwaan, M., & Mueller, A. (2011). The relationship between compulsive buying, eating disorder symptoms, and temperament in a sample of female students. *Comprehensive Psychiatry, 52,* 50–55.

Claydon, L. (2012). Are there lessons to be learned from a more scientific approach to mental condition defences? *International Journal of Law and Psychiatry, 35,* 88–98.

Cohen, C., Janicki-Deverts, D., Doyle, W. J., Miller, G. E., Frank, E., Rabin, B. S., & Turner, R. B. (2012). Chronic stress, glucocorticoid receptor resistance, inflammation, and disease risk. *Proceedings of the National Academy of Sciences, 109,* 5995–5999.

Cohen, D., & Leung, A. K. (2011). Violence and character: A CuPS (culture 3 person 3 situation) perspective. In P. R. Shaver & M. Mikulincer (Eds.), *Herzilya series on personality and social psychology. Human aggression and violence: Causes, manifestations, and consequences* (pp. 187–200). Washington, DC: American Psychological Association.

Cohen, S., & Lemay, E. P. (2007). Why would social networks be linked to affect and health practices? *Health Psychology, 26,* 410–417.

Cohen, S., Doyle, W. J., Alper, C. M., Janicki-Deverts, D., & Turner, R. B. (2009). Sleep habits and susceptibility to the common cold. *Archives of Internal Medicine, 169,* 62–67.

Cohen, S., Doyle, W. J., Turner, R. B., Alper, C. M., & Skoner, D. P. (2003). Sociability and susceptibility to the common cold. *Psychological Science, 14,* 389–395.

Cole, M., & Gajdamaschko, N. (2007). Vygotsky and culture. In H. Daniels, J. Wertsch, & M. Cole (Eds.), *The Cambridge companion to Vygotsky* (pp. 193–211). New York: Cambridge University Press.

Coleborne, C., & MacKinnon, D. (2011). *Exhibiting madness in museums: Remembering psychiatry through collection and display.* New York: Routledge.

Coleman, M. D. (2013). Emotion and the ultimate attribution error. *Current Psychology, 32,* 71–81.

Collins, J., & Lidz, F. (2013). Why NBA center Jason Collins is coming out now. *SI: The Magazine.* Retrieved from: http://sportsillustrated.cnn.com/magazine/news/20130429/jason-collins-gay-nba-player/

Collins, R. (2011). Content analysis of gender roles in media: Where are we now and where should we go? *Sex Roles, 64,* 290–298.

Collins, R. O., & Adams, J. L. (2013). *Prefrontal cortex: Developmental, executive, and cognitive functions and role in neurological disorders.* Hauppauge, NY: Nova Science.

Colom, R., Burgaleta, M., Román, F. J., Karama, S., Álvarez-Linera, J., Abad, F., . . . Haier, R. J. (2013). Neuroanatomic overlap between intelligence and cognitive factors: Morphometry methods provide support for the key role of the frontal lobes. *NeuroImage, 72,* 143–152.

Colombo, J., Brez, C. C., & Curtindale, L. M. (2013). Infant perception and cognition. In R. M. Lerner, M. A. Easterbrooks, J. Mistry, & I. B. Weiner (Eds.), *Handbook of psychology, Vol. 6. Developmental psychology (2nd ed.,* pp. 61–89). Hoboken, NJ: Wiley.

Colrain, I. M. (2011). Sleep and the brain. *Neuropsychology Review, 21,* 1–4.

Columb, C., & Plant, E. A. (2011). Revisiting the Obama Effect: Exposure to Obama reduces implicit prejudice. *Journal of Experimental Social Psychology, 47,* 499–501.

Colzato, L. S., Ozturk, A., & Hommel, B. (2012). Meditate to create: The impact of focused-attention and open-monitoring training on convergent and divergent thinking. *Frontiers in Psychology, 3,* 116.

Conger, A. J., Dygdon, J. A., & Rollock, D. (2013). Conditioned emotional responses in racial prejudice. *Ethnic and Racial Studies, 35,* 298–319.

Conger, K. (2011). Embryonic stem cell therapy for paralysis given to first patient in western United States. *Stanford School of Medicine.* Retrieved from http://med.stanford.edu/ism/2011/september/geron.html

Connelly, B. S., & Hülsheger, U. R. (2012). A narrower scope or a clearer lens of personality? Examining sources of observers' advantages over self-reports for predicting performance. *Journal of Personality, 80,* 603–631.

Connelly, B. S., & Ones, D. S. (2012). An other perspective on personality: Meta-analytic integration of observers' accuracy and predictive validity. *Psychological Bulletin, 136,* 1092–1122.

Connolly, I., Zaleon, C., & Montagnini, M. (2013). Management of severe neuropathic cancer pain: An illustrative case and review. *American Journal of Hospice & Palliative Medicine, 30,* 83–90.

Constantino, M. J., Manber, R., Ong, J., Kuo, T. F., Huang, J. S., & Arnow, B. A. (2007). Patient expectations and therapeutic alliance as predictors of outcome in group cognitive-behavioral therapy for insomnia. *Behavioral Sleep Medicine, 5,* 210–228.

Conzen, P. (2010). Erik H. Erikson: Pionier der psychoanalytischen identitätstheorie [Erik H. Erikson: A pioneer of the psychoanalytic identity theory]. *Forum der Psychoanalyse: Zeitschrift für klinische Theorie and Praxis, 26,* 389–411.

Cook, M. (2013). *Levels of personality* (3rd ed.). New York: Cambridge University Press.

Cooper, J. A., Watras, A. C., Paton, C. M., Wegner, F. H., Adams, A. K., & Schoeller, D. A. (2011). Impact of exercise and dietary fatty acid composition from a high-fat diet on markers of hunger and satiety. *Appetite, 56,* 171–178.

Cooper, W. E. Jr., Pérez-Mellado, V., Vitt, L. J., & Budzinsky, B. (2002). Behavioral responses to plant toxins in two omnivorous lizard species. *Physiology and Behavior, 76,* 297–303.

Cordón, L. (2012). *All things Freud: An encyclopedia of Freud's world* (Vols. 1–2). Santa Barbara, CA: Greenwood.

Coren, S. (2013). Sensation and perception. In D. K. Freedheim & I. B. Weiner (Eds.), *Handbook of psychology, Vol. 1. History of psychology* (2nd ed., pp. 100–128). Hoboken, NJ: Wiley.

Corey, G. (2013). *Theory and practice of counseling and psychotherapy (9th ed.).* Belmont, CA: Brooks/Cole Cengage Learning.

Corkin, S. (2002). What's new with the amnesic patient H.M.? *Nature Reviews Neuroscience, 3,* 153–160.

Corr, C. A., Nabe, C. M., & Corr, D. M. (2009). *Death and dying: Life and living* (6th ed.). Belmont, CA: Wadsworth.

Correll, J., Park, B., Judd, C. M., & Wittenbrink, B. (2002). The police officer's dilemma: Using ethnicity to disambiguate potentially threatening individuals. *Journal of Personality & Social Psychology, 83,* 1314–1329.

Corsica, J. A., & Perri, M. G. (2013). Understanding and managing obesity. In A. M. Nezu, C. M. Nezu, P. A. Geller, & I. B. Weiner (Eds.), *Handbook of psychology, Vol. 9. Health psychology* (2nd ed., pp. 128–148). Hoboken, NJ: Wiley.

Costa, P. T., Jr., & McCrae, R. R. (2011). The five-factor model, five-factor theory, and interpersonal psychology. In L. M. Horowitz & S. Strack (Eds.), *Handbook of interpersonal psychology: Theory, research, assessment, and therapeutic interventions* (pp. 91–104). Hoboken, NJ: Wiley.

Cotter, D., Hermsen, J., & Vanneman, R. (2011). The end of the gender revolution? Gender role attitudes from 1977–2008. *American Journal of Sociology, 116*, 1–31.

Cougle, J. R., Bonn-Miller, M. O., Vujanovic, A. A., Zvolensky, M. J., & Hawkins, K. A. (2011). Posttraumatic stress disorder and Cannabis use in a nationally representative sample. *Psychology of Addictive Behaviors, 25*, 554–558.

Courage, M. L., & Adams, R. J. (1990). Visual acuity assessment from birth to three years using the acuity card procedures: Cross-sectional and longitudinal samples. *Optometry and Vision Science, 67*, 713–718.

Coyne, J. C., & Tennen, H. (2010). Positive psychology in cancer care: Bad science, exaggerated claims, and unproven medicine. *Annals of Behavioral Medicine, 39*, 16–26.

Craighead, W. E., Craighead, L. W., Ritschel, L. A., & Zagoloff, A. (2013). Behavior therapy and cognitive-behavioral therapy. In G. Stricker, T. A. Widiger, & I. B. Weiner (Eds.), *Handbook of psychology, Vol. 8. Clinical psychology (2nd ed.,* pp. 291–319). Hoboken, NJ: Wiley.

Creaven, A-M, Howard, S., & Hughes, B. M. (2013). Social support and trait personality are independently associated with resting cardiovascular function in women. *British Journal of Health Psychology, 18*, 556–573.

Crum, A. J., Salovey, P., & Achor, S. (2013). Rethinking stress: The role of mindsets in determining the stress response. *Journal of Personality & Social Psychology, 104*, 716–733.

Cuijpers, P., Geraedts, A., van Oppen, P., Andersson, G., Markowitz, J., & van Straten, A. (2011). Interpersonal psychotherapy for depression: A meta-analysis. *American Journal of Psychiatry, 168*, 581–592.

Culebras, A. (2012). Sleep, stroke and poststroke. *Neurologic Clinics, 30*, 1275–1284.

Cullen, D., & Gotell, L. (2002). From orgasms to organizations: Maslow, women's sexuality and the gendered foundations of the needs hierarchy. *Gender, Work and Organization, 9*, 537–555.

Cummins, R. A. (2013). Positive psychology and subjective well-being homeostasis: A critical examination of congruence. In A. Efklides & D. Moraitou (Eds.), *Quality of life: A positive psychology perspective* (pp. 67–86). New York: Springer.

Cunningham, M. R., Barbee, A. P., & Philhower, C. L. (2002). Dimensions of facial physical attractiveness: The intersection of biology and culture. In G. Rhodes & L. A. Zebrowitz (Eds.), *Facial attractiveness: Evolutionary, cognitive, and social perspectives. Advances in visual cognition* (Vol. 1, pp. 193–238). Westport, CT: Ablex Publishing.

Cunningham, M. R., Roberts, A. R., Barbee, A. P., Druen, P. B., & Wu, C. (1995). "Their ideas of beauty are, on the whole, the same as ours": Consistency and variability in the cross-cultural perception of female physical attractiveness. *Journal of Personality and Social Psychology, 38*, 181–192.

Curry, O., Roberts, S. G. B., & Dunbar, R. I. M. (2013). Altruism in social networks: Evidence for a 'kinship premium'. *British Journal of Psychology, 104*, 283–295.

Curt, A. (2012). Talk given at the Interdependence 2012 Global SCI Conference, Vancouver, British Columbia, May 15–17, 2012.

Curtiss, S. (1977). *Genie: A psycholinguistic study of a modern-day "wild child."* New York: Academic Press.

Cushman, F., & Greene, J. (2012). The philosopher in the theater. In M. M. P. R. Shaver (Ed.), *The social psychology of morality: Exploring the causes of good and evil* (pp. 33–50). Washington, DC: American Psychological Association.

Cusimano, M., Biziato, D., Brambilla, E., Donegà, M., Alfaro-Cervello, C., Snider, S., . . . Pluchino, S. (2012). Transplanted neural stem/precursor cells instruct phagocytes and reduce secondary tissue damage in the injured spinal cord. *Brain: A Journal of Neurology, 135*, 447–460.

Cutler, B. l., & Kovera, M. B. (2013). Evaluation for eyewitness identification. In R. Roesch & P. A. Zapf (Eds.), *Best practices in forensic mental health assessment. Forensic assessments in criminal and civil law: A handbook for lawyers* (pp. 118–132). New York: Oxford University Press.

Cvetkovic, D., & Cosic, I. (Eds.). (2011). *States of consciousness: Experimental insights into meditation, waking, sleep and dreams*. New York: Springer.

Daan, S. (2011). How and why? The lab versus the field. *Sleep and Biological Rhythms, 9*, 1–2.

Dalal, S., & Bruera, E. (2013). Access to opioid analgesics and pain relief for patients with cancer. *Nature Reviews Clinical Oncology, 10*, 108–116.

Dalenberg, C., Loewenstein, R., Spiegel, D., Brewin, C., Lanius, R., Frankel, S., . . . Paulson, K. (2007). Scientific study of the dissociative disorders. *Psychotherapy and Psychosomatics, 76*, 400–401.

Dana, R. H. (2005). *Multicultural assessment: Principles, applications, and examples*. Mahwah, NJ: Erlbaum.

Dandekar, M. P., Nakhate, K. T., Kokare, D. M., & Subhedar, N. K. (2011). Effect of nicotine on feeding and body weight in rats: Involvement of cocaine- and amphetamine-regulated transcript peptide. *Behavioural Brain Research, 219*, 31–38.

Danner, F., & Phillips, B. (2008). Adolescent sleep, school start times, and teen motor vehicle crashes. *Journal of Clinical Sleep Medicine, 4*, 533–535.

Danso, K., & Lum, T. (2013). Intergroup relations and predictors of immigrant experience. *Journal of Ethnic and Cultural Diversity in Social Work, 22*, 60–75.

Dantzer, R., O'Connor, J. C., Freund, G. C., Johnson, R. W., & Kelley, K. W. (2008). From inflammation to sickness and depression: When the immune system subjugates the brain. *Nature Reviews Neuroscience, 9*, 46–57.

Darwin, C. (1872). *The expression of emotions in man and animals*. New York: Appleton & Company.

Dattilio, F. M., & Nichols, M. P. (2011). Reuniting estranged family members: A cognitive-behavioral-systemic perspective. *American Journal of Family Therapy, 39*, 88–99.

David, S. P., McClure, J. B., & Swan, G. E. (2013). Nicotine dependence. In A. M. Nezu, C. M. Nezu, P. A. Geller, & I. B. Weiner (Eds.), *Handbook of psychology, Vol. 9. Health psychology (2nd ed.,* pp. 149–181). Hoboken, NJ: Wiley.

Davies, G., Tenesa, A., Payton, A., Yang, J., Harris, S. E., Liewald, D., . . . Deary, I. J. (2011). Genome-wide association studies establish that human intelligence is highly heritable and polygenic. *Molecular Psychiatry, 16*, 996–1005.

Davies, I. (1998). A study of colour grouping in three languages: A test of the linguistic relativity hypothesis. *British Journal of Psychology, 89*, 433–452.

Dawson, D. A., Goldstein, R. B., Moss, H. B., Li, T. K., & Grant, B. F. (2010). Gender differences in the relationship of internalizing and externalizing psychopathology to alcohol dependence: Likelihood, expression and course. *Drug and Alcohol Dependence, 112*, 9–17.

Dawson, D., Noy, Y. I., Härmä, M., Åkerstedt, T., & Belenky, G. (2011). Modelling fatigue and the use of fatigue models in work settings. *Accident Analysis and Prevention, 43*, 549–564.

De Leersnyder, J., Boiger, M., & Mesquita, B. (2013). Cultural regulation of emotion: individual, relational, and structural sources. *Frontiers in Psychology, 4, 55.*

De Smet, H. J., Paquier, P., Verhoeven, J., & Mariën, P. (2013). The cerebellum: Its role in language and related cognitive and affective functions. *Brain and Language.* Advance online publication. doi: 10.1016/j.bandl.2012.11.001

De Sousa, A. (2011). Freudian theory and consciousness: A conceptual analysis. *Brain, Mind and Consciousness, 9*, 210–217.

De Vos, J. (2010). From Milgram to Zimbardo: The double birth of postwar psychology/psychologization. *History of the Human Sciences, 23*, 156–175.

Deaner, R. O. (2013). Distance running as an ideal domain for showing a sex difference in competitiveness. *Archives of Sexual Behavior, 42*, 413–428.

DeAngelis, T. (2012). Practicing distance therapy, legally and ethically. *Monitor on Psychology, 43*, 52.

Deary, I. J., Ferguson, K. J., Bastin, M. E., Barrow, G. W. S., Reid, L. M., Seckl, J. R., . . . MacLullich, A. M. J. (2007). Skull size and intelligence, and King Robert Bruce's IQ. *Intelligence, 35*, 519–528.

Deci, E. L., & Moller, A. C. (2005). The concept of competence: A starting place for understanding intrinsic motivation and self-determined extrinsic motivation. In A. J. Elliot & C. S. Dweck (Eds.), *Handbook of competence and motivation* (pp. 579–597). New York: Guilford.

Deci, E. L., & Ryan, R. M. (2012). Self-determination theory. In P. A. M. Van Lange, A. W. Kruglanski, & E. T. Higgins (Eds), *Handbook of theories of social psychology* (Vol. 1, pp. 416–436). Thousand Oaks, CA: Sage Publications.

Decker, S. E., Nich, C., Carroll, K. M., & Martino, S. (2013). Development of the therapist empathy scale. *Behavioural and Cognitive Psychotherapy*, 6, 1–16.

DeClue, G. (2003). The polygraph and lie detection. *Journal of Psychiatry and Law, 31*, 361–368.

Dekel, S., & Farber, B. A. (2012). Models of intimacy of securely and avoidantly attached young adults. *The Journal of Nervous and Mental Disease, 200,* 156–162.

Del Giudice, M., Booth, T., & Irwing, P. (2012). The distance between Mars and Venus: Measuring global sex differences in personality. *PLoS ONE, 7*, e29265.

DeMaria, S. (2012). Club drugs. In E. O. Bryson & E. A. M. Frost (Eds.), *Perioperative addiction: Clinical management of the addicted patient* (pp. 111–128). New York: Springer Science + Business Media.

Dement, W. C., & Wolpert, E. (1958). The relation of eye movements, bodily motility, and external stimuli to dream content. *Journal of Experimental Psychology, 53*, 543–553.

Demeyer, I., De Lissnyder, E., Koster, E., & De Raedt, R. (2012). Rumination mediates the relationship between impaired cognitive control for emotional information and depressive symptoms: A prospective study in remitted depressed adults. *Behaviour Research and Therapy, 50*, 292–297.

Dempster, M., McCorry, N. K., Brennan, E., Donnelly, M., Murray, L. J., & Johnston, B. T. (2011). Do changes in illness perceptions predict changes in psychological distress among oesophageal cancer survivors? *Journal of Health Psychology, 16*, 500–509.

Denmark, F. L., Rabinovitz, V. C., & Sechzer, J. A. (2005). *Engendering psychology: Women and gender revisited* (2nd ed.). Boston, MA: Allyn and Bacon.

Denson, T. F. (2011). A social neuroscience perspective on the neurobiological bases of aggression. In P. R. Shaver & M. Mikulincer (Eds.), *Herzilya series on personality and social psychology. Human aggression and violence: Causes, manifestations, and consequences* (pp. 105–120). Washington, DC: American Psychological Association.

Depue, B. E. (2012). A neuroanatomical model of prefrontal inhibitory modulation of memory retrieval. *Neuroscience and Biobehavioral Reviews, 36*, 1382–1399.

Derntl, B., Schöpf, V., Kollndorfer, K., & Lanzenberger, R. (2013). Menstrual cycle phase and duration of oral contraception intake affect olfactory perception. *Chemical Senses, 38*, 67–75.

DeRobertis, E. M. (2013). Humanistic psychology: Alive in the 21st century?. *Journal of Humanistic Psychology.* doi:10.1177/00221678 12473369.

Desbordes, G., Negi, L. T., Pace, T. W. W., Wallace, B. A., Raison, C. L., & Schwartz, E. L. (2012). Effects of mindful-attention and compassion meditation training on amygdala response to emotional stimuli in an ordinary, non-meditative state. *Frontiers in Human Neuroscience, 6*, 292.

Dessalles, J. (2011). Sharing cognitive dissonance as a way to reach social harmony. *Social Science Information/Sur Les Sciences Sociales, 50*, 116–127.

Deutscher, G. (2010). *Through the language glass: Why the world looks different in other languages.* New York: Metropolitan Books/Henry Holt & Company.

DeWall, C. N., Anderson, C. A., & Bushman, B. J. (2013). Aggression. In H. Tennen, J. Suls, & I. B. Weiner (Eds.), *Handbook of psychology, Vol. 5. Personality and social psychology* (2nd ed., pp. 449–466). Hoboken, NJ: Wiley

Dewan, M. J., Steenbarger, B. N., & Greenberg, R. P. (2011). Brief psychotherapies. In R. E. Hales, S. C. Yudofsky, & G. O. Gabbard (Eds.), *Essentials of psychiatry* (3rd ed., pp. 525–539). Arlington, VA: American Psychiatric Publishing.

Dewar, M., Alber, J., Butler, C., Cowan, N., & Della Sala, S. (2012). Brief wakeful resting boosts new memories over the long term. *Psychological Science, 23*, 955–960.

Dhikav, V., Aggarwal, N., Gupta, S., Jadhavi, R., & Singh, K. (2008). Depression in Dhat syndrome. *Journal of Sexual Medicine, 5*, 841–844.

Di Iorio, C. R., Watkins, T. J., Dietrich, M. S., Cao, A., Blackford, J. U., Rogers, B., . . . Cowan, R. L. (2012). Evidence for chronically altered serotonin function in the cerebral cortex of female 3,4-methylenedioxymethamphetamine polydrug users. *Archives of General Psychiatry, 69*, 399–409.

Dickens, W. T., & Flynn, J. R. (2001). Heritability estimates versus large environmental effects: The IQ paradox resolved. *Psychological Review, 108*, 346–369.

DiDonato, T. E., Ullrich, J., & Krueger, J. I. (2011). Social perception as induction and inference: An integrative model of intergroup differentiation, ingroup favoritism, and differential accuracy. *Journal of Personality and Social Psychology, 100*, 66–83.

Diego, M. A., & Jones, N. A. (2007). Neonatal antecedents for empathy. In T. Farrow & P. Woodruff (Eds.), *Empathy in mental illness* (pp. 145–167). New York: Cambridge University Press.

Diener, E., & Chan, M. Y. (2011). Happy people live longer: Subjective well-being contributes to health and longevity. *Applied Psychology: Health and Well-Being, 3*, 1–43.

Dierdorff, E. C., Bell, S. T., & Belohlav, J. A. (2011). The power of "we": Effects of psychological collectivism on team performance over time. *Journal of Applied Psychology, 96*, 247–262.

DiFeliceantonio, A. G., Mabrouk, O. S., Kennedy, R. T., & Berridge, K. C. (2012). Enkephalin surges in dorsal neostriatum as a signal to eat. *Current Biology, 22,* 1918–1924.

DiGrazia, J., McKelvey, K., Bollen, J., & Rojas, F. (2013). More tweets, more votes: Social media as a quantitative indicator of political behavior. *Social Science Research Network.* Advance online publication. doi .org/10.2139/ssrn.2235423

Dillard, D. A., Smith, J. J., Ferucci, E. D., & Lanier, A. P. (2012). Depression prevalence and associated factors among Alaska native people: The Alaska education and research toward health (EARTH) study. *Journal of Affective Disorders, 136*, 1088–1097.

Dimberg, U., & Söderkvist, S. (2011). The voluntary facial action technique: A method to test the facial feedback hypothesis. *Journal of Nonverbal Behavior, 35*, 17–33.

DiPietro, J. A. (2000). Baby and the brain: Advances in child development. *Annual Review of Public Health, 21*, 455–471.

Dirks-Linhorst, P. A. (2013). An analysis of Missouri's insanity acquittee population, 1980–2009: Differences within African American insanity acquittees. *Journal of Ethnicity in Criminal Justice, 11*, 44–70.

Distel, M. A., Middeldorp, C. M., Trul, T. J., Derom, C. A, Willemsen, G., & Boomsma, D. I. (2011). Life events and borderline personality features: The influence of gene-environment interaction and gene-environment correlation. *Psychological Medicine: A Journal of Research in Psychiatry and the Allied Sciences, 41*, 849–860.

Doane, L. D., Kremen, W. S., Eaves, L. J., Eisen, S. A., Hauger, R., Hellhammer, D., . . . Jacobson, K. C. (2010). Associations between jet lag and cortisol diurnal rhythms after domestic travel. *Health Psychology, 29*, 117–123.

Doghramji, K. (2000, December). *Sleepless in America: Diagnosing and treating insomnia.* Retrieved from http://psychiatry. medscape.com/Medscape/psychiatry/Clinical Mgmt/CM.v02/public/indexCM.v02.html.

Dolev-Cohen, M. & Barak, A. (2013). Adolescents' use of instant messaging as a means of emotional relief. *Computers in Human Behavior, 29*, 58–63.

Domhoff, G. W. (2003). *The scientific study of dreams: Neural networks, cognitive development, and content analysis.* Washington, DC: American Psychological Association.

Domhoff, G. W. (2007). Realistic simulation and bizarreness in dream content: Past findings and suggestions for future research. In D. Barrett & P. McNamara (Eds.), *The new science of dreaming: Volume 2. Content, recall, and personality correlates* (pp. 1–27). Westport, CT: Praeger.

Domhoff, G. W. (2010). Dream content is continuous with waking thought, based on preoccupations, concerns, and interests. *Sleep Medicine Clinics, 5*, 203–215.

Domjan, M. (2005). Pavlovian conditioning: A functional perspective. *Annual Review of Psychology, 56*, 179–206.

Donnerstein, E. (2011). The media and aggression: From TV to the internet. In J. P. Forgas, A. W. Kruglanski & K. D. Williams (Eds.), *The psychology of social conflict and aggression* (pp. 267–284). New York: Psychology Press.

Donovan, D. M., Daley, D. C., Brigham, G. S., Hodgkins, C. C., Perl, H. I., Garrett, S.B., . . . Zammarelli, L. (2013). Stimulant abuser groups to engage in 12-step: A multisite trial in the National Institute on Drug Abuse Clinical Trials Network. *Journal of Substance Abuse Treatment, 44*, 103–114.

Doornbos, M. M., Zandee, G. L., DeGroot, J., & Warpinski, M. (2013). Desired mental health resources for urban, ethnically diverse, impoverished women struggling with anxiety and depression. *Qualitative Health Research, 23*, 78–92.

Dotsch, R., Wigboldus, D. H. J., & van Knippenberg, A. (2011). Biased allocation of faces to social categories. *Journal of Personality and Social Psychology, 100*, 999–1014.

Dougall, A. L., Wroble Biglan, M. C., Swanson, J. N., & Baum, A. (2013). Stress, coping, and immune function. In R. J. Nelson, S. J. Y. Mizumori, & I. B. Weiner (Eds.), *Handbook of psychology, Vol. 3. Behavioral neuroscience (2nd ed.*, pp. 440–460). Hoboken, NJ: Wiley.

Douglass, A. B. & Pavletic, A. (2012). Eyewitness confidence malleability. In B. L. Cutler (Ed.), *Conviction of the innocent: Lessons from psychological research* (pp. 149–165). Washington DC: American Psychological Association.

Dovidio, J. F., Eller, A., & Hewstone, M. (2011). Improving intergroup relations through direct, extended and other forms of indirect contact. *Group Processes and Intergroup Relations, 14*, 147–160.

Drapeau, V., & Gallant, A. R. (2013). Homeostatic and circadian control of food intake: Clinical strategies to prevent overconsumption. *Current Obesity Reports, 2*, 93–103.

Drew, L. (2013). What is the point of sleep? *New Scientist, 217*, 38–39.

Drew, L. J., Crabtree, G. W., Markx, S., Stark, K. L., Chaverneff, F., Xu, B., . . . Karayiorgou, M. (2011). The 22q11.2 microdeletion: Fifteen years of insights into the genetic and neural complexity of psychiatric disorders. *International Journal of Developmental Neuroscience, 29*, 259–281.

Drucker, D. J. (2010). Male sexuality and Alfred Kinsey's 0–6 Scale: Toward "a sound understanding of the realities of sex." *Journal of Homosexuality, 57*, 1105–1123.

Ducci, F., Bevilacqua, L., Landi, P., & Goldman, D. (2013). Genetic variation within serotonin genes, hormones, and aggression. In D. W. Pfaff & Y. Christen (Eds.), *Multiple origins of sex differences in the brain* (pp. 81–102). Berlin, Germany: Springer.

Duffey, K. J., & Popkin, B. M. (2013). Causes of increased energy intake among children in the US, 1977–2010. *American Journal of Preventive Medicine, 44*, e1-e8.

Dufresne, T. (2007). *Against Freud: Critics talk back.* Palo Alto, CA: Stanford University Press.

Duncan, B. L., & Reese, R. J. (2013). Empirically supported treatments, evidence-based treatments, and evidence-based practice. In G. Stricker, T. A. Widiger, & I. B. Weiner (Eds.), *Handbook of psychology, Vol. 8. Clinical psychology (2nd ed.*, pp. 489–513). Hoboken, NJ: Wiley.

Dunlosky, J., Rawson, K. A., Marsh, E. J., Nathan, M. J., & Willingham, D. T. (2013). Improving students' learning with effective learning techniques: Promising directions from cognitive and educational psychology. *Psychological Science in the Public Interest, 14*, 4–58.

Dunn, D. S., Saville, B. K., Baker, S. C., & Marek, P. (2013). Evidence–based teaching: Tools and techniques that promote learning in the psychology classroom. *Australian Journal of Psychology, 65*, 5–13.

Dunn, D., & Goodnight, L. (2014). *Communication: Embracing difference* (4th ed.). Upper Saddle River, NJ: Pearson.

Dunn, E. W., Aknin, L. B., & Norton, M. I. (2008). Spending money on others promotes happiness. *Science, 319*, 1687–1688.

Dunning, D., & Balcetis, E. (2013). Wishful seeing how preferences shape visual perception. *Current Directions in Psychological Science, 22*, 33–37.

Durgin, F. H., Ruff, A. J., & Russell, R. C. (2012). Constant enough: On the kinds of perceptual constancy worth having. In G. Hatfield & S. Allred (Eds.), *Visual experience: Sensation, cognition, and constancy* (pp. 87–102). New York: Oxford University Press.

Durrant, R., & Ellis, B. J. (2013). Evolutionary psychology. In R. J. Nelson, S. J. Y. Mizumori, & I. B. Weiner (Eds.), *Handbook of psychology, Vol. 3. Behavioral neuroscience (2nd ed.*, pp. 26–51). Hoboken, NJ: Wiley.

Duval, D. C. (2006). The relationship between African centeredness and psychological androgyny among African American women in middle adulthood. *Dissertation Abstracts International: Section B: The Sciences and Engineering, 67*, 1146.

Eagly, A. H., Karau, S. J., & Makhijani, M. G. (1995). Gender and the effectiveness of leaders: A meta-analysis. *Psychological Bulletin, 117*, 125–145.

Eaton, N. R., Keyes, K. M., Krueger, R. F., Balsis, S., Skodol, A. E., Markon, K. E., . . . Hasin, D. S. (2012). An invariant dimensional liability model of gender differences in mental disorder prevalence: Evidence from a national sample. *Journal of Abnormal Psychology, 121*, 282–288.

Eckel-Mahan, K., & Sassone-Corsi, P. (2013). Metabolism and the circadian clock converge. *Physiological Reviews, 93*, 107–135.

Ecker, U. K. H., Lewandowsky, S., & Apai, J. (2011). Terrorists brought down the plane!—No, actually it was a technical fault: Processing corrections of emotive information. *The Quarterly Journal of Experimental Psychology*, *64*, 283–310.

Edele, A., Dziobek, I., & Keller, M. (2013). Explaining altruistic sharing in the dictator game: The role of affective empathy, cognitive empathy, and justice sensitivity. *Learning and Individual Differences, 24,* 96–102.

Edelstein, B. A., Martin, R. R., & Gerolimatos, L. A. (2013). Assessment in geriatric settings. In J. R. Graham, J. A. Naglieri, & I. B. Weiner (Eds.), *Handbook of psychology, Vol. 10. Assessment psychology (2nd ed.*, pp. 425–447). Hoboken, NJ: Wiley.

Ehrenreich, B. (2004, July 15). *All together now*. Retrieved from http://select.nytimes.com/gst/abstract.html?res5F00E16FA3C5E0C768DDDAE0894DC404482.

Eichenbaum, H. (2013). Memory systems. In R. J. Nelson, S. J. Y. Mizumori, & I. B. Weiner (Eds.), *Handbook of psychology, Vol. 3. Behavioral neuroscience* (2nd ed., pp. 551–573). Hoboken, NJ: Wiley.

Eisenberger, R., & Armeli, S. (1997). Can salient reward increase creative performance without reducing intrinsic creative interest? *Journal of Personality and Social Psychology, 72*, 652–663.

Eisenberger, R., & Rhoades, L. (2002). Incremental effects of reward on creativity. *Journal of Personality and Social Psychology, 81*, 728–741.

Ekas, N. V., Haltigan, J. D., & Messinger, D. S. (2013). The dynamic still-face effect: Do infants decrease bidding over time when parents are not responsive? *Developmental Psychology, 49,* 1027–1035.

Ekman, P., & Friesen, W. V. (1971). Constants across cultures in the face and emotion. *Journal of Personality and Social Psychology, 17,* 124–129.

Ekman, P., & Keltner, D. (1997). Universal facial expressions of emotion: An old controversy and new findings. In U. C. Segerstrale & P. Molnar (Eds.), *Nonverbal communication: Where nature meets culture* (pp. 27–46). Mahwah, NJ: Erlbaum.

Elkind, D. (1967). Egocentrism in adolescence. *Child Development, 38,* 1025–1034.

Elkind, D. (2000). A quixotic approach to issues in early childhood education. *Human Development, 43,* 279–283.

Ellis, A. (2008). Rational emotive behavior therapy. In K. Jordan (Ed.), *The quick theory reference guide: A resource for expert and novice mental health professionals*, (pp. 127–139). Hauppauge, NY: Nova Science Publishers.

Ellis, A., & Ellis, D. J. (2011a). *Rational emotive behavior therapy.* Washington, DC: American Psychological Association.

Ellis, A., & Ellis, D. J. (2011b). *Theories of psychotherapy. Rational emotive behavior therapy*. Washington, DC: Amreican Psychological Association.

Elsesser, K., Wannemüller, A., Lohrmann, T., Jöhren, P., & Sartory, G. (2013). Attention focusing versus distraction during exposure in dental phobia. *Behavioural and Cognitive Psychotherapy, 41,* 173–187.

Emdin, M., Passino, C., & Giannoni, A. (2013). Breathless heart: Only when the neck is deep in water? *Journal of the American College of Cardiology, 61,* 1167–1168.

Emery, C. F., Anderson, D. R., & Goodwin, C. L. (2013). Coronary heart disease and hypertension. In A. M. Nezu, C. M. Nezu, P. A. Geller, & I. B. Weiner (Eds.), *Handbook of psychology, Vol. 9. Health psychology* (2nd ed., pp. 340–364). Hoboken, NJ: Wiley.

Emmett, J., & McGee, D. (2013). Extrinsic motivation for large-scale assessments: A case study of a student achievement program at one urban high school. *The High School Journal, 96,* 116–137.

Endendijk, J. J., Groeneveld, M. G., van Berkel, S. R., Hallers-Haalboom, E. T., Mesman, J., & Bakermans-Kranenburg, M. J. (2013). Gender stereotypes in the family context: Mothers, fathers, and siblings. *Sex Roles*, 68, 577–590.

Eng, P. M., Rimm, E. B., Fitzmaurice, G., & Kawachi, I. (2002). Social ties and change in social ties in relation to subsequent total and cause-specific mortality and coronary heart disease incidence in men. *American Journal of Epidemiology, 155,* 700–709.

Enoch, M.-A. (2011). The role of early life stress as a predictor for alcohol and drug dependence. *Psychopharmacology, 214,* 17–31.

Epley, N. (2008) Rebate psychology. *New York Times.* Retrieved from http://select.nytimes.com/mem/tnt.html?tntget2008/01/31/opinion/31epley.html.

Epstein, L. H., Handley, E. A., Dearing, K. K., Cho, D. D., Roemmich, J. N., Paluch, R. A., . . . Spring, B. (2006). Purchases of food in youth: Influence of price and income. *Psychological Science, 17,* 82–89.

Erlacher, D., & Schredl, M. (2004). Dreams reflecting waking sport activities: A comparison of sport and psychology students. *International Journal of Sport Psychology, 35,* 301–308.

Ersche, K. D., Jones, P. S., Williams, G. B., Robbins, T. W., & Bullmore, E. T. (2012). Cocaine dependence: A fast-track for brain ageing? *Molecular Psychiatry, 18,* 134–140.

Espy, K. A., Fang, H., Johnson, C., Stopp, C., Wiebe, S. A., & Respass, J. (2011). Prenatal tobacco exposure: Developmental outcomes in the neonatal period. *Developmental Psychology, 47,* 153–169.

Esquivel, G. B., & Acevedo, M. (2013). Testing for language competence in children and adolescents. In K. F. Geisinger, B. A. Bracken, J. F. Carlson, J.-I. C. Hansen, N. R. Kuncel, S. P. Reise, & M. C. Rodriguez (Eds.), *APA handbooks in psychology. APA handbook of testing and assessment in psychology, Vol. 3. Testing and assessment in school psychology and education* (pp. 213–230). Washington, DC: American Psychological Association.

Essau, C. A., & Petermann, F. (Eds.). (2013). *Anxiety disorders in children and adolescents: Epidemiology, risk factors and treatment* (Vol. 4). New York: Routledge.

Ethical Principles of Psychologists and Code of Conduct. (2010). *American Psychologist, 65,* 493.

Eysenck, H. J. (1967). *The biological basis of personality*. Springfield, IL: Charles C Thomas.

Eysenck, H. J. (1982). *Personality, genetics, and behavior: Selected papers*. New York: Prager.

Eysenck, H. J. (1990). Biological dimensions of personality. In L. A. Pervin (Ed.), *Handbook of personality: Theory and research* (pp. 244–276). New York: Guilford Press.

Fabre, B., Grosman, H., Mazza, O., Nolazco, C., Machulsky, N. F., Mesch, V., . . . Berg, G. (2013). Relationship between cortisol, life events and metabolic syndrome in men. *Stress: The International Journal on the Biology of Stress, 161,* 16–23.

Faddiman, A. (1997). *The spirit catches you and you fall down*. New York: Straus & Giroux.

Farber, I., & Banks, W. P. (2013). Consciousness. In A. F. Healy, R. W. Proctor, & I. B. Weiner (Eds.), *Handbook of psychology,*

Vol. 4. Experimental psychology (2nd ed., pp. 3–31). Hoboken, NJ: Wiley.

Fazio, L. K., Barber, S. J., Rajaram, S., Ornstein, P. A., & Marsh, E. J. (2013). Creating illusions of knowledge: Learning errors that contradict prior knowledge. *Journal of Experimental Psychology: General, 142*, 1–5.

Fein, S., & Spencer, S. J. (1997). Prejudice as selfimage maintenance: Affirming the self through derogating others. *Journal of Personality and Social Psychology, 73*, 31–44.

Feinstein, J. S. (2013). Lesion studies of human emotion and feeling. *Current Opinion in Neurobiology, 23*, 304–309.

Feldman, R. (2014). Synchrony and the neurobiological basis of social affiliation. In M. Mikulincer & P. R. Shaver (Eds.), *Mechanisms of social connection: From brain to group. The Herzliya series on personality and social psychology* (pp. 145–166). Washington, DC: American Psychological Association.

Fenn, K. M., & Hambrick, D. Z. (2012). What drives sleep-dependent memory consolidation: Greater gain or less loss? *Psychonomic Bulletin & Review, 20*, 501–506.

Fennis, B. M., & Stroebe, W. (2010). *The psychology of advertising*. New York: Psychology Press.

Ferguson, C. J. (2010). Violent crime research: An introduction. In C. J. Ferguson (Ed.), *Violent crime: Clinical and social implications* (pp. 3–18). Thousand Oaks, CA: Sage.

Ferguson, C. J. (2012). Violence in video games: Advocating for the wrong cause? *Child and Family Policy and Practice Advocate, 35*, 16–18.

Ferguson, M. J., & Porter, S. C. (2013). An examination of categorization processes in organizations: The root of intergroup bias and a route to prejudice reduction. In Q. M. Roberson (Ed.), *Oxford library of psychology. The Oxford handbook of diversity and work* (pp. 98–114). New York: Oxford University Press.

Fernández-Dols, J. M. (2013). Advances in the study of facial expression: An introduction to the special section. *Emotion Review, 5*, 3–7.

Ferreira, G. K., Rezin, G. T., Cardoso, M. R., Gonçalves, C. L., Borges, L. S., Vieira, J. S., . . . Streck, E. L. (2012). Brain energy metabolism is increased by chronic administration of bupropion. *Acta Neuropsychiatrica, 24*, 115–121.

Ferrucci, L. M., Cartmel, B., Turkman, Y. E., Murphy, M. E., Smith, T., Stein, K. D., & McCorkle, R. (2011). Causal attribution among cancer survivors of the 10 most common cancers. *Journal of Psychosocial Oncology, 29*, 121–140.

Festinger, L. A., & Carlsmith, J. M. (1959). Cognitive consequences of forced compliance. *Journal of Abnormal and Social Psychology, 58*, 203–210.

Field, K. M., Woodson, R., Greenberg, R., & Cohen, D. (1982). Discrimination and imitation of facial expressions by neonates. *Science, 218*, 179–181.

Fields, A., & Cochran, S. (2011). Men and depression: Current perspectives for health care professionals. *American Journal of Lifestyle Medicine, 5*, 92–100.

Figlewicz, D. P., & Sipols, A. J. (2010). Energy regulatory signals and food reward. *Pharmacology, Biochemistry & Behavior, 97*, 15–24.

Figueredo, A., Jacobs, W., Burger, S., Gladden, P., & Olderbak, S. (2011). The biology of personality. In G. Terzis & R. Arp (Eds.), *Information and living systems: Philosophical and scientific perspectives* (pp. 371–406). Boston, MA: MIT Press.

Filipović, D., Zlatković, J., Gass, P., & Inta, D. (2013). The differential effects of acute vs. chronic stress and their combination on hippocampal parvalbumin and Hsp70i expression. *Neuroscience, 236*, 47–54.

Fink, G. (2011). Stress controversies: Post-traumatic stress disorder, hippocampal volume, gastroduodenal ulceration. *Journal of Neuroendocrinology, 23*, 107–117.

Finkel, E. J., Slotter, E. B., Luchies, L. B., Walton, G. M., & Gross, J. J. (2013). A brief intervention to promote conflict-reappraisal preserves marital quality over time. *Psychological Science, 24*, 1595–1601.

Fischer, P., Krueger, J. I., Greitemeyer, T., Vogrincic, C., Kastenmüller, A., Frey, D., . . . Kainbacher, M. (2011). The bystander-effect: A meta-analytic review on bystander intervention in dangerous and non-dangerous emergencies. *Psychological Bulletin, 137*, 517–537.

Fischer, S., Peterson, C. M., & McCarthy, D. (2013). A prospective test of the influence of negative urgency and expectancies on binge eating and purging. *Psychology of Addictive Behaviors, 27*, 294–300.

Fisher, J. O., Birch, L. L., Zhang, J., Grusak, M. A., & Hughes, S. O. (2013). External influences on children's self-served portions at meals. *International Journal of Obesity, 37*, 954–960.

Fisher, M. A. (2013). *The ethics of conditional confidentiality: A practice model for mental health professionals*. New York: Oxford University Press.

Fishman, I., & Ng, R. (2013). Error-related brain activity in extraverts: Evidence for altered response monitoring in social context. *Biological Psychology, 93*, 225–230.

Fisk, J. E., Bury, A. S., & Holden, R. (2006). Reasoning about complex probabilistic concepts in childhood. *Scandinavian Journal of Psychology, 47*, 497–504.

Fiske, S. T. (1998). Stereotyping, prejudice, and discrimination. In D. T. Gilbert, S. T. Fiske, & G. Lindzey (Eds.), *The handbook of social psychology* (4th ed., Vol. 2, pp. 357–411). New York: Oxford University Press.

Fitzgerald, C. S., & Clark, S. (2013). Work locus of control and perceptions of practice. *Journal of Public Child Welfare, 7*, 59–78.

Fitzpatrick, D., & Mooney, R. D. (2012). The somatic sensory system: Touch and proprioception. In D. Purves, G. J. Augustine, D. Fitzpatrick, W. C. Hall, A.-S. LaManita, & L. E. White (Eds.), *Neuroscience* (5th ed., pp. 189–208). Sunderland, MA: Sinauer Associates.

Fivush, R., Bohanek, J. G., Zaman, W., & Grapin, S. (2012). Gender differences in adolescents' autobiographical narratives. *Journal of Cognition and Development, 13*, 295–319.

Flaherty, S. C., & Sadler, L. S. (2011). A review of attachment theory in the context of adolescent parenting. *Journal of Pediatric Health Care, 25*, 114–121.

Flavell, J. H., Miller, P. H., & Miller, S. A. (2002). *Cognitive development* (4th ed.). Upper Saddle River, NJ: Prentice-Hall.

Fleischhaker, C., Böhme, R., Sixt, B., Brück, C., Schneider, C., & Schulz, E. (2011). Dialectical Behavioral Therapy for Adolescents (DBT-A): A clinical trial for patients with suicidal and self-injurious behavior and borderline symptoms with a one-year follow-up. *Child and Adolescent Psychiatry and Mental Health, 5*, Article ID 3.

Fletcher, B. R., & Rapp, P. R. (2013). Normal neurocognitive aging. In R. J. Nelson, S. J. Y. Mizumori, & I. B. Weiner (Eds.), *Handbook of psychology, Vol. 3. Behavioral neuroscience (2nd ed.*, pp. 643–663). Hoboken, NJ: Wiley.

Fletcher, G. J. O., & Simpson, J. A. (2000). Ideal standards in close relationships: Their structure and functions. *Current Directions in Psychological Science, 9*, 102–105.

Flint, M. S., Baum, A., Episcopo, B., Knickelbein, K. Z., Liegey Dougall, A. J., Chambers, W. H., & Jenkins, F. J. (2013). Chronic exposure to stress hormones promotes transformation and tumorigenicity of 3T3 mouse fibroblasts. *Stress: The International Journal on the Biology of Stress, 16*, 114–121.

Flo, E., Pallesen, S., Åkerstedt, T., Magerøy, N., Moen, B. E., Grønli, J., . . .

Bjorvatn, B. (2013). Shift-related sleep problems vary according to work schedule. *Occupational and Environmental Medicine 70*, 238–245.

Flor, H. (2013). Cultural influences on perceptions of pain. In S. Barnow & N. Balkir (Eds.), *Cultural variations in psychopathology: From research to practice* (pp. 173–183). Cambridge, MA: Hogrefe Publishing.

Flynn, J. R. (1987). Massive IQ gains in 14 nations: What IQ tests really measure. *Psychological Bulletin, 101*, 171–191.

Flynn, J. R. (2007). *What is intelligence?: Beyond the Flynn Effect*. New York: Cambridge University Press.

Flynn, J. R. (2010). Problems with IQ gains: The huge vocabulary gap. *Journal of Psychoeducational Assessment, 28*, 412–433.

Foa, E. B., Gillihan, S. J., & Bryant, R. A. (2013). Challenges and successes in dissemination of evidence-based treatments for posttraumatic stress: Lessons learned from prolonged exposure therapy for PTSD. *Psychological Science in the Public Interest, 14*, 65–111.

Foell, J., & Flor, H. (2012). Phantom limb pain. In R. J. Moore (Ed.), *Handbook of pain and palliative care* (pp. 417–430). New York: Springer.

Foerde, K., & Shohamy, D. (2011). The role of the basal ganglia in learning and memory: Insight from Parkinson's disease. *Neurobiology of Learning and Memory, 96*, 624–636.

Fok, H. K., Hui, C. M., Bond, M. H., Matsumoto, D., & Yoo, S. H. (2008). Integrating personality, context, relationship, and emotion type into a model of display rules. *Journal of Research in Personality, 42*, 133–150.

Font, E., & Carazo, P. (2010). Animals in translation: Why there is meaning (but probably no message) in animal communication. *Animal Behaviour, 80*, e1–e6.

Forgas, J. P., & Eich, E. (2013). Affective influences on cognition: Mood congruence, mood dependence, and mood effects on processing strategies. In A. F. Healy, R. W. Proctor, & I. B. Weiner (Eds.), *Handbook of psychology, Vol. 4. Experimental psychology (2nd ed.*, pp. 61–82). Hoboken, NJ: Wiley.

Forshaw, M. (2013). *Critical thinking for psychology: A student guide*. Malden, MA: Wiley-Blackwell.

Forsyth, D. R. (2013). Social influence and group behavior. In H. Tennen, J. Suls, & I. B. Weiner (Eds.), *Handbook of psychology (Vol. 5). Personality and social psychology* (2nd ed., pp. 305–328). Hoboken, NJ: Wiley.

Fortune, E. E., & Goodie, A. S. (2012). Cognitive distortions as a component and treatment focus of pathological gambling: A review. *Psychology of Addictive Behaviors, 26*, 298–310.

Fouladi, D. B., Nassiri, P., Monazzam, E. M., Farahani, S., Hassanzadeh, G., & Hoseini, M. (2012). Industrial noise exposure and salivary cortisol in blue collar industrial workers. *Noise & Health, 14*, 184–189.

Foulkes, D. (1993). Children's dreaming. In D. Foulkes & C. Cavallero (Eds.), *Dreaming as cognition* (pp. 114–132). New York: Harvester Wheatsheaf.

Fraley, R. C., & Shaver, P. R. (1997). Adult attachment and the suppression of unwanted thoughts. *Journal of Personality and Social Psychology, 73*, 1080–1091.

Fraley, R. C., Roisman, G. I., Booth-LaForce, C., Owen, M. T., & Holland, A. S. (2013). Interpersonal and genetic origins of adult attachment styles: A longitudinal study from infancy to early adulthood. *Journal of Personality and Social Psychology, 104*, 817–338.

Francis, G. (2012). Publication bias and the failure of replication in experimental psychology. *Psychonomic Bulletin & Review, 19*, 975–991.

Franconeri, S. L., Alvarez, G. A., & Cavanagh, P. (2013). Flexible cognitive resources: competitive content maps for attention and memory. *Trends in Cognitive Sciences, 17*, 134–141.

Franklin, A., Bevis, L., Ling, Y., & Hurlbert, A. (2010). Biological components of color preference in infancy. *Developmental Science, 21*, 346–354.

Franko, D. L., Lovering, M. E., & Thompson-Brenner, H. (2013). Ethnicity, race and binge eating disorder. *A Clinician's Guide to Binge Eating Disorder, 14*, 93–112.

Freedheim, D. K., & Weiner, I. B. (Eds.). (2013). *Handbook of psychology, Vol. 1. History of psychology* (2nd ed.). Hoboken, NJ: Wiley.

Freeman, J. B., & Ambady, N. (2011). A dynamic interactive theory of person construal. *Psychological Review, 118*, 247–279.

Frenda, S. J., Knowles, E. D., Saletan, W., & Loftus, E. F. (2013). False memories of fabricated political events. *Journal of Experimental Social Psychology, 49*, 280–286.

Frew, J., & Spiegler, M. D. (Eds.). (2013). *Contemporary psychotherapies for a diverse world (1st rev. ed.)*. New York: Routledge/Taylor & Francis Group.

Fridlund, A. J., Beck, H. P., Goldie, W. D., & Irons, G. (2012). Little Albert: A neurologically impaired child. *History of Psychology, 15*, 302–327.

Friedberg, R. D., & Brelsford, G. M. (2011). Core principles in cognitive therapy with youth. *Child and Adolescent Psychiatric Clinics of North America, 20*, 369–378.

Friederich, H.-C., Wu, M., Simon, J. J., & Herzog, W. (2013). Neurocircuit function in eating disorders. *International Journal of Eating Disorders, 46*, 425–432.

Friedlander, M. L., Escudero, V., Heatherington, L., & Diamond, G. M. (2011). Alliance in couple and family therapy. *Psychotherapy, 48*, 25–33.

Friedman, D. D., Ertegun, L., Lupi, T., Beebe, B., & Deutsch, S. (2013). Securing attachment: Mother–infant research informs. In J. E. Bettmann & D. D. Friedman (Eds.), *Attachment-based clinical work with children and adolescents* (pp. 45–60). New York: Springer.

Fryer, R. G., Jr. (2010). Financial incentives and student achievement: Evidence from randomized trials. *National Bureau of Economic Research*, Working Paper No. 15898.

Fujimura, J. H., Rajagopalan, R., Ossorio, P. N., & Doksum, K. A. (2010). Race and ancestry: Operationalizing populations in human genetic variation studies. In I. Whitmarsh & D. S. Jones (Eds.), *What's the use of race? Modern governance and the biology of difference* (pp. 169–183). Cambridge, MA: MIT Press.

Fukase, Y., & Okamoto, Y. (2010). Psychosocial tasks of the elderly: A reconsideration of the eighth stage of Erikson's epigenetic scheme. *Japanese Journal of Developmental Psychology, 21*, 266–277.

Fuller-Rowell, T. E., Doan, S. N., & Eccles, J. S. (2012). Differential effects of perceived discrimination on the diurnal cortisol rhythm of African Americans and Whites. *Psychoneuroendocrinology, 37*, 107–118.

Fulton, L. V., Ivanitskaya, L. V., Bastian, N. D., Erofeev, D. A., & Mendez, F. A. (2013). Frequent deadlines: Evaluating the effect of learner control on healthcare executives' performance in online learning. *Learning and Instruction, 23*, 24–32.

Fumagalli, M., Ferrucci, R., Mameli, F., Marceglia, S., Mrakic-Sposta, S., Zago, S., . . . Priori, A. (2010). Gender-related differences in moral judgments. *Cognitive Processing, 11*, 219–226.

Funder, D. C. (2000). Personality. *Annual Review of Psychology, 52*, 197–221.

Furguson, E., Chamorro-Premuzic, T., Pickering, A., & Weiss, A. (2011). Five into one does go: A critique of the general factor of personality. In T. Chamorro-Premuzic, S. von Stumm, & A. Furnam (Eds.), *Wiley-Blackwell handbook of individual differences* (pp. 162–186). Chichester, UK: Wiley-Blackwell.

Furukawa, T., Nakano, H., Hirayama, K., Tanahashi, T., Yoshihara, K., Sudo, N., . . . Nishima, S. (2010). Relationship between snoring sound intensity and daytime blood pressure. *Sleep and Biological Rhythms, 8*, 245–253.

Fusar-Poli, P., & Meyer-Lindenberg, A. (2013). Striatal presynaptic dopamine in schizophrenia, Part I: Meta-analysis of dopamine active transporter (DAT) density. *Schizophrenia Bulletin, 39*, 22–32.

Gabry, K. E., Chrousos, G. P., Rice, K. C., Mostafa, R. M., Sternberg, E., Negrao, A. B., . . . Gold, P. W. (2002). Marked suppression of gastric ulcerogenesis and intestinal responses to stress by a novel class of drugs. *Molecular Psychiatry, 7*, 474–483.

Gacono, C. B., Evans, F. B., & Viglione, D. J. (2008). Essential issues in the forensic use of the Rorschach. In C. B. Gacono (Ed.), F. B. Evans (Ed.), N. Kaser-Boyd (Col.), & L. A. Gacono (Col.), *The handbook of forensic Rorschach assessment (pp. 3–20). The LEA series in personality and clinical psychology.* New York: Routledge/Taylor & Francis Group.

Gaetz, M., Weinberg, H., Rzempoluck, E., & Jantzen, K. J. (1998). Neural network classifications and correlational analysis of EEG and MEG activity accompanying spontaneous reversals of the Necker Cube. *Cognitive Brain Research, 6*, 335–346.

Galak, J., LeBoeuf, R. A., Nelson, L. D., & Simmons, J. P. (2012). Correcting the past: Failures to replicate psi. *Journal of Personality & Social Psychology, 103*, 933–948.

Gallagher III, B. J., & Jones, B. J. (2013). Childhood stressors and symptoms of schizophrenia. *Clinical Schizophrenia & Related Psychoses*, 8, 1–19.

Gallup Wellbeing. (2013). *Snapshot: Obesity rate ticking up.* Retrieved from http://www.gallup.com/poll/163205/snapshot-obesity-rate-ticking.aspx

Ganis, G., & Schendan, H. E. (2013). Cognitive neuroscience of mental imagery: Methods and paradigms. In S. Lacey & R. Lawson (Eds.), *Multisensory imagery* (pp. 283–298). New York: Springer.

Ganis, G., Rosenfeld J. P., Meixner, J., Kievit, R. A., & Schendan, H. E. (2011). Lying in the scanner: Covert countermeasures disrupt deception detection by functional magnetic resonance imaging. *Neuroimage, 55*, 312–319.

Gans, J. J., O'Sullivan, P., & Bircheff, V. (2013). Mindfulness based tinnitus stress reduction pilot study: A symptom perception-shift program. *Mindfulness, 12*(Suppl. 1): P76.

García, E. E., & Náñez, J. E., Sr. (2011). Education circumstances. In E. E. García & J. E. Náñez, Sr. (Eds.), *Bilingualism and cognition: Informing research, pedagogy, and policy* (pp. 103–114). Washington, DC: American Psychological Association.

Gardner, H. (1983). *Frames of mind.* New York: Basic Books.

Gardner, H. (1999, February). Who owns intelligence? *Atlantic Monthly*, pp. 67–76.

Gardner, H. (2008). Who owns intelligence? In M. H. Immordino-Yang (Ed.), *Jossey-Bass Education Team. The Jossey-Bass reader on the brain and learning* (pp. 120–132). San Francisco, CA: Jossey-Bass.

Gardner, H. (2011). *Frames of mind.* New York: Basic Books.

Garfield, A.S., Cowley, M., Smith, F.M., Moorwood, K., Stewart-Cox, J.E., Gilroy, K. . . . Ward, A. (2011). Distinct physiological and behavioural functions for parental alleles of imprinted Grb10. *Nature, 469*, 534–538.

Gasser, S., & Raulet, D. H. (2006). The DNA damage pathway regulates innate immune system ligands of the NKG2D receptor arouses the immune system. *Cancer Research, 66*, 3959–3962.

Gazendam, F. J., Kamphuis, J. H., & Kindt, M. (2013). Deficient safety learning characterizes high trait anxious individuals. *Biological Psychology, 92*, 342–352.

Gazzaniga, M. S. (2009). The fictional self. Personal identity and fractured selves: Perspectives from philosophy, ethics, and neuroscience. In D. J. H. Mathews, H. Bok, & P. V. Rabins (Eds.), *Personal identity and fractured selves: Perspectives from philosophy, ethics, and neuroscience* (pp. 174–185). Baltimore, MD: Johns Hopkins University Press.

Geangu, E., Benga, O., Stahl, D., & Striano, T. (2010). Contagious crying beyond the first days of life. *Infant Behavior and Development, 33*, 279–288.

Geisinger, K. F. (2013). Reliability. In K. F. Geisinger, B. A. Bracken, J. F. Carlson, J.-I. C. Hansen, N. R. Kuncel, S. P. Reise, & M. C. Rodriguez (Eds.), *APA handbooks in psychology. APA handbook of testing and assessment in psychology, Vol. 1. Test theory and testing and assessment in industrial and organizational psychology* (pp. 21–42). Washington, DC: American Psychological Association.

Gelder, B. D., Meeren, H. K., Righart, R. Stock, J. V., van de Riet, W. A., & Tamietto, M. (2006). Beyond the face: Exploring rapid influences of context on face processing. *Progress in Brain Research, 155*, 37–48.

Geller, P. A., Nelson, A. R., & Bonacquisti, A. (2013). Women's health psychology. In A. M. Nezu, C. M. Nezu, P. A. Geller, & I. B. Weiner (Eds.), *Handbook of psychology, Vol. 9. Health psychology* (2nd ed., pp. 477–511). Hoboken, NJ: Wiley.

Gellerman, D. M., & Lu, F. G. (2011). Religious and spiritual issues in the outline for cultural formulation. In J. R. Peteet, F. G. Lu, & W. E Narrow (Eds.), *Religious and spiritual issues in psychiatric diagnosis: A research agenda for DSM-V* (pp. 207–220). Washington, DC: American Psychiatric Association.

Geniole, S. N., Carré, J. M., & McCormick, C. M. (2011). State, not trait, neuroendocrine function predicts costly reactive aggression in men after social exclusion and inclusion. *Biological Psychology, 87*, 137–145.

Gerber, A. J., Posner, J., Gorman, D., Colibazzi, T., Yu, S., Wang, Z., . . . Peterson, B. S. (2008). An affective circumplex model of neural systems subserving valence, arousal, and cognitive overlay during the appraisal of emotional faces. *Neuropsychologia, 46*, 2129–2139.

Giacobbi, P., Jr., Foore, B., & Weinberg, R. S. (2004). Broken clubs and expletives: The sources of stress and coping responses of skilled and moderately skilled golfers. *Journal of Applied Sport Psychology, 16*, 166–182.

Gibb, B. E., Grassia, M., Stone, L. B., & Uhrlass, D. J. (2012). Brooding rumination and risk for depressive disorders in children of depressed mothers. *Journal of Abnormal Child Psychology, 40*, 317–326.

Gibbs, N. (1995, October 2). The EQ factor. *Time*, pp. 60–68.

Gibson, E. J., & Walk, R. D. (1960). The visual cliff. *Scientific American, 202*, 67–71.

Giles, L. C., Glonek, G. F. V., Luszcz, M. A., & Andrews, G. R. (2005). Effect of social networks on 10 year survival in very old Australians: The Australian longitudinal study of aging. *Journal of Epidemiology and Community Health, 59*, 574–579.

Gilles, F. H., & M. D. Nelson (2013). *The developing human brain: Growth and adversities.* Hoboken, NJ: Wiley.

Gillies, D., Taylor, F., Gray, C., O'Brien, L., & D'Abrew, N. (2012). Psychological therapies for the treatment of post-traumatic stress disorder in children and adolescents. *Cochrane Database of Systematic Reviews 2012*, Issue 12.

Gilman, S. R., Chang, J., Xu, B., Bawa, T. S., Gogos, J. A., Karayiorgou, M., & Vitkup, D. (2012). Diverse types of genetic variation converge on functional gene networks involved in schizophrenia. *Nature Neuroscience, 15*, 1723–1728.

Gilmour, D. R., & Walkey, F. H. (1981). Identifying violent offenders using a video measure of interpersonal distance. *Journal of Consulting and Clinical Psychology, 49*, 287–291.

Gimbel, S. I., & Brewer, J. B. (2011). Reaction time, memory strength, and fMRI activity during memory retrieval: Hippocampus and default network are differentially responsive during recollection and familiarity judgments. *Cognitive Neuroscience, 2*, 19–26.

Gini, M., Oppenheim, D., & Sagi-Schwartz, A. (2007). Negotiation styles in mother-child narrative co-construction in middle childhood: Associations with early attachment. *International Journal of Behavioral Development, 31*, 149–160.

Giummarra, M., & Moseley, L. (2011). Phantom limb pain and bodily awareness:current concepts and future directions. *Current Opinions in Anesthesiology, 24*, 524–531.

Glavis-Bloom, C., Alvarado, M. C., & Bachevalier, J. (2013). Neonatal hippocampal damage impairs specific food/place associations in adult macaques. *Behavioral Neuroscience, 127*, 9–22.

Glenn, A. L., Kurzban, R., & Raine, A. (2011). Evolutionary theory and psychopathy. *Aggression and Violent Behavior, 16*, 371–380.

Glicksohn, A., & Cohen, A. (2011). The role of Gestalt grouping principles in visual statistical learning. *Attention, Perception, and Psychophysics, 73*, 708–713.

Glikson, E., & Erez, M. (2013). Emotion display norms in virtual teams. *Journal of Personnel Psychology, 12*, 22–32.

Glover, V. (2011). Annual research review: Prenatal stress and the origins of psychopathology: An evolutionary perspective. *Journal of Child Psychology and Psychiatry, 52*, 356–367.

Go, A. S., Mozaffarian, D., Roger, V. L., Benjamin, E. J., Berry, J. D., Borden, W. B., . . . Turner, M. B. (2013). Heart disease and stroke statistics—2013 update: A report from the American Heart Association. *Circulation, 127*, e6-e245.

Goldfield, G. S. (2012). Making access to TV contingent on physical activity: Effects on liking and relative reinforcing value of TV and physical activity in overweight and obese children. *Journal of Behavioral Medicine, 35*, 1–7.

Goldstein, A. M., Morse, S. J., & Packer, I. K. (2013). Evaluation of criminal responsibility. In R. K. Otto & I. B. Weiner (Eds.), *Handbook of psychology, Vol. 11. Forensic psychology* (2nd ed., pp. 440–472). Hoboken, NJ: Wiley.

Goldstein, E. B. (2014). *Sensation and perception*. Belmont, CA: Wadsworth Publishing.

Goldstein, G., Brown, L. H., Haas, G. L., & Allen, D. N. (2013). Schizophrenia. In C. A. Noggle & R. S. Dean (Eds.), *Contemporary neuropsychology. The neuropsychology of psychopathology* (pp. 325–343). New York: Springer.

Goldstein, I. (2010). Looking at sexual behavior 60 years after Kinsey. *Journal of Sexual Medicine, 7*, 246–247.

Goldstone, R. L., Kersten, A., & Carvalho, P. F. (2013). Concepts and categorization. In A. F. Healy, R. W. Proctor, & I. B. Weiner (Eds.), *Handbook of psychology, Vol. 4. Experimental psychology (2nd ed.*, pp. 607–630). Hoboken, NJ: Wiley.

Gómez-Restrepo, C. (2007). 'Nada más que la verdad': Muchos cuestionamientos, pocas respuestas, parcas acciones. Dónde quedan la ética, los derechos fundamentales y la salud mental? Una opinión desde la academia. / 'Nothing but the Truth': Many questions, few answers, little action. What happened to ethics, human rights and mental health? An opinion from the academy. *Revista Colombiana de Psiquiatría, 36*, 675–690.

Gonzalez, S., Xu, C., Ramirez, M., Zavala, J., Armas, R., Contreras, S. A., . . . Escamilla, M. (2013). Suggestive evidence for association between L-type voltage-gated calcium channel (CACNA1C) gene haplotypes and bipolar disorder in Latinos: A family-based association study. *Bipolar Disorders, 15*, 206–214.

Goodson, J. L. (2013). Deconstructing sociality, social evolution and relevant nonapeptide functions. *Psychoneuroendocrinology, 38*, 465–478.

Goodwin, C. J. (2011). *Research in psychology: Methods and design* (6th ed.). Hoboken, NJ: Wiley.

Goodwin, C. J. (2012). *A history of modern psychology* (4th ed.). Hoboken, NJ: Wiley.

Goodwin, C. J. (2012). United States. In D. B. Baker (Ed.), *Oxford library of psychology. The Oxford handbook of the history of psychology: Global perspectives* (pp. 571–593). New York: Oxford University Press.

Goodwin, K. A., Kukucka, J. P., & Hawks, I. M. (2013). Co-witness confidence, conformity, and eyewitness memory: An examination of normative and informational social influences. *Applied Cognitive Psychology, 27*, 91–100.

Gooneratne, N. S., Edwards, A. Y. Z., Zhou, C., Cuellar, N., Grandner, M. A., & Barrett, J. S. (2012). Melatonin pharmacokenetics following two different oral surge-sustained release does in older adults. *Journal of Pineal Research: Molecular, Biolgical, Physiological, and Clinical Aspects of Melatonin, 52*, 437–445.

Gorelick, D. A., Goodwin, R. S., Schwilke, E., Schwope, D. M., Darwin, W. D., Kelly, D. L., . . . Huestis, M. A. (2013). Tolerance to effects of high-dose oral Δ9-tetrahydrocannabinol and plasma cannabinoid concentrations in male daily cannabis smokers. *Journal of Analytical Toxicology, 37*, 11–16.

Gosling, S. D., & John, O. P. (1999). Personality dimensions in non-human animals: A cross-species review. *Current Directions in Psychological Science, 8*, 69–75.

Gosling, S. D., Vazire, S., Srivastava, S., & John, O. P. (2004). Should we trust Web-based studies? A comparative analysis of six preconceptions about Internet questionnaires. *American Psychologist, 59*, 93–104.

Gottesman, I. I. (1991). *Schizophrenia genesis: The origins of madness*. New York: Freeman.

Gottman, J., & Silver, N. (2012). *What makes love last? How to build trust and avoid betrayal*. New York: Simon & Schuster.

Gracely, R. H., Farrell, M. J., & Grant, M. A. (2002). Temperature and pain perception. In H. Pashler & S. Yantis (Eds.), *Steven's handbook of experimental psychology: Vol. 1. Sensation and perception* (3rd ed., pp. 619–651). Hoboken, NJ: Wiley.

Graham, J. M. (2011). Measuring love in romantic relationships: A meta-analysis. *Journal of Social and Personal Relationships, 28*, 748–771.

Graham, J. R. (1991). Comments on Duckworth's review of the Minnesota Multiphasic Personality Inventory-2. *Journal of Counseling and Development, 69*, 570–571.

Grand, A. P., Kuhar, C. W., Leighty, K. A., Bettinger, T. L., & Laudenslager, M. L. (2012). Using personality ratings and cortisol to characterize individual differences in African elephants (*Loxodonta africana*). *Applied Animal Behaviour Science, 142*, 69–75.

Granillo, M. T., Perron, B. E., Jarman, C., & Gutowski, S. M. (2013). Cognitive behavioral therapy with substance use disorders: Theory, evidence, and practice. In M. G. Vaughn & B. E. Perron (Eds.), *Social work practice in the addictions* (pp. 101–118). New York: Springer.

Granrud, C. E. (2012). Judging the size of a distant object: Strategy use by children and adults. In G. Hatfield & S. Allred (Eds.), *Visual experience: Sensation, cognition, and constancy* (pp. 13–34). New York: Oxford University Press.

Grant, J. A., Courtemanche, J., & Rainville, P. (2011). A non-elaborative mental stance and decoupling of executive and pain-related cortices predicts low pain sensitivity in Zen meditators. *Pain, 152*, 150–156.

Grave, R. D. (2013). *Multistep cognitive behavioral therapy for eating disorders: Theory, practice, and clinical cases*. Lanham, MD: Jason Aronson.

Graven, L. J., & Grant, J. S. (2013). Coping and health-related quality of life in individuals with heart failure: An integrative review. *Heart & Lung, 42,* 183–194.

Green, A. J., & De-Vries, K. (2010). Cannabis use in palliative care—An examination of the evidence and the implications for nurses. *Journal of Clinical Nursing, 19,* 2454–2462.

Greenberg, D. L. (2004). President Bush's false "flashbulb" memory of 9/11/01. *Applied Cognitive Psychology, 18,* 363–370.

Greenberg, J. (2002). Who stole the money, and when? Individual and situational determinants of employee theft. *Organizational Behavior and Human Decision Processes, 89,* 985–1003.

Greenberg, L., Elliott, R., Lietaer, G., & Watson, J. (2013). The humanistic-experiential approach. In G. Stricker, T. A. Widiger, & I. B. Weiner (Eds.), *Handbook of psychology, Vol. 8. Clinical psychology* (2nd ed., pp. 320–344). Hoboken, NJ: Wiley.

Greene, C. A., & Murdock, K. K. (2013). Multidimensional control beliefs, socioeconomic status, and health. *American Journal of Health Behavior, 37,* 227–237.

Greenfield, P. M., & Quiroz, B. (2013). Context and culture in the socialization and development of personal achievement values: Comparing Latino immigrant families, European American families, and elementary school teachers. *Journal of Applied Developmental Psychology, 34,* 108–118.

Gregory, R. J. (2011). *Psychological testing: History, principles, and applications* (6th ed.). Boston, MA: Allyn & Bacon.

Gregory, S., Ffytche, D., Simmons, A., Kumari, V., Howard, M., Hodgins, S., & Blackwood, N. (2012). The antisocial brain: Psychopathy matters. *Archives of General Psychiatry, 69,* 962–972.

Gremore, T. M., Baucom, D. H., Porter, L. S., Kirby, J. S., Atkins, D. C., & Keefe, F. J. (2011). Stress buffering effects of daily spousal support on women's daily emotional and physical experiences in the context of breast cancer concerns. *Health Psychology, 30,* 20–30.

Griffin, R., & Moorhead, G. (2012). *Organizational behavior: Managing people and organizations* (10th ed.). Mason, OH: South-Western Cengage.

Griffith, R. M., Miyagi, O., & Tago, A. (1958/2009). The universality of typical dreams: Japanese vs. Americans. Retrieved from http://onlinelibrary.wiley.com/doi/10.1525/aa.1958.60.6.02a00110/pdf

Grills-Taquechel, A. E., & Ollendick, T. H. (2013). *Advances in psychotherapy. Phobic and anxiety disorders in children and adolescents.* Cambridge, MA: Hogrefe Publishing.

Groch, S., Wilhelm, I., Diekelmann, S., & Born, J. (2013). The role of REM sleep in the processing of emotional memories: Evidence from behavior and event-related potentials. *Neurobiology of Learning and Memory, 99,* 1–9.

Grossman, T. (2013). The early development of processing emotions in face and voice. In P. Belin, S. Campanella, & T. Ethofer (Eds.), *Integrating face and voice in person perception* (pp. 95–116). New York: Springer Science + Business Media.

Gruber, T. R. (2013). Nature, nurture, and knowledge acquisition. *International Journal of Human-Computer Studies, 71,* 191–194.

Grubin, D. (2010). The polygraph and forensic psychiatry. *Journal of the American Academy of Psychiatry and the Law, 38,* 446–451.

Guastello, S. J., Guastello, D. D., & Craft, L. L. (1989). Assessment of the Barnum effect in computer-based test interpretations. *Journal of Psychology: Interdisciplinary and Applied, 123,* 477–484.

Guenzel, F. M., Wolf, O. T., & Schwabe, L. (2013). Stress disrupts response memory retrieval. *Psychoneuroendocrinology, 38,* 1460–1465.

Gupta, M. A., & Gupta, A. K. (2013). Sleep-wake disorders and dermatology. *Clinics in Dermatology, 31,* 118–126.

Gurven, M., von Rueden, C., Massenkoff, M., Kaplan, H., & Lero Vie, M. (2013). How universal is the big five? Testing the five-factor model of personality variation among forager-farmers in the Bolivian Amazon. *Journal of Personality and Social Psychology, 104,* 354–370.

Guse, B., Falkai, P., Gruber, O., Whalley, H., Gibson, L., Hasan, A., . . . Wobrock, T. (2013). The effect of long-term high frequency repetitive transcranial magnetic stimulation on working memory in schizophrenia and healthy controls—A randomized placebo-controlled, double-blind fMRI study. *Behavioural Brain Research, 237,* 300–307.

Haab, L., Trenado, C., Mariam, M., & Strauss, D. J. (2011). Neurofunctional model of large-scale correlates of selective attention governed by stimulus-novelty. *Cognitive Neurodynamics, 5,* 103–111.

Hackley, C. (2007). Marketing psychology and the hidden persuaders. *The Psychologist, 20,* 488–490.

Haghighi, A., Schwartz, D. H., Abrahamowicz, M., Leonard, G. T., Perron, M., Richer, L., . . . Pausova, Z. (2013). Prenatal exposure to maternal cigarette smoking, amygdala volume and fat intake in adolescence. *Journal of the American Medical Association Psychiatry, 70,* 98–105.

Haines, R., & Mann, J. (2011). A new perspective on de-individuation via computer-mediated communication. *European Journal of Information Systems, 20,* 156–167.

Halbesleben, J. R. B., Wheeler, A. R., & Paustian-Underdahl, S. C. (2013). The impact of furloughs on emotional exhaustion, self-rated performance, and recovery experiences. *Journal of Applied Psychology, 98,* 492–503.

Hall, E. T. (2008). Adumbration as a feature of intercultural communication. In D. C. Mortensen (Ed.), *Communication theory* (2nd ed., pp. 420–432). Piscataway, NJ: Transaction Publishers.

Hall, P. A., & Schaeff, C. M. (2008). Sexual orientation and fluctuating asymmetry in men and women. *Archives of Sexual Behavior, 37,* 158–165.

Hall, W., & Degenhardt, L. (2010). "Adverse health effects of non-medical cannabis use"— Authors' reply. *The Lancet, 375,* 197.

Hallvig, D., Anund, A., Fors, C., Kecklund, G., Karlsson, J. G., Wahde, M., & Åkerstedt, T. (2013). Sleepy driving on the real road and in the simulator—A comparison. *Accident Analysis and Prevention, 50,* 44–50.

Hamby, S., & Grych, J. (2013). Implications for research: Toward a more comprehensive understanding of interpersonal violence. In S. Hamby & J. Grych (Eds.), *The web of violence* (pp. 67–79). New York: Springer.

Hamilton, G. F., Boschen, K. E., Goodlett, C. R., Greenough, W. T., & Klintsova, A. Y. (2012). Housing in environmental complexity following wheel running augments survival of newly generated hippocampal neurons in a rat model of binge alcohol exposure during the third trimester equivalent. *Alcoholism: Clinical and Experimental Research, 36,* 1196–1204.

Hamlett, J., & Hoskins, L. (2013). Comfort in small things? Clothing, control and agency in county lunatic asylums in nineteenth-and early twentieth-century England. *Journal of Victorian Culture, 6,* 1–22.

Hammack, P. L. (2003). The question of cognitive therapy in a postmodern world. *Ethical Human Sciences and Services, 5,* 209–224.

Hammen, C., & Keenan-Miller, D. (2013). Mood disorders. In G. Stricker, T. A. Widiger, & I. B. Weiner (Eds.), *Handbook of psychology, Vol. 8. Clinical psychology* (2nd ed., pp. 121–146). Hoboken, NJ: Wiley.

Hammond, J. L., & Hall, S. S. (2011). Functional analysis and treatment of aggressive behavior following resection of a craniopharyngioma. *Developmental Medicine and Child Neurology, 53,* 369–374.

Han, S., Mao, L., Qin, J., Friederici, A. D., & Ge, J. (2011). Functional roles and cultural modulations of the medial prefrontal and parietal activity associated with causal attribution. *Neuropsychologia, 49,* 83–91.

Handler, M., Honts, C. R., Krapohl, D. J., Nelson, R., & Griffin, S. (2009). Integration of pre-employment polygraph screening into the police selection process. *Journal of Police and Criminal Psychology, 24,* 69–86.

Haney, C., Banks, C., & Zimbardo, P. (1978). Interpersonal dynamics in a simulated prison. *International Journal of Criminology and Penology, 1,* 69–97.

Hardy, G., Barkham, M., Shapiro, D., Guthrie, E., & Margison, F. (Eds.). (2011). *Psychodynamic-interpersonal therapy.* Thousand Oaks, CA: Sage.

Harkness, K. L., Alavi, N., Monroe, S. M., Slavich, G. M., Gotlib, I. H., & Bagby, R. M. (2010). Gender differences in life events prior to onset of major depressive disorder: The moderating effect of age. *Journal of Abnormal Psychology, 119,* 791–803.

Harlow, J. (1868). Recovery from the passage of an iron bar through the head. *Publications of the Massachusetts Medical Society, 2,* 237–246.

Harriger, J. A., Calogero, R. M., Witherington, D. C., & Smith, J. E. (2010). Body size stereotyping and internalization of the thin ideal in preschool girls. *Sex Roles, 63,* 609–620.

Hart, C., & Ksir, C. (2013). *Drugs, society, and human behavior (15th ed.).* New York: McGraw-Hill.

Hart, J., Kraut, M. A., Womack, K. B., Strain, J., Didehbani, N., Bartze, E., . . . Cullum, C. M. (2013). Neuroimaging of cognitive dysfunction and depression in aging retired National Football League players: A cross-sectional study. *JAMA Neurology, 70,* 326–335.

Harvey, P. D., & Bowie, C. R. (2013). Schizophrenia spectrum conditions. In G. Stricker, T. A. Widiger, & I. B. Weiner (Eds.), *Handbook of psychology, Vol. 8. Clinical psychology* (2nd ed., pp. 240–261). Hoboken, NJ: Wiley.

Hasan, Y., Bègue, L., Scharkow, M., & Bushman, B. J. (2013). The more you play, the more aggressive you become: A long-term experimental study of cumulative violent video game effects on hostile expectations and aggressive behavior. *Journal of Experimental Social Psychology, 49,* 224–227.

Hashimoto, T., Mojaverian, T., & Kim, H. S. (2012). Culture, interpersonal stress, and psychological distress. *Journal of Cross-Cultural Psychology, 43,* 527–532.

Hassan, S., Karpova, Y., Baiz, D., Yancey, D., Pullikuth, A., Flores, A., . . . Kulik, G. (2013). Behavioral stress accelerates prostate cancer development in mice. *The Journal of Clinical Investigation,* 123, 874–886.

Hasson, D., Theorell, T., Bergquist, J., & Canlon, B. (2013). Acute stress induces hyperacusis in women with high levels of emotional exhaustion. *PloS one, 8,* e52945.

Hatemi, P. K., & McDermott, R. (2012). The genetics of politics: Discovery, challenges and progress. *Trends in Genetics, 28,* 525–533.

Hatfield, E., & Rapson, R. L. (1996). *Love and sex: Cross-cultural perspectives.* Needham Heights, MA: Allyn & Bacon.

Haukkala, A., Konttinen, H., Laatikainen, T., Kawachi, I., & Uutela, A. (2010). Hostility, anger control, and anger expression as predictors of cardiovascular disease. *Psychosomatic Medicine, 72,* 556–562.

Hauner, K. K., Mineka, S., Voss, J. L., & Paller, K. A. (2012). Exposure therapy triggers lasting reorganization of neural fear processing. *Proceedings of the National Academy of Sciences, 109,* 9203–9208.

Hauser, S. L., & Johnston, S. C. (2013). DSM-V: Psychodrama on the public stage. *Annals of Neurology, 73,* A5–A6.

Hay, D. F. (1994). Prosocial development. *Journal of Child Psychology and Psychiatry, 35,* 29–71.

Haynes, S., O'Brien, W., & Kaholokula, J. (2011). *Behavioral assessment and case formulation.* Hoboken, NJ: Wiley.

Hazan, C., & Shaver, P. (1987). Romantic love conceptualized as an attachment process. *Journal of Personality and Social Psychology, 52,* 511–524.

Hazler, R. J. (2011). Person-centered theory. In D. Capuzzi & D. R. Gross (Eds.), *Counseling and psychotherapy* (5th ed., pp. 143–166). Alexandria, VA: American Counseling Association.

Hazlett, E. A., Collazo, T., Zelmanova, Y., Entis, J. J., Chu, K.-W., Goldstein, K. E., . . . Byne, W. (2012). Anterior limb of the internal capsule in schizotypal personality disorder: Fiber-tract counting, volume, and anisotropy. *Schizophrenia Research, 141,* 119–127.

Heaner, M. K., & Walsh, B. T. (2013). A history of the identification of the characteristic eating disturbances of bulimia nervosa, binge eating disorder and anorexia nervosa. *Appetite, 65,* 185–188.

Heider, F. (1958). *The psychology of interpersonal relations.* Hoboken, NJ: Wiley.

Heine, S. J., & Renshaw, K. (2002). Interjudge agreement, self-enhancement, and liking: Cross-cultural divergences. *Personality and Social Psychology Bulletin, 28,* 578–587.

Heinicke, M. R., Carr, J. E., Eastridge, D., Kupfer, J., & Mozzoni, M. P. (2013). Assessing preferences of individuals with acquired brain injury using alternative stimulus modalities. *Brain Injury, 27,* 48–59.

Hellström, P. M. (2013). Satiety signals and obesity. *Current Opinion in Gastroenterology, 29,* 222–227.

Herbert, H. S., Manjula, M., & Philip, M. (2013). Resilience and factors contributing to resilience among the offsprings of parents with schizophrenia. *Psychological Studies, 58,* 80–88.

Hergovich, A., & Olbrich, A. (2003). The impact of the Northern Ireland conflict on social identity, groupthink and integrative complexity in Great Britain. *Review of Psychology, 10,* 95–106.

Herholz, S. C., Halpern, A. R., & Zatorre, R. J. (2012). Neuronal correlates of perception, imagery, and memory for familiar tunes. *Journal of Cognitive Neuroscience, 24,* 1382–1397.

Herman, C. P., & Polivy, J. (2008). External cues in the control of food intake in humans: The sensory-normative distinction. *Physiology and Behavior, 94,* 722–728.

Herman, L. M., Richards, D. G., & Woltz, J. P. (1984). Comprehension of sentences by bottlenosed dolphins. *Cognition, 16,* 129–139.

Hernandez, I., & Preston, J. L. (2013). Disfluency disrupts the confirmation bias. *Journal of Experimental Social Psychology, 49,* 178–182.

Herrenkohl, T. I., Hong, S., Klika, J. B., Herrenkohl, R. C., & Russo, M. J. (2013). Developmental impacts of child abuse and neglect related to adult mental health, substance use, and physical health. *Journal of Family Violence, 28,* 191–199.

Hervé, H. F., Cooper, B. S., & Yuille, J. C. (2013). Biopsychosocial perspectives on memory variability in eyewitnesses. In B. S. Cooper, D. Griesel, & M. Ternes (Eds.), *Applied issues in investigative interviewing, eyewitness memory, and credibility assessment* (pp. 99–142). New York: Springer.

Hervé, H., Mitchell, D., Cooper, B. S., Spidel, A., & Hare, R. D. (2004). Psychopathy and unlawful confinement: An examination of perpetrator and event characteristics.

Canadian Journal of Behavioural Science, 36, 137–145.

Hess, T. M., Popham, L. E., Emery, L., & Elliott, T. (2012). Mood, motivation, and misinformation: Aging and affective state influences on memory. *Aging, Neuropsychology and Cognition, 19*, 13–34.

Higley, E. R. (2008). Nighttime interactions and mother-infant attachment at one year. *Dissertation Abstracts International: Section B: The Sciences and Engineering, 68*, 5575.

Hilgard, E. R. (1978). Hypnosis and consciousness. *Human Nature, 1*, 42–51.

Hilgard, E. R. (1992). Divided consciousness and dissociation. *Consciousness and Cognition, 1*, 16–31.

Hill, J. S., Robbins, R. R., & Pace, T. M. (2012). Cultural validity of the Minnesota Multiphasic Personality Inventory–2 empirical correlates: Is this the best we can do? *Journal of Multicultural Counseling and Development, 40*, 104–116.

Hill, P. L., & Lapsley, D. K. (2011). Adaptive and maladaptive narcissism in adolescent development. In C. T. Barry, P. K. Kerig, K. K. Stellwagen, & T. D. Barry (Eds.), *Narcissism and Machiavellianism in youth: Implications for the development of adaptive and maladaptive behavior* (pp. 89–105). Washington, DC: American Psychological Association.

Hills, J. (2013). *Basic texts in counselling and psychotherapy. Introduction to systemic and family therapy: A user's guide.* New York: Palgrave Macmillan.

Hines, M. (2013). Gonadal hormone influences on human neurobehavioral development: Outcomes and mechanisms. In D. W. Pfaff & Y. Christen (Eds.), *Multiple origins of sex differences in brain* (pp. 59–69). New York: Springer.

Hirst, W., Phelps, E. A., Buckner, R. L., Budson, A. E., Cuc, A., Gabrieli, J. D. E., . . . Vaidya, C. J. (2009). Long-term memory for the terrorist attack of September 11: Flashbulb memories, event memories, and the factors that influence their retention. *Journal of Experimental Psychology: General, 138*, 161–176.

Hiscock, H., & Davey, M. J. (2013). Sleep disorders in infants and children. *Journal of Paediatrics & Child Health*. Advance online publication. doi: 10.1111/jpc.12033

Hoar, S. D., Evans, M. B., & Link, C. A. (2012). How do master athletes cope with pre-competitive stress at a "Senior Games?" *Journal of Sport Behavior, 35*, 181–203.

Hobson, J. A., Sangsanguan, S., Arantes, H., & Kahn, D. (2011). Dream logic—The inferential reasoning paradigm. *Dreaming, 21*, 1–15.

Hobson, J. A., & Silvestri, L. (1999). Parasomnias. *The Harvard Mental Health Letter, 15*, 3–5.

Hodges, S. D., & Biswas-Diener, R. (2007). Balancing the empathy expense account: Strategies for regulating empathic response. In T. Farrow & P. Woodruff (Eds.), *Empathy in mental illness* (pp. 389–407). New York: Cambridge University Press.

Hodson, G., & Hewstone, M. (Eds.). (2013). *Advances in intergroup contact.* New York: Psychology Press.

Hoff, E. (2013). *Language development* (5th ed.). Belmont, CA: Wadsworth Publishing.

Hoffman, M. L. (1993). Empathy, social cognition, and moral education. In A. Garrod (Ed.), *Approaches to moral development: New research and emerging themes* (pp. 157–179). New York: Teachers College Press.

Hogan, T. P. (2006). *Psychological testing: A practical Introduction (2nd ed.).* Hoboken, NJ: Wiley.

Hogg, D. (2013). Application of groupthink to Generation Y decision making processes within a professional services context in New Zealand. *International Journal of Business and Management, 8*, 69.

Hollander, J., Renfrow, D., & Howard, J. (2011). *Gendered situations, gendered selves: A gender lens on social psychology* (2nd ed.). Lanham, MD: Rowman and Littlefield.

Hollon, S. D. (2011). Cognitive and behavior therapy in the treatment and prevention of depression. *Depression and Anxiety, 28*, 263–266.

Hölzel, B. K, Carmody, J., Vangel, M., Congleton, C., Yerramsetti, S. M, Gard, T., & Lazar, S. W. (2011). Mindfulness practice leads to increases in regional brain gray matter density. *Psychiatry Research: Neuroimaging, 191*, 36–43.

Honig, A. S., & Nealis, A. L. (2012). What do young children dream about? *Early Child Development & Care, 182*, 771–795.

Honts, C. R., & Kircher, J. C. (1994). Mental and physical countermeasures reduce the accuracy of polygraph tests. *Journal of Applied Psychology, 79*, 252–259.

Hooley, J. M., Maher, W. B., & Maher, B. A. (2013). Abnormal psychology. In D. K. Freedheim & I. B. Weiner (Eds.), *Handbook of psychology, Vol. 1. History of psychology* (2nd ed., pp. 340–376). Hoboken, NJ: Wiley.

Hopfer, C. (2011). Club drug, prescription drug, and over-the-counter medication abuse: Description, diagnosis, and intervention. In Y. Kaminer & K. C. Winters (Eds.), *Clinical manual of adolescent substance abuse treatment* (pp. 187–212). Arlington, VA: American Psychiatric Publishing.

Hoppe, A. (2011). Psychosocial working conditions and well-being among immigrant and German low-wage workers. *Journal of Occupational Health Psychology, 16*, 187–201.

Hopwood, C. J., & Wright, A. G. (2012). A comparison of passive–aggressive and negativistic personality disorders. *Journal of Personality Assessment, 94*, 296–303.

Hora, M., & Klassen, R. D. (2012). Learning from others' misfortune: Factors in influencing knowledge acquisition to reduce operational risk. *Journal of Operations Management, 31*, 52–61.

Houlfort, N. (2006). The impact of performance-contingent rewards on perceived autonomy and intrinsic motivation. *Dissertation Abstracts International Section A: Humanities and Social Sciences, 67*, 460.

Howe, M. L., & Malone, C. (2011). Mood-congruent true and false memory: Effects of depression. *Memory, 19*, 192–201.

Hrobjartsson, A., Ravaud, P., Tendal, B., Thomsen, A. S. S., Boutron, I., Emanuelsson, F., . . . Brorson, S. (2013). Observer bias in randomized clinical trials with measurement scale outcomes: A systematic review of trials with both blinded and nonblinded assessors. *Canadian Medical Association Journal, 185*, E201-E211.

Hsiao, S. S., & Gomez-Ramirez, M. (2013). Neural mechanisms of tactile perception. In R. J. Nelson, S. J. Y. Mizumori, & I. B. Weiner (Eds.), *Handbook of psychology, Vol. 3. Behavioral neuroscience* (2nd ed., pp. 206–239). Hoboken, NJ: Wiley.

Huang, M., & Hauser, R. M. (1998). Trends in Black–White test-score differentials: II. The WORDSUM Vocabulary Test. In U. Neisser (Ed.), *The rising curve: Long-term gains in IQ and related measures* (pp. 303–334). Washington, DC: American Psychological Association.

Huang, X., Zhu, X., Zheng, J., Zhang, L. & Shiomi, K. (2012). Relationships among androgyny, self-esteem, and trait coping style of Chinese university students. *Social Behavior and Personality, 40*, 1005–1014.

Huber, G., & Malhotra, N. (2012). Political sorting in social relationships. Working paper. Retrieved from http://huber.research.yale.edu/materials/38_paper.pdf.

Huesmann, L. R., Dubow, E. F., & Yang, G. (2013). Why it is hard to believe that media violence causes aggression. *The Oxford handbook of media psychology, Oxford library of psychology* (pp. 159–171). New York: Oxford University Press.

Hulette, A., Freyd, J., & Fisher, P. (2011). Dissociation in middle childhood among foster children with early maltreatment experiences. *Child Abuse and Neglect, 35*, 123–126.

Hull, C. (1952). *A behavior system.* New Haven, CT: Yale University Press.

Hull, E. M. (2011). Sex, drugs and gluttony: How the brain controls motivated behaviors. *Physiology and Behavior, 104*, 173–177.

Hülsheger, U. R., Alberts, H. J., Feinholdt, A., & Lang, J. W. B. (2013). Benefits of mindfulness at work: The role of mindfulness in emotion regulation, emotional exhaustion, and job satisfaction. *Journal of Applied Psychology, 98*, 310–325.

Hunsley, J., & Lee, E. M. (2010). *Introduction to clinical psychology* (2nd ed.). Toronto, ON: Wiley.

Hunt, E. (2011). *Human intelligence.* New York: Cambridge University Press.

Hupbach, A., & Fieman, R. (2012). Moderate stress enhances immediate and delayed retrieval of educationally relevant material in healthy young men. *Behavioral Neuroscience, 126*, 819–825.

Husain, M. M., & Lisanby, S. H. (2011). Repetitive transcranial magnetic stimulation (rTMS): A noninvasive neuromodulation probe and intervention. *The Journal of ECT, 27*, 2.

Hutchison, P., & Rosenthal, H. E. S. (2011). Prejudice against Muslims: Anxiety as a mediator between intergroup contact and attitudes, perceived group variability and behavioural intentions. *Ethnic and Racial Studies, 34*, 40–61.

Hyde, J. S. (2005). The genetics of sexual orientation. In J. S. Hyde (Ed.), *Biological substrates of human sexuality* (pp. 9–20). Washington, DC: American Psychological Association.

Hyman, R. (1981). Cold reading: How to convince strangers that you know all about them. In K. Fraizer (Ed.), *Paranormal borderlands of science* (pp. 232–244). Buffalo, NY: Prometheus.

Hyman, R. (1996). The evidence for psychic functioning: Claims vs. reality. *Skeptical Inquirer, 20*, 24–26.

Iacono, W. G. (2008). Accuracy of polygraph techniques: Problems using confessions to determine ground truth. *Physiology and Behavior, 95*, 24–26.

Imada, T., & Ellsworth, P. C. (2011). Proud Americans and lucky Japanese: Cultural differences in appraisal and corresponding emotion. *Emotion, 11*, 329–345.

Inden, M., Takata, K., Nishimura, K., Kitamura, Y., Ashihara, E., Yoshimoto, K., . . . Shimohama, S. (2013). Therapeutic effects of human mesenchymal and hematopoietic stem cells on rotenone-treated Parkinsonian mice. *Journal of Neuroscience Research, 91*, 62–72.

Inostroza, M., Binder, S., & Born, J. (2013). Sleep-dependency of episodic-like memory consolidation in rats. *Behavioural Brain Research, 237*, 15–22.

Insel, T. (2012). Director's blog: Spotlight on eating disorders. *National Institute for Mental Health (NIMH).* Retrieved from http://www.nimh.nih.gov/about/director/2012/spotlight-on-eating-disorders.shtml

Inui, K., Urakawa, T., Yamashiro, K., Otsuru, N., Takeshima, Y., Nishihara, M., . . . Kakigi, R. (2010). Echoic memory of a single pure tone indexed by change-related brain activity. *BMC Neuroscience, 11*, Article ID 135.

Inzlicht, M., & Al-Khindi, T. (2012). ERN and the placebo: A misattribution approach to studying the arousal properties of the error-related negativity. *Journal of Experimental Psychology: General, 141*, 799–807.

Irish, M., Lawlor, B. A., O'Mara, S. M., & Coen, R. F. (2011). Impaired capacity for autonoetic reliving during autobiographical event recall in mild Alzheimer's disease. *Cortex: A Journal Devoted to the Study of the Nervous System and Behavior, 47*, 236–249.

Irvine, E. (2013). The scientific study of consciousness: Consciousness as a scientific concept. *Studies in Brain and Mind, 5*, 1–14.

Irwin, K., & Simpson, B. (2013). Do descriptive norms solve social dilemmas? Conformity and contributions in collective action groups. *Social Forces, 91*, 1057–1084.

Irwin, M. (2008).There's no good proof the real *Medium*, Allison DuBois, has ever cracked a case, but her fans don't care. *Phoenix New Times.* Retrieved from http://www.phoenixnewtimes.com/2008-06-12/news/there-s-no-good-proof-the-real-medium-allison-dubois-has-ever-cracked-a-case-but-her-fans-don-t-care/

Iwata, Y., Suzuki, K., Takei, N., Toulopoulou, T., Tsuchiya, K. J., Matsumato, K., . . . Mori, N. (2011). Jiko-shisen-kyofu (fear of one's own glance), but not taijin-kyofusho (fear of interpersonal relations), is an east Asian culture-related specific syndrome. *Australian and New Zealand Journal of Psychiatry, 45*, 148–152.

Izard, C. E. (1971). *The face of emotion.* New York: Appleton-Century-Crofts.

Jackendoff, R. (2003). Foundations of language, brain, meaning, grammar, evolution. *Applied Cognitive Psychology, 17*, 121–122.

Jackson, J. W., & Rose, J. (2013). The stereotype consistency effect is moderated by group membership and trait valence. *The Journal of Social Psychology, 153*, 51–61.

Jackson, M. L., Croft, R. J., Kennedy, G. A., Owens, K., & Howard, M. E. (2013). Cognitive components of simulated driving performance: Sleep loss effects and predictors. *Accident Analysis & Prevention, 50*, 438–444.

Jacobs Bao, K., & Lyubomirsky, S. (2013). Making it last: Combating hedonic adaptation in romantic relationships. *The Journal of Positive Psychology, 8*, 196–206.

Jaeger, A., Cox, J. C., & Dobbins, I. G. (2012). Recognition confidence under violated and confirmed memory expectations. *Journal of Experimental Psychology: General, 141*, 282–301.

Jaeger, M. (2011). "A thing of beauty is a joy forever"? Returns to physical attractiveness over the life course. *Social Forces, 89*, 983–1003.

Jaehne, E. J., Majumder, I., Salem, A., & Irvine, R. J. (2011). Increased effects of 3, 4-methylenedioxymethamphetamine (ecstasy) in a rat model of depression. *Addiction Biology, 16*, 7–19.

Jaffe, S. L., & Kelly, J. F. (2011). Twelve-step mutual-help programs for adolescents. In Y. Kaminer & K. C. Winters (Eds.), *Clinical manual of adolescent substance abuse treatment* (pp. 269–282). Arlington, VA: American Psychiatric Publishing.

James, W. (1890). *The principles of psychology* (Vol. 2). New York: Holt.

Jamieson, G. A., & Hasegawa, H. (2007). New paradigms of hypnosis research. In G. A. Jamieson (Ed.), *Hypnosis and conscious states: The cognitive neuroscience perspective* (pp. 133–144). New York: Oxford University Press

Jang, K. L., Taylor, S., & Livesley, W. J. (2006). The University of British Columbia Twin Project: Personality is something and personality does something. *Twin Research and Human Genetics, 9*, 739–742.

Janis, I. L. (1972). *Victims of groupthink: A psychological study of foreign-policy decisions and fiascoes.* Boston, MA: Houghton Mifflin.

Janis, I. L. (1989). *Crucial decisions: Leadership in policymaking and crisis management.* New York: Free Press.

Jaremka, L. M., Glaser, R., Loving, T. J., Malarkey, W. B., Stowell, J. R., & Kiecolt-Glaser, J. K. (2013). Attachment anxiety is linked to alterations in cortisol production and cellular immunity. *Psychological Science, 24*, 272–279.

Jarvis, S. (2011). Conceptual transfer: Crosslinguistic effects in categorization and construal. *Bilingualism: Language and Cognition, 14*, 1–8.

Jenkins, P. E., Meyer, C., & Blissett, J. M. (2013). Childhood abuse and eating psychopathology: The mediating role of core beliefs. *Journal of Aggression, Maltreatment & Trauma, 22*, 248–261.

Jensen, K. B., Kaptchuk, T. J., Kirsch, I., Raicek, J., Lindstrom, K. M., Berna, C., ... Kong, J. (2012). Nonconscious activation of placebo and nocebo pain responses. *Proceedings of the National Academy of Sciences, 109*, 15959–15964.

Jensen, L. A. (2011). The cultural-developmental theory of moral psychology: A new synthesis. In L. A. Jensen (Ed.), *Bridging cultural and developmental approaches to psychology: New syntheses in theory, research, and policy* (pp. 3–25). New York: Oxford University Press.

Jensen, M. P., Hakimian, S., Sherlin, L. H., & Fregni, F. (2008). New insights into neuromodulatory approaches for the treatment of pain. *The Journal of Pain, 9*, 193–199.

Jern, A., & Kemp, C. (2013). A probabilistic account of exemplar and category generation. *Cognitive Psychology, 66*, 85–125.

Jeste, D. V., Savla, G. N., Thompson, W. K., Vahia, I. V., Glorioso, D. K., Martin, A. S., . . . Depp, C. A. (2012). Association between older age and more successful aging: Critical role of resilience and depression. *American Journal of Psychiatry, 170,* 188–196.

Jewkes, R. (2013). Intimate partner violence as a risk factor for mental health problems in South Africa. In C. Garcia-Moreno & A. Riecher-Rössler (Eds.), *Violence against women and mental health. Key issues mental health* (pp. 65–74). Switzerland: Basel, Karger.

Ji, G., Yan, L., Liu, W., Qu, J., & Gu, A. (2013). OGG1 Ser326Cys polymorphism interacts with cigarette smoking to increase oxidative DNA damage in human sperm and the risk of male infertility. *Toxicology Letters, 218,* 144–149.

Jinap, S., & Hajeb, P. (2010). Glutamate: Its applications in food and contribution to health. *Appetite*, 55, 1–10.

Joanisse, M., Gagnon, S., & Voloaca, M. (2013). The impact of stereotype threat on the simulated driving performance of older drivers. *Accident Analysis and Prevention, 50,* 530–538.

Joeng, J. R., Turner, S. L., & Lee, K. H. (2013). South Korean college students' Holland Types and career compromise processes. *The Career Development Quarterly, 61*, 64–73.

Johns, M. M., Zimmerman, M., & Bauermeister, J. A. (2013). Sexual attraction, sexual identity, and psychosocial wellbeing in a national sample of young women during emerging adulthood. *Journal of Youth and Adolescence, 42*, 82–95.

Johnson, D. M., Delahanty, D. L., & Pinna, K. (2008). The cortisol awakening response as a function of PTSD severity and abuse chronicity in sheltered battered women. *Journal of Anxiety Disorders, 22*, 793–800.

Johnson, S. C., Dweck, C. S., & Chen, F. S. (2007). Evidence for infants' internal working method of attachment. *Psychological Science, 18*, 501–502.

Johnson, W., & Bouchard Jr., T. J. (2007). Sex differences in mental ability: A proposed means to link them to brain structure and function. *Intelligence, 35*, 197–209.

Johnston, C. C., Campbell-Yeo, M., & Filion, F. (2011). Paternal vs. maternal kangaroo care for procedural pain in preterm neonates: A randomized crossover trial. *Archives of Pediatrics & Adolescent Medicine, 165*, 792–796.

Johnston, L., Titov, N., Andrews, G., Dear, B. F., & Spence, J. (2013). Comorbidity and internet-delivered transdiagnostic cognitive behavioural therapy for anxiety disorders. *Cognitive Behaviour Therapy*, 42, 180–192.

Johnston, M. E., Sherman, A., & Grusec, J. E. (2013). Predicting moral outrage and religiosity with an implicit measure of moral identity. *Journal of Research in Personality, 47,* 209–217.

Jolliffe, C. D., & Nicholas, M. K. (2004). Verbally reinforcing pain reports: An experimental test of the operant conditioning of chronic pain. *Pain, 107,* 167–175.

Jones, D. A. (2013). The polarizing effect of a partisan workplace. *PS: Political Science & Politics, 46*, 67–73.

Jones, D. E., Hammond, P., & Platoni, K. (2013). Traumatic event management in Afghanistan: A field report on combat applications in regional command-south. *Military Medicine, 178*, 4–10.

Jones, E. E., & Nisbett, R. E. (1971). *The actor and the observer: Divergent perceptions of the causes of behavior.* Morristown, NJ: General Learning Press.

Jones, S. G., & Benca, R. M. (2013). Sleep and biological rhythms. In R. J. Nelson, S. J. Y. Mizumori, & I. B. Weiner (Eds.), *Handbook of psychology, Vol. 3. behavioral neuroscience (2nd ed.,* pp. 365–394). Hoboken, NJ: Wiley.

Jopp, D. S., & Schmitt, M. (2010). Dealing with negative life events: Differential effects of personal resources, coping strategies, and control beliefs. *European Journal of Ageing, 7*, 167–180.

Jost, K., Bryck, R. L., Vogel, E. K., & Mayr, U. (2011) Are old adults just like low working memory young adults? Filtering efficiency and age differences in visual working memory. *Cerebral Cortex, 21*, 1147–1154.

Jung, C. G. (1946). *Psychological types*. New York: Harcourt Brace.

Jung, C. G. (1959). The archetypes and the collective unconscious. In H. Read, M. Fordham, & G. Adler (Eds.), *The collected works of C. G. Jung, Vol. 9.* New York: Pantheon.

Jung, C. G. (1969). The concept of collective unconscious. In *Collected Works* (Vol. 9, Part 1). Princeton, NJ: Princeton University Press (Original work published 1936).

Jung, J., & Kim, Y. (2012). Causes of newspaper firm employee burnout in Korea and its impact on organizational commitment and turnover intention. *The International Journal of Human Resource Management, 23*, 3636–3651.

Jung, R. E., & Haier, R. J. (2007). The Parieto-Frontal Integration Theory (P-FIT) of intelligence: Converging neuroimaging evidence. *Behavioral and Brain Sciences, 30*, 135–154.

Jurado-Berbel, P., Costa-Miserachs, D., Torras-Garcia, M., Coll-Andreu, M., & Portell-Cortés, I. (2010). Standard object recognition memory and "what" and "where" components: Improvement by post-training epinephrine in highly habituated rats. *Behavioural Brain Research*, *207*, 44–50.

Kahneman, D., & Tversky, A. (1973). On the psychology of prediction. *Psychological Review, 80*, 237–251.

Kaida, K., Akerstedt, T., Takahashi, M., Vestergren, P., Gillberg, M., Lowden, A., . . . Portin, C. (2008). Performance prediction by sleepiness- related subjective symptoms during 26-hour sleep deprivation. *Sleep & Biological Rhythms, 6,* 234–241.

Kalat, J. W. (2013). *Biological psychology* (11th ed.). Belmont, CA: Wadsworth, Cengage Learning.

Kalnin, A. J., Edwards, C. R., Wang, Y., Kronenberger, W. G., Hummer, T. A., Mosier, K. M., . . . Mathews, V. P. (2011). The interacting role of media violence exposure and aggressive–disruptive behavior in adolescent brain activation during an emotional Stroop task. *Psychiatry Research: Neuroimaging, 192*, 12–19.

Kan, K.-J., Dolan, C. V., Nivard, M. G., Middeldorp, C. M., van Beijsterveldt, C. E., Willemsen, G., & Boomsa, D. I. (2013). Genetic and environmental stability in attention problems across the lifespan: Evidence from the Netherlands Twin Register. *Journal of the American Academy of Child & Adolescent Psychiatry, 52*, 12–25.

Kanayama, G., & Pope, H. G., Jr. (2011). Gods, men, and muscle dysmorphia. *Harvard Review of Psychiatry, 19*, 95–98.

Kandler, C., Bleidorn, W., Riemann, R., Angleitner, A., & Spinath, F. (2012). Life events as environmental states and genetic traits and the role of personality: A longitudinal twin study. *Behavior Genetics, 42*, 57–72.

Kang, H. J., Voleti, B., Hajszan, T., Rajkowska, G., Stockmeier, C. A., Licznerski, P., . . . Duman, R. S. (2012). Decreased expression of synapse-related genes and loss of synapses in major depressive disorder. *Nature Medicine*, 18, 1413–1417.

Kang, S.-M., & Lau, A. S. (2013). Revisiting the out-group advantage in emotion recognition in a multicultural society: Further evidence for the in-group advantage. *Emotion, 13*, 203–215.

Kar, B. R. (Ed.). (2013). Development of selection and control. In B. R. Kar, N.K. Srinivasan, & R. Bhoomika (Eds.), *APA human brain development series. Cognition and brain development: Converging evidence from various methodologies* (pp. 11–32). Washington, DC: American Psychological Association.

Karatsoreos, I. N., Bhagat, S., Bloss, E. B., Morrison, J. H., & McEwen, B. S. (2011). Disruption of circadian clocks has ramifications for metabolism, brain, and behavior. *Proceedings of the National Academy of Sciences, 108*, 1657–1662.

Karavolos, S., Stewart, J., Evbuomwan, I., McEleny, K., & Aird, I. (2013). Assessment of the infertile male. *The Obstetrician & Gynaecologist, 15*, 1–9.

Kariuki, C. M., & Stein, D. J. (2013). Social anxiety disorder. In S. M. Stahl & B. A. Moore (Eds.), *Anxiety disorders: A guide for integrating psychopharmacology and psychotherapy* (pp. 221–258). New York: Routledge.

Kark, R., Waismel-Manor, R., & Shamir, B. (2012). Does valuing androgyny and femininity lead to a female advantage? The relationship between gender-role, transformational leadership and identification. *The Leadership Quarterly, 23*, 620–640.

Karpicke, J. D., & Bauernschmidt, A. (2011). Spaced retrieval: Absolute spacing enhances learning regardless of relative spacing. *Journal of Experimental Psychology: Learning, Memory, and Cognition,* 37, 1250–1257.

Karpicke, J. D., & Smith, M. A. (2012). Separate mnemonic effects of retrieval practice and elaborative encoding. *Journal of Memory & Language, 67*, 17–29.

Karpowitz, C. F., Mendelberg, T., & Shaker, L. (2011). Gender inequality in deliberative participation. *American Political Science Review, 106*, 533–547.

Karra, E., O'Daly, O. G., Choudhury, A. I., Yousseif, A., Millership, S., Neary, M. T., . . . Batterham, R. L. (2013). A link between FTO, ghrelin, and impaired brain food-cue responsivity. *Journal of Clinical Investigations, 123*, 3539–3551.

Kato, K., Zweig, R., Barzilai, N., & Atzmon, G. (2012). Positive attitude towards life and emotional expression as personality phenotypes for centenarians. *Aging, 4*, 359–367.

Katz, I., Kaplan, A., & Buzukashvily, T. (2011). The role of parents' motivation in students' autonomous motivation for doing homework. *Learning and Individual Differences, 21*, 376–386.

Kaukiainen, A., Björkqvist, K., Lagerspetz, K., Österman, K., Salmivalli, C., Rothberg, S., & Ahlbom, A. (1999). The relationships between social intelligence, empathy, and three types of aggression. *Aggressive Behavior, 25*, 81–89.

Kaye, W. H., Wierenga, C. E., Bailer, U. F., Simmons, A. N., & Bischoff-Grethe, A. (2013). Nothing tastes as good as skinny feels: The neurobiology of anorexia nervosa. *Trends in Neurosciences, 36*, 110–120.

Keats, D. M. (1982). Cultural bases of concepts of intelligence: A Chinese versus Australian comparison. In P. Sukontasarp, N. Yongsiri, P. Intasuwan, N. Jotiban, & C. Suvannathat (Eds.), *Proceedings of the second Asian workshop on child and adolescent development* (pp. 67–75). Bangkok, India: Burapasilpa Press.

Keen, E. (2011). Emotional narratives: Depression as sadness—Anxiety as fear. *The Humanistic Psychologist, 39*, 66–70.

Keller, J., & Bless, H. (2008). The interplay of stereotype threat and regulatory focus. In Y. Kashima, K. Fiedler, & P. Freytag (Eds.), *Stereotype dynamics: Language-based approaches to the formation, maintenance, and transformation of stereotypes* (pp. 367–389). Mahwah, NJ: Erlbaum.

Kellogg, R. (2011). *Fundamentals of cognitive psychology* (2nd ed.). Thousand Oaks, CA: Sage.

Keltner, D., Kring, A. M., & Bonanno, G. A. (1999). Fleeting signs of the course of life: Facial expression and personal adjustment. *Current Directions in Psychological Science, 8*, 18–22.

Kendler, K. S., & Prescott, C. A. (2006). *Genes, environment, and psychopathology: Understanding the causes of psychiatric and substance use disorders*. New York: Guilford Press.

Kennedy, S. H., Giacobbe, P., Rizvi, S. J., Placenza, F. M., Nishikawa, Y., Mayberg, H. S., & Lozano, A. M. (2011). Deep brain stimulation for treatment-resistant depression: Follow-up after 3 to 6 years. *American Journal of Psychiatry, 168*, 502–510.

Kerr, N. L., Feltz, D. L., & Irwin, B. C. (2013). To pay or not to pay? Do extrinsic incentives alter the Köhler group motivation gain? *Group Processes & Intergroup Relations, 16*, 257–268.

Kershaw, S. (2008). Sharing their demons on the Web. *New York Times*. Retrieved from http://www.nytimes.com/2008/11/13/fashion/13psych.html

Kessler, R. C., McGonagle, K. A., Zhao, S., Nelson, C. B., Hughes, M., Eshleman, S., . . . Kendler, K. S. (1994). Lifetime and 12-month prevalence of DSM-IIIR psychiatric disorders in the United States. *Archives of General Psychiatry, 51*, 8–19.

Khaleque, A., & Rohner, R. P. (2011). Transnational relations between perceived parental acceptance and personality dispositions of children and adults: A meta-analytic review. *Personality and Social Psychology Review, 16*, 103–115.

Kiefer, F., & Dinter, C. (2013). New approaches to addiction treatment based on learning and memory. In W. H. Sommer & R. Spanagel (Eds.), *Current topics in behavioral neurosciences: Vol. 13. Behavioral neurobiology of alcohol addiction* (pp. 671–684). New York: Springer Science + Business Media

Kihlstrom, J. F. (2005). Dissociative disorders. *Annual Review of Clinical Psychology, 1*, 227–253.

Kilmann, P. R., Finch, H., Parnell, M. M., & Downer, J. T. (2013). Partner attachment and interpersonal characteristics. *Journal of Sex & Marital Therapy, 39*, 144–159.

Kilpatrick, L. A., Suyenobu, B. Y., Smith, S. R., Bueller, J. A., Goodman, T., Creswell, J. D., . . . Naliboff, B. D. (2011). Impact of mindfulness-based stress reduction training on intrinsic brain connectivity. *NeuroImage, 56*, 290–298.

Kim, J-H., & Park, E-Y. (2012). The factor structure of the Center for Epidemiologic Studies Depression Scale in stroke patients. *Topics in Stroke Rehabilitation, 19*, 54–62.

Kim, K-S., Kim, H. S., Park, J-M., Kim, H. W., Park, M-K., Lee, H-S., . . . Moon, J. (2013). Long-term immunomodulatory effect of amniotic stem cells in an Alzheimer's disease model. *Neurobiology of Aging, 34*, 2408–2420.

King, B. M. (2012). *Human sexuality today* (7th ed.). Boston, MA: Allyn & Bacon.

Kircher, T., Arolt, V., Jansen, A., Pyka, M., Reinhardt, I., Kellermann, T., . . . Straube, B. (2013). Effect of cognitive-behavioral therapy on neural correlates of fear conditioning in panic disorder. *Biological Psychiatry, 73,* 93–101.

Kirisci, L., Tarter, R., Ridenour, T., Zhai, Z. W., Fishbein, D., Reynolds, M., & Vanyukov, M. (2013). Age of alcohol and cannabis use onset mediates the association of transmissible risk in childhood and development of alcohol and cannabis disorders: Evidence for common liability. *Experimental and Clinical Psychopharmacology, 21,* 38.

Kirkbride, J. B., Jones, P. B., Ullrich, S., & Coid, J. W. (2012). Social deprivation, inequality, and the neighborhood-level incidence of psychotic syndromes in East London. *Schizophrenia Bulletin.* doi: 10.1093/schbul/sbs151

Kite, M. E. (2013). Teaching about race and ethnicity. In D. S. Dunn, R. A. R. Gurung, K. Z. Naufel, & J. H. Wilson (Eds.), *Controversy in the psychology classroom: Using hot topics to foster critical thinking* (pp. 169–184). Washington, DC: American Psychological Association.

Kivimäki, M., Nyberg, S. J., Batty, G. D., Fransson, E. I., Heikkila, K., Alfredsson, L., . . . Theorell, T. (2012). Job strain as a risk factor for coronary heart disease: A collaborative meta-analysis of individual participant data. *Lancet, 380,* 1491–1497.

Kivlighan Jr, D. M., London, K., & Miles, J. R. (2012). Are two heads better than one? The relationship between number of group leaders and group members, and group climate and group member benefit from therapy. *Group Dynamics: Theory, Research, and Practice, 16,* 1–13.

Kleider, H. M., Pezdek, K., Goldinger, S. D., & Kirk, A. (2008). Schema-driven source misattribution errors: Remembering the expected from a witnessed event. *Applied Cognitive Psychology, 22,* 1–20.

Klein, S. B. (2012). *Learning: Principles and applications* (6th ed.). Thousand Oaks, CA: SAGE.

Kluger, J., & Masters, C. (2006, August 28). How to spot a liar. *Time,* 46–48.

Kneeland, R. E., & Fatemi, S. H. (2013). Viral infection, inflammation and schizophrenia. *Progress in Neuro-Psychopharmacology & Biological Psychiatry, 42,* 35–48.

Knutson, K. L. (2012). Does inadequate sleep play a role in vulnerability to obesity? *American Journal of Human Biology,* 24, 361–371.

Kobeissi, J., Aloysi, A., Tobias, K., Popeo, D., & Kellner, C. H. (2011). Resolution of severe suicidality with a single electroconvulsive therapy. *The Journal of ECT, 27,* 86–88.

Kohl, J. V. (2012). Human pheromones and food odors: Epigenetic influences on the socioaffective nature of evolved behaviors. *Socioaffective Neuroscience & Psychology, 2*: 17338.

Kohlberg, L. (1964). Development of moral character and moral behavior. In L. W. Hoffman & M. L. Hoffman (Eds.), *Review of child development research* (Vol. 1, pp. 383–431). New York: Sage.

Kokkoris, M. D., & Kühnen, U. (2013). Choice and dissonance in a European cultural context: The case of Western and Eastern Europeans. *International Journal of Psychology.* Advance online publication. doi: 10.1080/00207594.2013.766746

Kolb, B. (2013). *Introduction to brain and behavior.* New York: Worth.

Kolen, M. J., & Hendrickson, A. B. (2013). Scaling, norming, and equating. In K. F. Geisinger, B. A. Bracken, J. F. Carlson, J.-I. C. Hansen, N. R. Kuncel, S. P. Reise, & M. C. Rodriguez (Eds.), *APA handbooks in psychology. APA handbook of testing and assessment in psychology, Vol. 1. Test theory and testing and assessment in industrial and organizational psychology* (pp. 201–222). Washington DC: American Psychological Association.

Kontak, A. C., Victor, R. G., & Vongpatanasin, W. (2013). Dexmedetomidine as a novel countermeasure for cocaine-induced central sympathoexcitation in cocaine-addicted humans: Novelty and significance. *Hypertension, 61,* 388–394.

Koopmann-Holm, B., & Matsumoto, D. (2011). Values and display rules for specific emotions. *Journal of Cross-Cultural Psychology, 42,* 355–371.

Koran, L. M. (2007). Obsessive-compulsive disorder: An update for the clinician. *Focus, 5,* 299–313.

Kotagal, S., & Kumar, S. (2013). Childhood onset narcolepsy cataplexy-more than just a sleep disorder. *Sleep, 36,* 161.

Kotowski, A. (2012). Case study: A young male with auditory hallucinations in paranoid schizophrenia. *International Journal of Nursing Knowledge, 23,* 41–44.

Kracher, B., & Marble, R. P. (2008). The significance of gender in predicting the cognitive moral development of business practitioners using the Socioemotional Reflection Objective Measure. *Journal of Business Ethics, 78,* 503–526.

Kraft, T. L., & Pressman, S. D. (2012). Grin and bear it: The influence of manipulated positive facial expression on the stress response. *Psychological Science, 23,* 1372–1378.

Krahé, B. (2013). *The social psychology of aggression (2nd ed.).* New York: Psychology Press.

Krebs, D. L. (2007). Deciphering the structure of the moral sense: A review of moral minds: How nature designed our universal sense of right and wrong. *Evolution and Human Behavior, 28,* 294–296.

Kreger Silverman, L. (2013). *Psych 101: Giftedness 101.* New York: Springer.

Kreipe, R. E., Starr, T. B., & Simeone, R. E. (2012). Eating disorders. In O. J. Z. Sahler, J. E. Carr, J. B. Frank, & J. V. Nunes (Eds.), *The behavioral sciences and health care* (3rd ed., pp. 199–205). Cambridge, MA: Hogrefe.

Kress, T., Aviles, C., Taylor, C., & Winchell, M. (2011). Individual/collective human needs: (Re) theorizing Maslow using critical, sociocultural, feminist, and indigenous lenses. In C. Malott & B. Porfilio (Eds.), *Critical pedagogy in the twenty-first century: A new generation of scholars (*pp. 135–157). Charlotte, NC: Information Age Publishing.

Kress, V. E., Hoffman, R. M., Adamson, N., & Eriksen, K. (2013). Informed consent, confidentiality, and diagnosing: Ethical guidelines for counselor practice. *Journal of Mental Health Counseling, 35,* 15–28.

Krettenauer, T., Campbell, S., & Hertz, S. (2013). Moral emotions and the development of the moral self in childhood. *European Journal of Developmental Psychology,* 10, 159–173.

Kring, A. M., Johnson, S. L. , Davison, G. C., & Neale, J. M. (2012). *Abnormal psychology* (12th ed.). Hoboken, NJ: Wiley.

Krohne, H. W., & Slangen, K. E. (2005). Influence of social support on adaptation to surgery. *Health Psychology, 24,* 101–105.

Krug, S. E. (2013). Objective personality testing. In K. F. Geisinger, B. A. Bracken, J. F. Carlson, J.-I. C. Hansen, N. R. Kuncel, S. P. Reise, & M. C. Rodriguez (Eds.), *APA handbooks in psychology. APA handbook of testing and assessment in psychology, Vol. 1. Test theory and testing and assessment in industrial and organizational psychology* (pp. 315–328). Washington, DC: American Psychological Association.

Krugman, H. E. (2013). *Consumer behavior and advertising involvement: Selected works of Herbert E. Krugman.* New York: Routledge Academic.

Krukowski, K., Eddy, J., Kosik, K. L., Konley, T., Janusek, L. W., & Mathews, H. L. (2011). Glucocorticoid dysregulation of natural killer cell function through epigenetic modification. *Brain, Behavior, and Immunity, 25,* 239–249.

Krusemark, E. A., Campbell, W. K., & Clementz, B. A. (2008). Attributions, deception, and event related potentials: An investigation of the self-serving bias. *Psychophysiology, 45,* 511–515.

Krypel, M. N., & Henderson-King, D. (2010). Stress, coping styles, and optimism: Are they related to meaning of education in students' lives? *Social Psychology of Education, 13,* 409–424.

Kteily, N. S., Sidanius, J., & Levin, S. (2011). Social dominance orientation: Cause or 'mere effect'?: Evidence for SDO as a causal predictor of prejudice and discrimination against ethnic and racial outgroups. *Journal of Experimental Social Psychology, 47,* 208–214.

Kubiak, T., Vögele, C., Siering, M., Schiel, R., & Weber, H. (2008). Daily hassles and emotional eating in obese adolescents under restricted dietary conditions—The role of ruminative thinking. *Appetite, 51,* 206–209.

Kubota, M., Miyata, J., Sasamoto, A., Sugihara, G., Yoshida, H., Kawada, R., . . . Murai, T. (2013). Thalamocortical disconnection in the orbitofrontal region associated with cortical thinning in schizophrenia thalamocortical disconnection. *Journal of the American Medical Association Psychiatry, 70,* 12–21.

Kuchenbrandt, D., Eyssel, F., & Seidel, S. K. (2013). Cooperation makes it happen: Imagined intergroup cooperation enhances the positive effects of imagined contact. *Group Processes & Intergroup Relations, 16,* 636–648.

Kukucka, J., & Kassin, S. M. (2012). *Do confessions taint juror perceptions of handwriting evidence?* Paper presented at the annual meeting of the American Psychology-Law Society, San Juan, Puerto Rico.

Kullmann, D. M., & Lamsa, K. P. (2011). LTP and LTD in cortical GABAergic interneurons: Emerging rules and roles. *Neuropharmacology, 60,* 712–719.

Kumar, S., & Mellsop, G. (2013). Burnout: Gender aspects. In S. Bährer-Kohler (Ed.), *Burnout for experts: Prevention in the context of living and working* (pp. 99–117). New York: Springer Science + Business Media.

Kvavilashvili, L., Mirani, J., Schlagman, S., Erskine, J. A. K., & Kornbrot, D. E. (2010). Effects of age on phenomenology and consistency of flashbulb memories of September 11 and a staged control event. *Psychology and Aging, 25,* 391–404.

Kyaga, S., Landén, M., Boman, M., Hultman, C. M., Långström, N., & Lichtenstein, P. (2012). Mental illness, suicide and creativity: 40-year prospective total population study. *Journal of Psychiatric Research, 47,* 83–90.

Kyriacou, C. P., & Hastings, M. H. (2010). Circadian clocks: Genes, sleep, and cognition. *Trends in Cognitive Sciences, 14,* 259–267.

Lageman, S. K., Mickens, M., Verkerke, T., & Holloway, K. (2013). Deep brain stimulation for Parkinson's disease. In A. R. Block & D. B. Sarwer (Eds.), *Presurgical psychological screening: Understanding patients, improving outcomes* (pp. 127–149). Washington, DC: American Psychological Association.

Laier, C., Schulte, F. P., & Brand, M. (2013). Pornographic picture processing interferes with working memory performance. *Journal of Sex Research, 50,* 642–652.

Lakein, A. (1998). *Give me a moment and I'll change your life: Tools for moment management.* New York: Andrews McMeel Publishing.

Lambert, A. J., Good, K. S., & Kirk, I. J. (2010). Testing the repression hypothesis: Effects of emotional valence on memory suppression in the think—no think task. *Consciousness and Cognition, 19,* 281–293.

Lambert, M. J. (2013). Outcome in psychotherapy: The past and important advances. *Psychotherapy, 50,* 42–51.

Lammers, J., & Stapel, D. (2011). Power increases dehumanization. *Group Processes and Intergroup Relations, 14,* 113–126.

Lamy, D., Leber, A. B., & Egeth, H. E. (2013). Selective attention. In A. F. Healy, R. W. Proctor, & I. B. Weiner (Eds.), *Handbook of psychology, Vol. 4. Experimental psychology* (2nd ed., pp. 267–294). Hoboken, NJ: Wiley.

Lancaster, R. S. (2007). *Stop Sylvia Browne: Sylvia Browne's best evidence.* Retrieved from http://www.stopsylvia.com/articles/ac360_brownesbestevidence.shtml.

Landsbergis, P. A., Schnall, P. L., Belkic, K. L., Baker, D., Schwartz, J. E., & Pickering, T. G. (2011). Workplace and cardiovascular disease: Relevance and potential role for occupational health psychology. In J. C. Quick & L. E. Tetrick (Eds.), *Handbook of occupational health psychology* (2nd ed., pp. 243–264). Washington, DC: American Psychological Association.

Lanfer, A., Bammann, K., Knof, K., Buchecker, K., Russo, P., Veidebaum, T., . . . Ahrens, W. (2013). Predictors and correlates of taste preferences in European children: The IDEFICS study. *Food Quality and Preference, 27,* 128–136.

Langenecker, S. A., Bieliauskas, L. A., Rapport, L. J., Zubieta, J-K., Wilde, E. A., & Berent, S. (2005). Face emotion perception and executive functioning deficits in depression. *Journal of Clinical and Experimental Neuropsychology, 27,* 320–333.

Langlois, J. H., Kalakanis, L., Rubenstein, A., Larson, A., Hallam, M., & Smoot, M. (2000). Maxims or myths of beauty? A meta-analytic and theoretical review. *Psychological Bulletin, 126,* 390–423.

Langmeyer, A., Guglhör-Rudan, A., & Tarnai, C. (2012). What do music preferences reveal about personality: A cross-cultural replication using self-ratings and ratings of music samples. *Journal of Individual Differences, 33,* 119–130.

Långström, N., Rahman, Q., Carlström, E., & Lichtenstein, P. (2010). Genetic and environmental effects on same-sex sexual behavior: A population study of twins in Sweden. *Archives of Sexual Behavior, 39,* 75–80.

LaPointe, L. L. (Ed.) (2005). Feral children. *Journal of Medical Speech-Language Pathology, 13,* vii–ix.

Lapsley, D. K. (2006). Moral stage theory. In M. Killen & J. Smetana (Eds.), *Handbook of moral development* (pp. 37–66). Mahwah, NJ: Erlbaum.

Lara-Sacido, A., Crego, A., & Romero-Maroto, M. (2012). Emotional contagion of dental fear to children: The fathers' mediating role in parental transfer of fear. *International Journal of Paediatric Dentistry, 22,* 324–330.

Lariscy, R. A. W., & Tinkham, S. F. (1999). The sleeper effect and negative political advertising. *Journal of Advertising, 28,* 13–30.

Larkby, C. A., Goldschmidt, L., Hanusa, B. H., & Day, N. L. (2011). Prenatal alcohol exposure is associated with conduct disorder in adolescence: Findings from a birth cohort. *Journal of the American Academy of Child and Adolescent Psychiatry, 50,* 262–271.

Larrick, R. P., Timmerman, T. A., Carton, A. M., & Abrevaya, J. (2011). Temper, temperature, and temptation: Heat-related retaliation in baseball. *Psychological Science, 22,* 423–428.

Lasnier, G. (2013). Popping the question is his job. *Newscenter.* Retrieved from http://news.ucsc.edu/2013/01/marriage-traditions.html

Latane, B., & Darley, J. M. (1968). Group inhibition of bystander intervention in emergencies. *Journal of Personality and Social Psychology, 10,* 215–221.

Lavner, J. A., & Bradbury, T. N. (2012). Why do even satisfied newlyweds eventually go on to divorce? *Journal of Family Psychology, 26,* 1–10.

Lawrence, C., & Andrews, K. (2004). The influence of perceived prison crowding on male inmates' perception of aggressive events. *Aggressive Behavior, 30,* 273–283.

Lawrence, V., Murray, J., Klugman, A., & Banerjee, S. (2011). Cross-cultural variation in the experience of depression in older people in the UK. In M. Abou-Saleh, C. Katona, & A. Kumar (Eds.), *Principle and*

practice of geriatric psychiatry (3rd ed., pp. 711–716). Hoboken, NJ: Wiley.

Lazar, S. W., Kerr, C. E., Wasserman, R. H., Gray, J. R., Greve, D. N., Treadway, M. T., . . . Fischl, B. (2005). Meditation experience is associated with increased cortical thickness. *Neuroreport, 16,* 1893–1897.

Lazarus, R. S. (1991). *Emotion and adaptation.* New York: Oxford University Press.

Lazarus, R. S. (1998). *The life and work of an eminent psychologist.* New York: Oxford University Press.

Leaper, C. (2013). Gender development during childhood. In P. D. Zelazo (Ed.), *Oxford handbook of developmental psychology* (pp. 327–377). New York: Oxford University Press.

Lebow, J., & Stroud, C. B. (2013). Family therapy. In G. Stricker, T. A. Widiger, & I. B. Weiner (Eds.), *Handbook of psychology, Vol. 8. Clinical psychology* (2nd ed., pp. 384–407). Hoboken, NJ: Wiley.

LeDoux, J. E. (1998). *The emotional brain.* New York: Simon & Schuster.

LeDoux, J. E. (2002). *Synaptic self: How our brains become who we are.* New York: Viking.

LeDoux, J. E. (2003). The emotional brain, fear, and the amygdala. *Cellular and Molecular Neurobiology, 23,* 727–738.

LeDoux, J. E. (2007). Emotional memory. *Scholarpedia, 2,* 180.

Lee, A. M., & Messing, R. O. (2011). Protein kinase C epsilon modulates nicotine consumption and dopamine reward signals in the nucleus accumbens. *Proceedings of the National Academy of Sciences, 108,* 16080–16085.

Lee, J., Jiang, J., Sim, K., Tay, J., Subramaniam, M., & Chong, S. (2011). Gender differences in Singaporean Chinese patients with schizophrenia. *Asian Journal of Psychiatry, 4,* 60–64.

Lee, J-H., Chung, W-H., Kang, E-H., Chung, D-J., Choi, C-B., Chang, H-S., . . . Kim, H-Y. (2011). Schwann cell-like remyelination following transplantation of human umbilical cord blood (hUCB)-derived mesenchymal stem cells in dogs with acute spinal cord injury. *Journal of the Neurological Sciences, 300,* 86–96.

Leichsenring, F., Leibing, E., Kruse, J., New, A., & Leweke, F. (2011). Borderline personality disorder. *The Lancet, 377,* 74–84.

Leichtman, M. D. (2006). Cultural and maturational influences on long-term event memory. In L. Balter & C. S. Tamis-LeMonda (Eds.), *Child psychology: A handbook of contemporary issues* (2nd ed., pp. 565–589). New York: Psychology Press.

LePage, P., Akar, H., Temli, Y., Sen, D., Hasser, N., & Ivins, I. (2011). Comparing teachers' views on morality and moral education, a comparative study in Turkey and the United States. *Teaching and Teacher Education, 27,* 366–375.

Leslie, M. (2000, July/August). The Vexing Legacy of Lewis Terman. *Stanford Magazine.* Retrieved from http://www.stanfordalumni.org/news/magazine/2000/julaug/articles/terman.html.

Lessov-Schlaggar, C. N., Agrawal, A., & Swan, G. E. (2013). Behavior genetics. In J. A. Schinka, W. F. Velicer, & I. B. Weiner (Eds.), *Handbook of psychology, Vol. 2. Research methods in psychology* (2nd ed., pp. 342–365). Hoboken, NJ: Wiley.

Leung, A. K. Y., Kim, Y. H., Zhang, Z. X., Tam, K. P., & Chiu, C. Y. (2012). Cultural construction of success and epistemic motives moderate American-Chinese differences in reward allocation biases. *Journal of Cross-Cultural Psychology, 43,* 46–52.

LeVay, S. (2003). Queer science: The use and abuse of research into homosexuality. *Archives of Sexual Behavior, 32,* 187–189.

Levine, J. R. (2001). *Why do fools fall in love: Experiencing the magic, mystery, and meaning of successful relationships.* New York: Jossey-Bass.

Levinson, D. B., Smallwood, J., & Davidson, R. J. (2012). The persistence of thought: Evidence for a role of working memory in the maintenance of task-unrelated thinking. *Psychological Science, 23,* 375–380.

Levinthal, C. (2011). *Drugs, behavior, and modern society (7th ed.).* Boston, MA: Prentice Hall.

Leyfer, O., Gallo, K., Cooper-Vince, C., & Pincus, D. (2013). Patterns and predictors of comorbidity of DSM-IV anxiety disorders in a clinical sample of children and adolescents. *Journal of Anxiety Disorders, 27,* 306–311.

Li, Y., Li, Y., McKay, R., Riethmacher, D., & Parada, L. F. (2012). Neurofibromin modulates adult hippocampal neurogenesis and behavioral effects of antidepressants. *The Journal of Neuroscience, 32,* 3529–3539.

Li, Y., Liu, J., Wang, W., Yong, Q., Zhou, G., Wang, M., . . . Zhao, D. (2012). Association of self-reported snoring with carotid artery intima-media thickness and plaque. *Journal of Sleep Research, 21,* 87–93.

Libby, D. J., Worhunsky, P. D., Pilver, C. E., & Brewer, J. A. (2012). Meditation-induced changes in high-frequency heart rate variability predict smoking outcomes. *Frontiers in Human Neuroscience, 6,* Article ID 54.

Libon, D. J., Xie, S. X., Moore, P., Farmer, J., Antani, S., McCawley, . . . Grossman, M. (2007). Patterns of neuropsychological impairment in frontotemporal dementia. *Neurology, 68,* 369–375.

Liem, D. G., Toraman Aydin, N., & Zandstra, E. H. (2012). Effects of health labels on expected and actual taste perception of soup. *Food Quality & Preference, 29,* 192–197.

Lien, Y-W., Chu, R-L., Jen, C-H., & Wu, C-H. (2006). Do Chinese commit neither fundamental attribution error nor ultimate attribution error? *Chinese Journal of Psychology, 48,* 163–181.

Lilienfeld, S. O., Lynn, S. J., Ruscio, J., & Beyerstein, B. L. (2010). *50 great myths of popular psychology: Shattering widespread misconceptions about human behavior.* Malden, MA: Wiley-Blackwell.

Lilienfeld, S. O., Waldman, I. D., Landfield, K., Watts, A. L., Rubenzer, S., & Faschingbauer, T. R. (2012). Fearless dominance and the U.S. presidency: Implications of psychopathic personality traits for successful and unsuccessful political leadership. *Journal of Personality and Social Psychology, 103,* 489–505.

Lim, L., Chang, W., Yu, X., Chiu, H., Chong, M., & Kua, E. (2011). Depression in Chinese elderly populations. *Asia-Pacific Psychiatry, 3,* 46–53.

Lim, S. S., Vos, T., Flaxman, A. D., Danaei, G., Shibuya, K., Adair-Rohani, H., . . . Degenhardt, L. (2013). A comparative risk assessment of burden of disease and injury attributable to 67 risk factors and risk factor clusters in 21 regions, 1990–2010: A systematic analysis for the Global Burden of Disease Study 2010. *The Lancet, 380,* 2224–2260.

Lin, C. S., Niddam, D. M., Hsu, M. L., & Hsieh, J. C. (2013). Pain catastrophizing is associated with dental pain in a stressful context. *Journal of Dental Research, 92,* 130–135.

Lin, C.-C. J., Chen, W.-N., Chen, C.-J., Lin, Y.-W., Zimmer, A., & Chen, C.-C. (2012). An antinociceptive role for substance P in acid-induced chronic muscle pain. *Proceeding of the National Academy of Sciences, 109,* E76–E83.

Lin, T.-C. E., Dumigan, N. M., Dwyer, D. M., Good, M. A., & Honey, R. C. (2013). Assessing the encoding specificity of associations with sensory preconditioning procedures. *Journal of Experimental Psychology: Animal Behavior Processes, 39,* 67–75.

Lindner, I., Echterhoff, G., Davidson, P. S. R., & Brand, M. (2010). Observation inflation: Your actions become mine. *Psychological Science, 21,* 1291–1299.

Liu, H. (2009). Till death do us part: Marital status and US mortality trends, 1986–2000.

Journal of Marriage and Family, 71, 1158–1173.

Liu, J. H., & Latané, B. (1998). Extremitization of attitudes: Does thought- and discussion-induced polarization cumulate? *Basic and Applied Social Psychology, 20*, 103–110.

Livingston, J. A. (1999). Something old and something new: Love, creativity, and the enduring relationship. *Bulletin of the Menninger Clinic, 63*, 40–52.

Lo, P. C., & Chang, C. H. (2013). Effects of long-term Dharma-Chan meditation on cardiorespiratory synchronization and HRV behavior. *Rejuvenation Research, 16*, 115–123.

Lobban, F., Postlethwaite, A., Glentworth, D., Pinfold, V., Wainwright, L., Dunn, G., . . . Haddock, G. (2013). A systematic review of randomised controlled trials of interventions reporting outcomes for relatives of people with psychosis. *Clinical Psychology Review, 33*, 372–382.

LoBue, V., & DeLoache, J. S. (2008). Detecting the snake in the grass: Attention to fear-relevant stimuli by adults and young children. *Psychological Science, 19*, 284–289.

Loftus, E. F. (2000). Remembering what never happened. In E. Tulving (Ed.), *Memory, consciousness, and the brain: The Tallinn Conference* (pp. 106–118). New York: Psychology Press.

Loftus, E. F. (2001). Imagining the past. *Psychologist, 14*, 584–587.

Loftus, E. F. (2007). Memory distortions: Problems solved and unsolved. In M. Garry, & H. Hayne (Eds.), *Do justice and let the skies fall* (pp. 1–14). Mahwah, NJ: Erlbaum.

Loftus, E. F. (2011). How I got started: From semantic memory to expert testimony. *Applied Cognitive Psychology, 25*, 347–348.

Loftus, E. F., & Cahill, L. (2007). Memory distortion from misattribution to rich false memory. In J. S. Nairne (Ed.), *The foundations of remembering: Essays in honor of Henry L. Roediger, III* (pp. 413–425). New York: Psychology Press.

Longino, H. (2013). *Studying human behavior: How scientists investigate aggression and sexuality*. Chicago: University of Chicago Press.

Loo, C. K., Mahon, M., Katalinic, N., Lyndon, B., & Hadzi-Pavlovic, D. (2011). Predictors of response to ultrabrief right unilateral electroconvulsive therapy. *Journal of Affective Disorders, 130*, 192–197.

Lopez, K. (2013). *"Silver Linings" hits close to home for director Russell*. Retrieved from http://www.usatoday.com/story/news/nation/2013/02/08/silver-lining-playbook-mental-illness/1891065/

Lopez-Munoz, F., & Alamo, C. (2011). *Neurobiology of depression*. Boca Raton, FL: CRC Press.

Lotem, A., & Halpern, J. Y. (2012). Coevolution of learning and data-acquisition mechanisms: A model for cognitive evolution. *Philosophical Transactions of the Royal Society B: Biological Sciences, 367*, 2686–2694.

Lovibond, P. (2011). Learning and anxiety: A cognitive perspective. In T. Schachtman & S. Reilly (Eds.), *Associative learning and conditioning theory: Human and non-human applications* (pp. 104–120). Oxford, UK: Oxford University Press.

Luby, J. L., Barch, D. M., Belden, A., Gaffrey, M.S., Tillman, R., Babb, C., . . . Botteron, K. N. (2012). Maternal support in early childhood predicts larger hippocampal volumes at school age. *Proceedings of the National Academy of Sciences, 109*, 2854–2859.

Luchies, L.B., Wieselquist, J., Rusbult, C. E., Kumashiro, M., Eastwick, P.W., Coolsen, M. K., & Finkel, E.J. (2013). Trust and biased memory of transgressions in romantic relationships. *Journal of Personality and Social Psychology, 104*, 673–694.

Luo, S., Romero, A., Hu, H. H., Monterosso, J, & Page, K. A. (2013). Abdominal fat is associated with a greater brain reward response to high-calorie food cues in Hispanic women. *Obesity, 21*, 2029–2036.

Luppa, M., Sikorski, C., Luck, T., Ehreke, L., Konnopka, A., Wiese, B., . . . Riedel-Heller, S. G. (2012). Age- and gender-specific prevalence of depression in latest-life – Systematic review and meta-analysis. *Journal of Affective Disorders, 136*, 212–221.

Lyn, H., Greenfield, P. M., Savage-Rumbaugh, S., Gillespie-Lynch, K., & Hopkins, W. D. (2011). Nonhuman primates do declare! A comparison of declarative symbol and gesture use in two children, two bonobos, and a chimpanzee. *Language and Communication, 31*, 63–74.

Lynam, D. R., Miller, J. D., Miller, D. J., Bornovalova, M. A., & Lejuez, C. W. (2011). Testing the relations between impulsivity-related traits, suicidality, and nonsuicidal self-injury: A test of the incremental validity of the UPPS model. *Personality Disorders: Theory, Research, and Treatment, 2*, 151–160.

Lynn, S. J., Condon, L., & Colletti, G. (2013). The treatment of dissociative identity disorder: Questions and considerations. In W. O'Donohue & S. O. Lilienfeld (Eds.), *Case studies in clinical science* (pp. 329–351). New York: Oxford University Press.

Lynn, S. J., Rhue, J. W., & Kirsch, I. (Eds.). (2010). *Handbook of clinical hypnosis* (2nd ed.). Washington, DC: American Psychological Association.

Lyubimov, N. N. (1992). Electrophysiological characteristics of sensory processing and mobilization of hidden brain reserves. *2nd Russian-Swedish Symposium New Research in Neurobiology*. Moscow: Russian Academy of Science Institute of Human Brain.

Maas, J., B., Wherry, M. L., Axelrod, D. J., Hogan, B. R., & Bloomin, J. (1999). *Power sleep: The revolutionary program that prepares your mind for peak performance*. New York: HarperPerennial.

Macmillan, M. (2000). *An odd kind of fame: Stories of Phineas Gage*. Cambridge, MA: MIT Press.

Macmillan, M. (2008). Phineas Gage — Unravelling the myth. *Psychologist, 21*, 828–831.

Macmillan, M., & Lena, M.L. (2010). Rehabilitating Phineas Gage. *Neuropsychological Rehabilitation, 20*, 641–658.

Madden, K., Middleton, P., Cyna, A. M., Matthewson, M., & Jones, L. (2012). Hypnosis for pain management during labour and childbirth. *Cochrane Database of Systematic Reviews*, 11:CD009356.

Madras, B. K. (2013). History of the discovery of the antipsychotic dopamine D2 receptor: A basis for the dopamine hypothesis of schizophrenia. *Journal of the History of the Neurosciences, 22*, 62–78.

Mahn, H., & John-Steiner, V. (2013). Vygotsky and sociocultural approaches to teaching and learning. In W. M. Reynolds, G. E. Miller, & I. B. Weiner (Eds.), *Handbook of psychology, Vol. 7. Educational psychology (2nd ed.*, pp. 117–145). Hoboken, NJ: Wiley.

Maier, S. F. (1970). Failure to escape traumatic electric shock: Incompatible skeletal-motor responses or learned helplessness? *Learning and Motivation, 1*, 157–169.

Main, M., & Solomon, J. (1986). Discovery of an insecure-disorganized attachment pattern. In T. Brazelton & M. W. Yogman (Eds.), *Affective development in infancy* (pp. 95–124). Westport, CT: Ablex Publishing.

Maisto, S. A., Galizio, M., & Connors, G., J. (2014). *Drug use and abuse* (7th ed.). Belmont, CA: Cengage.

Majer, J. M., Jason, L. A., Aase, D. M., Droege, J. R., & Ferrari, J. R. (2013). Categorical 12-step involvement and continuous abstinence at 2 years. *Journal of Substance Abuse Treatment, 44*, 46–51.

Mak, A. S. P., & Lam, L. C. W. (2013). Neurocognitive profiles of people with borderline personality disorder. *Current Opinion in Psychiatry, 26,* 90–96.

Makinodan, M., Rosen, K. M., Ito, S., & Corfas, G. (2012). A critical period for social experience–dependent oligodendrocyte maturation and myelination. *Science, 337,* 1357–1360.

Malhi, G. S. (2013). DSM-5: Ordering disorder? *Australian and New Zealand Journal of Psychiatry, 47,* 7–9.

Malinowski, P. (2013). Neural mechanisms of attentional control in mindfulness meditation. *Frontiers in Neuroscience, 7,* 8.

Malti, T. (Ed.). (2013). *New directions for youth development: Theory practice research. Adolescent emotions: Development, morality, and adaptation.* San Francisco, CA: Jossey-Bass.

Mancia, M., & Baggott, J. (2008). The early unrepressed unconscious in relation to Matte-Blanco's thought. *International Forum of Psychoanalysis, 17,* 201–212.

Maner, J. K., & Menzel, A. J. (2013). Evolutionary social psychology. In H. Tennen, J. Suls, & I. B. Weiner (Eds.), *Handbook of psychology, Vol. 5. Personality and social psychology (2nd ed.,* pp. 487–506). Hoboken, NJ: Wiley.

Manganelli, F., Dubbioso, R., Pisciotta, C., Antenora, A., Nolano, M., De Michele, G., . . . Santoro, L. (2013). Somatosensory temporal discrimination threshold is increased in patients with cerebellar atrophy. *Cerebellum, 12,* 456–459.

Manna, G., Faraci, P., & Como, M. R. (2013). Factorial structure and psychometric properties of the Sensation Seeking Scale-Form V (SSS-V) in a sample of Italian adolescents. *Europe's Journal of Psychology, 9,* 276–288.

Mansukhani, M. P., Kolla, B. P., Surani, S., Varon, J., & Ramar, K. (2012). Sleep deprivation in resident physicians, work hour limitations, and related outcomes: A systematic review of the literature. *Postgraduate Medicine, 124,* 241–249.

Mapayi, B., Makanjuola, R. O. A., Mosaku, S. K., Adewuya, O. A., Afolabi, O., Aloba, O. O., & Akinsulore, A. (2013). Impact of intimate partner violence on anxiety and depression amongst women in Ile-Ife, Nigeria. *Archives of Women's Mental Health, 16,* 11–18.

Marazziti, D., Masala, I., Baroni, S., Polini, M., Massimetti, G., Giannaccini, G., . . . Mauri, M. (2010). Male axillary extracts modify the affinity of the platelet serotonin transporter and impulsiveness in women. *Physiology and Behavior, 100,* 364–368.

Marcia, J., & Josselson, R. (2013). Eriksonian personality research and its implications for psychotherapy. *Journal of Personality.* Advance online publication. doi: 10.1111/jopy.12014

Marcotte, K., Perlbarg, V., Marrelec, G., Benali, H., & Ansaldo, A. I. (2013). Default-mode network functional connectivity in aphasia: Therapy-induced neuroplasticity. *Brain & Language, 124,* 45–55.

Mares, M. L., & Woodard, E. (2005). Positive effects of television on children's social interactions: A meta-analysis. *Media Psychology, 7,* 301–322.

Marks, D. F., Murray, M. D., Evans, B., & Estacio, E. V. (2011). *Health psychology: Theory, research and practice* (3rd ed.). London, UK: Sage.

Markus, H. R., & Kitayama, S. (2003). Culture, self, and the reality of the social. *Psychological Inquiry, 14,* 277–283.

Marques, L., Robinaugh, D., LeBlanc, N., & Hinton, D. (2011). Cross-cultural variations in the prevalence and presentation of anxiety disorders. *Expert Review of Neurotherapeutics, 11,* 313–322.

Martella, D., Casagrande, M., & Lupiáñez, J. (2011). Alerting, orienting and executive control: The effects of sleep deprivation on attentional networks. *Experimental Brain Research, 210,* 81–89.

Marti, F., Arib, O., Morel, C., Dufresne, V., Maskos, U., Corringer, P-J., . . . Faure, P. (2012). Smoke extracts and nicotine, but not tobacco extracts, potentiate firing and burst activity of ventral tegmental area dopaminergic neurons in mice. *Neuropsychopharmacology, 36,* 2244–2257.

Martin, C. L., & Fabes, R. (2009). *Discovering child development* (2nd ed.). Belmont, CA: Cengage.

Martin, L. J., & Carron, A. V. (2012). Team attributions in sport: A meta-analysis. *Journal of Applied Sport Psychology, 24,* 157–174.

Martinko, M. J., Harvey, P., & Dasborough, M. T. (2011). Attribution theory in the organizational sciences: A case of unrealized potential. *Journal of Organizational Behavior, 32,* 144–149.

Martin-Storey, A., Serbin, L. A., Stack, D. M., Ledingham, J. E., & Schwartzman, A. E. (2012). Self and peer perceptions of childhood aggression, social withdrawal and likeability predict adult personality factors: A prospective longitudinal study. *Personality and Individual Differences, 53,* 843–848.

Marusich, J. A., Darna, M., Charnigo, R. J., Dwoskin, L. P., & Bardo, M. T. (2011). A multivariate assessment of individual differences in sensation seeking and impulsivity as predictors of amphetamine self-administration and prefrontal dopamine function in rats. *Experimental and Clinical Psychopharmacology, 19,* 275–284.

Marx, D. M., Ko, S. J., & Friedman, R. A. (2009). The "Obama effect": How a salient role model reduces race-based performance differences. *Journal of Experimental Social Psychology, 45,* 953–956.

Maslow, A. H. (1954). *Motivation and personality.* New York: Harper & Row.

Maslow, A. H. (1970). *Motivation and personality* (2nd ed.). New York: Harper & Row.

Maslow, A. H. (1999). *Toward a psychology of being* (3rd ed.). Hoboken, NJ: Wiley.

Master, S. L., Eisenberger, N. I., Taylor, S. E., Naliboff, B. D., Shirinyan, D., & Lieberman, M. D. (2009). A picture's worth: Partner photographs reduce experimentally induced pain. *Psychological Science, 20,* 1316–1318.

Masters, W. H., & Johnson, V. E. (1961). Orgasm, anatomy of the female. In A. Ellis & A. Abarbonel (Eds.), *Encyclopedia of sexual behavior,* Vol. 2. New York: Hawthorn.

Masters, W. H., & Johnson, V. E. (1966). *Human sexual response.* Boston, MA: Little, Brown.

Masters, W. H., & Johnson, V. E. (1970). *Human sexual inadequacy.* Boston, MA: Little, Brown.

Mathis, J., & Hess, C. (2009). Sleepiness and vigilance tests. *Swiss Medical Weekly, 139,* 214–219.

Matlin, M. W. (2012). *The psychology of women* (7th ed.). Belmont, CA: Cengage.

Matlin, M. W. (2013). *Cognition* (8th ed.). Hoboken, NJ: Wiley.

Matsumoto, D. (2000). *Culture and psychology: People around the world.* Belmont, CA: Wadsworth.

Matsumoto, D. (2010). *APA handbook of interpersonal communication.* Washington, DC: American Psychological Association.

Matsumoto, D., & Hwang, H. S. (2011). Cooperation and competition in intercultural interactions. *International Journal of Intercultural Relations, 35,* 677–685.

Matsumoto, D., & Hwang, H. S. (2012). Culture and emotion: The integration of biological and cultural contributions. *Journal of Cross-Cultural Psychology, 43,* 91–118.

Matsumoto, D., & Juang, L. (2008). *Culture and psychology* (4th ed.). Belmont, CA: Cengage.

Matsumoto, D., & Juang, L. (2013). *Culture and psychology (5th ed.).* Belmont, CA: Wadsworth Publishing.

Maxson, S. C. (2013). Behavioral genetics. In R. J. Nelson, S. J. Y. Mizumori, & I. B.

Weiner (Eds.), *Handbook of psychology, Vol. 3. Behavioral neuroscience* (2nd ed., pp. 1–25). Hoboken, NJ: Wiley.

May, A. C., Rudy, B. M., Davis, T. E. III, & Matson, J. L. (2013). Evidence-based behavioral treatment of dog phobia with young children: Two case examples. *Behavior Modification, 37,* 143–160.

May-Collado, L. J. (2010). Changes in whistle structure of two dolphin species during interspecific associations. *Ethology, 116,* 1065–1074.

Mazur, A. (2013). Dominance, violence, and the neurohormonal nexus. In D. D. Franks & J. H. Turner (Eds.), *Handbooks of sociology and social research* (pp. 359–368). New York: Springer Science + Business Media.

McAllister, K. A., Saksida, L. M., & Bussey, T. J. (2013). Dissociation between memory retention across a delay and pattern separation following medial prefrontal cortex lesions in the touchscreen TUNL task. *Neurobiology of Learning and Memory, 101,* 120–126.

McArthur, L. Z., & Berry, D. S. (1987). Cross-cultural agreement in perceptions of babyfaced adults. *Journal of Cross-Cultural Psychology, 18,* 165–192.

McCauley, J. L., Killeen, T., Gros, D. F., Brady, K. T., & Back, S. E. (2012). Posttraumatic stress disorder and co-occurring substance use disorders: Advances in assessment and treatment. *Clinical Psychology: Science and Practice, 19,* 283–304.

McClelland, D. C. (1958). Risk-taking in children with high and low need for achievement. In J. W. Atkinson (Ed.), *Motives in fantasy, action, and society* (pp. 306–321). Princeton, NJ: Van Nostrand.

McClelland, D. C. (1987). Characteristics of successful entrepreneurs. *Journal of Creative Behavior, 3,* 219–233.

McClelland, D. C. (1993). Intelligence is not the best predictor of job performance. *Current Directions in Psychological Science, 2,* 5–6.

McClure, J., Meyer, L. H., Garisch, J., Fischer, R., Weir, K. F., & Walkey, F. H. (2011). Students' attributions for their best and worst marks: Do they relate to achievement? *Contemporary Educational Psychology, 36,* 71–81.

McColl, R., & Truong, Y. (2013). The effects of facial attractiveness and gender on customer evaluations during a web-video sales encounter. *Journal of Personal Selling and Sales Management, 33,* 117–128.

McCrae, R. R. (2004). Human nature and culture: A trait perspective. *Journal of Research in Personality, 38,* 3–14.

McCrae, R. R., & Costa, P. T., Jr. (2013). Introduction to the empirical and theoretical status of the five-factor model of personality traits. In T. A. Widiger & P. T. Costa, Jr. (Eds.), *Personality disorders and the five-factor model of personality* (3rd ed., pp. 15–27). Washington, DC: American Psychological Association.

McCulloch, M., Turner, K., & Broffman, M. (2012). Lung cancer detection by canine scent: Will there be a lab in the lab? *European Respiratory Journal, 39,* 511–512.

McDougall, D. (2013). Applying single-case design innovations to research in sport and exercise psychology. *Journal of Applied Sport Psychology, 25,* 33–45.

McFarlane, W. R. (2011). Integrating the family in the treatment of psychotic disorders. In R. Hagen, D. Turkington, T. Berge, & R. W. Gråwe (Eds.), *International Society for the Psychological Treatments of the Schizophrenias and Other Psychoses. CBT for psychosis: A symptom-based approach* (pp. 193–209). New York: Routledge/Taylor & Francis Group.

McGeehan, P. (2012). Driver fatigue and speed caused fatal bus crash, investigators say. *The New York Times,* June 5. Retrieved from http://www.nytimes.com/2012/06/06/nyregion/fatal-bronx-bus-crash-caused-by-driver-fatigue-board-says.html?gwh=3D1913CEAAD0A9F19130A6E6C337ED84

McGue, M., & Christensen, K. (2013). Growing old but not growing apart: Twin similarity in the latter half of the lifespan. *Behavior Genetics, 43,* 1–12.

McIntyre, C. K., McGaugh, J. L., & Williams, C. L. (2012). Interacting brain systems modulate memory consolidation. *Neuroscience and Biobehavioral Reviews, 36,* 1750–1762.

McKee, A. C., Stein, T. D., Nowinski, C. J., Stern, R. A., Daneshvar, D. H., Alvarez, V. E., . . . Cantu, R. C. (2013). The spectrum of disease in chronic traumatic encephalopathy. *Brain, 136,* 43–64.

McKellar, P. (1972). Imagery from the standpoint of introspection. In P. W. Sheehan (Ed.), *The function and nature of imagery.* New York: Academic Press.

McKinney, C., Donnelly, R., & Renk, K. (2008). Perceived parenting, positive and negative perceptions of parents, and late adolescent emotional adjustment. *Child and Adolescent Mental Health, 13,* 66–73.

McKoon, G., & Ratcliff, R. (2012). Aging and IQ effects on associative recognition and priming in item recognition. *Journal of Memory and Language, 66,* 416–437.

McLoyd, V. C. (2011). How money matters for children's socioemotional adjustment: Family processes and parental investment. In G. Carlo, L. J. Crockett, & M. A. Carranza (Eds.), *Nebraska symposium on motivation. Health disparities in youth and families: Research and applications* (pp. 33–72). New York: Springer.

McNally, R. J. (2012). Searching for repressed memory. *Nebraska Symposium on Motivation, 58,* 121–147.

McNamara, J. M., Barta, Z., Fromhage, L., & Houston, A. I. (2008). The coevolution of choosiness and cooperation. *Nature, 451,* 189–201.

Mead, E. (2012). *Family therapy education and supervision.* Hoboken, NJ: Wiley.

Mead, M. (1928). *Coming of age in Samoa: A psychological study of primitive youth for western civilisation.* New York: Morrow.

Mednick, S. C., Makovski, T., Cai, D. J., & Jiang, Y. V. (2009). Sleep and rest facilitate implicit memory in a visual search task. *Vision Research, 49,* 2557–2565.

Mehrabian, A. (1968). A relationship of attitude to seated posture orientation and distance. *Journal of Personality and Social Psychology, 10,* 26–30.

Mehrabian, A. (1971). *Silent messages.* Belmont, CA: Wadsworth.

Mehrabian, A. (2007). *Nonverbal communication.* New Brunswick, NJ: Aldine Transaction.

Mehta, P. H., Goetz, S. M., & Carré, J. M. (2013). Genetic, hormonal, and neural underpinnings of human aggressive behavior. In D. D. Franks & J. H. Turner (Eds.), *Handbooks of sociology and social research. Handbook of neurosociology* (pp. 47–65). Dordrecht, Netherlands: Springer Science + Business Media B.V.

Mehta, P. H., & Gosling, S. D. (2006). How can animal studies contribute to research on the biological bases of personality? In T. Canli (Ed.), *Biology of personality and individual differences* (pp. 427–448). New York: Guilford.

Mehta, R., Zhu, R. J., & Cheema, A. (2012). Is noise always bad? Exploring the effects of ambient noise on creative cognition. *Journal of Consumer Research, 39,* 784–799.

Meier, M. H., Caspi, A., Ambler, A., Harrington, H., Houts, R., Keefe, R. S. E., . . . Moffitt, T. E. (2012). Persistent cannabis users show neuropsychological decline from childhood to midlife. *Proceedings of the National Academy of Sciences, 109,* E2657–E2664.

Melas, P. A., Wei, Y., Wong, C. C., Sjöholm, L. K., Åberg, E., Mill, J., . . . Lavebratt, C. (2013). Genetic and epigenetic associations of MAOA and NR3C1 with depression and childhood adversities. *The International Journal of Neuropsychopharmacology/Official Scientific*

Journal of the Collegium Internationale Neuropsychopharmacologicum (CINP), 1, 1–16.

Melton, J. (2011). Organizational training in Japan: A case study of the spaces localization. *Technical Communication, 58*, 19–33.

Meltzoff, A. N., & Moore, M. K. (1985). Cognitive foundations and social functions of imitation and intermodal representation in infancy. In J. Mehler & R. Fox (Eds.), *Neonate cognition: Beyond the blooming buzzing confusion* (pp. 139–156). Hillsdale, NJ: Erlbaum.

Melzack, R. (1999). Pain and stress: A new perspective. In R. J. Gatchel & D. C. Turk (Eds.), *Psychosocial factors in pain: Critical perspectives* (pp. 89–106). New York: Guilford Press.

Mendelson, T., Turner, A. K., & Tandon, S. D. (2010). Violence exposure and depressive symptoms among adolescents and young adults disconnected from school and work. *Journal of Community Psychology, 38*, 607–621.

Menegaux, F. Truong, T., Anger, A., Cordina-Suverger, E., Lamkarkach, F., Arveux, P., . . . Guenel, P. (2013). Night work and breast cancer: A population-based case-control study in France (the CECILE study). *International Journal of Cancer, 132*, 924–931.

Mennella, J. A., Jagnow, C. P., & Beauchamp, G. K. (2001). Prenatal and postnatal flavor learning by human infants. *Pediatrics, 107*, E88.

Mercadillo, R. E., Díaz, J. L., Pasaye, E. H., & Barrios, F. A. (2011). Perception of suffering and compassion experience: Brain gender disparities. *Brain and Cognition, 76*, 5–14.

Messer, S. B., & Gurman, A. (2011). *Essential psychotherapies: Theory and practice* (3rd ed.). New York: Guilford Press.

Messer, S. B., Sanderson, W. C., & Gurman, A. S. (2013). Brief psychotherapies. In G. Stricker, T. A. Widiger, & I. B. Weiner (Eds.), *Handbook of psychology, Vol. 8. Clinical psychology* (2nd ed., pp. 431–453). Hoboken, NJ: Wiley.

Meyer, L. H. (2011). Making sense of differently able minds. *PsyCRITIQUES*. Retrieved from http://psycnet.apa.org/critiques/56/9/6.html.

Mieg, H. A. (2011). Focused cognition: Information integration and complex problem solving by top inventors. In K. L. Mosier & U. M. Fischer (Eds.), *Expertise: Research and applications. Informed by knowledge: Expert performance in complex situations* (pp. 41–54). New York: Psychology Press.

Milgram, S. (1963). Behavioral study of obedience. *Journal of Abnormal and Social Psychology*, 67, 371–378.

Milgram, S. (1974). *Obedience to authority: An experimental view*. New York: Harper & Row.

Miller, B. J., Culpepper, N., Rapaport, M. H., & Buckley, P. (2013). Prenatal inflammation and neurodevelopment in schizophrenia: A review of human studies. *Progress in Neuro-Psychopharmacology & Biological Psychiatry, 42*, 92–100.

Miller, F. M., & Allen, C. T. (2012). Corrigendum to "How does celebrity meaning transfer? Investigating the process of meaning transfer with celebrity affiliates and mature brands." *Journal of Consumer Psychology, 22*, 606.

Miller, J. G., & Bersoff, D. M. (1998). The role of liking in perceptions of the moral responsibility to help: A cultural perspective. *Journal of Experimental Social Psychology, 34*, 443–469.

Miller, K. B., Lund, E., & Weatherly, J. (2012). Applying operant learning to the stay-leave decision in domestic violence. *Behavior and Social Issues, 21*, 135–151.

Miller, P. K., Rowe, L., Cronin, C., & Bampouras, T. M. (2012). Heuristic reasoning and the observer's view: The influence of example-availability on ad-hoc frequency judgments in sport. *Journal of Applied Sport Psychology, 24*, 290–302.

Miller, S. D., Hubble, M. A., Chow, D. L., & Seidel, J. A. (2013). The outcome of psychotherapy: Yesterday, today, and tomorrow. *Psychotherapy, 50*, 88–97.

Miller, W. J. (2013). The polarized America: Coverage, characters, and issues in the new decade. *American Behavioral Scientist, 57*, 3–7.

Millings, A., Walsh, J., Hepper, E., & O'Brien, M. (2013). Good partner, good parent: Responsiveness mediates the link between romantic attachment and parenting style. *Personality and Social Psychology Bulletin, 39*, 170–180.

Millon, T. (2004). *Masters of the mind: Exploring the story of mental illness from ancient times to the new millennium*. Hoboken, NJ: Wiley.

Miltenberger, R. G. (2011). *Behavior modification: Principles and procedures.* (5th ed.). Beverly, MA: Wadsworth.

Mineka, S., & Oehlberg, K. (2008). The relevance of recent developments in classical conditioning to understanding the etiology and maintenance of anxiety disorders. *Acta Psychologica, 127*, 567–580.

Minnameier, G., & Schmidt, S. *(2013).* Situational moral adjustment and the happy victimizer. *European Journal of Developmental Psychology, 10*, 253–268.

Miranda-Contreras, L., Gómez-Pérez, R., Rojas, G., Cruz, I., Berrueta, L., Salmen, S., . . . Osuna, J. A. (2013). Occupational exposure to organophosphate and carbamate pesticides affects sperm chromatin integrity and reproductive hormone levels among Venezuelan farm workers. *Journal of Occupational Health, 55*, 195–203.

Mischel, W., Shoda, Y., & Ayduk, O. (2008). *Introduction to personality: Toward an integrative science of the person* (8th ed.). Hoboken, NJ: Wiley.

Mischel, W. (1968). *Personality and assessment*. Hoboken, NJ: Wiley.

Mischel, W. (1984). Convergences and challenges in the search for consistency. *American Psychologist, 39*, 351–364.

Mischel, W. (2004). Toward an integrative science of the person. *Annual Review of Psychology, 55*, 1–22.

Mischel, W., & Shoda, Y. (2008). Toward a unified theory of personality: Integrating dispositions and processing dynamics within the cognitive-affective processing system. In O. P. John, R. W. Robins & L. A. Pervin (Eds.), *Handbook of personality: Theory and research* (3rd ed., pp. 208–241). New York: Guilford Press.

Mita, T. H., Dermer, M., & Knight, J. (1977). Reversed facial images and the mere-exposure hypothesis. *Journal of Personality and Social Psychology, 35*, 597–601.

Mitchell, J. M., O'Neil, J. P., Janabi, M., Marks, S. M., Jagust, W. J., & Fields, H. L. (2012). Alcohol consumption induces endogenous opioid release in the human orbitofrontal cortex and nucleus accumbens. *Science Translational Medicine, 4*: 116ra6.

Mitchell, P., & Ziegler, F. (2013). *Fundamentals of developmental psychology* (2nd ed.). New York: Psychology Press.

Miyamoto, Y, & Ryff, C. D. (2011). Cultural differences in the dialectical and non-dialectical emotional styles and their implications for health. *Cognition & Emotion, 25*, 22–39.

Moayedi, M., & Davis, K. D. (2013). Theories of pain: From specificity to gate control. *Journal of Neurophysiology, 109*, 5–12.

Moghaddam, F. M. (2013). Conformity, obedience, and behavior regulation. In F. M. Moghaddam (Ed.), *The psychology of dictatorship* (pp. 123–139). Washington, DC: American Psychological Association.

Moghaddam, F. M. (2013). From torture to cognitive dissonance: Varieties of coercion in dictatorship. In F. M. Moghaddam (Ed.), *The psychology of dictatorship* (pp. 141–158). Washington, DC: American Psychological Association.

Mohamad, O., Song, M., Wei, L., & Yu, S. P. (2013). Regulatory roles of the NMDA receptor Glun3A subunit in locomotion, pain perception and cognitive functions in adult mice. *The Journal of Physiology, 591*, 149–168.

Mohr, D. C., Ho, J., Duffecy, J., Reifler, D., Sokol, L., Burns, M. N., . . . Siddique, J. (2012). Effect of telephone-administered vs face-to-face cognitive behavioral therapy on adherence to therapy and depression outcomes among primary care patients: A randomized trial. *Journal of the American Medical Association, 307*, 2278–2285.

Moilanen, J., Aalto, A.-M., Hemminki, E., Aro, A. R., Raitanen, J., & Luoto, R. (2010). Prevalence of menopause symptoms and their association with lifestyle among Finnish middle-aged women. *Maturitas, 67*, 368–374.

Moitra, E., Beard, C., Weisberg, R. B., & Keller, M. B. (2011). Occupational impairment and social anxiety disorder in a sample of primary care patients. *Journal of Affective Disorders, 130*, 209–212.

Mokrova, I. L., O'Brien, M., Calkins, S. D., Leerkes, E. M., & Marcovitch, S. (2013). The role of persistence at preschool age in academic skills at kindergarten. *European Journal of Psychology of Education.* Advance online publication. doi:10.1007/s10212-013-0177-2

Molenaar, D., Sluis, S., Boomsma, D. I., Haworth, C. M. A., Hewitt, J. K., Martin, N. G., . . . Dolan, C. V. (2013). Genotype by environment interactions in cognitive ability: A survey of 14 studies from four countries covering four age groups. *Behavior Genetics, 43*, 208–219.

Moline, R. A. (2013). *The diagnosis and treatment of dissociative identity disorder: A case study and contemporary perspective.* Lanham, MD: Jason Aronson.

Moll, J., Bado, P., de Oliveira-Souza, R., Bramati, I. E., Lima, D. O., Paiva, F. F., . . . Zahn, R. (2012). A neural signature of affiliative emotion in the human septohypothalamic area. *The Journal of Neuroscience, 32*, 12499–12505.

Mommersteeg, P. M. C., & Pouwer, F. (2012). Personality as a risk factor for the metabolic syndrome: A systematic review. *Journal of Psychosomatic Research, 73*, 326–333.

Monin, B. (2003). The warm glow heuristic: When liking leads to familiarity. *Journal of Personality and Social Psychology, 85*, 1035–1048.

Montangero, J. (2012). Dreams are narrative simulations of autobiographical episodes, not stories or scripts: A review. *Dreaming, 22*, 157–172.

Montgomery, G. H., Schnur, J. B., & Kravits, K. (2013). Hypnosis for cancer care: Over 200 years young. *CA: A Cancer Journal for Clinicians, 63*, 31–44.

Montoro-García, S., Shantsila, E., & Lip, G. Y. H. (2011). Platelet reactivity in prolonged stress disorders—A link with cardiovascular disease? *Psychoneuroendocrinology, 36*, 159–160.

Moodley, R., & Sutherland, P. (2010). Psychic retreats in other places: Clients who seek healing with traditional healers and psychotherapists. *Counselling Psychology Quarterly, 23*, 267–282.

Moon, C., Lagercrantz, H., & Kuhl, P. K. (2013). Language experienced in utero affects vowel perception after birth: A two-country study. *Acta Paediatrica, 102*, 156–160.

Moore, D. L. (2013). USA's Manteo Mitchell runs 4x400 relay on broken leg. USA Today Sports. Retrieved from http://usatoday30.usatoday.com/sports/olympics/london/track/story/2012–08–09/usa-man teo-mitchell-runs-4x400-relay-on-broken-leg/56915070/1

Moore, F., Filippou, D., & Perrett, D. (2011). Intelligence and attractiveness in the face: Beyond the attractiveness halo effect. *Journal of Evolutionary Psychology, 9*, 205–217.

Moore, T. S., Lapan, S. D., & Quartaroli, M. T. (2012). Case study research. In S. D. Lapan, M. T. Quartaroli, & F. J. Riemer (Eds.), *Qualitative research: An introduction to methods and designs* (pp. 243–270). San Francisco, CA: Jossey-Bass.

Moran, T., & Dailey, M. (2011). Intestinal feedback signaling and satiety. *Physiology and Behavior, 105*, 77–81.

Moreno, J. P., & Johnston, C. A. (2013). The role of confirmation bias in the treatment of diverse patients. *American Journal of Lifestyle Medicine, 7*, 20–22.

Morey, L. C. (2013). Measuring personality and psychopathology. In J. A. Schinka, W. F. Velicer, & I. B. Weiner (Eds.), *Handbook of psychology, Vol. 2. Research methods in psychology* (2nd ed., pp. 395–427). Hoboken, NJ: Wiley.

Morgan, C. A., Southwick, S., Steffian, G., Hazlett, G. A., & Loftus, E. F. (2013). Misinformation can influence memory for recently experienced, highly stressful events. *International Journal of Law and Psychiatry, 36*, 11–17.

Morgan, C. D., & Murphy, C. (2010). Differential effects of active attention and age on event-related potentials to visual and olfactory stimuli. *International Journal of Psychophysiology, 78*, 190–199.

Morgan, T. B., Crane, D. R., Moore, A. M., & Eggett, D. L. (2013). The cost of treating substance use disorders: Individual versus family therapy. *Journal of Family Therapy, 35*, 2–23.

Mori, K., & Arai, M. (2010). No need to fake it: Reproduction of the Asch experiment without confederates. *International Journal of Psychology, 45*, 390–397.

Morin, C. M., Savard, J., & Ouellet, M.-C. (2013). Nature and treatment of insomnia. In A. M. Nezu, C. M. Nezu, P. A. Geller, & I. B. Weiner (Eds.), *Handbook of psychology, Vol. 9. Health psychology (2nd ed.*, pp. 318–339). Hoboken, NJ: Wiley.

Morton, P. M., Schafer, M. H., & Ferraro, K. F. (2012). Does childhood misfortune increase cancer risk in adulthood? *Journal of Aging and Health, 24*, 948–984.

Moshman, D. (2011). *Adolescent rationality and development: Cognition, morality, and identity* (3rd ed.). New York: Psychology Press.

Moskowitz, J. T., Epel, E. S., & Acree, M. (2008). Positive affect uniquely predicts lower risk of mortality in people with diabetes. *Health Psychology, 27*, S73–S82.

Moss-Racusin, C. A., Dovidio, J. F., Brescoll, V. L., Graham, M. J., & Handelsman, J. (2012). Science faculty's subtle gender biases favor male students. *Proceedings of the National Academy of Sciences, 109*, 16474–16479.

Mota, N. P., Medved, M., Wang, J., Asmundson, G. J. G., Whitney, D., & Sareen, J. (2012). Stress and mental disorders in female military personnel: Comparisons between the sexes in a male dominated profession. *Journal of Psychiatric Research, 46*, 159–167.

Motyl, M., Hart, J., Pyszczynski, T., Weise, D., Maxfield, M., & Siedel, A. (2011). Subtle priming of shared human experiences eliminates threat-induced negativity toward arabs, immigrants, and peace-making. *Journal of Experimental Social Psychology, 47*, 1179–1184.

Moulin, C. (Ed.). (2011). *Human memory* (Vols. 1–4). Thousand Oaks, CA: Sage.

Moutinho, A., Pereira, A., & Jorge, G. (2011). Biology of homosexuality. *European Psychiatry, 26*, 1741–1753.

Muehlenkamp, J. J., Ertelt, T. W., Miller, A. L., & Claes, L. (2011). Borderline personality symptoms differentiate non-suicidal and suicidal self-injury in ethnically diverse adolescent outpatients. *Journal of Child Psychology and Psychiatry, 52*, 148–155.

Muenssinger, J., Matuz, T., Schleger, F., Kiefer-Schmidt, I., Goelz, R., Wacher-Gussmann, A., . . . Preissl, H. (2013). Auditory habituation in the fetus and neonate: An fMEG study. *Developmental Science, 16*, 287–295.

Müller, B., Kühn, S., van Baaren, R., Dotsch, R., Brass, M., & Dijksterhuis, A. (2011). Perspective taking eliminates differences in co-representation of out-group members' actions. *Experimental Brain Research, 211*, 423–428.

Mundia, L. (2011). Social desirability, nonresponse bias and reliability in a long self-report measure: Illustrations from the MMPI-2 administered to Brunei student teachers. *Educational Psychology, 31*, 207–224.

Murayama, K., Perkrun, R., Lichtenfeld, S., & vom Hofe, R. (2012). Predicting long-term growth in students' mathematics achievement: The unique contributions of motivation and cognitive strategies. *Child Development, 84*, 1475–1490.

Murray, A. D., Staff, R. T., McNeil, C. J., Salarirad, S., Starr, J. M., Deary, I. J., & Whalley, L. J. (2011). Brain lesions, hypertension and cognitive ageing in the 1921 and 1936 Aberdeen birth cohorts. *Age, 34*, 451–459.

Murty, V. P., Ritchey, M., Adcock, R. A., & LaBar, K. S. (2011). Reprint of: fMRI studies of successful emotional memory encoding: A quantitative meta-analysis. *Neuropsychologia, 49*, 695–705.

Mussweiler, T., Rüter, K., & Epstude, K. (2004). The ups and downs of social comparison: Mechanisms of assimilation and contrast. *Journal of Personality & Social Psychology, 87*, 832–844.

Myers, K., & Turvey, C. L. (Eds.). (2013). *Elsevier insights. Telemental health: Clinical, technical, and administrative foundations for evidence-based practice.* Amsterdam: Elsevier.

Nabi, R. L., & Moyer-Gusé, E. (2013). The psychology underlying media-based persuasion. In K. E. Dill (Ed.), The *Oxford handbook of media psychology, Oxford library of psychology* (pp. 285–301). New York: Oxford University Press.

Nadal, K. L. (2013). Sexual orientation, microaggressions: Experiences of lesbian, gay, and bisexual people. In K. L. Nadal (Ed.), *That's so gay! Microaggressions and the lesbian, gay, bisexual, and transgender community. Contemporary perspectives on lesbian, gay, and bisexual psychology* (pp. 51–79). Washington, DC: American Psychological Association.

Nadel, L. (2013). Cognitive maps. In D. Waller & L. Nadel (Eds.), *Handbook of spatial cognition* (pp. 155–171). Washington, DC: American Psychological Association.

Nagy, T. F. (2012). Competence. In S. J. Knapp, M. C. Gottlieb, M. M. Handelsman & L. D. VandeCreek (Eds.), *APA handbook of ethics in psychology, Vol 1: Moral foundations and common themes* (pp. 147–174). Washington, DC: American Psychological Association.

Nairne, J. S., & Neath, I. (2013). Sensory and working memory. In A. F. Healy, R. W. Proctor, & I. B. Weiner (Eds.), *Handbook of psychology, Vol. 4. Experimental psychology* (2nd ed., pp. 419–445). Hoboken, NJ: Wiley.

Nakamura, K. (2006). The history of psychotherapy in Japan. *International Medical Journal, 13*, 13–18.

Narasimamurthy, R., Hatori, M., Nayak, S. K., Liu, F., Panda, S., & Verma, I. M. (2012). Circadian clock protein cryptochrome regulates the expression of proinflammatory cytokines. *Proceedings of the National Academy of Sciences, 109,* 12662–12667.

Nasehi, M., Piri, M., Jamali-Raeufy, N., & Zarrindast, M. R. (2010). Influence of intracerebral administration of NO agents in dorsal hippocampus (CA1) on cannabinoid state-dependent memory in the step-down passive avoidance test. *Physiology and Behavior, 100*, 297–304.

National Organization on Fetal Alcohol Syndrome (2012). *FASD: What everyone should know.* Retrieved from http://www.nofas.org/wp-content/uploads/2012/10/NOFAS-FASD-What-Everyone-Should-Know-2012.pdf

National Sleep Foundation. (2012). Sleepy pilots, train operators, and drivers. Retrieved from www.sleepfoundation.org/article/press-release/sleepy-pilots-train-operators-and-drivers

Neal, D., & Chartrand, T. (2011). Embodied emotion perception: Amplifying and dampening facial feedback modulates emotion perception accuracy. *Social Psychological and Personality Science, 2*, 673–678.

Neale, J. M., Oltmanns, T. F., & Winters, K. C. (1983). Recent developments in the assessment and conceptualization of schizophrenia. *Behavioral Assessment, 5*, 33–54.

Negri, R., Di Feola, M., Di Domenico, S., Scala, M. G., Artesi, G., Valente, S., . . . Greco, L. (2012). Taste perception and food choices. *Journal of Pediatric Gastroenterology & Nutrition, 54*, 624–629.

Neher, A. (1991). Maslow's theory of motivation: A critique. *Journal of Humanistic Psychology, 31*, 89–112.

Neisser, U. (1967). *Cognitive psychology.* New York: Appleton-Century-Crofts.

Nelson, E.-L., Davis, K., & Velasquez, S. E. (2013). Ethical considerations in providing mental health services over videoteleconferencing. In K. Myers & C. L. Turvey (Eds.), *Elsevier insights. Telemental health: Clinical, technical, and administrative foundations for evidence-based practice* (pp. 47–62). Amsterdam: Elsevier.

Nelson, N. L., & Russell, J. A. (2013). Universality revisited. *Emotion Review, 5*, 8–15.

Nelson, T. D. (2013). The neurobiology of stereotyping and prejudice. In D. D. Franks & J. H. Turner (Eds.), *Handbooks of sociology and social research* (pp. 349–358). New York: Springer Science + Business Media.

Nemoda, Z., Szekely, A., & Sasvari-Szekely, M. (2011). Psychopathological aspects of dopaminergic gene polymorphisms in adolescence and young adulthood. *Neuroscience and Biobehavioral Reviews, 35*, 1665–1686.

Neri, A. L., Yassuda, M. S., Fortes-Burgos, A. C., Mantovani, E. P., Arbex, F. S., de Souza Torres, S. V., . . . Guariento, M. E. (2012). Relationships between gender, age, family conditions, physical and mental health, and social isolation of elderly caregivers. *International Psychogeriatrics, 24*, 472–483.

Neria, Y., Bromet, E. J., Sievers, S., Lavelle, J., & Fochtmann, L. J. (2002). Trauma exposure and posttraumatic stress disorder in psychosis: Findings from a first-admission cohort. *Journal of Consulting and Clinical Psychology, 70*, 246–251.

Nestor, P. G., & Schutt, R. K. (2012). *Research methods in psychology: Investigating human behavior.* Thousand Oaks, CA: Sage.

Nettle, D. (2011). Normality, disorder, and evolved function: The case of depression. In P. Adriaens & A. de Block (Eds.), *Maladapting minds: Philosophy, psychiatry, and evolutionary theory* (pp. 198–215). New York: Oxford University Press.

Neubauer, A. C., Grabner, R. H., Freudenthaler, H. H., Beckmann, J. F., & Guthke, J. (2004). Intelligence and individual differences in becoming neurally efficient. *Acta Psychologica, 116*, 55–74.

Newby, J. M., & Moulds, M. L. (2011). Intrusive memories of negative events in depression: Is the centrality of the event important? *Journal of Behavior Therapy and Experimental Psychiatry, 42*, 277–283.

Newman, M. L., & Roberts, N. A. (Eds.). (2013). *Health and social relationships: The good, the bad, and the complicated.* Washington, DC: American Psychological Association.

Nguyen, T., & Szymanski, B. (2012). Using location-based social networks to validate human mobility and relationships models. *Proceedings of the 2012 IEEE/ACM International Conference on Advances in Social Networks Analysis and Mining*, pp. 1247–1253.

Nickerson, R. (1998). Confirmation bias: A ubiquitous phenomenon in many guises. *Review of General Psychology, 2*, 175–220.

Nicolaidis, S. (2011). Metabolic and humoral mechanisms of feeding and genesis of the ATP/ADP/AMP concept. *Physiology and Behavior, 104*, 8–14.

Nielsen, T. A., Zadra, A. L., Simard, V., Saucier, S., Saucier, S., Stenstrom, P., . . . Kuiken, D. (2003). The typical dreams of Canadian university students. *Dreaming, 13*, 211–235.

Nieto, F. J., Peppard, P. E., Young, T., Finn, L., Hla, K. M., & Farre, R. (2012). Sleep disordered breathing and cancer mortality: Results from the Wisconsin Sleep Cohort Study. *American Journal of Respiratory and Critical Care Medicine, 186*, 190–194.

Nikolaou, A., Schiza, S. E., Chatzi, L., Koudas, V., Fokos, S., Solidaki, E., & Bitsios, P. (2011). Evidence of dysregulated affect indicated by high alexithymia in obstructive sleep apnea. *Journal of Sleep Research*, 20, 92–100.

Nishitani, S., Miyamura, T., Tagawa, M., Sumi, M., Takase, R., Doi, H., . . . Shinohara, K. (2009). The calming effect of a maternal breast milk odor on the human newborn infant. *Neuroscience Research, 63*, 66–71.

Noggle, C. A., & Dean, R. S. (Eds.). (2013). *Contemporary neuropsychology: The neuropsychology of psychopathology*. New York: Springer.

Noggle, C. A., Rylander, M., & Soltys, S. (2013). Personality disorders. In C. A. Noggle & R. S. Dean (Eds.), *Contemporary neuropsychology. The neuropsychology of psychopathology* (pp. 343–388). New York: Springer.

Nolan-Poupart, S., Veldhuizen, M. G., Geha, P., & Small, D. M. (2013). Midbrain response to milkshake correlates with ad libitum milkshake intake in the absence of hunger. *Appetite, 60*, 168–174.

Norcross, J. C., & Wampold, B. E. (2011). Evidence-based therapy relationships: Research conclusions and clinical practices. *Psychotherapy, 48*, 98–102.

Northcote, J., & Livingston, M. (2011). Accuracy of self-reported drinking: Observational verification of "last occasion" drink estimates of young adults. *Alcohol and Alcoholism, 46*, 709–713.

Northup, T., & Mulligan, N. (2013). Conceptual implicit memory in advertising research. *Applied Cognitive Psychology, 27*, 127–136.

Nusbaum, F., Redouté, J., Le Bars, D., Volckmann, P., Simon, F., Hannoun, S., . . . Sappey-Marinier, D. (2011). Chronic low-back pain modulation is enhanced by hypnotic analgesic suggestion by recruiting an emotional network: A PET imaging study. *International Journal of Clinical and Experimental Hypnosis, 59*, 27–44.

O'Boyle, E.H., Forsyth, D.R., Banks, G.C., & McDaniel, M.A. (2012). A meta-analysis of the Dark Triad and work behavior: A social exchange perspective. *Journal of Applied Psychology, 97*, 557–579.

O'Brien, C. W., & Moorey, S. (2010). Outlook and adaptation in advanced cancer: A systematic review. *Psycho-Oncology, 19*, 1239–1249.

O'Connell, K. L. (2008). What can we learn? Adult outcomes in children of seriously mentally ill mothers. *Journal of Child and Adolescent Psychiatric Nursing, 21*, 89–104.

O'Farrell, T. J. (2011). Family therapy. In M. Galanter & H. D. Kleber (Eds.), *Psychotherapy for the treatment of substance abuse* (pp. 329–350). Arlington, VA: American Psychiatric Publishing.

O'Neil, D. P. (2007). Predicting leader effectiveness: Personality traits and character strengths. *Dissertation Abstracts International: Section B: The Sciences and Engineering, 68*, 4178.

O'Neill, J. W., & Davis, K. (2011). Work stress and well-being in the hotel industry. *International Journal of Hospitality Management, 30*, 385–390.

Oberauer, K., Souza, A. S., Druey, M. D., & Gade, M. (2013). Analogous mechanisms of selection and updating in declarative and procedural working memory: Experiments and a computational model. *Cognitive Psychology, 66*, 157–211.

Obschonka, M., Schmitt-Rodermund, E., Silbereisen, R. K., Gosling, S. D., & Potter, J. (2013). The regional distribution and correlates of an entrepreneurship-prone personality profile in the United States, Germany, and the United Kingdom: A socioecological perspective. *Journal of Personality and Social Psychology, 105*, 104–122.

Ogedegbe, G. O., Boutin-Foster, C., Wells, M. T., Allegrante, J. P., Isen, A. M., Jobe, J. B., & Charlson, M. E. (2012). A randomized controlled trial of positive-affect intervention and medication adherence in hypertensive African Americans. *Archives of Internal Medicine, 172*, 322–326.

Ogilvie, R. D., Wilkinson, R. T., & Allison, S. (1989). The detection of sleep onset: Behavioral, physiological, and subjective convergence. *Sleep, 12*, 458–474.

Ohayon, M. M., Mahowald, M. W., Dauvilliers, Y., Krystal, A. D., & Leger, D. (2012). Prevalence and comorbidity of nocturnal wandering in the US adult general population. *Neurology, 78*, 1583–1589.

Olds, J., & Milner, P. M. (1954). Positive reinforcement produced by electrical stimulation of septal area and other regions of rat brains. *Journal of Comparative and Physiological Psychology, 47*, 419–427.

Ollendick, T. H., Thomas, M., Sherman, P. M., & King, N. (2012). Beyond Watson and Rayner's Little Albert. In A. M. Slater & P. C. Quinn (Eds.), *Developmental psychology: Revisiting the classic studies* (pp. 38–97). Thousand Oaks, CA: Sage.

Oller, J. W., Jr., Oller, S. D., & Oller, S. N. (2014). *Milestones: Normal speech and language development across the life span* (2nd ed.). San Diego, CA: Plural Publishing.

Olsen, L. R., Jensen, D. V., Noerholm, V., Martiny, K., & Bech, P. (2003). The internal and external validity of the Major Depression Inventory in measuring severity of depressive states. *Psychological Medicine, 33*, 351–356.

Olson, I. R., Berryhill, M. E., Drowos, D. B., Brown, L., & Chatterjee, A. (2010). A calendar savant with episodic memory impairments. *Neurocase, 16*, 208–218.

Olsson, C. A., McGee, R., Nada-Raja, S., & Williams, S. M. (2012). A 32-year longitudinal study of child and adolescent pathways to well-being in adulthood. *Journal of Happiness Studies, 14*, 1069–1083.

Oram, S., Trevillion, K., Feder, G., & Howard, L. M. (2013). Prevalence of experiences of domestic violence among psychiatric patients: Systematic review. *The British Journal of Psychiatry, 202*, 94–99.

Orne, M. T. (2006). The nature of hypnosis. artifact and essence: An experimental study. *Dissertation Abstracts International: Section B: The Sciences and Engineering, 67*, 1207.

Orta, I. M. (2013). The impact of cross-group romantic relationships on intergroup prejudice. *Social Behavior and Personality, 41*, 1–6.

Ortony, A., & Turner, T. J. (1990). What's basic about basic emotions? *Psychological Review, 97*, 315–331.

Orzel-Gryglewska, J. (2010). Consequences of sleep deprivation. *International Journal of Occupational Medicine and Environmental Health, 23*, 95–114.

Ost, J., Wright, D. B., Easton, S., Hope, L., & French, C. C. (2013). Recovered memories, satanic abuse, dissociative identity disorder and false memories in the UK: A survey of clinical psychologists and hypnotherapists. *Psychology, Crime & Law, 19*, 1–19.

Ostir, G. V., Markides, K., S., Peek, M. K., & Goodwin, J. S. (2001).The association between emotional well-being and the incidence of stroke in older adults. *Psychosomatic Medicine, 63,* 210–215.

Ottenheimer, H. J. (2013). *The anthropology of language* (3rd ed.). Belmont, CA: Wadsworth Cengage Learning.

Oudiette, D., Dealberto, M.-J., Uguccioni, G., Golmard, J.-L., Merino-Andreu, M., Tafti, M., . . . Arnulf, I. (2012). Dreaming without REM sleep. *Consciousness and Cognition: An International Journal, 21,* 1129–1140.

Overstreet, M. F., & Healy, A. F. (2011). Item and order information in semantic memory: Students' retention of the "CU fight song" lyrics. *Memory and Cognition, 39,* 251–259.

Owens, J. A., Belon, K., & Moss, P. (2010). Impact of delaying school start time on adolescent sleep, mood, and behavior. *Archives of Pediatric & Adolescent Medicine, 164,* 608–614.

Owens, J., & Massey, D. S. (2011). Stereotype threat and college academic performance: A latent variables approach. *Social Science Research, 40,* 150–166.

Owens, S., Rijsdijk, F., Picchioni, M., Stahl, D., Nenadic, I., Murray, R., & Toulopoulou, T. (2011). Genetic overlap between schizophrenia and selective components of executive function. *Schizophrenia Research, 127,* 181–187.

Oz, M. (2011). Bath salts: "Evil" lurking at your corner store. *Time.* Retrieved from http://www.time.com/time/magazine/article/0,9171,2065249,00.html

Ozawa-de Silva, C. (2007). Demystifying Japanese therapy: An analysis of Naikan and the Ajase complex through Buddhist thought. *Ethos, 35,* 411–446.

Ozturk, O., Shayan, S., Liszkowski, U., & Majid, A. (2013). Language is not necessary for color categories. *Developmental Science, 16,* 111–115.

Pace, T. W. W., & Heim, C. M. (2011). A short review on the psychoneuroimmunology of posttraumatic stress disorder: From risk factors to medical comorbidities. *Brain, Behavior, and Immunity, 25,* 6–13.

Pachur, T., Hertwig, R., & Rieskamp, J. (2013). The mind as an intuitive pollster: Frugal search in social spaces. In R. Hertwig & U. Hoffrage (Eds.), *ABC research group, evolution and cognition series. Simple heuristics in a social world* (pp. 261–291). New York: Oxford University Press.

Paciello, M., Fida, R., Tramontano, C., Cole, E., & Cerniglia, L. (2013). Moral dilemma in adolescence: The role of values, prosocial moral reasoning and moral disengagement in helping decision making. *European Journal of Developmental Psychology, 10,* 190–205.

Pagano, M. E., White, W. L., Kelly, J. F., Stout, R. L., & Tonigan, J. S. (2013). The 10-year course of AA participation and long-term outcomes: A follow-up study of outpatient subjects in Project MATCH. *Substance Abuse, Special Issue, 31,* 51–59.

Palmer, S., & Williams, H. (2013). Cognitive behavioral approaches. In J. Passmore, D. B. Peterson, & T. Freire (Eds.), *Wiley-Blackwell handbooks in organizational psychology. The Wiley-Blackwell handbook of the psychology of coaching and mentoring* (pp. 319–338). Hoboken, NJ: Wiley-Blackwell.

Panagopoulos, C. (2013). Extrinsic rewards, intrinsic motivation and voting. *The Journal of Politics, 75,* 266–280.

Panlilio, L. V., Zanettini, C., Barnes, C., Solinas, M., & Goldberg, S. R. (2013). Prior exposure to THC increases the addictive effects of nicotine in rats. *Neuropsychopharmacology, 38,* 1198–1208.

Papathanassoglou, E. D., Giannakopoulou, M., Mpouzika, M., Bozas, E., & Karabinis, A. (2010). Potential effects of stress in critical illness through the role of stress neuropeptides. *Nursing in Critical Care, 15,* 204–216.

Pardini, M., Krueger, F., Hodgkinson, C., Raymont, V., Ferrier, C., Goldman, D., . . . Grafman, J. (2011). Prefrontal cortex lesions and MAO-A modulate aggression in penetrating traumatic brain injury. *Neurology, 76,* 1038–1045.

Park, L., Troisi, J., & Maner, J. (2011). Egoistic versus altruistic concerns in communal relationships. *Journal of Social and Personal Relationships, 28,* 315–335.

Parker, R. & McCaffree, K. (Eds.). (2013). *Alcohol and violence: The nature of the relationship and the promise of prevention.* Lanham, MD: Lexington Books.

Partanen, E., Kujala, T., Näätänen, R., Liitola, A., Sambeth, A., & Huotilainen, M. (2013). Learning-induced neural plasticity of speech processing before birth. *Proceedings of the National Academy of Sciences, 110,* 15145–15150.

Paterson, H. M., Kemp, R. I., & Ng, J. R. (2011). Combating co-witness contamination: Attempting to decrease the negative effects of discussion on eyewitness memory. *Applied Cognitive Psychology, 25,* 43–52.

Pathman, T., & Bauer, P. J. (2013). Beyond initial encoding: Measures of the post-encoding status of memory traces predict long-term recall during infancy. *Journal of Experimental Child Psychology, 114,* 321–338.

Patra, B. N., & Balhara, Y. P. (2012). Creativity and mental disorder. *British Journal of Psychiatry, 200,* 346.

Patterson, F., & Linden, E. (1981). *The education of Koko.* New York: Holt, Rinehart and Winston.

Paul, M. A., Gray, G. W., Lieberman, H. R., Love, R. J., Miller, J. C., Trouborst, M., & Arendt, J. (2011). Phase advance with separate and combined melatonin and light treatment. *Psychopharmacology, 214,* 515–523.

Pause, B. M. (2012). Processing of body odor signals by the human brain. *Chemosensory Perception, 5,* 55–63.

Payne, J. D., Chambers, A. M., & Kensinger, E. A. (2012). Sleep promotes lasting changes in selective memory for emotional scenes. *Frontiers in Integrative Neuroscience, 6,* Article 108. doi: 10.3389/fnint.2012.00108

Payne, J. D., Tucker, M. A., Ellenbogen, J. M., Wamsley, E. J., Walker, M. P., Schacter, D. L., & Stickgold, R. (2012). Memory for semantically related and unrelated declarative information: The benefit of sleep, the cost of wake. *PLoS ONE, 7,* e33079

Paz, R., & Pare, D. (2013). Physiological basis for emotional modulation of memory circuits by the amygdala. *Current Opinion in Neurobiology,* 23, 381–386.

Pearson, J. L., Abrams, D. B., Niaura, R. S., Richardson, A., & Vallone, D. M. (2013). Public support for mandated nicotine reduction in cigarettes. *American Journal of Public Health, 103,* 562–567.

Pechtel, P., & Pizzagalli, D. A. (2011). Effects of early life stress on cognitive and affective function: An integrated review of human literature. *Psychopharmacology, 214,* 55–70.

Pedrazzoli, M., Pontes, J. C., Peirano, P., & Tufik, S. (2007). HLA-DQB1 genotyping in a family with narcolepsy-cataplexy. *Brain Research, 1165,* 1–4.

Peer, E., & Rosenbloom, T. (2013). When two motivations race: The effects of time-saving bias and sensation-seeking on driving speed choices. *Accident Analysis & Prevention, 50,* 1135–1139.

Peleg, G., Katzir, G., Peleg, O., Kamara, M., Brodsky, L., Hel-Or, H., . . . Nevo, E. (2006). Hereditary family signature of facial expression. *Proceedings of the National Academy of Sciences, 103,* 15921–15926.

Peng, A. C., Riolli, L. T., Schaubroeck, J., & Spain, E. S. P. (2012). A moderated mediation test of personality, coping, and health among deployed soldiers. *Journal of Organizational Behavior, 33,* 512–530.

Pepe, A., Zhao, L., Koikkalainen, J., Hietala, J., Ruotsalainen, U., & Tohka, J.

(2013). Automatic statistical shape analysis of cerebral asymmetry in 3D T1-weighted magnetic resonance images at vertex-level: Application to neuroleptic-naïve schizophrenia. *Magnetic Resonance Imaging, 31*, 676–687.

Pergola, G., Bellebaum, C., Gehlhaar, B., Koch, B., Schwarz, M., Daum, I., & Suchan, B. (2013). The involvement of the thalamus in semantic retrieval: A clinical group study. *Journal of Cognitive Neuroscience, 7*, 1–15.

Pergola, G., Güntürkün, O., Koch, B., Schwarz, M., Daum, I., & Suchan, B. (2012). Recall deficits in stroke patients with thalamic lesions covary with damage to the parvocellular mediodorsal nucleus of the thalamus. *Neuropsychologia, 50*, 2477–2491.

Perkmen, S., & Sahin, S. (2013). Who should study instructional technology? Vocational personality approach. *British Journal of Educational Technology, 44*, 54–65.

Perry, B. D. (2002). Childhood experience and the expression of genetic potential: What childhood neglect tells us about nature and nurture. *Brain and Mind, 3*, 79–100.

Perugi, G., Medda, P., Zanello, S., Toni, C., & Cassano, G. B. (2012). Episode length and mixed features as predictors of ect nonresponse in patients with medication-resistant major depression. *Brain Stimulation, 5*, 18–24.

Petrosini, L., Cutuli, D., & De Bartolo, P. (2013). Environmental influences on development of the nervous system. In R. J. Nelson, S. J. Y. Mizumori, & I. B. Weiner (Eds.), *Handbook of psychology, Vol. 3. Behavioral neuroscience (2nd ed.*, pp. 461–479). Hoboken, NJ: Wiley.

Petry, Y. (2011). 'Many things surpass our knowledge': An early modern surgeon on magic, witchcraft and demonic possession. *Social History of Medicine*, 25, 47–64.

Pezdek, K. (2012). Fallible eyewitness memory and identification. In B. Cutler (Ed.), *Conviction of the innocent: Lessons from psychological research* (pp. 105–124). Washington, DC: American Psychological Association.

Pfeiffer, P. N., Valenstein, M., Hoggatt, K. J., Ganoczy, D., Maixner, D., Miller, E. M., & Zivin, K. (2011). Electroconvulsive therapy for major depression within the Veterans Health Administration. *Journal of Affective Disorders, 130*, 21–25.

Pharoah, F., Mari, J. J., Rathbone, J., & Wong, W. (2011). Family intervention for schizophrenia. *Cochrane Database of Systematic Reviews 2010,* Issue 12.

Phillips, S. T., & Ziller, R. C. (1997). Toward a theory and measure of the nature of non-prejudice. *Journal of Personality and Social Psychology, 72*, 420–434.

Pietschnig, J., Voracek, M., & Formann, A. K. (2011). Female Flynn effects: No sex differences in generational IQ gains. *Personality and Individual Differences, 50*, 759–762.

Pilati, N., Ison, M. J., Barker, M., Mulheran, M., Large, C. H., Forsythe, I. D., . . . Hamann, M. (2012). Mechanisms contributing to central excitability changes during hearing loss. *Proceedings of the National Academy of Sciences, 109*, 8292–8297.

Pilcher, J. J., Burnett, M. L., & McCubbin, J. A. (2013). Measurement of sleep and sleepiness. In R. R. Sinclair, M. Wang, & L. E. Tetrick (Eds.), *Research methods in occupational health psychology: Measurement, design, and data analysis* (pp. 49–60). New York: Routledge/Taylor & Francis Group.

Pilecki, M. W., Józefik, B. & Sałapa, K. (2012). Kontekst kulturowy zaburzeodywiania si—Badania własne. / The cultural context of eating disorders—Own research. *Psychiatria Polska, 46*, 189–200.

Pina e Cunha, M., Rego, A., & Clegg, S. R. (2010). Obedience and evil: From Milgram and Kampuchea to normal organizations. *Journal of Business Ethics, 97*, 291–309.

Ping-Delfos, W., & Soares, M. (2011). Diet induced thermogenesis, fat oxidation and food intake following sequential meals: Influence of calcium and vitamin D. *Clinical Nutrition, 30*, 376–383.

Pinho, N., Moreira, K. M., Hipolide, D. C., Sinigaglia-Coimbra, R., Ferreira, T. L., Nobrega, J. N., . . . Oliveira, M. G. M. (2013). Sleep deprivation alters phosphorylated CREB levels in the amygdala: Relationship with performance in a fear conditioning task. *Behavioural Brain Research, 236*, 221–224.

Piper, W. E., & Hernandez, C. A. S. (2013). Group psychotherapies. In G. Stricker, T. A. Widiger, & I. B. Weiner (Eds.), *Handbook of psychology, Vol. 8. Clinical psychology* (2nd ed., pp. 367–383). Hoboken, NJ: Wiley.

Plassmann, H., O'Doherty, J., Shiv, B., & Rangel, A. (2008). Marketing actions can modulate neural representations of experienced pleasantness. *Proceedings of the National Academy of Sciences, 105*, 1050–1054.

Platt, T., Hofmann, J., Ruch, W., & Proyer, R. T. (2013). Duchenne display responses towards sixteen enjoyable emotions: Individual differences between no and fear of being laughed at. *Motivation and Emotion.* Advance online publication. doi: 10.1007/s11031-013-9342-9

Plöderl, M., Wagenmakers, E.-J., Tremblay, P., Ramsay, R., Kralovec, K., Fartacek, C., & Fartacek, R. (2013). Suicide risk and sexual orientation: A critical review. *Archives of Sexual Behavior, 42*, 715–727.

Plomin, R. (1990). The role of inheritance in behavior. *Science, 248*, 183–188.

Plomin, R., & Spinath, F. M. (2004). Intelligence: Genetics, genes, and genomics. *Journal of Personality & Social Psychology, 86*, 112–129.

Plucker, J., & Esping, A. (2013). *Intelligence 101*. New York: Springer.

Plumbe, L., Peters, S., Bennett, S., Vicenzino, B., & Coppieters, M. W. (2013). Mirror therapy, graded motor imagery and virtual illusion for the management of chronic pain. *Cochrane Database of Systematic Reviews*. doi: 10.1002/14651858.CD010329.

Plutchik, R. (1980). A general psychoevolutionary theory of emotion. In R. Plutchik & H. Kellerman (Eds.), *Emotion: Theory, research, and experience: Vol. 1. Theories of emotion* (pp. 3–31). New York: Academic Press.

Pohl, R. F., Erdfelder, E., Hilbig, B. E., Liebke, L., & Stahlberg, D. (2013). Effort reduction after self-control depletion: The role of cognitive resources in use of simple heuristics. *Journal of Cognitive Psychology*, 25, 267–276.

Pokhrel, P., Herzog, T. A., Black, D. S., Zaman, A., Riggs, N. R., & Sussman, S. (2013). Adolescent neurocognitive development, self-regulation, and school-based drug use prevention. *Prevention Science, 14*, 218–228.

Polley, K. H., Navarro, R., Avery, D. H., George, M. S., & Holtzheimer, P. E. (2011). 2010 updated Avery-George-Holtzheimer Database of rTMS depression studies. *Brain Stimulation, 4*, 115–116.

Pomerantz, A. (2013). *Clinical psychology: Science, practice, and culture (3rd ed.)*. Thousand Oaks, CA: Sage.

Pomerantz, E. M., & Kempner, S. G. (2013). Mothers' daily person and process praise: Implications for children's theory of intelligence and motivation. *Developmental Psychology*. Advance online publication. doi: 10.1037/a0031840

Pomponio, A. T. (2002). *Psychological consequences of terror*. Hoboken, NJ: Wiley.

Pope, K. S., & Vasquez, M. J. T. (2011). *Ethics in psychotherapy and counseling: A practical guide* (4th ed.). Hoboken, NJ: Wiley.

Popma, A., Vermeiren, R., Geluk, C. A. M. L., Rinne, T., van den Brink, W., Knol, D. L., . . . Doreleijers, T. A. H. (2007). Cortisol moderates the relationship between testosterone and aggression in delinquent male adolescents. *Biological Psychiatry, 61,* 405–411.

Portnoy, J., Gao, Y., Glenn, A. L., Niv, S., Peskin, M., Rudo-Hutt, A., . . . Raine, A. (2013). The biology of childhood crime and antisocial behavior. In C. L. Gibson & M. D. Krohn (Eds.), *Handbook of life-course criminology: Emerging trends and directions for future research* (pp. 21–42). New York: Springer Science + Business Media.

Post, J. M. (2011). Crimes of obedience: "Groupthink" at Abu Ghraib. *International Journal of Group Psychotherapy, 61,* 49–66

Posthuma, D., de Geus, E. J. C., & Boomsma, D. I. (2001). Perceptual speed and IQ are associated through common genetic factors. *Behavior Genetics, 31,* 593–602.

Potenza, M. N. (2013). Biological contributions to addictions in adolescents and adults: Prevention, treatment, and policy implications. *Journal of Adolescent Health, 52,* S22-S32.

Poulin, M. J., Holman, E. A., & Buffone, A. (2012). The neurogenetics of nice: Receptor genes for oxytocin and vasopressin interact with threat to predict prosocial behavior. *Psychological Science, 23,* 446–452.

Pournaghash-Tehrani, S. (2011). Domestic violence in Iran: A literature review. *Aggression and Violent Behavior, 16,* 1–5.

Prasada, S., Hennefield, L., & Otap, D. (2012). Conceptual and linguistic representations of kinds and classes. *Cognitive Science, 36,* 1224–1250.

Pressman, S. D., & Cohen, S. (2005). Does positive affect influence health? *Psychological Bulletin, 131,* 925–971.

Preston, S. D. (2013). The origins of altruism in offspring care. *Psychological Bulletin.* Advance online publication. doi:10.1037/a0031755

Price, J., Lefgren, L., & Tappen, H. (2013). Interracial workplace cooperation: Evidence from the NBA. *Economic Inquiry, 51,* 1026–1034.

Prkachin, K. M., & Silverman, B. E. (2002). Hostility and facial expression in young men and women: Is social regulation more important than negative affect? *Health Psychology, 21,* 33–39.

Protzko, J., Aronson, J., & Blair, C. (2013). How to make a young child smarter: Evidence from the database of raising intelligence. *Perspectives on Psychological Science, 8,* 25–40.

Pruett, D., Waterman, E. H., & Caughey, A. B. (2013). Fetal alcohol exposure: Consequences, diagnosis, and treatment. *Obstetrical & Gynecological Survey, 68,* 62–69.

Pu, S., Yamada, T., Yokoyama, K., Matsumura, H., Kobayashi, H., Sasaki, N., . . . Nakagome, K. (2011). A multichannel near-infrared spectroscopy study of prefrontal cortex activation during working memory task in major depressive disorder. *Neuroscience Research, 70,* 91–97.

Pullum, G. K. (1991). *The great Eskimo vocabulary hoax and other irreverent essays on the study of language.* Chicago, IL: University of Chicago Press.

Purves, D., & Piatt, M. L. (2012). Sleep and wakefulness. In D. Purves, G. J. Augustine, D. Fitzpatrick, W. C. Hall, A.-S. LaManita, & L. E. White (Eds.), *Neuroscience* (5th ed., pp. 625–646). Sunderland, MA: Sinauer Associates.

Qian, Z., Zhang, D., & Wang, L. (2013). Is aggressive trait responsible for violence? Priming effects of aggressive words and violent movies. *Psychology, 4,* 96–100.

Quick, J. C., Wright, T. A., Adkins, J. A., Nelson, D. L., & Quick, J. D. (2013). Primary prevention for individuals: Managing and coping with stressors. In J. C. Quick, T. A., Wright, J. A. Adkins, D. L. Nelson, & J. D. Quick (Eds.), *Preventive stress management in organizations (2nd ed.,* pp. 147–163). Washington, DC: American Psychological Association.

Quinn, J., Barrowclough, C., & Tarrier, N. (2003). The Family Questionnaire (FQ): A scale for measuring symptom appraisal in relatives of schizophrenic patients. *Acta Psychiatrica Scandinavica, 108,* 290–296.

Quinn, P. D., Stappenbeck, C. A., & Fromme, K. (2013). An event-level examination of sex differences and subjective intoxication in alcohol-related aggression. *Experimental and Clinical Psychopharmacology, 21,* 93–102.

Raaska, H., Elovainio, M., Sinkkonen, J., Stolt, S., Jalonen, I., Matomaki, J., . . . Lapinleimu, H. (2013). Adopted children's language difficulties and their relation to symptoms of reactive attachment disorder: FinAdo study. *Journal of Applied Developmental Psychology, 34,* 152–160.

Raggi, A., Plazzi, G., Pennisi, G., Tasca, D., & Ferri, R. (2011). Cognitive evoked potentials in narcolepsy: A review of the literature. *Neuroscience and Biobehavioral Reviews, 35,* 1144–1153.

Rai, T. S., & Fiske, A. P. (2011). Moral psychology is relationship regulation: Moral motives for unity, hierarchy, equality, and proportionality. *Psychological Review, 118,* 57.

Raison, C. L., & Miller, A. H. (2013). The evolutionary significance of depression in Pathogen Host Defense (PATHOS-D). *Molecular Psychiatry, 18,* 15–37.

Ramsay, C. E., Stewart, T., & Compton, M. T. (2012). Unemployment among patients with newly diagnosed first-episode psychosis: Prevalence and clinical correlates in a US sample. *Social Psychiatry and Psychiatric Epidemiology, 47,* 797–803.

Ratner, K. G., & Amodio, D. M. (2013). Seeing "us vs. Them": Minimal group effects on the neural encoding of faces. *Journal of Experimental Social Psychology, 49,* 298–301.

Rattaz, C., Goubet, N., & Bullinger, A. (2005). The calming effect of a familiar odor on full-term newborns. *Journal of Developmental and Behavioral Pediatrics, 26,* 86–92.

Read, D., & Grushka-Cockayne, Y. (2011). The similarity heuristic. *Journal of Behavioral Decision Making, 24,* 23–46.

Redd, S. B., & Mintz, A. (2013). Policy perspectives on national security and foreign policy decision making. *Policy Studies Journal, 41,* S11–S37.

Redish, A. D., & Ekstrom, A. (2013). Hippocampus and related areas: What the place cell literature tells us about cognitive maps in rats and humans. In D. Waller & L. Nadel (Eds.), *Handbook of spatial cognition* (pp. 15–34). Washington, DC: American Psychological Association.

Reel, J. J. (2013). Mortality rates. In J. J. Reel (Ed.), *Eating disorders: An encyclopedia of causes, treatments, and prevention* (pp. 283–284). Goleta, CA: ABC-CLIO.

Regan, P. (1998). What if you can't get what you want? Willingness to compromise ideal mate selection standards as a function of sex, mate value, and relationship context. *Personality and Social Psychology Bulletin, 24,* 1294–1303.

Reinhard, M.-A., & Dickhäuser, O. (2011). How affective states, task difficulty, and self-concepts influence the formation and consequences of performance expectancies. *Cognition and Emotion, 25,* 220–228.

Reivich, K., Gillham, J. E., Chaplin, T. M., & Seligman, M. E. (2013). From helplessness to optimism: The role of resilience in treating and preventing depression in youth. In S. Goldstein & R. B. Brooks (Eds.), *Handbook of resilience in children* (pp. 201–214). New York: Springer Science + Business Media.

Remer, P. (2013). Feminist therapy. In J. Frew & M. D. Spiegler (Eds.), *Contemporary psychotherapies for a diverse world* (1st rev. ed., pp. 317–414). New York: Routledge/Taylor & Francis Group.

Rentfrow, P. J., Gosling, S. D., & Potter, J. (2008). A theory of the emergence, persistence, and expression of geographic variation in psychological characteristics. *Perspectives on Psychological Science, 3,* 339–369.

Rest, J., Narvaez, D., Bebeau, M., & Thoma, S. (1999). A neo-Kohlbergian approach: The DIT and schema theory. *Educational Psychology Review, 11*, 291–324.

Reyes-Jaquez, B., & Echols, C. H. (2013). Developmental differences in the relative weighing of informants' social attributes. *Developmental Psychology, 49*, 602–613.

Rhee, S. H., & Waldman, I. D. (2011). Genetic and environmental influences on aggression. In P. R. Shaver & M. Mikulincer (Eds.), *Herzilya series on personality and social psychology. Human aggression and violence: Causes, manifestations, and consequences* (pp. 143–163). Washington, DC: American Psychological Association.

Rimmele, U., Davachi, L., & Phelps, E. A. (2012). Memory for time and place contributes to enhanced confidence in memories for emotional events. *Emotion, 12*, 834–846.

Ripoll, L. H., Snyder, R., Steele, H., & Siever, L. J. (2013). The neurobiology of empathy in borderline personality disorder. *Current Psychiatry Reports, 15*, 1–11.

Risman, B. J., & Davis, G. (2013). From sex roles to gender structure. *Current Sociology, 61*, 733–755.

Riva, M. A., Tremolizzo, L., Spicci, M., Ferrarese, C., De Vito, G., Cesana, G. C., & Sironi, V. A. (2011). The disease of the moon: The linguistic and pathological evolution of the English term "lunatic." *Journal of the History of the Neurosciences, 20*, 65–73.

Rivers, S. E., Brackett, M. A., Reyes, M. R., Elbertson, N. A., & Salovey, P. (2013). Improving the social and emotional climate of classrooms: A clustered randomized controlled trial testing the RULER approach. *Prevention Science, 14*, 77–87.

Rizvi, S. L., & Salters-Pedneault, K. (2013). Borderline personality disorder. In W. O'Donohue & S. O. Lilienfeld (Eds.), *Case studies in clinical psychological science: Bridging the gap from science to practice* (pp. 301–322). New York: Oxford University Press.

Rizzolatti, G. (2012). The mirror mechanism: A mechanism for understanding others. *International Journal of Psychophysiology, 85*, 282.

Robbins, L. (2013). Neuralstem's stem cells give spinal injury patients hope. Retrieved from http://www.gazette.net/article/20130114/NEWS/130119667/neuralstem-x2019-s-stem-cells-give-spinal-injury-patients-hope&template=gazette

Robertson, D. (2013). *The practice of cognitive-behavioural hypnotherapy: A manual for evidence-based cinical hypnosis.* London: Karnac Books.

Robichaud, M. (2013). Generalized anxiety disorder: Targeting intolerance of uncertainty. In G. Simos & S. G. Hofmann (Eds.), *CBT for anxiety disorders: A practitioner book* (pp. 57–85). Oxford, UK: Wiley.

Robnett, R. D., & Leaper, C. (2013). "Girls don't propose! Ew.": A mixed-methods examination of marriage tradition preferences and benevolent sexism in emerging adults. *Journal of Adolescent Research, 28*, 96–121.

Rodkey, E. N., & Riddell, R. P. (2013). The infancy of infant pain research: The experimental origins of infant pain denial. *The Journal of Pain, 14*, 338–350.

Rodrigues, A., Assmar, E. M., & Jablonski, B. (2005). Social-psychology and the invasion of Iraq. *Revista de Psicología Social, 20*, 387–398.

Roehrs, T., & Roth, T. (2012). Sleep and sleep disorders. In J. C. Verster, K. Brady, M. Galanter, & P. Conrod (Eds.), *Drug abuse and addiction in medical illness: Causes, consequences and treatment* (pp. 375–384). New York: Springer Science + Business Media.

Roelofs, J., van Breukelen, G., de Graaf, L. E., Beck, A. T., Arntz, A., & Huibers, M. J. H. (2013). Norms for the Beck Depression Inventory (BDI-II) in a large Dutch community sample. *Journal of Psychopathology and Behavioral Assessment, 35*, 93–98.

Roeser, R. W., Schonert-Reichl, K. A., Jha, A., Cullen, M., Wallace, L., Wilensky, R., . . . Harrison, J. (2013). Mindfulness training and reductions in teacher stress and burnout: Results from two randomized, waitlist-control field trials. *Journal of Educational Psychology, 105*, 787–804.

Roisko, R., Wahlberg, K.-E., Hakko, H., Wynne, L., & Tienari, P. (2011). Communication deviance in parents of families with adoptees at a high or low risk of schizophrenia-spectrum disorders and its associations with attributes of the adoptee and the adoptive parents. *Psychiatry Research, 185*, 66–71.

Rood, L., Roelofs, J., Bogels, S. M., & Arntz, A. (2012). The effects of experimentally induced rumination, positive reappraisal, acceptance, and distancing when thinking about a stressful event on affect states in adolescents. *Journal of Abnormal Child Psychology, 40*, 73–84.

Rooke, S. E., Norberg, M. M., Copeland, J., & Swift, W. (2013). Health outcomes associated with long-term regular cannabis and tobacco smoking. *Addictive Behaviors, 38*, 2207–2213.

Rosch, E. (1978). Principles of organization. In E. Rosch & H. L. Lloyd (Eds.), *Cognition and categorization.* Hillsdale, NJ: Erlbaum.

Rose, S. A., Feldman, J. F., Jankowski, J. J., & Van Rossem, R. (2011). The structure of memory in infants and toddlers: An SEM study with full-terms and preterms. *Developmental Science, 14*, 83–91.

Roselli, C., Reddy, R., & Kaufman, K. (2011). The development of male-oriented behavior in rams. *Frontiers in Neuroendocrinology, 32*, 164–169.

Rosenström, T., Hintsanen, M., Kivimäki, M., Jokela, M., Juonala, M., Viikari, J. S., . . . Keltikangas-Järvinen, L. (2011). "Change in job strain and progression of atherosclerosis: The cardiovascular risk in young Finns study": Correction to Rosenström et al. (2011). *Journal of Occupational Health Psychology, 16*, 201.

Rosenzweig, M. R., Bennett, E. L., & Diamond, M. C. (1972). Brain changes in response to experience. *Scientific American, 226*, 22–29.

Roskies, A. L., Schweitzer, N. J., & Saks, M. J. (2013). Neuroimages in court: Less biasing than feared. *Trends in Cognitive Sciences, 17*, 99–101.

Ross, A. (2013). Handbook of counseling and psychotherapy in an international context. *European Journal of Psychotherapy & Counselling, 5*, 1–4.

Ross, D., Kincaid, H., Spurrett, D., & Collins, P. (Eds.). (2010). *What is addiction?* Cambridge, MA: MIT Press.

Ross, L. (1977). The intuitive psychologist and his shortcomings. Distortions in the attribution process. In L. Berkowitz (Ed.), *Advances in experimental social psychology* (Vol. 10, pp. 173–220). New York: Academic Press.

Rossi, S. L. (2011). The characterization and transplantation of human embryonic stem cell-derived motor neuron progenitors following bilateral cervical spinal cord injury. *Dissertation Abstracts International: Section B. The Sciences and Engineering, 71*, 59–63.

Roth, R. M., Lavoie, M. E., Mason, E. A., & O'Connor, K. P. (2013). Obsessive-compulsive disorder. In C. A. Noggle & R. S. Dean (Eds.), *Contemporary neuropsychology. The neuropsychology of psychopathology* (pp. 261–286). New York: Springer.

Roth, T. (2012). Appropriate therapeutic selection for patients with shift work disorder. *Sleep Medicine, 13*, 335–341.

Rotter, J. B. (1954). *Social learning and clinical psychology.* Englewood Cliffs, NJ: Prentice Hall.

Rotter, J. B. (1990). Internal versus external control of reinforcement: A case history of a variable. *American Psychologist, 45*, 489–493.

Rotter, J. B. (1996). Generalized expectancies for internal versus external control of reinforcement. *Psychological Monographs: General & Applied, 80*, 1–28.

Rouder, J. N., Morey, R. D., & Province, J. M. (2013). A Bayes factor meta-analysis of recent extrasensory perception experiments: Comment on Storm, Tressoldi, and Di Risio (2010). *Psychological Bulletin, 139*, 241–247.

Rowe, B., & Levine, D. (2011). *Concise introduction to linguistics* (3rd ed.). Upper Saddle River, NJ: Prentice Hall.

Rowe, R., Maughan, B., Gregory, A. M., & Eley, T. C. (2013). The development of risky attitudes from pre-driving to fully-qualified driving. *Injury Prevention, 19*, 244–249.

Rozencwajg, P., Cherfi, M., Ferrandez, A. M., Lautrey, J., Lemoine, C., & Loarer, E. (2005). Age related differences in the strategies used by middle aged adults to solve a block design task. *International Journal of Aging and Human Development, 60*, 159–182.

Rumbaugh, D. M., von Glasersfeld, E. C., Warner, H., Pisani, P., & Gill, T. V. (1974). Lana (chimpanzee) learning language: A progress report. *Brain and Language, 1*, 205–212.

Ruocco, A. C., Amirthavasagam, S., Choi-Kain, L. W., & McMain, S. F. (2013). Neural correlates of negative emotionality in borderline personality disorder: An activation-likelihood-estimation meta-analysis. *Biological Psychiatry, 73*, 153–160.

Ruscheweyh, R., Albers, C., Kreusch, A., Sommer, J., & Marziniak, M. (2013). The effect of catastrophizing self-statements on pain perception and the nociceptive flexor reflex (RIII Reflex). *The Clinical Journal of Pain, 27*, 578–586.

Rushton, P., & Irwing, P. (2011). The general factor of personality: Normal and abnormal. In T. Chamorro-Premuzic, S., von Stumm, & A. Furnam (Eds.), *Wiley-Blackwell handbook of individual differences* (pp. 132–161). Chichester, UK: Wiley-Blackwell.

Russ, T. C., Stamatakis, E., Hamer, M., Starr, J. M., Kivimäki, M., & Batty, G. D. (2012). Association between psychological distress and mortality: Individual participant pooled analysis of 10 prospective cohort studies. *British Medical Journal, 345*, e4933.

Ruzek, J. I., Schnurr, P. P., Vasterling, J. J., & Friedman, M. J. (2011). *Caring for veterans with deployment-related stress disorders: Iraq, Afghanistan, and beyond.* Washington, DC: American Psychological Association.

Ryan, A. M., & Sackett, P. R. (2013). Stereotype threat in workplace assessments. In K. F. Geisinger, B. A. Bracken, J. F. Carlson, J.-I. C. Hansen, N. R. Kuncel, S. P. Reise, & M. C. Rodriguez (Eds.), *APA handbooks in psychology. APA handbook of testing and assessment in psychology, Vol. 1. Test theory and testing and assessment in industrial and organizational psychology* (pp. 661–673). Washington, DC: American Psychological Association.

Rymer, R. (1993). *Genie: An abused child's first flight from silence.* New York: HarperCollins.

Sachdev, P. S. (2013). Is DSM-5 defensible? *Australian and New Zealand Journal of Psychiatry, 47*, 10–11.

Sack, R. L. (2010). Jet lag. *The New England Journal of Medicine, 362*, 440–447.

Sacks, O. (1995). *An anthropologist on Mars.* New York: Vintage books.

Salgado-Pineda, P., Fakra, E., Delaveau, P., McKenna, P. J., Pomarol-Clotet, E., & Blin, O. (2011). Correlated structural and functional brain abnormalities in the default mode network in schizophrenia patients. *Schizophrenia Research, 125*, 101–109.

Salpeter, L. R., & Swirsky, J. I. (2012). Historical and legal implications of subliminal messaging in the multimedia: Unconscious subjects. *Nova Law Review, 36*, 497–555.

Samnani, A. K., Boekhorst, J. A., & Harrison, J. A. (2012). Acculturation strategy and individual outcomes: Cultural diversity implications for human resource management. *Human Resource Management Review, 22*, 323–335.

Sanbonmatsu, D. M., Uchino, B. N., & Birmingham, W. (2011). On the importance of knowing your partner's views: Attitude familiarity is associated with better interpersonal functioning and lower ambulatory blood pressure in daily life. *Annals of Behavioral Medicine, 41*, 131–137.

Sánchez-Villegas, A., Toledo, E., de Irala, J., Ruiz-Canela, M., Pla-Vidal, J., & Martínez-González, M. A. (2011). Fast-food and commercial baked goods consumption and the risk of depression. *Public Health Nutrition, 15*, 424–432.

Sanday, L., Zanin, K. A., Patti, C. L., Fernandes-Santos, L., Oliveira, L. C., Longo, B. M., . . . Frussa-Filho, R. (2013). Role of state-dependent learning in the cognitive effects of caffeine in mice. *The International Journal of Neuropsychopharmacology, 16*, 1547–1557.

Sander, D. (2013). Models of emotion: The affective neuroscience approach. In J. Armony, & P. Vuilleumier (Eds.), *The Cambridge handbook of human affective neuroscience* (pp. 5–53). New York: Cambridge University Press.

Sanderson, C. A. (2010). *Social psychology.* Hoboken, NJ: Wiley.

Sanderson, C. A. (2013). *Health psychology* (2nd ed.). Hoboken, NJ: Wiley.

Sangwan, S. (2001). Ecological factors as related to I.Q. of children. *Psycho-Lingua, 31*, 89–92.

Sanjuán, P., & de Lopez, K. J. (2013). Relationships between self-serving attributional bias and subjective well-being among Danish and Spanish women. In H. H. Knoop & A. Delle Fave (Eds.), *Cross-cultural advancements in positive psychology* (Vol. 3, pp. 183–194). New York: Springer Science + Business Media.

Sanjuán, P., & Magallares, A. (2013). Coping strategies as mediating variables between self-serving attributional bias and subjective well-being. *Journal of Happiness Studies.* Advance online publication. doi:10.1007/s10902-013-9430-2

Sara, S. J. (2010). Reactivation, retrieval, replay and reconsolidation in and out of sleep: Connecting the dots. *Frontiers in Behavioral Neuroscience, 4*, Article ID 185.

Sarafino, E. P. (2012). *Applied behavior analysis: Principles and procedures for modifying behavior.* Hoboken, NJ: Wiley.

Sargent, J. D., Tanski, S., & Stoolmiller, M. (2012). Influence of motion picture rating on adolescent response to movie smoking. *Pediatrics, 130*, 228–236.

Sarkhosh, K., Switzer, N. J., El-Hadi, M., Birch, D. W., Shi, X., & Karmali, S. (2013). The impact of bariatric surgery on obstructive aleep apnea: A systematic review. *Obesity Surgery, 2393*, 414–423.

Satler, C., Garrido, L. M., Sarmiento, E. P., Leme, S., Conde, C., & Tomaz, C. (2007). Emotional arousal enhances declarative memory in patients with Alzheimer's disease. *Acta Neurologica Scandinavica, 116*, 355–360.

Savage, R. (2013). Modern genocidal dehumanization: a new model. *Patterns of Prejudice, 47*, 139–161.

Savage-Rumbaugh, E. S. (1990). Language acquisition in a nonhuman species: Implications for the innateness debate. *Developmental Psychobiology, 23*, 599–620.

Saxton, M. (2010). *Child language: Acquisition and development.* Thousand Oaks, CA: Sage.

Sbarra, D. A., & Nietert, P. J. (2009). Divorce and death: Forty years of the Charleston Heart Study. *Psychological Science, 20*, 107–113.

Scarborough, P., Nnoaham, K. E., Clarke, D., Capewell, S., & Rayner, M. (2012). Modelling the impact of a healthy diet on cardiovascular disease and cancer mortality. *Journal of Epidemiology and Community Health, 66*, 420–426.

Schachter, S., & Singer, J. E. (1962). Cognitive, social, and physiological determinants of emotional state. *Psychological Review, 69*, 379–399.

Schaefer, R. T. (2008). Power and power elite. In V. Parillo (Ed.), *Encyclopedia of* *social problems*. Thousand Oaks, CA: Sage.

Scheele, D., Striepens, N., Güntürkün, O., Deutschländer, S., Maier, W., Kendrick, K. M., & Hurlemann, R. (2012). Oxytocin modulates social distance between males and females. *The Journal of Neuroscience, 32*, 16074–16079.

Scheiermann, C., Kunisaki, Y., & Frenette, P. S. (2013). Circadian control of the immune system. *Nature Reviews Immunology, 13*, 190–198.

Schiffer, B., Muller, B., Scherbaum, N., Hodgins, S., Forsting, M., Wiltfand, J., . . . Leygraf, N. (2011). Disentangling structural brain alterations associated with violent behavior from those associated with substance use disorders. *Archives of General Psychiatry, 68*, 1039–1049.

Schilling, C., Kühn, S., Romanowski, A., Banaschewski, T., Barbot, A., Barker, G. J., . . . IMAGEN Consortium. (2013). Common structural correlates of trait impulsiveness and perceptual reasoning in adolescence. *Human Brain Mapping, 34*, 374–383.

Schilling, T. M., Kölsch, M., Larra, M. F., Zech, C. M., Blumenthal, T. D., Frings, C., & Schächinger, H. (2013). For whom the bell (curve) tolls: Cortisol rapidly affects memory retrieval by an inverted U-shaped dose–response relationship. *Psychoneuroendocrinology, 38*, 1565–1567.

Schirmer, A. (2013). Sex differences in emotion. In J. Armony & P. Vuilleumier (Eds.), *The Cambridge handbook of human affective neuroscience* (pp. 591–610). New York: Cambridge University Press.

Schmid, P. F. (2013). Whence the evil? A personalistic and dialogic perspective. In A. C. Bohart, B. S. Held, E. Mendelowitz, & K. J. Schneider (Eds.), *Humanity's dark side: Evil, destructive experience, and psychotherapy* (pp. 35–55). Washington, DC: American Psychological Association.

Schmidt, A. M., Beck, J. W., & Gillespie, J. Z. (2013). Motivation. In N. W. Schmitt, S. Highhouse, & I. B. Weiner (Eds.), *Handbook of psychology, Vol. 12. Industrial and organizational psychology* (2nd ed., pp. 311–340). Hoboken, NJ: Wiley.

Schmidt, S. R. (2012). *Essays in cognitive psychology. Extraordinary memories for exceptional events*. New York: Psychology Press.

Schmitz, M., & Wentura, D. (2012). Evaluative priming of naming and semantic categorization responses revisited: A mutual facilitation explanation. *Journal of Experimental Psychology: Learning, Memory, and Cognition, 38*, 984–1000.

Schneider, C., Charpak, N., Ruiz-Peláez, J. G., & Tessier, R. (2012). Cerebral motor function in very premature-at-birth adolescents: A brain stimulation exploration of kangaroo mother care effects. *Acta Paediatrica, 101,* 1045–1053.

Schneidman, E. S. (1981). Suicide. *Suicide and Life-Threatening Behavior, 11*, 198–220.

Schott, B. H., Wüstenberg, T., Wimber, M., Fenker, D. B., Zierhut, K. C., Seidenbecher, C. I., . . . Richardson-Klavehn, A. (2013). The relationship between level of processing and hippocampal–cortical functional connectivity during episodic memory formation in humans. *Human Brain Mapping, 34*, 407–424.

Schredl, M. (2010). Nightmare frequency and nightmare topics in a representative German sample. *European Archives of Psychiatry and Clinical Neuroscience, 260*, 565–570.

Schroeder, K., Fisher, H. L., & Schäfer, I. (2013). Psychotic symptoms in patients with borderline personality disorder: Prevalence and clinical management. *Current Opinion in Psychiatry, 26*, 113–119.

Schulze, L., Domes, G., Krüger, A., Berger, C., Fleischer, M., Prehn, K., . . . Herpertz, S. C. (2011). Neuronal correlates of cognitive reappraisal in borderline patients with affective instability. *Biological Psychiatry, 69*, 564–573.

Schunk, D. H., & Zimmerman, B. J. (2013). Self-regulation and learning. In W. M. Reynolds, G. E. Miller, & I. B. Weiner (Eds.), *Handbook of psychology, Vol. 7. Educational psychology (2nd ed.,* pp. 45–68). Hoboken, NJ: Wiley.

Schwabe, L., & Wolf, O. T. (2013). Stress and multiple memory systems: from 'thinking' to 'doing'. *Trends in Cognitive Sciences, 17*, 60–68.

Schwartz, S. D., Hubschman, J. P., Heilwell, G., Franco-Cardenas, V., Pan, C. K., Ostrick, R. M., . . . Lanza, R. (2012). Embryonic stem cell trials for macular degeneration: A preliminary report. *Lancet, 379*, 713–720.

Schweitzer, N. J., & Saks, M. J. (2011). Neuroimage evidence and the insanity defense. *Behavioral Sciences & the Law, 29*, 592–607.

Scott, L. N., Levy, K. N., Adams, R. B., Jr., & Stevenson, M. T. (2011). Mental state decoding abilities in young adults with borderline personality disorder traits. *Personality Disorders: Theory, Research, and Treatment, 2*, 98–112.

Segal, N. L. (2013). *Born together—reared apart: The landmark Minnesota Twin Study*. Cambridge, MA: Harvard University Press.

Segerstrom, S., C., & Miller, G. E. (2004). Psychological stress and the human immune system: A meta-analytic study of 30 years of inquiry. *Psychological Bulletin, 130*, 601–630.

Seligman, M. E. P. (1975) *Helplessness: On depression, development, and death*. San Francisco, CA: Freeman.

Seligman, M. E. P. (2003). The past and future of positive psychology. In C. L. M. Keyes & J. Daidt (Eds.), *Flourishing: Positive psychology and the life well-lived* (pp. xi–xx). Washington, DC: American Psychological Association.

Seligman, M. E. P. (2007). Coaching and positive psychology. *Australian Psychologist, 42*, 266–267.

Seligman, M. E. P. (2011). *Flourish: A visionary new understanding of happiness and well-being*. New York: Free Press.

Seligman, M. E. P., & Csikszentmihalyi, M. (2000). Positive psychology: An introduction. *American Psychologist, 55,* 5–14.

Seligman, M. E., & Maier, S. F. (1967). Failure to escape traumatic shock. *Journal of Experimental Psychology, 74*, 1–9.

Senko, C., & Hulleman, C. S. (2013). The role of goal attainment expectancies in achievement goal pursuit. *Journal of Educational Psychology, 105*, 504–521.

Serlin, I. (2011). The history and future of humanistic psychology. *Journal of Humanistic Psychology, 51*, 428–431.

Shaffer, D., & Kipp, K. (2013). *Developmental psychology: Childhood and adolescence* (9th ed.). Belmont Park, CA: Wadsworth Publishing.

Shaffer, R., & Jadwiszczok, A. (2010). Psychic defective: Sylvia Browne's history of failure. *Skeptical Inquirer*, 34. 2.

Shand, G. (2013). Culture and the self: a comparison of attitudes to study among English and Japanese students in state secondary education. *Compare: A Journal of Comparative and International Education*. Advance online publication. doi: 10.1080/03057925.2012.752623

Sharf, R. S. (2012). *Theories of psychotherapy and counseling: Concepts and cases* (5th ed.). Pacific Grove, CA: Brooks/Cole.

Sharkey, P. (2010). The acute effect of local homicides on children's cognitive performance. *Proceedings of the National Academy of Sciences, 107*, 11733–11738.

Sharpe, D. I., Walters, A. S., & Goren, M. J. (2013). Effect of cheating experience on attitudes toward infidelity. *Sexuality & Culture, 7*, 1–16.

Shaw, N. D., Butler, J. P., McKinney, S. M., Nelson, S. A., Ellenbogen, J. M., & Hall, J. E. (2012). Insights into puberty: The relationship between sleep stages and pulsatile LH secretion. *Journal of Clinical Endocrinology & Metabolism, 97*, E2055–E2062.

Sheard, M. (2013). *Mental toughness: The mindset behind sporting achievement* (2nd ed.). New York: Routledge/Taylor & Francis Group.

Shedler, J. (2010). The efficacy of psychodynamic psychotherapy. *American Psychologist, 65,* 98–109.

Shepperd, J. A., Malone, W., & Sweeny, K. (2008). Exploring causes of the self-serving bias. *Social and Personality Psychology Compass, 2,* 895–908.

Sheridan, M. A., Fox, N. A., Zeanah, C. H., McLaughlin, K. A., & Nelson, C. A. III. (2012). Variation in neural development as a result of exposure to institutionalization early in childhood. *Proceedings of the National Academy of Sciences, 109,* 12927–12932.

Sherman, G. D., Lee, J. J., Cuddy, A. J. C., Renshon, J., Oveis, C., Gross, J. J., & Lerner, J. S. (2012). Leadership is associated with lower levels of stress. *Proceedings of the National Academy of Sciences, 109,* 17903–17907.

Shimane, T., Hidaka, Y., Wada, K., & Funada, M. (2013). Ecstasy (3, 4-methylenedioxymethamphetamine) use among Japanese rave population. *Psychiatry & Clinical Neurosciences, 67,* 12–19.

Shin, R.-M., Tully, K., Li, Y., Cho, J.-H., Higuchi, M., Suhara, T., & Bolshakov, V. Y. (2010). Hierarchical order of coexisting pre- and postsynaptic forms of long-term potentiation at synapses in amygdala. *Proceedings of the National Academy of Sciences, 107,* 19073–19078.

Shinfuku, N., & Kitanishi, K. (2010). Buddhism and psychotherapy in Japan. Religion and psychiatry: Beyond boundaries. In P. J. Verhagen, H. M. van Praag, J. J., J. Jr. López-Ibor, J. L. Cox, & D. Moussaoui (Eds.), *Religion and psychiatry: Beyond boundaries* (pp. 181–191). Malden, MA: Wiley-Blackwell.

Shweder, R. A. (2011). Commentary: Ontogenetic cultural psychology. In L. A. Jensen (Ed.), *Bridging cultural and developmental approaches to psychology: New syntheses in theory, research, and policy* (pp. 303–310). New York: Oxford University Press.

Sias, P. M., Heath, R. G., Perry, T., Silva, D., & Fix, B. (2004). Narratives of workplace friendship deterioration. *Journal of Social and Personal Relationships, 21,* 321–340.

Sidhu, M., Malhi, P., & Jerath, J. (2010). Intelligence of children from economically disadvantaged families: Role of parental education. *Psychological Studies, 55,* 358–364.

Sieber-Blum, M. (2010). Epidermal neural crest stem cells and their use in mouse models of spinal cord injury. *Brain Research Bulletin, 83,* 189–193.

Siegala, M., & Varley, R. (2008). If we could talk to the animals. *Behavioral and Brain Sciences, 31,* 146–147.

Siegel, A. B. (2010). Dream interpretation in clinical practice: A century after Freud. *Sleep Medicine Clinics, 5,* 299–313.

Siegel, J. M. (2000, January). Narcolepsy. *Scientific American,* pp. 76–81.

Siegel, J. M. (2008). Do all animals sleep? *Trends in Neurosciences, 31,* 208–213.

Siegler, I. C., Elias, M. F., Brummett, B. H., & Bosworth, H. B. (2013). Adult development and aging. In A. M. Nezu, C. M. Nezu, P. A. Geller, & I. B. Weiner (Eds.), *Handbook of psychology, Vol. 9. Health psychology (2nd ed.,* pp. 459–476). Hoboken, NJ: Wiley.

Signorielli, N. (2013). Gender-role socialization in the twenty-first century. *The international encyclopedia of media studies.* Advance online publication. doi: 10.1002/9781444361506.wbiems116

Sillén, A., Lilius, L., Forsell, C., Kimura, T., Winblad, B., & Graff, C. (2011). Linkage to the 8p21.1 region including the CLU gene in age at onset stratified Alzheimer's disease families. *Journal of Alzheimer's Disease, 23,* 13–20.

Silverstein, M. L. (2013). *Personality and clinical psychology. Personality assessment in depth: A casebook.* New York: Routledge/Taylor & Francis Group.

Simmons, A. L. (2012). Distributed practice and procedural memory consolidation in musicians' skill learning. *Journal of Research in Music Education, 59,* 357–368.

Simpson, T. L., Stappenbeck, C. A., Varra, A. A., Moore, S. A., & Kaysen, D. (2012). Symptoms of posttraumatic stress predict craving among alcohol treatment seekers: Results of a daily monitoring study. *Psychology of Addictive Behaviors, 26,* 724–733.

Sinason, V. (Ed.). (2011). *Attachment, trauma, and multiplicity: Working with dissociative identity disorder* (2nd ed.). New York: Routledge.

Sinclair, L. (2011). Designer drug's rapid spread causes alarm on several fronts. *Psychiatric News, 46,* 8.

Skinner, R., Conlon, L., Gibbons, D., & McDonald, C. (2011). Cannabis use and non-clinical dimensions of psychosis in university students presenting to primary care. *Acta Psychiatrica Scandinavica, 123,* 21–27.

Slater, L. Z., Moneyham, L., Vance, D. E., Raper, J. L., Mugavero, M. J., & Childs, G. (2013). Support, stigma, health, coping, and quality of life in older gay men with HIV. *Journal of the Association of Nurses in AIDS Care, 24,* 38–49.

Slutske, W. S., Cho, S. B., Piasecki, T. M., & Martin, N. G. (2013). Genetic overlap between personality and risk for disordered gambling: Evidence from a national community-based Australian twin study. *Journal of Abnormal Psychology, 122,* 250–255.

Smink, F. R. E., van Hoeken, D., & Hoek, H. W. (2012). Epidemiology of eating disorders: Incidence, prevalence, and mortality rates. *Current Psychiatry Reports, 14,* 406–414.

Smith, B. (2011). Hypnosis today. *Monitor on Psychology, 42,* 6.

Smith, C. V., & Shaffer, M. J. (2013). Gone but not forgotten: Virginity loss and current sexual satisfaction. *Journal of Sex & Marital Therapy, 39,* 96–111.

Smith, K. C. (2012). The Obama effect on African-American students' academic performance. *Dissertation Abstracts International: Section B: The Sciences and Engineering, 72,* 7114.

Smith, K. D. (2007). Spinning straw into gold: Dynamics of Rumpelstiltskin style of leadership. *Dissertation Abstracts International Section A: Humanities and Social Sciences, 68,* 1760.

Smith, M. L. (2012). Rapid processing of emotional expressions without conscious awareness. *Cerebral Cortex, 22,* 1748–1760.

Smith, M. L., & Glass, G. V. (1977). Meta-analysis of psychotherapy outcome studies. *American Psychologist, 32,* 752–760.

Smith, M. L., Glass, G. V., & Miller, T. I. (1980). *The benefits of psychotherapy.* Baltimore: Johns Hopkins University Press.

Smith, M. T., Huang, M. I., & Manber, R. (2005). Cognitive behavior therapy for chronic insomnia occurring within the context of medical and psychiatric disorders. *Clinical Psychology Review, 25,* 559–592.

Smith, M., Robinson, L., & Segal, R. (2012). How much sleep do you need? Sleep cycles and stages, lack of sleep, and getting the hours you need. Retrieved from http://helpguide.org/life/sleeping.htm

Smith, M., Wang, L., Cronenwett, W., Goldman, M., Mamah, D., Barch, D., & Csernansky, J. (2011). Alcohol use disorders contribute to hippocampal and subcortical shape differences in schizophrenia. *Schizophrenia Research, 131,* 174–183.

Snijders, T. J., Ramsey, N. F., Koerselman, F., & van Gijn, J. (2010). Attentional modulation fails to attenuate the subjective pain experience in chronic, unexplained pain. *European Journal of Pain, 14,* e1–e10.

Soares, S. C., & Esteves, F. (2013). A glimpse of fear: Fast detection of threatening targets in visual search with brief stimulus durations. *PsyCh Journal, 2*, 11–16.

Soderberg, C. K., & Sherman, J. W. (2013). No face is an island: How implicit bias operates in social scenes. *Journal of Experimental Social Psychology, 49*, 307–313.

Sokoloff, P., Leriche, L., Diaz, J., Louvel, J., & Pumain, R. (2013). Direct and indirect interactions of the dopamine D3 receptor with glutamate pathways: implications for the treatment of schizophrenia. *Naunyn-Schmiedeberg's Archives of Pharmacology, 386*, 107–124.

Solms, M. (1997). *The neuropsychology of dreams*. Mahwah, NJ: Lawrence Erlbaum.

Somerville, L. H., Wagner, D. D., Wig, G. S., Moran, J. M., Whalen, P. J., & Kelley, W. M. (2013). Interactions between transient and sustained neural signals support the generation and regulation of anxious emotion. *Cerebral Cortex, 23*, 49–60.

Son, H., Banasr, M., Choi, M., Chae, S. Y., Licznerski, P., Lee, B., . . . Duman, R. S. (2012). Neuritin produces antidepressant actions and blocks the neuronal and behavioral deficits caused by chronic stress. *Proceedings of the National Academy of Sciences, 109*, 11378–11383.

Sonnenberg, C. M., Deeg, D. J. H., van Tilburg, T. G., Vink, D., Stek, M. L., & Beekman, A. T. F. (2013). Gender differences in the relation between depression and social support in later life. *International Psychogeriatrics, 25*, 61–70.

Sowell, E. R., Mattson, S. N., Kan, E., Thompson, P. M., Riley, E. P., Edward, P., & Toga, A. W. (2008). Abnormal cortical thickness and brain-behavior correlation patterns in individuals with heavy prenatal alcohol exposure. *Cerebral Cortex, 18*, 136–144.

Spano, R., Koenig, T. L., Hudson, J. W., & Leiste, M. R. (2010). East meets west: A nonlinear model for understanding human growth and development. *Smith College Studies in Social Work, 80*, 198–214.

Spearman, C. (1923). *The nature of "intelligence" and the principles of cognition*. London, England: Macmillan.

Spears, R. (2011). Group identities: The social identity perspective. In S. Schwartz, K. Luyckx, & V. Vignoles (Eds.), *Handbook of identity theory and research* (Vols. 1–2) (pp. 201–224). New York: Springer.

Speisman, R. B., Kumar, A., Rani, A., Pastoriza, J. M., Severance, J. E., Foster, T. C., & Ormerod, B. K. (2013). Environmental enrichment restores neurogenesis and rapid acquisition in aged rats. *Neurobiology of Aging, 34*, 263–274.

Spiegler, M. D. (Ed.). (2013). Behavior therapy II: Cognitive-behavioral therapy. In J. Frew & M. D. Spiegler (Eds.), *Contemporary psychotherapies for a diverse world (1st rev. ed.,* pp. 301–337). New York: Routledge/Taylor & Francis Group.

Spindler, M. A., Galifianakis, N. B., Wilkinson, J. R., & Duda, J. E. (2013). Globus pallidus interna deep brain stimulation for tardive dyskinesia: Case report and review of the literature. *Parkinsonism & Related Disorders, 19*, 141–147.

Sprecher, S., & Fehr, B. (2011). Dispositional attachment and relationship-specific attachment as predictors of compassionate love for a partner. *Journal of Social and Personal Relationships, 28*, 558–574.

Spurling, L. (2011). Review of Off the Couch: Contemporary psychoanalytic approaches. *Psychodynamic Practice: Individuals, Groups and Organisations, 17*, 99–100.

Stadlbauer, U., Arnold, M., Weber, E., & Langhans, W. (2013). Possible mechanisms of circulating PYY-induced satiation in male rats. *Endocrinology, 154*, 193–204.

Stafford, J., & Lynn, S. J. (2002). Cultural scripts, memories of childhood abuse, and multiple identities: A study of role-played enactments. *International Journal of Clinical and Experimental Hypnosis, 50*, 67–85.

Stalder, T., Kirschbaum, C., Heinze, K., Steudte, S., Foley, P., Tietze, A., & Dettenborn, L. (2010). Use of hair cortisol analysis to detect hypercortisolism during active drinking phases in alcohol-dependent individuals. *Biological Psychology, 85*, 357–360.

Stefanek, E., Strohmeier, D., Fandrem, H., & Spiel, C. (2012). Depressive symptoms in native and immigrant adolescents: The role of critical life events and daily hassles. *Anxiety, Stress and Coping: An International Journal, 25*, 201–217.

Stegmann, U. E. (2013). *Animal communication theory: Information and influence*. New York: Cambridge University Press.

Steiger, H., Bruce, K. R., & Israël, M. (2013). Eating disorders: Anorexia nervosa, bulimia nervosa, and binge eating disorder. In G. Stricker, T. A. Widiger, & I. B. Weiner (Eds.), *Handbook of psychology, Vol. 8. Clinical psychology* (2nd ed., pp. 73–93). Hoboken, NJ: Wiley.

Stein, D. J., Denys, D., Gloster, A. T., Hollander, E., Leckman, J. F., Rauch, S. L., & Phillips, K. A. (2009). Obsessive-compulsive disorder: Diagnostic and treatment issues. *Psychiatric Clinics of North America, 32*, 665–685.

Stein, J. L., Medland, S. E., Vasquez, A. A., Hibar, D. P., Senstad, R. E., Winkler, A. M., . . . Thompson, P. M. (2012). Identification of common variants associated with human hippocampal and intracranial volumes. *Nature Genetics, 44*, 552–561.

Steinhart, P. (1986, March). Personal boundaries. *Audubon*, pp. 8–11.

Stephens, N. J., & Swartz, T. A. (2013). Beliefs of Chinese buyers of pirated goods. *Journal of Consumer Behaviour, 12*, 42–48.

Steptoe, A., & Kivimäki, M. (2013). Stress and cardiovascular disease: An update on current knowledge. *Annual Review of Public Health, 34*, 337–354.

Sternberg, R. J. (1986). A triangular theory of love. *Psychological Review, 93*, 119–135.

Sternberg, R. J. (1988). *The triangle of love*. New York: Basic Books.

Sternberg, R. J. (2006). A duplex theory of love. In R. J. Sternberg & K. Weis (Eds.), *The new psychology of love* (pp. 184–199). New Haven, CT: Yale University Press.

Sternberg, R. J. (2012). *Cognitive psychology* (6th ed.). Belmont, CA: Cengage.

Sternberg, R. J. (2013). Contemporary theories of intelligence. In W. M. Reynolds, G. E. Miller, & I. B. Weiner (Eds.), *Handbook of psychology, Vol. 7. Educational psychology* (2nd ed., pp. 23–44). Hoboken, NJ: Wiley.

Sternberg, R. J. (2013). Intelligence. In D. K. Freedheim & I. B. Weiner (Eds.), *Handbook of psychology, Vol. 1. History of psychology (2nd ed.,* pp. 155–176). Hoboken, NJ: Wiley.

Sternberg, R. J., & Grigorenko, E. L. (2008). Ability testing across cultures. In L. Suzuki (Ed.), *Handbook of multicultural assessment* (3rd ed., pp. 449–470). New York: Jossey-Bass.

Sternberg, R. J., & Lubart, T. I. (1992). Buy low and sell high: An investment approach to creativity. *Current Directions in Psychological Science, 1*, 1–5.

Stets, J. E., & Carter, M. J. (2012). A theory of the self for the sociology of morality. *American Sociological Review, 77*, 120–140.

Stickgold, R., & Walker, M. P. (2013). Sleep-dependent memory triage: Evolving generalization through selective processing. *Nature Neuroscience, 16*, 139–145.

Stiles, W. B. (2013). The variables problem and progress in psychotherapy research. *Psychotherapy, 50*, 33–41.

Stock, M. L., Gibbons, F. X., Peterson, L. M., & Gerrard, M. (2013). The effects of racial discrimination on the HIV-risk cognitions and behaviors of Black adolescents and young adults. *Health Psychology, 32*, 543–550.

Stoll, E. E., & Ha-Brookshire, J. E. (2012). Motivations for success: Case of U.S. textile and apparel small- and medium-sized enterprises. *Clothing & Textiles Research Journal, 30*, 149–163.

Stollhoff, R., Jost, J., Elze, T., & Kennerknecht, I. (2011). Deficits in long-term recognition memory reveal dissociated subtypes in congenital prosopagnosia. *PLoS ONE, 6*, Article ID e15702.

Stoltzfus, G., Nibbelink, B., Vredenburg, D., & Hyrum, E. (2011). Gender, gender role, and creativity. *Social Behavior and Personality: An International Journal, 39*, 425–432.

Stoner, J. A. (1961). *A comparison of individual and group decisions involving risk.* Unpublished master's thesis, School of Industrial Management, MIT, Cambridge, MA.

Stoodley, C. J. (2012). The cerebellum and cognition: Evidence from functional imaging studies. *The Cerebellum, 11*, 352–365.

Stopa, L., Denton, R., Wingfield, M., & Taylor, K. N. (2013). The fear of others: A qualitative analysis of interpersonal threat in social phobia and paranoia. *Behavioural and Cognitive Psychotherapy, 41*, 188–209.

Storsve, A. B., McNally, G. P., & Richardson, R. (2012). Renewal and reinstatement of the conditioned but not the unconditioned response following habituation of the unconditioned stimulus. *Behavioural Processes, 90*, 58–65.

Stowell, J. R., Robles, T. F., & Kane, H. S. (2013). Psychoneuroimmunology: Mechanisms, individual differences, and interventions. In A. M. Nezu, C. M. Nezu, P. A. Geller, & I. B. Weiner (Eds.), *Handbook of psychology, Vol. 9. Health psychology (2nd ed.,* pp. 79–101). Hoboken, NJ: Wiley.

Strack, F., Martin, L. L., & Stepper, S. (1988). Inhibiting and facilitating conditions of the human smile: A nonobstrusive test of the facial feedback hypothesis. *Journal of Personality and Social Psychology, 54*, 768–777.

Strange, D., Garry, M., Bernstein, D. M., & Lindsay, D. S. (2011). Photographs cause false memories for the news. *Acta Psychologica, 136*, 90–94.

Straub, R. O. (2011). *Health psychology: A biopsychosocial approach* (3rd ed.). New York: Worth.

Strauss, J. R. (2010). The baby boomers meet menopause: Attitudes and roles. *Dissertation Abstracts International Section A: Humanities and Social Sciences, 70*, 3196.

Strayer, D. L., Wartson, J. M., & Drews, F. A. (2011). Cognitive distraction while multitasking in the automobile. In B. H. Ross (Ed.), *The psychology of learning and motivation: Advances in research and theory* (Vol. 54, pp. 29–58). San Diego, CA: Elsevier Academic Press.

Stricker, G., Widiger, T. A., & Weiner, I. B. (Eds.). (2013). *Handbook of psychology, Vol 8: Clinical Psychology (2nd ed.).* Hoboken, NJ: Wiley.

Stroebe, W., & Stroebe, M. S. (1996). The social psychology of social support. In E. T. Higgins & A. W. Kruglanski (Eds.), *Social psychology: Handbook of basic principles* (pp. 597–621). New York: Guilford Press.

Strozier, C. B. (2011). Torture, war, and the culture of fear after 9/11. *International Journal of Group Psychotherapy, 61*, 67–72.

Sugarman, H., Impey, C., Buxner, S., & Antonellis, J. (2011). Astrology beliefs among undergraduate students. *Astronomy Education Review, 10.* Retrieved from http://aer.aas.org/resource/1/aerscz/v10/i1/p010101_s1?view=fulltext

Sullivan, M. J. L., Tripp, D. A., & Santor, D. (1998). *Gender differences in pain and pain behavior: The role of catastrophizing.* Paper presented at the annual meeting of the American Psychological Association, San Francisco, CA.

Suls, J., Davidson, K., & Kaplan, R. (Eds.). (2010). *Handbook of health psychology and behavioral medicine.* New York: Guilford Press.

Sundram, F., Deeley, Q., Sarkar, S., Daly, E., Latham, R., Barker, G., & Murphy, D. (2011). White matter microstructural abnormalities in antisocial personality disorder: A pilot diffusion tensor imaging study. *European Psychiatry, 26*, 957.

Surtees, P. G., Wainwright, N. W. J., Luben, R. N., Khaw, K-T, & Bingham, S. A. (2009). No evidence that social stress is associated with breast cancer incidence. *Breast Cancer Research and Treatment, 120*, 169–174.

Susilo, T., & Duchaine, B. (2013). Advances in developmental prosopagnosia research. *Current Opinion in Neurobiology, 23*, 423–429.

Suthana, N., Haneef, Z., Stern, J., Mukamel, R., Behnke, E., Knowlton, B., & Fried, I. (2012). Memory enhancement and deepbrain stimulation of the entorhinal area. *New England Journal of Medicine, 366*, 502–510.

Sutin, R., Terracciano, A., Milaneschi, Y., An, Y., Ferrucci, L., & Zonderman, A. B. (2013). The effect of birth cohort on well-being: The legacy of economic hard times. *Psychological Science, 24*, 379–385.

Suzuki, L. A., Onoue, M. A., & Hill, J. S. (2013). Clinical assessment: A multicultural perspective. In K. F. Geisinger, B. A. Bracken, J. F. Carlson, J.-I. C. Hansen, N. R. Kuncel, S. P. Reise, & M. C. Rodriguez (Eds.), *APA handbooks in psychology. APA handbook of testing and assessment in psychology, Vol. 2. Testing and assessment in clinical and counseling psychology* (pp. 193–212). Washington, DC: American Psychological Association.

Svrakic, D. M., Zorumski, C. F., Svrakic, N. M., Zwir, I., & Cloninger, C. R. (2013). Risk architecture of schizophrenia: the role of epigenetics. *Current Opinion in Psychiatry, 26*, 188–195.

Swami, V. (2012). Mental health literacy of depression: Gender differences and attitudinal antecedents in a representative British sample. *PLoS ONE, 7:* e49779.

Swami, V., & Harris, A. S. (2012). Evolutionary perspectives on physical appearance. In T. F. Cash (Ed.), *Encyclopedia of body image and human appearance* (Vol. 1, pp. 404–411). San Diego, CA: Elsevier Academic Press.

Swanson, S. A., Saito, N., Borges, G., Benjet, C., Aguilar-Gaxiola, S., Medina-Mora, M. E., . . . Breslau, J. (2012). Change in binge eating and binge eating disorder associated with migration from Mexico to the US. *Journal of Psychiatric Research, 46*, 31–37.

Sylvestre, A., & Mérette, C. (2010). Language delay in severely neglected children: A cumulative or specific effect of risk factors? *Child Abuse & Neglect, 34*, 414–428.

Szanton, S. L., Rifkind, J. M., Mohanty, J. G., Miller, E. R., Thorpe, R. J., Nagababu, E., . . . Evans, M. K. (2011). Racial discrimination is associated with a measure of red blood cell oxidative stress: A potential pathway for racial disparities. *International Journal of Behavioral Medicine, 19*, 489–495.

Szasz, T. (2012). Varieties of psychiatric criticism. *History of Psychiatry, 23*, 349–355.

Takahashi, A., Quadros, I. M., de Almeida, R. M. M., & Miczek, K. A. (2011). Brain serotonin receptors and transporters: Initiation vs. termination of escalated aggression. *Psychopharmacology, 213*, 183–212.

Takahashi, E., Ohki, K., & Kim, D.-S. (2013). Dissociation and convergence of the dorsal and ventral visual working memory streams in the human prefrontal cortex. *NeuroImage, 65*, 488–498.

Tang, Y. Y., & Posner, M. I. (2013). Tools of the trade: Theory and method in mindfulness neuroscience. *Social Cognitive and Affective Neuroscience, 8*, 118–120.

Tang, Y.-P., Wang, H., Feng, R., Kyin, M., & Tsien, J. Z. (2001). Differential effects of enrichment on learning and memory function in NR2B transgenic mice. *Neuropharmacology, 41*, 779–790.

Tarter, R. E., Kirisci, L., Mezzich, A., Cornelius, J. R., Pajer, K., Vanyukov, M., . . . Clark, D. (2003). Neurobehavioral disinhibition in childhood predicts early age at onset of substance use disorder. *American Journal of Psychiatry, 160*, 1078.

Tatkin, S. (2011). *Wired for love: How understanding your partner's brain and attachment style can help you defuse conflict and build a secure relationship.* Oakland, CA: New Harbinger Publications.

Taub, D. J., & Thompson, J. (2013). College student suicide. *New Directions for Student Services, 141*, 5–14.

Taub, E. (2004). Harnessing brain plasticity through behavioral techniques to produce new treatments in neurorehabilitation. *American Psychologist, 59*, 692–704.

Taub, E. (2012). The behavior-analytic origins of constraint-induced movement therapy: An example of behavioral neurorehabilitation. *The Behavior Analyst, 35*, 155–178.

Taylor, J. Y., Caldwell, C. H., Baser, R. E., Matusko, N., Faison, N., & Jackson, J. S. (2013). Classification and correlates of eating disorders among Blacks: Findings from the National Survey of American Life. *Journal of Health Care for the Poor and Underserved, 24*, 289.

Taylor, L., Fiore, A., Mendelsohn, G., & Cheshire, C. (2011). "Out of my league": A real-world test of the matching hypothesis. *Personality and Social Psychology Bulletin, 37*, 942–954.

Taylor, S. E. (2006). Tend and befriend: Biobehavioral bases of affiliation under stress. *Current Directions in Psychological Science, 15*, 273–277.

Taylor, S. E., & Sherman, D. K. (2008). Self-enhancement and self-affirmation: The consequences of positive self-thoughts for motivation and health. In J. Y. Shah & W. L. Gardner (Eds.), *Handbook of motivation science* (pp. 57–70). New York: Guilford Press.

Tellegen, A. (1985). Structures of mood and personality and their relevance to assessing anxiety with an emphasis on self-report. In A. H. Tuma & J. D. Maser (Eds.), *Anxiety and the anxiety disorders* (pp. 681–706). Hillsdale, NJ: Erlbaum.

Tennen, H., Suls, J., & Weiner, I. B. (Eds.). (2013). *Handbook of psychology, Vol. 5. Personality and social psychology (*2nd ed.). Hoboken, NJ: Wiley.

Terhune, D. B., Cardeña, E., & Lindgren, M. (2011). Dissociative tendencies and individual differences in high hypnotic suggestibility. *Cognitive Neuropsychiatry, 16*, 113–135.

Terman, L. M. (1906). Genius and stupidity: A study of some of the intellectual processes of seven "bright" and seven "stupid" boys. *Pedagogical Seminary, 13*, 307–373.

Terracciano, A., Löckenhoff, C. E., Zonderman, A. B., Ferrucci, L., & Costa, P. T. Jr. (2008). Personality predictors of longevity: Activity, emotional stability, and conscientiousness. *Psychosomatic Medicine, 70*, 621–627.

Terrace, H. S. (1979, November). How Nim Chimpsky changed my mind. *Psychology Today*, pp. 65–76.

Tesarz, J., Schuster, A. K., Hartmann, M., Gerhardt, A., & Eich, W. (2012). Pain perception in athletes compared to normally active controls: A systematic review with meta-analysis. *Pain, 153*, 1253–1262.

Teunissen, H. A., Spijkerman, R., Prinstein, M. G., Cohen, G. L., Engles, R. C., & Scholte, R. H. (2012). Adolescents' conformity to their peers' pro-alcohol and anti-alcohol norms: The power of popularity. *Alcoholism: Clinical and Experimental Research, 36*, 1257–1267.

Thaler, J. P., Yi, C. X., Schur, E. A., Guyenet, S. J., Hwang, B. H., Dietrich, M. O., . . . Schwartz, M. W. (2012). Obesity is associated with hypothalamic injury in rodent models and humans. *Journal of Clinical Investigations, 122*, 153–162.

Thaler, N. S., Allen, D. N., & Goldstein, G. (2013). Bipolar disorders. In C. A. Noggle & R. S. Dean (Eds.), *Contemporary neuropsychology. The neuropsychology of psychopathology* (pp. 221–242). New York: Springer.

Thoits, P. A. (2010). Stress and health: Major findings and policy implications. *Journal of Health and Social Behavior, 51*, S41–S53.

Thomas, B. (2012). What's so special about mirror neurons? Retrieved from http://scientificamerican.com/2012/11/06/whats-so-special-about-mirror-neurons/

Thompson, D. (2013, July 15). Could a gene help make you obese? US News. Retrieved from http://health.usnews.com/health-news/news/articles/2013/07/15/could-a-gene-help-make-you-obese

Thompson, R. F. (2005). In search of memory traces. *Annual Review of Clinical Psychology, 56*, 1–23.

Thomson, C. J., Hanna, C. W., Carlson, S. R., & Rupert, J. L. (2013). The– 521 C/T variant in the dopamine 4 receptor gene (DRD4) is associated with skiing and snowboarding behavior. *Scandinavian Journal of Medicine & Science in Sports, 23*, 108–113.

Thornton, B., & Tizard, H. J. (2010). "Not in my back yard": Evidence for arousal moderating vested interest and oppositional behavior to proposed change. *Social Psychology, 41*, 255–262.

Thornton, M. A., & Conway, A. R. (2013). Working memory for social information: Chunking or domain-specific buffer?. *NeuroImage, 70*, 233–239.

Thurstone, L. L. (1938). *Primary mental abilities*. Chicago: University of Chicago Press.

Thyer, B. A., & Myers, L. L. (2011). The quest for evidence-based practice: A view from the United States. *Journal of Social Work, 11*, 8–25.

Thyssen, A., Stavermann, M., Buddrus, K., Doengi, M., Ekberg, J., A., St John, J. A., . . . Lohr, C. (2013). Spatial and developmental heterogeneity of calcium signaling in olfactory ensheathing cells. *Glia, 61*, 327–337.

Tindale, R. S., Talbot, M., & Martinez, R. (2013). Decision making. In J. M. Levine (Ed.), *Frontiers of social psychology. Group processes* (pp. 165–192). New York: Psychology Press.

Tindale, S., & Posavac, E. (2011). The social psychology of stakeholder processes: Group processes and interpersonal relations. In M. Mark, S. Donaldson, & B. Campbell (Eds.) *Social psychology and evaluation* (pp. 189–209). New York: Guilford Press.

Todd, A. R., Bodenhausen, G. V., Richeson, J. A., & Galinsky, A. D. (2011). Perspective taking combats automatic expressions of racial bias. *Journal of Personality and Social Psychology, 100*, 1027–1042.

Todd, P. M., & Gigerenzer, G. (2000). Precis of simple heuristics that make us smart. *Behavioral and Brain Sciences, 23*, 727.

Tomasetto, C., & Appoloni, S. (2013). A lesson not to be learned? Understanding stereotype threat does not protect women from stereotype threat. *Social Psychology of Education, 16*, 199–213.

Tomash, J. J., & Reed, P. (2013). The generalization of a conditioned response to deception across the public/private barrier. *Learning and Motivation, 44*, 196–203.

Tomkins, S. S. (1962). *Affect, imagery, consciousness: Vol. 1. The positive effects.* New York: Springer.

Tompkins, T. L., Hockett, A. R., Abraibesh, N., & Witt, J. L. (2011). A closer look at co-rumination: Gender, coping, peer functioning and internalizing/externalizing problems. *Journal of Adolescence, 34*, 801–811.

Topham, G. L., Hubbs-Tait, L., Rutledge, J. M., Page, M. C., Kennedy, T. S., Shriver, L. H., & Harrist, A. W. (2011). Parenting styles, parental response to child emotion, and family emotional responsiveness are related to child emotional eating. *Appetite, 56*, 261–264.

Torry, Z. D., & Billick, S. B. (2011). Implications of antisocial parents. *Psychiatric Quarterly, 82*, 275–285.

Trawick-Smith, J., & Dziurgot, T. (2011). 'Good-fit' teacher–child play interactions and the subsequent autonomous play of preschool children. *Early Childhood Research Quarterly, 26*, 110–123.

Tronci, V., & Balfour, D. J. K. (2011). The effects of the mGluR5 receptor antagonist 6-methyl-2-(phenylethynyl)-pyridine (MPEP) on the stimulation of dopamine release evoked by nicotine in the rat brain. *Behavioural Brain Research, 219*, 354–357.

Trost, S., Platz, B., Usher, J., Scherk, H., Wobrock, T., Ekawardhani, S., . . . Gruber, O. (2013). The DTNBP1 (dysbindin-1) gene variant rs2619522 is associated with variation of hippocampal and prefrontal grey matter Vols. in humans. *European Archives of Psychiatry and Clinical Neuroscience, 263*, 53–63.

Trull, T. J., Carpenter, R. W., & Widiger, T. A. (2013). Personality disorders. In G. Stricker, T. A. Widiger, & I. B. Weiner (Eds.), *Handbook of psychology, Vol. 8. Clinical psychology* (2nd ed., pp. 94–120). Hoboken, NJ: Wiley.

Trzaskowski, M., Davis, O. S. P., DeFries, J. C., Yang, J., Visscher, P., M., & Plomin, R. (2013). Dna evidence for strong genome-wide pleiotropy of cognitive and learning abilities. *Behavior Genetics*, 43, 267–273.

Trzaskowski, M., Yang, J., Visscher, P. M., & Plomin, R. (2013). DNA evidence for strong genetic stability and increasing heritability of intelligence from age 7 to 12. *Molecular Psychiatry*. Advance online publication. doi: 10.1038/mp.2012.191

Tsien, J. Z. (2000, April). Building a brainier mouse. *Scientific American*, pp. 62–68.

Tsoukalas, I. (2012). The origin of REM sleep: A hypothesis. *Dreaming, 22*, 253–283.

Tulving, E., & Thompson, D. M. (1973). Encoding specificity and retrieval processes in episodic memory. *Psychological Review, 80*, 352–373.

Turnbull, D. L., Cox, B. J., Oleski, J., & Katz, L. Y. (2013). The effects of borderline personality disorder and panic disorder on suicide attempts and the associated influence of affective dysregulation in the general population. *The Journal of Nervous and Mental Disease, 201*, 130–135.

Turner, M., & Barker, J. B. (2013). Examining the efficacy of rational-emotive behavior therapy (REBT) on irrational beliefs and anxiety in elite youth cricketers. *Journal of Applied Sport Psychology, 25*, 131–147.

Tversky, A., & Kahneman, D. (1974). Judgment under uncertainty: Heuristics and biases. *Science, 185*, 1124–1131.

Tversky, A., & Kahneman, D. (1993). Probabilistic reasoning. In A. I. Goldman (Ed.), *Readings in philosophy and cognitive science* (pp. 43–68). Cambridge, MA: MIT Press.

Tyson, P. J., Jones, D., & Elcock, J. (2011). *Psychology in social context: Issues and debates*. Malden, MA: Wiley-Blackwell.

Ueno, M., Uchiyama, I., Campos, J. J., Dahl, A., & Anderson, D. I. (2012). The organization of wariness of heights in experienced crawlers. *Infancy, 11*, 376–392.

Ulrich, R. E., Stachnik, T. J., & Stainton, N. R. (1963). Student acceptance of generalized personality interpretations. *Psychological Reports, 13*, 831–834.

Unsworth, N., Spillers, G. J., & Brewer, G. A. (2012). Dynamics of context-dependent recall: An examination of internal and external context change. *Journal of Memory and Language, 66*, 1–16.

Urry, H. L., Roeser, R. W., Lazar, S. W., & Poey, A. P. (2012). Prefrontal cortical activation during emotion regulation: Linking religious/spiritual practices with well-being. In A. E. A. Warren, R. M. Lerner, & E. Phelps (Eds.), *Thriving and spirituality among youth: Research perspectives and future possibilities* (pp. 19–29). Hoboken, NJ: Wiley.

Vaillancourt, T. (2013). Students aggress against professors in reaction to receiving poor grades: An effect moderated by student narcissism and self-esteem. *Aggressive Behavior, 39*, 71–84.

Van de Carr, F. R., & Lehrer, M. (1997). *While you are expecting: Your own prenatal classroom*. New York: Humanics Publishing.

Van Der Kloet, D., Giesbrecht, T., Franck, E., Van Gastel, A., De Volder, I., Van Den Eede, F., . . . Merckelbach, H. (2013). Dissociative symptoms and sleep parameters—an all-night polysomnography study in patients with insomnia. *Comprehensive Psychiatry, 54*, 658–664.

van der Laan, L. N., de Ridder, D. T. D., Viergever, M. A., & Smeets, P. A. M. (2011). The first taste is always with the eyes: A meta-analysis on the neural correlates of processing visual food cues. *NeuroImage, 55*, 296–303.

Van Gordon, W., Shonin, E., Sumich, A., Sundin, E. C., & Griffiths, M. D. (2013). Meditation awareness training (mat) for psychological well-being in a sub-clinical sample of university students: A controlled pilot study. *Mindfulness*. Advance online publication. 10.1007/s12671-012-0191-5.

Van Horn, J. D., Irimia, A., Torgerson, C. M., Chambers, M. C., Kikinis, R., & Toga, A. W. (2012). Mapping connectivity damage in the case of Phineas Gage. *PLoS ONE, 7*. Article ID e37454.

Van Iddekinge, C. H., Roth, P. L., Raymark, P. H., & Odle-Dusseau, H. N. (2012). The critical role of the research question, inclusion criteria, and transparency in meta-analyses of integrity test research: A reply to Harris et al. (2012) and Ones, Viswesvaran, and Schmidt (2012). *Journal of Applied Psychology, 97*, 543–549.

van Ijzendoorn, M. H., Bakermans-Kranenburg, M. J., Pannebakker, F., & Out, D. (2013). In defence of situational morality: Genetic, dispositional, and situational determinants of children's donation to charity. *Journal of Moral Education, 39*, 1–20.

van Laar, M. (2012). Epidemiology of alcohol and drug use. In J. C. Verster, K. Brady, M. Galanter, & P. Conrod (Eds.), *Drug abuse and addiction in medical illness: Causes, consequences and treatment* (pp. 3–23). New York: Springer Science + Business Media.

Vandenbosch, L., & Eggermont, S. (2011). *Temptation Island, The Bachelor, Joe Millionaire*: A prospective cohort study on the role of romantically themed reality television in adolescents' sexual development. *Journal of Broadcasting & Electronic Media, 56*, 563–580.

Vasey, M. W., Vilensky, M. R., Heath, J. H., Harbaugh, C. N., Buffington, A. G., & Fazio, R. H. (2012). It was as big as my head, I swear! *Journal of Anxiety Disorders, 26*, 20–24.

Vaughn, D. (1996). *The Challenger launch decision: Risky technology, culture, and deviance at NASA*. Chicago, IL: University of Chicago Press.

Vaz-Leal, F., Rodríguez-Santos, L, García-Herráiz, A., & Ramos-Fuentes, I. (2011). Neurobiological and psychopathological variables related to emotional instability: A study of their capability to discriminate patients with bulimia nervosa from healthy controls. *Neuropsychobiology, 63*, 242–251.

Verleger, R., Ludwig, J., Kolev, V., Yordanova, J., & Wagner, U. (2011). Sleep effects on slow-brain-potential reflections of associative learning. *Biological Psychology, 86*, 219–229.

Vernon, A. (2011). Rational emotive behavior therapy. In D. Capuzzi & D. R. Gross (Eds.), *Counseling and psychotherapy* (5th ed., pp. 237–261). Alexandria, VA: American Counseling Association.

Veselka, L., Schermer, J. A., & Vernon, P. (2011). Beyond the big five: The dark triad and the Supernumerary Personality Inventory. *Twin Research and Human Genetics, 14*, 158–168.

Vidal, S. G. M., Hornik, A., & Morgan, C. (2012). Cocaine induced hippocampi infarction. *BMJ Case Reports*, Retrieved from http://casereports.bmj.com/content/2012/bcr.03.2012.5998.full

Viena, T. D., Banks, J. B., Barbu, I. M., Schulman, A. H., & Tartar, J. L. (2012). Differential effects of mild chronic stress on cortisol and S-IgA responses to an acute stressor. *Biological Psychology, 91*, 307–311.

Vitulano, N., Di Marco, B. A., Re, A., Riccioni, G., Perna, F., Mormile, F., . . . Bellocci, F. (2013). Obstructive sleep apnea and heart disease: the biomarkers point of view. *Frontiers in Bioscience (Scholar edition), 5*, 588.

Vokey, J. R., & Read, J. D. (1985). Subliminal messages: Between the devil and the media. *American Psychologist, 40*, 1231–1239.

Völker, S. (2007). Infants' vocal engagement oriented towards mother versus stranger at 3 months and avoidant attachment behavior at 12 months. *International Journal of Behavioral Development, 31*, 88–95.

Völlink, T., Bolman, C. A., Dehue, F., & Jacobs, N. C. (2013). Coping with cyberbullying: Differences between victims, bully-victims and children not involved in bullying. *Journal of Community & Applied Social Psychology*, *23*, 7–24.

von Dawans, B., Fischbacher, U., Kirschbaum, C., Fehr, E., & Heinrichs, M. (2012). The social dimension of stress reactivity: Acute stress increases prosocial behavior in humans. *Psychological Science, 23*, 651–660.

von Hofsten, C. (2013). Action in infancy: A foundation for cognitive development. In W. Prinz, M. Beisert, & A. Herwig (Eds.), *Action science foundation of an emerging discipline* (pp. 255–280). New York: Oxford University Press.

Voss, C., & Sandercock, G. R. H. (2013). Associations between perceived parental physical activity and aerobic fitness in schoolchildren. *Journal of Physical Activity and Health, 10*, 397–405.

Vrticka, P., Simioni, S., Fornari, E., Schluep, M., Vuilleumier, P., & Sander, D. (2013). Neural substrates of social emotion regulation: A fMRI study on imitation and expressive suppression to dynamic facial signals. *Frontiers in Psychology, 4*, Article 95. doi: 10.3389/fpsyg.2013.00095

Wachholtz, A. B., & Austin, E. T. (2013). Contemporary spiritual meditation: Practices and outcomes. In K. I. Pargament, J. J. Exline, & J. W. Jones (Eds.), *APA handbooks in psychology. APA handbook of psychology, religion, and spirituality (Vol. 1): Context, theory, and research* (pp. 311–327). Washington, DC: American Psychological Association.

Wachlarowicz, M., Snyder, J., Low, S., Forgatch, M., & DeGarmo, D. (2012). The moderating effects of parent antisocial characteristics on the effects of Parent Management Training-Oregon (PMTOTM). *Prevention Science, 13*, 229–240.

Wachtel, P. L. (2011). *Inside the session: What really happens in psychotherapy.* Washington, DC: American Psychological Association.

Waller, N. G., & Ross, C. A. (1997). The prevalence and biometric structure of pathological dissociation in the general population: Taxometric and behavior genetics findings. *Journal of Abnormal Psychology, 106*, 499–510.

Walsh, E., Hooven, C., & Kronick, B. (2013). School-wide staff and faculty training in suicide risk awareness: Successes and challenges. *Journal of Child and Adolescent Psychiatric Nursing, 26*, 53–61.

Walsh, K., & Cross, W. (2013). Depression: Classification, culture and the westernisation of mental illness. In N. Kocabasoglu (Ed.), *Mood disorders*. Retrieved from http://cdn.intechopen.com/pdfs/42233/InTech-Depression_classification_culture_and_the_westernisation_of_mental_illness.pdf

Walton, G. M. & Cohen, G. L. (2011). A brief social-belonging intervention improves academic and health outcomes of minority students. *Science, 331*, 1447–1451.

Wamsley, E. J., Hirota, Y., Tucker, M. A., Smith, M. R., Doan, T., & Antrobus, J. S. (2007). Circadian and ultradian influences on dreaming: A dual rhythm model. *Brain Research Bulletin, 71*, 347–354.

Wamsley, E. J., & Stickgold, R. (2010). Dreaming and offline memory processing. *Current Biology, 20*, 1010–1913.

Wang, H., Fang, H., Dai, J., Liu, G., & Xu, Z. J. (2013). Induced pluripotent stem cells for spinal cord injury: Current status and perspective. *Neurological Sciences, 34*, 11–17.

Wang, J., Yuan, W., & Li, M. D. (2011). Genes and pathways co-associated with the exposure to multiple drugs of abuse, including alcohol, amphetamine/methamphetamine, cocaine, marijuana, morphine, and/or nicotine: A review of proteomics analyses. *Molecular Neurobiology, 44*, 269–286.

Wansink, B., & van Ittersum, K. (2012). Fast food restaurant lighting and music can reduce calorie intake and increase satisfaction. *Psychological Reports, 111*, 228–232.

Warneken, F., & Tomasello, M. (2008). Extrinsic rewards undermine altruistic tendencies in 20-month-olds. *Developmental Psychology, 44*, 1785–1788.

Warren, K. R., & Murray, M. M. (2013). Alcohol and pregnancy: Fetal alcohol spectrum disorders and the fetal alcohol syndrome. In P. Boyle, P. Boffetta, A. B. Lowenfels, H. B. Burns, O. Brawley, W. Zatonski, & J. Rehm. (Eds.), *Alcohol: Science, Policy and Public Health* (pp. 307–347). *New York: Oxford University Press.*

Warren, P. (2013). *Introducing psycholinguistics*. Cambridge, UK: Cambridge University Press.

Warrington, N. M., Wu, Y. Y., Pennell, C. E., Marsh, J. A., Beilin, L. J., Palmer, L. J., . . . Briollais, L. (2013). Modelling BMI trajectories in children for genetic association studies. *PloS ONE, 8*, e53897.

Wasserman, S., Weisman, A., & Suro, G. (2013). Nonreligious coping and religious coping as predictors of expressed emotion in relatives of patients with schizophrenia. *Mental Health, Religion & Culture, 16*, 16–30.

Watkins, M. W., & Smith, L. G. (2013). Long-term stability of the Wechsler Intelligence Scale for Children—Fourth Edition. *Psychological Assessment, 25*, 477–483.

Weaver, J. (2012). A new look at "filler cells" in the brain reveals their role in learning. *PLoS Biology, 10*, Article e1001263.

Weber, M. T., Rubin, L. H., & Maki, P. M. (2013). Cognition in perimenopause: The effect of transition stage. *Menopause, 20*, 511–517.

Wechsler, D. (1944). *The measurement of adult intelligence* (3rd ed.). Baltimore, MD: Williams & Wilkins.

Wechsler, D. (1977). *Manual for the Wechsler Intelligence Scale for Children* (Rev.). New York: Psychological Corporation.

Weems, C. F., Scott, B. G., Banks, D. M., & Graham, R. A. (2012). Is T.V. traumatic for all youths? The role of preexisting posttraumatic-stress symptoms in the link between disaster coverage and stress. *Psychological Science, 23*, 1293–1297.

Weinberger, D., & Harrison, P. (Eds.). (2011). *Schizophrenia* (3rd ed.). Hoboken, NJ: Wiley.

Weiner, B. (1972). *Theories of motivation.* Chicago, IL: Rand-McNally.

Weiner, B. (1982). The emotional consequences of causal attributions. In M. S. Clark & S. T. Fiske (Eds.), *Affect and cognition.* Hillsdale, NJ: Erlbaum.

Weiner, B. (2006). *Social motivation, justice, and the moral emotions: An attributional approach.* Mahwah, NJ: Erlbaum.

Weinstein, N., Ryan, W. S., DeHaan, C. R., Przybylski, A. K., Legate, N., & Ryan, R. M. (2012). Parental autonomy support and discrepancies between implicit and explicit sexual identities: Dynamics of self-acceptance and defense. *Journal of Personality and Social Psychology, 102,* 815–832.

Weisberg, R. & Reeves, L. (2013). *Cognition: From memory to creativity.* Hoboken, NJ: Wiley.

Weisman, O., Zagoory-Sharon, O., & Feldman, R. (2012). Oxytocin administration to parent enhances infant physiological and behavioral readiness for social engagement. *Biological Psychiatry, 72,* 982–989.

Weiss, A., Gartner, M. C., Gold, K. C., & Stoinski, T. S. (2013). Extraversion predicts longer survival in gorillas: An 18-year longitudinal study. *Proceedings of the Royal Society B.* doi: 10.1098/rspb.2012.2231

Weitlauf, J. C., Cervone, D., Smith, R. E., & Wright, P. M. (2001). Assessing-generalization in perceived self-efficacy: Multidomain and global assessments of the effects of self-defense training for women. *Personality and Social Psychology Bulletin, 27,* 1683–1691.

West, R., Meserve, R., & Stanovich, K. (2012). Cognitive sophistication does not attenuate the bias blind spot. *Journal of Personality and Social Psychology, 103,* 506–519.

Westen, D. (1998). Unconscious thought, feeling, and motivation: The end of a centurylong debate. In R. F. Bornstein & J. M. Masling (Eds.), *Empirical perspectives on the psychoanalytic unconscious* (pp. 1–43). Washington, DC: American Psychological Association.

Weyandt, L. L., Verdi, G., & Swentosky, A. (2011). Oppositional, conduct, and aggressive disorders. In S. Goldstein & C. R. Reynolds (Eds.), *Handbook of neurodevelopmental and genetic disorders in children* (2nd ed., pp. 151–170). New York: Guilford Press.

Whalen, P. J., Kim, M. J., Neta, M., & Davis, F. C. (2013). Emotion. In R. J. Nelson, S. J. Y. Mizumori, & I. B. Weiner (Eds.), *Handbook of psychology, Vol. 3. Behavioral neuroscience (2nd ed.,* pp. 422–439). Hoboken, NJ: Wiley.

Whalen, P. J., Raila, H., Bennett, R., Mattek, A., Brown, A., Taylor, J., . . . Palmer, A. (2013). Neuroscience and facial expressions of emotion: The role of amygdala–prefrontal interactions. *Emotion Review, 5,* 78–83.

Whaley, A., Smith, M., & Hancock, A. (2011). Ethnic/racial differences in the self-reported physical and mental health correlates of adolescent obesity. *Journal of Health Psychology, 16,* 1048–1057.

Whalley, L. J. (2011). Brain lesions, hypertension and cognitive ageing in the 1921 and 1936 Aberdeen birth cohorts. *Age, 34,* 451–459.

Wheaton, A. G., Perry, G. S., Chapman, D. P., & Croft, J. B. (2012). Sleep disordered breathing and depression among U.S. adults: National Health and Nutrition Examination Survey, 2005–2008. *Sleep, 35,* 461–467.

Whitbourne, S. K. (2011). *Adult development and aging: Biopsychosocial perspectives* (4th ed.). Hoboken, NJ: Wiley.

White, H. R., Fite, P., Pardini, D., Mun, E.-Y., & Loeber, R. (2013). Moderators of the dynamic link between alcohol use and aggressive behavior among adolescent males. *Journal of Abnormal Child Psychology, 41,* 211–222.

White, T., Andreasen, N. C., & Nopoulos, P. (2002). Brain volumes and surface morphology in monozygotic twins. *Cerebral Cortex, 12,* 486–493.

Wickramasekera, I., II. (2008b). Review of hypnotizability, absorption and negative cognitions as predictors of dental anxiety: Two pilot studies. *American Journal of Clinical Hypnosis, 50,* 285–286.

Widiger, T. A. (Ed.). (2013). Diagnosis and classification. In G. Stricker, T. A. Widiger, & I. B. Weiner (Eds.), *Handbook of psychology, Vol. 8. Clinical psychology* (2nd ed., pp. 3–18). Hoboken, NJ: Wiley.

Wiener, H., Klei, L., Calkins, M., Wood, J., Nimgaonkar, V., Gur, R., . . . Go, R. (2013). Principal components of heritability from neurocognitive domains differ between families with schizophrenia and control subjects. *Schizophrenia Bulletin, 39,* 464–471.

Wikgren, M., Maripuu, M., Karlsson, T., Nordfjäll, K., Bergdahl, J., Hultdin, J., . . . Norrback, K-F. (2011). Short telomeres in depression and the general population are associated with a hypocortisolemic state. *Biological Psychiatry, 71,* 294–300.

Wille, B., De Fruyt, F., & De Clercq, B. (2013). Expanding and reconceptualizing aberrant personality at work: Validity of Five-Factor Model aberrant personality tendencies to predict career outcomes. *Personnel Psychology, 66,* 173–223.

Williams, J. E. (2010). Anger/hostility and cardiovascular disease. In M. Potegal, G. Stemmler, & C. Spielberger (Eds.), *International handbook of anger: Constituent and concomitant biological, psychological, and social processes* (pp. 435–447). New York: Springer Science 1 Business Media.

Williams, M. R., Chaudhry, R., Perera, S., Pearce, R. K. B., Hirsch, S. R., Ansorge, O., . . . Maier, M. (2013). Changes in cortical thickness in the frontal lobes in schizophrenia are a result of thinning of pyramidal cell layers. *European Archives of Psychiatry and Clinical Neuroscience, 263,* 25–39.

Williams, S. C. P. (2013, July 15). Obesity gene linked to hunger hormone. *Science NOW.* Retrieved from http://news.sciencemag.org/sciencenow/2013/07/obesity-gene-linked-to-hunger-ho.html?ref=em#.UeTHLsf3tP0.email

Williams, S. S. (2001). Sexual lying among college students in close and casual relationships. *Journal of Applied Social Psychology, 31,* 2322–2338.

Williamson, A., Lombardi, D. A., Folkard, S., Stutts, J., Courtney, T. K., & Connor, J. L. (2011). The link between fatigue and safety. *Accident Analysis and Prevention, 43,* 498–515.

Williamson, J. M., Lounsbury, J. W., & Han, L. D. (2013). Key personality traits of engineers for innovation and technology development. *Journal of Engineering and Technology Management, 30,* 157–168.

Williamson, M. (1997). Circumcision anesthesia: A study of nursing implication for dorsal penile nerve block. *Pediatric Nursing, 23,* 59–63.

Willingham, D.B. (2001). *Cognition: The thinking animal.* Upper Saddle River, NJ: Prentice Hall.

Willyard, C. (2011). Men: A growing minority. *gradPSYCH, 9,* 40–44.

Wilner, B. (February 5, 2011). Vick wins Comeback Player award. *Associated Press.* Retrieved from http://news.yahoo.com/s/ap/20110206/ap_on_sp_fo_ne/fbn_comeback_player.

Wilson, G. T. (2011). Behavior therapy. In R. J. Corsini & D. Wedding (Eds,), *Current psychotherapy* (9th ed., pp. 235–275). Florence, KY: Cengage Learning.

Wilson, S., & Nutt, D. (2008). *Sleep disorders.* London, England: Oxford University Press.

Winder, G. S., Stern, N., & Hosanagar, A. (2013). Are "bath salts" the next generation of stimulant abuse? *Journal of Substance Abuse Treatment, 44,* 42–45.

Winerman, L. (2004). Sleep deprivation threatens public health, says research award winner. *Monitor on Psychology, 35,* 61.

Wirtz, D., & Chiu, C-Y. (2008). Perspectives on the self in the East and the West: Searching for the quiet ego. In A. H. Wayment & J. J. Bauer (Eds.), *Transcending self-interest: Psychological explorations of the quiet ego. Decade of behavior* (pp. 149–158). Washington, DC: American Psychological Association.

Wiste, A. K., Arango, V., Ellis, S. P., Mann, J. J., & Underwood, M. D. (2008). Norepinephrine and serotonin imbalance in the locus coeruleus in bipolar disorder. *Bipolar Disorders, 10*, 349–359.

Witelson, S. F., Kigar, D. L., & Harvey, T. (1999). The exceptional brain of Albert Einstein. *The Lancet, 353*, 2149–2153.

Wolpe, J., & Plaud, J. J. (1997). Pavlov's contributions to behavior therapy. *American Psychologist, 52*, 966–972.

Wood, B., Rea, M. S., Plitnick, B., & Figueiro, M. G. (2012). Light level and duration of exposure determine the impact of self-luminous tablets on melatonin suppression. *Applied Ergonomics, 44*, 237–240.

Wood, J. M., Nezworski, T., Lilienfeld, S. O., & Garb, H. N. (2011). *What's wrong with the Rorschach: Science confronts the controversial inkblot test.* Hoboken, NJ: Wiley/ JosseyBass.

Wood, J. T. (2013). *Gendered lives*. Belmont, CA: Wadsworth.

Wood, R. L., & Thomas, R. H. (2013). Impulsive and episodic disorders of aggressive behaviour following traumatic brain injury. *Brain Injury, 27*, 253–261.

Woods, R. J., & Wilcox, T. (2013). Posture support improves object individuation in infants. *Developmental Psychology, 49*, 1413–1424.

Wright, A. J. (2011). *Conducting psychological assessment: A guide for practitioners.* Hoboken, NJ: Wiley.

Wright, D. S., Wade, K. A., & Watson, D. G. (2013). Delay and déjà vu: Timing and repetition increase the power of false evidence. *Psychonomic Bulletin & Review*, 20, 812–818.

Wryobeck, J. M., Haines, M. E., Wynkoop, T. F., & Swanson, M. M. (2013). Depressive disorders. In C. A. Noggle & R. S. Dean (Eds.), *Contemporary neuropsychology. The neuropsychology of psychopathology* (pp. 201–220). New York: Springer.

Wu, T., Liu, J., Hallett, M., Zheng, Z., & Chan, P. (2013). Cerebellum and integration of neural networks in dual-task processing. *NeuroImage, 65*, 466–475.

Wulandari, L. P. L., Craig, P., & Whelan, A. K. (2013). Foetal health locus of control and iron supplementation adherence among pregnant women in Bali. *Journal of Reproductive & Infant Psychology, 31*, 94–101.

Wyman, A. J., & Vyse, S. (2008). Science versus the stars: A double-blind test of the validity of the NEO five-factor inventory and computer-generated astrological natal charts. *Journal of General Psychology, 135*, 287–300.

Wyse, C. A. (2012). Does human evolution in different latitudes influence susceptibility to obesity via the circadian pacemaker? *BioEssays, 34*, 921–924.

Xia, Q., & Grant, S. F. (2013). The genetics of human obesity. *Annals of the New York Academy of Sciences, 1281*, 178–190.

Xu, L., & Barnes, L. (2011). Measurement invariance of scores from the inventory of school motivation across Chinese and U.S. college students. *International Journal of Testing, 11*, 178–210.

Xu, Y., Schneier, F., Heimberg, R. G., Princisvalle, K., Liebowitz, M. R., Wang, S., & Blanco, C. (2012). Gender differences in social anxiety disorder: Results from the national epidemiologic sample on alcohol and related conditions. *Journal of Anxiety Disorders, 26*, 12–19.

Yamada, H. (1997). *Different games, different rules: Why Americans and Japanese misunderstand each other.* London, England: Oxford University Press.

Yantis, S. (2013). *Sensation and perception*. New York: Worth.

Yin, F., Tian, Z-M., Liu, S., Zhao, Q-J., Wang, R-M., Shen, L., . . . Yan, Y. (2012). Transplantation of human retinal pigment epithelium cells in the treatment for Parkinson disease. *CNS Neuroscience and Therapeutics, 18*, 1012–1020.

You, S., Hong, S., & Ho, H. Z. (2011). Longitudinal effects of perceived control on academic achievement. *Journal of Educational Research, 104*, 253–266.

Young, R. M., Connor, J. P., & Feeney, G. F. X. (2011). Alcohol expectancy changes over a 12-week cognitive–behavioral therapy program are predictive of treatment success. *Journal of Substance Abuse Treatment, 40*, 18–25.

Young, S. G., Brown, C. M., & Ambady, N. (2012). Priming a natural or human-made environment directs attention to context-congruent threatening stimuli. *Cognition & Emotion, 26*, 927–933.

Young, T. (1802). On the theory of light and colours. *Philosophical Transactions of the Royal Society, 92*, 12–48.

Yu, C. K.-C. (2012). Dream motif scale. *Dreaming, 22*, 18–52.

Yu, J.-T., Ma, X.-Y., Wang, Y.-L., Sun, L., Tan, L., Hu, N., & Tan, L. (2013). Genetic variation in clusterin gene and alzheimer's disease risk in han chinese. *Neurobiology of Aging, 34*, e17-e23.

Yuen, E. Y., Wei, J., Liu, W., Zhong, P., Li, X., & Yan, Z. (2012). Repeated stress causes cognitive impairment by suppressing glutamate receptor expression and function in prefrontal cortex. *Neuron, 73*, 962–977.

Zampieri, M., & Pedrosa de Souza, E. A. (2011). Locus of control, depression, and quality of life in Parkinson's Disease. *Journal of Health Psychology, 16*, 980–987.

Zandi, T. (2013). Possible misclassification of psychotic symptoms among Moroccan immigrants in the Netherlands. In S. Barnow & N. Balkir (Eds.), *Cultural variations in psychopathology: From research to practice* (pp. 219–229). Cambridge, MA: Hogrefe Publishing.

Zarate, C. A. Jr., Brutsche, N. E., Ibrahim, L., Franco-Chaves, J., Diazgranados, N., Cravchik, A., . . . Luckenbaugh, D. A. (2012). Replication of ketamine's antidepressant efficacy in bipolar depression: A randomized controlled add-on trial. *Biological Psychiatry, 71*, 939–946.

Zelazo, P. D., Chandler, M., & Crone, E. (Eds.). (2010). *The Jean Piaget symposium series. Developmental social cognitive neuroscience*. New York: Psychology Press.

Zentner, M., & Mitura, K. (2012). Stepping out of the caveman's shadow: Nations' gender gap predicts degree of sex differentiation in mate preferences. *Psychological Science, 23*, 1176–1185.

Zerr, A. A., Holly, L. E., & Pina, A. A. (2011). Cultural influences on social anxiety in African American, Asian American, Hispanic and Latino, and Native American adolescents and young adults. In C. A. Alfano & D. C. Beidel (Eds.), *Social anxiety in adolescents and young adults: Translating developmental science into practice* (pp. 203–222). Washington, DC: American Psychological Association.

Zhang, L. F., & He, Y. F. (2011). Thinking styles and the Eriksonian stages. *Journal of Adult Development, 18*, 8–17.

Zhaoping, L., & Guyader, N. (2007). Interference with bottom-up feature detection by higher-level object recognition. *Current Biology, 17*, 26–31.

Zhou, J., & Urhahne, D. (2013). Teacher judgment, student motivation, and the mediating effect of attributions. *European Journal of Psychology of Education, 28*, 275–295.

Zhu, B., Chen, C., Loftus, E. F., He, Q., Chen, C., Lei, D., . . . Dong, Q. (2012). Brief exposure to misinformation can lead to long-term false memories. *Applied Cognitive Psychology, 26,* 301–307.

Zhu, D. H. (2013). Group polarization on corporate boards: Theory and evidence on board decisions about acquisition premiums. *Strategic Management Journal, 34,* 800–822.

Zhu, L., & Zee, P. C. (2012). Circadian rhythm sleep disorders. *Neurologic Clinics, 30,* 1167–1191.

Zimbardo, P. G. (1993). Stanford prison experiment: A 20-year retrospective. *Invited presentation at the meeting of the Western Psychological Association,* Phoenix, AZ.

Zink, D. N., Ojeda, C., Hernandez, M., & Puente, A. E. (2013). Generalized anxiety disorder and panic disorder. In C. A. Noggle & R. S. Dean (Eds.), *Contemporary neuropsychology. The neuropsychology of psychopathology* (pp. 243–260). New York: Springer.

Zuckerman, M. (2011). Psychodynamic approaches. In M. Zuckerman (Ed.), *Personality science: Three approaches and their applications to the causes and treatment of depression* (pp. 11–45). Washington, DC: American Psychological Association.

Zuckerman, M. (2013). Biological bases of personality. In H. Tennen, J.Suls, & I. B Weiner (Eds.), *Handbook of psychology, Vol. 5: Personality and social psychology* (2nd ed., pp. 27–42). Hoboken, NJ: Wiley.

Zvyagintsev, M., Clemens, B., Chechko, N., Mathiak, K. A., Sack, A. T., & Mathiak, K. (2013). Brain networks underlying mental imagery of auditory and visual information. *European Journal of Neuroscience, 37,* 1421–1434.

Zweig, J. (2007). *Your money and your brain: How the new science of neuroeconomics can help make you rich.* New York: Simon & Schuster.

Name Index

D

Subject Index

Note: Page numbers followed by a "t" indicate the entry may be found within a table. Page numbers followed by an "f" indicate the entry may be found within a figure.

50 GREAT MYTHS OF POPULAR PSYCHOLOGY

Shattering Widespread Misconceptions about Human Behavior

Scott O. Lilienfeld
Steven Jay Lynn
John Ruscio
Barry L. Beyerstein

WILEY-BLACKWELL
A John Wiley & Sons, Ltd., Publication

This edition first published 2010

Blackwell Publishing was acquired by John Wiley & Sons in February 2007. Blackwell's publishing program has been merged with Wiley's global Scientific, Technical, and Medical business to form Wiley-Blackwell.

Registered Office
John Wiley & Sons Ltd, The Atrium, Southern Gate, Chichester, West Sussex, PO19 8SQ, United Kingdom

Editorial Offices
350 Main Street, Malden, MA 02148-5020, USA
9600 Garsington Road, Oxford, OX4 2DQ, UK
The Atrium, Southern Gate, Chichester, West Sussex, PO19 8SQ, UK

For details of our global editorial offices, for customer services, and for information about how to apply for permission to reuse the copyright material in this book please see our website at www.wiley.com/wiley-blackwell.

Library of Congress Cataloging-in-Publication Data
50 great myths of popular psychology : shattering widespread misconceptions about human behavior / Scott O. Lilienfeld . . . [et al.].
p. cm.
Includes bibliographical references and index.
ISBN 978-1-4051-3111-7 (hardcover : alk. paper) — ISBN 978-1-4051-3112-4 (pbk. : alk. paper) 1. Psychology—Popular works. 2. Human behavior. I. Lilienfeld, Scott O., 1960– II. Title: Fifty great myths of popular psychology.
BF145.A15 2010
150—dc22
2009020179

A catalogue record for this book is available from the British Library.

Set in 10/12.5pt Sabon by Graphicraft Limited, Hong Kong
Printed in Singapore

1 2010

1 BRAIN POWER

Myths about the Brain and Perception

Myth #1 Most People Use Only 10% of Their Brain Power

Whenever those of us who study the brain venture out of the Ivory Tower to give public lectures or media interviews, one of the questions we're most likely to encounter is, "Is it true that we only use 10% of our brains?" The look of disappointment that usually follows when we respond, "Sorry, I'm afraid not," strongly suggests that the 10% myth is one of those hopeful truisms that refuses to die simply because it would be so darn nice if it were true (Della Sala, 1999; Della Sala & Beyerstein, 2007). Indeed, this myth is widespread, even among psychology students and other well-educated people. In one study, when asked "About what percentage of their potential brain power do you think most people use?," a third of psychology majors answered 10% (Higbee & Clay, 1998, p. 471). Fifty-nine percent of a sample of college-educated people in Brazil similarly believe that people use only 10% of their brains (Herculano-Houzel, 2002). Remarkably, that same survey revealed that even 6% of neuroscientists agreed with this claim!

Surely, none of us would turn down a hefty hike in brain power if we could achieve it. Not surprisingly, marketers who thrive on the public's fond hopes for a self-improvement breakthrough continue to peddle a never-ending stream of dubious schemes and devices premised on the 10% myth. Always on the lookout for a "feel-good" story, the media has played a big role in keeping this optimistic myth alive. A great deal of advertising copy for legitimate products continues to refer to the 10% myth as fact, usually in the hopes of flattering potential customers who see themselves as having risen above their brain's limitations. For example, in his popular book, *How to Be Twice as Smart*, Scott Witt

(1983) wrote that "If you're like most people, you're using only ten percent of your brainpower" (p. 4). In 1999, an airline tried to entice potential flyers by informing them that "It's been said that we use only 10% of our brain capacity. If, however, you're flying ____ (name of company deleted) Airlines, you're using considerably more" (Chudler, 2006).

Yet an expert panel convened by the U.S. National Research Council concluded that (alas!), in this, as with other miraculous self-improvement claims, there's no good substitute for hard work when it comes to getting ahead in life (Beyerstein, 1999c; Druckman & Swets, 1988). This unwelcome news has done little to discourage millions who comfort themselves with the belief that the shortcut to their unfulfilled dreams lies in the fact that they just haven't quite caught up with the secret for tapping their vast, allegedly unused cerebral reservoir (Beyerstein, 1999c). That desired promotion, stellar grade point average, or authorship of the next bestselling novel is within your grasp, say the sellers of cerebral miracle remedies.

Even more questionable are the offerings of New Age entrepreneurs who propose to hone the psychic skills we allegedly all possess with obscure gizmos for the brain. Self-proclaimed psychic Uri Geller (1996) claimed that "In fact, most of us use only about 10 percent of our brains, if that." Promoters like Geller imply that psychic powers reside in the 90% of the brain that simple folk forced to subsist on the drudge-like 10% haven't yet learned to use.

Why would a brain researcher doubt that 90% of the average brain lies silent? There are several reasons. First of all, our brain has been shaped by natural selection. Brain tissue is expensive to grow and operate; at a mere 2–3% of our body weight, it consumes over 20% of the oxygen we breathe. It's implausible that evolution would have permitted the squandering of resources on a scale necessary to build and maintain such a massively underutilized organ. Moreover, if having a bigger brain contributes to the flexibility that promotes survival and reproduction—which are natural selection's "bottom lines"—it's hard to believe that any slight increase in processing power wouldn't be snapped up immediately by existing systems in the brain to enhance the bearer's chances in the continuous struggle to prosper and procreate.

Doubts about the 10% figure are also fueled by evidence from clinical neurology and neuropsychology, two disciplines that aim to understand and alleviate the effects of brain damage. Losing far less than 90% of the brain to accident or disease almost always has catastrophic consequences. Look, for instance, at the much-publicized controversy surrounding the nonconscious status and ultimate death of Terri Schiavo, the young Florida woman who lay in a persistent vegetative state for 15 years (Quill, 2005). Oxygen deprivation following a cardiac arrest in 1990 had destroyed about 50% of her cerebrum, the upper part of the brain responsible for conscious awareness. Modern brain science argues that "mind" equals brain function. Therefore, patients like Ms. Schiavo had permanently lost the capacity for thoughts, perceptions, memories, and emotions that are the very essence of being human (Beyerstein, 1987). Although some claimed to see signs of consciousness in Schiavo, most impartial experts found no evidence that any of her higher mental processes had been spared. If 90% of the brain is indeed unnecessary, this shouldn't have been the case.

Research also reveals that no area of the brain can be destroyed by strokes or head trauma without leaving patients with serious deficits in functioning (Kolb & Whishaw, 2003; Sacks, 1985). Likewise, electrical stimulation of sites in the brain during neurosurgery has failed to uncover any "silent areas," those in which the person experiences no perception, emotion, or movement after neurosurgeons apply these tiny currents (neurosurgeons can accomplish this feat with conscious patients under local anesthesia because the brain contains no pain receptors).

The last century has witnessed the advent of increasingly sophisticated technologies for snooping on the brain's traffic (Rosenzweig, Breedlove, & Watson, 2005). With the aid of brain imaging techniques, such as electroencephologram (EEGs), positron emission tomography (PET) scanners, and functional magnetic resonance imaging (MRI) machines, researchers have succeeded in localizing a vast number of psychological functions to specific brain areas. With nonhuman animals, and occasionally with humans undergoing neurological treatment, researchers can insert recording probes into the brain. Despite this detailed mapping, no quiet areas awaiting new assignments have emerged. In fact, even simple tasks generally require contributions of processing areas spread throughout virtually the whole brain.

Two other firmly established principles of neuroscience create further problems for the 10% myth. Areas of the brain that are unused because of injuries or disease tend to do one of two things. They either wither away, or "degenerate," as neuroscientists put it, or they're taken over by nearby areas that are on the lookout for unused territory to colonize for their own purposes. Either way, perfectly good, unused brain tissue is unlikely to remain on the sidelines for long.

All told, evidence suggests that there's no cerebral spare tire waiting to be mounted with a little help from the self-improvement industry. So, if the 10% myth is so poorly supported, how did it get started? Attempts to track down this myth's origins haven't uncovered any smoking guns, but a few tantalizing clues have materialized (Beyerstein, 1999c; Chudler, 2006; Geake, 2008). One stream leads back to pioneering American psychologist William James in the late 19th and early 20th centuries. In one of his writings for the general public, James said he doubted that average persons achieve more than about 10% of their *intellectual potential.* James always talked in terms of underdeveloped potential, never relating it to a specific amount of the brain engaged. A slew of "positive thinking" gurus who followed weren't as careful, though, and "10% of our capacity" gradually morphed into "10% of our brain" (Beyerstein, 1999c). Undoubtedly, the biggest boost for the self-help entrepreneurs came when journalist Lowell Thomas attributed the 10% brain claim to William James. Thomas did so in the 1936 preface to one of the bestselling self-help books of all time, Dale Carnegie's *How to Win Friends and Influence People.* The myth has never lost its steam since.

The popularity of the 10% myth probably also stems partly from authors' misunderstandings of scientific papers by early brain researchers. In calling a huge percentage of the human cerebral hemispheres "silent cortex," early investigators may have fostered the mistaken impression that what scientists now call "association cortex" had no function. As we now know, association cortex is vitally important for our language, abstract thinking, and performance of intricate sensory-motor tasks. In a similar vein, early researchers' admirably modest admissions that they didn't know what 90% of the brain did probably contributed to the myth that it does nothing. Another possible source of confusion may have been laypersons' misunderstanding of the role of glial cells, brain cells that outnumber the brain's neurons (nerve cells) by a factor of about 10. Although neurons are the scene of the action with respect to thinking and other mental activities, glial cells perform essential support functions for the neurons that do the heavy lifting, psychologically speaking. Finally, those who've searched for the origins of the 10% myth frequently came across the claim that Albert Einstein once explained his own brilliance by reference to the myth. Nevertheless, a careful search by the helpful staff at the Albert Einstein archive on our behalf yielded no record of any such statement on his part. More likely than not, the promoters of the 10% myth simply seized on Einstein's prestige to further their own endeavors (Beyerstein, 1999c).

The 10% myth has surely motivated many people to strive for greater creativity and productivity in their lives, which certainly isn't a bad thing.

The comfort, encouragement, and hope that it's generated almost surely help to explain its longevity. But, as Carl Sagan (1995) reminded us (see *Introduction*, p. 11), if something sounds too good to be true, it probably is.

Myth #2 Some People Are Left-Brained, Others Are Right-Brained

The next time somebody tries to sell you a book or device for retraining your allegedly flabby right hemisphere, reach for your wallet. Then clasp it firmly to your chest and run as fast as you can. Like some other myths in this book, the one you're about to encounter has a grain of truth to it. Nevertheless, this grain can be a bit hard to find amidst the mounds of misinformation that bury it.

Are some people left-brained and others right-brained? There's good evidence that the two sides of the brain, called *hemispheres*, differ in their functions (Springer & Deutsch, 1997). For example, different abilities are more affected by injuries to one side of the brain than the other, and brain imaging techniques demonstrate that the hemispheres differ in their activity when people engage in various mental tasks. By far the most dramatic evidence for *laterality of function*—the superiority of one or the other hemisphere for performing certain tasks—comes from patients who've undergone a "split brain" operation. In this rarely performed procedure, surgeons sever the nerve tracts connecting opposite points in the brain's left and right hemispheres in a last-ditch attempt to control severe epilepsy. The large pathway connecting these hemispheres, the main target of the split-brain operation, is the corpus callosum ("colossal body").

Roger Sperry shared the Nobel Prize in 1981 for his landmark studies of split-brain patients, and a fascinating lot they are (Gazzaniga, 1998). Once they'd recovered from surgery, they appeared deceptively normal in their everyday activities. But once Sperry tested them in the laboratory, it became apparent that the two halves of their brains were working independently. Each side operated without awareness or knowledge of the other.

In Sperry's laboratory tests, patients fixate their eyes at the center of a screen, on which the researcher briefly flashes words or pictures. With the eyes immobilized, information flashed to the left of the fixation point goes to the right hemisphere and the opposite is true of information presented to the right of the fixation point (that's because the optic pathways on each side of the visual field cross over to the other side). In more ordinary situations, this separation of information doesn't occur because patients constantly move their eyes about their surroundings. As a result, the input normally reaches both hemispheres eventually. When it doesn't, though, some decidedly peculiar things can happen.

The right hemisphere receives input from and controls the movements of the left side of the body, and the left hemisphere does the same for the right. In almost all right-handers, and most lefties as well, the primary areas for language reception and production are in the left hemisphere. Thus, if we restrict new information to the right hemisphere, the left hemisphere—which is more verbal than the right—will be unable to tell us what the input was, and it may be perplexed to see the left hand acting on the segregated knowledge, for reasons it can't fathom.

For example, if the researcher shows the right hemisphere of a split-brain subject a photograph of a naked man, she may giggle. Yet when asked what she's giggling about, the subject (her left hemisphere, that is) won't be able to say. Instead, she may cook up a plausible-sounding reason ("That photo reminds me of my uncle George, who's a really funny guy"). Split-brain subjects may even do something with their right hand, like assemble a group of blocks to fit a pattern, utterly oblivious of the fact that their left hand is following a few seconds behind, undoing all the good work. This much is well established. The dispute concerns the uniqueness of the kinds of tasks handled by the two hemispheres and how they go about it. In this regard, brain researchers have become more cautious in recent years while many pop psychologists have run wild.

Using Sperry's techniques, researchers have confirmed that the left and right hemispheres are relatively better at different mental activities. Note, however, that we wrote *relatively* better. The two halves of the brain differ in how they process tasks rather than what they process (McCrone, 1999). Let's take language, for example. The left hemisphere is better at the specifics of speech, such as grammar and word generation, whereas the right hemisphere is better at the intonation and emphases of speech (what's known as "prosody"). Although the right hemisphere is better at nonlinguistic functions that involve complex visual and spatial processes, the left hemisphere plays some role in these capacities if we give it the chance. The right brain is better at dealing with a general sense of space, whereas corresponding areas in the left brain become active when the person locates objects in specific places. In many cases, it's not that one hemisphere or the other can't perform a given task; it's just that one of them can perform it faster and better than the other. So it tends to grab the assignment first.

Of course, ordinary people aren't, as left-brain/right-brain aficionados suggest, just split-brain patients who haven't gotten around to having their corpus callosums snipped. In the normal brain, the side that's first off the mark will call for help from across the way. As long as the left–right pathways are intact, the two hemispheres share information extensively. Indeed, brain imaging research shows that the two hemispheres routinely communicate during most tasks (Mercer, 2010). After a split-brain operation, this cooperation isn't possible, so the separated systems limp along as best they can.

Therefore, the ways in which the two sides of brain differ are far more limited than pop psychology's "hemisphericity" entrepreneurs suggest (Aamodt & Wang, 2008; Corballis, 1999, 2007; Della Sala, 1999). On balance, the two hemispheres are much more similar than different in their functions (Geake, 2008). Modern neuroscientists have never agreed with many New Age "hemisphere trainers," who claim that the brain's two halves house totally dissimilar minds that approach the world in radically different ways, with one (the left) side an accountant and the other (the right) side a veritable Zen master. Robert Ornstein was among those to promote the idea of using different ways to tap into our "creative" right brains versus our intellectual left brains in his 1997 book, *The Right Mind: Making Sense of the Hemispheres*. Moreover, scores of educational and business programs de-emphasize getting the "right" answers on tests in favor of harnessing creative ability. Such programs as the *Applied Creative Thinking Workshop* have trained business managers to develop the untapped capacities of their right brains (Hermann, 1996). Furthermore, the enormously successful book, *Drawing on the Right Side of the Brain* (Edwards, 1980), which has sold over 2.5 million copies, encourages readers to unleash their artistic abilities by suppressing their "analytical" left hemispheres. Even cartoonists have jumped on the bandwagon; one shows a student holding an exam emblazoned with a big "F" who tells his professor, "It's not fair to flunk me for being a right-brain thinker."

The urge on the part of pop psychologists to assign all mental abilities to unique left and right compartments probably owes more to politics, social values, and commercial interests than to science. Its detractors have dubbed this extreme view "dichotomania" because of pop psychologists' tendency to dichotomize the two hemispheres' functions (Corballis, 1999). The notion was embraced enthusiastically by New Age proponents of the 1970s and 1980s, largely because it offered a rationale for worldviews that were mystical and intuitive.

Pop psychologists further embellished genuine differences in how the hemispheres process information, proclaiming the allegedly cold and rational left hemisphere "logical," "linear," "analytical," and "masculine." In contrast, they proclaimed the allegedly warm and fuzzy right hemisphere "holistic," "intuitive," "artistic," "spontaneous," "creative," and "feminine" (Basil, 1988; Zimmer, 2009). Arguing that modern society undervalues the right hemisphere's touchy-feely mode of approaching the world, dichotomizers touted fanciful schemes for boosting this hemisphere's activity. Their books and seminars promised to free us of the barriers to personal growth imposed by an inflexible school system that favors "left hemisphere thinking."

Yet an expert panel, assembled by the U.S. National Academy of Sciences, concluded that ". . . we have no direct evidence that differential hemispheric utilization can be trained" (Druckman & Swets, 1988, p. 110). The panel concluded that behavioral training could probably enhance different styles of learning or problem solving, but that such improvements were not due to differences in the two hemispheres' functioning.

If the behavioral exercises promoted for right hemisphere calisthenics might yield a few benefits, we can't say the same for the far-fetched "brain tuners" sold for the same purposes (Beyerstein, 1985, 1999a). Numerous devices of this sort allegedly harmonize or synchronize the activity of the two hemispheres. One of the most successful of these schemes was invented by a former public relations executive with no formal training in neuroscience. Like others of its ilk, the device supposedly synchronizes brain waves across the hemispheres by means of feedback signals. Probably because of the placebo effect (see *Introduction*, p. 14), the product found scores of satisfied customers. Yet even if the devices synchronized left–right brain waves, there's no reason to believe that making the two hemispheres resonate in this fashion would be good for us. In fact, if the brain is working optimally, this is probably exactly what you *wouldn't* want it to do. Optimal psychological performance usually requires differential activation rather than synchronization of the hemispheres (Beyerstein, 1999a).

The bottom line: Don't be taken in by the claims of dichotomizers with a seminar to sell or marketers of hemispheric synchronization gizmos that sound too good to be true. Current research on hemispheric differences, even by those responsible for discovering left–right specializations, focuses on showing how the normal brain works in an integrated fashion (Corballis, 2007; Gazzaniga, 1998; McCrone, 1999).

Myth #3 Extrasensory Perception (ESP) Is a Well-Established Scientific Phenomenon

Having trouble with your love life? How about money problems? Call Miss Cleo's Psychic Hotline for Free! The operators of Miss Cleo's Psychic Hot Line charged callers an astonishing $1 billion before a 2002 settlement with the Federal Trade Commission (FTC) required that they cancel $500 million in customer bills and pay a $5 million fine (Miss Cleo's psychic powers apparently failed to warn her of the FTC's impending legal action). Nearly 6 million viewers of late-night television commercials featuring the purported Jamaican soothsayer were moved to speak with her or one of her "trained psychics" by the promise of receiving 3 free minutes of revelations about their future. Callers had no reason to suspect that Miss Cleo had American parents, that she was born in Los Angeles, and that her real name was Youree Dell Harris. Nor did they realize that their calls were being charged at the rate of $4.99 a minute from the outset, and that the goal of the "psychic" on the other end of the line was to keep them talking as long as possible, thereby running up their phone bills.

Some readers skeptical of psychic abilities might assume that callers, who ended up paying an average of $60 for each call, were simply suckers. Yet this judgment doesn't consider the fact that belief in psychic abilities and extrasensory perception (ESP) is firmly entrenched in modern society. The millions of callers to "Miss Cleo" were but a tiny fraction of the Americans who believe that ESP is a firmly established scientific fact. Coined in 1870 by Sir Richard Burton, the term ESP has come to mean knowledge or perception without the use of any of the senses. According to the most recent Gallup poll on this topic (Moore, 2005), 41% of the 1,002 U.S. adults surveyed believe in ESP, 31% in the existence of "telepathy/communication between minds without using traditional senses," and 26% in "clairvoyance/the power of the mind to know the past and predict the future." Among 92 introductory psychology students, 73% said they believed that the existence of ESP was well documented (Taylor & Kowalski, 2003).

The types of experiences assessed by these surveys are also known as paranormal, or psi-related experiences. Many parapsychologists (psychologists who study the paranormal) also describe *psychokinesis*—the ability to influence physical objects or processes by the power of thought—as a paranormal ability. Nevertheless, psychokinesis is typically excluded from ESP, which includes the three capacities of (1) *telepathy* (mind reading), (2) *clairvoyance* (knowing the existence of hidden or far-away objects or people), and (3) *precognition* (predicting the future using paranormal means).

Believers in ESP aren't limited to the general public. More than half of natural scientists polled (Wagner & Monnet, 1979) reported that they believed that ESP is an established fact or a likely possibility. Starting in 1972, the U.S. government shelled out $20 million of taxpayer money to fund a program known as "Stargate" to study the ability of "remote viewers" to acquire militarily useful information from distant, inaccessible places (using clairvoyance), such as a nuclear facility in the then Soviet Union. Government agents gave remote viewers the geographical coordinates (longitude, latitude) of a specific person, place, or document, and these viewers then wrote down, drew, or described whatever they could glean mentally about the target. The government discontinued the Stargate program in 1995, apparently because it yielded no useful military information. Amidst the debate over whether the government was wasting taxpayer money on this project, a blue-ribbon subcommittee of the U.S. National Research Council reviewed the world literature on ESP and concluded that the case for psychic powers was feeble (Alcock, 1990; Druckman & Swets, 1988; Hyman, 1989). Still, the mere fact that such a program was established in the first place highlights the widespread acceptance of ESP among educated people.

If the scientific support for ESP is so weak—and we'll soon provide evidence for this verdict—why do so many people believe in it? From childhood, most of us are bombarded by favorable and unskeptical media accounts of paranormal experiences. Such television shows as the *X-Files*, *Medium*, *Fringe*, and *America's Psychic Challenge* and, before that, *Twilight Zone* and the *Outer Limits*, have portrayed ESP as part of the fabric of everyday life. Movie plots encourage belief in a wide range of paranormal powers, including clairvoyance (such as *Minority Report*, *The Dead Zone*, *Stir of Echoes*, *The Butcher's Wife*, *The Sixth Sense*), telepathy (such as *Scanners*, *Dreamscape*, *The Sender*, and *Ghostbusters*), and psychokinesis (such as *Carrie* and *X-Men*). Many popular self-help books (Hewitt, 1996; Manning, 1999) declare that we all harbor latent psychic talents and tout simple techniques to liberate these powers and achieve ESP success. The Internet features innumerable pitches for courses that promise to develop and enhance our psychic abilities. For example, an advertisement for the *Silva Ultra Mind Seminar* (2005) tells participants that they'll be paired up with other people, taught to harness their ESP following meditation, and given the skills to guess astonishing facts about each other by means of paranormal powers.

preliminary testing by a neurologist revealed that Ross' eyeblinks created a brain wave artifact that was inadvertently triggering the tone (False Memory Syndrome Foundation, 2008).

Psychologists still don't understand why so many of us hold extramission beliefs, but they have a few tantalizing leads. First, popular culture, as exemplified by Superman's X-ray vision with its power to attack villains and slice through steel (Yang, 2007), may have contributed to some modern extramission beliefs, although this influence of course can't explain the origins of these beliefs in ancient culture (see Figure 1.1). Second, most of us have experienced "phosphenes," perceptions of light —often consisting of dots or patterns—created by excitation of the retina, the light-sensitive layer at the back of the eye (Neher, 1990). Pressure phosphenes, which we most often see after rubbing our eyes after awakening, are almost certainly the most common. Some writers have conjectured that phosphenes may contribute to the belief that the eye emits tiny particles to detect objects (Gross, 1999). Third, the eyes of many animals that possess good night vision contain a "tapetum lucidum," a reflective layer behind or within the retina. Many of us have seen the gleaming light generated by this layer, sometimes called "eyeshine," in cats or raccoons at night (Ollivier et al., 2004). Some have suggested that this experience may foster the misimpression that the eyes generate emissions (Yang, 2007). Nevertheless, all three speculations, although intriguing, are just that—speculations—and none has been tested systematically. The reasons for extramission beliefs remain poorly understood (Winer et al., 2003).

Can we modify extramission beliefs by education? At first blush, the answer appears to be "no." Remarkably, exposure to lectures on sensation and perception in introductory psychology courses seems to make no difference in the percentage of college students who endorse beliefs in extramission (Gregg, Winer, Cottrell, Hedman, & Fournier, 2001; Winer et al., 2002). Nevertheless, there may be a "ray" of hope, if we can be forgiven for the pun. Research suggests that presenting college students with "refutational" messages, those designed not merely to explain how the eye works but how it *doesn't* work, in this case that the eye doesn't emit rays or particles, leads to short-term reductions in extramission beliefs (Winer et al., 2002). Even here, though, these reductions aren't especially long-lasting—they've largely dissipated by 3 to 5 months—suggesting that a one-shot exposure to a refutational message may not do the trick. Repeated exposure may be needed.

In many respects, research on refutational messages mirrors the approach we're adopted throughout this book: first debunking the fictions

Image not available in this digital edition.

Figure 1.1 Superman's "X-ray vision" captures many people's intuitive beliefs regarding visual emissions.
Source: Superman #37.

about the mind and brain before unveiling the facts. As Mark Twain reminded us, learning often first requires unlearning.

Myth #5 Subliminal Messages Can Persuade People to Purchase Products

Many of us know that psychologists and advertisers can present sights and sounds so briefly or so faintly that we fail to perceive them. But can those feeble stimuli influence our behavior in powerful ways? There's a profitable industry that hopes you believe the answer is "yes."

Some promoters push this kind of ultra-weak or "subliminal" messaging in the realm of advertising, whereas others have become leaders in the burgeoning self-help movement. The Internet, New Age fairs and magazines, supermarket tabloids, late-night TV "infomercials," and bookstores market subliminal audiotapes and CDs that promise to make the purchaser healthy, wealthy, and wise. Among our personal favorites we include audiotapes that promise to enlarge women's breasts, relieve constipation, improve one's sex life, or cure deafness (although the mechanism by which a deaf person could detect subliminal sounds remains truly mysterious). Given the widespread promotion of subliminal persuasion in the popular psychology world, it's hardly surprising that 59% of the psychology undergraduates sampled by Larry Brown (1983), and 83% of those sampled by Annette Taylor and Patricia Kowalski (2003), said they believed it works.

Interestingly, there's evidence that under tightly controlled laboratory conditions, psychologists can demonstrate short-lived and modest subliminal effects. In these experiments, researchers flash *priming* words or pictures on a screen so briefly that observers are unaware of what the flashes contain. In psychological lingo, priming stimuli increase the speed or accuracy with which we'll identify a later stimulus. Experimenters then determine whether the meanings or emotional content of the priming stimuli influences people's responses to the task, like completing a word with missing letters or judging the emotion of a person in a photograph. For instance, Nicholas Epley and his colleagues (Epley, Savitsky, & Kachelski, 1999) described an experiment in which researchers asked psychology graduate students to generate ideas for research projects. The investigators then exposed the students to extremely brief flashes featuring either the smiling face of a familiar colleague or the scowling face of their faculty supervisor. The students perceived the stimuli as nothing but flashes of light. Next, they rated the quality of the research ideas they'd produced. Without knowing why, subjects exposed to the flash featuring the scowling face of their supervisor rated their own ideas less favorably than those exposed to the smiling colleague's face.

Investigators can similarly influence verbal behaviors, as when a shared theme in a series of subliminally flashed priming words increases the odds that a person will choose a related word from a list of alternatives (Merikle, 1992). For example, if we present a subject with the word stem "gui _ _" and ask her to form a complete word, "guide" and "guile" are both options. Research shows that we can boost the probability of subjects choosing "guide" by priming them subliminally with words like "direct," "lead," and "escort," whereas we can boost the probability of their choosing "guile" by priming them subliminally with words like "deceit," "treachery," and "duplicity."

"Subliminal" means "under the limen." The *limen*, better known as the "sensory threshold," is the narrow range in which a diminishing stimulus goes from being just barely detectable to being just barely undetectable. If the stimulus happens to be a word or phrase, the first hurdle it must pass is the *simple detection threshold.* That's the point at which people first become dimly aware that the researcher has presented anything, even though they can't identify *what* they saw or heard. The researcher must present the stimulus for a longer interval and at a higher intensity to reach the next stage of awareness, the *recognition threshold.* At that point, people can say precisely what they heard or saw. If a stimulus has so little energy, or is so thoroughly obscured by noise that it can't trigger a physiological response in the eye's or ear's receptors, it can't affect anything the person thinks, feels, or does. Period. Messages that inhabit the gray zone between the detection and recognition thresholds, or that we simply aren't attending to, sometimes influence our emotions or behavior.

The subliminal self-help industry hopes you'll swallow the claim that your brain understands and acts on the complex meanings of phrases that are presented at vanishingly weak levels or overshadowed by stronger stimuli. Moreover, they claim that these sneaky subliminal stimuli are especially effective because they worm their way into your unconscious, where they can pull your strings like a hidden puppeteer. Should you be worried? Read on.

Modern psychology accepts that much of our mental processing goes on outside of our immediate awareness—that our brains work on many tasks at once without monitoring them consciously (Kihlstrom, 1987; Lynn & Rhue, 1994). Nevertheless, this is a far cry from the kind of non-conscious processing envisioned by pop psychology proponents of subliminal effects. Subliminal entrepreneurs are holdovers from the heyday of strict Freudian views of the unconscious, which most scientific psychologists have long abandoned (Bowers, 1987). Like Freud, subliminal enthusiasts see the unconscious as the seat of primitive and largely sexual urges that operate outside of our awareness to compel our choices.

Writer Vance Packard popularized this view of the unconscious in his 1957 smash bestseller, *The Hidden Persuaders.* Packard accepted uncritically the story of marketing consultant James Vicary, who supposedly conducted a successful demonstration of subliminal advertising at a Fort Lee, New Jersey movie theatre. Vicary claimed that during a movie, he repeated exposed cinema patrons to messages flashed on the screen for a mere 1/3,000 of a second, urging them to buy popcorn and Coca-Cola. He proclaimed that although movie-goers were unaware of these commands, sales of popcorn and Coca-Cola skyrocketed during the six-week duration of his "experiment." Vicary's findings achieved widespread popular acceptance, although he never submitted them to the scrutiny of a scientific journal, nor has anyone been able to replicate them. After much criticism, Vicary finally admitted in 1962 that he'd made up the whole story in an effort to revive his failing consulting business (Moore, 1992; Pratkanis, 1992).

Vicary's confession failed to discourage even more far-fetched accusations that the advertisers were subliminally manipulating the unsuspecting public. In a series of books with such titillating titles as *Subliminal Seduction* (1973), former psychology professor Wilson Brian Key claimed that advertisers were conspiring to influence consumer choices by embedding blurred sexual images into magazine and TV renderings of ice cubes, plates of food, models' hair-dos, and even Ritz crackers. Key gravely warned that even a single exposure to these camouflaged images could affect consumer choices weeks later. Although Key presented no real evidence to back up his claims, public alarm led the U.S. Federal Communications Commission (FCC) to look into his allegations. Although the FCC couldn't find any evidence that subliminal advertising worked, they declared it "contrary to the public interest" and warned licensed broadcasters to steer clear of it. Moreover, in an attempt to soothe public jitters, several advertising trade associations imposed voluntary restrictions, asking their members to refrain from attempts to punch below the liminal belt.

Although Vicary was an admitted fraud and Key never put his strange ideas to a proper test, some still believed that subliminal persuasion claims were worth examining. So in 1958, the Canadian Broadcasting Corporation (CBC) performed an unprecedented nationwide test. During a popular Sunday night TV program, it informed viewers that the network was about to conduct a test of subliminal persuasion. The CBC then flashed subliminally the message "phone now" on the screen 352 times throughout the show. Telephone company records indicated that phone usage didn't increase, nor did local television stations report a big upsurge in calls. Nevertheless, a few viewers, who may have known about Vicary's alleged results, called in to say they felt hungrier and thirstier following the program. The results of more carefully controlled tests of the ability of subliminal messages to influence consumer choices or voter attitudes were also overwhelmingly negative (Eich & Hyman, 1991; Logie & Della Sala, 1999; Moore, 1992; Pratkanis, 1992). To this day, there's no good evidence that subliminal messages can affect purchasers' decisions or voters' choices, let alone yield perfect memories or larger breasts.

Perhaps most bizarre of all were claims that heavy metal rock bands, such as Judas Priest, were inserting *backward* recordings of Satanic messages in their music. Alarmists claimed these messages encouraged suicidal behavior, although what conceivable purpose entertainers might have in killing off potential album buyers remains unclear. Some even asserted that it was all a plot to subvert the morality of youthful music fans. Many would maintain that youth generally manage this feat quite well without any special subliminal help, but no matter.

John Vokey and J. Don Read (1985) put the idea of subliminal backward messages to a controlled test. In one particularly amusing demonstration, they found that participants with prudish leanings, given subtle suggestions as to what they were about to hear, were likely to perceive nonexistent pornographic material in reverse-played Biblical passages. These results suggest that people who claim to hear Satanic messages embedded in commercial sound tracks are allowing their overheated imaginations to read the lewd material into meaningless sound patterns. It's all in the ear of the beholder.

Tests of self-help subliminal products have been equally discouraging. Anthony Greenwald and his colleagues (Greenwald, Spangenberg, Pratkanis, & Eskenazi, 1991) conducted a double-blind test of commercially marketed subliminal audiotapes that purport to enhance memory or self-esteem. They told half of the participants they were getting the memory boosting tapes, the other half they were getting the self-esteem boosting tapes. Within each of these groups, half got the tapes they were expecting and half got the tapes with the other message. Participants reported that they improved in ways consistent with whichever kind of tape they *believed* they received. Those who received the self-esteem tapes, believing they were the memory boosters, were just as happy with their apparent memory improvement as those who got the real McCoy, and vice versa. This curious finding led Greenwald and his colleagues to refer to this phenomenon as an *illusory placebo effect*: People didn't improve, but they thought they had.

Despite convincing debunking of the concept by the scientific community, subliminal advertisements still pop up occasionally. During the 2000 U.S. presidential election, sharp-eyed Democrats spotted, in a Republican TV attack ad aimed at candidate Al Gore, an extremely brief flash of the word "RATS" superimposed on Gore's face (Berke, 2000). The ad's creator claimed that the fact that the last four letters of the intended word "BUREACRATS" just happened to become detached from this longer word was entirely accidental (see Figure 1.2). Nevertheless, advertising production experts said that given the advanced technology used to prepare the ad, an unintentional insertion of this kind was unlikely.

Image not available in this digital edition.

Figure 1.2 Was the inclusion of the word ("RATS"), which appeared subliminally in this 2000 Republican campaign advertisement against Democratic candidate Al Gore, intentional?
Source: Reuters/Corbis.

Perhaps the final word should go to a spokesperson for the industry that lives or dies by its ability to persuade people to buy things they may—or may not—need. Bob Garfield (1994), a columnist for *Advertising Age* magazine, summed up many people's views on the matter: "Subliminal advertising does not exist except in the public consciousness, at least not in consumer advertising. Nobody bothers with it because it's hard enough to impress people by hitting them upside the head with [blatant] images."

Chapter 1: Other Myths to Explore

Fiction	**Fact**
We need a full brain to function effectively.	Some people who've had one brain hemisphere surgically removed in childhood due to illness can function reasonably well in adulthood.
Modern humans have larger brains than Neanderthals.	Neanderthals' brains were probably slightly larger than ours.
Areas of activation on brain scans mean that brain regions are becoming more active.	Areas of activation on brain scans sometimes mean that some brain regions are inhibiting other regions.

Fiction	Fact
"Alpha consciousness" is associated with states of relaxation.	There's no evidence that boosting the brain's alpha waves increases relaxation; moreover, some people who aren't relaxed, such as children with attention-deficit/hyperactivity disorder, have high levels of alpha waves.
Adult humans don't grow new neurons.	Relatively recent research points to the growth of new neurons in parts of the adult brain, especially the hippocampus.
As adults, we lose about 100,000 neurons each day.	We do lose neurons each day, but the actual number is probably only about one tenth of that.
Blind people have especially well-developed senses of hearing and touch.	There's little evidence that the blind have superior abilities in other senses, including hearing, touch, or smell.
Blind people can detect obstacles at a distance by sensing heat and pressure on their foreheads.	There's no evidence for this claim.
A coma is a state of deep sleep.	People in comas are not asleep.
We can "awaken" people from comas by playing their favorite songs.	There's no scientific evidence that people can be brought out of comas by presenting them with their favorite songs or other familiar stimuli.
Biofeedback is a uniquely effective means of reducing tension.	Most studies indicate that biofeedback is no more effective than relaxation for reducing anxiety.
Humans have an invisible "body energy" that can cause psychological problems when blocked.	There's no scientific evidence for invisible energy fields in or around the human body.
Alcohol kills brain cells.	Alcohol appears not to kill brain cells themselves, although it can damage neuronal "dendrites," which are portals that bring messages into neurons.
Alcohol's primary effect is stimulating the brain.	Alcohol is primarily a depressant, and is typically a stimulant only at low doses.
Alcohol enhances sexual arousal.	Alcohol tends to inhibit sexual arousal and performance, especially at high doses.
One can always detect alcohol on the breath.	One can't always detect alcohol on the breath.

Fiction	Fact
Alcohol promotes sleep.	Although alcohol typically results in falling asleep more quickly, it usually suppresses deep sleep, often producing awakenings later in the night.
Alcohol warms the body.	Although drinking alcohol in cold temperatures can make us feel warmer, it actually results in a loss of body heat and therefore cools the body.
It's easier to get drunk at high altitudes, such as while flying in an airplane.	Studies show that higher altitudes don't result in greater intoxication.
Impaired judgment after drinking occurs only after obvious signs of intoxication.	Impaired judgment can occur well before drunkenness is apparent.
Drinking coffee is a good way to sober up after heavy drinking.	Drinking coffee won't help with a hangover; it just turns us into a "wide awake drunk."
A cold shower or exercise is a good way to sober up after heavy drinking.	Same as above.
Switching among different types of alcohol is more likely to lead to drunkenness than sticking to one type of alcohol.	The total amount, not the type, of alcohol predicts the risk of intoxication.
One can't become an alcoholic by drinking beer only.	Not true.
There's good evidence that people who smoke marijuana for many years end up apathetic.	The evidence for "amotivational syndrome" is mixed, largely in part because heavy marijuana smokers frequently use other drugs.
Most people with brain injury look and act disabled.	Most people with brain injury appear normal and act normally aside from subtle deficits on neuropsychological tests.
Following a head injury, the best prescription is rest.	Following a head injury, the best prescription is a gradual return to activity.
A head injury can't produce brain damage unless the person is knocked unconscious.	Brain damage that's detectable on neurological and neuropsychological tests can occur even with no loss of consciousness.
Prefrontal lobotomies (more popularly called "lobotomies") turn people into human "vegetables."	Most people who've received lobotomies are far from "vegetables," although they are typically apathetic.

Fiction	Fact
Humans have five senses.	Humans have several senses in addition to sight, hearing, smell, taste, and touch, including body position, temperature, and pain.
Most color-blind people see the world in black and white.	Almost all color-blind people can see at least some colors; "monochromats," who see the world in black and white, comprise only about 0.005% of the population.
Dogs see the world in black and white.	Dogs have red–green color blindness, but can perceive a number of colors, including blue and yellow.
Reading in dim light can ruin our eyesight.	Research offers no support for this claim.
The human tongue's tastes can be described as a "map" of four tastes.	Although some textbooks present a human "taste map," this map is grossly oversimplified, because receptors for the four tastes are spread throughout most of the tongue.
Consuming ice cream of other cold substances too quickly causes pain in our brains.	"Brain freeze" is caused by a constriction of blood vessels in the roof of the mouth, followed by an expansion of these vessels, triggering pain.
Magnets, like those embedded in shoe insoles, can reduce pain.	Controlled studies reveal that such magnets are useless for pain reduction.
Eating lots of turkey can make us tired.	There's no evidence that turkey is any more sleep-inducing than other foods; but because we often eat turkey on major holidays when we eat a lot and drink alcohol—both of which contribute to fatigue—we may mistakenly perceive a causal association.

Sources and Suggested Readings

To explore these and other myths about the brain and perception, see Aamodt and Wang (2008); Bausell (2007); Beyerstein (1990); Della Sala (1999, 2007); El-Hai (2005); Herculano-Houzel (2002); Hines (2003); Juan (2006); Lilienfeld and Arkowitz (2008); Vreeman and Carroll (2007).

Notes

Notes

Notes

Notes

Notes

Notes

Notes

Notes

THE MEANINGS OF MODERN ART

THE MEANINGS OF MODERN ART

JOHN RUSSELL

T&H

THAMES AND HUDSON

First published in Great Britain in 1981
by Thames and Hudson Ltd, London
Reprinted 1985.

Printed and bound in Japan

To the memory of THOMAS B. HESS 1920-1978

CONTENTS

PREFACE

This book is built upon two beliefs. One is that in art, as in the sciences, ours is one of the big centuries. The other is that the history of art, if properly set out, is the history of everything. As the case for these beliefs is argued on every page of this book, either directly or by implication, I shall not defend them here. But I owe it to the reader to explain that this book itself has an unusual history.

Rather more than ten years ago I was asked by The Museum of Modern Art and the Book-of-the-Month Club if I would write for them a general survey of modern art. It was to cover the period from 1875 to the present day. It was to be acceptable to the Museum, in terms of art history, and it was to be acceptable to the Club, in terms of general interest and readability. Beyond that, I was on my own.

The book that resulted was published in 1974–75 in twelve monthly parts. It was distributed by the Book-of-the-Month Club and could be had by mail subscription only. In preparing the present edition, which appears under the joint imprint of The Museum of Modern Art and Harper & Row, I have made a radical change in the presentation of the text. While the earlier edition had captions which in many cases were so lengthy and so elaborate as almost to constitute a parallel text, I have now eliminated them. I have, however, felt free to integrate them, wherever it seemed desirable, in the text proper. That text is therefore substantially longer—and, I hope, richer—than it was in the original edition. I have also revised and updated the text here and there, though this is not a text for which I would claim a fugitive up-to-dateness.

As work on the original edition proceeded, the true nature of the book seemed to me to declare itself more and more clearly. It was intended to meet the severe standards of the College Art Association, which subsequently was kind enough to present me with its Frank Jewett Mather Award for art criticism, but it was not a mainline art history. Nor was it a directory, a dictionary or an encyclopedia. Whole countries, whole schools, whole categories of artists (some of them individually dear to me) appeared in it either momentarily or not at all. In art, as in most other things, I hold by what André Gide once said: "The world will be saved by one or two people."

Insofar as *The Meanings of Modern Art* is modeled upon any other book or books, they date from quite some time ago and have nothing to do with art history. They are examples, that is to say, of the democratic Enlightenment that came into being in Victorian times and was a force for good at least until the outbreak of World War I. It had to do with the notions of self-help and of adult education, but it also had to do with a moral obligation that was felt by many good writers, even if they did not always put it into words.

It was a point of honor with these writers to make the best of themselves available to the largest possible public at the lowest possible cost. John Ruskin, the greatest of all English writers on art, was wholeheartedly of that persuasion. The ideal of universal education was at hand: how could good writers address themselves to the privileged only?

In the first years of our century, book after book was animated by this noble ambition. Three that I cherish especially are *Our Knowledge of the External World* by Bertrand Russell, *Landmarks in French Literature* by Lytton Strachey and *An Outline of Russian Literature* by Maurice Baring. These could have been no more than primers, but in point of fact they have quite another character: and it was that character, or something like it, that I hoped to annex for *The Meanings of Modern Art.*

It was fundamental to that character that every book should be an act of commitment. We never doubt that Ruskin would have put his hand in the fire for J. M. W. Turner. Freshness and lightness of touch are fundamental also: Bertrand Russell made us aware not of the hard work that had gone into his book, but merely of the barely audible hiss of glee with which the final formulations were set down on paper.

These books had, finally, an element of covert

autobiography. Their authors did not write as deskmen or as high-grade copyists. They wrote as men made and marked by what they were writing about. When Lytton Strachey wrote about the terrible insights of Racine, he did not make us think of Racine as "a classic," but as a friend and confidant whose every word left a brand. When Maurice Baring wrote of the great Russian novelists, it was not as a man who had graduated from a language laboratory. He wrote as someone who had sat long and late over the table in Russian country houses, and argued this way and that with Russians on weeklong railway journeys, and plunged into Russian rivers at the time of year when bathing in those rivers was like bathing, he tells us, in hot tea.

These things were not paraded, but they were present. They did not validate what was said, but they brought with them a sense of involvement that communicated itself as the single most desirable characteristic in books of that kind. I have no illusions as to how far *The Meanings of Modern Art* may fall short in this matter, but I like to think that its subject matter has been as much lived as studied. My opinion of Gustav Klimt was formed in Vienna before World War II. My opinion of Henry Moore was formed in the early 1940s, at a time when he could barely keep himself in stone or wood. My opinion of the great masters of the School of Paris was formed during visits beyond number to that city from 1946 onward, and my opinion of the Russian avant-garde was formed in Moscow and Leningrad during the 1950s. I hope that in dealing with more recent art—and in particular with art that originates in New York City, where I now live—I am as attentive as ever to considerations of time and place and cultural context. Immediacy is not everything in such matters, but where it exists it should be put to work.

None of the things I have mentioned can make a foolish man wise or a bad book good. But when they are properly used they remind us that the act of reading is an act of confidence, and almost of conspiracy, between one human being and another. That conspiracy can get nowhere, and that confidence can be betrayed. But if all goes well the reader may put down the book at the end and say what the author—and this author is no exception—most wants to hear: "I learned a lot from your book, but what is more to the point is that I had a very good time."

Perhaps I might add that the human conditions in which I worked on the original edition were outstandingly happy. It is a grief to me that among the officers of the Book-of-the-Month Club who did so much to make those years agreeable neither Warren Lynch nor that most stringent of editors, Ralph Thompson, is here to see the book in the stores. At The Museum of Modern Art I benefited beyond measure from the professionalism of Frances Keech, Patricia White (now Mrs. Bradford A. Warner, Jr.), Nora Sheehan, Francis Kloeppel and Clive Phillpot.

THE MEANINGS OF MODERN ART

Edouard Manet.
The Folkestone Boat, Boulogne. 1869.
Oil on canvas,
23½ × 28⅞ inches.
Philadelphia
Museum of Art.
Mr. and Mrs. Carroll
S. Tyson Collection

THE SECRET REVOLUTION

When art is made new, we are made new with it. We have a sense of solidarity with our own time, and of psychic energies shared and redoubled, which is just about the most satisfying thing that life has to offer. "If that is possible," we say to ourselves, "then everything is possible"; a new phase in the history of human awareness has been opened up, just as it was opened up when people first read Dante, or first heard Bach's 48 preludes and fugues, or first learned from *Hamlet* and *King Lear* that the complexities and contradictions of human nature could be spelled out on the stage.

This being so, it is a great exasperation to come face to face with new art and not make anything of it. Stared down by something that we don't like, don't understand and can't believe in, we feel personally affronted, as if our identity as reasonably alert and responsive human beings had been called into question. We ought to be having a good time, and we aren't. More than that, an important part of life is being withheld from us; for if any one thing is certain in this world it is that art is there to help us live, and for no other reason.

It was always so. Art is there to tell us where we are, and it is also there to tell us who we are. It gives pleasure, coincidentally, but primarily it is there to tell the truth. For hundreds of years, and on many matters of supreme importance, it had the edge over all other sources. It gave out the truth about this world and the next one. It encapsulated history. It told us what people wiser than ourselves were thinking. It told the stories that everyone wanted to hear, and it fixed, once and forever, the key moments in our evolution. Art answered the great riddles, filled in the gaps in our general knowledge, and laid Eternity on the line. Above all, it gave reassurance; it told us what we wanted to hear—that experience was not formless and illegible, that man could speak to man without the obstructions of language, and that we were at home in the world, and with one another.

That was long the function of art. Art restored

to us the lost wholeness, the sensation of being at one with Nature, and at one with society, which we crave from the moment of birth. Many and desperate are the expedients which we devise for the recapture of that lost wholeness; art restores it completely and forever. So we are quite right to be dismayed when art seems to shift its ground in ways that we find difficult to follow. Still less do we like to think that art might one day peter out. We do not care to echo what was written more than three hundred years ago by Sir Thomas Browne: " 'Tis too late to be ambitious. The great mutations of the world are acted." We should prefer to think—and in my opinion we are quite right to think—that the masterpieces of our own day can perfectly well stand comparison with the great achievements of the past.

But the anxiety remains. And art *has* shifted its ground, and recoded its messages, and questioned its own nature, and reshaped the ordeal by initiation to which we are subjected before we can understand it completely. Indignation at all this masks feelings to which we dare not give their true name. E. H. Gombrich, with his *The Story of Art,* has taught millions of people how to look at old pictures; and he put this point very well when he said that European Expressionism before 1914 sprang from the fear of "that utter loneliness that would reign if art were to fail and each man remained immured in himself." If the two words "modern art" are enough to start an argument almost anywhere, it is because this fear of the eventual and hypothetical failure of art has come to haunt even people who have never been to a museum, let alone bought a picture.

It was in the second half of the 19th century that art was relieved of certain of the duties which it had been carrying out on society's behalf and became free to look into its own nature. The duties in question had been many and varied. Philip IV of Spain never doubted that when his troops won a famous victory his court painter Velázquez was the best man to commemorate it. When Marat was murdered in his bath in 1793, it was by popular demand, almost, that Jacques-Louis David made haste to paint *Marat Assassinated.* When the Houses of Parliament burned down in London in 1834, art gave us our most memorable account of what happened: J. M. W. Turner was on hand to tell how the great scarf of flame unwound itself high in the night sky. Art had no rival on such occasions. It gave us what we could get nowhere else. Nor was the artist simply a passive recorder: when the French frigate *Méduse* was lost in particularly ghastly circumstances in 1816, it was a painter, Théodore Géricault, who brought the matter out of the newspapers and onto a deeper level of concern.

In paintings such as the ones I have named, people were told what they wanted to know, and told it in a way that allied power to concision and eloquence to understanding. These traits in combination inspired a collective confidence in art. A recent example of that confidence is the first line of a poem by W. H. Auden: "About suffering they were never wrong, the Old Masters." Though not wholly true—some Old Masters were platitudinous and histrionic, others had an attitude toward suffering that was distinctly equivocal—this line does indicate one of the ways in which art helps us to live.

That is to say that we have a deeper understanding of old age and are the readier to meet it ourselves if we have studied Joseph Wright of Derby's *The Old Man and Death.* We have a deeper understanding of what it means for one person to give himself to another if we have studied Rembrandt's *The Jewish Bride.* We have a deeper understanding of what it means to love the world and lose it if we have studied the valedictory images of the dying Watteau. Marcel Proust was one of the most observant men who ever lived, but he spoke for all of us when he wrote, "Until I saw Chardin's paintings I never realized how much beauty lay around me in my parents' house, in the half-cleared table, in the corner of a tablecloth left awry, in the knife beside the empty oyster-shell."

Behind this collective confidence in art is our

trust in the archetypal attitude, the stance before life, which is exemplified for us by each of the great masters in turn. It is a common dream that one man's life should be the measure of all things and that it should make sense of the complexity of experience in ways which are valid for everyone. Reading Tolstoy, watching a play by Shakespeare, working our way through the canon of Schubert's songs, looking at a Titian, or at a Dürer, or at Poussin's *Four Seasons,* we find that dream fulfilled. One man can master life. He cannot shield us from misfortune, but he can teach us to bear it better. And while we are under the spell of his art we feel invulnerable, as Brünnehilde was invulnerable when Wotan spread around her the magic circle of fire.

Invulnerability: that is what people ask of art. It would be a bad day if such achievements, and such men, could be talked about only in the past tense. No one likes to think that there lies before us only a long littleness. If rage and dismay enter so often into reactions to new art it is because of what is at stake: our capacity to make sense of life as it now presents itself. The Old Masters are still there, and they may well be present to us more vividly than many people whom we meet in "real life"; but we need the new masters, too, and it is very uncomfortable to feel that they may not be there.

The poet Charles Baudelaire realized this as early as the 1840s. He foresaw that the conditions of life were going to change faster and faster, and that the duty of modern art would be "to express that specific beauty which is intrinsic to our new emotions." Our *new* emotions, he said; for there were going to be new emotions to make new sense of. Baudelaire knew that there would be drastic readjustments for all, both in the public and in the private domain, and that art would have to come to terms with them. And that is what has happened; Tolstoy in his novels said all that there is to say about many aspects of life, but we needed Solzhenitsyn to tell us in *Cancer Ward* and *The First Circle* how much of human dignity can survive when a great adventure is perverted and the vision of a just world brought to nothing. Beethoven in *Fidelio* gave us once and forever an ideal image of human loyalty; but not until Schoenberg's *Erwartung,* more than one hundred years later, did music yield a definitive image of the dissolution of personality under stress.

In art, equally, we had needs which could not be satisfied by the Old Masters, because those needs did not exist when the Old Masters were around. Poussin in his *Massacre of the Innocents* gave us an unforgettable image of a human mouth wide open in a scream; but because he was a great classical artist that scream was incidental to his Olympian overview of the scene as a whole. It fell to Edvard Munch, in 1893, to give us an image of a shriek which (in Munch's own words) "pierced the whole of Nature" and stood for a sudden, vast and quite irresistible sensation of panic and dismay. Europe needed just that picture at just that time, and nothing from the past could have taken its place. In 1945, when the complete facts about the Nazi concentration camps were available for the first time, Europe needed Picasso's *The Charnel House,* which was the more powerful for its sobriety of color, its condensed, pressed-down, claustrophobic imagery and its refusal to itemize what was so readily to hand in print. The best art of the past hundred years came into being on occasions when nothing from the past would fill the bill. What those occasions were, and what art did about them, is the subject of this book.

As to exactly when new art came in and old art went out, several opinions can be upheld. There is a case for those who believe that the change came in the second half of the 1860s. Those five years were pregnant with the future: these were the years when Marx began to publish *Das Kapital,* Nobel invented dynamite and Bismarck drew nearer, step by step, to the domination of Europe. In painting, not-yet-named Impressionism was beginning to dissolve the Old Master tradition of modeling from dark to light in a simulated deep space. The "subject," as previously conceived, was

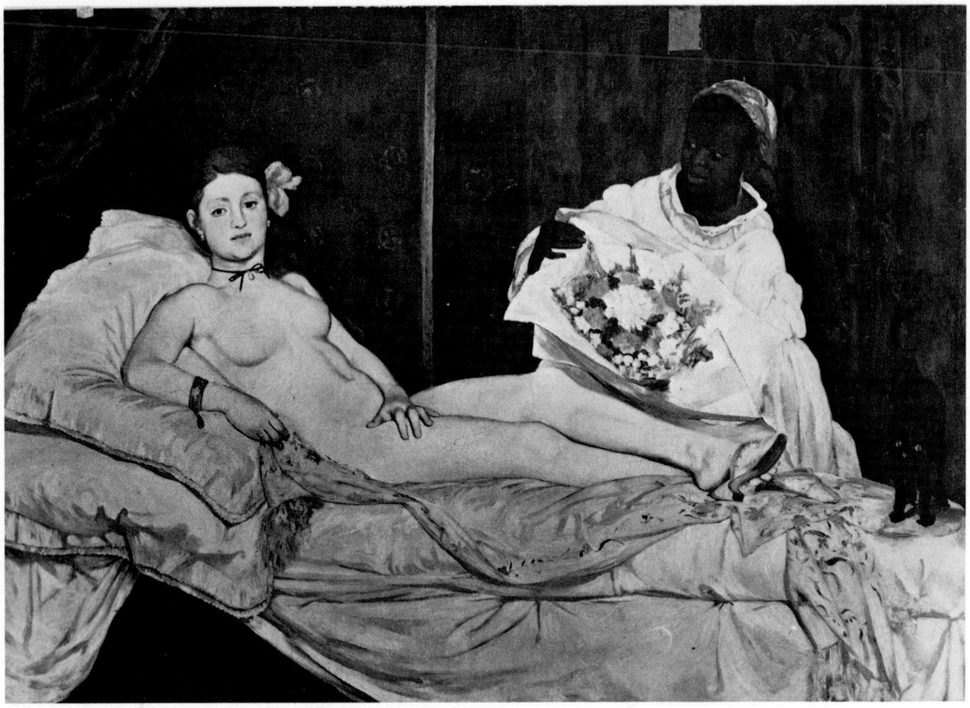

Edouard Manet.
Olympia. 1863.
Oil on canvas,
51⅜ × 74¾ inches.
Musée du Louvre,
Paris

giving way to a new conception of painting, in which the artist's sensations *were* the subject, no other being needed. One of the most challenging pictures of the century was put on view at the Paris Salon in 1865: *Olympia* by Edouard Manet. *Olympia* was challenging in every possible way. It stood for a new kind of candor as between the painter and painting, as between the painter and his subject matter and as between the painter and his public. Manet in 1863 had annoyed people very much by transposing motifs from the Old Masters into modern life and showing, in his *Le Déjeuner sur l'herbe*, how it was possible for a pretty young girl to take off all her clothes while picnicking in the open air with two fully dressed men. That painting had been rejected by the official Salon; but two years later *Olympia* was hung among the 3,559 canvases which had officialdom's sanction.

We do not, of course, see *Olympia* as our great-great-grandfathers would have seen it had they chanced to be in Paris in 1865. The picture has aged, as a physical object. Where once it looked blank and blatant it now looks what it is: an Old Master of our time. More than a hundred years of rougher, more coarsely provocative painting of the female nude has made us aware that Manet was essentially an aristocrat. We also know, as the public of the 1860s mostly did not, that the pose is taken from Titian's *Venus of Urbino,* which Manet had copied nine years earlier. The treatment of the naked figure now seems to us a model of tenderness and delicacy; but at the time it looked two-dimensional and incomplete ("Like the Queen of Spades just out of her bath," said Gustave Courbet). We enjoy the cat, and we find it wonderfully true to the facts of feline behavior, and we know the symbolic role of the cat in the poetry of Manet's friend Baudelaire. In fact, we find the whole picture strongly Baudelairean in its frankness, its overtones of luxury and indulgence, and in the contrast between the white of the flesh, the white of the sheets, the dazzling still life of the bouquet of flowers, and the dark face and hands of the attendant. We relish the uninhibited way in which the naked girl looks straight at us, as much as to say, "Here I am. What are you going to do about it?" The public of the 1860s sensed that the girl was saying it. But they also sensed, even if unconsciously, that the way of painting was saying it, too. *Olympia* was a declaration of war. The public was presented with a new way of seeing and a new way of setting down the thing seen. "Here I am," was the message, "and what are you going to do about it?" The mid-1860s were crucial in that respect. In 1867 both Manet and Courbet exhibited on their own at the World's Fair in Paris, thereby indicating that an alternative must soon be found to the art circuits of officialdom. These were the years in which Claude Monet and Pierre-Auguste Renoir began to paint regularly in the open air; and in which Camille Pissarro put it about that black and bitumen should be outlawed by every painter worthy of the name; and in which the young Zola began to champion the young Paul Cézanne. If we are simply looking for the new, we need look no further.

The case for the late 1860s is the stronger in that Impressionist paintings of the top class have made so great a contribution to human happiness. Looking at them, we think better of life and better of ourselves. Nor are they simply a school of pleasure, and one from which we have all graduated; they are also a school of truth. Impressionist painting

Pierre-Auguste Renoir. *Luncheon of the Boating Party.* 1881. Oil on canvas, 51⅜ × 69¼ inches. The Phillips Collection, Washington

Claude Monet.
Bazille and Camille.
c. 1865.
Oil on canvas,
36⅝ × 27⅛ inches.
National Gallery of
Art, Washington.
Ailsa Mellon Bruce
Collection

was true to everyday experience in a way that painting had not been true before. This is how light falls, this is how color is broken up, this is how the fugitive moment presents itself. These pictures have a physical beauty, but they have a moral beauty as well: free and independent human beings have said "No" to pictorial tradition and set themselves instead to tell the truth about what happens when they set up their easels in front of Nature. It was the truth about what the eye saw, and it was also the truth about what happened on the canvas. The allover flicker of Impressionism mimed the very act of putting paint on canvas, where the suaver, blander and, in intention, seamless procedures of earlier painting had tended to conceal it. Impressionism said "No" to the mind, with its apparatus of received values, and put its trust in intuition. That does not sound, in today's terms, like too momentous an undertaking. But then we say things every day which would have got us banished or burned alive in earlier times; in art, equally, we take it for granted that we can do just as we like, with impunity. The painters of the 1860s were the prisoners of a very different set of historical conditions. Edmond Duranty, one of the most discerning of French writers on art, had said in 1855 that "It takes immense genius to represent, simply and sincerely, what we see in front of us." That had never been what art was about; for the tens of thousands of people who went every year to the official Salons in Paris, art was one of the learned professions, and it was not the function of the artist to teach people to look around them.

The Impressionists thought just the contrary. They were living in an extraordinary time: a time when the conditions of life were changing more radically than in any previous era. They saw, for instance, that between them the steam train and the steamboat were putting a completely new style of life at the disposal of everyone. At once rakish and imposing, convenient and yet the emblems of an imperious masculinity, they were the great new subjects of the day. When Gustave Flaubert began to write *A Sentimental Education* in 1865, he chose for his opening scene the departure of a steamboat, with all its attendant bustle and activity, as a symbol for the way in which human relationships are continually forming and re-forming. Manet in his *The Folkestone Boat, Boulogne,* 1869, and Monet in his painting of *The Gare Saint-Lazare, Paris,* 1877, found in the steam age an ideal subject matter. The scene on the quayside allowed Manet to employ what looked at the time like an almost improvisational method of composition; the rapid, nervous movement of the brush corresponded exactly to the vibration of the ship's engines, the brisk to-and-fro of passengers and crew and the sense—never absent from the most conventional departure—that a decisive moment in life was at hand. People were about to pass from the known to the unknown, from *terra firma* to the open sea; and painting was in the same situation.

In Impressionist painting, the eye has a new

Pierre-Auguste Renoir. *Monet Painting in His Garden at Argenteuil.* 1873. Oil on canvas, 18⅜ × 23½ inches. Wadsworth Atheneum, Hartford, Conn. Bequest of Anne Parrish Titzell

privilege: that of concentrating on aspects of experience which had previously been thought to be too disorderly, too freakish, too seemingly accidental to qualify as material for art. Manet found this material on the quayside, where the spectacle changed from moment to moment. Monet, in the Gare Saint-Lazare series, took the huge iron-and-glass structure of the station, which had only lately been opened; he took the locomotives, which a generation earlier would have seemed like visions from an unimaginable future; and he took the element of steam itself—the mysterious, tinted exhalations which ballooned up and up beneath the unprecedented roof. The Gare Saint-Lazare was a startling enough sight even in the 1930s, when the steam locomotive had not yet been ousted; in the 1870s, and for painters who had known the countrified look of a preindustrial Paris, there can have been nothing to cushion the shock of modernity.

But if Monet was painting the new world, he was also painting the new way. He was using the element of shock in the experience of the Gare Saint-Lazare to cover and justify the element of shock in Impressionism itself. In the painting now in the Fogg Art Museum, for example, he used the swerving movement of the right-hand set of tracks in the foreground to draw the observer into the center of the painting. That center is defined as a space like a diamond laid on its side, with the flattened and inverted V of the roof as its top; the

Claude Monet.
The Gare Saint-Lazare, Paris.
1877.
Oil on canvas,
32½ × 39¾ inches.
Fogg Art Museum, Harvard University, Cambridge, Mass.
Bequest the Collection of Maurice Wertheim

lower half of the diamond is formed by two invisible lines that run through the upper section of the two locomotives in the foreground and meet up in the spectral locomotive that can be glimpsed in the center and at the rear. Within this diamond is the true subject of the painting: the play of light on something never before recorded—the iridescent cloudscape of steam as it forms and re-forms within a confined space. Such a thing had never been seen before, and it will now never be seen again.

No one relished the new subject matter of Impressionism more completely than Edgar Degas, in the series of music-hall and café-concert studies which he made in the second half of the 1870s. In the café-concert he found an ideal combination of the things that most prompted his imagination—faces and bodies in vigorous movement, artificial lighting that turned the most humdrum scene into carnival, strange and aggressive combinations of color. The scene lent itself to abrupt, asymmetrical, snapshotlike images which threw the emphasis everywhere but where it was expected. It was a continual challenge; faced with hardworking professionals, Degas in his turn gave all that he had.

A capital example of this is the *Café Singer Wearing a Glove* of 1878. Degas at this time was using tempera mixed with pastel to produce little paintings, at once astringent and feather-soft, which he could carry through quickly after long and careful preparation. "Pastel colors" in every-

Edgar Degas.
Café Singer Wearing a Glove.
1878.
Pastel and distemper,
20⅞ × 16⅛ inches.
Fogg Art Museum, Harvard University, Cambridge, Mass.
Bequest the Collection of Maurice Wertheim

Camille Pissarro.
The Climbing Path.
1875.
Oil on canvas,
24½ × 25¾ inches.
The Brooklyn Museum. Gift of Dirkan G. Kelekian

day speech have connotations of the washed-out and the effete; but there was nothing of that when Degas matched palest lilac against salmon pink, as here, and set up a sharp apple green to sing out against the black of the glove. Where other painters might have portrayed the singer as a dignified figure in the middle distance, Degas gives us a dentist's view of her wide-open mouth, allows her to slip sideways as if at any moment she would move out of the frame altogether, turns her black glove into the most powerful single image in the picture and makes of her outstretched and bent-back thumb an unforgettable image of effort and strain. Degas spared nobody; but he didn't diminish anybody, either.

Man as a seeing animal has few monuments that can compare with the masterpieces of Impressionism. But man is not only a seeing animal. He is also a thinking, an imagining, a cross-referring and a systems-making animal; and none of these latter traits could be accommodated by pure Impressionism.

Impressionism was by definition dependent on the fugitive and the contingent in human experience. The beauty of the sunlight on the climbing path in the painting of that name by Pissarro is something that once seen is never forgotten; we see such things, ever after, as he saw them. But there are other kinds of experience, and other ways of marshaling them; and to the extent that Impressionism cannot deal with them it has, in the end, its limitations.

When Cézanne said of Monet that he was "only an eye—but what an eye!" he did not mean to put Monet down. An uncorrupted eye is a wonderful thing, and many a later painter has set a very high value on Monet's robust energy, on his open and candid procedures and on his readiness to break with the past when instinct told him that it was the right thing to do. Where Manet hedged his bets on modernity with learned allusions to this great master or that, Monet simply went ahead on his own. He did much more editing than was formerly supposed, but fundamentally he was a master of the

the painting is the irresponsibility, the ignorance of destiny, the general lack of focus and understanding, which leads human beings to go on living in an aimless day-to-day way while inscrutable forces, stronger than ourselves, look down on us.

It was, Gauguin said, "a philosophical work, comparable to the Gospels." He admitted that it had "enormous mathematical faults"; but he refused to adjust them, prizing above any mere correctness the fact that the big picture had been done "direct from imagination, straight from the brush, on sackcloth full of knots and wrinkles." In a letter written some years after the picture was completed, Gauguin summarized the subject matter by saying that in the left-hand section an old woman sits, near to death; that in the central section "the man of instinct," still in his prime, meditates on the meaning of human existence; and that in the right-hand section life begins again with a little child lying beside a stream. Not the least touching thing about this huge ramshackle painting is that in time of supreme stress Gauguin, the Parisian know-all, should have reverted to so old-fashioned a scheme.

Tolstoy's *What I Believe In* came out in French in 1882, and one of the people to whom its ideas appealed especially was van Gogh. "Tolstoy suggests," he wrote to his brother Theo, "that whatever may happen in the way of a violent revolution there will also be a private and secret revolution in man. From this there will be born a new religion—or rather something entirely new, for which we do not have a name. It will give comfort, and make life possible, in the way that Christianity once did."

This idea mattered a great deal to van Gogh, who had tried his very best to be an evangelist and had had no success at all. Better than many a more worldly individual, he understood the apocalyptic implications of industrialization. He was convinced that "through revolutions, through war, through the bankruptcy of worm-eaten states, disasters are bound to fall like a terrible lightning on the modern world and on civilization." But what if art could bring about the "private and secret revolution" which Tolstoy had in mind? What if he, van Gogh, could help to avert disaster by touching men's hearts with his paintings as he had once hoped to touch them with his words? Van Gogh died before he could see his pictures put on show; but when we look at the lines of people that stretch round the block when those pictures are on exhibition today, we know that he did indeed get through to them.

More could be got out of art: as to that, the dreamer and the scientist were of one mind with the student of society. Art's potential had been underrated, underused, undersystematized. Art was not a boutonniere to be worn once a year; it was, on the contrary, one of the most fundamental of human activities. So that Seurat was aiming high, but not too high, when he said that he wanted his studies of metropolitan life to be the modern equivalent of the Panathenaic frieze on the Parthenon. The Parisians, like all other peoples, revealed themselves in their pleasures; and it was in their pleasures that Seurat sought them out —*en masse* on a hot summer Sunday afternoon, in *La Grande Jatte,* in ones and twos in *Une Baignade à Asnières,* at the theater in *Le Chahut,* at the circus in the painting of that name and at the street fair in *La Parade.*

Seurat was only 31 when he died. His output of oil paintings was small by comparison with that of van Gogh or Gauguin, and he has none of their universal celebrity. There are those who find his speckly procedures mechanical; even in his lifetime he is reputed to have been called "the little chemist" on account of the deliberate, laboratory-like manner in which he calculated the dosage of this color or that. Nor did the dot prove to be in itself a very rewarding instrument in the hands of others.

There is, even so, a grotesque injustice in this view of Seurat. Of course he was an eager theoretician. Like many another clever man in the 1880s, he believed that applied science could do a great

Georges Seurat. *Invitation to the Sideshow (La Parade).* 1887–88. Oil on canvas, 39¼ × 59 inches. The Metropolitan Museum of Art, New York. Bequest of Stephen C. Clark

deal for art. To that end, he studied the composition of color, and the emotional properties of mathematics, and the significance of ascending and descending lines and many another para- or pseudo-scientific formulation. Above all, he believed that, as the French theoretician David Sutter had argued in his *Phenomena of Vision* in 1880, "the laws of color harmony can be learned as one learns the laws of harmony in music." In this Seurat followed a number of earlier French 19th-century theoreticians, but with the difference that where their vision of a grammar of the arts did not really get off the printed page, Seurat was one of the great picture-architects of all time. He was also a penetrating social observer, with a particularly keen eye for the compulsive pranks to which his contemporaries subjected themselves in the name of pleasure. The governing principle behind his metropolitan subjects was this: that places do things to people, and that new kinds of places do new kinds of things to them and that it is the painter's privilege to sort all this out.

La Parade is full of scientific devices. The idea of using the dot as a basic unit agreed with the 19th century's many attempts to estimate the size of the smallest unit of matter into which physical phenomena can be broken down. Baudelaire in 1846 was already analyzing Nature in terms of its molecular structure and likening it, in its color relations, to "a spinning-top which revolves so rapidly that it looks gray, even though it embraces within itself the entire gamut of color"; and Seurat's contemporaries noted that although he applied his colors in small touches of the utmost purity and intensity, the optical mix which resulted often had the grayish look which Baudelaire attributed to Nature in its molecular aspect.

In its architectural construction, *La Parade* is based on mathematical theories put forward in 1885 by a Frenchman called Charles Henry, who was regarded at that time as a universal genius, as ready to pronounce on the best method of training for a bicycle race as on whatever lofty and abstract question was the topic of the day. A pleasure-pain

Georges Seurat.
Sunday Afternoon on the Island of La Grande Jatte.
1884–86.
Oil on canvas, 6 feet 9 inches × 10 feet.
The Art Institute of Chicago.
Helen Birch Bartlett Memorial Collection

theory much in favor in the 1880s can be linked to Seurat's use of a meandering line here and there, just as the form of the gas lamps at the top of the painting corresponds to the idiosyncratic, flower-like forms that Seurat prized as an emblem of festivity.

Art history thrives on details such as this. But the real message of the painting relates more to the dehumanization of big-city life than to systematic ingenuities of color and line. Anyone who compares an earlier treatment of the same theme—Gabriel de Saint-Aubin's *La Parade du boulevard* in the National Gallery in London, for instance—will see that where Saint-Aubin speaks for genuine, unforced, unsophisticated enjoyment, Seurat is almost ghoulish in his detailing of the metropolitan scene. His trombone player might be an executioner, and his auxiliary musicians defendants on the stand, while the director of the circus, in his cutaway coat, might be a prison warden ready to strike out at the nearest offender with his cane. Artificial light pollutes the environment, and the scene as a whole reminds us of what had lately been published in Rimbaud's *Illuminations*—the portrait of a big modern city as a place where trees bear no leaf, where people prefer not to know one another, and where the air is fouled by the leavings of industry. (On this last subject, Seurat's drawings of Paris have much to say.) *La Parade* is a masterpiece of ordered statement; but it also calls for a change of heart before the big city gets out of hand.

Seurat looked in many directions: back to Piero della Francesca, out of the studio window to the posters by Chéret which were turning the boulevards into one enormous picture gallery and forward toward kinds of art as yet unimagined. The ramifying tendrils of Art Nouveau derived in part from Seurat's use of arabesque; Marcel Duchamp, in his *Nude Descending a Staircase,* developed an idea of serial representation which was already present in Seurat's *Le Chahut;* Paul Klee by 1912 had mastered Seurat's color doctrine, even though his own work was then still primarily in black and white; Robert Delaunay took the systemic use of pure divided color and worked it up into Orphism; Wassily Kandinsky wrote that Seurat had aimed to show "not a fragment of Nature chosen at random, but Nature complete and entire in all her splendor"; and although Henri Matisse did not go along with the programmatic element in Seurat's work, he saluted "those other, truer values—those human painterly values which today seem ever more profound."

It would be hard to work up much opposition today to the proposition that Cézanne was one of the greatest painters, and by extension of that one of the greatest men, who ever lived. No one has had more influence on later art. Yet a mature painting by Cézanne has neither the immaculate and inexorable organization of a painting by Seurat nor the importunate pull of a painting by van Gogh or Gauguin. The subject matter is likely to be sober and conventional; the manner was for a long time thought to be tentative and overlaid with second thoughts. (Cézanne "couldn't draw," people said.)

This was because Cézanne had dismantled, one by one, the beliefs on which the practice of art had previously been based. That was in itself so momentous an ambition that he did not need, and could not have encompassed, the hectic high color and the patently symbolical subject matter of Gauguin or van Gogh.

There was nothing in Cézanne of the willful iconoclast. He revered the French classic tradition—as it had been exemplified by Poussin, above all. He revered it for its clarity, its complex, masterful organization, its noble and fastidious utterance, its disdain for the private and the accidental. Everything in Poussin happens the way it is meant to happen; never does he permit himself a loose end, a second thought, a momentary whim or caprice. A price was paid for all this, as it was paid in the plays of Poussin's near-contemporary, Racine. In Racine, nobody sneezes; the disorder of everyday life is outlawed by classic tradition. In Poussin, equally, we never come across a passage that is awkward or unfinished or a piece of drawing that has been flubbed.

Cézanne was alive to all this, but he knew that it was his destiny both to let in the things that had been left out of the French classic tradition and to let drop, one by one, its grave certainties. "Is that really how we look at the world? Or is there something in the nature of painting itself which has not yet been explored?" Those were the questions which Cézanne was to ask, and to answer, in the paintings of his last 29 years. He did not ask them in an abstract or schematic way. He *lived them,* in front of the motifs which Nature provided. No painter was ever more attentive to the outward and ostensible subject of his paintings: the portraits, the still lifes, the Provençal landscapes whose beauty Cézanne hoped to reveal for the first time. But fundamentally from the late 1870s onward he was also preoccupied with the notion of painting as a constructive act.

Cézanne took nothing for granted. He knew that style in art is like style in life: there is a moment at which it allows us to do what we have never done before, and there is a later moment at which it simply walls up the unknown and cuts us off from our own potentialities. Cézanne took down that wall; and he worked not as a dynamiter works but minutely and patiently, chip by chip, until in the end everything could come in. Prizing above all things a certain equilibrium of the vital faculties, Cézanne never aimed to let instinct rip.

It must, for instance, have been very painful for him when he gradually came to realize that traditional perspective would have to go. He knew how for more than four hundred years perspective had been the painter's automatic pilot, marshaling on his behalf no matter how large a quantity of visual information. By taking as its first premise a single point of vision, perspective had stabilized visual experience. It had bestowed order on chaos; it allowed elaborate and systematized cross-referencing, and quite soon it had become a touchstone of coherence and evenmindedness. To "lose all sense of perspective" is to this day a synonym for mental collapse. Yet perspective, before Cézanne, was fundamentally one of the sanctified frauds that keep the world turning: a conspiracy to deceive, in other words.

Of course it had brought great rewards. The expressive potential of perspective had been enormous. Cézanne acknowledged that his ambition was "to do Poussin over again from Nature"; and nothing in Western art is more moving than the godlike assurance with which Poussin argues that perspective is the right and natural way, the harmonious and logical way, in which complex statements can be spelled out on canvas. Yet Cézanne had in mind something more truly and more completely expressive of human capacities. Whether or not he knew it, his stance before life was characteristic of his time—and, more especially, of the attitude defined by Henri Bergson in a famous essay of 1889 on the nature of intuition: *Les Données immédiates de la conscience.* "We have to express ourselves in words," Bergson begins, "but most often we think in space." In French the word *conscience* means "conscience" in our sense, and it also means both "consciousness" and "knowledge." To a Frenchman, therefore, consciousness *is* knowledge, and to be conscious is to be learning, continuously. Bergson's ideas about duration and contingency, and about the interrelations and interpenetrations of objects, are often strikingly similar to Cézanne's procedures. We soon realize that whereas Tolstoy in the 1880s was asking "What Then Must We Do?" Cézanne was asking, "What can we know?" and asking it in terms which will always be relevant.

He let in, one by one, the things that had been kept out of painting: the fact, for instance, that in our knowledge of a given object time plays a part. We do not see it once and for all from a given point; nor does the given object have a given identity, once and for all. Monet also was aware of this, in his Cathedrals series of 1894; but the particularity of Cézanne was that he could work the effects of serial vision into a single canvas, thereby showing how everything is relative, in questions of identity, and subject to time, and movement, and change. Renaissance and post-Renaissance practice had given art stability; but stability and equilibrium are not necessarily the same, and when stability is spurious—willed, that is to say, and arbitrary—bluff enters into it. Cézanne called that bluff.

It was the same bluff that lay behind all the other pseudo-immutable systems—Euclidean geometry, for one, and Newtonian physics, for another. All the bluffs got called, between 1880 and 1914, and nowhere more thoroughly than in art.

Cézanne rebuilt the experience of seeing. He rebuilt it on the canvas, touch by touch, and he made each touch do a threefold duty. It had to be true to the object seen. It had to be true to the experience of seeing it. And it had to play its part in a grand overall design. That design was not carried out in the sweeping, unified and clearly eloquent style of the earlier masters. It was *built up,* piecemeal. All this is shown to perfection in his *Still Life with Peppermint Bottle,* which is a majestic amalgam of traits derived from French classical tradition, on the one hand, and forays into completely new territory, on the other. Since the 17th century French still-life painting had been remarkable for the weight, the solidity and the sense of a classical equilibrium with which household objects were rendered. Cézanne was faithful to this: never was fruit more monumental, never glass more artfully transparent, never the neck

Paul Cézanne.
Still Life with Peppermint Bottle.
1890–92.
Oil on canvas,
26 × 32⅜ inches.
National Gallery of Art, Washington.
Chester Dale Collection

and shoulder of a bottle more thoughtfully aligned to their surroundings.

But there was no authority in classical French painting for the peremptory way in which the top of the table had become invisible and illegible; for the way in which the decanter was made to belly out on the right; for the tumult of the drapes, which rear up from the top of the table like waves on a rough day at sea; or for the way in which the composition as a whole is both a portrait of stability, in which everything is balanced, somewhere and somehow, by every other thing, and at the same time a portrait of perpetual motion. Those drapes did not come from earlier painting but from the recesses of a riotous imagination; and yet, as always, Cézanne was minutely attentive to such details as the particular shiny red of the seal at the top of the bottle. There are portents of later painting in the way, for instance, in which the drapes mysteriously form, in the lower right-hand folds, into the likeness of a musical instrument much favored by the Cubists. There is a quick-moving, widely ranging system of echoes in the patterning of the drapes; Matisse was to pick this up and use it to great effect before 1914. Paintings such as this one stand on a high plateau between the past and the future of European painting. Cézanne was always true to what Bergson called *la conscience immédiate:* the facts of his own awareness. Anyone who doubts this should look at his monumental and yet totally human paintings of card players: everyone in them is, as D. H. Lawrence said of one of his characters, "like a piece of the out-of-doors come indoors." Cézanne never took a formula

Paul Cézanne.
The Card Players.
1890–92.
Oil on canvas,
25½ × 32 inches.
The Metropolitan
Museum of Art,
New York.
Bequest of Stephen
C. Clark

from stock; every mark on the canvas had to prove itself. But he also personified the organizing intelligence; and as he grew older there developed an ever greater tension between the demands of this organizing intelligence and the evidence which was brought to an eye that grew continually more acute. It was a part of the French tradition that order and stillness and lucidity should be bestowed on scenes which in themselves were in continual flux. When Louis Le Nain painted his *Peasants in a Landscape,* for instance, he devised a grand mathematical structure for his figures; his picture is a triumph of the grand style, and yet it does not abate the individuality of his subjects. Their dignity as human beings is enhanced by it. When Corot painted his *Breton Women at a Well,* he too gave the scene a severe, pyramidal structure in which the element of chance was ruled out. Cézanne, in the big *Grandes Baigneuses* now in Philadelphia, was as concerned as either of his predecessors with the august harmonies of triangular form—in fact he used the triangle three times over: once in the trees and twice among the bathers—but he also let in all the paradoxes, the contradictions and the irrational emphases which abound in our everyday experience. Cézanne included these too, and in doing so he gave an altogether grander dimension both to art itself and to the cognitive act. It is for this reason that Cézanne now seems to have given us, in words used by Henry James in another context, "the strongest dose of life that art can give, and the strongest dose of art that life can give."

That quotation might seem to relate, and in its original context in *The Tragic Muse* did relate, to a key moment in classical drama, when violent emotion is made bearable, but only just, by art. In Cézanne it might seem to apply more to the early imaginative subjects, where rape and murder are taken for granted, than to the work of the later years. But Cézanne from the 1880s onward was on to one of the fundamental truths about our life on

Paul Cézanne.
Grandes Baigneuses.
1898–1905.
Oil on canvas, 6 feet 10 inches × 8 feet 3 inches.
Philadelphia Museum of Art.
W. P. Wilstach Collection

earth: that *an idea is the most exciting thing there is.* Imagined melodramas about one man killing another cannot compete for enduring interest with the restructuring of the act of cognition which was Cézanne's deepest concern during the last years of his life. In one way or another, there is hardly an artist of consequence in the 20th century who was not affected by Cézanne's handling of the fundamental question "What can a man know?"

Gauguin was a very good judge of painting, and when he had the money, between 1876 and 1880, he formed a collection of Impressionist paintings which would have got him into art history even if he himself had never touched a brush. But when he became a painter himself his instinct told him that European art needed reinvigoration and that that reinvigoration would come from sources untapped in the schools. His memories of a sojourn in Peru in childhood had convinced him that in so-called primitive art there were inherent forces that could somehow revitalize the European imagination. Working in Brittany in the 1880s, and trying to build a picture language that would be distinctly his own, he remembered the hieratic and antinaturalistic presence of the Egyptian, Assyrian and Far Eastern sculptures which he had seen in the Louvre. He had Japanese prints pinned up in his room, alongside reproductions of Manet's *Olympia* and paintings by Botticelli and Fra Angelico; he looked hard at the Romanesque carvings which were to be seen in Brittany near Pont-Aven. Painting his *Breton Eve* in 1889, he took her pose from a Peruvian mummy which he had seen in Paris; painting his *Yellow Christ,* in the same year, he took both color and pose from a polychrome wooden sculpture in the chapel at Tremalo, near Pont-Aven. By taking the statue out of the chapel and putting it in the Breton landscape he gave it, however, something specifically Gauguinesque, the sense that mysterious forces, sometimes Christian in origin and sometimes not, are at work in landscape. Where the Impressionists saw landscape as fundamentally wholesome and benign, Gauguin saw it as the henchman of the unknown, and he made us aware of this by treating the landscape, as in the *Yellow Christ,* in terms of flat bands of color that had none of the Impressionists' regard for probability. "The mysterious centers of thought" were what Gauguin wanted to reach; and with that in mind he deliberately broke with the conventions of visual experience, circumscribing the principal elements of the picture with a firm, bold line, heightening and sharpening the color and flattening the planes until we are in no doubt that a new experience in a new kind of country is at hand.

Gauguin's personality in general was strong to the point of aggressiveness. But in one very beautiful painting done in Brittany in 1890, Gauguin subordinated his own edgy, incisive and at times almost hectoring approach to portraiture. *Marie Lagadu* is in fact an act of creative homage to Cézanne. More than anything that could be said or written, it shows with what a tender submission Cézanne was regarded by those of his fellow painters who had got close to him. Gauguin gave his sitter the monumental stillness and solidity for which Cézanne strove in his own portraits. He modeled her with a sculptural fullness and firmness, building the head with rich, fat color areas. Just behind her he placed a still life by Cézanne himself. ("I cling to that picture," he once said, "as I cling to my own life.") Re-creating a part of that still life on his own canvas, he went on to modulate almost imperceptibly from it to the real still life—the fruit and the tablecloth—in front of it. With a noble reticence quite foreign to his own nature, he integrated the real still life and the interpreted still life into a single, unbroken image. There was nothing of Gauguin's arbitrary, heavily outlined handling of color; the color was Cézanne's, just as the majesty of the pose was Cézanne's. Gauguin for once did not think of himself.

Marie Lagadu was an act of creative assimilation. If Gauguin's methods were usually more abrupt, it was because he believed that desperate situations called for desperate remedies. When he went to the South Seas it was not to "escape forever" but to save himself—and perhaps Europe too—from inanition. "A great thought-system is written in gold in Far Eastern art," he wrote in June, 1890. "The West has gone to rot, but a strong man could redouble his strength, like Antaeus, just by setting foot in the Far East. A year or two later he could come back as a new man."

Gauguin did not come back as "a new man," but the idea of the transplantable energies inherent in primitive art was to spread to Picasso, to Matisse, to Derain, to Kirchner and his colleagues in the group called Die Brücke (The Bridge) in Dresden, and to many another young artist before 1914. Gauguin saw the artist as a lord of life who could pick and choose from the past whatever would best release his own inmost nature. In this he pioneered one of the archetypal attitudes of the 20th century.

Gauguin also showed how color could be heightened in the interests of truth to individual human feeling; and in this, once again, his example was of primary importance to later painters. It is crucial to remember that what we call "influences" in art are not always linear. The people who profited most from Gauguin's example were not his immediate followers. Nor were they the people who tried to imitate what he had done. They were artists of quite other persuasions: Edvard Munch, most evidently, Bonnard and Vuillard in the 1890s, Picasso in his Blue Period, Matisse in 1905, Kandinsky in the years 1908–10. "Heighten color, simplify form" was the essence of what Gauguin told his admirers. It was Maurice Denis who said later: "The idea of having to copy Nature had been a ball and chain for our pictorial instincts. Gauguin set us free."

What Gauguin did in the last years of the 1880s was to specify the conditions in which the artist of the future could go to work. "My own work may be only relatively good," he said later, "but I have tried to vindicate the right to dare anything." Like Nietzsche in *Beyond Good and Evil,* he wanted to

Paul Gauguin.
Marie Lagadu. 1890.
Oil on canvas,
25⅝ × 21½ inches.
The Art Institute of Chicago.
The Joseph Winterbotham Collection

Paul Gauguin.
The Moon and the Earth (Hina Tefatu).
1893.
Oil on burlap,
45 × 24½ inches.
The Museum of Modern Art, New York.
Lillie P. Bliss Collection

get back to "the terrible original text, *Homo natura.*" "Two natures dwell within me," he wrote to his wife in 1888, "the Indian and the sensitive being. And now the sensitive being has dropped out and left the Indian to stride out ahead on his own." But the "sensitive being" in Gauguin kept coming back, unbidden, even if the Indian agreed with Nietzsche that Christian principles were "mere enfeeblement: witchcraft and sugar." But Gauguin was in touch with Paris till the end; the pictures he painted in the South Seas owed as much to Puvis de Chavannes (1824–98) and the tradition of European pastoral as to anything he picked up in Tahiti. This is true even of paintings which, like *The Moon and the Earth,* seem at first sight entirely non-European in their terms of reference. Gauguin did not like people to press him for a literal "explanation" of his South Seas paintings. He preferred on such occasions to quote the poet Stéphane Mallarmé: "Music needs no libretto." "The essence of a work," he wrote to one of his critics, "lies precisely in what is not expressed. . . . It has no material being."

So we may not be a great deal further forward for the knowledge that *The Moon and the Earth* represents an encounter between Hina, the moon, and Fatou, the earth. Hina stretches to her full height in order to ask Fatou if man cannot be reborn after death. When he says "No," she replies, "As you wish, but the moon will be reborn." The two figures dwarf the surrounding jungle. Gauguin has in fact given Hina the full-bodied power of one of Courbet's forest girls, while rendering the landscape in summary and miniature style, thereby reinforcing the suggestion that these are superhuman beings, personified Fates whose dialogue affects every one of us. But, once again, elements from earlier French painting keep coming in. The giant head of Fatou, for instance, is a descendant of the statues that look down on the mortals' goings-on in more than one major painting by Watteau. Degas bought this picture when it got to Paris in 1893; and as no one could have been less interested in images of the supernatural, I suspect that what he responded to was the strength and assurance with which Gauguin had reinvented the notion of pastoral.

The breakthrough that mattered to later art was the one he made in Brittany in 1888—to an abrupt, peremptory, self-willed sort of painting, in which perspective was flattened, forms were outlined with none of the continuous modeling of earlier times and color was used with unprecedented simplicity and force.

That is what Matisse, for one, took from Gauguin: flat tones, radical contouring and the readiness to let unaccented color areas overwhelm the

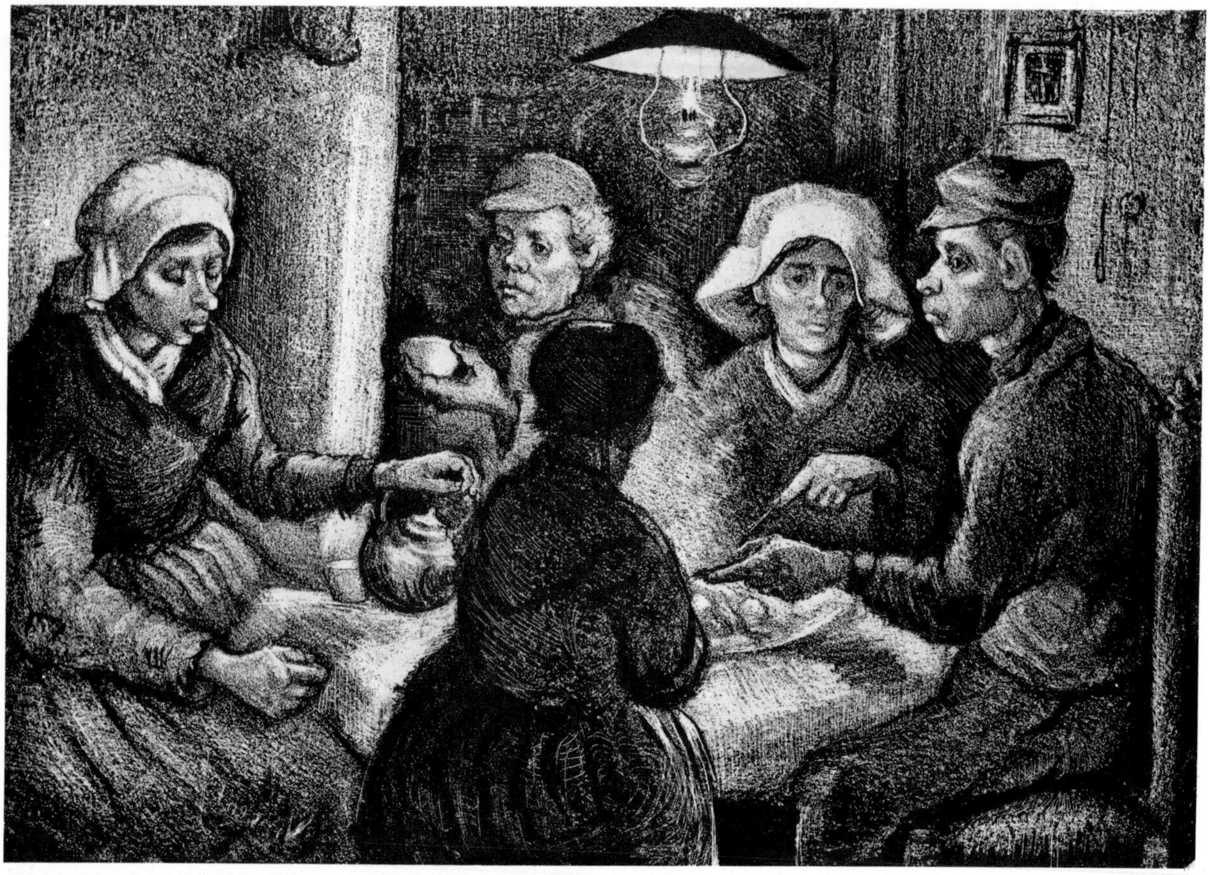

Vincent van Gogh.
The Potato Eaters.
1885.
Lithograph,
12¼ × 15¾ inches.
The Museum of Modern Art, New York.
Gift of Mr. and Mrs. A. A. Rosen

spectator. Bonnard and Vuillard could not have been less like pre-Columbian Peruvians, but they saw what could be made of Gauguin's arbitrary flat patterning and disregard for conventional perspective. When Gauguin used heightened color to express emotional truth, he got through to Kirchner and his colleagues in Dresden not as an "experimenter" but as a free spirit who used painting to redefine the dignity of man. We know now what Picasso meant when he said, many years later, that from a certain time onward "every man could re-create painting as he understood it from any basis whatever. . . ."

Gauguin in later years did not demur if people thought that van Gogh was fundamentally a simpleton, a Dutch dunce who had been picked up and put on the right road by him, Gauguin. Some of the facts were on his side: Gauguin knew the Impressionists when van Gogh was still toiling over his perspective-frame in The Hague, watching the workmen shambling out into their courtyards at four o'clock in the morning while the first fires were starting to smoke all over the town. In 1885–86, when Gauguin was about to make the decisive jump toward an arbitrary, inner-directed manipulation of color, van Gogh was still pondering how, in Dutch painting, "one of the most beautiful things has been the painting of *black,* which nevertheless has *light* in it." Black, which Pissarro had outlawed 20 years before!

Yet van Gogh in his Dutch years was already, even if only in intuition, the progenitor of much that is best in the art of our century. The year 1885 was, for instance, the year of the *Potato Eaters,* the dusky masterpiece of his years in Holland. But it was also the year in which instinct told him that color could be set free. Before he had ever seen what we call "modern painting"—that was reserved for his arrival in Paris in February, 1886—

Vincent van Gogh. *Street in Les Saintes-Maries.* 1888. Ink and reed pen, 9⅝ × 12½ inches. The Museum of Modern Art, New York. Abby Aldrich Rockefeller Bequest

he was writing to his brother in terms that even today have kept their explosive power. Holed up in the Dutch village of Nuenen, where his father had been a pastor, he developed on his own the idea-structure which gives him so firm a hold on later art.

"Color expresses something by itself," he wrote. "Let's say that I have to paint an autumn landscape with yellow leaves on the trees. If I see it as a symphony in yellow, does it matter whether the yellow that I use is the same as the yellow of the leaves? *No, it doesn't."* So much for the ancient convention by which every object has its "local color" and must bring it everywhere as evidence of its identity.

The culmination of van Gogh's views about the moral potential of color is *The Night Café,* which he painted in Arles in 1888. For the Impressionists, the café was a place where people went to enjoy themselves; Degas, for one, looked at it from the standpoint of an unshakable social assurance. Van Gogh saw it quite differently: partly because it was in his nature to solidarize with the poor and the lonely, partly because he was never rich enough or assured enough to go to places where the customers did not have to count their every penny. He saw the café as "a place where one can ruin oneself, or run mad, or commit a crime." He sensed "the powers of darkness" in what was probably a straightforward French working-class drink shop; and he tried, when painting it, "to express the terrible passions of humanity by means of red and green." His account of the painting is explicit enough to deserve quotation. The room, he said, was "blood red and dark yellow, with a green billiard table in the middle." Four lemon yellow lamps cast a glow of orange and green. The blood red and the yellow and the sharp green of the billiard cloth contrasted with "the tender, soft, Louis XV green of the counter, with its pink bouquet of cut flowers." The atmosphere was full—or so it seemed to van Gogh—of pale sulphur, "like a devil's furnace"; and the owner's white coat was changed to "lemon yellow, or a pale, luminous green," as he stood on duty in the corner.

Now, it is quite clear from a painting which Gauguin made of this same café that van Gogh misrepresented its basic nature, which was that of a place where people sat not too far apart and stared boldly around them. Van Gogh's inner distresses caused him to present the café as a place where a few cheerless patrons were swept to the perimeter of the scene, the way snow is swept into the gutters of a roadway. All possibility of an amiable human intercourse seems excluded, and we genuinely feel, as he wished us to feel, that "the terrible passions of humanity" have run their course behind the half-drawn curtain at the back of the room. Even the billiard table, that robust old stand-in for a more active and constructive way of life, suddenly looks like a bier. Van Gogh achieves all this in part by manipulations of perspective; but it is above all the color that projects a sense of the most penetrating inner anguish. Truth to feeling had never come out more strongly in painting. By setting truth to individual feeling above truth to objective fact, van Gogh gave the colorist his charter. Those words of his in 1885 are the beginnings of much of Matisse, much of Munch, much of early Derain and Vlaminck, much of Kandinsky, much of Chagall in his early years, much of Klee. To this day, when artists talk about color, they owe something, directly or indirectly, to van Gogh.

Vincent van Gogh.
The Night Café.
1888.
Oil on canvas,
28½ × 36¼ inches.
Yale University Art Gallery, New Haven, Conn.
Bequest of Stephen Carlton Clark

Van Gogh was also coming to terms at that time with what is for the layman one of the most bothersome aspects of modern art: distortion. Distortion is, or was, a sore subject with young and old alike. We remember, for instance, how in 1913 the art students of Chicago burned Matisse's *Blue Nude* in effigy when it came to the city as part of the Armory Show. And it was an "artist" who complained to van Gogh's brother about the distortions in the *Potato Eaters.* "Tell him," van Gogh wrote, "that I should be in despair if my figures were 'correct,' in academic terms. I don't want them to be 'correct.' Real artists paint things not as they are, in a dry, analytical way, but as *they* feel them. Tell him that I adore Michelangelo's figures, though the legs are too long and the hips and backsides too large. Tell him that what I most want to do is to make of these incorrectnesses, deviations, remodelings or adjustments of reality something that is—yes, 'untrue,' if you like, but more true than literal truth."

This was, once again, written in the year 1885, and in the depths of the Dutch countryside. Again van Gogh hit on just the turn of phrase that could stand as a motto for the century that is now in its last decades. To "paint things not as they are . . . but as *they* feel them" is an ambition so nearly universal in our time that van Gogh would deserve immortality for that phrase alone. Yet he went on finding, to the end of his short life, the right words for the kind of work which would bring to light the buried life of man. Before how many great paintings of this century do we not remember van Gogh saying that "the painter of the future will be a colorist such as there has never been," and that the unit of expression for the new art would be "a form of brushwork that would cut out stippling, and the rest, and offer simply the varied stroke"?

In pictures like *The Starry Night,* painted in Saint-Rémy in June, 1889, van Gogh showed what he meant. The paint in *The Starry Night* is not applied in polite, well-judged, art-school style. It forms itself into ideograms of convulsion: emblems of an apocalyptic vision which includes stars brighter than the sun at midday, a huge horned moon that seems to hold the sun in its embrace, and a spiral nebula that flies through the air like a serpent from the Book of Revelations. Even the moonlit woodlands behind the little town are rendered with a ferocious, nonstop, over-and-over movement of the loaded brush. Just once or twice before, others had got somewhere near to the intensity of *The Starry Night:* Leonardo da Vinci in his drawings of a storm, the German Old Master Altdorfer in his portrayals of a tormented northern sky. But van Gogh was out on his own for the sheer visionary intensity of his new "unit of expression." This is painting that refers not to earlier painting but to areas of our experience to which art had not previously had access.

To Cézanne's "What can a man know?" van Gogh added a question of his own: "How can we best unlock the valves of feeling?" To one or the other of these questions, or to both of them in conjunction, modern art has the answers.

Vincent van Gogh.
The Starry Night.
1889.
Oil on canvas,
29 × 36¼ inches.
The Museum of Modern Art, New York.
Acquired through the Lillie P. Bliss Bequest

THE EMANCIPATION OF COLOR

Between 1890 and 1905 the emancipation of color was completed.

Like most of history's upheavals, this one looks inevitable when surveyed from a safe distance. Emancipation had been in the air for a long time: you couldn't open a newspaper, sit through a play by George Bernard Shaw or put your nose inside a factory without realizing that radical changes—some peaceful, some not—were on the way. The 1860s had provided the Grand Design: people remembered 1861 for the emancipation of the serfs in Russia, 1863 for the emancipation of the slaves in the United States, 1867 for the emancipation of the Jews—in principle, at any rate—throughout the Austro-Hungarian Empire. The emancipation of women would take longer, but by the late 1880s it had become clear that society was moving toward it. It was unthinkable that in art, that most sensitive area of life, equivalent emancipations should not occur.

And occur they did, though not quite fast enough to save Pissarro and Monet from near-martyrdom by poverty in the late 1860s. Gradually it became clear that the traditional patronage of the state and the church was giving way to a freer and more informal relationship between the painter, his dealer and just one or two informed collectors. The tyranny of the big annual official exhibition loosened around the same time, and a new tradition began: that of the little back room to which the fortunate few were admitted by pioneer dealers like Ambroise Vollard and *le père* Tanguy. Subject matter was set free, now that the favor of a frock-coated official was no longer essential to an artist's advancement. The fine arts were released from obligations to society which could better be carried out by photography; as a result, their natures could be explored without either inhibition or surveillance.

In all this, color was the conspicuous element. Its emancipation was foreshadowed as early as 1885, when van Gogh put it in writing that "color expresses something by itself." That color could send coded messages in a cipher not yet cracked was clear to Gauguin by 1888 and quickly got through to his disciples. That color could make volume and define form was being proved by Cézanne all through the 1880s and 1890s. That patches of color laid flat on the canvas were the prime constituent of painting, and should take rank as such, was argued by Maurice Denis, then just 20 years old, in a now-classic article, "A Definition of Neo-Traditionism," first published in August, 1890. The more men looked into the fundamentals of art, the more consistently did color turn up at the center of their inquiries.

But when color finally came out strongly at the Salon d'Automne of 1905—in the room given over to Henri Matisse, André Derain, Maurice Vlaminck, Albert Marquet, Henri-Charles Manguin and others—people were dumbfounded, all the same. They were dumbfounded all over again in Dresden in 1906, and in Munich in 1911, and at the Armory Show in New York in 1913. As in other departments of life, it is one thing to talk about emancipation and quite another to meet it face to face. There were local and auxiliary motives for their stupefaction: many of those who were appalled by Matisse's paintings at the Salon d'Automne in Paris in 1905 had never seen a Gauguin or a van Gogh and knew nothing of the historic fatality which had brought those particular Matisses into being. But there was also a general and a more rational reason to raise the alarm.

Color is a constant: one of the standards of excellence and normality by which we judge Nature, judge much that is of our own making and judge one another. Color is also a differential: one of the things that help us to find our way about the world. We don't like to feel that either of these two main functions of color is subject to alteration. Color is fundamental to life: to call a man "colorless" is as rude as we can get without descending to particulars. Color has a hot line to instinct, and its messages take priority even over those of language: the hunter doesn't need to speak if he can point to fresh blood in the snow. Our first reaction to change in all this is one of defensive rigidity; if the traffic lights turned blue at the next intersection, a conservative driver would put the gears into neutral and sit by the side of the road.

But we also know, and our predecessors knew already in 1905, that color is one of the affirmative elements in life. Color is energy made visible. Energy in itself is not necessarily good; anyone who has been within range of a hurricane will have seen for himself that energy can be vicious and destructive. But in the context of art, heightened color usually brings heightened energy of a euphoric sort; and I don't think it was an accident that Matisse in 1905 was painting in a world that wanted to get more out of life than people had been getting before. What was the message of Henry James in *The Ambassadors*, first published just two years before? "Live all you can—it's a mistake not to."

Heightened color came into art at just the time when heightened energy of an environmental kind was becoming available to everyone. This is not to say that there was a self-evident relationship between science and art from the 1880s onward. Gauguin in Pont-Aven and van Gogh in Arles were about as innocent of up-to-date scientific knowledge as intelligent human beings can be. But they knew that there was more to color than had yet been got out of it, and that somewhere in color there was energy, waiting to be released. Color had to be made to work for everyone as electricity was working for Edison, as the gasoline engine was working for Gottlieb Daimler, and as Niagara Falls was beginning to work for those who knew how to tame it. These things had to have their equivalent in art; and Gauguin knew before he died that he had opened new color options for painting, just as van Gogh knew that the great artist of this century would be a colorist of a kind never seen before.

Matisse, as much as anyone, was that colorist. By 1909, when he painted the first version of his *Dance*, he was able to make a plain, bald, unhesitating affirmation of color-as-energy. *Dance*

Vincent van Gogh.
Bedroom at Arles.
1888.
Oil on canvas,
28¾ × 36 inches.
The Art Institute of Chicago.
Helen Birch Bartlett Memorial Collection

looked (and still looks) so spontaneous that many people believed that Matisse had simply trusted to instinct and let rip, like a "great artist" in a movie. When Matisse opened a private art school in Paris in 1908, his students thought to please him on the first day of the term by daubing their canvases at random with the hottest colors they could lay their hands on—only to find that Matisse disliked this very much indeed and sent them right back to the formal beginnings of art education.

He also knew that the Old Masters were neither ignorant nor timid when it came to the use of color. Everyone has heard of Titian's way with red, Veronese's way with green and Vermeer's way with a lapislike blue. But the conditions of art in their day were such that color had to stay down in the kitchen as the servant of form and the henchman of design.

There was even a socio-philosophical prejudice against color. Immanuel Kant, in his *Critique of Judgment,* first published in 1790, gave classic expression to the subjection of color. "In painting and sculpture," he said, "the *design* is the essential thing. . . . The colors which give brilliance to the

Maurice Vlaminck.
The Blue House.
c. 1905.
Oil on burlap,
21½ × 25½ inches.
The Minneapolis
Institute of Arts.
Bequest of Putnam
Dana McMillan

sketch are part of its charm and they may, in their own way, give an added liveliness to what we are looking at. But they can never, in themselves, make it beautiful." This was, admittedly, a philosophical position rather than the view of a man who had spent much of his life looking at pictures. Kant had hardly ever left his native city of Königsberg and was so indifferent to the pleasures of sight that it was several years before he even noticed that he had gone blind in one eye. Kant was predominantly cerebral in his orientation, and he ran true to psychological type in preferring line to color; the sensitory freedom for which color stood was of no interest to him. But, quite independently of this innate predisposition, he spoke for educated European opinion at a time when color was thought of as a dispensable additive; and Matisse could almost have had Kant in mind when in 1945 he looked back, as a man in his late 70s, on the evolution of color.

"The whole history of color," Matisse said then, "lies in the recapture of its powers of expression. For centuries it was no more than the complementary of drawing. Raphael, Dürer and Mantegna were like all the painters of the Renaissance in that they built their pictures on drawing and added the local color later. The case was quite different with the Italian primitives and with the painters of the Orient. With *them*, color was the principal means of expression. . . . From Delacroix to van Gogh (and, in particular, to Gauguin) by way of the Impressionists, who cleared the ground, and by way of Cézanne, who gave the definitive push when he showed us how to make volumes with pure color, we can trace the rehabilitation of color and the recovery of its power to work upon us directly."

Matisse, when he said that, had been painting and drawing and sculpting for over half a century. There lay before him, in his 80s, a terminal period as fruitful as any in the history of modern art. No one ever knew more about color than he. So what he has to say has great weight with us and, once again, the upheaval which he describes now looks inevitable.

But changes of this sort correspond to profound, hard-won changes in social attitudes. The long subjection of color stood, for instance, for a fear, or at the very least, a distrust of the instinctual life. By the 1890s Nietzsche had spread throughout Europe a contrary point of view: instinct was marked *plus* in his work, whereas for centuries it had been marked *minus.* When Kant wrote his *Critique of Judgment* it was with art as it was with property, and with monogamy, and with authority in all its forms: the instinctual life had to be kept down, lest anarchy should supervene. There was no such thing in the 1790s as a "pure colorist," in our modern sense; but any such person would at that time have been put on the official list of subversives, along with the seducer, the freethinker and the democrat. If such people were not kept under control there would not be in all Europe a great house unsacked, a church without its Tree of Liberty or a husband without horns: that was the idea.

Like most ideas, this one was thoroughly raked over in the 19th century. It wasn't altogether foolish, by the way. There really is such a thing as the demagogy of color: Hitler's use of black and red at the Nuremberg rallies soon proved that. But the 19th century's investigations into color were conducted for the most part in a liberationist spirit: the question to be answered was "Can color set men free, and if so how?" It seemed to Goethe, and to those who came after him, that the understanding of color was an important subdepartment of self-knowledge. Color might provide the grammar that was needed if we were to speak a new language and the keyboard that we needed if we were to draw new music from our life on earth. Ingres spoke for a steely and unalterable rearguard when he reiterated that "drawing is the probity of art"; but John Ruskin carried the century before him when he wrote in 1851 that "the purest and most thoughtful minds are those which love color the most."

The emancipation of color was linked, moreover, to the emancipation of art in general from social duties which had by then become obsolete. If we look at a masterpiece of Kant's day like David's *The Oath of the Horatii,* 1784, we shall see at once that it carries a load of anecdote, of precise documentation and of learned pictorial reference which could not be borne by the color language of 1905, even had that language been available. Interiors painted by Edouard Vuillard in the 1890s now seem to us not only ravishing in themselves but remarkably precise in their references to costume and decoration; and if, at the time they were painted, they seemed sketchy and approximate even to quite sensitive people the reason is that those people were conditioned to expect color of a tight, predictable sort. Every painting is a duet, after all. If the man who is looking at it can't keep time with the man who painted it, then the painting is incomplete; even the most radical moves in modern art were always made to an audience of not less than one.

So color was not set free in any one moment of time, as Florestan is set free in *Fidelio.* It took well over a hundred years to resolve the antithesis between the English connoisseur Sir George Beaumont, who said, "A good picture, like a good fiddle, should be brown," and a painter like Derain, who in 1905 took a plain red, a plain blue and a plain yellow from the tube and put them straight on the canvas in rectangular dabs that subverted the whole notion of "good painting." Color was set free in a disorderly and coincidental way: by Constable when he set out to show things that "exist in Nature but have not been seen before"; by Delacroix when he noted in the 1850s that painters should "banish all earthen colors" and remember that shadows cast on the ground, by no matter what object, are violet; by Turner when he came back from his first visit to Italy and prompted Constable to say that "Turner is stark mad with ability

André Derain. *Three Trees, L'Estaque.* c. 1906. Oil on canvas, 39½ × 31½ inches. Art Gallery of Ontario, Toronto. Gift of Sam and Ayala Zacks

much as Gauguin's or van Gogh's, an exemplary destiny. He spoke, as they did not, for certain permanent traits of the French genius: the inspired conservatism, the power of lucid analysis, the ability to objectify. When instinct said "Drop all that and think only of yourself!" Matisse could always say "No."

Among Matisse's friends and contemporaries before 1901, none were of his own caliber. But in 1901 he happened to see Derain at an exhibition of van Gogh's work in Paris, and through Derain he met Vlaminck. Matisse had never looked young, and in the company of Derain and Vlaminck, who were extraverted giants of a generation later than his own, he must have had an almost exaggeratedly careworn and professorial look. (Derain captured something of this in the portrait of Matisse which he painted in 1905.) The encounter was important to Matisse because he soon found that Derain and Vlaminck had arrived at a position very similar to his own. They wanted to let color come through, in other words, without any of the constraints which the history of art had imposed upon it. Derain wanted this because he was an immensely well-educated young man who had looked at everything in the museums and decided that that was the way art had to go. Vlaminck wanted it because he was a coarse brute with just one brief spark of genius, and he wanted to prove that the art of the museums and the Salons was all washed up and could be ignored without loss. Matisse did not go along with Vlaminck in this, but he did undoubtedly derive very great comfort from the allegiance of his two juniors. (One of them wrote that Matisse "looked ten years younger" at the end of his first visit to them.)

Those first meetings in 1901 led eventually to what is called Fauve painting. ("Fauve" is the French word for a wild and dangerous beast.) It is in some ways a silly name, and it certainly does not suit Matisse; but it does suggest the ferocious energy with which the public as a whole was confronted, head-on, at the Salon d'Automne of 1905.

(This was, by the way, the last confrontation of its kind that Paris was to see. Later developments in painting were first shown in dealers' galleries, and some were not shown at all: Picasso's *Les Demoiselles d'Avignon,* probably the most famous painting of this century, was not seen in public until 30 years after it was painted, while some of Matisse's greatest works went to Moscow before 1914 and were not seen in a French museum until 1970.)

Chromatic energy found in Fauvism its strongest and least ambiguous expression. An aesthetic of pure exhilaration could ask for no finer monument than Derain's Fauve landscapes. In them, a robust and for the moment undivided nature fulfills itself completely. But as Derain was a deeply intelligent man he may have sensed that only at that moment in his life, and only at that moment in the history of art, was such a fulfillment possible. For just two or three years the compass needle of painting turned toward an art that was all spontaneity, all heightened and simplified sensation. Nuance was banished, and the order of the day was "All systems go!" Derain and Vlaminck at

Balthus.
André Derain. 1936.
Oil on wood,
44⅜ × 28½ inches.
The Museum of
Modern Art, New
York.
Acquired through
the Lillie P. Bliss
Bequest

that time disdained the gloss of "fine art": their paintings had to be seen as what they were—and for what they were.

That was never quite Matisse's position, and even Derain and Vlaminck could not maintain it for long. The rest of Derain's long career was a 40-year attempt to recapture the qualities for which Fauvism had no place: long-pondered composition, Old Masterly craftsmanship, learned allusion to the art of the past and the search for a well-carpentered equilibrium. Only rarely, and above all in his stage designs and illustrated books, did the delicious, unballasted chromatic energy of 1905–07 return to Derain's art in later years. Derain, for almost all his life, was a man mismated with his time and mismated with himself: something of his wracked intelligence, his overwhelming but somewhat tumbledown physical presence and his tendency to smother self-doubt with histrionics comes out in Balthus's portrait of him.

Fauvism was like a forest fire: everyone who was anywhere near got singed. This applied as much to Georges Braque, a painter of supreme gifts, as it did to minor masters like Albert Marquet and Raoul Dufy. It also applied to someone like Kees van Dongen, who for just a year or two was hoisted right out of his class by the fact of participating in an important moment of art history. That moment could not be prolonged, however. Fauvism was an art of maximum statement, and although its crashing, undifferentiated oppositions of pure color were thrilling in the hands of Derain and Vlaminck, the thrill was bought at a very high price.

Braque put this clearly when he discussed many years later the period in the fall of 1906 when he followed the example of Derain (and of Cézanne before him) and went down to paint at L'Estaque, near Marseilles. He had responded, just for one season, to the violent change of color and light. "But I couldn't have done it again," he went on. "I'd have had to go to the Congo the next time to get the same effect." Of course this was in part a temperamental reaction; Braque was one of the most fastidious men who ever touched a brush, and he could neither think, feel nor act to the drumbeat of pure Fauvist practice. But he adapted it, all the same, to his own nature. He brought in lavender blue as well as Prussian blue, Veronese green as well as emerald green, pink as well as vermilion, violet as well as orange. With all these, and with ivory laid on a priming of white lead, he nuanced his way across the canvas and yet stayed loyal to the Fauvist ethic: there was nothing on the canvas but the approved lozenges of unbroken color. Yet a Fauve landscape by Braque is never aggressive in the way that a landscape by Vlaminck can be aggressive; the return route to other kinds of expression is always kept open.

Braque at that time—1906—was barely 24 years old; one of the most fruitful careers in 20th-century painting had hardly begun. He was young enough and inexperienced enough not to chafe at his compositional skill, and defeated Ingres, whose *The Golden Age* looks congested and unspontaneous when set beside Watteau. The subject preoccupied many of Matisse's contemporaries; André Derain, for one, expressly gave the title of *The Golden Age* to the ambitious, energetic but finally quite incoherent painting which he produced in 1905. It was left to Matisse to restate the subject in terms of the 20th century.

His *Joy of Life* was by no means a break with the past. Those who got over their first astonishment might soon see that the piping boy in the rearground on the right derives from the Titian/Giorgione *Pastoral*, which Matisse had seen hundreds of times in the Louvre. They could go on to acknowledge that the *Joy of Life* is, from beginning to end, a derivative of those major paintings by Watteau in which figures are grouped in landscapes. Finally, they would remember that Matisse admired Ingres for the freedom with which he would reinvent the female anatomy when it suited him to do so. They would think especially of Ingres's *The Golden Age*—stilted as it may be —and they would see that the two paintings are closely allied in their readiness to violate academic anatomy in the interests of a broad, flowing arabesque set against a heavily wooded landscape that was cut open in the center to give depth and admit of a far blue distance.

The *Joy of Life* hung for years in Gertrude Stein's drawing room in Paris, where Picasso was a frequent visitor. He must, consciously or not, have seen the big picture as a challenge to his own capacities; and when he came to paint *Les Demoiselles d'Avignon* he began from a compositional scheme which was strikingly akin to that of the *Joy*

Pablo Picasso. *Family of Saltimbanques.* 1905. Oil on canvas, 6 feet 11¾ inches × 7 feet 6⅜ inches. National Gallery of Art, Washington. Chester Dale Collection

Henri Matisse.
The Red Studio.
1911.
Oil on canvas, 71¼ inches × 7 feet 2¼ inches.
The Museum of Modern Art, New York.
Mrs. Simon Guggenheim Fund

of Life. Les Demoiselles d'Avignon will dominate a later chapter in this book, and I need say here only that, like the *Joy of Life,* it has to do with grouped human figures set in a tripartite formal design that varies in color from warmth on the left to a cooler, sharper climate on the right. Again like the *Joy of Life,* though in a way that is altogether more trenchant, it treats the figures in a variety of styles, with no attempt at internal consistency.

Meanwhile Picasso, in his 25th year, was working on two monumental projects which had in common an instantly identifiable pinkish tonality. Picasso's Rose Period would seem to have begun in March, 1905, with a painting in gouache and watercolor of a young acrobat. Thereafter he produced a substantial corpus of paintings and drawings of circus- and street-perfomers, in costume and out of it. Their general subject was the contrast between the beauty and fragility of the human body and the feats of strength and endurance which it can be trained to carry out. With this came a subsidiary contrast: between the enclosed world of the performers and the world which we ourselves inhabit. The poet Rainer Maria Rilke knew Picasso's *Family of Saltimbanques* very well, and he wrote about it in one of his "Duino Elegies." He saw the little family as having been tormented from childhood onward by the will toward a brief, hard-won perfection: a fugitive beauty which few would notice and fewer still would stay to applaud. The *Family of Saltim-*

Henri Matisse.
Dance (1st version).
1909.
Oil on canvas, 8 feet 6½ inches × 12 feet 9½ inches.
The Museum of Modern Art, New York.
Gift of Nelson A. Rockefeller in honor of Alfred H. Barr, Jr.

banques was intended in this sense, beyond a doubt; but it is also a metaphor for the painter's position in society.

Picasso in the *Saltimbanques,* and in the never-finished project of 1906 for a large painting of horses and their attendants, was carrying forward a tradition in which Manet, in particular, had excelled: that of the complex figure composition in which people, often costumed beyond the demands of everyday, were grouped in an informal manner. The paintings in question can be read as portraits of disconnection, though there is no reason to think that Manet (or Watteau before him, in his theatrical paintings) so intended them. "Alienation" is, even so, our current name for the look of apartness which Manet gives to the old musician and his companions; and it recurs in Picasso's *Family of Saltimbanques.* Color in the big Picasso defines the emotional climate of the picture—and how subtly! Those faded pinks and subdued terra cottas, those echoing blues are picked up by the colors of earth and sky; the flowers in the child's basket index them all over again; even the pitcher on the ground plays along.

We would suppose that all this was as much a product of Picasso's imagination as the recurrent washes of moon blue in his paintings of a year or two earlier. But it has been pointed out that some of the Rose Period paintings deal—in terms of straightforward local color—with the facts of life among circus performers. It was a matter of literal truth that the interior of the most popular circus in Paris was painted "a tender red, shading slightly into gray," and that acrobats traditionally wore what one writer called "pink tights tinted the color of fresh roses." Indeed, Degas and Seurat had treated that same circus building in tones of rose, pink and red. There is therefore no reason to think of the color in these paintings as a bid to preempt our sympathies. Touching as it is, it remains primarily descriptive.

The delectable paintings of circus performers

which figure so largely in Picasso's Rose Period were linked to life, therefore, by their use of color which was, in effect, a mark of professional identification: circus pink was as specific, in this context, as "navy blue." But the Rose Period also corresponded to a basic change of mood in Picasso's output; and that change of mood persisted in the more directly autobiographical work of the period —the self-portraits, the affectionate variations on the looks of his best friends and the sideways allusions to the role of the artist in society. Matisse was altogether more detached—more cool-hearted, many would say—in his choice of subject matter. And whereas Picasso could manipulate circumstantial detail to most poignant effect, Matisse tended between 1905 and 1910 to eliminate more and more of those elements in his figure paintings which could detract from the central role of color.

When Matisse's Russian patron Shchukin asked him, for instance, for a decorative panel on the theme of music, he began with a sketch which showed people in the standard attitude of enraptured concertgoers; standard flowers grew at their feet, and a standard mastiff completed the scene. But before long he cut out the flowers, cut out the dog, cut out the self-awareness of the listeners. Color had been set free, and now it must be *left* free: that was the message of the two big decorations, *Dance* and *Music,* which Matisse sent to Moscow.

The Museum of Modern Art possesses the first version (1909) of *Dance.* From the study of this, and more particularly from the study of *The Red Studio* of 1911, we can see exactly what "color for color's sake" could mean at that time. It meant— as Matisse told his students—building the picture in terms of color. It meant getting the colors to support one another without anecdotal references or any resorting to "local color." Nature must be made to submit to "the spirit of the picture"; and that spirit was to be expressed in terms of pure color, as intense as the painter could make it. Color must do all the talking.

Matisse decided to build *Dance* with three colors: in his own words "a beautiful blue for the sky, the bluest of blues (the surface was colored to saturation, that is to say, up to a point where the blue, the idea of absolute blue, appeared conclusively) and a like green for the earth, and the vibrant vermilion for the bodies." Matisse had experimented with maximum saturation the year before with a single bathing figure. Now he took a group of dancers from the middle ground of the *Joy of Life* and brought them up front, on the kind of anonymous promontory that Picasso had used for his *Family of Saltimbanques.* The Museum of Modern Art's version has not quite the chromatic intensity of the Moscow version, and some of the drawing is more felt than realized: the detailing of hands and feet, for instance. The New York painting is about an uncomplicated form of high spirits; the Moscow one, about what could almost be a dance to the death, such as was to be portrayed in the music of Stravinsky's *The Rite of Spring.* But the two big paintings should be contrasted rather with the classic bacchanalia of European painting than with one another. Poussin's *Bacchanalian Scene* in the National Gallery in London has, for instance, a comparable round dance, with comparable positioning of hands and feet and a comparable circular pounding swing, round and round, as if naked figures had picked up Energy itself, as one might pick up a ball, and were flinging it from hand to hand. But Poussin upholstered the image with allegorical byplay in ways which Matisse by 1909 felt free to discard; in *Dance* there are no garlanded satyrs, no overhanging foliage, no distant mountains, no bunches of symbolic grapes and no cherubs to lap up the symbolic juices. The picture is presented to us undressed, just as the dancers themselves are undressed; whatever is not indispensable has been dispensed with. Both dance and dancers burst out of the frame; and in the simplifying and concentrating of the image the role of color is primary.

As much as any of the great altarpieces of the past, Matisse's *Dance* is a painting that can be seen

Henri Matisse.
Music. 1910.
Oil on canvas, 8 feet 5⅝ inches × 12 feet 9½ inches.
The Hermitage, Leningrad

from a great distance and still dominate the surroundings. But it differs from those altarpieces in that there is reserved for each of us a place in the very middle of the dance: it is for us, if we feel like it, to fill the gap between the outstretched hands of the two foreground figures.

Even more irresistibly are we drawn into the picture space of *The Red Studio,* 1911: the box of crayons in the foreground seems in some mysterious way to be already under our hand, and we wouldn't be surprised to see our own two familiar feet somewhere on view along the lower rim of the canvas. Color in *The Red Studio* is used to bend space in a way more radical than had been seen before in painting. Matisse takes the classic, rectangular deep space of the studio and treats it as we treat a miscellany of objects presented to us on a jeweler's tray. Certain things he picks up and puts under our noses. To others he says, "Keep your distance!" On the far wall, four identifiable pictures face us frontally, setting up a clear idea of the distance involved. Two identifiable statues by Matisse define, again, the space immediately in front of the far wall; but the double-A shape of the stools on which they stand is not related to the floor beneath them, any more than we can identify, in the top half of the picture, the point at which the left-hand wall meets the far one. Matisse's own paintings, and his own ceramic plate in the foreground, retain their own chromatic identity. But other objects in the room have been bled of that identity and restated in terms of the glorious, uniform red which gives the picture its name. What we see is, in fact, an unbroken field of red on which certain incidents have been laid, or incised. Delectable as they are in themselves, these incidents are the captives of that one resonant, imperious, inescapable field of red. It is a crucial moment in the history of painting: color is on top, and making the most of it.

Edvard Munch.
The Dance of Life.
1899–1900.
Oil on canvas,
50 inches × 6 feet
4 inches.
Nasjonalgalleriet,
Oslo

HISTORY AS NIGHTMARE

One of the key remarks of this century occurs in a very long novel which was begun in 1914 by an Irish writer who had yet to make a name. James Joyce was the writer, the novel was *Ulysses*, and the remark was all of 11 words long. "History," said Joyce's Stephen Dedalus, "is a nightmare from which I am trying to awake."

I take "history" to mean, here, a sense of the past as something that determines the present to an intolerable degree. To be born in a certain place, at a certain time, and of a particular parentage, can be a disadvantage from which it is impossible to recover completely. I take "nightmare" to mean, here, the state of mind defined in 1931 by Ernest Jones, the eminent psychoanalyst and biographer of Sigmund Freud. Jones described the classic symptoms of nightmare as "agonizing dread, a sense of oppression or weight at the chest which alarmingly interferes with respiration, and a conviction of hopeless paralysis." A sense of history as nightmare, thus interpreted, is as severe an affliction as can be wished upon us.

Yet we can all think of times at which that sense was mandatory among intelligent and sensitive people. The calendar of the recent past is full of such times, and very often they are linked to particular places: Prague in 1968, Dallas in 1963, Budapest in 1956, Hiroshima in 1945, Leningrad during the seige of 1941–43, Pearl Harbor in 1941, Paris in 1940, Berlin in 1933. To be aware of what was going on in those places at those moments was to experience in our waking life the terrors attributed in 1834 by a Scottish savant, Dr. Robert Macnish, to the nightmare state: "The whole mind is wrought up to a pitch of unutterable despair; a spell is laid upon the faculties which freezes them into inaction; the wretched victim feels as if pent alive in his coffin, or overpowered by resistless and unmitigable pressures."

At such times, and in the face of such thoughts, we realize how high van Gogh was aiming when he said that he wanted his paintings "to retain their calm even in the midst of catastrophe." Art and literature are there at such times to steady us: to remind us that night thoughts, even when warranted, are not the whole of life. But art and literature are also there to remind us of aspects of existence, and of ourselves, with which we have not dared to come to terms.

Someone who knew this was Franz Kafka. Kafka in 1903 was only 20 years old, and he was still some way from writing the novels and the stories—among them *The Trial, The Castle* and *The Metamorphosis*—which were to earn him a unique place in the history of the European imagination. But he already knew what was worth writing (and reading) and what wasn't. He sensed that a state of emergency would shortly be declared within the European psyche, and that a new kind of awareness would be needed to deal with it. The old order might seem to be intact in the Austro-Hungarian Empire of 1903, and the concept of the collective unconscious had not yet been formulated by C. G. Jung. But Kafka also sensed that someone would have to force that new kind of awareness upon us. Meanwhile, it was not the writer's first duty to help the reader to pass the time as agreeably as possible. "A book must be an ice axe," Kafka wrote to a friend, "to break the sea frozen within us." "If the book in our hands does not wake us, as with a fist that hammers on the skull, then it just isn't worth reading." That was the message.

Kafka and his ice axe could remind us of a German painting which, though not modern in date, is both a classic of clear-sightedness and the ancestor of much that is memorable in the art of the last hundred years: *The Frozen Sea,* which was painted by Caspar David Friedrich in 1822. This was a new kind of picture, with a new echo to it, and it is still the best image we have of the way in which human hopes and human ambitions can have the life crushed out of them by forces beyond our control. Friedrich took one of the vicissitudes of early Arctic exploration and turned it into a symbol of "history as nightmare." Such was the force of his emotional commitment, when allied to a steadfast and pellucid form of expression, that his private anxieties took on a universal and timeless validity.

Like all the great symbols, *The Frozen Sea* will bear many interpretations and yield something new to all of them. It is a painting to which every age reacts in a different way. Friedrich never sold it. The sailing ship was for him, throughout his career, a symbol for all that was vulnerable and nerve-ridden in human affairs; but I believe that *The Frozen Sea* had a secret meaning for him, and one so poignant that he could not bear to part with the painting. It had an inner subject: the events of the immediate past in Germany. The disaster to which it refers is political as much as maritime. Friedrich was still the man who had painted, ten years earlier, a picture called *The Grave of One Who Fell for Freedom;* and when he painted *The Frozen Sea* he must have had in mind the Carlsbad Decrees of 1819, by which freedom of the press was abolished over a large part of Germany, political agitation was suppressed, the universities were brought under state control and the free-spirited individual laid under suspicion of "conspiracy." That was "history as nightmare" in the 1820s. In how many countries is it not still with us?

Friedrich was the first major European artist to acknowledge the role in his work of the as-yet-unnamed unconscious. "Close your physical eye" was his advice to other painters. "Look first at your picture with the eye of the spirit, and bring to the light of day what you have seen in darkness." It is as if he knew, ahead of his time, that the documentary, illustrative function would soon be wrested from art. Art had still the power, however, to come up with symbols so telling, so universal in their application, that they take rank among the experiences that orient us in life. One such was Goya's *The Colossus.* As much as anyone who ever lived, Goya carried within him the sense of history as nightmare. The offhand brutality of our own times is something to which Goya, in 19th-century Spain, gave definitive expression. Where he trod, it is pointless for other painters to follow; what has been done completely need not be done again.

Caspar David Friedrich.
The Frozen Sea.
1822.
Oil on canvas,
38½ × 46½ inches.
Hamburger Kunsthalle, Hamburg

Goya had in an extreme degree the premonitory sense: he knew what kinds of behavior had come to stay. "No one," said Baudelaire of Goya, "has ventured further in the direction of the *possible* absurd." Now that the absurd is everywhere—in behavior so appalling that we have to give it an ironical name before we can bear to think about it all—we realize that to explore the "possible absurd" in such depth was as great a service to mankind as art can perform.

The Colossus gave us a new metaphor for nightmare. Just who the giant was, and just what he was doing, Goya left it to us to decide. He is an archetypal figure of dread; each generation gives him a new set of identity papers. To have some idea of the powers of art we have only to set *The Colossus* beside a comparable image from the 1930s: a still from *King Kong*. *King Kong* was a good movie, and its image of a giant gorilla standing on top of a skyscraper has entered into the folk-memory of our times. But beside the Goya how flat it is, how banal, how pedestrian! How much less terrifying is King Kong's petulant stance, with its conventional baring of the teeth, than the indifference of Goya's colossus, who does not even deign to look back at the scene of panic and terror beneath him!

Both *The Colossus* and *The Frozen Sea* stand for an important shift in the activities of the human imagination: the shift from allegory to symbol. Allegory in this context is the use of art to tell a story which is already familiar but cannot be told too often. Anyone who went to the Doges' Palace in Venice in the 1580s and was shown the new paintings by Veronese would immediately see that most of the paintings in question were about power, and about the fact that the Venetian Republic had power and intended to keep it. Allegory, in this instance, was doing its job well; Mars and Neptune were on the ceiling, and very fine they looked; but the implication was that Venetian power had the sanction of the gods and woe betide anyone who presumed to challenge it. Allegory had for centuries been one of the prime functions of art. Allegory in public places was confirmatory, by its very nature. If a painting was put up in church, or in the law courts, or in one of the seats of government, it was a safe bet that it would tell people that things were quite all right as they were. The painter was not going to say that religion was a hoax, or that the judges were ignorant and corrupt, or that the ruler was not fit to rule. When Tintoretto worked in the Doges' Palace, and Rubens worked for Marie de Médicis when she was Queen of France, and Tiepolo painted the great ceiling in the Bishop's Palace in Würzburg, they were being asked to uphold the status quo; and they did it, without demur. If they thought that the Doges had got above themselves, or that the Bishops were too free with the excellent local wine, they never said so.

By the 19th century the structure of obeisance, long shaken, fell apart. So did the structure of shared learning on which allegory could draw. The old confidence in society and its rulers, already undermined by the revolutions of the 18th century, was collapsing. ("Casca il mondo"—"The world is coming apart"—said the Papal Secretary of State in 1866, when the Prussians defeated the Austrians at the battle of Königgrätz.) Allegory in its great days depended on shared beliefs, and shared expectations, and allusions universally recognizable. But in the 19th century a new world was coming into being: a world in which many thoughtful people had not read Virgil and Ariosto, and didn't know one saint from another, and were convinced that the only thing in which they could believe completely was their own private emotional experience. Whole sections of humanity felt themselves orphaned. To accommodate all this—to express the poetry of dissent and the politics of disquiet—a new kind of art had to come into being.

Friedrich's had been a preindustrial sensibility: one that functioned in perfect unselfconsciousness before what now seems to us the second Fall of Man. By the 1880s the role of the imagination was in the ascendant, in that symbols alone could stand for thoughts too long repressed in made-to-order painting. Symbol was the free man's revenge upon authority. It was the essence of the symbol, in this context, that it did not tell a familiar story. In fact it didn't tell a story at all. It sowed a seed: of disquiet, wonder, speculation, doubt. It was an invaluable way of saying something very important without pinning oneself down. No tyrant was immune to the symbol; and the 1880s had their full share of tyrants and would-be tyrants. The time was approaching when James Joyce could say that "silence, exile and cunning" were the only conditions in which a major artist could go to work. The silence could be conditional, the exile a matter of inner adjustment, the cunning a strategy to keep out of authority's way. The essential was to keep the work intact. The symbol was the mine with which outdated ideas would be blown sky-high; meanwhile, the vagrant imagination did better to shun company. It is significant that the life style of Symbolist painters like Gustave Moreau and Odilon Redon was private and obsessional, with none of the hearty, outgoing quality which had characterized Monet and Renoir in their youth.

But if the vagrant imagination did not have company in the Paris of the 1880s, it had backers. In poetry and painting alike, it was defended by masters of language: Stéphane Mallarmé, above all, and his fellow poets Jules Laforgue, Tristan Corbière and Jean Moréas. Symbolism is so much a matter of the individual imagination, and so little a matter of theory and doctrine, that groupings of this sort are valid primarily as a matter of historical convenience. Much of what is called Symbolist

Edvard Munch.
The Voice. 1893.
Oil on canvas,
34½ × 42½ inches.
Museum of Fine Arts, Boston. Ernest Wadsworth Longfellow Fund

into old age. But these endowments did not save him from the most lurid and melodramatic of private entanglements. When he was 40, for instance, he was involved with a girl who had herself laid out, as if on her deathbed, in an attempt to prevent him from leaving her; and when she threatened to shoot herself and Munch tried to restrain her, the gun went off accidentally and he lost one of his fingers in the struggle. Two or three years later he had to leave Norway after a public brawl with another man. As late as the 1930s Munch was still reliving that day in his work—still picturing the look of his bloodied antagonist as he staggered along the narrow lane toward Munch's house, and still picturing the reflex of instinct with which he himself had picked up a gun as if to ward off a second attack.

Munch was able to share these experiences with us in a way that is neither garrulous nor self-pitying. He was also able to give them a universal implication. (A later painter, Oskar Kokoschka, said that Munch had been the first man to enter "the modern Inferno" and come back to tell how it was.) Art was for Munch what the theater was for Strindberg: "a *Biblia pauperum*, or Bible in pictures." He could have said, with Strindberg, that he "found 'the joy of life' in life's cruel and mighty conflicts"—and in the colossal discharges of psychic energy to which they gave rise. In dealing with those "cruel and mighty conflicts," Munch undressed feelings the way bodies are undressed in the act of love.

All this is made clear in such classic Munch subjects as *The Death Chamber*, *Jealousy* and *The*

Edvard Munch.
Jealousy. 1896.
Lithograph,
18¾ × 22⅝ inches.
The Museum of Modern Art, New York.
The William B. and Evelyn A. Jaffe Collection

Dance of Life. In a painting like the *Virginia Creeper* of 1898, Munch uses a perfectly ordinary aspect of suburban horticulture to make us feel that the whole of Nature is hemorrhaging in sympathy with the tormented man in the foreground. Munch came from a part of the world in which Nature often seems to side with the extremes of human feeling; and Nature in his paintings is neither indifferent nor hostile. She figures, rather, as the accomplice of mankind and as a commentator who gives a new amplitude (and what Rodin had called "an unlimited development") to emotions which in life are often repressed.

For the greater part of his life Munch was preoccupied with the idea of painting a series of pictures which, when put together, would constitute a complete panorama of human life. He completed a modest version of it for the foyer of a theater in Berlin. Later, in 1922, he tried to compress the idea into a series of 12 paintings for a chocolate factory in Oslo; and sometimes there were single paintings which, like *The Dance of Life,* tried to show the whole gamut of human existence at once. Munch felt so strongly and so deeply for this subject that he was ready to adopt a system of cues which another artist would have rejected as too banal: as in *The Dance of Life,* for instance, where the white dress of the girl on the left stands for an as yet unblemished purity, the black dress and tortured demeanor of the woman

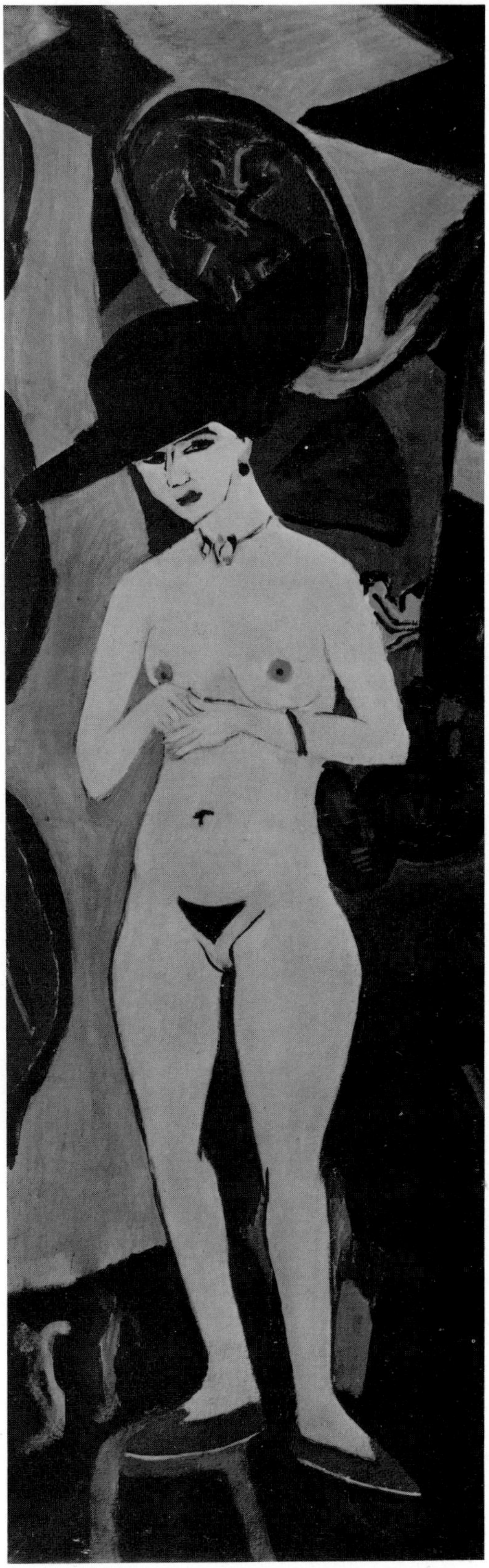

Ernst Ludwig Kirchner. *Standing Nude with Hat.* 1910–20. Woodcut, 6 feet 10 inches × 26 inches. Städtische Galerie, Frankfurt

to bear witness as best he could. This might seem to rule out—and in the case of Kirchner and his friends it did rule out—those grand panoramic adventures which had always been the supreme ambition of the allegorical painter.

Adventures of that kind were not likely to come the way of radical painters in Germany while Kaiser Wilhelm II was on the throne; but they did come the way of Munch, who spent some of the best years of his life (1909–14) on mural paintings —some of them as much as 38 feet in length—for Oslo University. And a comparable opportunity was given in Vienna to Gustav Klimt when, in October, 1894, he was invited to paint three large panels—*Jurisprudence, Medicine* and *Philosophy* — for the great hall or Aula of the University of Vienna. It must have seemed quite a safe choice; Klimt was known as a reliable young man who could work to order. He was practiced, docile, meticulous, and he turned in his work on time. There was every reason to suppose that his work for the University would go through without incident.

Klimt was in human terms the exact opposite of almost all the artists with whom we have lately dealt. Easy and convivial by nature, he was accepted throughout his life as a man who did honor to his generation: not for him the subterranean political motivation and the eventual exile of Goya. He strode into life as a champion swimmer strides into the sea. Of course such looks can be deceptive, and Klimt in point of fact had his full share of inner anxieties; but these never compared with the alienation of Munch, who in 1908–09 was restored to mental stability only after eight months of intensive care in a clinic, or with the slow decline of Kirchner, who died by his own hand in Switzerland in 1938 after a long period in exile. The crippled emotional life of the mother-bound Moreau was at a far extreme from the royal freedom with which Klimt appeared to move from one attachment to another. Klimt was at one with the world.

Or was he? It did not seem so when the first of

Gustav Klimt.
Judith I. 1901.
Oil on canvas,
33½ × 16½ inches.
Osterreichische
Galerie, Vienna.
© Galerie Welz,
Salzburg

the three panels, *Philosophy*, was put on view in 1900. *Medicine* was shown in 1901; and in 1903 all three were shown together, though *Jurisprudence* was still not finished. There was in every case a most terrible uproar—so much so that in the fall of 1903 the contract was annulled. The three paintings were never installed in the University; and, as they were destroyed in a fire during the last phase of World War II, we can judge them only by the old and imperfect photographs which have survived and by a few working drawings in Viennese public collections. It is clear from these, however, that Klimt did not represent philosophy, jurisprudence and medicine in terms of superior wisdom, or of an intellectual majesty that stood high above the battle, or of a long view that put all our earthly concerns in perspective. The imagery in general was nearer, if anything, to that of Rodin's *Gates of Hell.* What had philosophy to do with families twirling in limbo? Or medicine with an over-decorated temptress who was feeding her pet snake from a glass saucer? Or jurisprudence with the seductive young women, dressed only in their superabundant hair, who fixed the spectator with looks that were anything but judicial? It was all too much for the Ministerial committees, and too much for the outraged faculty members of the University, and too much for the general public.

Klimt had, of course, changed a great deal since the contract came his way. In 1892 he had lost both his father, an engraver by profession, and his younger brother Ernst, who had worked with him on more than one laborious decoration. In ways not yet disentangled, these misfortunes seem to have liberated Klimt; after several years' silence he emerged in 1898 as an artist of a completely different kind and a vastly greater stature. The docile journeyman-decorator became the spokesman of his age—or, more exactly, of that age's unconscious longings and fears. In the Vienna of Gustav Mahler, Arnold Schoenberg and Sigmund Freud, Gustav Klimt was a person of consequence. He was present at table on the occasion when Mahler first set eyes on his future wife, and he was

Max Beckmann.
Family Picture.
1920.
Oil on canvas,
25⅝ × 39¾ inches.
The Museum of
Modern Art, New
York.
Gift of Abby Aldrich
Rockefeller

He himself went on to serve in the medical corps on the Russian front and in Flanders. It was at this point that history caught up with him, and the well-built, untroubled young man became a neurasthenic who had to be discharged from the army, after barely a year, as unfit for further service. When he began to paint again it was, as he said in 1917, "to reproach God for his errors." A great part of his new material came from the notes which he had taken during month after month of close contact with men who had been hideously wounded. This experience had given him a phantasmagorical insight into the casual indignities which come the way of the human body; and when the war came to an end in 1918, and it turned out that those indignities did not come to an end with it, Beckmann was able to sum up the situation in a big painting called *The Night.*

The Night is not an objective statement, like *Declaration of War.* It is a symbolic statement: "history as nightmare" is everywhere present in it. It has in it elements from the news of the day: the killing in furtive and underhand ways of people who should have played a lofty part in German life; the swinish conduct of the defeated military; the stealth with which evil deeds were done, and the readiness with which wicked men found accomplices, and the equanimity with which people would stand around and watch. All these things were a part of German life during the months—August, 1918, to March, 1919—that Beckmann toiled away at the picture; and it is, to that extent, a "document of the times." There is, in *The Night,* enough circumstantial detail to flesh out a novel;

Max Beckmann.
The Night. 1918–19.
Oil on canvas,
53 × 61½ inches.
Kunstsammlung
Nordrhein-
Westfalen,
Düsseldorf

but the peculiar and lasting force of the picture is owed to its pre-echoes of an even more bestial era. This was how it would be when torture was taken for granted as the instrument of state policy, and when millions of people would live in dread of a knock on the door in the night. "You may live to see this" is the message of *The Night.* As in all Symbolist paintings of real quality, the artist spoke truer than he knew.

It is not, however, a self-pitying picture. Beckmann's was not a negative nature. He believed that if the case were put in the right way, and with sufficient force, the course of history might just possibly be changed. But he did not underestimate the role of habit, and of ingrained obedience, in the German nature. In 1920, for instance, he painted his *Family Picture:* a portrait of an enclosed world, a shallow Gothic space updated to the 1920s and inhabited by six human beings, each one of them locked in his own concerns. These are the people who will have to choose, one way or the other. Beckmann himself lies brooding on the piano bench. The auguries do not look promising. His mother-in-law hides her face. His wife thinks only of the possible fading of her good looks. His sister-in-law has drifted into dreamland. The servant is content to sponge up the small print in the local newspaper. Beckmann's young son alone shows something of resolution in the avidity with which he pores over his book. Elsewhere the concept of *Gemütlichkeit* has turned rancid.

Family Picture is not much fun to look at. As for *The Night,* it is one of the most disagreeable images which the art of our century has to show. Yet Beckmann nowhere exaggerates: he makes his effects by enumeration, and by a certain steadiness of mind, and above all by the exact and unsparing draftsmanship which made him so fine a printmaker. One can admire these things and yet feel that these paintings bring bad news. What could be more rash, after all, than to assume that what happened in 1918–19, and what happened thereafter, will never happen again? If we have lived through even part of all that, we can be forgiven for not wanting to think about it. If we are young enough to know it only from hearsay, we are likely to have problems of our own time to preoccupy us. In either case, we may well be glad to let the ice form again over those particular seas. If all this were a matter of record—of keeping a particular body of knowledge in being—we could leave it to the libraries; art could find its material elsewhere. But what if the symbols which art has to offer are vital to our understanding of the world and cannot be found elsewhere? If that is so—and in the case of the works here discussed it is so, beyond a doubt—then what Kafka said about books is no less true about pictures. Here it is again: "What we need are books which come upon us like ill-fortune, and distress us deeply. . . . A book must be an ice axe, to break the sea frozen within us."

Pablo Picasso.
Les Demoiselles d'Avignon. 1907.
Oil on canvas, 8 feet × 7 feet 8 inches.
The Museum of Modern Art, New York.
Acquired through the Lillie P. Bliss Bequest

which gave off an almost palpable sense of elemental energies for which no definitive use had been found. It was at this point that Braque with his composed and impregnable nature and his steady, consistent methods of work began to play an ever larger part in Picasso's life. Braque had for some time been awed by the beauty and dignity of Cézanne's achievement; L'Estaque was a favorite workplace of Cézanne's, and had Braque been an everyday "follower of Cézanne" he would have seized, in that summer of 1908, on the first facts about the landscape there, which were the devouring brilliance of the light and the saturated blue of the sky. But in fact he did nothing of the kind. The landscapes which he brought back with him were filled with a hooded light of his own devising. In their compositional scheme the sky played no part. They were severe, tightly constructed paintings in which color was restricted to the most sober of greens and ochres. Contours were broken, contrasts of "near" and "far" were often contradicted, forms opened up into one another, and houses were splayed out in such a way that more was seen of them than could have been seen from any one point of view in life.

It was with respect to these paintings that the critic Louis Vauxcelles wrote that Braque "reduces everything—places, figures, houses—to geometrical schemas, to cubes." The name was never apt, since there are no cubes in Cubist painting, but it stuck. One column-inch in a newspaper dated November 14, 1908, established Braque as the pioneer of the movement; and as he went on his ruminative way he produced *Still Life with Fruit* in late 1908 in which intersecting planes were dramatized by the quite arbitrary fall of the light, and early in 1909 a *Harbor in Normandy,* painted in Paris, which was fundamental to the development of Cubism. The memory of Cézanne still presides over it; the repeated triangles which form up in the sky, the sails of the boat on the left and the detailing of the jetty are related to the lofty, echoing, triangular forms in the *Grandes Baigneuses.* But Braque had evolved on his own a method of unifying the painting by causing the sky, the sea, the boats, the lighthouses and the harbor itself to run on into one another—each coaxing the other, as it were, to take over the burden of structuring the picture. Braque's ambition was to remake space in such a way that each

Georges Braque.
Still Life with Fruit.
1908.
Oil on canvas,
21½ × 26 inches.
Moderna Museet,
Stockholm

object would come forward in turn—to be stroked, almost, as antelopes are stroked in a zoo. (The art historian John Golding says of the *Harbor in Normandy* that "the optical sensation produced is comparable to that of running one's hand over an immensely elaborate, subtly carved sculpture in low relief.")

In the preface which Apollinaire wrote for Braque's first one-man show at Kahnweiler's, in November, 1908, he rightly singled out the element of "angelic moderation" in Braque's nature. But to be angelic is not to be characterless; Braque in 1908–09 defined the immediate ambitions of Cubism in a way that testified to the operation of a most powerful and resourceful intelligence. "Angelic" remains the right word, however, for the final effect of Braque's early Cubist work, which is that of a peaceable kingdom of forms, each of which submits with total docility to its presentation in a continually changing space. That kind of thing was quite foreign to Picasso's nature, and when in the summer of 1909 he produced his first group of completely realized Cubist paintings they had quite another character. Alike in landscape and in portraiture, he displayed a power-mindedness and a drive toward total possession which were quite absent in Braque.

Something of the difference between Picasso and Braque comes out in the contrast between Braque's *Still Life with Fruit,* 1908, and Picasso's *Still Life with Liqueur Bottle,* 1909. If the Braque is more broadly and generally conceived, it is more a matter of generous forms generously modeled, and if it has touches of much higher color, that may be in part because it is the earlier picture of the two and because Cubism was not yet so distinctly based on sharp-edged, prismatic planes and near-monochromatic color. But there is something peculiar to Picasso in the use of idiosyncratic objects like the many-faceted bottle of Spanish anisette that is in the lower left-hand half of the painting and the rather less legible ceramic bottle in the form of a cock that is above and to the right of it. Picasso had by this time proceeded much further toward the adoption of an all-purpose, prismatic form, like a folded sheet of writing paper, which paces the image and determines the speed at which information is given to the observer; and it is already quite difficult to read the individual objects in the picture. It is an indication of the dynamic of Picasso's career that the year 1909, which produced such fidgety, prismatic Cubist paintings as the *Still Life with Liqueur Bottle,* should also have prompted the *Still Life with Bread and Fruit Dish on a Table.* Everything here seems larger, grander and more stable than in everyday life. The majesty of the hinged table, the bare, strong outline of the bread, the total lack of fuss or histrionics—all relate back to the ancient traditions of Spanish still-life painting; it is as if, after the agitations of the *Demoiselles,* Picasso had come through to the kind of calm, clear, exact statement which proves all over again that absolute dignity can characterize the fundamentals of everyday. (It is, by the way, in character with the metamorphic energy of Picasso's procedures that this most austere of still lifes should have evolved

Pablo Picasso.
Still Life with Liqueur Bottle.
1909.
Oil on canvas,
32⅛ × 25¾ inches.
The Museum of Modern Art, New York.
Mrs. Simon Guggenheim Fund

Georges Braque.
La Roche-Guyon: The Château. 1909.
Oil on canvas,
31¾ × 23⅝ inches.
Moderna Museet,
Stockholm

and houses to windowless canisters drawn in with an unwavering straight black line. The painting is as much a "contrast of forms" as any one of the paintings which actually bear that name, but the contrasts are tied to everyday reality.

Cubism as a joint effort came to an end with the outbreak of World War I in August, 1914. It was never reintegrated. The friendship between Picasso and Braque had been too intense, and had been lived through at too great an imaginative pressure, to be taken up again like a friendly game of chess. Phases in life cannot be relived, and when Braque came back from being trepanned in a military hospital his once-great strength had been diminished forever. But in his work of 1918–19 he produced what is in effect an elegy—and one of the most poignant things of its kind—for the lost oneness of the Cubist effort.

It was after a long and slow convalescence that Braque returned to painting toward the end of World War I. In *Café-Bar* 1919, he applied the methods of Synthetic or "late" Cubism to subject matter derived from popular life. The overlapping, flat planes defy conventional perspective and put us within touching distance of the basic elements of French café-life: the guitar, the sheet music, the white clay pipe on the table, the fruit in its dish, the diamond-patterned floor, the sharp-toothed decorative surround of door and window, the dado, the speckled wallpaper, the folded newspaper, the windowpane with its sprawly, outmoded lettering and the unpainted, rough-grained wood of the table. The lettering suggests that we are looking in from the street; but in reality we are neither inside nor out, but "in touch" with the scene in all its aspects. In its detail, the picture recalls the Cubist works of before 1914, with their stenciled letters and scraps of real newspaper; but in the majesty of its proportions, in the fullness and richness of its color, and in its ambitious and equivocal exploration of space, *Café-Bar* looks forward to the symphonic interiors of 1939–55 which were to be the crowning glory of Braque's long career.

Picasso likewise produced, at the very end of the decade, at least one major work in which the preoccupations of the previous ten years were given monumental and, in one way or another, definitive expression. The point of *Guitar,* 1919, lies not so much in the guitar, painted on torn paper, which is attached to the canvas by two real and all but invisible pins, as in the tall, thin diamond which lies behind it. William Rubin argued in 1972 that the subject of the picture is not "a guitar," but a guitarist. The diamond-shape represents, in other words, an immensely simplified human figure, with just one or two very discreet clues as to its pose and location. Thus read, the picture would constitute a late if not final contribution to Cubist iconography. The use of a paper nail with a simulated shadow at the top of the guitar is an echo, also, of the ways in which nails were used in Cubist painting to point the difference between depicted reality and "the real thing." Picasso in 1919 was able to use both of them simultaneously and in the same context.

Fernand Léger.
Contrast of Forms.
1913.
Oil on canvas,
39½ × 32 inches.
The Museum of
Modern Art, New
York.
Philip L. Goodwin
Collection

Picasso and Braque had not set out with any specific program in mind, and Picasso in 1923 rejected the idea of research in art with words which soon became famous: "To search is meaningless, in painting. To *find*—that is the thing." It will be clear by the end of this book that a very large proportion of what is best in this century's art has been predicated in one way or another on what Picasso and Braque "found" between 1907 and 1914. They had liquidated, one by one, the problems which had been left unsolved at the time of the death of Cézanne in 1906. They had given altogether new answers to the question, "What can a picture be?" They kept alive the idea of the masterpiece and on many occasions lived up to it. In 1914 their careers had still a long way to go, in that they were still giving new resonance to the idea of Cubism in the late 1940s and '50s; but it could be said that by the end of that fateful year there was already in existence what the art historian Edward Fry has rightly called the "greatest single aesthetic achievement of this century."

Georges Braque.
Café-Bar. 1919.
Oil on canvas,
64 × 32¾ inches.
Kunstmuseum, Basel

THE COSMOPOLITAN EYE

Shortly before 1914 modern art began to matter, all over Europe, in ways in which it had never mattered before.

No one date, no one place, no one name can be brought forward as proof of this; but there came about a general awareness that there was such a thing as a modern sensibility, and that that sensibility had the key to modern life. People were learning to live with the fact—well put by Fernand Léger in the summer of 1913—that "the modern conception of art is the total expression of a new generation, whose condition it shares and to whose aspirations it responds."

To be modern, in this sense, was to take due note of all the changes which were being brought about in the conditions of life. It involved an acceptance of the elements of the unconscious and the irrational in human affairs. It meant overturning the tyranny of high art and high culture, and realizing that great art was just as likely to arise from close scrutiny of other areas of human activity. It meant looking at the art of other times and other peoples than those of Athens and Florence, Venice and Rome. It meant believing, with Léger again, that a billboard stuck up in the middle of a field could enrich the landscape and not desecrate it. It meant accepting the airplane and the telephone and the steel-framed building as instruments of liberation. It meant seeing our human inheritance as a whole, without fear or prejudice.

Life in those years was dipped in the dyes of the new. After 1900, when Sigmund Freud published his *Interpretation of Dreams,* the role of the unconscious was bound to come sooner or later into the forefront of art. Between 1893 and 1914 museums in Leipzig, Brussels, Cologne, Stockholm, Paris, Frankfurt, Basel and Essen installed permanent exhibitions of primitive art. In each case a whole new vocabulary was made available to young artists. In 1910 Henri Matisse was one of many attentive visitors to the great exhibition of Islamic art in Munich. The Italian Futurist Umberto Boccioni spoke for a whole generation when he wrote in his diary in 1907 that "I want to paint

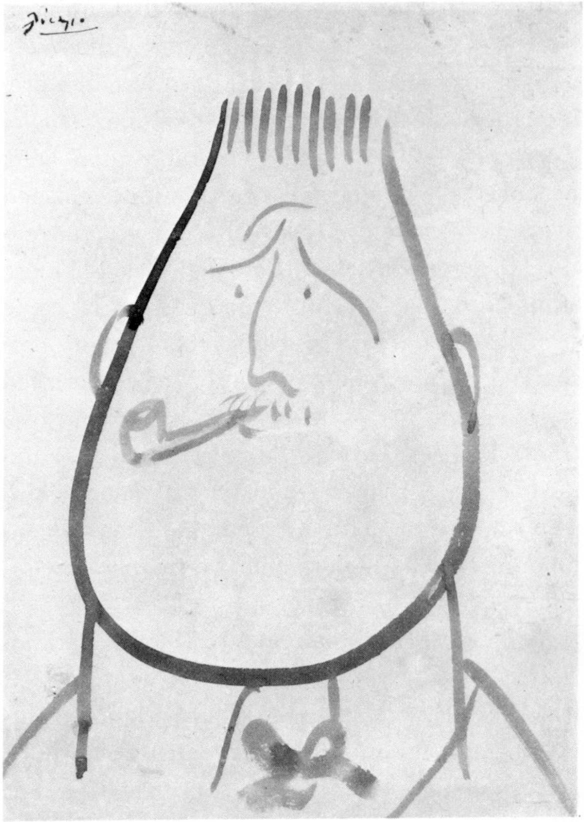

Pablo Picasso.
Portrait of Apollinaire. 1905.
Ink and wash,
12½ × 9¼ inches.
Private collection,
Washington

the new, the fruits of our industrial age. Old walls and old palaces, old motifs and old memories nauseate me. Our feverish era makes yesterday's productions obsolete and useless." The skirl and thump of Stravinsky's *The Rite of Spring* spoke in 1913 for elemental forces too long excluded from art. Radical changes were imminent—changes as radical as those set out in the Special Theory of Relativity, which Einstein had published in 1905, or in Rutherford's experiments with the atom in the years that followed.

News of these changes was carried, where art was concerned, by word of mouth, by the magazines, by one or two farsighted dealers and collectors, and by the huge conglomerate exhibitions in Paris, Berlin, London, Cologne, Munich and elsewhere, which operated before 1914 as a pacific International: a collective force which broke down national barriers, argued for a new openness of spirit, and exemplified a superabundant curiosity as to what was being done, anywhere and everywhere, in the name of the new. By 1913, when New York had a first taste of it, that pacific International had made itself felt all over Europe as the free expression of a genuinely modern sensibility.

The poet Guillaume Apollinaire (1880–1918) was, as much as anyone, the epitome of that sensibility. He had a position peculiar to himself, in that unlike most of the people who write or lecture about art he was in his own right a man of genius. In his poetry he made sense of modern life in a completely new way. Endowed with a lyrical gift of the rarest, most irresistible sort, he gave the new century the new tone for which it had been waiting; and his fragmented, unpunctuated, free-associating manner of speech became one of the basic elements in the creative practice of the 20th century. The closing section of *The Waste Land* could not have been written if T. S. Eliot had not read Apollinaire; Apollinaire stood, equally, as godfather to the best lyrics of Cole Porter and to the verbal agility which made the Beatles' song "Lucy in the Sky with Diamonds" so great a success in the late 1960s. It is well over 50 years since his two books of poems, *Alcools* and *Calligrammes,* were published; yet the poems still come across in a direct and confidential way which convinces us that Apollinaire is telling us the truth, without reserve or humbug.

In life, Apollinaire was never the high-collared Great Man. He was the involved, vulnerable, supremely human individual who got into scrapes because of the openhearted and guileless nature which made him everyone's favorite companion. When he was in love, he was unsuccessful as often as not. When society needed a scapegoat—as happened when two little statues were stolen from the Louvre—it was Apollinaire, the archetypal innocent, who was jailed on suspicion of the theft. Life made things difficult for him from the moment that he was born in Rome in 1880 of a young unmarried Polish lady and a well-connected but ne'er-do-well Italian officer, already in his middle 40s, who not long afterward disowned the relationship.

Reared first in Rome, then in Monte Carlo, and later in one or another of the towns by the Mediterranean where his mother hoped to find a protector, Apollinaire in first youth took the whole of Europe for his birthright. A natural cosmopolitan, he looked at every new place, every new book and every new person in terms of a potential adventure. If he found Nick Carter and Buffalo Bill more stimulating than Milton's *Paradise Lost,* he came straight out and said so. He was spontaneity personified: "Almost all my poems have been printed as they were first written down," he wrote to a friend in 1913. He was a natural identifier, and never happier than when instinct signaled to him —in a book or a picture or a human being—a genuine life force, or a perfection not paralleled elsewhere.

All this was invaluable to him when he was introduced to Picasso in 1904. From that day onward he saw more and more of painting and painters. From 1905 until his death in 1918, he spoke up in defense of just about everyone who was going to last on the European art scene. What he said was often rather silly; but there is no denying the record, which is that he was right in there in defense of Picasso (1905), Matisse (1907), Braque (1908), the Douanier Rousseau (1910), Robert Delaunay (1911), Kandinsky, Duchamp, Picabia, Gris and the Italian Futurists (1912), Chagall and Mondrian (1913), Larionov, Gontcharova and de Chirico (1914). Not all of them needed him; I have heard one protégé of Apollinaire say that he would write anything to fill up a page, and another that he could not tell Rubens from Rembrandt. But once again the record speaks for itself. Who introduced Picasso to Braque? Apollinaire. Who worked hardest to make Cubism acceptable to the general public? Apollinaire. Who was at the top of the visiting list for every informed foreigner who came to Paris? Apollinaire. The illustrated books on which Apollinaire worked with Derain in 1909 and with Dufy in 1911 are classics of their kind. Apollinaire gave Orphism its name in 1913. From February, 1912, onward he edited *Les Soirées de Paris,* as brilliant a review of art and literature as has ever existed. When he and Delaunay went to Germany in 1913 he made an unforgettable impression on the young Max Ernst. In 1917 he invented the word "Surrealism." When he got married in 1918 Picasso was a witness at the ceremony; and nothing in Picasso's work bespeaks a more heartfelt affection than the long series of portrait drawings of Apollinaire—Apollinaire plain, Apollinaire fantasized, Apollinaire in health and strength, and Apollinaire with the head wound he sustained as a willing soldier in 1916. Apollinaire was not always right about art—who ever was?—but one of the greatest periods of European art bears the mark of his passage over and over again.

He did more for art and for artists than just write about them. The conditions of his life had made him the most adroit of persuaders—who else has had a plaque put up in his honor on the wall of a hotel which he left without paying the bill?—and he never begrudged time spent on behalf of the new. When the minor or auxiliary Cubists (among them Gleizes, Metzinger, Delaunay, Léger and Le Fauconnier) determined to show together at the Salon des Indépendants in April, 1911, it was Apollinaire who acted as their champion. When they were invited to Brussels, again as a group, two months later, it was Apollinaire who prefaced the catalogue. What he said was not all true, but it did very clearly indicate what Gleizes, for one, was aiming to do. He was getting ready, Apollinaire said, to tackle "the vast subjects which yesterday's painters in their timidity had never dared to wrest from the presumptuous, outdated and tedious daubers of the official Salons." Today we know that "vast subjects" played no part in Cubist painting as it was brought to perfection by Picasso, Braque and Gris. Their subject matter was limited, concise, and most often emotionally neutral. Apollinaire unwittingly let slip the fact that Gleizes and Metzinger had no idea of what Cubism was really about and were using it simply as a way of giving a look of modernity to undertakings which funda-

Robert Delaunay.
Homage to Blériot.
1914.
Distemper on canvas, 8 feet 4 inches × 8 feet 4½ inches.
Kunstmuseum, Basel

Munich before 1914 was a stronghold of the pacific International. It had always been a city open to great ideas and eager, often in a deadpan, literal way, to annex them. Visitors found echoes of Athens and Florence in its architecture and of English landscape gardening in the huge park which came right into the middle of the city. There was a tradition of the new in Munich, also. Wagner had been performed there when theaters elsewhere were closed to him. In 1893, the year in which Thomas Mann settled in Munich, a new exhibiting society called the Munich Secession brought together Franz von Stuck, Arnold Böcklin, Lovis Corinth, Max Liebermann, Max Slevogt and others who were then regarded as advanced artists. In 1895–96 three important magazines were founded there: *Pan, Jugend* and *Simplicissimus*. Art Nouveau produced one of its most celebrated triumphs in the façade which August Endell designed for a Munich photographer's studio in 1898. Good acting has always been treasured in Munich, and in 1901 the new Schauspielhaus set a new standard for theater architecture.

All this attracted foreigners; and the Munich art world was remarkable above all for its large Russian contingent. This was made up for the most part not of beginners but of mature men and women who had had experience of other cities and had finally fixed on Munich as the most stimulating place in which to live. The leader of this large group was Wassily Kandinsky, who had arrived in Munich in 1897 at the age of 30. He had not always meant to be an artist; only a few months before he arrived in Munich he had been offered a professorship in law at a Russian university, and whereas his fellow Russians in Munich had mostly been art students in Moscow or St. Petersburg, Kandinsky had followed a wide range of interdisciplinary interests before settling for painting as his main activity. He was, for instance, something of an amateur ethnographer, and he had traveled in parts of Russia in which a timeless folk-world was still intact. In those remote provinces, color was everywhere: houses were painted inside and out with a richness, a power of invention, and a spiritual energy which were deeply impressive to Kandinsky. He felt while there as if he were living in a world that was all art; and when he became an artist himself his ambition was not to produce beautiful and lucrative objects but to communicate something that was of vital importance to the spiritual well-being of mankind.

Kandinsky's maternal grandmother had come from the Baltic provinces of Russia, where the traditional culture was markedly Germanic, and from her he had learned not only the German language but the elaborate mythic structures of German folklore. This predisposed him to feel at home in Munich, which had the further advantage of having, in those days, a great deal of the emblematic color—canary-yellow mailboxes, bright blue streetcars, apricot-yellow baroque façades and burnished gold cupolas—which Kandinsky had prized in Moscow. Fixed, recurrent color was

Wassily Kandinsky. *Russian Beauty in a Landscape.* 1905. Tempera on black paper, 16½ × 11¼ inches. Städtische Galerie im Lenbachhaus, Munich

Wassily Kandinsky. *Study for "Landscape with a Tower."* 1908. Oil on board, 13 × 17⅝ inches. The Solomon R. Guggenheim Museum, New York

a necessity of life to him; from his childhood in Moscow he needed to be assured that at a certain time, every day, certain colors would be on hand. He found all this in Munich; and from Bavaria in general he got a parallel reassurance: the knowledge that certain ancient crafts—painting on glass, above all—were still being carried on with undiminished poetry. Munich was absolutely right for Kandinsky, and he lost no time in making an impression there.

He had, among other things, a very good sense of timing. He knew when situations were ripe for himself, and he knew when they were ripe for others. He knew when to start a liberal art school in Munich called the "Phalanx," just after the turn of the century, and he knew when to close it up (in 1902) and go on his travels. He knew when to start an association of artists in Munich (the Neue Künstlervereinigung, in 1909), and he knew when to secede from it (two years later) and found The Blue Rider. He was ideally open-minded—in its second exhibition, in the winter of 1910–11, the Neue Künstlervereinigung gave Picasso, Braque, Derain, Rouault, Vlaminck and van Dongen the freedom of its walls—and when The Blue Rider came to publish its *Almanac*, in December, 1912, the table of contents read like an index to modern sensibility. Everything was there: the perfected internationalism, the cross-references to theater and music, the sharp focus on primitive art, the total rejection of cultural hierarchies, the belief that much could be learned from children's art, and from peasant crafts, and indeed from anything at all that was done without thought of academic sanction.

Kandinsky was alive to all this, but he was also alive to his own particular needs. Even the name of The Blue Rider corresponded to them; he said later that "Franz Marc loved horses, and I loved riders, and we both loved blue. It was as simple as that." Kandinsky wrote later in his fragmentary memoirs: "The horse carries the rider with strength and speed, but it is the rider who guides the horse. Talent can bring an artist to great heights, again with strength and speed, but it is for the artist to direct his talent." Timing was vital: "There comes a predestined hour," he wrote in The Blue Rider *Almanac*, "when the time is ripe for decisions." What Kandinsky was waiting for in the first years of this century was the moment at which new values could be promulgated and mankind set on the path toward redemption.

It was in the course of this, and not as an aesthetic exercise, that Kandinsky came to paint abstract pictures. Such is our historical conditioning that for years it was very difficult to think of abstract painting as dictated rather by inner necessity than by one episode or another in a holy war between abstraction and figuration. Abstract painting was something that people had to be for or against, as they were for or against corporal punishment or universal free trade. To have "painted the first abstract picture" became a brevet of honor, like being the first man to step onto the moon. Even Kandinsky in later years staked out his claim, for fear that someone would boast of having beaten him to it.

But there was nothing willed or doctrinaire about Kandinksy's abstract paintings. Nor was there a Monday on which he was painting representational pictures and a Tuesday on which he gave them up forever. His development is vastly more complicated than that, and not the least of its complications is the fact that Kandinsky actually desiderated an element of mystery in the whole matter. In the winter of 1911–12 he defined

Wassily Kandinsky. *Study for "Composition II."* 1909–10. Oil on canvas, 38⅜ × 51⅝ inches. The Solomon R. Guggenheim Museum, New York

Marc Chagall.
Over Vitebsk (after a painting of 1914). 1915–20.
Oil on canvas, 26⅜ × 36½ inches.
The Museum of Modern Art, New York.
Acquired through the Lillie P. Bliss Bequest

as far as he was concerned; and he certainly had no reason to feel that conditions in Russia had been hostile to his personal development.

In this, he was in striking contrast to Marc Chagall, who arrived in Paris from Russia in 1910 and in time became a friend of both Apollinaire and Delaunay. The pacific International was very much in operation at this time in Franco-Russian artistic relations; by 1914 a young painter in Moscow, in particular, had easy access to the great paintings by Matisse and Picasso which two Russian collectors, Shchukin and Morosov, had brought together, and there had been loan shows of recent French painting which have never been surpassed for quality and discernment. For the well-bred, well-fed, much-traveled and personally not seldom irresistible aesthetes who made up the art world of Moscow and St. Petersburg, life had just about every advantage. It was very pleasant before 1914 to go to Paris as the countryman of Diaghilev, who had given Western Europe a new idea of what the ballet could be, and of Chaliapin, who was acclaimed as the greatest singer-actor in history, and of Scriabin, who had given a new dimension to concert life. (Scriabin's tone-poem *Prometheus* was the subject of a close and eulogious analysis in The Blue Rider *Almanac.*)

Among the Russians who visited Paris at that time were Mikhail Larionov and Nathalie Gontcharova, who between them were about to set Russian painting on a new path. They would have found it much harder to do so without the enlightened patronage of Diaghilev, who sent them to Paris in 1906—and, in a more general way, without the atmosphere of informed curiosity which the pacific International had created in Moscow. That curiosity was ubiquitous at that time, and

Marc Chagall.
Homage to Apollinaire.
1911–12.
Oil on canvas,
6 feet 10 inches × 6 feet 6 inches.
Stedelijk van Abbe Museum, Eindhoven

when Larionov and Gontcharova came to live in Paris in 1914 Apollinaire wrote about them in *Les Soirées de Paris* as established and substantial figures, partners in the creation of "a universal art in which painting, sculpture, poetry, music and even science in all its manifold aspects will be combined." To be a gifted young artist in such conditions was to be one of a privileged brotherhood for whom national frontiers had no meaning.

Diaghilev almost always chose well. He knew for instance that Rimsky-Korsakov was a master of spangled and glittering orchestral timbres; and in her designs for his opera *Le Coq d'or* Nathalie Gontcharova found a precise visual equivalent for the intoxicating sounds which carried all before them when they were heard for the first time in Western Europe. It was to be quite sure of this kind of authenticity that Diaghilev had invited Larionov and Gontcharova to Paris. Nor did Larionov fail him, as a painter. At a crucial stage in his career Larionov had to spend nine months (1908–09) in the Russian army. From this he derived a wealth of new subject matter which was ideally suited to what he wanted to achieve: the mingling of Russian folk art with sophisticated European attitudes to color and form.

Things did not however look quite so well if, like Chagall, you were Jewish, came from a town in the sticks, and could not even get permission to live in St. Petersburg, much less to study there, unless you were registered as a domestic servant. Chagall survived all this, but he survived by using his art as a charm against alienation. In other words, he kept sane by painting an alternative world. It was in some respects a world of the most faithful realism; the township in *Over Vitebsk* is "true to life" in a way that strikes us at once as authentic, and the wooden house in *Burning House* could not sit more squarely on the canvas. Chagall in first youth had a way of hugging fact—of holding it ever more closely to him—as if by hugging it tight enough he could remake the world. He was a wonderful storyteller—later he became one of the great book illustrators—but his first purpose was to heal the hurt of living in a society which denied him certain fundamental human rights.

He did this in two ways. First, he used color to say to the observer, "This is not the world as you know it." Second, he used fantasy to show that at a given moment the events portrayed on the canvas became a revision of the known life and an emblem of a better one. The Jew in life, in the little town of Vitebsk, was a tethered man. He had none of the mobility, social and geographical, which was the birthright of the European Gentile before 1914. He was not precisely a captive, but he was not a free man either. Chagall dealt with this by positing an alternative world in which the Jew had supernatural powers. He could soar above the rooftops like a Montgolfier balloon, he could cross the town in one easy stride, he could make life dance to the tunes which he drew from his green violin, and when he met the girl of his dreams he could put the whole of Vitebsk to sleep as he and she whirled around it and above it as prince and princess. Imagination was the outcast's revenge in Vitebsk; and the paintings came from an inner necessity as strong as Kandinsky's and a good deal more immediate in its action. Later—much later—Chagall fell back on winsome repli-

Gino Severini. *Dynamic Hieroglyph of the Bal Tabarin.* 1912. Oil on canvas with sequins, 63⅝ × 61½ inches. The Museum of Modern Art, New York. Acquired through the Lillie P. Bliss Bequest

the here-and-now got through in Italy and a re-thought and radical approach to design was adopted not long after Mussolini (much admired by Marinetti, by the way) had brought the country near to ruin and been hung up by a meathook for his pains.

In the spring of 1910 five Italian painters made common cause with Marinetti. The painters concerned were Umberto Boccioni, Carlo Carrà, Giacomo Balla, Gino Severini and Luigi Russolo. Severini lived in Paris and knew what was going on there; he had seen, therefore, with what a delicate and continuous historical awareness French painting had been brought into the 20th century. He must have known also that it was one thing for his colleagues to stand up and talk their heads off on the stage of a theater in Turin, and quite another for them to come across with paintings that would hold their own in the context of what was being done in Paris. It was for this reason, and at Severini's suggestion, that Marinetti sent Boccioni and Carrà to Paris, at his own expense, in October, 1911.

Once again, Marinetti was quite right. It would not do at all for the Futurist painters to make fools of themselves in Paris; there was far too great a gap between their ambitions, as set out in March–April, 1910, and their performance. From our point of view, however, the interesting thing is not that they should have fallen short of their aims, but that those aims should have been so concisely and so cogently formulated. A great part of modern sensibility is foreshadowed in the "Technical Manifesto of Futurist Painting," to which Boccioni, Carrà, Balla, Severini and Russolo put their names in April, 1910. Before long there was a large international audience for what they had to say: notably for such pugnacious opinions as that "all forms of imitation are to be despised," that "all subjects previously used must be discarded," and that "what was truth for the painters of yesterday is falsehood for the painters of today." It was the power of these ideas, and not the degree of their fulfillment, which spread the name of Futurism all over Europe and made it a constructive force even after Marinetti himself had been discredited.

What Boccioni and his friends had to say was comparatively free from the militaristic verbiage with which Marinetti seasoned his public appearances. It had affinities of a more exalted sort: with Henri Bergson, for instance, and especially with his *Matter and Memory.* Bergson believed that there was something ridiculous in the idea—fundamental to most pre-Futurist painting—of an object stilled and isolated. Not only was the interpenetration of past and present one of the cornerstones of his philosophy, but he believed that an object owes its essence and existence to its environment and could not possibly exist by itself. A fixed object in a fixed space was an academic fiction, therefore. Boccioni and his friends were saying meanwhile that "space no longer exists. . . . Our bodies penetrate the sofas on which we sit, and those sofas penetrate our bodies. The motorbus rushes into the houses which it passes, and the houses in turn throw themselves on the motorbus and mingle with it." Insofar as previous art had concerned itself with the "universal dynamism" which seemed to the Futurists the basic principle of life, it had focused on a notional fixed moment within it. Futurism aimed to set down on the canvas "the dynamic sensation itself, eternalized." Previous art had given a restricted and pedestrian account of man's potential; now that the full extent of that potential had been revealed by science, it was for art to catch up. The material nature of bodies had been revealed by science as no more than a convenient figure of speech; art should forthwith admit that, in the words of the Technical Manifesto, "movement and light destroy the materiality of bodies."

To all this there had seemed to be no natural Italian ancestor. At most the sculptor Medardo Rosso could be advanced as having once said that "in space, nothing is material." Rosso was reported in 1909 as having made mock of conventional sculpture, in which "forms are shaved off from the whirling center of universal life, remaining there

Carlo Carrà.
Funeral of the Anarchist Galli.
1911.
Oil on canvas,
6 feet 6¼ inches × 8 feet 6 inches.
The Museum of Modern Art, New York.
Acquired through the Lillie P. Bliss Bequest

stiff and still, to be gaped at by the inquisitive spectator." Far better, he said, that the intensity of feeling in a work should "impel it out into space, radiating out to infinity in the way that an electric wave flies out to rejoin the eternal force of the universe." Rosso was, therefore, on the Futurists' side; but Rosso lived in Paris and was in virtual retirement. The Futurists had said what they were going to do; now they had to go out and do it, on their own.

If Paris gave them a rough ride at the first exhibition of Futurist painting in February, 1912, it was partly because they attempted to prejudge their own exhibition by saying that it established them as "the leaders of the European movement in painting." In particular, they derided Cubism for its reliance on the idea of the motionless object. Now, it is perfectly true that Cubism is an art of equilibrium, and that in the hands of second-rate artists an art of equilibrium becomes an art of stasis. It was not only the Italian Futurists who were to complain in time of the restrictions of the Cubist grid. But in several of the paintings which he showed in Paris, Boccioni, for one, borrowed heavily from the Cubist paintings by Gleizes and Metzinger which he had seen in the Salon d'Automne a month or two before; this was not quite, therefore, the moment at which to make fun of them.

"Sheer idiocy" was how Apollinaire summed up the Futurists' pretensions; and there were others in Paris who said that if the Futurists wanted to burn down the Italian museums it was because they couldn't stand the competition. And of course many of the key works of Italian Futurism certain rhythm of life, a certain circumambient culture; himself and one suitcase would have to be enough.

Such an art did come about, from 1915 onward. It came about in New York, initially, and it came about later in Zurich, in Cologne, in Hanover, in Berlin and, eventually, in Paris. It was an odd, extreme and sometimes desperate art; but then those were odd, extreme and desperate times. It was not at all unified; its attitudes ranged from a wholehearted political commitment to a dandified rejection of the outer world *in toto*. There were people who risked lynching for their beliefs, and there were others who thought, with Picabia, that they should change their ideas as often as they changed their shirts. The art in question produced, in Marcel Duchamp's *Large Glass*, what has rightly been called "the most elaborately fabricated art object of this century"; it also produced at least one periodical of which no copy survives and art objects which the observer was invited to destroy. Tempers can still run hot when this alternative art is under discussion; but if any one thing about it is beyond dispute it is the fact that for a year or two, from 1915 onward, its headquarters was in New York.

Three things made this possible: the presence in New York of Marcel Duchamp and, intermittently, of Francis Picabia, the emergence of a new kind of American artist (Man Ray, above all), and the enthusiasm of a small group of new-style American collectors. (There was also, of course, the fact that until April, 1917, the United States remained neutral in World War I.) Collecting modern art in North America was pioneered at just this time by John Quinn, the beaky, pertinacious lawyer who had been one of the prime movers of the Armory Show; by Walter Arensberg, eventually to have a wing of his own at the Philadelphia Museum; by Arthur Jerome Eddy, one of the great benefactors of The Art Institute of Chicago; by the bizarre and redoubtable Dr. Alfred Barnes, founder of the Barnes Collection in Merion, Pa.; and by Miss Lillie P. Bliss, one of the founders of The Museum of Modern Art in New York. Add to these Miss Katherine Dreier, who, with Marcel Duchamp's help and support, formed the avant-garde collection which is now at Yale, and it becomes clear that New York from 1915 was exceptionally alert to the new.

The Armory Show traditionally gets the credit for this, and it is perfectly true that in 1913 it assembled in record time a panorama that on the European side ran from Ingres and Delacroix to Kandinsky's *Improvisation No. 27* and Brancusi's *The Kiss*. It updated enthusiasms, all around. The Metropolitan Museum of Art bought its first Cézanne from the Armory Show, for instance, and there was not an American artist of any quality who did not find it in one way or another a tremendous experience. But it should also be said that the bulk of the Armory Show represented a solid, safe taste. If the "new" was naturalized in New York by 1915, Alfred Stieglitz deserves much of the credit. An artist in his own right—with the camera—he had, since 1905, been running a little gallery at the top of a brownstone house at 291 Fifth Avenue. By 1913 regular visitors would have seen sizable shows by Rodin, Toulouse-Lautrec, Matisse (twice) and Picasso. Stieglitz had a nose for the new in American art, too, and he sponsored the debuts of John Marin, Max Weber, Arthur Dove and Georgia O'Keeffe (whom he married). "I am trying," he once said, "to establish an America in which I can breathe as a free man." He believed that America would not always be one of the outer provinces of art: a place from which moneyed people journeyed to France to buy Degas and Renoir. Out of America, something great would come. Stieglitz would have agreed in that context with Ezra Pound, who wrote to a friend in August, 1912, that the American awakening, when it finally came, would "make the Italian Renaissance look like a tempest in a teapot."

Intimations of this awakening were many, both in Paris and New York, in the years of Stieglitz's activity. In Paris before 1914 Patrick Henry Bruce

Patrick Henry Bruce.
Composition II.
c. 1916–17.
Oil on canvas,
38¼ × 51 inches.
Yale University Art Gallery, New Haven.
Gift of Collection Société Anonyme

was a student of Matisse and a friend of Robert Delaunay. As much as any American of his generation, he understood what had happened to painting, and more especially to color, in the 20th century. With his intelligence, his carefully nurtured gifts, and his close personal contacts in Paris, he could have been one of the leaders of a new American art; but he preferred to remain in Paris, where he pursued an increasingly isolated course. In 1932 he gave up painting and destroyed all but a few of his canvases; in 1937 he committed suicide.

Among the young American painters who abounded in Paris before 1914, Stanton Macdonald-Wright was outstanding for the energy with which he adapted to the theories of color which were propagated by Robert Delaunay. He brought to the exploitation of Delaunay's theories a largeness of feeling which can truly be called American; and after years of careful study he was able to use color, in itself and by itself, to blast off into an empyrean of his own devising. While still adhering to what he called "the fundamental laws of composition (placements and displacements of mass as in the human body in movement)" he avoided all direct reference to identifiable forms; the soft voluptuous shapes floated freely, defining and redefining themselves in terms of pure color.

There were also gifted Americans who had been to Paris and come back again. Max Weber, an American born in Russia, had studied painting in Paris, where he became engrossed with Cubism. But he also prized very highly the brilliant and unequivocal coloring of American Indian dolls, quilts and blankets; and when he took, as in his *Chinese Restaurant,* a subject from everyday life in Manhattan, he gave it a crisp, allover sparkle which derived as much from American sources as from the graver, more slow-moving procedures of Cubism.

Paris was not the only European city to tempt the American avant-garde. In his middle 30s Marsden Hartley spent much of his time in Germany. Stieglitz paid for him to go to Paris in 1912, but in 1913–14 he was in Munich and came to know Kandinsky and his colleagues in the Blue Rider group. Having seen the German military machine at close quarters, he was able in his *Portrait of a German Officer* to suggest to what an extent the uniform was the man. The little picture also dem-

Stanton Macdonald-Wright. *Abstraction on Spectrum (Organization 5).* 1914. Oil on canvas, 30 × 24 inches. Des Moines Art Center. Nathan Emory Coffin Memorial Collection

Max Weber.
Chinese Restaurant.
1915.
Oil on canvas,
40 × 48 inches.
Whitney Museum of American Art, New York

Marsden Hartley.
Portrait of a German Officer.
1914.
Oil on canvas,
68¼ × 41⅜ inches.
The Metropolitan Museum of Art, New York.
The Alfred Stieglitz Collection

onstrates the uses of a pictorial shorthand in which shapes are abstracted from nature and fitted together in such a way as to make an image as striking as it is concise.

But in point of fact an American artist at that time did not have to go anywhere to sense what was going on, both in art and in a more general sense. Man Ray was not the only artist to be haunted in 1914 by the notion of an army on the move; but there is something particularly vivid about the faceless and monolithic horde that obeys the order to march in his *A.D. MCMXIV.* As for *The Rope Dancer* of 1916, it could be called the last in the canon of circus paintings which began with Degas, Seurat and Toulouse-Lautrec. What Man Ray did was to chart the dancer's progress along the rope in terms of the different shadows that she cast from her lofty perch. By rendering the shadows in terms of flat panels of pure color he was able to divide up the canvas in a way that can be read either as abstract painting of an incisive and astringent sort or as a veracious portrait of the dancer's unsteady progress.

Sometimes the transmission of ideas from one continent was as mysterious to the layman as is the pollination that results from transoceanic winds. For instance, Arthur Dove was neither learned nor widely traveled, but by 1911 he was able to symbolize the forces of Nature as vividly as any of his contemporaries in Germany or elsewhere. With highly energized tusk-and-comma forms he could epitomize the look of an upland landscape traversed by high winds, marked out alternately by sun and shadow, sharply accented by hillock and tall tree.

New York by 1916 was the kind of forcing-house, in a smaller and more intimate way, that Paris and Munich had been before 1914. At the time of her New York debut in that year, Georgia O'Keeffe already had at her command a highly simplified vocabulary of form. With just one or two shapes, sumptuous in color and dreamlike in the way that they oozed slowly across the paper, she produced images which were peculiar to herself.

the fall of 1911. He just hadn't thought it possible that such people existed. Picabia by the spring of 1913 had become so much a New Yorker by adoption that Duchamp was beyond doubt wide open to suggestion when Walter Pach, coorganizer of the Armory Show, declared in the winter of 1914–15 that he, too, should cross the Atlantic. Duchamp had been excused from military service because of a weak heart. He was bored by the seedy, depleted, unsmiling character of Parisian art life in wartime. He took the boat for New York in June, 1915, and he lived there, on and off, until his death in 1968.

Duchamp at that time was known to thousands of Americans as "the man who painted the *Nude Descending a Staircase.*" That painting had been beyond question the great success of the Armory Show. It had been lampooned and caricatured day after day in the newspapers; it had been bought, sight unseen, by telegram from Albuquerque; at the Armory itself the crowd around it was so thick that many visitors never got to see it at all. Duchamp in 1915 had a celebrity in North America which he was never to acquire in the country of his birth. Walter Pach was at the dock when he arrived. They went straight to Walter Arensberg's apartment at 33 West 67th Street, and Duchamp stayed there not for an afternoon but for a month. Unlike Picabia, he had no visible needs, was not interested in possessions, and never put himself forward. But when it became clear that he had no new paintings to sell and that even to breathe the air of New York cost money, it was John Quinn above all who came to the rescue. Quinn was not rich by the standards of a Mellon or a Morgan, but when it came to man-to-man patronage he did more for art and literature in our century than anyone, anywhere. If it had not been for John Quinn, it is quite possible that T. S. Eliot would never have completed *The Waste Land* nor James Joyce seen *Ulysses* in the bookstores. Ezra Pound and Joseph Conrad were among the others who had reason to be grateful to Quinn; and when Quinn sensed that Marcel Duchamp could use a little money he hired him, part-time and with all possible discretion, to look after his French correspondence for an honorarium of $100 a month. With this, Duchamp could live as he liked to live and get on with his work.

What work? Duchamp in that respect was the opposite of his close friend Picabia. Picabia had the instincts of a top-class vaudeville performer. He liked to "make it new" continually, and he liked his ideas to get across on the instant. Like Duchamp, he liked to think of the human anatomy in terms of emblematic machinery. But whereas Duchamp took great care to cover his tracks and to present his findings in terms that were close to abstraction, Picabia came out into the open. *I See Again in Memory My Dear Udnie* was prompted by Picabia's admiration for a dancer whom he had met on the boat on his way to New York in 1913. Petal shapes, clearly expressive of uplifted skirts, open themselves to nozzle-like forms, no less clearly expressive of the male sexual organ at a moment of strenuous activity. Picabia at that time owned Duchamp's *The Bride* of 1912, and there are evident affinities between the two, but Picabia was explicit by nature and was determined to remain so.

Where living was concerned, Duchamp learned a great deal from Picabia, but in his work he was indifferent to direct contact with the public. If anything, he disliked the idea of the work of art as something that could be comprehended directly and instantaneously. He was insistent that the enormous work on which he had been engaged since 1912 was not "a picture" in the traditional sense and that immediate retinal effect was not its aim. Painting since Courbet had gone steadily downhill, in his view, by substituting retinal satisfaction—the "pleasures of the eye"—for the more complex mingling of image and idea, delectation and close study, which gives true dignity to art.

Duchamp acted on this belief with characteristic pertinacity. In his progress from conventional painting to something more like map- or diagram-making an important part was played by a choco-

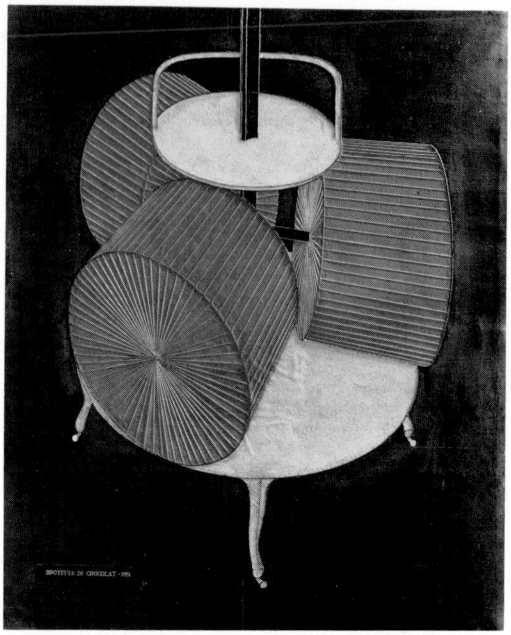

Marcel Duchamp.
Chocolate Grinder, No. 1. 1913.
Oil on canvas,
24⅜ × 25½ inches.
Philadelphia Museum of Art. The Louise and Walter Arensberg Collection

Marcel Duchamp.
Chocolate Grinder, No. 2. 1914.
Oil, thread and pencil on canvas,
25½ × 21¼ inches.
Philadelphia Museum of Art. The Louise and Walter Arensberg Collection

late grinder which he had seen in the window of the best confectioner in Rouen. Initially in 1913 he produced a traditional still-life painting *(No. 1)* varied only by the application of a leather label in the upper right-hand corner. Then in 1914 he produced an entirely different version *(No. 2)* in which the image was built rather than painted—and built quite frankly in three dimensions, with an emphatic use of glued string to make it clear that this was not "a painting," in the standard sense, but a constructed object of a new kind.

The Duchamp who disembarked in New York in June, 1915, was no longer, in any but a historical sense, "the man who painted the *Nude Descending.*" He had decided to demystify the act of painting, with its patient handcrafting, its pervasive smell of turpentine, and its courtship of the eye. New ways of conjugating experience were at hand, and it was for the artist to make use of them. A work of art was not simply something to look at; it was also, and much more, something to think about. And the way to force people to think about it was to take it out of the traditional contexts of art.

All this meant a break with art, as it was then understood (and nowhere more so than in Duchamp's family circle, where just about everyone was an artist and the theory, practice and politics of art were continually to the fore). Whether or not the break was prompted in part by a period of intense private emotion is a matter over which controversy has waxed hot and shows no signs of waning. But in any case Duchamp was, like everyone else, a product of his time. He grew up at a time when there seemed to be no limit to the number of ways in which machines could change life for the better. Machines made fresh miracles every day. And it seemed to Duchamp that the taut, impersonal procedures of the machine could also be carried over into art, and above all into the archaic procedures of freehand drawing. ("An absolutely precise coordinate drawing, with no relation to arty handwork," was his own description of what he was after at that time.)

In the late fall of 1911 Duchamp had been with Apollinaire and Picabia to see a stage production in Paris of Raymond Roussel's *Impressions of Africa;* in October, 1912, he made a motor trip from Paris to the Jura mountains, again with Apollinaire and Picabia. These were two capital experiences for him. From the Roussel he got a reinforced delight in the possibilities of the pun as a

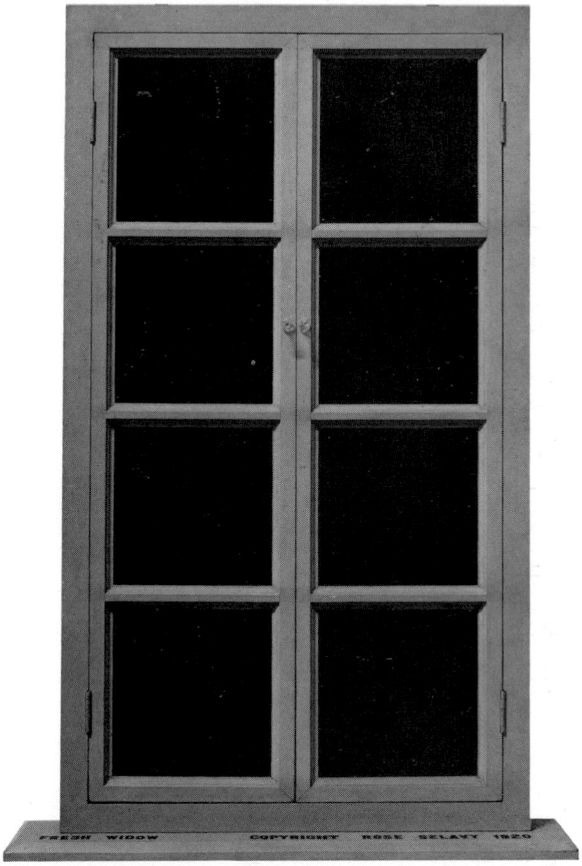

Marcel Duchamp. *Fresh Widow.* 1920. Miniature French window: painted wood frame with 8 panes of glass covered with black leather, 30½ × 17⅝ inches. The Museum of Modern Art, New York. Katherine S. Dreier Bequest

sual. The title of *Fresh Widow* combines the notions of (i) a French window, (ii) a woman recently and still deeply bereft and (iii) a widow already eager for masculine attentions. "Fresh," "French," "widow" and "window" form, that is to say, a kind of verbal conglomerate, which we may assemble as we think fit. In visual terms, what we see is a window in mourning: a standard French frame in which eight panels of polished black leather have been substituted for clear glass. The black has obvious overtones of widowhood—the "panes" could be there to protect the mourner from the curiosity of passers-by—but Duchamp wanted a high polish on the black leather, so that it could also seem that we are looking out, as we look out in times of mourning, upon nothingness.

Duchamp was fascinated by chance. As much as any of his works, he liked the *Three Standard Stoppages* of 1913–14, which was based on a chance operation: the outline of three threads, each one meter long, dropped from a height of one meter onto a canvas painted Prussian blue. It amused him very much to build an elaborate structure around these random marks, just as it also amused him to start from a ready-made verbal statement and gently take it apart, as happened in the piece called *Apolinère Enameled* of 1916–17. He gave such things an overlay of meaning upon meaning that was all his own, but the basic ambition had a wide currency at the time. In Zurich, it was taken for granted among the writers and artists who formed from 1916 onward the Dada group that the liberation of chance was one of the best things that had come out of the new century. "Chance appeared to us as a magical procedure by which we could transcend the barriers of causality and conscious volition, and by which the inner ear and eye became more acute. . . . For us, chance was the 'unconscious mind,' which Freud had discovered in 1900." The voice here is that of Hans Richter, painter, collagist, photographer and filmmaker, but the opinions are those of the Zurich Dada group as a whole. Dada was not, strictly speaking, an art movement—in fact, it stood for the repudiation and abolition of art—and its energies related for the most part to poetry, typography, public relations and an idiosyncratic subspecies of the performing arts. Nurtured in a neutral country and galvanized by occasional visits by Picabia, Zurich Dada established prototypes of avant-garde activity which have still to be superseded: among them café-theater, the mixed-media happening, concrete poetry, automatic writing and the use of aleatory procedures in art, poetry and music. When the Rumanian poet Tristan Tzara composed a Dada poem he would cut up newspaper articles into tiny fragments, shake them up in a bag, and scatter them across the table. As they fell, they made the poem; little further work was called for. When Jean Arp, the German-born sculptor-poet, tore up a drawing in despair and threw it on the studio floor he realized after a time that that, too, was a perfectly valid way to start a picture. And in

Jean (Hans) Arp. *Madame Torso with a Wavy Hat.* 1916. Wood relief, 16 × 10 inches. Kunstmuseum, Bern. Hermann and Margrit Rupf Foundation

1917 Arp got into the habit of closing his eyes, underlining words or sentences in the newspaper with a pencil, and going on from there to write a complete poem. "A sentence from a newspaper gripped us as much as one from a prince among poets," he wrote in 1953.

Implicit in all this was contempt for the discredited bourgeois society which had allowed language to be debased by the mendacities of wartime and art to become a matter of routine. "In that wonderful Dada time," Arp wrote later, "we hated and despised finicky, laborious habits of work. We couldn't stand the otherworldly look of the 'titans' as they wrestled with problems of the spirit." Oil painting, in particular, had a rough ride with Dada. "When closely and sharply examined, the most perfect picture"—Arp is again the speaker—"is a warty, threadbare approximation, a dry porridge, a dismal moon-crater landscape."

History has not always been kind to the Dadaists, and much of what they did now looks what they least wanted it to be: arty. In Zurich particularly the fact of Swiss neutrality makes the big talkers seem, in retrospect, both sheltered and effete. What still commands our respect is the constructive element; and that was provided by artists who would have come through in any case. Arp spoke for them when he said later that "we were looking for an art based on fundamentals, one which would cure the madness of the age. We wanted a new order of things to restore the balance between heaven and hell. Something told us that power-crazed gangsters would one day use art itself as a way of deadening men's minds."

It was a formidable program. Arp's work has survived not so much for its specifically Dada qualities as because he was equipped by his heredity, and by several years of intensive solitary effort, to decide for himself in which directions art needed to go. Born and reared in Strasbourg, he had, like Strasbourg itself, a dual nationality. (Strasbourg, by turns French and German for centuries, was German till 1919, French thereafter.) Arp for years called himself Hans Arp when in Germany and Jean Arp when in France; and in all his activities there was a mingling of German lyricism with down-to-earth French logical analysis. This paladin of modernity never lost the hot line to the German Middle Ages which he had acquired in first youth from a prolonged study of *Des Knaben Wunderhorn,* the anthology of German folksongs which had been published by Brentano and von Arnim in 1805–08. But at a very early age Arp became acquainted with Robert and Sonia Delaunay in Paris, and with Kandinsky and his friends in Munich, and with Herwarth Walden, the editor of *Der Sturm* in Berlin. By 1914 he was a valued though still youthful member of the pacific International: the gifted group who believed that creativity made nonsense of nationalism. And what he did under the aegis of Dada was, largely, to go on as before. There is an obvious contradiction between the grandiose program of Dada and

Jean (Hans) Arp. *Squares Arranged According to the Laws of Chance.* 1917. Collage of cut and pasted papers, gouache, ink and bronze paint, 13⅛ × 10¼ inches. The Museum of Modern Art, New York. Gift of Philip Johnson

the sweet good taste which is uppermost in the so-called Dada collages of Arp. In his painted wooden reliefs of the same period he indulged a play instinct which, once again, has nothing to do with an aesthetic of desperation. But the point of these beguiling little works is that they reintroduce into serious art a repertory of forms for which Cubism had had no place. Whimsy of a superior kind stood behind the shorthand ideograms for "bird," "forest," "water" and "human being"; and the shorthand in question was expressed in biomorphic terms. Arp's floppy, joky, wayward, curvilinear forms took the stress out of art at a time when the major Cubists were mostly off duty and it had become clear that art was in need of an alternative formal alphabet. In his case, that alphabet was in the service of a relaxed humor; but over the next 50 or 60 years it was destined to run the whole gamut of human expression.

It was fundamental to an alternative art that magic could be made from the humblest of materials. "We 'painted,'" said one of the pioneers of Zurich Dada, "with scissors, adhesive plaster, sacking, paper." In Zurich this sprang from a conscious polemical preference; but the time was approaching when art would simply be compelled, in a defeated Germany, to work from an aesthetic of scarcity—in other words, with just about anything that came to hand. This applied as much to artists like Kurt Schwitters, who stood aloof from politics, as to those who stood for a committed point of view. If magic was made in Cologne, in Hanover and in Berlin, it was because artists were able to release the buried life within disregarded materials, just as Duchamp had released the buried life within the bicycle wheel.

As with Duchamp, language played its part in all this: sometimes in caption form, sometimes by unexpected conjugations of printed matter which made the observer jump back and forth between the act of looking and the act of reading. Duchamp had raided both domains in a spirit of detached inquiry; but German Dada was carried on in a society that was teetering toward total collapse. It was the work of men with nothing to lose, and its notional trajectory was not at all that of the traditional work of art: dealer → collector → museum. Its life span was estimated as nearer to that of the newspaper, or the public meeting, or the telegram marked "Urgent." Its function was to negotiate with chaos for terms of truce. It borrowed from the techniques of the handbill and the poster, and it counted on the cooperation of observers whose situation was so desperate that they just couldn't afford not to understand. We should remember this when we try to imagine how the steeplechase of image and idea must have looked to those who had run it in the heyday (1919–22) of German Dada.

German Dada had nothing but the name in common with Zurich Dada. Fundamentally, Zurich Dada was a sub-department of the entertainment industry. Genuine revolution was not to be expected from evenings on which the young Arthur Rubinstein played the piano music of Saint-Saëns and other performers evoked the Parisian

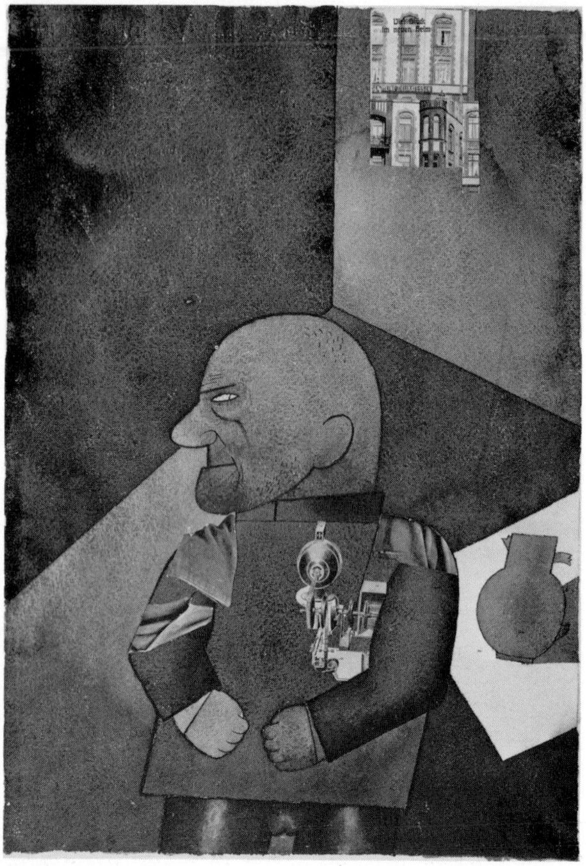

George Grosz. *The Engineer Heartfield.* 1920. Watercolor and collage, 16½ × 12 inches.
The Museum of Modern Art, New York.
Gift of A. Conger Goodyear

café-chantant as it had been in the lifetime of Toulouse-Lautrec. "In Zurich," Richard Hülsenbeck wrote later, "people lived as they would have lived in a health resort, running after women and longing for the coming of night that brought with it pleasure barges, colored lights and music by Verdi." Hülsenbeck had arrived in Zurich from Berlin in the winter of 1915–16 as a 23-year-old medical student to whom the war was abhorrent. He was a versatile young man with a talent for insolence, and he turned out to play a leader's role in Zurich Dada. He was poet, performer, coeditor with Hugo Ball of the Dada periodical *Cabaret Voltaire,* and a most ferocious champion of what in Switzerland passed for jazz. He fancied himself as a writer of nonsense verse ("The whole Monist Club is gathered on the steamship Meyerbeer," one passage ran, "but only the pilot has any conception of high C"), but he did not agree with another Dadaist, Tristan Tzara, that "Dada means nothing." And when he got back to Berlin in January, 1917, he saw to it that, as he said, "in Germany Dada lost its art-for-art's-sake character with its very first move."

Evenings at the Galerie Dada in Zurich were frankly eclectic: new music by Arnold Schoenberg and Alban Berg took its turn with readings from Jules Laforgue and Guillaume Apollinaire, demonstrations of "Negro dancing" and a new play by the Expressionist painter and playwright Oskar Kokoschka. Hülsenbeck would have none of that in Berlin. The Expressionists, in particular, seemed to him like "those famous medical quacks who promise that 'everything will soon be back to normal.' " He goes on, "Under the pretext of turning inward, the Expressionist painters and writers have banded together into a generation which already looks forward to honorable mention in the history books and a chestful of civic distinctions." The Expressionists stood for subjectivity, for the spiritual life, for the old-German Gothic world; to that extent they backed up the status quo. "Dada was not a 'made' movement," George Grosz wrote; "it was an organic product, which began as a reaction against the head-in-the-clouds attitudes of so-called high art, whose disciples brooded over cubes, and over Gothic art, while the generals were painting in blood."

This was the state of mind in which Hülsenbeck and Raoul Hausmann wrote their Dada manifesto in Berlin in April, 1918. It called for an international revolutionary union of all creative men and women; for progressive unemployment through the mechanization of all fields of activity; for the abolition of private property; for the provision of free daily meals for creative people and intellectuals; for the remodeling of big-city life by a Dadaist advisory council; and for the regulation of all sexual activity under the supervision of a Dadaist sexual center. These proposals were put forward at what George Grosz called "the time of the turnip": a period in which it was nothing unusual for the supply of potatoes to give out and be replaced by turnips normally used as cattle fodder. The Allied blockade brought starvation daily nearer; the German Army was getting more and more demoralized; there had been the beginnings of mutiny in the German Navy as early as July, 1917; 400,000 munition workers had been on strike in Berlin. It was, if ever, a time for desperate measures; and we cannot blame the Berliners who thought of Zurich as a city not so much neutral as neutered.

Much of Berlin Dada is a matter of legend. There were bold single acts which nobody followed up, as when Johannes Baader climbed up to the pulpit in Berlin Cathedral and treated the congregation to a Dadaist harangue. There were projects well over the frontiers of fantasy, as when that same Baader planned a five-story-high "Dio-Dada-Drama" which was to encapsulate "The Greatness and the Fall of Germany." There were prosecutions for antimilitarist activity. There were publications which have clung to history as burrs cling to the jacket of a hunter. Alternative art reached its point of maximum immediacy in the Berlin of 1918–20; and though not much of it survived as museum material something of its quintessence can be seen in the photomontages which were produced by John Heartfield, George Grosz, Johannes Baader, Raoul Hausmann and Hannah Höch. (In his witty little portrait of Heartfield, Grosz used some of the techniques that Heartfield had perfected. The printed message on the cut-out section of a Berlin street reads, "The best of luck in your new home"; but the new home in question is clearly a prison cell. Heartfield at that time was constantly in danger of arrest for subversive activities.) Berlin is a quick-witted, skeptical city in which a certain lapidary derision stands high among conversational qualities; and in the photomontages in question that trait is carried over into art.

In any account of international Dada an invidious distinction must be made between the people who went on to be major artists of a more general sort and the people whose association with Dada is really their only claim upon us. Cologne Dada, like Berlin Dada, had its full share of glorious human oddities; but it is on Max Ernst, finally, that our attention rests. When Ernst returned to Cologne as a demobilized soldier in 1918 he sized up the situation not as a social revolutionary, like his friend Johannes Baargeld, but as an artist who had proved himself a considerable painter as early as 1906. He had been a member of August Macke's

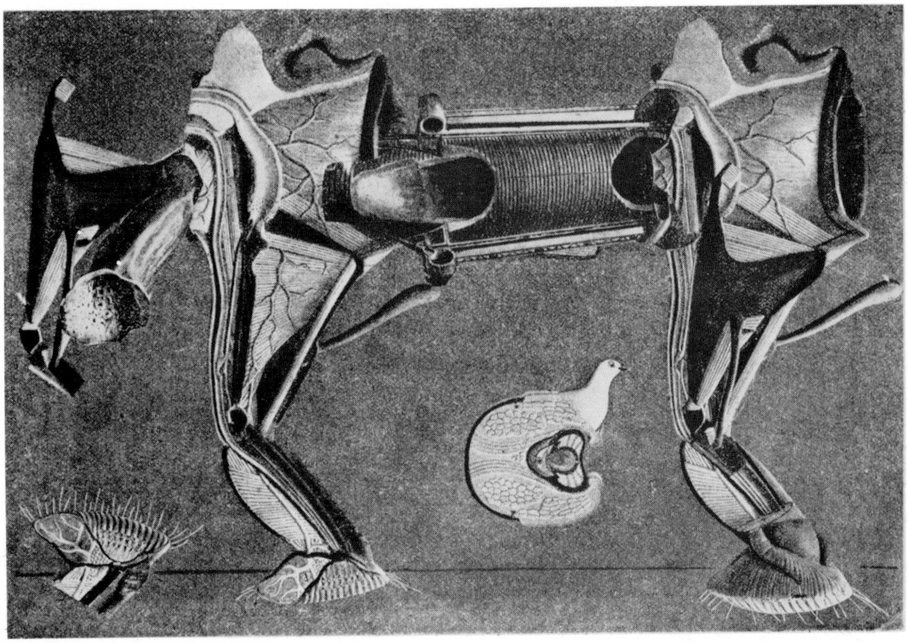

Max Ernst.
The Horse, He's Sick.
1920.
Pasted papers, pencil and ink, 5¾ × 8½ inches.
The Museum of Modern Art, New York. Purchase

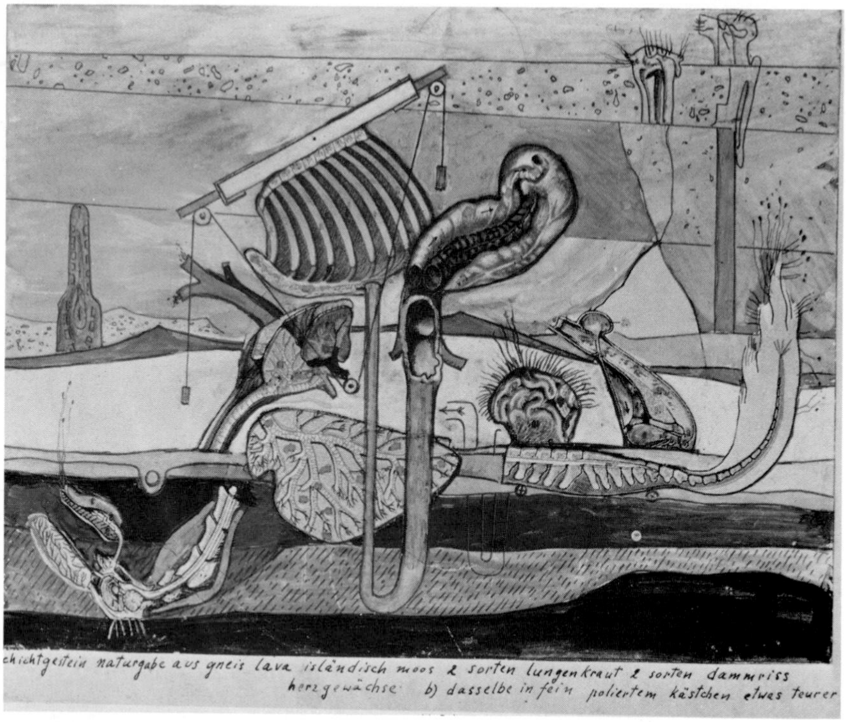
chichtgestein naturgabe aus gneis lava isländisch moos 2 sorten lungenkraut 2 sorten dammriss
herzgewächse b) dasselbe in fein poliertem kästchen etwas teurer

Max Ernst. *Stratified Rocks, Nature's Gift of Gneiss Lava Iceland Moss 2 Kinds of Lungwort 2 Kinds of Ruptures of the Perineum Growths of the Heart (b) The Same Thing in a Well-Polished Box Somewhat More Expensive.* 1920. Anatomical engraving altered with gouache and pencil, 6 × 8⅛ inches. The Museum of Modern Art, New York. Purchase

Young Rhineland group in Bonn before the war, he had known Jean Arp since 1914 and he had made himself familiar with the prewar art scene in Paris, Cologne and Berlin. Already as a student he had realized that the untaught scribblings of children, mad people, obsessives of all kinds might have more to contribute to modern art than anything that was taught in the academies. So it was by extension of a long-held opinion that Max Ernst spoke out in 1919 against "Everyman," who "loves Everyman's expressionists but turns away in disgust from the graffiti in public lavatories."

He was still only 28 in that year, and he had arrears of experience to make up. Until he and Baargeld went to Munich on a visit, he had no idea of the role that Arp had played in Zurich Dada; and it was from a magazine picked up by chance in a Munich bookshop that he learned what Carlo Carrà and Giorgio de Chirico had been doing in Italy. He was a convinced Dada member, who enjoyed the nickname of "Dadamax," was cofounder with Baargeld of the Rhineland branch of Dadaism (address: W/3 West Stupidia), edited its Dadaist review, *Die Schammade,* and took a leading role in the Dada exhibition which opened in Cologne in April, 1920, and was almost immediately shut down by the police. Dada owed a great deal to Max Ernst by the time he left Germany for Paris in 1921; but he owed something to Dada, too, and to the notion of a general strike for art which Dada had been mooting since 1916. He spoke of himself in November, 1918, as "a young man who aspired to find the myth of his own time"; he had studied abnormal psychology at an early age, and he knew that what had applied to individuals before 1914 might well apply to whole societies when World War I at last came to an end. In life he was antipaternalism personified and had an especial horror of the word "duty"; if Dada could do away with the structures of obedience which had for so long been mandatory among Germans, so much the better.

Max Ernst was not so anxious to do away with art as to extend full membership to forms of statement which had previously been denied admission. This was, of course, typical of Dada; but he brought to his Dada works a steely determination, a malicious humor with overtones of intellectual

Francis Picabia.
Plumes.
c. 1923–27(?).
Ripolin, feathers, macaroni, cane and corn plasters on canvas in a doweled frame, 46⅞ × 30⅞ inches.
Private collection

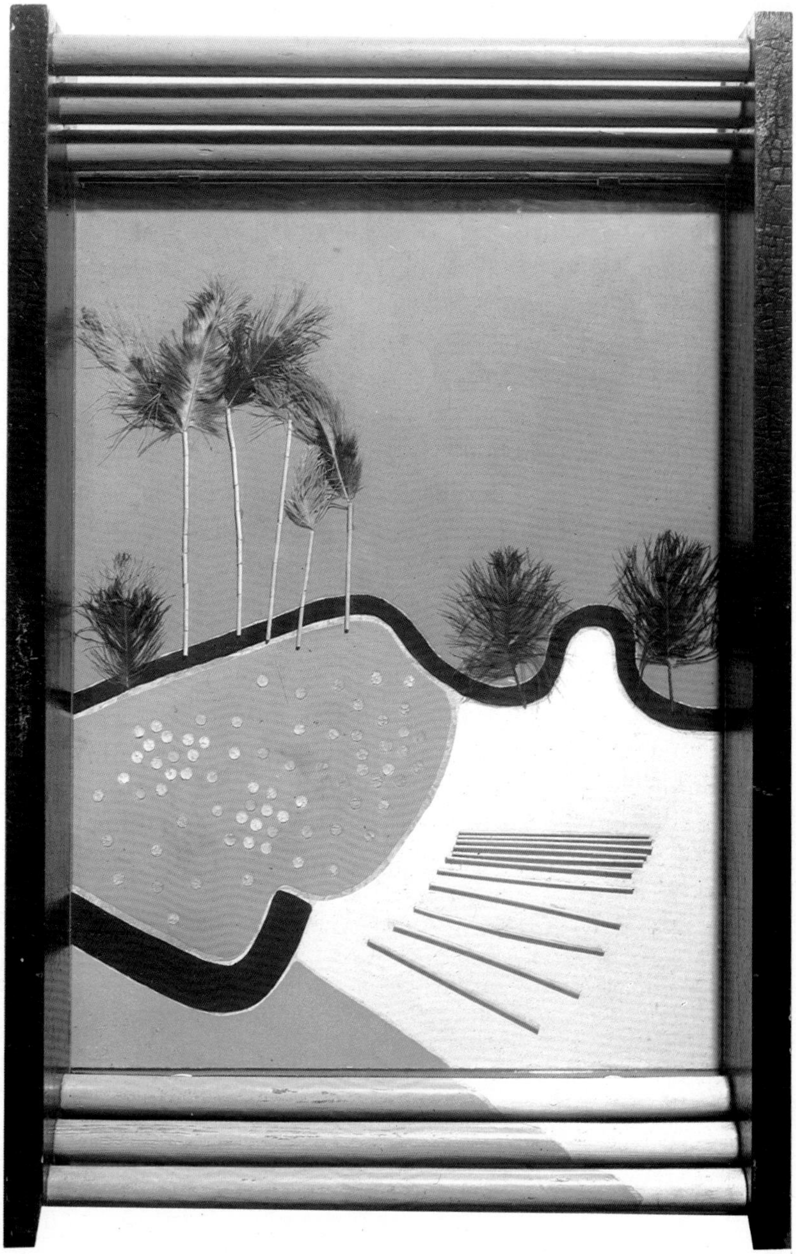

terrorism, and a gift for verbal embellishment which was quite the equal of anything that had been done in that line elsewhere. At the same time he had an existence of his own outside of Dada, and interests which were independent of it. As much as Duchamp, he had that flair for irreverent conjunction which had been pioneered by Lautréamont and carried onward by Jules Laforgue, Alfred Jarry and Guillaume Apollinaire. Above all, his work was quintessentially modern in that he used, to still unsurpassed effect, the device of the quick cut.

The quick cut was a combination of ellipsis, on the one hand, and a well-calculated jump in the dark, on the other. Fernand Léger was quite right when he said in 1914 that modern man could be distinguished from earlier man by the fact that the number of impressions with which he had to deal was a thousand times greater. Léger himself tackled this problem both by rigorous selection and by the fragmentation or overlapping of images which would formerly have been shown complete. But only after a complete break with previous pictorial tradition could the kind of quick cutting which was perfected by Max Ernst become incorporated in the act of reading a picture. To that extent, and by making a certain nimbleness of mind mandatory among those who looked at new art, Dada created a climate in which Max Ernst could go to work.

It was in art that the quick cut and the well-calculated jump imposed themselves most vividly at this time. Anyone who looked at Max Ernst's *Here Everything Is Still Floating* had to adjust to an underwater scene in which a steamship was fathered by an anatomical drawing of a beetle seen upside down; above and to the right was a fish, seen as if in an X-ray photograph, which could also be read as a primitive airship. Air and water, soaring and swimming, anatomy and engineering —all exchanged roles in this tiny and mysterious picture, and yet all were still present as themselves. In such pictures as these Max Ernst restructured the act of reading a work of art. He was not alone in doing it—it could be said to have begun, like so much else, with Cubism—and the acts both of reading and of looking were, of course, being restructured in other forms of human activity also.

Max Ernst.
Here Everything Is Still Floating. 1920. Pasted photoengravings, 4⅛ × 4⅞ inches. The Museum of Modern Art, New York. Purchase

Kurt Schwitters.
Merz 83: Drawing F.
1920.
Collage of cut paper wrappers, announcements and tickets, 5¾ × 4½ inches.
The Museum of Modern Art, New York. Katherine S. Dreier Bequest

At its most inventive, the silent cinema of the 1920s demanded of its audiences such acrobatics of attention as had never been performed before. Max Ernst knew when to tease, when to present an image directly, and when to spike the whole adventure with a long caption that darted in and out of common sense as a lizard darts in and out of the shade. What he made was not "a Dada picture" but an accelerated statement for which Dada had given the go-ahead.

Max Ernst was against Authority, as such, and it never worried him that Cologne Dada was more than once in trouble with the police. But he was not a political activist. He stood somewhat apart, therefore, from the Berlin Dadaists when they took (often from the most innocent of motives) a straight Communist line. He was his own man.

Kurt Schwitters in Hanover was his own man, too, much to the exasperation of Hülsenbeck, who called him "a highly talented petit-bourgeois." One of Schwitters' closest friends was nearer to the point when she said that he "simply didn't have a conventional bone in his body." But he did, admittedly, sit out the vicissitudes of postwar Germany in his house in Hanover, unaffected by the commitments of Dadaists elsewhere. This was the more enraging to the activists in that Schwitters was in many ways the ideal (and potentially the supreme) Dadaist. Others got up on platforms and made fools of themselves, more or less. Schwitters survives, through a gramophone recording, as one of the most extraordinary performers of the century. When he read his "Primeval Sonata"—a long poem made up entirely of wordless sounds—it was as if there had come into existence a completely new mode of human expression, by turns hilarious and terrifying, elemental and precisely engineered. Others dreamed of reconciling art and language, music and speech, the living room and the cathedral, the stage and the unspoiled forest. Schwitters had the sweep of mind not only to dream of these things but to carry them out, within the physical limits available to him. All this he did in the name of an invented concept which he called "Merz."

Merz (derived from the second syllable of the German word *Kommerz*) was a working name which Schwitters used to identify all his activities (and himself, also, at times: one of his publications was signed Kurt Merz Schwitters). "Everything had broken down," Schwitters wrote of the beginnings of Merz, "and new things had to be made out of fragments. It was like an image of the revolution within me—not as it was, but as it might have been." Schwitters was a one-man encyclopedia of Dada preoccupations. He was painter, collagist, sculptor, poet, performer, typographer, visionary architect. He was the consummation of Dada. As much as anyone, he completed the union of art and nonart which had always been fundamental to Dada. In intention he was one of our century's great reconcilers: as a roller-back of boundaries he has still to be surpassed. It was never easy, and it is now impossible, to see his achievement in its totality. That achievement was summed up in the union of the arts which he

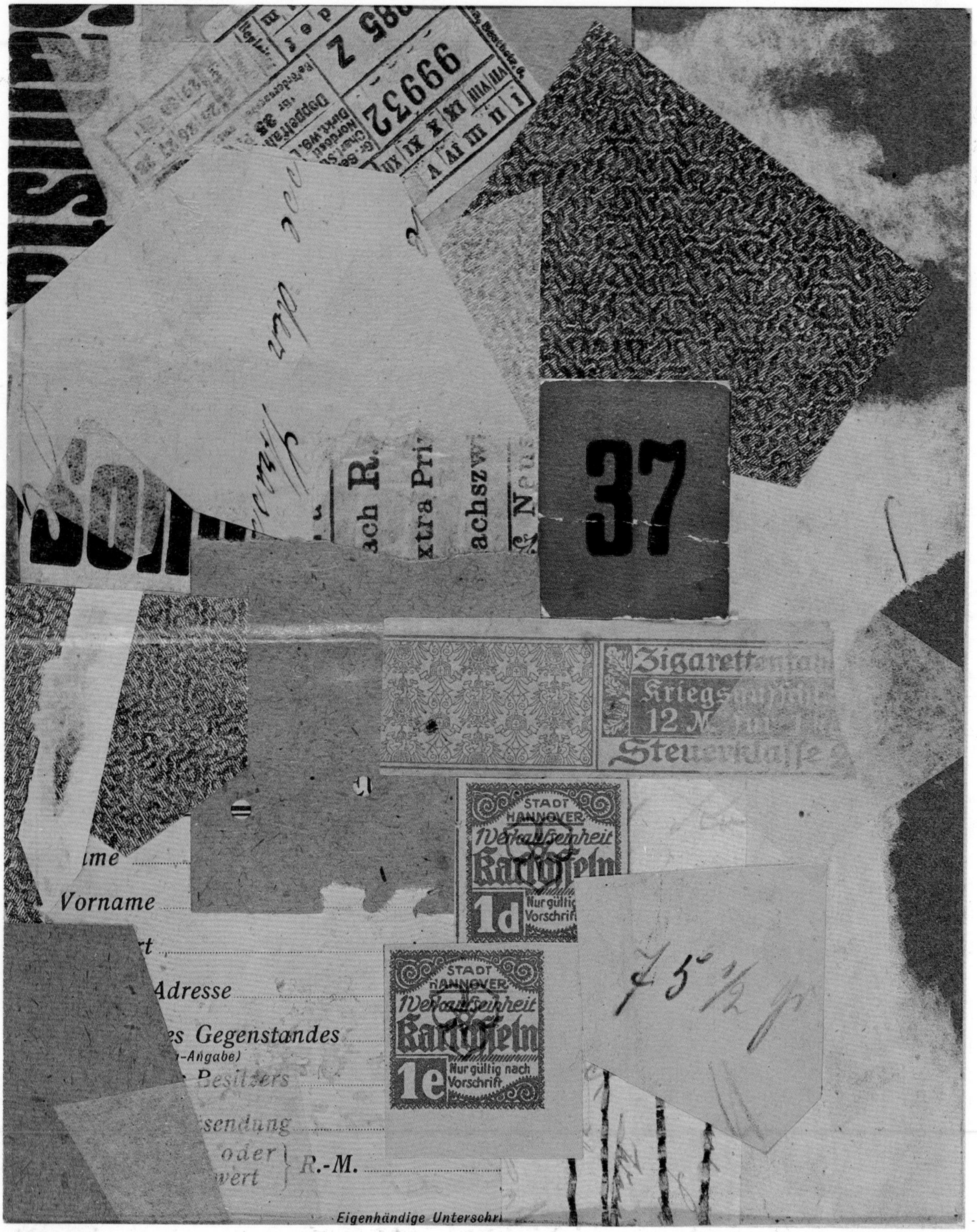

Kurt Schwitters.
Merz 19. 1920.
Collage,
7¼ × 5⅞ inches.
Yale University Art Gallery, New Haven.
Gift of Collection Société Anonyme

belief which were the equivalent of his "religious past."

Art was slower to adapt itself, and for a good reason. In an age of great storytellers—perhaps the last great age, in fact, of the printed narrative—there was not much for art to do in that domain. Art's traditional subjects were far from exhausted when Jules Verne was at the height of his powers. Between 1880 and 1914 the waking life provided quite enough material for the constructive imagination of a Cézanne or a Matisse to get to work on. But when life began to patch itself together again after the end of World War I there was a case for saying that new art must fulfill new needs, and that the most urgent of new needs was to find ways of dealing with the liberated unconscious.

It was in response to this imperative that Surrealism came into being. The role of the Surrealists was to go where almost no one had gone before: to disentangle the dream and to present it—"infantile, grotesque or immoral as it may be"—complete and unaltered. The spokesmen for Surrealism were frankly and markedly imperialistic, in that they annexed terrain to which they had no exclusive right and dismissed, unheard, arguments of great weight and cogency. Paintings and sculptures which were not Surrealist in their allegiance were derided as sterile, outmoded, timid and effete. The dream was *everything* at that time. After 50 years we can see that a bathroom scene by Bonnard or an abstract painting by Mondrian was every bit as much of an imaginative achievement as any of the masterpieces of Surrealism. But at the time preconscious fancies stood on their own as the new subject matter of art, and he who was not with the Surrealists was against them. The dream *was* the imagination: or was at any rate the imagination's only rightful outlet. The sense of life stilled and suspended had always been present in art, and sometimes it had come out with a particular radiant gravity in parts of the world which could strictly have been called provincial—what better example than the *Mourning Picture* which was painted in the late 1880s by a little-known American, Edwin Romanzo Elmer?—but in the 1920s a small group of gifted people suddenly put forward the idea that this was the thing, and the only thing, on which the dignity of art would thereafter depend.

Like the earlier confederation of the dream of which I have just spoken, this one was international. Its most conspicuous members were Max Ernst, a German; Jean Arp, an Alsatian; Joan Miró, a Spaniard; André Masson, a Frenchman; René Magritte, a Belgian; Man Ray, an American; Alberto Giacometti, a Swiss; and Salvador Dali, another Spaniard. Insofar as they had a joint ancestor, he was Giorgio de Chirico, an Italian born in Greece. Most of the masterpieces of Surrealism were made in Paris, but the Surrealists did not rely, as Cézanne and Matisse had relied, on the almost unbroken evolutionary thrust of French painting as it had existed for several hundreds of years. Their allegiances derived from literature, from medicine, from psychoanalysis, and from the ideology of political revolution. "Beauty must be convulsive," wrote their chief spokesman, poet and critic André Breton, "or it will cease to be."

Because Surrealism overlapped with the last days of Dada, and because some of the same people took part in both, it is convenient to treat the one as the outcome of the other. But the truth is that they have almost nothing in common. In the First Surrealist Manifesto as it was published by Breton in 1924 there was none of that hostility to the past, that wish to ignore or abolish "art" and "literature" as they had previously existed, which was basic to Dada. Surrealism was fundamentally the continuation by other means of activities which could be traced back to the late 18th century. In 1936, when Breton was invited to introduce Surrealism to an English audience, he traced its origins to the summer of 1764, when Horace Walpole wrote his novel, *The Castle of Otranto,* under the influence of a dream in which he found himself on the great staircase of an ancient castle and saw on the topmost banister "a gigantic hand in armor." Walpole went on, "In the evening I sat down and began to write, without knowing in the least what I wanted to say or relate." In this way there was initiated the idea that Surrealism had one foot in automatism and the other in the dream.

Another English novel, Charles Maturin's *Melmoth the Wanderer* (1820), was among the ancestors of the book which is most often quoted in connection with the methodology of Surrealism. Maturin's demonic adventurer found his French counterpart in *Les Chants de Maldoror,* which was written in Paris in 1868 by the 22-year-old Isidore Ducasse, self-styled Comte de Lautréamont. The key passage in this context is one in which Lautréamont speaks of an English boy as being "as beautiful as the chance meeting on a dissecting table of a sewing machine and an umbrella." The famous passage is very much stronger, in point of fact, if it is read in full. We need, for instance, the image of the deserted Paris street along which the boy is walking while overhead "a screech-owl with a broken leg flies dead straight above the Madeleine"; and we also need the crescendo of oddity by which the boy's beauty has already been likened to "the retractility of the claws of birds of prey," to the specific effects of "wounds in the soft parts of the lower cervical region," and to the mechanism of a self-operating rat trap. But even in its diminished form the phrase upholds that fundamental principle of Surrealism by which seemingly unrelated objects turn out, when set side by side, to have an unexpected significance. The umbrella, the sewing machine and the dissecting table symbolize the improbable encounters in inappropriate places that can play so decisive a role in human life; and when André Breton wanted to justify the picturing of such encounters it was Edgar Allan Poe whom he called in as chief witness. Poe had written in his *Marginalia* that "the pure imagination chooses from either Beauty or Deformity only the most combinable things hitherto uncombined." He went on, "As so often happens in physical chemistry, so not unfrequently does it occur in the chemistry of the intellect that the admixture of two elements results in something that has nothing of the qualities of one of them, or even nothing of the qualities of either."

Reactions of this kind had been set up in painting since 1911 by Giorgio de Chirico. The paintings in question were first exhibited in Paris before 1914, and Apollinaire for one got the point of them immediately. De Chirico became a familiar though quietly mutinous attender at Apollinaire's weekly receptions, and before long he assumed a place which he has never lost: that of the acknowledged forerunner of the new visionary painting. There was something almost supernatural about the initiatory powers which his work seemed to possess, and about the seemingly accidental ways in which it imposed itself on those who were predestined to make use of it. Breton first saw it in a shop window, Max Ernst in a bookshop in Munich, Yves Tanguy from the top of a bus, René Magritte when a friend chanced to show him a reproduction of the *Song of Love.* These were "chance encounters," but each came at a moment of maximum need for the artists in question.

We can still see why this was. A de Chirico of the period 1911–17 gives classic and definitive expression to anxieties characteristic of our century. With its unexpected jumps in scale, its backward glance at antiquity, its unfathomable architecture, its locomotive with a head of steam up and its bizarre conjunction of unrelated objects, de Chirico's *Song of Love* is a painting that took its time by the throat. Such has been the proliferation of the image over the last 80 years that we have to apply to every new work of art a terrible question: "Who needs it?" Only if the answer is "Everybody" do we accept the work unreservedly; and I hope to make it clear that in the case of a de Chirico of those years we can still return that answer.

If these pictures make so much of Surrealism look feeble, contrived, or superfluous it is partly because de Chirico set himself so stringent a criterion. It was that the basic idea of each painting must give the painter "such joy or such pain that he has no alternative but to paint it and is driven on by a force greater even than that which drives a starving man to bite into the first piece of bread that comes his way." The observer must identify, equally, with the first man in the world, "who must have seen auguries everywhere, and trembled with every step that he took."

De Chirico had a very low opinion of the accredited Surrealists when they eventually materialized, and there is nothing in his work of the invalidish imaginings which run wild in Lautréamont. His compound images derive from identifiable elements in his own life, even if they have been edited and recombined in ways for which "dreamlike" is as good a word as any. He had also looked with great intelligence both at the union of disparate elements in the pasted-paper works of Picasso and Braque and at the use of flat silhouette in Synthetic Cubism; these helped him to present his ideas with measured coherence and a logic that was not of the waking world.

He did not wait in passivity for the dream to put subjects in his way. "The methods of people like Thomas De Quincey do not tempt us," he wrote in 1919. He saw the artist as someone who used the gift of clairvoyance to reappraise the objects of everyday, and to release from within them a mysterious and ominous element which normally passes unnoticed. "Metaphysical" was the name which he gave to this element. "We who know the signs of the metaphysical alphabet," he went on, "are aware of the joy and the solitude which are enclosed by a portico, by the corner of a street, or even in a room, on the surface of a table, or between the sides of a box.... The minutely accurate and prudently weighed use of surfaces and volumes constitutes the canon of the metaphysical aesthetic." De Chirico had a pan-European inheritance, and his education was as much German as Italian; in his student days in Munich he had learned from Schopenhauer that "to have original, extraordinary and perhaps even immortal ideas one has only to isolate oneself from the world for a few moments in such a way that even the most commonplace happenings seem new and unfamiliar, and so reveal their true essence."

He remained loyal to this idea: "The daemon in everything must be discovered." Sometimes it was enough simply to displace an object from the environment in which we expect to see it, "like an armchair, a divan and some chairs, grouped together on the traditionless prairies of distant America." Sometimes a change of scale did the trick, as when he noticed how, outside a little workshop in a Parisian side street, "a huge glove made of painted zinc, with terrible gilded nails, was pointing with its index finger at the stones of the sidewalk." Sometimes the image was carried forward like a mascot from his childhood: a huge and archaic cannon, for instance, which he remembered from the harbor in Volos, the Greek seaport where he had first been brought up. Sometimes he stayed even nearer to the facts of his youth. His father had been a railway engineer; and

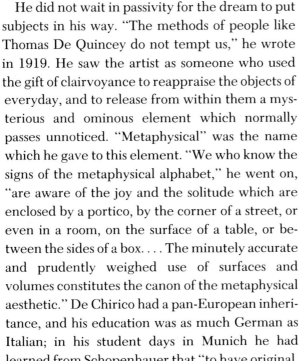

Giorgio de Chirico.
The Philosopher's Conquest. 1914.
Oil on canvas,
49½ × 39¼ inches.
The Art Institute of Chicago.
The Joseph Winterbotham Collection

the town terminal, the station clock and the locomotive with its plumes of steam were early members of the "metaphysical alphabet." Sometimes he drew upon the grander, more spacious elements of Greek or Italian town planning, sometimes on specific works of ancient art (notably an antique statue of Ariadne), sometimes on fragments of the Italian industrial scene: factory chimneys above all. A tireless window shopper, he found metaphysics in the shapes of the biscuits put out by specialized pastry cooks and metaphysics again in the relief maps of Europe which were in vogue after the outbreak of World War I.

The belching factory chimney, the symbols of imminent departure (locomotive and sailing ship), the phallic artillery with its accompaniment of two huge balls, the mysterious cowled figures whose shadows appear beneath the clock—all these make *The Philosopher's Conquest* one of the most dense, as well as one of the most cryptic, of de Chirico's paintings. Where other painters strove for infinity with pictures of mountain ranges and distant horizons, de Chirico from 1914 onward aimed to induce in the observer a systematic disorientation. He did nothing that was not personal to himself; yet the result has a universal resonance, and we can agree with what de Chirico said of it in 1919—that it arose from "a fatality of the human spirit which is governed by fixed mathematical laws. It ebbs, flows, departs, returns and is reborn like everything else on our planet." He was to turn up everywhere. Something of his vocabulary—his menacing way with architecture, his delight in relief maps, his ability to see the human body half as a lay figure, half as automaton—was taken up in 1917 by the Futurist painter Carlo Carrà in his *Metaphysical Muse.* The painting is, moreover, an anthology of themes which were to preoccupy other artists many years later: the target (Kenneth Noland and Jasper Johns), the map (Johns, once again) and the summary, schematic automaton (Oskar Schlemmer in the 1920s). After World War I George Grosz exploited elements from de Chirico's vocabulary to press home a satirical point about the people who had served like robots in the German Army and lost no time in adapting to a change of political regime.

Giorgio de Chirico invented as valid a metaphor as painting has to show for the anxiety, the sense of unfocused guilt and dread, which has been common to almost every thinking individual throughout the 20th century. In his world nothing is what it seems; our relationship to our environment is warped at every turn; normal life is suspended. Omens are everywhere: we cannot see the little girl bowling her hoop in *The Mystery and Melancholy of a Street* without being reminded by her two-dimensional silhouette of how running figures were turned into flattened and calcinated profiles when Dresden was destroyed by fire in 1945.

What de Chirico did, between 1911 and 1917, was to create a modern mythology—a compound of private guilt and the externals of big-city life—which has never been superseded. Proud and re-

Carlo Carrà.
Metaphysical Muse.
1917.
Oil on canvas,
36 × 26¼ inches.
Emilio Jesi, Milan

throw of authority as represented by the father. De Chirico was haunted by the withdrawn, authoritarian figure of his father. Max Ernst was marked for life by the imperious rhythm of child-bearing which his father imposed on his mother, and by the hallucinatory intimations of this which came to him in dreams. Fathers in general stood for authority, for repression, for conjugal rights exercised with a brutish regularity; and the Surrealists turned with a particular ferocity on public men whose activity seemed to them to be paternalist in character. One such was Paul Claudel, the playwright and poet who for many years held high rank in the French diplomatic service. Claudel was strong on duty, strong on obedience, strong on the letter of the law. He would have been anathema to the Surrealists even if in 1925 he had not been imprudent enough to say that "neither Dada nor Surrealism can lead to anything new; they are for pederasts only." The Surrealists replied with a long collective letter that ended, "We ask for ourselves the 'dishonor' of having treated you once and for all as the trash that you are." Claudel deserved it; but the riposte was addressed as much to the institution of fatherhood as to the prepotent rhetorician, then in the prime of life, who was the French ambassador in Tokyo.

In such contexts, art was the best possible way of paying off old scores. Oedipal feelings ran berserk throughout the 1920s. Imaginary misfortunes were constantly being wished on the representatives of fatherhood, and not least on God the Father himself. The prototypical Surrealist title is *Mama, Papa Is Wounded!* and it would stick in our minds even if the painting in question (by Yves Tanguy) were not one of the finest of its date. Salvador Dali returned over and over again to the image of the son castrated by his father. The father, everywhere, was seen as having done his son an irreparable mischief; and his presence, whether in de Chirico's *The Child's Brain* or in Max Ernst's *Pietà or Revolution by Night* or in one of their many derivatives, was seen as granitic, oppressive, unyielding.

As a comment on intergenerational hostility, these things were memorably vivid. Insofar as several of the artists concerned did genuinely still bear the wounds of childhood, the works in question had an immediacy which can no longer be recaptured. The mid-1920s were the first moment in time at which it was possible for an artist to interpret his early experience in the light of psychoanalysis: they were also the last moment in time at which this could count as authentic pioneering. On a more general and less private level many taboos which now seem to us impossibly archaic were then still taken for granted.

Surrealism stood in all this for the restatement of the rights of man. Breton had always in his mind what he called "the future continent": a landmass, as yet unlocated, on which all men would tread freely and as equals. All women, too: many years before Women's Liberation was heard of, Breton laid it down as an integral part of Surrealism that "not only must we put an end to the exploitation of men by other men, but we must review—from top to bottom, in a totally unhypocritical spirit and as a matter of the first urgency—the problem of men's relations with women." In this, the Surrealists ranged themselves behind Charles Fourier (1772–1837), the Utopian socialist, who said that the essential prerequisite for social change was that women should be free to dispose of themselves as independent human beings.

The masterpieces of Surrealism have long ago been tamed and ticketed. But it is still very well worthwhile to look at them in the light of what the English historian G. M. Young once had to say about the writing of history. "The real central theme of history," he said, "is not what happened but what people felt about it when it was happening." Time and the museums combine to flatten what was for the artist and his contemporaries the most urgent aspect of his work: its either/or quality. For those who live by them, beliefs are nonetheless tenacious for being unfounded. It seemed to the Surrealists that there was, for instance, a straight choice, a clear-cut either/or, be-

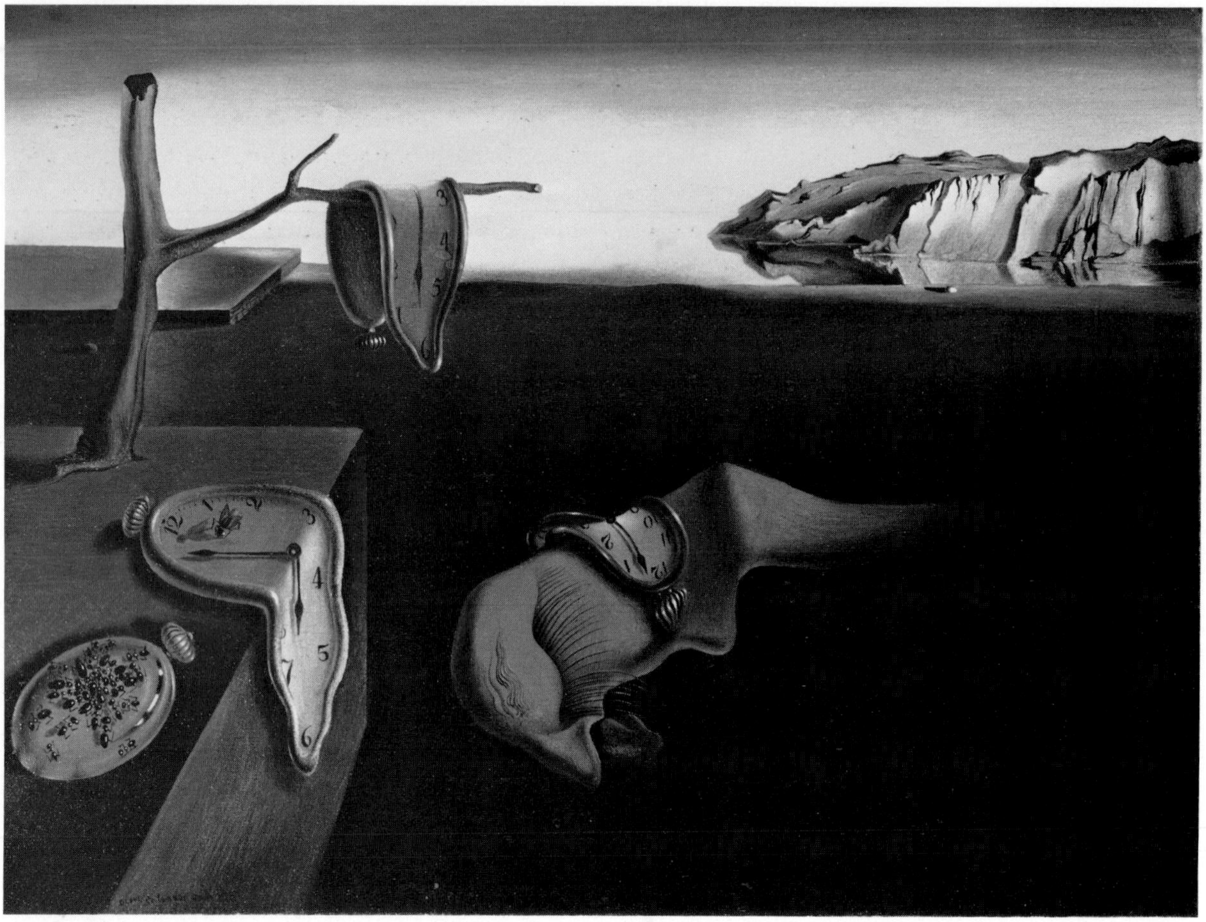

Salvador Dali. *The Persistence of Memory.* 1931. Oil on canvas, 9½ × 13 inches. The Museum of Modern Art, New York. Given anonymously

tween the liberated imagination and the drudgery of copying appearances; a straight choice between liberated sexuality and the shams and compromises authorized by society; and a straight choice between the steeplechase of image and idea which the Surrealists had in mind and the predictable manufacturing of standard subject paintings which was to turn much of French painting into a subdepartment of the souvenir trade.

In all this the truth was bent, much as it is bent in time of war when the overriding consideration is to keep the reader, or the listener, in good heart. Time sorts all things out: and time has already told us that the dosage of poetic imagination in a great Matisse is as high as in the finest of Surrealist paintings; that the sexual content of Ingres and Courbet has as much weight and resource as can be found anywhere in Surrealism; and that it was not the Surrealists but Mondrian, with his search for a constructive and immutable truth, who put forward the most audacious alternative to traditional painting in the 1920s. But this is quite immaterial: artists believe what they have to believe, and in the 1920s and '30s this was as true in the private domain—the management of their own gifts, that is to say—as it was in matters of universal principle. Max Ernst had so strong a creative identity that whatever he did was distinctly his own, even if it began from the automatic imprint of a piece of graining on the floorboards of a country hotel. What resulted was specifically, unmistakably, peremptorily his own. But when he was asked to define Surrealism in 1934 he said that there was no such thing as individual talent, and that the legend of individual creativity was one of the last and most ridiculous of the superstitions with which the civilization of the Occident was encumbered. The active, constructive, initiatory role of the artist fresh start in the new Russia; and he must truly have felt, as the young man in the picture feels, that with one elastic stride he could step over the rooftops and be off and away.

The young man in the picture may of course have expected far too much of a momentary exhilaration. Certainly Chagall's career during the years from 1917 onward was by no means a story of uninterrupted success. In Vitebsk he was outmaneuvered and forced to resign after less than a year in office. Anti-Semitism in Russia was not so much abolished as in abeyance. By 1922 he had given up and gone back to Western Europe with 50 years and more of exile before him. His little painting might now seem to stand for an overconfidence more ludicrous than poignant—a last match struck in a hurricane. What was there to be so cheerful about in 1917, with Russia on the edge of famine and civil war, with nearly a million men, French and German, lately killed around Verdun, and with the United States newly committed to a European war?

And yet Chagall's spring-heeled young man really does stand for something that can be traced to the year 1917: the beginnings of a reconciliation between art and society. After about a hundred years in which the two had pulled different ways there was a real chance of their reintegration. Initially the idea of the artist as builder and healer must have seemed ridiculous to those who remembered how for generations art had only to come up with new ideas for society to turn them down flat. (We think of Courbet in jail, Cézanne walled up within his own thoughts, Matisse among the cackling crowds at the Salon d'Automne.) If the people whom Ibsen called "pillars of society" looked to art for confirmation of their importance, they too could count on a rebuff; from Honoré Daumier to George Grosz, art made mock of them. Art and society were in a state of war, declared or undeclared; and even the supposedly safe men, the bemedaled architects and the official portraitists, could not be relied on.

There were exceptions, of course—times when the arts and society worked well together. But it was not through governmental foresight that Henry Hobson Richardson gave a marvelous plain grandeur to the Marshall Field Wholesale Store in Chicago, and when *Harper's Weekly* commissioned wood engravings from Winslow Homer no one at the office knew that they would perpetuate the quintessence of rural America. When Hector Guimard designed entrances for the Paris subway in 1900 the result was art; but that was not because the city fathers had had art in mind. The posters designed in England in the 1890s by James Pryde and William Nicholson were also art—more so, in fact, than most English paintings of their date—but once again it would be too much to say that the advertisers had planned on getting museum material for their money. What happened from 1917 onward was something quite different—a systematic attempt, all over Europe, to reconcile art with society.

Such things do not happen overnight. The time and the man have to be in collusion, for one thing, and meanwhile the points of departure may pass almost unnoticed. Who would have thought in 1917 that the look of the world would be changed in the end by the publication in neutral Holland, a country then almost phantomatic in its isolation, of a little magazine called *De Stijl?* What possible importance could have been placed on the arrival in Paris of a Swiss architect called Charles-Edouard Jeanneret who had not yet taken the name of Le Corbusier? A notional union of the arts had been much talked about in Germany before 1914; but with defeat drawing steadily nearer it was hardly likely that the aristocratic patrons of the original idea would be in a position to go on with it. Russia was known to have some gifted painters with a firm grasp of general ideas; but at the moment in November, 1917, when Lenin got control of the entire country, it must have seemed the merest fantasy that the new government would have time for such people.

A partisan of the new might, in fact, have made a two-word note in his diary—"conditions hope-

Marc Chagall.
Forward! 1917.
Gouache,
15 × 9¼ inches.
Art Gallery of
Ontario, Toronto.
Gift of Sam and
Ayala Zacks

less"—at any time, and at almost any place, in the year 1917. But he might also have taken comfort from something said many years earlier by Victor Hugo and almost too often repeated since: "No army in the world can hold out against the strength of an idea whose time has come." When the idea is right, and the man is right, though political and social upheavals do their worst, the idea will make its way. That was what Hugo believed, and history from 1917 on bore him out.

Nothing great can be done in a hurry, and almost all the people who concern us here had gone through a slow and thorough seasoning by 1917. The magazine *De Stijl* had been thought of as early as August, 1914, by a many-sided near-genius, Theo van Doesburg, who was its animator and ideas man. Already in 1912, at the age of 29, van Doesburg had defined one of the governing principles of De Stijl: "Disengage form from Nature," he wrote, "and what remains is style." What he meant was that the artist should not aim to reproduce—and still less should he aim to rival—the wayward, luxuriant, ever-varying charms of Nature. He should think his way through to the simplest, the fundamental, the irreducible elements of form. Having found them, he should stick with them. It was not his business to imitate, or to ornament, or to tell stories. The question to be asked of his work was not "Is it beautiful?" but "Is it true?"

This was an aesthetic question. Where architecture and design were involved it was also a practical question; but above all it was a moral question. Truth and falsehood, not beauty and ugliness, were the criteria to bear in mind. Truth in architecture meant a style purified of ornament and idiosyncrasy, and one which declared its function from the outset and used new materials and new building techniques quite openly. Truth in painting meant the end of painting as it had previously existed and the substitution of an art based on equilibrated relationships which owed nothing to Nature.

Van Doesburg shared this point of view with his colleagues of De Stijl: the painters Piet Mondrian and Bart van der Leck; the architects J. J. P. Oud, Gerrit Rietveld and Jan Wils; the sculptor Georges Vantongerloo; the designer Vilmos Huszár. It was fundamental to all their activity. But it was not a point of view that they had invented. Already in the 1890s the Belgian painter, architect and designer Henry van de Velde had said that the architecture then in favor was "a lie; all posturing and no truth." The Dutch architect H. P. Berlage, who built the revolutionary Stock Exchange building in Amsterdam in 1898–1903, said much the same thing: the prevailing style was "sham architecture —i.e. imitation, i.e. lying." Berlage went on, "Lying is the rule, and truth the exception. That is why our parents, our grandparents and we ourselves have had to live in surroundings more hideous than any that human beings have known before."

Lying in architecture is the same as lying in life —it means covering up, faking motives, evading, pretending, misleading. As to what form a truthful architecture should take, much was owed before 1914 both to the writings and to the exemplary finished work of an American, Frank Lloyd Wright. As they walked through Paris and Brussels, Berlin and London, European architects could turn in loathing from the fidgety, overblown office buildings that had sprung up on every hand and console themselves with what Wright had had to say: "Simplicity and repose are the qualities that measure the true value of any work of art." Confronted in Wright's own country with the New York Racquet and Tennis Club (an imitation Italian palazzo) or with the domineering portico of the Metropolitan Museum, they could remember what Wright had said in 1910: "The old structural forms, which up to the present time have been called architecture, are decayed. Their life went from them long ago and new conditions industrially—steel and concrete, in particular—are prophesying a more plastic art." The United States had what Europe had not: a plainspoken tradition in architecture and design. If there was such a thing as a North American norm, a common standard to which American design should revert instinctively, it was the tradition of Pennsylvania Dutch barns and Shaker furniture. Such things were truth made visible; and it should be remembered that when a new magazine called *House Beautiful* began publication in Chicago in 1896 it stood for an honest simplification in matters of decoration and design.

But if there was a moral imperative behind all this, there was also—from 1914 onward, especially—a practical one as well. Le Corbusier was a Swiss, and he grew up in La Chaux-de-Fonds in the Jura, which from a cosmopolitan point of view was a long way from anything that mattered. But he had traveled; he had made it his business to get to know the most inventive of living European architects—Josef Hoffmann in Vienna, Auguste Perret in Paris, Peter Behrens in Berlin— and he had taught himself to respond to any given situation by asking himself, "What can architecture do?" As early as 1910 he set down on paper his plans for a new kind of art school: a school strikingly similar, as it turned out, to the one which still had the force of novelty when it was set up by Walter Gropius in Weimar in 1919 and christened the Bauhaus. In the fall of 1914, when most people were still wringing their hands in despair at the destruction to which World War I had already given rise in Flanders, Le Corbusier came up with an idea which, if adopted, would have cut reconstruction time by nine-tenths.

He devised a standard two-story framework, independent of any floor plan, which carried both floors and staircases. Truth, in this context, lay with the methods of the assembly line, the standardized design ingredient, and the mass-produced prefabricated living unit. The architect was no longer restricted to forms that huddled together as if for warmth, or propped one another up in ways that had hardly varied since the building of Stonehenge. The monolithic, earth-oriented forms of earlier architecture could be discarded, just as single-point perspective was being discarded in painting; as early as 1909 Frank Lloyd Wright's Robie House in Chicago had shown how cantilevering made it possible for forms to fly outward and onward without visible support. Nothing but neurosis could justify continued subjection to such fundamentals of old-style architectural practice as the load-bearing wall, the small fixed window, or the design that was thickest and fattest at the point of its junction with the earth. The time was approaching when houses could be flown in the air on stilts; when inner space could be adjusted at will; when houses need have no front and no back but could be experienced from every point of the compass as fully energized living spaces.

Le Corbusier behaved all his life as if this could be taken for granted. Circumstances did not always run his way, but—to take one example only—his Villa Savoye of 1929–31 is on more than one count a classic of modern architecture. Where earlier houses sat heavily on the ground, this one stood on legs slender as a gazelle's. Where earlier houses had a front and a back, this one presented itself with equal eloquence in all four directions. Where earlier houses had gardens attached to them at ground level, this one had its garden slung above the living area. The conditions of building and the conditions of living were alike turned upside down.

The fundamental prerequisite for buildings such as this was that people acknowledge the truth: that architecture had changed as radically as painting and sculpture, that new materials and new methods of construction should serve new ideas and not old ones, and that the pioneer moves in these directions were manifestations of a collective will to make the world a better, simpler and more rewarding place to live in. It was the De Stijl group who got closest, fastest, to this general idea. They knew that painting and building could have a great deal in common, and that a house could be very like a sculpture and all the better for it. Theirs was an art of first principles; Mondrian wrote in 1922 that "Theo van Doesburg brought *De Stijl* into being not to 'impose a style,' but to discover and disseminate in collaboration what in the future will be *universally valid.*" Mondrian at that time and later very much disliked what he called "art as ego expression"; his ambition was to break through to a kind of painting which would make known to everyone the fundamental characteristics of the cosmos. His subject matter was the workings of the universe, not the workings of his own temperament.

This was not an idea that he took up from one day to the next, in a doctrinaire way. He was driven to it in part by the results of his 20 years' investigation of the modes of art—from Symbolism to Cubism—that were current in his youth, and in part by the conversation of the Dutch philosopher M. H. J. Schoenmaekers, whom he met in Holland in 1914.

Piet Mondrian.
Self-Portrait.
c. 1900.
Oil on canvas mounted on composition board, 19⅞ × 15½ inches.
The Phillips Collection, Washington

In looking at a Mondrian of no matter what period it is important to remember that he was a man of almost angelic purity, a high-souled mystic who put up uncomplainingly with a long lifetime of isolation and near-penury. (Something of this comes out in the self-portrait now in the Phillips Collection in Washington, which dates from his late 20s.) In the work of the young Mondrian there were echoes of the Symbolist movement and, also, of van Gogh's sometimes sententious way with still life. A dying sunflower would be turned, for instance, into an image of insistent poignancy. But there were also times when, as in *Red Amaryllis*, Nature looks her finest and firmest; and if the lofty, cruciform image of the lily has mystical overtones it also has affinities with the forms of Art Nouveau glass as it was brought to its point of maximum fulfillment by Louis Comfort Tiffany and others.

Piet Mondrian.
Red Amaryllis with Blue Background.
c. 1907.
Watercolor, 18⅜ × 13 inches.
The Museum of Modern Art, New York.
The Sidney and Harriet Janis Collection

As much as Edvard Munch, and as much as van Gogh in his more somber moments, Mondrian in his early years would call upon Nature to abet him in the portrayal of states of turbulent emotion. His *Woods near Oele* of 1908 may well remind us of those Scandinavian forests, lit by the unearthly glow of a northern night, into which Munch sent

Piet Mondrian.
Woods near Oele.
1908.
Oil on canvas,
51 × 63 inches.
Gemeentemuseum,
The Hague

men and women in search of their destiny. It is, moreover, in a wood such as Mondrian sets before us that the woman in Arnold Schoenberg's opera *Erwartung* stumbles upon the body of her dead lover. What we have here is not the peaceable Dutch countryside but a primeval forest ringed with an unnatural fire: a place of trial and torment, in which a whole generation lived out an important part of its emotional life.

It was in the fall of 1911 that Mondrian first saw Cubist paintings by Picasso and Braque. In May, 1912, he went to live in Paris and set himself to relive, in his own work, the evolution of French painting since Cézanne. (The motif that dominates Mondrian's *Still Life with Ginger Pot* was a favorite theme of Cézanne's.) Four years after the frantic emotionalism of his *Woods near Oele*, Mondrian was concerned with something entirely different: the reduction of still-life material to severe, blocklike forms, with echoes here and there of architecture (see the majestic, portal-like forms to the right of the ginger pot) and of Cézanne's preoccupation with the cube, the cylinder and the cone.

Living in the Montparnasse district of Paris, and scrutinizing day after day the battered gray façades of the buildings adjacent to his own, Mondrian gradually extracted from them what he needed: a motif in which both verticals and horizontals presented themselves quite naturally, with occasional notes of blue, in the rounded forms of chimney pots, to offset flat, pigeon-gray walls and space, moving faster and faster as the eye followed it upward. The monument was intended to make visible to everyone, on the largest imaginable scale and with all possible versatility, the reintegration of art and society. Quite apart from the inventive magic of the building itself, its functioning would serve as an encyclopedia of the ways in which the poetic imagination of the artist could enrich the life of everyday. Tatlin envisaged the use of giant loudspeakers, for instance, and messages beamed onto the clouds when the weather was bad, and a gigantic cinema screen, clearly visible from below, on which the news of the day would be available to all.

Some of these notions were carried over into the design for the *Pravda* building in Moscow, which was prepared by the Vesnin brothers in 1923–24. They had what may now seem to us an unfounded belief in the impartiality and total openness of the Soviet news services; the *Pravda* building is, in effect, a hymn to transparency. It suggests by implication that *Pravda* has nothing to hide; the elegant inner workings of the Vesnin brothers' design are as open to us as the workings of a specimen watch in a Swiss shop window; the entire building functions as an instrument of communication. Eye, ear and mind were to be seduced in turn; what the Vesnins had on the drawing board was an architecture which would serve up "the truth, and nothing but the truth."

Pravda did not turn out to be that kind of newspaper; nor did the Vesnins' building get built. But if projects like these still haunt our imagination it is because they stand for the hope of a better world in which all the news will be good news and the last of the tyrants will have been shipped off to some maximum-security playpen. Not to have shared at least momentarily in that hope is to have fallen short of our potential as human beings, and it is not surprising that Tatlin's monument has so often been built and rebuilt in scale-model form by architectural students. It symbolizes the fulfillment of the aim which Lunacharsky once set himself—the acceptance at government level of a cultural policy in which everything was possible.

El Lissitzky. "The New One" from the portfolio *Victory over the Sun.* 1923. Lithograph, 21 × 13¾ inches. The Museum of Modern Art, New York. Purchase

In the conditions then prevailing in Russia it would have been out of the question to initiate an avant-garde of the kind which was already in existence. It was Lunacharsky's good fortune that the people in question not only knew what they wanted to do but in most cases had already been doing it for years. One of the most controversial achievements of the pre-Revolutionary avant-garde in Russia was for instance the opera *Victory over the Sun,* which was produced in St. Petersburg in 1913. The text, music and scenery (the last by Malevich) were all equally daunting to conventional taste; the theme had a prophetic interest in that it described how technology would change the conditions of life by discovering new sources of energy. After the Revolution Lissitzky adapted this same theme for what he called an "electro-mechanical peepshow" or mechanized puppet theater. A portfolio of prints on the same subject, published in 1923, included a classic image of man as he might one day be: alert and indestructible, a mechanized version, in fact, of the young man in Chagall's *Forward!*

El Lissitzky. Model of the set for *I Want a Child* (by Sergei Tretyakov), commissioned by Meyerhold for production at his Moscow theater. 1926–29. Photograph courtesy the Arts Council of Great Britain

If the political revolution and the aesthetic revolution could work together very closely, for just a year or two, it was not because the one brought the other about. It was because the political revolution had no aesthetic identity and was prepared to settle for whatever lay within reach, just as a man in a hurry to leave for the tropics will buy the featherweight suit that hangs nearest on the rack. There were artists like Tatlin, who genuinely identified himself with Communism and did all that he could to foster its advance; but there were others —Kandinsky, Gabo, Chagall—who were completely apolitical. It is part of the mythology of the period that Lunacharsky's protégés worked together as a band of brothers; but the truth is that if they were brothers it was in the way that Cain and Abel were brothers. Tatlin and Malevich had literally come to blows already in 1915 and never ceased to represent antithetical points of view. Malevich did not scruple to intrigue against Chagall in Vitebsk at a time when Chagall was away in Moscow. Kandinsky's draft plans for the remodeling of art education in Russia were turned down by a majority vote of his colleagues in 1920. Art life in Czarist Russia had always been a ferocious affair, with faction pitted against faction, and all this was if anything intensified after 1917. It was to Lunacharsky's credit that he made no attempt to produce a homogenized official line in such matters, but maintained a watchful impartiality throughout what Naum Gabo has called "the oral period"—the years 1917–20 during which open forums and seminars were available in Moscow to an audience totaling in all several thousand. It was in these discussions, rather than in any formal teaching sessions, that ideas were hammered out and tested in debate.

If these things are still worth talking about, it is because so much of what still passes for the latest thing in the arts was pioneered in Russia at that time. The internal situation of the country was so desperate between 1917 and 1921 that literally anything could be tried out on the assumption that Authority was far too busy to object. If someone sympathetic observer was back with the notion of truth, just as he was back with it in Western Europe and back with it in the Chicago of Frank Lloyd Wright; truth meant defining the quintessence of the painting experience. When Malevich put a black square in the middle of a white canvas he meant the square to stand for sensation and the white surround to stand for the blank state of awareness and expectation on which sensation impresses itself. Even that came to seem to him too obvious, and in the *White on White* painting, first shown in 1919, color dropped out altogether; sensation and its surround merged into one another, distinguished only by a change of texture and by the spectral pivoting of a white square which hovered, weightless, within the confines of a larger square of its own color.

We may feel, in commonsense terms, that such paintings give us nothing to look at. But Malevich took exactly the opposite point of view. In his Suprematist pictures (as he called them) there is, for the first time in the history of art, nothing to distract or deceive. The experience comes to us pure and entire. The square on a square, thus interpreted, stands for primary, irreducible emotional structure: the power to set one element in our experience against another, and to define the relationship between them. These paintings provide, in other words, a schema or pilot system which helps us to find our way among our own feelings. Malevich and Kandinsky did not always see eye to eye; but fundamentally Malevich was carrying on with the mystic or intuitional line of thought which Kandinsky had pioneered in his book *On the Spiritual in Art.* Once again, and without falling back on any stereotyped view of the Russian nature, one could say that the speculations of both men had an all-or-nothing character, a compulsive inwardness and a disdain for ridicule which are not common in other countries. The square, the circle and, to a lesser degree, the triangle are fundamental to much of the abstract painting of the last 50 years; but nobody has quite felt about the square in the way that Malevich felt about it, any

Kasimir Malevich. *Suprematist Composition: White on White.* 1918(?). Oil on canvas, 31¼ × 31¼ inches. The Museum of Modern Art, New York

Kasimir Malevich. *Suprematist Painting.* After 1920.
Oil on canvas, 33½ × 27½ inches.
Stedelijk Museum, Amsterdam

more than anyone has felt about the circle in the way that Kandinsky did in the 1920s. ("If I have used the circle so often and so passionately in the last years," he wrote in 1929, "it is not because of the geometrical shape of the circle, or of its geometrical attributes, as because of my overwhelming recognition of its inner strength and its limitless variations.")

Malevich did not think of these paintings as objects of luxury to be sold to the highest bidder. Still less did he regard them as addressed to a cultivated elite. He thought of them as terminal statements. If they signaled the end of art as it had previously been known—if "art," thus understood, was a casualty of evolution—that seemed to him a perfectly fair exchange for the new spirituality which his paintings made available to everyone. Those simplified flat shapes afloat on a plain background stood, in his eyes, for the new life that was opening up for the human spirit. And the coming of that new life was overdue. "Their bodies may fly in airplanes," he said of his contemporaries, "but they live by the beauty of ages long past."

The Malevich who wrote those words was not a peripheral crank to whose ravings no importance was attached. He had established himself among his fellow artists as early as December, 1915, as a leader with whom it was rash to quarrel. Nor was he a man to put his head in the clouds by way of escape from the realities of life after 1917. He saw nothing contradictory in calling on the one hand for a new and exalted degree of spirituality and in promoting on the other a future bound up with automated, electrified and prefabricated housing. It may seem that at a time of extreme national emergency the one might have precluded the other. But that is to misunderstand what Edmund Wilson in *A Window on Russia* called "the Russian perception of time—a sense of things beginning, of things going on, of things to be completed not at the present moment but in the future, of things that have happened in the past all relegated to the same plane of pastness with no distinction between perfect and pluperfect: a sense, in short, entirely different from our Western clock time, which sets specific events with exactitude in relation to an established and unvarying chronology."

Our Western clock time did catch up, even so, both with Malevich and with Lunacharsky's regime as a whole. By the end of 1921 Lunacharsky's policy of humane tolerance had been dismantled in favor of a program which admitted only those forms of art which had an immediate social utility. A Russia in which anything was possible gave way, step by step, to a Russia in which nothing was possible. To have some idea of the personal suffering which was inflicted on people who had much to give to the world, the reader should turn to the poems of Anna Akhmatova and Nadezhda Mandelstam's two volumes of memoirs, or to those late compositions in which Shostakovich turns a bleak and unforgetting eye upon the ordeals of his generation. What we are concerned with here is something quite different: the continued existence in other countries, and into other decades, of that same pacific International which had been active before 1914, and of which the Lunacharsky regime was a distinguished and highly localized offshoot. It was thanks to this pacific International, and to the extreme receptivity of its most prominent members, that the contribution of Russia between 1917 and 1921 should be seen not as an isolated and foredoomed experiment, but rather as one episode in an ongoing process that made itself felt all over Europe in the 1920s and later spread to the United States.

As early as 1910, when he was in his late 20s, Walter Gropius was arguing that aesthetic creativity and industrial mass-production were perfectly compatible. Noting how in the United States Thomas Edison had made extensive use of poured concrete and standard components made of iron, he foresaw a time when the bricklayer and the carpenter would play no part in architecture. In 1911 his factory for the shoe-last firm of Fagus proved that exterior walls need no longer bear heavy loads and could, on the contrary, be no more than transparent shields against the weather. Even in the worst days of World War I Gropius went on planning for a school that would synthesize the arts and the crafts and see to it that the best ideas of the age were made available cheaply and to everyone. Himself a Berliner, he would have preferred to have a school in Berlin, one of the great capitals of the world, rather than in Weimar, a small country town best known for its associations with Goethe, Schiller, Liszt and Nietzsche. It is one of the ironies of history that the Bauhaus, which was finally dreamed up in a Berlin on the very edge of a proletarian revolution, should have its first home in a set of buildings designed in 1904 by Henry van de Velde at the request of the Grand Duke of Saxony. A comparable irony was built into the inaugural prospectus of the Bauhaus, which was written by Walter Gropius in April, 1919. "We must all return to the

Wassily Kandinsky.
Composition 8.
1923.
Oil on canvas, 55½ inches × 6 feet 7⅛ inches.
The Solomon R. Guggenheim Museum, New York

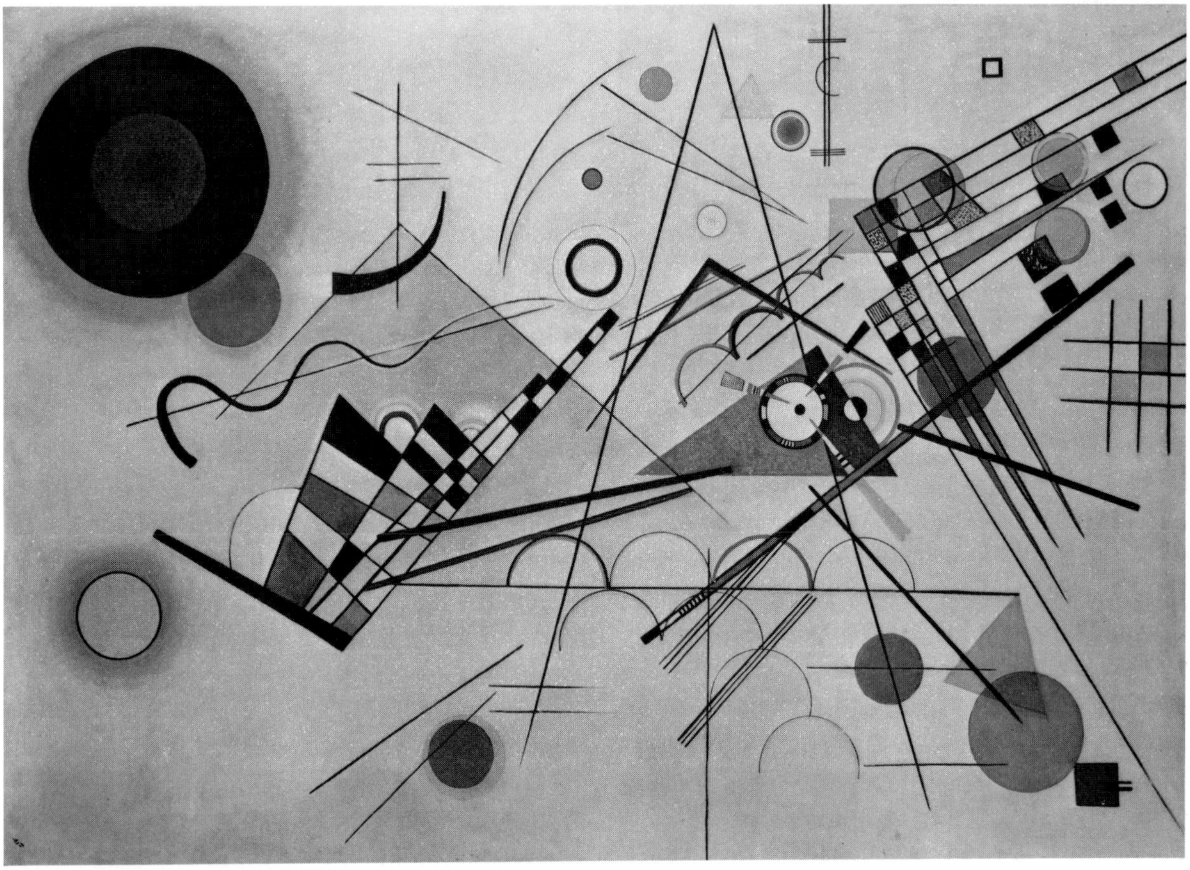

Oskar Schlemmer. *Bauhaus Stairway.* 1932. Oil on canvas, 63⅞ × 45 inches. The Museum of Modern Art, New York. Gift of Philip Johnson

crafts!" was its theme; and although Gropius looked forward to "the new structure of the future" which was to "rise toward heaven from the hands of a million workers like the crystal symbol of a new faith," the structure which appeared on the program itself was of purely medieval inspiration.

Between 1919 and 1933 the Bauhaus had on its staff, at one time or another, as brilliant a group of men as ever taught. The New Yorker who wishes to realize the extent of their radiation has only to walk around midtown Manhattan. The Seagram Building is by Mies van der Rohe (Bauhaus, 1930–33) and Philip Johnson; the Whitney Museum is by Marcel Breuer (Bauhaus, 1920–28); the Pan Am Building above the train shed at Grand Central Station is by Walter Gropius (Bauhaus, 1919–28) and his partners. The collection of the Solomon R. Guggenheim Museum is dominated by Wassily Kandinsky (Bauhaus, 1922–33).

It is difficult to go into an office that calls itself modern and not find chairs designed at the Bauhaus by either Breuer or Mies. In a more general way, Moholy-Nagy (Bauhaus, 1923–28) produced a revolution in communications techniques and Herbert Bayer (Bauhaus, 1921–28) a revolution in graphic design, which still influence every American who wants to get a message across. Generations of American students owe much to the painter Josef Albers (Bauhaus, 1920–33), who began teaching at Black Mountain College in 1933 and was teaching classes at Yale as recently as 1960. Not merely the example but the name of the Bauhaus crossed the Atlantic when, in 1937, Moholy-Nagy founded The New Bauhaus: American School of Design (since 1939 The Institute of Design) in Chicago. It would be fair to say that American life is permeated by the influence of the Bauhaus and that even those who have never heard of the original school have had reason to be grateful to it.

This is not to say that the history of the Bauhaus was either consistent or glorious. There were changes of internal policy, changes of personnel, changes of orientation. Though outwardly nonpolitical, the school depended for its existence on support from whatever party was in power; the times were turbulent, as often as not, and things were done which would not have been done had the school been functioning with ample funds in a stable society. Internal disputes set individual against individual, and discipline against discipline. Sometimes students complained that they did not see their famous teachers for months on end. A regime which aimed at the updating of the medieval guild system would be followed by one which crossbred lectures on Gestalt psychology with compulsory physical training. It is easy to speak ill of a school which aimed in 1919 to "build the cathedral of Socialism," only to peter out in August, 1933, with the announcement that it was closing down not because of any reluctance to make concessions to the Nazis but because it simply hadn't the money to go on.

been drawn from antiquity five hundred years earlier for the same purpose. . . . It was re-created in *The Three Dancers* to fill the same need, to epitomize the agonizing incongruity between death and sensual life, which is the source of grief."

History had also caught up with *The Three Dancers* by the late 1960s, insofar as we had had continual reminders from news photography of the way in which people react in real life to unexpected and appalling situations. In the light of such reminders the left-hand figure in Picasso's painting is not at all histrionic in her bodily contortions, in the disorder of her dress, or in the grimace which tears her face in two. This is what grief does to people. We had seen it in art before —in Gothic sculpture, for instance, where the sculptor spares us nothing of the physical impact of mourning—but before we could *feel* it again someone had to reinterpret it.

To say the last word about a great painting is always a vain endeavour; it will look different, in any case, to those who come after us. *The Three Dancers* is about the dance, but the dance seen as convulsion. It is about the crucifixion image—a tall thin figure with upstretched arms, outlined against a T-shaped cross. It is about mourning and about the aggressivity, the wish to take Destiny by the throat, to which mourning notoriously gives rise. It is about Cubism, and about the way in which Cubism can operate within a complex system of allusion. And it is about the painter's job, part of which is to bear witness to the worst that can happen to human beings.

The *Studio with Plaster Head* at first sight seems much less complex in its implications. Its subject matter is straightforward enough—the table itself (cut foursquare to steady the composition); the tumbled cloth, a triangular fold of which reappears beneath the table to balance the many triangular forms in the upper half of the canvas; the insistent, repeated pattern of the wallpaper; the mass-produced woodwork, here given a most powerful thrust and counterthrust; the Chardinesque group of evocative objects. The only thing that speaks loud and clear for the 1920s is, in fact, the toy theater—a precise rendering of a recent gift from Picasso to his four-year-old son—which makes us wonder if we are indoors or out-of-doors as we explore the top left quarter of the painting. (Even the sky looks like a painted sky and seems to be both outside the window and inside the theater.)

A tour de force, therefore, of ingenuity and high spirits: a working model of a world in which reality and make-believe change places and nothing can ever go wrong. But something more than that, as well. Those severed arms and hands, for instance, and the big sculptured head which we see three times (in shadow, in profile and in a half-hidden frontal view): are they just decorative additions to an already crowded scene? Certainly the hand meant enough to Picasso for him to remake it on its own many years later, in sculpture, and with an effect of peculiar poignancy. And what about that sprig of laurel, soon to wither? Picasso in the summer of 1925 was living quietly in a still unspoiled Juan-les-Pins, and as he was not at all a political person nothing is less likely than that he consciously foresaw the downfall of Europe. But there is in great art a clairvoyance for which we have not yet found a name, and still less an explanation; and there is no doubt that in the *Studio with Plaster Head* Picasso was making ready the language which he would need both for *Guernica*, 1937, and for the expression of more private exasperations in years to come. More exactly, as William Rubin has pointed out, the look of the plaster head in the painting of 1925 forecasts the rictus of dismay which we see on the severed head of the soldier in *Guernica*. And the severed arm reappears, holding a broken spear, in that same formidable picture. The *Studio with Plaster Head* looks brisk enough, open enough, pellucid enough; but it runs a gamut of experience that ranges from civilized recreation (reading, drawing, the stage) to pre-echoes of *The Charnel House* of 1944–45. But then Picasso was someone who could keep a

Pablo Picasso.
Studio with Plaster Head. 1925.
Oil on canvas,
38⅝ × 51⅝ inches.
The Museum of Modern Art, New York. Purchase

dozen ideas going at a time. In *Painter and Model* he showed his awareness of Matisse in the patterning (white on yellow) of the painter's chair in the lower right-hand corner. He remembered the ferocious reworking of the human face in Oceanic art when it came to his presentation both of the painter's own face and of the face of his model. Reversing the traditional procedures of modern art, he metamorphosed the head of the model into a naturalistic profile on the canvas. He also remembered the decorative flat patterning of Art Deco (then at its height) when he came to organize the picture in terms of interlocking flat planes. These planes rhymed with the natural flatness of the chair back, the chair's tasseled fringe, the picture on the wall, the wall itself, and the stylized dado which traverses the wall at shoulder height. The use of bright flat color relates, also, to current practice in architecture (see, for this, the workings of De Stijl; Chapter 8). When we are faced with paintings such as this, which can be thought over for a lifetime, it is more than ever difficult to see the 1920s as a period of secondary achievement in art.

If the 1920s have that reputation it is because the best work of the period so often turns up in isolation, with none of the armature of chronology with which we can find our way, week by week, through the heroic age of modernism. Even the best artists have dry periods: no one can make history every day of his life. A long patience and a strategy of withdrawal or concealment may be the best way of coping with these periods. The great Europeans with whom we are dealing were prepared to lie low, or to shift their ground, or to withhold all news of their activity in ways that

Georges Braque.
Le Guéridon (Th
Round Table). 19
Oil on canvas,
58 × 45 inches.
The Phillips
Collection,
Washington

tween the painter and a given number of square feet of space. If Matisse was "born to simplify painting," as his teacher had told him in the 1890s, this was one of the ways in which he passed on his mandate to posterity. He was to do it to even more spectacular effect at the very end of his life in big cut-paper decorations where painting was dematerialized and color was as near as not made incorporeal. Meanwhile the Barnes mural set an august precedent.

Matisse went on renewing himself, even into the 1950s, by finding new solutions for new tasks. This was never the case with Braque. Everything that Braque did in middle and later life turned out in the end to be a way of nursing painting along; and as he grew older and frailer his studio became the whole world for him and he reacted hardly or not at all to the outside involvements—exhibitions, major commissions, polemics in print—on which art history battens. He painted for himself, not for the historian. Interpretation of his work seemed to him at best superfluous, at worst actively harmful. "The only valid thing in art is the one thing that cannot be explained," he once wrote; and in the 1950s he said that "to explain away the mystery of a great painting would do irreparable harm, for whenever you explain or define something you substitute the explanation or the definition for the real thing."

It takes a rash man to ignore a warning of that sort. But it ought to be said that these remarks apply above all to Braque's paintings of the 1940s and '50s, in which he went all out for what he called a metamorphic ambiguity; in other words, he blurred the distinction between the real and the imaginary, the literal and the metaphorical, the named and the unnamed. In those late paintings identities melt like butter in the pan; where ambiguity is fundamental to the picture it is reasonable enough that the artist should resent any attempt to explain it away. Even in a relatively early painting like the *Café-Bar* of 1919 there are passages where the images overlap in such a way that we are hard put to disentangle them. Braque at that time prepared his canvases with what the art critic John Richardson calls "a thickish sandy layer of matt black paint, which Braque compared to coffee grounds or tea leaves because, like a fortune teller, 'he can divine there things which others cannot see.' " This dense black foundation conferred upon his images a kind of immunity: press them too hard to declare their identity and they vanish.

But, like the other great Frenchmen of his generation, Braque was a strategist. It was not at all his style to peak in his 20s or 30s and thereafter go into a long decline. He was also anxious to nurse painting, as I said earlier, through a difficult period in its evolution. What Léger aimed to do by close attention to the Aviation Show, and what Matisse hoped to do by a sage diversification of his activities, Braque did by staying still in one place and counting up the things that he could do better than anyone else. He had the true French feeling for continuity; he would never have talked as Arnold Schoenberg talked when he said to a visitor in 1922 that he had "discovered something that will guarantee the supremacy of German music for the next one hundred years." But he did undoubtedly intend to put French painting beyond the reach of rivalry. *Le Guéridon (The Round Table)*, 1929, is one of the grandest and most completely realized paintings of our century. In it, Braque summed up once and for all the traditional preoccupations of Cubism: the splay-footed table with its arcaded support, the piece of sheet music, the pipe, the musical instrument, the labeled bottle, the scrolled dado, the still life of fruit. He also introduced the knife which from Edouard Manet onward had been an important element in still life. And at the top of the canvas, where the con-

Georges Braque.
The Black Rose.
1927.
Oil on canvas,
20 × 37 inches.
Mr. and Mrs. Burton Tremaine, Meriden, Conn.

Georges Braque.
Studio (with Wooden Stool).
1939.
Oil on canvas,
45½ × 58¼ inches.
Lucille Simon, Los Angeles

vergence of walls and ceiling can make for dullness, he brought the whole matter down to within an inch or two of the observer's nose and animated it with shifts of perspective and changes of color.

Braque had an unequaled sense of touch. No one has ever put on canvas a more varied or more consistently delectable substance than he. Next, he had a sense of the space in his paintings as being infinitely adjustable: something that could be bent back, folded over, hinged, cut into slivers and made transparent or opaque as suited him best. In particular, he learned to maximize the impact of his sense of touch by bringing the objects in his still lifes within reach, one and all. He carried over from Synthetic Cubism the practice of distributing color without regard for its local allegiances, and he felt at liberty to reorder the shapes of things in the interest of a majestic harmony of his own devising.

All this went in tandem, throughout his career, with a total appreciation of the still uncorrupted countryside of France, and of the things which it could produce for the still-life table top. Looking at a picture like his *The Black Rose,* 1927, we remember what the Goncourt brothers said of Chardin: that he could reproduce for us "the shaggy velvet of the peach, the amber transparency of the white grape, the sugary rime of the plum, the moist crimson of strawberries, the hardy berry of the muscatel and its smoke-blue film, the wrinkles and tubercles of an orange skin, the embroidered guipure of melons and the copperas of old apples. . . ." But when we look more closely it turns out that what Braque sets before us is an equivalent, not an imitation; in this context Braque evokes, but does not specify. As he grew older, indeed, Braque began to pit the identities of art against the identities of everyday life. In a painting like the *Studio Interior with Black Vase* of 1938, everything has equal status: the paneled wall, the grained wood of the easel, the vivid wallpaper, the palette with dabs of paint still wet, the canvas on the easel and the framed canvas on the wall. Braque practiced, as between each and every one of these surfaces, a perfect equality: none had precedence over the others. Each form, each plane, each texture, each nicely contrasted patch of color slid into its place.

When ruminating on the nature of art, and on the tasks which art could still validly undertake,

Pablo Picasso. *Painter and Model.* 1928. Oil on canvas, 51⅛ × 64¼ inches. The Museum of Modern Art, New York. The Sidney and Harriet Janis Collection

Braque was at one with Matisse and Picasso in that he turned again and again to the studio itself for his subject matter. The best way to think about art was to see what actually happened when someone was making it. The act of painting was a metaphor for creativity in its purest, most absolute form, and a lot of irrelevance could be avoided if the scrutinies of art were turned inward, upon art itself; that was the idea, and it lent itself to the widest possible range of statement. Picasso in the late 1920s most often took an aggressive and schematic point of view, emphasizing the polarization of artist and sitter and the ways in which the information given by the sitter's appearance is censored (or added to, or transformed) by the time it reaches the canvas. Matisse enjoyed playing with our expectations in such a way that we are never for instance quite sure (as in *The Artist and His Model,* 1936) whether we are looking out of a window onto a real landscape or whether we are looking at a picture that has been hung on the wall in just the right place. (In this case it's a picture: a cartoon for a tapestry in which Matisse drew on his memories of a visit to Tahiti.) Braque did not align himself with either, but went quietly ahead with his own inquiries, which were about the extent to which objects can lose their identities and yet retain them. He wanted to find out how many kinds of reality could live together within a single picture and in ways that only painting could bring about.

All this took him a long way from the Cubism of 1910–12, which was fundamentally an art of plain statement about a small number of identifiable facts. But Braque in the 1930s was a very different person from the enormously strong young man who before 1914 could overturn a carnival float with his own two shoulders. There is in great art an element of historical fatality; but something is also owed to the private evolution of an individual human being. Braque's health never recovered from the wounds which he sustained in 1915, and in middle life he had none of the power of attack which made Picasso react instantaneously to whatever happened around him. "A picture is not a snapshot," Braque said in 1939; and in the late 1930s he began to treat the world in terms of a consciousness which took as much account of what was not as of what was. He was still interested in fact, and was as ready as ever to evoke a specific kind of graining in wood or the precise outline of a bottom-heavy jug. But if mystery entered into his experience—if there was a bird on the canvas on the easel, for instance, and if that bird seemed to take off and fly around the room—Braque did not demur. Nor did it at all disturb him if objects went adrift from their presumed positions in space and floated around the room in a state of transparency. This vision of a world in a state of perpetual flux, motion and change was, after all, no more unreal than the traditional picture image of a world artificially stilled and categorized according to a single unvarying canon.

These late Braques are philosophical paintings, even if the manner of their presentation is irresistibly voluptuous. Such a gamut of sanded tans, so close a conjunction of purple and violet had rarely been seen before. As surely as the Surrealists, but with none of their sensational or pathological subject matter, Braque in the 1930s reintroduced the irrational into painting. (In 1935 he said that "writing a poem, painting a picture, carving a stone—all three of them are irrational acts.") What he wanted at that time was to achieve an equipoise, peculiar to himself, between logic and the free

Georges Braque. *Studio Interior with Black Vase.* 1938. Oil and sand on canvas, 38¼ × 51 inches. Mr. and Mrs. David Lloyd Kreeger, Washington

play of instinct—and between the strict scaffolding of Cubism as it had evolved before 1914 and the fluidity and irrationality of life as it actually presents itself.

As in Picasso's *Painter and Model* of 1928, the studio in Braque's *Studio (with Wooden Stool)* of 1939 is represented mainly in terms of tall flat rectangular panels. But Braque allowed himself an infinitely greater license in the matter of textures, in the scale on which individual objects are presented and in the way in which space is reordered. Objects move forward and back, turn opaque or transparent, at the painter's whim. Real flowers are set off against simulated ones; imitation wood is set off against the real thing. As with the splay-footed table in Matisse's *The Window* of 1916, the spokelike interweaving of the seat of the stool on the right is used to guide us gently from one point of the compass to the next. As for the bird on the easel, it is the forerunner of many others in Braque's later work. Is it a picture of a bird? Or is it a real bird that has flown into the studio from outside and is posing in front of the easel? Or is it a painted bird that has "chosen liberty" and refused to stay on the canvas? Braque isn't telling: this is just the kind of poetic ambiguity which he most enjoyed.

It could be argued from 1933 onward that philosophical inquiry might well be suspended, in deference to the steadily worsening condition of Europe. Braque did not agree. "We must insist," he said in 1939, "on a categorical distinction between act and actuality." This belief has sometimes got him into trouble with self-appointed moralists, most of whom have never seen a shot fired in anger, let alone fought as gallantly as

Paul Klee.
Fear (Angst). 1934.
Oil on burlap,
20 × 21⅞ inches.
The Museum of
Modern Art, New
York. Gift of Nelson
A. Rockefeller

Braque. Where the future of Europe was concerned Braque saw as clearly, and felt as deeply, as any other intelligent and humane observer. But in his art he was an armored man, and the pictures went their own way without interruption until France herself was brought almost to a standstill during the later stages of the German occupation.

Throughout the 1930s Braque was free, moreover, to wall himself up in his studio if he so wished. The case was very different for Paul Klee, who in 1933 was deprived of the right to teach in Germany and in 1934 learned that the Nazis had ordered the confiscation of a book on his work which had been written by his old friend Will Grohmann. Switzerland was the country of Klee's birth, and to that extent his misfortunes were mitigated; but he felt them acutely, nonetheless, and his son Felix has described how one of his first actions on arriving in Switzerland as a refugee was to make a little picture called *Struck off the List.* Klee was sensitive to every vibration of the world around him—after the outbreak of World War I in 1914 he wrote in his diary, "For a long time I have carried this war within me"—and between 1933 and his death in June, 1940, he referred over and over again in his work to the all-encompassing persecution which was the lot of so many of his friends and colleagues.

He never did this in a literal or a descriptive way. It was not his role to duplicate what could be seen on the newsreels or read about in those newspapers which could still report freely. He was there to find what he had so often found before in happier contexts: the perfect metaphor for what everyone was feeling but no one knew as well as he how to express. He set before us the idea of fear, at a time when virtually every European had fear as his daily companion. Klee saw fear in terms of an inescapable intrusion. In an oblique but unforgettable image, he made us feel that a man was trying to escape from his terrors in sleep, only to find that fear had impregnated the very blankets that he tries to pull up to his chin. Klee imagined his *Letter Ghost* at a time when not to get a letter

Paul Klee.
Letter Ghost. 1937.
Gouache, watercolor and ink on newspaper, 13 × 19¼ inches. The Museum of Modern Art, New York. Purchase

Paul Klee.
Imprisoned Animal. 1940.
Gouache on paper, 12¼ × 19¼ inches. Private collection, Switzerland

often meant the arrest, if not the death, of the person who had gone to the mailbox as a free human being the week before. Waiting for a letter that does not come is torture, as we all know. What could be more natural, to Klee's way of thinking, than that letters should have ghosts—white-faced presences that take on the look of a human head and a pair of shoulders? The image of an imprisoned animal in 1940 was as poignant to Klee, and therefore to ourselves, as was the image of the imprisoned unicorn to the people who made *The Hunt of the Unicorn* tapestries in the 15th century. Klee did not apply himself in literal terms to the history of his own times. But we know, all the same, that this imprisoned animal with its huge staring eyes is a metaphor for the millions of people who were to experience imprisonment in one form or another in the 1940s. It is thanks to people like him, as much as to commentators of a more straightforward kind, that posterity knows what it was like to live in Europe at that time.

Yet there is a case for saying that in terms of immediate public impact Picasso's *Guernica* was a greater service to humanity, at the time it was painted, than any other single painting of the period. It was in April, 1937, that the Spanish city of Guernica was destroyed by German aircraft under the order of General Franco. The world has seen many such things since, and seen them on a bigger scale and with more calamitous weapons. But at the time there was something uniquely chilling about the deliberate obliteration of a historic city. Six days later Picasso began work on the huge monochromatic painting which bears the name *Guernica.* This painting was shown from July, 1937, onward in the Spanish Pavilion at the Paris International Exhibition; and as a contribution to the poetics of outrage it had a colossal effect.

It is a tribute to the power of *Guernica*—and a comment, also, on the confusion of the times—that we still find it difficult to place the picture once and for all in the context of Picasso's output. He himself said in 1965 that as between *Guernica* and *The Three Dancers* of 1925, "I much prefer *The Three Dancers.* It's more a real painting—a painting in itself without any outside considerations." And there is in *Guernica* something descriptive—something of the "Agit-prop" wall-newspaper raised to the scale of epic—which lays it open to comprehensive explanation in just the way that Braque regarded as unworthy of high art. But there are moments in history at which it is more important to strike hard and strike soon than to aim at the privileged status of high art, and the summer of 1937 was one of them.

In painting *Guernica* Picasso took up a challenge—that of the specific event from recent history—which for one reason and another is now often regarded as being outside the province of serious art. Its affinities in that respect are with the 19th century: with Goya's *The Third of May, 1808,*

Delacroix's *Liberty Leading the People,* Manet's *The Execution of the Emperor Maximilian.* Beyond these it looked back to a classic figure subject from still earlier days—the Massacre of the Innocents. At the same time it has characteristics which relate it to our own era: the image is put before us in the blacks and whites of the 1930s newsreel, and the scale and format foreshadow the sprawling animation of the wide-screen movies of the 1960s. There is something of everything in *Guernica,* from the tabloid headline to distant echoes of 11th-century Spanish illuminated manuscripts. On one level the imagery is as explicit as that of a news photograph; on another it secretes layer upon layer of recondite allusion, some of it conscious, some of it most probably not.

There are in existence 45 preliminary studies for *Guernica,* all but one of them dated. There are also seven photographs of successive phases during the painting of the picture itself. We know a great deal about *Guernica,* therefore. We know that the figure of the wounded horse derives from a drawing made by Picasso in 1917, and that the striped skirt and flung-back head of the woman on the left derive from the mourning Maenad in *The Three Dancers* of 1925. The broken spear and the head of the dead soldier in *Guernica* hark back, as we also know, to the *Studio with Plaster Head,* again of 1925. There are many pre-echoes in Picasso's work for the figure of the bull, bemused and stationary despite all the tumult around him. If the arm that holds the lamp seems to be 15 feet long, and if the necks of the four women seem to be made of elastic, these elongations were initiated in the 1920s, when Picasso spent a lot of time at the seaside and noticed how people seem to deny their normal dimensions when they get to run and jump around the beach.

Every great artist carries much of the past of art within him, and when he is under exceptional pressure the past is likely to break in, unbidden, in ways not to be foreseen. When the English art historian Anthony Blunt published a book on *Guernica* in 1969 he had no difficulty in tracing the formalized masks of Picasso's women to massacre subjects painted in the 17th century by Guido Reni and Nicolas Poussin. But along with identifiable borrowings of this kind there came allusions of an oblique and perhaps involuntary sort. On the ground in the middle of the picture, beneath the forefeet of the horse, there is for instance a flower for which no logical reason can be adduced in a purely metropolitan scene. "Is it permissible," Blunt asked, "to see in this an allusion to the anemone which sprang from the blood of Adonis and became a symbol of his resurrection?"

Pablo Picasso. *Guernica.* 1937. Oil on canvas, 11 feet 6 inches × 25 feet 8 inches. The Museum of Modern Art, New York. On extended loan

Pablo Picasso.
Still Life with Red Bull's Head. 1938.
Oil on canvas,
38⅛ × 51 inches.
The Museum of Modern Art, New York.
Promised gift of Mr. and Mrs. William A. M. Burden, New York

Guernica is, therefore, on one level a polemical painting that goes all out for quick results. On another, it stands for that general mobilization of the European past which was art's last line of defense in the 1920s and '30s. It can be seen as a magniloquent patchwork, and it can also be seen as one of the instances in which a major modern artist has faced directly up to his responsibilities as a social being. As to precisely where the truth lies, opinions are likely to vary from one age to another. My own view is that as larger lunacies efface the memory of the destruction of Guernica, the picture is likely to look more and more like an isolated phenomenon in Picasso's work: one that by the standards of the highest art relies too much, as Picasso himself said, on "outside considerations." It stands out, all right; but does it quite stand up? Does it do something that could not be done in any other medium, or is there in the end too much of illustration in it?

When Picasso painted his *Still Life with Red Bull's Head* in November, 1938, he must have had this problem on his mind. For what he did was to carry over from *Guernica* the steady flame which stands for reason and truth; with it, he carried over the head of the bull. Between the two are a palette and a book, symbols of the power to make truth visible. There are changes, since *Guernica.* Not only has the bull's head been skinned, but it has taken on an unmistakable look of Picasso himself. The huge helpless head glares across at the flame; the painter's tools lie to hand; the picture has a message: it is that it is one thing to see the truth and quite another to know how to put it on canvas. Nothing in this picture is explicit; but like so much that we have considered here it is a delaying action on behalf of a European tradition far gone in decline.

Thomas Eakins.
The Gross Clinic.
1875.
Oil on canvas,
8 feet × 6 feet
6 inches.
Jefferson Medical
College of
Philadelphia

AMERICA REDEFINED

Between 1945 and 1970 there was acted out in New York City a considerable human adventure: the emergence after nearly 300 years of an independent, self-generating and specifically American art.

Why *then,* and not before? Why *there,* and not somewhere else? These questions deserve an answer. For there had of course been art in America before, and some of it had been very good. But it had stood in the shadow of European art. Such independence as it had was owed sometimes to its American subject matter, sometimes to the American turn of mind which lay behind it, sometimes to the irresistible complicity which links a painter to his public. There had also, as we have seen, been instances in America from 1913 onward of an art which could be called "new." But these were phenomena without progeny; the artists in question did not, for one reason or another, produce that continuing body of distinctly new work which was the mark of the great Europeans. Sometimes they died young, sometimes they turned conservative, sometimes they gave up hope, sometimes they went so far as to destroy their earlier and more experimental work.

It is for these reasons that American painting remained until 1945 in what might be called a colonial situation. It was dominated, in other words, by the art of other times and older places. Thomas Eakins was a first-rate human being, but something in his art came to him at second hand —from Rembrandt, in the case of *The Gross Clinic,* from Gustave Courbet, from Thomas Couture. *The Gross Clinic* is one of the noblest pictures ever painted by an American. Though clearly based on Rembrandt's *Anatomy Lesson,* it is specifically of the American 19th century in its determination to get at the truth, no matter how awkwardly. Medical studies were not for the squeamish, as we can judge from the attitude of the man in the foreground on the left; and art was not for the squeamish either. It demanded the same degree of dedication and that same insensibility to ridicule which distinguished the great pioneers in other disciplines. Anatomy was as fundamental to art in Eakins's day as it was to medicine: whence the gravity with which he recorded the attitudes of those who, like himself, were looking for the truth at no matter what cost to themselves.

Eakins was probity personified; there are paintings by him which stand out as landmarks in the history of American self-awareness; nothing in his work is fudged or faked. But if we put an Eakins on the wall beside a great Courbet it ends by looking limited, local, and in the noblest sense provincial. We have to remind ourselves that for an American painter to come so far in the 1870s and '80s was already a prodigious achievement.

Yet America had already a literature of the kind, and of the stature, which stamps and defines a great nation at a crucial stage in its development. In the France of the 1850s Edgar Allan Poe was one of the most influential of all English-speaking writers; and a nation which had produced, in that same decade, Melville's *Moby Dick*, Whitman's *Leaves of Grass*, Thoreau's *Walden*, Hawthorne's *The Scarlet Letter*, Emerson's *Representative Men* and Motley's *The Rise of the Dutch Republic* did not have to bother about being called "provincial." Every one of these books was unmistakably and irreducibly American; and so firmly did Melville, Whitman and Hawthorne probe the sensitive places of American awareness that they can be said to have usurped the prerogatives, and to a real degree the idiom, of art. Clement Greenberg

Thomas Eakins.
Max Schmitt in a Single Scull. 1871.
Oil on canvas,
32¼ × 46¼ inches.
The Metropolitan Museum of Art, New York.
Alfred N. Punnett Fund and gift of George D. Pratt

Arshile Gorky.
Agony. 1947.
Oil on canvas,
40 × 50½ inches.
The Museum of
Modern Art, New
York.
A. Conger Goodyear
Fund

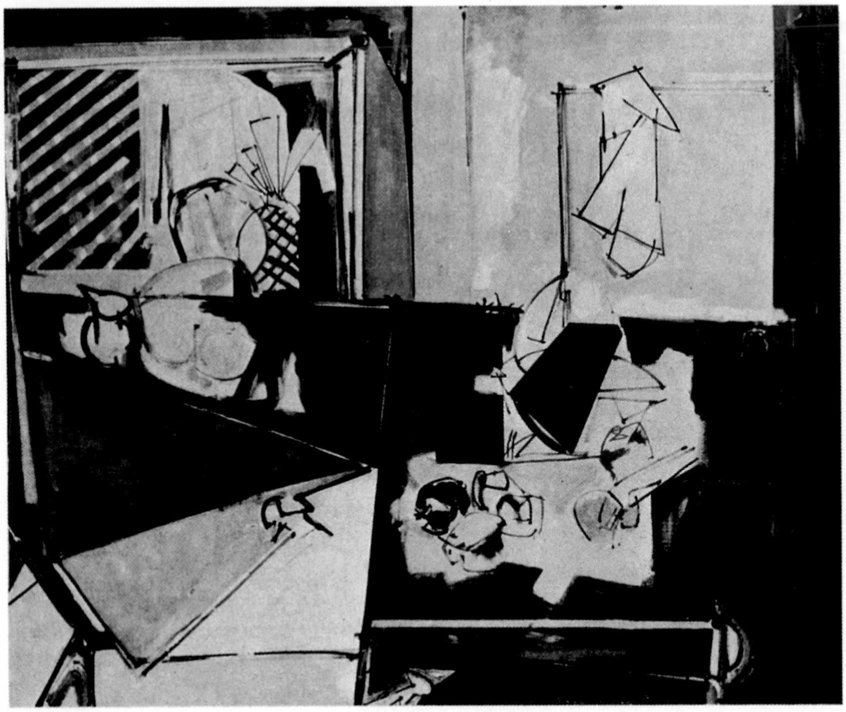

Hans Hofmann.
Magenta and Blue.
1950.
Oil on canvas,
48 × 58 inches.
Whitney Museum of American Art, New York

doubtless correct in citing Soutine—above all, Soutine's Céret landscapes—as the source of this element in Hofmann's teaching. In the landscapes which Soutine painted in Céret, in southern France, there is foreshadowed one of the chief characteristics of the First New York School: an intense nervous energy which communicated itself to the movement of the brush. Soutine painted what looks to us like a world in convulsion; but the convulsion in question was in his own fingers' ends, and in the rapid and purposeful to and fro of the brush. As much as in anything painted by Jackson Pollock, the canvas becomes what Harold Rosenberg in 1952 called "an arena in which to act, rather than a space in which to reproduce, redesign, analyze or 'express' an object, actual or imagined." Insofar as any one man could set up the conditions for the new American painting, that man was Hans Hofmann. He was the complete cosmopolitan; but whereas the cosmopolitan has often more knowledge than drive, Hofmann had in the highest possible degree the German's will to win. And he kept at it with the kind of big, square-built ambition that made it possible for him to peak toward the end of his long life, rather than 30 years earlier. *Magenta and Blue,* 1950, looks back to the classic French interiors which Matisse for one had brought to perfection; but it also looks forward to the day when Hofmann would be able to structure his paintings in terms of large flat rectangles of pure color.

Early in 1939 Picasso's *Guernica* arrived in New York. With the outbreak of World War II, and more especially with the fall of France in the summer of 1940, New York began to harbor not only the masterpieces of modern European art but quite a few of the men who had made them. The men in question included Piet Mondrian, Fernand Léger, Max Ernst, Yves Tanguy, László Moholy-Nagy, André Masson and the Chilean-born Sebastian Matta Echaurren. André Breton was there to assure the continuity of a certain idea of Surrealism, and Peggy Guggenheim was there to open, in 1942, a gallery called Art of This Century. In World War II, as in World War I, the European avant-garde was in and out of New York all the time.

Somewhere in the mid-1940s the notion of a

specifically American modern art began to be discussed, and what history calls the First New York School came into being. The name is unhistorical, in more ways than one. There was no one school, in the sense of a teaching institution, in the sense of an orthodoxy or shared body of beliefs, or in the sense of a group of artists who showed together, like the French Impressionists. There was not even the kind of unified activity which the word generally implies. The artists were as unlike one another, as human beings, as it is possible for artists to be. Yet the words "First New York School" stand for men who do undeniably belong together: Jackson Pollock, Arshile Gorky, Willem de Kooning, David Smith, Hans Hofmann, Franz Kline, Mark Rothko, Barnett Newman, Adolph Gottlieb, Philip Guston, Clyfford Still. It is thanks to them that feelings of wonder and acceptance took the place of the defeatism which had been so widespread among the public for American art in the 1920s and '30s.

These feelings were generated by men who were not young, at the critical moment, as Picasso and Braque were young when they broke through to Cubism. To one degree or another they had all taken a battering from life. Beyond that, what was there in common between Arshile Gorky, who was born in Turkish Armenia of a family of village tradesmen, and Clyfford Still, who was born in North Dakota of Scottish and Irish ancestry? Gorky learned the European masters by heart, the way an aspirant actor learns "To be or not to be"; Still thought of the Armory Show as "that ultimate in irony" which "had dumped upon us the combined and sterile conclusions of Western European decadence." There were close friendships among the artists concerned—Pollock and Guston, de Kooning and Gorky, Rothko and Gottlieb—but there were also divergences of experience and of origins, which were so extreme as to exclude anything more than a wry and intermittent admiration.

For instance, Willem de Kooning was born in Rotterdam, Holland, and he was going on 22 when he got into the United States with false papers at the third time of trying. He did not have, therefore, the sense of an American-ness within him that cried out for redefining. "It is a certain burden, this American-ness," he said in 1963. "If you come from a small nation, you don't have that. When I went to the Academy in Rotterdam and I was drawing from the nude, *I* was making the drawing, not Holland." In the 1930s and early '40s very dull things were done in the name of American-ness. ("Art in America today," Barnett Newman wrote in 1942, "stands at a point where anything that cannot fit into the American Scene label is doomed to be completely ignored"; de Kooning spoke of "making art out of John Brown's body." Just about the only artist who used specifically and unmistakably American subject matter without falling into an isolationist aesthetic was Stuart Davis, who loved France and French art and yet never reneged on his wiry, sinewy, plainspoken nature. He cut the descriptive element in painting to essentials that could be reduced no further; and then he put them together again in ways that owed much to French mentors but were also quintessentially American in their throwaway wit. It was Davis, as much as anyone, who deprovincialized American painting. This was acknowledged already in 1931 by Arshile Gorky, then 26 years old, when he paid tribute to Davis as "this man, this American, this pioneer, this modest painter, who never disarranges his age, who works to perfect his motives, who renders—clear, more definite, more and more decided—new forms and new objects." The phrase that matters here is that Davis "never disarranges his age"; the art and the age were one, in his work, and a painting like his *Lucky Strike* of 1921 has about it not only an after-echo of Fernand Léger but a specifically American form of plain statement.

To those who wondered if American painters would ever manage to modernize themselves in Ezra Pound's sense, Stuart Davis brought reassurance. But it was not enough for one man and one picture, here and there, to have exceptional status.

Clyfford Still.
Painting. 1951.
Oil on canvas,
7 feet 10 inches × 6 feet 10 inches.
The Museum of Modern Art, New York.
Blanchette Rockefeller Fund

Mark Rothko.
Number 10. 1950.
Oil on canvas,
7 feet 6⅜ inches ×
57⅛ inches.
The Museum of
Modern Art, New
York. Gift of Philip
Johnson

What was dreamed of in the 1930s, and what found all too little in the way to support it, was a state of affairs like the one described by Harold Rosenberg in an article first published in 1940. Inspired by the entry of the German armies into Paris, it began with the sentence: "The laboratory of the 20th century has been shut down." Rosenberg went on to look back to the period immediately before 1914, when "suddenly, almost in the span of a single generation, everything buried underground was brought to the surface. The perspective of the immediate was established—or rather, a multiple perspective, in which time no longer reared up like a gravestone or flourished like a tree but threw up a shower of wonders at the will of the onlooker."

That was exactly what people were beginning to ask of New York in the 1940s: a shower of wonders, in which everything buried underground was brought to the surface and a perspective of the immediate was established. This could not be one man's doing, any more than what happened in Paris before 1914 was one man's doing. Picasso and Matisse, Braque and Delaunay, Bonnard and Mondrian, late Cézanne and continuing Monet—all had contributed to Paris at that time, sometimes in the closest collaboration but most often with no interconnections whatever. Frenchmen like Braque played their part; but so did new arrivals from abroad, like Juan Gris and Constantin Brancusi, and visitors who stayed only a season, like Kandinsky. A bit of everything, in human terms, and all of it good: that was the idea.

And New York in the 1940s carried it through. Even more than St. Petersburg before 1917, or Paris in the 1920s, New York is the completely cosmopolitan city: the place in which no one need feel a complete outsider or despair of finding someone of his own race, color, tastes and beliefs with whom to strike up acquaintance. New York has something of Athens, something of Shanghai, something of Odessa, something of Dublin, something of Tel Aviv. It's all there: there is no tune that cannot be played on the human keyboard that this city provides.

New York is also very good at processing new arrivals and making them its own. First- and second-generation immigrants made up the greater part of the New York School, along with country boys from Wyoming (Jackson Pollock) or from the coal-mining part of Pennsylvania (Franz Kline). Willem de Kooning was born in Holland, Mark Rothko in Russia, Arshile Gorky in Armenia, Hans Hofmann in Bavaria, and Barnett Newman's parents came over from Polish Russia at the turn of the century; yet in the 1940s all these people were complete Americans. They were as committed to America as if their forefathers had come over with Columbus. What Thomas B. Hess had to say about Newman is true of all of them: that Newman was "a quintessential American. His passion to move with pragmatic curiosity and idealist self-confidence into the modern experience came not only from living an experience of freedom and independence in a new country, but also from an understanding of, and holding onto connections with, a European tradition."

Even so, major art can come about only when the tradition in question is the one that can most fruitfully be carried further. And there was no doubt in the 1940s that the future for art lay in a working alliance between the reasoned order of Cubist painting, with its emphasis on the virtues of equilibrium, and the demands of the liberated unconscious. Cubism in itself seemed to have nowhere to go (though Braque was to prove this mistaken); the heyday of European Surrealism seemed, equally, to be a thing of the past. Somehow the two might be made to work together by a mysterious multiplication. Hans Hofmann, for one, believed this: after spending years "sweating out Cubism," by his own account, he said in 1944 that "the highest in art is the irrational." The task of the irrational was to release "the potential inner life of a chosen medium, so that the final image resulting from it expresses the *all* of oneself."

As far as any one sentence could define the mandate of the New York School, that one does it: the task of the painter was to release the potential inner life of his chosen medium, and in so doing to produce a final image that expressed "the *all* of oneself," unprecedentedly. As to the who, the when and the how of all this, the historian is free to tidy the record as he pleases: or, as Hess once said, to "make a seamless web of process out of what had been a shambles of false moves, happy accidents, and precious insights gained through heartbreaking labors." The artists themselves knew better. Willem de Kooning said in 1949 that "it is impossible to find out how a style began. I think that it is the most bourgeois idea to think that one can make a style beforehand."

And it is of course true that every member of the New York School (and one or two other very fine painters who cannot be so categorized) negotiated quite freely in the late 1940s and early 1950s between the promptings of his own nature and his individual sense of what remained for painting to do. Like many another American artist of his generation, Mark Rothko came under the influence of European Surrealism in the 1940s. But even when he was using hybrid forms derived from that source he enveloped them in a fluid, dimensionless space of his own invention. By 1950 the hybrid forms had dropped out of sight and Rothko had arrived at the compositional device which he employed for the rest of his life: the juxtaposition of rectangular areas of paint in which color was allowed to bloom undisturbed either by drawing, by any suggestion of deep space, or by anything that could be called geometry. Within this basic schema, which might have appeared limited, he produced a huge and unexpectedly varied body of work. The enveloping poetry of his best paintings is owed not only to a superfine color sense but to shifts of emphasis, shifts of proportion, and a continual give and take between one floating shape and another.

Mark Rothko and Clyfford Still at that time were just about as unlike one another as it is possible for human beings to be: in looks, in their ethnic origin, in temperament and in their general experience of life. Still looked like what he was: an irreducible homegrown American. Rothko, too, looked like what he was: a transplanted Eastern European in whom the sense of loss was never quite subdued. But they did have one thing in common: a conviction that their paintings should keep no company but their own. There is about Still's vast fissured shapes, and also about his stark and intransigent writings, something that rejects absolutely the idea of art as a superior distraction. "This is the most serious thing there is," he seems to say. As the art historian Robert Rosenblum pointed out in 1961, there is in this an echo of that craving for the sublime which is perhaps the strongest of all motives for the making of art. There is also something of the archetypal American belief that no limits need be set to human ambition.

Nothing can replace the testimony, in such matters, of the painters. But it is also worthwhile to listen to a very intelligent observer who was around at the time. Thomas B. Hess set out the general position as follows: "Like all artists in the decade 1935–45, the New York painters were faced by a crisis in modernism that took the dramatic form of a clamping down on art—the Paris masters had stamped each approach with so personal a style that it seemed impossible to grow around, much less to move beyond them. . . . The Americans, like their contemporaries in Europe, faced what one artist has called a hotel full of rooms each marked 'Occupied.' "

Hess went on to say that "the solution that de Kooning and his colleagues (including such artists as Pollock, Motherwell, Newman, Kline, Rothko, Still, Gottlieb) attempted was to confront the European masters on their own ground and to work through their styles by changing the hypotheses. A shorthand way of expressing it would be to say that the Americans would base their art on ethical rather than aesthetic pressures. They would turn their concentration inward, focus on the personal experience, express it as forcefully as possible and as efficiently as possible in pictorial

Franz Kline.
Two Horizontals.
1954.
Oil on canvas,
31⅛ × 39¼ inches.
The Museum of Modern Art, New York. The Sidney and Harriet Janis Collection

terms." The question to be answered was "What can a man still do, with paints and canvas, to express the *all* of himself?"

As to the results of this, a large and ferocious literature is already in being. In situations of this kind the best thing is always to look at the work; for it was the work that made its way from 1943 onward. Between 1943 and 1950 there were substantial one-man shows in New York by Hofmann, Pollock, Gorky, Rothko, Still, Kline, Gottlieb, Newman, de Kooning and David Smith. What matters is to examine major works by these artists in the context of their first appearance.

Even the look of the city at a given time can be important in this context. Franz Kline knew New York when the elevated railway was still a fact of everyday life and the crisscross of black girders high above a construction site was just beginning to replace the terraced houses of the last century. His mature paintings were in no sense portraits of that city; but in paintings like *Two Horizontals,* 1954, the headlong power of the slashed black-on-white derived from a townscape in which ruthless change was beginning to be taken for granted.

"I think," de Kooning once wrote, "that innovators come at the end of a period. Cézanne gave the finishing touches to Impressionism before he came face to face with his 'little sensation.' " De Kooning was 44 when he wrote that, and 45 when he painted his *Excavation* in 1950. He had at that time been concerned with art, part-time or full-time, for 33 years. His first one-man show had been in April, 1948; and as a man in his 40s he had had plenty of time to put the "finishing touches" to the art of the immediate past. Now, with *Excavation,* he was completely himself. The painting is already set fast in history, but it is worthwhile to try to see it as it looked in 1950: a picture unlike any other.

It is a big picture, by the standards of its day. It came immediately after a long series of paintings in which de Kooning had expressly avoided the emotional associations of color. He had used these black-and-white paintings as a way of crossing over, as it were, from drawing to painting. De Kooning is one of the great draftsmen of this century, with a variety of attack and a range of subject matter which are almost beyond comparison. He can do anything that he wants with line; and the line in question can be as thin as a silk thread or

Arshile Gorky.
Garden in Sochi.
1941.
Oil on canvas,
44¼ × 62¼ inches.
The Museum of
Modern Art, New
York. Gift of Mr.
and Mrs. Wolfgang
S. Schwabacher

make their wishes come true. They could look, finally, for the "Holy Tree," which was hung with strips of cloth that pilgrims had torn from their own clothes. This Holy Tree, itself leafless, had therefore a covering of pseudo-leaves which seemed to the young Gorky to rustle in the wind "like the silver leaves of poplars."

Chagall, for one, would have got a great deal of mileage out of detail of this sort; but the case of Gorky was more complicated. In the hybrid forms of these three paintings the things he spelled out for the catalogue reader were both *there* and *not there.* This is an extreme instance of the fact that no two people see the same picture. We can read into it what we will. Or, more exactly, it will summon, from our own unconscious, kindred but idiosyncratic memories with which we can complete the image. All pictures do this, in a varying degree; what is special about Gorky is that he unlocks the valve of private feeling with a particular sureness. It is a mistake, as Breton said, to read his pictures literally. They should be to us what Nature was to Gorky: a springboard.

It is legitimate, even so, to take up one or two of the clues which he offers us. Most commentators agree that the strong vertical form at the top of the *Garden in Sochi* is the Holy Tree; some see a porcupine, to the right below, and blue rock and black earth in the lower part of the picture to the left. The idea, part visual, part tactile, of a human female breast held in the hand and rubbed against a rock is pure Gorky in its alliance of the unexpected with the voluptuous; and I don't see why we should not find echoes of it in the *Garden in Sochi.* Gorky did not define his images, and he defies us to define them for him; but when we concentrate on his paintings as intensely as he concentrated upon Nature we shall find that memo-

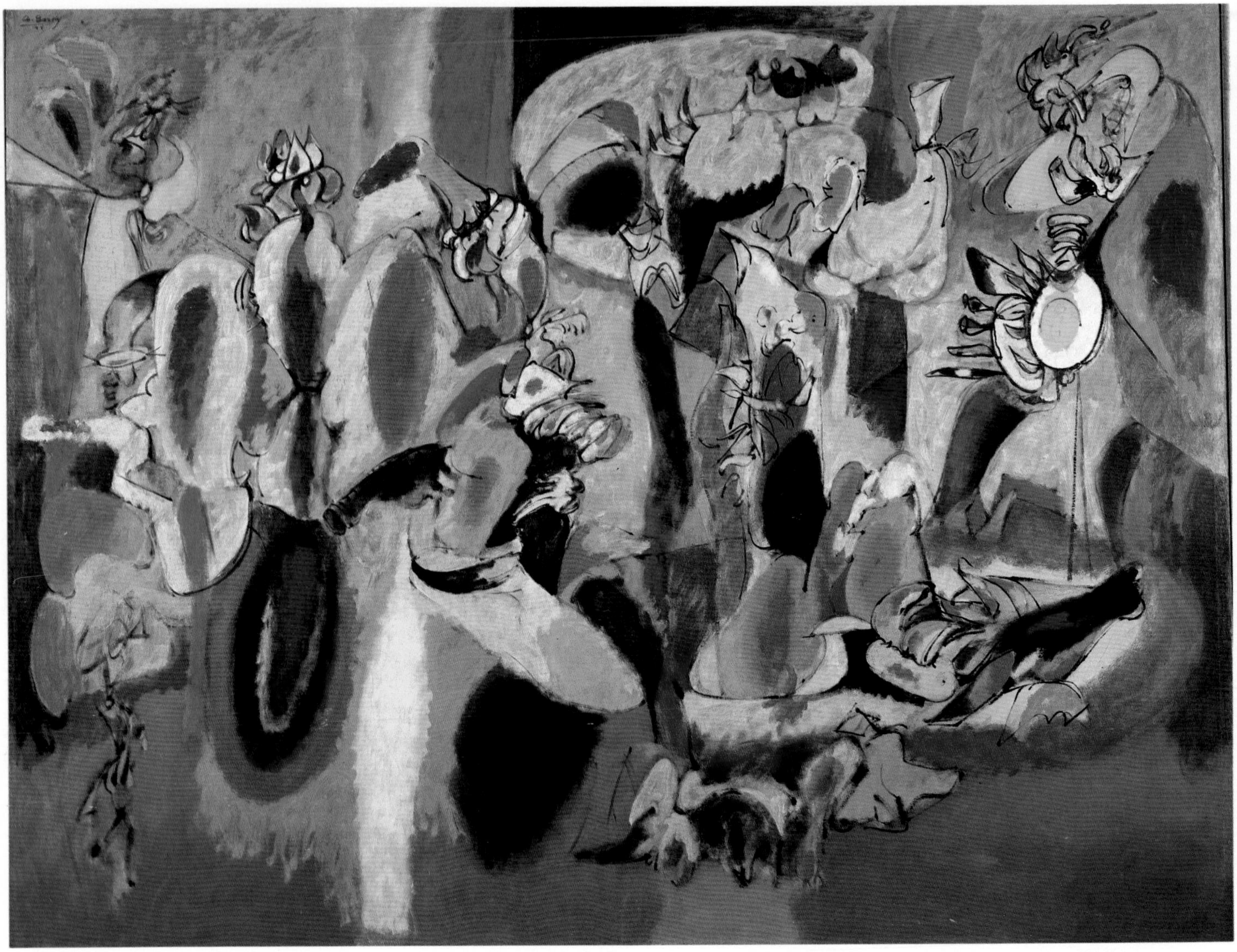

Arshile Gorky.
The Liver Is the Cock's Comb. 1944.
Oil on canvas,
6 feet × 8 feet 2 inches.
Albright-Knox Art Gallery, Buffalo. Gift of Seymour H. Knox

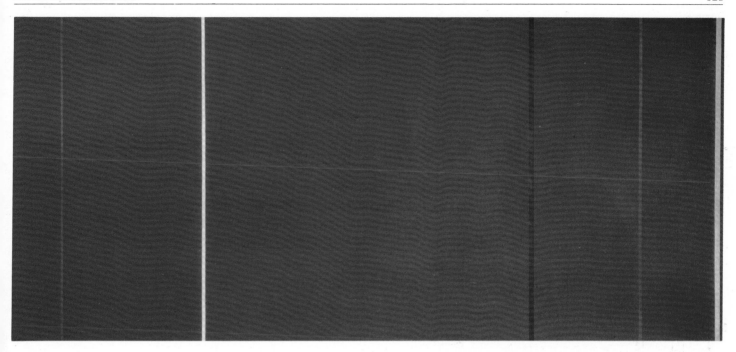

Barnett Newman.
Vir Heroicus Sublimis. 1950–51.
Oil on canvas, 7 feet $11\frac{3}{8}$ inches × 17 feet $9\frac{1}{4}$ inches.
The Museum of Modern Art, New York. Gift of Mr. and Mrs. Ben Heller

Barnett Newman. *Concord.* 1949. Oil on canvas, 7 feet 5¾ inches × 53⅝ inches. The Metropolitan Museum of Art, New York. George A. Hearn Fund

ries long "forgotten" come back to us and that, as in a successful psychoanalysis, we make constructive connections between aspects of our experience which had previously seemed to us quite unrelated.

Gorky does this for us because he was prepared to risk himself. He opened himself out, where earlier artists had kept themselves shut. Like one of Arthur Miller's heroes, he allowed himself "to be completely known." His work had nothing of the grand public quality which was the mark of Hofmann and Pollock in their major statements. It was addressed to one pair of eyes at a time, and it set up an ideal of human intercourse in which everything can be said: without fear and without reserve. Gorky took from other artists and never tried to deny it; but where Picasso and Miró, Matta and André Masson in the last resort defended their own privacy—with wit, with panache, with masks borrowed from other places and other times—Arshile Gorky was the man who kept nothing back. Like John Berryman in poetry, he allowed art to eat him alive.

In his last paintings, of which *Agony* is an outstandingly fine example, Gorky was able to ally painterly eloquence to forms which epitomize the hurts which life had inflicted upon him. On the one hand, he opens the door upon the charnel house in which all human hopes and ambitions have their end; on the other, he achieved a fullness and subtlety of color that then were only just beginning to be within the reach of Abstract Expressionism.

Gorky's was an art of private reference: more so than Hofmann's, more so than de Kooning's, more so even than Pollock's. The other three had by implication a heroic stance which went beyond autobiography; and this was true, equally, of Barnett Newman.

Newman doubtless had, in private, his full share of those sensations of loss and unease which were mandatory among responsible human beings in the dark middle of this century. But in his art he was concerned with healing, and with restoration, and with the ways in which an individual human nature can be at one with itself and with the universe. *Onement* was the title he chose for the painting with which he broke through in 1948 to a way of painting that was entirely his own. *Concord* was the title of a major painting of the following year. Now, Newman was very sensitive to language, and he knew that *Onement* has overtones both of being "at one with the world" and of atonement in a specifically religious sense. *Concord* sets up likewise a complex vibration in our minds: concord as the aim of a fulfilled and humane society, Concord as a place-name that means much in American history, Concord the village as part of a pastoral New England still not too much contaminated. Newman thought every-beauty, the ideal content—tragedy." It seemed to him that in that context the European artist was "nostalgic for the ancient forms, hoping to achieve tragedy by depicting his self-pity over the loss of the elegant column and the beautiful profile." The American artist had by contrast "an opportunity, free of the ancient paraphernalia, closer to the sources of the tragic emotion." Alike in *Achilles* and *Broken Obelisk*, Newman gave a new twist (literally, in the case of the obelisk) to formulae which long use had made flaccid. In *Achilles*, the hero's giant stature and broken sword are hinted at but not described. As for the obelisk, it is a potent symbol of man's flawed, divided nature.

I cannot claim in these few pages to have done more than touch on certain major figures of the New York School. Even in the period under review, which ends in 1951, other men, other works and other media should ideally be included. Other dialogues—with the American past, with the European masters, with the notion of an art that would lie beyond the range of the art market—could also be spelled out in detail. Something could also be said about the coincidence (if it is one) by which these artists came to fulfillment at the apogee of American power: political, military, economic. What I have tried to suggest is that art, like nature, abhors a vacuum; that there was a job to be done in the United States in the late 1940s, just as there had been a job to be done in Paris between 1885 and 1914; and that for the first time American artists proved equal to a span of involvement that ranged from the most intimate disorders of the psyche to what is called in Jewish mysticism "the everlasting unity and presence of Transcendence."

Jasper Johns.
Flag. 1954–55.
Encaustic on newsprint over canvas mounted on plywood, 42¼ × 60½ inches.
The Museum of Modern Art, New York.
Gift of Philip Johnson in honor of Alfred H. Barr, Jr.

THE GREAT DIVIDE 1950-70

The art of the second half of this century treads everywhere on tender ground. For what is true of people and of public events is also true of works of art: we have a special feeling toward the ones we grew up with.

This feeling is rooted in reason, for it is in first youth that we establish the modes of feeling, the canons of beauty, and the standards of truth and integrity by which we are to live for the rest of our lives. But it also goes beyond reason. We are committed, every one of us, in ways that are sometimes welcome, sometimes repugnant, to what is done in our own day. Its face is our face, its ways are our ways, its echo is the twin of our own. We may demur—"It has nothing to do with me," we may say, whether from modesty or from disgust—but posterity will not believe us. Posterity will say that to be alive at a given time and not to be marked by the events of the day is a disgrace and a diminution. We were there; this and that happened; how could we not bear the mark forever?

This is true above all of those moments in history at which a shift of sensibility occurs or the potential of human capacities is redrafted. People who come to maturity at such times are by that much the more alive. It would, for instance, be a very dull American who did not feel that the first years of the presidency of Harry S. Truman were a time unlike any other. In terms of political, economic and military power the United States dominated the rest of the world as never before or since. It had a primacy of the sort which can turn to tyranny; but the use made of it was more often than not both farsighted and responsible. It was also magnanimous: how often in history has a nation offered to renounce a decisive military superiority in the interests of the common good? Yet this is what happened in 1946. Had the Baruch plan been accepted by the United Nations, the United States would have destroyed her stock of atomic weapons and manufactured no more of them, in return for a general agreement that atomic power should be used for peaceful purposes only, with regular worldwide inspection to confirm that this was being done.

United States policy was magnanimous in other ways also. We should not forget that twelve million American men and women were given the chance of further education under the G.I. Bill of Rights; that relief to the devastated countries of Europe ran at around $700,000,000 a year; and that when George C. Marshall was Secretary of State, in 1947, he made it possible for those same countries to establish, by their own exertions but with American financial backing, "the political and social conditions in which free institutions can exist." That such institutions should exist was much to the advantage of the United States: to that extent the Marshall Plan can be interpreted in terms of American self-interest. But anyone who traveled in Europe in 1946 will know that the condition of victors and vanquished alike was appalling; and to both of them at that time the large-heartedness of the United States seemed as genuine as it was prompt.

It could be a coincidence, but I don't think it was, that American Action Painting came to the fore at precisely that time. Action Painting was not, as some people supposed, melodramatic or self-indulgent. It arose from an intelligent examination, on the part of people who had been serious artists for nearly half a lifetime, as to just why so much of European painting had run itself into the ground. And it stood for an idea current in public life also: that human nature had not said its last word.

Many of its manifestations had an evangelical character. In a major Jackson Pollock, as in a slashing, man-sized, black-on-white Franz Kline, painting comes into the open, baring its essential nature with a mimetic vivacity that can still carry us away. When Arshile Gorky unbandaged the wounds with which life had left him, he did it in such a way that we found new courage to face our own hurts. It was a time for the undefeated spirit. What was called an "American sublime" was brought into being: a mode of expression from which the contingent and the equivocal were banished. A painting like Barnett Newman's *Day One* is typical of that moment in history. Already its title suggests the beginning of a new era for all humanity; and it was typical of its time in being, as Thomas B. Hess pointed out, "not only unsaleable, but unexhibitable. There was no chance at all, with its 11-foot height, that it could be sold, or even seen by anybody but the artist and the friends he invited to his studio."

The all-or-nothing, backs-against-the-wall character of work such as this answered to experience of life not only during the Depression and during World War II, but even in the late 1940s, when the audience for radically new art in a country of 140,000,000 people was estimated at around 50: "a small circle," as Clement Greenberg described it in the fall of 1947, "of fanatics, art-fixated misfits who are as isolated in the U.S. as if they were living in Paleolithic Europe." Greenberg went on to describe their isolation as "inconceivable, crushing, unbroken, damning"; and it is natural that those who lived through that period either as participants or as sympathizers should consider that later generations of American artists have had a much easier ride. Certainly they have not had to draw for so long on the reserves of moral energy which were demanded of Pollock, de Kooning, Gorky and Newman. Nor were they called upon to make the kind of breakthrough to public acknowledgment which has to be made once and once only; by 1956, the year of Pollock's death, that job had been done. Thereafter it was taken for granted that painting and sculpture had a new rank among American modes of expression, and that they were redefining America as distinctly as it had been redefined by Emerson in the 1830s, by Herman Melville in the 1850s, and by Whitman in the laconic penetrations of his *Specimen Days in America* (first published in 1882–83).

It was a lot to ask of any artist that he do this; but in their different ways—and no group of men could have been more different, one from the other—the American Action Painters had trained ments which would "make available for musical purposes any and all sounds that can be heard." Musical expression would be set free from the tyranny of existing musical instruments; "we can compose and perform," Cage went on, "a quartet for explosive motor, wind, heartbeat, and landslide."

As between Johns and Rauschenberg, there is no doubt that it was Rauschenberg who took over the Cage position in a wholehearted and single-minded way. In an often-quoted statement he said that he wanted to work "in the gap between art and life"; and in 1961 he told an interviewer that "there is no reason not to consider the world as one gigantic painting." So far from treating the picture as something set apart from the world, he welcomed the world into it. He saw it as the function of the artist to work with what is given; and in paintings like *Charlene* he sieved the dredged filth of New York City as a prospector sieves the sand of the riverbed: for gold. *Charlene* is as American, and as much a part of the American life of its epoch, as is the page in *Specimen Days* where Whitman describes Manhattan as he knew it in 1879. It is, in fact, a contribution to the roomy, meandering, accumulative tradition of American autobiography.

"Combine-paintings" was Rauschenberg's name for pictures of this sort; and they do, in effect, combine unaltered materials of the most heterogeneous kind with passages of straightforward paintwork. So far from making fun of Action Painting, they are the work of someone for whom the Abstract Expressionist brush stroke and the look of paint dripped straight from the can are an important part of art: but a part to be taken into the work as a phenomenon among others. It is not for them to bear sole responsibility for the picture; and they are, if anything, all the more eloquent for being made to coexist with newsprint, reproductions of Old Master painting, half-obliterated comic strips and (in *Charlene*) the outstretched spokes of an umbrella which have been fleshed out and painted over and can be spun around like the

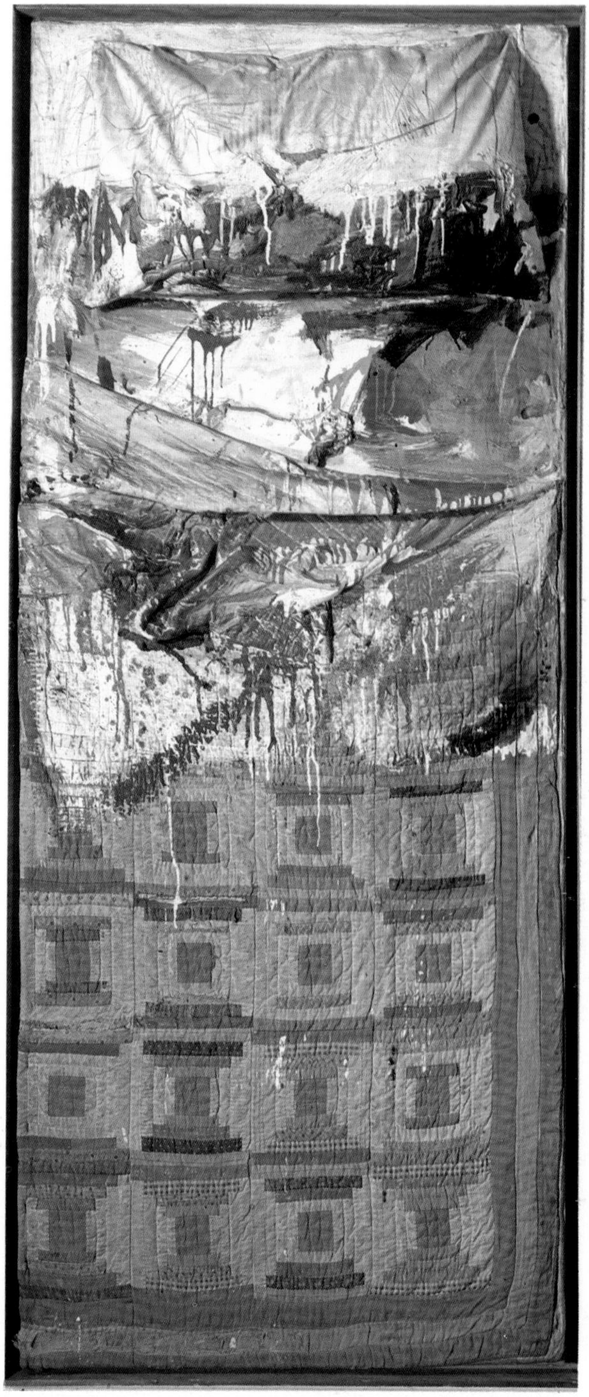

Robert Rauschenberg.
Bed. 1955. Combine painting,
6 feet 2 inches × 31½ inches × 6½ inches.
Mr. and Mrs. Leo Castelli, New York

arms of a windmill.

So dense is the deposit of allusion and association in *Charlene* that we can stay with it for weeks on end and still find new points of entrance, new appeals to memory, new combinations of sight and touch and feel and remembered smell. It is a part of the continuum of big-city experience; and as I said before it treats earlier, preexisting art as a part of that experience. Art is accorded equality with the rest: no less, and no more. A lost tradition of narrative painting reasserts its rights as we track back and forth in the accumulation of one man's experience. There are elements of abstract painting also in the tall thin vertical panels which structure the painting as a whole; and in the flattened umbrella in the top right-hand corner there is an after-echo of the severe geometrical painting of Europe in the 1930s—a time when *Circle* seemed a predestined name for a good art magazine. *Charlene* is a picture to live in, not to look at; and among the qualities for which it speaks is an open trust in the way things are.

The case of Rauschenberg's *Bed* is comparatively simple, though few works of art have caused so much exasperation. *Bed* is about paint's power to survive, as the instrument of human expression, in surroundings no matter how far removed from those of high art. Action Painting had claimed for the artist, and for what he produces, a place set apart. It relied on materials, and on a specific type of physical construction, that asserted the continuity of high art. Pollock may have spread his canvas on the floor and worked on it in ways that were quite new, but when the picture got up on the wall it was stretched taut and trim on a rectangular wooden support, just like an easel painting by Rubens or Velázquez. *Bed* gets away from all that and asserts, by contrast, that the eloquence of paint can be bestowed on the apparatus of everyday life. The bed in *Bed* is still a bed, but it is also a painting; Rauschenberg here works literally in "the gap between art and life," and he contrives to close it, so that art and life merge into one single experience and can no longer be separated one from the other.

These were difficult ideas, when they were first mooted. Too much was risked, too much was questioned, too much familiar ground was ruled "off limits." It was not immediately clear to what an extent the epic scale and the exuberant physicality of *Charlene* and the other combine-paintings of Rauschenberg were specifically American qualities that had found a completely new outlet. The facts of American abundance had always tempted American writers, poets, composers and painters, and many of them had tried one variant or another of the cumulative approach: Charles Ives piling one orchestra on top of another, Whitman listing his allegiances for page after page, John Dos Passos aping the crosscutting of the cinema in *U.S.A.*, Joseph Stella in 1913 working his heart out to get all Coney Island down on canvas. Rauschenberg was in the listing business, too; but he realized, as no one had realized before him, that raw material can be served up raw and that art and life could be made to interlock in the mid-1950s as they had never quite interlocked before. In *Rebus*, for instance, he took the detritus of the New York street—a political poster, two news photographs of track events, a comic strip and some objects of more mysterious provenance—and allied them to a small reproduction of Botticelli's *The Birth of Venus* and a page from an art magazine. The great art of the past took its chance, in other words, with metropolitan graffiti and with the kind of images to which no one gives more than a moment's attention. For all its chaotic appearance the picture is tautly organized and bound together with passages of pure painting.

Rauschenberg at this stage in his career was still very much the boy from out of town who had made it into the big city. He had just discovered the poetics of glut, and he couldn't wait to tell us about them. The paintings were a way of dealing with the unprecedented input that came the way of everyone in the postwar metropolis: and not merely "a way," but the only way of coming to terms with it without censorship or dilution. Raus-

Robert Rauschenberg. *Rebus.* 1955. Combine painting, 8 feet × 12 feet. Mr. and Mrs. Victor W. Ganz, New York

chenberg gave himself, too: openhandedly. It is the paradox of his combine-paintings that although there is nothing so bizarre or so recalcitrant that it could not find a place in them (a stuffed hen, a deflated inner tube, a radio in full operation) Rauschenberg marks them all with his own identity. He is them, and they are him: the ancient sorceries of art are still in operation.

Rauschenberg's activity is basically outgoing in character. He has a gift for communication and an inbred sense of performance. Extravagances no matter how hazardous turned out to end well when he was in charge of them; and when he encroached upon the performing arts—whether as dancer, as artistic adviser to the Merce Cunningham Dance Company, as a founder-member of EAT (Experiments in Art and Technology), and as the inventor of art works that depended in part on activation by their audiences—it was with a consistent optimism. Rauschenberg worked for years with Merce Cunningham and his dance company. Cunningham is the agile figure in the top right-hand area in *Trophy I.* And Rauschenberg makes the most of Cunningham's seemingly effortless balance by introducing into the lower left-hand area of the painting an image which is the epitome of ungainliness—a fallen horse and its unseated rider. The point is rammed further home by the sign that reads "Caution: Watch Your Step." In *Empire II* Rauschenberg perpetuates the kind of image which he would improvise from whatever materials came to hand as Merce Cunningham and his company moved from city to city. An object familiar from the New York skyline in its less pretentious days is given a new and altogether grander identity by being mounted on

Robert Rauschenberg. *Trophy I (for Merce Cunningham).* 1959. Combine painting, 66 × 41 inches. Galerie Beyeler, Basel

what looks, in this context, to be a rough-and-ready chariot.

The case of Jasper Johns is entirely different. He stands for the lapidary, as against the garrulous; for ideas laid one on top of another, as against ideas spread out laterally; and for the thing thought over week after week, as against an overflowing generosity that can survive occasional lapses. Rauschenberg in the mid-1950s was like a faucet of ideas that just couldn't be turned off; Johns was, and is, more deliberate, more self-critical, more apt to say, "Is this really worth doing?"

His work presented from the first the kind of many-layered difficulty which is the surest indication that important art is on the way. The flag, for instance: was it a hoax? An affront to Old Glory? An inscrutable private joke? Discussion waxed hot. In point of fact it was none of those things. It was an intelligent man's response to the fact that the admired painting of the day had to do with images of an entirely idiosyncratic sort: signs never made before. Painting of this kind was running itself breathless by the time of Johns's first New York show in 1958, and in many cases it looked like self-indulgence. It seemed to Johns to be a good idea to see what could be made with an image which was, on the contrary, readymade and immutable. Such an image would ideally have length and breadth but no depth, since the flatness of the canvas was fundamental to painting at that time. If the basic image was so familiar as to bring about a virtual anaesthesia of the aesthetic faculty, people might be confronted as never before with the pure essence of painting: the primal shock, for which others had aimed in ways that had begun to look merely rhetorical. The American flag was just right, in this context. It was an image which in itself left no one indifferent; yet its associations were so far outside the domains of art as to suspend altogether the traditional art-gallery habits of mind. There occurred to every single person, when he first saw one of Johns's flags, a moment of disbelief; and in that moment he was accessible as never before to the primal shock of painting.

As it happened, no two of his flags were the same. People who said "Seen one, seen them all" were put in their places when it turned out that the unchanging face of Old Glory masked a series of raids upon the traditional uses of oil paint, together with a revival of the use of encaustic and a number of forays into territory not yet mapped. There was a ghost-flag—a huge, phantomatic expanse of whites on whites and grays on grays—and there were flags in which faces half-surfaced through the familiar red-and-white horizontals. There were flags on flags, most monumentally superimposed. There were flags which had a private reference, and as late as 1973 there was a double flag which came across with a brilliant, extroverted, public effect. There were flags which re-

Robert Rauschenberg. *Empire II.* 1961. Construction, 61 × 29 × 58 inches. Philip Johnson, New Canaan, Conn.

flected the large areas of melancholy in Johns's own nature; and there were flags which stood for the elemental cachinnations with which in private life he seems to reinvent the notion of laughter.

The flags did, however, have one thing in common: they were all painted on a flat, unbroken surface, and they were to that extent traditional pictures with no adjuncts or annexes. This was not the case with the *Target with Four Faces* of 1958, and it was not the case with many other, later works by Johns. The target, like the flag, was ideal subject matter, in that flatness was of its essence. It was readymade and immutable, like the flag; and in its everyday appearances it, too, probed the limits of impersonality. A target which showed individuality would be by that much the less of a target.

A target is made up, on the other hand, of concentric circles, and Johns was far too astute an observer of modern art not to know that concentric circles had been a favorite motif with abstract painters since the days of Robert Delaunay and the youthful Stanton Macdonald-Wright. Concentric circles did away with the necessity for composition, since the form of the image was dictated from the start. They made it possible for colors to "tell" with an intensity that would be modified and weakened if they had to overlap or interlock. In a fine-art context they also raised problems which in the past had been solved by giving the circles not the blank, frontal look of a target, but a fragmented or interrupted fine-art look. (This continued to be the case in the late 1950s and early 1960s when Kenneth Noland, for one, was working with concentric circles; he repudiated the unvarying readymade form of the target by varying the internal relationships of one circle to another.) Johns made no claims for this target as art. It was what the title said it was: two pairs of yellow and blue circles, centering onto a red bull's-eye. Their physical substance was mysterious, as was that of the wall-like surface of which they formed a part. There could hardly be a less personal image, and yet the impression which stayed with the observer could be owed to one man only.

Flag and target make demands upon us which have nothing to do with the demands of art, though with the one as with the other we associate an exceptional degree of involvement. When Johns paints them we shift to and fro, involuntarily, between the kind of recognition which is owed to a flag, or to a target, and the kind of recognition which is owed to art. Noticing this, we learn something new about living. In *Target with Four Faces,* Johns thickens this particular plot, and we come to know what John Cage meant when he wrote in his notes on Johns that "I thought he was doing three things (five things he was doing escaped my notice)." For the upper part of this picture is really very peculiar. Where the lower part has the total flatness of a paving-slab, the upper part has real three-dimensional recession: genuine depths in which plaster casts of a sightless head are secreted. This section is hinged, moreover, and has a lid which can be swung down at will. The four heads are identical, and they present themselves to us with an identical frontality. There is the sharpest possible contrast between the shadowed recesses, in which the heads sit in retreat from the world, and the light of open day which floods across the target. The one is a complex scale-model, in full working order, of an inscrutable situation; the other one of the simplest of man-made objects, and one of the most easily explicable. The complete image, as haunting as any in 20th-century art, has overtones of fairground and firing squad, jury box and old-style pharmacy.

It is basic to the work of Jasper Johns that he makes us question not only what we are looking at but what is entailed in the act of looking. All looking has to do with cognition; but do we look in order to know something completely? Or do we stop looking, in any real sense, as soon as we have made an initial act of recognition? Johns never lets us off that particular hook. Defying us to give in to laziness, he chips away at the sloven in all of us. Take the printed word "Blue," for instance. It is so keyed to our expectations of a certain color that if it happens to be colored red, as may well be the case in a painting by Johns, then we see it as if we had never seen it before.

In the 1960s Jasper Johns began to tackle these questions in bulk and simultaneously, in paintings on the scale of epic which have none of the small-scale concision of his earlier work. But in 1958–59, in his *Numbers in Color,* he was still working with a finite image drawn from the experience of everyday. The series of numerals that runs from 1 to 0 is a sign language so complete and so nearly universal that it would really be very difficult to get through life without it. Its rival, in this, is the alphabet (and Johns did once make a very beautiful painting called *Gray Alphabet*); but there are several kinds of alphabet, whereas the series 1–0 is as valid for a Russian as for an American, and as valid for a Pakistani as for a Moroccan. It is one of the great instruments of negotiation; without it, we should be stuck with the abacus.

What Johns did in his *Numbers in Color* was to set out the complete sequence from 1 through 0 eleven times over. The subject was *given,* and it recurred with an absolute regularity, just as in a passacaglia the bass line recurs unaltered over and over again. The paradox of *Numbers in Color* is that by accepting this fixed and immutable subject Johns gave himself a freedom of maneuver and an openness of expression which were total and unlimited. We can see just what this means if we compare *Numbers in Color* with Pollock's *White Light.* In the Pollock, freedom of expression is preordained. The painter has no obligations to anything except the dictates of his own psyche. The picture is the paint, and the paint is the picture: nothing else intrudes. And *White Light* is undeniably a beautiful picture, with all the luxuriance which we associate with a major artist who knows exactly what he is doing and is comfortably inside the limits of his potential. It might seem to be enough, and in terms of the embellishment of life it certainly is enough; but art has a higher and a more strenuous function, and a part of that function is to go on questioning the terms of art's validity. Art survives not because it gives pleasure, but because it goes on asking questions to which we need to know the answer. Pollock in *White Light* was giving pleasure of an exalted, hard-won kind. Johns in *Numbers in Color* gave that same pleasure—the delight of seeing paint handled superlatively well—plus something else. He used the alphabet of numerals to redraft the alphabet of feeling. *Numbers in Color* sets out the gamut of human emotion with reference (and herein lies the contribution of Johns) to an ordered schema from which feeling is traditionally excluded. Emotion plays no part in mathematics. Neither love nor hate will make 2 × 2 equal 5. Numerals are weightless, incorporeal, independent of time and place, above and beyond individual feeling. They form a closed system to which feeling has no access. The impersonal single subject, so valuable to Johns in 1954, was succeeded in 1958 by the impersonal system, with its even greater potential.

Questions of identity have always preoccupied Johns, and he is perfectly well aware that each of the ten numerals in question has a personality which is clearly defined. "Number One" stands for leadership, in common parlance, and Johns's number 1 has a broad, upstanding shaft, a sharp downward turn at the top (like the peaked cap of some archetypal field-marshal), and a square-built plinth-type base: all stand up for an impregnable solidity. Zero has also its associations; and Johns drafts a broad-bellied vacancy, an echoing oval that signals a moment of repose after the clattering activity of numbers 1–9. Himself conspicuous in life for sensitivity toward the identity of others, he gave each intervening numeral its own character: we remember, for instance, the enlarged teardrop which forms the stem of his number 7 and the swanlike curve of his number 2. But he tells us explicitly that the picture is about numbers in *color;* and as every word counts in a title by Johns we are warned that the picture is as much about color as it is about numbers.

What Johns does is to animate the entire surface of the canvas with an allover, in-and-out paint structure which has the vitality of Action Painting but is keyed to something outside itself. There are two separate and independent structures here: on the one hand 11 rows of numerals with their recurrent subliminal crescendo from 1 to 0, on the other the continually varied skeins and loops of paint which sometimes menace, and sometimes give way to, the mathematics of the basic design. Every great painting carries within itself the history of other great paintings; and in *Numbers in Color* we see something of the fugitive and vagabond humors of landscape painting, something of the verticals and horizontals of Mondrian, and something of the patient monitoring which we associate with still life. Everything is there, and every kind of statement. Looking at it, we realize all over again that it is not from the unsupported ego that great art is most likely to come.

There is, of course, an alternative hazard: the artist may fail to impose upon heterogeneous material that imaginative order which is the essence of what we call "art." If too much material is given the right of entry, and if the operating imagination is too weak to deal with it, chaos and triviality will result. The challenge of new and complex subject matter had to be met, even so; the highly energized character of new art in the 1950s made it mandatory. And it was not only Rauschenberg and Johns who gave the signal; on the contrary, the expansiveness, the limitless ambition and the bodily involvement for which Pollock set the definitive example were an inspiration to artists who wanted to get more and more of the world into their art. In 1958 this point was put by Allan Kaprow, artist and theoretician, when he wrote that "Pollock left us at the point where we must become preoccupied with and even dazzled by the space and objects of our everyday life. . . . Not satisfied with the *suggestion* through paint of other senses, we shall utilize the specific substances of sight, sound, people, movement, odors, touch. Objects of every sort are the material for the new art."

It was in this belief that from 1954 onward art made raid after raid into territory which it had traditionally disdained. The great divide grew ever wider between those who believed, with

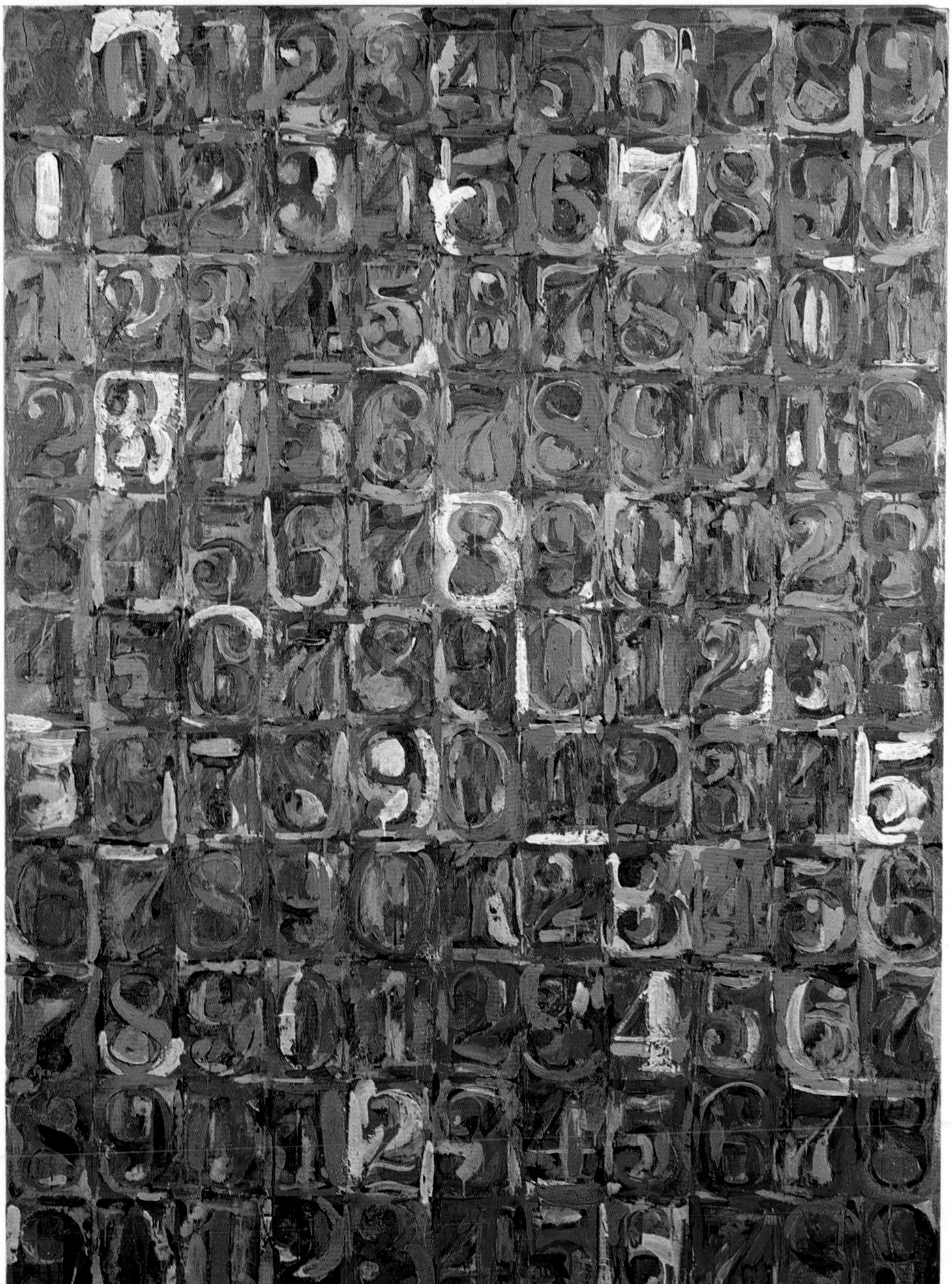

Jasper Johns.
Numbers in Color.
1959.
Encaustic and collage on canvas,
66½ × 49½ inches.
Albright-Knox Art Gallery, Buffalo.
Gift of Seymour H. Knox

Thomas B. Hess, that the only art worth talking about was "difficult, serious, remote, aristocratic" and those who believed that, no matter where the action was, art should get a piece of it. The two points of view looked to be irreconcilable, and many of the participants were determined that they should remain so. "Avoid a polar situation," Johns had said: but what common ground could there be between Ad Reinhardt, who said that "a museum is a treasure house and a tomb, not a countinghouse or an amusement center," and Claes Oldenburg, who said that he was for "an art which does something other than sit on its ass in a museum"?

The truth is that by the mid-1950s too much new energy had come into everyday life, and too many new forms of awareness were available to the artist, for any but the most steadfast of gifted natures to look neither to right nor to left. What Reinhardt called "Art-as-something-else" was irresistibly attractive when the world as it had previously existed was turning out to be obsolete and new ways of life were calling out for comment. Reinhardt stood, on the contrary, for what he called "Art-as-only-itself." In May, 1957, he wrote that "the first rule and absolute standard of fine art, and of painting, which is the highest and freest art, is the purity of it. The more uses, relations, and 'additions' a painting has, the less pure it is. The more stuff in it, the busier the work of art, the worse it is. More is Less."

Reinhardt himself acted on these principles, with an evergrowing stringency, till his death in 1967. "Looking is not as simple as it looks," he had said in 1946. And he went on to prove it with a long series of paintings which culminated in the black paintings of which *Number 119, 1958,* is one. It takes time and patience to decipher the cruciform image which lies within the matt, light-absorbing surface of the canvas; but Reinhardt's intention was to free the observer from the conventional time-span within which we look at art. A lifelong polemicist, cartoonist, demonstrator and writer of enraged letters on subjects that were dear to him, Reinhardt in his late paintings aimed at a terminal statement: a point beyond which easel painting could go no further.

One or two others, as we shall see, did the same and are still doing it with a singular scorn for compromise. Sometimes superb work resulted, with a critical follow-up remarkable for both cogency and conviction: the thing written and the thing done were one, almost. But the work that got itself talked about by laymen in the 1960s originated for the most part in what Rauschenberg had called the gap between art and life; and it overturned three of Thomas B. Hess's requirements by being not remote, not difficult, and not aristocratic. (Whether it was not serious would have to be debated case by case.) At the highest level there were points of contact—Johns and Noland both painted targets, as I said earlier, and the panoramic and environmental scale of Action Painting was common both among Pop painters (James Rosenquist, above all) and among sculptors of several persuasions (Louise Nevelson, George Segal)—but fundamentally the great divide was never deeper or wider than in the 1960s.

If the world can be thought of as one gigantic painting, as Rauschenberg had suggested in 1961, it follows that we can cut into it almost at random and come up with something that hangs together as art. "If I call it art, it's art," had been the implication of what Marcel Duchamp did when he signed a urinal in 1917 and sent it in for an exhibition. Pop art (as it came to be called) did not quite do that; its impact was owed to the combination of unprocessed material from everyday life with traditional fine-art procedures (paint on canvas, adjustments of scale, adroit reemphasis and the use of isolated details in the interest of irony or pathos). In fact it claimed for itself the privileges (and, eventually, the financial rewards) of high art, while sticking closely to subject matter with which high art had never associated before. "To think that I have been speaking prose all my life and never knew it!" says Monsieur Jourdain in

Ad Reinhardt. *Number 119, 1958 (Black).* 1958. Oil on canvas, 7 feet × 6 feet 3 inches. Hirshhorn Museum and Sculpture Garden, Smithsonian Institution, Washington

Molière's *Le Bourgeois Gentilhomme;* in the same way, people learned from Andy Warhol and Roy Lichtenstein that they had lived amidst art all their lives and never known it.

Lichtenstein was always a great forager. The source material of *Girl with Ball* was an advertisement for vacations in the Poconos. Lichtenstein introduced into the painting allusions both to the technology of printing (the benday dots which serve as skin tone for the vacationing girl) and to the recent history of art (the curvilinear Art Nouveau forms which designated her hair, the cropping of the whole image at top and bottom to bring it closer to the spectator, and the firmly drawn line which unites the profile of the wave to the outline of the girl's body). What looks crude and simplistic to eyes nurtured on French Impressionism results in reality from a series of conscious and intelligent decisions. In the early 1960s Lichtenstein probed one after another the kinds of image we acknowledge, cherish, or in some cases have simply got used to and no longer notice. One such was the likeness of George Washington as it turns up over and over again in post-Colonial times. Another was the stylized notion of gods and goddesses.

Pop art was rooted, furthermore, in certain perennial aspects of American life: the element of insistent repetition, for instance. Repetition of this kind gives off a visual drumbeat that calls on us to stop and pay attention. It was always so: witness the photograph of a provincial druggist's shop which Charles Ellis Johnson took in the year 1888. That druggist knew his public; no matter what he had to sell—canker syrup, essence of ginger, "Essence of Life" or an all-purpose medicine called the "Valley Tan Remedy"—he knew that people wanted to get the message over and over again.

Roy Lichtenstein.
Girl with Ball.
1961.
Oil on canvas,
60½ × 36½ inches.
Philip Johnson, New Canaan, Conn.

Roy Lichtenstein.
George Washington.
1962.
Pencil and frottage,
18¾ × 14½ inches.
Mr. and Mrs. Ned Owyang, New York

In Andy Warhol's *Green Coca-Cola Bottles,* 1962, ancestral memories of this kind were drawn upon. Whereas Jasper Johns in his *Numbers in Color* renewed the great tradition of oil painting with subject matter that seemed to be entirely impersonal, Warhol with his Coca-Cola bottles aimed at the effect of a print run that was not quite perfect. And it is with what would elsewhere be looked at askance, as errors of registration, that he sustains our interest from row to serried row. Further, Warhol was always interested in the demystification of art: in its reduction, in other words, to something that at first glance could be done by anyone. His *Numbers,* 1962, an adaptation of a do-it-yourself painting manual, is a particularly crisp and jaunty example; and it is one of the many paradoxes of Warhol's career that this image should be so inescapably his own.

Pop art could also operate with metamorphic effect upon objects of current use that would not at other times have been the material of art. New Yorkers look at the zip codes of Manhattan every day of their lives, for instance, and they also regard a juicer as indispensable to a well-furnished kitchen. It was left to Claes Oldenburg to wreak his peculiar white magic with these things. He took the zip-code map of Manhattan and built it, block by block, as a sculpture, with the tall thin shape of Central Park conspicuous in the center. We became conscious as never before of the interlocked segments which make up a mailman's Manhattan; and the piece also works as a work of art, to be hung from a nail on the wall and quizzed, day after day, for what it has to offer.

In the case of the juicer, Oldenburg took metamorphosis a step further. With vinyl, kapok and fake fur he produced a sculpture which is two things in one. It is the portrait of the way a juicer might look if it melted like wax while halfway through juicing an orange. And it is a self-portrait of the artist himself, complete with cap, a few strands of untidy fair hair, a half-hidden face, and what might be a parka several sizes too big for him.

Roy Lichtenstein.
Drowning Girl.
1963.
Oil and synthetic polymer paint on canvas, 67⅝ × 66¾ inches.
The Museum of Modern Art, New York. Philip Johnson Fund and gift of Mr. and Mrs. Bagley Wright

Andy Warhol. *Do It Yourself—Seascape.* 1962. Liquitex on canvas, 54 inches × 6 feet. Dr. Erich Marx, Berlin

Richard Lindner, though not a Pop artist, was related to Pop in his shrewd observation of American mores. For some years he lived on East 69th Street in New York City. His apartment was only a few doors away from the headquarters of the F.B.I.; and Lindner was much taken with the idea that on his very own street tabs were being kept on the mobsters and hoodlums in whom he had taken a lifelong and an immensely sardonic interest. *East 69th Street* has to do with the imagined arrest of a king of the underworld, a kid-gloved Lucifer for whom only the newest and most stylish men's wear will do. It has the relish with which George Grosz and Bertolt Brecht would seize on people of the same sort; but it also has a flat heraldic quality which is one of Lindner's contributions to the American painting of our day.

So Pop art had complex motives. One of them was to see just how far it could flout the expectations of the "cultivated" public (Roy Lichtenstein said that his ambition had been to produce a picture so hideous that no one would hang it). What was put to the test was the automatic reverence, the white flag of immunity from comment, which is accorded to the large framed painting *as such*, no matter how bitterly the status of individual paintings may be contested.

Next came an important social change, and one not yet definitively acknowledged. Generation after generation had taken for granted that the categories proposed by the novelist Sinclair Lewis in his *Babbitt* (1922) were eternal and unchangeable. They believed that there was such a thing as the cultivated life, on the one hand, and that on the other hand there was life as it was led by the vast majority of Americans. That majority was dis-

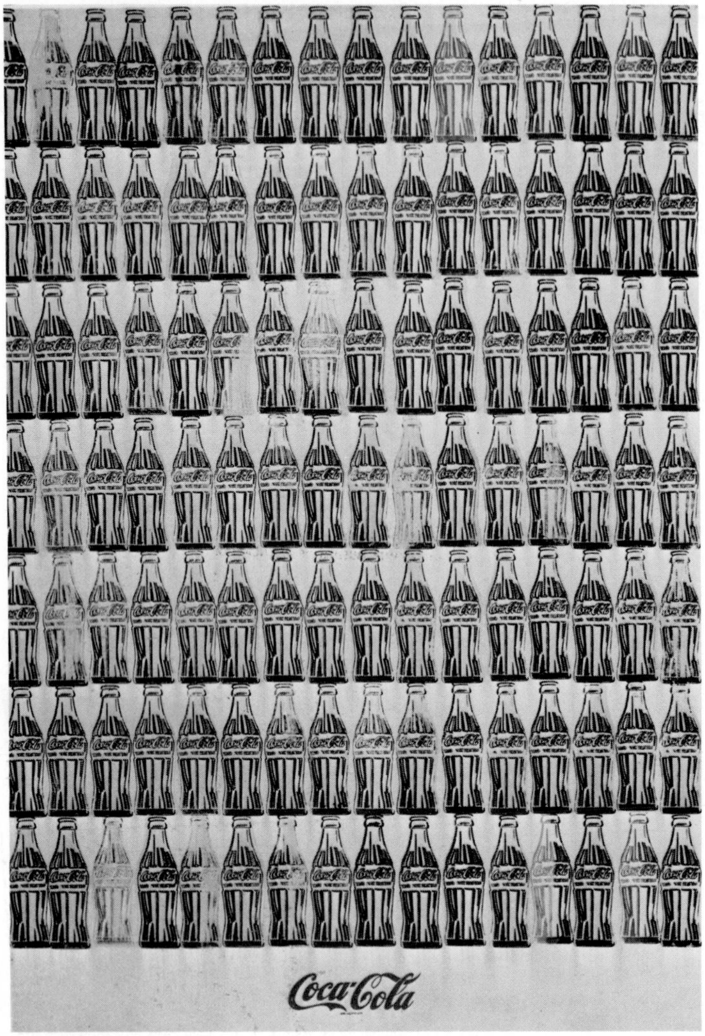

Andy Warhol.
Green Coca-Cola Bottles. 1962.
Oil on canvas,
6 feet 10¼ inches × 57 inches.
Whitney Museum of American Art, New York.
Gift of the Friends of the Whitney Museum of American Art

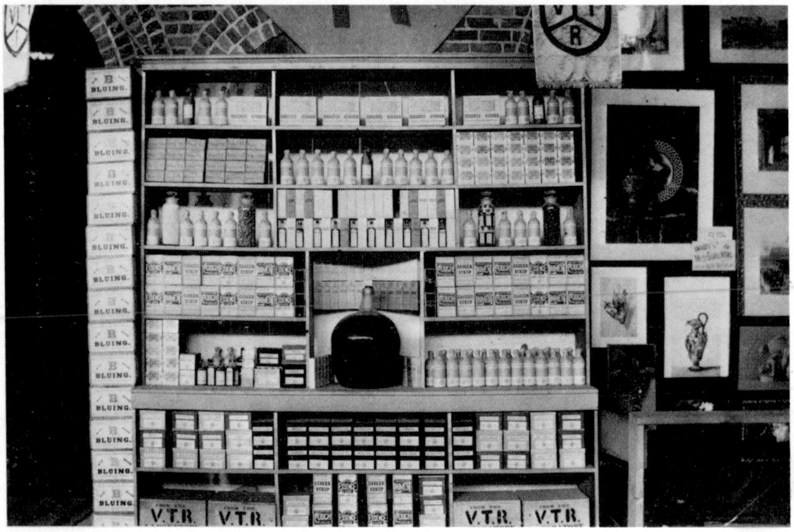

Charles Ellis Johnson.
Druggist's Display, Featuring Valley Tan Remedy. 1888.
Photograph.
Museum of Fine Arts, Boston. Photo courtesy of Dr. and Mrs. Avard T. Fairbanks

Claes Oldenburg.
Soft Manhattan #1 (Postal Zones). 1966.
Stenciled canvas and kapok,
6 feet 8 inches × 30 inches × 8 inches.
Albright-Knox Art Gallery, Buffalo.
Gift of Seymour H. Knox.

counted as mediocre, undiscriminating, herd-minded, all but illiterate. One of the best things that ever happened to America is that between 1950 and 1970 this idea got a thorough going-over and was to a large degree discredited. Of course there were still plenty of Babbitts around; but there was a new self-awareness on the part of other generations, and one of the rewards of this was the realization that there is such a thing as popular culture and that it is primarily in relation to the popular culture of the day that each generation defines itself. Anyone who happened to read J. D. Salinger's *The Catcher in the Rye* on the day of its publication in 1951 will have recognized not only the portrait of a new archetypal young American but the arrival of a new attitude to popular culture. Popular culture from that day onward was neither something to be overinflated, in fan-club style, nor something to be put down by set-faced heads of families: it was just *there,* once and for all, as a complete structure in relation to which young people could find out who they were.

Pop art had its place in all this. It was also one of its functions to demystify the procedures of fine art. One of the monuments of Pop is George Segal's *The Butcher Shop,* 1965—a reconstruction, as it happens, of the shop owned by Segal's father: the locus, therefore, of his deepest and earliest intimations of how life is carried on from one day to the next. *The Butcher Shop* has the stillness of the image of an ancient Greek stele, but it is also direct, immediate and actual in a way that is akin to the black-and-white movies of Segal's youth. It is of yesterday, but it is also of all time. It speaks for the ancient ritual by which we take life so that we ourselves may survive: but it has none of the stylization with which the sculptors of the 19th century hoped to make their work last forever. A complete society is somewhere there inside it, and yet it is made up of plaster casts and a summary architecture, with no pretensions to high art. (It is worth noting that *The Butcher Shop* has a hieratic, abstract quality—a feeling for ritual on an almost bare stage—which is in striking contrast to Bere-

George Segal.
The Butcher Shop.
1965.
Plaster, wood, vinyl, metal and plexiglas, 7 feet 10 inches × 8 feet 3¼ inches × 48 inches.
Art Gallery of Ontario, Toronto. Gift from the Women's Committee Fund

nice Abbott's photograph of the real thing as it was in the 1930s. The Segal has the look of classical drama; the Abbott—one of many in which she recorded a New York now largely vanished—has a Dickensian delight in detail.)

There was in Pop art an element of exorcism. It was made to banish evil memories, or to hoist them to a level on which they would lose their power to degrade. Segal's father, in effigy, has a dignity which society did not always accord him in life. Robert Indiana's numerals have none of the philosophical implications of Johns's; they are based on the memory of a time when the great numbered highways of the United States meant the possibility of escape from the grinding meanness of life in the Depression. James Rosenquist's *F-111* puts as cogently as anyone could wish the case against the uses to which the American Air Force was beginning to be put; "If I spell it out large enough," he seems to say, "someone's going to read it." With his panoramic *F-111* Rosenquist renewed the tradition of outrage which had produced Picasso's *Guernica* and Miró's *Head of a Woman.* The picture is polemical in intent; and it suggests, among much else, that something is wrong with a world in which the production of a new kind of aircraft allows one little girl to sit laughing under the hair-dryer while other little girls in a distant country will be burnt to death when that same aircraft gets into service. It is more difficult to ascribe any one motive to Andy Warhol, since Warhol operates behind a mask of inarticulacy, but his Electric Chair and his Car Crash series undoubtedly reminded people of what was being done in their name, in the one case, and of what they may well end up doing themselves, in the other. In the Happenings pioneered by Jim Dine, Claes Oldenburg and Allan Kaprow in 1959–60 there was, equally, a strong element of social protest.

Much in all this was subject before long to what the poet and novelist James Agee called "the emasculation of acceptance." It was difficult to sustain that point of maximum tension—fundamental

Berenice Abbott.
New York Shopfront.
c. 1936–37.
Photograph.
Museum of the City of New York

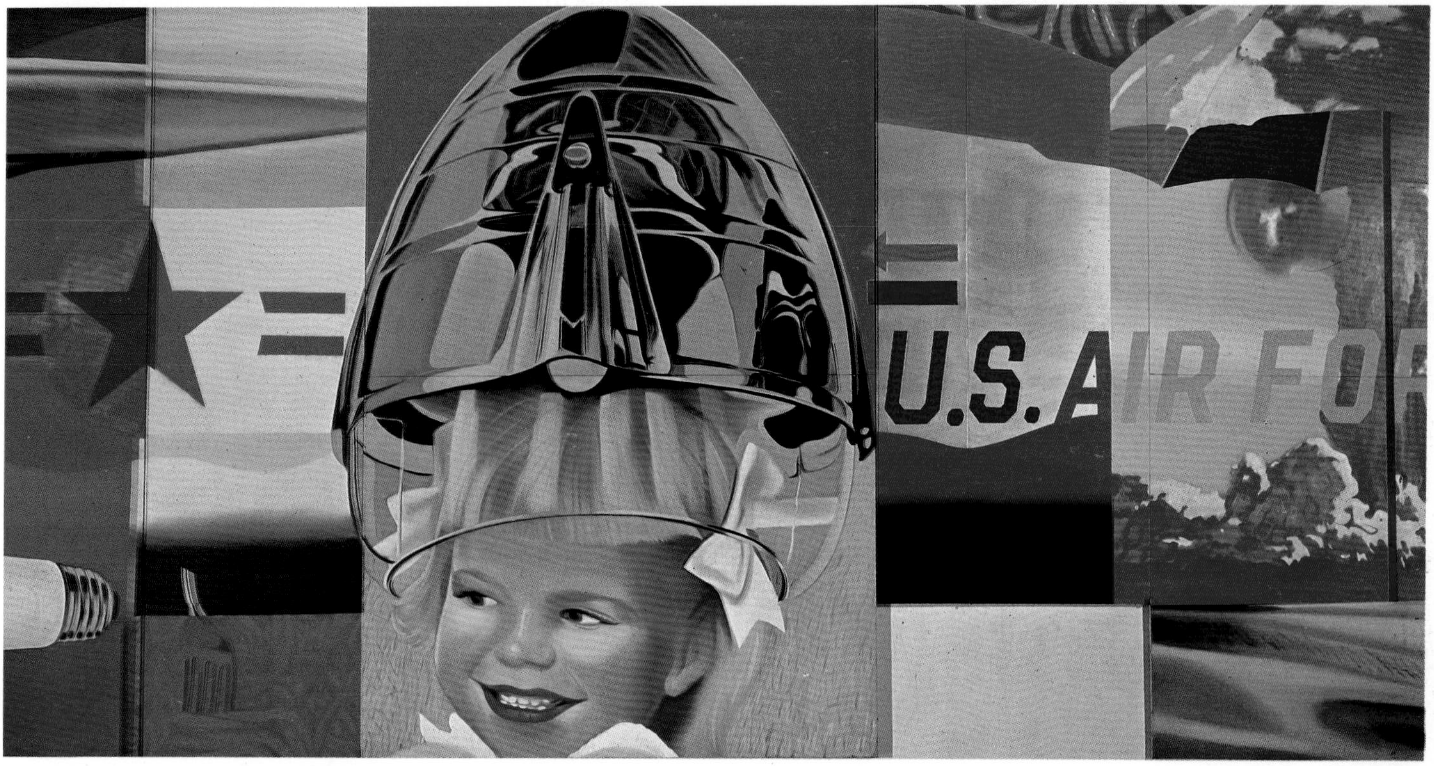

James Rosenquist.
F-111 (partial view).
1965.
Oil on canvas with aluminum, entire work 10 feet × 86 feet.
Robert C. Scull, New York

to the creation of a valid art—between what needs to be said and the means which are available for saying it. "Don't bother with that—just do it all over again" is the message of the market; and it was difficult in the mid-1960s to recapture the élan which powered Pop art when Claes Oldenburg rented a real store to sell his simulated pieces of pie. It was a time for evolution. Sometimes the evolution was merely toward the tactics of merchandising; in such cases the moral thrust of the work quite withered away.

Sometimes, on the other hand, it turned out that artists had been double agents for high art all the time. Jasper Johns, for one—though never a Pop artist in any strict sense—had been the source of much that was later taken over from him by other artists in simplified form, and when he produced his *Painted Bronze* in 1960 many people took it as an affront: the *Bed* all over again. How could two beer cans be art? Surely it was all part of a wager? (Someone had said of Johns's dealer, Leo Castelli, that "that so-and-so could sell beer cans as art if he put his mind to it.") People who went to see the work itself before making up their minds soon realized that the two cans had their place in high art, as securely as did Picasso's *Glass of Absinthe*, so clear at every point was the mark of Johns's governing hand. It turned out, equally, that Roy Lichtenstein was as capable of working from Monet's Cathedrals, or from his Haystack series, as from the comic strips which had made his name. As for the direct reproduction of objects of common use—well, it was plain to any unprejudiced person that Alex Hay's five-foot-high enlargement in paper, epoxy, fiberglass and paint of an E-ze brown paper bag, done in 1968, was one of the most elegant of art objects and not at all the put-on that it would have been assumed to be ten years earlier.

The great divide was in no way narrowed, however, by the fact that Reinhardt's "Art-as-only-itself" had infiltrated the enemy camp. These incidents were thought of, indeed, as gross improprieties. Historical allusions had at most a

Richard Lindner.
The F.B.I. on East 69th Street. 1972.
Oil on canvas,
6 feet 8 inches × 70 inches.
Museum Boymans-van Beuningen, Rotterdam

parasitic function: a play element quite out of place in serious art. As to that, a firm opinion was forthcoming from the Viennese-born philosopher Ludwig Wittgenstein, whose later books were required reading for all ambitious people in the 1960s (not least for those whose first and last experience of philosophy they were). Wittgenstein had said that "something new (spontaneous, 'specific') is always a language game"; and this was in line with the general trend of fashionable thought in the 1960s, when linguistics was all the rage in the paperback bookshops.

Play has, however, a quality of reaching outward. Play is a dramatization of our deepest concerns. In play, we mime the strategies for survival which are so fundamental to our equilibrium that we dare not reveal them in any other way. Chess, tennis, golf, baseball, football in its various guises —all serve to externalize our anxieties. ("No chess playing" was one of Ad Reinhardt's rules and regulations for a new art.) When Jasper Johns wanted to emphasize that the painter is the prisoner of a perfectly flat surface which can only be concealed by obsolete make-believe, he put a real drawer, complete with knobs, in the middle of the picture. But this was a device from outside of art, and as such unacceptable to those who believed that high art must ensure its continuance within the terms of its own physical existence and in no other way.

Clement Greenberg was an embattled supporter of this point of view, and what he had to say is worth quoting at length. He saw the predicament of art in the late 1950s and '60s as a part of a historical process that had begun with the German philosopher Immanuel Kant. It was by self-criticism that art survived; and around the beginning of our century, at a time when many of art's prerogatives were being taken away, a process of radical self-criticism began. The survival of art would depend on the thoroughness with which artists defined the areas in which art could still do incomparably well.

"What had to be made explicit," Greenberg wrote, "was that which was unique and irreducible not only in art in general but also in each particular art. Each art had to determine, through the operations peculiar to itself, the effects peculiar and exclusive to itself. By doing this, each art, would, to be sure, narrow its area of competence, but at the same time it would make its possession of this area all the more secure."

"It quickly emerged," Greenberg went on, "that the unique and proper area of competence of each art coincided with all that was unique to the nature of its medium. The task of self-criticism became to eliminate from the effects of each art any and every effect that might conceivably be borrowed from or by the medium of any other art. Thereby each art would be rendered 'pure,' and in its 'purity' find the guarantee of its standards of quality as well as of its independence. 'Purity' meant self-definition, and the enterprise of self-criticism in the arts became one of self-definition with a vengeance."

Whether or not Greenberg was aware of the overtones of the word "vengeance" in this context, the program that he set out had undeniably a punitive quality. Old scores were to be settled,

Jasper Johns.
Painted Bronze.
1960.
Painted bronze,
5½ × 8 × 4¾
inches.
Kunstmuseum,
Basel.
The Ludwig
Collection

old wrongs put right, sham heroes toppled from their pedestals, and the one true faith upheld. Good art—or "strong art," as it was called—was to be made within a set of conditions that grew ever more stringent until eventually everything that was not prohibited would be mandatory. One of the things to be said about all this is that it actually worked: good art and strong art were made, year by year, on the basis of a reductive program, a series of logical and ruthless decisions, that concentrated on the essential practicalities of art: the size and shape of the stretcher, the physical characteristics of the paint, the extent to which the final image was free from the taint of illusionism.

Fundamental to all of this was the role of color. Color had been set free, as we all know, by 1914. But was there such a thing as freer than free? The dying Matisse proved that there was, with the cut-paper paintings that he had produced in 1950–53. But those paintings were still not well known, and they were in any case a function of terminal illness, on the one hand, and of 60 years of research on the other. The problem was to make color freer than free as a logical next step forward from what had been done by Mark Rothko, for one, in America. It could be done, and it was done to stunning effect by Kenneth Noland in paintings like *Bend Sinister.* In the sideways thrust of that colossal image (it measures 7 feet 8 inches by 13 feet 5 inches) it seems as if color, incorporeal and unsupported, were pulling itself free from the absolute flatness: with just one unprecedented heave, the thing was done.

When seen by itself, *Bend Sinister* impresses by the authority with which a unified and seemingly quite simple image is made to carry the whole burden of art. It is even more arresting, however, if we know the paintings which immediately preceded it: chevron images which hang down with a perfect symmetry, blasting off from the two top corners of the canvas and hurtling straight on down toward the exact center of the canvas's lower edge. These centered chevrons have an added meaning, in their turn, if we know what came before *them:* and so on back to the beginning of Noland's career.

Even then, we need to know more: for Noland is one of the painters who bear out van Gogh's prediction that no one man could bring the art of the future into being. It would have to be done, van Gogh thought, by groups or teams, or at the very least by paired enthusiasts (like Gauguin and himself in their more harmonious days). Van Gogh was proved right by the history of subsequent art, in which not one consequential movement has been the work of a man on his own. Bonnard and Vuillard; Matisse, Derain, Vlaminck; Picasso and Braque; Kirchner and his friends in Dresden; Kandinsky and his friends in Munich; Lunacharsky's protégés in the U.S.S.R.; the Dadaists and the Surrealists in their heyday—in every case there was a collective impulse. How it was in New York in the 1940s we have seen; and although it is easy to exaggerate the degree of complicity which joins one coeval to another there is no doubt that in the 1950s the friendship of Kenneth Noland with Morris Louis, and to a lesser extent with the sculptor David Smith, was fundamental to the development of American art.

Louis and Noland met in 1952 in Washington, D.C., where they both lived. Morris Louis was by 12 years the older of the two, but it was Noland who had the kind of outgoing, combative temper-

Kenneth Noland.
Bend Sinister. 1964.
Acrylic on canvas,
7 feet 8¾ inches ×
13 feet 5¾ inches.
Hirshhorn Museum
and Sculpture
Garden, Smithsonian
Institution,
Washington

Kenneth Noland.
Beginning. 1958.
Acrylic on canvas,
7 feet 6 inches × 8
feet.
Hirshhorn Museum
and Sculpture
Garden, Smithsonian
Institution,
Washington

ament which thrives on the definition of ideas: and for the three years—1952–55—of their close friendship they were able to effect a joint hammering-out of their intentions such as had rarely been paralleled since the first alliance of Picasso and Braque. (At one time they even painted on the same canvas.)

What were they doing? Well, they wanted to find out what was the predestined next thing in art: the step which history dictated, but which it was left to individual men and women to riddle out. As friends of Clement Greenberg, they proceeded by elimination: by defining their "area of competence," no matter how narrow it might turn out to be. Noland had spent some time at Black Mountain College as a student of the Russian-born painter Ilya Bolotowsky, who brought to his raw young audiences something of the European abstract tradition. He had worked in Paris, where the sculptor Ossip Zadkine (then one of the most famous artists in Europe) had singled him out in 1949 as someone of exceptional promise. Noland had steam up, by the end of the 1940s, but he had nowhere to go—until, that is, he and Morris Louis began to work on the impressions they had brought back from Helen Frankenthaler's studio in 1953. In her *Mountains and Sea* they found an answer to the question "What is it that art can still do, *and that nothing else can?*" In paintings like *Mountains and Sea* and *Other Generations* Frankenthaler in the 1950s was onto something all her own: the alliance of delicate freehand drawing with paint that was allowed to stain its way into the canvas rather than to sit, like a skin, on top of it. Hers was not the only answer: Matisse and Braque in France had lately come upon quite different ones, for instance. But it was an answer that they followed through to spectacular effect: Louis until he died in 1962, Noland to this day.

Certain things were eliminated from the start, as having lately exhausted their usefulness. One of them was the manual element in painting: the evident motion of the hand, whether with brush or tube or can, which left its mark on the canvas in the form of motor energy. Another was drawing, in any of its accepted forms, since anything

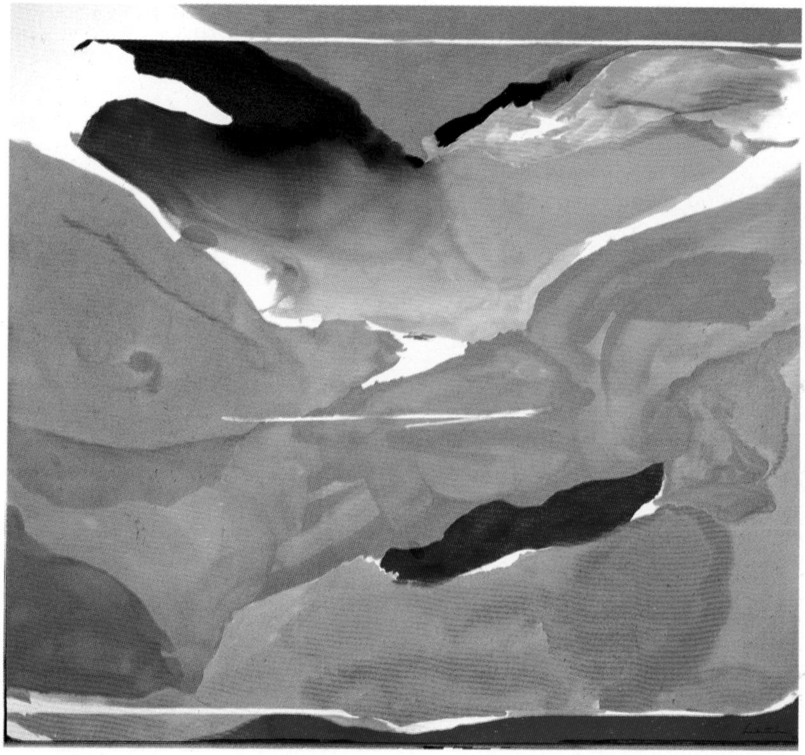

Helen Frankenthaler. *Nature Abhors a Vacuum.* 1973. Acrylic on canvas, 8 feet 7½ inches × 9 feet 4 inches. Private collection, New York

that could be read as drawing could also be read as illusion, or as metaphor: the pounding rhythms of a major abstract Pollock demand, for instance, to be described in terms of loops and skeins and lassos. A third thing to be eliminated was composition, as it was generally understood; for composition in Action Painting as often as not looked back to composition as it had evolved in Cubist painting, even down to the uneasiness which seized the Cubist painters as they got further and further from the closely argued central image and had to decide what to do at the edges of the canvas.

So a lot was going out. What was coming in? New ways of applying paint, to begin with: after that, new ways of structuring the image. Thinned pigment (the new synthetic paint called "acrylic") was to be soaked and stained into unsized canvas. Instead of building up on the surface of the canvas, in traditional style, the paint sank into the canvas and became one with it. Just how this was to be done—how the artist was to govern the nature of the image without being seen to direct it—was a matter for discussion. The paint could be poured onto a canvas laid flat on the floor; it could be allowed to run down a canvas that was held up as one holds up a sheet for folding; it could be rubbed in with a sponge; and it could be rolled on with a commercial paint roller. The important thing was that none of the traditional signs of "handling" should be present: no mark should be seen to result from a strong forward movement of the arm, a turn of the wrist, a well-judged dab with the brush held between two fingers and thumb. Color should seem to act spontaneously and of its own nature.

As to the structuring of the image, Louis and Noland proceeded according to their own very different natures. Louis was physically frail, and by temperament he was a quiet, inward sort of person. Noland liked to bring everything into the open, and to go to work from a position of armored certainty. Louis at more than one stage of his career echoed the aspirations of the American sublime; Noland did not want overtones of any kind, anywhere. In a top-class Morris Louis—in one of the "unfurled" paintings, for instance—color seems to go its own way, freer than ever before or since, down runnels which are never the same twice over. In a Noland, we know who's boss, down to the last millimeter of the surface. Louis

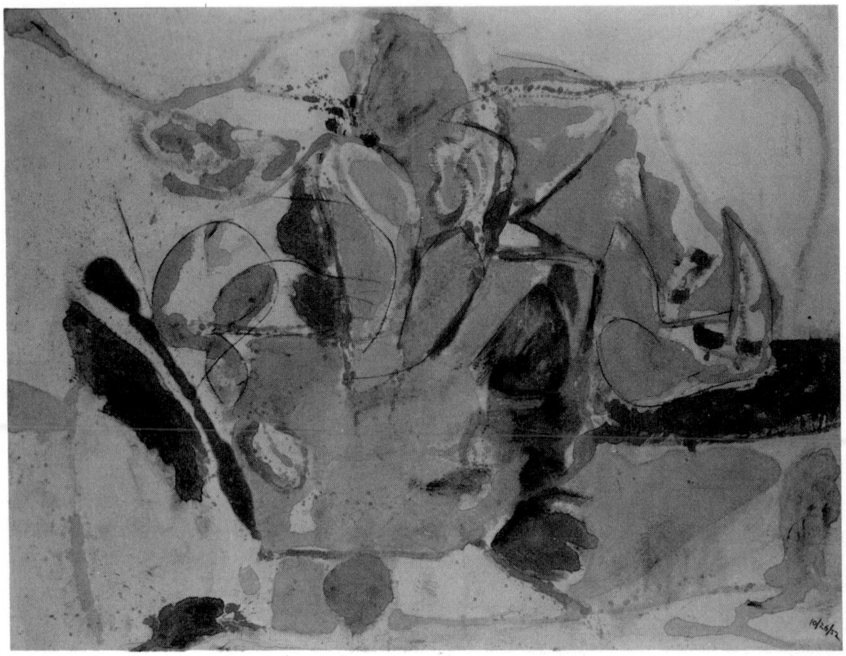

Helen Frankenthaler. *Mountains and Sea.* 1952. Oil on canvas, 7 feet 2⅜ inches × 9 feet 9¼ inches. Collection the artist, New York

ler in Germany in 1933, Giacometti began to turn to quite another aspect of art.

"I knew that one day," he said later, "I'd have to sit down on a stool in front of a model and copy what I saw." His colleagues among the Surrealists were appalled—"As if everyone didn't know what a head is!" was André Breton's reaction—but to Giacometti it seemed that the most adventurous thing which remained for art to do was to reinvent the idea of likeness. On this one card, as Simone de Beauvoir said in her memoirs, he staked everything. He sat down and tried to say exactly what it was like to be in the presence of another human being. And he tried to do it as if no one had ever done it before: to start from zero. He did it, as he said himself, "with no hope of succeeding." What do we really see? What do we mean by likeness? What are we to do with the formless, blubberlike space which separates us from the person we are looking at? How can we possibly recapture the total experience? What if the sculpture, even if passable in itself, is falsified by its relation to the world around it? These were the problems which Giacometti tried to deal with. While dealing with them from 1935 to 1947 he never had an exhibition. Nothing satisfied him: his aim was, as Sartre wrote, to "cut the fat off space" until only the lean meat of experience was left; unlearning was as important as learning, in this context, and the work was bound to go through some peculiar phases. (Among other things, it got very small: the complete surviving work of the years 1942–45 could be transported in six matchboxes.)

It was as a result of these preoccupations that Giacometti eventually found three-dimensional equivalents for things that sculpture had not previously dealt with: the fugacity of sense-impressions, for instance, the unstable or at any rate unseizable nature of human personality, and the arbitrary deformations which are imposed on the human figure by memory, by its surroundings at any given time, or by the chance involvements of looking. We can see today that the break with the sculpture of the past was not as complete as it once seemed; the *Man Pointing* of 1947 had a look of Rodin, for instance. Nor did Giacometti

Alberto Giacometti. *The Nose.* 1947. Plaster, paint and iron, 32¾ × 16¾ × 16 inches. Alberto Giacometti Foundation. Deposed at the Kunstmuseum, Basel

Alberto Giacometti. *City Square.* 1948. Bronze, 8 ½ × 25⅜ × 17¼ inches. The Museum of Modern Art, New York. Purchase

lose altogether the Gogol-like feeling for the grotesque which had marked some of his Surrealist pieces; the plaster version of *The Nose,* 1947, is a telling example of this. But in general what Giacometti had to say about the poignancy and the incompleteness of human relations was altogether new—as were, equally, his ways of saying it. Big-city life looks different when we have seen Giacometti's *City Square,* 1948; and as for the act of offering oneself, whether from love or for money, it was reimagined in the *Four Figures on a Pedestal* of 1950, just as it had been reimagined in Manet's *Olympia.* "Here we are. What are you going to do about it?" is what the four girls have to say: as with Dubuffet, the central themes of European art are recalled and furthered, even if the immediate obsessions are of an unprecedented sort.

Giacometti was the last person to make claims for his own work—he would invariably say, in fact, that it was a disaster from start to finish—but in his actions he was true to the European notion that a career in art should be cumulative and that ideally the work should grow in weight, and in density, and in its power of commitment, year by year. The remains of a great name were not enough; recruitment was for life, or not at all. This was what Matisse had believed, and Braque, and Klee. It was what Picasso lived up to, with a determination to put all of himself on record, no matter what the consequences. It was what Piet Mondrian thought, too; and of the Europeans who came to live in the United States in the 1940s it was perhaps Mondrian who best exemplified the principle—one could almost say the duty—of continual growth.

Mondrian was quite specific on this point. Already in 1924 he had written, "We are at a turning point in the history of culture. We are at the end of everything *old,* in a total and all-comprehensive sense. The divorce between the old and the new is now absolute and definitive." In 1942, when he was living in New York, he wrote: "Art must not only move parallel to human purposes. It must advance ahead of them." He believed, with the Indian mystic Krishnamurti, that it was the duty of every man to be "a force for evolution," and to do what he could to bring about a better world. "It is in human nature," Mondrian said toward the end of his life, "to love a static balance; the great struggle, and the one which every artist must undertake, is to annihilate a static equilibrium."

Piet Mondrian.
Victory Boogie-Woogie.
1943–44.
Oil on canvas,
70¼ × 70¼ inches
(on the diagonal).
Mr. and Mrs. Burton
Tremaine, Meriden,
Conn.

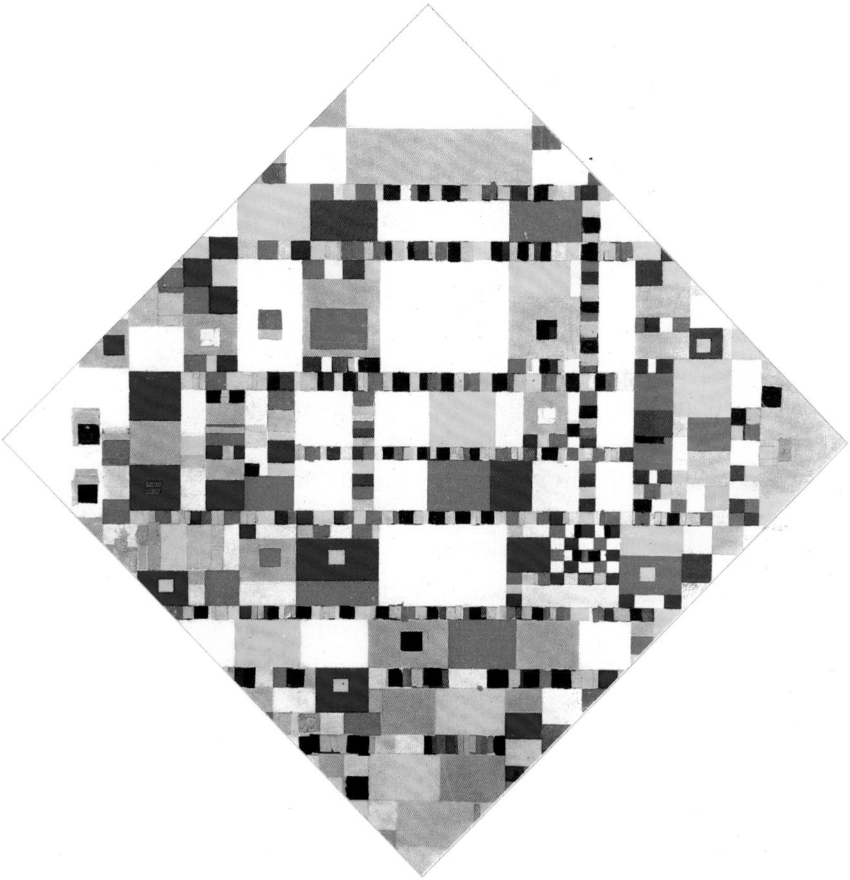

Mondrian had always abhorred "a static balance" in his own work. To avoid it, he went to enormous though largely invisible pains, working over and over until the finished painting was at every point the expression of a free man's hand—and, beyond that, of a free man's existence in the world. When he arrived in the United States he took the risk that every exile takes: that of total disorientation. There were Europeans in New York at that time who ate exiles' food, read exiles' newspapers, chased all over town for exiles' tobacco, and sought no company but that of other exiles. Mondrian was the opposite. "I feel here is the place to be," he said in 1943, "and I am becoming an American citizen. Where you live you belong to it, and when you feel a place is the nearest to you, you should become part of it."

Mondrian saw the new as a process of continual evolution. When he lived in New York, he felt that the best way for him to "advance ahead of human purposes" was to annihilate the "static equilibrium" which for many years had characterized the means which he allowed himself: the rectangular areas of red, blue and yellow, separated from one another by unbroken black lines of varying thicknesses. What if the black lines were to go, and unbroken lines of pure color—still red, blue and yellow—were to be allowed to overlap? What if he were to move on from there and work from a completely new constituent unit, the small square or rectangle, while retaining the linear crisscross as the basic compositional schema? Would not these changes correspond to evolutionary developments in other domains of life?

Behind these thoughts lay the conviction that life could still be mastered. This has now become something of a historical curiosity: a belief that it is very difficult to put forward with confidence. In the 17th century, and even in the 18th, people believed that everything worth knowing could be put within the covers of a single publication. Nor need that publication overtax a trained intelligence. It was in this belief that the Encyclopedia of Diderot and d'Alembert began publication in 1751. Everything was in that book, from the best way to make a pair of gloves to the latest thing in scientific research. Such a project today would make no sense. Not only is there more to know than any one person can encompass, but mankind has gone so far wrong in so many directions that it may already be too late to arrest the consequences of our errors. Life may be not only unmastered but unmasterable. The evolution which Mondrian believed in may lead only toward disaster. The role of the artist may become purely consolatory: that of a cool-fingered nurse at the bedside of someone who will never recover.

This was not how it looked at the time of Mondrian's death in February, 1944. But, given the premonitory nature of art, we should not see it as a mark of old age and declining health that Mondrian in more than one case was unable to complete his New York paintings. They were more complex than any he had attempted before—in fact they make many of his paintings of the 1920s and early '30s look almost epigrammatic—and they raised problems of resolution which it remained for a later generation to tackle completely. But their incompleteness was not of the kind that halted Michelangelo when he was carving his late *Pietà*, or of the kind that brought Haydn to a stop after the first two movements of his last string quartet. It was an echo of that incapacity to bring great undertakings to a formal conclusion which is one of the marks of this century. In this context we remember Arnold Schoenberg, who broke off his opera *Moses and Aaron* at the end of act II; Marcel Duchamp, who never quite finished the *Large Glass;* Ezra Pound, with his open-ended series of *Cantos;* Robert Musil, whose three-volume novel, *The Man without Qualities,* ends in midair. These were not men of puny energies; they had an intimation that a time was coming when the world could no longer be mastered, and that for that reason the 19th-century ideal of the well-rounded masterpiece was no longer true to the facts of life. Marcel Proust may have been the last man in history to undertake a complete survey of life as it presented itself to a supremely intelligent observer and bring it to a majestic and shapely conclusion; and he was only able to do it from a point of view that was by turns stoical and deeply pessimistic.

Mondrian had quite other ideas, and at the end of his life he wanted to devise a more complex metaphor for the encounters, the misadventures and the mutual accommodations of which life is made up. Once or twice, he succeeded. Art exists, as we know, to negotiate with life on our behalf, and if possible to come to terms with it in ways that will help us live. But if those negotiations cannot be brought to a successful conclusion, it is the duty of the artist to bring back a true bill: an unfinished work in which we glimpse both the nobility of the initial program and the point beyond which no one, no matter how gifted, could go further. That is the significance of Mondrian's unfinished paintings.

Art as an instrument of mediation between ourselves and the world was never in safer hands than during the first half of this century. Modern art as it then existed was the quintessence of modernity, if by modernity we mean an alert, resourceful and unprejudiced enquiry into those aspects of life which are specifically of our own day. But there is a fundamental difference between the art of the first half of this century and the art of earlier periods of high achievement. If we look at the art of the Italian Renaissance, or at Baroque art, or at Neo-Classical or Romantic art, we can go quite a long way down the ladder and still find work that commands our interest and our respect. The little masters of 17th-century Holland are not in the class of Rembrandt or Cuyp or Frans Hals, but they are good enough to look at, and to think about, and to talk about, year after year. Minor artists in these periods were lifted above and beyond themselves by collective and impersonal forces: a shared level of technical proficiency, a shared and luxuriant subject matter, a shared sense that art was speaking for the age in a way that nothing else did, a documentary interest now taken over by other forms of expression. We have none of these things. Such is our belief in individual and inimitable genius that, by definition, only a very few people at any one time can be accepted as artists of consequence. When André Gide was the most famous writer in Europe in the mid-1940s, he wrote that "the world will be saved by one or two people." Gide was born in 1869 and was the contemporary, therefore, of Matisse and Proust. He took it for granted, as they did, that the burdens of art and literature would be shouldered for eternity, as they had been shouldered in his own long lifetime, by "one or two people." He also believed that that elite could not, in the nature of things, be enlarged.

It was then taken for granted that the finite and stationary structure was the highest form of art. When Matisse and Picasso and Braque and Mondrian painted their last pictures, the norms to which they conformed were exactly what they had been in the days of Raphael and Titian. If it surprised Marshall McLuhan that the form of the printed page should not have changed in the five centuries that had passed since the printing of the Gutenberg Bible, it should have been equally surprising to those who cared about such things that the formats and the materials in use among the First New York School in 1947–52 were virtually identical with those of the panoramic landscapes of Rubens.

If this was taken as perfectly natural, it was in part because the work in question was so good as to delay any enquiry as to whether other formats and other materials would not be more apt for the time. It was also because the best new art still had, at most, the kind of almost clandestine success which had been the lot of serious new art since the time of the first Impressionist exhibition in 1874. There was continuity in that fact. Not only was art being made by "one or two people," but it was being admired and bought by one or two people, just as D.-H. Kahnweiler had only one or two clients when he began to show Cubist paintings in Paris in 1908.

And there was, finally, the question of quality. Quality is what matters most in new art, and it is the only sure guarantee for its continuance. Where quality is present in a very high degree, it usually results from a secret alliance with the past. That alliance may be concealed, as it was when Dubuffet literally dragged painting through the mud with his Corps de Dame series in 1950, or when the English painter Francis Bacon around the same time was producing what were then regarded as gratuitous scenes of horror, or when Roy Lichtenstein said that his ambition had been to paint pictures which were so despicable that nobody would put them on the wall. The secret was well kept in all three cases; but each had used a hot line to the past, even so.

Dubuffet had things to say about women's bodies that at first glance seemed merely coarse and derisive; but in point of fact he had truths to tell that had not been told in art before, and the final effect of these truths was to heal and not to wound. History caught up with Francis Bacon when every newspaper in the world carried photographs—presidential candidates in full spate, Adolf Eichmann on trial in his glass box in Jerusalem, unnamed prisoners in their cells—that looked like nothing so much as diluted Bacon. Before long it was clear, moreover, that Bacon's affinities were as much with Old Master painting as with the purely instinctive procedures which he freely acknowledged. Bacon in the 1970s was out to combine the grand formal statements of Old Master painting with a continual awareness of the imagery that is fed into us in our every waking moment: the police photographs, the standard portraits of political leaders (many times life-size), the discarded fragments of newsprint, the raised oval that sets the scene for high drama in theaters all over the

Francis Bacon.
Painting. 1978.
Oil on canvas,
6 feet 6 inches × 58 inches.
Private collection

Roy Lichtenstein. *Artist Studio—The Dance.* 1974. Oil and magna on canvas, 8 feet × 10 feet 8 inches. Mr. and Mrs. S. I. Newhouse, Jr., New York

world. He also drew upon the memory of Michelangelo's incomparable evocations of male voluptuousness and upon that element of the irrational that has played so large a part in 20th-century art. From all these he fashioned compound images that move to and fro, like captive tigers, between the known and the unknown, the clear and the ambiguous, the dreamed and the real. After Roy Lichtenstein had been driving conservative connoisseurs to apoplexy for years it turned out that he had developed a subtle amalgam between an analytical awareness of past art and the modification of the image by industrial techniques. Remembering how in a famous painting which is now in the U.S.S.R. Henri Matisse took a part of his *Dance* and made it incidental to another composition, Lichtenstein took up this same idea more than 60 years later. After draining *Dance* of the color, which is its most spectacular attribute, he got the image to work with other elements from Matisse, and with memories of his own earlier preoccupations. In this way he was able to carry on a conversation with one of the supreme masters of modern art. His laconic manner of speech should not delude us as to the daring of the enterprise. The mid-1970s did not witness a more complex pictorial achievement.

In painting, at any rate, the finite and stationary structure—the picture that stayed flat on the wall, complete and in one of a few standard formats—had the advantage that no one had thought of anything better. Throughout the second quarter of this century, painting had all it could do to cope with what had been initiated by "one or two people" between 1900 and 1925. If we take what had been done by Matisse, Picasso, Braque and Mondrian by 1920, and if we add what came in with the Surrealists between 1920 and 1925—the element of automatism, that is to say, and the freedom to draw upon the unconscious—the basic energy sources of painting in the first half of this century are complete.

Such was the momentum of those energies that it was possible to feel even in the 1950s that they were operating in Europe at an undiminished pressure. If painting had to a large extent turned in upon itself for subject matter, it had plenty to turn in upon. If there was self-evidently a big gap between the best artists and the next best, the answer was that the same had been true of the Impressionists, the Post-Impressionists, the Fauves, the Cubists and the Surrealists. Inequality is intrinsic to life. Meanwhile living art as a whole seemed to have reserves of energy which were in no danger of becoming exhausted. As the 1940s turned into the 1950s, it seemed to Europeans and Americans alike that a great era for art might well be at hand. There was an element of self-satisfaction, as always, in prognoses of this kind. But it is not ignoble to wish for our grandchildren the specific excitement, the sense of invigoration and renewal, with which we first set eyes on the last works of Matisse and the first works of Jasper Johns.

Yet we should be rash to count on a continuity of this kind. We have to remember, disagreeable as it may be, that the great age of Athenian drama lasted only 70 years and that the great age of verse drama in England was even shorter. Between the middle age of Haydn and the death of Brahms, sonata form was one of the loftiest modes of human expression; how often since then has it been used to comparable effect? The great ages of Venetian painting, Dutch painting, Flemish painting went out as if at the turn of a switch. We have very good novelists today, but who could argue that the novel as a form has lately been renewed? In every age there are those who agree with Friedrich von Schiller, greatest of German dramatists, that "beauty too must die, though it holds gods and men in thrall." Change is the law of life. What we once needed, we need no more. What we once made, we make no more. Why should modern art be exempt from these cruel laws?

"Because we'd miss it," is one answer. "Because it still has a lot to give us," is another. Both could be upheld throughout the 1950s and '60s. The sheer intensity of intergenerational friction during those decades was significant: the future of art was very much a live issue. Painting might be referred to as "bow and arrow art" by those who thought of the future of art in terms of a typewritten message, a ditch in the desert, a suitcase filled with rotting cheese, or free access to an electronic toyshop; but the thralldom of color, in particular, was as strong as ever. There was color as extension, in the stripe paintings of Kenneth Noland; color liberated from drawing, as in the tinted vapors that were as if breathed onto the canvas by Jules Olitski; and color as conspiracy, in paintings by Ad Reinhardt in which time was recruited as an ally and only a long, slow look would reveal the true nature of the picture.

What people called "the mythic drive behind high art" was still in evidence, and it took many different forms. At a time for instance when abstract painting in the United States was much occupied with unequivocal statements conceived in terms of the straight line, a young British artist was concerned with just the opposite: the extent to which curved lines could act out a complete psychodrama which moved with an intransigent eloquence from initial statement to conflict, and from conflict to resolution. Bridget Riley's *Fall* has nothing to do with the trumpery distractions of "Op" art. It is about the ways in which inner stresses can be faced and worked out to our eventual advantage. It takes the formal language which Edvard Munch used in the background of his *The Shriek*, drains away the emotive color, strips the image of its anecdotal element, and ends up with a statement which is as terse as it is compelling.

The priority of painting was, however, much in dispute throughout the 1960s. There were many reasons for this. There was the argument that it was in sculpture that truly revolutionary work was

Bridget Riley.
Fall. 1963.
Acrylic on board,
55½ × 55¼ inches.
The Tate Gallery,
London

being done. There was the argument that a new world needed not "a new art" but new kinds of art. There was the argument that the fixed and finite physical nature of painting was bound to rule it out as the locus of some of the deepest of human concerns at a time when human expectations and motivations were in a state of radical change. There was the argument that both painting and painters were being exploited by economic forces of a detestable sort. There was the argument, finally, that the self-exploratory activities of painting were entering their terminal phase. Ad Reinhardt, for one, believed that he was painting the last pictures which would ever need to be painted. Frank Stella in the late 1970s renewed the potential of painting by annexing for it the energies inherent in the third dimension. What resulted was a form of painted sculpture which in its impact on the view was both galvanic and unsettling.

There was something in each and all of these arguments. Painters are people, before and after they are painters. They are as dismayed as the rest of us by what is being done to other people, and to the world, in our name. Painting is an edgy, lonely, uncertain business, and it is very disagreeable to feel that the end product of it is being used to make big money fast for a pack of speculators. It is legitimate in times of crisis for a painter to crave something more direct in the way of communication with other people. In bad times the to-and-fro of human contact is more than ever essential to us, and if that to-and-fro can have something of the urgencies of art, so much the better. Traditional art has a traditional audience, and that audience still excludes a large part of the human race. We should not ignore one of the central facts of our time: that new populations and new publics are coming of age all over the world. Such people have the same rights, in matters of art, as the handful of poets, connoisseurs and fellow artists who alone appreciated the best new art before 1914.

So it is natural to speculate as to whether the future of art may not lie in the new forms of communication in which our age has specialized. As recently as 1945 we were still deeply conservative in such matters. The formulas of the art world had set fast, like pack ice, and showed no signs of melting. The rituals of the opera house and the symphony orchestra had not changed for more than half a century. Going to the theater meant sitting in an auditorium in attitudes unchanged since the time of Sophocles and gazing across the footlights at a play that lasted exactly two and a half hours. A book bound in paper had something wrong with it. A phonograph record was both heavy and fragile and stopped after four minutes. Films were something you saw in a movie house; and movie houses, like the Moscow subway, were vast, ornate, and designed to blind the customer to the drabness of life outside.

All these things were accepted as immutable. Yet it took a bare 25 years for us to adapt to improvised theater, aleatory music, free-form architecture, magnetic tapes that run for three hours or more, and dance dramas that owed nothing to the formalized miming of *Swan Lake.* In all these and many other domains we saw what Mondrian had meant when he said almost 50 years earlier that "we are at the end of everything *old.*" Sitting through the 25-minute monologue which constitutes Samuel Beckett's play *Not I,* listening to Karlheinz Stockhausen's electronic *Hymnen,* watching Merce Cunningham and his dance company give a completely new idea of the ways in which life can be spelled out on the stage, we might find it really rather odd that much of painting and sculpture should still be stuck with the materials of Rembrandt and Rodin. Perhaps it is hardly less odd that so many of us should still think

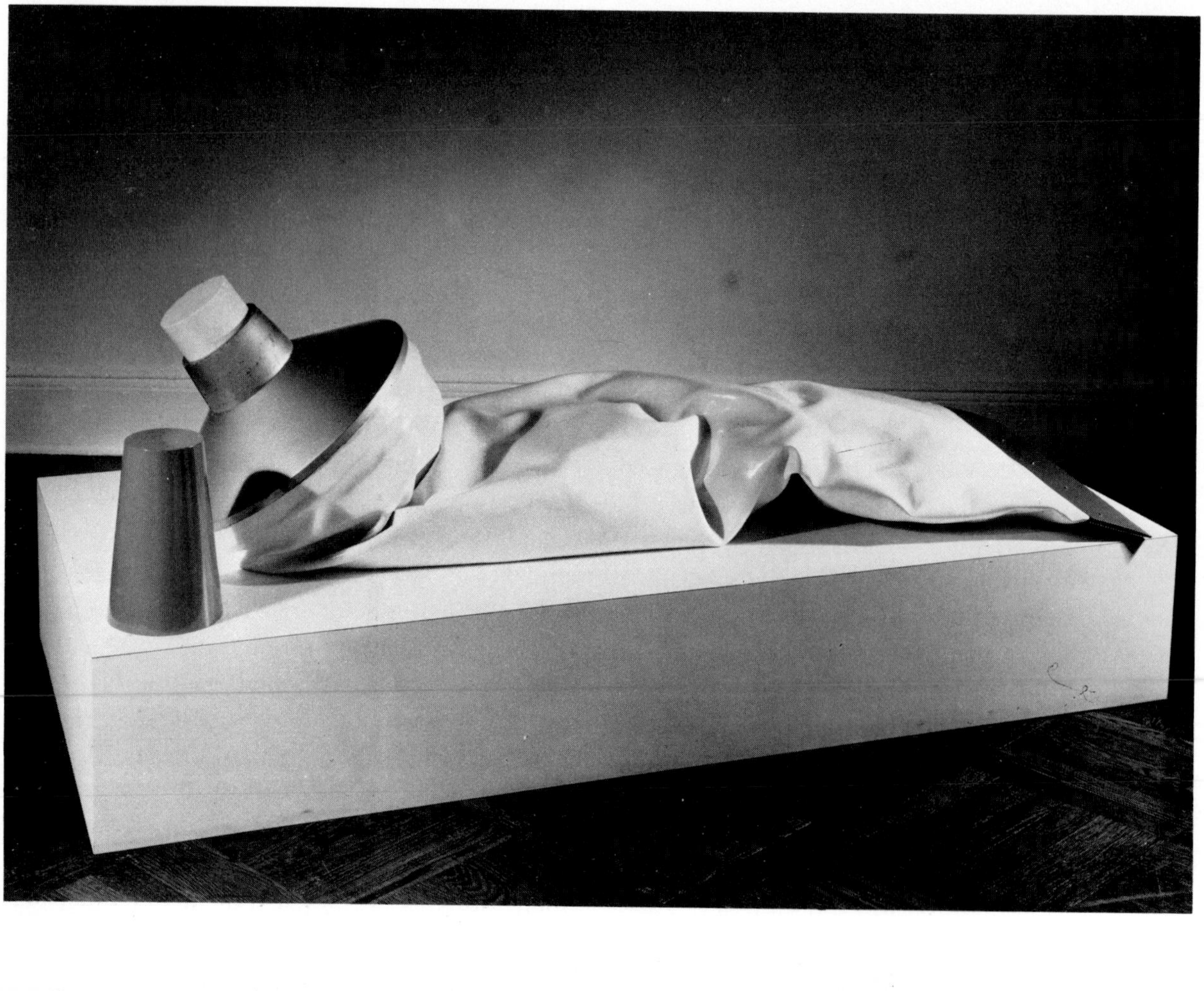

Claes Oldenburg. *Giant Toothpaste Tube.* 1964. Vinyl over canvas filled with kapok, 25½ × 66 × 17 inches. Private collection, Fort Worth, Texas

of painting and sculpture as separate entities, defined once and forever, when we acknowledge that the future of music may depend on new sources of sound and the future of the theater on modes of expression that owe nothing to theater as it was understood by the public of Alfred Lunt and Lynn Fontanne.

What we have witnessed, in this context, is the normalization of the avant-garde on the one hand and the abhorrence of existing conventions on the other. There is nothing new about new sources of sound: the symphony of factory chimneys as it was performed in Russia not long after the Revolution is evidence enough of that. There is nothing new about the boredom which many people feel when faced with the sterotyped subscription concert, the ritual "gallery opening" with its herd of free-loading nonentities, or the evening at the theater which costs a fortune and offers very lean pickings in terms of pleasure or enlightenment. Nor is there anything new about the freedom to restructure the arts, or to borrow freely and at will from one discipline in the service of another. To hear Kurt Schwitters recite his wordless poem was one of the great oratorical experiences of the 1920s and '30s. Poetry has arrogated to itself a total liberty on the page ever since Mallarmé published "Un Coup de Dés" in 1897. The Douanier Rousseau fancied himself as a playwright, and so did Picasso. Kandinsky wrote a drama to be performed by music, light and moving stage parts alone. But all these activities were incidental to a strenuous creativity in other domains; and they were done in a world which had not yet learned to exploit art for immediate advantage.

That is where the difference lies. There is something radically wrong with a world in which the effective life of most new books is between two and three weeks and in which works of art which are part of our universal inheritance can be hidden in vaults until the bankers' consortium which owns them can make a sufficient return on its investment. Things of this kind create a climate in which it is inordinately and unnecessarily difficult

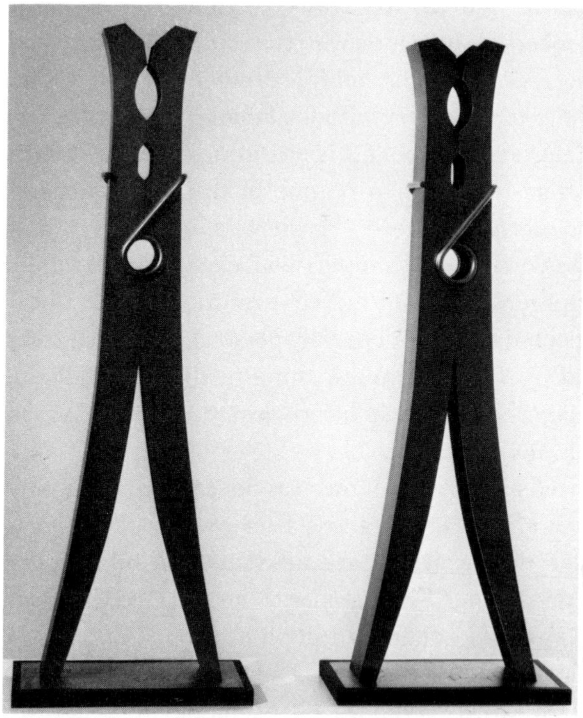

Claes Oldenburg. *Clothespin-4.* 1974. Bronze and steel (edition of 9), 48¾ inches high, including base. Courtesy Leo Castelli Gallery, New York

to produce good new work. They are the enemies of art; and in the 1960s artists began to fight back in the only way that was available to them—by making art that in one way or another was immune to the system.

The new art in question was of many kinds. Much of it was, and is, no good at all. How could it be otherwise? Art cannot function without an agreed social context. There must be some kind of contract, formulated or not, between the artist and the public which he wishes to reach. Contrary to popular belief, no art of consequence was ever produced in isolation. But there are times when both art and its audience are refugees from an environmental madness: this was the case with Dada in its Swiss and German phases, and it was the case with many manifestations of the new in the 1960s. When Claes Oldenburg set up his "Store" at 107 East Second Street, New York City, in the winter of 1961–62 and sold his simulated ray guns, wedding bouquets, wristwatches, pieces of pie, gym shoes, jelly doughnuts, airmail envelopes and inscribed birthday cakes, as a standard store would sell the real thing, he got under the guard of the system. Art was flourishing, but in what looked to be a nonart situation. Oldenburg had solved one of the central problems of the 1960s: how to make art without falling prey to the system, and he spelled it out in *Store Days* (1967), which deserves to be one of the classic texts of modern literature: "I know," he wrote, "that down to the last simple detail experience is totally mysterious." And he went on to assert an unexpected kinship: "The only person I know that tried to prove the simplest thing in the world, like a piece of candy, was utterly mysterious was Chirico (in his early days)."

Oldenburg in all this was not taking the dignity out of art. He was giving back to everyday objects the dignity which everyday life had taken away from them. "I am for an art," he said, ". . . that does something other than sit on its ass in a museum. I am for an art that grows up not knowing it is art at all, an art given the chance of having a starting point at zero. I am for an art that is smoked, like a cigarette, smells, like a pair of shoes. I am for an art that flaps like a flag, or helps blow noses, like a handkerchief. I am for an art that is put on and taken off, like pants, which develops holes, like socks, which is eaten, like a piece of pie, or abandoned with great contempt, like a piece of shit."

Nothing could be less like a recipe for an old-style masterpiece. But, as with Dubuffet, high art ended by getting its way; and those tiny and resolutely demotic pieces by Claes Oldenburg have an imaginative vitality which is very rare in mainstream scupture of their period.

Initially in 1964 the *Giant Toothpaste Tube* came across as an act of defiance. What could such an object have to do with high art? But in time the almost empty tube of toothpaste took shape in our minds as a traditional reclining figure. And if the detached top of the tube still contradicted this—well, there remained the parallel of the Crusaders' tombs of the 14th century in Europe, where the dead warrior was sometimes portrayed with his helmet at his side. Besides, Oldenburg knew that changes of scale always bring with them changes of implication. The humble clothespin when magnified and cast in bronze and steel assumes an imperious hominoid look, as if it were halfway through changing into the image of a born leader of men, with his two feet set firmly apart, his left hand tucked into his belt and his big ears cocked to catch the latest news. The toothpaste piece and the clothespin piece are ten years apart, but the aesthetic behind them is the same.

That we have to give the name of "sculpture" to the *Giant Toothpaste Tube* is in itself instructive, by the way. If we consider that that same word is applied to a Calder mobile, a fluorescent light piece by Dan Flavin, a totem in stainless steel by David Smith and a length of felt hung from a nail by Robert Morris, it will be clear that the word "sculpture" now has wider connotations than the word "painting." The emancipation of sculpture is one of the discreeter romances in the cultural life of our century.

Sometimes the new sculpture had a long ancestry. At a first glance Donald Judd's *Untitled,* 1970, might seem to be a work without precedent in art, so completely does it outlaw the traditional elements of sculpture: variety, surprise, "composition," personal handling and evidence of effort. But in point of fact Judd here draws upon the measured regularity and the austere plainness of statement which are fundamental to a certain specifically American aesthetic. That aesthetic turns up all over the place: in the high-backed chair made in the first half of the 19th century, in the Navajo blanket made some 50 years later, and in Charles Sheeler's painting of 1925, where the stately movement of the staircase is echoed in the ribbing of the ceiling on the right and turns up all over again in the roof. A recurrent America stands, therefore, behind Judd's sculpture, for all its deliberate modernity.

Meanwhile there was still a demand for public sculpture. Sculpture in a public context has both advantages and drawbacks. It was a drawback to its emancipation that for centuries it had a clearly defined public function. There are millions of people on this earth who have never seen an original painting of any quality; but it is difficult to live in a big city anywhere in the world and not have daily contact with sculptures to which at any rate a certain ambition must be conceded. (Even the badness of those sculptures can liberate the imagination; Giorgio de Chirico took a great deal, for instance, from the public monuments of Turin, in Italy, where the 19th century excelled itself in terms of absurdity.) Sculpture is built into big-city experience in a way that other kinds of art are not, and for that reason it has associations with officialdom which have lately fallen into disrepute.

As against this, sculpture in a private context is very much a minority art. A picture on the wall is part of an almost universal currency of good living. By contrast, a sculpture in the living room very often causes dismay and embarrassment. Backs can be turned to a bad painting; a bad sculpture sits there and defies us to ignore it. Sculpture is apart from the mainstream of living in ways which ensure for it a certain privacy. Its mutations are not monitored as closely as are the mutations of painting. Until recently there was, moreover, a fundamental untractability about the materials of sculpture; this called for a degree of dedication and perseverance which does not arise in the case of the amateur painter. Making sculpture was real work, and the chances of a happy accident of the kind which enriches the life of the Sunday painter were very small. Sculpture has always had, finally, a magical quality—witness the myth of Pygmalion, the sculptor, whose statue of Galatea came to life—and the traditional sculptor stood next to God in his ability to create an unmistakable human being where none had existed before.

This apartness and this implicitly superior status have continued into our own time. Sculpture is a crusading art. The degradation of public sculpture in the second half of the 19th century drove the more thoughtful among younger sculptors to renew and purify the sculptural act. Raymond Duchamp-Villon, the brother of Marcel Duchamp, saw it as fundamental before 1914 that sculpture should be "a reaction against our business era, where money is the master." The great painter-sculptors—Degas, Matisse, Boccioni, Picasso, Giacometti—used sculpture with a freedom and an audacity and a determination to try something quite new. As for the sculptor-sculptors —Medardo Rosso, Naum Gabo, Julio Gonzalez,

Donald Judd. *Untitled.* 1970. Anodized aluminum, 8 boxes (6 shown), each 9 × 40 × 31 inches. Courtesy Leo Castelli Gallery, New York

Henry Moore, David Smith, Anthony Caro—they inspired loyalty of a kind which few painters experience. People went to Brancusi's studio in Paris as they would have gone to visit a hermit in the desert. Something fundamental to human dignity was being carried on there: the search for an absolute perfection. In a general way Duchamp-Villon had been quite right when he said in 1913 that "In an era of floating ideas and aspirations, there can be no such thing as a definitive or durable monument"; but this is the sign of a decay in human affairs that must somehow be arrested. Whence the peculiar urgency of modern sculpture at its best; whence, equally, the fascination for sculptors of many kinds, before 1914, of what the art historian Albert E. Elsen has aptly called "the image of the powerful figure whose legs scissor space, whose past and future are measurable only by his tread and not by his name."

If sculpture produced, against all the odds, a definitive and durable monument in the 20th century it was not in the form of a striding figure. Nor did it have the public function which earlier ages had assigned to it. Much of the best sculpture went underground. The full extent of Picasso's activity as a sculptor was not revealed till the 1980s. Matisse's sculpture was always regarded as auxiliary to his painting, though he devoted an immense amount of time to it. Much significant work was lost or destroyed: above all, what was done by Tatlin and others in Russia after 1917. Brancusi's monumental works in Rumania must be the least readily accessible of all the major achievements of modern art. From Medardo Rosso to Joseph Cornell, the making of three-dimensional objects has kept an element of privacy.

Still, there are worse things than privacy when it comes to the making of great art. (When did Cézanne live in the limelight?) Original sculpture in the 20th century had the advantage that no publicity machine was behind it. Brancusi lived off the enthusiasm of "one or two people." Moore in his early 40s could rarely afford the materials for a major work. Henri Laurens lived and died on the edge of penury. David Smith in his studio at Bolton Landing, New York, was never favored (or oppressed, according to one's point of view) by the adulation which surrounded painters without a fraction of his gifts. It would almost be true to say that sculpture in our century has been the secret weapon of art.

This is not a mere form of words. At any time in

(left)
Charles Sheeler.
Staircase, Doylestown. 1925.
Oil on canvas, 24 × 20 inches.
Hirshhorn Museum and Sculpture Garden, Smithsonian Institution, Washington

(center)
Man's Shoulder Blanket. Navajo Indian, 1875–90.
Tapestry weaving, wool yarns, 6 feet 8 inches × 52 inches.
Museum of Fine Arts, Boston. Gift of John Ware Willard

(right)
Side Chair, from Nacogdoches, Texas. c. 1830–45.
Turned ash and elm, with hickory-bark seat.
San Antonio Museum Association Collection, San Antonio, Texas

Alexander Calder. *Black Widow.* 1959. Painted sheet steel, 7 feet 8 inches × 14 feet 3 inches × 7 feet 5 inches. The Museum of Modern Art, New York. Mrs. Simon Guggenheim Fund

the recent history of art there is likely to have been one area which functioned as a touchstone of probity. "Drawing is the integrity of art," said Ingres when faced with the rivalry of Delacroix; he meant that drawing was the department of art in which no one can fake. In our own century, painting has carried the banner for modernism; and it is with painting above all that the public associates the idea of the new. But it can be argued that on many an important occasion sculpture darted ahead of painting. And sculpture endures to this day a degree of physical hostility which painting is spared; sculptures in public places attract a peculiarly mindless hostility. Sculpture is difficult to show and difficult to talk about. Sculptors incline to be pugnacious—often with good reason—and even if many bronzes are now cast in quite large editions there is still something about the firsthand experience of sculpture which cannot be counterfeited. Sculpture is immune, therefore, from the vulgarization which lies in wait for painting.

At the same time, a bad sculpture is one of the most blatant forms of environmental pollution. Thomas Mann in his essay on Wagner said that no one can make himself smaller than his true size—the point being that Wagner could not plan a light romantic comedy without turning out *Die Meistersinger,* which runs for five hours—and it is equally true that no one can make himself larger than his true size; a big sculpture which doesn't come off is intolerable. The case for the moral grandeur of sculpture in our century rests on the number and scope of the conventions which had to be overthrown before sculpture could regain its dignity. David Smith put the sculptor's point of view when talking to Thomas B. Hess in 1964. "Sculpture has been a whore for many ages," he said. "It had to be a commissioned thing. Sculpture was not sculpture till it was cast in bronze. Before it was cast, the man who paid for it had certain reservations and designations as to subject matter."

Initially, before 1914, the dignity of sculpture was reclaimed by an isolated piece here and there. Later, where a large body of work existed, it was

Henry Moore.
Reclining Figure.
1969–70.
Bronze, 13 feet long.
Schlesinger Organization, Johannesburg

overshadowed by the priority accorded to painting. If sculpture impinged on the general consciousness, it was likely to be in the form of artifacts remote from our own culture, such as those from pre-Columbian Mexico, from Benin or from Easter Island. One of the novelties of the last 50 years, in this context, is the emergence of modern sculptors with whom a whole generation could identify itself. Instances of this are Alexander Calder, Henry Moore and David Smith, all three of whom in their work got through to the public with a physical immediacy that is very rare.

Something in this is owed to personality. Calder, Moore and Smith come across in their work as men of open, straightforward, downright character, with a contempt for anything mean or evasive: whence comes our confidence in them as human beings. When Calder first made inert materials get up and dance, the world danced with them. Some of the ideas in his mobiles may have come from Joan Miró, whom Calder knew well for many years; but Calder was the master of a dynamic, free-running humor, and his feeling for life was distinctively that of the most glorious type of American. Quite apart from the contagious amusement of his work, he was in himself one of humanity's more presentable possessions.

At a time in history when it was possible to despair of human nature, Henry Moore likewise said in effect, "There is an alternative." Everything in his experience of childhood, everything in his education, everything in his watchful and undeceived understanding of adult life has suggested to him that if human nature is given the right opportunities it may even now redeem itself. This has lately been a very difficult case to argue. A discouraged "No" has been much easier to justify than a constructive "Yes"; and in Moore's affirmative position there was something of that earlier epoch in which D. H. Lawrence in one way and H. G. Wells in another looked forward to a radical change in the prospects for humanity. Lawrence in particular wanted people to know their rights, as human beings, and to act upon them. He wasn't too far, in this, from Henry Moore.

Moore throughout his long career has functioned as a concerned citizen. In the 1930s he was a master of the cryptic three-dimensional image

Ellsworth Kelly.
Red Blue Green.
1963.
Oil on canvas,
7 feet × 11 feet 4 inches.
La Jolla Musem of Contemporary Art.
Gift of Dr. and Mrs. Jack Farris

is fundamental to them. So is their scale, which dominates but does not dwarf us. Smith's was, at the last, an optimistic art: one that suggests to us that there is nothing human beings cannot do if they put their minds to it.

David Smith may have been the last major artist to have an absolutely explicit, constructive and sanguine conception of the future of art. In this, as in everything else, he came on as one of Nature's frontiersmen. Art "has existed from the minds of free men for less than a century," he once said. Thus "the freedom of man's mind to celebrate his own feeling by a work of art parallels his social revolt from bondage. I believe that art is yet to be born and that freedom and equality are yet to be born."

Modern art could have no nobler charter than that. Written in 1950, it stands for a large-heartedness, a freedom from corruption and a breadth of ambition which have largely ceased to characterize the world of art. Smith at that time was as unsuccessful, in worldly terms, as an artist can be. (His income from the sale of his work in 1951 was $333. In 1952 it was nothing at all.) The boom years for art were yet to come, and conditions—for sculpture, at any rate—were roughly as they had been in 1937, when Smith was prompted by the example of the Spanish sculptor Julio Gonzalez to begin making welded sculptures: the work was done to define the sculptor's identity as a free human being, and with no rational prospect of financial success.

Smith was killed in 1965 when his truck overturned on the road. He had no successors, but he did have a friend and colleague whose work is in some respects a continuation of his. Anthony Caro began as an Expressionist figure sculptor: a manipulator of weighty full-bodied human forms that spread and sprawled in space. But by 1962 he had turned to loose-jointed lateral conjunctions of man-made forms which made no reference to nature. Not only gravity but function was denied—as in *Atlantic*, where the monumental I-beam stands at an angle which it would not conceivably adopt in "real life." The emphasis is on open and transparent sequences of form that get clear away from the monumental, earthbound associations of earlier sculpture. Not forms, but the relations between them, had become the true subject of art. Caro's contacts with David Smith in 1963–64 were fruitful for both of them. Working in the United States at that period, Caro at times used the square or near-square forms which Smith built up to such effect in his Cubi series. But where Smith used them to develop ever more imposing emblems of masculinity, Caro took the weight out of them and made them relate to one another, as in *Rainfall*, with a rare elegance. Where Smith worked by concentration, Caro worked by dispersion, setting his forms free from any overtone of menace and devising for them a whole new set of delicate relationships. Often he gave his collocations of form the sculptural equivalent of slender wrists and ankles. Fine-drawn in themselves, they are so lightly connected with one another as to make us wonder if they have not just floated together by mutual attraction. In a piece like *Crosspatch*, Caro explores the poetics of adjacency in ways that make us newly aware of the balance that should be inherent in our own bodies. In 1972–73 Caro paid three visits to Veduggio, Brianza, Italy, where he worked with a material quite new to him: soft-edged steel. Using scraps from plates and joists, he held fast to their ruddy, worked-over quality, so that the sculpture which resulted has none of the immaculateness of *Crosspatch*. The forms have on the contrary a flamboyant, eaten-into and yet spreading outward look, which is perhaps nearer to the paintings of Helen Frankenthaler (who had worked in Caro's studio in 1972) than to anything that Caro had done before. Yet the elements which lie flat on the ground are unmistakably Caro's, as is the flexible syntax of the piece as a whole. In this, as in the whole corpus of his work to date, Caro is the most creative sculptor to have emerged in any country since World War II.

By 1970 a vast machinery of promotion and speculation had fastened onto the making of art, which for most of David Smith's lifetime had been almost as private a matter as theology or pure mathematics. How this came about is a complex question. In part it was an authentic and justified tribute to the new role of art in the imaginative life of the United States. People acknowledged that something extraordinary had happened in art. They might not like it, any more than they liked the music of Elliott Carter or the prose of Gertrude Stein, but they knew that these things resounded to the credit of the United States. To wish to get a piece of the action is intrinsic to human nature. It is fundamental to the seduction of art that we hope to become what we look at; and if we can look at it every day in our own house the process may perhaps be accelerated. That was the most reputable of the motives which led people to pay high prices for modern art.

Other factors should be spelled out. New money breeds new collectors, and new collectors do not always have the patience, the knowledge and the discrimination which are basic to the enjoyment of Old Master painting. Much of the best modern art calls for these attributes, but in the art of the 1960s there was much that was altogether readier of access. Ambiguity and complexity played no part in it. There was no question of lingering before it as we linger before Giorgione or Vermeer. Frank Stella was categorical about that in 1964: "One could stand in front of any Abstract Expressionist work for a long time, and walk back and forth, and inspect the depths of the pigment and the inflection and all the painterly brushwork for hours. But I wouldn't ask anyone to do that in front of my paintings. To go further, I would like to prohibit them from doing that in front of my paintings. That's why I make the paintings the way they are." About much of the art of the 1960s there was a bluntness and a blankness which in time gave it the status of an ostentatious form of traveler's check.

Something in this bluntness and blankness came from a revulsion against the art of the 1940s and early '50s. Among the ideas most in disfavor were that of the heroic but foredoomed failure, the approximation that could never become complete, and the acting out, either on the canvas or in three dimensions, of any kind of private drama. There was believed to be something almost obscene about personalized brushstrokes, about sculpture that bore the mark of the shaping hand and about the traditional European idea of the balanced composition. ("With so-called advanced painting you should drop composition," said Stella.) Much of this was a natural reaction against the extreme subjectivity and the secular mysticism of much that had been made famous since 1950. But it was exploited by a public that did not want to look hard for more than a few moments and by promoters who preferred work that avoided the classic stance—the "now and never again," the "here and nowhere else"—of European art. From this emerged the impersonal series-painting of the 1960s, and the graphics industry which was often no more than an expensive form of souvenir hunting, and the multiples which cashed in on the prestige of art but ran none of art's risks. The remarkable thing was not that this situation should have come about, but rather that good work was done from time to time in spite of it.

And good work was done, right through the 1960s and the 1970s. The wish to make a monumental statement did not die out, either. Whether in the Ocean Park series of Richard Diebenkorn, or in the outsize provocations of Frank Stella, or in the three-dimensional autobiography of Joseph Beuys, or in the enormous paintings in which Jennifer Bartlett took image after image to the very point of disintegration, only to bring them safely back again, there were statements of a grand, searching, unsubdued sweep that spoke up for mankind as clearly as they spoke up for art. There were also compound statements, in which art raided archaeology, raided natural history, raided cartography, raided the skies and raided the seabed. Someone who did all this and much else besides, in painting and sculpture alike, was Nancy Graves. In her *Trace* an informed viewer will find

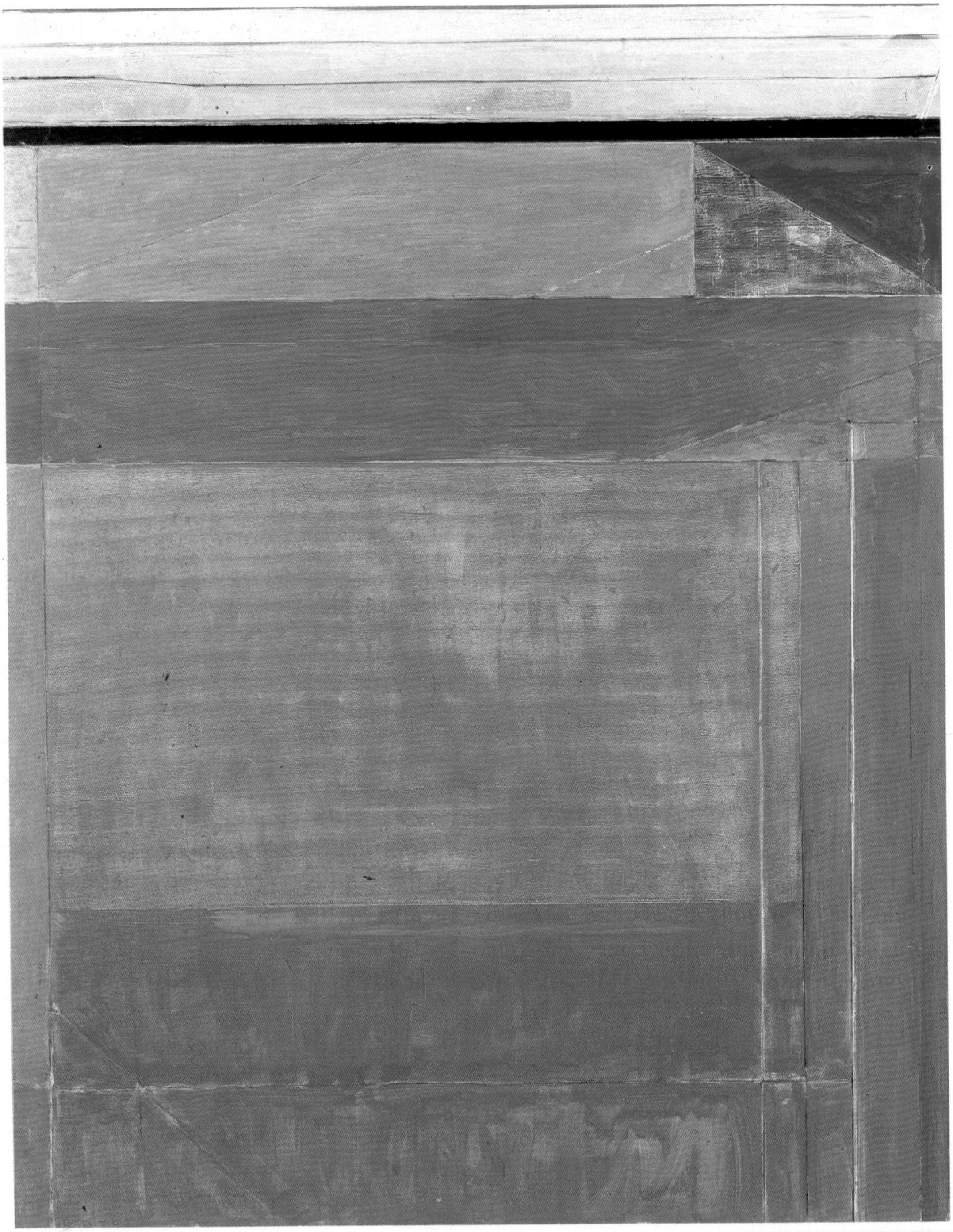

Richard Diebenkorn.
Ocean Park 115.
1979.
Oil on canvas,
8 feet 4 inches × 6 feet 9 inches.
The Museum of Modern Art, New York. Mrs. Charles C. Stachelberg Fund

Frank Stella.
New Caledonian Lorikeet II. 1977. Lacquer, oil, glitter, paintstick on metal relief, 10 feet × 13 feet × 30 inches. Courtesy Leo Castelli Gallery, New York

Nancy Graves.
Trace. 1979–80. Bronze, steel, patina and paint, 9 feet 7 inches × 8 feet 11 inches × 50 inches. Graham Gund, Cambridge, Mass.

the new openness of form that we expect from sculpture since David Smith and Anthony Caro. He will find an incorporeal lightness and radiance of color to which neither Smith nor Caro aspired. And he will also find a marriage, well and truly consummated, between art and natural history.

So there were people who stayed with gallery art, museum art, continuity art. But art did go underground, all the same. It had gone underground before, when nobody wanted it: when the audience for the best art numbered six or seven people and the artist—Picasso, at his very best, and Matisse, at his very best—did not even think of putting it on show. Now it went underground for the opposite reason: because everybody wanted it. As insistently as before 1914, the times called for an alternative art. It took many forms; but what these forms had in common was that they questioned the nature of art—and, more especially, of art that was susceptible to instant marketing. Art was to go about its own concerns, in private, and if necessary take forms that denied what was fundamental to marketed art: the possibility of possession.

No one can buy a work of art that consists in the temporary and all but invisible readjustment of the city that we live in. If a work of art exists in idea form only, the idea in time will belong to everyone, and the typewritten statement that can be bought and sold is no more than an outdated token. The alternative art of the late 1960s and early '70s took forms that were ephemeral, impalpable, sometimes purely notional. Sometimes it depended on the participation of the viewer: and although this in itself was not new—every work of art has always been completed by the person who looks at it—there was often a willed ephemerality about the new art which had not been met with before.

The instruments of art had never before been so varied. At one extreme there was brought into play every newest refinement of technology: the video-tape, the hologram that hung in the air, the android or humanized robot that clanked and stumbled along the streets of New York, the computer-generated environment, the labyrinth of light and sound that is activated by the public that penetrates it, the crystals in a glass sphere that turn from solid to gas in response to atmospheric conditions. At the other extreme, there were artists who made art with pebbles picked from the foreshore and a worn-down piece of chalk, or with a folded sheet of carbon paper and a few lines ruled in pencil. There were people who went further still and said, with Joseph Kosuth, "I want to remove the experience from the work of art." ("Actual works of art," he also said, "are little more than historical curiosities.") On this last reading, art as it had existed previously was a tautology: an acting-out, in other words, of something that existed already, in definition form, and did not need to be made visible.

These were heady matters, as tempting to the near-genius as to the charlatan, and as accessible to the near-saint as to the ravening opportunist. Among the technophiles there were some who simply ran wild, like small boys let loose in a candystore. Among the pseudo-philosophers there were some who could not tell "its" from "it's," let alone master Plato or Kant. Sometimes the wish that art once again become private was simply overridden by society. Claes Oldenburg once described how this came about; and his remarks ring true in other and later contexts. "I really don't think you can win. . . . The bourgeois scheme is that they wish to be disturbed from time to time, they like that, but then they envelop you and that little bit is over, and they are ready for the next. . . ." Sometimes, also, elements from marketed art, and from the market situation, made their way in, unbidden. The promotion of personality is as repulsive in this context as the promotion of art. The aesthetics of undifferentiated experience had been put forward to great effect by John Cage, in many of his later compositions, and by Andy Warhol (above all, in his films). It was dismal when the same point of view motivated people who had neither talent nor spontaneous impulse. Where something humbler and more conventionally human. It is what is called in German *Torschlusspanik:* the terror of the closing door. The end of art, as art has hitherto been conceived, is more than "the end of an era." It is the end of a god: the death of something which brought reassurance, and brought consolation, and brought an unshakable equanimity. It is very disagreeable, as I said at the outset of this survey, to think that art will one day come to an end. And it is particularly disagreeable when the art of the recent past has been of very high quality.

It is for this reason that the status of art has been claimed for activities which in themselves might seem to be no more than novelty hunting of a particularly fatuous kind. It is for this same reason, and to relieve the strain upon those rare individuals who still produce finite works of art at the highest level, that such efforts have been made to bring the notion of art into a public (if not actually into an anonymous) domain. If everything is art, and if the life of everyday can be monitored in terms of art, then we shall no longer have to apply to individual exertions the dreaded words "not good enough." We should aim, therefore, to arouse in every human being the kind of superior awareness which is in itself a form of creativity. If this were to become universal—so the argument runs—the gap between art and life would be closed once and for all.

That everyone should be an artist is, on one level, the noblest of dreams: the enfranchisement of one man in a million would give way to the enfranchisement of everyone, without exception. On a less conscious level it stands, however, for something quite different: the wish to spread among all mankind, and therefore to spread very thin, the responsibility for what is considered in the Bible, and in mythology, as a blasphemous act. It is not for mankind—so the primeval belief ran—to rival the gods. When Marsyas with his reed pipes challenged Apollo to a trial of skill, Apollo had him flayed alive. When Orpheus made music so beautiful that it overthrew the existing order of things, the gods saw to it that he lost his beloved Eurydice and was torn apart by Maenads. When the Hebrews got above themselves and tried to build a tower that would reach to Heaven, Jehovah put an end to it by destroying the unity of language that alone made possible the control of the vast and heterogeneous work force.

Somber warnings, these. Yet in bad times we need to believe that the problems before mankind are not insoluble. We know that the breakdown of art, like the breakdown of literacy, may portend a more general breakdown, and one that is irreversible. If it is forbidden to rival the gods, it is also despicable not to attempt it. That particular rivalry, with all that it involves in the way of risk and terror and possible retribution, may well be the supreme human act: the one that best justifies our existence and may prevent it from coming to an end.

This is not a belief that we need to abandon. Rarely in human history can a decade have begun less well than the 1980s. On every hand, and in every country in the world, the present is matter for misgiving and the future a matter for dread. It is natural that at such a time people should think of art as a thing of the past. But what is natural is not always laudable, and it is a pointless diminution of our status on earth to assume that "art as we knew it" can no longer be counted upon. "Art as *who* knew it?" is the answer to that. Now more than ever we need to remember that art is the constructive act, and that the artist is the person who puts the world together after everyone else has let it go to pieces.

For what is the alternative? The silence of the German poet Friedrich Hölderlin. The silence of the French poet Arthur Rimbaud. The silence in old age of the American poet Ezra Pound. The silence of Moses, in Arnold Schoenberg's unfinished opera, when he realized that people were turning away from the truths for which he, Moses, could not find the right words. We may never know why Hölderlin went mad, why Rimbaud left Europe to eke out a living in Africa or why Pound

Max Ernst.
The Voice of the Holy Father. 1930.
Paper on paper, collage, 5¾ × 6¾ inches.
Private collection, New York

abjured the gift of tongues that he had used so unwisely. But we know that one of the last poets in classical Latin literature was right when he said that civilization lives by speech and dies by silence. For "speech," in our present context, we should substitute the image in all its forms, finite or variable.

It is difficult to think of today's world in terms other than those of crisis and emergency. What is at stake is the survival of the earth as a place fit to live on, and of the human race as something that will bear scrutiny. It was not in conditions such as these that the masters of early modern art grew to manhood; and a certain sympathetic indulgence should, I think, be accorded to those who aspire to be their successors. "What can we know for certain?" is a question which has haunted modern art ever since it was first posed by Cézanne. If it has lately been answered primarily in terms of art's own nature—if art, in other words, has aspired primarily to define itself—the lesson in self-knowledge which we can draw from it is nonetheless valid for being metaphorical. Art has provided us with models of our environment ever since cave paintings conjured up the bulls and the bisons that shook the earth as they passed overhead. It is still fulfilling this same function, whether in the panoramic and posthumous masterpiece of Marcel Duchamp which is now in the Philadelphia Museum, or in such more restricted studies as the miniature forest, to be viewed from what felt like a refrigerated trench, which Robert Morris contributed to an exhibition at The Museum of Modern Art in New York. Art is there to make sense of the world, and it should surprise nobody if over the last 50 years this has become progressively more difficult. In 1930, when Max Ernst made his *Voice of the Holy Father*, many of the secrets of our century were still intact. To open the book of the future was a perilous act: one to be watched, as it is watched in that little picture, with every symptom of dismay. But art could do it, and art until now has dared to do it.

It is possible, too, to be unduly discouraged. The French poet Paul Valéry was very bright indeed as a young man at the turn of this century, and he mixed with people in Paris whose business it was to know what was going on. But, like other very bright people who have been close to the work of their immediate seniors, he took a gloomy view of what was to come. To feel that nothing can be the same again is the most natural of human instincts, and Valéry may well have drawn only assent when he wrote to a friend in 1908 and said, "Will anything great ever again come out of Europe?" I shall have failed in my purpose if I have not convinced the reader that this question called for a full-throated "Yes!" The best art of our century may well remind us of what was written not long ago by the British scientist and Nobel prizewinner P. B. Medawar: "To deride the hope of progress is the ultimate fatuity, the last word in poverty of spirit and meanness of mind."

For no one can foresee in what forms of art the next generation will see itself fulfilled and justified. The poet William Carlos Williams spoke ideally well of the effect of great painting when he said that "It is ourselves we seek to see on the canvas, as no one ever saw us, before we lost our courage and our love." This sense of ourselves redeemed and made whole is the greatest gift which one human being can make to another. Art has always been there to give us that sense of ourselves, and never more so than since the springs of feeling were made over to us, unmuddied, by the Impressionists. Over and over again it has reminded us that all art consoles, and that great art consoles absolutely. What form art will take in the future no one can say; but no sane society will wish to be without it.

SUGGESTED READINGS

GENERAL

Arnason, H. H. *History of Modern Art.* New York, Abrams, 1968.

Ashton, Dore. *A Fable of Modern Art.* New York, Thames & Hudson, 1980.

Baigell, Matthew. *History of American Painting.* New York, Praeger, 1971.

Banham, Reyner. *Theory and Design in the First Machine Age.* New York, Praeger, 1960.

Barr, Alfred H., Jr., ed. *Masters of Modern Art.* 2nd. ed. New York, The Museum of Modern Art, 1955.

Bowness, Alan. *Modern European Art.* New York, Harcourt, Brace, Jovanovich, 1972.

Breunig, LeRoy C., ed. *Apollinaire on Art: Essays and Reviews, 1902–1918.* New York, Viking, 1972.

Brown, Milton W., and others. *American Art: Painting, Sculpture, Architecture, Decorative Arts, Photography.* New York, Abrams, 1979.

Brown, Milton W. *American Painting from the Armory Show to the Depression.* Princeton, N.J., Princeton University Press, 1955.

Buckle, Richard. *Diaghilev.* New York, Atheneum, 1979.

Burnham, Jack. *Beyond Modern Sculpture: The Effects of Science and Technology on the Sculpture of This Century.* New York, Braziller, 1968.

Chipp, Herschel B. *Theories of Modern Art: A Source Book by Artists and Critics.* Berkeley and Los Angeles, University of California Press, 1968.

Clay, Jean. *Modern Art, 1890–1918.* New York, Vendome Press (distributed by Viking), 1978.

Elsen, Albert E. *Modern European Sculpture 1918–1945, Unknown Beings and Other Realities.* New York, Braziller, 1979.

Elsen, Albert E. *Origins of Modern Sculpture: Pioneers and Premises.* New York, Braziller, 1974.

Gablik, Suzi. *Progress in Art.* New York, Rizzoli, 1977.

Geldzahler, Henry. *American Painting in the Twentieth Century.* New York, The Metropolitan Museum of Art, 1965.

Giedion, Sigfried. *Space, Time and Architecture.* Rev. and enl. 5th edition. Cambridge, Mass., Harvard University Press, 1973.

Gombrich, E. H. *The Story of Art.* London, Phaidon, 1972.

Greenberg, Clement. *Art and Culture: Critical Essays.* Boston, Beacon Press, 1961.

Haftman, Werner. *Painting in the Twentieth Century.* New ed. New York, Praeger, 1965.

Hamilton, George Heard. *19th and 20th Century Art.* New York, Abrams, 1970.

Hamilton, George Heard. *Painting and Sculpture in Europe 1880–1940.* Rev. ed. Baltimore, Penguin Books, 1972.

Hammacher, A. M. *The Evolution of Modern Sculpture: Tradition and Innovation.* New York, Abrams, 1969.

Herbert, Robert L., ed. *Modern Artists on Art.* Englewood Cliffs, N.J., Prentice-Hall, 1964.

Holt, Elizabeth Gilmore, ed. *From the Classicists to the Impressionists: A Documentary History of Art and*

Architecture in the Nineteenth Century. Garden City, N.Y., Doubleday, 1966.
Hunter, Sam, and Jacobus, John. *American Art of the 20th Century: Painting, Sculpture, Architecture.* New York, Abrams, 1974.
Kramer, Hilton. *The Age of the Avant-Garde: An Art Chronicle of 1956–1972.* New York, Farrar, Straus & Giroux, 1973.
Kuh, Katharine, ed. *The Artist's Voice.* New York, Harper & Row, 1962.
Lynton, Norbert. *The Story of Modern Art.* Ithaca, Cornell University Press, 1980.
Malraux, André. *The Psychology of Art.* New York, Pantheon, 1949.
Malraux, André. *Museum without Walls.* (Vol. 1 of *The Psychology of Art.*) Garden City, N.Y., Doubleday, 1963.
Porter, Fairfield. *Art in Its Own Terms: Selected Criticism, 1935–1975.* Rackstraw Downes, ed. New York, Taplinger, 1979.
Read, Herbert. *A Concise History of Modern Painting.* Rev. and enl. ed. New York, Praeger, 1968.
Read, Herbert. *A Concise History of Modern Sculpture.* New York, Praeger, 1971.
Rose, Barbara. *American Art since 1900: A Critical History.* Revised edition. New York, Praeger, 1975.
Schapiro, Meyer. *Modern Art, 19th and 20th Centuries: Selected Papers.* New York, Braziller, 1978.
Shattuck, Roger. *The Banquet Years: The Origins of the Avant-Garde in France, 1885 to World War I.* Rev. ed. New York, Vintage Books, 1968.
Steinberg, Leo. *Other Criteria: Confrontations with Twentieth-Century Art.* New York, Oxford University Press, 1972.
Walker, John A. *Glossary of Art, Architecture and Design since 1945.* 2nd. rev. ed. Hamden, Conn., Linnet Books, 1977.

MOVEMENTS

Impressionism, Post-Impressionism

Herbert, Robert L. *Neo-Impressionism.* New York, Solomon R. Guggenheim Foundation, 1968.
Lövgren, Sven. *The Genesis of Modernism: Seurat, Gauguin, van Gogh and French Symbolism in the 1880s.* 2nd. rev. ed. Bloomington, Indiana University Press, 1971.
Pool, Phoebe. *Impressionism.* New York, Praeger, 1967.
Rewald, John. *The History of Impressionism.* 4th rev. ed. New York, The Museum of Modern Art, 1973.
Rewald, John. *Post-Impressionism: From van Gogh to Gauguin.* 3rd ed. rev. New York, The Museum of Modern Art, 1978.
Roskill, Mark. *Van Gogh, Gauguin and the Impressionist Circle.* Greenwich, Conn., New York Graphic Society, 1970.

Symbolism

Delevoy, Robert L. *Symbolists and Symbolism.* New York, Rizzoli, 1978.
Jullian, Philippe. *Dreamers of Decadence: Symbolist Painters of the 1890s.* New York, Praeger, 1971.
Lucie-Smith, Edward. *Symbolist Art.* London, Thames & Hudson, 1972.
Milner, John. *Symbolists and Decadents.* London and New York, Studio Vista/Dutton Paperbacks, 1971.
Symons, Arthur. *The Symbolist Movement in Literature.* (First publ. 1899.) New York, Dutton, 1958.

Fauvism

Crespelle, Jean-Paul. *The Fauves.* Greenwich, Conn., New York Graphic Society; London, Oldbourne, 1962.
Duthuit, Georges. *The Fauvist Painters.* New York, Wittenborn, 1950.
Elderfield, John. *The "Wild Beasts": Fauvism and Its Affinities.* New York, The Museūm of Modern Art, 1976.

Expressionism, Die Brücke, Der Blaue Reiter

Grohmann, Will. *Expressionists.* New York, Abrams, 1957.
Kandinsky, Wassily, and Marc, Franz, eds. *The Blaue Reiter Almanac.* New York, Viking, 1974.
Manvell, Roger, and Fraenkel, Heinrich. *The German Cinema.* New York, Praeger, 1971.
Miesel, Victor H., ed. *Voices of German Expressionism.* Englewood Cliffs, N.J., Prentice-Hall, 1970.
Myers, Bernard S. *The German Expressionists: A Generation in Revolt.* New York, McGraw-Hill, 1963.
Roethel, Hans K. *The Blue Rider.* New York, Praeger, 1972.
Roh, Franz. *German Art in the 20th Century.* Rev. ed. Greenwich, Conn., New York Graphic Society, 1968.
Selz, Peter. *German Expressionist Painting.* Berkeley and Los Angeles, University of California Press, 1957.

Cubism

Apollinaire, Guillaume. *The Cubist Painters.* New York, Wittenborn, 1962.
Barr, Alfred H., Jr. *Cubism and Abstract Art.* Reprint. First publ. 1936. New York, Arno for The Museum of Modern Art, 1967.
Cooper, Douglas. *The Cubist Epoch.* London, Phaidon Press (distributed by Praeger), 1971.
Fry, Edward F. *Cubism.* London, Thames & Hudson; New York, McGraw-Hill, 1966.
Golding, John. *Cubism: A History and an Analysis, 1907–1914.* Rev. ed. New York, Harper & Row, 1972.
Rosenblum, Robert. *Cubism and Twentieth-Century Art.* New York, Abrams, 1968.

Futurism

Apollonio, Umbro, ed. *The Futurist Manifestos.* New York, Viking, 1973.
Kirby, Michael. *Futurist Performance.* New York, Dutton, 1971.
Marinetti, Filippo Tommaso. *Selected Writings.* R. W. Flint, ed. New York, Farrar, Straus & Giroux, 1971.
Martin, Marianne W. *Futurist Art and Theory, 1909–1915.* New York, Oxford University Press, 1968.

Taylor, Joshua C. *Futurism.* New York, The Museum of Modern Art, 1961.
Tisdall, Caroline, and Bozzolla, Angelo. *Futurism.* New York, Oxford University Press, 1978.

ORPHISM
Spate, Virginia. *Orphism: The Evolution of Non-Figurative Painting in Paris, 1910–1914.* New York, Oxford University Press, 1979.

VORTICISM
Cork, Richard. *Vorticism and Abstract Art in the First Machine Age.* Berkeley, University of California Press, 1976.

DADA
Barr, Alfred H., Jr. *Fantastic Art, Dada, and Surrealism.* Reprint. First publ. 1937. New York, Arno for The Museum of Modern Art, 1970.
Bigsby, C. W. *Dada and Surrealism.* London, Methuen, 1972.
Foster, Stephen C., and Kuenzli, Rudolf E., eds. *Dada Spectrum: The Dialectics of Revolt.* Madison, Wisc., Coda Press, and Iowa City, Ia., University of Iowa, 1979.
Hülsenbeck, Richard, ed. *Dada Almanach.* Millerton, N.Y., Something Else Press, 1966.
Lippard, Lucy R., ed. *Dadas on Art.* Englewood Cliffs, N.J., Prentice-Hall, 1971.
Motherwell, Robert, ed. *Dada Painters and Poets.* New York, Wittenborn, 1951.
Richter, Hans. *Dada: Art and Anti-Art.* New York, McGraw-Hill, 1965.
Rubin, William S. *Dada, Surrealism, and Their Heritage.* New York, The Museum of Modern Art, 1968.
Rubin, William S. *Dada and Surrealist Art.* New York, Abrams, 1969.
Tashjian, Dickran. *Skyscraper Primitives: Dada and the American Avant-Garde 1910–1925.* Middletown, Conn., Wesleyan University Press, 1975.
Verkauf, Willy, ed. *Dada: Monograph of a Movement.* New York, Wittenborn, 1957.

SUPREMATISM, CONSTRUCTIVISM
Bann, Stephen, ed. *The Tradition of Constructivism.* New York, Viking, 1974.
Barron, Stephanie, and Tuchman, Maurice, eds. *The Avant-Garde in Russia, 1910–1930: New Perspectives.* Exhibition catalogue, Los Angeles County Museum of Art. Cambridge, Mass., MIT Press, 1980.
Bowlt, John E. *Russian Art 1875–1975: A Collection of Essays.* New York, MSS Information Corporation, 1976.
Bowlt, John E., ed. *Russian Art of the Avant-Garde: Theory and Criticism, 1902–1934.* New York, Viking, 1976.
Gray, Camilla. *The Russian Experiment in Art: 1863–1922.* London, Thames & Hudson, 1971.
Shvidkovsky, O. A., ed. *Building in the USSR, 1917–1932.* New York, Praeger, 1971.

DE STIJL
Jaffé, Hans L. C. *De Stijl.* New York, Abrams, 1971.
Jaffé, H. L. C. *De Stijl, 1917–1931: The Dutch Contribution to Modern Art.* Amsterdam, Meulenhoff, 1956.
Overy, Paul. *De Stijl.* New York, Dutton, 1969.

BAUHAUS
Bayer, Herbert; Gropius, Ise; and Gropius, Walter. *Bauhaus, 1919–1928.* Introduction by Alfred H. Barr, Jr. New York, The Museum of Modern Art, 1938.
Gropius, Walter. *The New Architecture and the Bauhaus.* Shand, P. Morton, tr. First publ. 1936. Boston, Charles T. Branford, 1955.
Itten, Johannes. *Design and Form: The Basic Course at the Bauhaus.* New York, Reinhold, 1964.
Naylor, Gillian. *The Bauhaus.* London, Studio Vista; New York, Dutton; 1968.
Neumann, Eckhard, ed. *Bauhaus and Bauhaus People.* New York, Nostrand Reinhold, 1970.
Roters, Eberhard. *Painters of the Bauhaus.* New York, Praeger, 1969.
Wingler, Hans M. *The Bauhaus: Weimar, Dessau, Berlin, Chicago.* Cambridge, Mass., MIT Press, 1969.

SURREALISM
Breton, André. *Manifestoes of Surrealism.* Seaver, Richard, and Lane, Helen, tr. Ann Arbor, University of Michigan Press, 1972.
Breton, André. *Surrealism and Painting.* Watson Taylor, Simon, tr. New York, Harper & Row, 1972.
Gershman, Herbert S. *The Surrealist Revolution in France.* Ann Arbor, Mich., University of Michigan Press, 1969.
Jean, Marcel, ed. *The Autobiography of Surrealism.* New York, Viking, 1980.
Jean, Marcel. *The History of Surrealist Painting.* New York, Grove, 1960.
Levy, Julien. *Surrealism.* Reprint. First publ. 1936. (Co-publ. by Worldwide Reprints.) New York, Arno, 1968.
Lippard, Lucy, ed. *Surrealists on Art.* Englewood Cliffs, N.J., Prentice-Hall, 1970.
Read, Herbert. *Surrealism.* New York, Praeger, 1972.
Waldberg, Patrick. *Surrealism.* New York, McGraw-Hill, 1966.

NEW YORK SCHOOL
Ashton, Dore. *The New York School: A Cultural Reckoning.* New York, Viking, 1973.
Geldzahler, Henry. *New York Painting and Sculpture: 1940–1970.* New York, The Metropolitan Museum of Art, 1969.
Hess, Thomas B. *Abstract Painting: Background and American Phase.* New York, Viking, 1951.
Janis, Sidney. *Abstract and Surrealist Art in America.* Reprint. First publ. 1944. New York, Arno, 1970.
Motherwell, Robert, and Reinhardt, Ad, eds. *Modern Artists in America: First Series.* New York, Wittenborn, Schultz, 1951.
O'Doherty, Brian. *American Masters: The Voice and the Myth.* New York, Random House, 1974.

INDEX

A page number preceded by an asterisk indicates an illustration; if the number is boldfaced, the illustration is in color.

PHOTOGRAPHY CREDITS

Photographs reproduced in this volume have been provided, in the majority of cases, by the owners or custodians of the illustrated works of art (see captions). The following list, keyed to page numbers, applies to photographs for which a separate acknowledgment is due: E. Irving Bloomstrann, New Britain, Conn.: 19; Brigdens, Toronto: 154; Bulloz, Paris: 50, 55 bottom; Rudolph Burckhardt, New York: 181, 341, 347 top, 355, 383; Richard Cheek, Cambridge, Mass.: 384 right; Geoffrey Clements, Staten Island, N.Y.: 162 top, 298, 300, 302, 350, 356 top and bottom, 359, 388 bottom; Prudence Cuming Associates, London: 376; Eeva-Inkeri, New York: 392 bottom; André Emmerich, New York: 390; Jonathan L. Fairbanks, Boston: 350; Frequin-Photos, Voorburg, Holland: 219, 354; Claude Gaspari, St-Paul, France: 283; Giraudon, Paris: 16, 73; Gianfranco Gorgoni/Contact, New York: 400; Greenberg-May Prod. Inc., Buffalo: 155, 351; Hickey & Robertson, Houston: 325; Colorphoto Hinz, Basel: 125, 133; Bruce C. Jones, Huntington, N.Y.: 339, 349, 401; Jones-Gessling Studio, Huntington, N.Y.: 380; Peter A. Juley & Son, New York: 37, 299; Kate Keller, New York: 204, 229 top and bottom, 237; Robert E. Mates, New York: 136, 137, 266; James Mathews, New York: 38, 54, 147, 169, 190, 215, 227 bottom, 231, 284, 333, 372; O. E. Nelson, New York: 335; Mali Olatunji, New York: 116; Fotostudio Otto, Vienna: 88; Mario Perotti, Milan: 198; Hans Petersen, Copenhagen: 57; Rolf Petersen, New York: 131 bottom, 150, 178 bottom; Eric Pollitzer, New York: 377, 381, 385, 397 top; Sandak, Inc., New York: 64, 65, 81, 85, 91, 93, 96, 109, 117, 124, 129, 132, 145, 148, 165, 193, 205, 212, 220, 241, 252, 301, 305, 321; Soichi Sunami, New York: 39, 41, 78, 79, 92, 103, 106, 112, 115 top, 146, 151 bottom, 166, 179, 182, 183, 184, 186, 187, 200, 202, 203, 208, 209, 211, 214, 215, 217, 232, 233, 234 top, 242, 243, 246, 250 bottom, 263, 264, 265 bottom, 266, 267 top, 279, 287 left, 288, 310, 311, 312, 319, 368, 369, 370; Joseph Szaszfai, New Haven, Conn.: 188, 189; Taylor & Dull, Inc., New York: 295; Rodney Todd-White & Son, London: 235; Charles Uht, New York: 55 top, 108 top, 289; O. Vaering, Oslo: 68; Malcolm Varon, New York: 121, 164, 261, 304, 316, 328, 348, 364; John Webb, London: 141, 236, 238, 239; A. J. Wyatt, Philadelphia: 58, 114 top and bottom, 163 top, 168 right, 254, 260.